658·1625

D1579878

BPP Professional Education
32-34 Colmore Circus
Birmingham B4 6BN
Phone: 0121 345 9843

Creating Value from Mergers and Acquisitions

The Challenges

Visit the *Creating Value from Mergers and Acquisitions*, 2nd edition, Companion Website at **www.pearsoned.co.uk/sudarsanam** to find valuable **student** learning material including:

- Chapter learning objectives to help you track your progress
- Answers to some chapter review questions to check your understanding

BPP University

087807

Reviews of the first edition

'Simply a "must read" for all persons who require a broad understanding of the various issues involving planning and executing acquisitions and mergers.'
Tom Berglund, Professor of Finance, Swedish School of Economics and Business Administration, Helsinki, Finland

'The book is extremely comprehensive and current. I think you really have done an excellent job summarizing so much of the literature. It is a very nice piece of work.'
Henri Servaes, Professor of Finance, London Business School

'This weighty, well-written, well-researched and easy-to-read tome is set to become a standard work.'
The Times Higher Education Supplement

'An excellent textbook . . . One of the many strengths of this book is that it truly takes an international perspective and does not just stick to the US viewpoint. An excellent overview of the empirical research findings . . . clarity of presentation makes this book a very attractive textbook on both undergraduate and MBA level.'
European Financial Management

'This is a big book in more ways than one. It is the first that tries to provide encyclopaedic coverage of M & A for practitioners and students alike . . . an authoritative guide to the theory and practice of M & A.'
Professional Investor

'If you apply the findings of a recent book, things may not be too awful. Within a comprehensive and very readable survey of the theory and practice of mergers and acquisitions, . . . reviews the transatlantic literature on whether M & A works.'
John Plender, *Financial Times*

'As well as synthesising academic work on takeovers [the book] presents a common-sense approach to the consideration of M & A that might constitute a noisier conscience for over-optimistic boardrooms.'
Ed Warner, *The Guardian*

2nd edition

Creating Value from Mergers and Acquisitions

The Challenges

Sudi Sudarsanam

**Financial Times
Prentice Hall
is an imprint of**

Harlow, England • London • New York • Boston • San Francisco • Toronto • Sydney • Singapore • Hong Kong
Tokyo • Seoul • Taipei • New Delhi • Cape Town • Madrid • Mexico City • Amsterdam • Munich • Paris • Milan

Pearson Education Limited

Edinburgh Gate
Harlow
Essex CM20 2JE
England

and Associated Companies throughout the world

Visit us on the World Wide Web at:
www.pearsoned.co.uk

First published 2003
Second edition published 2010

© Pearson Education Limited 2003, 2010

The right of P.S. Sudarsanam to be identified as author of this work has been asserted
by him in accordance with the Copyright, Designs and Patents Act 1988.

All rights reserved. No part of this publication may be reproduced, stored in a
retrieval system, or transmitted in any form or by any means, electronic, mechanical,
photocopying, recording or otherwise, without either the prior written permission of
the publisher or a licence permitting restricted copying in the United Kingdom issued
by the Copyright Licensing Agency Ltd, Saffron House, 6–10 Kirby Street, London EC1N 8TS.

All trademarks used herein are the property of their respective owners. The use of any trademark
in this text does not vest in the author or publisher any trademark ownership rights in such trademarks,
nor does the use of such trademarks imply any affiliation with or endorsement of this book by such owners.

ISBN: 978-0-273-71539-9

British Library Cataloguing-in-Publication Data
A catalogue record for this book is available from the British Library

Library of Congress Cataloging-in-Publication Data
Sudarsanam, P. S.
    Creating value from mergers and acquisitions : the challenges / Sudi
Sudarsanam. -- 2nd ed.
        p. cm.
      ISBN 978-0-273-71539-9 (pbk.)
    1. Consolidation and merger of corporations.   2. Corporations --
Valuation.   I. Title.
      HD2746.5.S83 2010
      658.1′62--dc22
                                                  2009052003

10 9 8 7 6 5 4 3
14 13

Typeset in 10/12pt Minion by 35
Printed by Ashford Colour Press Ltd., Gosport

To Nandhini, the memory of Alfred Kenyon and
the numerous scholars who have enriched my understanding of M & A

I have stood upon many a tall scholarly shoulder
To raise my gaze and see farthest
Yet my vision is short and
I am searching for shoulders taller still

(adapted from Sir Isaac Newton)

CONTENTS

Preface to the second edition   xiii
Preface to the first edition   xvi
Author's acknowledgements   xix
Publisher's acknowledgements   xxi

1 Introduction   1

Do mergers and acquisitions add or
    destroy shareholder value?   2
The five-stage (5-S) model   3
Stage 1: How good is the corporate
    strategy development process?   3
Stage 2: How well does the company
    organize for acquisitions?   5
Stage 3: What are the pitfalls in deal
    structuring and negotiation?   6
Stage 4: Don't count the chickens yet!
    Post-acquisition integration   8
Stage 5: How did the merger go? Post-
    acquisition audit and organizational
    learning   9
Objectives of the book   9
Outline of the book   9
Notes and references   11

PART ONE
HISTORIC, CONCEPTUAL AND
PERFORMANCE OVERVIEW OF
MERGERS AND ACQUISITIONS

2 Historical overview of mergers and acquisitions activity   15

Objectives   15
Introduction   15
The wave pattern of takeovers in the US   16
Takeover activity in the European Union   22
Historical overview of takeover activity
    in the UK   26
Mergers in emerging markets   30
Overview of the merger waves   31
Why do merger waves happen?   31
Rational economic models of merger waves   32
Impact of industry changes on M & A
    activity   33
Behavioural models of merger waves   39

It's not all 'high buys low'; 'low buys
    high' too   41
Strategic implications of industry
    clustering of M & A   41
Case Study: Pharmaceuticals suffer from
    the urge to merge   42
Overview and implications for practice   44
Review questions   44
Further reading   45
Notes and references   45

3 Alternative perspectives on mergers   49

Objectives   49
Introduction   49
The economic perspective on mergers   50
Industry analysis of competition   54
Game theory and competitive moves   57
Strategy perspective on mergers   62
Dynamic capabilities and mergers   69
Corporate and business strategies   71
Finance theory perspective on mergers   72
Managerial perspective on mergers   78
Organizational perspective on mergers   79
Summary of the multiple perspectives on
    mergers   80
Case Study: 'The Best a Man or a Woman
    Can Get' – P&G and Gillette bridge the
    gender gap in their brands!   81
Overview and implications for practice   82
Review questions   83
Further reading   83
Notes and references   83

4 Are acquisitions successful?   86

Objectives   86
Introduction   86
Defining success of mergers and
    acquisitions   87
Measuring the impact of acquisitions on
    shareholder returns   88
Review of stock market assessment of
    acquisition performance   91
Results of empirical studies of merger
    impact on stock returns   94

Assessing the operating performance of
  acquirers   101
Overview of the operating performance
  studies   107
Post-merger performance of alternative
  corporate strategies   107
Mergers, managers and corporate
  governance   108
Post-merger performance and M & A
  deal characteristics   109
Overview and implications for practice   110
Review questions   111
Further reading   111
Notes and references   111
Appendix 4.1: Abnormal returns
  methodology to study the impact of
  mergers on shareholder value   113
Appendix 4.2: Studies cited in Tables 4.1
  to 4.9   117

PART TWO
CORPORATE STRATEGY AND
ORGANIZING FOR ACQUISITIONS

**5 Sources and limits of value
   creation in horizontal and
   related mergers**   **123**
Objectives   123
Introduction   123
Motivations for horizontal mergers in
  mature industries   124
Revenue enhancement through mergers   126
Cost savings as a source of value creation
  in acquisitions   131
New growth opportunities as a source
  of value   140
Resource-based view (RBV) of
  acquisitions and value creation   141
Evidence of lack of sustainable
  competitive advantage   147
Case Study: Heavy truckers trundle their
  way to market dominance   149
Overview and implications for practice   150
Review questions   151
Further reading   151
Notes and references   151

**6 Sources and limits of value
   creation in vertical mergers**   **156**
Objectives   156
Introduction   156

Vertical integration   157
Benefits and costs of buying in markets   159
Benefits and costs of long-term contracts   160
Benefits and costs of vertical integration   162
Vertical mergers and value creation   165
Empirical evidence on vertical mergers
  and their value effects   166
Vertical mergers that blur industry
  boundaries   167
Outsourcing through acquisitions   170
Case Study: Hospital, heal thyself   172
Overview and implications for practice   177
Review questions   178
Further reading   179
Notes and references   179

**7 Sources and limits of value
   creation in conglomerate
   acquisitions**   **180**
Objectives   180
Introduction   180
Pattern of conglomeration in different
  countries   181
Why do firms diversify?   184
Resource-based view of conglomerate
  acquisition   187
Finance theory of conglomerate
  diversification   189
Managerial perspective on conglomerate
  diversification   192
Organizational perspective on
  conglomerate diversification   194
Summary of alternative perspectives   195
Review of empirical evidence on the
  value of conglomerate diversification   196
Valuation of conglomerates in other
  countries   201
Evidence on operating performance   202
Is the internal capital market efficient?   203
Case Study: Messier bets Vivendi on
  his grand vision and pushes it towards
  bankruptcy!   208
Overview and implications for practice   212
Review questions   212
Further reading   212
Notes and references   213

8 Cross-border acquisitions   **217**
Objectives   217
Introduction   217
Alternative overseas expansion strategies   218

Recent trends in cross-border
acquisitions 218
Factors influencing cross-border mergers 221
Why do corporations undertake cross-
border acquisitions? 224
Barriers to cross-border takeovers 230
Valuation and financing of overseas
acquisitions 234
Post-acquisition integration 234
Empirical and survey evidence on CBA
performance 236
Case Study: Cross-border acquisitions
bring power to companies 240
Overview and implications for practice 241
Review questions 242
Further reading 242
Notes and references 242

9 Strategic alliances as an
alternative to mergers and
acquisitions 245
Objectives 245
Introduction 245
Types of strategic alliance 247
International joint ventures 250
Model of a joint venture 251
Structuring a joint venture 256
Performance evaluation of joint
ventures 259
Critical success factors in strategic
alliances 262
Choosing between an acquisition and
an alliance 263
Case Study: General Motors (GM) and
Ford drive on different roads to same
town 265
Overview and implications for practice 266
Review questions 266
Further reading 267
Notes and references 267

10 Corporate divestiture 270
Objectives 270
Introduction 270
Rationale for corporate divestitures 271
Forms of corporate divestiture 274
Corporate sell-offs 275
Corporate spin-offs 282
Equity carve-outs 292
Stock market arithmetically challenged in
pricing equity carve-outs? 295

The downside of downsizing 296
Tracking stock 296
Overview of the divestiture methods 298
Case Study: Marriott's bondholders taken
for a spin (or for a ride?) 299
Overview and implications for practice 301
Review questions 301
Further reading 302
Notes and references 302

11 Leveraged buyouts 306
Objectives 306
Introduction 306
Leveraged buyout 307
Organizational and legal structure of
the private equity firm 308
Types of LBO 313
Overview of the LBO markets in the US
and Europe 315
Sources of LBO targets 319
Exit from LBOs 320
Characteristics of optimal LBO targets 323
Organizing the buyout and role of the PE
sponsor 323
LBOs in major European countries 332
Managerial motivations for an MBO 335
LBO as a superior business organization 336
Value creation performance of LBOs 341
Future of the LBO market in the US and
Europe 344
Case Study: The tale of two stores:
Safeway and Kroger 345
Overview and implications for practice 347
Review questions 348
Further reading 348
Notes and references 348

12 Acquisition decision process:
organizational, psychological
and governance perspectives 351
Objectives 351
Introduction 351
Acquisition decision-making process:
organizational perspective 352
Acquisition decision process:
psychological perspective 355
Narcissistic CEOs and acquisitions 359
Imitative acquisitions: institutional theory
perspective 361
Acquisition decision-making process:
compensation incentive perspective 362

Acquisition decision-making process: governance structure impact	366
Managing acquisition decision-making	372
Survey evidence on the acquisition process	376
Case Study: Deutsche Boerse CEO and Chairman pay with their jobs for lesson on shareholder activism!	378
Overview and implications for practice	382
Review questions	383
Further reading	384
Notes and references	384

13 Target selection for acquisition   389

Objectives	389
Introduction	389
Target selection process	390
Strategic choices and acquisition	391
Platform strategies	400
Serial acquisitions	402
Deal considerations	404
Profiling desirable targets	408
Due diligence	411
Case Study: How Beecham approached its merger with SmithKline Beckman	411
Overview and implications for practice	413
Review questions	414
Further reading	414
Notes and references	414

PART THREE
DEAL STRUCTURING AND
NEGOTIATION

14 Target valuation   419

Objectives	419
Introduction	419
Sources of value in acquisitions	420
Valuation models	424
Estimating target equity value using the RI model	428
Estimating target value using the PER model	429
Enterprise value multiple	434
Asset-based valuation	436
Valuation using other multiples	436
Discounted cash flow model	437
Impact of tax on target valuation	448

Real options framework for valuing targets	449
Financial options and real options	450
Case Study: 'They also lose who only stand and wait' – when option value is eroded by competition	455
Overview and implications for practice	456
Review questions	457
Further reading	457
Notes and references	457
Appendix 14.1: Real options in mergers and acquisitions	459

15 Accounting for mergers and acquisitions   466

Objectives	466
Introduction	466
Consolidated accounts	467
Types of business combination	467
Accounting for business combinations	468
Accounting for goodwill	473
Overview and implications for practice	479
Review questions	480
Further reading	480
Notes and references	480

16 Paying for the acquisition   482

Objectives	482
Introduction	482
Methods of payment for acquisitions	483
Tax aspects of acquisition financing	486
Impact of bidder's financial strategy	490
Earnings dilution in a share exchange	490
Valuation risk and payment currency	496
Equity derivatives and risk management in equity offers	497
Payment currency versus financing	502
Leveraged cash financing	503
Deferred consideration financing	509
Factors determining financing method choice	511
Empirical evidence on the impact of payment method on financial performance	513
Case Study: Choosing the better acquirer: MCI faces a dilemma!	518
Overview and implications for practice	522
Review questions	522
Further reading	523
Notes and references	523

17 Antitrust regulation   528

Objectives   528
Introduction   528
Economic rationale for antitrust regulation   530
Assessing the effects of mergers on competition   533
Competitive constraints on merging firms   536
Merger regulation in the European Union   537
The UK merger control regime   545
Merger regulation in the US   551
Antitrust regulation in continental Europe   555
Critique of merger control regimes   555
Regulatory risk to M & A deals   557
International Competition Network   559
Stock market reaction to merger references   560
Case Study: William Hill takes a bet on Stanley Leisure and swallows OFT remedy   560
Overview and implications for practice   563
Review questions   563
Further reading   564
Notes and references   564

18 Regulating takeover bids   568

Objectives   568
Introduction   568
Rationale for takeover regulation   569
Takeover regulation in the UK   569
European Union Takeover Directive   583
Regulation of takeover bids in continental Europe   588
Takeover regulation in the US   590
Takeover regulation and takeover activity   596
Case Study: UK Takeover Panel doesn't buy the Big MAC   597
Overview and implications for practice   598
Review questions   599
Further reading   599
Notes and references   600

19 Advisers in takeovers   602

Objectives   602
Introduction   602
Role of advisers in acquisitions   603
Role of investment banks   604
Lawyers   620
Accountants   621
Other advisers   621
Public and investor relations   622

Case Study: What are investment banks' duties and to whom are they owed?   622
Overview and implications for practice   624
Review questions   624
Further reading   625
Notes and references   625

20 Bid strategies and tactics   627

Objectives   627
Introduction   627
Bid strategies   628
Bid tactics   636
Developing a negotiation strategy   637
Negotiating a friendly bid   641
Post-acquisition integration and deal negotiation   643
Hostile bid tactics   646
Institutional investors and bid outcome   647
Bid strategies and tactics in the US   651
Empirical evidence on bid strategies and value creation   655
Bid strategies and tactics in continental Europe: impact of the Takeover Directive   657
Case Study: Mittal breaks Arcelor's steely defence and becomes the Emperor of Steel!   658
Overview and implications for practice   663
Review questions   664
Further reading   664
Notes and references   664

21 Defences against takeovers   669

Objectives   669
Introduction   669
Bid resistance motives   669
Bid defence strategies   670
Impact of defensive strategies   675
Takeover defences outside the UK   676
Takeover defences in continental Europe   676
Takeover defences in the US   683
Case Study: State anti-takeover laws in the US and how they protect targets   688
Overview and implications for practice   690
Review questions   691
Further reading   691
Notes and references   691

PART FOUR POST-ACQUISITION INTEGRATION AND ORGANIZATIONAL LEARNING

22 Organizational and human aspects of post-acquisition integration 695

Objectives	695
Introduction	695
From strategy to integration	696
A post-acquisition integration model	698
Political and cultural perspectives on integration	700
Change management perspective on post-acquisition integration	709
Human resource management issues during integration	711
Problems in integration	716
Stages in the integration process	722
Project management approach to integration	723
What do managers think about acquisition integration and performance? Survey evidence	725
Survey evidence on acquisitions and the human factor	726
Critical success factors	728
Case Study: Spanish conquistador arrives in England: Santander the new Armada?	731
Overview and implications for practice	735
Review questions	736
Further reading	737
Notes and references	737

23 Post-acquisition audit and organizational learning 740

Objectives	740
Introduction	740
Do acquirers assess acquisition performance?	741
What are the performance metrics?	742
Organizational learning perspectives	747
Exploitative and exploratory learning	751
Acquisition-making as a core competence	758
Case Study: Learning from past acquisitions	760
Overview and implications for practice	761
Review questions	762
Further reading	762
Notes and references	762

24 Meeting the challenges of mergers and acquisitions 765

Objectives	765
Introduction	765
Importance of the five-stage model	766
Challenges in competitive strategy planning	769
Challenges in organizing for acquisitions	771
Challenges in deal structuring and negotiation	772
Challenges in post-acquisition integration	773
Challenges in post-acquisition audit and organizational learning	775
Notes and references	776

Index 777

Supporting resources

Visit **www.pearsoned.co.uk/sudarsanam** to find valuable online resources

Companion Website for students
- Chapter learning objectives to help you track your progress
- Answers to some chapter review questions to check your understanding

For instructors
- Instructor's Manual containing an overview of each chapter along with solutions to review questions, additional questions and end of chapter cases
- PowerPoint slides highlighting key concepts, figures and tables from the book
- References to additional case studies highlighting key issues
- Teaching hints on how students can learn the practical aspects of M & A

Also: The Companion Website provides the following features:
- Search tool to help locate specific items of content
- E-mail results and profile tools to send results of quizzes to instructors
- Online help and support to assist with website usage and troubleshooting

For more information please contact your local Pearson Education sales representative or visit **www.pearsoned.co.uk/sudarsanam**

PREFACE TO THE SECOND EDITION

The first edition published in 2003 has been well received and numerous reviewers and users have commended its structure, scope, comprehensiveness and clarity of writing. They have also welcomed the focus on mergers and acquisitions (M & A) in Europe and the presentation of empirical evidence along with theory. The first edition has been translated into Chinese as was its predecessor, *The Essence of Mergers and Acquisitions*. Since its publication, the M & A market has undergone a number of interesting developments. The meltdown in 2000–2001 was followed, contrary to expectations, by a rapid resumption of M & A activity that surged to its peak in 2007. Private equity sponsored M & A was a major contributor to this surge and it was aided enormously by the torrent of liquidity in credit markets. The credit crunch of 2007 stopped this surge in its tracks and the deepening credit crisis and the drying up of liquidity brought this latest M & A wave to an end in 2008. This recent wave was much more global than before with emerging market firms spreading out their wings to become global players through acquisitions. This revised edition traces these developments.

The continuing Europa project of enlarging the European Union to bring within its fold more and more Nordic, Central and Eastern European, and Southen European states has resulted in an economic region that is now larger than the USA. This is reflected in the larger value of M & A deals involving companies in the EU than the value of US deals. At the time of writing the EU includes 27 member states with a population surpassing that of the US. An important legislative milestone in the EU was the approval of the Takeover Directive by the European Parliament in 2004. Since then the Directive has been incorporated into the UK domestic law and into the domestic laws of other member states. Regulation of takeovers in the EU now therefore derives from law, although in the UK the City Takeover Panel has retained its self-regulatory character.

Our understanding of the M & A process has grown thanks to new scholarship in different disciplines that influence the framework used in this book. In the last edition I described the merger waves that had taken place in the US, the UK and continental Europe over the previous century or more. Several scholars have attempted to develop new theories of merger waves and test them with empirical data. The results, while answering some questions, still leave others, about the timing of mergers and the relationship between industry merger waves and aggregate merger waves, unanswered. Nevertheless they allow us to think of more comprehensive theories of merger waves. Both theoretical and empirical research on the structure and evolution of corporate governance provides new insights into the relationship between corporate governance and takeovers. There is now much greater empirical evidence on the impact of executive compensation contracts on manager's risk incentives in undertaking M & A. There is also much more evidence on the consequences of good or bad acquisitions for managerial incentives and jobs.

An exciting new development is the behavioural and psychological perspective on CEO's and other top managers' motivations and incentives for making high risk and value-destroying acquisitions. Clinical psychology applied to organizations provides us with more insights into M & A transactions and their value outcomes that cannot be explained on the basis of rational economic models alone. More recent research in the areas of corporate divestitures, leveraged buyouts, and the financing of acquisitions has given us a better understanding of the M & A process. Theoretical developments and empirical research in post-acquisition integration processes drawing from a range of disciplines concerned with individual, group and organizational behaviour provides new insights into the factors that can undo good acquisitions and make M & A more of a challenge.

In addition to drawing upon new theoretical and empirical research mentioned above, I have also used the opportunity of the revision to improve the exposition of the regulatory issues. I have covered more US antitrust and takeover regulations to provide a balanced comparative analysis of mergers in the US and Europe. In discussing bid strategies and defence strategies I have again enhanced the coverage of US laws, regulations and recorded transactions to achieve a better balance between the two regions.

Users of the previous edition have commented very favourably on the logic and cogency of the structure of the chapters built around the five-stage model. This structure is therefore retained. While the number of chapters has been kept at 24, the old chapter 6 on consolidating mergers has now been dropped and much of its content where still relevant is now included in Chapter 13. Chapter 2 now includes new merger wave theories and discusses the empirical evidence for them and its limitations. I have expanded discussion of game theory and real options as frameworks for explaining various M & A characteristics such as merger waves and serial acquisitions in Chapters 3 and 14. A new chapter, Chapter 12, provides the organizational, psychological and governance perspectives on M & A. Chapter 13 now deals with target selection and provides many practical analytical tools for identifying the right target/s to bid for. Chapter 14 now covers a wider range of valuation models with illustrations. Chapter 17 (antitrust regulation) and Chapter 18 (takeover regulation) have been updated and expanded to provide more in-depth coverage of the US and continental European laws and regulations. Chapter 20 (bid strategies) and Chapter 21 (defence strategies) have been similarly updated and expanded. Since the first edition, I have been working as a member of the UK Competition Commission (CC) and have sat on inquiries into the competition effects of mergers. This experience has deepened my understanding of not only antitrust issues in mergers and but also how merger regulation works. In revising Chapter 17 on antitrust regulation I have been able to draw upon my experience as a regulator. The content of this chapter, however, in no way reflects the views or opinions or position of the CC except where they are explicitly acknowledged and cited. Chapter 21 (post-acquisition integration) now reflects the recent literature on the organizational, cultural and sociological aspects of integration and Chapter 22 similarly draws upon the insights provided by new research on organizational learning.

In addition to updating the relevant information in various chapters, I have also sought to improve the clarity of presentation and its reader-friendliness. Several new illustrations and case studies have been included while some have been retained from the previous edition because of their continued value to the reader. I have also used figures and diagrams to present the ideas in the book in a more accessible way.

The book is primarily intended for MBA and Master's level programmes in management as well as advanced undergraduate courses in industrial organization, finance, business strategy, and corporate governance, plus those preparing for professional exams. However, the structure is modular and different chapters from the book can be used on courses that include substantial discussion of M & A such as courses on strategic management, industrial economics, finance and regulation. On such courses some overview of M & A (e.g. Chapters 1 and 3) may be combined with more specific focus on the strategic, economic, finance and regulatory aspects of M & A. I have used this book on M & A courses on MBA, executive MBA and Master's in Finance programmes by following the modular approach. I have also used parts of the book on executive programmes.

The book is accompanied by a web-based source of supplementary teaching resources for lecturers using this book as the main text book. These resources include answers to review questions and questions for the end-of chapter cases. Powerpoint slides for the chapters are also available. References to additional cases from sources such as the Harvard Business School with a brief description of the main issues dealt with in those cases are also provided. How such extended cases complement the material in the book is also indicated. Lecturers who wish to supplement the illustrations and short cases in the chapters with longer cases may therefore be able to locate such cases easily. Hints on how students can be taught to learn about the practical aspects of M & A through, for example, simulated games are provided. There is a similar web-based supplementary resource bank for students with answers to selected review questions and additional sources of information on M & A deals.

Sudi Sudarsanam

PREFACE TO THE FIRST EDITION

This book builds on and extends the author's previous title *The Essence of Mergers and Acquisitions* (Prentice Hall International, 1995). This title has been translated into Spanish, Polish, Chinese, Indonesian and Thai. Since that book was published, we have experienced perhaps the most sweeping merger wave in history. At the peak of the wave in 1999, the value of mergers and acquisitions in the US alone was about $2 trillions (where a trillion is equal to 10^{12}). Europe similarly witnessed historically unprecedented levels of mergers and acquisitions reaching a peak of $1.5 trillions in 1999. Asian countries have also experienced high levels of merger activity. Since the publication of the *Essence* book, the merger phenomenon has also been examined by scholars extensively and our understanding of the causes and consequences has advanced as a result.

Mergers and acquisitions (M & A) are undertaken by companies to achieve certain strategic and financial objectives. They involve the bringing together of two organizations with often disparate corporate personalities, cultures and value systems. Success of mergers may, therefore, depend on how well the organizations are integrated. There are a variety of stakeholders in the merging companies who have an interest in the success of mergers. Shareholders and managers are two of the most important stakeholders, but others include employees, consumers, local communities and the economy at large. Mergers can have anti-competitive implications, and hence in many countries they attract rigorous antitrust scrutiny.

One of the most puzzling aspects of the merger phenomenon is the widespread perception that mergers and acquisitions do not create value for the stakeholders and in fact destroy value. If so, given the stupendous scale of the investment that mergers represent and the losses to stakeholders, including possible welfare losses to the community as a whole, we need a serious investigation of the reasons for such failure. In some cases, the feverish atmosphere, the inexorable momentum and thrill of the chase of a hostile bid may drive managers to foolish excess in the bid premium they pay. The causes of failure may, in other cases, stem from the fragmented perspective that managers and other players in the acquisition game have of the M & A process. The book's central focus, reflected in the title, is on the challenges to the corporate strategy of using mergers and acquisitions as an instrument to create shareholder value. Challenges mean both threats and opportunities. This book is about both.

What is the approach?

The book regards M & A as a process, rather than as a transaction, which requires insights from a number of disciplines to understand and effectively carry out. It considers that this process is a multi-stage one and that a holistic view of the process is necessary to appreciate the inter-stage links and develop effective value creating M & A strategies. To develop this holistic view, the book draws upon multiple perspectives developed by scholars in different disciplines. The book emphasizes critical examination and empirical validation of the predictions and prescriptions from these perspectives. It seeks to signpost risks and potential problems and improve the odds of successful M & A. Because of the increasing importance of M & A in individual countries, in regions and across countries, the book deals with the above issues from an international perspective. The book seeks to provide a balanced treatment of M & A drawing upon the conceptual, empirical and practitioner perspectives.

The specific themes and structure of the book

The book consists of four parts, in addition to the Introduction to the broad themes of the book:

- **Part 1** provides an overview of M & A, a five-stage model of the M & A process, historic overview of merger waves, five different but complementary perspectives on mergers and assessment of the success of mergers in the US and Europe.
- **Part 2** deals with stages 1 and 2 of the five-stage model – the framework for competitive strategies and the place of M & A in those strategies, the different types of M & A, their value creation potential, the empirical evidence on value creation and the risks in different acquisition types. Part 2 draws on evolving paradigms such as game theory, shareholder value management, resource-based view of competition, network externalities, real options and change management. It incorporates the recently revised perspectives on several established paradigms, including corporate governance, modern industrial revolution, vertical integration, antitrust regulation and conglomerate diversification. Part 2 is also concerned with corporate restructuring through divestitures, and leveraged and management buy-outs. It discusses strategic alliances as an alternative to M & A and also the issues involved in how firms organize themselves for acquisitions.
- **Part 3** deals with stage 3 of the M & A process model – fundamentals of M & A deal structuring and negotiation, target valuation models, accounting rules, paying for the acquisition, antitrust and takeover regulations, the role of advisers, bid strategies and tactics, and defences against hostile takeover bids.
- **Part 4** of the book deals with the fourth and fifth stages of the M & A process model, the organizational and human aspects of acquisitions, the organizational challenge of change management and creating organizational processes and systems to ensure organizational learning about M & A.
- The book concludes by identifying factors that contribute to acquisition failure and those that increase the odds of acquisition success.
- In each part, the book covers M & A in North America and Europe, the two most active M & A markets in the last two decades.

The style of the book is to a large extent non-technical, and the accent is on the practical aspects of mergers and acquisitions. This practical orientation is strengthened by the copious use of illustrative examples from actual acquisitions and mergers carried out in the last few years. Quantitative areas of the subject such as valuation are explained with worked examples. To increase reader friendliness, complex information, such as reviews of empirical studies and regulatory rules, is presented in tables. Major points and conclusions are presented as bullet points to focus the reader's attention. Technical issues such as empirical methodology are located in appendices to chapters. Where necessary, graphics are used to highlight complex information and facilitate reader access. At the end of each chapter the implications for the practice of M & A are drawn and presented as bullet points. A companion website to help readers and instructors with additional discussion material and references to case study material will be set up.

Target readership

Both the *Essence* title and this book have evolved out of a specialist MBA elective course on Mergers, Acquisitions and Divestments (MAD) which I have been teaching at the Cranfield School of Management in the UK and had previously taught at City University (now Cass) Business School, London. MAD is generally one of the most popular electives on the MBA menu. The book is intended to be used by MBA students of mergers and acquisitions. At the MBA level, the book may be used in courses in corporate finance, business strategy, industrial economics, corporate restructuring, organizational change and corporate governance. It may also be used in similar courses at the undergraduate level and by students preparing for professional examination bodies, such as the Stock Exchange and the Association of Corporate Treasurers. It will be of use to managers, investment bankers and other practitioners in corporate finance, strategy, organizational change and law looking for a rigorous integration of the conceptual, empirical and practical aspects of M & A as well as a holistic view of the M & A process. I have used different parts of the book on executive training courses on M & A or specific aspects of M & A such as financing and negotiation.

Sudi Sudarsanam

AUTHOR'S ACKNOWLEDGEMENTS

It has been a long and arduous task to revise this book for its second edition and in the process I have received much support from friends and colleagues, which lightened the burden. The very favourable response to my first book, *The Essence of Mergers and Acquisitions*, and the first edition of this book, upon whose foundations rests the current revision, encouraged me to prepare the revised edition. With the help and cooperation of Isabella Barnard, my secretary at Cranfield School of Management, I was able to gather hundreds of journal articles, upon which I have drawn. She also helped with the final preparation of the manuscript. I received further data collection help from Dzung Nguyen and Tim Broadhurst, my doctoral students both at Cranfield School of Management. I would very much like to thank the staff at the Cranfield School of Management library, in particular Mary Betts-Gray, for the help they have provided in collecting the material for the book. Part of the work for the revision was completed while I was visiting Santa Clara University in California in 2008 and 2009. I wish to thank Professor Sanjiv Das, Chair of the Finance Department at the Leavey School of Business there and Professor Meir Statman for facilitating my visit. I wish to thank Nandhini and her husband Radhakrishnan for providing me with a 'home away from home' during that time and making the writing of this book a less daunting task. My tedium in writing the book was many times relieved by the delights of watching their baby daughter Ananya grow.

Professor Hersh Shefrin of the Leavey School of Business, a world authority on behavioural finance, kindly spared his time to comment on the psychological perspectives on M & A in Chapter 12. Professor Richard Taffler of Edinburgh University read parts of the manuscript relating to the same aspects of M & A and I benefited from his suggestions. Among my colleagues at Cranfield, I wish to thank Dr Tarik Diouchi for his comments on parts of the manuscript, especially those relating to real options. Dr Paul Guest offered suggestions, based on his use of the first edition on his courses, to improve the book. Leonidas Barbopoulos of St. Andrews University in Scotland read large parts of the book and updated me on some of the more recent literature in different areas.

Professor Scott Moeller, Director of the Mergers & Acquisitions Research Centre at Cass Business School in London, having used the first edition on his M & A courses, made numerous suggestions for improvement, which I have taken on board in revising the text. Professor Luc Renneboog of Tilburg University reviewed the first edition for *European Financial Management* and his suggestions have enhanced the presentation in the new edtion and led to enlarged coverage of topics like valuation models and real options. Russell Sparkes, reviewing the last edition for *Professional Investor*, suggested more coverage of corporate governance. The revised edition provides more detailed discussions of the impact on M & A of corporate governance in both bidders and targets in various chapters including Chapter 12. I took heart from the highly complimentary anonymous reviewers of the first edition, who made excellent suggestions for its improvement. I hope that I have incorporated most of these.

I received numerous and substantive comments on the first edition of this book and have sharpened the intellectual rigour and focus of the second edition in the light of those comments. Among those that provided the comments are:

- Professor Colin Mayer of the Said Business School at Oxford University;
- Professor Henri Servaes of the London Business School;

- Professors Georges Selim and Mez Lasfer of the Cass Business School at City University London;
- Professor Nick Travlos of the ALBA Graduate Business School, Athens, Greece;
- Professor Nikhil Varaiya of the San Diego State University;
- Professor Tom Berglund of the Swedish School of Economics, Helsinki;
- Professor Rezaul Kabir of Tilburg University;
- Professor Raghu Rau of Purdue University;
- Professor Jay Dahya of Baruch College at City University, New York;
- Professor Arie Melnik, Haifa University, Israel; and
- Dr Dimitri Kyriazis of the University of Piraeus, Athens.

I owe special thanks to Professor Alfred Kenyon, formerly of Cass Business School, London. He read the manuscript of the first edition with a great deal of enthusiasm and zest and came forward with very incisive comments. His combative, but good-natured, arguments about my presentation of the material concerning corporate strategy models and their implications for mergers and acquisitions not only made me think more critically about the issues he raised but also renewed my faith in the book and its usefulness. As a former corporate treasurer of Plessey Plc, Alfred combined his practical insights with a robustly conceptual approach. Sadly, Alfred passed away after the publication of the first edition and the revised edition is the poorer for the loss of his wise and perceptive comments. I dedicate this edition to his memory.

I have used the previous edition in teaching courses on M & A on full time MBA programmes, executive MBA programmes, executive programmes and Masters in Finance programmes at Cranfield School of Management, Santa Clara University in California, ALBA Graduate Business School in Greece, the Mangement Centre, University of Innsbruck in Austria and the University of Szczecin in Poland. The questions my students raised about the various aspects of M & A have led me to think more deeply about them and the revised edition has benefited from such a reflection.

Above all, I wish to thank my wife Padhma for her continued support and endurance of my pre-occupation with writing this edition.

Sudi Sudarsanam

PUBLISHER'S ACKNOWLEDGEMENTS

We are grateful to the following for permission to reproduce copyright material:

Figures

Figure 2.1 from *Diversification through Acquisitions: Strategies for Creating Economic Value*, The Free Press (Salter, M. S. and Weinhold, W. A.) Fig. 1.2, p. 10, Reprinted with the permission of The Free Press, a Division of Simon & Schuster, Inc., copyright © 1979 by Malcolm S. Salter and Wolf A. Weinhold. All rights reserved; Figure 3.2 adapted from *Competitive Advantage: Creating and Sustaining Superior Performance*, The Free Press (Porter, M. E.) Fig. 1.1, p. 5, Reprinted with the permission of The Free Press, a Division of Simon & Schuster, Inc., copyright © 1985, 1998 by Michael E. Porter. All rights reserved; Figure 3.3 from Coopetition by Adam M. Brandenburger and Barry J. Nalebuff, copyright © 1996 by Adam M. Brandenburger and Barry J. Nalebuff. Used by permission of Doubleday, a division of Random House, Inc. and the Rees Literary Agency; Figure 3.4 adapted from *Economics of Strategy*, John Wiley & Sons, Inc. (Besanko, D., Dranove, D. and Shanley, M.) F3.4, p. 39, copyright ©. 2000 John Wiley & Sons, Inc., Reproduced with permission of John Wiley & Sons, Inc.; Figure 3.8 from *Competitive Advantage: Creating and Sustaining Superior Performance*, The Free Press (Porter, M. E.) Fig. 2.2, p. 37, Reprinted with the permission of The Free Press, a Division of Simon & Schuster, Inc., copyright © 1985, 1998 by Michael E. Porter. All rights reserved; Figure 3.10 from *Hypercompetition: Managing the Dynamics of Strategic Maneuvering*, The Free Press (D'Aveni, R. A.) Fig. 1–2, p. 12, Reprinted with the permission of The Free Press, a Division of Simon & Schuster, Inc., copyright © 1994 by Richard A. D'Aveni. All rights reserved; Figure 3.11 from *Business Analysis and Valuation*, 4/ed, Thomson Learning (Palepu, K., Healy, P. and Peek, E.) Fig. 6.1, copyright © 2008 South-Western, a part of Cengage Learning, Inc. Reproduced by permission www.cengage.com/permissions; Figure 5.4 from Paths to creating value in pharmaceutical mergers, *Mergers and Productivity* (Ravenscroft, D. J. and Long, W. F. 2000) (Ed. Kaplan, S. N.) copyright © University of Chicago Press; Figure 7.3 from The BCG Portfolio Matrix from the Product Portfolio Matrix copyright © 1970, The Boston Consulting Group; Figure 11.1 from *The new demography of private equity*, The Global Economic Impact of Private Equity Report 2008 *(The Global PE Report)*, 2008, Fig. 1b (Stromberg. P.), World Economic Forum, copyright © World Economic Forum; Figure 11.3 from *The British Private Equity and Venture Capital Association Submission to the Treasury Select Committee of the UK Parliament*, May, BVCA (BVCA 2007) Appendix 1, copyright © The British Equity and Venture Capital Association; Figure 11.5 from European management buy-outs Jan–Dec 2008, *The Centre for Management Buyout Research*, February, Fig. 1.15 (The Centre for Management Buyout Research (CMBOR), University of Nottingham 2009), copyright © CMBOR/Barclays Private Equity; Figures 11.7, 11.9, 11.10, 11.11 from *'Defaults and returns in the high yield bond market: The year 2007 in review and outlook'*, in Special Report from the New York University Salomon Center (Altman, E. I. and Karlin, B. J. 2008) copyright © Leonard N. Stern School of Business; Figure 11.8 from *European Quarterly High Yield and Leveraged Loan Report*, First Quarter 2009, European High Yield Association (2009) Fig. 15, copyright © Association for Financial Markets in Europe (AFMA); Figure 12.3 adapted from Executive compensation and managerial overconfidence: Impact on risk taking and shareholder value in corporate acquisitions, *International Mergers and Acquisitions Activity Since 1990: Recent Research and Quantitative Analysis*, pp. 223–260 (Sudarsanam, S. and Huang, J. (eds. Gregoriou, G. N. and Renneboog, L.) 2007), copyright © 2007 Elsevier Inc. All rights reserved; Figure 13.2 from Strategies of diversification *Harvard Business Review*, 25(5), pp. 113–25 (Ansoff, I. 1957), Sept/Oct, copyright © Harvard Business School; Figures 14.4a, 14.4b from *Business Analysis and Valuation*, 4/ed, Thomson Learning (Palepu, K. G.,

Healy, P. M., Bernard, V. L., Peek, E.) copyright © 2008 South-Western, a part of Cengage Learning, Inc. Reproduced by permission www.cengage.com/permissions; Figure 14A.2 from *Strategic Investment: Real Options and Games*, Princeton University Press (Smit, H. and Trigeorgis, L. 2004) Fig. 8.4, Reprinted by permission of Princeton University Press, copyright © Princeton University Press; Figure 16.5 from Business combination: An exchange ratio determination model, *The Accounting Review*, 44 (Larson, K. and Gonedes, N. 1969), copyright © American Accounting Association; Figure 16.6 from *Corporate Finance*, McGraw-Hill (Ross, S. A., Westerfield, R. W. and Jaffe, J. F. 2002) pp. 640–642; Figure 16.7 from What determines the financing decision of corporate takeovers? Investor protection, asymmetric information or method of payment?, *Journal of Corporate Finance*, Vol 15 (3), pp. 290–315 (Martynova, M. and Renneboog, L. 2009), Copyright © 2009 Elsevier B.V. All rights reserved; Figures 16.8a, 16.8b from 'Mergers and acquisitions in Europe', *Advances in Corporate Finance and Asset Pricing* (Martynova, M. and Renneboog, L. 2006), eds L. Renneboog, copyright © Emerald Group Publishing Limited; Figure 20.3 from Whither hostility?, *Corporate Governance and Regulatory Impact on Mergers and Acquisitions* pp. 103–129 (Bratton, W. W. (Gregoriou, G. and Renneboog, L. (eds.)) 2007), Copyright © 2007 Elsevier Inc. All rights reserved; Figure 22.2 adapted from *Strategy Synthesis: Resolving Strategy Paradoxes to Create Advantage*, Thomson Learning (de Wit, B. and Meyer, R. 2005) Fig. 4.3; Figure 22.4 from *Managing Mergers, Acquisitions and Strategic Alliances: Integrating People and Cultures*, Butterworth-Heinemann (Cartwright, S. and Cooper, S. L. 1996) p. 50, copyright © 1996, Elsevier; Figure 22.8 from The influence of intellectual capital on the types of innovative capabilities, *Academy of Management Journal*, 48(3), pp. 450–463 (Subramaniam, M. and Youndt, M. A. 2005), copyright © American Accounting Association, permission conveyed through Copyright Clearance Centre.

Tables

Table 2.1 from Evolution of national, community and international M&A transactions in the EU (% of all transactions including divestitures), Thomson Reuters, www.thomsonreuters.com, copyright © Thomson Reuters; Tables 2.2, 2.3 from Table on M&A in major overseas markets outside the US, *Mergers & Acquisitions*, February (2008), SourceMedia, Inc., copyright © SourceMedia, Inc.; Table 2.4 from What drives merger waves?, *Journal of Financial Economics*, Vol 77 (3), pp. 529–60 (Harford, J. 2005), copyright © 2005, Elsevier Ltd. All Rights Reserved; Table 2.5 from Sectoral and geographical breakdown of M&A operations with a US or EU target 2006–07 (%), Thomson Reuters, www.thomsonreuters.com, copyright © Thomson Reuters; Table 3.3 adapted from *Economics of Strategy*, John Wiley & Sons, Inc. (Besanko, D., Dranove, D. and Shanley, M.) T3, pp. 36–40, copyright © 2000 John Wiley & Sons, Inc., Reproduced with permission of John Wiley & Sons, Inc.; Table 4.2 adapted from Wealth destruction on a massive scale? A study of acquiring-firm returns in the recent merger wave, *The Journal of Finance*, Vol 60 (2), pp. 757–782 (Moeller, S., Schlinegemann, F. P. and Stulz, R. M. 2005), John Wiley and Sons, copyright © 2005 by The American Finance Association; Table 8.1 from Cross-border acquisitions of, and by, US corporations, Thomson Reuters, www.thomsonreuters.com, copyright © Thomson Reuters; Table 8.2 from Cross-border acquisitions involving EU companies, Thomson Reuters, www.thomsonreuters.com, copyright © Thomson Reuters; Table 8.3 from Cross-border acquisitions involving EU member states in 2007, Thomson Reuters, www.thomsonreuters.com, copyright © Thomson Reuters; Table 8.4 adapted from *Mergers & Acquisitions: The Dealmakers' Journal*, February, p. 59 (2009), SourceMedia, Inc., copyright © SourceMedia, Inc.; Table 10.3 from Spinoffs in individual European countries (excluding UK) 1990–2007, Thomson Reuters, www.thomsonreuters.com, copyright © Thomson Reuters; Tables 11.2, 11.4 from European management buy-outs Jan–Dec 2008, *The Centre for Management Buyout Research*, February (The Centre for Management Buyout Research (CMBOR), University of Nottingham 2009), copyright © CMBOR/Barclays Private Equity; Table 11.5 from Leveraged buyouts in the UK and continental Europe: Retrospect and prospect, *European Corporate Governance Institute Discussion Paper*, 2006–70 (July), Table 6 (Wright, M., Renneboog, L., Simons, T. and Scholes, L. 2006), copyright © Tilbery University (CentER); Table 11.6 adapted from *BVCA Private*

Equity and Venture Capital Performance Measurement Survey 2008, PriceWaterhouseCoopers (BVCA, PriceWaterhouseCoopers and Capital Dynamics 2008), copyright © PriceWaterhouseCoopers; Table 11.7 from 'Leveraged buyouts in the UK and continental Europe: Retrospect and Prospect', *European Corporate Governance Institute Discussion Paper*, 2006–70 (July), Table 6 (Wright, M., Renneboog, L., Simons, T. and Scholes, L. 2006), copyright © Tilbery University (CentER); Table 14.5 from The Worldwide Equity Premium: A Smaller Puzzle, *EFA 2006 Zurich Meetings Paper. AFA 2008 New Orleans Meetings Paper* (Dimson, E., Marsh, P. and Staunton, M. 2006), http://ssrn.com/abstract=891620, copyright © Elsevier, granted with kind permission from Professors E. Dimson, P. Marsh and M. Staunton; Table 14.10 from *Real Options: Managerial Flexibility and Strategy in Resource Allocation*, MIT Press (Trigeorgis, L. 1996) Table 1.1, copyright © 1996 Massachusetts Institute of Technology, by permission of The MIT Press; Table 16.8 adapted from Moody's Financial Metrics™: Key Ratios by Rating and Industry for Global Non-financial Corporations: 2008, www.moodys.com, Published January 2009, copyright © Moody's Investors Service, Inc. and/or its affiliates. Reprinted with permission. All Rights Reserved; Table 17.4 adapted from 'Notifications and decisions under the Merger Regulation during 1990–May 2009' European Commission, http://ec.europa.eu/competition/mergers/statistics.pdf, copyright © European Communities, 2009; Table on p. 631 adapted from Do auctions induce a winner's curse? New evidence from the corporate takeover market, *Journal of Financial Economics*, Vol 89 (1), pp. 1–19 (Boone, A. and Mulherin, J. 2008), Copyright © 2008 Elsevier B. V. All rights reserved; Table 20.5 adapted from Are performance based arbitrage effects detectable? Evidence from merger arbitrage, *Journal of Corporate Finance*, Vol 13 (5), pp. 793–812 (Officer, M. S. 2007), Copyright © 2007 Elsevier B. V. All rights reserved; Table 20.11 adapted from *Mergers & Acquisitions*, p. 26 (2008), February, copyright © SourceMedia, Inc.; Table 21.2 adapted from Defensive strategies of target firms in UK contested takeovers, *Managerial Finance*, 17(6), pp. 47–56 (Sudarsanam, P. S. 1991), copyright © Emerald Group Publishing Ltd, permission conveyed through Copyright Clearance Centre; Table 21.3 adapted from Less than lethal weapons: Defense strategies in UK contested takeovers, *Acquisitions Monthly*, January, pp. 30–32 (Sudarsanam, P. S. 1994), copyright © Thomson Reuters; Table 21.6 adapted from An overview of the takeover defense economy, *Mergers and Acquisitions* (Ruback, R. 1988), Auerbach, A. (ed.) copyright © University of Chicago Press; Tables 21.7, 21.8 adapted from Corporate governance, corporate control and takeovers, *Advances in Mergers and Acquisitions*, Vol 1, pp. 119–155 (Sudarsanam, S., C. Cooper and A. Gregory (eds.) 2000), Copyright © 2000, Emerald Group Publishing Limited; Table 22.3 from *Making a Success of Acquisitions*, Coopers & Lybrand (Coopers & Lybrand 1993), copyright © PriceWaterhouseCoopers.

Text

Exhibit 6.6 from The outsourcing of R&D through acquisitions in the pharmaceutical industry, *Journal of Financial Economics*, Vol 80 (2), pp. 351–383 (Higgins, M. J. and Rodriguez, D. 2006), Copyright © 2005 Elsevier B. V. All rights reserved; Chapter 6 Case study from 'Hospital, heal thyself', McKinsey Quarterly, 1, 2000, 91, 93 (Figliuolo, M. L., Mango, P. D. and McCormick, D. H.). This article was originally published in *McKinsey Quarterly*, www.mckinseyquarterly.com, February 2000. Copyright © 2010 McKinsey & Company. All rights reserved. Reprinted by permission. Exhibit 7.2 adapted from Why do managers diversify their firms? Agency reconsidered, *The Journal of Finance*, Vol 58 (1), pp. 71–118 (Aggarwal, R. K. and Samwick, A. A. 2003), John Wiley and Sons, copyright © 2003, 2003 by the American Finance Association; Exhibit 7.3 adapted from 'Does corporate diversification destroy value?, *The Journal of Finance*, Vol 57 (2), pp. 695–720 (Graham, J. R., Lemmon, M. L. and Wolf, J. G. 2002), John Wiley and Sons, copyright © 2002, The American Finance Association 2002; Exhibit 8.6 based on 'A learning perspective on sociocultural integration in cross-national mergers', *Mergers and Acquisitions: Managing culture and Human Resources* (Bjorkman, J., Tienari, J. and Varra, E. 2005), Stahl, G. and Mendenhall, M. (eds.) Stanford University Press; Exhibit 9.1 adapted from *Alliances and Joint Ventures: Fit, Focus and Follow-through*, KPMG International (KPMG 2005) pp. 8–9, www.kpmg.ca, Reprinted with permission of KPMG LLP (Canada);

Exhibit 10.11 from Extra helpings on the gravy train: Tracking stocks let some execs double up on their options, *Business Week*, 22 April 2002 (Byrne, J.); Case Study 10 from Spin-offs and wealth transfers: The Marriott case, *Journal of Financial Economics*, Vol 43 (2), pp. 241–274 (Parrino, R. 1997), Copyright © 1997 Published by Elsevier Science B.V.; Exhibit 11.3 from *European management buy-outs Jan–Dec 2008*, The Centre for Management Buyout Research, February, Table 1.1 (The Centre for Management Buyout Research (CMBOR), University of Nottingham 2009), copyright © CMBOR/Barclays Private Equity; Exhibit 11.6 adapted from Leveraged buyouts in the UK and continental Europe: Retrospect and Prospect, *European Corporate Governance Institute Discussion Paper*, 2006–70 (July) (Wright, M., Renneboog, L., Simons, T. and Scholes, L. 2006), copyright © Tilbery University (CentER); Exhibit 11.7 adapted from *Acquisitions Monthly*, September, p. 52 (2007), copyright © Thomson Reuters; Exhibit 11.11 adapted from Perform or perish, *Business Week*, pp. 38–45 (Thornton, E.); Exhibit 12.4 adapted from Article Alcatel-Lucent dumps chairman, CEO, www. infotech.indiatimes.com, 29 July 2008, All rights reserved. Republication or redistribution of Thomson Reuters content, including by framing or similar means, is expressly prohibited without the prior written consent of Thomson Reuters. Thomson Reuters and its logo are registered trademarks or trademarks of the Thomson Reuters group of companies around the world. Copyright © Thomson Reuters 2009; Exhibit 13.1 adapted from The five competitive forces that shape strategy, *Harvard Business Review*, January, p. 89 (Porter, M. 2008), copyright © Harvard Business School; Case Study 13 from *From Promise to Performance: A Journey of Transformation at SmithKline Beecham*, Harvard Business School Press (Bauman, R. P., Jackson, P., Lawrence, J. T. 1997) pp. 51–55, copyright © Harvard Business School; Exhibit 15.2 adapted from *Goodwill Impairment in 2009* by Marc Castedello, 6 December 2009, http://www.kpmg.com/Global/en/Issues AndInsights/ArticlesPublications/Press-releases/ Pages/Press-release-Goodwill-impairment-12- Jun-09.aspx copyright © KPMG 2009; Exhibit 16.1 adapted from Equity issuance and adverse selection: A direct test using conditional stock offers, *Journal of Finance*, LII(1), pp. 197–219 (Houston, J. F. and Ryngaert, M. D. 1997), copyright © John Wiley &

Sons 1997; Exhibit 17.3 adapted from *Annual Report 2005/2006*, The Competition Commission (The Competition Commission) www.competition-commission.org.uk, Crown Copyright material is reproduced with permission under the terms of the Click-Use License; Exhibit 17.5 adapted from Press release 4 March 2009, http://ec.europa.eu/ competition/mergers/news.html, copyright © European Communities, 2009; Exhibit 17.6 adapted from Mergers: Commission refers proposed acquisition of Plus Discount by REWE to Czech Competition Authority, Press release IP/08/1102, 19 May 2008, http://ec.europa.eu/comm/competition/mergers/cases/ index/m102.html#m_5112, copyright © European Communities, 2008; Case Study 17 adapted from Review of merger decisions under the Enterprise Act 2002, *Report prepared for Competition Commission, Office of Fair Trading, and the Department for Business, Enterprise and Regulatory Reform* (Deloitte LLP), www.oft.gov.uk, Crown Copyright material is reproduced with permission under the terms of the Click-Use License; Exhibit 19.4 adapted from Investment banks as insiders and the market for corporate control, *The Review of Financial Studies*, Vol 22, pp. 4989–5026 (Bodnaruk, A., Massa, M., Simonov, A. 2009), Copyright © 2009 by the The Society for Financial Studies; Exhibit 19.5 adapted from Loan underpricing and the provision of merger advisory services, *Journal of Banking and Finance*, Vol 31, pp. 3539–3562 (Allen, L. and Peristiani, S. 2007), Copyright © 2007, Elsevier; Case Study 19 from Legal perils mount for M&A advisers, *Mergers & Acquisitions*, November pp. 37–41 (2005), SourceMedia, Inc., copyright © SourceMedia, Inc.; Exhibit 21.1 adapted from What's in it for me? CEOs Whose Firms are Acquired, *Review of Financial Studies*, Vol 17 (1), pp. 37–61 (Hartzell, J. C., Ofek, E. and Yarmack, D. 2004), Copyright © 2004 by the The Society for Financial Studies; Exhibit 21.6 adapted from *Mergers and Takeovers in the US and UK*, Oxford University Press (Kenyon-Slade, S. 2004) pp. 343–344, By permission of Oxford University Press; Exhibit 22.4 adapted from *From Promise to Performance: A Journey of Transformation at SmithKline Beecham*, Harvard Business School Publishing (Bauman, R., Jackson, P. and Lawrence, J. 1997) Chapters 7 and 8, copyright © Harvard Business School; Exhibit 22.10 adapted from The fine art of tech mergers, *Business Week*, July 10 (Hamm, S. 2006); Exhibit 23.1 adapted from

Reducing causal ambiguity in acquisition integration: Intermediate goals as mediators of integration decisions and acquisition performance, *Academy of Management Journal*, 51(4), pp. 744–767 (Cording, M., Christmann, P. and King, D. 2008), copyright © American Accounting Association, permission conveyed through Copyright Clearance Centre; Exhibit 23.2 based on 'A learning perspective on sociocultural integration in cross-national mergers', *Mergers and Acquisitions: Managing Culture and Human Resources*, pp. 155–175 (Bjorkman, I., Tienari, J. and Vaara, E. 2005), Stahl, G. and Mendenhall, M. (eds.) Stanford University Press; Exhibit 23.3 adapted from The intersection of organizational identity, knowledge and practice: Attempting strategic change via knowledge grafting, *Academy of Management Journal*, 50(4), pp. 821–847 (Nag, R., Corley, K. and Gioia, D. 2007), copyright © American Accounting Association, permission conveyed through Copyright Clearance Centre.

The *Financial Times*

Exhibit 3.1 adapted from Breuer's bet, *Financial Times*, 8 March 2000 (Barber, A.); Exhibit 3.2 adapted from NCS could be transforming purchase for Pearson, *Financial Times*, 1 August 2000 (O'Conner, A.); Exhibit 3.4 adapted from Bankers land a fortune, *Financial Times*, 9 May 2000 (Pretzlik, C. and Lewis, W.); Exhibit 3.5 adapted from Six continents may return cash early, *Financial Times*, 22 October 2002 (Daneshkhu, S.); Exhibit 5.2 adapted from P&G gets to the root of the problem, *Financial Times*, 22 May 2001 (Edgecliffe-Johnson, A.); Exhibit 5.3 adapted from Arcelor steels itself for fame *Financial Times*, 3 January 2002 (Marsh, P.); Exhibit 5.3 adapted from Steelmakers seek help with consolidation, *Financial Times*, 6 December 2001 (Bowe, C.); Exhibit 5.4 adapted from Shake-up may be just what the doctors ordered, *Financial Times*, 23 February 2001 (Pilling, D.); Exhibit 5.5 adapted from Where science and Mammon collide, *Financial Times*, 21 March 2000 (Pilling, D.); Exhibit 6.1 adapted from A sharp sense of the limits to outsourcing, The art of manufacturing: Part 1, *Financial Times*, 31 July 01 (Marsh, P.); Exhibit 6.2 adapted from A sharp sense of the limits to outsourcing, The art of manufacturing: Part 1, *Financial Times*, 31 July 2001 (Marsh, P.); Exhibit 6.3 adapted from Germany unwrapped, *Financial Times*, 30 March 2001 (Major, T. and Willman, J.); Exhibit 8.1 adapted from Roche deal with Chugai is model for co-operation, *Financial Times*, 14 December 2001 (Nakamato, M.); Exhibit 8.2 adapted from Tapping potential across the border, *Financial Times*, 12 February 2002 (Marsh, P.); Figure 8.2 from Gavazzi holds his position in heat of battle, *Financial Times*, 15 January 2002 (Barker, T. and Kapner, F.); Exhibit 8.3 adapted from Deal puts Finmeccanica firmly on global radar, *Financial Times*, 14 May 2008 (Dinmore, G. and Pfeifer, S.); Exhibit 8.4 adapted from Champagne heirs target raiders, *Financial Times*, 27 July 2001; Exhibit 8.5 adapted from Gavazzi holds his position in heat of battle, *Financial Times*, 15 January 2002 (Barker, T. and Kapner, F.); Case Study chapter 9 adapted from Carmakers take two routes to global growth, *Financial Times*, 11 July 2000 (Burt, T.); Exhibit 9.2 adapted from Electric effect of alliances, *Financial Times*, 15 January 1998 (Lester, T.); Exhibit 9.3 adapted from A corporate marriage made to last, *Financial Times*, 15 July 1992 (Butler, S.); Exhibit 9.4 adapted from Concert sounded off key almost from opening bars, *Financial Times*, 16 October 2001 (Waters, R. and Roberts, D.); Exhibit 9.5 adapted from Powered by a ten-tonne thrust, *Financial Times*, 1 February 1989 (Betts, P. and Kaletsky, A.); Exhibit 10.8 adapted from Siemens lowers its stake in Infineon to under 50%, *Financial Times*, 6 December 2001 (Benoit, B.); Exhibit 11.5 adapted from Plum deals shine out amid misty future, European Private Equity supplement, *Financial Times*, 21 June 2002 (Campbell, K.); Exhibit 11.5 adapted from Searching for a way out, European Private Equity supplement, *Financial Times*, 21 June 2002 (Harney, A.); Exhibit 11.5 adapted from Pearson wins MergerMarket in £101m deal, *Financial Times*, 9 August 2006 (Edgecliffe-Johnson, A.); Exhibit 12.1 adapted from Godfathers get control, *Financial Times*, 11 March 1992 (Baxter, A. and Bolger, A.); Exhibit 12.2 adapted from Boston Scientific executives win bonuses deal, *Financial Times*, 14 May 2006 (Bowe, C.); Exhibit 12.5 adapted from Fortis's woes lie with ABN Amro break-up, *Financial Times*, 29 September 2008 (Larsen, P.); Exhibit 13.3 adapted from RBS discovers the true cost of the ABN AMRO deal, *Financial Times*, 23 April 2008 (Larsen, P.); Exhibit 14.4 adapted from Pensions warning to ICI bidder, *Financial Times*, 18 June 2007 (Davoudi, S. and Burgess, K.); Exhibit 15.3 adapted from Media chiefs forced into a balancing act, *Financial Times*, 10 May 2002 (Waters, R.); Exhibit 16.4 from Reality check for Endemol lenders, *Financial Times*, 10 May 2008 (Edgcliffe-Johnson, A. and Sakoui, A.); Exhibit 16.5 from Torex expands into healthcare with acquisition, 23 November 2001 (Wendlandt, A.); Exhibit 19.1 adapted from Turning the tables on rivals, *Financial Times*, 18 February 2000 (Lewis, W.); Exhibit 20.1 adapted from Astellas drops hostile bid for CV Therapeutics, *FT.com*, 16 March 2009 (MacIntosh, J.); Exhibit 20.2 adapted from Standard Life could gatecrash merger, *Financial Times*, 20 September 2007 (Hughes, J. and Burgess, K.); Exhibit 20.3 adapted from Isoft takeover hits hurdle, *Financial Times*, 29 May 2007 (Fry, E.); Exhibit 20.4 adapted from GdF Suez merger overcomes two years of political roadblocks and diversions, *Financial Times*, 17 July 2008 (Hollinger, P.); Exhibit 20.6 adapted from Lawsuit ruins merger celebration, *Financial Times*, 2 July 2004 (Wighton, D.); Exhibit 20.7 adapted from Smith & Nephew's management premium in jeopardy, *Financial Times*, 2 May 2008 (Hughes, C.); Exhibit 20.10 adapted from Microsoft to target Yahoo investors, *FT.com*, 11 February 2008 (Nuttall, C. and Waters, R.); Exhibit 21.4 adapted from Two new investors buy into Air Berlin, *FT.com*, 29 March 2009 (Wiesman, G. and Done, K.); Exhibit 22.2 adapted from A good merger is all in the mind, *Financial Times*, 15 March 2006 (Maitland, A.); Exhibit 22.3 adapted from Bart Becht is strong on values, *Financial Times*, 16 March 2000 (Urry, M.); Exhibit 22.5 adapted from Ferrero departure casts doubt on merger, *Financial Times*, 16 December 2003 (Pretzlik, C.); Exhibit 22.7 adapted from A cultural shift in the gas works, *Financial Times*, 6 September 2006 (Milne, R.); Exhibit 22.8 adapted from Pioneer in need of protection, *Financial Times*, 29 January 2007 (Davoudi, S.).

In some instances we have been unable to trace the owners of copyright material, and we would appreciate any information that would enable us to do so.

CHAPTER 1

Introduction

Mergers and acquisitions, by which two companies are combined to achieve certain strategic and business objectives, are transactions of great significance, not only to the companies themselves but also to many other constituencies, such as workers, managers, competitors, communities and the economy. Their success or failure has enormous consequences for shareholders and lenders as well as the above constituencies. Companies invest billions of dollars in making acquisitions. Mergers and acquisitions (M & A) have happened in history in the last 110 years or more in waves. In the 1990s wave the value of M & A deals in the US rose from a mere \$200bn in 1992 to \$1.75 trillions (where a trillion is equal to 10^{12}) in 1999 before the market crashed. Some of the largest deals in history were done during that period. America Online (AOL) acquired Time Warner (TW) for about \$165bn in early 2000. But two years later AOL had to write off nearly \$60bn of the acquisition cost in goodwill write-down and restructuring charges. Goodwill is one of the intangible assets a firm acquires when it buys another company. The merger wave in the new millennium peaked in 2007 at \$1.2 trillions.

Europe experienced a merger wave no less spectacular in its magnitude than that on the other side of the Atlantic. The value of M & A deals in Europe at the height of the merger boom in 1999 was nearly \$1.5 trillions. The largest acquisition in European corporate history was the UK mobile telephone company Vodafone's hostile acquisition of the German telecom company Mannesmann in 1999 for over \$150bn. The new millennium witnessed a stupendous wave in the European Union, peaking in 2007 at \$1.2 trillions and matching the US wave of the same period.

Two years after acquiring Mannesmann, Vodafone wrote off several billion dollars to take account of impaired goodwill. There were several multi-billion dollar deals during the 1990s boom. With the meltdown in the M & A market and the stock market crash in 2000–2001, acquirers in many of these deals suffered enormous losses. Shareholders of these acquirers have suffered stupendous losses, not only from the stock market crash but also from the precipitous fall in the value of these acquisitions. The stock market crash of 2008 is also likely to have wiped off billions of dollars of value from the deals made before the crash.

Shareholders may lose their investment because of the imprudent acquisitions made by their companies. Acquiring companies are often motivated by the need to make efficiency savings in production and other activities. These are often achieved at considerable cost to workers, in the form of job losses, and to communities, in the form of terminated economic activity that plants and factories being shut down represent.

Do mergers and acquisitions add or destroy shareholder value?

Shareholder wealth gains are usually measured by abnormal returns, i.e. returns in excess of an appropriate benchmark return. An extensive review of the value-creating performance of acquisitions reported in numerous studies from the US, the UK and continental European countries provides clear evidence that shareholders of acquirers experience wealth losses on average or, at best, break even. On the other hand, shareholders of target companies are better off, with abnormal returns in the order of 20% to over 43%. The poor wealth experience of acquirers is common to many countries. In many of the studies there is a sharp deterioration in acquirer performance several years after deal completion.

Evidence from management surveys, reviewed in Chapter 22, confirms the view from the large-sample statistical studies that a high proportion, if not the majority, of acquisitions fail to deliver their objectives. Mergers and acquisitions more often destroy, rather than enhance, value for the acquirer shareholders. The odds of positive and significant value creation for acquirer shareholders may even be less than 50%, which is what one would get with the toss of a fair coin. Thus M & A transactions are high-risk corporate transactions. The cost of failure is egregious when one considers the value of M & A transactions, especially during merger waves, as noted above.

However, one striking aspect of the post-acquisition performance is that there is some variation in acquirer and target shareholder wealth performance across merger types. In the US, tender offers, i.e. offers to buy shares made directly to the target company shareholders, often without the support of the target management, generate more wealth for the acquirer shareholders than mergers made with management support. In the UK, hostile acquisitions generate larger wealth gains than friendly mergers. Relatively small acquisitions create more value than large acquisitions. These patterns suggest that certain types of acquisitions are more successful than others, and the transactional characteristics of an acquisition influence the performance outcome.

The more detailed literature review in Chapter 16 on payment currencies in acquisitions provides further evidence that deal structure makes a difference to value creation. Cash-financed acquisitions create more value than stock-for-stock acquisitions. Thus choice of deal type or payment currency has a significant effect on wealth outcomes for shareholders. This points to the risk attached to inappropriate deal structures, and the need for acquirers to choose the deal structure very carefully.

Can we identify the sources of failure?

The evidence presented above paints a rather unflattering picture of acquisitions, and raises important questions about the reasons for acquisition failure. To answer these questions we need a good understanding of the M & A process and its various stages. We need to understand the interconnectedness of these stages, and how weaknesses in prosecuting one stage can feed into the subsequent stages and erode the chances of overall success. We need to understand the motivations of different players, their expectations and their payoffs to determine their influence on the outcome of acquisitions. We need to understand not only the economic and strategic logic of acquisitions but also the organizational context of their conception and implementation. Above all, we need to avoid fragmented perspectives on different stages of M & A that regard each stage as the sole determinant of success or failure. There is often a 'disconnect' between the different stages of the M & A process, and managers 'lose the plot' about what the merger is about and how it is to be executed. We need an understanding of the economic and regulatory environment, and the process and systems in merging organizations, to define the limits of success. Such an understanding stems from systematic organizational learning built into the acquisition process.

Mergers, acquisitions, takeovers and buyouts

The terms 'merger', 'acquisition', 'buyout' and 'takeover' are all part of the mergers and acquisitions parlance. In a merger, the corporations come together to combine and share their resources to achieve common objectives. The shareholders of the combining firms often remain as joint owners of the combined entity. An acquisition resembles more of an arm's-length deal, with one firm purchasing the assets or shares of another, and with the acquired firm's shareholders ceasing to be owners of that firm. In a merger a new entity may be formed subsuming the merging firms, whereas in an acquisition the acquired firm becomes the subsidiary of the acquirer. A buyout is acquisition of a company or one of its component businesses, and generally implies that the acquirer is a group of investors, including specialist private equity firms and managers of the business being bought.

A 'takeover' is similar to an acquisition, and also implies that the acquirer is much larger than the acquired. Where the acquired firm is larger than the acquirer, the acquisition is referred to as a 'reverse takeover'. Although the terms 'merger' and 'acquisition' are often used interchangeably, they have precise connotations in certain contexts, such as when acquirers choose which accounting rules to apply in consolidating the accounts of the two firms involved. While the distinction is important for specific contexts, we shall, in general, use the terms interchangeably. We provide precise definitions of these different types of M & A in later chapters.

The five-stage (5-S) model

We divide the M & A process into five stages:

- corporate strategy development;
- organizing for acquisitions;
- deal structuring and negotiation;
- post-acquisition integration; and
- post-acquisition audit and organizational learning.

This model is shown in Figure 1.1. In this chapter we outline the important aspects of each of these stages and their links. The rest of the book is devoted to elaborating on these aspects.

Stage 1: How good is the corporate strategy development process?

M & A is a means to an end, and is an instrument for achieving the objectives of corporate and business strategies. Business strategy is concerned with ways of achieving, maintaining or enhancing competitive advantage in product markets. Corporate strategy is concerned with ways of optimizing the portfolio of businesses that a firm currently owns, and with how this portfolio can be changed to serve the interests of the corporation's stakeholders. M & A can serve the objectives of both corporate and business strategies, but M & A is only one of several instruments. The effectiveness of M & A in achieving these objectives depends on the conceptual and empirical validity of the models upon which corporate strategy is based. Given an

<table>
<tr><td>

Figure 1.1   Five stages of the M & A process
</td></tr>
</table>

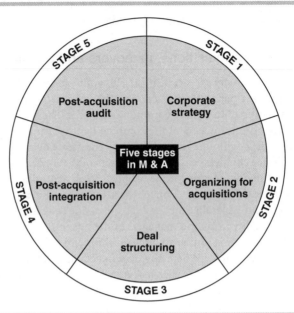

inappropriate corporate strategy model, M & A is likely to fail to serve the interests of the stakeholders, e.g. unrelated diversification for which the company brings no parenting advantage or the overhyped business to consumer (B2C) model of the dotcom era. With an unsustainable business strategy model M & A is likely to fail to deliver sustainable competitive advantage, e.g. a strategy that seeks easily replicable sources of competitive advantage.

Corporate strategy analysis has evolved in recent years through several paradigms – industry structure-driven strategy, competition among strategic groups, competence or resource-based competition, etc. Under the industrial organization model of competition firms choose cost leadership or product differentiation within narrow segments or broad segments (the range of focus), but in general they respond to Porter's five forces – current rivalry, threat of entry of new competitors, threat of substitutes, buyer power, and seller power[1]. Under this model, firms make acquisitions to gain market power, gain economies of scale and scope or internalize vertically linked operations to save on the cost of dealing with markets, thus adding further cost savings.

In recent years the resource-based view of competition has gained ground. The resource-based view is a conceptual framework for understanding firm-level growth, using resources as the basic building blocks. These resources may be financial, human, intangible, physical, organizational or technological. How a firm's management conceptualizes its resource base will define its strategy for growth. Competitive advantage is now regarded as deriving from unique and idiosyncratic organizational resources and capabilities rather than from industry and market factors. Sustainable competitive advantage grows out of those valuable, rent-generating capabilities that cannot be easily imitated or substituted. Some members of an organization may be unaware which resources give it its unique competitive advantage. The resources and capabilities that give a firm its distinct competitive advantage are also known as its core competences, postulated by Prahalad and Hamel as the source of sustainable competitive advantage[2]. These are embedded within organizational routines and cultures, i.e. 'our way of doing things', and remain tacit.

Acquisitions may be interpreted within the resource-based model as a search for partners with complementary resources and capabilities, which can be leveraged with those of the acquirer to the enhanced competitive advantage of both firms. This model can also explain different types of acquisitions – related and unrelated or conglomerate. The resource-based view of acquisitions raises important issues that may define the riskiness of those acquisitions. The acquiring firm may not be aware what its resources and capabilities are. It will be even less aware of the resources and capabilities of its intended merger partner. There will be further uncertainty about how complementary these capabilities are. Thus corporate strategy based on exploitation of resources, and acquisition strategy based on exploiting complementary resources, may run the risk of being based on incomplete knowledge. Traditional due diligence is unlikely to provide a reliable audit of the two firms' resources and capabilities and how they can leverage one another.

The tacit nature of resources and capabilities also means that it is difficult to quantify and value the benefits of the competitive advantage that they confer. Thus valuation may be seriously flawed. Post-acquisition integration of the complementary resources and capabilities is also a difficult exercise, since the related knowledge is tacit and embedded within the organizations. This difficulty raises the risk of integration failure. Acquirers can easily destroy the value of the acquired firm by attempting to gain non-existent synergies. Moreover, acquiring firms should pay at least as much attention to issues of cultural fit and organization dynamics during the pre-merger search and due diligence process as they do to issues of strategic fit and deal structuring.

Our review of acquisition performance in Chapter 4 also provides some evidence that post-acquisition operating performance, stockholder value creation and even the capacity for innovation are less likely in unrelated mergers than in related ones. Growth by unrelated acquisitions has resulted in the conglomerate firms being valued at a discount ('the conglomerate discount') to the sum of the values of the individual businesses. 'Unrelated diversification is a bad idea from the point of view of the bidding firm's shareholders in the 1980s'[3]. In this view, poor acquisitions are a manifestation of an agency problem in the acquirers, which is lacking in effective corporate governance. Thus poor acquisitions may be a consequence of, or aggravated by, governance failure.

Stage 2: How well does the company organize for acquisitions?

One of the major reasons for the observed failure of many acquisitions may be that firms lack the organizational resources and capabilities for making acquisitions. It is also likely that the acquisition decision-making processes within firms are far from the models of economic rationality that one may assume. Thus a precondition for a successful acquisition is that the firm organizes itself for effective acquisition-making. An understanding of the acquisition decision process is important, since it has a bearing on the quality of the acquisition decision and its value creation logic. Success of post-acquisition integration is determined at least partly by the thoroughness, clarity and forethought with which the value creation logic is blueprinted at the acquisition decision stage. Under certain circumstances the deficiency of the decision process can diminish the chance of a successful acquisition. Directors of companies who owe a fiduciary to their companies and/or their shareholders must remain vigilant against the behavioural biases of CEOs that cause them to overvalue acquisitions and under-estimate their risk.

Not all firms regard the M & A function as a separate function distinct from corporate development or corporate strategy. In some firms, however, separate M & A functions exist to provide an internal capability to undertake acquisitions on behalf of the firm as a whole or on behalf of business units that lack such a capability. A framework is developed in Chapter 12 for effective organization of the M & A function within acquisition-active firms. The aim of this framework is to develop the acquisition function as an important organizational capability and as a core competence of the firm. The various components of the acquisition function are described. Such a function serves as a repository of the firm's M & A-related skills, knowledge and capabilities. It also serves as a gatekeeper for ideas for M & A generated by the different parts of the firm and by external advisers. In the context of specific acquisitions, the acqui-sition function provides the strategic direction, organizes the resources for teams responsible for deal making, directs those teams, and ensures that deal-making leads to acquisitions that deliver the firm's strategic objectives and shareholder value. The salient characteristics of such an organization for acquisition are described and the obstacles to its creation highlighted. At this stage the firm lays down the criteria for potential targets of acquisitions consistent with the strategic objectives and value creation logic of the firm's corporate strategy and business model. We present a template for target selection in Chapter 13.

Stage 3: What are the pitfalls in deal structuring and negotiation?

This stage consists of:

- valuing target companies, taking into account how the acquirer plans to leverage its own assets with those of the target;
- choice of advisers to the deal, such as investment bankers, lawyers, accountants, and environ-mental consultants;
- obtaining and evaluating as much intelligence as possible about the target from the target as well as from other sources;
- performing due diligence;
- determining the range of negotiation parameters, including the 'walk-away' price, negotiat-ing warranties and indemnities;
- negotiating the positions of senior management of both firms in the post-merger dispensation;
- developing the appropriate bid and defence strategies and tactics within the parameters set by the relevant regulatory regime, etc.

The choice of advisers must be guided by the scope for conflicts of interests. Compensation contracts for advisers such as investment banks need to be drawn up, taking such conflicts into account, although custom and practice may influence the content of these contracts. Evidence shows that incentive contracts for investment banks may be perverse from the bidder's point of view. Whether investment banks add value to deals, and how their expertise and reputation influence takeover bid outcomes and shareholder wealth, are important questions for cor-porate deal-makers.

Negotiations are conducted in an atmosphere where the bidder and the target may have private information that the other party does not have. Each can use this information advan-tage to gain favorable terms during negotiation. Effective techniques developed for nego-tiations under such circumstances must be followed to avoid buying 'a lemon'. The negotiation team must be trained and experienced in these techniques. It must have the right balance among various relevant functions, top management and line management. It must operate with clear guidelines and well-defined limits so that overpayment is avoided.

The due diligence process is unlikely to provide a comprehensive view of the target firm, so the limits of due diligence must be borne in mind in assessing the information imbalance between buyer and seller. Traditionally, due diligence carried out by accountants and lawyers focused on accounting, tax, contractual liability issues, etc. However, in recent years the need to extend the scope of due diligence has become widely recognized. Due diligence is no longer just concerned with reducing risk. It should also contribute to effective management of the acquisition and the leveraging of the acquirer and acquired firms' resources and capabilities so that the goals of the acquisition can be realized.

In order to be useful in valuing and negotiating deals, and in effectively integrating and managing the acquired businesses, due diligence needs to cover the following aspects of the target company:

- commercial, e.g. competitive position, customer relations, patents;
- operational, e.g. production technology, processes and systems;
- financial and tax, e.g. historical accounting information, potential tax liabilities;
- legal, e.g. onerous contracts, product or environmental liabilities;
- human resource, e.g. compensation, training, employee relations;
- organizational, e.g. structure, management style, power distribution;
- information systems, e.g. performance, cost, complexity, compatibility.

Due diligence teams must therefore draw upon a wide range of competences, both from within the acquirer and from external sources. Coordinating a team of such diverse specialists is itself a demanding and specialized function. The coordinator contributes to the setting up of the due diligence team and to its functioning by identifying the areas that need focusing and by keeping the team to a more rounded and holistic, rather than a functional, view of the acquisition. While mapping the areas that due diligence should focus on is relatively simple, gaining access to the required information is a formidable challenge.

In hostile deals, and in deals with companies listed on the stock market, due diligence is likely to be deficient. Due diligence may also be inadequate in assessing the intangible assets of the target firm. Where the strategic logic is driven by such intangibles, and value realization depends on the ability of the firms to leverage their intangible resources and capabilities, due diligence may be particularly weak. Absence of intelligence about the target should not induce complacency or encourage excessive optimism and overpayment in the hope of some mythical real options that may not exist. The sorry tale of the dotcom and telecom boom of the late 1990s provides a salutary reminder of the scope for such exuberant follies. Intangibles depend on people, teams and organizational networks. Thus due diligence needs to include a human resource component.

We have noted that payment currency and type of acquisition – merger or tender offer, or hostile or friendly – have significant consequences for shareholders. The tendency to be over-generous with stock for stock offers, driven by current high stock valuation during a market boom, has to be checked, and stock exchange ratios must be determined by realistic expectations of future growth as well as by stock market conditions. The huge write-offs of goodwill by companies such as Vodafone, AOL and Vivendi, following their late 1990s acquisitions, are very good examples of companies being over-generous with their stock, believing that because the acquisition was carried out through the use of shares the company had not incurred any cost or value erosion. Risk of inappropriate payment currency or excessive acquisition premium must be mitigated by a careful justification based on realistic expectations. There needs to be a mechanism to provide this 'reality check'.

Stage 4: Don't count the chickens yet! Post-acquisition integration

At this very important stage the objective is to put in place a merged organization that can deliver the strategic and value expectations that drove the merger in the first place. Integration has the characteristics of a change management programme, but here three types of change may be involved:

- change of the target firm;
- change of the acquiring firm; and
- change in the attitude and behaviour of both to accommodate coexistence or fusion of the two organizations.

The integration process also has to be viewed as a project, and the firm must have the necessary project management capabilities and a programme with well-defined goals, teams, communication plans, deadlines, performance benchmarks, reward for meeting deadlines and benchmarks, and sanctions for failure, etc. Such a methodical process can unearth problems and provide solutions so that integration achieves the strategic and value creation goals. A company must discover a pattern of change that builds momentum and promotes the shared vision, confidence, leadership capacity and capabilities that will make the next change possible.

Merging firms' managers and employees may often be too distracted by the integration process to 'keep an eye on the ball', i.e. they may neglect to 'mind the store' and its customers, who then will turn to the firms' competitors – perhaps for good. The integration time is also a time of great uncertainty for the managers and the workforce. They may be lured away by the competitors. Thus the integration programme must assuage staff anxieties but also develop a key personnel retention policy. 'Executives from an acquired firm are an intrinsic component of the acquired firm's resource base and their retention is an important determinant of post-acquisition performance. There are strong economic motives for initiating acquisitions but there are also strong social processes at work that may seriously affect the outcomes'[4].

One of the major problem areas in post-merger integration is the integration of the merging firms' information systems (IS). This factor needs to be considered at the previous stages of the 5-S model. This is particularly important in mergers that seek to leverage each company's information on customers, markets or processes with that of the other company, as in a banking and insurance merger or in the merger of banks, e.g. the merger of the two largest Swiss banks, Union Bank of Switzerland and Swiss Bank Corporation. The compatibility of IS must be considered just as thoroughly as any strategic, operational, organizational or political issue. IS integration in M & A depends on a mix of both technical and organizational factors. Organizational culture compatibility must also be considered alongside IS synergies.

Acquisitive firms must also consider post-merger integrative capabilities as a core competence. 'GE Capital has been working to make acquisition a core capability'[5]. Development of such core competence requires the setting up of robust systems and processes for integration. It also requires systems and processes that allow the lessons from past integration exercises to be archived, diffused and internalized by the acquirer's organization. Each integration experience should not be lost in organizational amnesia so that history needs to repeat itself.

Stage 5: How did the merger go? Post-acquisition audit and organizational learning

This stage may often be neglected for several reasons:

- lack of organizational emphasis on learning;
- each deal considered so unique that past experience of mergers is deemed irrelevant;
- lack of centralized and ongoing function that is responsible for archiving the past and diffusion of learning;
- past learning not codified but resides in individuals' experience, with those individuals being co-opted into deal-making teams when necessary;
- individuals' past experience not systematically communicated but spread haphazardly through anecdotes and folklore within the organization;
- 'the trail gone cold' – difficult to trace the acquired or merged firm since it is now part of a larger strategic business unit or subsidiary, so lessons cannot be learnt.

The importance of organizational learning to the success of future acquisitions needs much greater recognition, given the high failure rate of acquisitions. Post-merger audit by internal auditors (IAs) can be acquisition specific as well as being part of an annual audit. IA has a significant role in ensuring organizational learning and its dissemination.

Objectives of the book

The various objectives of the book are as follows:

- To provide the reader with an overview of the subject of mergers and acquisitions.
- To provide a balanced treatment of M & A, drawing upon the conceptual, empirical and practitioner perspectives.
- To treat M & A as a *process*, rather than as a *transaction*, which requires insights from a number of disciplines to understand and carry out effectively.
- To describe the multi-stage character of M & A and underline the necessity for a holistic view of the process to appreciate the inter-stage links and develop effective value-creating M & A strategies.
- To provide a critical and empirical examination of the predictions and prescriptions from multiple perspectives on M & A.
- To identify the *challenges* to value realization through M & A as an instrument of corporate strategy.
- To signpost risks and potential problems and help improve the odds of successful M & A.

Outline of the book

The book is divided into four parts. **Part One** provides a historic overview of merger waves, five different but complementary perspectives on mergers, and an assessment of mergers based on numerous empirical studies from different countries. Chapter 2 traces the merger waves in the US, the UK and Europe. Chapter 3 sets out the different conceptual perspectives on M & A, providing the framework for the analysis of different M & A types in the rest of the book. These perspectives represent the economic, strategic, finance theory, managerial and organizational perspectives. Chapter 4 assesses the empirical evidence for the success or failure of mergers from the perspectives of different stakeholders.

Part Two deals with Stages 1 and 2 of the five-stages model. It provides a framework for examining the rationale for different types of mergers and acquisitions driven by different corporate and business strategies, their value creation potential, empirical evidence on such value creation, and the obstacles to value creation. Part 2 draws on the perspectives set out in Chapter 3 and adds to the overall empirical evidence on M & A by examining the empirical evidence relating to different M & A types.

The different merger types discussed in Chapters 5 to 8 include horizontal and related mergers, vertically integrating mergers, conglomerate mergers and cross-border mergers. Chapter 9 presents strategic alliances as alternatives to mergers, and sets out the conditions under which they are preferable to mergers. Corporate divestitures involve buying and selling of businesses as a way of increasing corporate business focus. These are analyzed in Chapter 10. Other forms of corporate-refocusing transactions are also discussed by way of comparison with divestitures. Chapter 11 traces the evolution of leveraged buyouts (LBOs) as an alternative to traditional strategic acquisitions by corporations, and contrasts the sources of value in strategic acquisitions and LBOs. Chapter 12 discusses the acquisition decision-making process within acquiring companies, and how this process may affect the success of the acquisition. It provides a psychological and governance perspective on the acquisition decision process. It identifies the obstacles to firms organizing themselves effectively for successful acquisition. Chapter 13 sets out a framework for target selection based on the acquisition strategy and the desirable characteristics of target firms.

Part Three deals with Stage 3 of the 5-S model and is concerned with deal structuring and negotiation in Chapters 14 to 21. Chapter 14 provides a framework for valuing target companies in acquisitions. Accounting rules for business combinations are set out in Chapter 15. How acquisitions are paid for, and the factors influencing the choice of payment currency, are examined in Chapter 16. Antitrust regulation and takeover regulation and their implications for deal structuring and conduct of takeover bids are discussed in Chapters 17 and 18 respectively. The roles of different advisers in M & A transactions, and potential conflicts of interest between acquirers/targets and these advisers, are highlighted in Chapter 19. Chapters 20 and 21 describe the various bid strategies and takeover defence strategies to fend off hostile takeover bids.

Part Four is concerned with Stages 4 and 5 of the 5-S model. Chapter 22 deals with the organizational and human aspects of acquisitions, the organizational challenge of change management, and the challenges to effective post-acquisition integration. It provides survey evidence on these issues and identifies critical success factors. Chapter 23 emphasizes the need for performance audit and organizational learning. It identifies several impediments to learning, and suggests how these may be overcome. Chapter 24 summarizes the main themes of the book, identifies the challenges to successful M & A, and provides guidance to increase the odds of success.

Because of the increasing importance of M & A in individual countries, in regions and across countries, the book deals with the above issues from an international perspective. We seek to provide comparative analysis of the various issues in M & A in the US, continental Europe and the UK. Discussion of cross-border acquisitions enhances this international perspective. Each chapter contains numerous short illustrations to exemplify practice or to elucidate complex issues. An overview of each chapter and the implications for M & A practice are presented at the end of each chapter. Short cases are included in chapters to highlight the main issues covered by that chapter, and to facilitate class discussion. Review questions are also provided for further class discussion. Throughout, the emphasis is on enunciating the ideas, concepts and principles that underlie M & A and on making them relevant to both scholars and practitioners.

The book is accompanied by a website that provides additional learning material for students. It also includes additional teaching materials and aids to instructors using this book for their teaching. PowerPoint® slides and answers to review questions are included. Links to more extended case studies are provided, with suggestions as to how they can be best used to highlight the issues raised in different chapters.

Notes and references

1. M. Porter, *Competitive Advantage* (New York: Free Press, 1985), Chapter 7.
2. C. K. Prahalad and G. Hamel, 'The core competence of the corporation', *Harvard Business Review*, May/June 1990, 79–91.
3. A. Shleifer and R. W. Vishny, 'Takeovers in the '60s and the '80s: Evidence and implications', *Strategic Management Journal*, **12**, 1991, 51–59.
4. A. A. Canella Jr and D. C. Hambrick, 'Effects of executive departures on the performance of acquired firms', *Strategic Management Journal*, **14**, Special Issue 1993, 137–152.
5. R. N. Ashkenas, L. J. DeMonaco and S. C. Francis, 'How GE integrates its acquisitions', *Harvard Business Review*, 1998, 165–178.

PART ①

Historic, conceptual and performance overview of mergers and acquisitions

As Chapter 1 argues, the mergers and acquisitions process needs to be viewed as a multi-stage process with each stage giving rise to distinct problems and challenges to companies undertaking such transactions. To understand the nature and sources of these problems we need a good understanding of the external context in which M & A take place. This context is not purely economic but includes political, sociological and technological contexts as well. The context is also ever-changing. Thus M & A could be regarded as a dynamic response to these changes. We need an understanding of the historical evolution of M & A and what factors have influenced the level and character of M & A activity in different time periods. In Chapter 2 we attempt a historical sweep of M & A activity over the past 120 years, and cover both the US and Europe.

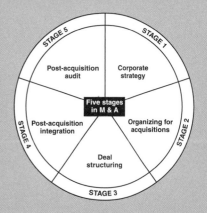

Our five-stage model conceptualizes the M & A process as being driven by a variety of impulses, not all of them reducible to rational economic paradigms. Both economic and non-economic factors affect the M & A process. We need an understanding of the M & A process informed by insights drawn from a broad range of disciplines and intellectual constructs. Without this underpinning we shall be unable to identify, let alone resolve, the problems associated with M & A. We provide a broad overview of five different conceptual frameworks that can elucidate the M & A process in Chapter 3.

Before embarking upon a detailed analysis of the M & A process and its putative challenges, we have to establish whether there is any credible evidence of performance failure. Since, as we shall describe in later chapters, there is a range of stakeholders in the M & A process, we need an understanding of what failure means and how it is measured.

This means that success of M & A can be assessed using a variety of perspectives and models. In Chapter 4 we review the historical evidence of the success of mergers and acquisitions primarily from the shareholder value point of view, but also from a wider perspective.

When we complete this review – historical, conceptual and performance-based – we shall be ready to undertake the detailed analysis of the various stages of the M & A process that this book is concerned with.

CHAPTER 2

Historical overview of mergers and acquisitions activity

Objectives

At the end of this chapter, this reader should be able to understand:

- the nature of merger waves and the possible reasons for the waves;
- the occurrence of mergers in industry-specific clusters, and the reasons for such occurrence;
- rational economic and behavioural models of merger waves; and
- the implications of merger waves and industry clusters for corporate strategy through mergers and acquisitions.

Introduction

One of the striking aspects of mergers and acquisitions as a phenomenon is that they occur in bursts interspersed with relative inactivity. This pattern is called the wave pattern of mergers and has been observed in the US with perhaps the longest history of mergers for over 100 years, in the UK from the early 1960s and, more recently, in continental Europe. What triggers these waves and why they subside are not fully understood, although alternative theories of merger waves have been propounded and several possible contextual explanatory factors have been identified. Another, possibly related, aspect of the phenomenon of merger waves is that mergers often happen in industry clusters. Different industries undergo abnormally intense merger activity at different times. This pattern points to some industry-specific factors that may trigger the clusters.

In this chapter we first provide evidence of merger waves, and highlight the increasingly global nature of the waves of the 1980s, the 1990s and the more recent burst of mergers in the new millennium, drawing upon published analyses. We identify the characteristics of the time periods and examine whether they may have any causal links to the merger waves. We review recent studies that have put forward alternative theories of merger waves. These may be broadly divided into rational economic or neoclassical theories and behavioural theories. The neoclassical theories explain merger waves as being triggered by economic upheavals that cause differences in valuation of corporate assets and hence reallocation of these assets from low-valued to high-valued uses. Such upheavals may be due to technological innovations or social or demographic changes, political changes etc. The behavioural theories posit that merger waves occur during times of stock market misvaluation of corporations. Managers of both acquirers and the targets of those acquisitions take advantage of such misvaluation and opportunistically engage in acquisitions. These alternative perspectives have implications for the timing of merger waves, what kinds of firms would be bought or sold to whom, how the acquisitions are paid for, and the value gains to those firms that engage in mergers at different stages of a merger wave.

Merger waves at the macro level hide another pattern, namely, industry-level waves or clusters. Arguably it is the industry-level clusters that aggregate to form waves at the macro level. We therefore focus also on the industry clustering of mergers, and review the empirical studies that have demonstrated a causal link between industry-specific developments and these clusters. We illustrate the impact of some of the environmental and industry-specific influences on takeover activity in certain industries.

The waves and clusters imply that firms implement their growth strategies or refocusing strategies fairly close on the heels of one another. Some of the firms may be first movers while others may be 'me-too' runners. This sequence of strategic moves and countermoves may raise or lower the risk and the chances of success of those moves. We elaborate on this and other implications of merger waves and industry clustering. Whether a firm is the first mover or a me-too runner influences the competitive outcomes of the restructuring game and the value gains to shareholders. There are competitive advantages and costs to being a first mover.

We review the empirical evidence for the macro-level wave theories and the industry shock theories. We defer discussion of the empirical evidence on the relative value gains of first movers and me-too players to Chapter 4, where evidence on the performance of buyers and sellers in M & A deals is presented.

The wave pattern of takeovers in the US[1]

Several countries have experienced high levels of takeover activity followed by a slump over the past decades. The US has perhaps the longest history of substantial takeover activity, going back to the 1890s. Figure 2.1 shows the level of merger activity in terms of number of mergers from the 1890s to 1978. We can observe three distinct peaks in (1) 1899, (2) 1929 and (3) 1970. In terms of value of the mergers the last peak actually occurred in 1968 rather than 1970. The three waves are characterized respectively as

- merging for monopoly (1890–1905);
- merging for oligopoly (1920s);
- merging for growth (1960s).

The first wave

The first peak was reached in a period of economic expansion following a decade of economic stagnation. Industrial production grew by 100%. This wave involved an estimated 15% of all manufacturing assets and employees. An important characteristic of this merger wave was the simultaneous consolidation of producers within industries, thus qualifying for the description 'horizontal consolidation'. Many of the giants of the US corporate world, such as General Electric, Eastman Kodak, American Can, American Tobacco and DuPont, were formed during the first wave through such consolidation. Approximately 71 important oligopolistic or near-competitive industries were converted into near monopolies by merger. More than

---

| Figure 2.1 | First three US merger waves, 1890–1978 |

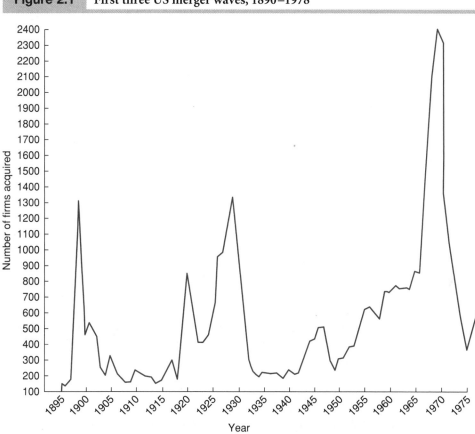

Year

Source: M. S. Salter and W. A. Weinhold, *Diversification Through Acquisitions* (New York: The Free Press, 1979)

1800 firms disappeared into consolidations. Of the 93 consolidations whose market shares could be traced, 72 controlled at least 40% market share and 42 controlled at least 70% of their industries. This massive restructuring of American industry remained intact for the next 50 years. For this reason, George Stigler described the first wave as merging for monopoly. Although the Sherman Act to control and prevent monopolies had come into effect in 1890, it had little immediate impact on the progress or ferocity of the first wave[2].

The second wave of the 1920s

This was a much smaller wave than the first in terms of its relative impact. In total it involved less than 10% of the economy's assets rather than the first wave's over 15%[3]. It followed the 1903–4 market crash and the First World War. During that fallow period, and following the enormous public concern over the huge increase in the monopoly power of big business that resulted from the first wave, stronger antitrust enforcement was effected. In 1911, in a land-mark judgement, the US Supreme Court ordered the break-up of Standard Oil, the Rockefeller empire formed during the first wave. Market monopolies were clearly established as illegal. Since the Sherman Act addressed only issues of substantial monopoly power, and generally did not apply to stock for stock mergers, the Clayton Act was passed in 1914 to 'arrest the creation of trusts, conspiracies and monopolies in their incipiency and before consummation'. (We discuss the antitrust regulations in more detail in Chapter 17.)

The second wave accompanied economic growth and stock market boom. An estimated 12,000 firms disappeared during this period. For several reasons, the impact on the market structure of industries was much less dramatic than during the first wave. In industries previously dominated by one giant firm, the mergers led to the formation of strong number two companies. In the manufacturing sector most mergers resulted in small market share increases for the merging firms, or in vertical integration. Thus the second wave represented a move towards oligopolistic structure in many industries. It collapsed in 1929 with the stock market crash of that year, and in the following four years of worldwide depression many of the utility-holding companies formed during the recent wave collapsed into bankruptcy.

The third wave of the 1960s

The end of the Second World War saw a steady increase in takeover activity until the middle of the 1960s, when it spurted to an explosive level. In 1950 Congress passed the Celler–Kefauver Amendments to the Clayton Act of 1914 to tighten up the antimerger regime, but by the mid-1950s the third wave was well under way. The third wave also surpassed in duration the two preceding waves, lasting until 1971 (see Figure 2.1). The mergers during the third wave were not large, and did not involve large acquirers. They were mostly unrelated mergers, aimed at achieving growth through diversification into new product markets. Whether this bias towards diversification was the result of the more stringent antitrust regime that precluded market power-increasing horizontal or vertical mergers remains a matter of inconclusive debate.

Among the Fortune 500 companies, the percentage of firms in the unrelated business category increased from about 4% in 1949 to about 9% in 1964 before reaching over 21% in 1974. In the related-business category during the same period the percentage of firms increased from under 26% to just over 42%. These dramatic increases contrasted with the declines over the same period in the percentage of single businesses (from 42% to 14%) and dominant businesses (from 15% to 10%)[4]. The third wave therefore resulted in a massive strategic shift in the business composition of US firms towards greater diversification. There was little impact on the market structure of individual industries, or on aggregate concentration by large firms[5]. Thus the third wave merits the description 'merging for growth'. Its end coincided with the great dislocation caused by the oil crisis induced by the Organization of Petroleum Exporting Countries (OPEC) in 1973 and the following inflationary spiral and economic slowdown.

Comparison of the three waves

The total numbers of mining and manufacturing acquisitions during the three waves were 2600 (1890–1905), 8000 (1920s) and 12,000 (1960s). In dollar (constant 1972 dollar) terms these acquisitions cost $6.4bn ($26bn), $12–15bn ($24–30bn) and $70bn ($69bn). Thus the 1960s wave was considerably bigger in value terms. On the other hand, in terms of assets acquired, as a percentage of total mining and manufacturing assets in the US, the 1890s wave was much more sweeping, with 15% of assets acquired compared with about 7–9% in the 1920s and 10% in the 1960s[6].

Gilson and Black identify four characteristics of the first three waves[7]:

● Relatively few mergers had market monopolization as their goal. The first wave increased the market power of merging firms, but this declined in the following two waves.

- All three occurred during sustained periods of economic prosperity and rapidly rising stock market levels, peaking almost with the stock market and then receding with the following economic recession.
- Many mergers were simply ordinary business transactions among entrepreneurs seeking to exit an industry profitably through a merger or through being acquired.
- Many mergers were accompanied or stimulated by massive changes in the economy's infrastructure, such as railroad building or the advent of electricity (see below for further discussion of the impact of these exogenous factors).

The fourth, fifth and sixth waves of the 1980s, 1990s and the new millennium

The late 1970s witnessed a small revival of takeover activity, but this did not last long, owing to the second oil crisis in 1979 and the deep recession of the early 1980s. It was in the middle of the 1980s that there was a fresh surge of takeover activity leading to the fourth merger wave in US history. This wave in fact consists of two waves: acquisitions (Figure 2.2a) and divestitures (see Figure 2.2b). To provide a comparison of the stock market levels during the merger waves the Standard and Poor's 500 index level is also shown. It is clear that merger waves seem to track the stock market level, either slightly leading or lagging the latter. We comment on this tracking below in the context of the merger wave theories.

The two types of corporate restructuring are very highly correlated, with a correlation coefficient of 0.93 (0.81) between number (value) of acquisitions and divestitures. Divestitures generally constitute about 21–129% of the acquisition activity during this period. The median is 63%. While divestitures in general rise and fall with acquisitions, in the years following the peak of the acquisition wave they tend to rise and stay high, for example in years 1989–92 and again in 2001–03. Thus many US corporations engage in simultaneous expansion and downsizing of their businesses, expanding those that offer scope for greater competitive advantage and exiting those in which their chances of gaining competitive advantage are limited, or their historic competitive advantage has been exhausted.

In contrast to the earlier periods, the period starting in the mid-1980s experienced an active market in corporate assets. Maksimovic and Phillips confirm this in their study of the plant level ownership changes through mergers and divestitures of partial and full segments by US corporations. Prior to 1984, asset divestitures represented a relatively flat percentage of plant reallocations, whereas after 1984 they rose and fell more in line with M & A[8]. Many US companies not only made numerous acquisitions but also sold off some of their component businesses in a move towards increasing the focus of their business portfolio and restricting it to what they deemed were core businesses in which they judged themselves to have a core competence and competitive advantage. In this sense, these firms were reversing many of the diversifying acquisitions they had made during the conglomerate wave of the 1960s. Shleifer and Vishny describe the initial conglomerate expansion and subsequent return to the core businesses as a 'round trip'[9]. The fourth wave subsided after 1989 by number (1988 by value) and the fifth wave enveloped the US economy from 1993 to 2000.

The fourth wave was characterized by a number of new developments on the M & A scene:

- The emergence of hostile tender offers.
- Predatory *bust-up* takeovers in which a 'predator' or 'raider' mounted a bid for a diversified underperforming firm and after the acquisition dismantled the portfolio by selling off the various parts of the acquired company[10].
- A high level of divestiture activity by diversified firms in pursuit of a strategy to focus on their core businesses.

Figure 2.2 | (a) US merger waves between 1985 and 2007; (b) US divestiture waves between 1985 and 2007

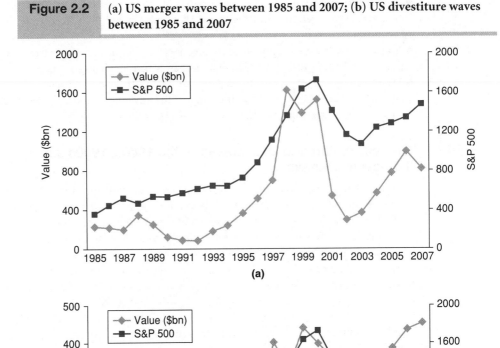

(a)

(b)

All deals completed and acquirers hold > 50% of targets share after deal; only deals with transaction value disclosed included; for acquisition deals either target or acquirer is a US firm. For divestitures, target is a US firm; deals categorized according to announcement year; deal value in 2007 US$. US Consumer Price Index – All Urban: All Items used to adjust for inflation.
Source: Thomson Reuters.

- A more benign antitrust regime towards related mergers than during the 1960s and 1970s. Many of the divestitures following bust-up takeovers were sold to related acquirers[11].
- The emergence of private equity firms encouraging and facilitating leveraged buyouts (LBOs), management buyouts (MBOs) and going-private (from public company status to private company status) deals that relied on heavy debt relative to equity and growth in the sub-investment grade debt instruments called junk bonds to finance LBOs.
- The average size of the acquisitions dwarfing the corresponding size of deals in the 1960s.

The 1990s wave

The fifth wave of the 1990s to some extent continued the theme of focus on core competences as the source of competitive advantage. As can be seen in Figure 2.2a, the fifth wave is the mother of all waves so far, assuming truly tsunamic proportions. At its height in 1998, the value of the M & A deals was $1.6 trillions compared with the previous peak of $343bn in 1988 (both in 2007 $). The value of divestitures in 1999 was $439bn compared with the previous peak of $199bn in 1988. Figure 2.2b shows that the 1990s divestitures were far more numerous than in the 1980s. In terms of value the 1990s peak does not dominate the 2007 peak[12].

The 1990s wave coincided with the re-emergence of the resource-based view of competitive strategy in the second half of the 1980s (see Chapter 3). Firms made acquisitions on the basis of the need to augment their resources and capabilities in order to enhance their competitive advantage. The 1990s saw the emergence of new technologies such as the Internet, cable television and satellite communication, which spawned new industries and firms with new technological capabilities. The fifth wave also was a period characterized by:

- shareholder value as a compelling imperative, and the emergence of shareholder activism with traditional institutional investors benchmarking corporate investment and financing decisions against shareholder value creation[13];
- globalization of product, services and capital markets;
- new supranational trading blocs such as the Single Market of the European Union, the North Atlantic Free Trade Association (NAFTA), which includes the US, Canada and Mexico, and creation of the World Trade Organization, which lowered barriers to trade and capital mobility and increased the opportunities for corporate growth;
- government policy changes in the area of healthcare, deregulation of industries such as banking and utilities, and privatization of public sector enterprises;
- government policy changes in antitrust enforcement and defence procurement;
- restructuring of mature industries such as automobiles, banking and food;
- the convergence of technologies in voice, video and data transmission, leading to blurred boundaries among industries selling goods and services based on these technologies;
- consolidation of fragmented industries by financial buyers and strategic buyers; and
- continuation of the move towards core businesses or specialization started in the 1980s[14].

Into the millennium

The great crash of the 1990s did not dampen the animal spirits of the takeover market for long. Soon takeover activity started its upward swing into a sixth wave that climaxed in 2007. This wave was much smaller than the 1990s wave but larger than the 1980s wave. The main drivers of this recent wave were the following:

- Private equity acquirers, who filled the void left by the strategic buyers, who had been bruised by the crash of the 1990s. This period, until 2007, saw a benevolent economic environment with enormous liquidity, low interest rates, and renewed incentives for leveraged buyouts (see Chapter 11 on private equity and leveraged buyouts).
- Hedge funds emerged as important players in the M & A market, often attacking firms making takeover bids and forcing them to drop their bids[15].
- They also, along with other traditional mutual funds, became active shareholders, often mounting highly publicized attacks on corporate managements for their failure to follow strategies that would enhance shareholder value, e.g. divestitures and share buybacks.

● Shareholder activism became a more important factor for corporate managements to consider in their acquisition and divestiture decisions.

An important development that might have a long-term impact on the level and nature of M & A deals was the passing of the Sarbanes-Oxley Act (SOX) in 2002 as a reaction to the scandals involving many acquisitive companies such as Worldcom, Tyco and Enron. The fraudulent and criminal shenanigans of the top managers of these companies, many of whom were convicted and imprisoned, gave rise to a strong legislative response in the form of SOX, which imposes more stringent corporate governance and disclosure rules on US-listed firms. It has increased the monitoring responsibilities of the board of directors, thereby seeking to constrain the excesses of deal-making during the dotcom bubble of the late 1990s. Whether boards will rise to the challenge and discharge their responsibilities effectively remains to be empirically verified.

Takeover activity in the European Union

The huge rise in takeover activity, including divestitures in the US during the 1980s and 1990s, was part of a global phenomenon, as evidenced by the experience of the European Union (EU) as a whole and, in particular, the UK, the second largest M & A market after the US. We survey the EU merger trends first, before focusing on the UK scene. The EU of 27 nation states of Europe is now the largest economic bloc in the world in terms of gross domestic product (GDP). In 2005 the GDP of the EU was over €11 trillion compared with over €10 trillion of the US[16].

The EU member countries have experienced increasing levels of takeover activity since 1984, as shown in Figure 2.3a. For the sake of continuity of comparison we provide data for all 27 member states, even though many of them were not members of the EU for the entire period, 1984–2007. To preserve comparison with the US merger waves, the value of deals is stated in 2007 US$. We can identify two waves, a small one during 1986–1992 and a vastly bigger one between 1996 and 2002. In the first wave the value of mergers rose from $50bn in 1986 to $147bn in 1989 before falling to $52bn in 1993. It then rose, in the second wave, to $1231bn in 1999 before a precipitous decline to just $237bn in 2002. Thus the two recent merger waves in the EU parallel those of the same period in the US. While the scale of the 1980s wave is much smaller than its US counterpart, the 1990s waves in the two regions are much closer in intensity.

In Figure 2.3a for comparison we show the European stock market level proxied by the *Financial Times Stock Exchange Western European Index* (FTSEWE) during 1984–2007. There is a striking parallel between the stock market movement and the merger waves in terms of value of deals. We return to this parallel in our discussion below of theories of merger waves.

Divestiture levels in the EU have shown much steadier growth in number, as shown in Figure 2.3b. The total value of divestitures increased from $4bn in 1985 to $115bn in 1990. After falling from this peak, they reached the next peak in 2000 at $401bn before falling off to $219bn in 2001. Divestitures as a proportion of mergers and acquisitions range from 2% (in 1984) to 208% (in 1993), but are about 30–70% in most years. The median is 65%. This level is not dissimilar to that in the US (63%). The correlation between number (value) of acquisitions and divestitures is 0.92 (0.86). Divestitures play a similar role in corporate restructuring in both the EU and the US. In the EU they are, however, increasingly more important for companies in restructuring their business portfolios than in the early 1980s, driven by a more

Figure 2.3   (a) EU merger waves, 1984–2007; (b) EU divestiture waves, 1984–2007

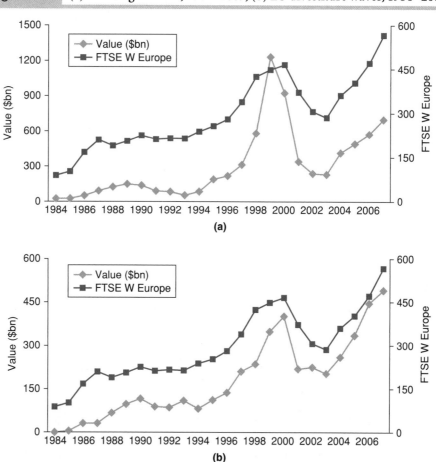

(a)

(b)

All deals completed and acquirers hold > 50% of target share after transaction; only deals with transaction value disclosed included; for acquisition deals either target or acquirer is a EU firm. For divestitures deals, the target is a EU firm; EU = 27 current members plus Switzerland; deals categorized according to announcement year; deal value in 2007 US$. US Consumer Price Index – All Urban: All Items used to adjust for inflation.
Source: Thomson Reuters.

pronounced emphasis on shareholder value and the more competitive markets promoted by the EU. These trends have forced firms in the EU to operate their businesses more efficiently.

In the new millennium there is strong revival of merger and divestment activity up to 2007. Indeed, divestments show a much stronger upward trend than acquisitions. In terms of deal value, whereas acquisition levels are still below the peak reached in 1999 (see Figure 2.3b), divestitures have hit a greater peak in 2007 at $490bn. This pattern mirrors the US pattern of divestitures (see Figure 2.2b). It points to the merger and divestment activity in these two regions as being part of a much larger global merger wave.

Analysis of the distribution of takeover activity in the EU further shows that during the 1990s purely domestic M & A, i.e. transactions involving two or more firms registered in the same member state, accounted for the bulk of the activity. As shown in Table 2.1, this proportion ranges from 65% in 1994 to 49% in 2007. Over the 17-year period there is a perceptible decline

Table 2.1 Evolution of national, community and international M & A transactions in the EU (% of all transactions including divestitures)

Year	National	Community	International EU target	International EU bidder	Total
1991	61.7	16.6	12.1	9.6	100
1992	63.6	14.7	13.3	8.4	100
1993	63.7	14.4	13.6	8.4	100
1994	65.3	11.9	12.6	10.2	100
1995	62.2	14.2	12.5	11.2	100
1996	61.6	13.8	12.8	11.7	100
1997	60.0	14.4	14.0	11.6	100
1998	59.2	13.0	14.9	12.9	100
1999	57.9	15.9	11.5	14.7	100
2000	54.9	18.9	10.1	16.2	100
2001	56.0	17.4	11.2	15.4	100
2002	59.3	16.4	12.3	12.0	100
2003	57.4	16.0	14.9	11.7	100
2004	55.6	15.4	16.0	13.1	100
2005	53.3	16.8	16.3	13.6	100
2006	52.6	17.2	15.2	14.9	100
2007	49.0	18.1	16.4	16.5	100

All deals completed and acquirers hold > 50% of target share after transaction; only deals with transaction value disclosed included; EU = 27 current members plus Switzerland; deals categorized according to announcement year; in national transactions, both target and acquirer are in same country; in Community transactions, target and acquirer are in different EU countries.
In international transactions, either target or acquirer is not in the EU.
Source: Evolution of national, community and international M&A transactions in the EU (% of all transactions including divestitures), Thomson Reuters, www.thomsonreuters.com.

in the proportion of national mergers, from about two-thirds to just under half of all M & A in the EU. Mergers of firms from different member states of the EU, the Community mergers, represent a more stable proportion, 12–19%. Similarly, non-EU international acquisitions of EU firms are also relatively stable, in the range 10–16%. By contrast, acquisitions of non-EU targets by EU firms increase from 8% in 1992 to 17% in 2007. International acquisitions including EU firms as either targets or as bidders grew from 22% in 1991 to nearly 33% in 2007.

The pattern of M & A activity suggests that, while takeover activity has increased within the EU, activity between the EU and the rest of the world has shown a more dramatic increase. This points to much greater globalization, but also to a more outward strategic thrust by EU firms. We discuss international and cross-border mergers and acquisitions in more detail in Chapter 9.

Main characteristics of the European merger waves

The late 1980s and the 1990s, which witnessed the two merger waves in the EU, were epochal and turbulent times in the history of the continent. This was a period of continual changes, with newer and ever more audacious (or foolhardy, according to Eurosceptics) initiatives being taken in the spheres of politics, economics and the social institutions to further European integration. Among them are the Single Market initiative, which came into effect in 1992, and the European Monetary Union project, which has ushered in monetary union among 12 out of 15 member states with the introduction of a single currency, the euro, from 1999. This was also the period when the Cold War ended, the Berlin Wall collapsed, and the countries of Central and Eastern Europe (CEE) started dismantling state control of their economies and adopting free markets and private enterprise with the enthusiasm and passion of the newly converted. This paved the way for integration of the CEE countries and the Baltic states into the EU. From 15 member states in 2002 the EU has now expanded to 27.

These historic events were also accompanied by the spread of deregulation and privatization by member states to improve the competitiveness of the EU economies, including the Central and East European member states. Although stock markets have traditionally been less important as a source of funding for non-UK EU firms than in the US, the stock markets experienced prolonged bull phases. In the 1990s, and in the recent years of the new millennium, technological changes in information technology, telecommunications and biotechnology provided new growth opportunities, which EU firms sought to exploit through mergers and acquisitions. Utility firms such as Deutsche Telecom, France Telecom and Vivendi, and French and Italian banks, recently privatized or part privatized, played an important role in creating the merger wave of the 1990s through domestic, intra-EU and extra-EU mergers and acquisitions.

A milestone in the history of European M & A was reached in 2004 when the EU Parliament approved the 13th Company Law Directive, which regulates takeovers in the EU. This takeover directive, implemented by member states in 2006, recognizes the rights of shareholders to determine the outcome of takeovers and, in particular, takeovers resisted by a target firm's incumbent management: that is, hostile takeovers. It lays down general principles and articles that would lower barriers to takeovers in the form of ownership structures that would impede hostile takeovers and the ability of incumbent managements to set up defences against such takeovers and pursue actions to frustrate them. The directive also provides for mandatory takeover bids triggered by an investor increasing its ownership above a critical threshold. This directive is indeed a momentous development, albeit born in the midst of controversy and, to a significant extent, compromised by various opt-out provisions. Its impact is yet to fully unfold (see Chapter 19 on takeover regulation in different countries).

In the 1990s companies such as Vivendi, originally a water and sewage utility in France, belied their history by taking to acquisitions, deal-making and diversification with breathtaking agility and panache. Financial services firms such as Deutsche Bank have dared to take on the Americans and barge their way into the bulge bracket of investment banks by acquiring targets such as Bankers Trust. Many EU firms, long accustomed to the comfort of their sheltered markets or state protection, were fearful of the winds of change, but others tasted the exhilaration of freedom borne by that wind[17]. These forays were not always very successful, and in some cases such as Vivendi brought the acquirers as well as their top managers to their knees. This experience has not deterred EU firms from exploiting the growth opportunities opened up by globalization and high economic growth around the world until 2007 (see Table 2.1 above).

Takeover activity in major EU member states

Traditionally, the UK has stood out among all the EU member countries in terms of the intensity of M & A activity and its exposure to international M & A. In the period 1991–2001 the UK accounted for 31.4% of the EU's M & A activity, although its share of the EU's GDP was only 13%. In contrast Germany (16% and 28% respectively), France (14% and 18%), Italy (6% and 13%), Spain (5% and 7%) had much smaller shares of M & A activity and less than their share of EU's GDP[18]. This dominance of the UK has continued in more recent years, as shown in Table 2.2, which reports the number and value of M & A deals involving a firm in the named country as target. Italy and Netherlands experienced mergers of some very large financial services firms, such as the US$88bn merger of Intesa and San Paolo in January 2007,

Table 2.2 M & A deals in 2006 and 2007 in major EU states plus Switzerland

Member state	2006		2007	
	Number	Value (US$bn)	Number	Value (US$bn)
UK	1247	269	1777	240
Netherlands	250	14	328	166
Italy	282	54	372	140
Germany	699	79	825	111
France	731	113	771	94
Spain	432	71	488	85
Switzerland	140	15	189	26
Sweden	271	28	404	22
Finland	127	6	143	15

Source: Mergers & Acquisitions, Table on M & A in major overseas markets outside the US, February 2008.

Unicredit's US$30bn acquisition of Capitalia in October 2007 in Italy, and the Dutch bank ABN-AMRO taken over by a consortium of European banks led by the Royal Bank of Scotland in a bitter hostile bid in 2007 for US$99bn, trumping a rival friendly bid by Barclays Bank. The ABN-AMRO deal accounts for the huge jump in deal value in the Netherlands between 2006 and 2007 in Table 2.2.

The UK also has a much longer history of merger transactions, and shares many similarities with the US in terms of governmental *laissez-faire* attitude to takeovers, importance of the stock market as a source of corporate finance, corporate governance and ownership structure. In the areas of privatization, takeover regulation and economic liberalization the UK has been a pacesetter. As Europe's prime centre for investment banking, the City of London plays a major role in influencing deal-making structures and in the financing of takeovers in Europe. For these reasons, we now focus on the historic M & A experience of the UK.

Historical overview of takeover activity in the UK

Active merger movement in the UK can be traced to the 1960s, although two mini merger booms happened in the 1890s and the 1920s[19]. Figure 2.4 presents the aggregate value of domestic takeovers and divestitures involving only UK companies from 1964 to 1992[20]. There are clearly peaks of takeover activity in 1968, 1972 and 1989 in terms of value. When allowance is made for the inflationary increase in company values, the peaks in those three years are unmistakable. There is a striking parallel in the incidence and timing of the 1960s and 1980s waves in the US and the UK.

The first, second and third waves

There was very little takeover activity between 1945 and the late 1950s in the UK, a period of post-war reconstruction. It then picked up and accelerated into a wave in the second half of the 1960s. After hitting a peak in 1968, the wave receded, only to surge again in the early 1970s to hit a second peak in 1972. The third merger wave was in the period 1984–89. The nominal value of the mergers in 1968 was £1.95bn. This increased to £2.5bn in 1972 and reached a dizzying £27bn in 1989. The average deal values at these peaks were £2m, £2m and £20.4m. The peaks of 1968 and 1972 were of a similar scale. However, the average deal value in 1989 was ten times the average size of a deal in 1968 or 1972, and the total value of acquisitions, at

Figure 2.4   UK merger waves during 1964–92

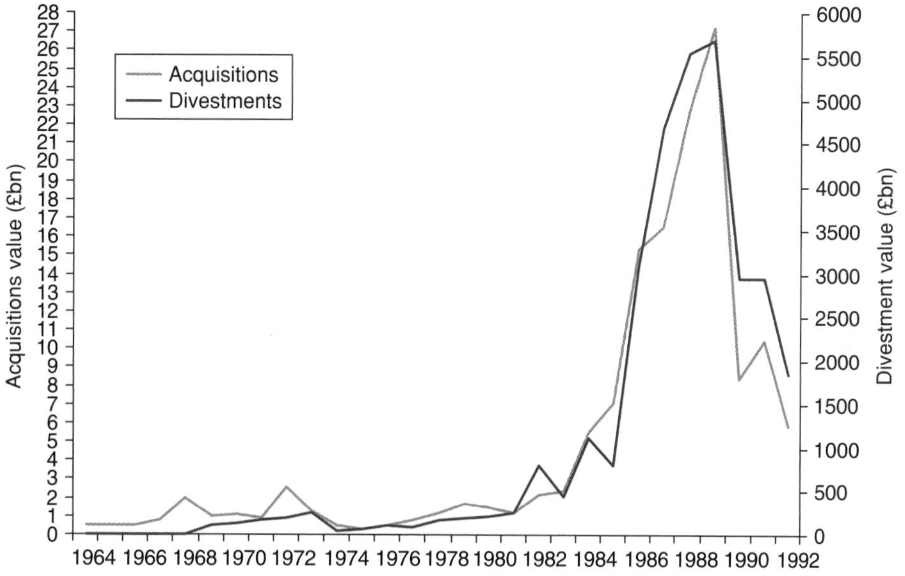

Source: Data from 'Acquisitions and mergers in the UK', *Central Statistical Office Bulletin*, London, May 1993

1990 prices, was twice the size of the earlier peaks. The second half of the 1980s thus represents a qualitatively different period from the earlier periods of high takeover activity.

Main characteristics of the first two UK merger waves

The first wave, peaking in 1968, was fuelled largely by horizontal mergers. This characteristic differentiates the UK wave from the US wave of the same period. The latter represented a shift from the monopolistic and oligopolistic mergers of the first two waves to conglomerate mergers. It was noted earlier that one of the possible reasons for this shift was a more rigorous enforcement of the antitrust rules following the Celler–Kefauver Act of 1950. The 1960s' wave in the UK is intriguing, since it followed closely the passing of the Monopolies and Mergers Act and the creation of the Monopolies and Mergers Commission (MMC) to enforce that Act in 1965. While the incipient nature of the antitrust regime might explain the unchecked incidence of horizontal mergers, there is an alternative reason for the paradox.

Under the Labour government of 1964 a new industrial policy was adopted to strengthen UK companies into 'national champions' that could take on competitors on world markets. The Industrial Reorganization Corporation (IRC) was the newly created instrument for bringing about this transformation. The IRC actively promoted and midwifed the merger of firms in the same lines of business[21]. The mergers sponsored by the IRC generally escaped antitrust scrutiny by the MMC[22]. Thus, during the first merger wave, the UK was 'hunting with the hounds and running with the hares', which may explain the paradox of a new antitrust regime accompanied by a massive horizontal merger boom. This shows how government industrial policy dictated merger activity in the past.

The second wave, which peaked in 1972, was also characterized by horizontal mergers but on a slightly smaller scale. There was also a greater incidence of conglomerate mergers. While horizontal mergers accounted for 89% of assets involved in mergers considered by the

Mergers Panel of the MMC during 1965–69, in the following wave, 1970–74, the corresponding figure was 65%. Diversifying mergers during the first wave accounted for 7% by value of the same merger sample, but they accounted for 27% during the second wave. Thus there is a perceptible shift towards diversifying mergers in the second wave[23]. The first merger wave may also have contributed to an increase in market concentration and aggregate concentration in the UK, although the relation between merger activity and market concentration is not empirically conclusive. Despite a large proportion of the second wave mergers being horizontal, their impact on merging firms' market power was very marginal[24].

Main characteristics of the 1980s wave

As noted earlier, this wave was of tidal proportions compared with the previous two. As in the US, this wave coincided with a stock market bull run from the recession of 1980–81 to the market crash in 1987. The merger boom did not screech to an immediate halt and, carried by momentum, peaked only in 1989. The 1980s wave enveloped massive restructuring not only in the manufacturing industries but also in the financial services sector.

The Big Bang deregulation of the financial services sector in the City of London heralded the arrival of US investment banks, which brought not only their huge capital-raising capabilities but also their investment banking expertise and techniques in the areas of mergers and acquisitions advisory work, corporate restructuring, risk management, securities trading and stockbroking. The impact of the Big Bang on the old City of London firms was little short of cataclysmic, with most of the British merchant banks, brokerage houses and securities firms being systematically swallowed up, initially by American and subsequently by continental European companies[25]. The City of London ('the City'), offering an immensely attractive venue for foreign banks to display their investment banking prowess, represents 'Wimbledonization'[26].

The expertise in hostile takeover tactics and defences was transplanted to the City by the newly arrived American investment banks, leading to more aggressive hostile bids than in the past, although hostile bids had been part of the UK scene from the late 1960s. Some of the predatory tactics of the US raiders were also tried in the UK[27]. New financing techniques, such as highly leveraged buyouts (LBOs), were also imported from the US into the UK takeover scene, although on a smaller scale. While the predators were on the prowl, many incumbent managements of their current or potential targets scrambled and unscrambled their businesses as a defence against these raiders.

The UK corporations and institutional investors, like their US counterparts, were undergoing a renewal of faith in shareholder value management – or at least that was the mantra and the rhetoric behind the 1980s' takeover wave. The resulting battle cry was return to specialization or 'sticking to the knitting', which led to divestitures on an unprecedented scale, as shown in Figure 2.5b.

The fourth merger wave

In the 1990s the UK experienced its fourth merger wave, as shown in Figure 2.5. For comparison with the US and EU merger waves the value of deals is expressed in constant 2007 US dollars. The fifth UK wave shares many of the characteristics of the merger wave of that period in the US, as well as the characteristics of the 1990s wave in the EU. Many new sectors in the UK were privatized, such as water, electricity and gas. Further deregulation of the telecom industry took place, increasing pressure on British Telecom, the previous monopoly, to restructure. Many firms undertook divestitures, such as ICI, which demerged into ICI and

Figure 2.5 (a) UK merger waves during 1984–2007; (b) UK divestiture waves during 1984–2007

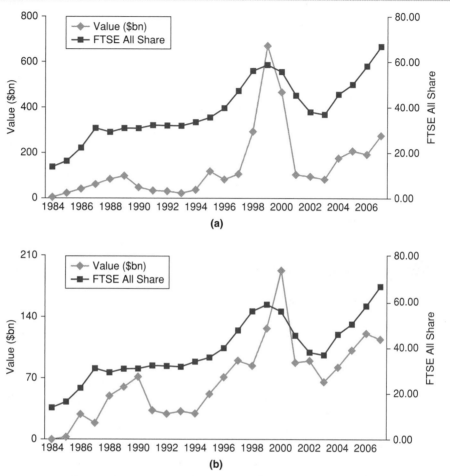

All deals completed and acquirers hold > 50% of target shares after transaction; only deals with deal value disclosed included; for acquisition deals either target or acquirer is a UK firm. For divestiture deals, target is a UK firm; deals categorized according to announcement year; deal value in 2007 dollars. US Consumer Price Index – All Urban: All Items is used to adjust for inflation.
Source: Thomson Reuters.

Zeneca, which then went on to merge with the Swedish pharmaceutical firm Astra to form AstraZeneca. Vodafone, born out of a demerger from Racal Electronics, has now become the largest mobile telephone company in the world after acquiring Airtouch in the US and Mannesmann in Germany. Thus, as in the US, the UK also experienced high-level divestiture activity as part of the merger boom.

The millennial merger wave

Figure 2.5a shows the number and value of acquisitions and divestitures during 1984–2007. For comparison the level of the UK stock market proxied by the FTSE All-Share Index is also shown. There is close movement of the merger waves and the stock market levels, as observed in the case of the US and EU merger waves above. The 1980s and 1990s waves are fairly comparable in terms of deal numbers, but in terms of value the 1980s wave is hugely dominated by the 1990s wave, indicating that the average size of acquisitions is considerably larger in the latter period. Again, as in the US and the EU, the new millennium sees a revival of acquisitions from the crash of 2001, but it hasn't achieved the same peak level as the 1990s wave. Thus in all three regions the 1990s merger wave is the largest in history. The millennial wave, while smaller than this wave, still substantially dominates all pre-1990 merger waves (see Figures 2.2a and 2.3a above). Thus there seems to be a step change in acquisition activity after the 1980s.

Figure 2.5b shows that divestiture activity in the UK has also occurred in waves. In terms of value of divestitures three waves are distinct. These waves happen around the same time as the acquisition waves, with the correlation between the two in terms of numbers (value) being 0.85 (0.79). But divestiture activity seems to be maintained at higher levels than acquisitions following the peaks. For example, after the fall off the acquisition peak in 1999, divestitures peak in value in 2000, and the decline from that peak is much gentler than in the case of acquisitions (see Figures 2.5a and 2.5b). This suggests that divestitures may be pursued even when acquisition activity has abated.

Mergers in emerging markets

Unlike the previous merger waves, the millennial wave has been reinforced by mergers, acquisitions and divestitures in major emerging markets. We focus here on merger activity in Brazil, the Russian Federation, India and China, the so called BRIC countries. These countries have experienced very strong economic growth rates in the last decade, accompanied by greater openness to foreign direct investment and, in particular, equity ownership of domestic companies by foreign corporations as well as by private equity firms. The private sector has played a major role in achieving high growth rates in these countries, which also undertook substantial privatization of previously state-owned enterprises. These privatized enterprises with enormous financial resources have engaged in domestic as well as foreign acquisitions.

New industries sprang up, such as mobile telecoms, and these have seen a number of cross-border M & A. The spectacular growth rates of many of these countries increased demand for infrastructure and the products of companies selling to infrastructure projects. As a result some industries once regarded as sunset industries, such as steel and cement, have found new vitality and manifested numerous cross-border mergers. The takeover trail of Mittal has swamped well-established steel makers in Europe (e.g. Arcelor), in the US, in Central and Eastern Europe (CEE), and in Asia. Many large companies from BRIC countries made bold forays into the developed countries and acquired companies in steel, (e.g. Tata Steel's $12bn acquisition in 2007 of Corus of UK-Netherlands after beating a rival bid from CSN, a Brazilian steel maker); in automobiles, e.g. Tata Motors' acquisition of Jaguar and Land Rover in the UK for $2.3bn in 2008; and in information technology sectors, e.g. Lenovo's $1.8bn acquisition of the personal computer business of IBM in 2004.

These examples demonstrate that many firms in BRIC countries have grown in size, resources and capabilities, including distinct technological capabilities, that have fuelled their ambitions and widened their strategic vision to become global players, e.g. Russian gas giant Gazprom's acquisitions in the CEE and seeking targets in the US. The cumulative outcome of these forces is the arrival of these countries as significant players on the world M & A scene. Table 2.3 provides the statistics on takeover activity in BRIC countries in 2005 to 2007. The major sectors experiencing these restructuring activities included automotive, financial services, oil and gas, and minerals.

Table 2.3 M & A deals in 2005–2007 in BRIC countries

Country	2005		2006		2007	
	Number	Value (US$bn)	Number	Value (US$bn)	Number	Value (US$bn)
Brazil	75	9	112	21	266	31
Russia	138	31	202	17	298	68
India	161	10	216	16	213	21
China	171	11	199	15	295	22

Source: *Mergers & Acquisitions*, Table on M & A in major overseas markets outside the US, February 2008.

Overview of the merger waves

Our survey of the merger waves around the world shows that while the early waves were influenced by conditions in the individual countries, and by firms seeking to alter their competitive position *vis-à-vis* their domestic rivals, the waves of the 1980s, 1990s and 2000s were characterized by similar trends in different countries, by increasing globalization of product and capital markets, by similarity of approaches to government's role in industry and regulation and corporate governance, and by shareholder value as an important determining factor in corporate decisions. The increasing importance of cross-border M & A (e.g. see Table 2.1) also reflects the strategies of companies to cope with the institutional changes in the EU, such as the Single Market and the Eurozone with a single currency, as well as the need to compete globally for markets, technologies and capabilities. Thus corporate M & A strategies seem to have evolved in response to these environmental changes as well as to changes affecting individual industries. There are, however, different perspectives on the causes of merger waves.

Why do merger waves happen?

Figures 2.2, 2.3 and 2.5 above show that merger waves seem to parallel the stock market movements. The correlation coefficients between stock market level and value of acquisitions in the same year (and between stock market level in a year and value of acquisitions in the following year) respectively are very high: 0.88 (0.94) for the US, 0.92 (0.86) for the EU, and 0.81 (0.79) for the UK. Thus merger waves occur during periods of high stock market valuation. High valuation of their stock may induce companies to use it as a payment currency and acquire target companies on the cheap if the latter are relatively undervalued. Thus high merger activity may reflect this opportunistic behaviour of managers rather than the economic rationale of acquisitions. High valuation may also increase the scope for high valuation errors that may lead target firms to overestimate potential synergies and accept takeover bids, thereby increasing the momentum of the waves.

In recent years alternative theories of merger waves have emerged and been subjected to empirical tests. These can be broadly divided into[28] *rational economic models* and *behavioural models*. Rational economic, also called neoclassical, models, assume that managers, in making acquisitions, are driven by the objective of maximizing the long-term value of their companies. Financial markets are assumed to be rational and to price up fairly the stock of firms that make value-creating acquisitions. By contrast, behavioral models impute opportunism to these managers, for example capitalizing on their stock's overvaluation at times of irrationally high stock market valuation. In the rest of this chapter we review these theories, their implications for merger waves, and the available empirical evidence in their support[29].

Rational economic models of merger waves

The Q theory

Michael Gort developed the economic disturbance theory of merger waves[30]. According to this model merger waves occur when a rise in general economic activity creates a disequilibrium in product markets. Some investors hold a more positive expectation of future demand than others, and value target firms higher. Mergers result from attempts to take advantage of such valuation differences. Once some leading firms make merger moves, their competitors follow suit and pursue 'me-too' mergers for fear of being left behind. Thus the momentum for a wave develops. Gort's model is consistent with the incidence of merger waves during periods of strong economic growth and rising stock markets in the US, the EU and the rest of the world.

In the same tradition, Boyan Jovanovic and Peter Rousseau formulate their Q-theory of merger waves and argue that 'mergers are a channel through which capital flows to better projects and better management'[31]. Thus the function of mergers is to ensure that corporate assets are redeployed to more efficient firms run by more competent managers, leading to higher value creation. Efficient use of assets is measured by the ratio of the market value of the firm that owns the assets to the replacement cost of such assets. This ratio is known as the Q ratio, with a higher value signifying more efficient use of assets. Thus the model predicts that high-Q firms will acquire low-Q firms ('*high buys low*'). This requires that firms have widely varying valuations of corporate assets. Such large inter-firm dispersion in valuation increases the incentives for mergers that reallocate corporate assets from low- to high-Q firms.

Such valuation dispersion is therefore a characteristic of merger waves that are essentially reallocation waves. While identifying two interesting characteristics of such waves – wide valuation dispersion and 'high buys low' – the Q-theory does not explain why valuation differences arise in concentrated time periods. We still need to identify the triggers not just of *mergers* but of *merger waves*. It is plausible that some economic disturbance or other acts as the triggers. We therefore need to understand the nature of these disturbances, and where they originate.

Environmental analysis of merger waves

While economic disturbances may partly account for merger waves, these disturbances and the merger waves may both be subject to wider influences. It is also plausible that an incipient merger wave itself creates new, or reinforces existing, economic disequilibrium. We have noted that many contextual factors also change just prior to or during these merger waves. In some cases firms undertake mergers in anticipation of changes of great import. For example, many European firms carried out mergers in the late 1980s in anticipation of the Single Market in the EU from 1992 so as to position themselves to competitive advantage in the new market. As a result, the growth in intra-EU mergers was much faster than the growth in purely national mergers[32]. Thus disturbances that trigger, or provide conditions for, large-scale merger activity can be traced to a wider range of sources.

A framework to explain merger waves is the PEST model of the environment, incorporating political, economic, social and technical (PEST) dimensions[33]. For example, the technological breakthroughs of the 1890s in mass production and transportation and the information technology breakthroughs of the 1990s provided the impetus for a number of mergers. Changes in tax regimes or government policy changes in pension provision for citizens are examples of changes in contextual factors that may provide firms with the opportunity to develop new sources of competitive advantage through mergers and acquisitions. Mergers of investment banks and commercial banks in the US during the 1990s were encouraged by a less stringent application of and finally the repeal of the Glass–Steagall Act, which had prevented such consolidation for more than 60 years.

The new rules adopted in 2001 by Germany to give relief from capital gains tax for banks such as Deutsche Bank and insurers such as Allianz when they unwind their investments in German companies were expected to lead to considerable restructuring of German companies through acquisitions, since a major disincentive to such liquidation had been removed. The increasing proportion of income spent by Europeans on leisure activities such as travel reflects a lifestyle change, and has spurred a number of mergers in the travel industry in the 1990s. The privatization of electricity in the UK in the 1980s attracted a number of US utility firms to acquire UK utilities as a way of diversifying out of the more restrictive regulatory regime in the US. Similarly, water privatization in the UK attracted French utility firms to acquire UK targets.

In the second merger wave of the 1920s in the US, political and regulatory factors influenced the direction of mergers away from monopolies to oligopolies, since popular disquiet over the monopolies created during the first wave led to stringent new antimonopoly laws and their trust-busting enforcement. New management models such as the multidivisional form (M-form) of management enabled managers to acquire unrelated businesses[34]. Managerial preference for growth during the 1960s and the new management tools probably spurred the conglomerate growth of the 1960s. In the 1980s, with a more relaxed antitrust regime, political factors receded, but economic factors and social factors such as globalization, shareholder activism and emphasis on shareholder value provided the impetus for the fourth merger wave in the US. Finally, political and ideological trends towards deregulation and privatization in member states of the EU and attempts at economic integration at both the regional and global levels impacted on the M & A scene. The phenomenal development of information technology and the convergence of technologies in Internet communication, media and telecommunication contributed to the 'new economy' mergers.

In the EU, in addition to the above technological and political factors, sociological factors such as the ageing profile of the populations and their longevity have led governments to change their policies on pension provision for their citizens. The move away from state provision for retirement benefits to private provision by individuals created new opportunities for financial services firms to sell their existing products in new markets, or to design new products to suit new customers. This in turn triggered an avalanche of mergers in the financial services sector, both nationally and across borders.

Environmental factors may have both direct and indirect influences on corporate investment decisions. The increasing concern over global warming and carbon dioxide emissions has led to greater awareness of the carbon footprints of individual and corporate activity. The emergence of carbon trading, which allows high polluters to buy carbon permits from low polluters, provides an economic solution to the problem of excessive carbon emission. More environmentally friendly cars, such as hybrid cars that run on both gas and electricity, manifest corporate responses to the pressure to minimize carbon emissions. Such pressures towards socially responsible corporate behaviour can alter the incentives to shift to new technologies, and encourage firms to access them through corporate mergers or strategic alliances.

Impact of industry changes on M & A activity

The PEST environmental analysis and the Gort model suggest that different industries may be affected differently by the forces generating disturbances. If these disturbances alter the competitive structure of an industry by, for example, lowering entry barriers or opening new markets for the industry's products, or by increasing the cost of operations through burdensome regulations, firms already operating in an industry need to cope with these challenges to their competitive position. Thus disturbances that have industry-wide impact also tend to trigger industry-wide competitive moves in a jockeying for a new competitive equilibrium[35].

While technology-based competitive changes may often be initiated by firms themselves when they create new technologies, political, economic and social changes are largely exogenous to individual firms. Changes in PEST dimensions can often confer first-mover advantages on firms that can anticipate these changes, or read the implications of these changes correctly. Thus merger decisions of firms are designed to cope with both the direct impact of PEST factors and the indirect impact of these factors through changes in the industry structure.

Industry clustering of mergers

One of the natural forces of change in an industry is the product life cycle of that industry, such as agricultural products or clothing. As these products become commoditized, there is fierce price competition with the industry characterized by excess capacity, and firms have to merge to 'take out' the excess capacity. Excess capacity may exist in several forms: in production capacity, in R & D, in marketing and distribution channels or in managerial expertise. For example, the automobile industry suffered from excess production capacity in the 1990s. The pharmaceutical industry had an excess of R & D capacity in the same period, and commercial banks had too many branches. The need to reduce this capacity drove many mergers in the 1980s and 1990s, such as the merger of Daimler-Benz with Chrysler in 1998, the merger of Union Bank of Switzerland with Swiss Banking Corporation in 1997, and the merger of Synthelabo SA with Sanofi SA in France in 1999 (see Chapter 5 for further discussion of such consolidating mergers).

In other industries mergers may be triggered by other forces, such as deregulation or the convergence of technologies. For example, deregulation and privatization have affected industries such as power, water, airports and telecommunications, leading to a surge in mergers in these industries. Technological changes drove new business models in the financial services industry, such as banking, insurance and investment management, and in the media and entertainment industries. Financial innovation such as junk bonds has facilitated the restructuring of mature industries with fairly predictable cash flows, such as oil and gas or food and drinks, a necessary condition for high-leverage financing. In the new millennium the development of credit derivatives has allowed the spread of credit risk and encouraged banks to accept higher levels of leverage in corporate acquisition deals, at least until the explosion of the subprime crisis in 2007 and financial meltdown in 2008.

The European Single Market has had an impact on the manufacturing industries, whereas European Monetary Union and the euro have impacted more strongly on the financial services sector[36]. The removal of restrictions on interstate banking in the US allowed the consolidation of regional banks into much larger national banks, for example the West Coast-based Bank of America merger with the southern Nations Bank. Thus mergers and acquisitions in different industries are triggered by different 'industry shocks'. The collapse of banks in the wake of the credit crisis led to the takeover of failed banks by stronger banks, such as the Bank of America takeover of Merrill Lynch and the JP Morgan Chase takeover of Bear Stearns in the US, and the Lloyds Bank takeover of HBOS in the UK.

Evidence for industry shocks causing merger waves

US evidence

Harford tests the industry shock theory of merger waves at the industry level using recent US data from 1981 to 2000[37]. He also examines partial acquisitions, e.g. acquisitions of

Table 2.4 Types of industry shocks in the US affecting M & A activity during 1981–2000

Industry affected	Date and 'cause' of wave
Banking	August 1985 – deregulation allowing interstate banking; October 1996 – deregulation and information technology
Candy and soda	April 1992 – Snapple and other non-carbonated beverages make strides leading to activity to beat or buy them
Communication	November 1987 – deregulation; break-up of AT&T in 1984 allowing entry into long-distance telephony, fibre optic technology; July 1997 – deregulation, Telecommunication Act of 1996, consolidation and technological changes
Computers	July 1998 – Internet
Entertainment	October 1987 – deregulation of radio station ownership; March 1998 – Telecom Act 1996 relaxes media ownership limits, allowing studios to seek diversified production sources and strong libraries
Healthcare	May 1996 – service providers consolidate to counter bargaining power of health management organizations (HMOs)
Shipbuilding	August 1998 – shrinking defence budget exposed overcapacity
Transportation	July 1997 – end of Interstate Commerce Commission, overcapacity in shipping, open skies agreement in aviation, railroad consolidation
Utilities	November 1997 – deregulation in some markets plus elimination of law prohibiting mergers between non-contiguous providers.

Source: J. Harford, 'What drives merger waves?', *Journal of Financial Economics*, 77(3), 2005, 529–560.

subsidiaries rather than whole firms. Merger activity in successive 24-month periods is examined, and benchmarked against expected activity in such periods generated by a simulation model. Harford finds:

- *35 waves in 28 industries*, seven of which have two distinct waves;
- the *average number of bids* experienced by any of these industries in a 24-month period is *7.8*; but
- in a similar period during a merger wave it is *34.3*!

Table 2.4, extracted from Harford, provides examples of industry shocks that influence takeover activity. These industry shocks arise from deregulation (air transport, broadcasting, utilities), political events (shipping), changing consumer tastes (candy and soda) and economic factors (healthcare), Internet technology (banking and computers), consistent with the PEST model.

The PEST framework suggests that the various factors can not only directly trigger merger waves but also indirectly facilitate them. One such facilitating factor is the availability of financing. In periods of high capital market liquidity, acquisitions, especially those paid for with cash rather than the acquirer's stock, are more likely. Harford argues that lack of liquidity may impede, delay or shorten merger waves. This is particularly relevant to partial firm acquisitions, since they are mostly financed with cash. Thus merger waves occur in periods of high liquidity. Using a variety of tests, and low commercial and industrial loan rate spread above the Federal Reserve funds rate as a proxy for liquidity, Harford finds strong support for his hypothesis. He also finds that deregulatory events, economic shocks and the combination of economic shocks and high liquidity in the previous year increase the likelihood of merger waves. The correlation between industry-specific waves and aggregate economy-wide waves is very high (correlation coefficient of 0.85). Thus industry-level merger waves drive the economy-wide merger waves. The corollary of this evidence is that while high liquidity – an economy-wide phenomenon – can facilitate mergers, the basic drivers are essentially industry-specific changes in competitive structure, and supply and demand side shocks.

Mitchell and Mulherin provide broadly similar evidence for the 1980s[38]. They find significant differences among industries in both rate and time-series clustering of mergers. The inter-industry patterns are directly related to the economic shocks borne by the industries, and show distinct timing effects. Generally, 50% of takeovers in a given industry cluster within two years. In a following study, Mitchell and Mulherin observe industry clustering of both acquisitions and divestitures during the 1990s[39]. Among all the sample industries, 29% of the member firms are acquired. The average level of divestitures in all sample industries is 21%. Thus divestiture intensity, while significant, is on average less than acquisition intensity in the 1990s.

Evidence from the EU

In the light of the increasing globalization of markets and products from the 1990s, one would expect a similar industry clustering in countries outside the US. Indeed, we find some striking similarities in the level of M & A activity in the US and the EU during 2006–07, as shown in Table 2.5. The level of industry aggregation in the table (at the one-digit level, the broadest industry grouping) may perhaps accentuate industry clustering. Nevertheless, we find broadly similar M & A patterns across the US and the EU. The main sectors affected by M & A within each region, as well as between regions, are:

- hotels, personal, business and recreational services (SIC 7);
- glass, plastics etc. (SIC 3);
- finance, insurance and real estate (SIC 6); and
- food, textiles, paper etc. (SIC 2).

This pattern suggests that industry-level clusters may be driving aggregate merger waves not only within a region but also globally through cross-border merger clusters. In other industries,

Table 2.5 Sectoral and geographical breakdown of M & A operations with a US or EU target, 2006–07 (%)

Sector SIC	Intra-US	Extra-US (US as target)	Intra-EU	Extra-EU (EU as target)
0 Agriculture, forestry, and fisheries	0.6	0.3	0.5	0.4
1 Mining and construction	7.7	12.4	4.4	3.7
2 Food, textiles, paper, chemicals, etc.	9.2	12.3	11.2	10.2
3 Glass, plastics, metals, machinery, computers, transport equipment, etc.	16.7	21.1	11.6	20.8
4 Network industries	9.8	6.7	10.8	7.8
5 Wholesale and retail trade	7.1	3.3	10.4	6.7
6 Finance, insurance, and real estate	19.0	14.3	20.8	22.1
7 Hotels, personal, business and recreational services, etc.	21.4	21.0	20.3	20.4
8 Health, legal, educational, social, engineering and management	8.6	8.6	9.8	7.7
9 Public administration	0.1	0.1	0.1	0.2
Total	100.0	100.0	100.0	100.0

All deals completed and acquirers hold > 50% of target shares after transaction; only deals with disclosed transaction values included; EU = 27 current members plus Switzerland; deals categorized according to announcement year.
Source: Sectoral and geographical breakdown of M&A operations with a US or EU target 2006–07 (%), Thomson Reuters, www.thomsonreuters.com.

such as wholesale and retail trade (SIC 5) and network industries (SIC 4), firms are concerned more with consolidation within each region than with cross-region clustering.

Evidence from the UK

In the UK, similar industry clustering of mergers in response to industry shocks has been observed. Powell and Yawson report, for their sample of about 1300 UK firms during 1986–2000, 947 acquisitions and 562 divestitures. Acquisitions exhibit significant clustering in the second half of the 1980s and 1990s[40]. They also cluster by industry. For example, over half of all takeovers in speciality chemicals, electricity and computer services take place in a two-year period. Interestingly, divestitures do not exhibit clustering in time, but cluster by industry, for example in builders' merchants, electricity, and clothing and footwear in a two-year period.

At the industry level, with an average of 18 firms in each industry, the median number of acquisitions over the sample period is 10, but for divestitures it is only 3. Thus acquisition intensity is greater than divestiture intensity, a pattern also observed in the US by Mulherin and Mitchell (see footnote 38). The study also shows that divestitures happen more evenly over time than takeovers. For example, the median annual value of takeovers as a percentage of the value of all sample takeovers is 2.6, but this level of takeover activity is exceeded only in 1988–89 and 1995–2000. By contrast, the corresponding figures for divestitures are 4.3% and years 1993–2000. Not only do divestitures become more important in value in the 1990s, but they also become a more regular feature of corporate restructuring. Unlike divestitures, takeovers seem to be more episodic and in the nature of sudden and large responses to discontinuous shocks[41].

Schoenberg and Reeves observe industry clustering of M & A among 200 industry sectors in the UK during 1990–95[42]. They find that deregulation is the single most important discriminator between industries with high and low acquisition activity. In insurance, national restrictions on underwriting by foreign companies were removed as part of the 1992 Single European Market programme. The resulting trend towards a single insurance market saw 18 UK insurance firms acquired by continental European companies, together with 41 acquisitions among UK competitors. In the electricity distribution industry, of the 12 regional electricity companies (RECs) privatized in 1990, eight were acquired by overseas investors and three by other British utilities; only one remained independent. In contrast, some US studies have not found deregulation on its own a significant determinant of takeover waves.

In an analysis of all mergers and acquisitions in UK two-digit industries during the period 1988–2006 reported by SDC Platinum, a Thomson Reuters Financial product, we find 21 industries with identifiable merger waves[43]. Figure 2.6 shows them for some of these industries. The bars represent the number of acquisitions in successive two-year periods. These figures suggest that the duration or amplitude of merger waves is not uniform across these industries. In pre-packaged software the wave is much sharper and shorter than in retail trade – eating and drinking places. Thus different intensities of shocks occur in different industries, or different strategic responses to industry shocks are adopted by firms in those industries.

As noted above in our discussion of industry waves in the US, Harford observes that an economy-wide merger wave is an aggregation of industry-wide merger waves. A similar conclusion holds for the UK, as shown in Figure 2.7, where the bars represent the total number of mergers in 21 industries experiencing merger waves as illustrated in Figure 2.6. The line curve in Figure 2.7 is the sum of these industry mergers. This aggregate merger wave is similar to that in Figure 2.5a, although the latter includes all industries, whereas this figure represents only 21 two-digit industries with distinct merger waves. While industry-level merger waves may have different spans, their peaks occur in fair temporal proximity. Thus economy-wide merger waves seem to be driven essentially by industry-level merger waves, although industry-level merger

Figure 2.6   Merger waves in UK industries: (a) retail trade – eating and drinking places; (b) hotels and casinos; (c) prepackaged software.

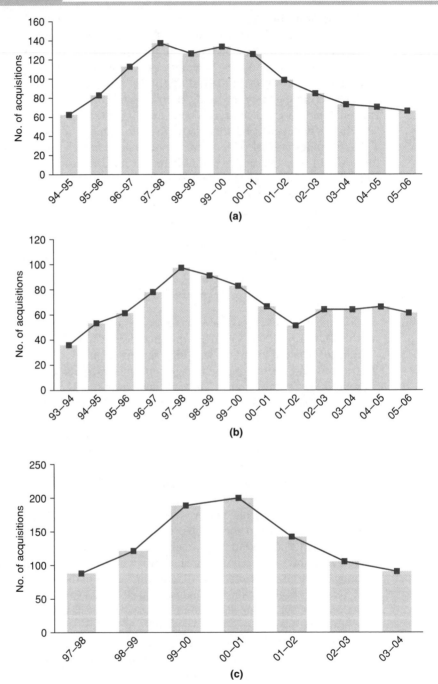

Source: SDC Platinum: A Thomson Reuters Financial Product

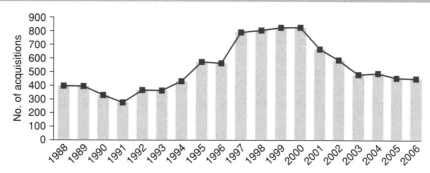

Figure 2.7 UK merger waves as aggregation of industry-wide merger waves during 1988–2006

Source: SDC Platinum: A Thomson Reuters Financial Product

waves are not perfectly synchronized (see Figure 2.6). Thus in seeking to understand aggregate merger waves we need to understand industry shocks and how firms respond to these.

Behavioural models of merger waves

In contrast to the rational models discussed above, behavioural models assume some inefficiency in capital markets, reflected in overvaluation of corporate stock. Andrei Shleifer and Robert Vishny argue that smart corporate managers perceiving these inefficiencies take advantage of them through acquisitions[44]. In periods of high stock market misvaluation of companies, companies can use their overvalued stock to acquire other companies: that is, they exchange their overvalued stock for the real assets of the acquired company. An incentive for acquirers to do so is the fear that when overvaluation is corrected their stock would decline in value unless they convert their stock into real assets. With conversion of overvalued stock into real assets, any subsequent correction of overvaluation would harm the acquirer less than if it had not made the acquisition. An implication of this is that acquirers that exploit overvaluation will outperform otherwise similar companies that do not, when the overvaluation is corrected.

Since, during these periods of overvaluation, the target firms' stock is also likely to be overvalued, the implication of this model is that bidders' stock is more overvalued than the targets'. This phenomenon is consistent with the '*high buys low*' strategy of the Q-theory. However, cash financing of acquisitions seems inconsistent with the desire to exploit stock overvaluation[45]. An interesting question is why target managers accept the overvalued stock of bidders. Shleifer and Vishny hypothesize that target managers do so out of selfish motives, that is, to cash out their accumulated stock and stock options. Thus target managers also exhibit opportunism[46].

Other implications of the model are that:

- managerial opportunism will be more evident in a stock exchange than in cash-financed takeovers;
- post-acquisition, target managers will sell their stock in the acquirer;
- targets are less overvalued than bidders; and
- long-run returns to stock acquirers are greater than to similar acquirers who acquire for cash, or to similarly overvalued non-acquirers.

Ang and Cheng find support for the overvaluation hypothesis and its many implications with US data consisting of more than 3000 mergers during 1981–2001[47]. In particular, they report the following results:

- Overvalued acquirers opportunistically make stock acquisitions.
- Overvaluation is correlated with stock market returns.
- Cash acquirers are less overvalued than stock acquirers.
- Cash acquirers are not overvalued relative to targets but stock acquirers are: the median difference between acquirer's overvaluation and target overvaluation is only 3% (statistically insignificant) in cash deals, but it is a significant 7.5% in the case of stock acquirers.

Ang and Cheng also report further results consistent with the behavioural model:

- Long-run performance up to three years of overvalued stock acquirers is superior to that of overvalued non-acquirers.
- Shareholders of overvalued acquirers are better off than those of overvalued non-acquirers[48].

However, not all stock acquirers are overvalued. In their sample, 330 out of 1574 stock acquirers are undervalued not overvalued. This suggests that the Shleifer and Vishny model does not explain all stock mergers.

Rhodes-Kropf and Viswanathan (RV) depart from Shleifer and Vishny (SV) by assuming that both bidder and target managers are rational value maximizers, and that targets may accept overvalued acquirer stock, not because of opportunism but because of limited information they have about the extent of overvaluation[49]. RV's model assumes market inefficiency in pricing corporate stock. In times of market-wide overvaluation there is a greater likelihood of target managers attributing any perceived overvaluation of the bidder stock to such market-wide overvaluation rather than to acquirer-specific overvaluation. These managers are unable to make accurate allowance for different sources of overvaluation, tend to overestimate the synergy between bidders and targets, and therefore will accept the bids. Thus high market valuation errors may go with high overestimation of synergy, giving rise to merger waves.

In a sequel to this model, Rhodes-Kropf, Robinson and Viswanathan (RRV) test its predictions empirically for a large sample of 4325 US mergers during 1997–2000. They decompose the error in valuation into market-wide errors, industry-wide errors and firm-specific errors. They estimate overvaluation using market-to-book value of equity (MB) as a valuation metric. The major findings of the study are:

- Overvaluation is much higher for merging than for non-merging firms, and mergers occur when both bidders and targets are overvalued.
- Acquiring firms are priced 20% higher than targets.
- Firm-specific valuation error is much larger than market-wide error, suggesting an overestimation of merger synergy. About 60% of the acquirer's MB is due to firm-specific error, but almost none of the target's is attributable to such error.
- Acquirers and targets cluster in sectors with high time-series sector error. They share a common misvaluation component. This suggests that industry shocks may not be the only factor explaining industry-level merger waves. These may occur because of overestimation of synergies in those sectors.
- Cash acquirers are less overvalued than stock acquirers.
- High firm-specific error makes acquisitions more probable by firms that use their stock as payment currency.

RRV conclude that

> even when the merger is part of a merger wave that is being driven by neoclassical considerations, most merger activity is the work of misvalued firms. . . . the vast majority of transactions (whether or not they occur during periods of economic shocks) involve highly overvalued bidders . . . Economic shocks could well be the fundamental drivers of merger activity, but misvaluation affects how these shocks are propagated through the economy. Misvaluation affects who buys whom as well as the method of payment.

These conclusions are broadly consistent with those from Ang and Cheng and from Harford discussed above. Corporate managers, even though driven by rational economic motives, may nevertheless time their acquisition moves to take advantage of overvaluation of their own firms and overestimation of potential merger synergies arising from market-wide overvaluation. Further support for the overvaluation model comes from Dong, Hirshleifer, Richardson and Teoh, who also empirically test the hypothesis with the US data for the 1980s and 1990s[50].

It's not all 'high buys low'; 'low buys high' too

Time-series merger data throw up interesting patterns not explained by the Q-theory or the behavioural model and empirical tests reviewed above. One such is that low-valued firms buy high-valued targets, or firms buy others of similar valuation, i.e. 'low buys low'. Rhodes-Kropf and Robinson provide evidence that in the US merger waves there is a significant proportion of high-Q firms merging with other high-Q firms as well as low-Q firms merging with other low-Q firms[51]. They call this type of mergers 'like buys like', and explain it on the basis of complementarity of the merging firms' assets or resources. This is consistent with the resource-based view of corporate strategy and mergers. We review this study in more detail in Chapter 3 on alternative perspectives on mergers.

Strategic implications of industry clustering of M & A

While industry-level analysis of M & A is useful, we need to remember that industry as a construct is too static, and assumes that firms are constrained to operate within their current industry structures. We must also note the following caveats:

- Not all the shocks are exogenous. Some are generated by the firms in an industry in order to alter the industry structure so as to gain competitive advantage, e.g. technological innovation in products or processes.
- The relation between shocks and takeovers is not linear. While some firms react to shocks by undertaking takeovers, these takeovers themselves lead to further structural changes to which other firms may react, thereby amplifying or moderating the impact of the initial shock.
- Some firms acquire resources and capabilities through mergers that enable them to escape the current industry structure and enter or create new industries.
- Industry boundaries are also in some cases blurred, as in the case of the Internet and media, or banking and insurance (see case study below). Firms pole-vault industry boundaries: for example, AOL, the Internet provider, merged with Time Warner in 2000 to gain access to content in terms of movies and music, although this strategy was a colossal failure and destroyed enormous value for the companies' shareholders.

- Industry clustering patterns suggest that some industries undergo turbulent restructuring, but on average nearly half of the firms in an industry may participate in mergers within a short time period (see review of Mitchell and Mulherin, and Powell and Yawson studies above).

- This industry clustering suggests copycat or 'follow my leader' moves. Some of these are countermoves to restore competitive equilibrium disturbed by the leader's move. In a game theory context the first mover must anticipate this countermove and factor the implications of the countermove in fashioning its first move (see Chapter 3 on game theory). The competitive advantage from the first move may be just ephemeral. This is consistent with the poor post-acquisition value creation performance of many acquirers (see Chapter 4 for review of the related evidence).

- Firms making copycat moves must consider whether it is the optimal strategy and the cost of being an 'also-ran'. The pay-off to being a 'fast second' may also often be good[52].

- While a vast majority of acquisitions are reallocating mergers, in which low-valued firms are taken over by high-valued firms, thereby enhancing operational efficiency, others exploit complementarity of resources to improve their competitive advantage and create value.

- Value creation from mergers requires a matching of corporate strategy and financial strategy, since payment currency in mergers is a determinant of value created for the stakeholders.

CASE STUDY

Pharmaceuticals suffer from the urge to merge

In recent years the pharmaceutical industry has been consolidating globally through a large number of mergers. Some of the mega deals in the last decade are listed in the table below.

Year	Target	Acquirer	Value ($bn)
1998	Astra (UK)	Zeneca (UK)	40
1999	Warner-Lambert (US)	Pfizer (US)	112
1999	Hoechst (France)	Rhone-Poulenc (France)	34
1999	Pharmacia & Upjohn (US)	Monsanto (US)	32
2000	SmithKline-Beecham (UK)	Glaxo Wellcome (UK)	80
2002	Pharmacia (US)	Pfizer (US)	60
2004	Aventis (France)	Sanofi-Synthelabo (France)	71
2008	Genentech (44%) (US)	Roche (Switzerland)	46
2009	Wyeth (US)	Pfizer (US)	68
2009	Schering-Plough (US)	Merck (US)	41

There have been numerous mid-size and small acquisitions as well. In addition to purely pharmaceutical acquisitions these firms have also acquired biotechnology firms, e.g. Roche acquiring Genentech, AstraZeneca acquired Cambridge Antibodies (see Chapter 22). Moreover in recent years many pharmaceutical companies have diversified into related businesses such as healthcare products in an attempt to reduce their dependence on prescription drugs. They have also diversified through acquisition into generics, over-the-counter-drugs and healthcare systems. Some pharma companies have followed the strategy of acquiring much smaller rivals that can help fill their fast-drying product pipelines. Bristol-Myers Squibb's acquisition of Imclone for $4.5bn in 2008 exemplifies such a strategy (called 'string of pearls' strategy).

What drives these consolidating and diversifying acquisitions by so many firms in the industry? We can identify many drivers that can be characterized as PEST factors:

● Political – pressure by publicly-funded healthcare systems in several European countries and healthcare management organizations in the US on pharma companies to lower drug prices; public perceptions that pharma companies put their profits before people and were selling drugs at too high prices for people to afford; more stringent regulation of clinical trials requiring longer trials and drug approval regimes; the healthcare reforms of the Obama administration are expected to put more pressure on prescription drug prices.
● Economic – tight budgetary constraints faced by several governments in financing their healthcare systems; the high cost of R & D; massive competition from me-too and copycat or generic producers selling unbranded drugs at considerably cheaper prices.
● Social – trend towards more healthcare products than curative drugs, for example nutritionals.
● Technological – the declining productivity of the drug discovery process at many of the big pharma companies.
● Legal – expiry or imminent expiry of patents on the blockbusters that have contributed high profits to pharma bottom lines in the past.

While these mergers seek to extract cost savings in various functional areas such as purchases, marketing, production, sales, etc., they are also aimed at improving the drug pipeline of the merging firms by improving their research productivity. There are also synergies in well established pharma firms acquiring newly formulated drugs from younger and smaller companies without the resources for prolonged drug trials, market and brand development and production infrastructure. Above all for many of the big pharma companies the imminent loss of patents would deal a serious blow to their profits and market valuation. They, therefore, desperately needed to replenish their pipelines with new blockbusters. One industry estimate put the value of patented drugs that would come off patent by 2011 at $60bn. Bristol-Myers Squibb faced the prospect that drugs accounting for 30% of its 2007 pharma revenue would lose protection by 2012.

The Merck-Schering Plough deal would double Merck's late-stage drugs to 18 and transform its R & D. Since R & D and marketing costs account for a high proportion (35% to 40%) of total costs, savings in these areas would add to the profitability of the merging firms. Merck also estimated that it would reduce costs, with planned annual savings of $3.5bn from 2011.

Discussion questions

1 What are the different subsectors of the pharmaceutical industry?

2 What are the types of mergers that have taken place in the industry?

3 What are the drivers of the mergers that have happened?

4 What are the sources of value in these different types of mergers?

Sources: A. Jack, 'A dose of pharmaceutical competitiveness', *Financial Times*, 9 March 2009; R. Mukherjee, 'Pharma M&A wave set to reach India', *Times of India*, 16 March 2009; 'Bristol Myers/Imclone', *Financial Times*, 31 July 2008.

Overview and implications for practice

- This chapter provides an historic overview of trend in mergers and acquisitions over the last 120 years in the US, 45 years in the UK, and 25 years in the rest of the EU. Takeover activity exhibits distinct wave patterns in both the US and Europe. The US has had six waves, the UK five, and continental Europe three.

- Merger waves are no longer limited to the USA or Western Europe. In BRIC countries there has been a surge of M & A in recent years.

- A number of contextual developments accompany merger waves. High economic growth, recovery from an economic downturn, rising stock market and new technologies alter the competitive advantage of firms, or open up new markets and trigger mergers.

- The character of merger waves is also crucially dependent on political, technological, regulatory, institutional and demographic changes.

- While mergers in the first decades of the last century increased market power enormously, leading to stronger antitrust enforcement in later years, market concentration of the largest firms has not increased, and has even declined following the merger waves after the 1970s.

- Merger waves have also increased in intensity and frequency. The 1980s, 1990s and 2000s waves were of a considerably larger magnitude and followed each other more rapidly than the first three waves.

- Takeover activity is characterized by industry clustering. In certain industries, corporations, in a seeming imitation of lemmings, pursue M & A as if on an autopilot in fast-forward mode.

- With industry clustering, the first-mover firms may become winners, and 'me-too' followers end up as losers. However, 'me-too' followers may also gain from the errors of the first movers. Industry clustering throws up both opportunities and risks of failure.

- Merger waves may be triggered by rational economic motivations as well opportunistic behavioural motivations of corporate managers to exploit temporary stock market mispricing. It appears that both motivations may explain the past merger waves in the US.

- In the next chapter we provide alternative conceptual perspectives drawn from a variety of analytical traditions. This provides the framework to explain the context and rationale for mergers. The merger waves and industry clusters we have observed in this chapter may also be interpreted using that framework.

Review questions

2.1 What is meant by a merger wave?

2.2 What merger waves has the US experienced?

2.3 What are the major characteristics of these merger waves?

2.4 Do you think economic activity and stock market level cause merger waves? Why?

2.5 Are merger waves part of a global phenomenon?

2.6 How do the PEST factors affect merger activity?

2.7 What may be the reasons for industry clustering of mergers?

2.8 What is the significance of high divestiture activity during merger waves?

2.9 What is the significance of industry clusters in mergers for companies seeking competitive advantage?

2.10 Explain the rational economic theories of merger waves. What is the empirical evidence to support them?

2.11 Explain the behavioural theories of merger waves. What is the empirical evidence to support them?

Further reading

M. C. Jensen, 'The modern industrial corporation, exit and the failure of internal control systems', in D. H. Chew (Ed.), *Studies on International Corporate Finance and Governance Systems* (New York: Oxford University Press, 1997).

J. Harford, 'What drives merger waves?', *Journal of Financial Economics*, **77**, 2005, 529–560.

M. Rhodes-Kropf and D. T. Robinson, 'The market for mergers and the boundaries of the firm', *Journal of Finance*, **63**, 2008, 1169–1211.

Notes and references

1. This section on the first three waves in the US draws upon M. S. Salter and W. A. Weinhold, *Diversification Through Acquisition* (New York: Free Press, 1979), Chapter 1; N. R. Lamoreaux, *The Great Merger Movement in American Business 1895–1904* (Cambridge: Cambridge University Press, 1988), Chapters 1, 6 and 7; R. J. Gilson and B. S. Black, *The Law and Finance of Corporate Acquisitions* (New York: Foundation Press, 1995), Chapter 1; and M. C. Jensen, 'The modern industrial corporation, exit and the failure of internal control systems', in D. H. Chew (Ed.), *Studies on International Corporate Finance and Governance Systems* (New York: Oxford University Press, 1997).
2. G. J. Stigler, 'Monopoly and oligopoly by merger', *American Economic Review*, **40**, May 1950, 23–34.
3. R. J. Gilson and B. S. Black, *ibid.*, 15.
4. R. Rumelt, 'Diversification strategy and profitability', *Strategic Management Journal*, **3**, 1982, 359–370.
5. Gilson and Black, *ibid.*, p. 18.
6. Gilson and Black, *ibid.*, p. 23.
7. Gilson and Black, *ibid.*, p. 18.
8. V. Maksimovic and G. Phillips, 'The market for corporate assets: Who engages in mergers and asset sales and are there efficiency gains?', *Journal of Finance*, **56**, 2001, 2019–2065. See their Figure 3.
9. A. Shleifer and R. W. Vishny, 'Takeovers in the '60s and the '80s: Evidence and implications', *Strategic Management Journal*, **12**, 1991, 51–59.
10. P. G. Berger and E. Ofek, 'Bustup takeovers and value-destroying diversified firms', *Journal of Finance*, **LI**(4), 1996, 1175–1200.
11. See S. Bhagat, A. Shleifer and R. W. Vishny, 'Hostile takeovers in the 1980s: The return to corporate specialisation', *Brookings Papers on Economic Activity: Microeconomics*, **1990**, 1–72. Shleifer and Vishny, *ibid.*, argue that rigorous antitrust enforcement in the 1960s caused US firms to diversify into unrelated lines of business. Matsusaka rebuts this argument with empirical evidence that diversifying acquisitions were made by small as well as large firms, with the former being less likely to face antitrust challenge. Further, in European countries such as Germany and the UK and in Canada, in the inter-war years, large firms undertook diversifying mergers although antitrust policy in these countries was less stringent than in the US. 'The bulk of the evidence, then, is inconsistent with the antitrust hypothesis.' See J. G. Matsusaka, 'Did tough antitrust enforcement cause the diversification of American corporations?', *Journal of Financial and Quantitative Analysis*, **31**(2), 1996, 283–294.
12. A possible reason why the number of divestitures and their value tell different stories is that in 2000–2006 private equity firms became major players and bought divested businesses rather than whole firms, and some of these divestitures were very large (see Chapter 10 for a discussion of divestitures). This may also explain why divestitures increased in value in 2007 while mergers had slumped by then.

13. For a review of these trends see B. Holstrom and S. Kaplan, 'Corporate governance and merger activity in the United States: Making sense of the 1980s and 1990s', *Journal of Economic Perspectives*, **15**(2), 2001, 121–144.

14. Roundtable discussion, 'Keeping score on the key drivers in M & A's future', *Mergers & Acquisitions*, May/June 1998.

15. Hedge funds make investments to exploit anticipated market movements using a variety of investment styles and derivative instruments to hedge risk. They exploit volatility of asset price movements as well as timing. They also invest in special situations such as merger arbitrage (see Chapter 20) and distressed debt. They raise funds from financial institutions, pension funds, sovereign wealth funds and high net worth individuals. In 2007 hedge fund assets amounted to $1.9 trillions ($491bn in 2000) and fell to $1.4 trillions in 2008 (Casey Quirk-Bank of New York Mellon Thought Leadership series, *The Hedge Fund of Tomorrow: Building an Enduring Firm*, April 2009. Hedge funds are generally regarded as short-term opportunistic investors, although in the last few years their investment strategies have evolved to include long-term strategies such as LBOs. Hedge funds are unregulated, and receive management fees and performance fees in excess of some minimum yield to their investors, by the so-called 2/20 rule (2% of capital as management fee and 20% as performance fee). They have been blamed for contributing to the credit crisis in 2007–08.

16. From http://europa.eu/abc/keyfigures/index_en.htm, downloaded on 3 June 2008.

17. J. Ratner, 'Global ambitions fuel a takeover boom', *Financial Times*, International M & A Survey, 30 June 2000.

18. See Table 2.3 of Sudi Sudarsanam, *Creating Value from Mergers and Acquisitions: The Challenges* (FT Prentice Hall, 2003).

19. G. Bannock, *The Takeover Boom: An International and Historical Perspective*, Hume Occasional Papers (Edinburgh: The David Hume Institute, 1990), p. 10.

20. Data for Figure 2.4 from 'Acquisitions and mergers in the UK', *Central Statistical Office Bulletin*, London, May 1993. Data up to 1969 include only listed companies. After 1969, figures include all industrial and commercial companies.

21. One of the most important examples of this state-sponsored cloning of corporate giants was GEC merging with two competitors, AEI and English Electric, and another was British Leyland, born of a merger of smaller automobile manufacturers. During 1965–69 the IRC sponsored approximately 50 horizontal mergers.

22. J. Fairburn, 'The evolution of merger policy in Britain', in J. A. Fairburn and J. A. Kay (Eds), *Mergers and Merger Policy* (Oxford: Oxford University Press, 1989), pp. 193–220.

23. A. Hughes, 'The impact of merger: A survey of empirical evidence for the UK', in Fairburn and Kay (Eds), *ibid.*, Table 1.4. A similar picture emerges, based on number of mergers.

24. Hughes, *ibid.*, Tables 1.7 and 1.8. The average five-firm sales concentration ratio increased only marginally from 46% in 1970 to 47% in 1975, before falling to 46% in 1979. The 100-firm concentration ratio was even more stable at about 25% through 1968 to 1980.

25. P. Augar, *The Death of Gentlemanly Capitalism* (London: Penguin, 2000).

26. Although Wimbledon in southwest London is the venue of the greatest of all tennis tournaments, the UK has produced very few champions over the years. The City of London is the world's premier financial centre, but it is not dominated by home-grown British financial institutions.

27. As discussed in Chapters 18, 20 and 21, many US-style bid and defence strategies were not possible under the UK Takeover Code.

28. The correlations between stock market level and number of acquisitions in the current year (and between stock market level and acquisitions in the following year) are also very high: 0.81 (0.64) for the US; 0.92 (0.91) for the EU; and 0.84 (0.84) for the UK.

29. In the M & A literature there are other behavioural models, e.g. where corporate managers are irrational but the financial markets are rational value maximizers. A conjunction of irrational managers and irrational financial markets is also possible. These models are discussed in later chapters.

30. M. Gort, 'An economic disturbance theory of mergers', *Quarterly Journal of Economics*, **11**, 1969, 241–273.

31. B. Jovanovic and P. Rousseau, 'The Q-theory of mergers', *American Economic Review*, AEA Papers and Proceedings, **92**(2), 2002, 198–204.

32. S. Davies and B. Lyons, *Industrial Organization in the European Union: Structure, Strategy and the Competitive Mechanism* (Oxford: Clarendon Press, 1996), pp. 17–19.

33. A variant of the PEST framework is PESTEL, i.e. political, economic, sociological, technical, environmental and legal. Since environmental and legal influences are likely to operate largely through the other four dimensions, we prefer the simpler framework.

34. A. Shleifer and R. W. Vishny, *ibid.*, discuss the contrasting influences that might have fuelled the 1960s and 1980s merger booms in the US. We discuss the M-form organizational structure further in Chapter 7 on diversifying acquisitions.

35. This suggests that when a firm in an industry becomes the target of an acquisition, it increases the probability that other firms in the same industry might also attract takeover bids. For evidence consistent with such an increase see M. H. Song and R. A. Walkling, 'Abnormal returns to rivals of acquisition targets: A test of the "acquisition probability" hypothesis', *Journal of Financial Economics*, **55**, 2000, 143–171; A. Akhigbe, S. F. Borde and A. M. Whyte, 'The source of gains to targets and their industry rivals: Evidence based on terminated merger proposals', *Financial Management*, 29(4), 2000, 101–118.

36. Directorate-General for Economic and Financial Affairs, European Commission, *European Economy, Supplement A, Economic Trends*, 2000, p. 14.

37. J. Harford, 'What drives merger waves?', *Journal of Financial Economics*, **77**, 2005, 529–560.

38. M. L. Mitchell and J. H. Mulherin, 'The impact of industry shocks on takeover and restructuring activity', *Journal of Financial Economics*, **41**, 1996, 193–229. Mitchell and Mulherin examine the impact of industry shocks on takeovers in the US during 1982–89 and define industry shock as any factor, whether expected or unexpected, that alters industry structure.

39. J. H. Mulherin and A. L. Boone, 'Comparing acquisitions and divestitures', *Journal of Corporate Finance*, **2**, 2000, 117–139. For example, 50% or more of the firms in banking, broadcasting/cable and petroleum are acquired during that period, whereas in household products, construction machinery, shoes, newspaper, semiconductor and homebuilding this is less than 10%. At least 40% of the firms in chemicals, petroleum, telecommunications, medical services and natural gas make divestitures, whereas there is no divestiture in banking in the Midwest, grocery stores, securities brokerage and toiletries/cosmetics.

40. R. Powell and A. Yawson, 'Industry aspects of takeovers and divestitures: Evidence from the UK', *Journal of Banking & Finance*, **29**, 2005, 3015–3040. Clustering is assessed by number of acquisitions or divestitures and not value of these deals.

41. Powell and Yawson, *ibid.*, based on their Tables A1 and 1. Supporting this conclusion is the greater volatility of the annual percentage value of takeovers (10.5%) than that of divestitures (6.9%) relative to the mean of 6.7% in each case (their Table 1). Numbers rounded to the nearest decimal place.

42. R. Schoenberg and R. Reeves, 'What determines acquisition activity within an industry?' *European Management Journal*, 17(1), 1999, 93–98.

43. A merger wave is identified by first identifying the year with the highest number of mergers and then locating the beginning and end of the wave defined as the year with one third of the peak number or less. This algorithm is similar to the one used by K. Carow, R. Heron and T. Saxton, 'Do early birds get the returns? An empirical investigation of early mover advantages in acquisitions', *Strategic Management Journal*, **23**, 2004, 781–794. The mergers are completed and involve UK firms as targets and acquirers who gain at least 50% stake in the targets from the merger. An initial sample of 25,591 deals is screened for this analysis.

44. A. Shleifer and R. Vishny, 'Stock market driven acquisitions', *Journal of Financial Economics*, **70**, 2003, 295–311. The following two paragraphs draw upon this paper.

45. If a bidder raises cash prior to the bid by selling its stock, say by a rights issue, such an issue can be construed as taking advantage of stock overvaluation. However, since equity issues are often made at a steep discount to the current stock price, and may involve underwriting costs, the degree of exploitation of market overvaluation is less than when a bidder uses its stock directly to make an acquisition.

46. Since in a tender offer in which the target shareholders are invited by the bidder to tender their shares directly to the bidder, target managers' opportunism is likely to be constrained (see Chapter 20 on difference between mergers and tender offers). This constraint is even more binding if the tender offer is a hostile tender offer where target shareholders have even more power relative to their managers. This implies that in times of stock market overvaluation, tender offers and hostile tender offers should be less frequent than in normal times. There is evidence that during the 1990s the incidence of hostile tender offers in the US was much less than in the 1980s (see Holmstrom and Kaplan, *ibid.*). This model does not assume information asymmetry between bidders and target managers who knowingly accept bidders' overvalued stock and therefore are not irrational.

47. J. S. Ang and Y. Cheng, 'Direct evidence on the market driven acquisition theory', *Journal of Financial Research*, 29(2), 2006, 199–216.

48. J. S. Ang and Y. Cheng, *ibid.* Market value is compared with the expected value estimated by the residual income (RI) model incorporating expected return based on the Fama–French three-factor model and industry-relative market-to-book ratio (MB) (see Chapters 4 and 16 on these models respectively).

Median overvaluation for the whole sample is 36% (RI model) and 31% (MB model). Cash acquirers are overvalued by (median) 20% but stock acquirers by 40%, with the difference being significant. Median buy and hold return of overvalued acquirers is higher by 4% (around deal completion) and 5–6% (over one to three years post-acquisition) than those of overvalued non-acquirers (see Chapter 4 on this return). Overvaluation is greater in successful than in failed mergers, with the median difference between acquirer and target overvaluations 9% in successful and 0.6% in failed mergers. Since, generally, it is tender offers and hostile tender offers that fail, rather than mergers that are negotiated between bidder and target managers, this result is consistent with target managements' opportunism being more constrained in failed bids (see footnote 41 above).

49. M. Rhodes-Kropf and S. Viswanathan, 'Market valuation and merger waves', *Journal of Finance*, **59**(6), 2004, 2685–2717. The authors tease out a number of implications of their model, which they empirically test for in a follow-up paper discussed below.

50. M. Dong, D. Hirshleifer, S. Richardson and S. Hong Teoh, 'Does investor misvaluation drive the takeover market?', *Journal of Finance*, **61**(2), 2006, 725–762.

51. M. Rhodes-Kropf and D. T. Robinson, 'The market for mergers and the boundaries of the firm', *Journal of Finance*, **63**(3), 2008, 1169–1211.

52. On advantages of being a fast second player, see C. Markides and P. Geroski, *Fast Second* (San Francisco, USA: Jossey-Bass, 2005).

CHAPTER 3

Alternative perspectives on mergers

Objectives

At the end of this chapter, the reader should be able to understand:

- the different perspectives on M & A, their focus and the major elements;
- the rationale for merger decisions under each perspective;
- the potential outcomes of merger decisions under each perspective;
- sources of value and risk in mergers; and
- M & A as a process rather than as a mere transaction.

Introduction

In the last chapter we traced M & A trends over the past 110 years and observed several peaks of activity. Takeover activity is also from time to time concentrated in certain industries, perhaps because of firms in those industries responding to exogenous factors and seeking to alter the competitive structure of their industries in their favour under the stimulus of these factors. The earliest wave we observed, the 1890s wave in the US, was described as merging for monopolies. Thus one possible framework to explain and predict the incidence of mergers is the economic perspective that covers monopoly power, economies of scale and scope, and relative transaction costs in markets and costs of internal organization.

We have also seen that technological changes often trigger corporate restructuring through mergers and acquisitions. This suggests that firms seek to alter the competitive structure of their markets through exploitation of technological resources and capabilities they have built up internally or acquired through M & A. We have also observed that although monopolistic mergers may have declined over the decades as a result of strict antitrust regimes, companies still carried out many related and unrelated or diversifying acquisitions. To explain these we need a corporate strategy perspective.

There are also other perspectives such as finance theory and managerial perspectives from which to view mergers and acquisitions. For example, the managerial perspective is useful in explaining the widespread evidence that most acquisitions do not generate value for their shareholders or other stakeholders. The finance perspective explains the conditions under which takeovers can provide discipline against the self-interested behaviour of top managers, and the relationship between takeovers as a disciplinary device and other corporate control mechanisms. Mergers occur in the context of their firms' political structure, culture and social processes, and these may impact on the merger decision as well as on its effectiveness. An organizational perspective may explain the quality of acquisition decisions and some of the risks involved in the merger process. Human aspects of the merger process also need to be kept in view.

These alternative perspectives provide a much richer set of models than any single perspective, and may explain not only the rationale for corporate acquisition decisions but also the organizational context and the processes that condition the decisions. The alternative perspectives are not always mutually exclusive. Since a modern corporation, especially a medium- or large-sized firm, tends to be a multi-product firm, we assume this model of the firm in the following discussion. This allows us to incorporate economies of scope, transactional costs, diversification and some of the managerial motives for mergers and other elements as being germane to our discussion. We can also examine organizational complexity as a factor in the M & A process.

The economic perspective on mergers

The rationale for mergers under the economic perspective generally rests on their impact on the various costs faced by the firms, and on their market power. Costs may be reduced or market power augmented, allowing firms to enjoy higher profits than under competitive conditions. Thus firms merge in order to gain competitive advantage over their rivals through cost reduction or increased market power. In the following analysis we discuss the various cost concepts underlying the economic perspective and how mergers enable firms to reduce their costs. We also examine how mergers enhance market power.

A firm is regarded as a homogeneous decision-making unit concerned with maximizing its long-run profitability through achieving or sustaining competitive advantage over its rivals. The ability of the firm to create or maintain its competitive advantage depends on the competitive structure of the market in which it sells its output–monopoly, monopolistic, oligopolistic or competitive. The competitive tool that the firm selects will depend on this structure, and on the expected reaction of the firm's rivals. In a competitive market selling a homogeneous product or service it has to compete on price, and can maintain its competitive advantage only by being the least-cost producer. In a situation of monopolistic competition it may differentiate its offerings sufficiently to avoid or minimize direct rivalry with other firms and achieve a degree of monopoly in a local market. In an oligopolistic structure the firm may avoid price rivalry and compete on non-price dimensions that again may have the effect of differentiating the product.

In the case of a single product firm competing in a single market, cost leadership may be achieved through economy of scale or vertical integration. Superior profitability may also be achieved through increase in market power, with the concomitant ability to dictate or influence the price and profits. We observed in Chapter 2 that the first merger wave in the US, between 1890 and 1905, was described as merging for monopoly, but subsequent antitrust laws reduced the opportunity for such mergers. Thus monopoly power is no longer a sustainable goal for mergers, albeit attractive for the merging firms.

Economy of scale

Where the firm is a multi-product firm selling a number of related or unrelated products, cost reduction may be achieved through both economy of scale and economy of scope. Economy of scale refers to the cost reduction in producing a product from increasing the scale of its production in a given period. Since production costs may have a fixed component that is largely invariant to volume of production, e.g. rents, administrative costs, the average cost of production falls when these fixed costs are spread over a larger volume. This results in scale economies. A limit to scale economies exists when the production volume reaches the minimum efficient scale (MES). Average production cost does not fall with increasing volume beyond that level.

Similar scale economies may also exist in the case of non-production costs associated with marketing, selling, distribution, storage or after-sales service, provided they have a fixed cost component invariant to volume. Since, in a merger, the merging firms jointly produce and sell a larger volume of their product than each on its own, there is opportunity for scale economies in both production and non-production costs. For this reason, many mergers and acquisitions are often justified on this basis (see Exhibit 3.1).

Exhibit 3.1

Scale economy in a merger

The German retail banking market is heavily dominated by the public sector savings banks and cooperatives, and for private banks, faced with this competition, retail banking is a low-returns operation. In March 2000 Deutsche Bank, the largest commercial bank in Germany, and Dresdner Bank, one of its oldest rivals and the third largest German bank, proposed a merger to address the sub-optimal size of each bank. Deutsche Bank judged that it needed 10m to 12m retail customers to achieve the critical mass necessary to generate decent profits in the retail business. The merger would have produced a retail business exceeding the critical size, and would have yielded scale economies. Although this logic was sound, the negotiation between the banks failed for other reasons.

Source: Adapted from A. Barber, 'Breuer's bet', *Financial Times*, 8 March 2000

Scale economies may, however, be limited for several reasons. Once the firm passes the minimum efficient scale there are no further efficiency gains. When the firm becomes very large, organizational control problems may lead to diseconomies of scale. Where large scale leads to substantial market power, antitrust regulations may come into play to check or roll back such power, e.g. the Clayton Act in the US or EU Merger Regulation (see Chapter 17 on antitrust regulation).

Economy of learning

A firm can reduce the costs of producing the same volume of output in successive production periods through the learning process. Such learning arises in the form of more efficient scheduling of production, minimizing wasteful use of materials, better teamwork, or avoidance of past mistakes. Japanese companies' continuous improvement processes exemplify the application of learning economy to production. Initial learning costs are high, but as the cumulative output over time increases, the learning curve gets less steep and the marginal value of learning with each additional unit of production increases.

While scale economy is concerned with scale of output in a *single period*, learning economy is concerned with cumulative volume of the same product over *several periods*. Scale economy requires the existence of fixed costs of production, but learning economy is not premised upon it; it is more about organizational capacity for learning. Mergers can bring about economy of learning through sharing of best practices based on accumulated knowledge and experience of the workforces of the merging firms, but the case for learning economy is perhaps much weaker than for scale economy as a rationale for mergers. After a merger the cumulative output of the merging firms' products increases, but the learning opportunities may be more limited than when a firm increases its cumulative output on its own from one period to the next.

Economy of scope

Scale economy and learning economy are characteristic of a single product. Most modern firms are, however, multi-product firms. In spite of a high volume of divestitures in the last two decades, the largest 500 firms in the US and in the world remain significantly diversified[1]. Thus it is appropriate to focus on multi-product firms. With multiple products, a firm can achieve scope economy. Scope economy exists when the total cost of producing and selling several products by the multi-product firm is less than the sum of the costs of producing and selling the same products by individual firms specializing in each of those products. Examples of economy of scope include costs of research and development, use of a single umbrella brand to sell several products, and selling several products through common distribution channels. Richard Branson's Virgin group exemplifies the use of an umbrella brand, e.g. Virgin Atlantic Airways, Virgin Music, Virgin Cola and Virgin Media. The bancassurance model pursued by many banks and insurance companies in the 1990s provides another example, with insurance companies using banking networks to sell their insurance and asset management products.

Scope economy depends on the existence of certain capabilities and resources that have a common applicability across several products. How common a firm's resources and capabilities are depends on the portfolio of products the firm is selling. Some products may share a common technological basis, some may share similar geographical markets or consumer groups, and some may share only managerial capabilities. The last provides a rationale for a firm making unrelated diversification.

Scope economy may also be manifested in the form of increased revenue and profits rather than unit cost reduction of the individual products in a multi-product firm. Thus it is effective use of existing common resources and capabilities that creates added value through increased volume and sales revenue, rather than through efficiency. Thus use of an umbrella brand or common marketing channels may serve to increase sales of existing or new products, and may provide the opportunity to sell them at a premium price, thereby increasing profitability. Selling two complementary products together, e.g. food and wine, increases the sales of both in a restaurant. Revenue enhancement through scope economies is often a strategic logic for mergers of firms selling related products, technologies or markets (see Exhibit 3.2).

In theory, scale, learning and scope economies are a function of size of the firm, i.e. 'big is beautiful and profitable', and give large firms a cost advantage over small firms. They give firms an incentive to grow. Since mergers are a quick way to increase firm size, firms may resort to these transactions to exploit scale, learning and scope economies. By the same token, acquirers often justify their acquisitions on the basis of these putative economies. We discuss the conditions for optimal exploitation of scale and scope economies through M & A in more detail in Chapters 5 to 7, along with the limits to such economies that often result in 'big is ugly'. Scope economies in unrelated mergers are discussed in Chapter 8.

Exhibit 3.2

Scope economy in a merger

Pearson plc, the UK firm that, *inter alia*, publishes the *Financial Times*, also produces several products for the education market, particularly the fast growing e-education market. It made several acquisitions and entered into alliances to expand its online product portfolio concerned with developing and distributing curriculum content. In August 2000 Pearson acquired the Minneapolis-based firm National Computer Systems (NCS) for $2.5bn. NCS provided software and Internet-based technologies for collecting, managing and interpreting education data, and was also leader in testing and assessment technology that had access to 40% of the US schools. The acquisition extended Pearson's product range, and allowed the merged companies to tailor individual learning programmes that enabled students to learn from home with the participation of their parents, while cutting the cost of reaching a wider number of students. Pearson estimated that the acquisition would deliver annual cost savings of $50m by 2002.

Source: Adapted from A. O'Conner, 'NCS could be transforming purchase for Pearson', *Financial Times*, 1 August 2000

Transaction cost economies and vertical integration

A firm may enter into arm's length transactions with its supplier to source its inputs or with a distributor to sell its output. Alternatively, it can set up production of those inputs or distribution of its outputs within its own organizational control. These alternatives represent the 'buy or make' decision of the firm. The make decision can be effected by acquisition of a supplier or a distributor, leading to a vertical merger or integration. Firms choose between the make and buy alternatives by evaluating the comparative transactional costs of dealing with independent parties in the market and internal organization.

Both the market relationship between buyer and seller and vertical integration of the two operations generate costs for both the transacting parties. In the case of the market relationship these costs include the return required by them for entering into the transaction, the cost of contracting, the cost of monitoring contract compliance, and the enforcement cost when either party breaches the contract. These costs may be difficult to estimate and even more difficult to recover in the event of a breach. The sources of these problems are varied, and rooted in the information asymmetry between the buyer and seller. In other cases, even a long-standing buyer–seller relationship could be strained by forces generated outside that relationship.

Until the late 1990s Marks and Spencer, once regarded as the flagship of the UK clothing retail market, had a close relationship with its UK-based suppliers. The suppliers, albeit independent, would tailor their clothing designs to the specifications supplied by M & S. The long and paternalistic relationship, however, precluded M & S from sourcing its supplies from cheaper markets overseas, whereas its high street competitors could. Moreover, the relationship also weakened the suppliers' incentive to innovate and produce competitive designs. These suppliers had developed too much dependence on M & S. At the end of the 1990s M & S's operating and stock market performance fell sharply, forcing it to start sourcing its merchandise from overseas to cut costs. This switching hurt M & S's traditional suppliers a great deal, with many of them unable to survive.

An alternative to market relationship is to internalize the transaction through vertical integration. Thus an organizational solution is proposed for market failure. In the case of a conglomerate firm, Oliver Williamson[2] also proposed that the firm plays an internal capital market role by allocating scarce capital resources to highest valued uses. The need for this internalization of the capital market function arises from the supposed failure of the external capital market, which also suffers from information asymmetry.

Firms can undertake mergers to bring about vertical integration of the adjacent stages from the inputs through production to retailing to the consumer. Firms can integrate vertically forwards or backwards through a merger. For example, an oil company owning refineries may acquire an exploration and production company to increase its access to oil to feed its refineries. Many Chinese steelmakers made vertical mergers to acquire captive iron ore mines, and Russian steel companies acquired small steel companies in Europe to gain technology and market access in 2006.

In addition to the cost reduction benefits of vertical integration, it can also give the firm a competitive advantage over its rivals that do not enjoy similar low-cost inputs or distribution channels. Thus it can also be used as an effective entry barrier. Vertical integration, however, is not free of problems. For example, the integrated supplier may sell only in-house and therefore not exploit possible scale economies. We discuss these potential problems in Chapter 6. Where a vertical merger encounters these problems it will not be an optimal decision, and it will fail to create value for its stakeholders. The 1980s and 1990s divestiture waves included many previously integrated operations, suggesting that the realized benefits did not exceed the costs of integration. The recent trend in large-scale outsourcing testifies to the excessive cost of integrated operations.

Industry analysis of competition

The above perspective describes the sources of economic value to the firm, but does not relate to the context of the firm's efforts at value creation. This context is the competitive environment of the firm. What this environment is, and how firms compete within it, are matters of relevance to whether or not they can create value. An economic perspective that provides a framework to analyze mergers is the traditional *structure–conduct–performance* paradigm of industrial economics shown in Figure 3.1, and Michael Porter's five forces model of industry competition as shown in Figure 3.2. In the SCP model industry structure plays a central role,

Figure 3.1   **Industry structure, firm conduct and firm performance**

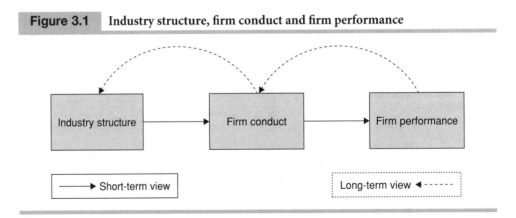

Figure 3.2　Porter's five forces model of competition

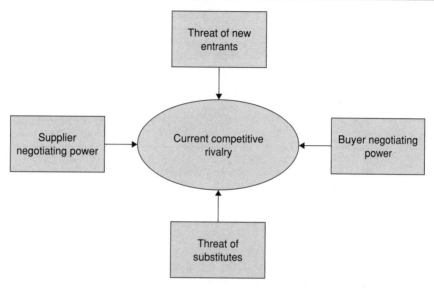

Source: Adapted from M. Porter, *Competitive Advantage: Creating and Sustaining Superior Performance* (New York: The Free Press, 1998), Figure 1.1.

and shapes firm conduct and determines firm as well as average industry profit performance. This is depicted by the continuous arrows.

Porter defines industry competitive structure by the interaction of these five forces: current competitive rivalry, threat of new entrants, relative bargaining power of the buyers of firm's output, relative bargaining power of the seller of the firm's inputs, and threat of substitutes. The strength of each competitive force is determined by a number of factors, as illustrated in Table 3.1.

These five forces determine the average profitability of firms in the industry and hence its attractiveness. They are not of equal strength within the same industry or across industries. An assessment of market attractiveness depends in turn upon an assessment of the strength of

Table 3.1 Determinants of strength of the five competitive forces

Competitive force	Strengthened by
New entrant	Low level of entry barriers (e.g. scale economies, capital requirements, absolute cost advantages from learning, access to distribution channels)
Product substitution	Low relative price of substitute, buyer propensity to substitute, low (product) switching costs to buyers, superior performance of substitutes
Supplier power	High (supplier) switching costs to buyers, non-availability of substitutes, supplier concentration, ability to integrate forwards
Buyer power	Buyer concentration, low cost of switching to other sellers, ability to integrate backwards, buyer information
Current rivalry	Low industry growth, high fixed operating costs, excess capacity, low product differentiation, seller concentration

Table 3.2 Competitive force level and industry attractiveness

Threat to firm from	*Level of threat makes industry*		
	Very unattractive	*Possibly attractive*	*Very attractive*
Current rivals	High	High	Low
Substitutes	High	Low	Low
New entrants	High	Low	Low
Buyers	High	High	Low
Seller	High	High	Low
Risk to profitability	High	Indeterminate, depends on relative force levels	Low

these factors. A market is more attractive the weaker the threat of the five forces, as illustrated in Table 3.2.

Five forces or six?

Brandenburger and Nalebuff have proposed a model of competitive forces faced by a firm that is conceptually similar to the five forces model of Porter but introduces an addition force, i.e. complementor. The value net represents these forces (see Figure 3.3)[3]. It represents the various players in a competitive game in which the firm is the focal player. It also represents the interdependencies among the players. The other players are the customers, suppliers, competitors and complementors. These players influence the value gains to a firm from being a player in the industry.

A player is a complementor if customers value your product more when they have the other player's product than when they have your product alone. Computer hardware and software, automobile and motor insurance, food and drinks are examples of complementors. On the other hand, a player is a competitor if your customers value your product less when they have the other player's product than when they have your product alone. Whereas in the Porter model suppliers, customers and competitors have in general an adversarial relationship with the firm, they can also be allies and enjoy a symbiotic relationship, e.g. the growth of DVD and movie studios, although DVD can threaten existing media of movie viewing, such as cinema, or joint advertising campaigns by a producer and its distributor. Thus the five forces model portrays the threats and the value net the opportunities that a firm faces[4].

Figure 3.3   **The value net**

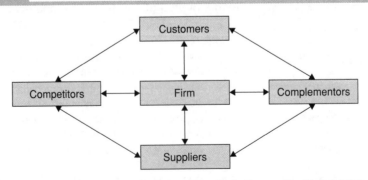

Source: A. Brandenburger and B. Nalebuff, *Co-opetition* (New York: Currency Doubleday, 1996), pp. 111–117.

Changing the industry structure and mergers

The Porter model is limited by its static nature, since it views industry structure as stable and externally determined. Structural changes are induced as much by environmental factors as by what the players in an industry themselves do. In the short term firm performance is driven by industry structure, and companies respond to industry structure and are constrained by it. In the long term, however, competition is a dynamic process, and firms can reshape the industry structure through creating new technologies, substitute products or distribution channels, e.g. Internet retail. Industry structure or the nature of the interrelationships among the five or six forces can also change in response to environmental changes, which can be viewed within the PEST framework discussed in Chapter 2. Firms responding to the threats and opportunities posed by the PEST changes may alter the industry structure and hence its attractiveness. Strategic innovation can also relieve firms from the suffocating effects of industry structure: for example, low-cost airlines such as Southwest in the US and easyJet and Ryanair in Europe are successful examples of innovations in new business models.

Firms faced with the five/six forces configuration may attempt to change the configuration to increase their competitive advantage and their profitability through mergers. It is, however, important to understand the key structural factors that need to be changed, and whether they are amenable to change through mergers. For example, if profitability is depressed because of the threat of new entrants, a merger that generates substantial scale economies to move the firm beyond the MES of production may raise the entry barrier to new entrants, which will operate below the MES threshold. A merger that gives privileged access to suppliers or distribution channels reduces current rivalry. Of course, the rivals may emulate the first firm and carry out copycat mergers to achieve the same scale economies or gain similar access.

A merger with a rival, for example a merger of two supermarkets, enhances the bargaining power of the merged firms against both firms' suppliers if the merger reduces the number of supermarkets. A merger in a mature industry suffering from overcapacity allows the firms to reduce that capacity, thereby reducing price competition and improving the profit margin for all firms. Thus mergers, by altering the configuration of the competitive forces in an industry, can trigger several rounds of subsequent mergers until a new competitive equilibrium is reached. This, as we saw in Chapter 2, is one of the reasons for mergers to occur in industry clusters. The case study at the end of this chapter illustrates how mergers among supermarkets increase buyer power, and how their suppliers counter-attack with their own mergers. Thus the players themselves often transform industry competition when they make strategic moves, a merger being one such move.

Game theory and competitive moves

The retailers, while making acquisitions to increase their buying power, may have anticipated the countermoves by the manufacturers. Thus players in a competitive market often evolve their strategies by taking into account the countermoves their rivals may make. Game theory is concerned with 'analysis of optimal decision making when all decision makers are presumed to be rational, and each attempts to anticipate the actions and reactions of its competitors'[5].

In a market with a small number of competitors, i.e. in a duopoly or oligopoly, each competitor recognizes the possibility that its rivals will make simultaneous or subsequent counter moves. For example, in a market with two suppliers, they have to decide whether to increase capacity. Capacity expansion increases output, and may lead to scale economies and cost efficiencies. The expanding player can exploit these cost savings to reduce prices and increase market share. The non-expanding player is faced with price pressure, and loss of market share

Table 3.3 Incremental payoff to Tweedledum and Tweedledee when they play the acquisition game (in $000 and total incremental value to both in parentheses)

		Tweedledee	
		Acquisition	No acquisition
Tweedledum	Acquisition	$80, $80 ($160)	$100, $75 ($175)
	No acquisition	$75, $100 ($175)	$90, $90 ($180)

Source: Adapted from D. Besanko, D. Dranove and M. Shanley, *Economics of Strategy* (New York: John Wiley & Sons, 2000), pp. 36–40.

and scale efficiencies, with a further squeeze on price. The first supplier may increase capacity and the second supplier may follow suit or not change its capacity level. The payoffs to the suppliers are known, and will depend on the action–reaction combination. Each player in this competitive game chooses the best course of action, given the actions of its rival. If both players follow this rule, they reach equilibrium, called Nash equilibrium, named after the Nobel Prize-winning mathematician–economist John Nash[6]. If a player moves away from that equilibrium strategy, he will be worse off.

Table 3.3 sets out the payoffs to two competitors, Tweedledum and Tweedledee, in the same industry playing the acquisition game[7]. Either can increase capacity by acquiring a competitor (not each other). The payoff is in the form of incremental economic value to each firm, conditional on its own decision to make or not make an acquisition. In the table Tweedledum's payoffs appear first. Each competitor makes his acquisition decision simultaneously but independently of the other. Assuming that Tweedledum is doing his best, given Tweedledee's strategies, and vice versa, the Nash equilibrium in the game is that both decide to acquire. This strategy maximizes the payoff to each player no matter what the other player does. This game has a dominant strategy, i.e. acquire, since the payoff to that strategy is superior to that of no acquisition, across all of the other player's strategies. Where there is a dominant strategy, it also represents a Nash equilibrium for the player. It can be seen that the total payoff to both is highest when neither acquires, but acquisition will be the preferred strategy because it maximizes the individual player's wealth.

Nash equilibrium has the following characteristics:

- It is reached by each player acting in his or her own best interest.
- It is self-enforcing, being based on each player's expectation that the other player will choose his or her Nash equilibrium strategy.
- It may not maximize the aggregate payoffs. In the first game in Table 3.3 the maximum aggregate payoff ($180k) results from both Tweedledum and Tweedledee not acquiring. Then they will be collectively better off, but this requires cooperation and agreement not to acquire, or a firm commitment by each firm to retaliate in kind if the other acquires, provided the commitment signal is credible[8].

Nash equilibrium can also exist in the absence of a dominant strategy, as shown in Table 3.4.

In this game the optimal outcome for each player depends on the move made by the other. If either player makes an acquisition and the other does not, the latter will be worse off than by both acquiring. Thus if Tweedledum acquires so should Tweeledee, and vice versa. If, however, either player does not acquire, the optimal move for the other is also not to acquire. Each player's move invokes a retaliatory or conciliatory countermove depending on the relative payoffs. Unlike in the game in Table 3.3, a player cannot expect to choose its strategic move in isolation[9]. Both 'acquisition–acquisition' and 'no acquisition–no acquisition' are Nash

Table 3.4 Incremental payoff to Tweedledum and Tweedledee in acquisition game (in $000 and total incremental value to both in parentheses) (no dominant strategy)

		Tweedledee	
		Acquisition	No acquisition
Tweedledum	Acquisition	$80, $80 ($160)	$90, $60 ($150)
	No acquisition	$60, $90 ($150)	$100, $100 ($200)

equilibria conditional on the first mover's decision. If one player acquires, the other player's pay-off declines without a matching acquisition. This is an example of negative externality for the other player. No acquisition has a positive externality if the other player also forgoes acquisition.

Nash equilibrium in a sequential acquisition game

Suppose the players can choose among three acquisition decisions: no acquisition ('No acq'), small acquisition ('Small'), and large acquisition ('Large'). Suppose Tweedledum makes the first move; Tweedledee would react to that move. The incremental value gains to the two players in a two-stage game are set out in Figure 3.4 in a decision tree format to reflect the sequential nature of the game. The value gains are the incremental payoffs for different action–reaction combinations. In making his first move, Tweedledum has to

- think forward and put himself in the position of Tweedledee;
- identify the latter's optimal choices conditional upon his initial choice; and
- make his own optimal decision conditional on Tweedledee's *expected* reaction.

Figure 3.4 Sequential acquisition game (value gains in $000)

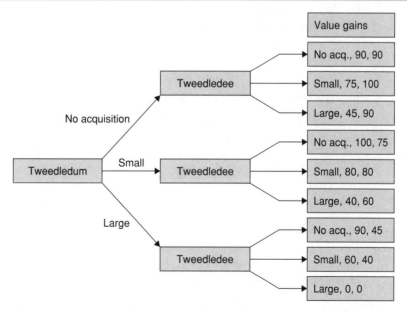

Source: Adapted from D. Besanko, D. Dranove and M. Shanley, *Economics of Strategy* (New York: John Wiley & Sons, 2000), p. 39.

This fast-forward and then rewind mode of thinking is known as *dynamic programming*. Of course, Tweedledee would rationally anticipate this line of thinking. Thus each player has to get inside the mind of the other.

For Tweedledee, the optimal reactive strategy is a small acquisition if Tweedledum either does not acquire or makes a small acquisition and no acquisition in response to a large acquisition. Anticipating this optimal strategy, Tweedledum will choose large expansion yielding profits of $90k, forcing Tweedledee to maintain its current capacity, which gives profits of $45k, rather than a small acquisition with a profit of $40k or a large acquisition with zero profits. The aggregate profits to both when Tweedledum elects large acquisition are $135k. The large expansion choice of Tweedledum is known as *subgame perfect Nash equilibrium* (SPNE). SPNE is the optimal action for a player at each stage that it reaches believing the other players will behave in the same way. Thus, given Tweedledum's choice, Tweedledee makes his optimal choice. This expected choice then determines the first-stage choice of Tweedledum.

By contrast, if the game were a simultaneous game, the Nash equilibrium would be (small, small) with an $80k payoff to each. For each player this strategy is clearly superior to the other two when the other player chooses no acquisition or small acquisition, and only slightly inferior to no acquisition when the other player chooses large acquisition ($40k against $45k). Given the higher probability of being better off with small acquisition, and given that neither player knows what the other player will do, (small, small) becomes the Nash equilibrium strategy. But it is not Tweedledum's dominant strategy for all three choices that Tweedledee could make. Thus SPNE produces a different optimal strategy for the first mover, i.e. large expansion, from that for a simultaneous mover, i.e. small acquisition.

By being the first mover, and by choosing a large acquisition strategy, Tweedledum has pre-empted Tweedledee's small acquisition choice. This requires a large-scale investment on Tweedledum's part. This large-scale investment signals commitment and forecloses its rival's choices. This coercive value of commitment is absent from the simultaneous game. This advantage to the first mover is one of several we discuss in Chapter 5. The large commitment also reduces the flexibility of the first mover to exploit any future and more valuable growth opportunity. We consider flexibility within the real options framework below. There is always tension between the strategic imperative of commitment to gain advantage conditional on the current industry structure and the strategic need for flexibility to shape the industry structure of the future.

Mergers as a sequential game – some illustrations

We encounter the sequential game in the M & A context. We observed in the previous chapter that mergers occurred in clusters, and that this pointed to moves and countermoves by competitors in the same industry. These mergers can be modelled by the sequential game outlined above. For example, the huge merger of BP and Amoco for $48bn in 1998 was fairly quickly followed by the even more stupendous merger of Exxon and Mobil for $79bn in 1999. BP Amoco then replied with the acquisition of Atlantic Richfield in 2000 for $27bn. This was followed by Chevron's acquisition of Texaco for $43bn in 2000 and then by the merger of Phillips Petroleum with Conoco in 2001 to create a combined entity with assets of $54bn. The mergers among supermarkets and food manufacturers illustrated in the case study below are also examples of sequential games. In many cases, mergers are made to pre-empt similar moves by rivals by taking a potential target out of play. The aborted takeover bid by Coca-Cola for Quaker Oats in November 2000 was in part an attempt to prevent its great rival Pepsi from acquiring Quaker. Another example is Microsoft (MS)'s strenuous attempts in 2001 to prevent the purchase of AT&T's cable business by AOL-Time Warner (AOLTW)[10]. MS feared that the combination of AOLTW's cable businesses with those of AT&T would create an industry giant with control over one of the most promising means of delivering advanced Internet services such as e-commerce, information and entertainment services to US consumers. MS was therefore prepared to join other bidders for the AT&T business. This strategy is particularly effective if suitable targets are in short supply, although in such an event the first mover needs to consider the regulatory risk of its bid being blocked by antitrust authorities.

Implications of game theory for M & A

In the sequential game in Figure 3.4 when the first mover, Tweedledum, undertakes a large commitment, Tweedledee is deterred from making even a small acquisition. The first mover's acquisition may not have such a strong deterrent effect on the other players as long as the latter can also undertake similar acquisitions, thereby negating or mitigating the advantage gained by the first mover. Thus a competitive acquisition game may leave the old rivals relatively no better off than before the round of acquisitions started. The whole industry becomes much more concentrated. Whether competitive rivalry abates as a result is not unequivocally predictable. Thus it is not clear that acquisition as a competitive tool can confer more than ephemeral advantage. If so, the first acquirers may not achieve any more value gains than the me-too acquirers. We review the empirical evidence on the relative performance of first and me-too acquirers during merger waves in Chapter 4. For the first acquirer advantage to be more than ephemeral, the acquisition may perhaps have to yield a competitive profile that cannot be easily replicated. This requires that the acquisition bring together two firms with uniquely complementary competitive strengths, resources and capabilities. A real test of the value creation potential of an acquisition is whether it consummates such a happy union.

Game theory's assumptions concerning the knowledge of options available to all the players and the associated payoffs may be limiting, especially where the game involves more than two players. The game also gets more complicated in a multi-period setting involving several moves. Moreover, mergers driven by search for access to resources and capabilities to generate future, and hitherto unknown, technologies and products pose complex valuation, i.e. payoff, issues. The decision variables are thus wider ranging than just capacity increase. Their valuation needs a different framework, such as the real options models introduced later in this chapter and discussed in more detail in later chapters.

How important is the industry factor for firm performance?

While industry factor seems relevant to firm conduct and performance, as indicated by the SCP model in Figure 3.1, its influence may be mitigated by firm-level factors that reflect firm conduct. Robert Grant summarizes the studies of differences in profitability (return on assets) among firms that break it down into its variance explained by industry effects and that explained by firm effects. Industry factors account for between 4% and 19% and firm-specific factors for between 36% and 55% of the variability in firm profits. Thus industry factors seem to be less important than firm specific factors in determining firm profitability[11]. One of these studies also finds that profit variance is also explained by year-to-year variations. This evidence points to the following:

- in the context of the SCP model, *conduct* is more important than *structure*;
- firms' competitive strategies can overcome structural constraints;
- profitability varies greatly within each industry; and
- profitability varies greatly over time.

Strategy perspective on mergers

The chemicals industry mergers in Exhibit 3.3 describe different motivations for mergers. In the bulk chemicals segment, scale economies drive the mergers, consistent with Porter's model of industry competition. However, in the speciality chemicals segment, mergers are motivated by the need to acquire products, technologies and businesses that complement core competences. In the life sciences segment, with rapid changes in technology, acquirers search for capabilities for innovation, product development and differentiation[12]. These acquisitions thus illustrate the contrast between cost-based competition and capabilities-based competition through mergers.

Exhibit 3.3

Chemical firms look for growth hormones in mergers

In recent years the chemicals industry experienced substantial restructuring through M & A. In 1998, 175 acquisition deals worth $18bn were done. This figure was surpassed in the first nine months of 1999 with 154 deals worth $23bn. The chemicals industry is made up of three segments: bulk or commodity chemicals, speciality chemicals, and life sciences. Commodity chemicals is a volume business with slow growth rates, tight margins and a high level of cyclicality, whereas the speciality segment is more of a niche market, often protected by patents and product differentiation. It is a relatively high-margin business. The life sciences segment, including pharmaceuticals, biological products and nutritional substances, is the most dynamic of the three segments, enjoying patents and intellectual property rights. Its profit margins are multiples of those of the bulk and speciality chemicals. Firms in the commodity end of the industry were merging to achieve scale economies by increasing their capacity. The US acquisition of ARCO Chemical Co. by Lyondell Petrochemical Co. in a deal worth $5.7bn and Ashland Co.'s acquisition of a petrochemical division of Dow Chemical Co. exemplified the competitive merger moves. In the speciality and life sciences segments, too, several firms merged to gain access to markets, products or capabilities. In all three segments firms were making acquisitions to improve their competitive position against one another and achieve profitable growth.

Source: J. Harrison, 'Unrelenting chemicals M & A reconfigures the industry', *Mergers and Acquisitions*, January 2000

Generic competitive strategies

Michael Porter has developed three generic competitive strategies, as shown in Figure 3.5[13]. Cost leadership is achieved through being the lowest-cost producer and seller. Lowest costs are achieved through an efficient combination of the value chain of the firm's activities, such as production, sales and marketing, and distribution. The firm differentiates its products by endowing them with such attributes as will induce consumers to pay a premium price well above the cost of producing and selling them. In the focused approach the firm chooses the segment of the market to compete in, and competes on the basis of either cost leadership or

Figure 3.5 Types of competitive strategy

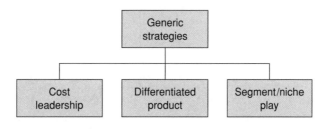

perceived customer benefits. We have seen that in the chemicals industry many firms have given up a broad market approach in favour of segmental competition. In the bulk chemicals segment competition is based on cost leadership, whereas in the speciality segment it is based on product differentiation.

The generic categories, however, do not explain how firms choose among them, or why they migrate from one generic strategy to another. They also do not identify which firms in an industry will follow which of the three strategies. As the chemicals industry restructuring indicated, firms may switch from one strategy to another through mergers. During this transition such firms may be 'stuck in the middle'[14]. Being stuck in the middle may also be a deliberate strategic choice. These choices can be explained only by understanding the bases on which firms compete, how over time these bases are eroded, and how they renew themselves through acquiring new bases of competition. Thus we need greater insights into how firms compete, and which firm-specific and external conditions allow them to compete in particular ways.

Resource-based view (RBV) of competitive strategy

Under this perspective, firms are not passive prisoners of external forces with only limited degrees of freedom, but are capable of proactively managing and shaping their environment. They compete on the basis of their resources and capabilities. The resources are tangible and intangible assets owned or controlled by the firm. Capabilities are the essential organizational competences that allow the firm to make effective use of its resources. Resources by themselves do not differentiate a firm's competitive advantages or strengths. Two firms with similar resource endowments may have different competitive profiles. These resources need to be leveraged by the firm's capabilities to generate a given competitive profile. It is the unique combination of resources and capabilities that confers a unique competitive advantage. This rests on the assumption that strategic resources and capabilities are heterogeneously distributed across firms, and these differences may often persist to give firms a sustained competitive advantage[15].

Resources of firms
Broad categories of resources available to a firm are shown in Figure 3.6. Some of these resources, e.g. tangible assets, may not be idiosyncratic to a firm, and may be easily replicated or bought and sold. Others, such as intangible assets, are firm specific but may be tradeable, e.g. patents, or replicable, e.g. R & D facilities. The human resources may be mobile, e.g. investment bankers migrating to other banks. But, in general, human resources may be embedded in organizations and not as valuable outside these organizations: for example, creativity may be team specific or culture specific. Resources that are easily imitated, replicated, substituted, traded or mobile are unlikely to confer sustainable competitive advantage.

Figure 3.6 Organizational resources of a firm

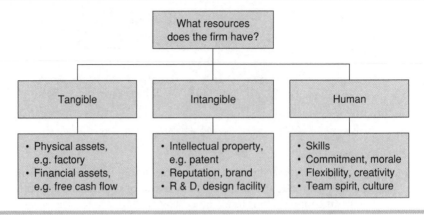

Figure 3.7 Organizational capabilities of a firm

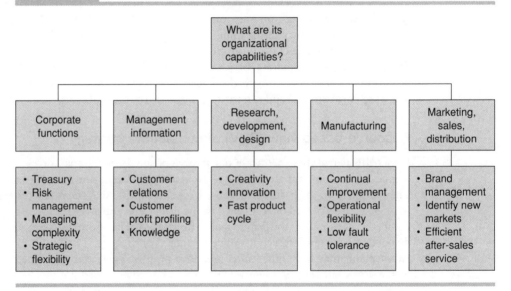

Organizational capabilities

These are distinct from organizational resources. Prahalad and Hamel consider these strategic capabilities a firm's 'core competences'. They represent the collective learning in the organization, especially how to coordinate diverse production skills and integrate multiple streams of technology[16]. We may trace the organization's capabilities to its various functional capabilities as shown in Figure 3.7[17].

Firms may have developed the resources and capabilities over time organically, or may have acquired them in the factor markets or through mergers, acquisitions, strategic alliances, etc. At any point in time the stock of resources and capabilities defines the firm's capacity to compete with other firms. Competitive advantage, however, depends on relative firm capacities *vis-à-vis* its competitors and sustainable competitive advantage depends on the

Exhibit 3.4

Look! Capabilities walk out of the door

In the heyday of the dotcom boom in 1999–2000 many investment banks were faced with an exodus of their star deal-makers to the dotcom start-up companies. One of them was Terry Kawaja, who left his position as a senior executive in Salomon Smith Barney, the bulge-bracket investment bank on Wall Street. He left his job at the bank to become chief financial officer of a little-known Internet service provider, Evoke, in April 2000, saying 'it feels great doing deals for yourself rather than as an adviser for someone else'. For many investment bankers the attraction of working for oneself, and the lure of huge stock options offered by the Internet companies, were quite irresistible. The banks were fighting to hold on to their employees with seductive pay packages including bonuses guaranteed for several years. One Wall Street headhunter remarked: 'It's like a hand-to-hand combat out there, recruiting at senior levels.' The technology start-ups created increased pressure on staff retention in banks. Sadly for the upstart start-ups, the dotcom bubble burst only a few months later and the disenchanted investment bankers had to look for jobs again.

Source: Adapted from C. Pretzlik and W. Lewis, 'Bankers land a fortune', *Financial Times*, 9 May 2000

firm's capacity to preserve its superior resources and capabilities. In a fiercely competitive world, firms will relentlessly seek to erode one another's superior resources and capabilities through poaching, imitation, replication or substitution. Furthermore, the factors that give rise to core competences should not be mobile[18]. Exhibit 3.4 shows how mobile resources and capabilities can be in certain businesses.

Path dependence of resources and capabilities: DNA to M & A

A firm develops its resources and capabilities over time. The evolutionary path of the firm itself therefore defines their characteristics. This path dependence of the current resource and capability profile of a firm does provide a degree of protection against replication[19]. Each firm carries its own corporate DNA, with its unique genetic code[20]. For other firms to replicate its profile they have to decode its DNA, map its genes, and perform some genetic engineering. Mergers offer an alternative pathway to resource and capability acquisition. However, whether genetic modification through merger will be successful depends on what sort of corporate genes are being spliced, and how. The genetically modified merged entity may not be robust.

Resource-based competition and mergers

While firms can develop their R & C to gain sustainable competitive advantage where the gap between their current endowments and the desired profile to accomplish their competitive goals is wide, firms may follow the M & A route to fill the gap. This suggests that the merging firms have complementary resources and capabilities. As is evident from Exhibit 3.4 on Internet companies poaching investment bankers from Wall Street, it is possible to hire resources.

However, where the required capabilities are embedded in organizations – i.e. their teams, routines and cultures – piecemeal acquisition of resources and capabilities and reassembling them may not replicate their unique profile. Hence mergers may be the only way.

Acquisition of resources through M & A may be easier than acquisition of capabilities, because of the latter's embedded nature. Thus capability acquisition and integration into a more harmonious whole within the merged entity pose particularly challenging organizational problems. Valuation of capabilities as opposed to tangible resources is also a formidable challenge. Capability acquisition and consequent leveraging to generate new technologies are in the nature of real options, and real option valuation is still at an incipient state of model development (see introduction to real options later in this chapter)[21]. We discuss these problems in Parts 3 and 4.

Value chains and R & C sharing

In the RBV of mergers, the merging firms share their R & C to create value. This means that the sharing should lead to cost reduction, sales revenue enhancement, or real option-type growth opportunities. The scope for R & C sharing, which of them can be shared, and whether the sharing will create value, are issues that can be examined within the framework of the value chain model developed by Porter and shown in Figure 3.8[22]. A comparison of the acquirer's and its target's value chains shows that the two differ in several components of the value chain, allowing scope for improvements in both operations and infrastructure, such as technology development. For example, the target incurs higher costs as a proportion of its revenue in inbound logistics and outbound logistics, but is more efficient in operations, and marketing

Figure 3.8   Comparative value chains of acquirer and target

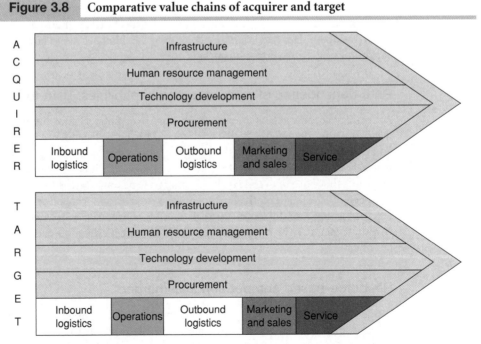

Source: Adapted from M. Porter, *Competitive Advantage: Creating and Sustaining Superior Performance* (New York: The Free Press, 1998), Figure 2.2.

and sales. Similarly, the target's spend on technology development is much larger than the acquirer's. This may be because the target business is more technology-intensive, requiring higher R & D spend.

In a horizontal merger there will be much wider overlap among the value chain elements than in a conglomerate merger, e.g. infrastructure such as top management, strategic consulting, and finance. In a related merger driven by scope economies, non-production elements of the value chain may dominate the integration. When the two value chains are combined, the value margin must increase to create value for shareholders. Which elements of the merger need to be merged depends on the type of business model that drives the merger, i.e. horizontal merger, vertical integration or conglomerate diversification and its value creation logic. In acquisitions representing real options, the technology and human resource elements may dictate the integration (see below for a description of real options). In the value chain framework the different merger types differ in the ways the value chain elements of the merging firms are related[23]. These are discussed in Chapters 5 to 11.

Value chain as activity system

A value chain is more than a mapping of the various sources of costs and revenue in a firm's income statement. It represents an 'activity system' and the underlying processes[24]. Two firms may differ in their activity systems even when their business models are the same and their endowments of R & C are also the same. To understand a firm's value chain, and how it contributes to the firm's competitive advantage, one needs to understand its context and content as well as the processes and procedures that link the activities in the value chain. These links may be formalized in routines, or embedded in tacit knowledge, or captured by a firm's culture. In the context of a merger the merging firms' activity systems must be integrated, leveraged and reconfigured to create an expanded set of resources and capabilities that will pass the VRINS test (see Figure 3.9). The two value chains can be reconfigured to suit

Figure 3.9	Acquisition, new core competences, sustainable competitive advantage and value creation

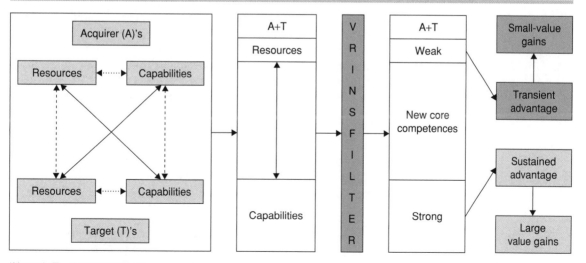

*Note: A+T = the merged entity

alternative competitive strategies such as cost leadership, product differentiation or narrow segmentation[25].

Sustainable competitive advantage through acquisitions

While firms endeavour to establish their competitive advantage over their rivals, how long can they maintain such advantage? The longer this *competitive advantage period (CAP)* is, the more valuable is the advantage, and this has implications for the valuation of a firm in the M & A context, since an acquirer has to value the target firm for the purpose of carrying out the acquisition. The CAP depends on a range of factors:

- the relative strengths and weaknesses of the forces in the value net;
- the uniqueness of the configuration of resources and capabilities assembled; and
- the speed with which new competitive forces emerge and render the above configuration obsolete.

R & C characteristics and competitive advantage: the VRINS test[26]

Jay Barney has argued that not all resources and capabilities can confer sustainable competitive advantage (SCA), and that only those that pass the VRINS test are likely to do so. VRINS stands for *valuable, rare, inimitable* (i.e. costly to imitate) and *non-substitutable*. Moreover, the organization must have the necessary policies and procedures to support exploitation of VRINS resources and capabilities, leading to VRIO (*valuable, rare, inimitable and organizationally underpinned*). When two firms have similar VRINS, they may still have differing competitive advantages owing to their different organizational structure, policy and practices as well as appropriate managerial incentives to pursue those policies.

What makes VRINS costly to imitate or non-substitutable? The factors that isolate R & C from imitation or substitution are called *isolating mechanisms*. These include the following:

- The firm's unique historical conditions that led to the creation of its R & C. For example, the firm has accumulated its R & C in a low-cost manner because of its past activities and the strategic decisions made in the past, and it is difficult for other firms to replicate the same historical conditions and processes. Current R & C are thus path dependent. *Corporate history matters!*
- Causal ambiguity. The firm's advantages are based on a complex web of inter-related R & C, and it is difficult for other firms to disentangle causality from this web and replicate the same cause-and-effect relationship.
- Social complexity. The firm's R & C involve interpersonal relationships, trust, culture and other social conditions that are costly to imitate in the short term. The firm's organizational and social context of the development and deployment of its R & C make them difficult for other firms to replicate.
- Tacitness of knowledge. Many of the intangible resources and capabilities are knowledge assets embedded in the firm's routines and relationships, and not susceptible to clear articulations or codification. This prevents diffusion of such knowledge by imitation or replication.

Causal ambiguity is a two-edged sword. It may often be the case that even the firm that possesses a competitive advantage may attribute it to the wrong set of R & C, which are often *tacit* in nature and not well articulated in established codes and manuals. This may lead to costly strategic errors. Isolating mechanisms, if effective, render a firm's R & C unique, but firms should guard against the '*illusion of uniqueness*' and overestimating the value or durability of such uniqueness.

Figure 3.9 depicts how, in an acquisition, the acquirer's and target's resources and capabilities are pooled and leveraged with one another to produce a new set of R & C. The dotted arrows indicate the *intra-firm* leveraging in the pre-acquisition firms, dashed arrows represent *inter-firm* pooling of R & C, and the unbroken arrows point to the leveraging between the acquirer and its target. An acquisition provides an enlarged set of resources and capabilities and opportunity, by mutual learning, to improve both *intra-firm* leveraging and *inter-firm* leveraging of this expanded set. Leveraging R & C in the post-acquisition period is thus both *additive*, i.e. pooling of resources or capabilities, and *multiplicative*, i.e. new ways of leveraging the pooled resources with the pooled capabilities. It is both *linear* and *non-linear* in its impact.

Acquisition, to be successful, requires understanding the new set of R & C in the combined firm and creating a new model for leveraging them. But it may also require re-examining the configuration of legacy R & C and the associated model of leveraging in the individual firms. The new R & C configuration, however, has to pass the VRINS filter before being transformed into new core competences and into a valuable source of incremental competitive advantage. The resulting configuration may be weak, and lead to a transient competitive advantage, or strong, and confer a sustained competitive advantage. Transient advantage results in small value gains (or even negative when transaction costs are taken into account), whereas sustained advantage generates large value gains to stakeholders.

Dynamic capabilities and mergers

As shown in Figure 3.9, an acquisition can be transformational and lead to a new or enhanced set of core competences, sustained competitive advantage and substantial value gains. M & A can thus serve as a vehicle for acquiring dynamic capabilities. Teece, Pisano and Shuen formulate a model of business strategy in which 'competitive success arises from the continuous development and reconfiguration of firm-specific assets'[27]. This model attempts to explain how firms develop and renew their internal competences. Acquisitions provide the motivation and opportunity to reconfigure acquirers' and targets' resources and capabilities in such a way as to create new core competences. Reconfiguration and renewal are a continuous, evolving and dynamic process. Acquiring dynamic capabilities through M & A may also be a way of adapting to hypercompetition.

It is worth remembering that 'advantage' is a relative term, and is determined as much by what a firm does as by what its competitors and complementors do. It is this competitive interaction that accelerates competition and shortens the competitive advantage period as suggested by game theory.

How sustainable is competitive advantage? Evidence

How durable is a firm's competitive advantage? Richard D'Aveni has argued that industries are characterized by *hypercompetition*, which shortens the duration of SCA. Hypercompetition may arise from rapid technological changes and rapid imitation of firms' R & C by other firms, or rapid adoption of one another's business models etc. In such an environment firms need to search continually for new sources of strategic advantage as the earlier ones become obsolete. Figure 3.10 shows how a firm can generate successive sources of competitive advantage in a hypercompetitive environment. Thomas and D'Aveni, in their study of shifts in

Figure 3.10 Hypercompetition and competitive advantage

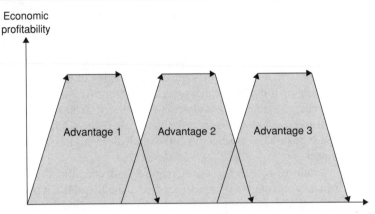

Source: R. D'Aveni, *Hypercompetition: Managing the Dynamics of Strategic Maneuvering* (New York: The Free Press, 1994), Figure 1–2, p. 12.

industry structure and competitive advantage between 1950 and 2002 in several manufacturing industries in the US, find a 'shift towards more temporary advantages as well as indicators of increasing structural instability', with this trend accelerating from 1980[28]. This finding implies a decreasing sustainability of competitive advantage and the imperative for firms to create value not with a single enduring advantage but with a series of transient and unsustainable advantages.

Further evidence of a sharp decline in competitive advantage is provided by Krishna Palepu and his co-authors for a sample of European firms with their sales growth performance assessed over 1989 to 2005 (see Figure 3.11). Sales growth rates of high performers in a year fall within 2 years to the average level, and from year 3 onwards their sales growth rates are similar

Figure 3.11 High sales growth doesn't last for long. Sales growth of European firms over time, 1989–2005

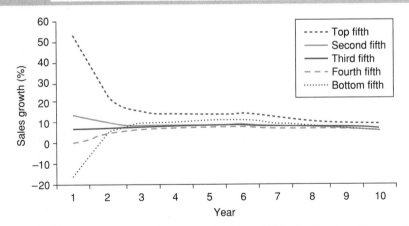

Source: K. Palepu, P. Healy and E. Peek, *Business Analysis and Valuation* (London: Thomson Learning, 4th edition, 2008), Figure 6.1.
*Note: Year on the horizontal axis refers to the year from the time of formation of the quintile portfolios

to those of the other sample firms[29]. While at the start of the sample period the gap between high and low growth performers is over 60%, by year 2 this range narrows to just 3%, and by year 10 the gap is wiped out. The authors report a similar pattern, but over a more prolonged period, of erosion in relative profitability of their sample firms[30].

Mueller provides contrary evidence that firms in many industries are able to maintain the superior profitability record for a long period. In his sample of 600 US manufacturing firms from 1950 to 1972, the high profit group's average return on assets (ROA) starts out at 12% and decreases over time, converging to less than 8% after 10 years. The low-profit group starts out at 0% and increases over time, converging to about 4.9% over the same period. Thus after 10 years the former outperforms the latter by 3.1%[31]. Thus while there is substantial mean reversion, the high-performing group still maintains a superior profit performance, indicating sustained competitive advantage.

Although a firm may achieve high revenue growth or high profit performance because of its competitive advantage, this is quickly eroded. Figure 3.11 depicts the average performance of a multi-industry sample, but in individual industries the erosion rates may be different, and individual firms may sustain their high performance. The caveat is that individual firms must identify what contributes to their superior competitive advantage in those circumstances, and find ways of maintaining their superiority.

Acquisitions, viewed in the context of hypercompetition, must therefore enhance the acquirers' competitive advantage quickly. Compared with other modes of market entry such as organic growth or a JV, acquisition can shorten the *'time to market'*. On the other hand, the enhanced competitive advantage must be realized by acquirers fairly quickly, since the competitive advantage period following an acquisition may not be very long. This also emphasizes the need for the post-acquisition integration process to be reasonably quick but effective. These conditions for successful acquisitions may be hard to satisfy, resulting in poor post-acquisition performance. The empirical evidence that we review in detail in the next chapter suggests as much.

Corporate and business strategies

Firms develop their strategies at two broad levels – the corporate level and the business (often referred to as strategic business) unit level (see Figure 3.12). Corporate strategy aims at building a portfolio of operating businesses that together will maximize value for the firm's stakeholders. Business strategy aims at achieving sustainable competitive advantage in individual operating business units, and hence long-term value. The linkages among the portfolio business units may be a source of competitive advantage through scope economies arising from the sharing and leveraging of their resources and capabilities. In the presence of such economies, the beneficial portfolio effects of enhancing the competitive advantage of one business unit on the other portfolio businesses need to be considered. These synergies add value, and hence need to be factored into individual business unit strategies. Adding a new business unit that is unrelated to the other existing business units in terms of non-generic functions, resources and capabilities such as technology, production process, markets etc. is called unrelated or conglomerate diversification.

M & As can be undertaken to achieve the firm's strategic objectives at either level. Conglomerate acquisitions have been a feature of the M & A scene for several decades. Business unit strategies may result in acquisition of businesses:

● in the same markets selling the same products or similar products broadly serving the same user needs, e.g. a merger of two airlines (horizontal merger); or

Figure 3.12 **Corporate and business strategies and acquisitions**

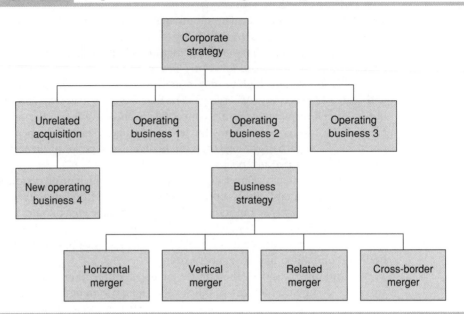

- related by sharing some inputs, functions, resources or capabilities (related merger), e.g. a merger of truck and car companies; or
- operating the successive stages in a value chain, e.g. a raw material producer or a wholesale distributor (vertical merger); or
- selling the same products but in different national geographical markets, e.g. banks acquiring banks in neighbouring countries (cross-border merger).

We develop this framework further in Chapters 5 to 8 and discuss the role of M & A in different types of strategy.

Finance theory perspective on mergers[32]

The finance theory perspective marks a point of departure from the economic and strategy-based perspectives. Its focus is firmly on the inside of the firm: internal systems, decision processes, decision-makers' motivations and their behaviour. While game theory does incorporate a behavioural perspective, it is concerned with intra-firm behaviour in a competitive strategic game context. Finance theory is concerned with the games that the stakeholders in a firm play in order to maximize the returns they earn from the capital they have invested in the firm.

Finance theory considers merger decisions of firms within the framework of the conflicts of interests among various financial claim holders of those firms. This framework rests on the following elements:

- shareholder wealth maximization as the paramount goal of corporate investment and financing decisions;
- the agency model of the firm as a nexus of contracts, and the characterization of managers as agents, agency costs and conflicts of interests between principals and agents;

- deviation from the shareholder wealth maximization objective due to agency problems;
- internal corporate governance constraints on managerial self-interest pursuit;
- external constraints imposed by the activism of institutional and large block shareholders; and
- external constraints imposed by the market for corporate control.

Shareholders owning a firm may also manage it. In this case there is no separation of ownership and control. Owner–managers make decisions that would maximize the value of the firm and their shareholding. Mergers and acquisitions undertaken to achieve sustainable competitive advantage through the strategies we have outlined above are consistent with shareholder wealth maximization. By definition, sustainable competitive advantage manifests itself in returns to the firm well in excess of the competitive cost of capital, and therefore can enhance shareholder wealth (see Chapter 14 on valuation of target firms). However, where control by managers is divorced from ownership, managers may undertake mergers that do not satisfy the shareholder wealth maximization criterion. Extensive empirical evidence reviewed in Chapter 4 suggests that this is more often the case. This raises questions about the motivation behind many of the mergers.

Berle and Means observed the increasing separation of ownership from control resulting from diffusion of share ownership and the small proportion of shares held by the managers[33]. Diffusion of ownership results in a large number of small shareholders that have no incentive or means to monitor the behaviour and performance of managers. This lack of monitoring leaves managers in effective control of their firms, and they may make decisions that enhance their private benefits at the expense of shareholder interests.

Agency model of the firm[34]

Jensen and Meckling develop a model of the firm as a nexus of contracts. Firms receive capital by issuing equity and debt. Shareholders as owners enter into a contract with managers delegating powers to manage the company on their behalf. The managers become agents of the shareholders, the principals. Managers may pursue their own interests and neglect the interests of shareholders, thereby destroying shareholder value. The divergence between shareholder and managerial interests represents the agency cost to the shareholders. Shareholders can reduce these agency costs of shirking, perquisite consumption and consumption of other private benefits of control by managers by writing, monitoring and enforcing detailed contracts with the managers. From the shareholders' point of view, the optimal agency relationship equates the monitoring costs with the savings from reduced agency costs.

Where the agency problem is extreme, investors may refrain from investing in the firm's shares, thereby denying managers the resources that would enable the firm to grow. The value of the shares in the company may fall so low that existing shareholders will be willing to sell their shares to a predatory bidder. To avoid these unfavorable outcomes managers may subject themselves to some external monitoring. For example, managers may agree to an external audit. The firm pays out the associated bonding costs, but if the reduction in agency costs exceeds the bonding costs, shareholders gain.

Agency costs of debt

Creditors provide debt capital to the firm and face similar agency costs, since the debt capital may be used by managers to enhance their private benefits. Creditors have less control over the managers, but a stronger, legally enforceable contract with the borrowing firm. Creditors also use devices such as covenants that allow them to monitor the borrowing firm's financial condition. The ultimate sanction that creditors have against defaulting borrowers is that they can force the latter into insolvency or liquidation. Free cash flow is the operating cash flow available to a firm after meeting its operating and tax commitments, and after it has exhausted all investment opportunities that would yield a return in excess of its cost of capital, i.e. in positive net present value (NPV) projects. Managers may invest this free cash flow in suboptimal projects with negative NPV if that would enhance their personal utility rather than maximize shareholder interests[35].

Michael Jensen argues that debt provides effective monitoring of management, and prevents them from over-investing in negative NPV such as ill-thought-out acquisitions that promote managers' own self-interest such as empire building. Jensen cites the example of many oil companies that spent vast sums of money in oil exploration and building up their oil reserves in the 1970s, but these over-investments led to their stock prices falling. In the mid-1980s many of these oil companies were subject to hostile takeovers financed with considerable amounts of debt. These gave rise to the adage that it was cheaper to buy oil on Wall Street than dig for oil. The proposition that debt compels managers to run their businesses more efficiently and in the interests of their principals, both equity and debt holders, has provided the intellectual underpinning for the extraordinary growth of leveraged buyouts from the 1980s to date (see Chapter 11 on leveraged buyouts).

Agency costs and corporate governance

While debt provides a mechanism for managerial monitoring and control, its focus is parochial, since it serves the creditors' interests more than the equity holders' interests. For equity holders, the beneficial effects of debt monitoring are incidental and due to overlapping interests, especially firm survival. Equity holders can set up more direct monitoring and control mechanisms since, after all, they appoint the board of directors, who, in turn, appoint the executive managers. While, in theory, shareholders are the ultimate arbiters of management performance, in practice, again because of diffusion of ownership, the corporate governance mechanisms may not be quite effective.

Corporate governance refers to the set of contractual devices that regulate, monitor and control the behaviour and performance of executive managers, who are agents of capital providers such as lenders and stockholders. These devices include:

- the board of directors;
- the large block shareholders, e.g. financial institutions such as pension funds and insurance companies;
- shareholder activism by traditional fund managers, specialist corporate governance monitors and hedge funds;
- a management compensation system that aligns managerial and stockholder interests, e.g. performance-related stock options or stock grants;
- managerial stock ownership that may align managerial and stockholder interests; and
- the rights of lenders to call default and enforce their claims.

Corporate governance and mergers and acquisitions

Mergers provide a fast lane to growth in size of the firm. If managerial utility is a function of firm size, e.g. when remuneration and private benefits to managers are size related, the urge to merge may be quite irresistible for managers. Apart from managerial self-interest driving them to make bad acquisitions, honest incompetence of managers or organizational inefficiencies, such as lack of requisite acquisition-related competences, may also result in bad acquisitions. Corporate governance has an important bearing both on the choice of M & A as a means of achieving the firm's growth and shareholder value objectives and on the outcome of those decisions. Exhibit 3.5 shows how alert and active shareholders can prevent managers from pursuing value-destroying acquisitions. Thus the corporate governance perspective can explain the nature and type of acquisitions that occur, and also the success or failure of those acquisitions. (See Chapter 12 for a more detailed discussion of the impact of corporate governance on the acquisition decision and performance.)

Exhibit 3.5

Don't go splashing in posh hotels

Six Continents was the world's second largest hotel group, and by January 2002 the group had built up a £3bn cash mountain and was ready to buy upmarket hotels around the world. However, the acquisition plan drew considerable criticism from investment analysts and large institutional shareholders. One activist shareholder, Hermes, wrote to the company, accusing it of destroying value, and demanded a return of cash. Another large shareholder said that the company had paid too much for its past acquisitions. A leisure analyst said that the company's shares were lowly rated because 'people do not have the confidence in their ability to buy well'. The company, under pressure of such criticism of its acquisition policy, offered to return cash to shareholders if hotels were to be too expensive to buy.

Source: S. Daneshkhu, 'Six Continents may return cash early', *Financial Times*, 22 October 2002

The market for corporate control

Failure of internal governance of corporations may activate an external control device. This is the market for corporate control first conceptualized by Henry Manne[36]. This market is where the right to manage corporate assets is traded between competing management teams. Operation of this market involves takeovers of firms that have failed to make the most efficient use of their resources and capabilities. This is a measure of the incumbent managers' failure. A competing managing team currently running another company then makes a bid for the failed target firm. The acquiring firm then puts the resources and capabilities of the acquired firm to more profitable uses to generate higher value for shareholders.

Where the incumbent management does not agree with the bidder's diagnosis of its ills or the prognosis for its revival without the acquisition, it will resist the takeover bid, turning it into a hostile bid. Hostile takeovers thus provide a corrective mechanism for replacing under-performing managers. Often the threat of a hostile bid can by itself engender a miracle cure for the ailing target. Sometimes a 'friendly' takeover is a barely disguised hostile one, a metaphorical equivalent of a rather amiable executioner who whispers sensitively that he is acting in the best interest of the (about to be) executed by putting him out of his misery.

Conceptually, the market for corporate control is an extension of the free market in products and services to a free market in corporations. However, the course of the market for corporate control does not always run smooth. Hostile takeovers are extremely rare outside the Anglo-Saxon region consisting of the US, the UK, Canada and Australia. These countries share common law systems, a high reliance on stock markets as a source of capital, a *laissez-faire* attitude of governments and a culture that accepts adversarial encounter as a means of settling relative claims of contending parties. In continental Europe and in Asia, particularly Japan, such an adversarial model has to compete with the more traditional consensual style of doing business.

Takeover regulation and the market for corporate control

Efficient operation of the market for corporate control requires a neutral, if not a benign, regulatory regime. Many countries have no explicit takeover regulation and rely on security laws and corporate laws to regulate takeovers, especially hostile takeovers. The European Union enacted, after an elephantine gestation of 20 years, a takeover directive in 2004, which came into force in member countries in 2006, that allows for a more level playing field for hostile bidders *vis-à-vis* the targets. This directive constrains the target managers' ability to frustrate a hostile bid. We review this directive, its implications and impact so far in Chapter 19 on takeover regulation. Among the EU countries the UK has the most elaborate and sophisticated takeover regime, which in a diluted form has provided the template for the EU directive. In the US the Williams Act has, since 1968, regulated tender offers that often assume a hostile character.

In the US, since the mid-1980s, hostile takeovers have been subject to a host of hostile anti-takeover statutes by states and an ingenious panoply of anti-takeover defences devised by companies. As a result, the incidence of hostile takeovers has been much reduced. By contrast, several continental European countries have witnessed hostile, often fierce, takeover battles. Examples include the acquisition of Telecom Italia by Olivetti in Italy, the acquisition of Paribas by Banque Nationale de Paris (BNP) in France and, most spectacularly of all, the hostile takeover of Mannesmann of Germany by the UK's Vodafone in 2000 for over $150bn. These deals point to a wider acceptance of the relevance of the market for corporate control. Nevertheless, the incidence of hostile takeover has declined from its heyday in the 1980s.

A well-developed regulatory regime for the market for corporate control increases the scope of competition for corporations, and empowers shareholders. This also means that acquirers may find that, in winning the competition for a target firm, they may be betting the store and have little to show to their own shareholders. Thus with an efficient market for corporate control, profitable acquisitions may be harder to accomplish. We discuss the characteristics of the market for corporate control in different countries, and how it impacts on deal structuring, negotiation and outcome, in Chapter 18.

Finance theory and real options perspective on acquisitions

The resource-based view outlined above considers acquisitions as a means and process of changing the firm's resources and capabilities through the acquisition of the target's resources and capabilities. Some of the acquisitions are exploitative in nature, since they involve combining the existing resources and capabilities of the two firms to greater effectiveness or efficiency to gain competitive advantage. Others may be in the nature of exploration, involving further research and development and growing new resources and capabilities that will confer competitive advantage at some future, but indeterminate, date. While exploitation requires the deployment of existing knowledge in newer and more effective ways, exploration requires the creation of new knowledge. The latter involves a larger gamble on the unknown than the former. Exploratory acquisition may herald follow-on investments if the punt proves right. Finance theory has developed the concept of real options to conceptualize and value such exploratory investments.

Real options are options on real investments as opposed to options on financial assets, such as common stock or a currency. They represent exploratory investments on a small scale in activities that carry with them options that can be exercised in the future. For example, a small investment in R & D to develop a new product may, if successful, afford the firm the opportunity to invest further in production of that product if at some time in the future the firm has the information to determine that the investment will be valuable. Real options may also include the option to sell off an initial investment (the abandonment or put option) if, on further information, the firm believes the initial investment is no longer sustainable.

Real options and strategic acquisitions

A strategic acquisition is one whose value depends not necessarily on the cash flows from that acquisition *per se* but accrues from the follow-on opportunities opened up by that acquisition. Thus the initial acquisition may *appear* to be value destructive, but such value loss is more than offset by the value created from the subsequent decisions. The essence of real options is that firms can acquire these options and gain greater strategic flexibility. The first-step investment is no longer irreversible. Acquisitions commonly include growth or expansion options, abandonment options and delaying options. Investment in a biotechnology company that researches a cure for cancer is an example of a real option. The drug discovery stage is followed by other stages of investment – in clinical trials, commercial development, production and so on – with each stage providing an option to proceed to, or abandon, the subsequent stages.

Acquisition of a company that can be subsequently sold off if it turns out to be a poor bet is another example of a real option. Acquisition of intangible-rich target firms has a strong real-option flavour to it. Many acquisitions may thus be driven by the search for future growth opportunities in the form of real options. Wernerfelt argues that candidates for product or resource diversification must be evaluated in terms of their long-term capacity to function as *stepping stones* to further expansion[37]. Platform acquisition, discussed in Chapter 5, and strategic alliances, discussed in Chapter 9, are examples of potentially multi-stage investments with real option characteristics. Firms may delay their acquisitions, awaiting a more opportune time or better market intelligence. Such delays may enhance the value of the follow-on investments. Recent developments in the valuation of real options provide a framework for analyzing these acquisitions and a means of valuing acquisition targets (see Chapter 14 on target valuation).

Game theory, real options and acquisitions

Acquisitions can also be viewed in a framework that combines both real options and game theory. You will recall that in sequential games the first mover can signal a huge commitment, for example a large acquisition that can forestall its rivals from eroding its advantage with copycat mergers (see Figure 3.4 and related discussion above)[38]. Large acquisitions are thus appropriate in competitive situations where the competitive structure is well known and the aim is to pre-empt rivals. On the other hand, a small acquisition of an exploratory nature offers greater flexibility, and allows the firm to exercise any real option with subsequent larger investment. Such small acquisitions are appropriate where the competitive structure of the industry is still evolving. Real-option-based acquisitions thus represent emergent, rather than deliberate, strategies[39]. Emergent strategies are characterized by opportunism, flexibility and learning[40]. Takeovers of different types and size of target may be dictated by commitment or flexibility. If a firm intends to make a series of acquisitions to strengthen its market position, its competitors' reaction to this strategy will determine its success. However, the firm may decide to make the first acquisition, await the competitor reaction, and then decide whether to make the second acquisition if the competitors do not engage in a copycat acquisition. Thus the first acquisition is an option on the second. Real-option-driven acquisitions present considerable challenges to the valuation of the related benefits to the acquirer, and hence to the acquisition price and the takeover premium paid to target shareholders. We discuss these challenges in Chapter 14.

Managerial perspective on mergers

This perspective is closely related to the agency model of the firm. Under this perspective, managerial motives for mergers are considered as crucial determinants of the incidence, rationale, type, deal structure and outcome of mergers. One of the important considerations for managers during mergers is the extent of their control loss. This is not just a psychological deprivation. Since control offers the opportunity to enjoy private benefits, its loss will have pecuniary connotations. Managers, in making acquisition decisions and in reacting to takeover bids, will be motivated by both pecuniary and non-pecuniary considerations. Desire for control may also dictate how they structure a deal. For example, they may make cash acquisitions to preserve control and reject a cash bid to avoid control loss. It may be recalled from our review in Chapter 2 of the 1960s merger wave in the US that managers were said to have undertaken conglomerate diversification to achieve growth rather than profitability.

In the context of takeovers, managers may act to maximize their own interests rather than those of the shareholders. They may settle for a low premium offer from a bidder in exchange for a share in management control of the merged entity or a more exalted managerial position. Shareholders need to devise appropriate incentive contracts to align managerial and their own interests. Contracts such as golden parachutes that allow compensation for managers in the event of losing their jobs are designed to minimize conflicts of interests. The existence or otherwise of such arrangements will influence the deal structure and the attitude of managers to a deal.

Behavioural perspectives on managerial motivations for mergers or the outcome of mergers include the hubris hypothesis developed by Richard Roll and the risk diversification hypothesis put forward by Amihud and Lev[41]. Infected with hubris, acquiring company managers overestimate their capacity to create value out of acquisitions, and often overpay for them. Richard Roll uses this argument to explain the failure of most acquisitions to create value for acquirer shareholders.

Managers' capital, human and financial, is invested in the firm. Stock options designed to align the interests of managers and shareholders further increase the proportion of managerial capital invested in their own firm. As a result, managers hold highly undiversified asset portfolios, in contrast to the well-diversified shareholders. This increases their exposure to firm-specific risk such as bankruptcy of their firm. They undertake diversifying acquisitions to minimize the volatility of the firm's earnings, thereby reducing the risk of bankruptcy and the risk to their own jobs and their investment in their firm.

Managers' psychological biases such as hubris, overoptimism and overconfidence may drive them to undertake high risk acquisitions or overpay for them, thereby increasing the chances of value destruction. Target managers may be more concerned with the financial benefits to themselves if they agree to an acquisition than with those of shareholders and other stakeholders. Target managers may also use a wide range of anti-takeover devices to entrench themselves. Thus takeovers provide a fertile ground for the emergence of managerial versus shareholder conflicts. We discuss these conflicts in Chapter 12 on corporate governance, Chapter 20 on bid strategies, and Chapter 21 on takeover defence strategies.

Organizational perspective on mergers

The managerial perspective rejects the view of the firm as a black box, and examines the motivations of managers. The organizational perspective takes this approach further. It considers the *decision-making processes* within a firm as being not entirely rational but subject to a wide variety of pressures and pulls of a political nature. Different actors within the firm have different perspectives, motives and expectations regarding a merger. The complex acquisition decision-making process needs to be managed. Similarly, in the post-acquisition period, the organizational dynamics and human aspects of the integration process determine its success. Mergers are also change programmes, giving rise to considerable turbulence, fear and resistance. The organizational perspective raises the importance of many 'soft' issues that tend to be assumed away in the more rationalist models but nevertheless have serious implications for the M & A process.

The organizational perspective plays a critical role in identifying the sources of competitive advantage that an acquisition may create for the merging firms. The R & C view of competition depends on a very good organizational perspective of the merging firms' R & C. Organizational structure, its governance, systems and procedures, and its soft characteristics such as resilience, absorptive capacity, adaptive ability and willingness to change, are important determinants of the effectiveness of the post-acquisition integration stage of M & A and hence its success.

The human aspects of M & A, and how they impact upon the merger process at various stages, have received much greater attention from scholars and practitioners in the last decade or more. Willingness to change, and a firm's resilience, are essentially rooted in human beings who are members of the organization, although the collective sociological factors within firms may influence individual human behaviour. Thus human behaviour at both the individual and group level can influence merger outcomes.

M & A is also a learning process, since to leverage one another's R & C after a merger the merging firms must learn about each other's R & C, and they can be leveraged to gain or create competitive advantage. The organizational learning perspective provides insights into this learning process, including what the impediments are to effective learning. This perspective also tells us that M & A is a change process, and tells us how it can be managed, and what human and other resources are required to implement the acquisition project effectively. The challenges faced by merging firms in achieving effective and value-creating integration, and in enhancing learning from an acquisition, are indeed formidable. We return to these topics in Chapters 22 and 23.

Intellectual/knowledge assets and mergers

Increasingly the value of a firm resides in its intellectual or knowledge assets more than in its physical or tangible assets, as reflected in valuation measures such as the market-to-book value of tangible assets (see Chapter 14 for the definition and interpretation of such measures). The various sources of intellectual assets are:

● individual – knowledge embedded in individuals;
● social – knowledge and capabilities embedded in networks and teams, in their interaction and in their culture, and manifested in their behaviour; and
● organizational – codified in systems, procedures, processes and routines.

Firm capabilities based on these different sources of intellectual assets influence its innovative capabilities differently: for example, organizational assets may facilitate exploitative innovation whereas social and individual assets may lead to exploratory innovations[42]. This has implications both for acquisition strategy – how it will enhance exploitative and exploratory innovation – and for post-acquisition integration (see Chapter 5 on exploitative and exploratory acquisitions and Chapter 22 on post-acquisition integration).

Summary of the multiple perspectives on mergers

Table 3.5 provides a summary of the above perspectives on mergers. The different perspectives show that M & A is a process subject to a variety of often conflicting forces, and the outcome of mergers is generally determined by the interplay of the external and firm-specific forces. In the chapters that follow we shall elaborate on these various perspectives in identifying the key challenges to creating value through mergers and acquisitions.

Table 3.5 Comparison of different perspectives on mergers

Perspective	Focus	Major elements
Economic	• External to firm, on competitors • Various market structures, e.g. monopoly and how firms compete in each • Vertical integration	• Competition based on cost and perceived benefits • Scale and scope economies • Relative transaction cost as determinant of market versus hierarchies • Mergers driven by above • Hypercompetition and short competitive advantage period
Strategy	• External • How to achieve sustainable competitive advantage • Firm's resources and capabilities (R & C) • How firms develop these	• Competitive advantage result of superior R & C • Sustainable advantage rests on R & C resistant to imitation and replication • R & C path dependent on and part of firm's evolution • Mergers a means to acquiring R & C
Finance theory	• Internal to firm • Shareholders, creditors and managers in a nexus of contracts • Diffusion of firm ownership • Agency conflicts and costs • Corporate governance • Market for corporate control • Real options	• Managers agents of equity and debt holders • Managers' interests diverge from principals' interests • Mergers motivated by managerial interests • Managers monitored and controlled by corporate governance • Hostile takeovers control managers • Real options framework for exploratory acquisitions
Managerial	• Internal to firm • Managerial utility • Control loss due to mergers	• Hostile takeovers • Incentives to align managerial and shareholder interests • Takeover defences • Managerial incentives in takeover context
Organizational	• Internal to merging firms • Political processes, cultures • Conflicts among groups • M & A as change process	• Acquisition decisions not always rational • Dilution of acquisition quality • Post-merger integration problems • Organizational learning perspective and impediments to learning

'The Best a Man or a Woman Can Get' – P&G and Gillette bridge the gender gap in their brands!

In January 2005 Procter & Gamble Company (P&G) selling women's personal care products such as Clairol, Olay and CoverGirl acquired Gillette selling men's personal care brands: Gillette razor blades, Right Guard deodorants and, hair and tooth care products for $57bn. Gillette's razors were popular and advertised on TV with the catchy slogan, 'The Best a Man Can Get'. P&G was number one and Gillette number five in the US household goods companies and, post-merger, the two companies would have annual sales of $60bn and 14,000 employees.

Strategic rationale for the merger

- The merged firm would also have a large portfolio of 22 brands with annual sales of $1bn or more – 16 from P&G and 6 from Gillette. Gillette brands were also growing at a good rate of 6 to 12%. Of the two companies, Gillette was much more international in its sales than P&G and its international marketing savvy would be of much value to the latter.
- The businesses were complementary in terms of the gender markets they served.
- The businesses were complementary in terms of the international geographical markets they served, for example P&G was strong in China and Gillette was strong in India and Brazil. This created opportunities for cross-selling each other's products in these markets.
- Enhance the power of merged firm *vis-à-vis* giant retailers like Wal-Mart.

Battling buyer power

In the 1990s mass retailers like Wal-Mart increased their scope geographically and across customer segments, gathering enormous strength against suppliers. To reach these markets, consumer products group (CPG) companies had to sell through the superstores. In 2003 Wal-Mart accounted for 13% of Gillette's sales. Such heavy dependence on a powerful buyer was a source of substantial business risk to Gillette. Wal-Mart's market power was such that it could extract large price reductions from CPG firms which considered its custom so important that many of them had established permanent offices near Wal-Mart's head-offices in Arkansas. Large retailers had similar buyer power against suppliers like P&G and Gillette. In part the merger of these two firms was aimed at resisting the retail squeeze.

Among the brands that P&G was acquiring were some 'non-core' brands such as Duracell batteries and the small appliances brand Braun and P&G itself included two food brands, e.g. Folger's coffee and Pringle's potato chips, and IAMS pet food. Analysts speculated that P&G would divest such brands and focus on the core. Thus the value of this acquisition was also dependent on the value of such divestitures. These potential divestitures were real abandonment options embedded in the merger.

Although this corporate marriage between P&G and Gillette received the blessing of the famous investor Warren Buffett, who described it as a dream deal, one analyst commented that P&G had overpaid for the acquisition. Valuation of brands that are intangible assets is fraught with valuation risk. This may explain why P&G might have overpaid to acquire Gillette's brands.

Discussion questions

1 How complementary are the brand portfolios of P&G and Gillette?

2 How does such complementarity create value?

3 How does the merger help the two companies counterbalance the power of mass retailers?

Source: D. Stowell, 'The Best Deal Gillette Could Get? Procter & Gamble's Acquisition of Gillette', Kellogg School of Management case study KEL 183, July 2007; B. Shearer, 'P&G seeks more sales to men by acquiring Gillette', *Mergers & Acquisitions: The Dealmaker's Journal*, March 2005, 30–31.

Overview and implications for practice

- This chapter sets out a framework for understanding mergers and acquisitions, and draws on five perspectives that are not mutually exclusive: economic, strategy, finance, managerial and organizational.

- Economic theory models are concerned with competition in different market structures. Important sources of competitive advantage are market power, and scale, scope and learning economies. Mergers allow firms to reap these economies and increase their competitive advantage. Relative transaction costs explain vertical integration.

- Porter's five forces model identifies current rivalry, threat of new entrants, threat of substitutes, buyer power and seller power as determining the competitive structure of an industry. Mergers enable firms to change the competitive structure in their favour.

- The game theory framework sets out how firms make competitive moves, given their expectation of the actions their rivals may take. Merger patterns in industries are consistent with game theory predictions.

- In Porter's strategy perspective firms compete on cost leadership, on product differentiation, or by segmental focus.

- The resource-based view (RBV) of strategy emphasizes a firm's unique resources and capabilities as the source of competitive advantage. Mergers can be a means to developing these.

- In the RBV model, mergers integrate the value chains of the merging firms to create added value. The competitive strategy model underlying the merger dictates the nature and extent of integration.

- Finance theory considers merger decisions within the agency model of the firm, the role of the market for corporate control, and the interaction between corporate governance and takeovers in resolving agency conflicts.

- The real options framework is useful in understanding acquisitions in the nature of options on future growth opportunities. This framework is now extended to understand the RBV of competition and acquisitions. It provides a means of valuing exploratory acquisitions.

- The managerial perspective is related to the agency model of the firm, and considers the motivations of managers in making or resisting acquisitions.

- The organizational perspective views acquisition as a organizational change process subject to a complex interplay of organizational politics, cultural clashes and resistance to change.

These factors may weaken merger decisions and frustrate smooth merger integration, causing mergers to fail.

● The incidence, nature and outcome of mergers are the result of these multiple factors, and therefore require a range of perspectives to manage them successfully.

Review questions

3.1 How do mergers help firms achieve scale and scope economies?

3.2 How does enhancing perceived customer benefits increase a firm's competitive advantage?

3.3 Describe the five forces model of industry competition, and explain how they influence the attractiveness of an industry for firms.

3.4 How do mergers help firms compete within the five forces framework?

3.5 What is the relevance of game theory to mergers and acquisitions?

3.6 What is the relevance of the resource-based view (RBV) of competition to mergers?

3.7 What is the link between RBV, value chains and value creation in mergers?

3.8 What is the relevance of the agency model and managerial perspective to mergers?

3.9 Do you agree that a merger represents an organizational change initiative?

3.10 How do organizational structures and processes affect the success of mergers?

3.11 Why is it important to develop an oganizational perpective of M & A?

3.12 What is organizational learning, and what factors could impede such learning in the M & A context?

Further reading

A. M. Brandenburger and B. J. Nalebuff, *Co-opetition* (New York: Currency Doubleday, 1996), pp. 111–117.

M. Jensen, 'Agency costs of free cash flow, corporate finance and takeovers', *American Economic Review*, **76**, 1986, 323–329.

M. A. Peteraf, 'The cornerstones of competitive advantage: A resource-based view', *Strategic Management Journal*, **14**, 1993, 179–191.

M. Porter, 'From competitive advantage to corporate strategy', *Harvard Business Review*, **May–June** 1987, 43–59.

Notes and references

1. C. A. Montgomery, 'Corporate diversification', *Journal of Economic Perspectives*, **8**(3), 1994, 163–178, and J. B. Barney and W. S. Hesterly, *Strategic Management and Competitive Advantage: Concepts and Cases* (Upper Saddle River, NJ: Pearson Prentice Hall, 2008), who note that 'vitually all of the 500 largest firms in the United States and the 500 largest firms in the world are diversified either by product or geographically. Large single business firms are unusual' (p. 208).
2. O. Williamson, *The Economic Institutions of Capitalism* (New York: Free Press, 1985).
3. A. M. Brandenburger and B. J. Nalebuff, *Co-opetition* (New York: Currency Doubleday, 1996), pp. 111–117.
4. D. Besanko, D. Dranove, M. Shanley and S. Schaefer, *Economics of Strategy* (New York: John Wiley & Sons, 2007), p. 319.

5. D. Besanko, D. Dranove and M. Shanley, *Economics of Strategy* (New York: John Wiley & Sons, 2000), p. 37.

6. The 2002 Oscar award-winning Hollywood movie *A Beautiful Mind*, with Russell Crowe starring in the title role, is based on John Nash's life. Miller, however, cautions that seeing the movie 'will not increase your knowledge of game theory'. See J. Miller, *Game Theory at Work* (New York: McGraw-Hill, 2003), p. 113.

7. Table 3.3 and Figure 3.2 are adapted from D. Besanko, D. Dranove and M. Shanley, *Economics of Strategy* (New York: John Wiley, 2000), pp. 36–40.

8. This is similar to the policy of 'no first use' of nuclear weapons that some countries proclaim. This policy is underpinned by the commitment to a massive retaliatory strike against the first striker. The credibility of the 'no first use' policy therefore depends on: (1) the possession of a second-strike capability; (2) its invulnerability to the first strike; and (3) whether the commitment to retaliatory strike is hard or soft.

9. If either player decides to be nasty and somewhat sadistic, it can choose to acquire when the other has chosen not to acquire. Even though this is not optimal for the acquirer it may hope to inflict on the non-acquirer greater pain than it bears, thereby hoping to drive out the former. This strategy, while irrational in the short term, may be quite rational in the long term. If, however, either player anticipates such 'irrational' behaviour of the other, it will also acquire. Thus both will settle for a suboptimal acquisition–acquisition solution.

10. L. Kehoe, 'Microsoft determined to foil AOL cable bid', *Financial Times*, 30 July 2001.

11. See Robert Grant, *Contemporary Strategy Analysis* (Oxford: Blackwell, 2008), Table 4.1. I have ignored the result from the Schmalensee study in that table as it relates to the 1980s, and the model has a weaker explanatory power (80% unexplained) than in the other studies (32%–52% unexplained). W. F. Misangyi, H. Elms, T. Greckhamer and J. A. Lepine, 'A new perspective on a fundamental debate: A multilevel approach to industry, corporate and business unit effects', *Strategic Management Journal*, **27**, 2006, 571–590.

12. J. Harrison, 'Unrelenting chemicals M & A reconfigures the industry', *Mergers and Acquisitions*, January 2000, 21–23.

13. M. Porter, *Competitive Advantage* (New York: Free Press, 1985), Chapter 7.

14. Michael Porter warns against being stuck in the middle although other strategy scholars find it attractive. See Besanko *et al.*, *ibid.*, pp. 374–379.

15. J. Barney, 'Firm resources and sustained competitive advantage', *Journal of Management*, **17**(1), 1991, 99–120.

16. C. K. Prahalad and G. Hamel, 'The core competence of the corporation', *Harvard Business Review*, May/June 1990, 79–91.

17. This figure draws on R. Grant, *Contemporary Strategy Analysis* (Oxford: Blackwell, 2002), Chapter 5.

18. D. Carey (moderator), 'Lessons from Master Acquirers: A CEO roundtable on making mergers succeed', *Harvard Business Review*, May/June 2000, 153.

19. M. A. Peteraf, 'The cornerstones of competitive advantage: A resource-based view', *Strategic Management Journal*, **14**, 1993, 179–191.

20. Gary Hamel also uses the metaphor of corporate DNA in discussing management innovation. See G. Hamel, *The Future of Management* (Boston, MA: Harvard University Press, 2007), pp. 151–159.

21. T. A. Luehrman, 'Investment opportunities as real options: Getting started on the numbers', *Harvard Business Review*, July/August 1998, 51–67.

22. M. Porter, *ibid.*, Chapter 2, p. 37.

23. M. Porter, 'From competitive advantage to corporate strategy', *Harvard Business Review*, May/June 1987, 43–59; S. Mathur and A. Kenyon, *Creating Value, Shaping Tomorrow's Business* (Oxford: Butterworth-Heinemann, 1997), pp. 335–337.

24. See B. de Wit and R. Meyer, *Strategy Synthesis* (London: Thomson Learning, 2005), p. 111.

25. R. Grant, *ibid.*, pp. 235–236 and 255–257.

26. See J. Barney and W. S. Hesterly, *ibid.*, pp. 86–88. This section also draws on S. Lipman and R. Rumelt, 'Uncertain imitability: An analysis of inter-firm differences in efficiency under competition', *Bell Journal of Economics*, **13**, 1982, 418–438.

27. D. Teece, G. Pisano and A. Shuen, 'Dynamic capabilities and strategic management', *Strategic Management Journal*, **18**(7), 1997, 509–533.

28. L. G. Thomas and R. A. D'Aveni, 'The rise of hypercompetition in the US manufacturing sector 1950–2002', Amos Tuck working paper, version 2.8, October 2004.

29. K. G. Palepu, P. M. Healy, V. L. Bernard and E. Peek, *Business Analysis and Valuation (IFRS edition): Text and Cases* (London: Thomson, 2007), Figure 6.1, p. 263.

30. This study is discussed in more detail in Chapter 14 in the context of target valuation.

31. D. C. Mueller, 'The persistence of profits above the norm', *Economica*, **44**, 1997, 369–380; cited in D. Besanko *et al.*, *Economics of Strategy* (New York: John Wiley & Sons, 2007), pp. 402–403.

32. This section and the following section on managerial perspectives on mergers draw on P. S. Sudarsanam, 'Corporate governance, corporate control and takeovers', in A. Gregory and C. Cooper (Eds), *Advances in Mergers and Acquisitions* (London: JAI Elsevier Science, 2000), pp. 119–156.

33. A. Berle and G. Means, *The Modern Corporation and Private Property* (New York: Macmillan, 1932).

34. M. Jensen and W. Meckling, 'Theory of the firm: Managerial behaviour, agency costs and ownership structure', *Journal of Financial Economics*, **3**, 1976, 305–360.

35. M. Jensen, 'Agency costs of free cash flow, corporate finance and takeovers', *American Economic Review*, **76**, 1986, 323–329. NPV is the present value of all future free cash flows from a project discounted at an appropriate cost of capital minus the investment in the project.

36. H. Manne, 'Mergers and the market for corporate control', *Journal of Political Economy*, **73**, April 1965, 110–120.

37. B. Wernerfelt, 'A resource-based view of the firm', *Strategic Management Journal*, **5**(2), 1984, 171–180.

38. In general, option value increases with waiting i.e. its time to maturity. This may seem to run counter to the game theory view of early commitment. However, while waiting may add value to proprietary options, early exercise may create more value or avoid value destruction where the option is a shared option. See Appendix 4.1 for a further discussion of different types of option.

39. Henry Mintzberg is an ardent critic of the traditional deliberate strategy school, and argues that business strategies are often unintended consequences of deliberate strategies that go wrong. See H. Mintzberg and J. A. Waters, 'Of strategies: Deliberate and emergent', *Strategic Management Journal*, **6**(3), 1985, 257–272.

40. For a further discussion of the contrasting deliberate and emergent strategies see R. de Wit and R. Meyer, *Strategy Synthesis: Resolving Strategy Paradoxes to Create Competitive Advantage* (London: Thomson Learning, 2005), Chapter 5.

41. R. Roll, 'The hubris hypothesis of corporate takeovers', *Journal of Business*, **59**(2), 1986, 197–216; Y. Amihud and B. Lev, 'Risk reduction as managerial motive for conglomerate mergers', *Bell Journal of Economics*, **12**, 1981, 605–617.

42. See M. Subramaniam and M. Youndt, 'The influence of intellectual capital on the types of innovative capabilities', *Academy of Management Journal*, **48**(3), 2005, 450–463.

Are acquisitions successful?

Objectives

At the end of this chapter, the reader should be able to understand:

- how success of mergers is assessed using a variety of perspectives;
- how shareholder value creation in mergers can be measured and assessed;
- the variety of empirical methodologies that have been developed for this purpose;
- the limitations of these methodologies;
- the results and conclusions from the empirical studies relating to the success of different types of mergers in different countries; and
- the possible sources of value destruction and how they relate to different merger perspectives.

Introduction

In Chapter 2 we examined the merger waves that have occurred in several countries since 1890. The intensity of merger activity over short periods, and the high acquisition premia often paid during the merger waves, have invited pejorative descriptions such as 'merger mania' or 'merger frenzy'. These reflect the widely held perception that mergers are often driven by irrational impulses and not by carefully constructed and honestly endorsed arguments for value creation. To what extent is this perception based on carefully assembled evidence? Who are the winners and losers in mergers and acquisitions?

In the last chapter we developed alternative perspectives on the causes of and motivations for mergers. The economic and strategy perspectives suggest that mergers may be driven by economic and strategic logic that seeks to establish competitive advantage, leading to value creation for shareholders. The finance perspective proposes shareholder wealth maximization as the pre-eminent objective of merger decisions, although contextual factors such as principal–agent problems, weak corporate governance structure and an imperfect market for corporate control may cause deviation from this objective.

The organizational perspective calls into question the assumption that acquisition decision process is a coldly logical process driven by considerations of economic rationality and shareholder value imperative. It also raises the possibility that the outcome of any merger may not deliver the *ex ante* merger objectives because of the difficulties in achieving the organizational change that is a precondition for their achievement. The managerial perspective, again drawing upon the agency model of the firm, points to managerial objectives that may conflict with shareholder objectives. Managerial incentives, designed to alleviate the agency conflicts, may also have perverse effects by encouraging managers to take more risk. The collapse of the stock markets and of the M & A waves in 2000–2001 have been attributed to such skewed incentives. These various perspectives suggest that merger outcomes may not always be beneficial to shareholders and other stakeholders.

Nevertheless, mergers and acquisitions are of considerable interest to all the stakeholders in the merging firms. These include shareholders, managers, employees, consumers and the wider community. Thus assessment of the 'success' of mergers depends on the particular stakeholder perspective adopted, and on the success criteria that flow from that perspective. Definition of the criteria for success as well as the measurement tools and benchmarks must therefore be carefully set out for a proper evaluation of merger outcomes.

There is a widely held view that a vast majority of mergers and acquisitions 'fail'. This view, if true, is a matter of grave concern to all stakeholders, since trillions of dollars are spent by firms on M & A, pointing to a horrendously wasteful investment of society's resources. Further, understanding the extent of failure of M & A and identifying the factors that contribute to such failure are important in meeting the risks and challenges of the M & A process and crafting successful M & A in future. The evidence assembled in this chapter thus defines the scope of our discussion in the rest of the book.

In this chapter we define several criteria for measuring merger success from different stakeholders' perspectives. We review the available empirical evidence of the outcomes of mergers and acquisitions in different countries and in different types of merger. The methodologies used to assess merger performance are described. The limitations of these methodologies and their impact on the assessment of merger success are indicated. Possible sources of failure of mergers, and the challenges of fixing them, are identified for further elaboration in later chapters. The main focus of the assessment in this chapter is whether mergers create shareholder value.

Defining success of mergers and acquisitions

A merger involves the coming together of two companies – the acquirer and the acquired. In each company there is a range of stakeholders, including the shareholders, managers, employees, consumers and the community at large. The antitrust authorities, e.g. the Federal Trade Commission (FTC) in the US, the Competition Commission in the UK, the European Commission in the EU or the Federal Cartel Office in Germany, are the custodians of the interests of the consumers and the community at large, and regulate mergers and acquisitions. These competition authorities generally follow the rule that mergers that lead to substantial lessening of competition (SLC) should be prohibited. We examine the role of antitrust authorities in Chapter 17.

In this chapter we are concerned with assessing the success of mergers from the perspectives of shareholders, managers, employees and the firms themselves. As noted above, the interests of these groups do not always coincide. One group can win at the expense of the others. For example, a takeover can lead to high shareholder returns, but loss of managerial jobs. This conflict often drives managerial resistance to takeover bids (see Chapter 21 on defences against hostile takeovers). Similarly, acquisitions motivated by efficiency considerations such as scale economies and rationalization of the merging firms' operations will result in redundancy, wage cuts, or loss of pension rights for the workforce. Managers may benefit from making or accepting takeovers, but the shareholders and other stakeholders may lose from those deals.

Our primary focus in this chapter is the shareholder value impact of mergers. We examine the empirical evidence for the success of mergers in terms of shareholder value created by them. This evidence comes from a number of countries. Since mergers and acquisitions are based on a range of value creation models (see Chapter 3 on merger perspectives), evidence relating to the success of different types of merger is presented. Both short-term and long-term wealth effects are germane to the assessment of success of mergers. The impact of mergers on productivity and innovation that have long-term welfare implications for shareholders as well as other stakeholders is also investigated. We then examine the impact of mergers on managers and other employees of the merging firms. In particular, we focus on whether mergers lead to managerial and employee job losses, or have other deleterious consequences for them. We also identify firm and deal characteristics that may cause acquisitions to succeed or fail.

Acquisitions and shareholder value

According to the finance theory perspective, managers' decisions are aimed at enhancing shareholder wealth. How do acquisitions stand up to this test? If we can show that shareholders are better off – that the value of their shares has increased as a result of the acquisition – then this test is satisfied. The term 'better off' is taken to mean that the shareholders' wealth gains are enough to compensate them for the risk they bear in being invested in the acquirer company following the acquisition. Technically, this means that the return they earn from investing in the acquirer's stock is at least equal to the cost of capital. If an acquisition fails this 'shareholder is better off' test, the shareholders would have been better off investing their capital in another investment opportunity, say, a better-performing company. The investors' required rate of return is thus equal to their opportunity cost.

Measuring the impact of acquisitions on shareholder returns

The benchmark problem: conceptual issues

While the above test is conceptually simple, in practice it poses a number of problems. The most fundamental problem is the appropriate benchmark for assessing the post-acquisition performance of the acquirer. The post-acquisition firm is different from the acquiring and acquired firms that existed prior to the acquisition. What would have been the shareholder value performance of the two firms had they not merged? Since they normally do not exist as separate entities after a merger, to answer this 'counter-factual' question requires some assumptions about how the two firms might have performed. For example, the two firms might have persisted in their pre-merger competitive strategies generating the same returns for the shareholders as before.

Suppose firms X and Y were of equal size and generating returns of 10% each in the pre-merger period. Extrapolating this performance on the assumption that they would have continued to pursue the same strategies and generated the same returns as before yields an expected performance of 10% (the weighted average of the pre-merger returns, weighted by the value of each firm). The merged firm Z (= X + Y) will satisfy our shareholder value creation test if it generates at least 10% return for the combined firms' shareholders. This benchmark poses at least two problems of a conceptual nature:

- X and Y might not have continued to perform as well as before.
- Z may perform better than X and Y combined, even if individually they would have only maintained their pre-merger performance.

The first objection to extrapolating the past arises from the argument that firms undertake mergers precisely to alter the extant strategy to gain competitive advantage. Failure to alter the strategy might have led to an erosion of their current competitive advantage and a decline in shareholder value performance. The second objection arises from the argument that the purpose of the merger is to create *new* sources of competitive advantage and thereby enhance shareholder value performance. In the first case extrapolation overstates the expected performance, and in the second it understates the expected performance of the merged firm. Thus one needs to incorporate the *expected* shareholder value improvements that the merger promises in the benchmark used to evaluate those promises.

Persistence of high profitability or stock market value

Another problem that makes choice of benchmark critical is the persistence of profitability or high stock market valuation of the acquirer from the pre-merger period to the post-merger period. Where such performance persists, any post-merger performance measure needs to be stripped of this persistent component to capture the true impact of the merger on performance. Several studies in both industrial organization and stock price behaviour indicate persistence. Some studies of post-merger performance have sought to control for this persistent component of the post-merger performance (see the review of these studies later in this chapter).

Forecast performance as a benchmark

Once the merger is consummated, the merging firm's trail may be lost, and it becomes difficult to see how well these firms might have performed: that is, the *counterfactual* is difficult to construct. One way to overcome this problem is to use the forecast performances of the merging firms on a stand-alone basis and then synthesize a measure of forecast performance for the two firms together. This synthetic portfolio's forecast performance provides a useful benchmark. This benchmark allows for changes in, say, market conditions or competitive reaction, and thus does not just extrapolate past performance. This benchmark, however, depends on the quality and reliability of analysts' forecasts of future performance, and may not be available for sufficiently long future periods. It is rarely employed in empirical research.

External benchmark

Extrapolation uses the merging firms as their own benchmark, and throws up the problems identified above. What about an external benchmark, i.e. a firm that is 'identical' to the acquiring firm except that it has not made an acquisition? Researchers assess the performance of merging firms against the benchmark of these non-merging firms, called 'control' firms. How does one pick a control firm or a set of control firms for each acquiring firm? Any pair of firms may share similarities as well as differences in their strategic posture, resources and capabilities, growth prospects, financial characteristics such as debt to equity ratio or cash resources, and corporate governance structures.

In picking the appropriate control firm we need to apply screening criteria based on one or more of the above characteristics of firms, e.g. growth opportunities or size. Both the screening criteria and the control firm chosen must be fit for the purpose, i.e. measuring post-merger performance. The test is whether the merging firms and the control firms would have produced the same shareholder value performance in the absence of the mergers. The assumption is that firms sharing the same characteristics would have produced the same performance.

Control firms are often chosen on the basis of shared characteristics that are a key or even perhaps the only determinant of shareholder returns. For example, consider the capital asset pricing model (CAPM), a model developed to value securities and based on the correlations or co-movement of returns among those securities. It yields the result that the return generated by an asset depends on the risk-free interest rate, the return on the capital market, and the market-related risk known as the systematic risk or beta. Of these, the first two are common to all firms whose stocks are traded in the same stock market. Therefore two firms with the same systematic risk are expected to yield the same return.

A firm that has the same systematic risk as the merging firms then provides a good control for estimating the post-merger performance. However, this procedure assumes that the systematic risk of the merged firm will continue to be the same as that of the control firm. This raises the question of whether the merger has altered the systematic risk profile of the merging firms. Strategic reconfiguration of firms often alters their risk profile. For example, a horizontal or vertical merger may change the cost structure, market share and volatility of earnings, thereby changing the risk profile. In this event the control may no longer be a valid benchmark if it does not undergo similar transformation.

More recent studies have cast doubt on systematic risk, i.e. beta being the only relevant parameter in determining the returns to individual firms. In a series of empirical papers Fama and French have shown that, in addition to beta, two other factors may be relevant: the size of a firm and its market value to book value of equity (referred to simply as market-to-book). Barber and Lyon have shown that matching by size, market-to-book and pre-event performance may provide adequate control. The importance of these factors as determinants of stock returns rests on extensively documented empirical evidence that realized returns from company stocks depend on the company size as well as on its market-to-book ratio[1].

Unlike the CAPM's beta, these additional variables, such as size and market-to-book, have been identified through empirical research rather than from first principles. Indeed, in the finance literature, the empirical relevance of variables such as size and market-to-book ratio is treated as an aberration or 'anomaly'. Such anomalies are attributed to market imperfections, investor biases or plain irrationality. They are often derided as *ad hoc* rationalizations or products of data mining, and as lacking in theoretical foundation. They may also capture risk factors that are as yet not clearly understood. Nevertheless in practice, in assessing post-merger performance, we need to control for these factors.

Other firms in the acquirer's and acquiree's industries as benchmark

Since firms in the same industry share many production and market characteristics and growth opportunities, an appropriate benchmark is the performance of other firms in the same industry. To start with, all firms in the same industry selling similar products face the same technological and demand conditions, and are subject to similar competitive pressures from rivals, suppliers and customers. If firms within that industry merge to gain greater competitive advantage, the non-merging firms provide a benchmark to assess the success of that strategy. The average or median performance of these non-merging industry rivals thus serves as a benchmark. As our discussion of industry clustering of mergers in Chapter 2 shows, firms facing the competitive pressures often follow 'me-too' competitive strategies. Thus another benchmark may be firms in the same industry following broadly similar competitive strategies[2].

Summary of the benchmark problem: conceptual issues

The above discussion, albeit brief, provides an indication of the perplexing diversity of benchmarks to determine the success of acquisitions. It is not always robust theoretical models, built from first principles, that guide the choice of benchmarks. Many benchmarks are chosen because their relevance to the value or return-generating process has been empirically demonstrated by several prior studies. Many, of course, are also intuitively meaningful even though the intuition lacks rigorous conceptual underpinning.

Measuring shareholder wealth impact: when is it felt and for how long?

The timescale for assessing the wealth increase is an important consideration. The need for the long-term analysis of shareholder returns also depends on one's view of the efficiency of the capital markets. If they are informationally efficient, they foresee all the future benefits and costs of a merger, and factor them into share prices at the time of the merger. Then the time interval ('event window') that exhausts all the valuation effects of the merger ('event') is short. Analysis of valuation changes outside this event window is therefore redundant, and such changes are due to other events unconnected to the acquisition, and random (called 'noise' in the literature).

This short event window places great reliance on a prescient, or even an omniscient, capital market that can fairly quickly, if not instantaneously, impound the full ramifications of the acquisition as well as the probability of realizing the acquisition benefits in the stock prices. However, several studies of stock market reaction to events such as release of accounting information, initial public offerings, rights issues, etc., have shown that stock markets continue to react after their impact day, i.e. their announcement day. This evidence of 'stickiness' in stock market pricing suggests that the market takes time to digest information about these events, or awaits more information to assess not only the extent of the benefits but also the probability of their realization[3]. Thus recent empirical studies have extended the event window to three, five or even seven years.

Lengthening the event window to several years may make good sense when capital markets have to wait and see how the acquisition drama unfolds and revise their judgement in the light of new information about the progress of acquisition integration and competitor reaction. However, long event windows create other problems. First, the longer the event window, the greater are the chances that other events such as strategic, operational or financial policy changes of the acquirer firms will impact on their valuation. Thus the water is muddied, and unambiguous evaluation of merger benefits becomes difficult. Second, long windows raise questions about the efficacy of statistical test procedures, and reduce the reliability of test results.

For the above reasons, finance researchers have employed a variety of test procedures that differ in benchmark, length of event window, return estimation, benchmark for 'normal' return, statistical test, etc. Some of the tests are parametric, that is, they assume normality of statistical distribution of the stock returns. Since this assumption is generally not true (because of skewed stock returns), other studies use non-parametric tests. These differences, indicated below, make comparison of the results of these studies difficult. Where, however, a similar pattern of post-acquisition performance emerges in spite of these differences, the conclusions are robust and reliable.

Review of stock market assessment of acquisition performance

Post-acquisition performance in stock return terms has been empirically assessed in several countries. The 1960s saw an intellectual explosion in the form of new asset-pricing models in capital markets based on the portfolio diversification theory developed by Harry Markowitz. The elegant and concise CAPM was derived by a number of researchers, including William Sharpe, John Lintner and Jack Treynor, and then refined by others such as Fisher Black. For their contribution to these conceptual breakthroughs Markowitz and Sharpe received a Nobel Prize in Economics.

Assuming that capital markets are competitive and efficient in quickly assimilating information, and allow transactions freely, the CAPM sets out the relationship between risk and expected return on a company's stock:

$$E(R_{it}) = R_{ft} + \beta_i[E(R_{mt}) - R_{ft}] \tag{4.1}$$

where $E(R_{it})$ = expected return in period t on stock i
$\qquad R_{it}$ = actual return in period t on stock i
$\qquad R_{ft}$ = risk-free return in period t
$\qquad \beta_i$ = beta of stock i
$\qquad E(R_{mt})$ = expected return on the market in period t

Beta is known as the systematic risk because of its sensitivity to the market and, in turn, the economy as a whole.

If the CAPM is correct, investors are exposed only to systematic and not firm-specific risk, since it is diversified away. Individual securities have different levels of specific risk, and by investing in a portfolio of diverse securities investors can eliminate the specific risk altogether. Since investors can, through diversification, eliminate firm-specific risk, they will not earn any return for bearing that risk. Thus only systematic risk is priced in the capital market. Hence only beta appears in the CAPM model (4.1) above. Any other variability in stock i's returns is assumed to be removed when investors hold a well-diversified portfolio (in theory, the market portfolio). Investors' expected risk premium for bearing the exposure to beta is equal to beta times the risk premium for investing in the market as a whole.

$$\text{Risk premium on } i = \beta_i[E(R_{mt}) - R_{ft}] \tag{4.2}$$

This, when added to the risk-free return, gives the return that investors expect from investing in the stock i.

The risk-free rate is the return an investor can receive from investment that is default free, e.g. a government treasury bill or bond.

What does CAPM mean for assessing merger impact?

The normal return we can expect from a stock in the absence of any unusual event such as a merger is given by equation 4.1. If the actual return at the time of a merger exceeds this normal return, that excess or abnormal return AR_{it} in time t for the stock of merging company i is a measure of the merger impact on the value of the stock to investors:

$$AR_{it} = R_{it} - E(R_{it}) \tag{4.3}$$

Since the critical determinant of the individual stock's normal return is the beta, given an estimate of beta we can estimate the normal return using the relevant information on the market return and the risk-free rate.

The beta estimate is generally based on the historical relationship between individual stocks' returns and the market returns and made using sophisticated econometric methods, i.e. time-series regression:

$$R_{it} = \alpha_i + \beta_i R_{mt} \tag{4.4}$$

where α_i, β_i are estimated parameters of the regression. Equation (4.4) is known as the market model. Since alpha and beta are estimated directly by using the historical relationship, researchers started to use the market model to estimate the normal return on stock i as well as the abnormal return. In a sense, the market model and the CAPM are related, and alpha can be related to the risk-free return and beta. Many early studies of stock market efficiency and the impact of numerous corporate events, such as acquisitions, dividend policy changes, accounting policy changes, new share issues and seasoned share issues, were conducted using the CAPM, the market model, or slight variations of these.

The market-adjusted model is one such variation. It assumes that alpha in the market model is 0 and beta equals 1. By construction, the beta of the market is 1. These assumptions imply that the individual stock *i* earns the same normal return as the market, i.e. the stock *i* is the same as the average stock in the market.

Oh, if only CAPM were true!

When the CAPM was put through its paces in numerous empirical tests, sadly it was found wanting. Beta, hitherto the exclusive key to the returns and hence the value of a stock, was found not to be so exclusive. For want of new theories to rival the CAPM, researchers have developed empirical models of asset returns and prices. These have resulted from attempts to explain the actually observed patterns of stock returns. First to breach beta's exclusivity was size measured by stock market capitalization of the stock. It was found that, over long periods, small capitalization firms ('small caps') generated higher returns than large caps. In other periods the relative outperformance was reversed.

Next to breach beta's ramparts were two widely used stock market indicators of relative value – the price earnings ratio (PER) and the book to market value ratio ('book-to-market'). PER is the ratio of the stock price to the earnings per share of the stock (see Chapter 14 on these valuation metrics). It represents the value placed on $1 of the firm's earning, and is widely used by analysts and investors to compare firms with different earnings patterns, e.g. in different industries and sectors. Book-to-market is the ratio of the accounting-rules-based value of the assets of a firm that belong to the equity shareholders (net asset value) and the market value of the company's equity capital. Market-to-book, discussed earlier, is the reciprocal of book-to-market. It represents the value placed on $1 of the net assets of a firm by the stock market.

Beta makes room for size and book-to-market

Fama and French in a series of articles have developed a model of asset returns that includes the sensitivities of these returns to the following three factors:

- beta;
- size; and
- book-to-market value of equity[4].

This three-factor model can therefore be used to estimate the normal returns and the abnormal returns to events such as acquisitions. This application of the Fama–French three factor (FFTF) model assumes that three factors are adequate to explain the observed returns. But Carhart found that there was another missing factor! This is the momentum in stock returns: that is, firms experiencing high returns in the past continue to earn high returns[5]. But the last word has perhaps not been said on this matter, since finance researchers have been engaged, long and hard, in a search for what are quaintly described as 'anomalies', i.e. aberrations from the CAPM. Other researchers have tried to explain asset prices by including, in addition to beta, size and book-to-market, other proxies for more obscure factors such as dividend yield, past performance or bankruptcy risk. Thus the enthusiastic search for the Holy Grail of *the* asset pricing model continues, and this search, as in the legend, may be interminable[6]. Appendix 4.1 provides a summary of the various models that researchers have employed in the past.

What does all this mean for measuring merger impact?

In simple terms, the measured impact is model sensitive, and no uniquely infallible model exists so far. The fallibility of the models also increases with the event window. That is, conclusions based on a model are more reliable in the short term than over the long term. A number of factors affect this trade-off between event window and model accuracy. Among these are the following:

- How the abnormal returns are measured, e.g. arithmetic or geometric returns. (Arithmetic return is a discrete-period return, whereas geometric return is continuously compounded.)
- How returns from one period to the next, say, over several years, are added up: is the return summed up ('cumulated'), or calculated over the entire holding period ('buy and hold')?
- How the statistical distribution properties of stock returns change with event window: for example, do they become more skewed?

In the following sections, where we present the evidence from numerous studies of merger impact, the reader is advised to bear in mind the complexity of the measurement process. As common sense would dictate, less reliance should be placed on small samples and more on results that seem fairly robust to alternative model specifications.

Results of empirical studies of merger impact on stock returns

We first review those studies that have examined US mergers and acquisitions, and then present those from the UK and other countries. We focus first on short-run performance and then on long-run performance. As discussed above, the short-run approach assumes stock market efficiency. Thus the stock market reaction to acquisitions when they are announced or completed provides a reliable measure of the expected value of the acquisition. The long-run performance assessment assumes that markets take time to evaluate the value implications of acquisitions, and await fresh information about the progress of the merger and the probability that merger benefits will be realized.

US studies: short-run performance

Table 4.1 presents the summary results of some of the major studies of short-term performance following the acquisition of control in target firms. The table reports the abnormal returns earned by shareholders. Abnormal returns are the actual returns in excess of the normal, i.e. benchmark, returns these shareholders might have received except for the takeover event. Normal returns are estimated as the returns earned during the same event period by portfolios of control firms. Tender offers in the US are offers from bidders to the target company shareholders to tender their shares. These are made directly to the shareholders with or without the target company management's agreement. Mergers are agreements made with the target firm management, and tend to be friendly deals (see Chapter 18 on takeover regulation concerning tender offers and mergers)[7]. Some studies report the combined abnormal returns to the pair of a bidder and its target. On average these are positive. For example, Bhagat, Dong, Hirshleifer and Noah report 11-day mean CARs of 0.2%, 30% and

Table 4.1 Announcement period abnormal returns to shareholders in US acquisitions

Study; sample period; sample size[a]	Event window (around announcement)[b]	Benchmark return model	Target abnormal return (%)[c]	Bidder abnormal return (%)[c]
Panel A: Tender offers				
Jensen and Ruback (1983) (summary of seven previous studies), 1958–81; 17 to 161	20 to 60 days	Market-adjusted	29	4
Jarrell, Brickley and Netter (1988); 1960–85; 405	31 days	Market-adjusted		2
Magenheim and Mueller (1988); 1976–81; 26	1 month	Market		1
Bradley, Desai and Kim (1988); 1963–84; 236	11 days	Market	32	1
Jarrell and Poulsen (1989); 1963–86; 526	31 days	Market-adjusted	29	1
Loderer and Martin (1990); 1966–84; 274	6 days	Market		1
Schwert (1996); 1975–91; 564	42 days before 126 days after	Market	16 20	
Datta, Iskandar-Datta and Raman (2001); 1993–98; 142	2 days	Market		0
Bhagat, Dong, Hirshleifer and Noah (2005); 1962–01; 1018 (includes offers for > 15% of target equity)	11 days	Market	30	0
Panel B: Mergers				
Jensen and Ruback (1983) (summary of seven previous studies); 1962–79; 60 to 256	1 month	Market	16	1
Magenheim and Mueller (1988); 1976–81; 51	1 month	Market		0
Loderer and Martin (1990); 1966–84; 1135	6 days	Market		1
Schwert (1996); 1975–91; 959	42 days before 126 days after	Market	12 5	
Datta, Iskandar-Datta and Raman (2001); 1993–98; 1577	2 days	Market		0
Panel C: Both tender offers and mergers				
Kaplan and Weisbach (1992); 1971–82; 271	11 days	Market	27	−2*
Andrade, Mitchell and Stafford (2001); 1973–98; 3688	3 days	Market	16	−1
Graham, Lemmon and Wolf (2002); 1980–95; 356	3 days	Market	23	−1*
Moeller, Schlingemann and Stulz (2004), 1980–01; 12,023	3 days	Market (median) (mean)		−1 1*
Cai and Vijh (2007); 1993–2001; 250	3 days 22 days	Market-adjusted	18 24	−3* 0
Masulis, Wang and Xie (2007); 1990–03; 3333	5 days	Market		0.2*
Sudarsanam and Huang (2007); 1993–2004; 2527, 16% tender offers	3 days	Market		−4*
Bouwman, Fuller and Nain (2009); 1979–2002; 380	3 days	Market-adjusted		−0.5*

[a]Publication details of the cited studies are given in Appendix 4.2.
[b]Event window generally spans the day or month of announcement of the tender offer or merger proposal. Days are stock market trading, not calendar, days.
[c]Returns rounded to nearest integer/decimal point. All target returns are statistically significant at 1% whereas bidder returns are insignificant unless indicated otherwise.
*Means significant at the 5% or lower level.

5.3% to tender offer bidders, targets and combined respectively. Cai and Vijh report 3-day CARs of −3%, 18% and 0.4% for their sample[8]. This is interpreted as the merger being overall value-additive, but means that all of the added value is grabbed by the targets, leaving little for bidder shareholders.

Some of the studies report what percentage of the sample acquirers earn positive abnormal returns. A statistically insignificant abnormal return also suggests that at least 50% of the sample acquirers earn negative or zero returns. Loderer and Martin found that only 49% of their sample of acquirers in tender offers and only 54% in mergers earn positive returns. This percentage implies that the chances of successful value creation for acquirer shareholders are at best even. This also suggests that a large minority of acquirers may be successful in creating value.

Some of the studies report the relative size of the acquirer and the target. In general, this is of the order of three or four times or even larger. When the abnormal returns are value weighted and added, we get the combined abnormal return to both acquirer and target shareholders. From these studies this overall return is significantly positive. This means that, overall, acquisitions add value.

Value destruction on a massive scale

In their study of the shareholder wealth gains to acquirers over the period 1980–2001, which covers both the fourth and fifth merger waves in the US, Moeller, Schlingemann and Stulz report some astonishing value losses experienced by shareholders of large acquirers at the peak of the latter wave[9]. These are shown in Table 4.2. Acquirer shareholders lost $240bn in the four years, and combined losses to acquirer and target shareholders were at least $134bn, both after adjusting for market movements and risk.

The authors trace the massive losses to large acquirer deals. During 1998–2001, out of 4136 acquisitions, 87 led to acquirer shareholders losing $1bn or more, with an aggregate loss of $397bn, whereas the remaining deals made $157bn. Thus a small proportion of large deal losses turned that period into one of incredible losses. Overall, the 1980s merger wave was mildly value destructive (loss of $4bn to acquirers) whereas the 1990s wave was hugely value destructive (loss of $216bn) and the peak period of that wave even more so (loss of $240bn).

US studies: long-run performance

Table 4.3 presents the results of various studies that have estimated the abnormal returns to acquirer shareholders over a range of windows from 24 months to 70 months. Again we show

Table 4.2 Value gains when the merger wave hits the peak

Period	Transaction value ($bn)	Acquirers' gain ($bn)	CAR %	Combined gain ($bn)	Combined CAR (%)
1998–2001	1992	−240	0.7	−134	0.3
1991–2001	2931	−216	1.2	−90	1.0
1980–1990	483	−4	0.6	12	2.4
1980–2001	3413	−221	1.1	−79	1.4

Aggregate $ gains rounded to the nearest billion; sample CAR is based on the market model over three days. Combined figures only for listed acquirers and listed targets.
Source: Adapted from S. Moeller, F. P. Schlingemann, and R. M. Stulz, 'Wealth destruction on a massive scale? A study of acquiring-firm returns in the recent merger wave,' The Journal of Finance, 60(2), John Wiley & Sons 2005, pp. 757–82.

Table 4.3 Post-acquisition abnormal returns to shareholders in the US

Study; sample period; sample size[a]	Event window (months)[b]	Benchmark return model	Bidder abnormal Return (%)
Panel A: Tender offers			
Dodd and Ruback (1977); 1958–76; 124	60	Market	−6
Franks, Harris and Mayer (1988); 1955–84; 127 (cash offers treated as tender offers)	24	Market, market-adjusted and CAPM	−4 to 9
Magenheim and Mueller (1988); 1976–81; 26	39	Market	9
Agrawal, Jaffe and Mandelker (1992); 1955–87; 227	60	Size- and beta-adjusted	2
Loderer and Martin (1992); 1965–86; 155	60	Size- and beta-adjusted	21
Loughran and Vijh (1997); 1970–89; 135	60	Size- and book-to-market-adjusted	43*
Rau and Vermaelen (1998); 1980–91; 316	36	Size- and book-to-market-adjusted	9*
Panel B: Mergers			
Mandelker (1974); 1941–62; 241	40	Market	−1
Langetieg (1978); 1929–69; 149	70	Four methods	−22* to −26*
Franks, Harris and Mayer (1988); 1955–84; 392 (stock exchange offers treated as mergers)[a]	24	Market, market-adjusted and CAPM	−2 to −18*
Magenheim and Mueller (1988); 1976–81; 51	39	Market	−28
Franks, Harris and Titman (1991); 1975–84; 399 (includes tenders)	36	Eight factors including beta, size	−11
Agrawal, Jaffe and Mandelker (1992); 1955–87; 937	60	Size- and beta-adjusted	−10*
Loderer and Martin (1992); 1965–86; 304	60	Size- and beta-adjusted	−1
Loughran and Vijh (1997); 1970–89; 788	60	Size- and book-to-market-adjusted	−16*
Rau and Vermaelen (1998); 1980–91; 2823	36	Size- and book-to-market-adjusted	−4*
Panel C: Both tender offers and mergers			
Mitchell and Stafford (2000); 1961–93; 2068	36	Beta-, size-, book-to-market-adjusted; calendar time portfolio	0
Moeller, Schlingemann and Stulz (2005); 1998–2001; only large loss acquirers (see Table 4.2 above)	24 months (BHAR)	Industry and size matched	−39
	Monthly AR	Beta-, size-, market-to-book- and momentum-adjusted	−0.8*c
Sudarsanam and Huang (2007); 1993–2004; 736	36 (mean) 36 (median) BHAR	Size-, book-to-market- and momentum-adjusted	−1 −12*
Bouwman, Fuller and Nain (2009); 1979–2002; 2944	24 (BHAR) Monthly AR	Size- and book-to-market-adjusted Beta-, size-, market-to-book and momentum adjusted	−7* 0.7*d

[a]Publication details of the cited studies are given in Appendix 4.2. BHAR is buy-and-hold return; AR is abnormal return. (See above and Appendix 4.1 for definitions.)
[b]Event window starts with the bid completion month, except that Dodd and Ruback, and Maggenheim and Mueller start earlier with the announcement date and 3 months prior to announcement month respectively.
[c]A rough estimate (without compounding) of the 2 year AR is $-0.8 \times 24 = -19\%$.
[d]Rough estimate of 2 year AR is 16%.
*Statistically significant at least at the 10% level. Other returns in this column are either insignificant or the studies do not report the significance level.

the results for tender offers and mergers separately. A range of benchmarks is employed in these studies. Overall, in tender offers acquirer shareholders earn returns from an insignificant −6% to a significant 43% (Panel A). Two of the studies report significant positive returns, but the other five show that acquirers break even. In Panel B we find that all of the studies report negative returns for acquirers in mergers, ranging from −26% to −1%. Five studies report significant negative returns and three report insignificant negative returns. These results suggest that tender offers create more value than mergers for their shareholders. Sudarsanam and Huang report a large median loss of 12%: that is, 50% of the sample experienced buy-and-hold abnormal losses of more than 12% (Panel C).

The above review results in the following broad conclusions of post-acquisition performance:

- In the short term, target firms' shareholders make substantial gains, and these gains are much larger in tender offers than in mergers.
- Bidder firms' shareholders make insignificant or small significant gains, and these are marginally larger in tender offers than in mergers[10].
- Since acquirers are substantially larger than targets, the above results translate to small positive overall gains when the two shareholders' groups are taken together. Tender offers create more value than mergers.
- In the long run, acquirers in mergers suffer wealth losses, significant in many studies, but in tender offers they earn insignificantly positive returns in many studies[11].

The result that acquisitions create overall value but almost all of the gains go to target shareholders suggests that acquirers lose out in bargaining with the targets. This reflects the way acquisition deals are structured and negotiated. We discuss this aspect further in Part 3. This distribution of gains is also consistent with a highly competitive market for corporate control (see Chapter 3 for a description of this market).

UK studies: short-run performance

Table 4.4 provides a summary of the studies that have examined the shareholder value impact of acquisitions in the short term using methodologies broadly similar to those employed in US studies. In the UK the distinction between tender offers and mergers is unimportant, since almost all of the offers are made to the shareholders, even in friendly mergers (see Chapter 18 on takeover regulations in different countries). The UK results for the short term are similar to those in the US, with substantial gains to target shareholders and zero, small positive or small negative gains to acquirer shareholders.

UK studies: long-run performance

Table 4.5 provides the long-run results. The long-term returns are also not dissimilar to the US results, at least for the mergers. The results are model sensitive but there is broad agreement across the models. In three of the four models in Sudarsanam and Mahate the abnormal returns are significantly negative. They also find that only a minority (35–45%) of acquirers earns positive returns. For all the six models, Gregory reports significant negative returns. Baker and Limmack find significantly negative returns for all the eight models. Michael Firth's is the only study to report break-even, but that is based on a single model, the market model. More recent studies by Cosh *et al.* and Antoniou *et al.* also report significant wealth losses to acquirers. Overall, the UK acquirers achieve value losses rather than value gains with their acquisition strategy.

Table 4.4 Announcement period abnormal returns to shareholders in UK acquisitions

Study; sample period; sample size[a]	Event window (around announcement)	Benchmark return model	Target abnormal return* (%)	Bidder abnormal return (%)
Firth (1980); 1969–75; 486	1 month	Market	28	−6*
Franks and Harris (1989); 1955–85; 1445	1 month	Market, market-adjusted and CAPM	22	0
Limmack (1991); 1977–86; 462	Bid period (about 3 months)	Market	31	0
Sudarsanam, Holl and Salami (1996); 1980–90; 429	−20 to +40 days	Market	29	−4*
Higson and Elliott (1998); 1975–90; 830	Bid period (about 3 months)	Size	38	0
Baker and Limmack (2002); 1977–90; 595	1 month	Eight methods		0
Sudarsanam and Mahate (2003); 1983–95; 519 public targets	−1 to +40 days	Size, market-adjusted, book to market, means-adjusted		−1 to −2
Goergen and Renneboog (2004); 1993–2000; 70 targets, 66 bidders	6 months 5 days	CAPM	29 17	−2 2*
Cosh, Guest and Hughes (2006); 1985–96; 363 public targets	3 days	Market-adjusted		−1*
Antoniou, Petmezas and Zhao (2007); 1987–2004; 1401 public and private targets	5 days	Market-adjusted		1*

[a]Publication details of the cited studies are given in Appendix 4.2. Goergen and Renneboog sample also includes some failed bids.
*All target returns are significant at 1% level and bidder returns at 5% level or lower. Other bidder returns insignificant.

Table 4.5 Post-acquisition abnormal returns to shareholders in the UK

Study; sample period; sample size[a]	Event window (months)	Benchmark return model	Bidder abnormal return (%)[b]
Firth (1980); 1969–75; 434	36	Market	0
Franks and Harris (1989); 1955–85; 1048	24	Market, market adjusted and size CAPM	−13 to 5
Limmack (1991); 1977–86; 448	24	Market, three methods	−5 to −15
Kennedy and Limmack (1996); 1980–89; 247	23	Size	−5
Gregory (1997); 1984–92; 452	24	Market, size, CAPM, three factor	−12 to −18
Higson and Elliott (1998); 1975–90; 722	36	Size	1
Baker and Limmack (2002); 1977–90; 595	60	Eight models including three factor, size, book to market	−26 to −31
Sudarsanam and Mahate (2003); 1983–95; 519	700 days (about 34 months)	Size, market adjusted, book to market, means adjusted	−9 to −22
Cosh, Guest and Hughes (2006); 1985–96; 363	36 months	Industry and profit matched control firms	−16
Antoniou, Petmezas and Zhao (2007); 1987–2004; 1061	36 months	Size and book to market portfolios (calendar time abnormal returns)	−0.43[c] (per month)

[a]Publication details of the cited studies are given in Appendix 4.2.
[b]Except for Firth and Higson and Elliott, the studies report abnormal returns from several of their models as significant. Kennedy and Limmack do not report level of significance. Returns rounded to the nearest integer.
[c]A rough estimate (ignoring compounding) of the 3-year return is −0.43 × 36 = −15.5%, comparable to the estimates from the other listed studies.

Studies from continental Europe

Information about the stock market performance of firms involved in mergers and acquisitions in other European countries is very scarce, at least in the English language media. As noted in Chapter 2, substantial takeover activity began in continental Europe from the mid-1980s. Empirical research into the shareholder wealth consequences of events such as mergers and acquisitions is not well established. Further, given the smaller number of companies listed on stock exchanges, acquisitions involving such listed companies are far fewer than those of private and unlisted companies. This perhaps explains the lack of interest in the shareholder wealth effects that require share prices for calculation. Thus there is paucity of research evidence – compared with the US and the UK – about the shareholder wealth performance of continental European mergers and acquisitions.

Table 4.6 reports the short-term abnormal returns in four countries: Sweden, Belgium, the Netherlands and France. The patterns of shareholder wealth gains in these countries are similar to those in the US and the UK. Target shareholders gain substantially, whereas acquirer shareholders just about break even. The pan-continental European study of Goergen and Renneboog (GR), based on the most recent acquisitions, yields a similar conclusion. Target shareholders are considerably better off in tender offers than in mergers where the distinction between the two types is allowed for in the test design. For acquirers the offer mode

Table 4.6 Announcement period abnormal returns to shareholders in European acquisitions

Study; sample period; sample size[a]	Country	Event window (around announcement)	Benchmark return model	Target abnormal return (%)	Bidder abnormal return (%)
Bergström, Högfeldt and Högholm (1993); 1980–92; 94 targets, 149 bidders (tender offers)	Sweden	11 days	Market	17	0
Doukas and Holmen (2000); 1980–95; 93 tender offers	Sweden	11 days	Market		1
Van Hulle, Vermaelen and de Wouters (1991); 63 tender offers	Belgium	6 weeks	Market	38	−1
Van Hulle, Vermaelen and de Wouters (1991); 76 acquirers and 48 acquired	Belgium	3 months	Market	6	−1
Eckbo and Langohr (1989), 1966–82; 90 targets and 52 acquirers in public tender offers	France	16 weeks	Market	14	−3
Goergen and Renneboog (2004); 1993–2000; 66 targets and 76 bidders	Several countries	6 months 5 days	CAPM	15* 9*	1 1*
Campa and Hernando (2004); 1998–2000; 262	EU	2 months 3 days	CAPM CAPM	9* 4*	1 0
Holmen and Knopf (2004); 1985–95; 121	Sweden	11 days	Market	17*	0
Martynova and Renneboog (2006); 2106 bidders and 760 targets	Europe	11 days	Market	16*	1*
Faccio, McConnell and Stolin (2006); 1996–2001; 735 acquirers of listed and 3694 acquirers of unlisted targets	Europe	5 days	Market-adjusted		1[b]
Kräussal and Topper (2007); 1980–2003; 269	Netherlands	3 days	Market model		1*

[a]Publication details of the cited studies are given in Appendix 4.2. Goergen and Renneboog sample also includes some failed bids. CARs can be calculated only for listed targets and bidders.
[b]Calculated from the separate subsample returns in their Table 3.
*Significant at 10% or lower level. Other returns either insignificant or significance level not reported.

makes little difference. Overall, mergers enhance target shareholder wealth without diminishing that of the acquirers, but tender offers are even more beneficial for the target shareholders.

In addition to the short-term perspective, van Hulle *et al.* also provided some post-acquisition performance figures. In the six months after the bid the acquirers earn 20.4% abnormal return. Taking into account the run-up in abnormal returns six months prior to bid announcement and the drift for six months after, they estimated that bidders earned on average BF12m (not significantly different from 0) and the targets realized BF45bn (significantly different from 0). The overall wealth created was BF3.5bn, with bidders, on average, 13 times the size of targets. GR find that targets earn significantly higher returns in the UK (29%) than in continental Europe (15%).

Assessing the operating performance of acquirers

A few researchers have examined the operating, rather than stock market returns-based, performance. Share price changes, i.e. stock returns, are based on expected benefits of the merger, the expectation being formed on the basis of the information available to the stock market investors. Share prices may often be swayed by other factors than the company's expected performance, e.g. market swings, fads, euphoria. Although the influence of these factors is controlled by careful research design that adjusts for a variety of benchmarks, there is nevertheless the possibility that share price movements may not reflect the underlying performance of the company.

Moreover, stock price changes do not provide a direct measure of the impact of the acquisition or merger on costs, revenues, profits and cash flows. After all, acquisition strategy is generally articulated in terms of the improvement in these variables as a result of the firm's enhancing its competitive advantage through that strategy. It is therefore appropriate to evaluate acquisitions on the basis of the changes in these variables, i.e. on the basis of operating performance improvement. Hence the focus on performance evaluation, using accounting data. Before the advent of the CAPM, notions of stock market efficiency and shareholder wealth enhancement as a central goal of corporate decisions in finance theory by the 1970s, evaluation of M & A was generally carried out using accounting data in company financial reports.

Evaluating acquisitions on the basis of operating performance provides additional insight into the impact of the acquisition. The accounting-based performance approach also allows the researcher to study private and unlisted target and acquirer companies for which stock price data are unavailable. However, we must bear in mind the limitations of relying on operating performance measures alone:

- Operating performance measures are subject to measurement problems, e.g. the use of different accounting rules to account for an acquisition (see Chapter 15).
- Operating performance measures are vulnerable to manipulative and discretionary choice of accounting rules, e.g. valuation of acquired assets, restructuring charges, goodwill estimates.
- Disentangling the impact of acquisition from that of other corporate decisions is difficult.
- The appropriate level at which performance is measured, e.g. at the operating income level or the earnings per share level, is ambiguous.
- The benchmark for performance measurement is ambiguous, as in the case of the abnormal returns approach.
- The relation between operating performance improvement and shareholder returns may be weak[12].

- The appropriate time lag in measuring performance improvement is not clear. Unlike stock prices, which are deemed to reflect the future quickly, operating performance may not be reflected in financial reports for several years.
- Accounting numbers are backward-looking and measure historical performance.
- Given evidence of persistence of profitability, post-merger performance needs to allow for this so that performance improvement due to the merger alone can be assessed.

Some of these problems are common to both operating performance and stock return performance. Accrual accounting allows firms the discretion to allocate revenues and costs such as depreciation to different accounting years, and provides scope for 'creative accounting' to project good performance in a given year. This vulnerability of profit measures to accounting rule manipulation renders them more suspect than measures based on cash flow accounting, which minimizes the effect of discretionary cost and revenue allocations. This subject is dealt with in Chapter 15. Despite the above weaknesses, operating performance assessment provides useful indicators of the value of acquisitions.

Operating performance assessment of US acquisitions

Table 4.7 presents the operating performance of US acquirers of domestic targets. A number of interesting patterns emerge. Ravenscraft and Scherer (1988) found, when measuring performance with accounting profitability, that mergers led to decline from the merging firms' pre-merger performance. This decline, however, crucially depends on how accounting rules have been applied. Where purchase accounting is applied, the performance is worse than

Table 4.7 Post-acquisition operating performance of acquirers in US studies

Study; sample period and sample size	Performance measure	Performance measure adjusted for effect of	Post-merger performance change
Ravenscraft and Scherer (1988); 2955 lines of business; 1974–77; mergers and tender offers during 1950–77	Operating income before interest, tax and extraordinary item/total assets	Market share, merger of equals, non-acquisition growth, accounting rules	Significant decline but depends on accounting method
Ravenscraft and Scherer (1987); 1974–77; 153 lines of business; tender offers	1. As above 2. Cash flow = Operating income + depreciation	As above	1. Significant 3% decline over years 2. No decline
Herman and Lowenstein (1988); 1975–83; hostile tender offers	Return on equity of targets	Pre-acquisition performance	No significant improvement
Healy, Palepu and Ruback (1992); 1979–84, 50 largest mergers	Pre-tax operating cash flow to market value of assets	Industry median performance; also controls for accounting method	Significant 3% improvement Asset productivity significantly up
Linn and Switzer (2001); 1967–87; 413	Pre-tax operating cash flow to market value of assets	Same industry firms	Significant 2% improvement over 5 years
Ghosh (2001); 1981–95; 315 acquiring and target firms	As above	Pre-bid performance and size	No evidence of significant improvement
Bouwman, Fuller and Nain (2009); 1979–2002; 2944	EBITDA/average total assets	Control firms of similar pre-merger performance, size and industry	Significant decline*

Publication details of the cited studies are given in Appendix 4.2.
*For tender offers it is 0.3% (not significant) and mergers –1.4% (significant at 1%). For both –1.2% (significant at 1%).

when pooling accounting is employed (see Chapter 15 for a discussion of these and other accounting rules for M & A). However, when performance is measured by cash flow, post-merger performance is unchanged in Ravenscraft and Scherer (1987), as well as in Ghosh. But Healy *et al.* reported significant operating performance improvement. This improvement is also positively and significantly related to stock returns.

Although Healy *et al.* report that pre-merger operating performance of the merging firms, relative to their industry medians, persists after the merger, they do not incorporate the pre-merger performance itself as a benchmark. Such incorporation is necessary if the pre-merger relative performance is due to permanent factors, e.g. sustained competitive advantage, and not due to temporary factors, e.g. windfall profits from temporary demand surge. Ghosh benchmarks post-acquisition operating performance against that of similarly performing, and also similarly sized, firms. With this adjusted benchmark, he finds that acquisition does not lead to any improvement in operating performance.

These conflicting results highlight the need for choosing the benchmark correctly based on the right counter-factual assumptions about what would happen in the absence of the acquisition. These assumptions in turn need to be based on an understanding of industry as well as individual firm competitive dynamics. Further, we observe that accrual accounting-based performance measures are less reliable than cash flow measures. The latter avoid many of the distortions caused by the discretionary accounting rule choices that companies can make (see Chapter 15 for discussion of the differences between the two). Cash flow measures are also conceptually better related to valuation, since the value of a company is the present value of its future cash flows, as the evidence of a positive and significant relation between operating cash flow changes and abnormal returns in Healy *et al.*'s study suggests (see Chapter 14 on valuing target firms). On the basis of cash flow measures of performance, we can conclude only that US acquirers, on average, perform at least as well as their industry counterparts or similar-sized firms.

How does acquisition impact on other performance indicators?

So far we have assessed operating performance by accrual-based profitability or cash flow measures. These are themselves derived from the company's performance in key activities that may give it competitive advantage. For example, productivity gains from an acquisition may enable the acquirer to attain cost leadership. Improved R & D may enable the acquirer to deliver new products or new processes, gain market share, or create new and profitable markets. These in turn may generate higher profits, cash flows and shareholder returns. What is the impact of acquisitions on such key activities of the acquirer and the acquired firms?

Acquisitions and innovation

Given the critical importance of innovation to successful corporate strategy as well as firm survival, acquisitions may provide a quick route to such innovation developed by the acquired firm and satisfy the acquirer's 'need for speed' (see Chapter 3 on the resource-based view of acquisitions). In this sense acquisition is a substitute for internal innovation by the acquirer. But such acquisition poses at least two challenges. The acquired innovative capabilities need to be effectively integrated and managed by the acquirer if they are to contribute to value creation. Innovation acquisition may supplant and erode the acquirer's own innovative capabilities, with portentous consequences for its future. Hitt *et al.* reported some evidence that both R & D intensity (a measure of input into innovation) and patent intensity (a measure of innovation output) decline after acquisition. Firms making acquisitions also introduce fewer new products into the marketplace[13].

On the other hand, if the acquisition provides the right technological inputs, and the acquirer manages the integration process creatively, innovation output may increase as a result. Ahuja and Katila found that the ability of the acquirer to leverage technological acquisitions to increase patent output in the global chemicals industry depended on a number of characteristics of the acquirer and the acquired companies, e.g. the relatedness of the two companies' knowledge bases or their relative size. Ahuja and Katila also highlight a number of impediments to increased innovation following acquisition[14]. Only acquirers with certain prerequisites benefit in terms of acquisition-led innovation. Thus the acquirer's learning and absorptive capacity determine the success of acquisitions as a conduit for new innovation. Similarity of knowledge between the acquirer and target helps post-acquisition innovation, but beyond a certain level dissimilarity, rather than similarity, stimulates innovation. Thus the breadth and width of the acquirer's pre-acquisition knowledge influence the ability of the acquirer to leverage the target firm's innovative capabilities[15]. The acquirer's intellectual capital and its types, i.e. whether individual, social or organizational, may shape the nature of subsequent innovation, i.e. whether exploitative or exploratory[16] (see Chapter 3 on the strategy perspective).

Acquisitions, productivity gains and employment

Acquirers generally argue that their acquisition decision rests on expected value gains through synergies, cost efficiencies, etc. Efficiency gains may arise from lowering the level of employment in the acquired firm. In the process of achieving these gains the acquirer, especially a hostile acquirer, may breach implicit contracts that the target firm had entered into with its customers, suppliers and workers prior to the acquisition. An implicit contract is an unwritten understanding between parties to a relationship that recognizes their mutual rights, obligations and expectations. In the case of workers, implicit contracts may concern expectations of future compensation or rewards in return for their commitment and loyalty to the employer. Implicit contracts are built on trust and awareness of mutual dependence rather than legally enforceable rights. Shleifer and Summers argued that gains to shareholders in hostile takeovers result from breach of implicit contracts with the target firm's workers[17].

In their extensive study of manufacturing plant productivity following ownership change during 1972–81 in the US, Lichtenberg and Siegel find that, compared with plants that do not undergo ownership change[18]:

- acquired plants exhibit lower initial levels of productivity and deterioration in relative performance in the years prior to acquisition;
- acquired plants improve their relative performance and eliminate the productivity gap over seven years; and
- productivity improvement in acquired plants contrasts with, and offsets, much of the productivity decline in the US economy in general observed during the sample period.

Lichtenberg and Siegel conclude that shareholder value gains appear to be social gains, not merely private gains to shareholders, and there is no evidence that ownership change is accompanied by the abrogation of implicit contracts with workers or suppliers.

While there is reduction in employment and wages following ownership change, this decline is three times as great in auxiliary establishments employing top managers, administrators and many R & D personnel, as in production establishments. There is, however, little difference between acquired and non-acquired control firms. Within production establishments, production workers suffer more unemployment than non-production workers.

In 62 successful and unsuccessful hostile takeovers between 1984 and 1986 analyzed by Bhagat *et al.*, the post-takeover layoffs were relatively small in number and could explain only 10–20% of the takeover premium on average[19]. Headquarters staff are the group most at risk of a layoff. Further, cuts in investments proposed by target firms are important in only nine of the sample cases. Schoar finds that, when firms diversify, productivity in their existing plants falls, but it increases in the newly acquired plants[20].

Operating performance assessment of UK acquisitions

Table 4.8 presents the post-merger operating performance of UK acquirers of other UK companies, based, as in the case of the US studies reviewed above, on both accounting accrual profitability and cash flow profitability. Manson *et al.* took an innovative approach to measuring post-acquisition performance by adjusting the industry average performance benchmark for the potential erosion of profitability of the merging firms, if the merger had not taken place. This erosion is due to competitive pressures when the rival firms play catch-up with their more profitable rivals. The decline is called regression to the mean. They found that after the merger the adjusted performance improves significantly. Overall, however, there is no consistent evidence of post-acquisition performance improvement, especially from recent, large sample studies.

Table 4.8 Post-acquisition operating performance of UK acquirers

Study; sample period and sample size[a]	Performance measure	Performance measure adjusted for effect of	Post-merger performance change
Meeks (1977); 1964–71; 164	Average net income/net assets over 3/5 years	Performance of same industry firms; average 5-year pre-merger performance	Significant decline over 3 and 5 years
Kumar (1984); 1967–74; 241	As above	As above	Decline over 3 years significant but not over 5 years
Cosh, Hughes and Singh (1980); 1967–70; 225	As above	Non-merged firms	Significant improvement over both 3 and 5 years
Manson, Stark and Thomas (1994); 1985–87; 38	Operating cash flow to total market value of firm	Industry but allows for profitability erosion due to competition	Improved performance; related to bid period stock returns
Dickerson, Gilson and Tsakalotos (1997); 1948–77; 2914	Return on assets	Size, firm, time specific	Significant performance decline
Gugler, Mueller, Yurtoglu and Zulehner (2003); 181	Return on assets	Predicted ROA	Insignificant improvement
Powell and Stark (2005); 1985–93; 191	Operating cash flow after working capital deflated by alternative size proxies[b]	Industry, size and 1-year pre-acquisition performance	Insignificant improvement; unrelated to bid period CARs
Cosh, Guest and Hughes (2006); 1985–96; 363	As above[b]	Industry, size and 3-year pre-acquisition performance	Insignificant improvement

[a]Publication details of the cited studies are in Appendix 4.2.
[b]Both these studies report significant improvement in an accrual-based performance measure that does not adjust for working capital. Powell and Stark also report such improvement to be sensitive to the size proxy.

Chapter 4 / Are acquisitions successful?

Acquisitions and employment decline

Conyon *et al.* investigated the impact of mergers on employment in merging firms during 1967–96[21]. There is significant rationalization in the use of labour as the merging firms increase post-merger efficiency, but they also found output decline. The latter may have resulted from substantial post-merger divestiture of some of the businesses of the merging firms. These results are 'supportive of the view that merger activity, particularly related and hostile merger activity, promotes efficiency', since employment decline is larger than output decline. The profit measures, subject to managers' discretionary accounting choices, are more noisy than the output and employment data used by Conyon *et al.* This may explain why enhanced efficiency is not reflected in improved operating performance reported in Table 4.8.

Operating performance of acquirers in continental Europe

Studies assessing performance changes after mergers in countries other than the US and the UK seem even scarcer than those assessing stock return performance. Table 4.9 summarizes the results of studies of mergers that took place in several continental European countries. The sample size in these is generally small, but the conclusions as regards the post-merger operating

Table 4.9 Post-acquisition operating performance of continental European acquirers

Study; sample period and sample size	Performance measure	Performance measure adjusted for effect of	Post-merger performance change
Cable, Palfrey and Runge (1980) *Germany*; 1962–74; about 50 mostly large horizontal mergers	Return on assets Return on equity Return on sales (3–5 years) pre- and post-merger mean	1. Matched non-merging firms 2. Industry average 3. Merging firm performance projected at industry average	Merging firms do not outperform benchmarks
Jenny and Weber (1980) *France*; 1962–72; 40 horizontal mergers	As above but average of 4 years before and after merger	As above	Merging firms underperform benchmarks but insignificantly
Peer (1980) *Netherlands*, 1962–73; 36 horizontal and conglomerate mergers	As above but average of 3 years	As above	Merging firms under-perform benchmarks
Ryden and Edberg (1980) *Sweden*, 1962–76; 40	As above	As above	Merging firms under-perform benchmarks marginally
Kumps and Wtterwulghe (1980) *Belgium*; 1962–74; 21	Return on assets Return on equity (average of 5 years)	As above	No significant outperformance
Gugler, Mueller, Yurtoglu and Zulehner (2003); *Several countries*	Return on assets	Predicted ROA	Insignificant improvement over 5 years
Martynova and Renneboog (2007); 1997–2001; 155; *Several countries*	Working capital adjusted EBITDA/ book value of assets	Industry, size and pre-acquisition performance	No significant improvement

Source: See Appendix 4.2 for the source of these papers.

performance of merging companies are uniform. In Germany, France, the Netherlands and Sweden these mergers did not significantly improve profitability relative to a number of benchmarks. This poor performance is also reflected in pan-European samples. It appears that poor or lacklustre post-merger operating performance is a multinational phenomenon.

Overview of the operating performance studies

In reaching any conclusion we need to bear in mind the differences among the above studies in terms of national environment, competitive market structure, accounting rules, sampling period, sample size, definition of performance measure, pre- and post-merger assessment period, and statistical methodology. Nevertheless, they suggest that accounting rules may distort performance measurement and lead to negative assessment of mergers: performance measures based on cash flow provide an indication of improved performance, at least in some studies.

Before we pronounce ourselves entirely satisfied with this assessment, we therefore need more evidence based on large samples from different countries from more recent time periods. Further, we also need to consider non-operating cash flows from disposal of non-core businesses, since, at least in the 1980s and 1990s, the strategic logic of acquisitions often encompassed selective divestitures to achieve a more coherent focus to the combined business of the acquirer and the acquired firms. An exclusive focus on operating cash flow gains is likely to understate the beneficial impact of acquisitions. Where we find significant operating performance improvement we lack evidence that this improvement is sufficient to meet the cost of capital incurred in financing the acquisitions. Thus significant operating performance improvement does not mean that the shareholders of acquirers are better off, the test we set up at the beginning of this chapter.

Post-merger performance of alternative corporate strategies

As was discussed in Chapter 3, acquisitions are undertaken to achieve certain strategic objectives, and different acquirers follow different corporate or business strategies. Success of an acquisition should therefore be judged in accordance with these strategies. The different acquisition types defined by the underlying strategy are broadly:

● related acquisitions, including horizontal mergers of businesses selling the same goods and services in the same markets and vertical mergers;
● unrelated or conglomerate acquisitions; and
● serial acquisitions reflecting buy-and-build strategies.

In general, vertical mergers are far less frequent than horizontal mergers. Horizontal mergers are motivated by the desire to achieve scale efficiencies or scope economies and sales revenue enhancement. Revenue growth is thus an important source of value creation, and can come from market share gains or from higher prices. Mueller documented evidence that merging firms in the US often failed to maintain market shares, and also lost them to rivals that had grown organically[22]. Efficiency gains leading to higher returns on equity are also difficult to achieve. Alberts and Varaiya showed that for US mergers during 1976–84 improvements in returns on equity and earnings growth rates implied by the acquisition premia paid by the acquirers were far beyond those achieved by over 90% of US companies. Given the competitive pressures on US companies, such a performance would be almost impossible to attain, and may explain some of the acquisition performance failures discussed above[23].

Many acquisitions fail to maintain the revenue growth rates at the average industry level of the acquirer and the target. A study by consultants McKinsey of mergers worth $100m or more in the US during 1990–97 found revenue growth to be fairly elusive. Most target firms achieved slower growth rates than their industry peers in the first year, but over three years only 12% of the acquired companies managed to accelerate growth. Acquisition integration-related problems such as unsettled customers and distracted staff contributed to the slow-down in revenue growth[24]. This view is consistent with the analysis in Chapter 22 of organizational problems that cause post-acquisition integration failure. Leading M & A practitioners also consider cost savings a less daunting challenge than revenue growth[25].

Empirical evidence on the performance of the different types of acquisition is presented in the following chapters that deal with them. Chapter 5 discusses the value creation rationale of horizontal mergers. Chapter 6 develops the vertical integration model, and assesses acquisition performance based on that model.

Post-acquisition performance of diversifying acquisitions

Both related and unrelated acquisitions have many distinct and some overlapping sources of value creation. Which type generates more value is an empirical issue, and the comparative performance of unrelated and related acquisitions is still unresolved. For example, Seth found that both related and unrelated acquisitions generated synergies and shareholder value gains. Neither group outperformed the other[26]. Economists researching the accounting-based performance of conglomerates have concluded that unrelated acquisitions underperform in terms of profitability selected benchmarks[27]. Finance researchers have reported a 'conglomerate discount', suggesting that the stock market values an unrelated bundle of businesses less than the sum of the values of component businesses on their own. However, more recent studies have provided support for the value creation properties of conglomerates[28]. We defer a detailed discussion of the empirical evidence to Chapter 7 after presentation of the rationale for diversifying acquisitions.

Mergers, managers and corporate governance

In the light of the foregoing evidence that mergers, on average, are not value creating, the way corporates are governed has become an important issue. The managerial perspective positing a conflict of interest between managers and shareholders suggests that acquisitions may be undertaken to promote managerial rather than shareholder interests. This is consistent with shareholder value losses from acquisitions. Several researchers have investigated the relation between corporate governance of acquirer and target firms and the performance outcomes. This investigation covers a wide range of issues:

- the structure of the board of directors and its independence;
- managerial compensation contracts, and whether they align conflicting interests; and
- behavioural biases of top management, and how directors respond to these.

Acquisitions affect the managers of the acquirer and the acquired companies differently. For the acquirer managers they offer new opportunities to enhance their company's competitive advantage, operational efficiency and financial performance, thereby increasing shareholder value. They also allow managers scope for maximizing their own utility by increasing remuneration and job security. For the acquired company managers a takeover causes uncertainty and stress because of the expected changes. They now have to adapt to the new bosses and their culture. For many, a takeover may mean loss of power, status and freedom to innovate, or redundancy. Change of control clauses in executive contracts allow target managers to 'cash out' their stocks and options and receive golden parachute payments. The size of such payments may influence target managers' incentives to agree to deals that may not benefit target shareholders (see Chapters 21 and 22 for further discussion).

Whether or not all of these dire consequences will be visited upon acquired firm managers depends upon the motivation and the strategic logic of the acquisition. For example, a merger based on expected revenue enhancement may not lead to redundancies, whereas one driven by rationalization in a mature industry is likely to. Similarly, a disciplinary takeover with its presumption of inefficient target management will, almost by definition, result in high turn-over of that management.

Empirical evidence on these issues is far from conclusive. We return to a detailed discussion of these issues and the empirical evidence in Chapter 12.

Post-merger performance and M & A deal characteristics

Empirical research has thrown interesting light on the role played by many of the transactional characteristics of acquisition deals. This role emphasizes the need to look beyond purely economic or strategic arguments for value creation in mergers and acquisitions and under-stand how deals are made and what impact deal characteristics have on post-acquisition performance. Some of these characteristics are as follows:

- Mood of the bid – is the takeover bid friendly or hostile?
- Mode of acquisition – tender offer or merger?
- Is the target firm small or large relative to the acquirer?
- Is the target firm a public, stock market-listed company or a private company?
- Is the acquirer regarded by the stock market very highly at the time of the bid? Glamour acquirers are highly valued and value acquirers are lowly valued.
- Is the acquisition financed with cash or the acquirer's equity stock, or a mixture of several payment currencies?

There is fairly uniform evidence that cash-financed acquisitions outperform stock acqui-sitions in terms of shareholder returns. Ghosh reports significant operating cash flow improve-ment for cash acquisitions but a decline for stock acquisitions[29]. Similarly, tender offers made directly to the shareholders of the target firm do better than mergers agreed in a friendly way with the target management (see Tables 4.1 and 4.2 above). Relatively small targets are in some studies conducive to better post-acquisition value creation. Glamour acquirers seem to be bad news for acquirer shareholders[30]. On the other hand, low-value acquirers turn out superior shareholder value performance. There is some evidence that hostile acquisitions are not necessarily bad news for shareholders, although hostile acquirers are often portrayed as grubby and greedy[31].

We discuss the evidence for the impact of these characteristics in Part 3. For now, it is important for the reader to keep in mind that deal structuring is not just atmospherics, full of sound and fury signifying nothing, as might be suggested by stories of takeover battles in newspapers. Deal characteristics do have a substantial impact on the success of acquisitions, and therefore need to be understood and carefully structured (see Chapters 13, 16 and 20).

Overview and implications for practice

- In this chapter we have reviewed the empirical evidence on the benefits of mergers and acquisitions for different stakeholders.

- Our main focus is to find the answer to the question whether shareholders of the acquirers and acquired companies are better off as a result of these transactions.

- We review the studies from the US, the UK and some continental European countries that investigate both the short-term and long-term effects on shareholder value.

- Since the effectiveness of acquisition strategies is expected to be reflected in revenue growth, cost saving and profitability enhancement, we also review the studies from these countries concerned with the post-merger profitability of mergers. We review evidence based on both accrual accounting profitability and cash flow profitability. We also review more direct evidence on productivity improvement and innovation growth in the post-merger period.

- Overall, mergers create shareholder value in the short term, but almost all of this value increase is enjoyed by target-firm shareholders. Acquirer shareholders experience significant wealth losses in the long term, and more so in mergers than in tender offers, where such a distinction exists.

- Profitability-based assessment shows that mergers either perform just as well as relevant benchmarks or experience significant profit decline. When profitability is reworked with cash flow rather than accrual accounting profit measures, merging firms record significant improvement or just break even. This points to some distorting influence of accounting policies and rules.

- Both shareholder value assessment and profitability assessment depend on benchmarks, assessment intervals, the sampling period and the nature of the transaction. Certain transactions, such as cash-financed ones, perform better than others.

- Performance also depends on the underlying corporate strategy, i.e. whether the acquisition is into same, related or unrelated businesses, with the latter underperforming in many studies.

- R & D intensity, patent output and the introduction of new products decline following acquisitions.

- Mergers generate productivity gains, and this is not necessarily due to large job losses. These gains are also larger in horizontal and hostile mergers.

- Top managers of target companies are more likely to lose their jobs after hostile than friendly acquisitions.

- Overall, this review points to a substantial failure of many mergers and acquisitions. However, there is also a large number of these transactions that lead to increased productivity, innovation, profitability and shareholder value. Acquisition success varies with the underlying business strategy for value creation.

- Deal characteristics affect the shareholder wealth gains and operating performance improvement after merger. The challenge for managers is to craft a winning business and acquisition strategy. Structuring the deal correctly is another challenge.

- In the following chapters we aim to highlight these challenges to value creation that arise at different stages of the M & A process. The risks associated with each of these stages, the sources of these risks and how these risks may be managed or mitigated are the subject of the remainder of the book.

Review questions

4.1 What are the different ways of measuring the success of M & A?

4.2 What is the rationale for shareholder maximization as a success criterion?

4.3 What are the issues in setting up an appropriate benchmark for assessing shareholder value performance of mergers?

4.4 What are the different benchmarks available for making such assessment?

4.5 What is benchmark return and what is abnormal return?

4.6 How is the CAPM used to assess merger performance? What are its limitations?

4.7 What is the link between abnormal returns and abnormal operating performance? How is the latter assessed?

4.8 What is short-run performance? What is long-run performance? Which is the appropriate measure of merger performance? Why?

4.9 What is the shareholder value performance of US and UK acquisitions in the short and long run?

4.10 What is the operating performance of US and UK acquirers?

4.11 What is the shareholder value and operating performance of continental European acquirers?

4.12 Comment on the differences in acquisition performance in the US, Europe and the UK.

Further reading

G. Andrade, M. L. Mitchell and E. Stafford (2001), 'New evidence and perspectives on mergers', *Journal of Economic Perspectives*, **15**(2), 2001, 102–120.

D. Carey, 'Lessons from master acquirers: A CEO roundtable on making mergers succeed', *Harvard Business Review*, **78**(3), 2000, 145–156.

A. Ghosh, 'Does operating performance improve following corporate acquisitions?', *Journal of Corporate Finance*, **7**, 2001, 151–178.

M. Goergen and L. Renneboog, 'Shareholder wealth effects of European domestic and cross-border takeover bids', *European Financial Management*, **10**(1), 2004, 9–45.

M. A. Hitt, R. E. Hoskisson, R. D. Ireland and J. S. Harrison, 'Are acquisitions a poison pill for innovation?', *Academy of Management Executive*, **5**(4), 1991, 22–34.

S. Moeller, R. P. Schlingemann and R. M. Stulz, 'Value destruction on a massive scale? A study of acquiring firm returns in the recent merger wave', *Journal of Finance*, **60**, 2005, 757–782.

Notes and references

1. See Appendix 4.1 for a brief review of the empirical work leading up to these conclusions. Fama and French argue that these factors capture some components of systematic risk.
2. In practice, however, researchers choose, as controls, firms that have not undertaken acquisitions in the relevant observation period. Thus comparison is made between merging and non-merging firms rather than between firms that follow similar competitive strategies.
3. Such stickiness is regarded as an indication of an inefficient stock market. However, Mitchell and Stafford attribute it to problems of statistical methodology, and when these are resolved the long-term stock returns are reduced to zero. See M. Mitchell and E. Stafford, 'Managerial decisions and long-term stock price performance', *Journal of Business*, **73**(3), 2000, 287–329.
4. Fama and French published a series of articles in developing and testing the three-factor model. See Appendix 4.1 for references to these.

5. See M. Carhart, 'On persistence of mutual fund performance', *Journal of Finance*, **52**(1), 1997, 57–82. Momentum may persist owing to the stickiness we mentioned earlier, or investors' irrational trading strategies of buying or selling based on past stock high or low prices respectively. See Appendix 4.1 for further discussion.

6. In a recent paper, Haim Levy defends the CAPM against attacks by behavioural economists and psychologists proposing the prospect theory that its theoretical foundations, i.e. the expected utility maximization and mean-variance rules, are not valid, and that the model lacks empirical support. See H. Levy, 'Behavioral economics and asset pricing', SSRN id 1361699 dated February 2009, downloaded from www.ssrn.com.

7. Percentage of shares owned and level of control in target resulting from a tender offer varies across the different studies in Panel A of Tables 4.1 and 4.2. In Schwert (1996) this percentage exceeds 50%. In Bradley, Desai and Kim (1998) it is, on average, 60%. In other studies the percentage is well below 50%.

8. See S. Bhagat, M. Dong, D. Hirshleifer and R. Noah, 'Do tender offers create value? New methods and evidence', *Journal of Financial Economics*, **76**, 2005, 5–60, and J. Cai and A. Vijh, 'Incentive effects of stock and option holdings of target and acquirer CEOs', *Journal of Finance*, **62**(4), 2007, 1891–1933. The bidder returns are generally higher the longer the pre-announcement period included in the event window, since bids often follow bidders' good stock price performance. Where the bidder holds shares in the target prior to bidding, the combined performance may be overstated because of double counting. Andrade *et al.* report −0.7% (insignificant), 16% and 1.8% (significant at 5%) respectively.

9. See S. Moeller, F. P. Schlinegemann and R. M. Stulz, 'Value destruction on a massive scale? A study of acquiring-firm returns in the recent merger wave', *Journal of Finance*, **60**, 2005, 757–782. The fact that the CAR is positive but the $ returns are negative suggests large losses for large acquirers. In technical language, $ returns are value (size) weighted whereas CAR is equally weighted. Value-weighted CAR for the 1980–2001 sample is −1.2% as reported by the authors in their 2004 paper, Table 2, consistent with the $ losses.

10. Bhagat *et al.* (2005) criticise the estimates based on short event CARs that do not encompass the whole offer period to deal completion. They argue that not all the announced bids will be completed because of target resistance, i.e. in hostile deals and the subsequent arrival of rival bids for the same target. After correcting for the reduced probability of initial bid success they report that CARs for tender offers are much higher than reported in other prior studies. Since this correction is probably larger for tender offers than for mergers, which face less hostility and perhaps less rivalry, tender offer returns are likely to be larger than those of mergers.

11. André *et al.* report for their sample of 267 Canadian acquisitions over 1980 to 2000 that the 36 month Fama–French calendar time abnormal return is −27% (significant at 1%). See P. André, M. Kooli and J. L'Her, 'The long-run performance of mergers and acquisitions: Evidence from the Canadian stock market', *Financial Management*, **33**(4), 2004, 27–43.

12. P. Healy, K. Palepu and R. Ruback, 'Does corporate performance improve after mergers?', *Journal of Financial Economics*, **31**, 1992, 135–175. They find significant positive correlation, but R^2 is only 0.30 (their Table 7).

13. M. A. Hitt, R. E. Hoskisson, R. D. Ireland and J. S. Harrison, 'Effects of acquisitions on D inputs and outputs', *Academy of Management Journal*, **34**, 1991, 693–706; 'Are acquisitions a poison pill for innovation?', *Academy of Management Executive*, **5**(4), 1991, 22–34.

14. G. Ahuja and R. Katila, 'Technological acquisitions and the innovation performance of acquiring firms: A longitudinal study', *Strategic Management Journal*, **22**, 2001, 197–220.

15. See J. C. Prabhu, R. K. Chandy and M. E. Ellis, 'The impact of acquisitions on innovation: Poison pill, placebo or tonic?', *Journal of Marketing*, **69**, 2005, 114–130. The authors' sample consists of 157 targets acquired by 35 pharmaceutical firms in the US during 1988–97. Their measure of innovation is the number of products in Phase 1 trials. They measure depth by the average number of approved patents per patent subclass, and breadth by the number of approved patent subclasses the firms held.

16. See M. Subramaniam and M. Youndt, 'The influence of intellectual capital on the types of innovative capabilities', *Academy of Management Journal*, **48**(3), 2005, 450–463.

17. A. Shleifer and L. Summers, 'Breach of trust in hostile takeovers', in A. Auerbach (Ed.), *Corporate Takeovers: Causes and Consequences* (Chicago, IL: University of Chicago Press, 1988).

18. F. R. Lichtenberg and D. Siegel, 'The concept of relative plant productivity and its measurement using Census LRD data' and 'Takeovers and corporate overhead', in F. R. Lichtenberg, *Corporate Takeovers and Productivity* (Cambridge, MA: MIT Press, 1992).

19. S. Bhagat, A. Shleifer and R. Vishny, *The Aftermath of Hostile Takeovers*, London School of Economics Discussion Paper 87, June 1990.

20. A. Schoar, 'Effects of diversification on productivity', *Journal of Finance*, **57**(6), 2002, 2379–2403. See Chapter 8 for further discussion.
21. M. J. Conyon, S. Girma, S. Thompson and P. W. Wright, 'The impact of mergers and acquisitions on company employment in the United Kingdom', *European Economic Review*, **46**, 2002, 31–49.
22. D. C. Mueller, 'Mergers and market share', *Review of Economics and Statistics*, **67**, 1985, 259–267.
23. W. W. Alberts and N. Varaiya, 'Assessing the profitability of growth by acquisition', *International Journal of Industrial Organization*, **7**, 1989, 133–149.
24. M. M. Bekier, A. J. Bogardus and T. Oldham, 'Why mergers fail', *The McKinsey Quarterly*, **4**, 2001, 6–9.
25. D. Carey, 'Lessons from master acquirers: A CEO roundtable on making mergers succeed, *Harvard Business Review*, **78**(3), 2000, 145–154.
26. A. Seth, 'Value creation in acquisitions: A re-examination of performance issues', *Strategic Management Journal*, **11**, 1990, 99–115.
27. D. Ravenscraft and F. Scherer, 'Mergers and managerial performance', in J. Coffee and C. Ackerman (Eds), *Knights and Raiders* (Oxford: Oxford University Press, 1988), pp. 194–210.
28. K. Lins and H. Servaes, 'International evidence on the value of corporate diversification', *Journal of Finance*, **60**(8), 1999, 2215–2239; J. R. Graham, M. L. Lemmon and J. G. Wolf, 'Does corporate diversification destroy value?', *Journal of Finance*, **63**, 2002, 695–720.
29. A. Ghosh, 'Does operating performance really improve following corporate acquisitions?', *Journal of Corporate Finance*, **7**, 2001, 151–178.
30. P. R. Rau and T. Vermaelen, 'Glamour, value and the post-acquisition performance of acquiring firms', *Journal of Financial Economics*, **49**, 1998, 223–253; S. Sudarsanam and A. Mahate, 'Glamour acquirers, method of payment and post-acquisition performance: The UK evidence', *Journal of Business Finance & Accounting*, **30**(1 & 2), 2003, 299–341. André *et al.*, *ibid*, report similar results for Canadian acquirers.
31. See S. Sudarsanam, 'Corporate governance, corporate control and takeovers', in C. Cooper and A. Gregory (Eds), *Advances in Mergers and Acquisitions* (New York: Elsevier Science, 2000), pp. 119–156, for a review of the evidence.

Appendix 4.1	Abnormal returns methodology to study the impact of mergers on shareholder value*

Event study methodology

The event study methodology introduced by Fama *et al.* (1969) has become the standard method of measuring security price changes in response to an event or announcement. It is a major research tool for examining market efficiency as well as for testing theories of corporate finance such as the impact of dividend policy, capital structure and corporate control changes. Event studies help address the fundamental question of how the flow of information to the market about an event affects stock returns, and are a powerful tool for assessing the impact of corporate changes on the value of the firms. Event studies are used for two purposes: to test the null hypothesis that the market efficiently incorporates new information, and to examine the wealth impact of an event. They involve determining whether there is an abnormal stock return following an unanticipated event. The methodology is popular, because it obviates the need to analyze accounting-based measures and instead focuses on stock price changes that are supposed to incorporate all relevant information. Post-event abnormal performance studies provide evidence on market efficiency. Systematically non-zero returns that persist after an event are inconsistent with the hypothesis that prices adjust quickly to fully reflect new information.

*I wish to thank Dr Vineet Agarwal of Cranfield School of Management for his expert knowledge and help in preparing this appendix.

Short- versus long-horizon studies

The short-horizon event studies assume that the response of prices to an event is quick – almost instantaneous – reflecting the stock market's informational efficiency. Hence researchers use a short event window of a few days around the event, e.g. a takeover bid announcement. A growing body of literature argues that stock prices adjust slowly to information, and therefore examines returns over longer horizons (typically 3–5 years) to get a full view of market inefficiency. The choice of an inappropriate model in short-horizon event studies vitiates conclusions less than in long-horizon studies, since daily expected returns are close to zero. When an event is a 'big impact' event, and the stock returns are large and concentrated in a few days, the bad model problem is negligible. For example, in mergers and tender offers the average stock return for target firms during a three-day event window is 15% where the normal average daily stock return is only about 0.04%. Use of daily stock returns not only captures the big impact, it also has the further advantage that the bad model problems are less severe. This allows cleaner tests of market efficiency than monthly returns. In studies that analyze long-run stock returns following major corporate events, there is considerable variation in the way abnormal returns are calculated and in statistical tests employed to detect abnormal returns.

Benchmark models and abnormal returns

A security's price performance can be considered abnormal only with reference to some benchmark, and therefore it is necessary to specify a return-generating model before abnormal returns can be measured. Normal returns can be generated in several different ways:

- *Capital asset pricing model*: The expected return for security i in time t is given by

$$R_{it} - R_{Ft} = \alpha_i + \beta_i(R_{Mt} - R_{Ft})$$

The parameters a_i and b_i are estimated by regressing the excess security returns on the excess market return for the estimation period.

- *Mean-adjusted model*: the *ex ante* expected return on a security is constant across time, but can differ across securities. The expected return for security i in time t is given by

$$E(R_{it}) = K_i$$

The model is consistent with CAPM under assumptions of constant systematic risk and a stationary optimal investment opportunity set for investors.

- *Market-adjusted model*: the *ex ante* expected return on a security is constant across securities and can differ across time. The expected return for security i in time t is given by

$$E(R_{it}) = E(R_{Mt})$$

where R_i is the return on security i, R_M is the return on the market index, and t is the time period. The model is consistent with CAPM under the assumption $\beta = 1$ for all securities.

- *Market model*: the expected return for security i in time t is given by

$$R_{it} = \alpha_i + \beta_i R_{Mt}$$

The parameters a_i and b_i are estimated by regressing the security returns on the market return for the estimation period.

- *Fama and French three-factor model (FFTF)*: the expected return R_{it} for security i in time t is given by

$$R_{it} - R_{Ft} = \alpha_i + \beta_i(R_{Mt} - R_{Ft}) + h_i\text{HML}_t + {}_i\text{SMB}_t$$

where R_F is the risk-free rate, R_M is the value-weighted return on the market index, HML is the return on the mimicking portfolio for the book-to-market factor, SMB is the return on the mimicking portfolio for the size factor, and t is the time subscript. HML is the difference in returns between high-market-to-book and low-market-to-book portfolios. SMB is the difference in returns between large-firm and small-firm portfolios.

- *Carhart four-factor model*:

$$R_{it} - R_{Ft} = \alpha_i + \beta_i(R_{Mt} - R_{Ft}) + h_i\mathrm{HML}_t + s_i\mathrm{SMB}_t + m_iM_t$$

where M_t is the momentum factor measured, for example, as the difference between the highest returns and lowest returns portfolios in the year preceding the event. The assumption is that historic stock returns tend to persist for a while i.e. stocks experiencing high (low) returns in the recent past will continue to experience high (low) returns. This factor captures the component of stock pricing due to momentum.

Both the FFTF and Carhart four-factor models are generally used to measure long term performance and estimated using monthly returns. α_i is a monthly excess return. It is also described as calendar time abnormal return. For an example of a study reporting such a return see Bouwman, Fuller and Nain (2009) listed in Table 4.3.

- *Reference portfolio*: this approach sorts the population of stocks on one or more predefined characteristics (e.g. size, book to market ratio, industry), and the expected return on the security i during time t is the realized return during time t on the reference portfolio to which the security belongs.
- *Matching with control firms on specific firm characteristics*: this approach matches each sample security to another non-event security on one or more predefined characteristics such as size, book-to-market, industry. The expected return on the sample security i during time t is the same as the realized return on the control security during time t.

Calculating abnormal returns

The abnormal return is the difference between the realized return and the expected return on the sample security:

$$\mathrm{AR}_{it} = R_{it} - E(R_{it})$$

where AR_{it} is the abnormal return, R_{it} is the realized return and, $E(R_{it})$ is the expected return on security i for period t.

There are two methods of computing abnormal returns:

- *Cumulative abnormal returns (CAR)*: these are computed as the sum of daily (or monthly) abnormal returns over the horizon of the study. CAR for security i during period T is given by

$$\mathrm{CAR}_{iT} = \sum_{t=1}^{T} \mathrm{AR}_{it}$$

- *Buy-and-hold abnormal returns (BHAR)*: this is computed as the return on buy-and-hold investment in the sample firm less the expected return on buy-and-hold investment in a control firm or reference portfolio. BHAR for security i during period T is given by

$$\mathrm{BHAR}_{iT} = \prod_{t=1}^{T}(1 + R_{it}) - \prod_{t=1}^{T}[1 + E(R_{it})]$$

Controversies over abnormal returns measures

Barber and Lyon (1997) argue that BHARs are theoretically superior to CARs because BHARs accurately capture the wealth effects of a long-term investor. Fama (1998), on the other hand, argues that CARs are theoretically superior because formal tests of abnormal returns should use the same returns metric as the model to estimate expected returns uses. Asset-pricing models are silent about the time interval, but they usually assume normally distributed returns, and normality is a better approximation for short-horizon returns such as monthly returns. Tests of asset-pricing models generally use monthly returns.

Mitchell and Stafford (2000) point out that BHARs can give false impressions of the speed of price adjustments, because they can grow with time even when there is no abnormal performance after the initial period. Kothari and Warner (1997) found that in their simulation results both CAR and BHAR produce misspecified test statistics, and Lyon *et al.* (1999) found that test statistics based on CARs were no less reliable than those based on BHARs. Fama (1998) also argued that CARs were better than BHARs on statistical grounds. Lyon *et al.* (1999) developed elaborate techniques to correct some of the inference problems of BHARs, but their elaborate methods did not produce more reliable inferences than simple methods used for CARs. Brav (1997) emphasized that not all BHAR models correct fully for cross-correlations of returns, and a full solution was typically not available. For average abnormal returns (AARs) there is a full solution to the problem of cross-correlations.

Using control firms alleviates these biases and gives well-specified test statistics in random samples. However, controlling for size and book-to-market ratio is not sufficient to yield well-specified test statistics when samples are non-random.

Event clustering and calendar time portfolio returns (CTPR)

To alleviate the problem of time clustering of events and the cross-correlation of their returns the calendar time portfolio return methodology constructs portfolios of event securities, e.g. takeover target stocks and benchmark control portfolios and estimates the abnormal returns over time. This procedure controls for event clustering and the correlation of event returns. For an example of a study employing this approach see Mitchell and Stafford (2000) listed in Table 4.3.

References and bibliography

Barber, B. M. and J. D. Lyon (1997), 'Detecting long-run abnormal stock returns: The empirical power and specification of test statistics', *Journal of Financial Economics*, **43**, 341–372.

Brav, A. (1997), 'Inference in long horizon event studies: A re-evaluation of the evidence', Unpublished working paper, Graduate School of Business, University of Chicago.

Brav, A., C. Geczy and P. A. Gompers (2000), 'Is the abnormal return following equity issuances anomalous?', *Journal of Financial Economics*, **56**, 209–249.

Brown, S. and J. Warner (1980), 'Measuring security price performance', *Journal of Financial Economics*, **8**, 205–208.

Brown, S. and J. Warner (1985), 'Using daily returns: The case of event studies', *Journal of Financial Economics*, **14**, 3–31.

Carhart, M. M. (1997), 'On persistence of mutual fund performance', *Journal of Finance*, **52**(1), 1977–1984.

Dimson, E. (1979), 'Risk measurement when shares are subject to infrequent trading', *Journal of Financial Economics*, **7**, 197–226.

Dravid, A. J. (1987), 'A note on the behaviour of stock returns around ex-dates of stock distributions', *Journal of Finance*, **42**, 163–168.

Fama, E. F. (1976), *Foundations of Finance*, Basic Books, New York.

Fama, E. F. (1991), 'Efficient capital markets II', *Journal of Finance*, **46**, 1575–1617.

Fama, E. F. (1998), 'Market efficiency, long-term returns, and behavioral finance', *Journal of Financial Economics*, **49**, 283–306.

Fama, E. F., L. Fisher, M. C. Jensen and R. Roll (1969), 'The adjustment of stock prices to new information', *International Economic Review*, **10**, 1–21.

Johnson, N. J. (1978), 'Modified *t* tests and confidence intervals for asymmetrical populations', *Journal of the American Statistical Association*, **73**, 536–544.

Kothari, S. P. and J. B. Warner (1997), 'Measuring long-horizon security price performance', *Journal of Financial Economics*, **43**, 301–340.

Lyon, J. D., B. M. Barber and C. Tsai (1999), 'Improved methods for tests of long-run abnormal stock returns', *Journal of Finance*, **54**(1), 165–201.

Mitchell, M. and E. Stafford (2000), 'Managerial decisions and long-term stock price performance', *Journal of Business*, **73**(3), 287–329.

Patell, J. and M. Wolfson (1979), 'Anticipated information releases reflected in call option prices', *Journal of Accounting and Economics*, **1**, 117–140.

Scholes, M. and J. Williams (1977), 'Estimating betas from nonsynchronous data', *Journal of Financial Economics*, **5**, 309–328.

Appendix 4.2   Studies cited in Tables 4.1 to 4.9

Agrawal, A., J. Jaffe and G. N. Mandelker (1992), 'Post-merger performance of acquiring firms: A re-examination of an anomaly', *Journal of Finance*, **47**, 1605–1621.

Andrade, G., M. L. Mitchell and E. Stafford (2001), 'New evidence and perspectives on mergers', *Journal of Economic Perspectives*, **15**(2), 102–120.

Antoniou, A., D. Petmetzas and H. Zhao (2007), 'Bidder gains and losses of firms involved in many acquisitions', *Journal of Business Finance and Accounting*, **34**(7&8), 1221–1244.

Baker, R. D. and R. J. Limmack (2002), 'UK takeovers and acquiring company wealth changes: The impact of survivorship and other potential selection biases on post-outcome performance', University of Stirling working paper, May.

Bergström, C., P. Högfeldt and K. Högholm (1993), 'Strategic blocking, arbitrageurs and the division of the takeover gains', *Multinational Financial Management*, **3**, 217–248.

Bhagat, S., M. Dong, D. Hirshleifer and R. Noah (2005), 'Do tender offers create value? New methods and evidence', *Journal of Financial Economics*, **76**, 3–60.

Bouwman, C., K. Fuller and A. Nain (2009), 'Market valuation and acquisition quality: Empirical evidence', *Review of Financial Studies*, **22**(2), 633–679.

Bradley, M., A. Desai and E. H. Kim (1988), 'Synergistic gains from corporate acquisitions and their division between the stockholders of target and acquiring firms', *Journal of Financial Economics*, **21**, 3–40.

Cable, J., J. Palfrey and W. Runge (1980), 'Federal Republic of Germany, 1964–74', in D. Mueller (Ed.), *The Determinants and Effects of Mergers: An International Comparison* (Oelgeschlager, Gunn & Hain: Cambridge, MA), pp. 99–132.

Cai, J. and A. Vijh (2007), 'Incentive effects of stock and option holdings of target and acquirer CEOs', *Journal of Finance*, **62**(4), 1891–1933.

Campa, J. M. and I. Hernando (2004), 'Shareholder value creation in European M&As', *European Financial Management*, **10**, 1, 47–81.

Cosh, A., A. Hughes and A. Singh (1980), 'The causes and effects of mergers: An empirical examination for the UK at the macroeconomic level', in D. C. Mueller (Ed.), *The Determinants and Effects of Mergers: An International Comparison* (Oelschlager, Gunn & Hain, Cambridge, MA), pp. 227–270.

Cosh, A., P. M. Guest and A. Hughes (2006), 'Board share-ownership and takeover performance', *Journal of Business Finance and Accounting*, **33**(3&4), 459–510.

Datta, S., M. Iskandar-Datta and K. Raman (2001), 'Executive compensation and corporate acquisition decisions', *Journal of Finance*, **56**, 6, 2299–2336.

Dickerson, A. P., H. D. Gilson and E. Tsakalotos (1997), 'The impact of acquisitions on company performance: Evidence from a large panel of UK firms', *Oxford Economic Papers*, **49**, 344–361.

Dodd, P. and R. Ruback (1977), 'Tender offers and stockholder returns', *Journal of Financial Economics*, **5**, 351–373.

Doukas, J. and M. Holmen (2000), 'Managerial ownership and risk reducing acquisitions', in C. Cooper and A. Gregory (Eds), *Advances in Mergers and Acquisitions*, Vol. 1 (JAI Press/Elsevier Science, New York), pp. 183–203.

Eckbo, E. and H. Langohr (1989), 'Information disclosure, method of payment and takeover premiums', *Journal of Financial Economics*, **24**, 363–403.

Faccio, M., J. McConnell and D. Stolin (2006), 'Returns to acquirers of listed and unlisted targets', *Journal of Financial and Quantitative Analysis*, **41**(1), 197–220.

Firth, M. (1980), 'Takeovers, shareholder returns and the theory of the firm', *Quarterly Journal of Economics*, **94**, 235–260.

Franks, J. and R. Harris (1989), 'Shareholder wealth effects of corporate takeovers: The UK experience 1955–85', *Journal of Financial Economics*, **23**, 225–249.

Franks, J., R. Harris and C. Mayer (1988), 'Means of payment in takeovers: Results for the United Kingdom and the United States,' in A. J. Auerbach (Ed.), *Corporate Takeovers: Causes and Consequences* (Chicago University Press, Chicago, IL).

Franks, J., R. Harris and S. Titman (1991), 'The post-merger share price performance of acquiring firms', *Journal of Financial Economics*, **29**, 81–96.

Ghosh, A. (2001), 'Does operating performance improve following corporate acquisitions?', *Journal of Corporate Finance*, 7, 2001, 151–178.

Goergen, M. and L. Renneboog (2004), 'Shareholder wealth effects of European domestic and cross-border takeover bids', *European Financial Management*, **10**(1), 9–45.

Graham, J., M. Lemmon and J. Wolf (2002), 'Does corporate diversification destroy value?', *Journal of Finance*, **57**, 695–720.

Gregory, A. (1997), 'An examination of the long-run performance of UK acquiring firms', *Journal of Business Finance and Accounting*, **24**(7&8), 971–1002.

Gugler, K., D. C. Mueller, B. B. Yurtoglu and C. Zulehner (2003), 'The effects of mergers: An international comparison', *International Journal of Industrial Organization*, **21**, 625–653.

Healy, P., K. Palepu and R. Ruback (1992), 'Does corporate performance improve after mergers?', *Journal of Financial Economics*, **31**, 135–175.

Herman, E. S. and L. Lowenstein (1988), 'The efficiency effects of hostile takeovers', in J. Coffee, L. Lowenstein and S. Ackerman (Eds), *Knights, Raiders and Targets* (Oxford University Press, Oxford).

Higson, C. and J. Elliott (1998), 'Post-takeover returns: The UK evidence', *Journal of Empirical Finance*, **5**, 27–46.

Holmen, M. and J. D. Knopf (2004), 'Minority shareholder protection and the private benefits of control for Swedish mergers', *Journal of Financial and Quantitative Analysis*, **39**(1), 167–191.

Jarrell G. A. and A. Poulsen (1989), 'The returns to acquiring firms in tender offers: Evidence from three decades', *Financial Management*, **18**, 12–19.

Jarrell, G. A., J. Brickley and J. Netter (1988), 'The market for corporate control: The empirical evidence since 1980', *Journal of Economic Perspectives*, **2**(1), 49–68.

Jenny, F. and A. Weber (1980), 'France, 1962–72', in D. Mueller (Ed.), *The Determinants and Effects of Mergers: An International Comparison* (Oelgeschlager, Gunn & Hain: Cambridge, MA), pp. 133–162.

Jensen, M. and R. Ruback (1983), 'The market for corporate control: The scientific evidence', *Journal of Financial Economics*, **11**, 5–50.

Kaplan, S. and M. Weisbach (1992), 'Success of acquisitions: Evidence from divestitures', *Journal of Finance*, **47**(1), 107–138.

Kennedy, V. and R. J. Limmack (1996), 'Takeover activity, CEO turnover, and the market for corporate control', *Journal of Business Finance and Accounting*, **23**, 267–285.

Kräussal, R. and M. Topper (2007), 'Size does matter: Firm size and the gains from acquisitions on the Dutch market', in G. N. Gregoriou and L. Renneboog (Eds), *International Mergers and Acquisitions Activity since 1990* (Elsevier, Amsterdam), pp. 279–294.

Kumar, M. S. (1984), *Growth, Acquisition and Investment* (Cambridge University Press, Cambridge).

Kumps, A. and R. Wtterwulghe (1980), 'Belgium, 1962–74', in D. Mueller (Ed.), *The Determinants and Effects of Mergers: An International Comparison* (Oelgeschlager, Gunn & Hain: Cambridge, MA).

Langetieg, T. (1978), 'An application of a three-factor performance index to measure stockholder gains from merger', *Journal of Financial Economics*, **6**, 365–384.

Limmack, R. (1991), 'Corporate mergers and shareholder wealth effects', *Accounting & Business Research*, **21**(83), 239–251.

Linn, S. C. and J. A. Switzer (2001), 'Are cash acquisitions associated with better postcombination operating performance than stock acquisitions?', *Journal of Banking and Finance*, **25**, 1113–1138.

Loderer, C. and K. Martin (1990), 'Corporate acquisitions by NYSE and AMEX firms: The experience of a comprehensive sample', *Financial Management*, Winter, 17–33.

Loderer, C. and K. Martin (1992), 'Post-acquisition performance of acquiring firms', *Financial Management*, Autumn, 69–79.

Loughran, T. and A. M. Vijh (1997), 'Do long term shareholders benefit from corporate acquisitions?', *Journal of Finance*, **52**(3), 1765–1790.

Magenheim, E. B. and D. C. Mueller (1988), 'Are acquiring firm shareholders better off after an acquisition?', in J. Coffee, L. Lowenstein and S. Ackerman (Eds), *Knights, Raiders and Targets* (Oxford University Press, Oxford).

Mandelker, G. (1974), 'Risk and return: The case of merging firms', *Journal of Financial Economics*, **1**, 303–335.

Manson, S., A. Stark and H. Thomas (1994), *A Cash Flow Analysis of the Operational Gains From Takeovers*, Research Report 35, Chartered Association of Certified Accountants, London.

Martynova, M. and L. Renneboog (2006), 'Mergers and acquisitions in Europe', *European Corporate Governance Institute*, Finance working paper 114/2006.

Martynova, M., S. Oosting and L. Renneboog (2007), 'The long-term operating performance in European mergers and acquisitions', in G. N. Gregoriou and L. Renneboog (Eds), *International Mergers and Acquisitions Activity since 1990* (Elsevier, Amsterdam), pp. 79–116.

Masulis, R., C. Wang and F. Xie (2007), 'Corporate governance and acquirer returns', *Journal of Finance*, **62**(4), 1851–1889.

Meeks, G. (1977), *Disappointing Marriage: A Study of the Gains from Mergers* (Cambridge University Press, Cambridge).

Mitchell, M. L. and E. Stafford (2000), 'Managerial decisions and long term stock price performance', *Journal of Business*, **73**, 287–320.

Moeller, S., R. P. Schlingemann and R. M. Stulz (2004), 'Firm size and the gains from acquisitions', *Journal of Financial Economics*, **73**, 201–228.

Moeller, S., R. P. Schlingemann and R. M. Stulz (2005), 'Value destruction on a massive scale? A study of acquiring firm returns in the recent merger wave', *Journal of Finance*, **60**, 757–782.

Peer, H. (1980), 'The Netherlands, 1962–73', in D. Mueller (Ed.), *The Determinants and Effects of Mergers: An International Comparison* (Oelgeschlager, Gunn & Hain: Cambridge, MA), pp. 163–191.

Powell, R. G. and A. W. Stark (2005), 'Does operating performance increase post-takeover for UK takeovers? A comparison of performance measures and benchmarks', *Journal of Corporate Finance*, **11**, 293–317.

Rau, R. and T. Vermaelen (1998), 'Glamour and the post-acquisition performance of acquiring firms', *Journal of Financial Economics*, **49**, 223–253.

Ravenscraft, D. and F. Scherer (1987), *Mergers, Sell-offs and Economic Efficiency* (Brookings Institution, Washington, DC).

Ravenscraft, D. and F. Scherer (1988), 'Mergers and managerial performance', in J. Coffee, L. Lowenstein and S. Ackerman (Eds), *Knights, Raiders and Targets* (Oxford University Press, Oxford).

Ryden, B. and J. Edberg (1980), 'Large mergers in Sweden, 1962–76', in D. Mueller (Ed.), *The Determinants and Effects of Mergers: An International Comparison* (Oelgeschlager, Gunn & Hain: Cambridge, MA), pp. 193–226.

Schwert, G. W. (1996), 'Markup pricing in mergers and acquisitions', *Journal of Financial Economics*, **41**, 153–192.

Sudarsanam, S. and J. Huang (2007), 'Executive compensation and managerial overconfidence: Impact on risk taking and post-acquisition performance', presented to the 10th Conference of the Swiss Society for Financial Market Research, Zurich, April (also Cranfield School of Management Working Paper).

Sudarsanam, P. S. and A. Mahate (2003), 'Glamour acquirers, method of payment and post-acquisition performance: The UK evidence, *Journal of Business Finance & Accounting*, **30**, 299–341.

Sudarsanam, P. S., P. Holl and A. Salami (1996), 'Shareholder wealth gains in mergers: Effect of synergy and ownership structure', *Journal of Business Finance & Accounting*, **23**(5&6), 673–698.

Van Hulle, C., T. Vermaelen and P. de Wouters (1991), 'Regulation, taxes and the market for corporate control in Belgium', *Journal of Banking & Finance*, **15**, 1143–1170.

PART 2

Corporate strategy and organizing for acquisitions

In Part One we provided an overview of mergers and acquisitions. This covered a historical survey of mergers and acquisitions since the 1890s. We identified several patterns of M & A activity, and in particular the wave pattern of mergers and industry clustering. These have important implications for firms that seek to achieve their strategic objectives through M & A.

In Chapter 3 we viewed M & A from a variety of perspectives. Some of these perspectives account for the generally poor performance of acquisitions to deliver shareholder value. Most acquirers are unable to enhance shareholder value for their shareholders, although a minority of them succeed. This suggests that while the underlying rationale for acquisitions may seem good, there are serious impediments to realizing the strategic goals of acquisitions.

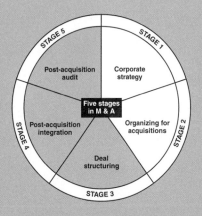

In Part Two we focus on the sources of value in different types of corporate acquisition, and examine the empirical evidence as to the limits on value creation in these acquisitions and how firms could organize themselves for effective and successful acquisitions. We cover Stage 1 of the five-stage M & A model outlined in Chapter 1 in Chapters 5 to 11. Chapter 5 deals with horizontal and related acquisitions of large firms. It also discusses the recent phenomenon of consolidating mergers aimed at integrating relatively small firms to create a firm with a critical size. In Chapter 6 we describe vertically integrating acquisitions, and examine their rationale and the limits to value creation. Chapter 7 deals with conglomerate acquisitions, which have often been held up as a value-destroying acquisition form. We find some new evidence to call this perception into question. Chapter 8 discusses cross-border acquisitions and the limits to value creation through them. In Chapter 9 we take a look at strategic alliance as an alternative to acquisition. Chapter 10 is concerned with the opposite of corporate acquisitions, i.e. corporate refocusing through various forms of divestiture.

The rationale for the divestitures and the empirical evidence on their performance are discussed. Chapter 11 discusses a special class of acquisitions, the leveraged buyouts or LBOs, distinguished by heavy reliance on debt as a source of funding for the acquisition.

Stage 3 of the five-stage model is covered in Chapters 12 and 13. Chapter 12 deals with the internal organization of the acquirers and targets and their influence on the acquisition process and acquisition performance. In particular it focuses on the corporate governance of acquirers and their targets and how it impacts on acquisitions. Chapter 13 provides a framework for identifying appropriate acquisition targets by setting up target selection criteria and a procedure for ranking potentially attractive targets.

CHAPTER 5

Sources and limits of value creation in horizontal and related mergers

Objectives

At the end of this chapter, the reader should be able to understand:

- the nature of horizontal or horizontally related mergers;
- the rationale for such mergers;
- how value may be created from such mergers;
- the limits on value creation; and
- the empirical evidence for the success of horizontal mergers.

Introduction

In Chapter 2 we reviewed the historical trend in mergers and acquisitions. The earliest merger wave in the US was characterized as merging for monopolies, and the second wave was described as merging for oligopolies. In both these instances the mergers were of firms selling the same products or the same range of products. We also observed similar mergers in Europe, including the UK. In recent years several firms in wide-ranging sectors such as electricity, utility, pharmaceuticals, banking, insurance, oil and gas, food and drinks, automobiles, steel and healthcare have merged with one another. Such mergers are called horizontally related mergers. Where firms selling the same products merge, we define it as a pure horizontal merger.

Where firms selling products that are not identical in terms of end use but nevertheless share certain commonalities, such as technology, markets, marketing channels, branding or knowledge base, merge, we refer to such mergers as related mergers. The term 'related' is thus more widely and loosely defined than 'horizontal'. In this chapter, for simplicity, we use the term 'horizontal merger' to refer to both pure horizontal mergers and related mergers of firms selling a range of 'similar' products. The merger of firms operating at successive stages of the same chain from creation to the sale of a product represents vertical integration/merger. Although vertical integration may also be considered a related merger, we defer discussion of it to Chapter 6. Merger of two pharmaceutical companies selling the same drugs is thus a horizontal merger, but merger of two pharmaceutical firms selling different drugs but through the same distribution channels or sharing R & D is a related merger. Merger of a drug manufacturer with a pharmacy benefit manager is vertical integration.

Horizontal mergers often characterize industries and markets whose products are generally in the mature or declining stages of the product life cycle. The overall growth rate of these markets is low, and firms have built up production capacity that far exceeds the demand. This combination of low market growth and excess capacity places pressure on firms to achieve cost efficiencies through consolidating mergers. Such efficiencies may result from scale, scope and learning economies, which we discussed in Chapter 3. Firms may also seek to achieve increased market share and revenue growth through mergers, leveraging each other's resources and capabilities for this purpose.

In this chapter we discuss the circumstances and forces that give rise to excess capacity and the pressure for consolidation. We set out the rationale for M & A as a means of coping with these pressures, and for value creation through consolidating mergers. After identifying the various sources of added value we illustrate how resources and capabilities are shared and transferred between horizontally merging firms. We then discuss the limits to value creation from a variety of sources, such as competitor reaction, and the limited duration of the competitive advantage gained from exploiting the various economies in horizontal mergers.

Motivations for horizontal mergers in mature industries

Characteristics of mature industries

Mature industries are characterized by:

- low overall growth in demand for the industry's products;
- excess capacity;
- a small number of large competitors; and
- considerable price pressure and pressure to reduce costs.

We first discuss how excess capacity arises, and the consequences of excess capacity for firms. This leads us to the rationale for some horizontal mergers. Such mergers may provide a means of 'taking out' excess capacity, increase scale and scope economies, and allow merging firms to gain market share at the expense of competitors. The limits to these gains through mergers are then outlined.

Causes of excess capacity

Jensen identifies various causes of excess capacity[1]:

- demand reduction;
- capacity-expanding technological change, e.g. microchip processor capacity;
- obsolescence-creating technological change;
- 'investment mania';
- government macro-policy changes, e.g. deregulation and privatization;
- organizational innovations that lower entry barriers and allow new but small competitors to compete on a level playing field, e.g. through virtual organization, networking; and
- globalization of production and trade, e.g. the steel industry in the US faced with cheaper imports from Asia.

Demand reduction arises during the recession episodes of the business cycle when demand falls below the level of output at which the existing capacity can be operated to yield the required rate of return. Where new production technology becomes available the current capital stock may be used to yield increased productivity and larger volume. This means that the currently installed capacity is in excess of that needed to meet the expected demand. New business models, or new organizational techniques or information technology deployed by new players, or some existing players, render the other players obsolescent. Firms endowed with these new technologies then increase capacity and gain market share from the obsolescent firms. Jensen cites the example from the US of Wal-Mart's strategy of entering a new retail market by increasing capacity and employing more intensive use of information technology, direct dealing with manufacturers, replacement of high-cost and restrictive work-rule union labour, etc.

New business models and the associated organization thus allow new players to increase capacity, to the detriment of current competitors. However, this strategy is not always a sure-fire winner. The failure of a large number of dotcom companies in 2000 shows that new technology does not always render existing players such as 'brick and mortar' retailers obsolescent. In this case the existing retailers could easily adapt the new technology and provide online shopping, e.g. Barnes and Noble when faced with competition from Amazon.com.

Finally, competitors in an industry may simultaneously rush to implement new technologies without considering whether the aggregate investment in new capacity will be supported by the demand for the final product. Exhibit 5.1 provides a cautionary tale of such lemming-like

---

Exhibit 5.1

Investment mania grips a third generation

In 1999 many European governments sold licences to operate the third generation (3G) broadband mobile telephone networks. Some of them, such as the UK, sold the licences in auctions. Many telecom companies considered the new broadband technology as heralding a spectacular revolution in communications, combining voice, visual and data transmission, and Internet technologies. They saw a hugely profitable market in services based on this new technology, and bid ferociously for the licences. Licensing governments saw pots of gold in these licences. Soon the licensing process assumed the character of a feeding frenzy. Bids by telecom started skyrocketing. The UK government would receive over the years €50.5bn, the German government €37.5bn. In all, the telecom operators would pay out €120bn to European governments over 15 to 20 years. The cost of building the networks would cost another €140bn. Many of the telecom operators also made acquisitions, paying fancy prices for mobile telephony companies or other telecom operators, whose stocks were also highly valued.

Financiers eagerly joined the party, and money flowed freely. Billions of dollars were raised in bonds, many of them high-yield or junk bonds (see Chapter 12 on these bonds). However, it was soon clear that if all the telecom operators built the networks there would be massive overcapacity. The 3G technology was also still being developed, and its introduction was delayed. It was becoming clear that the licences had been grossly overpriced. The telecom market collapsed. By the end of 2000 the total debt among Europe's six largest telecom companies reached €233bn. Many of the bonds issued by these companies were downgraded by the rating agencies, with some of them sinking into junk status as 'fallen angels'. This investment mania in the telecom sector matched that in the Internet business, and both – inspired by overhyped dreams – came to a grievous end for millions of investors.

Table 5.1 Sources of value in horizontal mergers

Category	Type of value source
Revenue enhancement	• Increased market power and increased market share • Network externalities • Leveraging marketing resources and capabilities
Cost savings	• Reduction of excess capacity • Scale economies in production, marketing, sales and distribution, logistics, branding, R & D • Scope economies in branding, marketing, distribution, production, logistics • Learning economies
New growth opportunities	• Creating new business models to compete • Creating new capabilities and resources • Creating new products, markets, processes

behaviour by telecommunication companies in winning the licences for the third generation mobile telecommunication services.

Internal restructuring through closures and shutdowns of plants or service centres may reduce overcapacity. Alternatively, firms may exit by becoming targets of acquisitions by other firms in the same industry, or by outside firms such as leveraged buyout or private equity firms. Thus takeover is an instrument of industry consolidation, leading to capacity reduction to match the demand for the industry's products.

Sources of value creation in horizontal/related mergers

We can divide these sources broadly into three categories:

• revenue enhancing while maintaining the existing cost base;
• cost reducing while maintaining the existing revenue level; and
• generating new resources and capabilities that lead to revenue growth or cost reduction, or crafting new business models to compete in the existing markets better or in new markets[2].

The first two sources are broadly based on leveraging the merging firms' current stock of resources and capabilities, whereas the third is derived from the creation of new resources and capabilities. Revenue enhancement and cost reduction are not necessarily exclusive of each other in a given merger. Increased sales volume may lead to various economies, which in turn can reduce the cost base. Similarly, reducing costs may allow the firm to compete on price and increase its market share. In either case the merger may lead to a virtuous cycle. Whether this virtuous cycle is triggered, and how long it will last, depend on a host of factors such as product characteristics, market segmentation, technology and level of current output. Table 5.1 summarizes the sources of revenue enhancement and cost savings from horizontal mergers.

Revenue enhancement through mergers

Increased market power and revenue growth

A horizontal merger of two firms selling in the same market increases the market share of those firms, conferring enhanced market power to dictate the output price or to compete more effectively on non-price terms. Revenue growth can be achieved by lowering prices for products that are highly price sensitive. Where the merger results in enhanced market power for the merging firms through a large increase in market share, and the price elasticity of their products is unchanged, the firms may also increase their revenue.

What is the impact of market share on firm performance? Studies from the 1980s suggest that higher market share is associated with higher profits[3]. While merging firms selling in the same market, by definition, increase their market share in the short term, maintaining their increased market share in the long term may not be easy. If, as we have seen in the case of industry clustering of mergers, rival firms replicate the merger strategy of the first mover, or pursue other and more aggressive competitive strategies, initial market share gains may not be sustained. Mueller found that, in a sample of US mergers during 1950–72, horizontally merging firms lost market share. Unacquired businesses on average retained 88% of their 1950 market share by 1972, whereas acquired businesses retained only 18%[4].

Horizontal merger may result in increased market concentration, but may not diminish the competitive rivalry among the residual players in the market. Thus increased market concentration may not lead to increased profits or value creation. Richard Schmalensee concluded that 'the relation, if any, between seller concentration and profitability is weak statistically and the estimated effect is usually small'[5]. From an extensive survey of concentration–profitability studies, Hay and Morris report: 'While very few studies suggest that concentration has a negative effect on profitability, only half of them find a significant positive relation and this is true for each of the USA, Canada and the UK separately'[6].

Do horizontal mergers lead to collusion among the remaining players in the market and increased profitability[7]? In a series of papers using US data, Eckbo addressed this question by examining the wealth gains made by shareholders of the merging firms and their rivals[8]. The alternative hypotheses tested were the collusion hypothesis and the efficiency hypothesis. Under the collusion hypothesis rivals of the merging firms benefit from the merger, since successful collusion limits output and raises product prices. Under the efficiency hypothesis the merger releases information about scope for productive efficiency, and the rivals may also benefit from that information. However, where the rivals are unable to implement the efficiency measures implicit in the new information, they lose. These gains and losses are measured in terms of gains or losses to the shareholders of the companies concerned. If the mergers are challenged by the antitrust authorities, such as the Federal Trade Commission (FTC) or the Department of Justice (DOJ) in the US (see Chapter 18 on antitrust regulation), the gains and losses observed at the time of the initial merger announcement will be reversed.

Eckbo finds evidence inconsistent with the collusion hypothesis. At the time of merger announcement the rival firm shareholders gain, but when the mergers are challenged these gains are not reversed. This outcome is consistent with the efficiency argument. Thus even horizontal mergers challenged by the FTC/DOJ, which potentially increase the chances of collusion, do not seem to give rise to market power. Wier and Stillman provide further evidence supporting the conclusions of Eckbo and his collegues[9]. Fee and Thomas, in a more recent study, report similar evidence[10]. They also find that returns to the customers of the merging firms at merger announcement and changes in their post-merger operating performance are negligible. These 'findings for rivals and customers suggest increased anticompetitive collusion is not a significant source of gains to mergers'.

However, there is evidence of gains arising from the increased buying power of the merging firms, since suppliers suffer significant declines in cash flow margins following downstream mergers[11]. The gains to merging firms are larger where they operate in more concentrated markets. Suppliers who are retained by the merging firms experience value gains, but those that are not suffer value losses. These patterns suggest that merging firms play off suppliers against one another. Scherer and Ross, after reviewing the evidence on the market power effects of horizontal mergers, concluded that these gains were small and rare under modern economic conditions, owing to contestability of markets, competitor reaction and replication of similar merger strategies, and antitrust restraints against monopolistic mergers[12].

Network externality and revenue growth

Another important source of revenue growth may be through network externalities (NWE). A network externality exists whenever the value of a product to an individual customer depends on the number of other users of the product, such as the Internet or email. Network externality arises from the creation of a customer base (also called an installed base), with customers sharing a common experience that can be facilitated, enriched or made more effective by interaction among themselves. This provides an incentive to intensify interaction and to join the installed base, which, in turn, provides the incentive to buy the product. What enhances the perceived customer benefit of the product is not the product's attributes *per se* but the gateway it provides to the network.

We can observe the working of NWE in a variety of contexts. Microsoft's dominance of the office software market is facilitated by users' access to the shared experience of other users through training, manuals, etc. Internet chatrooms and blogs create networks that increase the attraction of the Internet, as well as creating a network for the products forming the subject matter of the chatroom. Book clubs provide the forum for readers of certain types of book to share their anguish, agony, joy and ecstasy of reading the books, and induce many to buy books in order to join the club. Brandenburger and Nalebuff attribute the phenomenal success of Nintendo home video games to NWE[13].

NWE is like a hub and spokes wheel. While the spokes connect customers (C) to the hub (the product), the wheel (externality), as shown in Figure 5.1, also connects them to one

Figure 5.1   Hub and spokes of the externality wheel

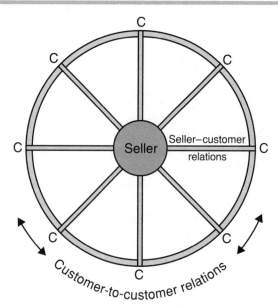

another. Multiplicity of spokes and their length lead to a giant wheel. An important source of value gains is through the learning economy that improves with the widening network (see section on learning economy below). Acquisition of a target with network externality potential can thus be a source of profitable revenue growth.

Revenue enhancement through acquisition of complementors

In Chapter 3 we introduced the idea of the value net and complementors (see Figure 3.3 and the related discussion). Firms can achieve revenue growth by introducing complementors into the game, since the demand for a product increases when the demand for its complement also increases. In the takeover context a firm may perceive the products of another firm as complementary, but the complementarity of the products of the two firms may have been under-exploited. The acquisition may enable the firm to leverage its competences to enhance and make more visible the latent complementarity. In the 1990s many utility companies in the UK acquired other utility companies. Water companies acquired electricity distribution companies. They offer price discounts to customers switching their custom from other water or electricity companies, thereby increasing the attractiveness of the utility bundle compared with the separate purchases of these services from different utilities. These strategies and acquisitions followed the deregulation of the UK utility sectors. For another example, GE Capital, by providing finance and credit to the customers of GE's aerospace division selling aero engines, acts as the latter's complementor. GE's avionics division is a complementor to its aero engine division[14].

A complementor is not just a product that shares certain commonalities, such as production process, components or a distribution network. The bundling of the complementors is not driven by the desire to economize on the cost of these commonalties. It is driven by the focus on topline growth, i.e. revenue enhancement. Whereas the former motive is based on the common activities within the firm, the latter is driven by customer perception of the value of bundling. In this sense acquisition of a complementor is a *related* acquisition.

Tanriverdi and Lee provide evidence that firms in the software industry can exploit increasing returns to scale due to the network effect by diversifying across operating system platforms and across software product markets. Implementing these two diversifying strategies together improves sales growth and market share. Implementing only one reduces either sales growth or both sales growth and market share[15]. This is consistent with firms that do not expand their installed base, fast becoming 'locked out' of competition in network industries[16].

Leveraging marketing resources and capabilities

Merging companies may be able to exploit each other's marketing resources and capabilities (R & C), including brand management, to augment the sales or revenue of each other's products. Distribution channels already established by each firm may be used to sell the other firm's products, thereby increasing the overall throughput of the products of both firms. Each firm's distribution capacity is thus more effectively used to enhance revenue. From the resource-based view, these economies may be exploited by redeploying the following marketing-related R & C:

● sales forces;
● brands; and
● general marketing expertise (GME).

Exhibit 5.2

Procter & Gamble waves the magic brand to grow Clairol's revenue

Procter & Gamble (P & G) sells a range of cosmetic and personal hygiene products, including shampoos, hair colour products, nappies and detergents. It has many leading brands and market leaders among these products, and considers managing brands and leveraging them to increase global sales as one of its core competences. In May 2001 P & G made a takeover bid worth $5bn for Clairol, which sold hair colouring dyes as well as shampoos. Clairol's market share in dyes had fallen from 44% in 1996 to just 36% in 2001. Its shampoo and colorant businesses had sales of $900m and $700m a year respectively.

P & G believed that its own brand management expertise applied to Clairol brands would lift the sales to $1bn plus within five years. The key to this growth was globalizing the brands, especially in developing countries, where ageing men, who did not consider grey hair a manifestation of their wisdom but only a painful reminder of their lost youth, would find Clairol's dyes the answer to their prayers. Clairol's global sales were small, but could be increased through P & G's global distribution network. Further, P & G's research and development capabilities could also be applied to Clairol's products to increase their attraction to potential customers. P & G would also exploit its new technology that allowed customers to see in the store what they would look like with a different hair colour. This would make customers' purchasing decision easier.

Thus P & G was hoping to apply its brand management expertise, R & D capabilities and distribution network to Clairol's under-exploited brands and achieve profitable revenue growth.

Source: Adapted from A. Edgecliffe-Johnson, 'P&G gets to the root of the problem', *Financial Times*, 22 May 2001

For example, in 2001, with its acquisition of Quaker Oats Co., PepsiCo gained ownership of a number of brands – Gatorade, Quaker Oatmeal, Cap'n Crunch, etc. LVMH acquired ownership of Donna Karan by buying Donna Karan International. The fight for Gucci between LVMH and Pinault Printemps Redoute lasted several years, because both companies were keen to have access to the famous Italian brand.

Redeployment may be a two-way process, and assumes that the merging firm with a surplus resource endowment or superior capability deploys it to increase the sales of the other firm's products. Exhibit 5.2 shows how Procter & Gamble's acquisition of Clairol was driven by the logic of leveraging the superior brand management capabilities of P & G to enhance Clairol's global sales. Redeployment of marketing R & C as a rationale for a merger needs to be carefully considered:

- Does it confer on the merged entity a sustainable competitive advantage?
- Can the firms' competitors replicate a similar strategy?
- What is the benefit-to-cost ratio of the strategy compared with other strategies, such as organic growth or other relationships between the merging firms?

Whether marketing R & C confer sustainable competitive advantage depends on their characteristics[17]. All the three marketing R & C are to varying degrees embedded within the host firms, and are path dependent. This invests them with varying degrees of rarity, inimitability, non-substitutability and immobility, i.e. non-tradeability of the above three R & C. In the context of horizontal acquisitions, Capron and Hulland rank the three marketing R & C on the above attributes[18]. While brands score highly in each of these attributes, sales forces are much less unique than brands, and GME is the least unique capability. Thus competitive advantage derived from the acquisition or sharing of brands is likely to be more sustained than that based on sales force pooling or transfer of general marketing expertise.

Sustaining the competitive advantage also rests on the availability of target firms for acquisition by competitors. Once again, target firms with competing brands may be more difficult to come by than targets with comparable sales forces or GME. As regards the benefit-to-cost ratio, incremental value can be created only when the revenue enhancement strategy leads to profits in excess of the associated costs on a long-term and sustainable basis. One of the important costs to consider is that of integrating the two firms' marketing R & C. As regards the brands, while it is plausible that the superior brand of one merging firm may lift the brand image of the other, there is also the risk that the latter will taint it. As already noted, the marketing R & C may be largely embedded within the teams, routines and cultures of the firms, and redeploying them may be a complex and challenging task, with a high risk of failure[19]. The value of the target firm's marketing R & C to the acquirers may also be subject to much error. Valuation models for brand valuation are as yet imprecise, and the embedded nature of the marketing R & C induces information asymmetry between the target and the acquirer, and consequently a large valuation error.

Online Internet and offline firms require different and non-overlapping resources and capabilities. A merger therefore allows them to leverage each other's resources and capabilities, thereby creating value. On the other hand, a merger of two online Internet firms allows the growth of their installed customer base and the network benefits. For a sample of 798 acquisitions of Internet firms during 1995 to 2001, Uhlenbruck, Hitt and Semadeni find that acquisition of offline firms by online firms generates a significant 0.9% abnormal returns ($9.7m for the acquirer) on the announcement day. For the subsample of online acquisitions by other online firms these returns are 1.1% ($8.7m). For the offline–offline mergers there was no significant value creation, suggesting that there was little scope for exploiting complementary resources and capabilities[20].

Cost savings as a source of value creation in acquisitions

One of the frequent arguments made by takeover bidders to justify the bid is the expected value creation that will flow from the cost savings resulting from the acquisition. Cost savings are derived from combining the acquirer and the acquired firms' activities in a number of functional areas, such as production, marketing, sales and distribution, R & D and head office operations, and generate efficiency savings as delineated in the value chain model discussed in Chapter 3. The same activities may be carried out at a lower cost than either firm would be able to achieve on its own. The unit cost of the output is thus reduced and, given unchanged unit price, the combined firm's profit is enhanced, thus creating value.

Reducing excess capacity

As discussed earlier in this chapter, excess capacity leads to price pressure and fierce rivalry, which squeezes profits. A horizontal merger can help the merging firms rationalize their production and take out the excess capacity. Such rationalization can reduce fixed production and other fixed costs. By reducing supply to match the demand it will also reduce the price pressure and improve profit margins. The surplus resources resulting from the rationalization will be laid off at a one-off cost in the form of, say, redundancy payoffs to the workforce. This kind of restructuring through merger is often episodic, with several firms in the same industry attempting the capacity reduction strategy fairly simultaneously or in quick succession. Thus we observe the industry-wide consolidation discussed in Chapter 2.

The steel industry worldwide has been suffering from excess capacity in many countries in Europe and Asia, and also in the US. It has undergone much consolidation through mergers in Europe, but less so in the US. The three-way merger resulting in the creation of Arcelor shows how European firms have responded to industry glut through mergers, and how consolidation generates cost savings and value (see Exhibit 5.3). The failure of the steel industry in the US to restructure meant that it continued to be a high-cost industry, and lost international competitiveness against imports. In March 2001 the US imposed tariffs to offset this loss, and the EU imposed retaliatory tariffs on US exports. Thus started the steel war.

Exhibit 5.3

Brittle steel: to consolidate or crumble?

In the last two decades or more, steel production has expanded around the world, leading to a global glut. Asian countries, such as Japan and South Korea, exported their relatively cheap steel into Europe and the US. Other countries, such as India and China, then joined the export bandwagon, thus putting pressure on steel producers in Europe and the US. In the US, integrated steel producers such as US Steel and Bethelehem Steel also faced competition from mini-mills using more efficient technologies and more flexible and lower-cost workforces.

In the 1980s and 1990s many European integrated steel makers consolidated through mergers or restructured by closing down or selling off their surplus production facilities. In 1999 two German steel producers, Thyssen and Krupp, merged in a consolidation move. In January 2002 steel makers Arbed of Luxembourg, Ulsinor of France and Aceralia of Spain merged to form the world's biggest steel maker against the backdrop of the lowest steel prices in 20 years. The merger was promoted to generate annual cost savings of $264m a year until 2003 and $616m a year by 2006.

Cost savings in the merger were to be achieved by concentrating steel production in fewer sites to achieve scale economies near coastal areas to reduce transportation costs of shipping in raw materials and transporting finished steel. Other sources of cost savings were:

- sharing efficient production know-how globally; and
- sharing quality control methods and standardizing steel products for all customers in a number of countries.

The European mergers in the steel industry are expected to be replicated by the large integrated steel producers in the US.

Sources: P. Marsh, 'Arcelor steels itself for fame', *Financial Times*, 3 January 2002; C. Bowe, 'Steelmakers seek help with consolidation', *Financial Times*, 6 December 2001

Scale economies

Consolidating horizontal mergers also provide opportunities for scale economies in the various functional activities listed in Table 5.1. Many of the activities carried out by the merging firms separately can now be combined and streamlined. A leaner workforce, a smaller sales team, a single head office rather than two, avoiding duplication in R & D, pooling of advertising expenditure to rejuvenate the old and acquired brands, etc., are sources of scale economies. In achieving these scale economies the following factors need consideration:

- associated costs;
- risks; and
- the extent of cost savings.

Associated costs include costs of plant or head office closures, such as redundancy costs and environmental clean-up costs. The indirect costs arise from the risk of losing the skills and capabilities that the departing workers or teams represent. There is the further risk that these workers and managers may carry their skills and capabilities to the merged firm's competitors. Since the achievement of scale economies requires a fairly extensive integration of the two firms, the risk of poor or ineffective post-merger integration is very relevant. As we shall see in Chapter 24, many mergers fail because of poor integration.

An important consideration in mergers driven by scale economies is the limit to such economies in the form of minimum efficient scale (MES). As the scale of production increases the cost of production falls initially steeply and then slowly before turning flat, as Figure 5.2 shows. Beyond the MES, further scale economies are unlikely. If the merging firms' plants are already operating at or beyond the MES, any production-based scale economy is difficult to achieve. Charles Hill points out that the MES in many industries is low, being of the order of 5% or less[21]. Thus production plant scale economies are very rapidly exhausted. This has two implications. First, competitive advantage gained through a production-based cost economy may not be significant[22]. Second, me-too mergers by rivals do not have to be large to catch up on the scale economy achieved by the first-mover merger.

Figure 5.2 **Plant-based minimum efficient scale (MES) of production**

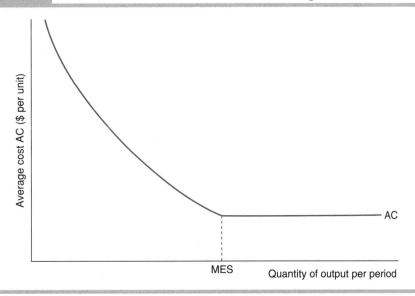

We have identified other sources of scale economies apart from the production function, e.g. marketing or R & D. These are firm-level, rather than plant-level, scale economies. While it is not known whether there is a MES associated with these non-production functions, or how small it is in relation to the revenue, it is likely that these scale economies are also subject to some level of MES. In that case, the incremental value due to these scale economies in mergers may be overstated.

Diseconomies of scale

While focusing on scale economies, firms should also be aware of diseconomies of scale, which arise from diffusion of control, complexities of monitoring, ineffectiveness of communication, and multiple layers of management. These diseconomies may be compounded by the process of scaling up through a merger, i.e. lumping two probably very dissimilar organizations. The post-merger integration problems discussed in Chapter 22 may exacerbate the sources of scale diseconomies.

Scaling up often involves codification of existing knowledge so that it can be applied and exploited on a larger scale. Such codification may, however, make the same knowledge easier to imitate, and thus allow its diffusion. Diffusion means loss of the esoteric nature of the firm's knowledge, its non-imitability, and hence a source of sustainable competitive advantage. This represents another downside of scale economies[23].

Scope economies

Economies of scope exist when the cost of joint production of two or more goods by a multi-product firm is less than the combined costs of separate production of those goods by firms specializing in those goods. Like scale economies, scope economies depend on firm size. Unlike scale economies, which are achieved when costs are spread over an *increased output of a single product*, scope economies are realized when costs are spread over an *increased range of output of different products*. Thus scope economies are available only for multi-product firms. Of course, both economies may be realized when the output of individual products as well as the total output of all the firm's products increases.

Which of the firm's costs can be spread over the different products of a multi-product firm depends on the commonality of the functions they share, the product characteristics, the markets in which they are sold, and the perceived customer benefits. The shared functions may include production, R & D, and marketing and distribution. Firms that have undertaken related diversification have a portfolio of products that share many of these functions. Indeed, the ability to spread the costs of these functions is often a justification for such acquisition.

Conditions for scope economies

Scope economies exist under the following conditions[24]:

● The products share the inputs or functions as illustrated above.
● The inputs, once acquired for producing one good, are costlessly available for use in producing other goods.
● There is surplus of inputs that cannot be traded out of the firm, i.e. the input or function is not perfectly divisible for such a trade.
● Inputs are reusable without reducing their value, e.g. know-how or technology.
● The transaction costs of organizing multi-product operations are less than the benefits.

Umbrella branding of several products using the corporate brand name or reputation, which otherwise have little in common, is an example of scope economy. Supermarkets, once built, need to fill their shelf space with as many goods as possible. For example, the forecourts of many supermarkets sell petrol to their customers. Supermarkets selling a wide range of products increase the scope economy but may lose the benefit of scale economies in buying, transportation, etc. Thus the store strategy involves a trade-off between scale economy and scope economy.

R & D activity often generates spillovers when ideas developed in one research project provide the stimulus for other projects. A firm with a wide range of R & D projects may offer greater scope for such creative cross-pollination than one with a narrow range. In the pharmaceutical industry such spillovers seem to increase the productivity of the firms' R & D. Rebecca Henderson and Iain Cockburn report that for an average firm with 19 research programmes, the addition of two research programmes raised the productivity of existing programmes by 4.5%. Thus the 'bang for buck' ratio is increased by scope economy in R & D[25]. In the merger of Glaxo Wellcome and SmithKline Beecham in 2000 to form GlaxoSmithKline (GSK), one of the drivers was the scope economy in drug research across several drug categories, and in the development and marketing of the drugs once discovered (see Exhibit 5.4).

Exhibit 5.4

GSK adopts a holistic scope to treating body parts

The merger of GlaxoWellcome (GW) and SmithKlineBeecham (SB) in 2000 brought together two companies that, in the tradition of many leading pharmaceutical firms, had specialized in developing drugs for a limited range of diseases affecting different parts of the body. It provided an opportunity to achieve scope economies by leveraging each other's R & D and marketing capabilities. In particular, SB's strength in genomics-based research was combined with GW's strength in the development and marketing of drugs. GSK expected to discover new blockbuster drugs, i.e. with sales of $1bn or more, to replace the drugs that had recently come off their patents and hence lost their monopoly of the prescription drugs market.

Following the merger, GSK reorganized its R & D activities to create a structure that would give autonomous space for the entrepreneurial drug discovery phase but take advantage of the scope economies in early-stage exploratory science, development, drug trials, regulatory clearance and marketing. The early stage, Genetics and Drug Discovery Research, works on understanding basic biology and on producing platform technology or drug discovery leads that feed into the six 'internal biotechs' designed to replicate the conditions of small entrepreneurial biotechnology companies. Clinical trials are undertaken on a massive scale, often across continents, and must comply with strict regulatory conditions. Thus corporate control, uniformity and scale economies are pre-eminent. The 'biotechs' benefit from scope economies at both the preceding and following stages, where huge resources are spent on developing a portfolio of drugs.

Source: Adapted from D. Pilling, 'Shake-up may be just what the doctors ordered', *Financial Times*, 23 February 2001

Diseconomies of scope

The extent for scope economy may often be very elusive. To get the same medical salespeople to sell drugs to physicians and hospitals (called 'detailing') aimed at different ailments may often be a prescription for even greater ailment for the firm. This may be the case if the drugs are highly specialized and require a considerable expert knowledge of them on the part of the sales force. Ability to sell also depends on the relationship with, and trust of, the physicians who prescribe[26]. Similarly, the same sales force or advertising strategy may not be appropriate in the premium segment and the price-sensitive mass segment of a market. This illustrates the problem of '*conflicting out*' when the mutually incompatible markets are approached with the same resource.

Capron and Hulland found, in their study of redeployment of marketing resources in European and US horizontal acquisitions already cited, that the effect of sales force redeployment on post-acquisition performance was disappointing. While transfers from the acquirer to the targets had no noticeable effect on either market share or profitability, transfers from the targets to the acquirers had a strong negative effect on both. 'A merger predicated primarily on the desire to acquire another firm's sales force resources is unlikely to succeed in the long run'[27].

Umbrella branding may be counterproductive if a product sold until recently under a low-valued brand is then marketed under a premium brand. When Volkswagen, the German car maker, acquired Skoda of the former Czechoslovakia, it retained the Skoda name and improved its image. Capron and Hulland again found that acquirers' use of the acquired brands has a negative effect on both their geographical coverage and market share without any effect on profitability. On the other hand, use of acquirer's brands by the acquired firms has a beneficial impact on post-acquisition product quality and geographical coverage.

Research on the extent of scope economies is scarce, in contrast to the literature on scale economies. One possible reason is that until recently product costing did not allocate costs to the various products correctly on the basis of the associated activities. Activity-based costing (ABC) alleviates this problem, but one still faces the problem of how to compare these product costs in the merged firm with the costs on the same products produced separately by different companies. Making this comparison while controlling for other contributors to costs, e.g. technology, economy of scale, is a formidable problem[28].

From a review of a number of empirical studies of commercial bank mergers in 13 countries in Europe and North America, Amel and his colleagues conclude that

> commercial bank M & As do not significantly improve cost and profit efficiency and, on average, do not generate significant shareholder value. There is evidence in favor of exploiting scale economies, but only up to a size well below that of the most recent large deals. Economies of scope are harder to pin down; there is no clear evidence of their existence.

Among the reasons they consider for these results are diseconomies of scale and scope, or that the deals have been subject to greater regulation, e.g. restrictions on the range of financial activities under the Glass-Steagal Act or on interstate banking in the US or due to poor choice of benchmarks, e.g. non-merging banks that might have nevertheless been indirectly affected by the mergers. Other reasons for the lack of significant benefits may be agency problems manifested in managerial behaviour (see Chapter 12 on the impact of managers' psychological biases on acquisition decisions and performance)[29].

Related diversification and, to a lesser extent, unrelated or conglomerate diversification into multi-product portfolios are rationalized on the basis of scope economies. Thus an indirect test of the existence of scope economies is a comparison of the profitability of related and unrelated diversified firms with that of single product firms that separately produce the same range of products. Our preliminary review of the performance of related diversifiers with that of single-product firms or unrelated diversifiers suggests that related diversifiers generally outperform unrelated diversifiers (see Chapter 4). This means that scope economies do exist, but they are limited to certain types of shared resources and not others (see also Chapter 7 on conglomerate acquisitions).

Beyond a certain level of related diversification, scope economies may give rise to scope diseconomies. In particular, the problem of coordinating the operations associated with a multi-product portfolio may be too serious. The trend towards focus as a strategic policy observed in the 1980s and 1990s (see Chapter 2) suggests that in many cases scope economies either did not exist or were exhausted easily. Thus there is a limit to scope economies, although the critical number of products in a multi-product firm that triggers diseconomies is not clear.

Further, scope economies may be easier to realize in certain functions than in others. Many drug companies have found that scope economies in large-scale R & D for drug discovery are too elusive, whereas they are easier to achieve in drug development and marketing, as exemplified in Exhibit 5.5. Thus the case for scope economies in mergers needs a close and sceptical approach[30].

Exhibit 5.5

Drug firms discover a cure sooner than scope!

Although many recent mergers in the pharmaceutical industry have been driven by putative scope economies in R & D, the results have not been very encouraging of this model. Despite pooling huge R & D investments, merging companies' R & D productivity in terms of success developing new drug, especially blockbusters, has not lived up to expectations generated at the time of those mergers. According to Dr Ed Scolnick, chief scientist of the US firm Merck, the largest pharmaceutical company in the world in 2000, scale of R & D does not translate into research efficiency. The size of an R & D site has nothing to do with its productivity. Organizing the increased R & D effort from the mergers and making it more efficient is 'not a trivial exercise'. He also felt that the drug discovery process, i.e. turning the drug leads in the form of chemicals into drugs, is what limits the rate of drug discovery. Dr Scolnick considered that 'mergers, by creating upheaval and management complications have dulled, rather than sharpened, the competitive edge of rival drug companies'.

Source: Adapted from D. Pilling, 'Where science and Mammon collide', *Financial Times*, 21 March 2000

Learning economy

Economy of learning arises when managers and workers become more experienced and effective over time in using the available resources of the firm, and help lower the cost of production. It is a function of the *cumulative output over several periods*. Increasing cumulative output increases the opportunity for the managers and workers to learn more efficient ways of producing each unit of the output. Workers learn not only from their own experience but

Figure 5.3 Learning curve and minimum efficient learning scale (MELS)

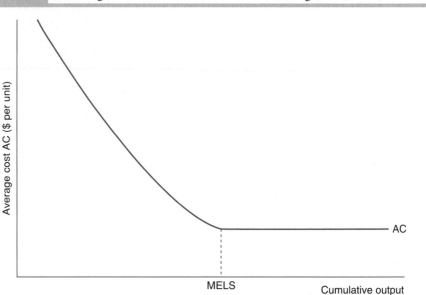

also from that of their fellow workers. There is, however, a limit to learning and its impact on cost reduction. The learning or experience curve shown in Figure 5.3 shows that there is a *minimum efficient learning scale (MELS)*. At this level, maximum learning has been achieved. Below this level of cumulative output there is scope for further learning and cost reduction.

Beneficial learning may be due to workers gaining understanding and confidence as they produce more. They may then speed up the production process and avoid wasteful use of inputs. Similar learning effects may be realized in product design, quality control, equipment maintenance, production scheduling, etc. Learning economies may also be available in other functions, such as R & D, marketing and distribution. Learning economy is in general due to the more efficient organization and coordination of the firm's activities over time. Learning economy is distinct from scale economy, which arises on size of the output in a single period. Scale economy arises from the indivisibility of fixed costs, whereas learning economy arises from experience and better organization of activities.

Learning economy is important in several industries. A study of seven generations of dynamic random access memory (DRAM) semiconductors from 1974 to 1992 found that the learning rates averaged about 20%. A 10% increase in cumulative production would then lead to a 2% decrease in cost. In the aircraft industry the learning rates may be as high as 40%. For example, the labor requirements for producing aircraft in Airbus Industrie fell sharply with cumulative output. At the initial output of, say, 20 aircraft the production hours per aircraft were well over 60, but at 200 aircraft they dropped to just 20 hours. However, the maximum learning was reached at this cumulative output level[31]. Learning curve efficiency requires that the firm have a large sales volume and therefore a relatively large market share. It is therefore a by-product of an increase in market share. The cost of acquisition of the increased market share therefore needs to be balanced against the subsequent cost savings from increased learning efficiency[32].

Learning economy and mergers

Horizontal mergers result in a sudden increase in the volume of output when the output of each merging firm is pooled. While each firm can learn from the experience of the other firm, this learning does not need the cumulative output of the merged entity to increase further. In the period following the merger this output may increase, thus creating opportunity for further learning. However, if the output of the merged entity is already large, it is likely to have passed the MELS of cumulative output.

The accumulated experience of the merging firms represents a part of their stock of R & C at the time of the merger. Sharing of that experience may lead to efficient reorganization of the merged entity's activities. To the extent that the experience is already embedded in organizational routines, teams and culture, sharing becomes a more complex process than when it is explicitly codified (see Chapter 22 on post-merger integration).

Charles Hill considers the joint impact of the age of the production process and its complexity[33]. In the case of established and low-complexity processes, learning economies may not be significant. With new and highly complex processes the learning effects can be quite substantial. Mergers of mature firms with standardized technologies serving mature markets are unlikely to be characterized by significant learning benefits. Related mergers offer a much greater scope. In particular, mergers involving complex technological processes such as drug discovery may yield potentially valuable learning opportunities, but they are also problematic because of the coordination and management problems referred to in Exhibit 5.5.

Overall, cost savings can improve profit margins substantially. David Ravenscraft and William Long, from a study of the value sources in horizontal pharmaceutical industry mergers, estimate the cost savings as shown in Figure 5.4. In their study several mergers result in substantial post-merger shareholder value gains while many others destroy value.

Figure 5.4 Cost savings in horizontal mergers

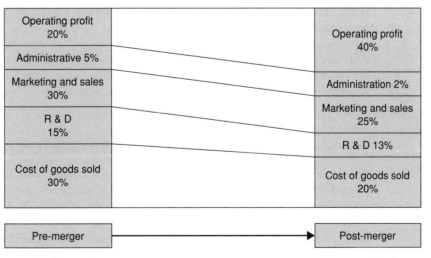

*Note: This figure shows the various costs and operating profit as percentage of sales revenue, representing the typical value chain of US and European pharmaceutical firms.
Source: D. J. Ravenscroft and W. F. Long, 'Paths to creating value in pharmaceutical mergers', in S. N. Kaplan (Ed.), *Mergers and Productivity* (Chicago: University of Chicago Press, 2000). pp. 287–326

New growth opportunities as a source of value

New growth opportunities arise from the creation of new technologies, products and markets. These are not just extensions or incremental modifications of existing technologies, products and markets. They are *discontinuous* changes that often emerge in serendipitous ways rather than as the outcome of a premeditated search process. Examples are televisions, video recorders, automobiles, the mapping of the human genes in the genome project, personal computers, the Internet, mobile telephones, and satellite or cable television.

Hamel and Prahalad describe two ways firms can compete[34]:

● race for the world; and
● race for the future.

Racing for the world is the search for competitive advantage in today's markets as they exist, including the global markets. The broad generic strategies such as cost leadership, product differentiation or focus in combination with either way are generally pursued by firms in the race for the world. The world of this race is relatively static. Racing for the future is to be the first mover to create a brave new world. It is to change the world as it is. It is about opportunity share, rather than market share. The strategy for the opportunity share represents a 'strategic stretch' from the present. Racing for the world requires knowledge, but racing for the future requires imagination. The former is about 'finding' whereas the latter is about 'inventing'[35].

Cost saving and revenue enhancement are strategies that exploit relatively familiar sources of efficiencies or growth. They are also focused on the short to medium term. Search for discontinuous new growth opportunities of the kind we have described is exploratory. It is a venture into the unfamiliar and a journey to the unknown. It is a gamble, and the investment made in the exploration activity is like buying an option similar to buying the licence to explore for underwater minerals. Neither the exploratory process nor the outcome of that process is known at the time the option is taken.

The exploratory investment is made in the absence of complete information about what investment opportunities will become available, although one may be able to attach some probabilities to alternative potential opportunities. Without the initial option-like investment, however, the firm will be unable to take advantage of potential opportunities when they materialize or make the follow-on investment. These exploratory investments are the real options described in Chapter 3. These can be modelled using tools borrowed from the valuation of financial assets, e.g. the Black–Scholes model for valuing currency or stock options discussed in Chapter 14.

Intellectual capital, acquisitions and new growth opportunities

The innovative capabilities of firms are affected by the nature of their intellectual capital (IC), distinct from their physical or financial capital. Subramaniam and Youndt divide IC into human, social and organizational capital. Organizational capital facilitates incremental and exploitative innovation, but human capital is capable of radical, out-of-the-box and often disruptive innovation. Interaction of these types of IC, e.g. the social and human, may also influence the type of innovation[36]. Organizations designed to increase space for individual creativity can facilitate exploratory innovation. In the context of acquisitions the interaction assumes great importance. Even if the target has the necessary human or social capital conducive to exploratory innovation, the organizational capital of the acquirer or the target or the merged entity may stifle the creativity necessary for exploration.

This means that acquirers must understand not only their own IC profile but also that of the target, and how they intend to interact the two in the post-acquisition organization. In addition to creating the right ambience for a fruitful interaction, the post-acquisition integration process also needs to provide for the right incentives for individual or teams of innovators to deploy their capabilities to increase the innovative efficiency of the merged entity[37]. We return to these issues in Chapter 22 on post-acquisition integration.

Horizontal mergers as exploratory investments

To what extent are mergers driven by cost saving and revenue enhancement or are in the nature of exploratory option-type investments? To the extent that most mergers are undertaken in the absence of complete information about the opportunities for value creation, there is an element of exploration. This certainly introduces uncertainty and risk in the estimation of the value of the merger. Nevertheless, cost saving and revenue enhancement opportunities are assessed on the basis, broadly, of existing technology, products, markets, resources and capabilities. They are not premised on new technologies, capabilities or resources of a major and discontinuous kind.

Certain types of merger, however, contain elements of exploration. For example, acquisition of biotechnology companies by established 'big pharma' firms or the taking of minority stakes in them is driven by the desire to explore the potentialities of the new science of genomics in the drug discovery process. This involves decoding of genes to understand the genetic characteristics associated with different diseases, in the expectation that such understanding will lead to therapeutic breakthroughs and new drugs or treatments. However, these investments are yet to bear fruit, and biotechnology firms are yet to deliver on their promises. In November 2000 Jon Leschley, the recently retired CEO of SmithKlineBeecham (SB), said that over the past 15 years over 1900 products developed by biotech companies had failed in clinical trials, while only 137 made it to the market[38]. Such a poor success rate came despite the billions of dollars spent by these companies on research. Such 'hit and miss' outcomes are, however, quite characteristic of exploratory investments, although the odds of success could be improved by better management of the drug discovery process. As Exhibits 5.4 and 5.5 show, mergers may actually get in the way of such management.

Resource-based view (RBV) of acquisitions and value creation

In the dynamic capabilities model of M & A, which we discussed in Chapter 3, acquisitions are driven by the sharing and transfer of complementary resources and capabilities between the acquirer and acquired firms. The resources exchanged, and the extent of that exchange, depend on particular sources of value driving an acquisition and on the characteristics of the R & C. In the RBV, mergers happen when:

- the merging firms need to reconfigure their R & C to achieve or maintain their competitive advantage;
- there is asymmetry in R & C between the two firms, and the firms consider merger a means of overcoming that asymmetry; and
- the deficit in R & C cannot be bridged through organic growth or market purchases.

Capacity for organic growth may be limited for a number of reasons. Firms may find it difficult to break out of the inherited routines, thereby constraining their ability to develop new capabilities, especially those far off the beaten track of inherited capabilities. Firms' core competences may have degenerated into 'core rigidities' that imprison them[39]. These old dogs cannot learn new tricks. Rapid competitive changes may give firms little time to develop their own R & C mandated by their new competitive paradigm. If they attempt to develop resources internally and too rapidly they may fall victim to 'time compression diseconomy'. Thus crash R & D programmes or advertising blitzes may be less effective than similar efforts performed over a longer period as part of the firm's evolution[40]. Markets for certain types of R & C may not exist where they are of an intangible nature, such as organizational culture. Even for recognizably distinct resources such as brands, the secondary markets do not exist, thereby making it difficult to value them.

A necessary condition of R & C transfers in acquisitions is that they result in value creation. The cost of these R & C acquisitions should be below the consequential benefits, and should generate a return that at least equals the cost of capital to the acquiring firm. We now review some of the recent empirical studies of R & C transfers in acquisitions, and their impact on firm performance.

Pattern of resource redeployment in horizontal acquisitions

In a carefully argued and rigorously constructed empirical study of resource redeployment, Capron *et al.* investigated 253 US and European horizontal mergers during 1988–92 based on survey data[41]. They classified the R & C redeployed into the following categories:

- R & D resources, i.e. technological capability, R & D capability and product development speed;
- manufacturing resources, i.e. production cost structure;
- marketing resources, i.e. brand management, distribution channels, buyer–seller relationships, user base, customer service and business reputation;
- managerial resources, i.e. management skills; and
- financial resources.

They investigated the extent of resource transfer from the acquirer to the target, and vice versa. They also tested for the impact of relative R & C strength of the two firms in each of the resource categories, and the influence of other factors such as market share, motives for the horizontal merger, the financial and other characteristics of the acquirer and the target. Table 5.2 reports a summary of their results on the extent of resource redeployment.

Table 5.2 Redeployment of various resources and capabilities in US, Canadian and European horizontal mergers

Resource	From target to acquirer		From acquirer to target	
	To some extent or greater (% of sample firms)	Mean level of redeployment (on a scale of 1 = none to 5 = large)	To some extent or greater (% of sample firms)	Mean level of redeployment (on a scale of 1 = none to 5 = large)
R & D	54	2.5	72	3.2
Manufacturing	48	2.5	80	3.4
Marketing	66	3.1	77	3.6
Financial	14	1.5	88	4.0
Managerial	19	1.7	90	4.1
Senior executives	22	1.8	53	2.7

Percentage of sample firms that reported no or little redeployment is 100 less than the number in columns 2 and 4.

The results show that:

- resource redeployment after acquisitions is quite substantial, and encompasses a range of capabilities;
- resource transfers from acquirers to targets are more pervasive than transfers from targets to acquirers (columns 2 and 4);
- in every category the acquirers redeploy more resources to targets than the other way round (columns 3 and 5); and
- transfers of specialized resources, i.e. R & D, manufacturing and marketing, are more similar in magnitude between acquirers and targets than transfers of generalized resources, i.e. managerial and financial.

Among the managerial resources, redeployment of senior executives is less intense and frequent than redeployment of all managers. This pattern suggests several possible reasons. Middle-level managerial capabilities are co-specialized and therefore necessarily bundled with the specialized resources being transferred. Prahalad emphasizes that involvement of the middle managers is a critical element in the strategy process[42]. Senior executive capabilities are perhaps more mobile and more easily obtained from the managerial labour market. The acquirers have no surplus senior management capability.

Similar resource redeployment patterns were also evident in the sample of horizontal acquisitions that might also be motivated by market power, excess capacity reduction and scale efficiency considerations. Capron and his colleagues conclude that while these traditional market power and scale efficiency arguments apply to many horizontal acquisitions, resource redeployment is common in practice and underemphasized in theory. They also conclude that acquisitions characterized by resource redeployment are part of the evolutionary process that allows firms to develop their distinctive and idiosyncratic resources. Other firms pursuing me-too acquisition strategies may not be able duplicate the same resource configurations as the first mover.

Resource transfers in acquisitions and new growth opportunities

How do resource transfers within horizontal mergers create real options and new growth opportunities? The answer depends on the type, nature and range of resources and capabilities redeployed between the acquirer and the acquired firms. Karim and Mitchell classified resource redeployment as serving[43]:

- path-dependent change; or
- path-breaking change.

Path-dependent change occurs when acquirers build on current capabilities instead of exploring new areas. They retain the acquired firm's resources and capabilities that are similar to their own, which have been derived from historic and path-dependent accumulation of learning, investments and other organizational activities. The greater the overlap of acquirer and target resources, the more likely it is that acquirers will retain targets' resources and their own resources.

Path-breaking change occurs when the acquirers and targets have different resource configurations and the differences can be exploited to create uniquely valuable synergy and new sources of competitive advantage. Acquirers may pursue path-breaking change and retain resources that are distinct from their own. These resources may help an organization to develop its core competences and dynamic capabilities further. Thus path-breaking acquisitions are much more exploratory than path-dependent acquisitions.

Karim and Mitchell examined the extent of change in the resource configuration of acquisitive firms in the US medical sector during 1978–95 and benchmarked it against non-acquisitive firms on the basis of product line addition, retention and deletion as forms of changing resources. The authors also compared resource-deepening (path-dependent) acquisitions with resource-extension (path-breaking) acquisitions. The sample included 3000 firms, offering more than 200 product lines. The results show that:

- acquisition activity is a key mechanism by which firms change their mix of business resources;
- acquirers are more likely than non-acquirers to possess resources that have only recently entered the industry;
- acquirers use acquisitions either for close reinforcement of existing skills or for substantial jumps into new skill sets, and much less for incremental move away from existing skills; and
- acquisitions often provide means for undertaking path-breaking changes, by stretching beyond existing absorptive capacity and seeking targets with markedly different resources.

Brand-driven acquisitions

There is evidence that firms with strong brands add shareholder value at lower risk than firms with weaker or no brands[44]. Brands have therefore become an important driver of acquisitions. Table 5.3 provides some recent examples of brands acquired in 2004–6. But do brand-driven acquisitions create shareholder value? We have already cited evidence from Capron and Hulland's study of redeployment of marketing resources in US and European horizontal mergers that sales force and brand redeployment does not always deliver profit improvement, and in many cases may actually destroy profitability. Consistent with this evidence, Knudsen *et al.* contend that only one in five attempts at brand consolidation succeeds[45].

There are numerous examples of brand corrosion following acquisitions in the automobile industry when mass-market firms acquire luxury brands or vice versa. These include the acquisition of Saab by General Motors, Jaguar by Ford and Chrysler by Mercedes-Benz. Štrach and Everett argue that the blending of luxury and mass-market automobile brands in one corporate portfolio, while rationalized on the basis of scale and scope economies, induces

Table 5.3 Brands changing hands through acquisitions

Acquirer	Target	Brands	Product category
Abbot Labs	Kos Pharmaceuticals	Niaspan, Advicor	Cholesterol drugs
Anheuser-Busch	Rolling Rock brand of InBev USA	Rolling Rock, Rock Green Light	Beer
Apollo Management	Jacuzzi Brands	Jacuzzi	Whirlpool baths, plumbing products
Blackstone Group	La Quinta	La Quinta	Hotels
H J Heinz	HP Foods and Lea Perrins of Groupe Danone	HP, Lea & Perrin and Rajah	Worcestershire sauce; sauces and spices
Coty	Prestige fragrance business of Unilever	Calvin Klein; Vera Wang; Chloe	Perfume
Ares Management	Maidenform division of Oaktree Capital	Maidenform	Lingerie

Source: *Mergers & Acquisitions*, February 2005, 2006 and 2007.

Exhibit 5.6

Morgan Stanley discovers it doesn't need Dean Witter

In 1997 Morgan Stanley (MS), the investment bank with a strong franchise in investment banking, acquired Dean Witter (DW) with a strong position in stock-broking and credit card services under the brand name of *Discover*. To capitalise on this brand strength, MS first transitioned the name of the merged entity to *MS Dean Witter Discover and Co*. This move was protested by MS's investment bankers, who were worried about any adverse impact on its reputation. Ten months later the *Discover* name was dropped from the corporate name, followed in April 2002 by the deletion of the *Dean Witter* name. MS was by then confident of participating in the new markets such as credit cards under the original brand. In the UK MS was able to build a successful credit card business issuing 1 million cards and building up receivables of $2bn.

Source: S. Kumar and K. H. Blomqvist, *ibid*.

potentially fatal brand corrosion. Mass-market producers build luxury cars using cheaper components to achieve scale economies, and this may deter consumers of the up-market brands. Thus in customer perception the high-quality brands may suffer from contamination by association[46].

Brand-driven acquisitions therefore need careful management, ranging from a strategy for managing acquirer and acquired brands after acquisition to brand due diligence and understanding the conditions that facilitate creation of a post-acquisition portfolio of brands that can yield sustainable competitive advantage. Post-acquisition brand management needs to consider both short-term (transitional) options and long-term (final) options (see Exhibit 5.6 on transitional management).

The value of the acquired brands depends on the way the acquirer leverages the acquired assets. Bahadir, Bharadwaj and Srivastava find that several acquirer and target firm characteristics enhance this value as disclosed in the acquirers' post-acquisition financial statements[47]. Among these are:

- acquirer and target marketing capabilities; and
- diversity of their brand portfolios prior to acquisition.

Brand diversity may also mean some overlap among brands: for example, they serve the same markets, and these brands can potentially cannibalize one another's sales and market share. Of course, such overlap is the basis of a synergistic acquisition. The authors find that synergistic acquisitions result in lower value attached to acquired brands.

Conditions for effective redeployment of other R & C

For effective redeployment of other R & C, however, several conditions need to be fulfilled. They must be fungible, and both firms must be capable of 'unlearning' their past and learn new skills, capabilities and routines. Such redeployment, especially of the path-breaking kind, also involves organizational change, and such change may not always be easily accomplished. Both firms must identify those R & C that can truly transform the merging firms and endow them with sustainable competitive advantage. It is often the case that firms themselves do not

Exhibit 5.7

Where is my company value? In your customer relations, stupid!

A consultant was hired by a UK-based linen supply company that was increasing its market share despite being in an industry driven by costs, and the firm was actually at a cost disadvantage. The consultant advised the firm to trim its costs, and the company decided to outsource its van delivery service. Then one day, by chance, the consultant joined a van delivery driver on his round to see how the company operated at its sharp end, i.e. in dealing with customers. Accompanying the driver was for the consultant indeed a journey on the road to Damascus. The driver had developed trusted relationships with his customers with his sincerity and friendliness. He knew his customers well, and had good knowledge of their businesses and even their personal lives. The consultant discovered that other drivers had developed similarly close customer relationships.

The consultant then met the company's directors and asked them to evaluate their core competences on the criteria of valuable, rare, inimitable and organized (VRIO). The relationship with customers developed through the drivers was the only item that figured on all criteria. The company's only source of competitive advantage was the very competence that the firm had planned to outsource! And it was discovered only by chance!

Source: M. J. Rouse and U. S. Dallenbach relate this anecdotal story in 'Rethinking research methods for the resource-based perspective: Isolating sources of sustainable competitive advantage', *Strategic Management Journal*, **20**, 1999, 487–494

know what makes them tick, let alone whether what makes them tick will also make another firm tick[48]. Exhibit 5.7 provides a cautionary tale.

Causal ambiguity

The link between a resource or capability and competitive advantage cannot always be established unambiguously. The latter is often the result of an array of resources leveraged in a multitude of ways using the firm's capabilities. There are two types of causal ambiguity:

- many-to-one; and
- one-to-many.

The first means that a single outcome, e.g. competitive advantage, is due to several contributing factors, each of which on its own cannot determine the outcome, and the contribution of each is conditional upon the contributions of other factors. Moreover, the relative contribution of each factor cannot be precisely measured. The second type means that a single factor can determine several outcomes, each of which cannot be determined *a priori*. The relative probabilities of these outcomes conditional on the incidence of that factor may not be precisely estimated. These ambiguities again make choice of a strategic action to achieve a certain strategic outcome a matter of chance. Causal ambiguity is a two-edged sword. While posing problems for the owner of given R & C in exploiting them effectively to create competitive advantage, causal ambiguity may also be an effective isolating mechanism that makes imitation of those R & C a fruitless exercise[49].

Applying the VRIO test

Firms may often hype just about everything as a potentially value-creating competence. They may be chasing a mirage[50]. This form of self-delusion may be compounded by the inability to assess:

- whether such competences actually exist and are transferable in a merger;
- whether the transfer will create a set of resources and capabilities that satisfy criteria such as the VRIO[51];
- whether the resulting resource configuration will confer sustainable competitive advantage; and finally
- whether the sustainable competitive advantage will create value after taking into account the investments that need to be made to realize it, and the risk-adjusted cost of capital.

Where these caveats are ignored or glossed over in the desperate search for synergy, acquirers may land in an expensive synergy trap that destroys rather than creates firm value[52].

Evidence of lack of sustainable competitive advantage

When a firm in an industry is acquired, other firms may also be targeted. This may happen when the value creation rationale of the first acquisition is replicable by the me-too acquirer. The potential replication will be reflected in the rising acquisition probability of other potential target firms in the industry, and this in turn raises their market value. Song and Walkling report that for US firms during 1982–91, initial acquisition in an industry leads to significant positive revaluation of potential targets in the same industry, and this revaluation is influenced by the revision in their acquisition probability[53]. The value gains are even higher when the potential targets subsequently become actual targets. This evidence is consistent with the value creation sources not being unique to the first merger. The evidence of industry clusters in mergers over a long period of time, discussed in Chapter 2, is also consistent with there being no unique sources of value in horizontal mergers, and with such mergers not conferring sustainable competitive advantage.

Mark Walker's empirical analysis of the wealth gains to shareholders from mergers driven by different strategic objectives provides further confirmation of the difficulty of gaining valuable competitive advantage[54]. In the case of a sample of 278 US acquisitions between 1980 and 1996, he finds that acquisitions motivated by geographical expansion, broadening of product line and market share increase are unable to outperform non-acquisitive firms in the same industry in terms of shareholder value gains. He concludes that it is difficult for acquiring firms to gain a competitive advantage over rival firms.

Many of the performance testing studies reviewed in Chapter 4 also examine the impact of horizontal, related and other types of merger. We summarize, in Table 5.4, the abnormal returns to the acquirers and, where reported, those to both acquirers and targets around bid announcements and over the post-acquisition period. The post-acquisition operating performance improvements are also reported. These results are in line with those of Walker discussed in the previous paragraph and Mueller discussed above (see footnote 4). The negative return reported by Macquiera seems to reflect the negative returns associated with stock for stock mergers (see Chapter 17 for a discussion). There is little evidence that horizontal and related mergers lead to revenue enhancement and efficiency savings in the long run. There is very little value gain to acquirer shareholders. There is little evidence of horizontal mergers leading to market power increases and high profit margins.

Table 5.4 Shareholder gains and operating performance of horizontal and related acquirers

Study[a]	Country, sample period, sample size	Event window	CAR[b] (%)	Post-acq. return[b] (%)
Panel A: Announcement period CARs and post-acquisition abnormal returns to bidders				
Leath and Borg (2000)	US; 1919–30; 417	Bid period	1	
Hubbard and Palia (1999)	US; 1961–70; 392	11 days	2	
Morck *et al.* (1988)	US; 1975–87	4 days	2 to 3	
Macquiera *et al.* (1998)	US; 1977–96; 47 stock offers	81 days	−5*	
Doukas *et al.* (2002)	Sweden; 1980–95; 46		3*	
Martynova and Renneboog (2006)	Europe; 1993–2001; 1334	11 days	1*	
Bae *et al.* (2002)	Korea; 1981–97; 66	11 days	4*	
Eckbo *et al.* (1986)	Canada; 1964–83; 215	12 months		1

Study	Country, sample period, sample size	Years	Benchmark[c]	Result
Panel B: Post-acquisition operating performance				
Linn and Switzer (2001)	US; 1967–87	5	Industry	Decline
Ghosh (2001)	US; 1981–95	3	Industry, size and BM	Sales and cash flow ROA decline
Meeks (1977)	UK; 1964–72; 73	3/5	ROA	Significant decline over both periods
Cosh *et al.* (1980)	UK; 1967–69; 109	3/5	ROE	Decline over both periods
Martynova and Renneboog (2007)	Europe; 1997–2001; 34	3	OCF/BV	No significant improvement

[a]Publication details of the cited references except for Leath and Borg are in Chapter 4. J. Leeth and J. Borg, 'The impact of takeovers on shareholder wealth during the 1920s merger wave', *Journal of Financial and Quantitative Analysis*, **35**(2), 2000, 217–238; B. E. Eckbo, 'Mergers and the Market for Corporate Control: The Canadian Evidence', *The Canadian Journal of Economics; Revue Canadienne D'Economique*; Malden, 1986, 236–260; R. Mørck, A. Shleifer and R. W. Vishny, 'Characteristics of targets of hostile and friendly takeovers' in Auerbach, Alan J. (Ed.) *Corporate takeovers: causes and consequences*, National Bureau of Economic Research, Chicago, IL, 1988, 101–136; C. Macquiera, W. Megginson and L. Nail, 'Wealth creation versus wealth redistribution in pure-stock-for-stock mergers', *Journal of Financial Economics*, **48**, 1998, 3–33; R. G. Hubbard and D. Palia, 'A re-examination of the conglomerate merger wave in the 1960s: An internal capital markets view', *Journal of Finance*, **54**, 1999, 1131–1152; K. Bae, J. Kang and J. Kim, 'Tunneling or value added? Evidence from mergers by Korean business groups', *Journal of Finance*, **57**(6), 2002, 2695–2740; M. Doukas, M. Holmen and N. Travlos, 'Diversification, Ownership and Control of Swedish Corporations', *European Financial Management*, **8**(3), 2002, 281–313.
[b]Returns rounded to nearest integer and based on a variety of benchmarks.
[c]BM = book to market value of assets; ROA = operating profit to net assets; ROE = net income to net assets; OCF = operating cash flow excluding working capital changes; BV = book value of assets.
*Significant at 5% or lower level. Significance of other returns not reported or they are insignificant.

CASE
STUDY

Heavy truckers trundle their way to market dominance

The heavy truck (HT) makers form part of the automobile sector along with the medium heavy vehicles and light commercial vehicles. They are, in general, part of automotive manufacturers that produce a spectrum of vehicles from small passenger cars to luxury passenger cars and from light commercial vehicles (LCVs) to vans and heavy trucks. Over the years some manufacturers have tended to focus on LCVs or medium duty trucks or heavy trucks to capitalise on scale economies, reduce production costs by using fewer platforms and reduce development costs. Increasingly stringent emission control regulations have raised the cost of compliances and forced truck makers, like car makers, to focus on developing fuel efficient engines. The research and development costs of such engines are therefore an important cost element for the truck manufacturers. Many of these costs are subject to scale and scope economies, for example fuel efficient engine technology can be applied across both car and truck manufacturing.

Thus the economics of mergers in the truck industry has been driven by these potential scale and scope efficiencies in costs of development, production, operations, marketing and regulatory compliance. The truck industry is also highly cyclical since its fortunes are driven by the demands of an industry which in turn follows the economic cycle. Given the capital intensive nature of HT manufacturing, high market share and high volume growth are important determinants of profitability in the industry.

Truck making has become a more concentrated industry over the years. In North America and Europe, where the number of major players has dropped to about seven, from about 40 in the 1960s. 'Where the consolidation will occur in the next 15 to 20 years will be in Asia, where there are about 40 manufacturers,' said Mr Mark Pigott, CEO of European truck maker DAF. In 2005, the global heavy truck manufacturers in terms of '000s of units sold were:

DaimlerChrysler (DC) (German-US)	245
Volvo (European)	150
Paccar (European)	125
Dongfeng (Chinese)	72
Navistar (US)	60
FAW	55
MAN (German)	50
Scania (Swedish)	50
Telco (India)	50
China National HT	40

Source: Data from Ibison, Nakamoto and Reed (full reference at end of study).

In 2006–07 the HT around the world was in for a major overhaul through mergers and alliances. In addition to the cost efficiencies referred to above, truck manufacturers were also looking to access new markets in Eastern Europe and Asia to gain market share and push revenue growth. The industry at that time was, as seen in the table above, dominated by the number one global player, DaimlerChrysler. Other truck makers were shaping up to challenge this dominance. Volvo acquired Nissan Diesel for $1.1bn in February 2007 and MAN the German truck maker owned by Volkswagen (VW) made a $13.4bn bid in January 2007 for Scania, the Swedish truck maker. Although this bid failed because Scania was determined to stay independent, the two companies later talked of exploring an alliance since cooperation between the two truck makers still had a compelling economic logic. Fiat the Italian car maker that also owned the heavy truck maker Iveco was considering alliances in North America.

Volvo's takeover of Nissan Diesel (ND) was justified by Leif Johansson the CEO of Volvo: 'Nissan Diesel holds a solid position in Japan and the rest of Asia where Volvo foresees substantial growth potential. A merger offers both parties possibilities to learn and benefit from each other'. The acquisition of ND was also a platform for further consolidation for Volvo since a merger of Volvo and ND with the Chinese manufacturer, Dongfeng was also on the cards. The merger of all three companies would catapult them to the first position above DC with total sales to 263,000 units compared to DC's 245,000 units. The merger would also make the merged entity second to DC in the medium duty trucks.

Volvo's acquisition of ND was well received by investors and analysts. Christer Gardell, partner in the Swedish activist fund Cevian had long campaigned for Volvo to distribute its accumulated cash balances to the shareholders or make value creating investments, said: 'Clearly this is a value-enhancing deal for Volvo. Financially and strategically it is a great deal'. An analyst from the rating agency, Moody's, said: 'It makes strategic sense. They get a good foothold in the Japanese market and hopefully in other Asian markets'. A Nomura analyst said that the merger 'could increase pressure on MAN and Scania to reach a deal and make them nervous that everyone around them appears to be getting bigger'.

Discussion questions

1 What is the competitive structure of the HT industry?

2 What are the sources of value creation in HT mergers?

3 What types of resource redeployment are possible in the merger of HT makers?

Sources: J. Mackintosh, 'Truckmakers look for more wheels on their wagons', 22 March 2006; D. Ibison and R. Milne, 'After failed MAN bid, Scania chief can see route to an alliance', 26 January 2007; D. Ibison, M. Nakamoto and J. Reed, 'Volvo bids SKr7.5bn for Nissan Diesel', 21 February 2007; J. Reed, 'Commercial vehicles: Truckmakers circle the wagons', 11 September 2007; all from *Financial Times*.

Overview and implications for practice

- We have identified three broad sources of value creation in horizontal mergers: revenue enhancement; cost savings; and new growth opportunities arising from changes in operational efficiency through scale, scope and learning economies, increased market power, market share and network externality, and through exploiting new growth opportunities.

- From the resource-based view of acquisitions, harnessing these sources of value requires redeployment of the merging firms' resources and capabilities.

- Empirical literature on the effect of mergers on cost savings through scale efficiencies and on market power suggests that accretion of market power is difficult to achieve, and scale economies may be easily exhausted and copied by rival firms following me-too mergers.

- Recent large-sample studies show that resources and capabilities redeployed include marketing resources such as sales force, brands and general marketing capabilities, manufacturing, R & D, general management and financial resources, but the impact of resource redeployment on financial performance is limited.

● Redeployment of some marketing resources may actually be detrimental to acquirers. This suggests that resource redeployment is a hazardous business, and the odds on success may not be high. This is so even when the resources transferred are well defined, such as brands.

● We have little evidence on how resource redeployment to generate real options influences post-acquisition performance, but the odds on this are probably even longer.

● The limited evidence on profit and value impact of resource redeployment is consistent with the overall evidence seen in Chapter 4 that mergers may not be sure-fire bets to creating value.

Review questions

5.1 What are the characteristics of horizontal mergers?

5.2 What are the characteristics of mature industries?

5.3 How does horizontal merger help firms in achieving competitive advantage?

5.4 What are the different sources of value in horizontal mergers?

5.5 What do you understand by network externality, and how is it relevant to a horizontal merger? Think of other mergers driven by NWE.

5.6 What are the benefits and problems of brand redeployment in mergers as a source of competitive advantage?

5.7 Do you think firms can achieve unlimited scale and scope economies? Or learning economies? Give reasons.

5.8 What kind of real options may be relevant to horizontal mergers?

5.9 Comment on the empirical studies of resource redeployment.

5.10 What are the problems associated with such redeployment?

Further reading

S. Bahadir, S. Bharadwaj and R. K. Srivatsava, 'Financial value of brands in mergers and acquisitions: Is value in the eye of the beholder?', *Journal of Marketing*, 72, 2008, 49–64.

C. Fee and S. Thomas, 'Sources of gains from horizontal mergers: Evidence from customer, supplier and rival firms', *Journal of Financial Economics*, 74, 2004, 423–460.

M. Jensen, 'The modern industrial revolution, exit and the failure of internal control systems', *Journal of Finance*, 48(3), 1993, 831–880.

D. Leonard Barton, 'Core capabilities and core rigidities', *Strategic Management Journal*, Summer, Special Issue, 1992, 111–126.

Notes and references

1. M. Jensen, 'The modern industrial revolution, exit and the failure of internal control systems', *Journal of Finance*, 48(3), 1993, 831–880.

2. There is a stream of literature that examines the value of horizontal mergers in the face of uncertainty confronting the merging firms that may have private information about uncertain demand or costs. In a merger this private information is shared, thereby allowing the merged firm to cope with the uncertainty

better and make output decisions in Cournot markets. See A. Banal-Estañol, 'Information-sharing implications of horizontal mergers', *International Journal of Industrial Organization*, **25**, 2007, 31–49. Zhou examines mergers motivated by the merging firms' desire to increase their flexibility to relocate production from high-cost to low-cost centres in order to manage uncertainty. See W. Zhou, 'Large is beautiful: Horizontal mergers for better exploitation of production shocks', *The Journal of Industrial Economics*, **56**(1), 2008, 68–93.

3. R. D. Buzzel and B. T. Gale, *The PIMS Principles* (New York: Free Press, 1987). PIMS is profit impact of market share.

4. D. C. Mueller, 'Mergers and market share', *Review of Economics and Statistics*, **67**, May 1985, 259–267. In a more recent paper Mueller and his colleagues examine the difference between actual post-merger profit increase and sales increase of horizontally merging firms (in the same four-digit industry) and projected levels based on the profits and sales of the median firms in the acquirer's and target's two-digit industries (the median serving as a proxy for the performance of non-merging firms) for a large multinational sample of mergers during 1981–98. They test for significant increases in $ profits and $ sales relative to the chosen benchmarks and find that in horizontal mergers by year $t + 5$ (t is merger year) sales decline is insignificant, but profit increase is significant. In years $t + 1$ to $t + 3$ profit increases are insignificant, but sales decline significantly (see their Table 5). Thus it is not clear whether such mergers conform to the pattern of increased market power posited by the authors, i.e. lower sales but increased profits. See K. Gugler, D. C. Mueller, B. B. Yurtoglu and C. Zulehner, 'The effects of mergers: An international comparison', *International Journal of Industrial Organization*, **21**, 2003, 625–653.

5. R. Schmalensee, 'Inter-industry studies of structure and performance', in R. Schmalensee and R. D. Willig (Eds), *Handbook of Industrial Organization* (Amsterdam: North-Holland, 1989).

6. D. A. Hay and D. J. Morris, *Industrial Economics and Organization* (Oxford: Oxford University Press, 1991), p. 261.

7. The price and welfare effects of such collusion are referred to as 'coordinating effects' of a merger in antitrust regulation, and are discussed further in Chapter 17.

8. B. E. Eckbo, 'Horizontal mergers, collusion and stockholder wealth', *Journal of Financial Economics*, **11**, 1983, 241–273; 'Mergers and the market concentration doctrine: Evidence from the capital market', *Journal of Business*, **58**, 1985, 325–349; 'Mergers and the value of antitrust deterrence', *Journal of Finance*, **47**, 1992, 1005–1029.

9. P. Wier, 'Costs of antimerger lawsuits: Evidence from the stock market', *Journal of Financial Economics*, **11**, 1983, 207–224, and R. Stillman, 'Examining antitrust policy towards horizontal mergers', *Journal of Financial Economics*, **11**, 1983, 225–240 support these conclusions.

10. C. Fee and S. Thomas, 'Sources of gains from horizontal mergers: Evidence from customer, supplier and rival firms', *Journal of Financial Economics*, **74**, 2004, 423–460. They examine 554 US deals announced between 1980 and 1997 and find evidence of monopsony power from the merger against the suppliers as a source of value gains. Buying power is particularly important among retailers.

11. Fee and Thomas, *ibid*.

12. F. M. Scherer and D. Ross, *Industrial Market Structure and Economic Performance* (Boston: Houghton Mifflin, 1990).

13. A. M. Brandenburger and B. J. Nalebuff, *Co-opetition* (New York: Currency Doubleday, 1996), pp. 111–117.

14. In 2001 GE, a seller of aero engines, made a takeover bid for Honeywell, which sold avionics. Such bundling of complementary products might give rise to market power and reduce competition in the market for either product. This was the basis on which the EU blocked the bid. Thus the potential anticompetitive effects of complementor acquisition need to be kept in view while contemplating such an acquisition. We discuss the GE–Honeywell bid in more detail in Chapter 17 on antitrust regulation.

15. H. Tanriverdi and C. Lee, 'Within industry diversification and firm performance in the presence of network externalities: Evidence from the software industry', *Academy of Management Journal*, **51**(2), 2008, 381–397. The authors argue that a platform-relatedness strategy enables the exploitation of direct network externalities by increasing application quality and reducing application development, maintenance and renewal costs. This attracts new customers and expands the installed base of the firm. A product-market-relatedness strategy allows exploitation of indirect network externalities by enabling a firm to leverage its existing customer relationships. Increased customer knowledge facilitates development of new applications that complement the installed base. As more complementary applications become available for the installed base, customer utility increases further and indirect network externalities emerge.

16. See M. A. Schilling, 'Technology success and failure in winner-take-all markets: The impact of learning orientation, timing and network externalities', *Academy of Management Journal*, 45, 2002, 387–398. This means that a merger that increases network externality can lead to dominant market power, and may attract antitrust investigation and even its prohibition. In 2000 the European Union prohibited the proposed merger of Worldcom and Sprint, the two US telecommunications firms, on the ground of the merger leading to a powerful network and large installed base. See Chapter 17 on antitrust regulation.

17. M. N. Clemente and D. S. Greenspan, 'Getting the biggest marketing bang from the merger', *Mergers and Acquisitions*, July/August 1996, 19–23.

18. L. Capron and J. Hulland, 'Redeployment of brands, sales forces and general marketing management expertise following horizontal acquisitions: A resource-based view', *Journal of Marketing*, 63(2), 1999, 41–54.

19. M. N. Clemente and D. S. Greenspan, *Winning at Mergers and Acquisitions: The Guide to Market-focused Planning and Integration* (New York: John Wiley & Sons, 1998), Chapter 9.

20. See K. Uhlenbruck, M. A. Hitt and M. Semadeni, 'Market value effects of acquisitions involving internet firms: A resource-based analysis', *Strategic Management Journal*, 27, 2006, 899–913.

21. C. W. L. Hill, 'Differentiation versus low cost or differentiation and low cost: A contingency framework', *Academy of Management Review*, 13(3), 1988, 401–412.

22. P. Holl and J. F. Pickering, 'Takeovers and other influences on economic performance: A plant level analysis', *Applied Economics*, 23, 1991, 1779–1788. They found with UK data on 972 plants surveyed in 1984 that while the plants achieved sales growth, they experienced below-average financial performance. This is consistent with the argument above that plant-level scale economies may be very small. The study does not, however, indicate whether the motivation behind the mergers was plant-level scale economy.

23. R. Coff, D. Coff and R. Eastvold, 'The knowledge-leveraging paradox: How to achieve scale without making knowledge imitable', *Academy of Management Review*, 2006, 31(2), 452–465. For the tension between scale and non-imitability.

24. D. J. Teece, 'Economies of scope and the scope of the enterprise', *Journal of Economic Behaviour and Organization*, 1(3), 1980, 223–247.

25. R. Henderson and I. Cockburn, 'Scale, scope and spillovers: Determinants of research productivity in the pharmaceutical industry', *RAND Journal of Economics*, 27(1), 1996, 32–59.

26. D. Pilling, 'Towards a medicine swap shop', *Financial Times*, 23 July 2001.

27. Capron and Hulland, *ibid.*

28. Exploiting scope economy is an exercise in *strategic stretch* of the merging firms' resources and capabilities to meet the strategic goals of a merger (see G. Hamel and C. K. Prahalad, *Competing for the Future* (Boston, MA: Harvard University Press, 1994), p. 146 on strategic stretch). However, many of the exemplars of such stretch put forward by Hamel and Prahalad subsequently generated below-average returns to shareholders as reported in P. Kontes and M. Mankins cited in D. Besanko, D. Dranove, M. Shanley and S. Schaefer, *Economics of Strategy* (New York: John Wiley & Sons, 2007), p. 434.

29. See D. Amel, C. Barnes, F. Panetta and C. Salleo, 'Consolidation and efficiency in the financial sector: A review of the international evidence', *Journal of Banking & Finance*, 28, 2004, 2493–2519. They, however, find scale and scope economies in insurance.

30. This is consistent with evidence that key inventors leave the acquired firms or they significantly reduce their patenting performance in Germany. See H. Ernst and J. Vitt, 'The influence of corporate acquisitions on the behaviour of key inventors', *R&D Management*, 30(2), 2000, 105–119. For similar evidence of fall in the innovation productivity in the US semiconductor industry, see Kapoor and Lim cited in footnote 37 below.

31. R. S. Pindyck and D. L. Rubinfeld, *Microeconomics* (Upper Saddle River, NJ: Prentice Hall, 2001), pp. 236–237.

32. For a critique of learning curve as a competitive strategy tool, see J. B. Barney and W. S. Hesterly, *Strategic Management and Competitive Advantage* (Upper Saddle River, NJ: Pearson Prentice Hall, 2008), p. 122.

33. C. W. L. Hill, 'Differentiation versus low cost or differentiation and low cost: A contingency framework', *Academy of Management Review*, 13(3), 1988, 401–412.

34. G. Hamel and C. K. Prahalad, *Competing for the Future* (Boston, MA: Harvard University Press, 1994), Chapter 2.

35. J. Liedka, 'In defence of strategy as design', *California Management Review*, 42(3), 2000, 8–30. In De Wit and Meyer's taxonomy, racing for the world requires a 'rational reasoning perspective', and racing for the future requires a 'generative reasoning perspective'. On the attributes of these perspectives see B. De Wit

and R. Meyer, *Strategy Synthesis: Resolving Strategy Paradoxes to Create Competitive Advantage*, (London: Thomson Learning, 2005), pp. 42–46.

36. M. Subramaniam and M. A. Youndt, 'The influence of intellectual capital on the types of innovative capabilities', *Academy of Management Journal*, **48**(3), 2005, 450–463. In their study, human capital is measured by the skill, expertise and knowledge levels of the employees, organizational capital by the firm's ability to appropriate and store knowledge in databases, manuals and patents as well structures and processes, and social capital by the organization's ability to share and leverage knowledge among and between networks of employees, customers, suppliers and alliance partners.

37. See R. Kapoor and K. Lim, 'The impact of innovations on the productivity of inventors at semiconductor firms: A synthesis of knowledge-based and incentive-based perspectives', *Academy of Management Journal*, **50**(5), 2007, 1133–1155. Also P. Puranam, H. Singh and M. Zollo, 'Organizing for innovation: Managing the coordination–autonomy dilemma in technology acquisitions', *Academy of Management Journal*, **49**(2), 2006, 263–280.

38. F. Guerrera and D. Firn, 'Leschly says biotech was a bad investment', *Financial Times*, 18 November 2000.

39. D. Leonard Barton, 'Core capabilities and core rigidities', *Strategic Management Journal*, **Summer** Special Issue, 1992, 111–126.

40. R. Grant, *Contemporary Strategy Analysis* (Oxford: Blackwell, 2008), p. 141.

41. L. Capron, P. Dussauge and W. Mitchell, 'Resource redeployment following horizontal acquisitions in Europe and North America, 1988–1992', *Strategic Management Journal*, **19**, 1998, 631–661.

42. C. K. Prahalad, 'Changes in the competitive battlefield', *Financial Times Mastering Strategy*, 4 October 1999.

43. S. Karim and W. Mitchell, 'Path-dependent and path-breaking change: Reconfiguring business resources following acquisitions in the US medical sector 1978–1995', *Strategic Management Journal*, **21**, 2000, 1061–1081.

44. T. Madden, F. Fehle and S. Fournier, 'Brands matter: An empirical demonstration of the creation of shareholder value through branding', *Journal of the Academy of Marketing* Science, **34**(2), 2006, 224–235. They calculate the abnormal returns to a portfolio of 111 US firms with the World's Most Valued Brands relative to returns on the market, size, book to market and momentum factors (see Chapter 4 Appendix 4.1 for a discussion of this approach). Whereas the strong brands portfolio generates abnormal return of 1.32% per month, other firms (called reduced portfolio) experience −0.25% and have higher systematic risks (see their Table 3). This evidence is consistent with the framework that relates market-based assets to firm volatility and shareholder value (see R. K. Srivastava, T. A. Shervani and L. Fahey, 'Market-based assets and shareholder value: A framework for analysis', *Journal of Marketing*, **62**, 1998, 2–18).

45. T. Knudsen, L. Finskud, R. Tornblom and E. Hogna, 'Brand consolidation makes a lot of economic sense but only one in five attempts succeed', *McKinsey Quarterly*, **4**, 1997, 189–194.

46. P. Štrach and A. Everett, 'Brand corrosion: Mass-marketing's threat to luxury automobile brands after merger and acquisition', *Journal of Product & Brand Management*, **15**(2), 2006, 106–120. Among the brand-diluting factors they are platform sharing, attempts to make luxury brands more affordable, and combining mass and niche strategies. The German car maker BMW, the premium niche market player, acquired the UK's Rover in the 1990s in order to combine luxury and mass-market segments, but this acquisition was a disaster and cost BMW several hundred million euros to unwind. After a fire sale of Rover, BMW retained only one enduring brand, the Mini, and turned it into a successful Mini Cooper brand. On the tension between increasing volume to achieve scale economies and keeping it low to preserve exclusivity of a luxury brand, see the case of Louis Vuitton Moët Hennessy (LVMH)'s acquisition of several brands in S. Kumar and K. H. Blomqvist, 'Mergers and acquisitions: Making brand equity a key factor in M & A decision making', *Strategy & Leadership*, **32**(2), 2004, 20–27.

47. S. C. Bahadir, S. G. Bharadwaj and R. K. Srivastava, 'Financial value of brands in merges and acquisitions: Is value in the eye of the beholder?', *Journal of Marketing*, **72**, 2008, 49–64.

48. 'Resources are difficult to categorize, but worse yet, often difficult to recognize . . . the *tacit* (non-articulated) nature of much organizational knowledge makes it difficult to identify the firm's knowledge base. The same is true for a firm's capabilities, which have developed in the form of organization routines', B. De Wit and R. Meyer, *ibid.*, pp. 114–115.

49. See S. Lippman and R. Rumelt, 'Uncertain imitability: An analysis of interfirm differences in efficiency under competition', *Bell Journal of Economics*, **13**, 1982, 418–438. See also M. Augier and D. J. Teece, 'An economic perspective on intellectual capital', in B. Marr (Ed.), *Perspectives on Intellectual Capital*, (Oxford: Elsevier, 2005), pp. 3–27, on the limits to imitation.

50. K. P. Coyne, S. J. D. Hall and P. G. Clifford, 'Is your core competence a mirage?', *McKinsey Quarterly*, **1**, 1997, 41–54.

51. See J. B. Barney and D. N. Clark, *Resource-Based Theory: Creating and Sustaining Competitive Advantage* (Oxford: Oxford University Press, 2007), pp. 69–74, Table 3.1, on the application of the VRIO test.

52. A. Campbell, 'Desperately seeking synergy', *Harvard Business Review*, **76**(5), 1998, 130–143; M. Sirower, *The Synergy Trap* (New York: Free Press, 1997).

53. M. H. Song and R. A. Walkling, 'Abnormal returns to rivals of acquisition targets: A test of the "acquisition probability hypothesis"', *Journal of Financial Economics*, **55**, 2000, 143–171. Also see, for similar results, A. Akhigbe, S. F. Borde and A. M. Whyte, 'The source of gains to targets and their industry rivals: Evidence based on terminated merger proposals', *Financial Management*, **29**(4), 2000, 101–118.

54. M. M. Walker, 'Corporate takeovers, strategic objectives and acquiring firm shareholder wealth', *Financial Management*, **29**(1), 2000, 53–66.

CHAPTER ⑥

Sources and limits of value creation in vertical mergers

Objectives

At the end of this chapter, the reader should be able to understand:

- the economic rationale for vertical integration;
- the alternatives to vertical integration;
- the costs and benefits associated with vertical integration and the alternatives;
- characteristics of industry-blurring mergers and the drivers of such mergers;
- the limits to value creation in vertical and industry-blurring mergers; and
- how acquisitions are used to outsource certain capabilities.

Introduction

In the broad framework we developed in Chapter 3 to analyze the rationale and consequences of M & A, firms seek to extend the scope of their activities in a number of ways:

- horizontal scope including segment or product scope;
- geographical scope;
- vertical scope; and
- industry scope;

In Chapter 5 we presented the framework for evaluating the sources of value in horizontal scope-enlarging mergers, focusing on mergers of large firms. The merging firms either sell the same products or services in the same markets, or sell products that share certain commonalities in terms of inputs, technology, marketing, sales and distribution, etc. Thus the essential drivers of these mergers are scale economies, scope economies, market power, revenue enhancement through leveraging the resources and capabilities of the two firms, and to some extent exploring future growth opportunities.

In this chapter we turn our attention to mergers of firms that produce goods or services that represent the output of successive stages of the same vertical chain. A vertical chain represents the various stages from raw material inputs to the final product sold to the customer, for example from iron ore to steel products sold to automobile manufacturers. The different stages of the vertical chain are also referred to as downstream or upstream activities in the flow of the production process. At any stage in the vertical chain the activities that precede that stage are upstream to that stage, and all activities that follow are downstream.

There is another type of vertical merger, which accounted for a substantial number and value of the M & A deals done in the 1990s, that merits a special focus. These mergers brought firms whose output was in one industry together with firms that provided the distribution channels originally designed for another industry. For example, the Internet, initially meant as a high-speed communication channel of information, now carries video and audio signals and has turned into a channel not only for information but also for entertainment and social networking. The controversial firm Napster, which allowed the downloading of music from its website, was pointing to this change in the medium by which music could be accessed and sold. Thus the Internet is vying with the print media and traditional audio and visual media as a channel for such transmission. The newly coined term 'infotainment' captures this crossover. This transformation has triggered a spate of multimedia mega mergers, e.g. AOL and Time Warner.

Similarly, in banking and insurance there is a blurring of industry boundaries, to the extent that we now have a new industry category 'bancassurance', with the products of one industry being sold through the other's distribution channels. The crossover extends beyond just the scope economy implied in the exploitation of each other's distribution channels to the creation of new savings, insurance and asset management products and new markets, for example the mass affluence customers. The objective is to serve the needs of these customers in all the above areas in a seamless and integrated manner. This has again set in motion a number of mergers of banks and insurance companies.

In this chapter we review the value creation logic of vertical mergers, including the industry-blurring mergers of the kind exemplified above. The conditions under which such mergers are likely to be value creating are then discussed. The limits to value creation are indicated. The phenomenal growth of outsourcing in the 1990s provides some evidence of such limits to vertical integration as a source of value. The huge post-acquisition write-offs and restructuring charges announced by some of the acquirers, such as AOL-Time Warner and Vivendi, are used to illustrate the perils of the 'new economy', industry-blurring mergers.

Vertical integration

Definition

The flow of production of goods in a traditional vertical chain is shown in Figure 6.1 for a manufacturing firm. It breaks down the sequential activities involved in the transformation of raw materials and other inputs into finished products and delivery of these products to the final consumer. This transformation process is supported by a number of infrastructure or support services. A firm operating at one stage of the vertical chain may restrict itself to that stage while sourcing the upstream activities from other providers, either through market-based transactions or through contractual or other arrangements. Similarly, the firm's output can be sold through market transactions or contractual or other arrangements. Vertical integration is the *combination of successive activities in a vertical chain under common coordination and control of a single firm*. Thus vertical merger *replaces* two or more independent firms with a single firm, and it *internalizes* the coordination of the successive activities rather than relying on arm's length market-based transactions or contractual dealings.

Figure 6.1   Vertical chain of production

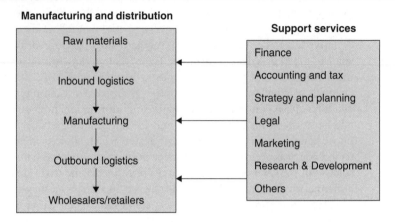

Manufacturing and distribution

- Raw materials
- Inbound logistics
- Manufacturing
- Outbound logistics
- Wholesalers/retailers

Support services

- Finance
- Accounting and tax
- Strategy and planning
- Legal
- Marketing
- Research & Development
- Others

Figure 6.2   Transaction modes for sourcing inputs

Spot purchase	Informal supplier relation	Long-term contract	Franchise	Strategic alliance	Vertical integration

Vertical integration as a make-or-buy decision

The decision to internalize production of an input rather than source it from an external supplier is akin to a 'make or buy' decision. The decision has to be made on the balance of costs and benefits of either alternative. The buy decision may be implemented in a variety of ways. In a spot market transaction the product is sold in a spot market characterized by a large number of sellers, from whom it could be bought for immediate delivery and at a known price in an arm's length transaction. For many products, such as specialized products or intangible products, spot markets are non-existent, or there may be only a small number of sellers. Where competitive spot markets do not exist, the buy decision may be executed by entering into formal and informal agreements between the buyer and the seller. The alternative modes of internal and external sourcing of the inputs are shown in Figure 6.2, which represents a continuum of transactional devices from spot market purchase to vertical integration.

Why does a firm seek to replace market-based transactions or supplier contracts with internal production? The choice between external arrangements and internalization through vertical merger is based on the relative costs and benefits of external versus internal coordination of the activities in a vertical chain. Choice of a particular transaction mode depends on a range of factors:

- the current and future availability of spot markets for arm's length transactions;
- the cost of sourcing from the spot market;

- the direct and indirect costs of contracts and informal arrangements;
- uncertainty and information asymmetry between buyer and seller; and
- the direct and indirect costs of internalizing production.

In the following sections we compare the costs and benefits of using markets, contracts and other arrangements, and vertical integration[1].

Benefits and costs of buying in markets

There are many pros and cons of using competitive spot markets to source the upstream activities in a vertical chain. The benefits essentially stem from the pressure and discipline of competition on the suppliers in a competitive market. Where the suppliers supply to a large number of buyers they can achieve scale and learning economies. Suppliers may also achieve efficient division of labour and specialization. Where the product is specialized, for example in terms of production technology and design attributes, the suppliers are probably few, and gain dominance in the bargaining game. Oliver Williamson describes the change from large numbers of suppliers bidding to sell the product to a small number bargaining with the buyers as a fundamental transformation[2].

In a small-numbers game the bargaining power may be loaded in favour of the supplier, depending on the product characteristics, such as complexity, access to resources to produce the product, the proprietary nature of production technology, or legal monopoly such as patents. Where the input is critical in the vertical chain, and the buyer firm cannot internalize the production, it is being 'held up' by the suppliers. In addition there may be problems of coordinating the supply and integration of the supplies into the subsequent stages of the vertical chain, e.g. transport bottlenecks and design incompatibility. Uncertainties about quality and delivery schedules may make internalization more attractive. Where market dealings reveal information of a strategic nature about the buyer's product, production process or technology, such dealings may be avoided.

Internalization also has a coordination cost. This is the cost of delegating the activities to another division or subsidiary of the firm, supervising and monitoring its activities, and rewarding its performance. These costs are known as agency costs, since the performing division is an agent of the buying division. Agency relationships give rise to opportunism in using information, shirking, and inflated (transfer) price of internally produced inputs to hide inefficiencies. Ambiguity in measuring performance and problems in attaching accountability for performance failure give rise to moral hazard, that is, lack of accountability and the breakdown of internal coordination.

Internalization may also generate disincentives for innovation. It may be difficult to assign specific responsibility for ideas or efforts that lead to breakthroughs and to reward them. Firms may then resort to easily observed and easily measured indicators of performance rather than the real indicators. This may bias innovation efforts towards low-level incremental improvements and away from riskier projects. This disincentive to innovate in the vertically integrated firm is indeed a double whammy. Internalization deprives the activity of the market discipline that spurs innovation, but it has perhaps a more insidious effect of rewarding the wrong kind of innovation.

Internalization may also become a victim of influence costs. An integrated firm serves as an internal capital market in allocating scarce capital resources to the various activities. The organization's political processes may distort such allocation, with some factions, divisions or managers being able to lobby for a more favourable allocation even though their economic case for such allocation may be relatively weak. For example, the in-house supplier of a component may try to thwart the user department, dissatisfied with the performance of the former, from sourcing from the market, even though market prices may be lower or market suppliers may be superior in terms of delivery schedule or quality of the component supplied. The in-house supplier may use its influence in doing so, and continue to produce in an unsatisfactory way. Womack *et al.* observed this process in General Motors (GM), and concluded that it explained 'how GM managed to have both the world's highest production volume and the world's highest costs in many of its components supply divisions' through much of the 1980s[3].

Benefits and costs of long-term contracts

Where there is market failure, a firm may source its inputs externally from suppliers by negotiating supply contracts. These contracts may be of a short-term or long-term nature. Contractual relations with suppliers again have benefits and costs attached to them, compared with the costs and benefits of vertical integration.

Benefits of contracts

Contracts may be of short or long duration. A short-term contract carries the uncertainty (from the supplier's point of view) that it may not be renewed. This uncertainty may deter the supplier from committing itself to the buyer and making relation-specific investment. On the other hand, it may encourage the supplier to make more diligent efforts to comply with the contract in the hope that such diligence will be rewarded with renewal of the contract. Where there is a prospect of repeat business from the buyer, a short-term contract may ensure greater contract compliance. Nevertheless, the uncertainty associated with renewal may deter the supplier from making long-term investment in enhancing product quality, development or cost reduction technology.

A long-term contract avoids the under-investment incentive of short-term contracts, since the supplier, now assured of a long-term business relationship, can make long-term investment plans. A long-term relationship allows the buyer and seller to go beyond a supplier–buyer relationship to understand each other's strategy, resources and capabilities and engender a partnership that allows the leveraging of these resources and capabilities. The supplier can use its knowledge of the production processes of the buyer to design better products, and the buyer can modify its production techniques to incorporate the improvements made by the supplier. The close relationship between component suppliers and many user firms such as Toyota or BAE Systems (the British aerospace company) exemplifies the benefits of such a close relationship[4].

A long-term contract allows the supplier to invest in information technology that facilitates the close scheduling of the supplies to meet the just-in-time needs of the buyer. The supplier develops a stake in the success of the buyer, and thus has an incentive to enhance the quality and pricing of its supplies, to the benefit of both parties.

Where the contract does not fully exhaust the economically useful life of the investments, such as plant or machinery, the residual rights to the assets rest with the supplier, who decides on how these assets will be used to serve other customers. If the supplier had been replaced by internalization, the buyer firm would then be faced with the risk of the residual assets even if secondary markets for such assets exist. Thus this residual risk to the buyer is minimized.

Costs of contracts

Contracts may be divided into complete and incomplete contracts. A complete contract specifies the terms of the contract, the process of contract monitoring, performance measurement, assessment of contractual default, the enforcement mechanism for contract compliance, and the damages and penalties for breach of contract in *complete* detail. All contingencies are foreseen, and there is no ambiguity. Alas, such contracts probably do not exist! Contracts in practice tend to be *incomplete*.

Contracts may be incomplete for the following reasons:

- uncertainty and inability to correctly anticipate and specify all the circumstances in the future under which the contract will have to be performed;
- bounded rationality;
- asymmetric information between the contracting parties; or
- disagreement on how to measure performance and how to define default, and the allocation of responsibility for breach or breakdown of contract.

The first condition is, of course, the pervasive human condition. This uncertainty may be alleviated by elaborate information search, modelling of all possible future contingencies and drawing up an exhaustive contract. Such an exercise is likely to be excessively costly and, while bringing a gleam to the eyes of the drafting lawyers, is unlikely to eliminate risk altogether. Human beings, when faced with uncertainty and limited information, act with bounded rather than absolute rationality. Their cognitive limitations restrict their capacity to process information, deal with complexity and make absolutely rational choices. Since human beings differ in their cognitive abilities, their bounds of rationality also differ. This means that two contracting parties can see and interpret the same information differently. With bounded rationality, contracting parties settle for contracts that seem to satisfy their *own* bounds of rationality.

The contracting parties may have access to different information sets, and, given uncertainty and the costs of information search, this information asymmetry may never be completely bridged. Information asymmetry may then be exploited opportunistically by the party that has access to superior or privileged information. This opportunistic behaviour gives rise to both *adverse selection* and *moral hazard*. *Adverse selection*, famously described as the lemon problem, is the choice of a contracting party that has an information advantage even prior to the contract – for example, a person who seeks a life insurance policy while concealing his serious illnesses, or the infamous and proverbial second-hand car dealer selling a car with a doctored speedometer or fresh paint that covers a rusty body. A supplier may likewise hype up its capacity to deliver, while concealing its lack of resources to do so or its dishonest intention not to deliver.

Moral hazard is associated with the inability to measure performance, and hence failure of performance, precisely. It may also arise from the inability to identify the causal factors in performance failure. In the presence of *moral hazard*, the defaulter can 'get away with it'. This possibility alters his behaviour, leading to perfunctory contract performance or fraudulent neglect of contractual obligations. While the contract may provide for monitoring of performance, this cannot be done costlessly. Moreover, information asymmetry may preclude effective monitoring. For example, the quality assurance procedures employed by the supplier may not be easily verifiable or accessible to the buyer.

Opportunistic behaviour

Under what conditions does opportunistic behaviour assume serious proportions, and what are the consequences of such behaviour? The scope for opportunism is much greater when the investment made to support the contract is relation specific. Such relation-specific investment increases the cost of switching to a new customer, thereby locking the supplier into that relationship. A supplier wary of such a lock-in may have to draw up a tighter contract with stiff penalties for walking away from the contract, or increase the price of the supplies to compensate for the risk of lock-in and the erosion in value of the relation-specific asset. Once the relation-specific contract comes into being, the game becomes a small-number or bilateral bargaining game rather than the large-number competitive suppliers game. Oliver Williamson describes this change as the fundamental transformation that results in shifting the bargaining power from one party to the other.

Relation-specific investment creates assets with different types of specificity:

● site specific;
● physical characteristics specific;
● dedicated assets; and
● human asset specific.

Site-specific asset refers to an investment located close to the buyer's production facility. Once located, the site may become captive to the buyer, and relocation may be costly. Selling the output from that site to other users who may require similarly proximate location may be too costly in terms of transportation costs and delivery time lags to be economically viable. Physical asset specificity refers to the product characteristics designed to match the exclusive specifications of the buyer. These idiosyncratic products may have few other uses. Asset specificity also makes switching to other suppliers by the buyer more difficult.

Dedicated assets are investments in production facilities that are made to satisfy the needs of a particular buyer, such as contract manufacturing facilities. Without the buyer's business, such dedicated investments will lose their economic value. Human asset specificity refers to investments made by managers and the workforce in acquiring skills and capabilities suited to a given relationship but less valuable in other uses.

Benefits and costs of vertical integration

Our review of the costs and benefits of spot market exchanges and long-term contracts indicates that they both carry costs. Table 6.1 lists the costs and benefits of vertical integration. These are the flip side of the benefits and costs associated with spot market exchanges and long-term contracts. Technical efficiency concerns the process of production, and coordination efficiency concerns the process of contracting, coordination, monitoring and enforcement. Vertical integration increases technical efficiencies in some ways, but may introduce inefficiencies in other ways. Similarly, it can improve coordination efficiency by avoiding costly contracting with external suppliers, reducing information asymmetry between supplier and user divisions, and reducing the scope for opportunism in contract enforcement. Enlightened organizational practices and culture as well as the prospect of a close and long-term relationship between divisions can reduce opportunism. Interdivisional conflict resolution can be achieved by administrative fiat, thereby avoiding costly litigation.

While many of the coordination inefficiencies of market exchange may be minimized through vertical integration, it is by no means free of other inefficiencies. Interdivisional rivalries that may lead to opportunism and influence costs are ever present in organizations. In the absence of external benchmarks such as market prices, internal transfer pricing between divisions becomes a matter of haggling, relative bargaining power and political intrigue. Aligning

Table 6.1 Benefits and costs of vertical integration

Benefits of vertical integration	Costs of vertical integration
Technical efficiencies	
• More control over quality and delivery of inputs	• Absence of market discipline makes internal production inefficient and costly
• Premium for branded products avoided if unbranded inputs are internally made	• Small production volume reduces opportunity for scale and learning economies
• Greater control over coordinating production flows through vertical chains	• Efficiency effects of division of labour and specialization forgone
• Leakage of private information to supplier and possibly rivals avoided	• Incentive to keep up with new technology diminished
	• Risk in disposal of residual assets where asset lives exceed project life
Coordination efficiencies	
• Small-numbers bargaining, when suppliers are too few, avoided	• Internal agency monitoring costs not insignificant
• Incomplete contracts avoided	• Incentive structure for managers may not match that in independent firms
• Scope for opportunism reduced through long-term relationships within firm, closer monitoring, organizational culture	• Formal contracts replaced by implicit contracts with workers
• Monitoring supplier performance easier since information asymmetry reduced	• Influence costs reduce capital allocation efficiency
• Contract enforcement costs minimized	• Internal performance evaluation not free of opportunistic behaviour
• Disputes resolved through administrative fiat and costly litigation avoided	• Pricing internal supplies subject to opportunistic behaviour
• Free-riding by distributors on the reputation of the manufacturers avoided	

the interests of different divisions is not a painless process[5]. Even in integrated firms, information asymmetry may exist between different levels of management and between divisions. Designing divisional incentives to share information may be a complicated exercise[6]. Formal employment contracts in firms are generally supplemented by implicit or relational contracts, and when a firm breaches the latter it may face high costs in the form of a demoralized workforce, lack of commitment, and other dysfunctional behaviour. Creative and inventive managers may feel that the organizational reward system does not recognize their contribution as much as the market would if they operated as independent firms.

The decision choice among the three options therefore depends on a number of trade-offs. Broadly, the trade-offs are between the relative technical efficiencies of external and internal production and between the relative coordination efficiencies of market exchange and long-term contracts, and internalization. Medtronic's decision to internalize much of its component manufacturing is based on such trade-offs, as shown in Exhibit 6.1.

Relative costs of external sourcing and internal production, as well as the need for quality and precision control, account for the Swiss firm Disetronic's decision to integrate vertically, as shown in Exhibit 6.2.

Exhibit 6.1

Medtronic relies on its own power

The Minneapolis-based Medtronic is the world's biggest maker of medical devices, including heart pacemakers and tiny implants that deliver drugs into the body. In July 2001 it had a market capitalization of $59bn and was the 39th most valuable company in the US. It also makes implantable defibrillators. In addition to making these highly specialized and sophisticated products, it also makes the much simpler but specialized lithium iodine batteries. The batteries power the medical devices for up to nine years. Medtronic makes these batteries in-house rather than outsource their production in order to guarantee quality and reliability. The rationale for the vertical integration decision is to exercise control over many parts of the production process, including the supply of important components.

Source: Adapted from P. Marsh, 'A sharp sense of the limits to outsourcing. The art of manufacturing, Part 1', *Financial Times*, 31 July 2001

Exhibit 6.2

Disetronic pumps work like (Swiss) clockwork

Disetronic is a Swiss maker of pumps and infusion devices for people with diabetes. It turns a supply of plastic granules and ink into small disposable 'pens' for injecting insulin. But rather than look for suppliers of plastic parts from China or Eastern Europe, Disetronic invested SFr 20m ($11m) in 2000 in a highly automated plant in Burgdorf in Switzerland. This production line employed only 20 people to make roughly 10 million pens a year. The company found it very cost-effective to use ultra-precise injection moulding machines to make the products without any involvement of parts suppliers.

Thomas Meyer, Disetronic chief executive officer, judged that the reliability and quality of the company's in-house manufacturing were two reasons behind the tripling of its annual sales in the previous years to SFr302m, during which the net profits also doubled.

In the case of Disetronic, the cost advantage of outsourcing the plastic parts from seemingly low-cost centres such as China was outweighed by the use of better technology such as automated production, even though the plant was located in a high-cost country, Switzerland. In addition to this cost advantage, the intangible benefits of high-precision manufacture also made internalization attractive.

Source: Adapted from P. Marsh, 'A sharp sense of the limits to outsourcing. The art of manufacturing, Part 1', *Financial Times,* 31 July 2001

Vertical mergers and value creation

Vertical mergers are mergers of firms that carry out the successive activities of a vertical chain. Where a firm merges with another that carries out the immediately preceding upstream activity it results in backward integration, for example the acquisition of an engine manufacturer by an automobile manufacturer. Where a firm acquires another that carries out the immediately following downstream activity in the vertical chain it results in forward integration, for example a manufacturing firm acquiring a wholesaler.

The economic rationale for vertical mergers is derived from the comparative efficiency of vertical integration in terms of technical and coordination efficiency. For vertical merger to create sustainable competitive advantage, in addition to these cost efficiencies, the merger must also lead to other sources of value, such as revenue enhancement, and new growth opportunities through leveraging the existing resources and capabilities of the merging firms and the creation of new resources and capabilities.

Revenue enhancement may arise from the ability to offer a package of services and products rather than just products alone. Thus the offer of consumer credit and insurance services, or garaging and repair services through dealership, may help automobile manufacturers gain competitive advantage. This may explain why firms such as Ford and General Motors have in the past acquired or built up consumer finance or dealership activities. However, this strategy of bundling car sales with associated services is not an inimitable strategy. Therefore it is doubtful that it can be a source of sustained competitive advantage.

Higher profitability may be realized through the increased market power that vertical integration can confer. Vertical mergers may have anti-competitive consequences. They may:

- provide opportunities for indirect price discrimination;
- squeeze non-integrated final product manufacturers by cutting the price of the final product, e.g. ready-mixed concrete, and not the price of the intermediate product, e.g. cement;
- remove firms such as suppliers or distributors with countervailing power; and
- raise entry barriers by raising the capital requirement for new entrants.

However, evidence of market power enhancement through vertical integration seems scarce. Whether it confers market dominance again seems a doubtful proposition[7]. Nevertheless, antitrust authorities do consider the anti-competitive aspects of specific vertical mergers, such as input or customer *foreclosure* to its competitors. We discuss these issues in Chapter 17 on antitrust regulation.

It is not clear that vertical integration as an exploratory strategy will generate growth opportunities through the creation of new technology, product or market. Since the end-product of the vertical chain remains the same, and it is the ownership and organization of the intermediate stages of production or distribution that get reshuffled through vertical integration, the scope for real options and breakthrough growth opportunities seems quite limited.

Whether integration is more efficient than market exchange or long-term contractual relationship depends on the governance structure within the integrated firm[8] (see case study below). The governance structure consists of various building blocks:

- the degree of autonomy versus centralization among the divisions;
- the locus of decision making, e.g. who makes transfer pricing decisions;
- how information asymmetry is resolved;
- the performance measurement system and incentive structure;
- the performance benchmarks to guide transfer pricing between supplier and user division; and
- how the acquired resources and capabilities are integrated into the vertical acquirer.

Empirical evidence on vertical mergers and their value effects

Empirical evidence on the incidence of vertical mergers and their value effects is scarce relative to those that have examined horizontal (see Chapter 5) and diversifying mergers (see Chapter 7). One of the reasons for this is the reliance of many researchers on the SIC codes for classifying mergers as horizontal, related or unrelated. In general, mergers of firms from the same SIC industry are regarded as horizontal or horizontally related mergers, whereas those of firms from different SIC industries are classified as diversifying or conglomerate. This may mean that mergers of firms in different SIC industries, but which have a buyer–seller relation, may not be categorized as vertical mergers but as diversifying mergers. The SIC classification is not adequate to capture the relation where the output of one industry provides the input to the other.

Fan and Goyal, in one of the few studies that address this misclassification issue, use the input–output (IO) accounts for the US economy, produced by the Bureau of Economic Analysis, to establish significant IO-related industries.[9] Where merging firms are from IO industries the merger is classified as a vertical merger. Under their method, not all cross-industry mergers are unrelated mergers. Some mergers between firms in the same IO industry may be vertically related (mixed vertical–horizontal) and some may be purely horizontal, as shown in Figure 6.3. It is based on a threshold of at least 1% (5%) vertical relatedness. Vertical mergers thus account for 35% (19%) of all sample mergers. This proportion increases from 30% in the 1960s to 45% in the 1990s.

In terms of shareholder wealth effects, the authors report the following 21-day announcement period combined bidder and target abnormal returns for the 5% cutoff sample:

All mergers	2.4%
Vertically related	3.7%
Pure horizontal	3.5%
Diversifying	1.7%

Figure 6.3 **Vertical mergers during 1962–1996 in the US**

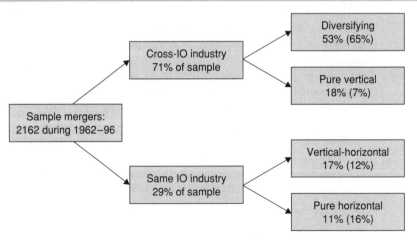

*Note: the percentage figure is the proportion of the sample classified into the given merger type. The figure within parentheses is based on the 5% cutoff. Percentage figures may not add up to 100 owing to rounding. IO refers to input–output-related industries.

Thus vertical mergers are value-creating transactions and are marginally more so than pure horizontal mergers. They also create more value for shareholders than purely diversifying mergers, but the latter are indeed value creating, as reported by many studies reviewed in Chapter 7 on conglomerate acquisitions. Vertical mergers generated significantly more value in the 1980s and 1990s than in the previous two decades.

Vertical mergers that blur industry boundaries

Vertical mergers integrate firms that carry out activities at successive stages of a vertical chain. Many mergers in the 1990s combined the activities of one vertical chain with those of another. The merger of a bank with an insurance company or an asset management company is based on the following premises:

- Banking has become a commodity business, and needs to offer value-added products to customers.
- Banks need to offer their customers not just banking products but also other savings and investment products.
- Banks can act as channels for the sale and distribution of savings products developed by insurance companies and investment products offered by the asset management firms.

The merger of this type transcends the traditional boundaries of the banking, insurance and asset management industries. Banks integrated 'backwards' to source the insurance industry's products. Insurance companies integrated 'forwards' to acquire distribution channels. For this reason the term 'bancassurance' has been coined to describe these boundary-blurring mergers. The combination of traditional commercial banking and investment banking offering investment products has been facilitated in the US by the repeal of the Glass-Steagall Act enacted in the 1930s, following the Great Crash, to prohibit such combinations[10].

Through a series of acquisitions in the 1990s, Travelers extended its coverage from insurance into the securities business by buying Smith Barney (a brokerage firm), Salomon Brothers (investment bank and securities trading firm) and Citibank (commercial banking) to emerge as a full-service financial institution called Citigroup. The full-service financial institution owes its origin to the German-Swiss concept of *Allfinanz*[11]. The cross-industry mergers carried out by Allianz of Germany (see Exhibit 6.3) exemplify it.

Exhibit 6.3

Allianz and Dresdner do a (banc)assuring deal

The traditional ownership pattern of large German corporations reflects significant holdings by banks and other financial institutions as well as cross-shareholdings among financial institutions. In 2001 Allianz, the giant insurer, held 21.4% of Dresdner Bank, 17.4% of Hypovereinsbank and 5.6% of Deutsche Bank, respectively the country's third, second and the largest banks. All three banks also held stakes in Allianz. Munich Re, the world's biggest insurer including reinsurance, held much smaller stakes of about 5% or less in the same three banks.

In March 2001 Allianz made a €24bn bid for Dresdner as part of interconnected deals to end the complex cross-shareholdings. The outcome of this bid and the deals was to create two giant bancassurance firms that offered banking

→

services, insurance and asset management products. Allianz was relatively weak in mutual funds, in bond and equity funds management, in the distribution of equity-linked investment products, and in the burgeoning private client businesses, and Dresdner had comparative and complementary strengths. Thus Allianz would be able to access on a larger scale the wealthy private client segment, and also sell a wider range of banking, insurance and investment products. Munich Re, by increasing its stakes in Hypovereinsbank, would also increase the opportunities for such market access and cross-selling.

In response to these developments, Deutsche Bank, which had already expanded from its base as a German retail commercial bank to being one of the top international investment banks, announced that it would form a closer relationship with Axa, the French insurer, although falling short of a merger. One of the drivers of the trend towards bancassurance was the shift from pension provision by governments through taxation to private provision through individual savings. Many governments in Europe have in recent years followed this policy of shifting the pension provision to reduce taxation and control public expenditure.

Source: Adapted from T. Major and J. Willman, 'Germany unwrapped', *Financial Times*, 30 March 2001

Another wave of mergers blurred the boundaries between telecommunications, cable transmission, media and the Internet. Broadband provides the conduit for the densely packed streams of digital data that can carry information and entertainment to homes and offices. It is a 'wide pipe' capable of delivering films, information, music and data to consumers that were previously delivered by different channels such as cable, television networks, print media and the Internet. With broadband these separate technologies now converge. This convergence enables the content produced for one medium to be delivered through other media. Bringing together different media platforms within a single company thus provides opportunities for growth. The opportunity for growth may arise from the merger of a content company with a company that controls different distribution channels. Firms that control distribution may gain access to content through mergers[12]. Exhibit 6.4 illustrates these value drivers in the series of multimedia mergers undertaken by AOL and Time Warner.

Exhibit 6.4

Warner makes a Hollywood Batman blockbuster

Time Warner was created by the merger in 1989 of Warner Communications, America's most powerful movie studio and music company at that time, with Time Inc., the country's largest magazine publisher. Their cable television assets fitted well, but the publishing and the movie businesses had little to do with each other. The merger was driven by the vision of a multimedia firm held by Steve Ross, who died in 1992. Gerald Levin, who succeeded Ross, then expanded this vision by merging in 1995 with Turner Broadcasting System (TBS) of Ted Turner, with TBS providing programming content for cable television, including Cable Network News (CNN), the 24-hour news programme started in 1980. Gerald Levin had in the meanwhile invested heavily in building up Time Warner's cable infrastructure. The merger of Time Warner with TBS thus married the programming content of TBS to the cable network of Time Warner. Richard Parsons, Time Warner's president, explained that the synergy logic of this deal was that it created a triangle of complementary businesses.

The movie studio, the publishing business and cable television could exploit a Warner brand, such as Batman. This multiple use of brands brings in new revenue streams and strengthens brand recognition. Batman is better known because he has been on television, in print and in the movies, and he has made more money for the company because he has been used in these different ways. Thus Turner cable systems were able to add value to Warner and Time content, and Warner and Time platforms could enhance Turner content. Being in both content and distribution, Time Warner was able to change the relationship between the two to its advantage. For example, movies did not have to wait several years before they could be shown on cable after being shown in cinemas.

In January 2000 America Online Inc. (AOL), the Internet service provider, merged with Time Warner in a $156bn deal. With this merger the merged company, AOL-Time Warner, would become the most dominant media company in the world, said an analyst. No other company had its powerful mix of online, cable, film, music and publishing assets. With the broadband, this combination of content and delivery channels would give AOL-Time Warner a massive competitive advantage over its rival media or Internet companies. The 12.6 million cable customers of Time Warner and AOL's even larger Internet customer base of over 26 million provided great opportunities for cross-selling products and services. Further, the merger also gave AOL-Time Warner the cross-platform marketing clout to sell advertising space in a variety of media. For the cable industry, the merger raised the possibility that it would become an enhanced delivery system, capable of interactive commerce, streaming video and music downloads on demand.

Source: Based on 'One house, many windows', *The Economist,* 19 August 2000; 'AOL/Time Warner sparks speculation on the future of media', *Mergers and Acquisitions*, March 2000; 'Making a package', *Financial Times* Creative Business, 5 February 2002

Challenges of industry-blurring mergers

While the value creation logic of these mergers rests on revenue enhancement through access to new markets and the opportunity to cross-sell each industry's products through the distribution channels of the other, realization of these putative benefits is by no means assured. While to some customers of the financial supermarkets their offerings may provide the convenience of one-stop shopping, other customers may find such shopping too restrictive of their choice. The bundling of banking, mortgage and insurance products may also evoke consumer suspicions of overpricing. Bundling services, such as investment analysis, and corporate finance services, such as underwriting IPOs and advising on M & A, has raised disturbing ethical issues in the wake of the collapse of Enron, Worldcom and other high flyers of the 1990s and the scandals involving leading investment banks. The financial supermarket model upon which corporations such as the Citigroup have been built therefore has come under much critical scrutiny (see discussion of Travelers' acquisition of Citibank above)[13]. These problems point to substantial coordination costs in financial supermarkets.

The potential for profitable revenue enhancement may also rest on over-optimistic assumptions about how fast or smoothly technologies will evolve and converge. This technology risk may be compounded by the market risk, that is, whether the market of the expected size and profitability will emerge. This expectation often assumes that consumers will be happy to pay premium prices for access to new technology-driven products. The post-acquisition performance of AOL-Time Warner is a cautionary tale of the dire consequences of ignoring the technological and market risks and the valuation risk of overestimating revenue growth and profit margins (see Exhibit 6.5).

Exhibit 6.5

Batman blockbuster bombs at the box office

Two years after the stupendous merger of AOL and Time Warner, AOL-Time Warner's (AOLTW's) stock price had fallen 70% from the time of the merger. Its rival media companies such as Viacom and Disney gained 10% in share price over the year to March 2002 whereas AOLTW fell by 30%. As Exhibit 6.4 shows, the transition to broadband was the technological underpinning of the merger in 2000. In March 2002 a successful transition seemed uncertain. AOLTW still had a tough job persuading its narrowband Internet customers to convert to higher-priced broadband services. Analysts judged that the company had to develop its broadband investment before being able to convert its existing customers. One analyst felt that broadband services would ultimately have a neutral effect on AOL's profits, as higher revenues might be offset by lower profit margins.

The poor performance of AOL evoked resentment from old Time Warner (TW) hands, who even suggested a spin-off of AOL! The cable business also came under strain. TW's minority partnership with the Newhouse family in cable business had to be renegotiated. The family controlled 2.3 million cable subscribers out of TW's 12.8 million. If the partnership ended, the subscriber base would fall by nearly 18%. AOL's Internet partnership with Bartelsmann of Germany ended with AOL paying $7bn to Bartelsmann. The financial crunch facing AOLTW meant that buying cable systems in Europe was also difficult. In April 2002, against these bleak developments, Wall Street talked about a possible spin-off of its cable systems!

AOLTW was playing out a bad script with the wrong plot. The script needed to change from 'lived happily ever thereafter' to one of severe matrimonial stress and possible break-up. This multibillion-dollar blockbuster bombed at the box office!

Source: Based on R. Waters and C. Grimes, 'A media giant finds the future less rosy', *Financial Times*, 28 March 2002; Reuters, 'AOL may spin off its cable business', reported in *The Economic Times*, India, 29 April 2002.

Outsourcing through acquisitions

Acquisition may be used as a vehicle for accessing certain capabilities in another firm although the acquirer also has some of them in-house. The need for this may arise if the in-house capabilities have become too costly to maintain, or they are not productive, in spite of the resources devoted to them. Quick time-to-market may be another driver of the search for out-of-house capabilities and resources. Research and development is one such capability often driving acquisitions. Here the acquirer may outsource all of its R & D to the target firms or retain some of it to preserve a limited capability for strategic reasons. Pharmaceutical company acquisitions of biotechnology firms (biopharma acquisitions) are examples of outsourcing through acquisitions. Exhibit 6.6 shows how weakness in a pharma company's future product pipeline drives it to a desperate search for biotech firms, and what effects the desperation-driven acquisitions have on shareholder wealth.

Exhibit 6.6

Don't despair. Relax, make an acquisition

M & A as a method for outsourcing research and development is one of the justifications for acquisition activity during the 1990s. Pharmaceutical companies began to supplement internal R & D efforts with acquisition of external technologies and address their research gaps. An acquisition can also enhance a firm's internal capability. For example, in discussing the December 2002 acquisition of Triangle Pharmaceuticals, a Gilead Sciences' spokeswoman said, 'We had a need to build our pipeline. This acquisition brings to Gilead not only a late-stage product that could launch next year, but a pipeline of other drugs in development.' In March 2002 Merck's chief executive officer lauded the company's pipeline of products, which numbered 11 potential treatments that were slated to launch over the next few years. However, as of November 2003, only two of the products had been launched. A third product was in the process of being filed for FDA approval. Two products' filings had been delayed until 2006, and six products were either cancelled or delayed indefinitely. These cancellations and failures caused Merck's pipeline to deteriorate significantly. Subsequently, in February 2004, Merck acquired Aton Pharmaceuticals Inc., a privately held biotechnology company. In describing the acquisition Merck said, 'The acquisition will enhance its [Merck's] internal research efforts to develop potential new medicines for the treatment of cancer.'

Mathew Higgins and Daniel Rodriguez examine the R & D motivation and performance of 160 pharmaceutical acquisitions from 1994 to 2001. A unique *Desperation Index* is employed to determine the current status of a firm's internal productivity and drugs pipeline. Firms experiencing serious declines in internal productivity, or which are more desperate, are more likely to engage in an outsourcing-type acquisition in an effort to replenish their research pipelines. Deteriorating R & D productivity motivates acquisition of research-intensive firms.

The authors find that the acquisitions effectively supplement acquirers' internal R & D efforts and R & D-focused alliances. They report highly significant and positive announcement period cumulative abnormal returns, on average, of 4% for the acquiring companies. These returns contrast with the zero or negative returns for acquirers in general (see Chapter 4). They are positively correlated with prior acquirer access to information about the R & D activities at target firms and a superior negotiating position. In addition, there are real measures of success. For example, 71% of the sample acquirers either maintain or improve their product pipelines or portfolios post-acquisition.

Source: M. Higgins and D. Rodriguez, 'The outsourcing of R & D through acquisitions in the pharmaceutical industry', *Journal of Financial Economics*, 80(2), 2006, 351–383. The quotes are from Smartmoney.com and *Wall Street Journal*. For details of these sources see the paper.

STUDY

Hospital, heal thyself

Michael L. Figliuolo, Paul D. Mango, and David H. McCormick

Hospitals bought up the practices of primary-care physicians to gain additional patient referrals, but instead they transformed those physicians from entrepreneurs into salaried, complacent bureaucrats. The damage can't easily be undone, but it can be mitigated in the present and avoided in the future.

Seeking a profitable and steady source of patient referrals, in the early 1990s US hospitals and hospital systems began hungrily acquiring primary-care physician practices (Exhibit 1, on the next spread).[1] By 1998, they owned roughly 10 percent of such practices, yet this strategy has done little, if anything, to increase their supply of patients. Moreover, proprietary primary-care practices have become a drain on their parent hospitals, which in 1998 lost a net average of roughly $80,000 per physician from them.[2] That adds up to more than $1 billion in losses, roughly 30 percent of the net revenue these doctors generated.

Such deals are not easily undone. But by thoughtfully applying two practical ideas from the world of marketing – segmentation and sound channel management – hospitals *can* increase the number of patients referred to them and turn this channel into a source of competitive advantage.[3]

A postmortem

Hospitals failed to improve their economic performance through the ownership of primary-care physician practices for several reasons. In the first place, most of the hospitals overestimated the ability of affiliated physicians to change their referral patterns. In a recent study of a large system-owned network of primary-care practices, for example, we found that even several years after the network had been acquired, referrals to it had actually increased by less than 10 percent. In absolute terms, fewer than half of the patients seen by the system's primary-care physicians received follow-up care from affiliated specialists or hospitals.

About 75 of 100 physicians in recently acquired primary-care practices told us that there were four main barriers to changing their referral patterns. Often, neither the doctors nor their patients were familiar with the affiliated specialists. Patients were unwilling to travel unusually long distances to see them. Payor incentives or policies sometimes encouraged

[1]Primary-care physicians are often the patient's entry point into the health-care system. They provide care for relatively straightforward diseases and injuries, encourage prevention, and refer patients to hospitals or specialists for further treatment or consultation. Specialists focus on a group of diseases (such as cancer), on a specific organ (the heart or liver, for example), or on a stage in the life cycle (childhood or old age). Most specialists are independent but affiliated with certain hospitals, where they refer the majority of their patients and perform surgical procedures.
[2]Medical Group Management Association, "Cost Survey: 1999 Report Based on 1998 Data."
[3]See Christine B. Bucklin, Stephen P. DeFalco, John R. DeVincentis, and John P. Levis III, "Are you tough enough to manage your channels?" *The McKinsey Quarterly*, 1996 Number 1, pp. 104–15.

The authors thank Martin Barkman, a McKinsey alumnus, for his contribution to this article.

David McCormick and **Michael Figliuolo** are consultants in McKinsey's Pittsburgh office, where **Paul Mango** is a principal. Copyright @ 2000 McKinsey & Company. All rights reserved.

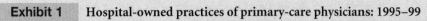

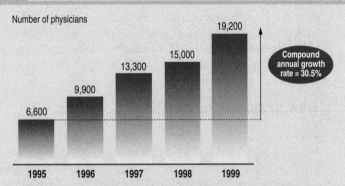

Exhibit 1   Hospital-owned practices of primary-care physicians: 1995–99

Number of physicians

6,600 — 1995
9,900 — 1996
13,300 — 1997
15,000 — 1998
19,200 — 1999

Compound annual growth rate = 30.5%

Source: Medical Group Management Association; American Medical Association

primary-care physicians to refer patients to unaffiliated hospitals and physicians. And affiliated hospitals suffered from shortages of critical technologies (such as CAT scanners) or surgical facilities, thus causing excessively long waits for patients and physicians alike.

Hospital systems **overestimated the ability** of affiliated physicians to change their referral patterns.

The second reason hospital systems could not improve their economic performance by purchasing practices of primary-care physicians was their new mode of compensation. Traditionally, primary-care physicians ran their own businesses and were paid for each patient they saw. Because every dollar they saved went straight into their own bank accounts, they had every incentive to keep their support staffs lean, to control other expenses, and to monitor billings and reimbursements closely. But hospitals encouraged primary-care physicians to join hospital systems by offering lump-sum payments over and above the value of the assets of the practices. The hospitals then put the physicians on salary. Assured of a certain income regardless of performance, the physicians' productivity declined by 15 to 20 percent in the two years after acquisition.

Finally, hospitals tended to overestimate the value of direct referrals from primary-care physicians into hospital systems – referrals that actually generate relatively little income

Exhibit 2   Primary-care physicians: A minimal contribution

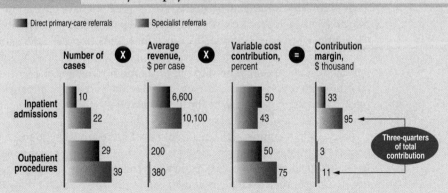

■ Direct primary-care referrals   ■ Specialist referrals

	Number of cases	X	Average revenue, $ per case	X	Variable cost contribution, percent	=	Contribution margin, $ thousand
Inpatient admissions	10 / 22		6,600 / 10,100		50 / 43		33 / 95
Outpatient procedures	29 / 39		200 / 380		50 / 75		3 / 11

Three-quarters of total contribution

(Exhibit 2). More than three-quarters of an average hospital's net income is derived from referrals by *specialists*. Specialists refer not only more patients than primary-care physicians do but also patients requiring more elaborate care – thus generating higher hospital bills and, potentially, more profit. Further enhancing the specialists' importance is the recent tendency of more informed and assertive patients to bypass primary-care physicians and go directly to specialists.

How to stanch the bleeding

Far from raising the profits of hospitals, the ownership of primary-care physician practices has clearly created an additional economic burden for them. Equally clear is the essential role specialists play in influencing the flow of patients and driving the economics of hospital systems. Moreover, it is telling that three of the four reasons primary-care physicians gave for declining to make referrals within their own hospital systems concerned their doubts about the quality, convenience, and availability of the services those systems offered patients and physicians. A successful channel management strategy must therefore acknowledge both the role of specialists and the importance of excellent service.

■ Segmentation

Good channel management begins with the segmentation of channel intermediaries, in this case primary-care physicians (independent or employed by the hospital) and specialists. Primary-care and specialist practices should be segmented according to their current and potential economic contribution to the system.

For practices owned by hospitals, the *current* contribution is the operating profit of the practice, plus any economic contribution its patient referrals (either to independent but affiliated specialists or directly to the hospital) make to the system. The current contribution of nonemployed practices excludes any consideration of their operating economics and is simply their contribution from referrals. The *potential* economic contribution of a practice is its ability to increase the number of referrals it makes to the system – an ability influenced by the local reputation of the practice, the number and quality of competing physicians and hospitals in the region, and the hospital's location, capabilities, and reputation.

Segmentation can help a hospital system devise appropriate strategies to improve the economic contribution of most practices. As Exhibit 3 shows, practices can be divided among four segments. Practices in the upper left quadrant ("grow the patient base") make a significant economic contribution to the hospital but have only a limited ability to refer more patients to it because of its distance from patients (compared with other hospitals), the number of competing practices, or constraints imposed by regional health plans. Members of a general-surgery practice in a rural area, for example, might have a hard time persuading patients of the need to bypass a local hospital for one farther away. Little can be gained from investing in efforts to increase the percentage of patients these practices refer to the parent system. What hospitals can do is help them enlarge their patient bases to increase the absolute number of referrals they make.

Practices in the upper right quadrant ("lock in referrals") also make a significant economic contribution to the affiliated hospital system but find it easier than practices in the upper left quadrant to shift their patient referral patterns. A cardiothoracic-surgery practice in a large urban area, for example, would probably fall into this category. Hospitals ought to manage such practices with a view to "locking in" their current referrals by

| Exhibit 3 | Approaches to segmentation |

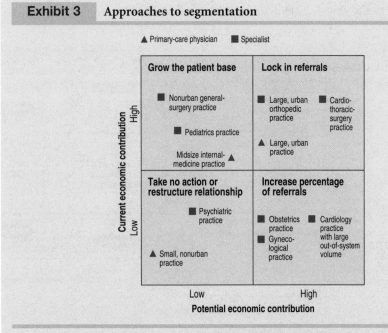

▲ Primary-care physician   ■ Specialist

Current economic contribution (High / Low) vs Potential economic contribution (Low / High)

Grow the patient base
- ■ Nonurban general-surgery practice
- ■ Pediatrics practice
- Midsize internal-medicine practice ▲

Lock in referrals
- ■ Large, urban orthopedic practice
- ■ Cardio-thoracic-surgery practice
- ▲ Large, urban practice

Take no action or restructure relationship
- ■ Psychiatric practice
- ▲ Small, nonurban practice

Increase percentage of referrals
- ■ Obstetrics practice
- ■ Gyneco-logical practice
- ■ Cardiology practice with large out-of-system volume

creating barriers that make it harder for them to shift their patients to alternative hospitals. A secondary objective should be to help the practices enlarge their referral bases.

Practices in the lower right quadrant ("increase percentage of referrals") make only a small current economic contribution to the system but have the ability to shift their patient referral patterns. Before locking in their referrals or helping such practices enlarge their patient bases, a hospital should take measures to increase the percentage of patients they refer to the hospital.

As for practices in the lower left quadrant ("take no action or restructure relation-ship"), they not only make a minimal contribution to the system but also have a limited ability to redirect the flow of patients – for the same reasons that make it hard for prac-tices in the top left quadrant to do so. Examples might include small, rural primary-care practices. If these practices are independent, a hospital need take no action, since they are not an economic burden. If the hospital owns them, it should change the relationship to improve the economics, perhaps by selling them or altering the way they are compensated.

Many primary-care practices fall in the lower left quadrant of the matrix. Most special-ist practices fall in the quadrants on the right side.

■ Four levers

McKinsey's channel management work across a multitude of industries has identified four key levers for enhancing performance: developing business skills, supporting infra-structure, improving coordination among channel players, and devising incentives. Applying these levers to the appropriate segments can help create an environment where practices are more successful and increase their contribution to the system (Exhibit 4).

Skills Practices can grow by developing better basic marketing and business skills, which even the most productive physicians and practices often have little time to improve. These skills are most valuable to practices in the top quadrants of the matrix.

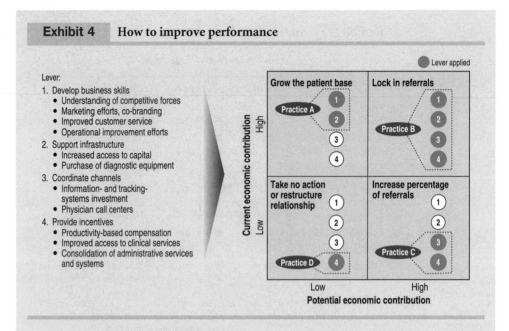

Exhibit 4   How to improve performance

Hospital systems can help practices grow and become more productive by improving their skills in four areas: strategy, marketing, services, and operations. Strategy might, for instance, encompass the ability to understand the potential of the local market, the competitive forces at work there, and the way patients choose physicians. Marketing efforts could include co-branding practices with their affiliated hospitals or devising advertisements to recruit physicians. Service development might involve efforts to identify new offerings, such as telemedicine or extended hours for the convenience of working patients. Operational skills include claims management, purchasing, and the automation of the physicians' key back-office processes.

Hospitals can help practices grow and become more productive by **raising their skills** in operations, marketing, services, and strategy.

Infrastructure   Practices of physicians are usually small businesses with little access to significant capital for investments. If hospitals could help practices buy imaging or diagnostic equipment, acquire office space, or establish nearby testing facilities, those practices could attract more patients. Spending on infrastructure would therefore not only help practices in the upper two quadrants increase their market share but also lock in referrals from practices in the top-right quadrant by creating switching costs for physicians.

Coordination   Better coordination is a useful lever for all physician practices but particularly for those in the two right quadrants of the matrix. Since referrals to specialists can slow to a trickle if the specialists don't continually update the referring physicians on the status of patients, hospitals should develop information systems to track and report their patients' progress throughout the entire care process. They can also improve coordination between specialists and primary-care physicians by, for example, investing in systems to inform primary-care physicians about the capabilities of affiliated specialists and in call centers to help primary-care physicians choose the right one.

Incentives   Particularly in the case of practices in the two right quadrants of the matrix, incentives are an important lever for maintaining and increasing the number of patients they refer to a hospital. Although federal regulations rightly prohibit hospital systems from paying practices for referrals, other kinds of incentives are allowed. Three in particular deserve mention.

First, our work with hundreds of physicians has impressed upon us the importance they place on the accessibility, efficiency, and quality of hospital services such as admitting, hotel services, and operating rooms, as well as clinical support services, including laboratories, imaging, and pharmacies. This suggests that enhanced customer service – both for patients and physicians – will not only maintain current referral levels but also raise them.

Second, whenever possible, hospitals should link the compensation of physicians to their productivity. For employed physicians, this would mean measuring the outcomes and efficiency of the care their patients receive. For independent physicians, it might mean forming partnerships – perhaps through jointly owned clinics or surgery centers – that would give them an incentive to maximize their own economic performance.

Third, to make it harder for practices to shift their referrals elsewhere, hospitals should, for example, consolidate purchasing for practices, handle their back-office work, and integrate their information systems.

The damage already wrought by the ill-advised acquisition and subsequent mismanagement of primary-care practices can't be undone, but it can be mitigated in the present and avoided in the future. The segmentation of physician practices – primary care and specialist alike – along the lines described here can help hospitals turn this channel into a source of competitive advantage.

Discussion questions

1 What is the economic and strategic logic of hospitals acquiring primary care practices?

2 How does such an acquisition represent vertical integration?

3 Why didn't the acquisition strategy work?

4 How can you fix the post-acquisition problems?

Source: M. L. Figliuolo, P. D. Mango and D. H. McCormick, 'Hospital, heal thyself', *McKinsey Quarterly,* **1**, 2000, 91–93. This article was originally published in *McKinsey Quarterly*, www.mckinseyquarterly.com, February 2000. Copyright © 2010 McKinsey & Company. All rights reserved. Reprinted by permission.

Overview and implications for practice

In this chapter we developed the framework for examining the value creation logic of vertical mergers that combined the successive stages of a vertical chain.

- A vertical chain links the various stages from the sourcing of raw materials and other inputs to production and delivery of output to final consumers.

- Activities in the vertical chain are divided into upstream and downstream activities. Upstream activities precede a given stage in the vertical chain, and downstream activities follow that stage.

- The vertical merger decision is contrasted with the decision to source from outside suppliers selling in a competitive market or through customized contracts with them. Thus vertical integration and sourcing from outside are akin to make-or-buy decisions.
- The benefits and costs of using competitive spot markets and those of long-term contracts with suppliers were examined. Two broad types of efficiencies were considered: technical efficiency and coordination (also called agency) efficiency.
- Technical efficiency is about production efficiency, whereas coordination efficiency is about the costs of contracting, monitoring and enforcing of contracts. Spot purchase, long-term contracts and vertical mergers have a range of technical and coordination costs and benefits.
- Vertical merger is optimal when it generates the best trade-off between the technical and coordination efficiencies compared with the buy decision. Where relative coordination costs exceed the relative technical efficiency benefits, outsourcing is preferable to vertical merger.
- We considered a more recent type of vertical integration that combines the vertical chains of firms operating in different industries. Vertical mergers of this type tend to blur industry boundaries. Examples of such mergers in recent times include those in the financial services industry, e.g. bancassurance mergers, and those in multimedia industries, e.g. mergers of Internet, cable, movie and music businesses.
- Industry-blurring mergers pose challenges that may destroy rather than create value in such mergers.
- Vertical mergers can be used to acquire capabilities such as R & D and access the resources of the target firms, e.g. drugs expected to complete clinical trials.

Review questions

7.1 Define and explain the following terms: vertical chain; vertical integration; upstream and downstream activities.

7.2 What are the alternatives to vertical integration?

7.3 What are technical and coordination efficiencies?

7.4 What is a spot market purchase, and what are the sources of technical and coordination efficiencies associated with spot market sourcing?

7.5 What are the costs and benefits of long-term contracts compared with spot market purchases?

7.6 What are the technical efficiencies of vertical integration compared with those of spot market and long-term purchase contracts?

7.7 What are the coordination efficiencies of vertical integration compared with those of spot market and long-term purchase contracts?

7.8 Comment on the empirical evidence for value creation in vertical mergers.

7.9 What is an industry-blurring merger? How does it differ from a traditional vertical merger?

7.10 What factors drive industry-blurring mergers?

7.11 What are the potential risks to firms contemplating such mergers?

7.12 What is the role of acquisitions in outsourcing key capabilities?

Further reading

J. Fan and V. Goyal, 'On the patterns and wealth effects of vertical mergers', *The Journal of Business*, **79**(2), 2006, 877–902.

M. Higgins and D. Rodriguez, 'The outsourcing of R & D through acquisitions in the pharmaceutical industry', *Journal of Financial Economics*, **80**, 2006, 351–383.

Notes and references

1. R. Coase pioneered the transactions cost analysis of market exchange in his paper 'The nature of the firm', *Econometrica*, **4**, 1937, 386–405. Oliver Williamson made subsequent and seminal contributions through his books *Markets and Hierarchies: Analysis and Antitrust Implications* (New York: Free Press, 1975) and *The Economic Institutions of Capitalism* (New York: Free Press, 1985).

2. O. Williamson, *ibid.*, 1975.

3. J. Womack, D. Jones and D. Roos, *The Machine that Changed the World: The Story of Lean Production* (New York: HarperCollins, 1990), p. 143.

4. T. Lester, 'Making it safe to rely on a single partner' *Financial Times*, 1 April 2002.

5. J. A. Brickley, C. W. Smith Jr and J. L. Zimmerman, *Managerial Economics and Organizational Architecture* (New York: McGraw-Hill, 2001), Chapter 17; C. Drury, *Management and Cost Accounting* (London: International Thomson Business Press, 1996), Chapters 21, 26 and 27.

6. R. S. Pindyck and D. L. Rubinfeld, *Microeconomics* (Upper Saddle River, NJ: Prentice Hall International, 2001), Chapter 17.

7. D. A. Hay and D. J. Morris, *Industrial Economics and Organization* (Oxford: Oxford University Press, 1991), Chapters 10.4 and 17.5.

8. D. Besanko, D. Dranove and M. Shanley, *Economics of Strategy* (New York: John Wiley & Sons, 2000), Chapter 5.

9. See J. Fan and V. Goyal, 'On the patterns and wealth effects of vertical mergers', *The Journal of Business*, **79**(2), 2006, 877–902. The vertical relatedness index is based on the value of the inputs provided by an industry as a proportion of the user industry output value for the industries from which the merging firms are drawn. It is calculated for flow of input from either firm, and the higher value of the index is taken. A 1% (5%) cutoff means this index is at least 1% (5%). The cumulative abnormal returns are weighted for the market capitalization of the bidder and target, and are based on the market model (see Chapter 4 on this methodology).

10. M & A Roundtable, 'Financial services acquisitions after the demise of Glass-Steagall, *Mergers and Acquisitions*, April 2000, 22–29.

11. A. Gart, 'The long reach of banking's acquisition wave', *Mergers and Acquisitions*, May/June 1998, 25–35.

12. M. J. Wolf, 'Media mergers: The wave rolls on', *McKinsey Quarterly*, **2**, 2002, Web exclusive.

13. G. Silverman, 'Simple virtues', *Financial Times*, 26 July 2002.

CHAPTER 7

Sources and limits of value creation in conglomerate acquisitions

Objectives

At the end of this chapter, the reader should be able to understand:

- the historical pattern of conglomerate business organization;
- the arguments for and against that organization form;
- their record in creating or destroying value for shareholders;
- the limitations of the conglomerates and;
- the conditions under which they may be able to deliver value.

Introduction

In the discussion of the merger waves in the US in Chapter 2 we identified the 1960s wave as a conglomerate wave and the 1980s wave as a partial reversal of that move towards conglomeration. In the words of Shleifer and Vishny[1] this pattern represents a 'round trip' to conglomeration. In the 1980s and the 1990s conglomerates fell into disrepute, and were often held up as an example of corporate managerial excess using the firm's free cash flows and leading to value destruction. In Chapter 4 we indicated that conglomerate firms suffer from 'conglomerate discount' in stock markets, reflecting the markets' judgement that these firms may generate higher shareholder value as stand-alone single business entities.

Despite this evidence, it is perhaps premature to write the obituary of conglomerate firms. For one thing, even in countries such as the US and the UK that have taken 'de-conglomeration' or 'return to focus' as wholesome and compelling corporate doctrines, large firms are still diversified. In continental Europe well-diversified firms still hold sway and account for a large part of national output and corporate value. In large parts of Asia large enterprises are controlled by families and within a conglomerate organization structure. This pattern may arguably be a lingering and fast-disappearing legacy from the age of corporate dinosaurs. Alternatively, diversified organizations may still perform a useful economic function in the allocation of resources to various business activities.

In this chapter we first examine the incidence of such firms, and then set out the conceptual arguments for and against conglomerate firms. These encompass their role as internal capital markets, in risk reduction, and in providing an alternative way of diversification for investors without relying on the stock market. We also consider conglomerate acquisition as a search for real options. We present empirical evidence for the success or failure of these firms in terms of both shareholder value creation and operating performance efficiencies. We highlight the obstacles to value creation in the conglomerate structure.

Pattern of conglomeration in different countries

Conglomeration represents one extreme of a continuum from a single-business firm, through a firm operating related businesses to exploit scope economies, to a firm that operates in a number of unrelated businesses with not a great deal in common by way of production technology, markets, etc. This continuum is shown in Figure 7.1. Between the single-business firm and the related diversified firm there may be another category where firms, although diversified to a small extent, still have a dominant business (see below).

Diversification is generally measured in terms of the number of industries in which a firm is operating: the larger this number, the more diversified the firm is. This measurement process depends on the industrial classification system by which industries are grouped. The classification is done at different levels of aggregation, with each level assigned a number. The lowest level of aggregation is often coded with a four-digit number, and at this level of grouping firms have the narrowest spread of businesses. They are almost single-business units. As we progress up the hierarchy of aggregation, through three-digit, two-digit and one-digit coded groupings, we find firms that are multi-business entities. But these multiple businesses may share certain inputs, such as technology, production process or raw materials, e.g. garments, textiles, clothing firms, but the degree of overlap among the businesses declines at lower digits. The lowest-digit level represents the most diversified business groups and the highest-digit level the least. This approach to industrial classification is followed in many countries, and is known as the standard industrial classification (SIC)[2].

Diversification pattern in the US

While many researchers have relied on the SIC system to identify single-business and diversified business firms, others have developed more refined typologies to take account of the nature of the overlap among the businesses[3]. Rumelt used the following scheme, which is meaningful albeit arbitrary, to study the changes in the diversification strategies of the Fortune 500 companies in the US during 1949–74[4]:

- single-business companies (95% or more of their sales in their main business);
- vertically integrated companies (70% or more of their sales in vertically related businesses; see Chapter 7 on vertical integration);
- dominant business companies (70–95% of their sales in their main business);

Figure 7.1   **Degrees of diversification**

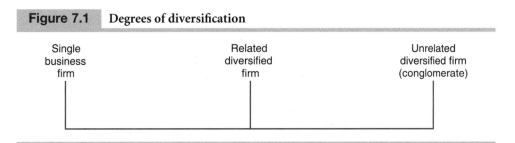

| Single business firm | Related diversified firm | Unrelated diversified firm (conglomerate) |

Table 7.1 Diversification in the top 500 US public companies (% of 500 firms)

Number of SIC industries firm is in	Number of four-digit SIC codes		
	1985	*1989*	*1992*
1	12	12	12
3 or less	23	23	22
More than 5	68	69	70
More than 10	42	44	44
Average	11	11	11

- related business companies (more than 70% of their sales in related businesses);
- unrelated business companies (less than 70% of sales in related businesses).

While single-business firms declined as a proportion of the 500 firms from 42% in 1949 to 14% in 1974, related business companies increased from 26% to 42% and unrelated business companies increased from 4% to 21% between the same years. In the last category the change accelerated from 9% in 1964 to 21% in 1974, reflecting the conglomerate merger wave of the 1960s. Henri Servaes also confirmed this trend in his study of the valuation of conglomerates during 1961–76[5].

Unrelated diversification did not peak after the 1960s wave. Even after the round trip of the 1980s wave, US firms were still well diversified in 1992, as shown in Table 7.1[6]. On average, the top 500 US public companies were involved in 11 four-digit industries. In 1992 this sample accounted for $3.2 trillion worth of goods and services, or approximately 75% of the output of all US public companies. The proportion of the sample firms operating in more than 10 industries was 44%, and that of firms in at least five industries was 70%. As Montgomery remarks, 'While the popular press and some researchers have highlighted recent divestiture activity among these firms, claiming a "return to the core", some changes at the margin must not obscure the fact that these firms are remarkably diversified'[7]. This analysis based on four-digit grouping does not, however, tell us the nature of diversification, i.e. related or unrelated. That nearly half of the sample firms had sales in more than 10 industries suggests significant unrelated diversification.

In two recent studies of the productivity and investment performance of US conglomerate firms, Maksimovic and Philips report that multi-segment firms (each segment equating to a three-digit industry), during 1972–87, account for between 63% and 69% of industrial output[8]. Further, the proportion of the output of single segment and multiple segment firms is as follows:

	Single segment firms	Multi-segment firms	
		Main segments	*Peripheral segments*
Beginning of 1980	22%	51%	28%
Beginning of 1990	27%	50%	24%

Main segments are those that represent at least 25% of the firm's total output. If we reasonably assume that peripheral segments represent unrelated businesses and main segments represent related businesses, these data suggest that, while unrelated diversification declined, related diversification is a significant phenomenon. In Schoar's study of the period 1977–95 in the US, highly diversified firms operating in about eight two-digit industries produced shipments of $4429bn (44%) and moderately diversified firms operating in about 2.9 such industries, $4650bn

Table 7.2 Diversification in large European companies, 1950–93 (% of sample)

Country	1950	1960	1970	1980	1993
France					
Single business	45	35	20	24	20
Dominant business	18	22	27	11	15
Related business	31	38	41	53	52
Unrelated business	5	5	9	12	14
Germany					
Single business	37	27	27	18	13
Dominant business	22	24	15	17	8
Related business	31	38	38	40	48
Unrelated business	9	11	19	25	32
UK					
Single business	24	18	6	7	5
Dominant business	50	36	32	16	10
Related business	27	48	57	67	62
Unrelated business			6	11	24

Figures do not add up to 100% owing to rounding.

(47%), whereas single-industry firms produced shipments of just $914bn (9%). Thus diversified US firms produced nearly 90%[9] and are a strong feature of the US corporate economy.

Diversification pattern in Europe

Table 7.2 shows the extent of related and unrelated diversification in the three largest European countries – France, Germany and the UK – over 1950–93[10]. In all the three countries related and unrelated diversification has increased at the expense of single and dominant business firms. Related business firms accounted for 48–62% of the sample firms and unrelated business groups accounted for 14–32%. The latter exhibited faster growth than the former over the period. You will recall from Chapter 2 that divestitures happened on a large scale in the UK during the 1980s wave, but this does not appear to have reduced the attractiveness of unrelated diversification, which increased from 11% in 1980 to 24% in 1993. Since divestitures were relatively more modest in the other two countries it is perhaps reasonable to conclude that diversifying acquisitions were still a preferred growth strategy for firms in France and Germany.

Recent trend in related and unrelated acquisitions

Andrade, Mitchell and Stafford, in their review of the 1973 to 1998 merger activity in the US, show how related mergers have increased (sample size 4256)[11]:

	1970s	1980s	1990s	1974–98
Own-industry acquisitions	30%	40%	48%	42%
Diversifying	70%	60%	52%	58%

The industry definition is based on the SIC two-digit code. Given that this is a very broad industry grouping, the diversifying mergers may be regarded as unrelated and the own-industry mergers as including horizontal, vertical and related mergers. Unrelated diversifying mergers, albeit declining in the three decades, still account for over 50% of American mergers. Sudarsanam and Huang report for a more recent US sample of 2527 majority share acquisitions during 1993–2004 that 64% of the sample are related acquisitions i.e. in the same two-digit SIC industry[12]. This continues the trend towards more related mergers observed by Andrade *et al.*, but nevertheless leaves a substantial 36% of merger as unrelated diversifying. This picture of some decline in unrelated acquisitions and an increase in related acquisitions is consistent with the results from Maksimovic and Philips discussed earlier.

For Europe, in a large sample of 2419 takeover announcements in Europe during 1993–2001, Martynova and Renneboog report that 36% are unrelated and 64% are related takeover bids. Industry is defined at the two-digit level[13]. It must be remembered that this analysis of the recent trend is in terms of number of acquisitions and not the value of acquisitions, which is likely to indicate an even larger share for unrelated acquirers. So, by Darwinian logic, what survives serves some economic or other purposes. In the next few sections we assess the rationale for diversified firms and for diversifying acquisitions.

Overview of diversification patterns in the US and Europe

It is clear that diversification has increased substantially over time in both regions. Most of this diversification has taken the form of related diversification, but a substantial part of it, say 15–20%, has been unrelated. It is a reasonable conclusion that at least large firms, and more so in Europe than in the US, are still substantially diversified. It is also reasonable to conclude that unrelated diversification is still a major characteristic of many large American and European firms. In the next section we set out the conceptual framework for examining the merits and demerits of diversification, before evaluating whether empirical evidence confirms the anticipated benefits.

Why do firms diversify?

Diversification may be explained in terms of the different merger perspectives that we set out in Chapter 3. These are the economic, the strategy-based, managerial, finance theoretic and organizational perspectives. In Chapter 5 we present the model of value creation in horizontally related mergers that represent related diversification (see Table 5.1 for a summary and the accompanying discussion in that chapter). In this chapter we develop a similar framework for assessing the value creation potential of acquisitions of unrelated businesses. As in Chapter 5, we adopt the multiple perspectives in identifying the sources of value.

Economic perspective on unrelated diversification

Conglomerate or unrelated diversification may create value as a result of

● increased market power; or
● operating an efficient internal capital market.

Market power is the ability of a firm in a market to pursue anticompetitive behaviour against its current rivals or potential entrants. This power does not derive from the monopoly position in that market but by virtue of the range of its activities and the size of the firm. We develop the arguments based on these sources of market power for conglomerates below.

A conglomerate firm, by definition, allocates investment funds to a number of individual businesses. If these businesses were independent, they would be receiving such funds directly from the capital markets – banks or equity markets. The conglomerate firm thus performs a capital market function. Where it performs this function more efficiently than the external capital market, it can create value. We examine below the conditions under which this internal capital market functions efficiently.

Conglomerates and market power

Economists have identified three ways in which conglomerates may wield power in an anti-competitive manner:

- cross-subsidizing;
- mutual forbearance; and
- reciprocal buying.

A conglomerate firm can follow a predatory, initially loss-making, pricing policy in a product market in which one of its divisions is competing, and finance this strategy with the profits it generates in its other markets. This type of cross-subsidy, of course, requires 'deep pockets', which may be provided by the size and range of activities of a conglomerate. A single-business firm competing in only that market will then be at a disadvantage. Once the firm sees off such a competitor and consolidates its market power, it can shift to more monopolistic pricing, recover the initial losses, and replenish its reserves before trying this strategy elsewhere.

Where competitors meet in several markets, and their relative competitive positions in some markets are mirror images of their positions in others, they may recognize their mutual dependence and adopt a policy of *live and let live*. A single-business competitor will not enjoy such forbearance and may be driven out. The remaining competitors bound by the *live and let live* code will then compete less vigorously among themselves. From mutual forbearance conglomerates may move to mutual support through reciprocal buying and selling among themselves in different markets. One conglomerate buys from another through one division but sells to the other through another division. In both markets other suppliers will be kept out. Greater diversification into a number of markets increases the opportunity for reciprocity. The existential code is rewritten from *live and let live* to *let us live together and bash the smaller guys*.

Constraints on conglomerates' market power

A number of factors may limit the extent and the benefits of market power potentially enjoyed by conglomerates. To wield power across markets a firm must first have some strength in its individual markets, otherwise the threat of deep pockets is not realistic. Similarly, for mutual forbearance, different conglomerates must have comparable strengths in their overlapping markets; otherwise any threat to breach the *live and let live* code is not realistic. It is a bluff that will be quickly called. Finally, size disparity between conglomerates in the individual markets in which they rub shoulders renders reciprocal buying and selling infeasible. Montgomery argues that market power may be incidental to the conglomerate diversification strategy rather than its primary driver[14]. Nevertheless, such power may allow the conglomerate to increase its profits and enhance shareholder value.

Empirical evidence on market power of conglomerates

There is very little empirical evidence of an association between diversification and the anti-competitive behaviour of conglomerates along the lines suggested above. Predatory pricing is seldom employed, and with mixed results. Predatory pricing may also be available for both narrowly diversified firms and conglomerates. Thus conglomerate acquisition confers no special advantage. Empirical evidence on reciprocal buying is also mixed at best. Thus, overall, there is not much support for the market power proposition[15]. We discuss the antitrust concerns with conglomerate mergers in more detail in Chapter 17.

Conglomerates as internal capital markets: financial synergy

In complete markets, where information is freely available and transaction costs are low, businesses should be able to raise whatever capital they need for projects that will yield the return the investors expect. For conglomerate firms to take over this capital allocation function:

● there must be capital market failure in some sense; and
● the internal market must have certain advantages over the external market.

In many countries, capital markets may not be well developed. The infrastructure of services such as banking, stock broking, accounting and legal services may be weak. The available statutory framework may not clearly define property rights of investors and promoters of businesses, and the judicial system for enforcement of these rights may lack credibility, increasing the reluctance of such investors to finance some businesses. Capital markets may be more risk averse or too short-termist in their expectation of rewards from the investment. They may be reluctant to provide capital to financially weak firms that nevertheless can be turned around. Under these market failure scenarios, capital allocation may have to be carried out internally by a firm[16].

An internal capital market may also have the advantage of better and easier access to information relevant to assessing the prospects of a component business that may be withheld from the capital market for proprietary or competition reasons. Ongoing internal monitoring of the investments already made, for the same reason, may be more rigorous and less costly than external market monitoring. The internal capital market may also be able to take a longer-term view of the attractiveness of a project[17]. Thus, in combination, these external market deficiencies and internal market strengths may allow a more efficient capital allocation of risk capital and reduce the cost of capital to the component businesses of a conglomerate. These relative advantages of conglomerates allow them to *pick winners* more cost-effectively than the external capital market.

What about the downside of the internal capital market?

The internal market is subject to tension on several fronts. The capital allocation process is subject to internal organizational politics, and may be distorted. Thus allocation is not always on the merits of an investment proposal but influenced by the more powerful barons within the corporate power structure. The head office may *pick favourites* rather than *pick winners*. Such misdirection of investment funds into relatively low-value projects when high-value projects are available to the firm leads to value diminution of the conglomerate as a whole. This value diminution represents the influence costs.

The strategic and selective use or provision of information may dilute even the information processing and monitoring efficiency of the conglomerate firm by the component divisions. The control hierarchy to administer the conglomerate requires two-way information flow through divisions, subsidiaries, the head office and the top management. It requires both vertical and lateral communication. Such information flow may not always be smooth or efficient unless the system creates incentives for transparency, integrity and speed in transmitting information. Where the hierarchy is complex because of the multitude of businesses within the conglomerate, or where the incentives are misaligned to corporate objectives, information flow will be impeded or manipulated to suit managers at different levels rather than the corporation as a whole. This control loss is a cost associated with the size and diversity of the conglomerate firm.

The assumption that the top management acts as an effective gatekeeper and a good monitor of investment decisions made by components businesses raises the question '*Who monitors the monitors?*' This issue concerns the corporate governance mechanisms available within the firm, the external governance mechanisms such as shareholder activism, and the interaction between internal and external governance devices (see Chapter 3 on the corporate governance aspects of the finance theory perspective). Michael Jensen's free cash flow model suggests that top managers derive private control benefits such as perks and empire building from running a corporation, and finance their extravagant fads and fancies with the free cash flow generated by their firms. This problem is perhaps more serious in conglomerates than in more focused firms because of the greater diversity and complexity of the former and the lack of internal benchmarks to evaluate the firm's investment decisions. These control loss problems associated with the conglomerate structure reduce the relative attractiveness of the internal capital market relative to the external.

Relative transaction costs of internal and external capital markets

The optimal choice between these two channels of capital allocation therefore depends on the relative transaction costs. From our discussion we can infer that these transaction costs depend on whether:

● the external capital market is complete in catering for small and more risky businesses;
● information about these businesses is available to the capital market; and
● incentives exist within hierarchical organizations to reduce the strategic and opportunistic use of information and attain efficient monitoring and allocation of investment to component divisions.

Further, the relative transaction cost advantages shift over time as capital markets become more complete, the associated infrastructure gets more sophisticated, and new and powerful information system capabilities emerge. Similarly, strengthened corporate governance regimes including activist shareholders help the internal capital market to be more efficient. Thus the round trip from the conglomerate merger obsession of the 1960s to the 'return to focus' passion of the 1980s and 1990s perhaps betrays no irrationality on the part of managers and investors in either period, but is a rational response to the shift in relative transactional cost dynamics.[18]

Resource-based view of conglomerate acquisition

We develop the resource-based view as part of our discussion of the strategic perspective of acquisitions in Chapter 3. In that perspective, firms undertake acquisitions to fill the gap between their current endowment of resources and capabilities and their desired competitive profile. Conglomerate acquisition may be driven by the same imperative. It may also be driven by the need for growth, and to exploit the excess capacity the firm has in certain resources or productive factors[19]. The firm may have exhausted profitable growth opportunities in its primary industry and have to look for pastures new[20]. The idle resources should therefore be redeployed to more productive and profitable uses. This line of argument presupposes one or more of the following characteristics of the resources:

- they are indivisible, and cannot be parcelled out and sold;
- there is no external market for excess resources, or they cannot be valued fairly for sale (*market failure*);
- they are easily put to uses other than those they were historically developed for (no *path dependence* problem);
- they can be easily mixed with the resources of the acquired firm to induce the value-creating chemistry (resources are *fungible*); and
- transfer of these resources is not subject to the *law of conservation*, i.e. value increase in the new use is at the expense of value reduction in the old use, but to the *law of synergy*, i.e. value in new use increases without eroding the value in the old use[21].

Types of resources that can be transferred

In Chapter 5 we identify the types of resources that satisfy the above criteria in the context of related horizontal mergers. In the case of conglomerate acquisitions, only some of the resources fit the bill. The internal capital market role under the economic perspective means that financial resources will be transferred from the acquirer firm to the acquired. This supposes either plenty of free cash flow in the acquirer or the ability to raise new capital externally more cheaply than the acquired company. Other physical resources such as plant and machinery need not be transferred.

Among the intangibles, resources such as brand name, reputation and goodwill may be exploited to enhance the value of the acquired company. The acquirer may redeploy some of the human resources and capabilities, such as top management, generic marketing and other functional management skills. The acquirer can also redeploy human resource management capabilities, such as techniques and incentives to motivate the acquired firm's workforce and managers.

Since firms are heterogeneous in their resource configuration, and in the intensity of their resource endowment, the excess capacity will also be heterogeneously distributed. For some firms this excess will be exhausted with a small number of unrelated acquisitions, whereas for others the optimal level will be higher. Such resource transfers and sharing are subject to the critical test – that the target firm cannot access these resources more cheaply elsewhere, i.e. organic development or in the relevant factor markets. Obviously, intangible assets such as brand name or reputation are not easily developed or purchased. Where the critical test fails, the conglomerate acquisition is more likely to destroy than create value.

Constraints on resource transfer in conglomerate acquisitions

In our discussion of related horizontal and consolidating mergers in Chapters 5 and 6 we highlight the obstacles to effective and efficient resource transfer and sharing between the acquirer and the acquired firms. These obstacles may be of a different order of magnitude with conglomerate acquisitions. A narrower range of physical and intangible resources may be shared in conglomerate acquisitions. This perhaps simplifies the sharing process. The greater the degree of familiarity the acquirer is likely to have with the acquired firm's products, markets, technology, the more growth opportunities in horizontal and consolidating mergers will ease the sharing process, but this familiarity is less likely with a conglomerate acquirer.

Corporate branding may be a source of value if the acquired company's products can, post-merger, be sold under the acquirer's superior corporate brand name. However, whether corporate or common branding will create value depends on the product characteristics and the consumer markets each company's products are sold to. Where the acquired company products are mass-market products whereas the acquirer's brands are upmarket, corporate branding may not work, and may end up damaging the acquirer's corporate brand. Thus corporate branding may be a high-risk exercise without adequate return. The risks exist even when the two companies sell similar products, such as cosmetics or hotel rooms, if they cater for different market segments or clientele. Where products are unrelated, as in a conglomerate merger, these risks may be considerably higher[22]. A careful risk and return analysis is therefore necessary.

Much of the value in conglomerate acquisitions may therefore come from, apart from the purely internal market role, the transfer of the superior management resources referred to above. Some companies may have developed strong parenting capabilities as a distinctive competence[23]. While these may be effectively redeployed to manage a portfolio of hetero-geneous businesses, they may soon be stretched beyond the optimal range of complexity. It would be facile to assume a capacity for infinite variety and elasticity. The law of diminishing returns may then set in. A careful inventory needs to be made of the acquirer's resources and the extent to which they are surplus.

Firms with a conglomerate acquisition strategy must have firm-specific organizational capabilities that can be deployed in different industries. However, these may not be equally valuable in every foray into a new industry. Firms may have to experiment to find out whether their organizational abilities have value in a specific industry. Such experimentation may generate long-term value after several experiments, but may also inflict short-term costs, since many of the experiments may fail[24]. Such experiments are in the nature of real options on future growth opportunities, which allow a firm to redeploy its resources and capabilities in related or unrelated diversification (see Chapter 3 on real options)[25]. Exhibit 7.1 on page 190 shows how the US company Corning Glass and the Italian conglomerate CIR took bets on emerging new businesses to diversify their business portfolio successfully.

Finance theory of conglomerate diversification

Pure financial rationale: cost-effective diversification

Corporate diversification may be a substitute for portfolio diversification across stocks of different companies by stock market investors. For example, instead of spreading investments in companies operating in 10 different businesses, an investor can buy the stock in a single conglomerate operating in the same businesses. In this case the assumption is that the con-glomerate is a replica of the stock portfolio, and the conglomeration, by itself, adds no extra value. This of course is not consistent with the economic or the strategy perspectives, which suggest that the conglomerate form can create value by exploiting market power, lowering capital-raising costs, and transferring organizational resources and capabilities. This added value should also exceed the cost of assembling the conglomerate firm. It must therefore add value net of this cost. Thus the rationale for a conglomerate is not as a mere replica of a stock portfolio but as a mechanism for exploiting synergies and market positioning in component markets.

The view that a conglomerate is a surrogate for a stock portfolio suggests that investing in the stock portfolio is more costly than assembling the conglomerate. Transaction costs in well-developed stock markets may probably be a small fraction of the costs of putting the 'conglomerate' together. In this case corporate diversification is a costly way of replicating the investor's stock portfolio. In some instances, though, this may not be true. Where some

Exhibit 7.1

Diversification driven by exploiting core competence

The American firm, Corning Glass, diversified to achieve growth through continual redeployment of a firm's resources and capabilities. Since starting in 1851, it has been a technology leader in a number of key areas – light bulbs, fibre optics, television screens, etc. Corning took bets on successful entry into new markets by extending its core competence in materials engineering. Such bets on new technology involved much experimentation with attendant risk of failure. In 2000, it was a world leader in optical fibres for telecommunications. In 2005 Corning produced about 60% of the glass required for liquid crystal display (LCD), far ahead of its closest rival. The glass making technology did not appear overnight; it was based on a process devised 40 years earlier for producing car windscreens – a product that Corning subsequently dropped.

Mr Wednell Weeks, CEO of Corning, explained the evolution: 'We spent 14 years working on LCD glass without making any money out of it. . . . There is a degree of technology risk about most things we do. At any one time we are examining a series of new ideas but we know that probably half of them won't work.' Over the years Corning had used its skills in glass chemistry and ceramics to develop products including cookware and laboratory instrumentation as well as TV screens and catalytic converters.

This case illustrates that although a snapshot of a company's business portfolio would suggest a diversified portfolio, it may conceal the dynamics of the change in that portfolio over time, driven by the firm's continual search for avenues to extend its core competencies to new processes, products and, hence, new markets.

Growth through unrelated diversification by an Italian conglomerate

Conglomerates in Italy have shown considerable staying power while they have attracted much odium elsewhere. In Italy, there was little stigma against good managers showing their skills in a variety of areas. CIR operated three businesses with sales of more than €1bn: Energia, the utility company, Espresso, the publisher of La Repubblica, and Sogefi, a car components manufacturer. In 2005 it added healthcare. Rodolfo De Benedetti, CIR's CEO, said it sat on the boards of its companies, appointed managers, decided their capital structure and dividend policies. But he also emphasized: 'the companies tend to be independent. Our role is in making sure that on a daily basis the management's decisions are fully consistent with the shareholder perspective of value creation.'

CIR's corporate strategy also involved starting its own operations, since the growth of private equity made value-creating acquisitions more difficult to find and expensive. Following privatization in Italy's health sector, CIR moved into healthcare. Liberalization of energy markets prompted the rise of Energia. New accounting standards and capital adequacy rules encouraged banks to sell tranches of their non-performing loans, and CIR saw this as a growth opportunity. De Benedetti stated, 'we can do half a dozen things really well and we have to go for things that can change the value of the CIR portfolio.' CIR exploited its general management, rigorous investment appraisal and corporate governance expertise in entering new businesses.

Sources: Adapted from P. Marsh, 'A careful giant behind the glass', FT.Com, 30 September 2005; A. Michaels, 'A rare breed alive and well in Italy', FT.Com, 2 November.

businesses are not listed on stock exchanges or (in some countries) the stock markets are not well developed or overseas investors are not allowed to invest, a diversified firm can provide a means of diversification into those businesses and countries. In this case conglomerate companies' stocks are likely to trade at a premium.

Pure financial rationale: risk reduction, increased debt capacity and tax benefit

Llewellyn puts forward another financial rationale for corporate conglomeration[26]. The income streams of the component businesses, by definition, are not highly correlated. For example, if one business does poorly in a recession but very well in boom time but another business is somewhat recession-proof, the combined income stream is likely to be more stable than that of each business. The portfolio effect of diversification of these income streams is to reduce the variability of the combined income stream. In general, a firm with a highly volatile income will find it more difficult to meet its commitments to pay interest on its borrowing. High volatility increases the risk of default and bankruptcy. Increasing bankruptcy risk increases the cost of borrowing as well as the cost of equity to the firm. If conglomeration reduces the volatility of income, the merged firm can meet its debt service obligations with greater certainty. Each firm now co-insures the debt of the other, thereby reducing the overall bankruptcy risk. Alternatively, if the firm wishes to maintain the same level of bankruptcy risk, it can afford to raise its borrowing: that is, its debt capacity is increased[27].

With increased borrowing, the conglomerate can reap the tax subsidy on interest payable on the borrowing, available in many tax regimes such as the US, the UK and Germany. Another form of tax benefit is the ability to offset tax losses of one business against the profits of other business within the same corporate tax group and reduce the overall tax charge. A single-business firm may have to wait to generate future profits before being able to apply the offset and recover the tax already paid. This benefit depends on the tax rules in the relevant jurisdictions (see Chapter 16 on the tax aspects of acquisitions)[28].

Agency perspective on conglomerate growth

We recall from Chapter 3 that, within the finance theory, firms make investment and financing decisions to maximize shareholder value, and agency problems may cause these decisions to deviate from that objective. The agency problems may be more severe in conglomerate firms than in firms with a relatively more homogeneous product range, because of the complexity of the firm's operations. The existing accounting reporting regimes may alleviate this information asymmetry by requiring disclosures of the operations of the different segments of the diversified firm. However, these accounting regimes differ from country to country, for example within the EU, where unrelated diversification, as observed at the beginning of this chapter, is substantial, although publicly listed companies have to switch to the International Financial Reporting Standards (IFRS) after 2005 (see Chapter 15 on Accounting for mergers and acquisitions). Second, the level of detail in segmental disclosures is restricted: for example, in the US and UK it is limited to a few income statement and balance sheet items, such as net assets, sales and profits. Segmental information is disclosed only if a segment is material, that is, has at least 10% of the group's above variables. Segmental disclosures may be tainted by strategic accounting practised by managers[29]. Thus a certain amount of opacity surrounds the conglomerate firm's true operations and performance. It is therefore more difficult for shareholders to monitor that firm than it is for them to monitor a single-business firm. As a consequence, such firms in many countries suffer from a 'conglomerate discount', being valued lower than the sum of the values of single-business firms that correspond to the component businesses. We report evidence of this discount in our review of empirical studies below. In this view the discount is the cost of lack of transparency[30].

This lack of monitoring, and the resultant conglomerate discount, may reflect the failure of both the internal and external corporate governance mechanisms that we described in Chapter 3[31]. We pursue this issue further in our discussion of the empirical studies below.

Managerial perspective on conglomerate diversification

Private control benefits

Managers may undertake conglomerate acquisitions to increase firm size for compensation and non-compensation reasons. If managerial compensation increases as the firm becomes larger, managers have the incentive to make the firm grow through acquisitions (see Chapter 4 for related empirical studies). Empire building or megalomania may also drive mergers. It is not unknown that, for some CEOs, acquisitions are ego trips (see Chapters 12 and 22, and the case study at the end of this chapter). Size may also confer private benefits, such as power, status and high public profile, and the ability to indulge their personal passions paid for by their company. Consumption of benefits outside formal compensation packages may also increase with firm size. Such incentives may influence the conglomerate acquisition decision, often with disastrous consequences for stock holders, as shown in Exhibit 7.2. The case shows how managerial ambition and weak corporate governance could lead to huge value destruction in diversifying acquisitions.

Exhibit 7.2

Glam Doll Barbie lost in conglomerate adventure

Mattel, the toy company and maker of the famous Barbie doll, announced in December 1998 that it was acquiring the Learning Company (LC). Mattel's toy business was stagnant, and the company planned to diversify into a non-toy business and leverage its brands in the toy market, such as Barbie, with a business in software, video games and the Internet. It was Mattel CEO and chairperson of the board Jill Barad's goal to achieve $1bn sales in the new business. Mattel had entered interactive software business but had sales of only $100m, and felt it could not build up a large business quickly without the merger. For Mattel, buying LC was very much a diversifying acquisition on a big scale. The acquisition would cost $3.5bn. Barad argued that the merger would provide tremendous opportunities for 'synergies, cross-branding, age expansion, consumer relevancy and channel expansion'. In terms of market share, LC was first in education and productivity software, second in reference software, and third in entertainment. Barad waxed eloquent about becoming 'the second largest consumer software company in the world, second only to Microsoft'.

By 2001, following the bursting of the Internet bubble, Mattel's earnings per share fell sharply from $1.11 in 1998 to a 29c loss in 1999 and a $1.01 loss in 2000. Its stock price fell 60% in two years from 1999. An important motive for this conglomerate acquisition was the dash for growth and the desire to run a larger and more glamourous high-tech business than a staid toy business. Apparently, Barbie wasn't glamoros enough!

The board of Mattel, which had approved of the merger with LC, was a deeply entrenched board, and was quite reluctant to fire Barad quickly. Eventually, in 2000, she was replaced by Robert Eckert, whose vision was to 'refocus' on Mattel's core business of toys. He said the company had quickly learnt that it 'did not need to own a software company to capitalize on the growth potential of the interactive games'. LC had not been a 'good fit'.

LC was sold in 2000 for no upfront consideration but only 50% share of future profits. Mattel wrote off $441m on the failed acquisition.

Source: Adapted from R. K. Aggarwal and A. A. Samwick, 'Why do managers diversify their firms? Agency reconsidered', *The Journal of Finance*, 58(1), 2003, 71–118. These authors draw upon reports that appeared in *Business Week* and other media

Pure managerial rationale: exploiting managers' firm-specific skills

Managers invest in developing their skills while working for a firm. As their association with their firm lengthens, the more firm specific these skills become. These skills may be valued less outside than in their current employer. Thus managers have an incentive to entrench themselves and increase the demand for those skills within the firm. Shleifer and Vishny argue that, in seeking to entrench themselves, managers invest beyond the value-maximizing level. Such investment often takes the form of conglomerate diversification. As firms grow and mature, profitable opportunities to invest in the same business or in related businesses become scarce, and managers tend to pursue increasingly far-flung opportunities[32].

Barney and Clark make a related, human-resource-based case for diversification[33]. They explain corporate diversification as a way for a firm to exploit its core competence to operate in multiple businesses simultaneously and to explain how it can be used to develop firm-specific human capital investments. Diversification reduces the risk faced by the firm, and this provides a reassuring environment in which employees can make their human capital investment to develop firm-specific knowledge and skills, that is, to develop the firm's core competence. Once developed, this competence needs to be deployed, thereby providing a rationale for diversification. In this scenario 'corporate diversification is both the effect of core competencies and the cause of core competencies'. Thus the decision to diversify and the decision to develop the core competence are endogenous decisions.

Pure managerial rationale: risk diversification

The risk reduction view of conglomerate diversification described above under the pure financial rationale has a managerial dimension as well. Unlike stockholders, managers hold undiversified portfolios with overwhelming concentration of investment in their employer firm. In addition to their human capital, much of their financial capital in the form of stock options or shares held in employee stock ownership plans (ESOPs) is also invested in the managers' own firm. This skewed distribution of their investments increases their risk exposure to the volatility of their firm's earnings and its bankruptcy risk. They have an incentive to reduce this exposure through risk-reducing conglomerate acquisitions, and weak agency monitoring by dispersed shareholders permits this behaviour[34]. Thus although stock options and stock ownership plans are motivated by the need to align stockholder and managerial interests, they may also provide the incentives to managers to pursue sub-optimal risk reduction strategies, possibly leading to value reduction rather than value addition[35]. Aggarwal and Samwick find empirical evidence to show that 'managers diversify their firms in response to changes in private benefits rather than to reduce risk'. Indeed, they may actually seek risk because of managerial optimism, overconfidence or hubris[36].

Conglomerate performance under the finance and managerial perspectives

While agency and pure managerial considerations lead to the prediction that conglomerate acquisitions will fail to create, and may even destroy, value, the pure financial rationale of providing an alternative to stock portfolio diversification may add value under certain conditions outlined above. Bankruptcy risk reduction may be a source of added value, leading to reduction in cost of debt and the overall cost of capital. Increased tax subsidy on debt again can add value.

Organizational perspective on conglomerate diversification

Our discussion of the control loss problem in diversified organizations, under the economic perspective above, points to the challenges in managing complex and heterogeneous organizations. The move from largely single-business organizations to diversified business organizations in the 1960s (see Rumelt's analysis above) was accompanied by new organizational innovations such as the multi-divisional (M-form) structure to manage complexity[37]. The M-form creates well-demarcated business units with significant within-unit cohesion and little between-unit overlap. The business units are given much autonomy and are monitored by the head office, which is separated from the operating divisions. The divisions are also distinct cost or profit centres, held accountable for their performance.

The M-form organizational design inspired faith in the ability of managers to manage highly diversified portfolios of operating businesses. The major tasks of the centre or head office encompassed:

- setting strategic objectives of the firm and for the divisions;
- ensuring harmony of these objectives;
- acting as an internal capital market to allocate centralized funds to highest-value use among the divisions;
- monitoring the performance of the divisions; and
- setting up incentive structures for the division managers to ensure desired performance.

This structure may, however, be dysfunctional for a variety of reasons, such as poor information systems to aid monitoring, interdivisional rivalry, or weak incentives that misalign divisional goals with the overall corporate goal of value maximization. One of the factors that may cause a dysfunctional outcome is the influence cost. Thus the political process of resource allocation within diversified firms may be as important as the seemingly rational economic process. Rajan *et al.* model this political process, the inefficiency of resource allocation process, and how it explains the widely observed 'conglomerate discount'[38]. In their model, extreme diversity in the growth opportunities of the component businesses and in their profitability may mean that the divisions scoring highly on these may see their profit surplus 'grabbed' by the centre and reallocated to divisions that score low on the criteria. This may act as a disincentive for the former to act to maximize the division's, and hence the firm's, value, causing value erosion and the conglomerate discount. Their model predicts that the discount will be larger, the greater the disparity among the divisions.

Summary of alternative perspectives

The above perspectives are summarized in Table 7.3. The implications of these arguments for the shareholder value impact of conglomerate acquisitions are indicated. Under certain conditions conglomerates can enhance shareholder wealth, although there are serious challenges to value realization.

Table 7.3 Summary of different models of value creation in conglomerate mergers

Perspective	Model focusing on	Concept	Implication for shareholder value
Economic	• Market power • Efficient internal capital market	• Through cross-subsidy, mutual forbearance and reciprocal buying • Failure of external capital market to appraise investments or risk or monitor performance increases cost of capital to single businesses; conglomerate allocates capital more efficiently	• Created in both cases
Strategy	• Resource and capabilities transfer • Core competence to manage diversified firm	• Diversifying acquirer redeploys excess of its resources and capabilities to target; resources cannot be sold but transfer cost-effectively • Managers have developed firm-specific skills to manage multi-business operations which need to be deployed • Risk reduction through diversification encourages managers to make firm-specific investment to develop its core competence	• Created
Finance theory	• Efficient diversification • Bankruptcy risk reduction • Agency cost	• Corporate diversification more efficient and cheaper than investor's stock portfolio diversification • Diversification of income and cash flow reduces volatility and default risk, and increases debt capacity and tax benefit (co-insurance benefit) • Conglomerate diversification manifests agency problem; managers waste free cash flow from current businesses for managerial reasons	• Created • Created • Reduced
Managerial	• Management entrenchment • Personal risk reduction • Private control benefits	• Managers exploit surplus firm-specific skills and make themselves indispensable • Most of managers' human and financial capital invested in their firm, so need to diversify risk • Managers want size-related benefits: monetary, i.e. large salary, and non-monetary, e.g. power and status	• Reduced • Reduced • Reduced
Organizational	• Coordination costs • Influence costs • Integration costs • M-form model	• Diversified firm costly to coordinate and monitor; scope for control loss • Allocation of capital within firm subject to political influences; hence inefficient • Resource and capability transfers across firms raises friction and risk of failure • Innovations like multidivisional organization improve efficient capital allocation	• Reduced • Reduced • Reduced • Increased

Review of empirical evidence on the value of conglomerate diversification

Researchers adopt three approaches:

- Compare the performance of already diversified firms with that of a matching portfolio of single-business firms and identify the conglomerate discount ('firm level cross-sectional' test).
- Test for significant and positive abnormal returns to acquirer shareholders following conglomerate acquisitions ('event period abnormal returns' test) (see Chapter 4 for this methodology).
- Test for evidence of inefficiency in investment decisions made by conglomerate segments compared with single-business firms.

The third is a test of whether segments with poor investment opportunities over-invest and those with good investment opportunities under-invest because of inefficient cross-subsidizing by the conglomerate head office. This procedure does not measure conglomerate discount, but may explain it. A separate stream of research has addressed the effect of diversification's mirror image, i.e. de-conglomeration or increase in business focus. This is achieved through divestiture or spin-off of what are regarded as non-core businesses. The results from this research generally indicate that stock market reaction to focus-increasing asset sales and spinoffs is positive, suggesting that they eliminate some of the conglomeration discount suffered by the parent firms undertaking these transactions. We review this research in more detail in Chapter 10.

The cross-sectional test and conglomerate discount

The basic methodology of this test is as follows.

1 For each conglomerate firm in the sample studied identify the segments in which it operates, and for each segment identify a group of firms in the same industry but non-diversified (also called single segment or focused).
2 Find the median or mean value multiplier, i.e. market value to assets or sales or operating profit, and use the multiplier of the group as the benchmark to calculate the value of each segment of the conglomerate (the 'imputed value').
3 Add up the imputed values of the conglomerate segments, weighted for their relative size, to arrive at the imputed value of the conglomerate firm as a whole.
4 Estimate the difference between actual market value and the imputed value of the firm as conglomerate discount or premium (also called 'excess value').
5 Interpret the discount (premium) as value destruction (creation) 'caused' by conglomeration.

Exhibit 7.3 shows how this calculation is made. Thus this conglomerate firm is said to be trading in the stock market at a discount of 5.7% to the 'true' value represented by the imputed value.

Let us remember that the following estimation of conglomerate discount depends on a number of caveats:

1 Is the industry classification system appropriate: for example, is the two-digit group too wide to capture the differences between the segment and the benchmark firms?
2 Is the benchmark group correctly identified: that is, do the benchmark (stand-alone) firms have the same prospects, i.e. growth opportunities, as the conglomerate segment they are compared with?

Exhibit 7.3

Estimating value destruction in a conglomerate

We estimate the excess value of a conglomerate firm AB made up of two segments A and B. AB is formed by the merging companies (now segments) A and
B. For each segment the benchmark is the median market-to-sales ratio of all
single-segment firms in the same industry.

	Segment A	Segment B	Combination
(a) Sales	$100.00	$65.00	$165.00
(b) Pre-merger market value	$115.00	$70.00	$185.00
(c) Benchmark market/sales	1.15	1.25	
(d) Imputed value (a × c)	$115.00	81.25	$196.25
Excess value (b − d)	0.00	−$11.25	−$11.25

Source: Adapted from J. R. Graham, M. L. Lemmon and J. G. Wolf, 'Does corporate diversification
destroy value?', *The Journal of Finance*, **57**(2), 2002, 695–720

---

3 Is the discount due to conglomeration, or did it exist before the two segments were merged?
That is, did Segment B in Exhibit 7.3 trade at a discount before being merged with A?

4 If the discount had existed before, perhaps this caused AB's 'conglomerate' discount: that
is, is the direction of causation reversed (this causes an endogeneity problem in estimating
the discount)?

The pedantic point is that value destruction *in* conglomerates is not the same as value destruction *by* them. Indeed, they may have mitigated or reversed some of the value destruction that
might have continued in the absence of the conglomerate merger. Thus the counterfactual is
that the firm would have done even worse. With these issues in mind we review the empirical
evidence for conglomerate discount.

Table 7.4 provides a summary of the results of many of the studies dealing with the stock
market valuation of conglomerate firms or conglomerate acquisitions, and using the above
methodology or its slight variants in terms of choice of value multiplier or benchmark firms[39].
They all report a significant conglomerate discount. Some of the studies have also controlled
for other factors that may influence the growth opportunities of different firms vary and hence
affect excess value. One of these factors is diversity in the investment opportunities, and in
the returns to these investments among the segments of a conglomerate firm in the Rajan
et al. study. We discuss this result in more detail below when we review the evidence for
the efficiency of internal capital markets.

The definition of conglomerateness in these studies merits careful attention (question 1
above). We observed above in discussing patterns of diversification that diversification
within a two-digit industry was roughly regarded as related and that outside was unrelated or
conglomerate. On this criterion, the three-digit system employed by Rajan *et al.* may not
measure unrelated diversification as well as the two-digit definition does. Nevertheless, the
discount they report is not out of line with that from Berger and Ofek for an overlapping
sample period.

Table 7.4 Summary of US studies estimating value destruction in conglomerates

Study; sample period; size	Value multiplier	Benchmark multiple	Conglomerate definition of firm: segments	Estimate of conglomerate discount	Discount decreases with	Other factors increasing discount
Berger and Ofek; 1986–91; 16, 181 single- and multi-segment firms	Asset multiple Sales multiple EBIT multiple	Industry median	In more than one two-digit industry	13–15%	Large company size High profit margin High capital expenditure Related segments	
Servaes; 1961–76, 1979; 266 to 518	Tobin's q Sales multiple	Industry mean and median	As above	19% (1960s) 6% (1970s)	High profit margin	Leverage
Rajan, Servaes and Zingales; 1980–93; 13, 947 segments	Tobin's q Sales multiple	Mean	In more than one three-digit industry	16–18%		Diversity of investment opportunities and investment returns among segments
Lamont and Polk 1980–97; 1987 firms	Asset multiple	Industry median	As above	3–6%		

Notes: Tobin's q is the ratio of market value of a firm to the replacement cost of its assets. It is an asset multiplier.
EBIT = earnings before interest and tax (operating profit).

Reverse Midas touch or just measurement error?

From these studies, it appears that conglomeration is associated with significant value destruction. However, our question 2 above remains. Use of industry median q or any other measure of the growth opportunity for a 'representative' firm of the industry that overlaps with a conglomerate segment does not mean that the two entities have the same growth opportunity. Suppose the segment, prior to being acquired by the conglomerate, had below-industry average q or was financially distressed[40]. In this case, to judge the result of this acquisition with the industry median benchmark would be a biased evaluation. Indeed, compared with the pre-acquisition q, the performance of the acquired segment may have improved.

Thus an alternative to an industry representative benchmark is a firm-level measure of growth opportunities. The pre-acquisition data may provide an indication of these. Graham *et al.* found that mean (median) excess value of targets, calculated using sales multiples, was about −21% (−15%) for related targets and, surprisingly, only −4% (−3%) for unrelated targets[41]. Thus these targets already suffer a value discount prior to their acquisition. If the pre-acquisition target and acquirer values are projected from the year prior to the acquisition to the year after, and then compared with the actual, the difference is negligible. Thus 'the addition of a discounted target explains most of the decline in excess value for the acquirer'. Moreover, consistent with the view that the characteristics of acquired units are an important factor in determining the conglomerate discount, the authors also find that the excess value is not reduced when a firm increases the number of its business segments organically and without making an acquisition.

Hubbard and Palia examined the 1960s conglomerate wave and showed that the targets of the conglomerate acquirers were financially constrained firms[42]. If so, the evidence from Servaes in Table 7.4 that conglomerates destroyed value during that wave may be reinterpreted as being due to the purchase of poorly performing targets rather than to the reverse Midas touch of conglomerate acquirers. What if a firm diversifies because of the need to balance its poor performance in an industry with poor growth prospects by diversifying into a more profitable and higher-growth industry? When this firm-specific strategy and prior performance are taken into account, Campa and Kedia find that the conglomerate discount disappears, and even turns into a premium[43].

Another concern with the studies that have used q of single-business firms as a proxy for the growth opportunities of conglomerate segments is that such a proxy may be measured with substantial error. The import of the measurement error is that it leads to inaccurate conclusions about the efficiency of investment by conglomerate firms. Toni Whited argues that the q as measured in the studies in Table 7.4 is a flawed proxy for marginal q: that is, it measures the average and not the marginal investment opportunities[44]. Using more refined econometric methodology to correct for this error, she reports that there is no evidence that conglomerate segments make inefficient investment decisions, or that there is inefficient cross-subsidizing by conglomerates. She concludes that 'much of the existing evidence of inefficiency is likely to be an artifact of measurement error'.

Another source of possible error is the use of segmented data to measure diversification. As noted above, segments reported by firms are self-selected, and may be subject to strategic accounting biases. Villalonga uses the Business Information Tracking Series (BITS) new census database of establishment (rather than firm-level) data. This database allows construction of business more consistently and objectively across firms. The author finds that, during the sample period 1989 to 1996, there was evidence of a conglomerate *premium* of about 28%, whereas segment data showed a discount of 18%, similar to that reported in Table 7.4. Since diversification across segments is likely to be less related than across BITS units, this difference is consistent with value creation in related mergers and value destruction in unrelated mergers.

Villalonga, in another paper, uses segmented data but more sophisticated econometric techniques to correct for the endogeneity problem discussed earlier. These enable control of the firm's propensity to diversify and the consequent selection bias. With this control, the author finds that the discount disappears, and concludes that 'diversification does not destroy value'[45]. In sum, while many studies have reported conglomerate discount, such a discount may to some extent be reflecting the pre-diversification characteristics of either the target or the acquirer, or both. If so, the observed discount is *not caused* by diversification.

How did the stock market react to conglomerate acquisitions?

Since the stock market was aware of the pre-acquisition characteristics of the target at the time of their acquisition, presumably any stock market reaction captures this knowledge. So what was the stock market's judgement at that time? Several studies reported that acquisition announcements by conglomerate acquirers during the 1960s and 1970s generated positive and significant abnormal returns, indicating market approval or enthusiasm for the deals[46]. These studies also reported that the combined acquirer and target value gains were positive, suggesting that the market anticipated value creation from the conglomerate acquisitions. As noted in our discussion in Chapter 2 of the round trip between the 1960s and 1980s merger waves, Shleifer and Vishny argue that the divestitures of the 1980s represent costly confessions of contrite conglomerates.

If so, the reaction to conglomerate acquisitions in the 1980s should be more damning than to related acquisitions. Morck *et al.* (MSV) compare the abnormal returns to related and unrelated acquirers during 1975–87[47]. Their measure of relatedness is that the acquirer and the target share a four-digit industry. This is perhaps a very narrow definition of relatedness, since firms that do not share a four-digit industry may still operate in non-overlapping four-digit industries that belong to the same three-digit or two-digit groups. Then an acquisition classified as unrelated may actually be related. Apart from this definitional problem, or because of it, the authors report no significant difference in mean three-day returns around bid announcement between related and unrelated acquirers in the 1970s or the 1980s. In their regression analyses they found only marginally significant superior returns for related acquirers in the 1980s. However, they did find that 68% of the unrelated acquirers earned negative returns on the purchase price of the targets in the 1980s but only 52% in the 1970s.

Agrawal *et al.* evaluated the post-merger shareholder value gains for acquiring firms in conglomerate and non-conglomerate mergers for a sample 765 mergers over 1955–87[48]. This sample is predominantly of conglomerate mergers. This is probably because the authors consider an acquisition in which the acquirer and the target are not in the same four-digit industry as unrelated. This is again a narrow definition of conglomeration, although consistent with MSV's definition above. Agrawal *et al.* reported that, 'in contrast with popular belief', non-conglomerates experience 60-month cumulative abnormal returns (CARs) of −26% and conglomerates only −9%. While the former is statistically significant, the latter is not. When the authors repeat their analysis for each of the three decades, they still observe conglomerate acquirers' superior performance. Walker also finds that related acquisitions (within the same two-digit industry) do not generate higher value than unrelated acquisitions (outside the two-digit industry)[49].

Does conglomerate acquisition create overall value?

Judith Chevalier provides evidence that contradicts MSV[50]. For her sample of acquisitions during 1980–87, using a three-digit industry definition of unrelatedness, she calculates an 11-day CAR using the market model. She reports mean acquirer abnormal returns of only −1.6%, compared with Morck *et al.*'s −4%. Chevalier also reports that the combined CAR to the bidders and targets in her sample is 3%, and 55% of the CARs are positive[51]. Macquiera *et al.* also reported that, in stock-for-stock mergers during 1963–96, overall median value gains, in the two-digit-based conglomerate merger sample, of 1% compared with 7% in the non-conglomerate sample[52]. They estimated a five-month market-adjusted CAR. Some 48% of the conglomerate mergers generate positive returns, while 64% of the non-conglomerates create value. Thus it is not conclusively established that conglomerate mergers are perceived as value destroying, at least around the time of their announcements.

In Europe, Martynova and Renneboog find for their large samples that related acquisitions generate a significant 1% CARs over −5 to + 5 days and diversifying acquisitions an insignificant 0.5%. Targets experience 15.2% and 17.4% respectively. The authors define diversifying acquisitions as those with bidder and target in different two-digit industries, and classify others as related. Thus diversifying mergers are not value destroying[53]. On the other hand, Doukas *et al.* report that in diversifying acquisitions, defined the same way but with a small sample of 46, acquirer shareholders experience CARs of −2.4% and related acquirers 2.7% (significant)[54]. Although diversifiers create less value, there is no strong evidence that they destroy value.

Reconciling the stock market reaction with the conglomerate discount

If the initial stock market reaction is at best positive and at worst neutral towards conglomerate acquisitions, how do we explain the cross-sectional evidence of conglomerate discount? One possibility is that the so-called discount is an artefact of a flawed methodological design that ignores the pre-acquisition characteristics of the targets. Once these are correctly incorporated, and correct methodology is applied, the discount either does not exist or is not attributable to conglomeration. Studies by Hubbard and Palia, Schoar, Villalonga, and Campa and Kedia provide some support for this view[55]. Another possibility is that the initial stock market reaction is based on unwarranted optimism, which is subsequently cured, and the conglomerate is seen for what it is – an inefficient corporate organization. Perhaps studies that combine both long-term stock return performance and internal organization and functioning of conglomerates may provide the answer to the paradox.

Valuation of conglomerates in other countries

Are conglomerates valued at a discount?

We have so far reviewed the empirical evidence based on US data. What about conglomerates in other countries? Table 7.2 tells us that different countries in Europe exhibit different levels of conglomerate diversification among their business enterprises. We also learn that this structure has gained in importance in the last few decades. Are conglomerates in these countries able to create value?

The case for conglomerate diversification rests on the economic gains (the economic perspective), strategic gains through resource and capability transfer, financial gains through tax and debt benefits and efficient internal capital markets, and governance gains through efficient internal monitoring and managerial incentive structures. Countries differ in the institutional and regulatory environment that affects the extent of these gains, for example a lax antitrust regime that allows more horizontal mergers and avoids the need for conglomeration, or tax rules that do not allow tax deduction on corporate debt or weak capital markets. Certain corporate organization structures may also have evolved for historical or cultural reasons. In some Asian countries conglomerates owned or controlled by founding families are common because of the scarcity of entrepreneurial or managerial talent.

Lins and Servaes examine the conglomerate discount in the UK, Germany and Japan. These countries differ in their traditional approach to conglomeration[56]. In Germany and Japan ownership concentration is much higher than in the UK. German companies and banks have traditionally held large cross-shareholdings in one another. The *Hausbank*, the main bank to an industrial group, has a close relationship with the group, often manifested in equity ownership by the bank. The *Hausbank* may also have representation on the group's supervisory board. German companies have relied on equity markets more than their counterparts in the UK and the US. In Japan companies belong to groups called *keiretsu*, which coordinate the activities of their members. Such a formal organization does not exist in other countries. Like German companies, Japanese companies rely less on equity capital markets and more on banks included in the *keiretsu*. These differences may mean that conglomerates in these two countries may have roles and performance constraints different from those in the UK, which, in turn, has considerable similarity to the US.

Lins and Servaes follow broadly the same empirical methodology as Servaes in his 1996 study of US conglomerates (see Table 7.4). They calculate the excess value for two years, 1992 and 1994, for samples from Germany (sample size 227 in 1994), Japan (778) and the UK (341). The proportion of sample firms that are diversified across two-digit industries is about 36–40% in these countries. These are higher than the unrelated diversification figures in Table 7.2 for Germany and the UK, perhaps because the samples comprise larger firms, and also because of the difference in defining conglomerate and unrelated diversification.

Lins and Servaes estimate the conglomerate discount after controlling for other factors such as profitability, firm size and capital expenditure. They find that:

- German conglomerates suffer no discount;
- Japanese companies experience 8–10% discount; and
- in the UK the discount is about 15%.

The UK discount falls in the range of discount in the US reported in all studies in Table 7.4 except for Lamont and Polk, although there are differences in sample size and sampling period among these studies.

Lins and Servaes relate the level of discount to other factors that represent different aspects of corporate governance in these countries (for a discussion of these aspects in general, see Chapter 3 on the finance theory perspective on mergers). These include ownership structure, for example whether, in Japan, the firm is a member of a *keiretsu*, and the joint effect of these factors with diversification. Lins and Servaes find that concentrated insider ownership (by directors and officers of the firm) enhances the value of German conglomerates, but has no effect in Japan or the UK. Only Japanese firms associated with a *keiretsu* suffer a discount. This study emphasizes the need to understand the contextual and environmental factors that determine the valuation of conglomerate firms. While some of these factors enhance value, others are detrimental[57].

Stock market reaction to conglomerate acquisition in the UK

For a sample of 429 acquisitions in the UK during 1980–90, Sudarsanam *et al.* estimated CARs over three months surrounding their announcements, and tested whether conglomerate acquisitions generate higher-value gains for shareholders[58]. Acquisitions with acquirer and target firms not being in the same two-digit industry were treated as conglomerate. After controlling for other factors affecting shareholder returns from acquisitions such as ownership structure, financial synergy and relative size, they found that these value gains were not affected by whether the acquisitions were conglomerate or not.

Gregory examined the impact of conglomerate acquisitions on the post-acquisition performance of a sample of 452 UK acquisitions during 1984–92[59]. He estimated the post-acquisition abnormal returns to acquirer shareholders 24 months after the acquisition. Conglomerate bids are those where the acquirer and the target firms are in different two-digit industries. He found that for the entire period the conglomerates produced abnormal returns of −11−−14%, whereas the non-conglomerates generated −4−−11% for six different models. These differences, and the differences in proportions of acquisitions with value gains, are not significant. Thus evidence for inferior performance or otherwise of conglomerate acquisitions is inconclusive.

Evidence on operating performance

Ravenscraft and Scherer analyzed the post-merger improvement in profitability of horizontal, related, vertical and conglomerate acquisitions in the US. They found that conglomerates improved performance, but not significantly[60]. In contrast, horizontal and related acquisitions enhanced profits significantly. Palich *et al.* reviewed both accounting-profitability-based research and stock-market-returns-based research of the last three decades[61]. They conducted a meta-analysis of the results of these studies to establish whether the diversification–performance linkage was linear or curvilinear (inverted U) or of an intermediate form, as shown in Figure 7.2.

Figure 7.2 (a) The linear model; (b) the inverted-U model; (c) the intermediate model

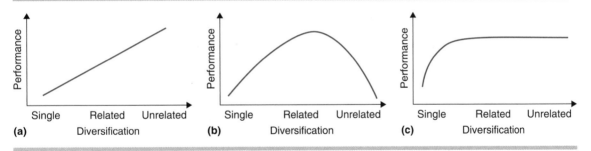

This meta-analysis exploited the correlation between diversification and performance derived from 71 different samples included in 55 of the 82 studies reviewed. Diversification was defined in terms of a number of proxies, e.g. count of industries or the Herfindahl–Hirschman index of industry concentration[62]. From this analysis the authors found support for the inverted-U pattern in Figure 7.2b. That is, profitability increases with related acquisition, but as the relatedness declines and unrelatedness increases, profitability declines. This suggests that control loss and other dysfunctional effects of conglomerate diversification may set in with increasing diversification. With stock return measures, however, the meta-analysis yielded no clear support for the same model.

Consistent with the curvilinearity view, the consulting firm McKinsey provides evidence that moderate diversification generates total shareholder returns as high as those of focused firms, and much higher than those of highly diversified firms. For example, the total returns to shareholders (TRS) during 1990–2000 were 8% per annum for focused firms and 4% for highly diversified firms, but 13% for moderately diversified firms[63].

Is the internal capital market efficient?

You will recall that one of the major arguments for the existence of the conglomerate firm is that it can be a more efficient capital market than the external market. How do we assess this superiority of the internal capital market? If efficient, the internal capital market, i.e. the conglomerate head office (HO), should be observed to allocate its scarce capital to the divisions or segments with the greatest growth opportunities and the highest expected returns. If, for any reason, a conglomerate deviates from this optimal rule, it may be deemed to operate an inefficient capital market. A possible manifestation of such suboptimal behaviour is cross-subsidizing segments with poor expected returns and prospects by diverting cash flows from segments that are relatively superior. Thus any observation that investment funds flow from efficient segments to inefficient segments may provide evidence of such behaviour. The next question is 'Why?' What are the organizational conditions that allow this behaviour? We first review the evidence of investment misallocation and then the evidence concerning the impact of organization structure on allocational efficiency.

Do conglomerates misallocate investments to inefficient segments?

To assess internal capital market efficiency we need to observe the cash flows across segments, how the segments differ in their profitable growth opportunities, and how sensitive the cash flows are to the disparity in growth opportunities of the segments. In the context of the Boston Consulting Group model (see Figure 7.3), investment funds should flow from cash cows with

Figure 7.3 **Boston Consulting Group business portfolio matrix**

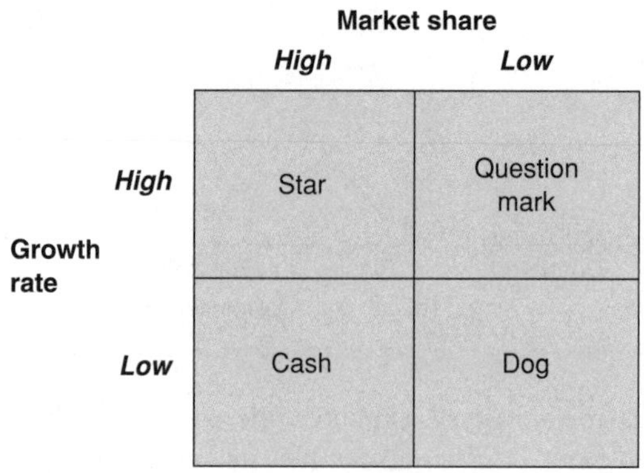

Market share

	High	Low
High	Star	Question mark
Low	Cash	Dog

Growth rate

Source: The BCG Portfolio Matrix from the Product Portfolio Matrix Copyright © 1970, The Boston Consulting Group.

limited growth opportunities to stars with superior growth opportunities, or to question marks with unknown but potentially superior opportunities. Similarly, funds should flow from dogs to the stars or question marks.

So the following types of internal cash flow can be regarded as inconsistent with an efficient internal capital market.

● There is little investment flow across segments, i.e. the internal market has broken down.
● Investment by high-growth segments is financed mostly by their own cash flows and less by other segments' cash flows, i.e. the internal capital market is superfluous.
● Investment by one segment is not sensitive to the other segments' valuable growth opportunities, i.e. the head office does not rank segments and then direct the investment funds.
● Funds do not flow from segments with the least valuable growth opportunities to those with the most valuable, i.e. the internal capital market fails.
● Funds flow from segments with the most valuable growth opportunities to those with the least valuable, i.e. the internal capital market is 'perverse' with this seeming perversity owing to organizational constraints.

Shin and Stulz tested some of the above implications for a sample of 2631 firms over 1980–92, which covered the 1980s merger wave[64]. Segments were identified with the two-digit industry. Each segment's investment opportunity set was measured by the median market-to-book value of total assets (a proxy for Tobin's q) of the single-segment firms in the same two-digit industry as the segment. Investment intensity in each segment was then regressed on proxies for its own cash flow, recent revenue growth, other cash flow, and other unknown segmental effects. They also estimated these relationships for single-segment firms for comparison.

Shin and Stulz concluded that:

● segments depend more on their own cash flow than on other segments' cash flows;
● there is active capital market with flow of funds among segments;
● segment investment is sensitive only to its own q;
● segments with the best and the worst investment opportunities show the investment-to-other-cash flow sensitivity; and
● if a segment with best opportunities suffers a cash shortfall, the HO does not protect it any more than it protects other segments.

On the whole, they argued that the internal capital market did not function efficiently.

One of the crucial data limitations of the Shin and Stulz study is the use of the single-segment firms' median q to proxy for the conglomerate segment's investment opportunities. As already noted in our discussion above, if the segment differs from the median firm systematically, the empirical conclusions are open to doubt. With a more appropriate proxy we may find evidence consistent with an efficient internal capital market. We review two studies that use different proxies and provide this evidence.

Evidence of efficient internal capital market

A similar approach to measuring the investment opportunity set was taken by Maksimovic and Philips[65]. They focused on how single- and multi-segment firms invest in plants, and take into account the relative productivity and growth prospects of these plants in the context of industry demand shocks, i.e. either acceleration or slowdown of demand. One of the important issues for them is the plant level investment behaviour of conglomerate firms in their sample of over 767,000 plant–year observations during 1974–92. The main conclusions from the study concerning conglomerates are that:

- investment is higher in plants that have higher productivity;
- growth of segments depends on the relative growth of other segments, i.e. a segment's growth is higher when the productivity of other segments is lower; and
- conglomerates that undergo restructuring grow efficiently across industries in which they operate.

The authors also noted that the results of papers using industry q to proxy for investment opportunities made the incorrect assumption that single-segment firms and their counterparts in the conglomerate firms had the same investment opportunities (see Shin and Stulz above and the studies cited in Table 7.5).

In their 2008 follow-on paper these two authors use similar plant-level data from 1974–2000 but examine acquisitions, rather than just capital expenditures, as the context for the evaluation of the relative allocational efficiencies of conglomerates and single-segment firms[66]. They find the following (in comparison with single-segment firms):

- conglomerates (based on three-digit industry classification) are more acquisitive than single-segment firms, whereas they have similar capital expenditure patterns;
- in high-growth industries conglomerates achieve 36% of their growth through acquisitions, whereas for single-segment firms this rate is only 9%;
- in high-growth industries conglomerates are better able to finance acquisitions from their internal resources, thus 'providing resources to segments with growth opportunities'; and
- conglomerates' most productive segments are more likely to make acquisitions if they also have segments in declining industries.

These results are consistent with the implication of the BCG matrix, i.e. re-allocation of investment capital from 'Dog' to 'Star', and contradict prior empirical studies or theoretical models suggesting inefficient cross-subsidizing of poor performers at the cost of high-performing segments.

Schoar, using the LRD, examines the productivity of conglomerate segments (based on two-digit segments) and stand-alone firms both cross-sectionally and over time. At a given time, the former are more productive than the latter. However, firms that diversify experience a net reduction in productivity. The acquired plants in the three pre-acquisitions had shown declining productivity, and it improved following ownership change. However, productivity gains in newly acquired plants are offset by declining productivity in incumbent plants. It seems that managers neglect the old plants and redirect their attention to the acquired plants, exhibiting a 'new toy' syndrome[67]. This study shows that conglomerates add value, but there are governance structures within conglomerate firms that cause a net decline in productivity, possibly over time.

Chevalier studied the investment behaviour of the acquirer and target firms involved in conglomerate mergers during 1980–95 *prior* to merger[68]. Using a methodology similar to Shin and Stulz's above, she found that investment patterns suggestive of inefficient cross-subsidy after the merger prevailed even before. A finding that investment in a segment was highly positively correlated with other segments' cash flows was interpreted by Shin and Stulz as indicative of cross-subsidy. Chevalier found such a positive relation before the merger between firms that subsequently become segments in a conglomerate. Thus it does not provide a reliable indicator of inefficient cross-subsidy. Exhibit 7.4 shows how diversified firms allocate capital when they are faced with a competitive threat. This suggests an efficient internal capital market in diversified firms.

In sum, the evidence for the misallocation of capital by conglomerate firms seems to be based on possibly weak proxies for investment opportunities at the firm level. Plant-level data provide evidence of efficient allocation of capital to growing businesses rather than to

Exhibit 7.4

When Wal-Mart drives you up the wall, how to respond?

Naveen Khanna and Sheri Tice examined the capital expenditure of two types of firm that faced a common competitive threat. These are specialized discount department store firms and the discount business segments of related-diversified retail firms. The common threat is the aggressive entry of Wal-Mart into their local markets. Is there a difference in the investment behaviour of the focused discounters and the segments in response to the change in their investment opportunities? If so, which of them makes optimal investment decisions in allocating capital?

Khanna and Tice used data between 1975 and 1996 for about 25 diversified firms and 24 focused firms with broadly similar characteristics, such as geographical dispersion, local market concentration and debt level. They found that:

- discount divisions of diversified firms were significantly more productive (in sales per square foot);
- diversified firms decided faster to stay in and fight Wal-Mart or quit;
- if they decided to stay, they invested more in the discount business and more in the high-productivity stores; and
- funds were transferred among divisions in an active internal capital market but away from divisions with worsening prospects, i.e. there is no inefficient cross-subsidy.

Khanna and Tice concluded that the related diversified firms in their sample made superior investment decisions, and 'the benefit from winner picking dominates the costs associated with the more complex organisational form of diversified firms'.

Source: N. Khanna and S. Tice, 'The bright side of internal capital markets', *Journal of Finance*, 56(4), 2001, 1489–1531

businesses with poor growth opportunities. Thus there is no clear-cut evidence of inefficient investment by conglomerates, but there seems to be more reliable evidence of efficient investment. Nevertheless, its is useful to understand the internal processes or the conditions under which misallocation of resources can occur. Future research needs to relate these processes and conditions to the outcomes of the investment process, that is, productivity and shareholder value creation. We turn to studies that shed some light on the internal capital allocations processes.

Why do conglomerates allocate capital inefficiently?

The inefficiency of the allocative process may be traced to the internal power configuration among the segments, the need to provide incentives to weak segments to improve their performance, a 'socialistic' approach that subsidizes the weak divisions at the expense of the strong ones, failure of corporate governance, etc. Rajan et al.[69] developed a model of the internal power distribution and politics and their influence on capital allocation based on the following assumptions:

- the headquarters (HQ) of a firm has limited power over its divisions; and
- divisions can affect the distribution of the surplus from their own and other divisions' investments in their negotiation with the HQ through choice of their own investment.

While allocating all investment funds to the best division may be the first-best solution, the HQ of a diversified firm may deliberately misallocate funds to small divisions with poor investment opportunities. Too little allocation may deprive these recipient divisions of any incentive to improve performance, and too much may be a disincentive to the larger and more productive divisions. Thus 'rational redistribution may be a rational second-best attempt to head off a third-best outcome'. HQ bribes the inefficient to prevent them from becoming even more so, a triumph of 'tyranny of equality', or blackmail by the banal! In this model the diversity of investment opportunities and resources among divisions is a critical determinant of the extent of misallocation and the size of the conglomerate discount. The need to balance allocational efficiency and the intra-firm political equilibrium distinguishes internal capital market allocation from the external. It is not clear, though, why the top management should succumb to tyranny or blackmail.

Rajan et al. tested their model with data on 157,000 firm-segment-years during 1979–93. They estimated excess value using both segmental q and market value to sales ratio, as Berger and Ofek discussed above, and tested its relation to inter-segment diversity proxied by the variability of the segments' asset-weighted investment opportunities (q). This diversity is also a measure of the dispersion of political power in the organization. They found that greater diversity made the conglomerate discount larger. However, the use of single-segment, focused firm q as a proxy for conglomerate segment investment opportunities raises the question of reliability of the estimates of conglomerate discount.

Conglomerate capitalism or camouflaged socialism?

Similar in spirit to the Rajan et al. model is the 'socialist' model of internal capital market that Scharfstein and Stein have developed[70]. Within the firm, divisional managers indulge in 'politicking' to get more compensation. This increases their bargaining power, but is also a wasteful activity. This 'rent-seeking' behaviour may also be more of a problem with the weaker divisions, since the opportunity cost to managers of these divisions of taking time away from productive work to engage in rent seeking is lower. This politicking is similar to the influence behaviour identified by Milgrom and Roberts[71].

Scharfstein and Stein also introduced the agency problem between outside capital market and the CEO. Thus this model covers two layers of agency. If the incentives for the CEO are focused on annual profits, for example, it makes sense for him or her to pacify the rent-seeking, but poorly performing, divisional managers by generous allocation of investment funds rather than a cash bonus that will reduce the firm's profits and his or her own compensation. This misallocation of investment may escape monitoring by outside shareholders, and can be carried out discreetly. Thus the CEO's dysfunctional internal allocation decisions result from the interaction of the two layers of agency problems. An implication of this model is that this inefficiency may be more serious when the productivity gap among divisions is large, i.e. there is considerable diversity in the firm.

Both the above models suggest that diversity aggravates internal politics with its wasteful lobbying, blackmail, shirking, scorched earth tactics, etc. It follows that it is a more serious problem for unrelated diversifiers than for related diversifiers. In the latter firms information used for ranking divisions is less noisy, and 'winner picking' is a more assured process. This is also consistent with the control loss problem in conglomerates that Oliver Williamson identified[72]. In his model, control loss arises from, *inter alia*, strategic use of information by divisional managers and creation of moral hazard for the top managers. Such strategic use of information may itself be part of the political power play.

CASE STUDY   # Messier bets Vivendi on his grand vision and pushes it towards bankruptcy!

In 1994, Jean-Marie Messier became the CEO of Compagnie Générale des Eaux (CGE), the French company that had started life providing water for irrigation and drinking water to cities in France. It then expanded into many related businesses and also abroad. It added heating services and a waste disposal service and in the 1970s it expanded into real estate promotion, construction and energy businesses. In the 1980s CGE also made significant acquisitions:

Business	Acquisition or joint venture (JV)
Heating and airconditioning services	Generale de Chauffe
Water management	Omnium de Triatement et de Valorisation (OTV)
Transport and waste management	Compagnie Générale d'Enterprise Automobiles (CGEA)
Pay television channel	JV with Agency Havas to form Canal Plus (15% stake)

It also expanded into telecom and media business by setting up Société Francaise de Radiotéléphone (SFR), a mobile telecom operator, and extended its water and utility services internationally to the US, Australia, and Latin America. Thus, by 1994 it was already a diversified group but still rooted in its origins as a water service utility.

Mr Messier arrived on the scene as CGE's CEO with a vision of transforming it into a 'leading global media company'. Messier was a product of the French elite *Ecole Polytechnique* in Paris and an *énarque* of the *Ecole Nationale d'Administration* (ENA), grooming its graduates for the upper echelons of French government. He had worked in the French ministry of finance where he was responsible for France's privatization programme. He then joined the prestigious investment bank, Lazard Frères. He was 37 when he became CEO of CGE. He was a man burning with a vision of 'Napoleonic' proportions to transform CGE into a global corporation*. His ambition was not limited to France

* paraphrased from Jo Johnson, 2009.

and Europe but extended to the US and, in particular, Hollywood. His chosen instrument for the transformation was a series of ever larger acquisitions financed with debt and Vivendi stock. He perhaps saw himself as a man of destiny and gave himself a nickname: J6M – Jean-Marie Messier, *moi-même, maître du monde* (*Myself, Master of the World*).

In the 1990s his acquisitions and joint ventures included:

Business	Acquisition or JV
Pay TV in Europe	NetHold acquired
Education and entertainment software	Cedent Software acquired in USA
Education and multimedia publishing	Anaya acquired in Spain
Pay TV in France	Havas, JV partner in Canal Plus acquired
Telecommunication network	JV with French national railways (SNFC) to establish Télécom Développement (TD)
Water services	United Water (48% stake) acquired in New Zealand
Telecom	30% stake in Polish telecom company
Satellite broadcasting	23% stake in Rupert Murdoch's BskyB

In 1998, CGE was re-named Vivendi and its worldwide sales revenue was 205bn FF.

In 2000 Messier made his big move and acquired Seagram, a leading alcoholic beverages company that also owned the Universal Entertainment (UE) – whose businesses included movie making and distribution, TV, multimedia, theme parks and books. This kind of merger was motivated by the desire of many multimedia and internet companies at that time to marry content with distribution channel (The most notorious and disastrous of such mergers being the $350bn AOL-Time Warner (AOL-TW) merger announced in 2000.) Following the merger with Seagram, the merged entity became known as Vivendi Universal (VU). VU now owned both Universal Studios, that made films, and Universal Music, that had on its roster many famous artists. Analysts at that time praised Messier for concocting a daring European response to AOL-TW. He also acquired a 3.5% stake in a Morocco telecom company and formed a JV with Vodafone, the major wireless telecom company, to create an internet portal, Vizzavi.

Messier made more acquisitions in 2001 and 2002, undeterred by the September 11, 2001 terrorist attack on the World Trade Center in New York which had a very negative economic impact. The US stock market was tumbling down. Nevertheless, VU paid $10bn in shares and cash to buy the entertainment business of USA Networks in December 2001. It also bought 10% of EchoStar, a US-based satellite broadcaster. Southern Water, a UK company, was bought in 2001–02. Analysts estimated that Messier had spent €100bn between 2000 and 2001 on acquisitions and predicted serious liquidity problems for the company.

In 2002 the 'acquisition party' came to a nasty end. Messier had accumulated huge debt in order to finance his acquisition binge. It amounted to net debt (net of cash and cash equivalent) of €35bn at the end of 2000 and €37bn at the end of 2001. Many of the acquired companies had not been well integrated and many were reporting large losses. VU reported a loss of €13.6bn for 2001, the largest in French corporate history. It was facing a severe liquidity crisis and was only a few days away from bankruptcy. French banks, Société Generale (SG) and BNP Paribas, refused to agree further loans to meet VU's liquidity crisis. Its long term debt had sunk to below BBB, the minimum investment grade given by rating agencies (see Chapter 16 on the rating of debt and the event risk to debt rating caused by debt-financed acquisitions). VU needed to raise cash fast in order to pay down its huge debt and improve its liquidity.

In July 2002, VU's share price had fallen to the level it was in 1989. VU as a conglomerate was valued lower than as a water utility company. This discount came to be known as the 'Messier discount'.

Messier's exit and VU restructuring

In July 2002, Messier was unceremoniously sacked from VU without any compensation (worth about $21m) for loss of office. He later sued VU for payment of the golden parachute and, although a US court ordered payment, VU and its shareholders refused to approve the payment. Jean-René Fourtou, Vice-Chairman of Aventis, the global pharmaceutical company and architect of the earlier merger of the French drug maker Rhône-Poulenc and its German counterpart, Hoechst, to create Aventis as a pharmaceutical giant, was considered a safe pair of hands and made CEO of VU. Fourtou described VU as a conglomerate of 6000 disparate companies. He said that it was 'an extremely fragmented, disorganized conglomerate with very limited internal synergies'. According to him, VU under Messier had been 'deluded'.

He started the long and arduous process of restructuring VU, reducing its excessive leverage and creating a more cohesive business. When Fourtou took over, VU's business portfolio looked like this: In August 2002 VU wrote off €11bn of goodwill included in the acquisition cost of $34bn for Seagram. It reported a net loss of €12.3bn for the first half of 2002 on top of the huge loss of €13.6bn reported earlier for 2001. In 2001 the goodwill write-off was €15bn. S&P downgraded VU's debt to junk status BB and Moody's pushed it even further into junk territory. Its shares had fallen 80% from January 2002 to just €11, a 15-year low. So times were desperate for VU. Fourtou's fire-fighting strategy was to sell off non-core assets and even divest some of the core assets. He had to re-define what VU would be like in the future. Fourtou said VU had about €10bn of debt above the level allowed by a triple BBB minimum investment grade rating and announced an asset disposal programme to raise €10bn in two years and half of that within about nine months. This target was raised to €12bn a few months later.

Disposal of VE interests

Messier had started the process of VU's divestment of its interest in the utility business, VE. In June 2002, VU had sold a 15% stake in VE to Deutsche Bank. Some of the VE shares were also sold in the market. In July that year VE's name was changed to Veolia Environnement (VE). In August 2002, Fourtou sold 20% of the stake to a group of investors. In December 2004, he sold a further 15%. VU's transition from a utility company to a media and telecom company was complete.

Divestiture of other assets

Over the next two years Fourtou divested a range of the earlier acquisitions made under Messier, often at huge losses. In 2004 Veolia, now independent of VU, sold US Filter Corporation for $933m. It had been bought by Messier in 1999 for $8bn. Houghton Mifflin (HM) was sold by the private equity acquirers in 2006 for €5bn to Riverdeep, an Irish software company, at three times the price they had paid VU in late 2002. Vivendi lost €500m when it sold HM.

What happened to Messier?

After Messier's exit from VU, both he and VU were the subject of criminal investigations in France and the US into allegations of accounting irregularities at the company and a class action suit in the US against both VU and Messier over misrepresentation of the group's financial position. He was arrested for fraud and violation of securities laws.

In November 2002, Messier published his *Mon Vrai Journal* (*My True Diary*) pouring his ire on a wide range of his detractors – journalists of the *Financial Times* and *Le Monde*, the rating agencies, the banks and the US directors on the VU board. He blamed the older French corporate establishment figures such as Claude Bébéar, the chairman of AXA who engineered his sacking and the installation of Fourtou as his successor and suggested that these old 'grandees' were jealous of his 'success' in challenging the US. He believed he had been the victim of a manhunt. In 2009, Messier published another book, this time offering prescriptions to solve the current credit crisis.

According to Jo Johnson, reporter on the *Financial Times* who had written a book about Messier's corporate misadventures, 'far from being the embodiment of "*la France qui gagne*", as he had hoped, Messier became a byword for executive egoism and managerial incompetence'. Johnson quotes Edgar Bronfman Jr, whose family lost a fortune on its Vivendi stock acquired when it sold Seagrams to Vivendi, as saying that the group suffered from two gigantic failures when one alone would have been fatal. 'First, we were too early, way too early, and that's the same as being wrong. Second, value creation is all about execution and we did not execute.'

In 2003, Messier was fined $1m by the US Securities and Exchange Commission and barred from holding directorships in the US for 10 years. Vivendi was fined $50m.

Discussion questions

1 What was the business portfolio of CGE before 1994?

2 What was Messier's business strategy?

3 What was Messier's acquisition strategy?

4 Do you agree with Fourtous' statement about the business portfolio of VU when he took over from Messier?

5 What is the cost of the diversification strategy to VU?

6 Do you agree that execution is as important as strategy? What was wrong with Messier's implementation of his acquisitions?

Sources: O. Gibson, 'Fourtou: Vivendi was "deluded"', *The Guardian*, 29 April 2003; S. Dutta, 'The turnaround of Vivendi Universal', ICFAI Centre for Management Research, Case Reference 306-187-1; R. Waters, 'Multimedia visionaries bid farewell to big dream', 10 January 2002; From the *Financial Times*: Jo Johnson, 'Vivendi Universal break up likely under new leader', 2 July 2002; Jo Johnson, 'Vivendi shares plunge 25% after debt downgrades', 15 August 2002; Jo Johnson and T. Burt, 'Vivendi needs firesale to service debt', 21 August 2002; Jo Johnson, 'Vivendi sells press and online assets', 31 August 2002; R. Budden, 'SFR war hots up on expiry of rights', 23 September 2002; M. Arnold, J. Ratner and R. Clow, 'Vivendi digs deep to keep Cegetel French', 25 October 2002; M. Arnold, 'Vivendi's former chief faces legal probe', 30 October 2002; Jo Johnson, 'A French revolutionary looks back in anger', 18 November 2002; B. Wassener and M. Arnold, 'Siemens buys Veolia filter division for $993m', 13 May 2004, FT; J. Poloti and J Brown, 'Houghton Mifflin agrees $5bn sale', 29 November 2006; Jo Johnson, 'Lunch with the FT: Jean-Marie Messier', 6 February 2009.

Overview and implications for practice

- In this chapter we reviewed the evidence for the prevalence of conglomerate firms. Firms representing a significant proportion of large firms continue to be well diversified into unrelated businesses in the US and Europe.

- The rationale for unrelated diversification comes from a variety of perspectives: economic, strategic, finance, managerial and organizational.

- We identified the sources of value in conglomerate acquisitions as well as the risks.

- Our review of empirical evidence on the value of conglomerate diversification shows that conglomerates are valued at a discount in the US, the UK and Japan but not in many other countries, such as Germany and India.

- Researchers differ as to the cause of the discount – in particular whether conglomerates underperform prior to the acquisition, pick underperforming targets, or destroy value after the acquisition.

- Stock market reaction to conglomerate takeover bids is not negative in all studies, especially not in the UK.

- One of the important justifications for the conglomerate form is that it provides an efficient internal capital market. Inefficient capital allocation seems to be related to excessive internal complexity, political and influence costs, etc.

- Firms must carefully identify their resources and capabilities and examine whether they are appropriate for the diversification strategy they wish to undertake. These are not limited to strategic resources but also to organizational resources and capabilities to manage diversity.

Review questions

7.1 What do you understand by conglomerate acquisition?

7.2 What are the implications of conglomerate diversification?

7.3 What is the rationale for a firm to follow conglomerate diversification? What is the rationale for related and unrelated diversification?

7.4 Why does the pattern of conglomerate diversification differ between countries?

7.5 What are the arguments against conglomerates?

7.6 What is the internal capital market? How is it different from the external capital market?

7.7 What are impediments to an efficient internal capital market?

7.8 Evaluate the evidence that internal capital market is inefficient.

7.9 Evaluate the stock market valuation of conglomerates.

Further reading

J. Baercovitz and W. Mitchell, 'When is more better? The impact of business scales and scope, while controlling for profitability', *Strategic Management Journal*, **28**, 2007, 61–79.

M. Dalby and T. Smit, 'A new look at diversification', *The McKinsey Quarterly*, 2004.

S. L. Gilson, J. W. Kensinger and J. D. Martin, 'Value creation and corporate diversification: The case of Sears, Roebuck & Co', *Journal of Financial Economics*, **55**, 2000, 103–137.

N. Khanna and S. Tice, 'The bright side of internal capital markets', *Journal of Finance*, **56**(4), 2001, 1489–1531.
C. Montgomery, 'Corporate diversification', *Journal of Economic Perspectives*, **8**(3), 1994, 163–178.

Notes and references

1. A. Shleifer and R. W. Vishny, 'Takeovers in the '60s and the '80s: Evidence and implications', *Strategic Management Journal*, **12**, 1991, 51–59.
2. Not all researchers use the same SIC level to define conglomeration or diversification. Some authors have relied on 'segments' as reported by firms in the financial statements, e.g. contained in the Compustat database to determine the extent of diversification, but a segment may include several four, three or even two-digit industries, since the definition is self-selected by the reporting firms. Not all of them differentiate between related and unrelated diversification. An admittedly rough-and-ready rule of thumb for readers is that a firm operating in only three-digit industries within the same two-digit industry is a related diversifier, whereas a firm operating in more than one two-digit industry is clearly an unrelated diversifier. A single-industry firm is one that operates in a single three-digit industry. The reader is advised to keep the caveat in mind that 'diversification' is an ill-defined term.
3. 'Relatedness' may also be defined by managers in a more subjective way than implied by these classification schemes. See A. Pehrsson, 'Business relatedness and performance: A study of managerial perceptions', *Strategic Management Journal*, **27**, 2006, 265–282.
4. R. P. Rumelt, 'Diversification strategy and profitability', *Strategic Management Journal*, **3**, 1982, 359–370.
5. H. Servaes, 'The value of diversification during the conglomerate merger wave', *Journal of Finance*, **51**(4), 1996, 1201–1225.
6. C. Montgomery, 'Corporate diversification', *Journal of Economic Perspectives*, **8**(3), 1994, 163–178.
7. Montgomery, *ibid*.
8. See V. Maksimovic and G. Philips, 'Do conglomerate firms allocate resources inefficiently across industries? Theory and evidence', *Journal of Finance*, **57**(2), 2002, 721–767, and 'The industry life cycle, acquisitions and investment: Does firm organization matter?', **63**(2), 2008, 673–708, for the data from 1972–87 and from 1980–90 respectively. Percentage figures are rounded to the nearest integer and hence may not add up to 100%.
9. Author's calculations based on Table 1 of A. Schoar, 'Effects of corporate diversification on productivity', *Journal of Finance*, **57**(6), 2002, 2379–2403. Output = no of firms × mean number of plants per firm × mean total value of shipments per plant. The single industry referred to is a two-digit industry. This may still include related diversifiers across three-digit industries within the same two-digit industry.
10. Adapted from R. M. Grant, *Contemporary Strategy Analysis, Concepts, Techniques and Applications* (Malden, MA: Blackwell, 2002), Table 15.2. Grant summarizes results based on previous studies.
11. G. Andrade, M. Mitchell and E. Stafford, 'New evidences and perspectives on mergers', *Journal of Economic Perspectives*, **15**(2), 2001, 103–120.
12. S. Sudarsanam and J. Huang, 'Gender diversity in US top management: Impact on risk-taking and acquirer performance', paper presented to the Strategic Management Society annual conference, San Diego, USA, October 2007. Cranfield School of Management working paper.
13. M. Martynova and L. Renneboog, 'Mergers and acquisitions in Europe', in L. Renneboog (Ed.), *Advances in Corporate Finance and Asset Pricing* (Amsterdam: Elsevier, 2006). pp. 13–75.
14. Montgomery, *ibid*.
15. L. E. Palich, L. B. Cardinal and C. C. Miller, 'Curvilinearity in the diversification–performance linkage: An examination of over three decades of research', *Strategic Management Journal*, **21**, 2000, 155–174, provides a brief review of this evidence.
16. Z. Fluck and A. W. Lynch, 'Why do firms merge and then divest? A theory of financial synergy', *Journal of Business*, **72**(3), 1999, 319–346.
17. O. Williamson, *Markets and Hierarchies: Analysis and Antitrust Implications* (New York: Free Press, 1975).
18. A. Bhide, 'Reversing corporate diversification', in D. H. Chew (Ed.), *Studies in International Corporate Finance and Governance Systems* (Oxford: Oxford University Press, 1997).
19. M. A. Peteraf, 'The cornerstones of competitive advantage: A resource-based view', *Strategic Management Journal*, **14**, 1993, 179–191.
20. L. H. P. Lang and R. M. Stulz, 'Tobin's q, corporate diversification and firm performance', *Journal of Political Economy*, **102**, 1994, 1248–1280.

21. D. J. Teece, 'Economies of scope and the scope of the enterprise', *Journal of Economic Behaviour and Organization*, **1**, 1980, 223–247.

22. For a case study and follow-on discussion of corporate branding in the luxury hotel business and its benefits and costs, see C. Dev, 'The corporate brand: Help or hindrance?' *Harvard Business Review*, February 2008, 49–58. Empirical evidence on the transferability of brands in horizontal mergers, reviewed in Chapter 5, again emphasizes the difficulty of realizing value from brand-driven mergers.

23. See M. Goold, A. Campbell and M. Alexander, *Corporate Level Strategy: Creating Value in a Multibusiness company* (New York: Wiley, 1994).

24. J. G. Matusaka, 'Corporate diversification, value maximisation and organizational capabilities', *Journal of Business*, **74**, 2001, 409–431.

25. A. E. Bernardo and B. Chowdhry, 'Resources, real options and corporate strategy', *Journal of Financial Economics*, **63**, 2002, 211–234, discuss diversifying and focused acquisitions as outcomes of such experiments within the real options framework.

26. W. G. Llewellyn, 'A pure financial rationale for the conglomerate merger', *Journal of Finance*, **26**, 1971, 521–535.

27. A. Melnik and M. A. Pollatchek, 'Debt capacity, diversification and conglomerate mergers', *Journal of Finance*, **28**(5), 1973, 1263–1273. For more recent and international evidence of a positive association between product market diversification and leverage, see P. E. Low and K. H. Chen, 'Diversification and capital structure: Some international evidence', *Review of Quantitative Finance & Accounting*, **23**, 2004, 55–71.

28. Mergers may not always generate financial synergies. Financial effects can also be negative, in which case maintaining the separate identities of the merging firms may yield optimal financial structures. One advantage of separation is the protection afforded by the multiplicity of limited liabilities. This is one of the rationales for structured finance, in which the borrowing entity is embedded in a special-purpose vehicle, which in turn is ring-fenced from the other entities in a group, a device often used to raise finance. For example, BAA plc, the UK airport company, was acquired in 2006 by the Spanish construction company Ferrovial in a leveraged buyout. When, subsequently, Ferrovial sought to refinance the acquisition, the designated airports – Heathrow, Gatwick and Stansted – were put into an SPV in 2008 and ring-fenced. This allowed Ferrovial to get a better credit rating and reduce its cost of debt. The purpose of ring-fencing is to reduce default risk, improve debt rating, and reduce the cost of debt. For a discussion of other conditions – volatilities and correlations of cash flows, default rates, tax rates and relative size – that may favour merger or separation, and the tradeoffs from a purely financial benefit perspective, see H. Leland, 'Financial synergies and the optimal scope of the firm: Implications for mergers, spinoffs and structured finance', *Journal of Finance*, **62**(2), 2007, 765–807.

29. Managers may have incentive to define segments for reporting so as to hide the real performance of the businesses within the segments, either to 'fool' the competitors or to obfuscate the investment analysts or their own board. See P. G. Berge and R. Hann, 'Segment profitability and the proprietary and agency costs of disclosure', *Accounting Review*, **82**(4), 2007, 869–906, on strategic accounting.

30. The evidence for lack of transparency in disclosures by diversified firms is weak. See S. Thomas, 'Firm diversification and asymmetric information: Evidence from analysts' forecasts and earnings announcements', *Journal of Financial Economics*, **64**, 2002, 373–396.

31. See D. J. Denis, D. K. Denis and A. Sarin, 'Agency problems, equity ownership and corporate diversification', *Journal of Finance*, **52**(1), 1997, 135–160, on how lack of alignment of managerial and shareholder interests through low managerial ownership encourages diversification. On the other hand, external monitoring by the market for corporate control reduces the proclivity to diversify. It may be the case that managers increase their ownership because their firm is highly diversified, and this reduces the risk to managers' stock holdings. Thus there may be an *ex post* positive correlation between diversification and ownership. See M. Goranova, T. Alessandri, P. Brandes and R. Dharwadkar, 'Managerial ownership and corporate diversification: A longitudinal view', *Strategic Management Journal*, **28**, 2007, 211–225, for a discussion of this reverse causation.

32. D. C. Mueller, 'A life cycle theory of the firm', *Journal of Industrial Economics*, **20**, 1972, 199–219; A. Shleifer and R. W. Vishny, 'Management entrenchment: The case of management-specific investments', *Journal of Financial Economics*, **25**, 1989, 123–139; D. O. May, 'Do managerial motives influence firm risk reduction strategies?', *Journal of Finance*, **50**(4), 1995, 1291–1308.

33. J. B. Barney and D. N. Clark, *Resource-based Theory, Creating and Sustaining Competitive Advantage* (Oxford: Oxford University Press, 2006), Chapter 9.

34. Y. Amihud and B. Lev, 'Risk reduction as managerial motive for conglomerate mergers', *Bell Journal of Economics*, **12**, 1981, 605–617. For an empirical analysis of the positive impact of diversification on firm survival, both independently and jointly with firm size, see J. Baercovitz and W. Mitchell, 'When is more better? The impact of business scale and scope on long term business survival, while controlling for profitability', *Strategic Management Journal*, **28**, 2007, 61–79.

35. Stock options, unlike stock grants or stock ownership, are designed to encourage managerial risk-taking. However, this may encourage excessive risk-taking, leading to value destruction.

36. See R. Aggarwal and A. Samwick, 'Why do managers diversity their firms? Agency reconsidered', *Journal of Finance*, **58**, 2003, 7–118. On empirical evidence for managerial biases driving risky acquisitions see Chapter 13.

37. Williamson, *ibid.*; A. Chandler, *The Visible Hand* (Cambridge, MA: Belknap, 1977).

38. R. Rajan, H. Servaes and L. Zingales, 'The cost of diversity: The diversification discount and inefficient investment', *Journal of Finance*, **55**(1), 2000, 35–80.

39. P. Burger and E. Ofek, 'Diversification's effect on firm value', *Journal of Financial Economics*, **37**, 1995, 39–65; Servaes, *ibid.*; Rajan, Servaes and Zingales, *ibid.*; O. A. Lamont and C. Polk, 'Does diversification destroy value? Evidence from industry shocks', *Journal of Financial Economics*, **63**, 2002, 51–77.

40. See Fluck and Lynch, *ibid.*

41. Graham, Lemmon and Wolf, *ibid.*

42. G. R. Hubbard and D. Palia, 'A re-examination of the conglomerate merger wave in the 1960s: An internal capital markets view', *Journal of Finance*, **54**, 1999, 1131–1152.

43. J. M. Campa and S. Kedia, 'Explaining the diversification discount', *Journal of Finance*, **57**(4), 2002, 1731–1762. The real options perspective of firms experimenting with alternative investment strategies to search for and identify eventual winners is consistent with this migration from low-performing to high-performing sectors. See Bernardo and Choudhry, *ibid.*

44. T. Whited, 'Is it inefficient investment that causes the conglomerate discount?', *Journal of Finance*, **56**(5), 2001, 765–806.

45. See B. Villalonga, 'Diversification discount or premium? New evidence from the Business Information Tracking Series', *Journal of Finance*, **59**(2), 2004, 479–506, and 'Does diversification cause the "Diversification Discount"?', *Financial Management*, **33**(2), 2004, 5–27.

46. K. Schipper and R. Thomson, 'Evidence on the capitalized value of merger activity for acquiring firms', *Journal of Financial Economics*, **11**, 1983, 85–119; J. Matsusaka, 'Takeover motives during the conglomerate merger wave', *Rand Journal of Economics*, **24**, 1993, 357–379; Hubbard and Palia, *ibid.*

47. R. Morck, A. Shleifer and R. Vishny, 'Do managerial motives drive bad acquisitions?', *Journal of Finance*, **45**(1), 1990, 31–48.

48. A. Agrawal, J. Jaffe and G. Mandelker, 'Post-merger performance of acquiring firms: A re-examination of an anomaly', *Journal of Finance*, **47**, 1992, 1605–1621. The authors report finding similar results with a three-digit industry classification, which still reflects related rather than unrelated mergers, according to our rule of thumb (see discussion *ante*).

49. M. M. Walker, 'Corporate takeovers, strategic objectives, and acquiring firm shareholder wealth', *Financial Management*, **Spring**, 2000, 53–66.

50. J. Chevalier, *What Do We Know About Cross-subsidization? Evidence from the Investment Policies of Merging Firms*, University of Chicago working paper, March 2000.

51. Akbulut and Matsusaka study diversifying acquisitions in the US during 1950 to 2006. They report that the announcement period median abnormal returns for the bidders and targets combined are positive (0.9%) and significant, thus attesting to value creation in diversifying acquisitions, defined as those across three-digit industries. They also find that there is no significant difference in these returns between related acquirers (across three-digit industries but within the same two-digit industry) and unrelated acquirers (across two-digit industries) (median return of 0.9% in both cases). Returns to acquirers alone are significantly negative, i.e. −0.6% for unrelated acquirers and −1.3% for related acquirers. Related acquirers perform worse than unrelated acquirers. See M. Akbulut and J. Matsusaka, '50+ years of diversification announcement', January 2008, SSRN id1081645, downloaded from www.ssrn.com.

52. C. P. Macquiera, W. L. Megginson and L. Nail, 'Wealth creation versus wealth redistributions in pure stock-for-stock-mergers', *Journal of Financial Economics*, **48**, 1998, 3–33.

53. Martynova and Renneboog, 2006, *ibid.*

54. J. Doukas, M. Holmen and N. Travlos, 'Diversification, ownership and control of Swedish corporations', *European Financial Management*, **8**(3), 2002, 281–314.

55. Hubbard and Palia, *ibid.*; Villalonga, *ibid.*; Campa and Kedia, *ibid.*

56. K. Lins and H. Servaes, 'International evidence on the value of corporate diversification', *Journal of Finance*, **54**, 1999, 2215–2239.

57. T. Khanna and K. Palepu, 'Is group affiliation profitable in emerging markets? An analysis of diversified Indian groups', *Journal of Finance*, **55**, 867–891. The authors report no discount.

58. S. Sudarsanam, P. Holl and A. Salami, 'Shareholder wealth gains in mergers: Effect of synergy and ownership structure', *Journal of Business Finance and Accounting*, **23**(5 & 6), 1996, 673–698.

59. A. Gregory, 'An examination of the long run performance of UK acquiring firms', *Journal of Business Finance and Accounting*, **24**(7), 1997, 971–1002.

60. D. Ravenscraft and F. M. Scherer: see details of their 1988 study in Table 4.6.

61. L. E. Palich, L. B. Cardinal and C. Chet Miller, 'Curvilinearity in the diversification–performance linkage: An examination of over three decades of research', *Strategic Management Journal*, **21**, 2000, 155–174.

62. The Herfindahl index is the sum of the squares of the market shares of firms in a market. The larger this sum, the more concentrated the market is. See Chapter 17 for a detailed definition and formula for the index.

63. N. Harper and S. Viguerie, 'Are you too focused?', *The McKinsey Quarterly*, Special Issue on Risk and Resilience, 2002, 29–37; M. Dalby and T. Smit, 'A new look at diversification', *The McKinsey Quarterly*, 2004. The TRS statistics are from the first paper.

64. H. Shin and R. M. Stulz, 'Are internal capital markets efficient?', *Quarterly Journal of Economics*, 1998, 531–552.

65. V. Maksimovic and G. Phillips, 'Do conglomerate firms allocate resources inefficiently across industries? Theory and evidence', *Journal of Finance*, **57**(2), 2002, 721–767.

66. V. Maksimovic and G. Phillips, 'The industry life cycle, acquisitions and investment: Does firm organization matter?', *Journal of Finance*, **63**(2), 2008, 673–708.

67. A. Schoar, 'Effects of corporate diversification on productivity', *Journal of Finance*, **57**(6), 2002, 2379–2403. The author also finds that stock prices track productivity changes in both conglomerates and single-business firms. This means that the conglomerate discount has some basis in productivity losses, and is not due to opacity in conglomerate performance data.

68. Chevalier, *ibid.*

69. *Ibid.*

70. D. S. Scharfstein and J. C. Stein, 'The dark side of internal capital markets: Divisional rent-seeking and inefficient investment', *Journal of Finance*, **55**(6), 2000, 2537–2564.

71. P. Milgrom and J. Roberts, 'Bargaining costs, influence costs and the organizations of economic activity', in J. Alt and K. Shepsle (Eds), *Perspectives on Positive Political Economy* (Cambridge: Cambridge University Press, 1990). pp. 57–89.

72. Williamson, *ibid.*

CHAPTER 8

Cross-border acquisitions

Objectives

At the end of this chapter, the reader should be able to understand:

- the extent of cross-border acquisitions (CBAs);
- the factors that influence CBA activity;
- the strategic and other motives for corporations to undertake CBAs;
- barriers to CBAs;
- post-acquisition integration management issues; and
- the empirical evidence on the performance of CBAs.

Introduction

In recent years the number of acquisitions made by companies in foreign countries has increased substantially. Such transnational or cross-border acquisitions (CBAs) have been motivated by a variety of strategic considerations, which often differ from those that drive purely domestic acquisitions. The approach to CBAs is not a straightforward extension of the approach to domestic acquisitions. CBAs are much more complex, owing to differences in political and economic environment, corporate organization, culture, tradition, tax rules, and law and accounting rules between the countries of the acquirer and the target company.

Acquirers need to have regard for these differences in considering, executing and managing overseas acquisitions. At first sight, the additional complexity of CBAs makes them very prone to failure, but this need not always be so. In this chapter we examine the motivations behind CBAs, the differences in the political and economic environment among different countries and their impact on CBAs, problems in negotiating foreign acquisitions, and the obstacles to efficient post-acquisition management.

This chapter provides some survey evidence on the success of CBAs, and on the approaches taken by successful acquirers overseas. From the evidence we draw together those factors that seem to contribute to successful acquisitions. Some of these are common to those relevant to domestic acquisitions, but there are several that are of particular significance to CBAs.

Alternative overseas expansion strategies

Where a firm sees profitable opportunities in serving an overseas market with its own products or service goods, an acquisition is not the only vehicle for achieving that aim. The firm has the following options:

- exporting from home to the overseas market;
- licensing an overseas company to produce the goods;
- greenfield investment in production facilities overseas;
- acquisition of, or merger with, a firm operating in the target overseas market; or
- joint venture or other strategic alliance with a firm operating in the target overseas market.

The last three modes are generally referred to as foreign direct investment (FDI). These methods entail different costs, benefits and risks to the firm, and the choice has to be made by a trade-off among these. This book is concerned with the last two modes of entry into a foreign market, and this chapter discusses acquisitions and mergers. Chapter 9 deals with strategic alliances.

Recent trends in cross-border acquisitions

Recent years have witnessed an enormous spurt in cross-border acquisitions and mergers, acquisitions of minority interests and joint ventures. These cross-border investments have become the overwhelming component of FDI made by corporations. M & A's share of global FDI has risen from 52% in 1987 to over 83% in 1999 and 85% in 2006. In 2007 it was 82%[1]. Investments have flown across countries that form a single economic unit, such as the EU, or between countries in different regions, for example between the US and the rest of the world. In value terms, CBAs rose from $200bn in 1990 to $1637bn in 2007. In relation to the world gross domestic product (GDP), the value of CBAs quadrupled from 0.1% in 1990 to 3% in 2007[2]. Thus CBAs represent a massive shift of capital and corporate control around the world, more than 80% of the deals occurring in the US, Europe and Japan and increasingly in China and India.

Cross-border acquisitions involving US corporations

Table 8.1 provides the statistics for foreign acquisitions of US companies and US companies' acquisitions of overseas targets during 1992–2007. As a percentage of the total value of all M & A deals involving a US company as either acquirer or target, these foreign acquisitions of US companies increased from about 6–7% in 1992–93 to about 20% in 2007. Thus foreign companies have increased their importance as contributors to US corporate restructuring. The US has been much less active in the opposite direction. Overseas acquisitions by US corporations have remained relatively low, below 9% until 2000 and then increasing to reach 15% in 2007. Given the relatively huge size of the US economy, it is not surprising that foreign companies spend more in the US than US companies spend abroad.

Table 8.2 provides the statistics for CBAs involving EU companies. Over the period 1992–2007 CBAs between EU and non-EU countries have increased, peaking at 42% in 1998 and remaining around 30% thereafter. By contrast the intra-EU CBA is of smaller magnitude by value, peaking at 32% in 1999 and remaining well below the non-EU acquisition levels. In 1999 the gap in total values is due to the stupendous €175bn acquisition of Mannesmann of

Table 8.1 Cross-border acquisitions of, and by, US corporations

Year	Foreign acquirer – US target deals			US acquirer – foreign target deals		
	Number	Value ($bn)	% of total value	Number	Value ($bn)	% of total value
1992	188	14	7	197	16	8
1993	181	20	6	194	18	6
1994	273	55	12	263	26	6
1995	274	66	10	314	65	9
1996	333	85	11	387	48	6
1997	446	81	7	506	83	7
1998	470	297	15	681	131	7
1999	525	330	17	550	146	8
2000	674	351	18	591	130	7
2001	439	137	15	428	110	12
2002	372	78	15	351	51	10
2003	344	71	11	362	80	12
2004	376	76	9	471	98	11
2005	452	134	11	509	108	9
2006	554	176	12	516	180	12
2007	602	271	20	503	198	15

All deals completed and the acquirers hold more than 50% of target share after transaction.
Only deals with disclosed transaction value included.
Deals categorized according to announcement year.
Deal value in 2007 US dollars.
US Consumer Price Index – All Urban: All Items used to adjust for inflation.
Source: Cross-border acquisitions of, and by, US corporations, Thomson Reuters, www.thomsonreuters.com.

Table 8.2 Cross-border acquisitions involving EU companies

Year	Between EU member countries			Between EU and non-EU countries		
	Number	Value ($bn)	% of total value	Number	Value ($bn)	% of total value
1992	249	46	26	367	30	17
1993	240	39	23	367	53	32
1994	234	29	16	451	66	36
1995	314	48	15	524	113	34
1996	322	50	13	573	109	28
1997	448	125	23	799	137	25
1998	476	146	17	1017	365	42
1999	655	522	32	1077	471	29
2000	811	356	25	1130	520	37
2001	556	141	23	848	206	34
2002	421	90	18	623	132	27
2003	410	61	14	682	118	27
2004	411	196	28	778	175	25
2005	543	263	30	966	285	32
2006	587	279	26	1025	355	33
2007	595	248	19	1085	459	35

All deals completed and acquirers hold more than 50% of target share after transaction.
Only deals with disclosed transaction value included.
Deals categorized according to announcement year.
Deal value in 2007 US dollars.
US Consumer Price Index – All Urban: All Items used to adjust for inflation.
EU means: 27 current members + Switzerland.
Source: Cross-border acquisitions involving EU companies, Thomson Reuters, www.thomsonreuters.com.

Germany by Vodafone of the UK. In both types of CBA the number and value of deals made quantum leaps, starting from 1997. Even after the meltdown in 2002–3, the total value of deals was in both cases still much higher than in 1992, indicating a longer-term trend towards more and bigger cross-border acquisitions and mergers.

Relative importance of EU- and non-EU-centred CBAs

For the 25 member countries of the EU, in 2006, domestic M & A accounted for 64% of all deals. CBAs within the EU represented 19% and CBAs involving a EU company and a non-EU company were about 17%. The US was the most important source of bidders for EU targets, with 7.5% of non-EU bidders being US and only 1.4% from Asia[3].

Cross-border acquisitions between European countries

Table 8.3 shows the top 10 European countries as originators or recipients of cross-border acquisitions in 2007. Relatively larger countries, such as the UK, France, Germany, Italy, Spain, the Netherlands, Sweden and Switzerland, witnessed both inward and outward acquisitions. The UK and the Netherlands were the most active in CBAs as both acquirers and targets. French, German, Italian and Swiss companies were more active as cross-border acquirers than as targets. Belgian and Spanish firms are more active as targets than as acquirers. In terms of the average deal value, the acquisition of ABN-AMRO, the Dutch financial services conglomerate, in 2007 by a consortium of European banks and insurance companies led by Royal Bank of Scotland for €72bn pushes the Netherlands to the top of the targets' league.

Table 8.3 Cross-border acquisitions involving EU member states in 2007

Country	As acquirer's country			As target's country		
	Number	Value ($bn)	Average value ($m)	Number	Value ($bn)	Average value ($m)
Belgium	31	4	118	31	10	311
Denmark	20	4	201	34	6	185
Finland	21	1	36	29	3	115
France	107	81	754	117	30	256
Germany	91	67	737	181	50	276
Italy	54	49	904	61	20	323
Netherlands	92	60	649	60	60	1001
Poland	9	0	53	20	2	124
Spain	72	18	245	68	57	836
Sweden	72	22	304	58	19	324
Switzerland	39	30	781	27	7	276
United Kingdom	390	145	372	299	136	455
Other EU countries	141	34	240	151	40	268

All deals completed and acquirers hold more than 50% of target share after transaction.
Only deals with disclosed transaction value included.
Deals categorized according to announcement year.
Deal value in 2007 US$. US Consumer Price Index – All Urban: All Items used to adjust for inflation.
EU means: 27 current members + Switzerland.
Figures rounded to the nearest $bn.
Source: Cross-border acquisitions involving EU member states in 2007, Thomson Reuters, www.thomsonreuters.com.

Factors influencing cross-border mergers

While there are company-specific motives for undertaking CBAs, there are also massive economic forces which have acted to unleash the tide of CBAs we have seen. These include the following:

- The economic integration of the EU represented by the Single Market, which began in 1992. European companies increasingly perceive the integrated market as their 'home' market.
- The establishment of european monetary union (EMU) and the introduction of the single currency euro in 12 member countries of the EU in 1999 (called the Eurozone or Euroland). This impacts on cross-border trade and investment not only in financial services such as banking, insurance and investment management, but also in product and services goods markets.
- Enlargement of the EU to include countries from Central and Eastern Europe including Poland and Hungary has created the opportunity for companies in Western Europe and from outside the EU to gain a foothold in these new markets.
- Globalization of product and service goods markets, with the convergence of consumer needs, preferences and tastes creating both the demand for and supply of goods and services by companies originating in different countries.
- Increase in competition, which has assumed a global character with companies competing in several markets, e.g. pharmaceuticals, investment banking.
- Explosion of technology based on massive investments in R & D, design, marketing and distribution. To recover these costs, companies have to sell to the largest market possible, which means globalization, e.g. automobiles, pharmaceuticals.
- Availability of capital to finance acquisitions and innovations in financial markets such as junk bonds (see Chapters 11 and 16).
- Privatization of state enterprises, as in many European countries, which have become targets for foreign acquirers or have felt liberated to follow more aggressive growth strategies both at home and abroad, e.g. in power, gas, telecommunications.
- A more benign and less hostile attitude to foreign ownership of national corporations, induced partly by the economic crisis and the need for corporate restructuring, e.g. the automobile industry or banking in Japan (see Exhibit 8.1)[4].
- Economic reforms undertaken by many developed and developing countries that emphasize competition and free markets and a positive and welcoming attitude to FDI and acquisition by foreign firms.
- The need for massive investments in infrastructure, e.g. gas, electricity, water and telecommunications, has forced many countries to open up these sectors for FDI, including cross-border acquisitions by MNCs.
- Strengthening of international institutions, e.g. the World Trade Organization (WTO), that promote international trade and capital flows, and relaxation or elimination of discriminatory conditions attached to FDI, e.g. local content requirements or export obligations imposed on foreign corporate investors in the automobile or food industries.

Some industries have experienced more upheaval in the form of cross-border takeovers than others. The extent of acquisition activity in an industry reflects the nature of competition in that industry, the product life cycle, changes in regulations, the current level of concentration, and technological changes (see Chapter 2 on industry clustering of M & A in the US and Europe).

Exhibit 8.1

Roche, a friendly 'wolf' at Japan's door?

Roche, the Swiss pharmaceutical company, merged its Japanese operations with those of the leading Japanese pharmaceutical company, Chugai, in December 2001. It acquired 50.1% of the equity in the US firm. Japanese corporations had in the past been very suspicious of European and US takeover bids. One of the reasons was the perceived loss of face in selling out. Another was fear of domination by the foreign partner. However, Osamu Nagayama, Chugai's chief executive, was much more open to Western influence and already had two foreigners on Chugai's board. Roche was nevertheless perceived by many in Japan as 'a wolf at the door'. Roche displayed much cultural sensitivity to Japanese misgivings by agreeing to a minority representation on the board and to preserving Chugai's autonomy, guided by its philosophy of self-governing subsidiaries. This deal reflected a more open attitude to foreign acquisitions by the Japanese.

Source: Adapted from M. Nakamato, 'Roche deal with Chugai is model for co-operation', *Financial Times*, 14 December 2001

Industry profile of CBAs in the US

We documented the cross-border mergers and acquisitions above and showed the deal flow within and between the US and Europe. As we have seen in our discussion of merger waves in general (see Chapter 2), different industries experience different levels of M & A activity.

Table 8.4 shows that, in both number and value of the deals, different industries experienced different levels of CBA activity in the US. Activity between the US and other countries is not uniform across the sectors. Acquisitions by US firms in some sectors are much greater than in others, and are also greater or smaller than acquisitions of US firms by foreign firms. This suggests that US and foreign firms seek to enhance their international competitive advantage in different sectors through M & A.

Industry profile of CBAs involving European Union companies

Table 8.5 provides the industry breakdown of CBAs in 2006 by number of deals involving EU targets and EU acquirers[6]. Overall, CBAs made by non-EU acquirers and those made by EU acquirers are similar, unlike in the US. The sectoral intensities of CBAs and purely domestic acquisitions are also similar. This suggests a broad-spread restructuring in the member countries of the EU through inward and outward CBAs as well as the domestic acquisitions.

Geographic versus product diversification

In 2006, in the 25 EU member states (EU25), domestic deals, i.e. both bidders and targets within the same member state, accounted for 63% whereas within-EU CBAs (hereafter EU CBAs) accounted for 19% and non-EU CBAs with the rest of the world (ROW) for the remaining 18%. In some member countries domestic deals dominated EU CBAs and non-EU CBAs, e.g. UK, France, Italy and Spain, and in others EU deals dominated others, e.g. new member states such as the Czech Republic, Hungary, the Slovak Republic and Lithuania. This pattern may be

Table 8.4 Industry distribution of CBAs (US bidders and targets)

Industry	US firm targets		US firm bidders		All deals	
	No.	Value ($bn)	No.	Value ($bn)	No.	Value ($bn)
Business services	173	14.6	234	7.1	1426	66.9
Chemicals	28	4.5	40	4.3	148	15.7
Drugs	53	35.5	31	2.4	174	54.3
Utilities	30	24.6	27	4.0	136	41.6
Electronic and electrical equipment	56	6.4	61	7.0	258	17.6
Food	26	64.7	46	5.6	162	101.8
Insurance	23	15.1	21	3.2	284	36.0
Investment and commodity trading	41	17.3	53	11.0	246	54.4
Oil and gas	44	9.8	24	13.6	240	53.3
Prepackage software	91	17.6	120	12.9	687	53.5
Real estate, mortgage	35	4.6	37	13.4	225	39.9
Personal care products	7	9.7	9	1.1	38	12.6
Wholesale trade: durables	41	4.9	50	5.5	230	15.8
Measuring, medical, photo equipment	51	27.3	61	2.8	242	44.0
Metal and metal products	54	11.5	29	0.5	201	21.7

Utilities include electricity, gas and water generation and distribution. All deals include purely US domestic deals. Only sectors with value of deals in excess of $5bn in either direction are shown.
Source: Adapted from *Mergers & Acquisitions: The Dealmakers' Journal*, February 2009, p. 59.

Table 8.5 Industry distribution of CBAs (EU bidders and targets) in 2006

Industry	EU firm targets		EU firm bidders		EU domestic	
	No.	%	No.	%	No.	%
Agriculture, forestry and fishing	28	0.7	7	0.2	47	0.7
Mining	194	5.0	75	2.6	80	1.2
Construction	74	1.9	40	1.4	233	3.5
Manufacturing	1306	33.6	991	34.9	1820	27.3
Network industries	397	10.2	240	8.4	787	11.8
Wholesale trade	213	5.5	86	3.0	340	5.1
Retail trade	115	3.0	64	2.3	380	5.7
Finance, insurance and real estate	646	16.6	409	14.4	1067	16.0
Other services	910	23.4	929	32.7	1906	28.6

Network industries include electricity, gas and water generation and distribution, and telecommunications. 'Public administration' is left out because of the negligible percentage of deals in that sector. 'EU domestic' is where both bidder and target are from the same member state.
Source: Author's calculations based on European Commission, 'Mergers & Acquisitions Note 4', *Directorate E, Economic Evaluation Service*, No. 4, April 2007, Table 7.

due to the stage of development of these economies, their size, exposure to internationalization, the competitive advantages of their firms, and any protective barriers they have raised against EU and non-EU bidders (for a discussion of such barriers see below). UK firms were more involved in non-EU than in EU CBAs as both bidders and targets, testifying not only to its being a very active M & A market but also as being the most open to international M & As.

Although, on the basis of comparative advantage of firms relative to firms in other geographic markets, one might expect CBAs to be limited to the sectors in which the bidders may have such advantages, we find that cross-sectoral CBAs, where such advantages may be less self-evident, are significant. At a global level, same-sector deals accounted for about 60% and within the EU for 58%. Such deals accounted for 57% of domestic deals but 66% of EU CBAs. This may be interpreted as a high level of market integration within the EU. However, it is important to note that cross-sector diversifying acquisitions are quite a substantial proportion (about 30–40%) of CBAs.

In terms of both EU and non-EU CBAs over 1986 to 2005, same-industry mergers, i.e. within the same two-digit industry, are about 56% in terms of deal value and 49% by number of deals[7]. This implies that diversifying mergers across two-digit industries are about half of the CBAs over a long period. Thus conglomerate diversification is very much a part of the M & A strategies of multinational firms. Thus many EU and non-EU firms engaging in CBAs seek to exploit their comparative advantages in their own industries but in overseas markets, or seek complementary resources and capabilities. Many also use their geographic diversification to achieve product diversification simultaneously. We discuss below the sources of value in diversifying and non-diversifying CBAs.

Impact of Economic and Monetary Union (EMU)

EMU was ushered in in 1999 with the introduction of the single currency, the euro, in 12 member countries of the European Union excluding the UK, Sweden and Denmark. The large number and value of deals in insurance and commercial banking in Europe may reflect the continuing restructuring of these industries in response to the creation of the Eurozone. However, analysis of the growth rates in the number of deals within and outside the Eurozone carried out by the European Commission for sectors such as banking and insurance, which may be regarded as sensitive to the advent of the single currency, suggests that many of the M & A deals represented domestic consolidation within each member state rather than consolidation across member states within the Eurozone. Thus the relationship between the introduction of the Eurozone and CBA in banking and insurance seems weak so far. This also seems true of the distribution sector, which may also be regarded as EMU sensitive[8].

Why do corporations undertake cross-border acquisitions?

Numerous theories seeking to explain the FDI decision in general and the foreign acquisition decision in particular have been developed over the last 40 years. These theories have been drawn from a wide range of disciplines – industrial economics, organizational economics, various competitive strategy models, finance, organizational theory, international economics and trade, and transaction cost economics. Dunning has developed an eclectic paradigm of the FDI decision process that envelops these numerous theories as to what motivates firms to invest in production outside their home countries[9]. We briefly summarize the essential characteristics of this model applied to the cross-border acquisition decision.

The eclectic model of the foreign acquisition decision

The eclectic model breaks down the foreign acquisition decision process into three stages concerned with evaluating:

- whether or not the firm possesses certain competitive advantages that can be exploited to create value through the foreign production decision (*Ownership* decision);
- whether or not the foreign location for production is superior to location in the firm's home country and subsequent export to the overseas market (*Location* decision); and

● whether or not foreign production based on the firm's ownership advantages should be carried out under the ownership and organizational control of the firm or through alternative modes, e.g. licensing or strategic alliance (*Internalization* decision).

This eclectic model is alternatively known as the *OLI model*.

If the location decision favours foreign production, then the firm has to select an appropriate entry mode – acquisition of an existing business in the 'host' country or a greenfield operation. The choice of entry mode depends on several factors, including the firm's international business strategy, and the firm's experience of the political, economic, regulatory, institutional and cultural aspects of the host country[10]. The FDI decision process leading to a cross-border acquisition is shown in Figure 8.1.

Figure 8.1   The eclectic model

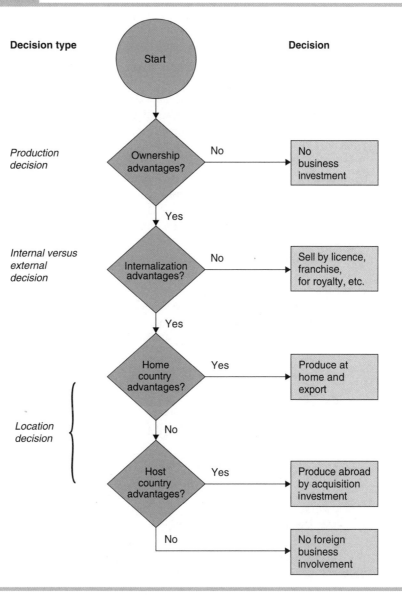

The ownership decision

The ownership decision has two dimensions: asset exploiting and asset augmenting. An asset-exploiting firm seeks to deploy its strategic assets that it considers the source of its competitive advantage in the home country to another country. These assets may include the resources and capabilities it has developed at home that can be deployed in the host country, such as brand name, reputation, design, production and management capabilities, engineering and technological expertise (e.g. Daimler-Benz's acquisition of Chrysler in 1998). The firm is essentially *market seeking* to exploit its pre-existing assets in new markets to fuel its growth. The predominance of same-industry/sector CBAs that we observed in our analysis of CBA trends above also suggests *market seeking*[11].

Firms may also seek to augment resources and capabilities from host countries. These may be natural resources such as minerals, intermediate goods such as components, or intangible assets such as technology. The host's resources and capabilities are leveraged with the acquirer's own to give the firm a competitive advantage, both in its home market and the host market, and perhaps even in third countries. The firm is essentially *resource seeking*. Since the acquired resources and capabilities need to be leveraged with the acquirer's own resources and capabilities, the value creation from the acquisition depends on the fungibility of the two sets of resources and capabilities.

In a study of 2175 capability-seeking acquisitions during 1974–91 by British, German and Japanese firms in the US, Anand and Delios found that the nature of the capability being sought and its fungibility determined whether acquisition or an alternative entry mode was likely to be chosen[12]. When downstream, less fungible capability such as sales force deployment or brands is sought, the mode of entry is acquisition. With upstream capabilities such as technology or R & D, the entry mode is more likely to be greenfield investment, since this capability is more fungible, and can be sourced locally and exploited globally. Thus the relative resource endowments of the acquirer and the host country, as well as the scope for redeployment and leveraging of these endowments, influence the cross-border acquisition decision.

Both *market seeking* and *resource seeking* can also serve purposes of scale and scope economies if they lead to an increase in the volume of the firm's output of finished or intermediate goods or in the range of related products (see Chapter 5 on these sources of value gains). Both searches can lead to revenue enhancement and market share growth. Exhibit 8.2 shows examples of *market-seeking* and *resource-seeking* cross-border acquisitions. Exhibit 8.3 shows how acquisition can open a market that would otherwise be closed to a foreign firm.

Exhibit 8.2

European integration facilitates cross-border merger

In 2001 Riello, a medium-sized company, was a market leader in machine tools in Italy. The global sales in the sector were €35bn. Riello's strategy was to grow organically and through acquisition. After a few acquisitions in Italy Riello had increased its Italian sales to 40% of turnover, but Germany accounted for only 3%. Riello also considered that its product range lacked breadth. Germany was Europe's biggest economy, the largest machine tool market in Europe, and a world leader in machinery manufacturing. Riello's search was for access to the large German market as well as for technology to enlarge the product range. For three years Riello had waited for an opportunity to acquire a suitable German target. Early in 2001 the opportunity came when Burkhardt & Weber (BW) was put up for sale while in bankruptcy. Riello bought BW in June 2001 against competitors. BW specialized in large machines for fashioning complex parts for engines, and was strong in selling to large companies. Riello then brought back Herr Mittermuller, who had worked earlier for BW, to head the acquired company. With Mittermuller's extensive network of customer contacts, Riello expected he would not only restore BW to health but also enable Riello to penetrate the German market for its own products. Riello also planned for the two companies to swap ideas in purchasing, product design and marketing. By early 2002 many of these expectations were beginning to be realized.

Source: Adapted from P. Marsh, 'Tapping potential across the border', *Financial Times*, 12 February 2002

Exhibit 8.3

Finmeccanica flies under the American radar on a strategic mission

Finmeccanica (FM), Italy's largest aerospace and defence group, acquired the US defence contractor DRS for $5.2bn in May 2008. DRS is a manufacturer of strategically sensitive electronics equipment such as sensors and radar that are used by the military and the US defence department. 'With this acquisition we have a large presence in defence,' said Pier Francesco Guarguaglini, chief executive of FM. 'This will give us a strong capability around the world to present not just European but also US products.' DRS acquisition complemented the 2005 presidential helicopter contract for its AgustaWestland subsidiary and its aeronautics division, which is working on Boeing's 787 Dreamliner and building the C27 cargo plane for the US armed forces. Mr Guarguaglini said he did not see any obstacle or political risk to the deal so far, noting the close relations between Italy and the US. Italian officials said a large defence acquisition in the US was seen as an important diplomatic boost for Italy in its competition against European Union rivals for a strong presence in the world's most important defence market. If approved, the deal would secure FM a big foothold in the lucrative American market and put it some way ahead of its continental European peers.

Thus the acquisition was a strategic move not only to access a lucrative market but also to leverage that advantage in other defence markets, since being a supplier to the US defence forces would boost FM's brand in other countries.

Source: Adapted from G. Dinmore and S. Pfeifer, 'Deal puts Finmeccanica firmly on global radar, *Financial Times*, 14 May 2008

The location decision

The location decision is a trade-off between the 'pull' factors in the host country that attract FDI and the 'push' factors in the home country that compel the firm to locate production abroad. Pull factors include the size of the market, demand for the firm's products, scale economies in local production and distribution, proximity to immobile resources, availability of complementary assets, host government incentives that promote FDI, and the presence of clusters. Walt Disney's decision in 1987 to locate its European theme park, Disneyland Paris, in Paris was influenced by its central location in Europe, excellent transportation network, easy accessibility, the lure of France as a great tourist destination, and French government subsidies.

A cluster brings together businesses engaged in the production of similar or related products and services within a small geographical space, e.g. a city or a region. It is characterized by excellent infrastructure in terms of physical facilities, human resources, communication structure and the presence of competitors. It facilitates local accumulation of knowledge, exchange of information and diffusion of learning. It augments the supply of physical and human resource inputs, and reduces transportation costs. Bangalore in India is a good example of such a cluster in software research and development, with a plentiful supply of software development skills and the presence of the major players such as Microsoft, Oracle and Intel, as well as major Indian and Chinese firms.

The push factors in the home country represent the maturity of the home market, intense competitive rivalry, poor infrastructure, government regulatory, fiscal and other policies, lack of access to cheap inputs, political and economic uncertainty, etc. Cultural distance between the home country and a potential host country also influences the location decision as well as the mode of entry. FDI is much higher among countries sharing common history, culture and traditions than among culturally disparate countries[13].

The internalization decision

The internalization decision is analogous to the *make-or-buy* decision that we discussed in the context of vertical mergers (see Chapter 6). The transaction and coordination costs of internalization versus external relationship such as joint venture and the potential for hold-up, loss of control over proprietary knowledge, risk of creating potential rivals, opportunistic behaviour by joint venture (JV) partners are the primary considerations in determining whether ownership and organizational control are preferred over looser cooperation arrangements. Other issues are the adverse selection of alliance partner, moral hazard, inability to enforce accountability for performance failure of the alliance, and inability to appropriate the benefits from the alliance commensurate with the contribution made and the risk borne by the firm in the alliance (see Chapter 9 for a discussion of strategic alliances and JVs).

Other motives for cross-border acquisitions

Firms may invest in foreign countries to provide home-country clients with service for their overseas subsidiaries, e.g. banks, law firms and accountancy firms. In some cases they may seek to exploit temporary advantages, e.g. a favourable exchange rate making foreign acquisition cheap. Depressed asset prices in a country may also attract foreign acquirers[14].

Survey evidence on the motivation for cross-border acquisitions

In a survey of 314 European firms concerning their cross-border acquisitions in Europe, the consulting firm KPMG found that the most important reasons for M & A activity (percentage of survey respondents indicating the reason) were[15]:

- to increase/protect market share (41%);
- to gain or increase presence in other geographical areas (28%);
- to acquire new products/services (11%); and
- scale economies (11%).

Other far less important reasons include company growth, opportunity to take advantage of a good deal, and diversification. These results are quite consistent with the implications of the eclectic model. Market seeking seems to dominate other motives.

Legal system, corporate governance and CBAs

Among the pull and push factors that drive CBAs are the bidder and target countries' legal system, and the protection it affords creditors and shareholders. The legal system provides the framework for corporate governance, but the latter includes other factors both at the macro and at the company level. The quality of the investor protection laws and corporate governance affects both the volume of CBA activity and the gains to shareholders and creditors. Countries differ in the strength of their corporate governance (CG) regimes along many dimensions:

- protection of shareholder rights so that shareholders can monitor the performance of executive management, and change it if there is performance failure;
- the power of the corporate board *vis-à-vis* the shareholders, i.e. whether they can vote out the directors who fail to act in shareholder interests;
- the independence and power of the corporate board *vis-à-vis* the executive management, i.e. whether the directors can effectively monitor and remove failing management;
- openness to market discipline through hostile takeovers, i.e. directors and large shareholders who are so entrenched that they can thwart value-creating hostile takeovers and preserve their private benefits of control;
- transparency of corporate behaviour and performance to stakeholders, e.g. through well-established accounting standards that are widely observed; and
- protection of minority shareholders against expropriation by majority shareholders.

These legal and CG characteristics influence not only the volume of CBAs and the direction of their flow but also the deal attributes, e.g. the payment currency. Rossi and Volpin argue that CBAs can channel best CG practices from acquirers originating from countries with strong CG regimes to targets located in countries with weak CG regimes. This transmission can happen without change in corporate law, and is characterized as functional convergence of CG across countries. They find that in 'cross-border deals, targets are typically from countries with poorer investor protection than acquirers' countries'. Moreover, shareholder protection in the acquirer country makes share exchange acquisitions more acceptable to target shareholders and hence makes cash acquisitions less likely[16].

Further, antitrust regulations and laws and their transparent enforcement create a level playing field for domestic acquirers, thereby facilitating greater CBA activity. Indeed, in many cases the foreign bidder may have the advantage that the acquisition may not increase market concentration and market power, whereas acquisition by a rival domestic bidder may raise antitrust issues. High-quality antitrust regulations increase the confidence of potential cross-border bidders and facilitate CBAs, thereby making the market for corporate control more efficient. This is likely to benefit both the firms and their shareholders[17]. We discuss antitrust regulation and its impact on M & A activity further in Chapter 17.

US companies making overseas acquisitions have to be mindful of the far reach of the Foreign Corrupt Practices Act 1977 (FCPA), which prohibits bribery as a means of obtaining foreign business. This was a response to widespread, post-Watergate allegations that US businesses were securing overseas contracts through bribery of foreign government officials. The statute generally prohibits US companies and their employees or agents from 'offering any-thing of value to foreign government officials in order to obtain or retain business or to secure any improper business advantage'. The statute also requires companies that issue debt or equity in the US to maintain internal accounting controls, and to keep books and records that accurately reflect the disposition of company assets. In 2004, as a result of the FCPA, Lockheed Martin Corporation terminated its planned merger with Titan Corporation, General Electric Co. delayed its acquisition of InVision Technologies Inc., and ABB Ltd delayed the divestiture of its two subsidiaries[18].

Barriers to cross-border takeovers

Takeovers face a variety of obstacles in different countries, in addition to those that may arise from weak legal and CG regimes outlined above. Many of these are the same whether or not the bidder is a domestic or a foreign company. Some major barriers are listed in Table 8.6. Use of many of these barriers by target companies to block takeover bids will be discussed and illustrated in Chapter 21 on takeover defences. Countries differ from one another in terms of the level and effectiveness of these barriers.

In continental Europe family control of companies, even the listed ones, is a formidable obstacle to hostile takeovers. In Italy even some of the largest companies are family owned and controlled through 'pyramid' structures that allow control of large groups of enterprises with only a small amount of equity investment in the holding company. Differential voting powers for different classes of shares mean that a small voting equity stake can thwart hostile bidders, as shown in Exhibit 8.4 in the case of Taittinger, the French champagne firm.

Corporate cross-shareholding is also a formidable obstacle to takeovers in Italy and Germany (see Exhibit 8.5 on how ownership of Fondiaria influenced takeover bids). In Germany recent tax changes have exempted profits from disposal of cross-shareholding from capital gains tax, and this has facilitated the unwinding of such holdings and consequently mergers, e.g. the merger of Allianz with Dresdner Bank (see Exhibit 6.3 in Chapter 6). This also reflects the wider disenchantment with these cross-holdings among banks such as Deutsche Bank[19]. Germany's industrial and commercial backbone is the Mittelstand, which is made up of family com-panies. Among these, the attitude to takeovers is one of reluctance and hostility, especially if any post-acquisition asset stripping is suspected (see Chapter 11 on the problems facing

---

Exhibit 8.4

No champagne for predators at Taittinger

In July 2001 more than 40 heirs to France's Taittinger champagne fortune struck a deal to ring-fence the company after defeating a hostile bid from foreign cor-porate raiders Guy Wyser-Pratt and Ascher Edelman. Under the deal no member of the family's seven branches could sell out during the next three years under the five-year pact without first offering their holdings to their relatives. Family members owned 46.25% of Taittinger's capital but 70% of voting rights. The family pact covered 43.52% of the shares and 65.6% of the voting rights.

Source: 'Champagne heirs target raiders', *Financial Times*, 27 July 2001

Table 8.6 Barriers to takeovers in different countries

Structural barriers

Statutory	• Strong powers for supervisory boards to block mergers. Unions and workers' councils have say on takeovers and strong redundancy rights
	• Issue of bearer shares, double voting or non-voting shares. Absence of one share, one vote (OSOV) principle
	• Discriminatory tax laws against foreign acquirers, e.g. withholding taxes on dividends, interest, thin cap rules (see Chapter 17)
Regulatory	• Antitrust regulation, foreign investment review, rules of stock exchange and professional self-regulatory bodies
	• Reciprocity rules that allow countries or firms to opt out of the EU Takeover Directive
	• Absence of statutory or voluntary bodies to regulate takeovers
Infrastructure	• Absence of M & A services, e.g. legal, accounting, investment banking services

Technical barriers

Management	• Two-tier boards that cannot be removed or changed quickly, e.g. the Netherlands
	• Families dominate shareholding (see Exhibit 8.4)
	• Powers to issue shares with differential voting rights or to friendly persons
	• Powers to limit maximum voting rights. Powers to override shareholders in company's interest

Information barriers

Accounting	• Accounting statements not available, quality of information poor
	• Low compliance with international generally accepted accounting principles (IFRS). Accounting practice biased to avoid tax liability, or conservative, hence accounting statements opaque
Shareholders	• Owing to issue of bearer shares, shareholding structure not known
Regulation	• Antitrust regulations favour local acquirers ('national champions') rather than foreigners
	• Takeover regulations used to block or delay foreign acquirers
	• Sectors declared of 'strategic interest' and made off-limits for foreign acquirers
	• Regulatory procedures not known or unpredictable

Culture and tradition

Attitude	• 'To sell is to admit failure' syndrome; dislike of hostile bids; dislike of institutional constraints on dividends or short-term profits. Xenophobia (see Exhibit 8.1)
	• Unwillingness to disclose information
Value system	• High premium on trust and confidence in negotiations rather than formal contracts

acquisitions through leveraged buyouts). For this reason British and US purchasers have gained a notoriety for their short-termism. For the owner-managers of Mittelstand companies, price is not everything, since they cherish their companies and wish them to be preserved[20].

According to Faccio and Lang, in Western Europe about 44% of firms are family controlled and 37% are widely owned. They report a variety of devices used in continental Europe to achieve corporate control with relatively small share ownership. These include the use of

Exhibit 8.5

Corporate Italy serves spaghetti

In January 2002 Fondiaria, the Italian insurer, was the subject of a three-way merger with rivals Toro and SAI. When the joint venture between Fiat and Électricité de France (EdF) acquired Italenergia, which owned Montedison, the power company, Montedison had a 24.4% stake in Fondiaria. SAI attempted to buy this stake and gain control of Fondiaria, but was prevented by the stock market regulator CONSOB, which required it to make a cash bid for all the shares of Fondiaria. The insurance regulator, however, declared that SAI was not financially strong enough to buy the minority stake from Montedison. SAI had been encouraged to buy the stake and bid for Fondiaria by Mediobanca, the Milan investment bank and a rival to the Fiat family. Montedison then sold 24.4% of its holding in Fondiaria to Toro, 98% owned by Fiat. Fondiaria's CEO, Roberto Gavazzi, owed his position to Mediobanca, which had a cross-shareholding with SAI and supported it. But Fiat and Toro were now in the driving seat. This is the tangled spaghetti web that Italian corporates and bankers weave that renders the ownership patterns so bewildering for potential acquirers (see Figure 8.2).

Figure 8.2   Fondiaria's ownership structure

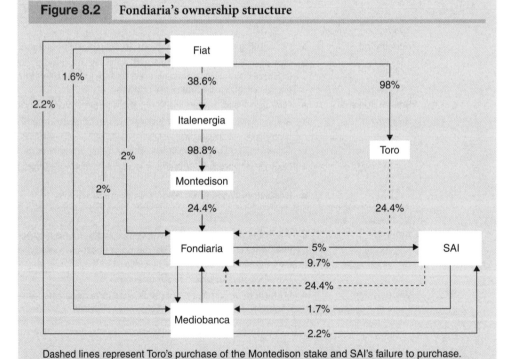

Dashed lines represent Toro's purchase of the Montedison stake and SAI's failure to purchase.

Source: Adapted from T. Barker and F. Kapner, Gavazzi holds his position in heat of battle, **FT** *Financial Times*, 15 January 2002. Figure 8.2 taken from that article.

multiple classes of shares with differential voting rights, pyramid structures, and cross-holdings between firms to achieve mutual control[21]. Exhibit 8.5 provides an example of such shareholding in Italy.

The absence of reliable accounting information hinders a proper valuation of the target company. In many countries, such as Spain and Greece, accounts may not be publicly available. Where they are, they might not have been prepared rigorously in accordance with internationally accepted accounting principles[22]. Moreover, in countries such as Germany and Japan accounts are prepared to satisfy the tax rules, and may tend to understate profits. In Germany, there has also been a traditional bias towards conservative valuation of assets and overprovisions, which again understates profits.

Recent scandals in the US have involved companies such as Enron and Worldcom violating accounting rules to falsely recognize revenues, understate costs, and use off-balance-sheet borrowing to hide liabilities. These suggest that, even in countries that have long-established and 'sophisticated' accounting regulatory systems, accounting statements are none too reliable. The conflict of interest in audit firms auditing the accounts and simultaneously providing non-audit services to the same clients renders the resulting accounting statements much less reliable than otherwise. The audit firm Arthur Andersen collapsed because of the impact of the Enron scandal.

Todd Guild observes that outsiders seeking to make acquisitions in Japan face three major difficulties: the lack of an M & A infrastructure; a scarcity of financial skills; and opposition from corporate boards, from vested interests outside the board such as regulators or corporate shareholders, and from executives[23]. It was only in April 2000 that fully consolidated accounting laws were introduced. Without these it would be impossible to assess a target company's assets, liabilities or performance.

In using the accounting information in those countries the bidder therefore needs to adjust the profits, assets and liabilities to realistic levels. Although within the EU many basic accounting rules have been harmonized, and the EU has decreed that from 2005 EU companies must follow International Financial Reporting Standards (IFRS), in practice there may be a very wide variation in the availability and quality of accounting information.

Overall, cross-border acquisitions may be considered riskier than purely domestic acquisitions because of the many barriers discussed above[24]. However, they also provide new opportunities for growth through asset-exploiting or asset-augmenting acquisitions. Further, they may provide opportunities for diversifying business, political and economic risks. Whether the benefits outweigh the costs and lead to value creation needs to be judged on the basis of empirical evidence, and this is reviewed below.

Cultural and political barriers to cross-border acquisitions often assume a high profile, and can cause adverse publicity for the acquirer. Firms from Japan, which is socioculturally distant from the US, prefer more greenfield investment to acquisitions on first entry than firms from culturally more proximate countries such as the UK or Germany, although in subsequent investments Japanese firms prefer joint ventures with US firms to greenfield investment[25].

Fear of foreign companies can arise even when the host and home countries have similar cultural profiles and speak the same language, as shown when the National Australia Bank (NAB) acquired the Bank of New Zealand (BNZ) for $787m in 1992. Many New Zealanders harbour deep-seated suspicions of their bigger neighbour. The acquisition was opposed by both politicians and shareholders, who even staged pickets outside BNZ branches[26]. Further, cultural difference does not always mean cultural antagonism that leads to value destruction in mergers. Very, Lubatkin, Calori and Veiga report, from a study of US companies' acquisitions of British and French targets, that cultural difference, obviously greater in the case of France than in that of Britain, has a neutral impact[27].

Morosini *et al.* found, from a survey of Italian acquirers or Italian targets of other European companies, that national cultural diversity might be a benign influence on performance (measured as percentage growth in sales for two post-acquisition years), as it presented an alternative set of routines and repertoires[28]. Norburn and Schoenberg, from a survey of 70 UK companies with acquisition experience in continental Europe, found that post-acquisition difficulties were likely to be compounded by cultural differences and the need to facilitate the transition from family to professional management[29]. However, in a more recent study Schoenberg did not find national cultural differences a significant determinant of performance in CBA[30].

Valuation and financing of overseas acquisitions

Acquisition of an overseas company raises important valuation and financing issues. Since the cash flows of the overseas company will be in a different currency from that of the acquirer (called the parent company post-acquisition), the cash flows for the purpose of valuation from the acquirer's point of view may have to be converted from the currency of the subsidiary to that of the parent. This introduces currency risk as a factor in valuation. (See Chapter 14 on target valuation.)

Financing of an overseas acquisition can be done in a variety of ways:

● raising equity in the acquirer's country and making a cash acquisition in the target's currency;
● raising debt in the acquirer's currency and making a cash acquisition in the target's currency;
● raising equity or debt in the local currency, i.e. the target country currency; or
● using the acquirer's own shares or loan stock to pay for the acquisition.

Sophisticated risk management tools such as currency swaps, options and futures are available to manage the currency risk associated with these alternatives. Other considerations in the choice of payment currency are:

● how to manage debt rating while financing with debt;
● which currency to borrow in;
● tax considerations, including thin capitalization rules where heavy debt financing is used; and
● equity flowback when target company shareholders are unable or unwilling to hold the acquirer stock and immediately sell it thereby, depressing the stock price significantly.

We revisit many of these financing issues in Chapter 16 on paying for the acquisition.

Post-acquisition integration

Integrating a foreign acquisition is generally complex, and often presents formidable problems. Many of the approaches to integration of domestic acquisitions discussed in Chapter 22 are relevant to foreign acquisitions. However, with the latter, the lack of familiarity with the target's environment demands that the acquirer has a well-thought-out programme of integration. This does not mean there will be no surprises, or that everything can be done according to this programme. Any expectation of that kind leads to the error of determinism.

Since the acquired company's managers and staff tend to be unfamiliar with the language, managerial behaviour and corporate custom of the acquirer, they need to be reassured, even more than in a domestic context, of the intentions of the acquirer. The acquirer must develop a vision for the target under the new dispensation, and communicate this vision with clarity. The benefits to the acquired company, its managers and staff must be explicitly outlined. The interface between the two companies must be handled with extra sensitivity. Compensation arrangements for the acquired managers must be designed in accordance with the host-country norms, and not transplanted from the acquirer.

In general, a foreign acquirer is likely to need the continued services of the incumbent management of the acquired company, since without them continuity may not be preserved. However, where the acquisition is based on a turnaround strategy, the management of the underperforming target will be dispensed with very quickly and a new management team put in its place. In carrying out rationalization and redundancies the local employment laws must be understood and complied with. Otherwise, the acquirer may be bogged down in a bitter and prolonged confrontation. We discuss the post-acquisition integration issues in more depth in Chapter 22.

CBAs present multi-stage problems

Very and Schweiger found, from interview-based research of 26 medium-size cross-border acquirers from France, Germany, Italy and the US, that problems with entering a new country are not just limited to national cultural differences during the integration stage[31]. They observed that lack of knowledge and experience of the target country affects the management of the entire acquisition process, from target selection to integration. Foreign acquirers in the sample faced problems in identifying acceptable targets, finding local advisers, and establishing first contact with targets. Lack of knowledge of currency regulations, local legal and tax systems, and local environmental regulations hindered effective evaluation of the acquisition opportunities.

Other difficulties identified in the survey are:

● different accounting systems – this problem may become less serious with most countries adopting the International Financial Reporting Standards (IFRS), but differences may still exist in the detail of the standards being implemented, in how they are implemented, and in how rigorous the enforcement mechanism is;
● overcoming local language barriers and communication problems because of differences in mentalities, cultures and management styles; and
● identifying ethical problems.

The solutions to these problems lie in developing good local knowledge, collecting reliable information, establishing a local presence to start with, and using employees with local knowledge. Further deals need to be structured to allow for the sharing of risk with the target, e.g. by using earn-out as a means of paying for the acquisition (see Chapter 16 on paying for acquisitions). Choice of payment currency is an important factor in determining the outcome of a takeover bid as well as its cost. Companies preparing for overseas acquisitions often list their shares in the home country of the target. This enables the bidder to offer to target shareholders shares that are listed on a local stock exchange. This is likely to reduce transaction costs for these shareholders. They may also have more information about the bidder if, following its listing, it is followed by many local analysts.

Intercultural management workshops, frequent visits by acquiring operational managers to the target, and communication strategies designed to make the acquired managers and staff feel they belong to a new company can facilitate smooth integration. Making organizational changes, such as relocation of the headquarters of an acquired business or improving the headquarters support structure through nomination of business unit controllers, is also helpful.

> **Exhibit 8.6**
>
> ## Two people divided by a common language: the Swedes and the Finns
>
> In 1997 the Swedish bank Nordbanken and the Finnish bank Merita were merged to form Merita Nordbanken. There is a significant minority of Finns for whom Swedish is the first language, a legacy of the time when Finland was ruled by Sweden. It is also compulsory at schools in Finland. In the negotiations prior to the merger the question of the language for the top management of the new bank was discussed. Vesa Vainio, the CEO of Merita and a Finn, suggested Swedish for that purpose. The entire Finnish top management of Merta spoke Swedish, some fluently. So the choice of Swedish was not surprising. Nevertheless, when the decision was announced it stirred a major controversy within the merged firm, and attracted adverse media comment in Finland. As a result, the top management had to justify the decision and explain that Swedish would be used only at high levels.
>
> Many Finnish managers perceived the choice as a shift in power balance to the Swedes, and felt inferior in their social interactions within the bank. For Finns the use of Swedish created a sense of professional incompetence. Both Finns in the bank and the Finnish media interpreted the choice of Swedish as yet another example of Swedish dominance. For the Swedes it was a non-issue, and they could not understand the symbolism for the Finns. Later, many senior managers conceded it was a strategic mistake.
>
> When Merita Nordbanken later merged with Unidanmark, a Danish bank, the management decided to use a neutral language, English! The Finns welcomed the switch from Swedish to English. Ironically, in everyday work-related and social interaction the language widely used among the Swedes, Norwegians and Danish was not English but 'Scandinavian', a mixture of all three, and the Finns may still feel 'inferior' to the Scandinavian speakers!
>
> *Source*: Based on I. Björkman, J. Tienari and E. Varra, 'A learning perspective on sociocultural integration in cross-national mergers', in G. Stahl and M. Mendenhall (eds), *Mergers and Acquisitions: Managing Culture and Human Resources* (Stanford, CA: Stanford University Press, 2005), pp. 155–175.

Wrong choice of official language for the merged entity may lead to feelings of inadequacy, inferiority and resentment, for example when the bidder company's language is chosen (see Exhibit 8.6).

Empirical and survey evidence on CBA performance

Shareholder wealth effects of CBAs

Table 8.7 lists the empirical studies that have investigated the shareholder wealth effects of cross-border acquisitions, focusing on the short term surrounding the takeover announcements, although two of the UK-centred studies have extended this period to five months after the takeover, and Gregory and McCorriston extend it to five years[32]. Shareholder wealth change is measured by abnormal return (see Chapter 4 on this methodology). In the first three

Table 8.7 Abnormal returns to acquirer shareholders in cross-border acquisitions

Study; sample period; sample size	Acquirer country (target country)[a]	Abnormal return (%) (days)[b] (benchmark)	Significant factors (effect on returns)
1. Cakici, Hessel and Tandon (1996); 1983–92; 195	Several (USA)	2 (21 days) (market model)	Only AUS, JP, NL and UK acquirers (+); no tax effect
2. Eun, Kolodny and Scheraga (1996); 1979–90; 103	Several (USA)	−1.2 (11 days) (mean adjusted)	JP & CND (+); UK (−); target's R&D (+)
3. Kang (1993); 1975–88; 119	JP (USA)	0.59 (2 days) (sig. at 5%) (market model)	Bank debt (+); strong yen (+); No tax effect
4. Markides and Ittner (1994) 1975–88; 276	US (several)	0.54 (5 days) (market model)	Strong $ (+); advertising (+); oligopoly (+); no country effect
5. Cakici, Hessel and Tandon (1996); 1983–92; 195	US (several)	0 (21 days) (market model)	
6. Danbolt (1995); 1986–91; 71	Several (UK)	−10 (6 months post-acquisition) (market model)	
7. Conn and Connell (1990); 1971–80; 35	US (UK)	−2.5 (6 months post-acquisition)	
8. Goergen and Renneboog (2003); 1993–2000; 56	Europe (Europe)	3.1 (5 days), −0.4 (121 days) (CAPM)	
9. Gregory and McCorrison (2005); 1985–94; 343	UK (several)	−0.02 (4 days) (ns) (market model) −3.9 (3 years) (ns) −9.3 (5 years) (ns) (Size and book to market)	Target region: US (−); Europe (0), ROW (+); acquirer R & D and advertising (+)
10. Moeller and Schlingemann (2005); 1985–95; 4430 CBAs and domestic	US (several)	0.31 (3 days) (ns) (market adjusted)	Domestic outperforms CBAs; target country's economic freedom (+); target country shareholder rights (+) global & product diversification increase (−)
11. Freund, Trahan and Vasudevan (2007); 1985–98; 194	US (several)	1.4 (3 days) (sig. 1%) (market model)	Low-q acquirers (+); shareholder rights in target country (+); geographic and product diversification increase (−)

[a]Key to countries: GER = Germany; FR = France; NL = Netherlands; SWD = Sweden; SWZ = Switzerland; IT = Italy; AUS = Australia; CND = Canada; JP = Japan; HK = Hong Kong; OT = Other; ROW = rest of the world.
[b]See Chapter 4 for a discussion of the event study methodologies for calculating abnormal returns; (ns = not significant).

studies US firms are targets of non-US acquirers, and the stock market reaction measured over very short event windows is quite mixed. While Cakici *et al.* report positive returns, this positive performance is limited to acquirers from Australia, Japan, the Netherlands and the UK. In the Eun *et al.* study UK acquirers experience wealth losses. Japanese acquirers, however, perform much better and more consistently, earning positive abnormal returns in the first three studies.

In studies 4 to 7 of Table 8.7 US acquirers of European targets earn marginally positive returns (in Markides and Ittner, significant at 10%), insignificant returns (Caciki *et al.*) or negative returns (Danbolt; Conn and Connell). European acquirers of UK targets also experience wealth losses. In study 8 within-Europe CBAs generate significant returns over a short window, but not over a longer one. Thus, with the exception of acquirers from certain countries, CBAs do not generate wealth gains for acquirers' shareholders in most cases. Thus acquirers' experience is no better in foreign acquisitions than in domestic acquisitions (see Chapter 4 for a review).

The last column of Table 8.7 indicates that certain contextual factors can improve the CBA performance. Where the acquisition is asset seeking in the form of the target's R & D capabilities or advertising or brand resources, the acquirer's performance is superior[33]. This supports the internalization argument that acquirers seek to internalize intangible assets. Acquirers also benefit from the strength of their home currency. Japanese acquirers subject to close monitoring by their bank lenders at home make more value-creating acquisitions.

Some country-specific legal and corporate governance characteristics also influence the wealth gains to acquirers, consistent with our earlier discussion of these factors (see above). Shareholder rights protection and the vigour of the takeover market in target countries help acquirers make value-creating acquisitions. Open economies as target firm locations also benefit acquirer shareholders.

The studies we have reviewed so far report the shareholder wealth performance of US and non-US acquirers. How well do the targets of foreign acquirers do? In a detailed study of 228 US targets of G7 country acquirers and a control group of 228 US targets of US acquirers Kang *et al.* find that the former earn median abnormal returns of 34% compared to 27% for the latter group[34]. The returns to foreign (acquisition) targets are significantly higher when the bidder is from a relatively high tax country, and the target has lower growth opportunities and higher advertising intensity. In the post-acquisition period:

- foreign acquirers make substantial acquisitions or investments (about $100m or 10% of the acquisition price vs $11m or 6% for domestic acquirers);
- layoffs account less for, at most, only 5% of the premium they pay and sell-offs for, at most, 6% of the acquisition price, compared with 37% and 23% respectively by US domestic acquirers; and
- foreign acquirers are more likely to lay off or sell off when the targets have low growth opportunities.

Overall, this study strongly supports the view that 'the sources of gains in foreign takeovers come mainly from this synergy and that the realization of synergy including tax benefits is the main motive' for such takeovers[35]. Future research is needed to identify the gains and their relationship to restructuring, target and deal characteristics and other factors such as corporate governance and legal regimes in bidder and target countries.

Survey evidence on CBA performance

Bleeke *et al.* examined the success of cross-border acquisitions[36]. Success was measured by (1) the improvement in the acquired company's return on equity and return on assets, and (2) whether the return on capital exceeded the acquirer's cost of capital. They reported on a sample of 28 foreign acquisition programmes by eight US, nine Japanese and eleven European corporations. These programmes represented 319 deals valued at $68bn.

The overall success rate for the sample was 57%, which is much better than for purely domestic acquisitions. Indeed, it compares favourably with the 55% reported by Hunt *et al.* (see Chapter 22) and the much gloomier evidence from statistical studies (see Chapter 4)[37]. The authors identify a number of critical success factors for this sample:

- Targets are in the core business of the acquirer.
- Targets are strong local performers in financial and capabilities terms.

- Acquirers focus on a few critical elements of the targets' business systems, especially those that are global.
- The acquirer and the acquired carry out significant mutual skill transfers.
- Acquirers integrate only the critical systems immediately.
- Acquirers learn from their experience.

Acquisition programmes in core businesses have a high success rate, with 14 out of 22 regarded as successful. Where the targets had strong local performance eight out of nine programmes succeeded, whereas without such performance seven out of ten failed. Successful acquirers typically focused on critical global functions such as R & D in pharmaceuticals to give them worldwide competitive advantage. Skills transferred included product management, selling and distribution management, and product development. These skills were generally embedded in the organization as a whole and not just in individuals.

The skill transfer mechanism was through moving a few senior managers between the acquirers and the acquired. In all 11 successful acquisitions skills transfer took place, whereas in 10 out of 13 unsuccessful programmes there was no transfer. Integration was done at a different pace depending upon how important the system element being integrated was. For example, a consumer products company rapidly patched its sales order entry system with the acquired, but delayed R & D integration.

Hoover focused on the experience of Scandinavian acquirers in the US. Out of 52 deals between 1970 and the mid-1980s, only 20 met the success criterion – that the return on capital exceeded the acquirer's cost of capital[38]. Hoover undertook a detailed study of 11 leading Scandinavian companies' acquisition experience and distilled the characteristics that made a difference between success and failure. Successful acquirers had a predetermined strategic programme for the US based on the following:

- The acquirers possessed a superior and transferable product or concept, focusing on a niche market to gain market share, targeting the relevant distribution channel, and making a proper assessment of industry risk.
- The acquirers aimed to achieve tight financial objectives, and the acquisition teams were driven by these objectives. The acquired managers were given aggressive goals to achieve.
- The acquisition teams had managers with multiple skills, and enjoyed the commitment of top management.
- Sources of synergy were estimated, with due allowance for the tendency to overestimate.
- Negotiations were hard-nosed, with a 'walk-away' price.
- Expectations and needs of US target managements were considered sensitively, with incentive-based compensation to retain them.
- A pre-planned integration programme was applied swiftly[39].

The above success characteristics of Scandinavian acquirers are similar to those observed by Hunt et al. in their study of British acquirers in the US[40]. They emphasized the need to mix with US managers at both business and social levels, to be tolerant of difference in management styles, to build trust and confidence, and to introduce executive share options. Such a compensation arrangement is particularly important for US managers.

What is the impact of cross-border diversification on innovation?

Since, as indicated by the eclectic model, search for new capabilities that can be leveraged with the acquirer's own resources and capabilities is one of the motives for CBA, the question is whether international diversification leads to greater accumulation of innovation. In a study of 295 US firms, both internationally and product diversified, with data from 1988 to 1990, Hitt *et al.* found that international diversification enhanced innovative capabilities proxied by R & D intensity[41]. R & D intensity is measured by R & D expenditure per employee. This effect is, however, weakened by excessive product diversification.

International diversification also impacts positively on firm performance (proxied by return on assets and return on equity) at low levels of diversification, but has a negative effect at high levels. The authors conclude that 'firms that achieve transnational capabilities may have advantages that are not readily imitable by competitors'. Interestingly, M & A activity of the firm, including CBA, reduces R & D intensity, whereas strategic alliances augment it once the effect of international diversification is taken into account. The interpretation of this result is, however, somewhat ambiguous, since these two variables are significantly correlated.

CASE STUDY   Cross-border acquisitions bring power to companies

In the early 1990s the UK government deregulated the electricity and water supply companies and privatized the previously government-owned utility companies. Prior to the deregulation the government companies generated electricity, transmitted it, and operated the supply to domestic and industrial consumers. To increase competition the power generation, distribution and supply activities were separated, and 14 regional electricity companies (RECs) were set up as independent companies to operate the supply business. To protect consumer interests, and to ensure that RECs did not abuse their local monopolies, a regulatory body was set up to oversee the RECs.

One of the consequences of the split-up was that the individual RECs as well as the power generators were relatively small, subject to politically sensitive regulatory monitoring and control, and unable to exploit any growth opportunity in the sectors. The power generator Powergen expanded through cross-border acquisitions, e.g. acquiring LG&E Energy in Kentucky in the US, and by diversifying into selling gas and telecommunications services. UK regulations did not allow it to acquire the RECs except by reducing its power generation capacity as a trade-off. As a result of the deregulation the UK has become the most liberalized energy market in the world. The natural gas industry also underwent a similar deregulation and privatization programme. British Gas, a sole government monopoly, was privatized and later split into a producer, British Gas (BG), and distributor, Centrica. With the liberalization of the electricity and gas markets, companies originally operating in either sector could operate in both.

Since privatization and deregulation the power sector has seen a spate of cross-border acquisitions of UK electricity companies. Since 1990 merger deals in the power sector have been worth £65bn. Power companies from the US, France and Germany have been the most active acquirers. At one time as many as eight of the RECs were owned by US utility companies. Soon, their foray into the UK brought much disappointment in terms of their profit performance, and most of them sold out. In June 2002 AEP, the American energy group, sold Seeboard to Électricité de France (EdF) for £1.4bn, and booked a loss of $440m on the sale.

The attraction of the UK market for the US energy companies rested on both 'push' and 'pull' factors. The highly restrictive regulatory regime under which the US corporations operated made the search for other growth opportunities imperative. Their experience of power sector competition in a regulated environment in the US perhaps provided them with the critical capabilities that would give them a competitive advantage in a similarly evolving UK and European power sector. However, the poor performance of US acquirers in the UK suggests that such capabilities may not have been sufficiently decisive. The original 14 RECs in the UK are now owned as follows:

- RWE of Germany – three RECs.
- Eon of Germany – one REC (it also recently acquired Powergen, the UK power generator).
- EdF of France – three RECs (it also has acquired 5000 MW of power generation capacity).
- TXU of the US – two RECs.
- Scottish Power – two RECs.
- Scottish & Southern – three RECs.

More than 55% of UK households now receive power from foreign-owned companies. Interestingly, privatization in the UK has increased the power of the state-owned EdF. EdF's predatory acquisitions in the UK, Spain and Italy have, however, generated much resentment because of the perceived lack of a level playing field for acquirers in the French power sector. Apart from the protection afforded by state ownership against foreign acquirers, EdF is further protected by the limits on private ownership to just 30%. The Spanish government's attempt to block foreign bids for its national electricity companies, however, fell foul of EU competition rules.

Thus deregulation and privatization have led to a free-for-all scramble, at least in some major EU member states in the hitherto protected power and utility markets. Much of the restructuring of these sectors has been due to massive cross-border acquisitions involving the US, French and German companies.

Discussion questions

1 What was the structure of the electricity supply industry in the UK?

2 Why did foreign companies find the UK an attractive place to make acquisitions in?

3 What were the barriers to foreign acquisitions in other European countries?

Sources: Financial Times, 7 February 2001, 17 June 2002 and 19 June 2002

Overview and implications for practice

- This chapter describes the increasing trend towards cross-border acquisitions and mergers. It has examined the industry-related factors that have contributed to this trend, and the corporate motivations behind cross-border acquisitions.
- The eclectic model classifies ownership advantages, location advantages and internalization advantages as factors that influence the overseas acquisition decision.
- There is a variety of barriers to takeovers in many European countries.
- Problems of post-acquisition integration are more complex in cross-border acquisitions than in purely domestic ones.
- Cross-border acquisitions in the US and Europe do not generate wealth gains for acquirer shareholders in most cases.

- Survey evidence, however, shows that cross-border acquisitions are successful in more than half the cases.
- Critical success factors in cross-border acquisitions have been identified from the survey evidence. Access to target's capabilities such as R & D, brands and management skills enhanced profitability and created value for shareholders.
- Acquisition is only one of several alternatives to service an overseas market. Strategic alliance is another. We discuss strategic alliances and joint ventures in Chapter 9.

Review questions

9.1 What are the factors that may account for the trends in cross-border acquisitions in the US and in Europe?

9.2 Are different industries affected differently by CBA? Why?

9.3 What is the impact of EMU on CBA?

9.4 What are the components of the eclectic model?

9.5 What are market-seeking and resource-seeking CBAs?

9.6 What are the different types of barrier to CBAs in different countries?

9.7 Do you see any special problems in integrating foreign acquired companies?

9.8 What are the critical success factors in CBAs?

Further reading

J. Anand and A. Delios, 'Absolute and relative resources as determinants of international acquisitions', *Strategic Management Journal*, **23**, 2002, 119–134.

J. H. Dunning, 'The eclectic paradigm as an envelope for economic and business theories of MNE activity', *International Business Review*, **9**, 2000, 163–190.

S. Moeller and F. Schlingemann, 'Global diversification and bidder gains: A comparison between cross-border and domestic acquisitions', *Journal of Banking and Finance*, **29**, 2005, 533–564.

Notes and references

1. UNCTAD, *World Investment Report 2000: Cross-border Mergers and Acquisitions and Development*, p. 14, and *World Investment Report 2008*, Table 1.4, p. 10 (New York: UNCTAD).
2. UNCTAD, 2008, *ibid*. Table 1.4.
3. See European Commission, 'Mergers & Acquisitions Note 4', *Directorate E, Economic Evaluation Service*, No. 4, April 2007, Table 1.
4. See also *Business Week*, 'Japan: Land of the hostile takeover?', 10 April 2000, on change in corporate attitudes to foreign hostile takeovers.
5. *Mergers & Acquisitions, The Dealmaker's Journal*, February 2009, p. 59.
6. In terms of deal value, the total value of deals with EU targets of CBAs was €943bn and with EU acquirers it was €918bn. Domestic, EU and non-EU CBAs accounted for about 55%, 29% and 18% of deal value. In terms of number of deals these were respectively 64%, 19% and 17%. This suggests that the average value of EU CBAs was much higher than that of domestic mergers. Non-EU CBAs are smaller than EU CBAs but larger than domestic mergers. See European Commission, 'Mergers & Acquisitions Note 4', *Directorate E, Economic Evaluation Service*, No. 4, April 2007, Tables 2 and 3.
7. See S. Brakman, H. Garretsen and C. van Marrewijk, 'Cross-border mergers and acquisitions: The facts as a guide for international economics', in G. N. Gregoriou and L. Renneboog (Eds), *International Mergers*

and Acquisitions Activity since 1990 (Amsterdam: Elsevier, 2007) pp. 23–50. The authors treat within-two-digit mergers as horizontal, whereas we have treated them as inclusive of horizontal, vertical and related industry mergers. See Chapter 7 for discussion of the use of industry classification codes to define related and unrelated mergers.

8. See European Commission, Directorate-General for Economic and Financial Affairs, *European Economy, Supplement A, Economic Trends*, No. 12 – December 2001 (from http://europa.eu.int//comm/economy_finance), pp. 12–14. For recent empirical evidence that EMU comprising 12 of the EU member states has stimulated intra-EU12 CBAs, see G. Garnier, 'European integration from the perspective of M & A activity', European Commission, 'Mergers & Acquisitions Note', *Directorate E, Economic Evaluation Service*, No. 4, April 2007.

9. J. H. Dunning, 'The eclectic paradigm as an envelope for economic and business theories of MNE activity', *International Business Review*, **9**, 2000, 163–190.

10. A. W. Harzing, 'Acquisitions versus greenfield investments: International strategy and management of entry modes', *Strategic Management Journal*, **23**, 2002, 211–227; S. J. Chang and P. M. Rosenzweig, 'The choice of entry mode in sequential foreign direct investment', *Strategic Management Journal*, **22**, 2001, 747–776.

11. See Brakman, Garretsen and van Maarewijk, *ibid*. To the extent that the two-digit industry classification used by these authors to identify same-industry CBAs includes not just horizontal mergers but also related mergers that seek to exploit scope economies, *market seeking* may not have motivated all the same industry CBAs. These authors also review the studies that develop competitive-advantage-based equilibrium models of international trade, FDI and CBAs, concluding that *market seeking* is an important driver of CBAs.

12. J. Anand and A. Delios, 'Absolute and relative resources as determinants of international acquisitions', *Strategic Management Journal*, **23**, 2002, 119–134.

13. B. Kogut and H. Singh, 'The effect of national culture on the choice of entry mode', *Journal of International Business Studies*, **19**, 1988, 414–432. Cartwright and Price also report, from a study of managerial preference while undertaking international acquisitions, that organizations would prefer to partner or be acquired by a foreign national culture that they perceive to be similar to their own, and are highly avoidant of cultural distance. See S. Cartwright and F. Price, 'Developing a framework for cultural due diligence in mergers and acquisitions', in G. Stahl and M. Mendenhall (Eds), *Mergers and Acquisitions: Managing Culture and Human Resources* (Stanford, CA: Stanford University Press, 2005) p. 256. For example, the two largest recipients of CBAs from the US are Canada and UK, owing to shared history, English language, common law system etc. See *Mergers & Acquisitions, The Dealmaker's Journal*, February 2009, p. 61.

14. G. M. Vasconcellos and R. J. Kish, 'Cross-border mergers and acquisitions: The European–US experience', *Journal of Multinational Financial Management*, **8**, 1998, 431–450. For evidence that the weakness of the US dollar increased FDI and foreign acquisitions of US targets during 1980 to 2007 see M. Fujita, *World Investment Report: Transnational Corporations and the Infrastructure Challenge*, UNCTAD, September 2008.

15. KPMG Management Consulting, *Colouring in the Map: Mergers and Acquisitions in Europe*, Research Report, 1997.

16. S. Rossi and P. Volpin, 'Cross-country determinants of mergers and acquisitions', *Journal of Financial Economics*, **74**, 2004, 277–304. We discuss the legal structure and CG regimes in more detail in Chapter 18 on takeover regulation.

17. A. Bris, C. Cabolis and V. Janowski, 'The effect of merger laws on merger activity: International evidence', in G. Gregoriou and L. Renneboog (Eds), *Corporate Governance and Regulatory Impact on Mergers and Acquisitions* (Amsterdam: Elsevier, 2007).

18. M. Koehler, 'Does your target have clean hands overseas?', *Mergers and Acquisitions*, **40**(4), 2005, 53–57.

19. A. Major and J. Wilman, 'Germany unwrapped', *Financial Times*, 30 March 2001. See also D. Bogler, 'At risk of losing gains', *Financial Times*, 13 June 2002, on the political threat of reversal of the CGT exemption law.

20. D. Waller, 'Now's the time to buy German', *Financial Times*, 9 November 1993.

21. See M. Faccio and L. H. P. Lang, 'The ultimate ownership of Western European corporations', *Journal of Financial Economics*, **65**, 2002, 365–395. They analyze a sample of 5232 European corporations.

22. E. Nowak, 'Recent developments in German capital markets and corporate governance', *Journal of Applied Corporate Finance*, **14**(3), 2001, 35–48.

23. T. Guild, 'Making M & A work in Japan', *McKinsey Quarterly*, **4**, 2000, 87–93.

24. Ernst & Young, *European Acquisitions: Getting it Right* (London: Ernst & Young, 1996).

25. Chang and Rosenzweig, *ibid.*

26. T. Hall, 'Public outcry fails to fend off bid for BNZ', *Financial Times*, 6 November 1992.

27. P. Very, M. Lubatkin, R. Calori and J. Veiga, 'Relative standing and performance of recently acquired European firms', *Strategic Management Journal*, **18**(8), 1997, 593–614.

28. P. Morosini, S. Shane and H. Singh, 'National cultural distance and cross-border acquisition performance', *Journal of International Business Studies*, **29**(1), 1998, 137–158.

29. D. Norburn and R. Schoenberg, 'European cross-border acquisition: How was it for you?', *Long Range Planning*, **27**(4), 1994, 25–34.

30. R. Schoenberg, 'The influence of cultural compatibility within cross-border acquisitions: A review', in C. Cooper and A. Gregory (Eds), *Advances in Mergers and Acquisitions*, vol. 1 (New York: Elsevier, 2000). pp. 43–60.

31. P. Very and D. Schweiger, 'The acquisition process as a learning process: Evidence from a study of critical problems and solutions in domestic and cross-border deals', *Journal of World Business*, **36**(1), 2001, 11–31.

32. N. Cakici, C. Hassel and K. Tandon, 'Foreign acquisitions in the United States: Effect on shareholder wealth of foreign acquiring firms', *Journal of Banking and Finance*, **20**, 1996, 307–329; C. S. Eun, R. Kolodny and C. Scheraga, 'Cross-border acquisitions and shareholder wealth: Tests of the synergy and internalization hypotheses', *Journal of Banking and Finance*, **20**, 1996, 1559–1582; J. Kang, 'The international market for corporate control: Mergers and acquisitions of US firms by Japanese firms', *Journal of Financial Economics*, **34**, 1993; C. C. Markides and C. D. Ittner, 'Shareholder benefits from corporate international diversification: Evidence from US international acquisitions', *Journal of International Business Studies*, **25**, 1994, 343–366; J. Danbolt, 'An analysis of gains and losses to shareholders of foreign bidding companies engaged in cross-border acquisitions into the United Kingdom', *European Journal of Finance*, **1**, 1995, 279–309; R. Conn and F. Connell, 'International mergers: Returns to US and British firms', *Journal of Business Finance and Accounting*, **17**, 1990, 689–711; M. Goergen and L. Renneboog, *Shareholder wealth effects of European domestic and cross-border takeover bids*, European Corporate Governance Institute, Brussels, 2003, Finance working paper 08; A. Gregory and S. McCorriston, 'Foreign acquisitions by UK limited companies: Short and long-run performance', *Journal of Empirical Finance*, **12**, 2005, 99–125; S. Moeller and F. Schlingemann, 'Global diversification and bidder gains: A comparison between cross-border and domestic acquisitions', *Journal of Banking & Finance*, **29**, 2005, 533–564; S. Freund, E. Trahan and G. Vasudevan, 'Effects of global and industrial diversification on firm value and operating performance', *Financial Management*, Winter 2007, 143–161.

33. See also R. Morck and B. Yeung, 'Why investors value multinationality', *Journal of Business*, **64**(2), 1991, 165–187. They report that the acquirer's R & D intensity enhances the positive impact of multinationality of US firms on their market value.

34. J. Kang, J. Kim, W. Liu and S. Yi, 'Post-takeover restructuring and the sources of gains in foreign takeovers: Evidence from US targets', *Journal of Business*, **79**(5), 2006, 2503–2538.

35. Danbolt reports similarly higher abnormal returns in the months −2 to +1 around takeover announcements by 116 CBAs and 514 domestic acquisitions of UK targets. The CBA target return is 31% and the domestic target return is 24%. He also finds that this is due to greater use of cash as payment currency in CBAs. See J. Danbolt, 'Target company cross-border effects in acquisitions into the UK', *European Financial Management*, **10**(1), 2004, 83–108.

36. J. Bleeke, D. Ernst, J. A. Isono and D. D. Weinberg, 'Succeeding at cross-border mergers and acquisitions' (Chapter 6) and 'The new shape of cross-border mergers and acquisitions' (Chapter 7) in J. Bleeke and D. Ernst (Eds), *Collaborating to Compete* (New York: John Wiley, 1993).

37. J. S. Hunt, S. Lees, J. J. Grumbar and P. D. Vivian, *Acquisitions: The Human Factor* (London: London Business School, 1987).

38. W. E. Hoover Jr, 'Making successful acquisitions: United States', in J. Bleeke and D. Ernst (Eds), *Collaborating to Compete* (New York: John Wiley, 1993), Chapter 12.

39. Hoover, *ibid.*

40. Hunt, Lees, Grumbar and Vivian, *ibid.*

41. M. A. Hitt, R. E. Hoskisson and H. Kim, 'International diversification: Effects on innovation and firm performance in product-diversified firms', *Academy of Management Journal*, **40**(4), 1997, 767–798.

Strategic alliances as an alternative to mergers and acquisitions

Objectives

At the end of this chapter, the reader should be able to understand:

- the economic logic of strategic alliances, and different typologies for classifying them;
- alternative models of a joint venture;
- the structure and management of different alliance types;
- how well strategic alliances have performed, and the reasons for performance failure;
- the critical success factors in alliances;
- comparative merits and demerits of strategic alliances and mergers; and
- the criteria for choosing among them.

Introduction

We have seen from Chapter 4 that acquisitions often fail to live up to the acquirers' expectations and objectives. Companies therefore need to explore alternative, and more successful, means of achieving the same objectives. In recent years there has been a surge of strategic alliances among companies across the globe. Most large companies have at least 30 alliances, and many have more than 100. Between 1973 and 2001 pharmaceutical and biotechnology firms had between 119 and 373 alliances[1]. These strategic alliances fall short of outright acquisitions, and take a variety of forms, from simple agreements between firms to buy or sell each other's goods, or co-marketing, to the creation of separate and legally distinct entities.

Strategic alliances are motivated by considerations such as cost reduction, technology sharing, product development, developing or accessing new resources and capabilities, market access or access to capital. Their objectives are not dissimilar to those in conventional acquisitions (see Chapter 3). Properly structured strategic alliances can be a less expensive alternative to acquisitions. The logic is that if two or more companies pool their resources, their joint objectives can be secured more easily and economically. Despite the attractions of strategic alliances, some estimates suggest that a large number of strategic alliances fail.

In this chapter we describe the different types of strategic alliance and their characteristics. The basic structure of an alliance and the motivations of partners to an alliance are delineated. The reasons for instability in alliances are explored. Evidence on the performance of strategic alliances from large-sample empirical studies and surveys is then presented. The chapter provides some guidelines for avoiding failure. We discuss the choice between a strategic alliance and a merger, and set out the criteria for making the choice.

A strategic alliance is an arrangement between two or more independent companies that choose to carry out a project or operate in a specific business area by coordinating the necessary skills and resources jointly rather than operating on their own or merging their operations[2]. Any arrangement or agreement under which two or more firms cooperate in order to achieve certain commercial objectives may be called a strategic alliance. A merger may be regarded as an extreme form of a cooperative venture in which one firm loses its identity and control to another, or both firms lose their identity to a new entity into which they are merged.

Doz and Hamel[3] identify two strategic imperatives behind strategic alliances (SAs):

● racing for the world; and
● racing for the future.

A firm racing for the world attempts to make the most of the extant global opportunities, and forms an alliance to do what it cannot do alone. A firm racing for the future attempts to create new products, new skills and resources and new competences. Either imperative is served by

● gaining competitive capabilities through co-option of partners;
● leveraging each other's co-specialized resources; and
● gaining competence through internalized learning from each other.

Whether racing for the world or for the future, the alliance partners aim to create a sustainable competitive advantage and thereby create value for their stakeholders. Exhibit 9.1 shows the key benefits to an alliance for developing fuel-cell technology.

Exhibit 9.1

Ford and DaimlerChrysler search for fuel and a cell

In 2004 Ford and DaimlerChrysler, the automobile rivals, formed a 50–50 joint venture to acquire the fuel-cell system division of Ballard Power Systems Inc. Ford, at that time, managed about 100 joint ventures and strategic alliances, and had relationships with competitors to produce such products as hydrogen fuel-cell vehicles, diesel engines, and transmissions. Kevin Cramton, Ford's director of corporate development said the reason for these competitor alliances was 'because of practical economics and the ability to leverage resources'. The fuel-cell alliance was formed 'to develop a new technology through shared efforts'. Automakers were exploring fuel-cell technology as an alternative to gasoline-powered engines. Automobiles powered by fuel-cell systems were being tested in several cities around the world. 'Developing this type of technology was an expensive and high-risk proposition that may be best approached through a partnership – in which costs and risks are shared'. The key benefits of the alliance with DaimlerChrysler were:

- to enter new markets/businesses based on the new technology;
- to share costs/risks, since R & D costs and risks are high;
- to leverage resources, i.e. each partner brings its competences;
- to gain speed/agility, i.e. working with partners using their specialist knowledge avoids having to reinvent the wheel and, shortens time to market;
- to overcome barriers – regulatory barriers, setting standards and winning their acceptance;
- divestiture/outsourcing, e.g. outsourcing activities to partners with the required capabilities;
- access to customers/distribution, e.g. alliance with integrated oil major BP to provide critical infrastructure for refuelling;
- access to technology and know-how, i.e. to learn about new technology and how to integrate it into automobiles;

Source: KPMG International, *Alliances and Joint Ventures: Fit, Focus and Follow-through*, 2005, downloaded from www.kpmg.com

Types of strategic alliance

Strategic alliances assume a variety of legal forms:

- supply or purchase agreement;
- marketing or distribution agreement;
- agreement to provide technical services;
- management contract;
- licensing of know-how, technology, design or patent;
- franchising;
- joint venture (JV).

These cooperative arrangements differ in the following respects:

- strategic objectives;
- logic of value creation;
- scope for joint decision-making;
- capital commitment;
- the way the risks and rewards are shared;
- organizational structure; and
- evolutionary trajectory, i.e. how the alliance evolves, and the balance of dependence of one partner on another changes over time.

Capital commitment often arises in the form of an equity investment. While joint ventures may be equity or non-equity ventures, the other types of cooperative arrangement are generally non-equity. For example, with a licence or a management contract, the partner giving the licence or providing the management service will receive a royalty or management fee. The royalty may in some cases be based on an agreed share of the profits accruing to the licensee. Non-equity arrangements do not normally create jointly owned entities distinct from the alliance partners. The scope for joint decision-making is also limited.

Classification by economic substance of alliance

Several authors have classified alliances in terms of their economic content, i.e. in terms of the strategic motivation of the partners and the pathways for achieving their strategic objectives. Yoshino and Srinivasa Rangan classify the strategic objectives of alliances into maintaining strategic flexibility, protecting core competences and strategic advantages, learning from the partner, and adding value to particular activities[4]. These objectives differ in importance across four alliance types:

- pre-competitive, e.g. between unrelated industry firms to develop new technology;
- competitive, e.g. between competitors in final markets, such as that between General Motors and Toyota;
- pro-competitive, e.g. vertical value chain relationship between manufacturers and suppliers; and
- non-competitive, e.g. between non-competing firms in the same industry but in different markets.

Koza and Lewin define two motivations for alliances: exploitative and exploratory[5]. An exploitative alliance seeks to leverage partners' resources and capabilities to enhance revenue or reduce costs, whereas in an exploratory alliance the partners seek to create new opportunities, resources, markets, products and technologies. The exploration/exploitation logic produces three basic kinds of strategic alliance, with each embodying a unique strategic intent, and each demanding a unique alliance management process[6]:

- *Learning alliances*, where partners have strong exploration intent but with limited or no exploitation intent. Learning alliances can be about markets, core competences or technologies. Learning alliances seek to reduce information asymmetry between partners.
- *Business alliances* link companies with strong exploitation intent but with little or no exploration intent. Their sole object is revenue enhancement, and they are typically structured as equity JVs. Business alliances structured as networks represent a new trend, e.g. the Star alliances in the airline business.
- *Hybrid alliances* join companies with strategic intents that incorporate both exploitation and exploration objectives. Partner companies seek to simultaneously maximize opportunities for capturing value from leveraging existing capabilities and assets as well as from new value creation through learning[7].

Alliances may also be classified as link alliances or scale alliances. Link alliances are inter-firm partnerships to which partners contribute different capabilities, where as scale alliances are partnerships to which the partners contribute similar capabilities[8]. Exhibit 9.2 shows how in 1998 UK group Johnson Matthey formed different types of strategic alliance with different partners.

Implication of classification types

The economic substance of the alliance determines the legal form, the management and organizational structure, the ability to manage the alliance, and the outcome of the alliance. The success or failure of an alliance depends upon the extent to which these aspects are married to the underlying economic substance and strategic motivation. For example, rigid bureaucratic structures may not be conducive to a learning alliance. Similarly, imposing a tight timetable may hinder an exploratory alliance. Cultural differences may precipitate crises or lack of trust. There are different critical success factors associated with each type of alliance, as discussed below.

Exhibit 9.2

Alliances are a catalytic converter for Johnson Matthey

Johnson Matthey (JM) in 1998 was a UK group specializing in precious metals, catalysts and electronic materials as well as in fuel cells. Its turnover was £2.6bn. It had built up a range of strategic alliances in a number of areas with varying degrees of financial and managerial commitments. These were both exploitative and exploratory:

- An *informal link* between its electronic materials division with Details, Inc. of California to produce small quantities of printed circuit boards used for testing and development work. It was a valuable additional service JM could offer to its major customers such as Sun and Motorola.
- A *partnership agreement* between its core electronic materials division and the largest manufacturer of ceramic chips, Kyocera of Japan. Technological developments within the two companies were complementary, and the two agreed to cross-license their know-how. An executive management committee managed the partner relationship.
- A *formal JV* with Mitsubishi Chemicals to supply materials for silicon chip production. JM took a 50% stake in Ryoka Matthey (RM), with an agreement to raise it to 66% in two years. With this JM gained access to the strategically critical Japanese market. RM had scope for territorial disputes with other JM units that needed to be resolved.
- Another *formal 50–50 JV* with the UK conglomerate Cookson to supply materials to the ceramic tableware and tile makers. The partners' cultures were different, and each partner would like to buy the other out.
- A *technology link* with Canadian Ballard Power systems. JM took a 3% stake in Ballard. JM contributed its platinum catalyst technology to solve Ballard's fuel cell problems. The original purpose having been served, JM was looking to redefine the relationship.

Source: Adapted from T. Lester, 'Electric effect of alliances', *Financial Times*, 15 January 1998

In this book we concentrate on joint ventures because of their great similarity to mergers and acquisitions. An equity joint venture (EJV) involves two or more legally distinct firms (the parents) investing in the venture and participating in the venture's management. The venture itself may be constituted as a separate entity distinct from the parents. A venture may come into being as a new activity, or may be created by transferring and pooling some or all of the existing interests of parents. An EJV is often very similar to a merger, and an example is given in Exhibit 9.3. A non-equity joint venture (NEJV) may also involve the pooling of resources, but no separate entity is created. The purpose of equity investment is twofold: first, to finance the operations of the joint venture (JV); second, to enhance the commitment of the parents to the venture.

The operations of the JV may sometimes overlap with those of the parents. For example, they may be targeting the same markets and selling the same or similar products. Such an overlap creates inevitable friction between the JV and the parent concerned (see Exhibit 9.4 below).

Exhibit 9.3

Advanced Micro Devices (AMD) and Fujitsu find a flash of romance

AMD, a US semiconductor manufacturer with a turnover of $1.2bn, entered into a production joint venture with Fujitsu, Japan's biggest computer company, in July 1992. The venture was formed to build a $700 million factory to manufacture flash memory devices. AMD had the flash technology, but needed a big partner to finance the investment and also bear the large risk involved. Fujitsu needed the technology.

A JV company in which AMD and Fujitsu owned equal shares was to be set up. In addition, each parent was to take about 5% equity stake in the other. From AMD's point of view this would ensure Fujitsu's interest in the financial success of AMD. The agreement forbade either parent from producing the devices outside the JV. This would ensure commitment and reduce opportunism.

Source: Adapted from S. Butler, 'A corporate marriage made to last', *Financial Times*, 15 July 1992

A parent may transfer some of its activities to the venture, but it may also enter into similar ventures with other parents. Again this may lead to a conflict of interest. Since the management of a venture is often shared between the parents, further conflicts may arise if the two parents are not compatible in terms of organizational objectives and culture. A joint venture has to be negotiated and structured in such a way as to minimize these conflicts. The sources of these frictions and conflicts, and how they may be guarded against, are discussed below.

Since a joint venture is a cooperative enterprise, the line between cooperation and a cartel may often be blurred. Thus JVs may give rise to concerns about their competitive implications, and are hence subject to the antitrust regulations in the UK, the rest of the EU, the US and other countries. The tax implications of different structures and locations of the JV must also be taken into account in formulating a JV, in order to maximize the benefits to the parents. How the JVs will be accounted for in the parents' published accounts also needs to be considered in structuring a JV.

International joint ventures

While JVs between companies operating within the same country (domestic JVs) are important, some of the largest JVs of recent years have been international, involving companies from different countries. The reasons for international joint ventures (IJVs) are many:

- globalization of product markets;
- globalization of competition;
- rapid technological change and short product life cycle;
- huge costs of research and development;
- high fixed costs of brand development, distribution networks and information technology;
- diffusion of technological capabilities and resources;
- relatively high cost of acquisitions and mergers.

Increasing globalization of product markets has resulted from the convergence of consumer tastes, preferences and lifestyles. This means that competition among companies to serve those product markets is also global. This has given opportunities for companies from one part of the world to market their products in another part. However, such global marketing and distribution cannot be undertaken by any company on its own: hence the strategic alliances aimed at marketing and distribution. For example, Allied-Lyons of Britain entered into an alliance with Suntory of Japan in 1989 to distribute each other's drinks products in the UK, the US and Japan. The two partners also entered into a joint sales and manufacturing operation for food products in Australia.

Many of today's products are based on complex technologies, some of them cutting edge. Competition has increasingly been shaped by technological innovations, which themselves are subject to intense competition. The cost of research and development leading to these innovations has mounted beyond the technical and material resources of any single company: hence the need for alliances aimed at technology sharing and development.

Technological competition has also meant that product life cycles have become shorter, thus escalating the pressure for new technologies and new products. Very few companies on their own can keep up with such a technological spiral: therefore companies have to share and pool their resources.

Technological capabilities are now much more diffused than in the past, with many more companies from many more countries being repositories of pockets of technological expertise and excellence. There is therefore an incentive for these companies to pool their expertise and achieve technological synergy. An example of this fragmentation of technological capabilities is in semiconductors. IBM's alliance with Toshiba of Japan and Siemens of Germany to develop a 256-megabit chip illustrates the alliance approach to overcoming this fragmentation.

The so-called multimedia products, combining voice, visual and information technologies, demonstrate that technology can no longer be neatly pigeonholed, and that boundaries between technologies are becoming irrelevant. This again demands that companies with capabilities in different areas come together by mergers or alliances to create these new products. This explains the scramble among telecommunications and computer companies to form alliances or to merge. British Telecom's alliance with MCI of the US to form Concert and the alliance between Sprint of the US and French Telecom and Deutsche Telecom are further examples.

The cost of cutting-edge technological research and development, of producing products for far-flung international markets, of distributing them and of information technology has led to very high fixed costs. One way of spreading these costs is to form alliances for research and development, production, distribution, etc. Thus alliances have become a common-sense method of spreading huge fixed costs.

Although many of the market access and cost reduction goals can be achieved by M & A, in many cases the cost and risks of M & A may be greater than with strategic alliances, although they could also avoid some of the problems of management control, conflict of interest and so on, which have plagued joint ventures.

Model of a joint venture

Cooperative model

International JVs reveal definite patterns in terms of industry, purpose and equity interest. This suggests that JVs are more appropriate in certain industries than in others. They can secure some purposes more effectively than others. Further, the existence of equity interest is

Figure 9.1   The prisoner's dilemma

Prisoner 2

	Confess	Not confess
Confess	Both get 5 years	P1 goes free P2 gets 7 years
Not confess	P1 gets 7 years P2 goes free	Both get 1 year

(Prisoner 1 labels the left side: Confess / Not confess)

deemed necessary in certain cases, but not in others. How do we explain the choices that JV partners make?

The choices are determined by the basic structure of a JV, which is a cooperative enterprise in which the motivations and payoffs of the partners may not always be congruent. In the case of JVs among companies who are also actual or potential competitors in the same markets, or in related markets, JVs can give rise to opportunistic behaviour: that is, cheating. Whether any partner in a JV can get away with cheating depends upon the negative payoff – the punitive sanction to such behaviour.

The incentives to cooperation and the sanction against cheating are captured by a famous model in game theory known as the prisoner's dilemma (PD). This dilemma arises when two prisoners jointly charged with an offence face different payoffs to confessing and not confessing to the offence, as shown in Figure 9.1. In this game, if both prisoners refrain from confessing, they are *collectively* better off than if one confesses and the other does not. In the latter case the confessor is rewarded with freedom, while the non-confessing partner gets seven years in prison. Thus the incentive to cheat on the partner is greater than the incentive to cooperate.

Each prisoner's decision problem is complicated by (1) lack of communication between them and (2) the possibility of getting away with 'squealing'. If each partner can trust the other – that is, if there is a form of non-verbal communication born of years of working together – then the chances of both prisoners not confessing are improved. Alternatively, if squealing does not lead to a happy ending in blissful freedom, but leads to sanctions from the non-confessing prisoner's friends or worse, again a cooperative behaviour will ensue.

Many JVs have built-in opportunities for cheating, and for one partner to gain at the expense of the other. For example, one partner can assiduously learn all the other can teach while withholding their own contribution. Early JVs between American and Japanese firms were often cited as examples of such behaviour, with the Japanese as the offending party. The JV then becomes a zero-sum, rather than a positive-sum, game. Luo, after investigating opportunism in 188 foreign JVs in China, concludes that it increases with difficulty in verifiability of information and in enforceability of law. Opportunism may be a way of managing environmental volatility[9].

The real trick in constructing a successful JV is therefore to increase the payoffs to cooperative behaviour and the sanctions to the 'beggar my partner' behaviour. Careful selection of a partner with a reputation for honest behaviour, and good communication between partners, will help. Further, mutual dependence between the partners is important. Such a mutual dependence in a JV context means that the partners bring complementary strengths to the venture. Where they have the same strengths and weaknesses, the tendency will be for them to gain from each other rather than work together.

Mutual dependence in a single, one-off venture may not, however, prevent a partner from learning as much as possible of the other partner's skills, technology and management systems, and making use of this learning subsequently to gain competitive advantage over the former partner. This is less likely to happen if the venture is of a long or indefinite duration, or where it is accepted by both partners as the beginning of a series of future ventures. In the latter case the expectation that the venture is a repetitive game dilutes the incentive to cheat the first time round. The aim is therefore to maximize the benefits to both parties from a long-term commitment.

One way of increasing the long-term mutual commitment is to provide for equity investment in the venture by both parties. In the alliance between Advanced Micro Devices and Fujitsu the mutual minority equity investment was clearly motivated by this consideration (see Exhibit 9.3 above).

Alliance failure or its instability may be critically determined by poor partner selection. Shah and Swaminathan summarize the criteria for partner selection after reviewing over 40 studies[10]:

- trust;
- commitment;
- complementarity; and
- financial payoff.

These may be more or less important depending on the nature of the alliance project, and the degree of uncertainty in measuring the partners' contribution, in performance assessment and in determining the payoffs to the partners. The relative importance of these four attributes of a good partner may depend on the manageability of the project and the ease of interpretation of the project outcome by the partners. For example, where a project is low on both these characteristics, trust may be more important than complementarity or commitment. Where it is high on both, financial payoff may be most critical determinant of alliance success[11].

It must be remembered that the four factors are not independent, and are often conditioned by one another. For example, trust building is more difficult in more complex alliances, and where the distribution of benefits to the partners lacks transparency. Smaller JVs are more conducive to trust development. Partner similarity may also enhance trust[12].

Transaction cost model

A joint venture requires an agreement between two or more parties, and leads to transaction costs, which include contracting, monitoring and enforcement costs. The venture partners must draw up a sufficiently detailed contract to cover the structure, mutual rights and responsibilities, performance measurement, and enforcement of contractual obligations and remedies. An inherent cost of a JV is that it increases the dependence between the partners, and the scope for one partner to hold up the other (see discussion of the hold-up problem in Chapter 6 in the context of vertical mergers). These transaction costs depend on the nature of the venture and the relationship between the venture partners. A complex venture such as in high-technology research and development needs a more elaborate contract than a service provision venture, since the future outcome of the R & D is less predictable and the attendant risk much greater, but for the same reasons such a contract is also more difficult to draft.

Transaction costs can be reduced if the venture is based on trust and commitment of the parties. Since, in a joint venture, a successful outcome depends on the interactions between people from the two parents, a relational contract based on trust and commitment is much more important than a formal, legally enforceable contract. An ideal venture is one in which the partners sign a contract and then put it away, never to be referred to again. A frequent reading of the contract signals lack of trust and commitment. Nevertheless, 'shotgun' clauses that threaten dire penalties for opportunistic behaviour may still be useful.

However, deals based on presumption of trust and without formal prior agreements on how the venture will be run or valued or on how assets on termination will be distributed may be quite costly for partner firms, as illustrated by the collapse of the JV Concert, between AT&T and British Telecom (BT) (see Exhibit 9.4).

Exhibit 9.4

Trust your partner but don't neglect the pre-nuptial

In 1994 British Telecom (BT) and the US telecom company MCI launched a JV called Concert. This was an attempt by BT to get a foothold in the US. The JV focused on providing international telecom service to large multinational corporations, and was a counter to a similar strategy being followed by other leading telecom groups. BT then made a full takeover bid for MCI but was outbid by Worldcom. When MCI was taken over, BT bought MCI out of Concert.

With its ambition to enter the US still not fulfilled, BT sought to leverage Concert again, this time in a JV with AT&T. Both AT&T and BT added some of their own operations to the JV, both to cement the JV relationship by increasing each partner's commitment to Concert and to give Concert a respectable and viable scale of operation. The two parents decided not to have a 'pre-nuptial agreement' that would have governed any future dissolution of the JV, as a show of their commitment to the marriage. But soon the marriage was on the rocks.

Excess capacity on many telecom routes put pressure on the JV. Further, the two parents still retained operations that competed with the JV. In the US, sales forces from both AT&T and Concert were pitching for the same clients. In the UK, BT had operations similar to those of Concert. AT&T was also disillusioned that BT had failed to 'deliver Europe' through its minority stakes in several continental telecom companies. It became difficult to maintain the JV relationship. The absence of a pre-nuptial agreement clearly setting out the terms of separation made the dissolution difficult[13].

Source: Adapted from R. Waters and D. Roberts, 'Concert sounded off key almost from opening bars', *Financial Times*, 16 October 2001

Real option model of JVs

JVs may be regarded as platforms on which to build the resources, capabilities and market positions to give the partner firms a sustainable competitive advantage. The value of the platform depends on how the underlying growth opportunities will evolve. When they evolve in the right direction, and the value of these opportunities increases, the JV partners can make follow-on investments in the venture or buy out the JV partner. This means that each partner, by entering the JV, acquires an option (a call option) to make follow-on investments. The follow-on option will be exercised when the value of the growth opportunity exceeds the follow-on investment (the exercise price). The initial investment in the JV is speculative, and increases in value with the value of the growth opportunities. It is also higher the more volatile the value of the growth opportunities is, and the longer the time the JV partner has to exercise the follow-on option.

These characteristics of JVs make them real options. Some researchers have therefore extended the real options framework to understand how JVs create value, and to value them (see Chapter 3 for an introduction to real options and Chapter 14 on real option valuation). The real option framework is particularly appropriate for exploratory alliances. These may be regarded as small bets on out-of-the-money, long-dated and highly speculative options. By contrast, exploitative alliances may be regarded as short-dated, more stable and in-the-money options.

Kogut investigates the proposition that JVs are designed as options that are exercised through divestment and acquisition decisions[14]. The divestment decision is analogous to the abandonment of real options. The decision to acquire the partner's equity stake is analogous to the exercise of a real call option. The decision to terminate a JV is to exercise the right to sell (a put option). Kogut analyzes the factors that increase the likelihood of an acquisition, using the real options model of valuation. He finds that an unexpected increase in the value of the venture, i.e. the value of the growth opportunity and the degree of concentration in the industry, increases the likelihood that a JV partner will exercise the acquisition option. In a concentrated industry, competitors are more likely to generate similar growth options through copycat JVs (see the case study at the end of the chapter for examples from the automobile industry). This decreases the potential value of the JV, and therefore forces an early exercise.

Folta and Miller argue that firms entering JVs have to choose between flexibility and commitment. Flexibility means delaying the exercise of the call option to make additional equity investment. Commitment means early exercise to pre-empt rival firms grabbing the growth opportunities. When the uncertainty about future value of the JV is resolved, i.e. volatility decreases, early exercise is more likely and a buyout of the JV partner occurs[15]. They find empirical support for this pattern from a study of JVs in the biotechnology industry in the US during 1978–99.

Tong, Reuer and Peng test for the conditions under which the growth options in IJVs are valuable. They argue that non-core product-market-based IJVs, a large number and greater spread (between emerging economies and others) of IJVs in the firms' portfolios generate more valuable growth options. Further, the partners can capture the growth option value better if the JVs are EJVs. The authors find support for diversifying IJVS (across two-digit industries) and equity investment in IJVs. However, there is no significant benefit from diversifying into emerging economies, perhaps because foreign IJV partners overpay for their share of the IJV, or because of greater implementation problems[16]. Thus factors that influence the various parameters of the real option model are important to understand whether JVs are valuable growth options or not.

An important insight from the real options framework of strategic alliances is that abandonment of the alliance is not necessarily a 'failure' Where an alliance is designed for a purpose, e.g. mutual learning and knowledge-sharing, and that purpose is accomplished, the alliance can be abandoned. However, where the partners are engaged in a *'learning race'* to acquire more knowledge from the partner, but deny or delay that partner's access to one's own knowledge, then the duration of the JV will be determined by the pace of the race. The winner of this race will then precipitate the abandonment of the JV[17]. A JV should be designed to factor in such abandonment, its likely timing, and the financial consequences of the partner's exit.

Structuring a joint venture

A joint venture involves the following stages[18]:

Pre-agreement:
1 Choice of joint venture as a strategic alternative.
2 Partner selection.
3 Negotiation and selection of contractual form.
4 Valuation of the JV's benefits.
5 Design of the organizational structure, e.g. new entity distinct from the parents.
Post-agreement:
6 Management of the venture.
7 Performance evaluation.
8 Feedback to strategy formulation and rethinking alliance strategy.

Pre-agreement aspects

At the first stage, the firm has to evaluate carefully whether a joint venture is the appropriate mechanism for achieving its strategic objectives. A joint venture should be compared with other options, such as a greenfield operation, an acquisition or a merger. In making the choice, the costs, benefits and risks of the alternatives must be considered (see discussion below).

Partner selection for a JV is a very important step, and partners should be evaluated on several criteria: the partner's strategic intent in a JV, the compatibility of partners' intents, the potential partner's commitment, resources, management style and organizational systems, and corporate culture. The track record of the potential partner in JVs must also be examined. Depending on the familiarity of the JV partners from previous alliances, they may be classified as '*friends, acquaintances or strangers*'. The choice of these partners does not always follow the same order. Where a partner is keen to protect valuable technological assets from appropriation by the other partner, it may even be the case that a stranger may be chosen in preference to a friendly partner[19].

Negotiating a JV agreement should be done with the utmost care. The objectives of the JV must be stated with clarity. The assumptions behind the expected performance must be explicitly articulated. Benchmarks for measuring performance and formulae for sharing the costs and profits of the venture must be agreed. Negotiation must also cover the arrangements for the management of the venture, the contribution each partner will make to the management, who will assume the leadership, and what the relationship will be between the parents and the venture as well as between the parents[20]. Mayer and Teece find, from a study of 15 alliance contracts to develop jet engines between a major aerospace manufacturer and its 11 alliance partners, that such contracts are 'designed to share risk, facilitate learning and exchange of knowledge, specify roles and responsibilities and provide administrative mechanisms for adapting and resolving disputes'[21].

Value gains from a joint venture

Partners to a joint venture have to evaluate the JV decision on the basis of a cost–benefit analysis. Both the costs and the benefits often depend on the future evolution of the alliance, particularly in the case of an exploratory or learning-type alliance, since the outcomes as well as future investments to further the objectives of the alliance are not easily foreseeable. A conventional discounted cash flow approach may not be helpful except in limited alliance types, e.g. in a cost-cutting exploitative alliance. A useful alternative model for exploratory alliances is the real options model, discussed above.

Doz and Hamel describe five valuation conundrums in alliances[22]:

- They bring together non-traded assets that are difficult to value.
- The relative contributions of each partner to alliance success are hard to assess.
- Value from the alliance may arise outside the relationship, i.e. the parents may be indirect rather than direct beneficiaries[23].
- The relative value of the partners' contribution may shift over time in ways that are difficult to anticipate and recognize (see Exhibit 9.6 below).
- Partners may conceal the real benefits they expect to receive or have received.

Often a company may spin off an existing business, say a subsidiary, into a JV by way of its contribution. This may be a tax-free spin-off (see Chapter 10 on spin-offs), but such a spin-off may also raise accounting reporting issues, i.e. whether the parent still retains control for accounting purposes. As in the case of mergers, there are also differences in accounting rules for JVs across countries that need to be considered while establishing cross-border JVs.

The above problems can to some extent be resolved by a careful definition of alliance scope, a robust pre-nuptial agreement, selection of appropriate organizational form for the JV, setting up objective performance benchmarks, assessment of both processes and outcomes, and increasing opportunities for repeated and long-term partner interaction.

Post-agreement management

Each partner will be concerned to ensure that access to its core technology is carefully regulated. It may be necessary to ring-fence such technology. Exhibit 9.5 highlights this problem in

Exhibit 9.5

GE ring-fences its core technology

American company GE and the French company Snecma formed a joint venture called CFM in 1974 to design and produce an engine for small civilian aircraft. The US government was reluctant to allow GE to use the top-secret design of the B1 engine core for the new engine development. However, after direct talks between Presidents Nixon and Pompidou, the US government agreed that the gas turbine core could be used, but GE could not give Snecma the technology. GE then built the gas turbine core and Snecma the low-pressure outer parts of the engine. Thus within the JV there were still significant proprietary technologies that the partners did not reveal to each other.

Source: Adapted from P. Betts and A. Kaletsky, 'Powered by a ten-tonne thrust', *Financial Times*, 1 February 1989

the joint venture between GE and Snecma. In other cases ring-fencing is necessary in order to prevent your partner emerging as a latter-day competitor; otherwise the venture will be reduced to a meaningless and 'hollowed-out' shell.

The duration of the venture and the exit must be agreed between the partners. How the assets, the technology and the profits and losses at the time of exit will be shared must form part of the pre-nuptial agreement (see Exhibit 9.4 above). The majority of JVs are terminated by the strong partner buying out the weak partner. Of course, such an end may be engineered by the buyer in an opportunistic way. The JV agreement must provide for alternative exit routes, including buyout of one partner by the other. In the case of a buyout the formula for valuation of each partner's stake and for a control premium will need to be agreed at the JV formation stage.

As with acquisitions, it is people who make joint ventures succeed. A venture normally involves managers and technical staff working together to achieve its common goals. The interface between the people from the two parents who come together in a venture therefore needs to be carefully managed. It may be necessary to evolve a new organization with its own value system and culture appropriate for the venture.

Over time, the relative strengths and weaknesses of the alliance partners may shift and cause friction in their relationship. Partners can use the time of renewal of the alliance to appropriate more value from the alliance or use it to exit from the alliance, causing it to break down (see Exhibit 9.6).

The linkages between the various stages of JV operation need to be kept in view. Mitchell emphasizes avoiding disconnection between corporate staff who negotiate an alliance and the business unit people lower down who carry out the day-to-day activities in executing the JV[24]. The latter should not be kept in the dark about the reasons why the alliance was formed and how it fitted the firm's broad objectives. In the post-alliance formation period there is a need for continual education answering the following questions:

- Who will be responsible for learning from your partner?
- Who will be responsible for teaching people in your own business?
- How will you reward alliance education?
- How is the alliance changing?
- What is your partner learning from you?
- Can you get out if you have to?

Even if a partner uses alliance as a key part of its strategy, it needs to have sufficient autonomy to operate independently, or at least be strong enough to attract a desirable new partner. Unlike good marriages, alliances are not for ever, and companies should be prepared to exchange partners if a better one emerges.

Corporate alliance management capabilities need to be developed. Where the firm relies on a large number of alliances to advance its strategic aims, it pays to develop these capabilities into a core competence[25]. This would avoid errors that often lead to alliance failure such as the following:

- *Kaleidoscope mistake* – treating each alliance as if it were the only relationship. It is critically important to create a dedicated alliance management unit, with corporate and business staff involvement. The alliance management unit must take the lead in assessing the composite needs and opportunities that arise from a portfolio of alliances, as well as the needs and value of each alliance.
- *Alliance a subsidiary mistake* – placing alliance management in a business development function focused on mergers and acquisitions. Acquisitions and alliances staff must communicate

Exhibit 9.6

Large Tom and Little Jerry switch roles

In 1994 Pixar, started by Steve Jobs, the founder of Apple Computers, was a struggling company making computer graphics animated motion pictures. This industry was nascent, and yet to grow into the multi-billion dollar entertainment industry segment it was to become. But in 1994 Pixar needed a partner to finance and distribute the new type of animated movies. Disney was already a world leader in animated films. So Pixar entered into a strategic alliance. In exchange for a share of the profits, Disney would finance Pixar and distribute its films. Disney acquired the right to make sequels to Pixar films if Pixar refused to do so. Disney also gained control of the characters that Pixar developed. At this stage Disney was the dominant partner; Pixar was the little Jerry to Disney's Tom.

Over the next 10 years Pixar produced blockbusters such as *Toy Story*, *A Bug's Life*, *Monsters, Inc.*, *Finding Nemo* and *The Incredibles*, generating aggregate revenue of well over $5 billion dollars. During the same period the performance of Disney's animated characters was lacklustre. They generated only a fraction of the revenues from Pixar's movies. Disney therefore eyed the Pixar-generated characters for sequels to generate revenues. But the robust performance of Pixar and the poorer performance of Disney had now shifted the balance of power to Pixar.

When the alliance was due for renewal in 2004, Pixar insisted on regaining control of its characters, and wanted Disney to be just a distributor. Disney's reluctance to agree to this term led to the collapse of the alliance. In the following two years Pixar attempted vainly to find a distributor of the same strength as Disney, but failed. In 2006 it accepted a takeover offer worth $7.4bn from Disney. Steve Jobs became the largest single investor in Disney, and John Lassiter – Pixar characters' creator – became its chief creative officer. Pixar, the little Jerry, outwitted big Tom!

Source: J. Barney and W. Hesterly, *Strategic Management and Competitive Advantage* (Upper Saddle River, NJ, USA: Pearson Prentice Hall), 2007, p. 290. They draw upon S. Levy and D. Jefferson, 'Hey Mickey, buzz off!', *Business Week*, 9 February 2004 and T. Lowry *et al.*, 'Megamedia mergers: How dangerous?', *Business Week*, 23 February 2004

and interact in a way that recognizes the different challenges of acquiring subsidiaries and managing partnerships.

In managing alliances a distinction must be made between *contracts* and *contacts* between alliance teams. The latter is very important in building confidence and trust, in problem solving, and in understanding how the alliance is performing and evolving.

Performance evaluation of joint ventures

How do we assess the success or failure of a strategic alliance? One possible yardstick is whether they create shareholder value in the short run and in the long run. Second is their mortality rate: that is, how soon after their formation they get dissolved or taken over. Dissolution or takeover *per se* does not signify failure, since an alliance that has served its purpose may be dissolved to the satisfaction of the partners, or sold to one of them (see Exhibit 9.7). Where dissolution or takeover is premature, failure may be inferred. After analyzing 1592 alliances that 200 US companies had formed between 1993 and 1997, Dyer, Kale and Singh find that 48% ended in failure in less than 24 months[26].

Exhibit 9.7

Romance wears off for AMD and Fujitsu

Ten years after establishing their JV called Spansion to devise and produce flash memory devices (see Exhibit 9.3 above), AMD decided in April 2005 to quit the venture. AMD said sales of $447m for the memory group in the first quarter were down 29% on a year earlier and 11% compared with the fourth quarter. Operating losses nearly tripled from the fourth quarter's $39m to $110m. 'The NOR Flash memory market continued to experience industry-wide oversupply and strong pricing pressure,' said Robert Rivet, chief financial officer. 'We experienced a rise in unit shipments, but our average selling price declined significantly, resulting in weaker than expected sales.' AMD's bigger rival, Intel, had made dramatic gains in market share with an aggressive pricing strategy for NOR flash memory devices. AMD was under pressure to act decisively to prevent Spansion becoming a permanent drag on earnings.

In December 2005 Spansion was spun off through an initial public offering (IPO) on the Nasdaq to raise $493m. Before the IPO, AMD had owned 60% of Spansion equity and Fujitsu 40%. After the IPO they owned 40% and 27% respectively. While they still had important stakes in Spansion, competitive pressures in the flash memory market had rendered the JV much less valuable than when it was conceived.

Source: Chris Nuttal, 'AMD plans to spin-off loss-making Spansion', 14 April 2005 and 'Spansion cuts price range of its IPO', 16 December 2005, both from *Financial Times*

When the alliance is in progress, purely financial metrics may be inadequate to assess its performance. It is therefore appropriate to include non-financial metrics as well. A more comprehensive score card may cover[27]:

- financial fitness – net income, cash flow, return on assets, expected net present value;
- strategic fitness – market share, new product launches, customer loyalty, access to new technologies and customers;
- operational fitness – quality of products, manufacturing thoughput, meeting operational milestones;
- relational fitness – cultural fit, trust, speed and clarity of decision-making, effective intervention to resolve disputes, adequacy of member contribution etc[28].

The all-important success measure is of course is the value that accrues to the alliance partners. The stock market returns in the short and long term provide this assessment.

Stock market reaction to JVs and alliances

Several studies investigate the impact of JVs and other forms of SAs on the market value of firms entering into them. These studies use data on alliances involving US companies. McConnell and Nantell reported a favourable stock market reaction to announcements of joint ventures[29]. Chan *et al.* reported that non-JV alliances also generate positive abnormal returns for partner firms' shareholders[30]. These returns are highest when the alliance involves the transfer or pooling of technical knowledge. Allen and Phillips find that the combination of equity ownership with JVs and other product market relationships increases stock prices and operating profitability for the partnering firms. This result is particularly true for alliances in R & D intensive industries[31].

Consistent with the exploratory nature of JVs, Chen *et al.* found that firms with promising investment opportunities had a significantly positive response to announcements of international JV investments, whereas firms with poor investment opportunities had an unfavourable response to such announcements[32].

These studies have, however, not examined the long-term stock return performance of alliances. It is therefore not clear whether the initial positive reaction to SA announcements is maintained over the longer term when problems with alliances come to the fore and they unravel. Surveys of managers of firms undertaking alliances may provide a clue in this regard.

Evidence of alliance performance from managerial surveys

Bleeke and Ernst from McKinsey, the consultants, examined a sample of 49 cross-border strategic alliances (CBSAs) made by companies in the top 150 in Europe, the US and Japan[33]. These CBSAs were motivated by the desire to speed entry into new markets, to develop and commercialize new products, to gain skills, or to share costs. Success was measured in terms of return on assets or on equity, and whether the return exceeded the cost of capital.

The survey revealed that 51% of the CBSAs were regarded as successful and 33% as failures by both partners. The remainder failed for at least one of the partners. Further, 67% of the CBSAs ran into trouble in the first two years. Some 78% of all the alliances that were terminated ended in acquisition by a partner, and 5% by a third party; 17% were dissolved.

Bleeke and Ernst identified characteristics that distinguished successful CBSAs. One of them is the geographical overlap in the operations of the partners. Whereas 62% of CBSAs with minimal overlap succeeded, only 25% of those with moderate or high overlap did so, and 37% of the latter failed. This result is consistent with our argument that complementarity, rather more than commonality, is conducive to a successful relationship between partners.

Alliances that provided for flexibility to broaden their scope were also more successful. Further, equal ownership reduced the scope for opportunism between partners, and enhanced cooperative behaviour, as suggested by the prisoner's dilemma model described earlier. For a sample of 20 CBSAs with a 50:50 ownership interest, 60% were successful, whereas for a sample of 13 with an uneven split of equity interest, only 31% were successful and 61% failed.

KPMG carried out a survey in 1997 of senior executives from 155 UK-based corporations that had been involved in either joint ventures or other strategic alliances over the previous few years. These were both domestic and international alliances. Some 34% of the respondents expressed the view that the JVs had performed a little or much worse than they had expected, and 27% found they had performed a little or much better than expected. For 29% the performance was as expected[34]. In a 1999 survey of 323 senior executives from the US, Europe and Asia, Andersen Consulting reported that 30% of alliances failed and 39% met or exceeded initial expectations of the partners. After analyzing over 2000 alliances formed over four years, Andersen estimated that the 15 most successful added \$72bn to their market capitalization while the 15 least successful partnerships lost \$43bn[35].

Critical success factors in strategic alliances

From the theoretical models of joint ventures as well as the survey evidence presented, we may draw up a list of factors potentially conducive to successful alliances:

- Partners should bring complementary skills, capabilities and market positions to the alliance.
- Market overlap between partners should be minimal to avoid conflict of interest.
- Partnership should be based on a balance of business strength and ownership interest among partners.
- The alliance must have a degree of autonomy, with strong leadership and continual commitment and support from the parents.
- The alliance must build up trust and confidence between the partners and not depend only on the contractual rights and obligations.
- Divergence of management styles and corporate cultures must be handled with sensitivity, and a new common style and culture distinct from the parents' must be evolved.

Risk factors in strategic alliances

Even long-standing strategic alliances can break down because of the divergence of strategies that the partners want to pursue. Thus the potential for rivalry and distrust between partners always exists in strategic alliances, as illustrated by the rift between Compaq and Intel in 1994 when Intel started its 'Intel inside' campaign to promote its semi-conductor. Compaq felt threatened as they felt this might undermine the Compaq brand name. The future evolution of a cooperative arrangement is not always linear and predictable. Both the duration and future shape of an alliance are uncertain, and depend on how the strategic priorities of the partners evolve. Where one partner learns from the other all it can or need to, that partner may walk out. Where one partner gains in power relative to the other, the weaker partner may be taken over[36].

For Koza and Lewin, the root cause of alliance failure is failure to grasp and articulate its strategic intent[37]. The second most common reason is lack of recognition of the close interplay between the overall strategy of the company and the role of an alliance in that strategy. Exploration alliances pool complementary resources that neither parent is interested in, or capable of, developing on its own in order to enhance revenue. Exploration alliances are generally implemented as open-ended co-development joint venture projects. They are intended to achieve learning of previously unknown technologies, new geographical markets, or new product domains. They are best for prospecting strategies. Their progress and outcomes are more difficult to measure. The seeds of alliance tension and instability are sown from the outset when alliances fail to recognize a mismatch in strategic intent. Alliances may evolve in ways that create divergence between original strategic intent and the present alliance outcomes. The JV may allow one of the partners to 'hold up' the other and increase the cost of following its own strategy.

Businesses also risk becoming dependent on their partners, creating serious problems when a partner shuts down and if a partner forms a relationship with a new partner. For a sample of software systems industry collaborations in the US during 1961–91, Singh and Mitchell found that businesses faced increased risk of dissolution if they did not form a new partnership after partners had shut down or formed relationships with new partners[38]. Collaboration is an imperfect process of acquiring resources. Businesses that are able to work closely with current partners while at the same time identifying possible new partners are likely to succeed in an industry marked by ongoing technological change.

JV partners also risk value losses when their partners become takeover targets[39]. This loss is due to expropriation of intellectual capital, and it increases with the R & D intensity of the non-targeted partner in the JV.

Choosing between an acquisition and an alliance

It is clear that acquisition and alliance, especially joint ventures, have considerable similarities and are often alternative modes of achieving the firm's strategic objectives. Do firms systematically evaluate the two options even if they view them as alternatives? A survey of 200 US companies reveals that, while 82% of these firms consider acquisitions and alliances as 'two different ways of achieving the same growth goals', only 24% had considered an alliance when they last executed an acquisition and only 14% have a specific policy guideline or criteria for choosing between the two options[40].

How then does a firm choose between the two? Although many of the market access and cost reduction goals can be achieved by acquisitions, in many cases the cost and risk of acquisitions may be greater than with strategic alliances. But acquisitions can also avoid some of the problems of management control, conflict of interest and so on that have plagued joint ventures. A disadvantage of an acquisition is that it involves the ownership of the entire target, whereas the acquirer's interest may be limited to some of the target's specific capabilities. Thus JVs allow parents to selectively access the target capabilities they need.

In an acquisition full control is achieved through ownership, whereas in a JV both ownership and control are shared. Thus a fundamental question is whether control through ownership is necessary. Of course, control through ownership is direct and unambiguous, whereas control through other means, e.g. exclusive access to technology or markets, is often much more subtle. Where the acquirer needs to protect its own competences from being copied by a potential alliance partner, or desires to throw a proprietary ring-fence around future development of competitive advantages, or wants to ensure the commitment of the partner firm, a merger is to be preferred to an alliance. Where a firm needs to control the 'road map' of technology evolution and its application, and avoid friction between partners over this roadmap, then acquisition is preferable[41].

Dyer, Kale and Singh provide a typology of five factors that determine the preferability of alliance over acquisition or vice versa. In some cases an equity alliance (EJV) is preferable to a non-equity alliance. These factors, and which growth strategy will suit each, are shown in Table 9.1[42].

Industry characteristics may also determine the suitability of either acquisition or alliance. Industry conditions, such as high specialized human asset intensity, a high level of tacit knowledge, and capital intensity are factors that determine the flexibility or commitment of firms and hence their choice of the organizational form for growth. Technological uncertainty may make alliances more likely. There is also a certain path dependence, since in industries where alliances have been dominant, firms may continue to prefer them. Antitrust regulations may be more benign to alliances than to acquisitions. Acquisitions may also follow from a platform built on alliances[43].

Reuer differentiates acquisitions and alliances along four dimensions, and identifies conditions under which an alliance may be preferred[44]:

Table 9.1 To ally or acquire? That is the question!

Factor	Acquisition, EJV or non-EJV
Synergy type	
• Modular (partners manage resources independently but pool the results)	• Non-EJV
• Sequential (one partner completes its tasks and passes results to another)	• EJV
• Reciprocal (partners execute tasks through interactive knowledge sharing)	• Acquisition
Nature of resources: relative value of soft to hard resources	
• Low	• Non-EJV
• Low/ medium	• Acquisition
• High	• EJV
Extent of redundant resources	
• Low	• Non-EJV
• Medium	• EJV
• High	• Acquisition
Market uncertainty	
• Low	• Non-EJV
• Medium	• Acquisition
• High	• EJV
Competition	
• Low	• Non-EJV
• Medium	• EJV
• High	• Acquisition

Source: KPMG International, *Alliances and Joint Ventures: Fit, Focus and Follow-through*, 2005, downloaded from www.kpmg.com.

- Infeasibility – acquisition may not be feasible for regulatory, political or legal reasons.
- Information asymmetry – the partners have access to different information sets, making it difficult to value their relative contributions.
- Indigestibility – post-acquisition integration of the acquirer and the acquired firms poses problems so severe as to prevent value creation from the acquisition.
- Investment in options where strategic flexibility is more important than commitment of the partners.

Indigestibility can be caused by resource indivisibility of target assets as well as cultural differences. It can also make it more difficult to judge the value of the combined entity in the first place. This provides the link between post-acquisition indigestibility and pre-acquisition valuation problems, i.e. information asymmetry[45].

Even with due diligence, the acquiring company may be very uncertain about the true value of target assets. Information asymmetry also arises when targeted assets are embedded and shared in the target company. Alliances can mitigate these valuation problems by enabling companies to combine complementary resources on a limited basis. They get a better idea of the assets' true value through repeated interaction with the partner. Once this learning occurs, the company can increase its commitment or quit the relationship as appropriate.

Are acquisitions less reversible than EJVs and in turn non-EJVs? Given the market for corporate assets (see Chapter 10), acquisitions can also be unwound the same way as JVs. However, the costs of unwinding may be higher.

The case study below discusses how General Motors and Ford preferred alternative growth strategies in the global automobile industry.

CASE STUDY

General Motors (GM) and Ford drive on different roads to same town

In the 1980s and 1990s both GM and Ford made a number of acquisitions, and formed a number of strategic alliances and joint ventures in Europe and Asia. Ford acquired majority controls of premium brands such as Jaguar, Volvo and Land Rover in Europe. Ford also made an offer for the near-bankrupt South Korean carmaker Daewoo. In Europe GM's strategy was to build up its presence in various markets through alliances.

About 12 years ago Ford acquired UK's ailing Jaguar luxury car company and sent in its restructuring team to revive the brand. Since then Jaguar has doubled its sales, and by 2000 was a profitable company. About the same time GM bought a 50% stake in Saab. Sweden's Wallenberg family retained the rest of the equity and some board seats. This JV failed to turn Saab around and stop its accumulation of losses. In early 2000 GM bought out the Wallenberg stake. In the same year Saab broke even.

Other leading automobile manufacturers such as Daimler-Benz, Volkswagen and Renault were also busy forming alliances or making acquisitions in the fast-consolidating industry. Volkswagen acquired Seat, Audi and Bentley. Daimler-Benz acquired Chrysler to become DaimlerChrysler and also took equity stakes in Mitsubishi. Renault formed an equity JV alliance with Nissan and took management control. Ford also took management control of Mazda. Why did these companies choose alliance in some cases and acquisition in other cases?

Non-availability of the target company for purchase leaves alliance as the only option to enter a market. Family ownership as well as nationalist sentiments against foreign ownership of an industry protected the automobile firms in some countries. Apart from these constraints, GM and Ford also had differing opinions about the merits of alliance versus acquisition. Rick Wagoner, GM's CEO, argued: 'Our alliance approach allowed us to realise synergies faster than we could in a full buy-out situation. In short we get most of the gain with a lot less of the pain. It is also a capital-efficient way to grow. Instead of pouring billions into acquisitions, we can spend that money on things like win–win product development programmes.' With a relatively small capital outlay, GM could gain access to technology, product areas and platforms.

GM also argued that alliances had other advantages. They minimized cultural clashes, and could safeguard employee morale. That its alliances were a serious business was demonstrated by the equity stakes that GM took in companies such as Fiat in Italy. Ford, on the other hand, felt that outright ownership offered several advantages. It could position its brands and products with a lot more strategic freedom, unencumbered by an alliance partner. It did not have to negotiate with an alliance partner. It could cut costs without the sentimental baggage of the previous owner turned alliance partner. It could exploit marketing and global positioning opportunities with speed. Where Ford wanted full control and full profits, outright acquisition was the better option.

Alliance management required great diplomatic skills of patience and compromise. Decision-making might be subject to paralyzing negotiations and cutting deals. Many of the alliances in the car industry had been big failures, e.g. Ford's JV with Volkswagen to develop people carriers, or Nissan's partnership with Ford in off-road vehicles. Alliances could succeed where both partners had clear goals and understood them, e.g. a takeover in the end or limited and well-defined scope, e.g. in diesel engines.

→

Discussion questions

1 What were GM's arguments for preferring alliance to acquisition?

2 What were Ford's arguments for preferring acquisition to alliance?

3 What factors influence the choice between the two growth pathways?

Source: Adapted from T. Burt, 'Carmakers take two routes to global growth', *Financial Times*, 11 July 2000

Overview and implications for practice

This chapter provides an introduction to strategic alliances, which, under certain circumstances, are preferable to conventional acquisitions and mergers. Recent years have seen hundreds of international and within-Europe alliances.

- Strategic alliances are of different types according to economic substance, legal structure and equity ownership. Joint ventures represent a major part of strategic alliances.

- Strategic alliances may be vulnerable to opportunism, inappropriate structure, and unsuitable or unreliable partners.

- Strategic alliances are subject to antitrust regulatory rules of each country as well as the EU.

- Stock markets on average react positively to strategic alliances.

- Survey evidence on strategic alliances formed by top companies in Europe, the US and Japan shows that a substantial number of them fail. A list of critical success factors is provided.

- Strategic alliance is an alternative to merger, provided a number of conditions are met. These include infeasibility of merger, information asymmetry between merging partners, indigestibility of the acquisition and need for strategic flexibility.

Review questions

9.1 What is the economic logic of strategic alliances? What is their economic substance?

9.2 How do alliances differ?

9.3 What are equity and non-equity joint ventures? What is the function of the equity investment?

9.4 What is the distinction between a learning alliance and a business alliance?

9.5 What are the problems associated with a JV?

9.6 In what sense is a strategic alliance a real option?

9.7 What are the problems in the valuation of JVs?

9.8 What factors cause strategic alliances to fail?

9.9 What factors contribute to their success?

9.10 Under what conditions is a merger preferable to a strategic alliance?

Further reading

J. Bamford and D. Ernst, 'Measuring alliance performance', *The McKinsey Quarterly*, October 2002.

S. Chan, J. W. Kensinger, A. J. Keown and J. D. Martin, 'Do strategic alliances create value?', *Journal of Financial Economics*, **46**, 1997, 199–221.

J. Dyer, P. Kale and H. Singh, 'When to ally and when to acquire', *Harvard Business Review*, 81(7&8), 2004, 109–115.

D. Li, L. Eden, M. Hitt and R. Ireland, 'Friends, acquaintances, or strangers? Partner selection in R & D alliances', *Academy of Management Journal*, **51**(2), 2008, 315–334.

Notes and references

1. See J. Bamford and D. Ernst, 'Measuring alliance performance', *The McKinsey Quarterly*, October 2002, and D. Besanko, D. Dranove, M. Stanley and S. Schaefer, *Economics of Strategy* (Hoboken, NJ: John Wiley & Sons, 2007), Table 4.1.

2. O. Dussauge, B. Garrette and W. Mitchell, 'Learning from competing partners: Outcomes and durations of scale and link alliances in Europe, North America and Asia', *Strategic Management Journal*, **21**, 2000, 99–126.

3. Y. L. Doz and G. Hamel, *Alliance Advantage: The Art of Creating Value Through Partnering* (Cambridge, MA: Harvard University Press, 1998). These may also be applied to mergers, as we did in Chapter 5.

4. M. Y. Yoshino and U. Srinivasa Rangan, *Strategic Alliances: An Entrepreneurial Approach to Globalisation* (Cambridge, MA: Harvard Business School Press, 1995).

5. M. P. Koza and A. Lewin, 'The co-evolution of strategic alliances', *Organization Science*, **9**, 1998, 255–264.

6. M. P. Koza and A. Lewin, 'Putting the S-word back in alliances', *Financial Times*, Mastering Strategy series, Part 6, 1 November 1999.

7. D. Lavie and L. Rosenkopf, 'Balancing exploration and exploitation in alliance formation', *Academy of Management*, **49**(4), 2006, 797–818, discuss the constraints on exploitation and exploration, and the challenges of balancing the two in forming alliances. For example, organizational inertia may limit the firm to exploitation, but the firm's absorptive capacity, i.e. learning from others and absorbing external knowledge, may facilitate exploration.

8. Dussauge, Garrette and Mitchell, *ibid.*

9. Y. Luo, 'Are joint venture partners more opportunistic in a more volatile environment?', *Strategic Management Journal*, **28**, 2007, 39–60.

10. R. Shah and V. Swaminathan, 'Factors influencing selection in strategic alliances: The moderating role of alliance context', *Strategic Management Journal*, 29, 2008, 471–494.

11. Shah and Swaminathan, *ibid.*

12. M. Robson, C. Katsikeas and D. Bello, 'Drivers and performance outcomes of trust in international strategic alliances: The role of organizational complexity', *Organization Science*, **19**(4), 2008, 647–665. Inter-partner trust is shown as improving alliance performance.

13. The delightful Hollywood romantic comedy *Intolerable Cruelty*, released in 2003, revolves round pre-nuptial agreements. George Clooney plays a clever, smooth but soulless lawyer who cares little for love, and boasts of his ability to draw up unbeatable pre-nuptial agreements for the benefit of his philandering clients, who can get away with offering little to their wronged spouses. He meets Catherine Zeta-Jones, a beautiful and scheming gold-digger, who marries wealthy men only to enjoy huge divorce settlements. She has not been beaten by pre-nuptial agreements so far. Her *modus operandi* is to sign a pre-nuptial but persuade the new husband to tear up the agreement in a moment of uncontrollable infatuation with the enchanting bride. Clooney foils her scheme but falls hopelessly in love with her. In revenge, Zeta-Jones gets him to sign a pre-nuptial before marrying him, and traps the lawyer. She beats him at his own game. Clooney finally finds 'love'.

14. B. Kogut, 'Joint ventures and the option to expand and acquire', in P. J. Buckley and P. N. Ghauri (Eds), *International Mergers and Acquisitions, A Reader* (London: Thomson, 2002). pp. 116–132.

15. T. B. Folta and K. D. Miller, 'Real options in equity partnerships', *Strategic Management Journal*, **23**, 2002, 77–88.

16. T. Tong, J. Reuer and M. Peng, 'International joint ventures and the value of growth options', *Academy of Management Journal*, **51**(5), 2008, 1014–1029. The sample size is 293 IJVs from 1989–2000.

17. Habib and Mella-Barral model the duration of a JV based on knowledge-sharing. In their model a JV can be terminated even when there is no learning race. See M. Habib and P. Mella-Barral, 'The role of knowhow acquisition in the formation and duration of joint ventures', *The Review of Financial Studies*, **20**(1), 2007, 189–233. See also Mayer and Teece below for similar arguments.

18. See S. Zahra and G. Elhagrasey, 'Strategic management of international joint ventures', *European Management Journal*, **12**(1), 1994, 83–98 for a discussion of some of these stages.

19. D. Li, L. Eden, M. Hitt and R. Ireland, 'Friends, acquaintances, or strangers? Partner selection in R & D alliances', *Academy of Management Journal*, **51**(2), 2008, 315–334.

20. Robinson and Stuart examine 125 strategic alliance contracts covering early-stage research at biotechnology firms sponsored by large pharmaceutical firms, and find that 'contracting problems posed in alliances are solved through a blend of ownership allocation, explicit contractual clauses and implicit contracts enforced through relational incentives'. Certain contractual clauses may 'inoculate' partners against hold-up, but other conditions exist. See D. Robinson and T. Stuart, 'Financial contracting in biotech strategic alliances', *Journal of Law and Economics*, **50**, 2007, 559–595.

21. K. Mayer and D. Teece, 'Unpacking strategic alliances: The structure and purpose of alliance versus supplier relationships', *Journal of Economic Behaviour & Organization*, **66**, 2008, 106–127.

22. Doz and Hamel, *ibid.*

23. Gulati describes them as network resources. See R. Gulati, *Managing Network Resources: Alliances, Affiliations and Other Relational Assets* (Oxford: Oxford University Press, 2007).

24. W. Mitchell, 'Alliances: Achieving long-term value and short-term goals', *Financial Times*, Strategy series, Part 4, 18 October 1999.

25. See J. Dyer, P. Kale and H. Singh, 'When to ally and when to acquire', *Harvard Business Review*, July-August 2004, 109–115.

26. *Ibid.* They further indicate that 40–55% of alliances break down prematurely and inflict financial damage on both partners.

27. J. Bamford and D. Ernst, 'Measuring alliance performance', *The Mckinsey Quarterly*, October 2002.

28. For an empirical survey-based assessment of alliance performance based on several of these measures, see R. Lunnan and S. Haugland, 'Predicting and measuring alliance performance: A multidimensional analysis', *Strategic Management Journal*, **29**, 2008, 545–556.

29. J. J. McConnell and T. J. Nantell, 'Corporate combinations and common stock returns: The case of joint ventures', *Journal of Finance*, **40**, 1985, 519–536.

30. S. Chan, J. W. Kensinger, A. J. Keown and J. D. Martin, 'Do strategic alliances create value?', *Journal of Financial Economics*, **46**, 1997, 199–221.

31. J. W. Allen and G. M. Phillips, 'Corporate equity ownership, strategic alliances and product market relationships', *Journal of Finance*, **55**(6), 2000, 2791–2815.

32. S. Chen, K. W. Ho, C. F. Lee and G. H. H. Yeo, 'Investment opportunities, free cash flow and market reaction to international joint ventures', *Journal of Banking and Finance*, **24**, 2000, 1747–1765.

33. J. Bleeke and D. Ernst, 'The way to win in cross-border alliances', in J. Bleeke and D. Ernst (Eds), *Collaborating to Compete* (New York: John Wiley, 1993).

34. KPMG, *Joint Ventures: A Triumph of Hope Over Reality* (London: KPMG, 1997).

35. A. Maitland, 'Diplomatic route to lasting relations', *Financial Times*, 30 September 1999. Details of performance measures, the period of stock market performance, etc. in the Andersen study are, however, not reported in this article.

36. Dussauge, Garrette and Mitchell, *ibid.*

37. Koza and Lewin, *ibid.*

38. K. Singh and W. Mitchell, 'Precarious collaboration: Business survival after partners shut down or form new partnership', *Strategic Management Journal*, **17**, 1996, 99–115.

39. S. A. Case, S. Lee and J. D. Martin, *Joint Venture and the Expropriation of Intellectual Capital*, Texas A & M University Working Paper, 2002.

40. Dyer, Kale and Singh, *ibid.*

41. Don McLellan, Corporate VP and Director of Business Development, Motorola, Inc. in interview with KPMG. See KPMG International, *Alliances and Joint Ventures: Fit, Focus and Follow-through*, 2005, downloaded from www.kpmg.com.

42. Dyer, Kale and Singh, *ibid.*

43. See X. Yin and M. Shanley, 'Industry determinants of the "merger versus alliance" decision', *Academy of Management Review*, **33**(2), 2008, 473–491, and W. Vanhaverbeke, G. Duysters and N. Noorderhaven, 'External technology sourcing through alliances or acquisitions: An analysis of the application-specific integrated circuits industry', *Organization Science*, **13**(6), 2002, 714–733.

44. J. Reuer, 'Collaborative strategy: The logic of alliances', *Financial Times*, Mastering Strategy series, part 2, 4 October 1999.

45. J. J. Reuer and M. P. Koza, 'Asymmetric information and joint venture performance: Theory and evidence for domestic and international joint ventures', *Strategic Management Journal*, **21**, 2000, 81–88.

CHAPTER 10

Corporate divestiture

Objectives

At the end of this chapter, the reader should be able to understand:

● the different forms of divestiture and their rationale;

● the structure of different divestiture types and their implications;

● the shareholder wealth effects of divestitures;

● the empirical evidence on the valuation of divestitures; and

● the limits to value creation through divestitures.

Introduction

In the last few chapters our focus has been on companies making acquisitions in pursuit of their corporate and business strategies. These result in new businesses being brought under ownership or control of the acquirer. We now turn to the opposite of acquisition – the divestiture phenomenon, in which a company sells a part of its business, say a division, or rearranges the ownership of some of its businesses so that they can be perceived as distinct and can be so evaluated by the stock market. Of course, for every sale there is a buyer. So divestitures form part of the M & A landscape.

Many large firms in the US and Europe sold off parts of their businesses for a variety of proximate reasons but in ultimate obeisance to the creed of shareholder value. In Chapter 8 we evaluated the performance of conglomerate acquisitions in the past four decades. Many of the empirical studies reviewed in that chapter show that conglomerate acquisitions may have led to shareholder value destruction. Although some of the recent studies record that the effect of conglomerate acquisition may have been less destructive of value, and may even have been neutral or significantly value enhancing, the general misgivings about unrelated corporate expansions led companies to reverse such expansion and reinvent themselves as focused business portfolios.

Outright sale of businesses represents one strategy in this reinvention process. In the last 20 years many companies also pursued other methods of restructuring, aimed at enhancing focus to their business portfolios and thereby shareholder value. Some sought to separate their businesses to reduce or eliminate the conglomerate discount by spin-off or demerger. Others have increased the visibility of some of their businesses to the stock market through equity carve-outs. This is argued to facilitate a more transparent view of the carved-out business and better valuation by the stock market. A more recent innovation with a similar motivation to an equity carve-out is the issue of tracking stock, in which a separate class of the parent's stock is issued to reflect the performance of a component business.

Innovative methods of financing acquisitions, such as leveraged buyouts (LBOs), were introduced into the M & A scene in the 1980s. In a large number of corporate sell-offs the buyers were the managers of the businesses being sold off. Such purchases by managers, called management buyouts (MBOs), have now become an established part of the M & A scene. MBOs are generally financed with a preponderance of debt. We defer our discussion of leveraged acquisitions, also called LBOs, to Chapter 11.

In this chapter we discuss the rationale behind corporate divestitures, their structure and characteristics. We use the term 'divestiture' to mean not only sell-offs but also transactions that are designed to increase focus, i.e. spin-off, equity carve-out and tracking stock. The empirical evidence on the impact of corporate restructuring on shareholder wealth is presented.

Rationale for corporate divestitures

That acquisitions and divestitures rise and fall fairly in tandem is not surprising, since acquisitions and divestitures may be part of the same strategy of firms in refocusing their portfolio of businesses. Often proceeds of divestments are used to finance the acquisitions. In a number of cases in the past acquirers unbundled the acquired firms, retained those parts that made strategic sense, and sold off the ones that did not fit.

Why do companies divest? In a small number of cases where a firm makes an acquisition it may be forced by antitrust authorities to divest those of its businesses that were deemed to lead to an anticompetitive market structure (see Chapter 17 on antitrust regulation, and divestiture as a remedy). This is an involuntary divestiture. In the context of voluntary divestitures there are a number of factors that motivate divestitures:

- The divested division is underperforming in relation to its industry competitors, or to other divestor businesses[1].
- The divested part is performing reasonably well, but it is not well positioned within its industry to give it long-term competitive advantage. For example, GE often divests businesses that are not among the top two or three in their industry, even though they may be profitable.
- The divested part has a poor fit with new strategy. The parent wants to concentrate on areas with the greatest competitive strengths. This process is known as 'sticking to the knitting'.
- The parent is too widely diversified, causing difficulties in monitoring the performance of divisional managers (see Chapter 7 for further discussion)[2].
- The parent is experiencing financial distress, and needs to raise cash to mitigate this and avoid eventual liquidation.
- The divested business has been bought as part of an acquired company, and the parent has no desire to keep it, i.e. unbundling to preserve focus.
- The divested business has been bought as part of an acquisition, and the parent needs to raise money to pay for the acquisition, i.e. unbundling to raise finance.
- The divested business has been bought as part of a 'bust-up' takeover in which unbundling and selling the target piecemeal to strategic buyers is the value creation strategy of the acquirer, i.e. buy low and sell high strategy[3].
- Acquisition and subsequent divestiture are part of a coherent strategy to buy an underperforming company, turn it around, and sell at a profit, i.e. buy–operate–sell strategy[4] (see Chapter 13).

- The parent feels the divested part will be valued higher if it is a 'stand-alone' entity, since more information about the divested company will be available to the stock market.
- The divested part has better strategic fit with another company, enabling the latter to create value. The divestor may then share some of the added value for the benefit of its own shareholders[5].
- A divestment may also be used as a defence against a hostile takeover: for example, sale of 'crown jewels' (see Chapter 21).

Does divestiture mean failure of prior acquisition?

Many researchers have traced the fate of acquired businesses to see whether and for how long they are retained as part of the acquirer. Porter found that 57% of the acquisitions made by 33 large US firms in unrelated industries before 1976 were divested by 1987. Ravenscraft and Scherer estimated that a third of the lines of business acquired by US companies in the 1960s and 1970s were sold off during 1974–81, and conglomerate acquisitions were more likely than related ones to be divested. Kaplan and Weisbach reported that from a sample of large acquisitions completed between 1971 and 1982, 44% were divested by 1989. But only 34% of the divested acquisitions were 'failures', e.g. sold at a loss[6]. In a more recent study of unrelated acquisitions, i.e. across the two-digit industry divide, made by US firms, Bergh (1997) reports that 66 out of 135 acquisitions in 1977 and 81 out of 140 acquisitions made in 1987 were retained after five years. Thus the retention rate has increased from 49% to 58%.

This evidence raises two important issues. First, a majority of even unrelated acquisitions are retained. This is consistent with the evidence presented in Chapter 7 that large US firms are still highly diversified. Second, the divestiture decision is not an unambiguous indictment of the original diversification decision. That decision may have been a reasonable value-enhancing one, given the conditions at that time. The evidence from Matsusaka that the stock market reaction to conglomerate acquisitions of the 1960s was positive supports this view (see Chapter 7)[7]. Subsequent developments in the product markets, technology, capital markets etc. may have rendered the original decision wrong, but only in hindsight. Thus to deploy divestiture as evidence of acquisition failure one needs to relate it to the motivation behind the original acquisition. Indeed, if some of the forays into unrelated businesses were of a speculative nature, it stands to reason that some of these exploratory (mis)adventures would fail. Thus unrelated acquisition may be a real option punt that in a minority of cases has failed (see Chapter 7 for a real option interpretation of conglomerate diversification, and Chapter 14 for valuation of real options).

Bergh tested a model that predicts divestitures based on the factors that constitute the rationale for the acquisitions in the first place[8]. These factors are drawn from the multiple perspectives that motivate conglomerate acquisitions, such as economic benefits, resource transfer and sharing (see Table 7.3). His results showed that the motives and conditions at the time of acquisition and changes in some of the factors were related to divestiture. For example, small acquisitions that fail to increase the acquirer's cash flow or fail to reduce the volatility of its sales are more likely to be divested.

Further, factors predicting the divestiture decisions in the two samples of acquisitions (from 1977 and 1987) are different. With the 1977 acquisitions the divestiture decisions seemed to be due to small size of acquisitions, lack of contribution to market power or other economic benefits and no co-insurance benefits. With the 1987 acquisitions divestiture was more likely with increased return on assets and borrowing, reduced liquidity and low level of diversification of the acquirer prior to the acquisition. Factors that make unrelated acquisitions desirable at one time may cease to be attractive at another time (see Chapter 7 for further discussion).

Divestiture as proactive strategic tool

Empirical evidence reviewed in Chapter 7 on conglomerate acquisitions suggests that diversification is an inescapable part of the corporate landscape in several countries. Further, there is also evidence that moderate diversification improves operating performance as well as shareholder returns. However, in practice, firm portfolios may be too little or too much diversified. Firms therefore need to constantly re-balance their business portfolios by selling those businesses that no longer create sufficient value and lack a strategic rationale for their retention. Having eliminated such businesses, firms can reinvigorate their portfolios by making strategically more meaningful acquisitions. Thus divestitures are an essential part of a *creatively destructive* and *continually self-renewing* corporate strategy[9].

Over time, as the firm expands its portfolio of businesses, the resources and capabilities (or the lack of them) that warranted diversification become inadequate or obsolete. For example, the head office or parenting capabilities may no longer be appropriate and therefore add little value to the component businesses. In this case divestiture of such businesses aligns the resources and capabilities of the parent to the needs of the remaining businesses. Having reduced what may be value-destroying misalignment, the parent can now acquire other businesses that can better align resources and capabilities and therefore add value. This approach is illustrated by the sell-offs and acquisitions undertaken by Philips, the Dutch electricals and semiconductor business, in recent years (see Exhibit 10.1).

Exhibit 10.1

Philips sees light at the end of the tunnel

Philips at the beginning of this decade was a conglomerate with operations in eletrical lighting, medical electronics, consumer electronics, domestic appliances and semiconductors, which left analysts often wondering what sort of a company it was. One analyst described it as 'one of the last great misunderstood conglomerates of Europe'. Its performance was mediocre. It had several high-cost, vertically integrated manufacturing operations in Europe. It was run on the Rhineland model, where shareholder interests were often neglected to balance their interests with those of other stakeholders, such as employees and the local community. Sell-offs with consequential downsizing, job losses etc. did not sit easily with that model. There was not much financial discipline in the company.

Gerard Kleisterlee became the CEO in 2001. He decided that Philips' portfolio needed to be shaken up. He undertook extensive cost-cutting, shutting down factories and outsourcing. The 60-year-old had spent all his career in the company, but did not feel too sentimental about such drastic pruning of operations that had for long been parts of Philips' portfolio. The semiconductor business was very volatile and, like the high-tech companies, experienced huge swings in sales in 2001–02. Although it bounced back in 2003 and 2004, Kleisterlee decided to shift focus to more predictable and stable businesses. Moreover, Philips' stock price performance was benchmarked by investors against the SOX semiconductor index, thus rendering the company's performance volatile. However, this business was the second most valuable in the firm. His father

→

had worked in the semiconductor business for decades. In spite of this, in the summer of 2006 Kleisterlee sold it off to private equity buyers for \$10bn.

Following the disposal, Kleisterlee said: 'The coming years will open a new chapter as important as the one we closed in 2006. We must see the results coming through in sustained profitable growth and in *making smart and sensible acquisitions*.' This approach exemplifies *creative destruction*.

Source: N. Schwartz, 'Lighting up Philips', *Fortune*, European edition, **155**(1), 22 January 2007

Behavioural perspective on divestitures

Parent firms often avoid or delay divestitures for a variety of reasons including:

- inertia until a crisis forces their hand;
- fear of stigma as sell-offs may be interpreted as admission of corporate failure; or
- the businesses are seen as making a contribution, however low it is.

Many of these reasons may stem from managers' psychological biases that influence human decision-making processes. Horn, Lovallo and Viguerie identify a number of such cognitive biases and the associated managerial behaviour patterns[10]:

- *confirmation bias* – seeking out information that supports the manager's predisposition and avoiding evidence that weakens or refutes it; playing up a division's strengths and playing down its more important weaknesses;
- *sunk-cost fallacy* – justifying incurring further costs as a way of recovering sunk, i.e. irrecoverable, costs; a bias towards 'hanging on to losers', the emotional sunk cost to managers making divestment a painful decision;
- *escalation of commitment* – continuing investments in a business with little prospect of turnaround, arguing that more investment will fix the problem; 'throwing good money after bad';
- *false optimism* – being in denial about the need to divest a poorly performing business; hoping that the problems that caused poor performance will 'go away'; attributing business-specific problems such as poor product quality/image to external factors such as the weather, recession etc.;
- *anchoring and adjustment* – tending to adjust estimates inadequately; setting the reservation price for divestment too high by choosing unrealistic benchmarks and not making realistic allowances for the bad condition of the business.

The authors suggest a number of built-in checks and balances to avoid such cognitive biases influencing divestiture decisions, including their timing, e.g. changing the top management, creating stronger accountability, using zero-based budgeting, or using independent evaluators.

Forms of corporate divestiture

Corporate divestitures can be carried out in a variety of ways, as shown in Figure 10.1:

- *Intercorporate sell-off*: that is, sale to another company, including a management buyout (MBO) and its variants, such as management buyin (MBI). We discuss these in Chapter 11 in the context of leveraged buyouts.

Figure 10.1   Types and characteristics of divestitures

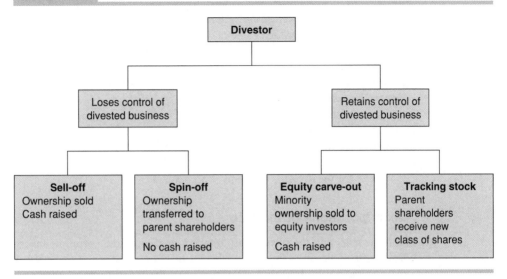

- *Spin-off or demerger*, where the divested part is floated on a stock exchange and the shares in that newly listed company are distributed to the shareholders of the parent.
- *Equity carve-out*, in which a subsidiary is floated on a stock exchange, but the parent retains the majority control.
- *Issue of tracking stock*, i.e. issue of a separate class of parent company shares designed to track the performance of a particular business or division.

What is common among spin-off, equity carve-out and tracking stock is that they are generally mediated by the stock market. Their aim is to lower the corporate veil and enable the stock market to 'see through' a component business of the corporation undertaking the transaction. In each case a new class of shares is created, with possibly some change of ownership of the concerned business. These three strategies differ from a sell-off, that is, a trade sale of the business to another corporate buyer, including that set up by the incumbent management in an MBO. Different factors motivate the choice of these alternative modes of divestiture. In the following sections we set out the specific rationale for these different types, and examine the empirical evidence as to whether they create value. We then provide a comparative overview of these alternatives. We refer to the divesting company as the parent (or divestor) and the divested unit as the offspring.

Corporate sell-offs

A sell-off is a transaction between two independent companies. The divestor may benefit from the cash flow proceeds, which could be put to more profitable use in other businesses within the group, or used to mitigate financial distress. Sell-off may also add value to the divestor by eliminating negative synergy, or by releasing managerial resources hitherto pre-empted by the divested business. It may also sharpen the strategic focus of the remaining businesses and enhance the divestor's competitive strengths.

For the buyer, the divested business may offer a better strategic fit than for the seller. Where the acquired business is related to any of its existing businesses, the buyer may enjoy increased market share and market power. This means that the business is more valuable to the buyer than to the seller. This added value may be creamed off by the buyer in full, or shared between the buyer and the seller. The sharing of the added value depends on the relative bargaining strength of the two parties, and this in turn depends upon the financial condition of the seller, the supply of divestitures, the relative size of the two companies, and the urgency of the divestor's need for cash.

If the divestor is in poor financial state, the divestment may be involuntary and thereby weaken its bargaining power. Nevertheless, the proceeds of sale may be used to regain financial strength. In that event the company is likely to receive a better rating from the stock and credit markets than before the divestment. Thus, for various reasons, a divestment may be good news for the divestor company shareholders.

Tax implications of the sale

Both the seller and the buyer need to take into account the corporate tax implications of the deal. For the seller the value of the sale may be reduced by any capital gains tax payable on the profit made. A sell-off or spin-off generally results in the divested member leaving the parent tax group. As part of the group, the divested business may have enjoyed or conferred benefits, e.g. absence of capital gains tax on intra-group assets sales, and offset of mutual losses and profits of group member firms. De-grouping leads to loss of such benefits, and can add to the tax burden of either the residual parent or the divested business. Another area that merits attention is how the tax liabilities of the group will be divided between the two. Such a division may have to be approved by the relevant tax authorities. These issues mean long and complicated preparatory work involving tax lawyers and accountants preceding the divestiture. To the buyer how much of the inherited or contingent tax liabilities are allocated to the divested business is of critical importance. The buyer may be able to step up the value of the assets bought from their book value to the purchase price, and it may be eligible for tax relief on the increased depreciation (or equivalent capital allowance in the UK). Whether the profit on sale is subject to capital gains tax depends on the tax regime, and on whether the buyer acquires the shares or assets of the divested business (see Chapter 14 on the tax aspects of acquisitions).

Five-stage process

Separation of the business to be divested is a long and complex *process* that needs to be managed with great skill. We can conceptualize it as a five-stage process in the same way as M & A, as shown in Figure 10.2. Whereas in an acquisition two firms/businesses are *integrated*, in a sell-off or spin-off two businesses are *separated*.

Figure 10.2   **Five-stage model of divestiture process**

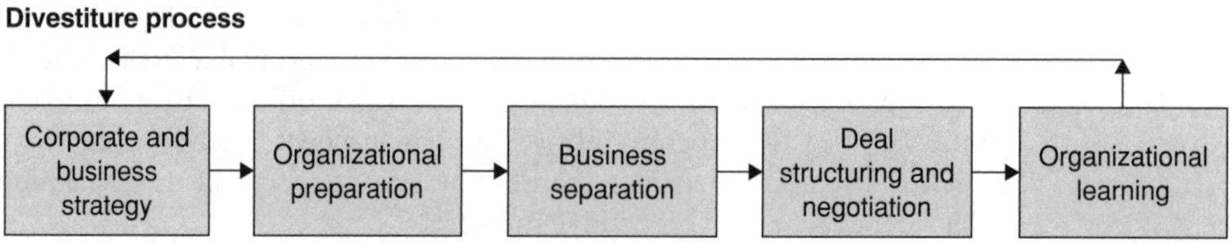

Divestiture process

| Corporate and business strategy | Organizational preparation | Business separation | Deal structuring and negotiation | Organizational learning |

The five stages of the divestment process involve[11]:

1 strategic evaluation of the current business portfolio to determine candidates for divestiture based on the fit of different constituent businesses, their past performance and future competitive prospects, and whether they satisfy key strategic and value creation criteria;
2 obtaining board approval for divestiture, and mobilizing internal and external resources to undertake business separation;
3 separating the to-be-divested business, preparing proforma financial statements, obtaining tax approvals; preparing and managing data rooms;
4 announcing intent to sell, finding suitable buyers, running an auction, negotiating sale agreement, closing the deal, and transferring the separated business to new owners; and
5 documenting transaction process, identifying learning points, and ensuring organizational diffusion of knowledge.[12]

As in the case of the five-stage M & A model, each of the five stages in the divestment process is characterized by its own risk.

Sale of a business

A business can be sold in a number of different ways. The divestor managers, if acting in the interests of their shareholder, would aim to maximize the sale value of the business. The sale can be negotiated with a buyer, but such a negotiated sale may not fetch the vendor shareholders the best price that reflects the intrinsic value of the divested business to the buyer. Negotiated deals are less transparent, and may arouse shareholder suspicions that they are 'sweetheart' deals that benefit the managers more than the shareholders. These suspicions may then take the form of class action lawsuits against the seller directors for failing their fiduciary duties to shareholders. Increasingly, therefore, sellers seek to run an auction.

The advantage of an auction is that it encourages competing bids from potential buyers and drives up the sale price. Buyers, for the same reason, prefer negotiated deals to sale by auction. Potential buyers in auctions include both 'strategic' buyers, i.e. firms operating in the same business as the divested one or a related business, or 'financial' buyers, i.e. private equity firms. Asset sell off by auction is illustrated in Exhibit 10.2. Investment banks play a crucial role in organizing such auctions. We discuss corporate auctions in more detail in the Chapter 11 on leveraged buyouts.

Empirical evidence of shareholder value creation from sell-offs in the US

Several empirical studies of voluntary divestments of different types have shown that they create value for the divestor's shareholders. The impact of sell-off announcements on divestor shareholders' wealth is generally positive and significant, as shown in Table 10.1[13]. Thus a divestment is greeted favourably by the stock market. The buying companies generally earn smaller returns than sellers, but these are positive. The buyers' gains are just as small as those that acquirers of whole companies receive (see Chapter 4 for evidence). The return to sellers is, however, very small, about 1–2%, compared with the target shareholder returns in full acquisitions (see Chapter 4). This is perhaps due to the small size of divestitures relative to the seller.

Do focus-increasing sell-offs create more value?

As noted above, one of the more popular corporate strategy themes of the 1980s and 1990s was focus and returning to the core business. If this proposition were true, divestitures that

Exhibit 10.2

Huntsman and Hexion divest by auction

In 2007 the two US chemical companies signed a merger agreement. Hexion was the bidder and was owned by the private equity firm, Apollo Management. The deal was worth $6.5bn. Because of antitrust concerns, the two companies agreed with the Department of Justice to divest the speciality epoxy chemicals businesses, where the two firms had considerable overlap and the merger would have led to a substantial lessening of competition (see Chapter 18 on anitrust regulations and remedies). To implement this divestiture remedy, in May 2008 the two companies started an auction process to sell the epoxy businesses. Since the merger agreement would expire on 4 July (unless both parties agreed to extend it), they were keen to get a firm offer for the divested businesses through the auction process. Several potential bidders – both financial and strategic buyers – evinced interest in bidding for the epoxy businesses.

The merger was, however, derailed later in 2008 as Hexion walked out of the deal, citing the deteriorating financial condition of Huntsman.

Source: C. Montoto, 'Huntsman/Hexion kick off epoxy divestiture sale in hopes of closing deal by 4 July – sources', *Financial Times*, 13 May 2008

Table 10.1 Cumulative abnormal returns (CAR) on sell-off announcements

Study; sample period; and size	Event window (days)	Benchmark model	% CAR for divestor	% CAR for buyer
Hearth and Zaima (1984); 1979–81; 58	11	Market model	3.6	
Rosenfeld (1984); 1969–81; 62	2	Mean adjusted	2.3	2.1
Jain (1985); 1976–78; 1064	1	Market model	0.1	0.3
Klein (1986); 1970–79; 202	3	Market model	1.1	
Hite, Owers and Rogers (1987); 1963–81; 55	2	Market model	1.7	0.8
Hirschey, Slovin and Zaima (1990); 1975–82; 170	2	Mean adjusted	1.5	
Sicherman and Pettway (1992); 1981–87; 278	2	Market model	0.9	0.5
Slovin, Sushka and Ferraro (1995); 1980–91; 179	2	Market model	1.7	
John and Ofek (1995); 1986–89; 321	3	Market model	1.5	0.4
Slovin, Sushka and Polonchek (2005); 258 cash sales and 69 stock for asset sales	2	Market model Cash Stock	1.9 3.2	−0.3 9.8

See Chapter 4 on abnormal returns methodology. Announcement day is Day 0. All CARs except Jain's for divestors and John and Ofek's for buyers, and Slovin *et al.* (2005) for cash buyers are statistically significant at the 5% level.

increase focus should create more shareholder value than those that do not. John and Ofek, in their study listed in Table 10.1, measured the change in focus with the change in the number of lines of business, the SIC industries and the Herfindahl–Hirschman index, a measure of dispersion of businesses. They found that when the focus of the remaining businesses of the seller increased, the shareholder gains also increased.

Impact of other factors on shareholder value gains

Among other factors that have been investigated are:

- relative size of the divestment;
- financial condition of the seller;
- management incentive structure of the seller; and
- how the proceeds of sale are used.

Companies divesting relatively large parts of their portfolio generate larger value[14]. This suggests that divestiture representing a substantial restructuring rather than a marginal or symbolic one is regarded more favourably by investors. Poor financial condition of the seller may suggest a sure-fire sale, and the seller may not have realized the true value of the divested business. Hearth and Zaima[15] report that sellers with high Standard & Poor's common stock rating generate 4% abnormal return, whereas those with low rating experience only 3.2%. But given the small sample size of each group reported, the difference may not be significant.

Management incentives affect the quality of decisions made by firms, and whether they are in shareholders' interest. Does this apply to divestment decisions? Sellers with long-term performance plans for their top managers generate 1.5% higher abnormal return over three days than those without such plans (0.9% compared with −0.6%), and the difference is statistically significant[16].

The divestor may use the proceeds in a number of ways – reinvest in other projects, pay higher dividends, buy back shares or pay down debt. While some of these uses may increase shareholder value, others, e.g. imprudent unrelated acquisitions, may destroy value. The latter is more likely if the agency problem in the seller is serious. Lang et al., however, found in their sample that sellers that paid out the proceeds as dividends experienced higher value gains especially if their pre-divestment financial performance had been much weaker[17]. Thus reinvestment by firms that have a poor track record seems to inspire much scepticism and negative valuation. This is consistent with the previous result that management incentive alignment leads to value-increasing divestiture decisions. However, John and Ofek did not find that the reported use of proceeds influenced the market reaction differently.

Empirical evidence of shareholder value creation from sell-offs in the UK

Table 10.2 summarizes the results of studies that have examined the shareholder wealth effects of divestiture announcements made by UK corporations[18]. All four studies report that these announcements generate significant value gains for the divestor shareholders. Alexandrou and Sudarsanam also reported that nearly 53% of their sample firms registered positive gains. In their study the abnormal wealth gain, i.e. after allowing for gains that the benchmark portfolios would yield, on average was £3.2m and the total was £6.2bn. This represents 9% of the value of the divestments by the sample, £70bn. For comparison, John and Ofek reported a gain of 10%. Thus value gains from divestitures to divestor shareholders are also economically significant.

Table 10.2 Cumulative abnormal returns (CAR) on sell-off announcements in the UK

Study, sample period and size	Event window (days)	Benchmark Model	% CAR for Divestor
Afshar, Taffler and Sudarsanam (1992); 1985–86; 178	1	Market model	0.9
Lasfer, Sudarsanam and Taffler (1996); 1985–86; 142	2	Mean adjusted	0.8
Kaiser and Stouraitis (2001); 1984–94; 590	2	Market model	1.2
Alexandrou and Sudarsanam (2001); 1987–93; 1941	3	Size and MV/BV	0.4

For abnormal returns methodology, see Chapter 4. MV/BV is market value to book value of equity. All the CARs are significant at 5% or better.

Do focus-increasing sell-offs by UK firms create more value?

Where the business being disposed of covers activities different from the core activities of the seller, it is treated as focus increasing. Otherwise it is focus decreasing. Kaiser and Stouraitis found that focus-increasing divestitures (defined by the *Financial Times* reported intention of the divestor) generated higher average abnormal returns (about 1–2%) than other divestitures (about 1%). Alexandrou and Sudarsanam, however, did not find any beneficial effect from a more focus increase, defined by the reduction in the overlap of the activities of the parent and offspring described by *Acquisitions Monthly*. This issue needs to be resolved with further analysis and more objective criteria for classifying the change in focus before the definitive impact of focus can be ascertained.

Impact of other factors on shareholder value gains

In both studies above, larger divestitures yield higher gains, consistent with the US studies. In Alexandrou and Sudarsanam the mean CAR for the quintile of the smallest divestitures is zero; it is 1.3% for the largest quintile. Lasfer *et al.* investigated the stock market reaction to divestitures by financially healthy firms and potentially bankrupt firms, and found that the reaction was more favourable for the latter. By divesting and (presumably) using the proceeds to reduce their debt burden, these firms might avoid bankruptcy and the associated dead-weight costs. However, for their much larger sample, Alexandrou and Sudarsanam reported a more positive reaction for healthy divestors. The difference between the two studies is probably due to differences in sample size and the sampling period. While Lasfer *et al.*'s sample covered the middle of an economic boom and the merger wave of the 1980s, Alexandrou and Sudarsanam's sample covered a short boom and a longer recessionary period.

Alexandrou and Sudarsanam also find that shareholder gains from divestitures are:

- higher during economic recession than during a boom (CAR of 0.61% versus 0.21%);
- higher for divestors with higher market-to-book value of equity (a proxy for higher growth opportunities); and
- higher when UK companies sell to non-UK buyers (0.8% against 0.1% with UK buyers)[19].

The last result seems to reflect the information advantage that the UK seller has over the non-UK buyer[20]. The combined impact of recession and greater growth opportunities suggests that investors react positively to divestiture as a means of coping with economic downturn, and as a means of financing strong future growth, consistent with the *creative destruction* view of divestitures (see discussion above).

Kaiser and Stouraitis find support for the view that divestiture is a means of:

- enhancing operating performance by getting rid of loss-making businesses;
- increasing payout to shareholders; or
- reducing the debt burden.

The last two results are similar to those reported by Lang *et al.* and discussed above.

Empirical evidence of shareholder value creation from sell-offs in continental Europe

Kaiser and Stouraitis carried out a similar analysis with divestitures drawn from the UK (sample size 76), France (46), Germany (36) and Sweden (30) during the period 1984–93. For the period 15 days before the announcement to the announcement date inclusive, shareholders experienced significant market model abnormal returns in the UK and Sweden (2–3%), but not in France and Germany (about 1%). The value gains increase with the size of the divestiture in all countries except Sweden. When French and German companies divest their foreign businesses they experience value losses that nearly offset the gains they make on their domestic divestitures. These differences across European countries may be due to a variety of factors, e.g. corporate tax liability for capital gains on sale of businesses, the liquidity of the market for divestitures, the active nature of the stock markets that evaluate these transactions, information disclosure about divestitures, and corporate governance structures. These potential sources of explanation for the observed differences in the valuation of divestitures need further research.

Overview and implications of the evidence on corporate sell-offs

We may summarize the major points that emerge from our analysis of sell-offs:

- The stock market generally perceives a sell-off as a value-creating decision, but in a large minority of cases the reaction may be negative.
- Sell-off size matters, with larger ones creating more value.
- Where sell-off increases the focus of the residual businesses, the valuation impact is generally positive.
- Sell-offs are viewed more favourably in the US, the UK and Sweden than in France or Germany, pointing to differences in regulatory, tax, corporate governance and other environmental factors.
- When the divestor's financial condition is poor, or the sold-off business has performed poorly, the market interprets the sell-off as performance enhancing and reacts positively.
- Where the divestor has strong growth opportunities, sell-offs even during a recession evoke positive market reaction.
- Where the seller has performed poorly, or has few good growth prospects, return of the sale proceeds to shareholders or creditors may enhance value more than retention and reinvestment.
- In interpreting sell-offs the markets have regard for the corporate governance, managerial incentive structure and lender monitoring as credible signals of potential value created.
- Transactional details, e.g. whether the buyer is a foreign buyer, influence the market valuation and should be disclosed. Thus information asymmetry seems to influence the division of sell-off gains between divestors and their buyers.

Corporate spin-offs

In a corporate spin-off a company floats off a subsidiary, which may be a small part of the parent company. The newly floated company now has an independent existence, and is separately valued in the stock market. Shares in the spun-off company are distributed to the shareholders of the parent company, and they own shares in two companies rather than just one. This is the exact reversal of a merger or acquisition. For this reason, in the UK the term 'demerger' is used in preference to spin-off, used in the US. Distribution of shares in a spin-off is somewhat similar to the distribution of a special cash dividend, since the receiving shareholders may be able to sell the newly issued shares, and 'cash out'. However, unlike a cash dividend, which is taxable at the hands of the receiving shareholders, the spin-off may be structured as a tax-free distribution, provided certain conditions are satisfied. We discuss the relevant tax considerations below.

Figure 10.3 shows the spin-offs carried out in the US, the UK and continental Europe during 1990–2007. The US has been the most active market for spin-offs, followed by the UK. There have been much fewer spin-offs in continental Europe.

Table 10.3 provides the spin-off activity data for many individual European countries. The most active market in spin-offs in continental Europe is Sweden, which as we saw in Chapter 2 is also one of the most active M & A markets. But in terms of value Switzerland's spin-off of Philip Morris by Altria for $108bn (see Exhibit 10.3 for details) places it at the top.

Figure 10.3 **Spin-offs from 1990–2007: (a) USA**

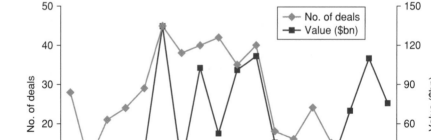

(a)

All deals are completed.
Only deals of which transaction value is disclosed are included.
EU means: 27 current members plus Switzerland.
Deals are categorized according to the announcement year.
Deal value is in 2007 dollars. US Consumer Price Index – All Urban: All Items is used to adjust for inflation.
Source: Thomson Reuters

Figure 10.3   Spin-offs from 1990–2007: (b) UK; (c) Europe (excluding UK)

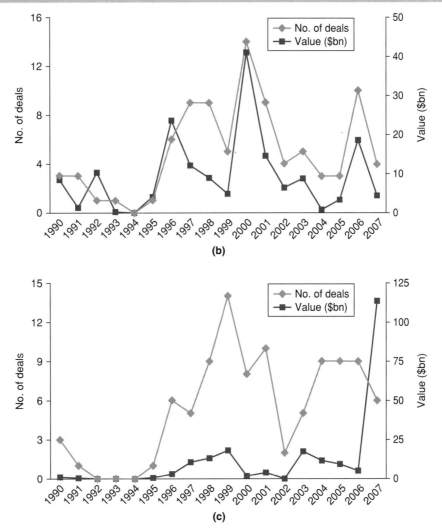

(b)

(c)

All deals are completed.
Only deals of which transaction value is disclosed are included.
EU means: 27 current members plus Switzerland.
Deals are categorized according to the announcement year.
Deal value is in 2007 dollars. US Consumer Price Index – All Urban: All Items is used to adjust for inflation.
Source: Spinoffs in individual European countries (excluding UK) 1990–2007, Thomson Reuters,
www.thomsonreuters.com.

Distinctive characteristics of a spin-off

Unlike in the other forms of divestiture the shareholders of the parent company take part
in the transaction directly. For example, in a sell-off the shareholders do not automatically
receive the sale proceeds, although, as we have seen in our review of empirical evidence on sell-
offs, companies may find it beneficial to do so. A second distinguishing feature of spin-offs is
that the parent does not raise any cash from the transaction. Third, the scale of a spin-off is

Table 10.3 Spin-offs in individual European countries (excluding UK) 1990–2007

Country	No. of deals	Value ($bn)
Belgium	5	6
Denmark	3	2
Finland	9	13
France	8	5
Germany	8	8
Italy	10	15
Netherlands	7	16
Sweden	34	17
Switzerland	6	124
Other EU countries	7	3
Total	97	210

Source: As for Figure 10.3.

generally larger than that of a sell-off or an equity carve-out. Like a sell-off, but unlike an equity carve-out, a spin-off represents a clean break with the divested business. It creates an independent company, a 'pure-play'.

Rationale for a spin-off

Why do companies undertake a spin-off? There are several benefits to the parent, the off-spring, the shareholders and managers. A spin-off may:

- like other forms of divestitures, lead to enhanced focus, reduced organizational complexity and control loss, and avoidance of negative synergy (see discussion above in the context of sell-offs);
- eliminate the conglomerate discount the parent may have suffered as a diversified company (see Chapter 7). In a demerger, typically, the separating firms have little synergy in terms of production, technology or markets;
- increase the transparency of both the parent and the spun-off business to the stock market through separate financial reports of the two firms to current shareholders;
- increase analyst and institutional investor following, create new shareholder interest and allow access to new capital;
- allow shareholders increased flexibility in their portfolio decisions, since they now have the freedom to alter the proportion of their portfolios invested in each company. Previously, their investment was indivisible because they could invest in the subsidiary only by investing in the parent;
- allow the firm to create more efficient capital structures for the constituent businesses in conformity with the economics of those businesses (see Exhibit 10.3 below); and
- ring-fence some division against the negative fallout from others: for example, Altria, the US cigarette manufacturer, exposed to expensive lawsuits by smokers spun off its international business Philip Morris, based in Switzerland.

Exhibit 10.3 lists some recent spin-offs in European countries that increase focus. A spin-off may also be a way of restructuring a diversified group so that distinct businesses can be sold off more easily. Potential buyers of these businesses not interested in other parts of the group are thus spared the risk, cost and tedium of buying the group and then unbundling it. Further, they may also avoid any capital gains tax payable on disposal of an unbundled business. Under

Exhibit 10.3

Corporate spin-offs in Europe to increase focus

Year	Parent (country) (activities)	Spun-off (activities)	Deal value
2008	Cadbury Schweppes **(UK)** (confectionary and soft drinks)	Dr Pepper Snapple Group (soft drinks)	£1.2bn
2007	Altria Group, Inc. **(US)** (global cigarette manufacturer)	Philip Morris International (Swiss-based cigarette manufacturer)	$108bn
2007	American Standard, Inc. **(US)** (vehicle controls, bath and kitchen products and air-conditioning)	WABCO (vehicle control systems)	$3.8bn
2006	GUS **(UK)** (retail of menswear, home retail, credit information service)	Home retail (Argos and Homebase); credit information (Experian)	£3.7bn £5.7bn
2001	Granada Compass plc **(UK)** (media, hotels and restaurants, catering)	Compass Group (catering, hotels and restaurant)	$17.9bn
2000	Barco NV **(Belgium)** (machinery, industrial and transport equipment distribution)	BarcoNet NV (construction)	$280m
1999	Gehe AG **(Germany)** (pharmaceuticals and healthcare)	Takkt AG (miscellaneous services)	$505m
1998	Instituto Nazionale delle Assicurazioni **(Italy)** (insurance real estate)	Union Immobiliare SpA (real estate)	$2.2bn
1998	Vendex International NV **(Netherlands)** (employment agency, business services)	Vedior International NV (business services)	$881m

what is known as the Morris Trust principle in the US, buyers of spun-off units would avoid the capital gains tax[21]. Unbundling prior to sale is likely to increase the sale value of individual businesses. Spinning-off may also facilitate a merger. These considerations have driven some of the European spin-offs, as shown in Exhibit 10.4. But spin-off may also be carried out as a defence against a hostile takeover, or to forestall one, as shown in Exhibit 10.5.

Exhibit 10.4

Go for a spin and then sell

In 1999 Hoechst AG (HT), the German pharmaceutical and chemicals group, spun off its chemicals businesses into Celanese AG (CN). HT shareholders received one CN share for every ten HT shares they held. The spin-off preceded HT's stock swap merger with Rhone-Poulenc SA to form Aventis.

In 1999 Alusuisse Lonza Group Ltd (AL) spun off its Lonza Group Ltd (LG). AL shareholders received one LG common share per one AL share they had. The value of LG based on the first trading day price on flotation was $3.9bn. The spin-off followed a stock swap merger agreement between AL and Alcan Aluminium.

> **Exhibit 10.5**
>
> ## To demerge or be merged?
>
> - In the case of ICI's demerger in 1992 into ICI (chemicals business) and Zeneca (pharmaceutical business), although the demerger decision was already in contemplation, Hanson's acquisition of a 2.8% stake in ICI earlier, regarded by the ICI board as hostile, added to the urgency of the plan.
> - In 1995 an investor group disclosed its intention to make a tender offer for Hafslund Nycomed (HN), the Norwegian diversified group. In response HN spun off its business manufacturing contrast media products and diagnostics into Nycomed ASA. HN was then renamed Hafslund ASA.

From the parent's point of view, the spin-off may be preferable to a sell-off, since in the latter case the parent has to decide what to do with the sale proceeds when it does not have any investment opportunities to finance. A spin-off may release the offspring from the centralized control of the parent and reliance on an inefficient internal capital market (see Chapter 8), and allow much greater strategic and operational autonomy. This autonomy may be reflected in new corporate governance structures, such as a new board of directors. The increased transparency to the stock market should also allow closer monitoring by block shareholders such as institutions.

In the case of others, underperformance of the spun-off subsidiary and changed strategic priorities led to the demergers, as in Pearson's decision to demerge Royal Doulton in 1994. An important reason for a demerger is that it gives the management of the demerged parts greater freedom and focus. Courtaulds, operating in chemicals, clothing and spinning, demerged its clothing and spinning businesses into Courtaulds Textiles in 1990. According to Courtauld's chairman, the demerger released a great deal of energy among the managers of the separate companies. The separation also allowed managerial incentive contracts that could be fine-tuned to the performance of the offspring or the parent without being held hostage to the underperformance of the other. The incentives could now be directly related to shareholder value performance through incentive share ownership schemes or stock options.

If the above rationale for a demerger is true, the combined market value of the demerged firms must be greater than that of the pre-demerger parent. Figure 10.4 illustrates the market value changes that followed the UK company GUS plc's 2006 demerger into Home Retail and Experian (see Exhibit 10.3 above). The combined value of the offspring was larger than that of the pre-spin-off parent by over £1bn a few months later.

Structure of spin-offs

A spin-off involves the *pro rata* distribution of shares in the newly floated company to the parent company shareholders (see Exhibit 10.4 above). In some cases the parent distributes less than 100% of equity in the divested unit. The ratio of shares held by a shareholder in the demerged companies is likely to reflect the ratio of the assets or values of the two companies. The allocation of assets and liabilities is often a complex process, and will affect the stock market valuation of the demerged companies. While the basic rationale of the demerger, i.e. the strategic need for separation, may dictate this allocation, other considerations are also relevant. The ownership structure of the parent may influence the allocation. For example, if

Figure 10.4　Value impact of GUS spin-off of its subsdiaries

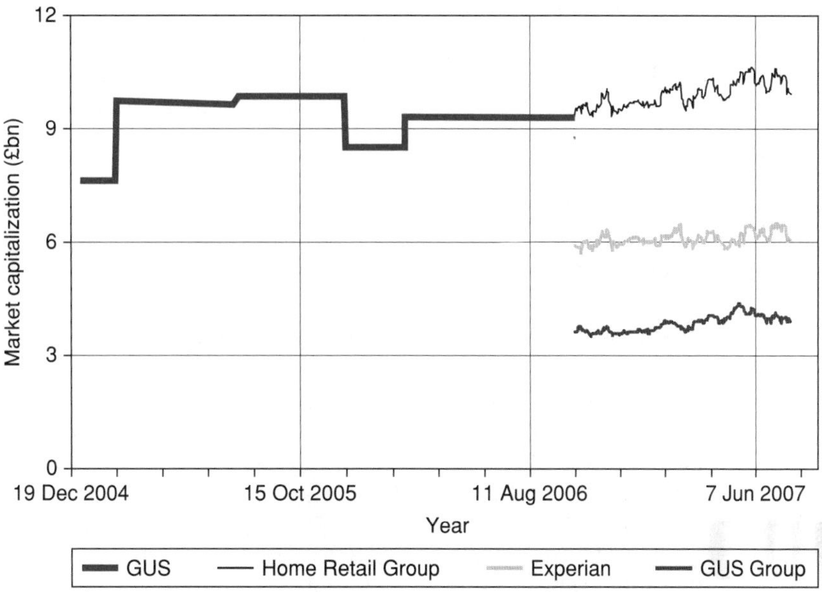

too much of the parent debt is loaded onto a demerged company, it may be seen as a more risky company and thus may be undervalued. Since there is scope for exploiting spin-off as an indirect way of distributing dividends, tax rules in certain jurisdictions may impose strict conditions for a tax-free spin-off.

Allocation of assets and liabilities: who gains and loses from spin-offs?

Spin-offs involve the allocation of assets and liabilities between the parent company and the spun-off business. In general, asset allocation follows the nature of the businesses being separated, but the parent company may have much more discretion to allocate liabilities. The resulting capital structure of the offspring should be consistent with the business risk profile of its business and its growth trajectory. High-risk and high-growth businesses cannot bear as much debt as more mature businesses. Available empirical evidence supports this tradeoff between business risk and leverage [22]. Montgomery, Hill and Moore illustrate the importance of the capital structure consideration.[23] Severn Trent (ST) consisted of:

● a water business, a regulated utility business with a stable cashflow and high debt capacity, and;
● a waste management business (Biffa), unregulated and more volatile.

In 2006 ST demerged and distributed shares in Biffa to ST shareholders. This allowed ST to raise its gearing level in the water business and return £600m of surplus cash to shareholders. After the demerger, ST shareholders held shares in two independent public companies. The demerger was tax-free to the shareholders.

Thus debt allocation may result in increasing the riskiness of certain corporate securities and diminishing that of other securities: for example if a group made up of a high-volatile and a low-volatile business is being demerged, and most of the debt is allocated to the business with high-volatile cash flows. This increases the default risk of debt, reduces its value, and leads to rating agencies marking down that debt. Parents are therefore anxious to ensure that debt allocated to the offspring or retained by themselves does not suffer any rating downgrade. For example, when in 2008 Land Securities, the UK's largest property company, wanted to spin-off its portfolio into retail and office properties, it sought the rating agencies' views as to the rating the debt would receive post-spin-off. Rating agencies indicated a AA rating, in line with the pre-spin-off rating[24]. Shareholders have gained from this transaction by reducing the protection that the creditors had enjoyed prior to the demerger. This of course upsets the debt holders (see Exhibit 10.6).

Exhibit 10.6

Bondholders hold up GUS demerger

As shown in Exhibit 10.3, in 2006 GUS plc demerged into Home Retail and Experian. The existing bondholders of GUS were unhappy with the allocation of all its debt to Experian, the credit-checking business. GUS would cease to exist. According to the bondholders, the liquidation of GUS amounted to a default on the bonds due to mature in 2013. GUS also had other bonds maturing in 2007 and 2009. GUS sought to persuade the bondholders to swap their bonds for those in Experian. While the 2007 and 2009 bondholders agreed, in exchange for insertion of a *change of control* clause and a consent fee of 0.5%, the 2013 holders, consisting of hedge funds and investment banks' proprietary trading desks, rejected the offer, and threatened to call default by GUS in the hope of extracting a high compensation to switch to the new bonds. Experian's bonds would be rated BBB+, the same as GUS's. Hence to the investors there was no increase in risk exposure. GUS also offered them an option to 'put' (redeem) the bonds at par. Nevertheless, the 2013 bondholders insisted on higher compensation.

Source: E. Rigby, 'Final curtain call for GUS', *Financial Times*, 9 October 2006, and 'Pistols at dawn as GUS defies recalcitrant bondholders angling to get more than par', *Euroweek*, 8 October 2006

Tax and accounting implications of spin-offs

A tax-free spin-off is one in which the distribution is not subject to immediate income tax at the hands of the receiving parent company shareholders. They become liable for capital gains tax (CGT) when they subsequently dispose of the received shares. There are two benefits to this arrangement. They defer tax, and the CGT rates in many jurisdictions tend to be lower than income tax rates. From the company's point of view in a taxable spin-off, it may become liable for any gains that arise from the divestiture.

In the US, for tax-free status, the spin-off needs to satisfy the requirements of Internal Revenue Service Section 355[25]. Briefly, these requirements are as follows:

- *Prior control* – the parent must possess control of the subsidiary prior to the spin-off.
- *Minimum voting control* – it must distribute to its shareholders a controlling amount of subsidiary stock, and control is defined as stock commanding at least 80% of the voting power and 80% of each class of non-voting stock.
- *Continuity of trade* – both parent and offspring must carry on active trade or business in which each has been actively engaged for at least five years before spin-off.

- *Continuity of interest* – parent shareholders must retain a significant continuing ownership in both parent and offspring following spin-off.
- *Not a tax avoidance device* – distribution is not used to distribute profits and convert dividend taxation into CGT.
- *Business purpose* – the offspring has a real and substantial business purpose separate from any tax saving, and the spin-off must bring about in a specific and immediate manner material and quantifiable cost savings or other benefits.

The UK tax rules are broadly similar. The Finance Act 1980 made demerger much easier to undertake without heavy tax penalties, provided it is not construed by the Inland Revenue as a tax avoidance scheme. Since a demerger results in a distribution of shares to the parent company shareholders, it has to be structured carefully to qualify as a tax-free arrangement both for the companies involved and for the shareholders.

An important consequence of the spin-off is that the offspring will no longer be included in the consolidated accounts of the parent. The parent suffers an immediate 'downsizing'. This shrinking may appear to reduce the liquidity of the parent's stock in the stock market, and may lead to its being 'dumped' from the constituents of major stock market indices, such as the *Financial Times* or Standard & Poor's indices. Such a deletion may influence the decisions of fund managers whether to hold or sell the parent stock. The deconsolidation of the offspring may also affect any debt covenant that governs the group's existing debt. If the spun-off entity is profitable, deconsolidation reduces the apparent profitability of the residual parent group. By the same token, spinning off a loss-making subsidiary provides an immediate boost to the bottom line of the parent.

Empirical evidence on the shareholder value gains from spin-offs

Several US studies have estimated the abnormal returns to shareholders of the parent firms over a short window. These are summarized in Table 10.4[26]. All the studies report significant value gains for shareholders of about 2–3% over just two days including the announcement day[27]. Thus the short-run stock market reaction to the spin-off decision is positive, and the parent shareholders gain.

Table 10.4 Summary of US studies of shareholder gains from spin-offs

Study, sample period and sample	Benchmark model	Two-day cumulative abnormal return (CAR) (%)
Hite and Owers (1983); 1963–81; 123	Market	3.3
Cusatis, Miles and Woolridge (1993); 1965–88; 146	Market-adjusted	2.1
Allen, Lummer, McConnell and Reed (1995); 1962–91; 94	Market	2.2
Slovin, Shushka and Ferraro (1995); 1980–91; 37	Not known	1.3
Seward and Walsh (1996); 1972–87; 78	Market	2.6
Allen, Lummer, McConnell and Reed (1995); 1962–91; 94	Market	2.2
Daley, Mehrotra and Sivakumar (1997); 1975–91; 85	Market-adjusted	3.6
Krishnaswamy and Subramaniam (1999); 1979–93; 118	Market	3.2
Maxwell and Rao (2003); 1974–97; 80	Market	3.6
Burch and Nanda (2003); 1979–96; 106	Market-adjusted	3.7[a]
Ahn and Denis (2004); 1981–96; 106	Market-adjusted	4.0[b]

See Chapter 4 for a discussion of the cumulative abnormal return as a measure of wealth gains to shareholders and the choice of benchmark models in estimating the CAR. All the CARs are statistically significant at least the 5% level.
[a]The event window is 4 days.
[b]The event window is 3 days.

Do both the parent and the offspring thrive in the long run?

Cusatis *et al.*, cited in Table 10.4, also investigated the value gains to shareholders of the parent and the offspring over 12, 24 and 36 months following spin-off. They measured these gains as abnormal returns against size- and industry-matched portfolios as benchmarks. For parents over 36 months the excess return was 18% but insignificant, but over the first 24 months it was 27% (significant at 1%). For the spun-off entities it was 34% and 25% respectively (both significant). These results suggest that the spin-off decision creates value, with the combined values of the parent and the offspring exceeding the value of the parent alone prior to spin-off.

However, as we know from Chapter 4, conclusions based on long-term returns are troubled by the benchmark problem. McConnell *et al.* replicated Cusatis *et al.*'s analysis for a sample of spin-offs from 1989–95, part of the Cusatis *et al.* period[28]. They found:

● Cusatis *et al.*'s result may have been driven by the impact of outlier firms; and
● when more appropriate benchmarks, i.e. size and market-to-book value benchmarks or the Fama and French three factors, are used, the abnormal returns are no longer significant.

Alas! All that glitters is not gold after all. It is therefore not clear that a spin-off generates long-term value benefits. It should be noted, however, that these studies concentrate on the overall sample, and do not consider the motivation behind the spin-off decision. Spin-offs driven by different motives may yield different results. The following analysis considers this possibility.

Value gains from focus-increasing spin-offs

Daley *et al.*, cited in Table 10.4, examined the differential performance of spin-offs that involved parents spinning off offspring operating in their own primary two-digit industry and spin-offs where the offspring and the parent belonged to different two-digit industries. The first type is 'own-industry' spin-off, which reduces focus of the parent's portfolio, and the second is 'cross-industry' spin-off, which increases focus. Of their sample, 60 spin-offs are cross-industry and 25 fall in the first category. Over a two-day announcement period they found that focus-increasing spin-offs generated highly significant 4% returns, but focus-decreasing spin-offs yielded an insignificant 1%. Daley *et al.* also found that this superior shareholder value performance was reflected in the post-spin-off profitability. The change in median return on assets (ROA) from the year before (of the parent) to the year after spin-off (parent plus offspring), adjusted for various benchmarks such as industry or similar-size firms, is 3% for focus-increasing spin-offs and zero for the focus-decreasing spin-offs. Desai and Jain confirmed the superior returns in the announcement period to focus-increasing spin-offs (4.5%) compared with focus-decreasing ones (2.2%)[29].

What about the long-term shareholder value performance? Desai and Jain extended their evaluation to a 36-month post-spin-off period for a sample of 111 focus-increasing and 44 focus-decreasing spin-offs. The abnormal returns for focus-increasing spin-offs were significant at 11%, 21% and 33% over 12, 24 and 36 months. For non-focus-increasing firms the corresponding returns were −1%, −8% and −14%. The superior performance persisted when focus was defined in different ways. Desai and Jain also confirmed the superior performance of focus-increasing spin-offs measured by operating cash flow return on assets. Moreover, the improvement in profit performance and shareholder value gains are positively related. This study used a size- and industry-based benchmark to estimate abnormal returns, and is therefore open to challenge because of potential benchmarking error. However, this problem is unlikely to be serious, since it involved comparing the performance of two sub-samples over the same period using the same methodology.

Thus overall, in both the short and the long term, shareholders gain much more from spin-offs that increase the parent companies' focus. Further, this gain seems to be driven by the underlying improvement in operating performance of both the parents and their offspring.

Other sources of value gains from spin-offs

One of the motivations for a spin-off may be to facilitate a subsequent merger of either the parent or the offspring (see Exhibit 10.2 above). Among the studies cited above, Cusatis *et al.* found that about 14% of their sample parents or offspring were taken over in the 36 months following spin-off. They estimated that takeover-related gains were about 4–9% in addition to the pure gains from spin-offs. McConnell *et al.* reported a gain of 1% or 2% for parents and 11–15% for offspring. On the other hand, Desai and Jain reported that their results were unaffected by takeover activity involving the spin-off firms.

One of the benefits of spin-offs is the increased analysis following a spin-off. This is due to the separation of the parent and offspring, and the reduction in information asymmetry between the firms and the stock market. Krishnaswami and Subramaniam[30] tested whether the latter occurred for a sample of 118 spin-offs during 1979–93 and found reduction in information asymmetry, and also that this reduction accounted for some of the post-spin-off value gains. Similarly, Gilson *et al.* found that analysts' individual and consensus forecasts of earnings became significantly more accurate following spin-offs, equity carve-outs and tracking stock offerings[31]. Analyst coverage of the parent and, not surprisingly, of the offspring increased.

Empirical evidence of value creation by European spin-offs

Evidence from Europe is quite scanty, perhaps because of the relatively low level of spin-offs in Europe, and the relatively new phenomenon that it represents. Veld and Veld-Merkoulova report, from a study of 156 spin-offs during 1987–2000 in 15 European countries, a three-day CAR of 2.7%. This increases to 3.6% for spin-offs that increase parent company focus, but falls to 0.8% for non-focus-increasing spin-offs.

For a larger but broadly similar sample of 170 European spin-offs during 1987–2005, Qian and Sudarsanam find that the mean three-day CAR to parents is 4.8%. UK parents enjoy 5.5% and the continental European parents 4.3%[32]. For the long run, over one to three years, Qian and Sudarsanam find no significant value gains to parent shareholders, and a small, and marginally significant gains to offspring shareholders. The long-run returns (up to 36 months post-spin-off) to parent shareholders are not significantly different from 0%. Veld and Veld-Merkoulova report lack of long-term value gains to both parents and offspring. These results contrast with those for US spin-off parents experiencing significant value gains. The reasons for the difference between the US and European spin-offs in terms of long-run returns require further examination[33].

Consistent with the previous US and European studies, short-run abnormal returns are significantly higher for focus-increasing spin-offs. However, Qian and Sudarsanam do not find this relation in the long run. These results hold for both UK and continental European spin-offs. Both returns are highly significant. Thus firms are able to create value through spin-offs, at least in the short term. In terms of operating performance, measured by industry-adjusted ROA and industry- and size-adjusted ROA, Qian and Sudarsanam find that over the three years following spin-off, glamour offspring significantly underperform non-glamour offspring[34].

Among other results, Qian and Sudarsanam also find that value gains to parents are greater when they spin-off subsidiaries in 'glamour' industries with high market valuation. They argue that this is consistent with the *catering theory* that managers seek to exploit stock market mispricing of glamour stocks, and time their spin-offs to cater to irrational investor preferences.

Do shareholders gain at the expense of bondholders?

Earlier in this chapter we highlighted the scope for expropriation of bondholders by shareholders of parents when they undertake spin-offs. In the context of abnormal returns this will be manifested in positive returns to shareholders and negative returns to bondholders. Maxwell and Rao report mean abnormal returns in the spin-off announcement month:

To bond investors in parent   −0.9% (68% of returns negative)
To shareholders in parent   2.9% (38% of returns negative)

Losses to bondholders are the greater, the larger the gains to shareholders. Other findings in this study are consistent with increased risk to bondholders. Bondholder losses are greater when:

- spin-off results in loss of collateral, e.g. when the offspring is from an unrelated industry (this reduces the coinsurance benefit – see Chapter 7 for a discussion);
- credit rating downgrading of bonds is more likely than an upgrade following a spin-off[35].

Veld and Veld-Merkoulova, however, find for their sample of European spin-offs that bondholders make a small gain.

Equity carve-outs

An equity carve-out is the sale of a minority or majority voting control in a subsidiary by its parent to outside investors. Exhibit 10.7 provides examples of US and European carve-outs. The case of Hoechst illustrates that parents use an equity carve-out to test the waters, and when the first carve-out is well received conduct further stages of the divestiture[36]. This flexibility may also be an advantage over a spin-off.

Why do firms undertake equity carve-outs? Equity carve-out is similar to a spin-off in many ways. Equity carve-outs are often motivated by the need to:

Exhibit 10.7

Sample equity carve-outs in the US and Europe

Year	Parent (country)	Subsidiary carved out	% equity in IPO	IPO raises*
2006	Haliburton (US)	KBR	17	$473
2006	Agilent Technologies (US)	Verigy	15	$128
2005	Thyssen-Bormemisza	HIS, Inc	25	$232
2005	AMD and Fujitsu (US & Japan)	Spansion Inc	33	$470
2004	Titan International (US)	Titan Europe	60**	£30
2000	Siemens AG (Germany)	Infineon Technologies	29	$11,709
2000	Zurich Financial Services Group (Switzerland)	PSP Swiss Property	52	$278
1999	Bayer AG (Germany)	Agfa-Gevaert NV	50	$1782

*Note that the amounts are in different currencies.

Source: Thomson Financial Services, The Economist and MSN Newsheets downloaded from www.google.co.uk.
**Majority ownership divested.

- increase the focus of the firm;
- improve the autonomy of component businesses;
- improve the managerial incentive structure by relating management performance directly to shareholder value;
- enhance the visibility of the component businesses being divested; and
- minimize the conglomerate discount through this enhanced visibility and increased information.

However, a carve-out differs in other ways:

- It is not a complete separation but a partial divestment. It does not create a pure play.
- The parent floats the subsidiary on a stock market, and may sell a minority stake to outside investors.
- The parent and the offspring may still have mutual synergies to exploit, and a complete separation is not strategically fruitful.
- The offspring receives cash from the sale (primary carve-out), and the parent may offload some of its equity in the offspring to raise cash (secondary carve-out).
- Raising cash may be an important motive for the carve-out, especially if the parent has been performing poorly and is in financial distress.
- The parent may benefit from including the offspring in the consolidated accounts if it still makes profit contribution or adds to balance sheet strength, so carve-out is preferable to a spin-off.
- Equity carve-out, unlike a spin-off, may not confer any corporate governance benefit, e.g. a new and independent board of directors, since the subsidiary may still be effectively controlled by the parent board (see Exhibit 10.8).

If the subsidiary is in a high-growth industry and outperforms its competitors, on flotation it is likely to be highly valued, and the parent has an incentive to opt for a carve-out. If the subsidiary underperforms its competitors, or is in a mature industry, it is likely to be valued low, and the parent may prefer a spin-off for its shareholders[37].

Tax and accounting implications of equity carve-outs

In a carve-out the parent loses some control over the subsidiary, and if the divestment takes the parent's shareholding to below 75% in the UK (80% in the US), group tax relief may cease to be available. Its ability to pass special resolutions could also be blocked. Since the parent continues to retain majority control, the minority stake may not be an attractive proposition to investors. In the US, if the parent sells some of its equity in the offspring in a secondary carve-out and realizes its investment, it becomes subject to capital gains tax. With a primary carve-out the parent has no tax liability. Thus firms with high marginal corporation tax rates may prefer a tax-free spin-off to a secondary carve-out[38].

Do equity carve-outs create value?

For the US data we find from Table 10.5 that parent company shareholders earn significant abnormal returns[39]. Thus the carve-out decision appears to be a value-enhancing decision, at least so far as the stock market assessment at the time of announcement is concerned. Anand Vijh examines the long-term returns to shareholders of the carved-out subsidiaries[40]. He finds no significant abnormal returns during the three years after they were made. The parent shareholders also earned no significant returns over the three-year period. At best, equity carve-outs seem to preserve the initial value gains and maintain their value subsequently.

Exhibit 10.8

Siemens loosens its grip on its carved-out offspring

As shown in Exhibit 10.7, Siemens, the German electronics and engineering conglomerate, carved out its high-technology chipmaker, Infineon Technology, in 2000. In December 2001 Siemens reduced its stake further by sale in the stock market to below 50%. This sale purported to give Infineon more independence by removing its status as a Siemens subsidiary, reducing its representation on Infineon's board, and possibly leading to the removal of board chairmanship from Siemens. Ulrich Schumacher, Infineon's CEO, had previously privately complained that Siemens' representatives had blocked some of Infineon's decisions, for example a proposal to issue convertible bonds. Thus the equity sale increased Infineon's freedom to pursue its own destiny.

Perhaps Siemens' motive in reducing its stake to a minority position had less to do with allowing Infineon greater autonomy. This reduction meant that Siemens did not have to consolidate Infineon's accounts, as it ceased to be a subsidiary. Investors had been wary of the impact of falling chip prices on Infineon's profit performance and, in turn, on Siemens' consolidated profits. James Stettler of investment bank Dresdner Kleinwort Wasserstein commented: 'This will have more of a psychological effect while also improving Siemens' cashflow.'

Given the benefits to both parent and offspring, the stock prices of both rose – Siemens' by 9% and Infineon's by 16% on the day of the share sale.

Source: Adapted from Benoit, B., 'Siemens lowers its stake in Infineon to under 50%', *Financial Times*, 6 December 2001

Table 10.5 Summary of US studies of shareholder gains from equity carve-outs

Study; sample period; and sample	Benchmark model	Two-day cumulative abnormal return (CAR) (%)
Schipper and Smith (1986); 1963–84; 76	Market model	1.83
Slovin, Shushka and Ferraro (1995); 1980–91; 36	NA	1.23
Vijh (2002); 1980–97; 336	Market model	1.9

See Chapter 4 for a discussion of the cumulative abnormal return methodology. CARs significant at 5% or better.
NA = not available.

More recent US studies find evidence of short-term gains but long-term wealth losses to parent and offspring shareholders (see Table 10.11). Some of these studies also report that the operating performance of firms emerging from carve-outs is also negative compared with relevant benchmarks[41].

Characteristics of value-creating carve-outs

Vijh finds that the following characteristics of his sample of carve-outs account for a significant part of the value gains:

- The market reaction is more positive when unrelated businesses are carved out.
- Many carve-outs are followed by complete spin-offs or third party acquisitions (see the Hoechst case in Exhibit 10.4 above), and the market seems to anticipate with some enthusiasm the follow-on divestitures.
- Use of proceeds to repay debt or meet other financial contingencies evokes a positive market reaction.
- The market reaction is more positive when the carve-out is interpreted as creating a pure-play.

Stock market arithmetically challenged in pricing equity carve-outs?

A very odd pricing anomaly has been observed in the context of many equity carve-out IPOs, casting doubt on the initial stock market valuation of the offspring: the parent's share of the market capitalization of the offspring exceeds the market value of the parent itself! Suppose parent P sells 25% of its stake in offspring OS and retains 75%. Following the IPO, P's market capitalization is V_P and that of OS is V_{OS}. Then the pricing anomaly results in

$$V_P < 0.75 \times V_{OS}$$

This is illustrated by the case of Palm, whose parent 3Com carried out in March 2000 an equity carve-out prior to its spin-off (see Exhibit 10.9). At that time high-tech and Internet stocks were in great demand. Investor sentiment about such stocks was quite frenzied. Clearly, investors were initially over-optimistic about the future growth of Palm. It seems that the

---

Exhibit 10.9

Glamour kid outshines the dowdy mom!

On 1 March 2000 3Com floated 5% of its shares in its subsidiary, Palm. 3Com offered a broad range of products, grouped into network systems products and personal connectivity products. Palm was a global designer and seller of hand-held computing devices, including the Palm III, Palm V and Internet-enabled Palm VII product families. Palm's smartphone held the promise of a revolution in personal communication. Following the IPO, Palm shares began trading on 2 March 2000. Prior to that, the ratio of 3Com's share of Palm's book value of equity and liabilities (owed to 3Com) to its own book value total assets was about 22%. On the first day of trading, however, the same ratio in terms of the equity market values of Palm and 3Com (and the book value of their liabilities) was 162%. This meant that 3Com's *95% share of Palm's equity* was 62% more valuable than *its own common stock*!

The market value of 3Com's holding in Palm ($50 billion) was substantially higher than the entire market value of 3Com ($28 billion), implying that 3Com's other businesses had a negative value (–$22 billion). Considering the size and profitability of the rest of 3Com's businesses, this result was astonishing, and indicated significant market mispricing of different businesses of 3Com at that time. Then, within three years, Palm's stock experienced a massive price decline from $104.13 per share to $0.10 per share.

Source: See footnote 41 for the relevant studies

general overvaluation of dotcom and high-tech stocks at that time caused the overvaluation of Palm. There were similar cases of equity carve-outs in which the parent's share of the off-spring's market value exceeded its own. Cornell and Liu call this anomaly '*the parent company puzzle*'. Many authors attribute it, at least partly, to stock markets' 'irrational exuberance' in the 1990s and in 2000[42].

The downside of downsizing

Post-divestiture challenges in spin-offs and carve-outs

Inappropriate allocation of assets and liabilities between the parent and offspring can expose either to inordinate risk. There are also further sources of post-divestiture risk. While a spin-off represents a complete separation of ownership of the parent and the offspring, and an equity carve-out a partial separation, the two firms may still maintain some links of a com-mercial, managerial or strategic nature. These links need careful structuring and handling so that the newly proclaimed autonomy of the offspring is more than an illusion, and the relation-ship between parent and offspring does not turn prickly and antagonistic. Risks of this nature must be carefully managed. This may involve a trade-off between continuity of links and the need for filial detachment in operational and strategic areas.

The following areas may be of concern[43]:

- Will the two firms be competitors, e.g. bidding for the same customers or projects?
- Will they have a supplier–user relationship: e.g. what will be the transfer pricing for such exchange?
- Will they share services, and what is the cost-sharing arrangement? Is it fair to both or is it imposed by the parent?
- Does the offspring have managerial autonomy, or is the parent still pulling the strings behind the façade of an independent board?
- How much support does the offspring need from the parent before it gets up and starts running its own show?

As argued in Chapter 7, one of the benefits of diversification is the spreading of risk and the consequent reduction in cost of capital. A spin-off or a majority carve-out eliminates this source of value. Thus the cost of capital of the parent and the offspring may increase if the divestiture is of unrelated businesses. Further, the reduction in size of the firm may reduce the market capitalization of the parent if it reduces the liquidity of the firm's shares in the stock market. In some cases downsizing may result in the parent losing its coveted place in a stock market index, thereby causing loss of interest among analysts and fund managers. For example, when GKN, the British engineering conglomerate, demerged its industrial services business in August 2001, it was feared that it would be dropped from the *Financial Times* (London) Stock Exchange (FTSE) 100 index. One analyst said: 'If you drop out of the FTSE 100, your stock will fall off the radar screens of larger index tracking funds. This could lead to a lower rating and could make access to capital more difficult'[44].

Tracking stock

In a tracking-stock restructuring the parent forms a separate subsidiary out of the busi-nesses that, it considers, could benefit from a separate profile and greater transparency. Instead of floating off this subsidiary on the stock market, the parent issues a new class of *its own* stock to track the performance of the newly created subsidiary, and gets this tracking stock listed on a stock market. For this reason it is also called targeted stock. Some of the newly created stock is issued to new investors. No pure-play is created, there is no change of control, and the owners of tracking stock do not own shares directly in the concerned subsidiary.

Tracking stock represents the least separation of the subsidiary from the parent, in contrast to spin-off and equity carve-out. It does not lead to a separate corporate governance structure, but can allow stock-market-based management incentives for the subsidiary, thus directly relating management compensation to shareholder value changes. Transparency of the subsidiary may be increased, since the parent is likely to produce separate accounts for it. This can then reduce the conglomerate discount, but less so than in the case of the other two types of restructuring.

Issue of tracking stock can increase the range of investments available to the investors, who can now invest in the tracking stock. There is no separation of debt between the parent and the tracking stock subsidiary. Thus debt rating is not likely to be affected. While analyst following may increase, it is likely to be marginal and not on the same scale as either equity carve-out or spin-off. There have been only a small number of tracking issues in the US. The number of completed issues during 1990–2002 was only 12, with a total market value of $26bn at the time of the IPO. In Europe there seems to have been no issue at all during the same period. Exhibit 10.10 gives examples of some recent tracking stock issues.

Exhibit 10.10

Examples of tracking stock issues in the US

Year	Parent	Spin-off	Share exchange Ratio	Deal value ($m)
2000	AT&T	AT&T Wireless Group		10,000
1999	Genzyme Corporation	Genzyme Surgical Products	1 for 6	
1999	Snyder Communications	Circle.com	1 for 4	
1999	Quantum Corporation	Hard Drive Disk Group	1 for 2	

Source: Thomson Financial and The Economist

How well did the tracking stocks do?

Tracking stocks have not been as popular as other forms of divestiture since, in essence, they hardly represent divestiture. Many high-technology companies have used them, especially in the telecom and Internet businesses. It is probably also the case that many of these tracking stocks covered businesses that were either underperforming or were highly speculative, with a considerable real option element to them. Many of these businesses were yet to generate sustained profits, and their value lay in their success in creating new product/markets[45]. With the dotcoms turning deathcoms, tracking stock as a restructuring device may have suffered a setback.

Empirical evidence on shareholder value performance of tracking stock issuers

Table 10.6 summarises the recent studies of the performance of parents issuing tracking stocks[46]. Tracking stocks are well received by the stock market on announcement.

Table 10.6 Summary of US studies of shareholder gains from tracking stocks

Study; sample period; and sample	Benchmark model	Two-day cumulative abnormal return (CAR) (%)
Billett and Mauer (2000); 1980–97; 24	Market-adjusted	2.6
Chemmanur and Paeglis (2001); 19	Market-adjusted	3.5
Harper and Madura (2002); 1984–99; 51	Market model	2.4
Billet and Vijh (2004); 1984–99; 29	Market-adjusted	1.1

All CARs significant at 5% or better.

Parents issuing tracking stocks, or their offspring tracked by them, do not improve their operating performance over the following two years compared with the year before the divestiture in terms of return on assets. The combined stock returns to the parent and off-spring are also significantly negative (about −30%) over three years. Tracking stock issues do not reduce information asymmetries, thereby leading to increased liquidity in the stock market for those stocks. The bid–ask spread, a measure of such liquidity, does not increase significantly for such stocks[47].

Managerial self-interest in higher executive compensation may motivate issue of tracking or an equity carve-out. CEOs may enjoy a 'double dip' by receiving stock options and other incentive pay in both the parent and the offspring (see Exhibit 10.11)[48].

Exhibit 10.11

Tracking stock an exec pay boondoggle?

In 1998 Sprint Corp. in the US issued a pair of tracking stocks to reflect its main-stream long-distance telephone business, Sprint FON Group, and its wireless operations, Sprint PCS Group. The manoeuvre was initially a big success, more than doubling the total market value of Sprint, to $105.8 billion within a year. How-ever, the combined stocks' value fell to just $25.2 billion in April 2002. Even so, in the three years after the Sprint restructuring, seven of the company's top executives realized gains of $185 million on PCS stock options alone. CEO Esrey had gains of $46.8 million, while President LeMay had $91.1 million. At the end of 2001 Esrey was also still holding options on 10.1 million shares of FON, while LeMay had 5.7 million. The company, however, justified the option awards on both, securities saying, 'Sprint is defined by two tracking stocks, both equally important.'

Source: J. Byrne, 'Extra helpings on the gravy train: Tracking stocks let some execs double up on their options', *Business Week*, 22 April 2002

Overview of the divestiture methods

All the four methods seek to achieve several overlapping objectives, such as:

● increase in focus of the parent's business portfolio;
● more robust corporate governance;
● greater managerial autonomy;

- more finely grained management incentive structures sensitive to stock price performance;
- enhanced liquidity impact on the parent and offspring;
- more efficient distribution of debt and associated risk rating among portfolio businesses; and
- greater visibility and transparency to the stock market, and the resultant stock rating investor interest and analyst following.

Nevertheless, they are not equally effective in achieving these objectives: hence the value gains to the announcements of divestitures are not sustained over time in all cases.

Chemmanur and Paeglis provide a comparative analysis of the shareholder value gains from spin-offs, carve-outs and tracking stocks, measured by market-adjusted abnormal returns (%)[49]:

Event window	Spin-off	Carve-out	Tracking stock
2 days	3.5	0.7	3.5
2 years (Parent)	−2.7	−57.8	−28.6
(Offspring)			−43.9

In our earlier review of empirical evidence on spin-offs and carve-outs we found that the latter underperformed their benchmarks in the long term. Tracking stocks and carve-outs generate smaller gains than spin-offs. This suggests that the benefits of increased transparency and lower information asymmetry are not enough to offset the negative synergies from continued control by the same parent. Divestment of control achieved by spin-offs seems to offer higher-value gains to parent shareholders. Equity carve-outs are generally preceded by parent's good stock price performance and may have been driven by smart managers taking advantage of investor sentiments and fads and timed the carve-outs accordingly. Tracking stocks are, however, generally preceded by poor stock return performance of the parents. Nevertheless, the issue of the vast majority of the tracking stocks in the studies we have reviewed at the top of the stock market boom in 1998–99 suggests that managerial timing to exploit investor sentiment may have been a motive. They may also have been motivated by managerial self-interest in boosting executive compensation.

CASE STUDY

Marriott's bondholders taken for a spin (or for a ride?)

In 1993 Marriott Corporation (MC) carried out a spin-off of its hotel management businesses to shareholders. In 1992, MC had revenues of $8.7bn and operating profits of $496m. The group consisted of two broad categories of businesses – the lodging management group including hotels that contributed 52% of group revenues and 68% of operating profits, and contract services catering and facilities management, airport and highway concessions that accounted for the rest. With two-thirds of its operating profit from lodging-related businesses, MC was generally viewed as a hotel company.

MC pursued ambitious growth and profitability objectives in the hotel business through a strategy of developing and then selling hotels while retaining the right to manage them. Management, separated from ownership of these properties, required smaller capital to fund growth but also reduced the volatility of cash flows. This low volatility allowed MC management to maintain high levels of debt. MC's operating profit increased yearly from 1986 to 1989 in both lodging management and contract services group. However, in

1990–91 recession hit the hotel occupancy rates and profits. The contract service businesses also suffered. MC had built up a large portfolio of hotel properties that were difficult to sell in the recession. It replaced high-risk senior debt with lower-risk subordinated debt against the background of falling credit rating of its debt.

Under the spin-off plan announced in October 1992, the lodging management, catering and other service businesses were to be spun off into Marriott International (MI). The parent, renamed Host Marriott (Host) retained ownership of the hotel and real estate interests. MI, under a long-term contract with Host, would manage the hotel properties. The Marriott family would continue to oversee all of the businesses and the senior management of MC would be split between MI and Host.

MC argued that the spin-off would benefit shareholders by:

- allowing MI to exploit its growth opportunities in the management business;
- allowing the capital markets to value MI more accurately because of better financial information;
- giving shareholders better investment options between a high-growth management company and a capital-intensive company with strong cash flow and long-term capital appreciation.

The initial spin-off proposal allocated most of MC's long-term debt to Host. When compared with the level of assets and operating cashflow, this allocation made Host vastly more risky than MI as shown below. This sparked considerable resistance from creditors who felt their debt was being put at high risk since most of it was being assigned to the cyclical property business and very little to the management business with more stable cash flows. The interest cover ratio shows this higher risk clearly. Such an allocation reduces the default risk faced by the shareholders and increases it for creditors, thereby transferring some of the corporate value from creditors to shareholders. Given the storm of protest from creditors and their class action suits, MC revised the spin-off proposal and reallocated more debt to the management business. This mitigated the additional risk faced by the creditors. MC was forced to accept several conditions, such as repurchase of debt, stricter covenants, higher coupon rate on new debt, etc. to the benefit of the creditors. The revised spin-off plan was implemented.

Robert Parrino estimated the market-adjusted bondholder loss at $195m and the industry-adjusted shareholder gains at $81m. Thus the spin-off caused a $114m decline in the total value of these securities from spin-off announcement to distribution. The spin-off failed to created shareholder value in the period surrounding the spin-off and destroyed bondholder value. What could be the reasons for this? There are several direct and indirect costs to a spin-off – direct transaction costs, loss of ability to offset Host's

Asset/liabilities	MC	First proposal		Final proposal	
		MI	Host	MI	Host
Total assets	6333	2360	4620	3017	3888
Property and equipment	3672	360	3310	772	2689
Current liabilities	1189	1130	210	1280	394
Long-term debt	2891	20	2870	899	2313
EBITDA/interest expense	2.6	20.3	1.3	6.5	1.8

EBITDA is earnings before interest, tax, depreciation and amortization.

losses with MI's profits and thereby save on corporation tax, the increased coupon on new debt, value of warrants issued to creditors, duplication of accounting and financial systems, higher costs of new security issues, etc.

The Marriott family continued to maintain control over the entire firm. The spin-off limited the potential losses to Marriott family from any default on debt. The separation improved the management business's debt capacity and this would allow the family to pursue growth in this business aggressively without losing control.

Discussion questions

1 Why did Marriott decide to go for a spin-off?

2 What is the initial structure of the spin-off?

3 Is there a conflict of interests in spin-offs among various stakeholders?

4 How were these resolved in the Marriott case?

Source: R. Parrino, 'Spin-offs and wealth transfers: The Marriott case', *Journal of Financial Economics*, 43(2), 1997, 241–274.

Overview and implications for practice

This chapter discusses various types of corporate refocusing, their rationale, their implications, and empirical evidence on shareholder wealth effects.

- Refocusing can take the form of sell-offs, spin-offs, equity carve-outs or tracking stocks.
- In a sell-off a division is sold to another company. In a spin-off the division becomes an independent company, with its shares distributed to the parent shareholders. In an equity carve-out the division's equity is partly floated. A tracking stock is new parent company stock that tracks the performance of a division.
- These refocusing alternatives differ in terms of cash flow, management control, corporate governance, visibility to stock market, analysts' following and other motives.
- They carry different personal and corporate tax implications, and have to be carefully structured for tax efficiency.
- Short-term stock market reaction to refocusing is generally positive, suggesting they are value-enhancing decisions.
- Downsizing through refocusing carries risks that must be factored into the decisions on refocusing.

Review questions

10.1 What is corporate refocusing?

10.2 What are the different types of refocusing? How do they differ in structure?

10.3 What are the motivations for a corporate sell-off?

10.4 Does divestiture mean failure of prior acquisitions? Why?

10.5 What are the implications of a corporate spin-off? What is the rationale for it?

10.6 What are the implications of an equity carve-out? What is the rationale for it?

10.7 What are the implications of a tracking stock? What is the rationale for it?

10.8 Compare and contrast the different refocusing methods.

10.9 Suggest circumstances in which you would choose one or other of the methods.

10.10 What is the stock market reaction to the different methods? What is your interpretation of it?

Further reading

M. Billett and A. Vijh, 'The wealth effects of tracking stock restructurings', *The Journal of Financial Research*, **27**(4), 2004, 559–583.

L. Dranikoff, T. Koller and A. Schneider, 'Divestiture: Strategy's missing link', *Harvard Business Review*, **80**(5), 2002, 75–83.

O. Lamont and R. Thaler, 'Can the market add and subtract? Mispricing in tech stock carve-outs', *Journal of Political Economy*, **111**, 2003, 227–268.

M. Mankins, D. Harding and R. Weddigen, 'How the best divest', *Harvard Business Review*, October 2008, 92–99.

C. Veld and Y. Veld-Merkoulova, 'Do spin-offs really create value? The European case', *Journal of Banking and Finance*, **28**(5), 2004, 1111–1135.

Notes and references

1. I. Duhaime and J. Grant, 'Factors influencing divestment decision-making: Evidence from a field study', *Strategic Management Journal*, **5**, 1984, 301–318.
2. C. C. Markides, 'Diversification, restructuring and economic performance', *Strategic Management Journal*, **16**(2), 1995, 398–412.
3. S. Bhagat, A. Shleifer and R. Vishny, *The Aftermath of Hostile Takeovers*, London School of Economics Discussion Paper 87, June 1990.
4. Z. Fluck and A. Lynch, 'Why do firms merge and then divest? A theory of financial synergy', *Journal of Business*, **72**(3), 1999, 319–346.
5. K. John and E. Ofek, 'Asset sales and increase in focus', *Journal of Financial Economics*, **37**, 1995, 105–126.
6. M. E. Porter, 'From competitive advantage to corporate strategy', *Harvard Business Review*, **65**, May/June 1987, 43–59; D. J. Ravenscraft and F. M. Scherer, *Mergers, Sell-offs and Economic Efficiency* (Washington, DC: Brookings Institution, 1987), Chapter 6; S. N. Kaplan and M. S. Weisbach, 'The success of acquisitions: Evidence from divestitures', *Journal of Finance*, **47**, 1992, 107–138.
7. J. Matsusaka, 'Takeover motives during the conglomerate merger wave', *Rand Journal of Economics*, **24**, 1993, 357–379.
8. D. D. Bergh, 'Predicting divestiture of unrelated acquisitions: An integrative model of ex ante conditions', *Strategic Management Journal*, **18**(9), 1997, 715–731. For a methodological challenge to the view that diversification and divestiture are linked, see D. D. Bergh, 'Assessment and redirection of longitudinal analysis: Demonstration with a study of the diversification and divestiture relationship', *Strategic Management Journal*, **18**(7), 1997, 537–571.
9. For a strong case for a creative destruction approach to divestitures, see L. Dranikoff, T. Koller and A. Schneider, 'Divestiture: Strategy's missing link', *Harvard Business Review*, May 2002, 74–83.
10. See J. Horn, D. Lovallo and S. Viguerie, 'Learning to let go: Making better exit decisions', *The Mckinsey Quarterly*, downloaded from www.mckinseyquarterly.com on 6 May 2006, for further discussion and examples of cognitive biases.
11. The five-stage model of divestment is somewhat different from that proposed by W. Cole and P. Hilger, 'Managing corporate divestiture transactions', *Journal of Accountancy*, August 2008, 48–51.

12. W. Cole and P. Hilger, *ibid.* See also Dranikoff, Koller and Schneider, *ibid.* On a strategic approach to divestitures and the importance of an efficient *process* for value creating divestitures see M. Mankins, D. Harding and R. Weddigen, 'How the best divest', *Harvard Business Review*, October 2008, 92–99.

13. D. Hearth and J. K. Zaima, 'Voluntary corporate divestitures and value', *Financial Management*, Spring 1984, 10–16; J. D. Rosenfeld, 'Additional evidence on the relation between divestiture announcements and shareholder wealth', *Journal of Finance*, **39**(5), 1984, 1437–1448; A. Klein, 'The timing and substance of divestiture announcements: Individual, simultaneous and cumulative effects', *Journal of Finance*, **41**(3), 1986, 685–697; G. L. Hite, J. E. Owers and R. C. Rogers, 'The market for interfirm asset sales: Partial selloffs and total liquidations', *Journal of Financial Economics*, **18**, 1987, 229–252; P. C. Jain, 'The effect of voluntary selloff announcements on shareholder wealth', *Journal of Finance*, **40**, 1985, 209–214; K. John and E. Ofek, 'Asset sales and increase in focus', *Journal of Financial Economics*, **37**, 1995, 105–126; M. B. Slovin, M. E. Shushka and S. R. Ferraro, 'A comparison of the information conveyed by equity carve-outs, spinoffs and assets sell-offs', *Journal of Financial Economics*, **37**, 1995, 89–104; N. W. Sicherman and R. H. Pettway, 'Acquisition of divested assets and shareholder wealth', *Financial Management*, **42**(5), 1992, 119–128; M. Hirschey, M. B. Slovin and J. K. Zaima, 'Bank debt, insider trading and the return to corporate selloffs', *Journal of Banking and Finance*, **14**, 1990, 85–98; M. B. Slovin, M. E. Sushka and J. A. Polonchek, 'Methods of payment in asset sales: Contracting with equity versus cash', *Journal of Finance*, **60**(5), 2005, 2385–2407.

14. See Klein, *ibid.*; Slovin *et al.* (2005), *ibid.*

15. *Ibid.*

16. N. Tehranian, N. Travlos and J. F. Waegelein, 'The effect of long-term performance plans on corporate sell-off induced abnormal returns', *Journal of Finance*, **42**, 1987, 933–942.

17. L. Lang, A. Poulsen and R. Stulz, 'Asset sales, firm performance and the agency costs of managerial discretion', *Journal of Financial Economics*, **37**(1), 1995, 3–37.

18. K. A. Afshar, R. J. Taffler and P. S. Sudarsanam, 'The effect of corporate divestments on shareholder wealth: The UK experience', *Journal of Banking and Finance*, **16**, 1992, 115–135; M. A. Lasfer, P. S. Sudarsanam and R. J. Taffler, 'Financial distress, asset sales and lender monitoring', *Financial Management*, **25**(3), 1996, 57–66; K. M. J. Kaiser and A. Stouraitis, 'Agency costs and strategic considerations behind sell-offs: The UK evidence', *European Financial Management*, **7**(3), 2001, 319–349; G. Alexandrou and S. Sudarsanam, 'Shareholder wealth effects of corporate selloffs: Impact of growth opportunities, economic cycle and bargaining power', *European Financial Management*, **7**(2), 2001, 237–258.

19. See also J. Coakley, H. Thomas and H. Wang, 'The short-run wealth effects of foreign divestitures by UK firms', *Applied Financial Economics*, **18**, 2008, 173–184. They report significant 21-day abnormal returns of 5% for UK divestors of their foreign subsidiaries.

20. In high-tech divestitures the buyer may be at an information disadvantage relative to the seller. Nevertheless, buyers experience higher returns than sellers, as reported in G. Benou, J. Madura and T. Ngo, 'Wealth creation from high-tech divestitures', *Quarterly Review of Economics and Finance*, **48**, 2008, 505–519.

21. T. H. Hudspeth and M. J. Kliegman, 'The intricate rules for crafting a spinoff', *Mergers and Acquisitions*, May/June 1996, 47–52.

22. The negative relation between high business risk and leverage is posited by the capital structure trade-off theory. For empirical evidence in support of this theory see A. Dittmar, 'Capital structure in corporate spinoffs', *Journal of Business*, **77**(1), 2004, 9–42; and V. Mehrotra, W. Mikkelson and M. Partch, 'The design of financial policies in corporate spin-offs', *Review of Financial Studies*, **16**(4), 2003, 1359–88. Mehrotra *et al.* find that post-spin-off firms have their leverage levels determined by their debt service capacity and ability to reduce debt-related costs. Higher leverage is associated with higher cash flows, a higher level of tangible fixed assets that provide collateral, and lower operating income volatility. They find no impact of managerial incentives on the choice of capital structure of the firms.

23. Demergers give rise to tax issues, and different types of demergers need to satisfy different conditions. In the UK, in a direct demerger, the parent pays a special dividend *in specie* satisfied by the issue of shares in the demerged business, like Biffa to its own shareholders. For example, the direct demerger illustrated below requires that the parent has enough distributable reserves to match the special dividend. Shareholder approval is necessary. The reduction in capital also needs to be approved by the court. Subject to these conditions this is a fairly simple procedure. In an *indirect* demerger, the demerged business is first transferred to a newly created company, *Newco*, which in turn issues shares in consideration to the parent

shareholders. Here, the parent declares a dividend *in specie* that is satisfied by these shares in *Newco*. A third demerger procedure is by way of a scheme of arrangement that is court-approved, and which requires that 75% of the shareholders vote in favour. For a more detailed discussion see A. Montgomery, D. Hill and R. Moore, 'Divesting control by demerger', a special *International Financial Law Review* supplement, 2007, downloaded from www.herbertsmith.com.

24. D. Thomas, 'Support for Land Securities demerger builds', *Financial Times*, 14 May 2008.

25. Hudspeth and Kliegman, *ibid.*

26. G. Hite and J. Owers, 'Security price reactions around corporate spinoff announcements', *Journal of Financial Economics*, **12**, 1983, 409–436; P. Cusatis, J. Miles and J. Woolridge, 'Restructuring through spinoffs: The stock market evidence', *Journal of Financial Economics*, **33**, 1993, 293–311; J. Allen, S. Lummer, J. McConnell and D. Reed, 'Can takeover losses explain spinoff gains?', *Journal of Financial and Quantitative Analysis*, **30**, 1995, 465–485; M. B. Slovin, M. E. Shushka and S. R. Ferraro, 'A comparison of the information conveyed by equity carve-outs, spinoffs and assets sell-offs', *Journal of Financial Economics*, **37**, 1995, 89–104; J. Seward and J. Walsh, 'The governance and control of voluntary corporate spinoffs', *Strategic Management Journal*, **17**, 1996, 25–40; L. Daley, V. Mehrotra and R. Sivakumar, 'Corporate focus and value creation: Evidence from spinoffs', *Journal of Financial Economics*, **45**, 1997, 257–281; S. Krishnaswami and V. Subramaniam, 'Information asymmetry, valuation and the corporate spin-off decision', *Journal of Financial Economics*, **53**, 1999, 73–112.

27. Other studies covering an almost identical sampling period and reporting a similar magnitude of CAR to Hite and Owers listed in Table 10.5 are the following: K. Schipper and A. Smith, 'Effects of recontracting on shareholder wealth, the case of voluntary spinoffs', *Journal of Financial Economics*, **12**, 1983, 437–467; J. A. Miles and J. D. Rosenfeld, 'The effect of voluntary spinoff announcements on shareholder wealth', *Journal of Finance*, **38**(5), 1983, 1597–1606; J. D. Rosenfeld, 'Additional evidence on the relationship between divestiture announcements and shareholder wealth', *Journal of Finance*, **39**(5), 1984, 1437–1448; W. Maxwell and R. Rao, 'Do spin-offs expropriate wealth from bondholders?', *Journal of Finance*, **58**(5), 2003, 2087–2108; T. Burch and V. Nanda, 'Divisional diversity and the conglomerate discount: Evidence from spinoffs', *Journal of Financial Economics*, **70**, 2003, 69–98.

28. J. J. McConnell, M. Ozbilgin and S. Wahal, 'Spinoffs, ex ante', *Journal of Business*, **74**(2), 2001, 245–280.

29. H. Desai and P. C. Jain, 'Firm performance and focus: Long-run stock market performance following spinoffs', *Journal of Financial Economics*, **54**, 1999, 75–101.

30. *Ibid.*

31. S. Gilson, P. Healy and K. Palepu, 'Corporate focus and the benefits from more specialized analysts coverage', Harvard Business School Working Paper, 1998. See also P. L. Anslinger, S. J. Klepper and S. Subramaniam, 'Breaking up is good to do', *McKinsey Quarterly*, **1**, 1999, 16–27.

32. See C. Veld and Y. Veld-Merkoulova, 'Do spinoffs really create value? The European case', *Journal of Banking and Finance*, **28**(5), 2004, 1111–1135; and B. Qian and S. Sudarsanam, 'Catering theory of corporate spinoffs: Empirical evidence from Europe', paper presented to the European Financial Management Association annual meeting, University of Vienna, June 2007, Cranfield School of Management Working Paper. See also H. J. de Vroom and R. van Frederikslust, 'Shareholder wealth effects of corporate spinoffs: The world-side experience', Rotterdam School of Management, Erasmus University, Working Paper, 2000, who, for a sample of 70 spin-off announcements during 1990–98, report an 11-day abnormal return, based on the market model, of 4.5%.

33. While the difference between US and European studies may be due to methodological differences, Qian and Sudarsanam, *ibid.*, report that their results are robust to a range of methodologies, including national versus world market indices, use of size and book-to-market benchmarks, industry- and size-adjusted benchmarks, and the-four factor model, and calendar time portfolio abnormal returns model. See Chapter 4, Appendix 4.1, for a discussion of these benchmarks.

34. For similar results with a UK-only sample, see L. Murray, 'Spin-offs in an environment of bank debt', *Journal of Business Finance & Accounting*, **35**(3&4), 2008, 406–433.

35. For a much smaller sample of 16 bonds in US spin-offs, Dittmar finds no evidence of bondholder gains or losses in terms of announcement period abnormal returns. She also finds that parent and offspring bonds do not suffer significant rating downgrade. See Dittmar, *ibid.*

36. A. Klein, J. Rosenfeld and W. Baranek, 'The two stages of an equity carve-out and the price response of parent and subsidiary stock', *Managerial and Decision Economics*, **12**, 1991, 449–460.

37. V. Nanda, 'On the good news in equity carve-outs', *Journal of Finance*, **46**(5), 1991, 1717–1737; L. Zingales, 'Insider ownership and the decision to go public', *Review of Financial Studies*, **62**, 1995,

425–448; M. B. Slovin, M. E. Shushka and S. R. Ferraro, 'A comparison of the information conveyed by equity carve-outs, spin-offs and assets sell-offs', *Journal of Financial Economics*, **37**, 1995, 89–104.

38. K. F. Frank and J. W. Harden, 'Corporate restructurings: A comparison of equity carve-outs and spinoffs', *Journal of Business Finance and Accounting*, **28**(3&4), 2001, 503–529.

39. K. Schipper and A. Smith, 'A comparison of equity carveouts and seasoned equity offerings: Share price effects and corporate restructuring', *Journal of Financial Economics*, **15**, 1986, 153–186; M. B. Slovin, M. E. Shushka and S. R. Ferraro, *ibid.*; A. M. Vigh, 'The positive announcements-period returns of equity carveouts: Asymmetric information or divestiture gains', *Journal of Business*, **75**(1), 2002, 153–190.

40. A. M. Vijh, 'Long-term returns from equity carveouts', *Journal of Financial Economics*, **51**, 1999, 273–308, with a sample of 628 carve-outs during 1981–95.

41. These studies include: A. Boone, D. Haushalter and W. Mikkelson, 'An investigation of the gains from specialized equity claims', *Financial Management*, **32**(3), 2003, 67–83; J. Madura and T. Nixon, 'The long-term performance of parent and units following equity carve-outs', *Applied Financial Economics*, **12**(3), 2002, 171–181; T. Chemmanur and J. Paeglis, 'Why issue tracking stock? Insights from comparisons with spin-offs and carve-outs', *Journal of Applied Corporate Finance*, **14**(2), 2001, 102–114.

42. See, for example, B. Cornell and Q. Liu, 'The parent company puzzle: When is the whole worth less than one of the parts?', *Journal of Corporate Finance*, **7**, 2001, 341–366; M. Schill and C. Zhou, 'Pricing an emerging industry: Evidence from internet subsidiary carve-outs', *Financial Management*, **30**(3), 2001, 5–33; and O. Lamont and R. Thaler, 'Can the market add and subtract? Mispricing in tech stock carve-outs', *Journal of Political Economy*, **111**, 2003, 227–268. These authors test a number of alternative hypotheses that could explain the mispricing: high costs of arbitrage that might have eliminated it; noise trading; managerial opportunism in timing the IPOs to exploit investor sentiment; investors' behavioural bias, such as anchoring and adjustment in extrapolating the recent spectacular performance of internet stocks; illiquidity; high agency costs in the parent, which discount the value of its holding in the offspring; taxes etc. These do not fully explain the anomaly.

43. P. Anslinger, S. Bonini and M. Patsalos-Fox, 'Doing the spin-out', *McKinsey Quarterly*, **1**, 2000, 98–105.

44. F. Gimbel, 'Dwindling engineers hang on in the FTSE-100', *Financial Times*, 6 August 2001.

45. M. Sikora, 'Tracking stocks: Do they create value?', *Mergers and Acquisitions*, **35**(7), 2000, 6.

46. See M. Billett & D. Mauer, 'Diversification and the value of internal capital markets: The case of tracking stock', *Journal of Banking and Finance*, **24**, 2000, 1457–1490; T. Chemmanur and I. Paeglis, 'Why issue tracking stock? Insights from a comparison with spin-offs and carve-outs', *Journal of Applied Corporate Finance*, **14**(2), 2001, 102–114; J. Harper and J. Madura, 'Sources of hidden value and risk within tracking stock', *Financial Management*, 2002, **31**(3); M. Billett and A. Vijh, 'The wealth effects of tracking stock restructurings', *Journal of Financial Research*, **27**(4), 2004, 559–583. In contrast, Clayton and Qian find positive announcement period returns and insignificant returns over three years for a small sample of tracking stocks.

47. See Boone *et al.*, footnote 39, *ante*; J. Elder, P. Jain and J. Kim, 'Do tracking stocks reduce information asymmetries? An analysis of liquidity and adverse selection', *Journal of Financial Research*, **27**(2), 2005, 197–213; Harper and Madura, footnote 44 *ante*; M. Clayton and Y. Qian, 'Wealth gains from tracking stocks: Long-run performance and ex-date returns', *Financial Management*, **33**(3), 2004.

48. A recent study links the poor long-term performance of both parents and offspring following tracking stock issues to such compensation-based incentives. See W. He, T. Mukherjee and P. Wei, 'Agency problems in tracking stock and minority carve-out decisions: Explaining the discrepancy in short- and long-term performances', *Journal of Economics and Finance*, **33**, 2009, 27–42. Top five parent firm managers in track stock issuers (in carve-outs) increase their total compensation by 121% (66%) in the year following the restructuring compared with the year before that. Their compensation in parent stock increased by 101% (34%) and in the offspring stock by 38% (1%). Thus exec compensation increases substantially following tracking stock issues and more so than following carve-outs.

49. See T. Chemmanur and I. Paeglis, 'Why issue tracking stock? Insights from a comparison with spin-offs and carve-outs', *Journal of Applied Corporate Finance*, **14**(2), 2001, 102–114, Tables 6 and 7. The sample sizes are not the same for the three divestiture types. The two-day returns to carve-outs and two-year returns to spin-offs are not statistically significant. All other returns are significant at at least 5%.

CHAPTER 11

Leveraged buyouts

Objectives

At the end of this chapter, the reader should be able to understand:

- what leveraged buyouts are, and how they are structured;
- the risk return characteristics and performance of junk bonds;
- what the different types of LBO are;
- the post-buyout structure and how this contributes to value creation;
- how private equity funds realize their investment, i.e. their exit strategy;
- the value creation performance of LBOs;
- how the LBO market has evolved in the 1990s, and where it stands today; and
- the probable staying power of the LBO as an efficient organizational form.

Introduction

In Chapters 5 to 10 we discussed acquisitions by corporate buyers. During the 1980s merger wave a new class of acquirers became prominent. These new buyers were financial investment firms, and they financed such acquisitions with a small amount of equity and a preponderance of debt. This mix gave rise to the name 'leveraged buyout' or LBO. They aimed to leverage the returns to their equity investment with substantial debt, and often earned astronomical returns over very short periods, say just one or two years. LBO acquirers are called *financial buyers* to distinguish them from *strategic buyers*, i.e. corporate acquirers motivated by expectations of strategic synergies. In an LBO the target may be a publicly listed corporation. As a result of the buyout it 'goes private', and equity provided by the investing public through stock markets is replaced by private equity by specialist buyout firms. The buyout specialist is also referred to as a private equity firm or LBO sponsor.

Michael Jensen has hailed leveraged buyout as a new organizational form that spelled the eclipse of the older and inefficient public corporation[1]. He has argued that an LBO organization is an effective remedy for the endemic agency problem in public corporations with a diffused ownership structure (see Chapter 3 for an introduction to the agency model). The defining characteristics of an LBO, such as concentrated equity ownership and monitoring by the LBO sponsor, and a high level of debt, are said to cure corporate management's waywardness and self-interest pursuit. Baker and Smith describe an LBO innovation as an 'entrepreneurial coup'[2]. In this chapter we delineate the sources of the therapeutic qualities of LBOs. Is an LBO a miracle cure, or just quackery that injects its own toxicity? Is it merely a transient organizational form whose trajectory reverts to a public corporation, or does it have much 'staying power'[3]?

A feature of the 1980s merger boom commonly associated with LBOs is the 'junk bond'. A junk bond is so called because it is rated below investment grade for certain types of financial institution in the US. They yield higher returns than investment-grade debt. The growth of the high-yield bonds made raising debt much easier, and led to substitution of bank financing with these bonds. The junk bonds in time came to embody the excesses of the 1980s takeover boom, and possibly contributed to its collapse after the 1989 peak. Names such as Drexel Burnham Lambert (DBL), the investment bank, and Michael Milken became synonymous with the junk bond market. The 1980s junk-bond-financed LBO boom ended with the conviction and liquidation of DBL and the conviction of Michael Milken for fraud.

Leveraged financing also made possible audacious takeover raids on large, well-established firms. The raiders, such as Boone Pickens, Carl Icahn in the US and Sir James Goldsmith in the UK, charged target firm managements with neglecting shareholder interests and following self-serving policies that destroyed shareholder value. The raid targets were stodgy companies in mature industries such as oil and gas, retail, food and drinks, tobacco and steel that had overdiversified in the 1960s and 1970s and become afflicted with the so-called conglomerate discount (see Chapter 8 on conglomerate discount). Since their value creation strategy generally necessitated job losses and sale of assets, the raiders and financial buyers gained notoriety as asset strippers that destroyed respected firms and their surrounding communities, dumped loyal workers on the scrap heap, and left devastation behind in their relentless trail of greed. The larger-than-life characters associated with hostile tender offers, junk bonds and raids, initially admired for their inventiveness and audacity, subsequently became the stuff of villains in novels and Hollywood movies[4].

In this chapter we track the growth of LBOs in the US and Europe. The major characteristics of LBOs are described. The characteristics of LBOs that not only distinguish them from strategic acquisitions and organization but also possibly contribute to their superior value creation performance are highlighted. The risk and return performance of junk bonds is assessed. We discuss LBO sponsors' exit strategies, and then review the performance record of LBOs and their variants.

Leveraged buyout

Definition

A leveraged buyout is an acquisition of a corporation as a whole or a division of a corporation mostly with cash, the cash being raised with a preponderance of debt raised by the acquirer. A special-purpose company, called Newco, is created to carry out the acquisition. This acquisition vehicle's financial structure consists of substantial debt, sliced into different types of debt, and equity. The equity component is provided by investors, who invest in a 'fund' raised by a specialist firm that finds suitable investment opportunities to invest the fund through one or more Newcos. Since the equity capital is contributed by investors privately, outside a public stock market, this source of finance is referred to as private equity, and the specialist firm is called a private equity firm.

The vast majority of LBOs carried out around the world are sponsored by PE firms. Over the period 1970 to 2007, out of 21,397 LBO transactions carried out around the world,

Figure 11.1 Global evolution of LBO deals by value 1970–2006

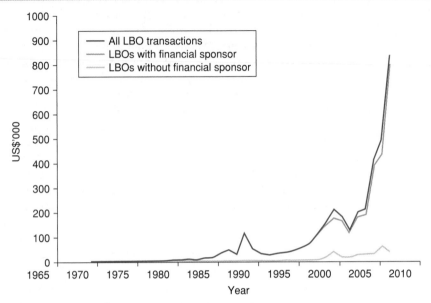

The values, in 2007 US$, are imputed enterprise values. See the source for computational details.
Source: P. Stromberg, 'The new demography of private equity', *The Global Economic Impact of Private Equity Report 2008*, Figure 1b, World Economic Forum.

80% were done by financial sponsors, i.e. by private equity firms. In terms of value, this share was even more overwhelming: that is, 92% of total enterprise value (EV) of US$ 3.9 trillions (in 2007 $). In recent years LBOs have grown exponentially, as shown in Figure 11.1[5].

A fund is normally organized as a limited liability partnership, with the fund investors being limited partners without any management responsibility. The LBO specialist is the general partner in the partnership with management responsibility. The role of the specialist is described in greater detail below. LBO specialist firms have their modern origin in the 1970s in the US, and two of the oldest of such firms are Kohlberg Kravis & Roberts (KKR) and Forstmann, Little from that period. In the 1970s and 1990s the relative weight of debt to equity in LBOs was often 9 to 1 or higher: hence the name 'leveraged buyout.' In the tougher competitive private equity markets of the 1990s this ratio fell to 3 to 1 or even 2 to 1. In the current credit crisis the ratio has again fallen from the highs reached during the mid-2000s.

Organizational and legal structure of the private equity firm

In the early 1980s LBOs generated some eye-popping returns for the equity investors because of the leverage effect. This naturally attracted avid competition. Many investment and commercial banks have since developed substantial private equity business, not only by drawing upon their own deep pockets for funds but also by inviting other investors to invest in funds for LBOs. Other financial institutions, such as insurance companies, have also developed private equity businesses.

Figure 11.2   Private equity firms' investment activities

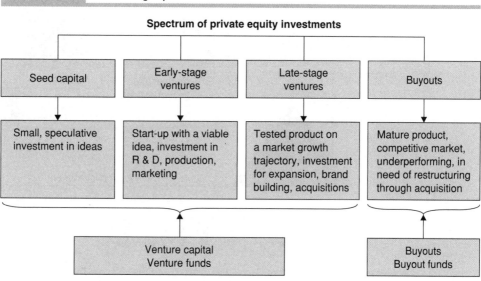

Private equity firms invest in early-stage ventures such as seed capital and start-ups, and expansion of early-stage investments and buyouts, as seen in Figure 11.2. Venture capital investment is much more speculative than buyout investments, since buyout targets are established firms with a track record of operating in fairly well-defined markets. Seed capital and early-stage investments are often in the nature of real options on subsequent investments if the early stage bears fruit (see Chapter 5 on the real option perspective on platform acquisitions). In general, the size of buyout investments is much larger than VC investment. In the rest of this chapter we shall focus on buyouts, since they are in the nature of mergers and acquisitions.

PE firms are legally structured as limited liability partnerships (LLPs) consisting of two classes of partners:

- *General partners (GPs)* (also called managing partners)
  - Raise funds, identify investment opportunities, negotiate investment deals, manage the investments portfolio, direct the operation of portfolio business, manage relations with investors, craft exit strategies, and ensure investors receive adequate returns.
  - Receive an *annual management fee* of about 2% per annum or 0.5% per quarter of the value of the fund (but can range from 1.5% to 2.5%) and an incentive fee of 20% of the *carried interest* or share of the profits made by the fund (this formula is known as *2-20*). The incentive fee kicks in when the fund makes a profit in excess of an agreed hurdle rate of return.
- *Limited partners (LPs)*
  - Commit to providing funds on call, pay annual management fee, and receive their share of the carried interest.

Figure 11.3 shows the sources and uses of funds raised by PE firms. Investors (LPs) in private equity funds include corporate and public pension funds, university endowments, foundations, banks, insurance companies, investment banks, non-financial corporations, and

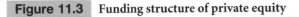

Figure 11.3 Funding structure of private equity

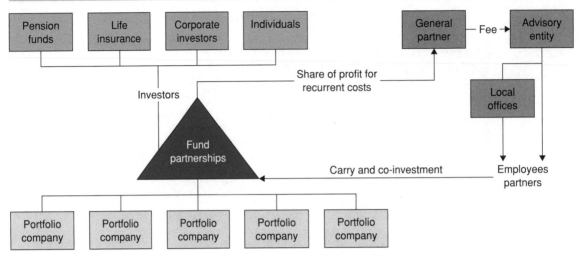

Source: *The British Private Equity and Venture Capital Association Submission to the Treasury Select Committee of the UK Parliament*, May 2007, Appendix 1

wealthy families and individuals. The equity funds raised from the LPs are invested by GPs in the range of investment opportunities discussed earlier. Funds have a finite life of 10 years, which may be extended by three years. At maturity, a fund is liquidated, and the LPs receive their original investment plus their share of the profits not already distributed during the fund's life. A single PE firm can set up a chain of funds with the same or new LPs for different investment purposes, for example investment in emerging markets. PE firms often invest their own funds ('co-invest') in the portfolio companies in addition to the investment made on behalf of LPs.

PEs are increasingly large global firms raising funds from international capital markets and investing in numerous countries in the US, Europe and increasingly on a large scale in Asia and Africa. In different countries they have set up their own offices, or work with local PE partners and banks. They set up advisory bodies made up of experienced corporate executives, investment bankers and other practitioners. PE firms have lured senior corporate executives from public corporations, including many very successful CEOs and investment bankers, over the years to broaden their human resources and capabilities.

What does an LBO look like?

In a typical buyout the financing package will consist of large chunks of debt, but in different layers, each characterized by different terms such as maturity, security, interest rate, i.e. coupon, whether the loan is amortized or is repaid by a single sum (bullet). Exhibit 11.1 explains this structure.

Table 11.1 presents the statistics on global leveraged buyouts from 1970 to 2007. North America is the dominant region for LBOs. However, its dominance has declined over time. Whereas in 1970–2000 the share of US and Canada was 57% by number of deals (66% by value), in 2001–07 it was only 38% (45%). On the other hand, continental Europe, Scandinavia and the UK increased their global market share from 39% (31%) to 50% (46%).

Exhibit 11.1

Financing structure of an LBO

Suppose the enterprise value of the target is £800m. The financing package for its buyout includes debt and equity. The purchase price is based on a multiple of 8 times the EBITDA of the target (earnings before interest, tax, depreciation and amortization, a measure of target's cash flow). Debt is normally priced at a certain margin over a benchmark return, generally the London Interbank Offered Rate (LIBOR). The margin or spread is a measure of the incremental risk of the debt and its seniority among the various categories of debt: that is, the higher the seniority, the lower the debt. Seniority is as regards payment of interest and repayment of the debt. Senior debt is normally secured. Junior or subordinated debt may have a second lien on the senior creditors' collateral (second lien debt) or may be unsecured (mezzanine debt). The level of each type of debt is expressed as a multiple of EBITDA. The higher the multiple, the larger the debt and the more risky the debt becomes. For this buyout, the financing structure may be as below.

Enterprise value			£800m
Debt		@margin	
Term loan A	£250m (amortized over 6 years)	2.0%	
Term loan B	£150m (8 year bullet repayment)	2.5%	
Total senior debt			£400m
2nd lien	£100m (10 year bullet)	5.0%	
Mezzanine	£100m	5% + 3% PIK*	
Total junior debt			£200m
Total debt			£600m
Equity			£200m

In addition, the package may include a revolving credit facility for working capital. This may rank along with senior debt. Senior debt is on a multiple of 4 times EBITDA and junior debt is on 2. Total debt is on a multiple of 6.

* *Payment in kind*, i.e. in the form of 3% equity in the new company. See below for its definition and role, and buyout financing. The significance of the EBITDA multiple is also discussed below.

The smaller regions also improved their market share in terms of both number and value of LBOs. Thus LBOS have increasingly become a global phenomenon.

In the 1980s and early 1990s buyout targets were generally firms operating in mature industries that would throw off steady operating cash flows. These companies had been undervalued by the conglomerate parent and their potential not fully exploited, perhaps owing to parental neglect. Such targets were therefore evocatively described as 'orphan children' or, more lugubriously, as 'the living dead'. The buyout specialists saw an opportunity to rescue the orphan and truly resurrect the living dead. Their under-performance often meant the targets also had surplus assets that could be sold off to raise cash to pay off some of the debt. However, the character of the targets changed significantly in the 1990s, as noted above. This trend continued in the new millennium with PE firms acquiring high-tech targets, such as satellite communication (e.g. Inmarsat), telecom (e.g. Deutsche Telecom), medical devices (e.g.

Table 11.1 LBOs in different regions of the world during 1970–2007

Region	Number of LBOs	% PE- sponsored	% of global	All LBOs ($bn)	% PE- sponsored	% of global
USA	9659	83	45.1	1948	93	49.7
Canada	471	71	2.2	81	94	2.1
Continental Europe	4619	85	21.6	864	95	22.0
Scandinavia	969	86	4.5	149	86	3.8
UK	4026	72	18.8	602	90	15.3
Eastern Europe	389	76	1.8	29	90	0.7
Asia	508	78	2.4	130	90	3.3
Australia	278	66	1.3	38	94	1.0
Africa and Middle East	284	63	1.3	38	65	1.0
Latin America	194	74	0.9	42	97	1.1
Total	21,397	80		3922	92	

The column figures don't add up to the 'Total global' owing to rounding to the nearest integer or nearest single decimal point. Value is enterprise value and, where not disclosed, is imputed by an approximation procedure. See the source for further details on the procedure. The term 'PE' includes all types of financial sponsor.
Source: As in footnote 5, *ante*.

Biomet), computer storage media (e.g. Seagate Technology in the US), and mobile technology (e.g. Bharti Tele-Ventures in India). Some of the LBO deals in the current decade have also run into several billion dollars, attesting to the great financial firing power of PE firms e.g. Biomet for $11bn by PE firms Blackstone, KKR, and TPG and the investment bank Goldman Sachs in late 2006. PE firms have shown increasing self-confidence to manage high-tech businesses. In 2006, while a KKR-led consortium bought the semiconductor subsidiary of the Dutch conglomerate Philips Electronics for $10bn, Blackstone beat KKR in winning the auction for the US firm Freescale Semiconductor for $17.6bn.

The private equity market is now a very crowded place indeed, with hundreds of firms, including both specialist firms and the arms of commercial and investment banks and other financial institutions. Hedge funds have also been muscling in on the PE territory as the hedge fund industry itself has become highly competitive and the opportunities for short-term profits through arbitrage have become harder to find, and they now fancy themselves as long-term investors that can turnaround ailing firms and help other firms grow. Nevertheless, the PE industry is dominated by a few giant firms with enormous financial power.

There is clear market segmentation in terms of firms and the size of the funds they raise. Leading PE firms have raised ever-larger funds. Before the market crash in the second half of 2007, the 12 largest US funds raised $155bn and seven European PE firms raised $60bn. These represented an average increase of 142% and 75% respectively over the previous funds that these firms had raised earlier[6]. Exhibit 11.2 lists the PE firms that raised these funds. Following the crisis, which rendered leverage financing impossible, these funds have remained largely underutilized. There is a lot of dry powder for PE firms to use when buyout shoot-outs erupt again in the next couple of years.

In recent years sovereign wealth funds (SWF) have become an important source of private equity investment. These funds are set up by governments of countries that have accumulated huge surplus reserves from their past trading in commodities, minerals or other goods, or fiscal surplus and want to invest them for the future benefit of their citizens. Such countries include China, Norway, and Middle Eastern oil sheikhdoms. For example, the Singapore fund Temasek invested in the equity capital to finance the acquisition of BAA plc, the British airport operator by Ferrovial in 2006. Another example was when Porsche sought investment from the Qatar Investment Authority when it sought to acquire Volkswagen in 2008 (see Exhibit 20.5). Other examples of SWF include: Abu Dhabi Investment Authority ($500–900bn), Saudi Arabia Monetary Authority ($247bn), China Investment Corporation ($200bn), and Australia Future Fund ($44bn).

They also invest in long-term funds. Due to high growth in the commodity prices, and high economic growth in many Asian emerging market countries, the size of these funds has grown spectacularly. Given their long term investment horizon they are particularly attractive for PE firms with long-term holding periods. Political sensitivities in the countries where they seek to invest may often prevent them from acquiring majority control. Thus, they may seek minority interests or invest in funds such as PE funds[7].

Exhibit 11.2

Mega funds raised in 2007 by leading PE firms

US PE firm	Fund size (US$ bn)[a]	European PE firm	Fund size (US$ bn)[a]
Blackstone 4	22	Permira	11
GS Capital Partners	20	Cinven	7
Carlyle	17	Apax 4	6
KKR	17	CVC Europe	6
TPG	15	BC Partners	6
Providence	12	Carlyle Europe	5
Apollo Management 5	10	KKR Europe 5	5

[a]Figures rounded to the nearest billion. The number after the PE firm name is the number of the fund in a series raised by that firm. Five other US funds – Hellman & Friedman, T H Lee 6, Silver Lake 6, Bain Capital, Warburg Pincus – raised about $8bn each.

PE firms differ in terms of their focus, with some specializing in certain sectors such as retail and chemicals; their ability to raise substantial funds; their ability to offer competitive prices to corporate vendors; their speed of execution; and their ability to generate attractive returns to both lenders and fund partners. Whereas in the early years LBOs created value through leverage, tax savings arising in part from the corporation tax deductibility of interest, and clever use of various financial instruments and financial market opportunities to lower the cost of capital, mere financial engineering of this kind is no longer sufficient. The LBO specialist needs to be able to add value through other resources and capabilities, e.g. spotting real winners among buyout candidates, and ability to work with the target company or new managers or through consolidation strategies (see Chapter 13)[8]. From being just equity investors and managers of those investments, their role has expanded to a strategic one, and many firms have built up strategic capabilities. These various sources of value creation in LBOs are discussed below.

Types of LBO

The different types of LBO are broadly the following:

- investor buyout (IBO);
- management buyout (MBO);

- management buyin (MBI);
- buyin management buyout (BIMBO);
- going private buyouts (also known as public to private, or PTP buyouts); and
- *club deals*, in which several PE firms form a consortium to buy out a target.

These types differ in the following aspects:

- whether the incumbent management of the target of the buyout is part of the team initiating the buyout and invests in the equity of Newco;
- whether the target firm is a company listed on a stock exchange and includes the public investors, both institutional and individual, as shareholders; and
- whether the management team consists of incumbent target management, or includes new managers from outside, or a mixture of both.

The management buyout initiative may come from the target's incumbent managers, who then arrange the support of a private equity firm. The parent may also run an auction for the target, and the target management then teams up with the winning sponsor. In an investor buyout the LBO sponsor buys the target without involving the target management. In some cases the management itself may be attempting a management buyout with the support of another LBO firm. For example, in the LBO of RJR Nabisco, KKR was pitted against the MBO proposal led by the then CEO, Ross Johnson. Thus the management was excluded from the IBO. In other cases the vendor corporation's directors may not allow the incumbent management to bid because of the conflict of interests between the managers and the shareholders. Directors have a fiduciary duty to the corporation and its shareholders, and so have the obligation to avoid a transaction that gives rise to a conflict of interest. Further, good corporate governance requires that directors avoid any decision that may engender such a conflict of interest. In the event of an MBO bid, the Securities and Exchange Commission (SEC) rules in the US require that the bid be evaluated by an independent committee of the board of directors. The corporate governance regime in the UK has a similar requirement.

In a management buyin the LBO sponsor replaces the incumbent management with a new management team of outsiders, perhaps because the incumbent management is not competent, or because new management will be more effective. Thus a new management is put in place to run the bought-out business. A BIMBO is a hybrid and combines some of the old target management with new outside managers. Many LBO sponsors keep a roster of executives with relevant operating experience in different industries and types of businesses, and draft them into MBIs and BIMBOs as appropriate. In a going-private buyout the public shareholders are bought out and the company becomes privately owned. In recent years managers or dominant shareholders have taken many medium-sized companies private, generally because they believe that the stock market undervalued their companies. A going-private deal may be one of the other types of LBO, i.e. MBO, MBI or IBO. After the deal the company is de-listed from the stock exchange.

In investor buyouts the sponsor, after the buyout, may negotiate with the target managers to retain them. Management in all these different buyout types is generally provided with performance incentives by being invited to contribute to equity, and by the offer of stock options.

Club deals are a recent phenomenon and have arisen because of the large deal size in recent buyouts, such as Biomet referred to earlier. Freescale Semiconductor was bought by a consortium of Blackstone, TPG, Carlyle and Permira for $17.6bn. PE firms pool their financial resources to acquire high-price targets and also spread their risks. Club deals obviously reduce the intensity of auction for a target, much to the disadvantage of the vendor. For this reason some vendors exclude consortium bidders: for example, when GE wanted to divest its plastics division worth about $10bn in January 2007, it disallowed consortium bids.

Overview of the LBO markets in the US and Europe

LBO growth in the 1980s

LBOs were very much a part, indeed one of the major drivers, of the 1980s merger wave in the US. The value of LBO deals in 1986 was $46bn, and in 1987, 1988 and 1989 it was $43bn, $58bn and $75bn respectively. The 1989 figure includes the RJR Nabisco buyout for $31bn. As a percentage of total M & A deals LBOs were about 21% in 1986–88, but this soared to 24% in 1989, before crashing, with the M & A market in general, to just 9% with a value of $18bn.[9] The reasons for the explosive growth of LBOs especially in the second half of the 1980s were the same forces that created the conditions for the merger wave of that time and the extensive restructuring through divestitures, discussed in Chapter 2 on merger waves and Chapter 10 on corporate divestitures.

In continental Europe LBOs did not catch on during the 1980s, although it was also experiencing a merger boom, as noted in Chapter 2. The number of MBOs and MBIs was less than 100 until 1985, and it increased to nearly 400 in 1989 and 1990. The annual value of these deals was very low, about $1bn until 1986. Even in 1989 and 1990 the value of the deals was very modest, about $5bn.

In the UK, however, MBOs became a more important source of M & A activity. The number of MBO and MBI deals increased from just 20 in 1979 (valued at $36m) to 152 ($402m) in 1981 and to 529 in 1989 ($11.3bn). The following year, as in the US, the value of MBO and MBI deals crashed to just $4.5bn. The average value of these deals increased from about $3m in 1981 to $21m in 1989.[10] The reasons for the rise in LBO activity in the UK during the 1980s were broadly similar to those that triggered the overall merger boom and those that accounted for the US LBO activity.

The LBO market in the 1990s and the new millennium

When the 1990s merger wave swept the US and Europe, LBO activity rode the crest. LBOs revived, although not on the same scale as some of the spectacular LBOs of the 1980s, such as RJR Nabisco. The deals of the 1990s tended to be much less leveraged, with debt accounting for about 75% of total financing rather than the 90–95% in the 1980s, and with lenders becoming more cautious after the failures or troubles of some of the large LBOs from the 1980s. However, the second half of the 1990s saw LBOs become an established component of the M & A market in the UK as well as in continental Europe, as shown in Figure 11.4. The UK is the second largest national LBO market, with a total value of deals from 1999 to 2007 of $424bn, after the US with $1066bn. The continental European deals over the same period amounted to $520bn. The UK boasts the best infrastructure in terms of specialist buyout or venture capital funds, the largest capital market in Europe, and the support services such as specialist law firms, but major European countries such as Germany, France and Italy and smaller countries such as Sweden have increasingly sophisticated infrastructures (we discuss the countrywide breakdown of LBOs below). Many of the UK and US buyout specialists, as well as commercial and investment banks with private equity arms, have been active in Europe.

For US buyout firms such as KKR, Blackstone, Carlyle, Texas Pacific Group (TPG) and Clayton, Dubilier and Rice (CDR), the competitive pressures in the US market and the diminishing opportunities for LBOs have been the 'push' factors driving them to Europe. The large-scale corporate restructuring taking place in Europe following the Single Market, European Monetary Union and the advent of the single currency € in the Eurozone, the increasing globalization of the capital markets and acceptance of the Anglo-American norms

Figure 11.4   Value of LBOs in various countries, 1990–2007 (in 2007 US$)

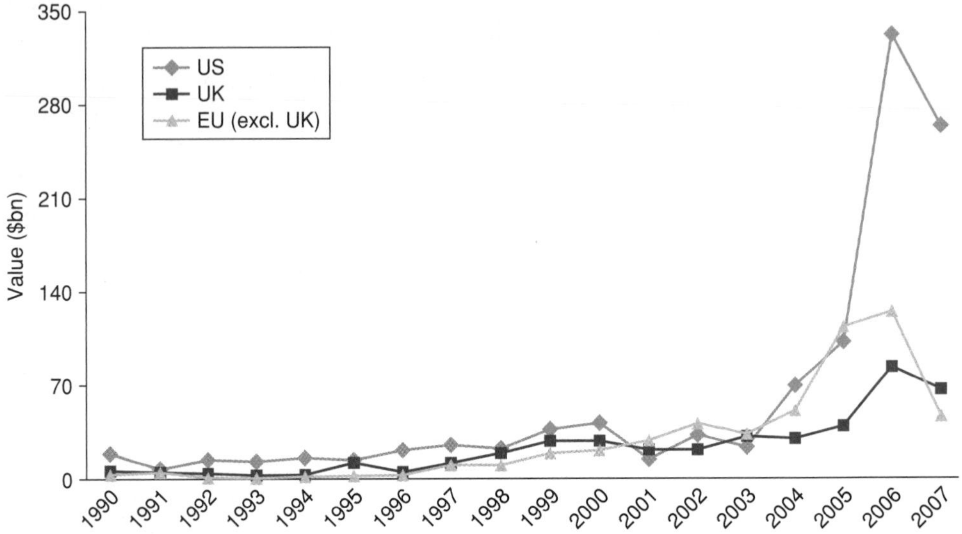

All deals are completed and the acquirers hold more than 50% of the target share after the transaction.
Only deals of which transaction value is disclosed are included.
All deals are completed and the acquirers hold more than 50% of the target share after the transaction.
Only deals of which transaction value is disclosed are included.
EU means: 27 current members plus Switzerland.
Deals are categorized according to the announcement year.
Deal value is in 2007 dollars. US Consumer Price Index – All Urban: All Items is used to adjust for inflation.
Source: Thomson Reuters

of shareholder value enhancement, have generated opportunities for deal-making for buyout and private equity firms. Moreover, these firms can also tap into their networks in the US to raise both private equity and high-yield debt to finance these deals.

In 2006 several of the largest European acquisitions were carried out by US PE firms, either alone or as a consortium. TDC, a Nordic telecom company, was bought out by Apax Partners, Blackstone, Providence Equity Partners, KKR and Permira Advisers for $10.6bn. A KKR-led consortium bought 80% of Philips Semiconductors for $9.5bn. A Blackstone-led consortium bought the Dutch publisher VNU for $9.6bn. In 2007 a consortium of US PE firms bought Alliance Boots, a UK pharmaceutical and retail group for $19.6bn. In 2008 Goldman Sachs led a consortium buyout of the German firm Xella for over $2bn (€2bn).

European LBOs

The European leveraged buyout market showed a massive growth during the 1990s. In the UK, the largest LBO market in Europe, the value of completed deals increased from about $3.6bn in 1993 to a peak of $84bn in 2006. In 2007 the value was still huge at $66bn. During the whole 1990–2007 period the value of deals in the UK was $424bn (in 2007 dollars) compared with $1066bn in the US. In the rest of Europe LBOs increased in popularity through the 1990s, having only recently been imported from the US and the UK. Over 1990 to 2007 LBO deals worth $520bn were completed, with a peak value of $33bn in 2002. In 2006 and 2007 alone European deals amounted to $114bn and $125bn respectively. Thus LBOs have truly

Table 11.2 European LBOs (including UK) by type from 1999 to 2008

Year	MBO		MBI		Going private	
	No. of deals	Value (€bn)	No. of deals	Value (€bn)	No. of deals	Value (€bn)
1999	804	20.4	366	32.0	46*	7.0
2000	787	25.5	344	49.0	62	21.6
2001	798	21.4	375	44.2	48	15.9
2002	839	17.8	371	52.3	36	11.0
2003	868	18.1	430	50.8	54	9.4
2004	810	24.7	527	62.0	31	14.2
2005	755	20.1	692	113.4	42	32.0
2006	728	20.7	775	15.3	45	40.9
2007	665	26.9	820	15.0	47	38.8
2008	670	16.6	528	52.4	28	13.2

Figures do not add up correctly owing to rounding.
Source: European Management Buy-outs Jan–Dec 2008, The Centre for Management Buyout Research (CMBOR), University of Nottingham, February 2009.

come of age in continental Europe, which, together with the UK, is now almost as big as the US LBO market.

Relative importance of different LBO types

Table 11.2 gives a breakdown of the LBO activity in Europe (including the UK) during 1999–2008 by three categories – MBO, MBI and going private. A going-private transaction is also known as a public-to-private (PTP) buyout. There is an overlap among these categories, since a PTP buyout could also be an MBO or an MBI. PTP buyouts are relatively few in number but, since the targets are public companies, are large in value. Many of the PTP buyouts are billion-dollar acquisitions. Many of the MBI and PTP deals may also be IBOs, since the initiative for the buyout may come from the LBO sponsors. MBIs tend to be larger in size, on average. They have also increased in relative importance compared with MBOs. The average deal value for MBOs ranges from €21m in 2002 to €41m in 2007. For MBIs it ranges from €88m in 1999 to €197m in 2006. In Europe, excluding the UK, going-private deals account for about 2–4% of all buyout deals by number and 9–24% by value. The average PTP value ranges from €174m in 2003 to €909m in 2006. PTP deals are, on average, much larger than MBIs and MBOs.

In the UK, all three categories hit their peaks in 2007. The average value of MBO deals ranges from €12m in 2003 to €40m in 2007. For the MBIs it ranges from €73m in 1999 to €197m in 2007. Going-private deals account for 3–7% of all buyouts by number and 17–42% by value. The average PTP value ranges from €152m in 1999 to €1.2bn in 2007. Thus, as in continental Europe, PTP deals in the UK are on average much larger than MBIs and MBOs. This pattern of relative deal sizes in the three categories was also observed in the 1980s and 1990s in Europe as well as in the US.[11]

Thus MBOs were increasingly being limited to small acquisitions, whereas MBIs were larger acquisitions. There may be several reasons for this trend. MBIs give sponsors more flexibility in selecting the management team, and this may be critical in large acquisitions that need a more experienced and versatile management. Sponsors, having built up a network of managers who specialize in running buyout targets, may be able to draw on this resource, and are not limited in their choice to the incumbent managements.

PTP has been a major feature of the UK LBO market in the last two decades. The growing acceptance and familiarity of PTP buyout in the UK have certainly helped it grow in the rest of Europe. For the best part of the 1990s PTP was a negligible part of LBOs there, but in the new millennium PTP deals have become much larger, and now, as in the UK, dominate MBIs and MBOs in terms of average deal size. In continental Europe shareholdings of even publicly listed companies are highly concentrated and family controlled. This may explain the relative unattractiveness of going private and why an LBO sponsor may prefer not to attempt a hostile PTP transaction.[12] Some of the largest deals in Europe in 2008 are shown in Exhibit 11.3. Some of the largest LBOs in the US in recent years are shown in Exhibit 11.4.

Exhibit 11.3

Mega LBOs in Europe in 2008

The following table illustrates some of the largest LBOs from different European countries, and also different sources of LBO targets. These sources are described in more detail below.

Country	Buyout target	Vendor	Value (€bn)
UK	EMAP	PTP	2.6
UK	Expro International Group	PTP	2.3
Germany	Xella	Haniel Group	2.0
Holland	Stork	PTP	1.7
Portugal	Enersis	Babcock & Brown	1.2
Sweden	Securitas Direct		1.1
Holland	Schuitema	Koninklije Ahold	1.0

Source: European Management Buy-outs Jan–Dec 2008, The Centre for Management Buyout Research (CMBOR), University of Nottingham, February 2009, Table 1.1

Exhibit 11.4

Mega LBOs in the US in recent years

Year	Target	PE firm/consortium	Value ($bn)[b]
2008	Harrah's Entertainment Inc	Investor Group	28
2008	Clear Channel Communication Inc	BT Triple Crown Co Inc	26
2007	Equity Office Properties	Blackstone Group LP	41
2007	TXU Corp	Investor Group	32
2007	First Data Corp	KKR	26
2007	Alltel Corp	Atlantis Holdings LLC	25
2007	Hilton Hotels Corp	Blackstone Group	20
2006	HCA, Inc	Bain, KKR[a], ML[a], Thomas Frist	33
2006	Freescale semiconductors	Blackstone, Carlyle, Permira, TPG[a]	18
2006	Albertsons, Inc	Supervalu, CVS, Cerberus Capital	17

[a]KKR = Kohlberg Kravis Roberts & Co; ML = Merrill Lynch; TPG = Texas Pacific Group.
[b]In some cases including liabilities assumed. Figures in last column rounded to the nearest $bn

Source: Mergers & Acquisitions, February 2007–2009

Sources of LBO targets

The major sources of target companies that are available for LBOs include:

- private and family-controlled firms that want to sell;
- divestitures by foreign companies (the orphans or 'living dead' divisions);
- divestitures by domestic companies;
- PTP;
- receivership or bankruptcy; and
- secondary buyout (SBO).

Figure 11.5 shows the relative importance of the above sources of LBOs for the UK and continental Europe in 2008.[13] The relative importance of the different sources is broadly the same across Europe, except that continental European divestitures are a greater source of LBOs than in the UK. Sourcing LBO targets from receivership is also more important in the UK than in continental Europe.

Factors influencing the supply of LBO targets

As Figure 11.5 shows, the most important source of targets is the family-controlled/private company. Family-controlled companies may wish to sell because of succession problems, with the younger generation of the founder's family not keen to carry on in the family business, top management retirement, or the need for the owners to raise cash and realize their investment. For example, the powerful *Mittelstand*, medium-sized companies in Germany, face problems of succession as well as the need to raise finance to fund the firm's growth. The founder managers, having worked long years to build up their firms, may want to retire. They may not like a trade sale if, after the sale, their beloved company loses its identity. The incentives for going private, or the disincentives for remaining as publicly listed firms, are identified above. Divestitures by foreign and domestic parents account for about 25–30% of the LBOs in Europe (see Figure 11.5). Thus there has been widespread corporate restructuring, with

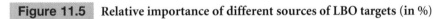

Figure 11.5　Relative importance of different sources of LBO targets (in %)

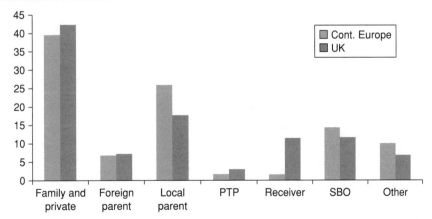

Source: *European Management Buy-outs Jan–Dec 2008*, The Centre for Management Buyout Research (CMBOR), University of Nottingham, February 2009, Figure 1.15

parents shedding component businesses that no longer fit their strategic focus, or divisions that underperform, or where the sale of divisions enables the parent to raise funds to finance other more profitable businesses in their portfolio. In Chapter 10 we offer other reasons for divestiture. A secondary buyout occurs when the sponsor sells its interest to another LBO sponsor. This is a possible exit strategy for the original sponsor, and is an alternative to a trade sale or doing an initial public offering (IPO) and becoming a publicly listed company. We discuss LBO exit strategies in more detail below.

Exit from LBOs

LBO investments by sponsors generally have a built-in programme of liquidation and exit. As noted above, this is an essential characteristic of such LBOs. Although LBO funds are generally raised for a life of 10 years, the majority of LBOs (57%) are exited within 5 years. Of the non-PE-sponsored LBOs, i.e. management buyouts financed by managers themselves, only 23% exit by the same time. These managers, of course, do not have the same exit pressure as the PE sponsors. The mean (median) holding period for PE-sponsored LBOS is 50 (42) months, and for the self-financed MBOs it is 40 (34) months. Median holding periods in both categories have fallen steadily from 1985–89 (72 and 80 months) to 2003–05 (24 and 22 months). Thus there seems to be some tendency to 'quick flip' (see Exhibit 11.8 below).

Exit options for LBOs

Exit is the process of realization of the investments made in an LBO. The following options exist for the LBOs:

- trade sale to a strategic buyer, e.g. a corporate in the same line of business that can reap scale or scope economies or leverage marketing capabilities;
- taking the company public through an IPO to public equity investors; and
- sale to another financial buyer through a secondary LBO.

A case of involuntary exit occurs when the buyout firms becomes insolvent and ends up in receivership or bankruptcy. Exhibit 11.5 presents some recent examples of different ways of exiting an LBO. Table 11.3 lists the LBO exits for a large global sample.

Table 11.3 LBO exits by their origin

Exit route	Number of exited LBOs	% of exited deals by original LBO type					
		PTP	Private company	Divisional	SBO	Distressed	Total
Strategic buyer	2728	34	37	44	37	41	38
SBO[a]	1980	33	27	28	37	21	28
IPO	966	16	13	15	11	9	14
Bankruptcy	488	9	7	5	7	16	7
MBO	115	2	1	2	2	1	2
Other	818	7	15	7	5	13	12
Total exited	7095	60	69	59	69	62	65
No exit	3752	40	31	41	31	38	35

[a]Includes LBO backed corporate buyers.
Source: See P. Strömberg, *The Global PE Report, ibid.*, Table 4.

Exhibit 11.5

Saying goodbye to LBO

Through IPO

Industrial Kapital, a private equity firm in Sweden, bought out Alfa Laval in 2000 for €1562m. In June 2002 it sought to exit from majority control of the target company through an IPO on the Stockholm stock market. In the depressed stock market conditions of 2002 selling the stake was quite an uphill struggle. Because of the unstable stock market conditions in 2001, Industrial could not offload its stake, and had to wait for another year. During the offer period the market sentiment was far from enthusiastic, and the offer period was extended and the initial offer price was cut from SKr108–140 to SKr90–95 to attract the punters. This price reduction made the offer successful.

Through SBO

CINVEN, a leading UK private equity firm, bought a number of pubs (public houses, bars) from Nomura, another leading private equity sponsor, for €3.2bn. BC Partners bought General Healthcare, a private hospital operator in the UK, for £1.29bn in a secondary buyout from CINVEN. For CINVEN the exit from one LBO allowed it to recycle its private equity funds to invest in another LBO.

Through trade sale

In 2006 Pearson, the owner of the *Financial Times*, won the £101mn auction for Mergermarket, an online financial information company specialising in providing news and data for investment bankers, merger arbitrageurs and distressed debt traders. Mergermarket's current investors made substantial returns on their investments on exit. Mr Hobbs and Mr Welsh, its founders, each held 15.8% of its ordinary shares. NewMedia Spark received £27.8m, making a return of almost 24 times its initial investment. Beringea, the private equity firm that helped fund Mergermarket's international expansion from 2001, received about £27m, or 14 times its original investment.

Sources: Through IPO: Adapted from Harney, A., 'Searching for a way out', European Private Equity Supplement, *Financial Times*, 21 June 2002; Through SBO: Adapted from Campbell, K. 'Plum deals shine out amid misty future', European Private Equity Supplement, *Financial Times*, 21 June 2002; Through trade sale: Adapted from Edgecliffe-Johnson, A., 'Pearson wins MergerMarket in £101m deal', *Financial Times*, 9 August 2006

From Table 11.3, we find that the most popular exit route is sale to a strategic (trade) buyer, followed by secondary or tertiary buyout, and then IPOs. Once a business falls into LBO ownership it is rarely exited by sale to the incumbent managers. A significant proportion of buyouts go bankrupt after PE ownership (7%). Financially distressed targets of the original LBOs are more likely to go bankrupt than other targets (16%). More than a third of the sample LBOs remain unexited after several years.

Figure 11.6 shows different exit types by region. The strategic buyer route dominates all exit types in all regions. This suggests that an important role of LBOs is to reallocate ownership of corporate assets, thereby facilitating the strategic restructuring of corporate economy. Second,

Figure 11.6   LBO exit patterns in various countries

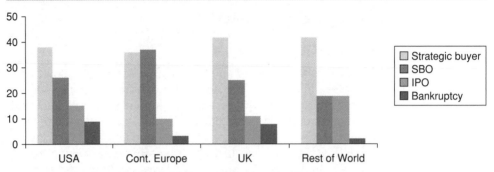

Source: Based on P. Strömberg, *The Global PE Report, ibid.*, Table 4

SBOs are a major exit route, but the target firms continue in PE ownership. IPO exits are much less important in developed economies than in developing economies of the rest of the world. Together, these point to the LBO universe being rather self-contained and able to circulate corporate assets among PE firms. Finally, bankruptcy is more often the fate of LBOs in the US and the UK than in other countries. In the UK, MBIs have a greater probability of such failure than buyouts.[14]

We have already identified the problems with one of the exit options, i.e. the IPO. The success of this route depends on stock market conditions. In volatile market conditions IPOs may not be well received. Moreover, in Europe, private equity IPOs are regarded with greater distrust than in the US. For institutional investors in stock markets such an IPO creates information asymmetry between the sponsor and the investors, whereas in the US, if a private equity firm brings a company to market, there is the perception that it is well scrubbed, well run and clean. European investors tend to think that a private equity firm has been hard run for cash. Further, the same institutional investor being asked to invest in the IPO may also have invested in the private equity fund of the sponsor. In the US the sponsor normally retains a significant holding in the IPO firm, whereas in Europe in the past the sponsor would prefer a clean get-out. However, increasingly in Europe too, sponsors continue to maintain equity interest, thereby inspiring greater trust among potential IPO buyers.[15] In IPOs shares are sold at a discount, but a trade sale normally includes a control premium.

Secondary buyouts have recently become a significant exit route for larger deals. Private equity firms have succeeded in raising huge funds, but have not been able to find matching investment opportunities to generate the required rates of returns. As noted in Exhibit 11.2, PE firms have been able to raise gigantic funds and, with limited opportunities for first time buyouts, have therefore turned to secondary buyouts (see Exhibit 11.5).

A secondary LBO buyer may face a number of problems in evaluating the deal:

- Has the first LBO squeezed the lemon dry already?
- What is the motivation for the exit?
- Were there no other exit routes open to the seller?
- What will be the reaction of the incumbent management, and will they have the enthusiasm and energy for a re-run of the buyout?

For these reasons there was a certain stigma attached to secondary buyouts.[16,17]

Exits need to be carefully managed to maximize the returns to management and the investors. Timing of the exit is an important consideration, and also determines the exit mode.

With the stock market in a bear phase, flotation is obviously not an attractive option. Exit policy may cause a conflict of interest between management and institutional investors, for whom exit crystallizes their returns and allows them to finance other MBO opportunities. On the other hand, a flotation may subject management to unnecessary pressure from the stock market. But an exit allows management to realize their investment. There is also a conflict of interest between equity investors and lenders, who dislike early exits on good deals. So some senior lenders require early repayment fees or an incentive in the form of equity kickers, i.e. warrants.

Characteristics of optimal LBO targets

Given the imperative of attaining the cash flow generation targets to meet the demanding debt service and repayment schedules, an obvious criterion is the ability to generate cash. This suggests a mature business that throws off regular operating cash flow that is not vulnerable to competitive threats. So businesses that operate within high entry barriers are attractive. They must be industries where demand for their products is not volatile. LBO targets may also be currently undervalued or underexploited by their parent. They have suffered neglect and been starved of investment funds or other support from the HQ. These orphan assets in the capable hands of the buyout specialist will, however, be able to realize their full and high value. The target must allow scope for efficiency savings in costs or redundant assets whose sale would generate cash flow.

In recent years, however, the business models of many PE firms have changed. LBO targets have been drawn from a wider range of industries including high tech industries (see Exhibit 11.6 on the Inmarsat buyout).[18] Easy availability of both equity and debt has led PE firms to accumulate huge amounts of funds that need to be invested. Investment opportunities in a wider range of industries therefore need to be exploited. Second, PE firms have accumulated significant operational expertise in running their portfolios businesses, and are therefore no longer deterred by the challenge of running high-tech and capital-intensive businesses.

To gather such expertise, PE firms have attracted some stars, such as Jack Welch and Lou Gerstner, former CEOs of GE and IBM, to their ranks as advisers or as CEOs of the portfolio businesses. Thus in terms of operational expertise PE firms can now mount a serious challenge to trade buyers. TPG, a PE firm specializing in finding the 'pony in the muck' and turning it into a thoroughbred, sets store as much by operational expertise as by deal-making and financial wizardry. The bonus pool is divided equally between the two categories of PE managers and partners.[19] It hired veteran Millard 'Mickey' Drexler, former CEO of Gap, to turn the cloth designer and retailer J. Crew around, and successfully floated it in 2006. PE firms now seek to enhance resources and capabilities to match the demands of their new business models.

Organizing the buyout and role of the PE sponsor

The organization of the buyout is the chief responsibility of the buyout specialist. Organization involves devising an efficient structure for the buyout vehicle to make the acquisition and raise the finance from various equity and debt providers. The buyout vehicle needs to be devised to minimize any tax liabilities to the vendor in the case of a divisional buyout, and the vendor shareholders in the case of a whole-company buyout. The structure is also designed to maximize the tax benefits to the buyout firm and the debt and equity providers.

Exhibit 11.6

Private equity ambitions soar into high orbit

Inmarsat, the UK mobile satellite communications company, was an inter-governmental organization (IGO) providing global safety and other communi-cations for the maritime community. Starting with a customer base of 900 ships in the early 1980s, it then grew rapidly to offer similar services to other users on land and in the air. In 1999 it became a private company. European PE firms Apax and Permira bought it in December 2003 for £921m. Their strategy was to continue to develop the company into the world's leading mobile satellite communications company by continuing with plans to launch the Inmarsat-4 satellites and the next generation of high-speed data and voice services – the Broadband Global Area Network (BGAN) service. The company was success-fully floated on the London Stock Exchange in June 2005 for a market capital-isation of £1120m, generating substantial profits in two years for the two PE owners. In 2006 Inmarsat supported links for phone, fax, and data communi-cations to more than 287,000 ship, vehicle, aircraft and other mobile users, and its BGAN service was accessible across 85% of the world's landmass and to 98% of the population.

Source: Adapted from M. Wright, L. Renneboog, T. Simons and L. Scholes, Leveraged buyouts in the UK and Continental Europe: Retrospect and Prospect, European Corporate Governance Institute Discussion Paper 2006–70 (July)

The self-liquidating nature of private equity funds (see the discussion at the start of this chapter) imposes a certain discipline and responsibility on the GPs to ensure that the buyouts they sponsor are sound and will generate attractive returns to the funds' investors.

While a specialist private equity firm depends on outside fund investors, the private equity arm of an investment bank such as Goldman Sachs, JP MorganChase, Morgan Stanley or Deutsche Bank may raise private equity funds from its own internal sources. From time to time they also raise dedicated buyout funds: for example, Morgan Stanley raised $5bn and Credit Suisse $2bn buyout funds in 2006. In the private equity market, banks with deep pockets have increased competition enormously over the past 20 years, to the utter delight and profit of vendor firms. Whereas in the early days of LBOs the vendors would have negotiated the sale of a division with a specialist firm, now they invite several PE firms and trade buyers to auctions. This competition has driven up buyout prices, increased acquisition premia, and lowered the returns to private equity investment, as we shall see below.

Organizing debt financing

The major source of financing in a buyout is in the form of debt, and the buyout sponsor raises the debt capital in a variety of ways. Debt in the form of loans is raised in the leveraged loan market.

The leveraged loan market

This is a market in bank loans of different types used to finance LBOs and other long-term investments, such as in infrastructure. The loans can be secured or unsecured, and rank according to their seniority in terms of repayment of principal and interest. Secured debt has the highest priority and, if it is a term loan, may have a prearranged repayment schedule, i.e. amortized. Where the repayment is at maturity it is called a *bullet loan*, and is more risky than a term loan with amortization. The interest rate is normally a floating rate at a margin of 2–3% over LIBOR (the London Inter-Bank Offer Rate), the wholesale rate for lending among banks. The margin or spread is generally expressed in *basis points* (bps, pronounced bips), equal to one hundredth of a percent (0.01%). Some part of the senior debt may be short term. Mezzanine debt, as the name suggests, is junior or subordinated to senior debt in terms of interest payment and capital repayment. It is generally unsecured, and is therefore more risky. Both debt components rank above equity.

The mezzanine layer is often in the form of preference shares or convertible loan stock or convertible preference shares. In the UK some firms specialize in providing mezzanine or intermediate finance. The interest rate is generally 400–500 bps above LIBOR (or Euribor, European inter-bank offered rate). Interest rate margins for both senior and mezzanine debt depend on the general level of interest rates, the demand for debt, and the competition among banks. A revolver is a revolving credit facility, generally provided to finance working capital. In many deals the sponsors also raise optional facilities to finance capital expenditure (capex).

Exhibit 11.7 provides an example of such a structure. The second lien may also be replaced by unsecured mezzanine debt as junior debt.[20] Mezzanine debt is often with interest rolled up in the form of *payment in kind* (PIK) and thus avoids the cash outflow from the buyout target.

Exhibit 11.7

Squeeze the banks until their bps squeak

In 2007 Apax and Cinven, the UK-based PE firms, exited their buyout of CBR Holdings, a German retailer, through a secondary buyout by EQT. The purchase price was €1.5bn. The table shows the financing package. When a loan package is oversubscribed by lenders, PE sponsors often ask them to *flex* their terms in favour of the sponsor. This leads to narrowing of the margins over LIBOR, or the amount of money lent in each debt class. In this case both senior and junior lenders offered significant price reductions. The mix between senior and junior lenders also changed, owing to flexing (not reported). In times of high credit liquidity the buyout sponsors force considerable flexing on lenders. 1 bps = 0.01%. The EBITDA multiple for the senior debt was 5.56 and for the total debt was about 6. EBITDA at the time of the buyout was €198m.

	Senior debt: term loan (€m)			Junior debt (€m)		Total debt (€m)	Equity (€m)
	A: 7 years	B: 8 years	C: 9 years	9½ years 2nd lien	7 years Revolver		
Amount	350	375	375	100	50	1,250	250
bps margin	200	212.5	237.5	400	200		
Margin flex in bps	0	−37.5	−50	−150	0		

Source: Adapted from *Acquisitions Monthly*, September 2007, p. 52

To the lender, PIK adds to the risk, since interest receipts are deferred to maturity rather than received every 6 months. For example, in the Cinven buyout of French clothing retailer Camaieu in 2007, the 10-year €140m mezzanine carried 14% for all PIK, and 8.5% for a mix of cash and PIK, reflecting the greater risk attached to an all PIK loan.

Mezzanine lenders are often given an equity kicker or sweetener to compensate them for the high risk they run. An equity kicker is an equity warrant, and it enables the mezzanine holder to partake of the upside potential of an MBO by exercising the warrants, and to receive shares in the company. Where there is a financing gap after tapping all the above sources, sometimes the vendor agrees to fill the gap. Vendor financing can take the form of unsecured loan notes or preference shares or convertibles. Vendor financing also demonstrates goodwill towards the management. Where the MBO maintains some trading links with the erstwhile parent, such as a supplier, vendor financing may smooth such links.

Banks often provide senior debt as syndicated loans to share the risk and to limit their exposure to individual borrowers, as required by prudential banking regulations. In addition to the interest they receive for lending, the participating banks are also paid fees up front at the time the loan is negotiated. The mezzanine debt is often provided by finance firms that specialize in that debt. Increasingly, however, investment banks and leveraged finance arms of commercial banks provide this layer of debt as well.

Mezzanine debt holders may be willing to give the issuer flexibility in terms of acquisitions and capital expenditure without running the risk of breaching covenants, thereby committing technical default on their loans. Such lending is *covenant-lite*, indicating that loan covenants are not as stringent as in *covenant-tight* loans. Junk or high-yield bonds often replace the mezzanine layer. In recent times the cash flows of the whole bought-out business have been ring-fenced, and the equity sponsors have been able to issue collateralized debt obligation (CDO) against these cash flows. Since a CDO receives greater protection from this ring-fencing, the sponsor can raise debt capital more cheaply.[21] Prior to the credit crisis in 2007–09, covenant-lite lending reflected strong competition among banks and hence quite aggressive lending.[22]

Levels of debt are generally determined as multiples of the expected cash flows of the bought-out business. Senior debt may be five times the expected earnings before interest and tax (EBIT) or its more recent variant, earnings before interest, tax, depreciation and amortization (EBITDA). Mezzanine, as more risky debt, tends to be a smaller layer than the senior debt (see Exhibit 11.6 above). The multiples vary with the economic conditions, level of interest rates, and expected prospects for the buyout. In times of economic downturn the multiples become conservative.

As noted earlier, LBO sponsors raise funds for private equity investment from time to time, with a normal liquidation timescale of about 10 years. Depending on the size of the fund and the size of individual deals, a fund may be invested in 10–20 deals at a time. Once a fund is raised, the sponsor needs to find investment opportunities and fill out the fund's portfolio. Any delay means the fund is underinvested, and it will fail to generate an adequate return to the investors. The average length of time for a fund is about five or six years.[23]

As noted earlier in this chapter, the LBO sponsor receives fees based on the 2-20 formula or its variants. The 20% profit-related fee represents the primary incentive for the sponsor to carry out successful buyouts. Both the management fee and carried interest rates vary from firm to firm, as well as over time, and have come under considerable pressure in recent years because of the competition among private equity firms. Whereas in the 1980s the profit-related fee was paid for each transaction, in recent years, again under competitive pressures and pressure from the investors, there has been a trend to pay the fee after netting of the profits and losses from all the deals in which the fund is invested. This means the sponsor shares the risk when a deal fails to deliver value to the investors.

In addition to the 2-20 fees a PE sponsor may receive an advisory fee for organizing the LBO, and an 'advisory service termination' fee if the LBO target returns to the public market via an IPO. PE sponsors in recent years have also shown some impatience to recover their equity investment from the target firm. The mechanism for this 'early return of capital', a rather anodyne description, is to get the target to load up with more debt and use the proceeds to pay 'special dividend' to the owner, i.e. the PE firm! Some PE firms like this special dividend so much that they return to ask for more of it, and the target firm obliges by levering up even more! Thus PE firms take a double or triple dip into the coffers of the target, filled by more and more levering. These repeated dips can lower the target's debt rating. In some cases PE firms have shown unseemly haste to return the targets to public ownership in reverse LBOs. Exhibit 11.8 shows examples of these exotic ways for PE firms to reduce their investment in the buyout by increasing the financial risk to lenders. The substitution of debt for the PE sponsors' equity is known as leveraged recapitalization or 'leveraged recap'.

Exhibit 11.8

Big fees, quick flips and triple dips!

In June 2006, after buying out the rental car company Hertz for $15bn with an equity investment of $2.3bn, the PE sponsors – Clayton, Dubilier & Rice, Carlyle Group and Merrill Lynch – received a special dividend of $1bn. Within six months, the PE owners reduced their investment by nearly 50%.

PE sponsors – Apax Partners, Apollo Management, MDP Global Investors and Permira Advisers – managed to receive dividends and fees worth $575m in multiple instalments within a year of buying the satellite operator Intelsat Global Services (IGS) for just $513m in 2005! IGS posted a loss of $325m in 2005, and its debt doubled to $4.79bn. The huge increase in leverage led to multiple credit downgrades of IGS's debt. IGS laid off 20% of its workforce.

Blackstone bought Celanese Corp. in April 2004, investing $650m in equity. In September 2004 it received $500m as special dividend, financed by Celanese raising new debt. In January 2005 it took Celanese to an IPO, and $800m of the proceeds was paid to Blackstone. After recovering twice its investment, Blackstone still owned 58% of Celanese common stock. All this within 10 months!

Blackstone charged Celanese Corp. $45m for its advisory work on its own deal in 2004. Bain Capital, Thomas H. Lee and Providence Equity were paid $75m for similar work by the target, Warner Music. PE firms charge portfolio firms for their management expertise in addition to the management fee charged to the LP partners. In 2005 three PE firms charged the target SMART Modular Technologies $3m, more than the $2m that the top five managers of the target earned that year.

When the target of their earlier buyout, Warner Chilcott (WC), a speciality pharmaceutical maker, went public in September 2006, the PE sponsors – Bain Capital, Donaldson, Lyfkin & Jenrette, JP Morgan Partners, and Thomas H Lee – collected $27m to compensate them for termination of their advisory services to

WC! Presumably, these PE owners decided to exit by taking WC public, and so the termination was a consequence of their own exit decision.

Three weeks after buying an 80% stake in Hawkeye Holdings, an ethanol producer, in May 2006, Thomas H. Lee Partners (THL) got the target ready for an IPO. During this quick flip, THL received $20m as advisory fee for negotiating the buyout, $1m 'management fee', and $6m to meet its tax bills.

Banks lent portfolio firms $71bn between 2003 and 2006 to pay dividends to PE owners, up from $10bn in the previous six years. Between January 2002 and September 2007, in 220 deals, PE sponsors extracted 20% of their investment in the first year, and in 39% of the deals more than 80% of the equity invested was recovered by new debt issues, causing 33% of the targets to suffer bond rating downgrades. Only 11% experienced upgrades.

Source: E. Thornton, 'Gluttons at the gate', *Business Week*, 30 October 2006; and W. Fruhan, *The company sale process*, Harvard Business School case 9-206-108, 16 April 2008.

Junk bonds

Corporate bond rating agencies have developed rating schemes to assess creditworthiness, that is, the ability and willingness of issuers to pay interest and repay the principal as agreed with the investors in the bonds. This assessment is based on both quantitative models and qualitative judgements. The grading systems divide corporate bonds into 'investment grade' and below-investment grade. The highest-quality bond receives the AAA rating from two agencies, Standard & Poor's and Fitch, and Aaa from Moody's. The medium or fourth grade is BBB for the first two agencies and Baa for Moody's. Within each of these grades three subgrades are used, e.g. BBB+, BBB, BBB– (in Moody's case this is Baa1, Baa2, Baa3). Bonds whose issuers are rated below this grade are sub-investment grade or junk bonds (JBs). The five below-investment grades run from 'somewhat speculative' category bonds to 'in default' bonds. (See Chapter 16 for a further discussion of credit rating and its impact on cost of capital in acquisition financing.)

To compensate investors buying junk bonds, the yield on these bonds is much higher than on the triple-A bonds. Hence the name high-yield bonds. For example, a triple-A bond with a 10-year maturity, i.e. due to be repaid after 10 years of issue, may offer a yield of 6%, whereas a single-B bond may need to offer a yield of 9–11%. In tougher economic conditions with high interest rate volatility and investor pessimism, this yield spread may be much higher. The minimum issue size is about $100m and the maturity period is 10 years, but often with a 'call' provision that allows the issuer to buy back the bonds after, say, five years. Bonds may also include a put option for buyers to sell them back to the issuer.

The significance of the lack of investment-grade rating is that certain financial institutions in the US, such as the savings and loan associations (SLAs), were prohibited from investing in them or restricted as to the amount they could invest in such bonds. Junk bonds may be new issues by small or high-risk firms that have not received investment-grade rating, or they may have started life as investment grade bonds that decline, following the issuing company's financial distress, into junk bond status. The latter bonds are known as *fallen angels*. Firms that have no access to the investment-grade bond market issue new junk bonds. So they pay a much higher-risk premium when they issue junk bonds. The issuing firms may have little track record by way of operating performance, they may be small firms, or they may be operating in high-risk businesses. Firms issuing junk bonds may then graduate to investment-

Figure 11.7	Value of outstanding high-yield bonds and default rates

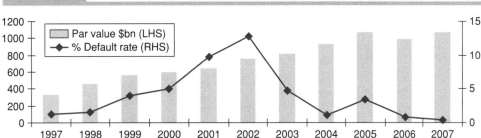

Source: E. I. Altman and B. K. Karlin, *Defaults and Returns in the High Yield Bond Market: The Year 2007 in Review and Outlook*, Special report from the New York University Salomon Center, Leonard N. Stern School of Business, February 2008, Figure 1

grade bonds when they become established, with a longer track record of profitability or access equity markets. Altman estimated the spread between high-yield (HY) bonds and US government Treasury (TREAS) with a 10-year maturity issued during 1978 to 2007[24]. The compound annual average return was 10.16% for HY bonds and 8% for Treasury bonds, with a spread of 2.2% over 1978–2007. The yield to maturity on HY bonds fell from a high 9.4% in 2000 following the dotcom bubble to 3.1% in 2006, before rising sharply to 5.7% in 2007.

Figure 11.7 shows the evolution of the US high-yield market from 1997 to 2007, along with the default rates. These figures show not only the phenomenal growth of the high-yield market but also that the default rates have declined substantially from the highs of 2000–02 and the earlier high of 10% in 1990–91 that followed the collapse of the junk bond market in the late 1980s. The junk has defied diagnoses of death and returned to rude health. The default rate rose sharply in 2008 and 2009. In Europe the default rate of HY bonds fell from about 11% in 2003 to almost 0% in 2008 before rising sharply to about 4% in the first quarter of 2009[25].

High-yield markets in Europe

Figure 11.8 shows the trend in European HY bond markets in contrast to the leveraged loan market discussed above. HY bond issues are used for wider purposes than just to finance acquisitions and LBOs. Leveraged loans are a much larger segment of the credit markets than HY bonds. As we have seen, leveraged loans are very substantially used for buyouts and takeovers. HY bonds are used for these purposes to a smaller extent, and a much smaller extent in terms of € value. Nevertheless, LBOs accounted for about 2% of HY issues in 2001, but this was about 32% in 2007 and 30% in 2008. Non-buyout acquisitions accounted for about 10% over the same period, peaking at about 15% in 2007.

LBOs hit by leveraged loan market melt down

The frenzied credit explosion of 2004–07 led to a price explosion for LBO targets. The EV to EBITA multiples rose very strongly, as shown in Figure 11.9. In the fourth quarter of 2007 it reached 10.2 for PTPs. Thus LBO deals were being done at very high, possibly unsustainable, multiples.

A much higher proportion of the purchase price was also financed with more risky, junk bonds, as shown in Figure 11.10, reaching or surpassing the levels last seen at the top of the

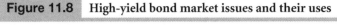

Figure 11.8 High-yield bond market issues and their uses

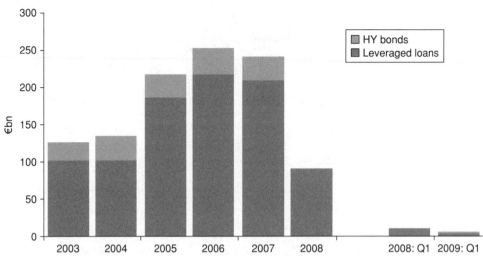

Source: European High Yield Association, *European Quarterly High Yield and Leverage Loan Report*, first quarter 2009, Figure 15, downloaded from www.ehya.com

Figure 11.9 Purchase price multiples excluding fees in LBO deals

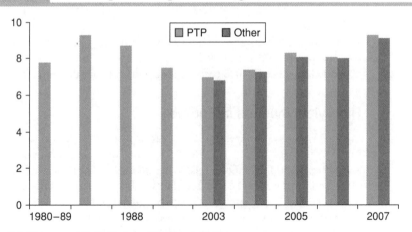

Source: E. I. Altman and B. K. Karlin, as for Figure 11.7

1990s merger wave, again reinforcing easy credit, and with PE firms making ever bolder, or reckless, buyouts on the back of aggressive bank lending. The capacity of the targets to support such high debt levels was becoming very stretched. Debt to EBITDA multiples was reaching unprecedented levels raising questions about the prudence of such high levels (see Figure 11.11). Many banks that lent money to buyouts on wafer-thin margins or on excessively generous EBITDA multiples began to feel the heat when the credit crisis exploded. They found few takers for the debt they had accumulated, as shown in Exhibit 11.9 below.

Figure 11.10   Percentage of new sub-investment-grade issues

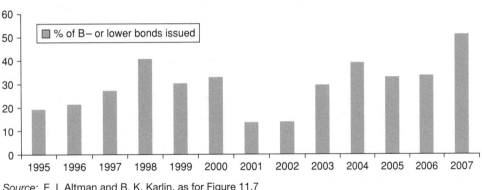

Source: E. I. Altman and B. K. Karlin, as for Figure 11.7

Figure 11.11   Average debt/EBITDA multiple in European and US LBOs

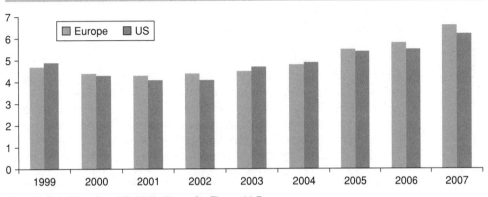

Source: E. I. Altman and B. K. Karlin, as for Figure 11.7

Exhibit 11.9

Banks fail to sell Alliance Boots debt

A 10-bank syndicate (that included Deutsche Bank, J P Morgan, Unicredit, Barclays, Bank of America, Merrill Lynch, RBS and Morgan Stanley) – that financed last year's £11bn buyout by KKR of Alliance Boots, planned to sell about £780m of the debt at about 91% of its original value. But the deal fell apart owing to growing tensions between investment banks over the terms of sale as they grappled with an overhang of private equity loans. Disagreement between the banks focused on a clause that would have required all eight lenders in the syndicate jointly to compensate buyers if any Alliance Boots debt was sold at a lower price in the future. The requirement, known as a 'most favoured nation' clause, would have made it harder for the banks to sell their debt aggressively if the market deteriorated. RBS wrote down the value of its leveraged loan port-folio to an average of 88% of its face value as the bank cleaned up its balance

→

sheet as part of its £12bn rights issue. Syndication of the £9bn of Boots debt was abandoned in 2007 after the crisis in US subprime mortgage lending triggered a liquidity crisis in debt markets.

Property market crash compounds credit crisis for senior lenders

Losses for lenders only months after they funded leveraged buyouts of retail and property companies suggest that debt investors fear these deals were priced too high, with excessive debt, and may now be facing trouble. Frits Prakke, managing director of Alchemy special opportunities fund, said: 'We are in a market that is still very overpriced. I think private equity buying companies at the top of the market with record amounts of debt, as it has been, is a recipe for disaster.' Some LBO debt gave companies breathing room, by including 'toggles' that allow borrowers to take interest payment holidays, or 'mulligans' forgiving missed debt repayments. But the most significant reason is the weight of underwritten leveraged loans in the pipeline ($100bn) that banks still have to sell, and the fear that some might be tempted or even forced to begin dumping holdings on the market.

Much of the European and UK loans to LBOS in recent years had 'retreads'. 'It is the same companies coming back to market again and again with higher leverage and higher earnings projections to pay as a new owner comes in or the current one takes out a dividend,' says Ed Eyerman, head of leveraged loans at Fitch Ratings, who estimated that new deals in 2008 would be lucky to see net debt to EBITDA leverage of more than five times. The average for single-B-rated deals in the market is getting on for 6.5 times. 'This means private equity will be holding companies for longer and getting back to the business of actually trying to run businesses rather than just looking for the exit,' Mr Eyerman adds.

Source: P. Larsen and M. Arnold, *Financial Times*, 2 May 2008; M. Arnold, P. J. Davies and J. Pickard, 'Private equity deals start to fray in sharp market', *Financial Times*, 20 November 2007

LBOs in major European countries

Figure 11.12 lists the MBO and MBIs in some major European countries. The UK is the most active buyout market in Europe, followed by Germany, France, Holland, Italy and Sweden. The UK alone accounts for 36% of all European MBO and MBI activity in 2008. Differences in LBO activity in different European countries depend on a range of factors:

- supply of divestitures by corporations, family companies and government privatization;
- corporate finance infrastructure, which includes funds and legal and accounting services;
- concentration of family-owned firms, and traditional reluctance to use institutional finance;
- quality of financial and accounting information about companies;
- reluctance to allow due diligence audit by outsiders;
- small and illiquid stock markets, which prevent exit by flotation;
- legal impediments to using the target's resources to finance buyouts, e.g. the UK and Italy;

Figure 11.12   Value of buyouts in European countries, 1999–2008

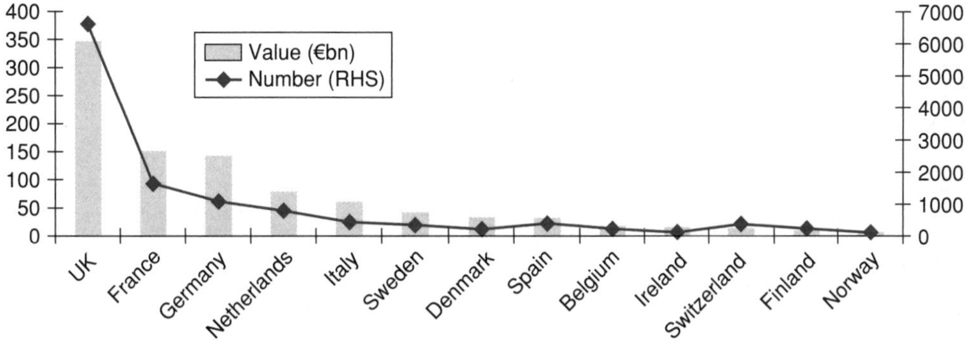

Source: Based on Centre for Management Buy-out Research, *European Management Buy-outs Jan–Dec 2008* (Nottingham, UK: Nottingham University Business School, 2009), Tables A3 and A4

- in small national markets, the ability of potential foreign buyers to make bids; and
- ability to squeeze out minorities in public companies, thus allowing high leverage.

Table 11.4 describes the main characteristics of LBOs in continental European countries. In France, Italy and Spain the most important source of MBOs is the family-owned or private

Table 11.4 Characteristics of LBOs in European countries (2004–08)

Country	Average deal value (€m)	LBO sources	Exit routes[a]	Most active sectors[b]
France	106	Family and private; local parent; SBO; foreign parent	SBO; trade sale; IPO	Manufacturing; business support services; retail; TMT; leisure; food and drinks
Germany	142	Local parent; family and private; SBO; foreign parent	SBO; trade sale; IPO	Manufacturing; TMT; business support services; retail
Netherlands	140	Local parent; family and private; SBO; foreign parent	SBO; trade sale; IPO	TMT; manufacturing; business support; retail; financial services
Italy	170	Family and private; local parent; SBO; foreign parent	SBO; trade sale; IPO	Manufacturing; TMT; retail; business support
Sweden	140	Local parent; family and private; SBO; foreign parent	Trade sale; SBO; IPO	Healthcare; manufacturing; business support; paper and print
Denmark	185	Family and private; local parent; foreign parent; SBO	Trade sale; SBO	TMT; business support; leisure; healthcare
Spain	111	Family and private; local parent; foreign parent; SBO	Trade sale; SBO; IPO	Leisure; business support; manufacturing; retail; healthcare

[a]Only for 2005–08.
[b]Industries listed in descending order of value of LBO deals in them.
Source: *European Management Buy-outs Jan–Dec 2008*, Centre for Management Buyout Research (CMBOR), University of Nottingham, February 2009.

Table 11.5 Factors influencing MBO market in Europe

	UK	France	Germany	CEE[a]
Panel A: Opportunities for LBO				
Family succession	Moderate need	High need	High need	Low need
Scope for PTP	Large market	Steady flow but family control issues	Small number of quoted companies	Many candidates but opportunities yet to grow
M & A developed?	Highly developed	Relatively active	Becoming active	Relatively active
Panel B: Demand for private equity				
Managers willing for MBO?	High	Moderate	Low but increasing willingness	Very active but lack financial means
Panel C: Infrastructure to complete deals				
PE and VC market	Highly developed	Fast growth but many small firms	Small and not MBO oriented	Small but developing
Supply of debt	High	High	Tradition of high leverage	Low but growing
Intermediaries network	Highly developed	Moderately developed	Fragmented	Highly developed
Legal framework	Favorable	Favorable	Moderately favorable	Favorable
Tax regime	Favorable	Favorable	Reforms in progress	Becoming more favorable under EU
Panel D: Exit routes				
Stock market exit	Receptive to PE companies but now more difficult	Development of second-tier market favorable	New issues sparse; second-tier market closed	Growing domestic capital pool
Trade sales	Highly active	Becoming more active	M & A market developing	Highly active
SBOs	Increasing interest	Favored route	Possible route	Possible exit route

[a]CEE: Central and Eastern Europe.
Source: M. Wright, L. Renneboog, T. Simons and L. Scholes, Leveraged buyouts in the UK and Continental Europe: Retrospect and Prospect', European Corporate Governance Institute Discussion Paper 2006–70 (July), Table 6.

company. The vendors are keen to ensure management succession, to preserve the firm they have built up and also to reward the incumbent management for their loyalty. In Germany, the Netherlands and Nordic countries corporate divestments are the major source of MBOs[26]. Average deal size differs across these countries. Going-private deals are much rarer in Europe than in the US, with the most active being the UK (see Tables 11.3, 11.4 and 11.5 above).

Countries also differ in terms of the sources of the targets in LBO deals. Some countries rely on family and private companies, whereas others rely on divestitures by local diversified firms. These countries also differ in terms of their exit routes. Trade sale and SBO are the most preferred. IPO is the least preferred, and not at all in Denmark. The industry intensity of LBO activity also differs across countries. TMT is important in France and Germany but not in Sweden or Spain. Leisure and healthcare are important in Spain and Sweden but not in other countries. Wright, Renneboog and Simons identify a number of factors affecting the LBO market in the UK, France, Germany and Central and Eastern Europe (CEE). Some of these are listed in Table 11.5.

Managerial motivations for an MBO

What drives managers to become owners of the businesses they have run under the direction and control of a parent? A survey of MBO managers by Wright et al.[27] revealed a number of reasons, of which the most important was the desire to run one's own business. In order of importance, managerial motivations in MBOs were as follows:

- opportunity to control own business;
- long-term faith in company;
- better financial rewards;
- opportunity to develop own talents;
- absence of head office constraints;
- fear of redundancy; and
- fear of new owner after anticipated acquisition.

Financial and investment constraints imposed by the head office in a group may result in under-exploitation of the full potential of a business, and may lead to frustration among the divisional managers.

Managerial incentives in MBO

Managers in MBOs invest in some of the equity. While this is normally a small fraction, often less than 1%, of the total funding for a buyout, it may still represent a substantial part of their individual wealth. Thus the incentive for managers to make a success of the MBO is compelling. Moreover, MBOs have in the past been structured to include an incentive for the management to achieve or exceed agreed levels of performance after the buyout. Such an incentive is known as a ratchet. There are three types of ratchet, related to targets based on:

- profit level;
- time of exit and value achieved on exit; and
- debt repayment.

The first two ratchets increase the amount or proportion of equity made available to the management when the targets are met. The last ratchet allows the interest margin on senior debt to be reduced if the MBO generates a sufficiently high level of cash flows. Reverse ratchets penalize management for failure to achieve targets.

Ratchets, though conceptually attractive as an incentive mechanism, may encounter severe problems in practice. First, profit-related ratchets require an agreed set of rules for measuring profits. Managements and the capital providers may disagree on the interpretation of these rules. Second, management may be forced to adopt expedient policies that maximize short-term profits but endanger the long-term prospects of the company, such as cutting down on R & D. Third, the timing of exit is determined at the time of investment, and may force an inopportune exit. From the institutional investors' and lenders' perspective, a ratchet is a means of reducing valuation errors, since the management's share of equity depends upon future performance of the company. In this sense, a ratchet is similar to earn-out, discussed in Chapter 16. They both serve to mitigate the problems of information asymmetry and uncertainty

Exhibit 11.10

What managers might gain from an MBO

Suppose the CEO and his top management team in partnership with a PE firm buys out his company for £1000m inclusive of transaction costs. This is based on an EV/EBITDA multiple of 10. Five years later the PE firm exits the investment by selling it at the same multiple. The exit enterprise value is £1300m. The payoffs to different investors on exit are shown below:

Enterprise value on exit			£1300m
		Debt repaid	
Senior lenders (bullet loan)	£700m @ margin of 2%	£ (700m)	
Mezzanine	£70m @ 15% plus equity kicker of 2%	£ (70m)	
Institutional loan	£220m @ 10%	£ (220m)	
Equity	£10m	Share of equity	£310m
Of which			
PE firm (90% of equity)	£9m	PE receives (88%)	£273m
Managers	£1m	Mezzanine kicker (2%)	£6m
Total	£1000m	Managers (10%)	£31m

The equity kicker to mezzanine comes from the PE's share. Return to managers is 99% per year. Return to PE is a blended return of the return on the insitutional loan of £220m and equity investment of £9m. It works out to 24% per year.

Without the ratchet the return to managers will be £30m, or an annual return of 99%! If managers receive additional equity of, say, 5% on exit (assuming the exit value equals or exceeds the target value under the ratchet agreement), its share will be £46.5 on exit. This works out to an annual return of 116% per year!

Here we have assumed that the market applies the same enterprise multiple. If the buyout improves the firm's long-term growth prospect, or its risk profile improves, the multiple may be higher, in which case the returns to PE and management will be even higher.

in valuation. Exhibit 11.10 shows the payoff to the LBO sponsor and the management in an MBO with and without a ratchet.

LBO as a superior business organization

As noted in the introduction to this chapter, LBO has been hailed by Michael Jensen[28] as an organizational innovation that would solve the agency problem, managerial excess and corporate performance failure. Baker and Smith[29] extol it as a 'classic entrepreneurial coup' and describe it as a dual revolution – one in corporate finance and another in corporate governance (p. 3). How well has this dual revolution done in terms of long-term value creation? Is LBO just an arbitrage operation to buy undervalued companies, improve short-term performance through efficiency savings, and then sell at a high price? Is it an organizational flash in the pan, a sprint rather than a marathon?

The arguments for the LBO association as a superior organizational form and a superior governance structure are based on the discipline of debt and the close monitoring of the acquired business by the LBO specialist.

Discipline of debt

The high leverage constrains the managers of the LBO target to make operating and investment decisions efficiently so that they generate adequate cash to meet interest and loan repayment schedules. Breach of covenants attached to the loans provide early warning signals to both lenders and the buyout firm. Any free cash flow that the firm generates is used to pay off debt rather than being squandered in empire-building acquisitions and other extravagant pursuits that boost managerial egos at the expense of value for shareholders. Since free cash flows generated by a target are returned to the LBO fund and are eventually returned to the fund investors, there is little opportunity for cross-subsidy between highly profitable businesses and poor performers, as might happen in a conglomerate firm. Thus the LBO specialist does not operate an internal capital market akin to that in a conglomerate. As discussed in Chapter 7, such an internal capital market may be one of the dysfunctional characteristics of a conglomerate firm.

Efficient corporate governance

The governance structure of an LBO association is efficient because it removes the dichotomy between ownership and control that is the source of the agency conflict. The general partners who have invested in the equity of the target firm are now in control, with majority seats on the board. They have accepted the obligation to limited partners to generate high returns and to lenders to pay interest and repay loans. Failure to discharge these obligations destroys the trust and confidence these investors have in the LBO specialist, and precludes any future access to them. This threat to future viability is a potent incentive for the LBO specialist to monitor the target management effectively. The reputational capital that the buyout specialist builds over time, by satisfying the expectations of investors as well as managers, is an important source of competitive advantage.

Further alignment between managers of the LBO target and the association is ensured by the huge incentives given to the managers in the form of equity ownership, stock options and ratchet payments. Thus managers expect to receive huge rewards by acting in the interest of the owners. Deviation from this optimal behaviour also entails punitive costs. Managerial failure will mean not only loss of jobs but also of their equity investment in the firm. The close monitoring of managers' strategy and investment decisions by the LBO specialist inhibits any waywardness (see Exhibit 11.11).

Is a private equity firm just a conglomerate in another guise?

Although a private equity firm holds investments in a number of businesses, it is not run like a typical conglomerate. In the early years of LBOs these investments were watertight, with little synergistic osmosis and little cross-subsidy. The general partner's continuing interest was defined by specific transactions, and by the portfolio of its businesses. Thus each individual LBO had to maintain a distinct identity. However, many LBO associations are even more diversified than many conglomerates. Baker and Montgomery, after surveying a small number of conglomerates and LBO associations, observe the following differences[30]:

Exhibit 11.11

'You can't hide from Mary'

In 2002 Wynnchurch Capital bought for $28m AxleTech, the ailing truck axles maker. Mary Petrovich, a former division head at autosupplier Dura Automotive, became the CEO. Mary, the second of eight children of a widowed Detroit hairdresser, was ready to pounce the moment she arrived at AxleTech at the end of 2002. In her first and most audacious move she persuaded hardened workers at the factory to sign a new United Auto Workers contract. Workers resigned themselves to a 33% cut in wages and benefits. It was a bitter medicine that angered the employees. Petrovich also forced executives to fly economy instead of business class. By 2005 such measures had worked, and the company was sold to Carlyle Group for $345m!

By November 2007 AxleTech had become a profitable company, with a turn-over of $400m and 300 customers including the US military. Carlyle estimated that it had already doubled the value of its investment. Its managing director, Gregory Ledford, said that Petrovich was 'about a year ahead of our investment plan'. But being ahead of plan was part of the brief for portfolio company CEOs. Many of Carlyle's CEOs were ahead of plan, and to stand out, Petrovich needed to push her people even harder. John Hatherly of Wynnchurch said of Petrovich, 'She is very demanding. You can't hide from Mary.'

Petrovich was toughest on her senior managers. In 2006 she said she had changed six of the seven top executives, and by May 2007 four of those recruits had gone. She added: 'Most senior leadership in private equity is driven by an inability to perform at the highest standards expected for value creation.'

Source: Adapted from E. Thornton, 'Perform or perish', *Business Week*, 5 November 2007, 38–45

- Both organizations grow by acquisition, but only the LBO associations regularly divest their operating units, as required by their limited partnerships.
- Both organizations rely on substantial use of pay for performance as part of their management compensation system, but the rewards and risks tend to be greater in LBOs because of the leveraged equity that managers hold.
- Expectations regarding performance, returns, cash flows and exit are set up front at the time of the LBO deals, unlike in conglomerate acquisitions. This sets out very clearly the relation between managers and the LBO association, and obviates the influence costs and costs of managerial opportunism in the post-buyout organization (see Chapter 8 on these issues).
- The exit imperative of the LBO association forces it to get rid of losers and not keep them as 'living dead' through ventilatory subsidies. This makes strategic change easier than for conglomerates.

Value creation through financial engineering

As noted earlier, debt is cheaper than equity, and by using high levels of debt LBO can create more value than a conventional firm with more modest levels of debt. Debt interest is also tax deductible in many tax regimes, including the US and the UK. Thus high debt levels increase the tax savings. One of the major advantages that financial buyers have in comparison with strategic buyers is the ability to access capital more cheaply because of their proximity to and participation in financial markets.

To summarize, LBOs are expected to create value through:

- the discipline of debt, which reduces the abuse of free cash flows;
- efficient management monitoring by buyout specialists;
- better alignment between managerial interests and equity and debt holder interests through incentive-intensive managerial contracts; the combination of harsh discipline and monitoring and hefty incentives is a major differentiator between LBOs and publicly listed firms (see Exhibit 11.7);
- expropriation of lenders through high leverage and through making high-risk investments;
- expropriation of government through tax subsidies on high debt levels;
- expropriation of government through passing default risk to federal savings and loans deposit insurance agencies that increased the incentives for SLAs to invest in high-leverage transactions.

LBOs, a sprint for the exit or a marathon?

We noted above that many of the LBO targets were held in the PE firms' portfolios for several years and were not exited. Moreover, a substantial proportion of exited ones pass into the ownership of other PE firms through secondary and tertiary buyouts. Strömberg, after studying global LBOs, concludes[31]:

- out of all firms entering LBO status during 1980–2007 (1980–2002), 69% (45%) are still in the LBO organizational form;
- the median firm in the sample remains in LBO status for more than nine years, and only 17% ever leave within three years;
- the number of firms entering LBO status is higher than the number leaving; and
- among the PTP group of LBOs, only 13% revert to public company status.

These results suggest that the LBO form is not merely a temporary stop on the round trip of public companies from, and back, into their public status.

What do general partners receive for their troubles?

Although funds are generally raised for 10 years, this *commitment* period is divided for fee purposes into the initial *investment* period of 5 years and a following *monitoring* period of about 5 years, or to exit if earlier. LPs may negotiate a lower fee for the monitoring period, since GPs now carry out a less onerous task of managing the investments already made and crafting the exit strategies. The basis of fee computation may also be either *committed* capital or *invested* capital. In general, invested capital is smaller than the committed, since funds may not be fully invested. LPs may negotiate a shift to the invested basis once the investment period is complete.

As noted at the beginning of this chapter, the general partners are compensated with different types of fees[32]:

1 the annual fund management fee from LPs:
   - flat or variable fee;
   - committed or invested basis;
   - provision for shift in basis;

2 the carry interest:
- generally 20% of *carried interest* but can be higher[33];
- carry basis either committed or invested capital;
- hurdle rate generally 8% return to LPs, but some LPs may not insist on it;
- *catchup* – GPs recover their share of carried interest only after LPs receive their invested capital + interest at hurdle rate;
- *early carry* – GPs can claim their share before LPs receive all their invested capital plus interest subject to claw back if subsequent fund performance is poor;

3 transaction fee from LBO targets, e.g. 1.37%:
- shared between LPs and GPs, e.g. on 50:50 basis but the sharing formula may vary;

4 annual portfolio company management fee from portfolio companies, e.g. about 2% of EBITDA. This fee may again be shared, e.g. 20:80 in favour of the GPs.

Fixed fees to GPs consist of fees 1 and 3, and their variable fees consist of fees 2 and 4.

Metrick and Yasuda estimate these fees for a sample of 144 LBO funds raised in 1993 to 2006. They report, for every $100 fund:

- the carry of $5.3 per $100;
- fund management fee of $10.4;
- fixed revenue of $11.6;
- variable revenue of $6.2; and
- total revenue of $17.8[34].

This means that over two thirds of the compensation to GPs is made up of fixed revenue, and only a third depends on performance-related variable revenue. This reduces the risk exposure of GPs and the incentives for making value-creating investments.

Critique of LBOs

In the late 1980s detractors of LBOs characterized them as no more than financial legerdemain helped by benign tax incentives for debt. LBOs came to be associated with high failure rates. Their value creation strategy was also disparaged as 'slash and burn', meaning savage cost cuts, asset stripping and job losses. Such a strategy could not provide the foundation for great businesses that require technological innovations and breakthroughs. The focus of LBOs, constrained by overwhelming debt and expectations of high returns by partners and managers, was too short term to create enduring new organizational forms. Thus the revolution in corporate finance was no more than a ride on the government tax gravy train, and the corporate governance revolution was perhaps a 'storm in a tea cup' that would not displace the traditional organization structures.

While the LBO association's organizational form may have eliminated the inefficient internal capital market that is blamed for the conglomerate discount in conglomerates (see Chapter 7), it may also represent a lost opportunity to exploit synergies between the same or related businesses among the private equity firm's investments. In more recent years, however, private equity firms have adopted consolidation strategies such as add-on, leveraged build-up or roll-up strategies (see Chapter 13). These require exploitation of synergies among successive LBOs, such as scale or scope economies. Moreover, the argument that LBO associations regularly churn their investments and get rid of the losers while conglomerates hang on to their losers seems weak in the light of the substantial divestitures many firms have undertaken in the 1980s and the 1990s. Indeed, the chief source of LBO targets is these divestitures. Evidence presented by Strömberg above also shows that a substantial proportion of LBO firms remain in PE ownership for several years. To resolve these contending claims for and against LBO associations we now turn to the empirical evidence of LBO performance.

Value creation performance of LBOs

Returns to limited partners of LBO funds in the US

The National Venture Capital Association (NVCA) of the US reported short- and long-term returns to private equity investors in buyouts over different investment horizons. As at 31 December 2001, all buyouts generated average annual returns of −14.5% over one year, 0.5% over three years, 5% over five years, 10.8% over 10 years and 14.4% over 20 years[35]. These returns are net of fees and carried interests of the general partners, and are based on 1400 US venture capital and buyout funds formed since 1969. These returns are particularly sensitive to the market downturn in 2000 and 2001 and the particularly terrible performance of the new economy stocks. Another study based on returns until 31 December 1999 presented a more positive picture of LBO performance[36]. Over five, 10 and 20 years the net compound average annual returns for LBOs were 18.6%, 16.6% and 20%. The corresponding returns to Standard & Poor's S & P 500 index are 28.3%, 18.1% and 17.8%. Thus private equity returns are inferior to investment in a broad-based stock market index over the five- and ten-year investment horizons and marginally superior over 20 years. These results may also overstate the performance of LBOs, since their higher risk than that of S & P 500 is not adjusted for.

Up to 30 September 2007, buyout funds generated net-of-fees IRR of 27.5 (over 1 year), 15.3 (3 years) 14.1 (5 years), 8.6 (10 years) and 12.3 (20 years). For the five-year period the S&P 500 return was 10.8%[37]. Although buyouts seem to outperform the public market it must be remembered that the cash flows to the funds include the net asset value estimate as a terminal value. Since such an estimate produced by the LPs may be optimistic, the outperformance may be overstated. Moreover, if buyout funds are more risky than S&P 500, again the outperformance will be overstated. Academic studies that have made adjustments for these two factors are now reviewed.

Kaplan and Schoar investigate the returns to buyout funds from 1980–2001 and focused on liquidated funds to avoid any upward bias due to general partners' optimistic valuation of companies still remaining in their portfolios. They report median returns of 13% for these funds, net of fees and carry. The higher, mean return of 18% suggests a very high performance of top funds. When compared with the performance of the S&P 500 index (as a proxy for the US public equity market), PE investors earn slightly less – about 93–97% of the index returns. Gross of fees, the PE funds outperformed the index, pointing to high GP fees draining the returns to LPs. Lerner, Schoar and Wongsunwai report in their study of funds started in 1991–98 that the mean (median) excess IRR over IRR to similar funds is −2% (−0.8%). They also report that certain types of fund are smarter, and generate considerably higher returns – for example, endowment funds generate 21% more than the average – and conclude that investors vary in their sophistication. Phalippou and Gottschalg also report that buyout funds underperform the S&P 500 index in the case of funds raised during 1980–2003[38]. Overall, buyout funds seem to underperform their benchmarks, especially when the GPs' fees are taken into account[39].

Operating and other performance of LBOs

Kaplan and Strömberg review the performance of LBOs in terms of other performance measures that numerous researchers have studied, such as profitability, innovation, productivity and growth in employment. They conclude as follows:

- The empirical evidence is consistent overall with significant operating improvements in e.g. operating income to sales, significant productivity gains, improved work practices.
- Employment grows at LBO targets, but at a slower rate than at other similar firms: this evidence is not consistent with the view that LBOs lead to job destruction.
- There is little evidence of any superior information that the PE acquirer possesses about the target's potential because of the association of the target management with the buyout, e.g. in MBOs.

Other findings from this review are that:

- PE firms seem to be able to bargain well, or take advantage of market timing and market mispricing;
- PEs raise funds following good prior performance of PE funds, and their performance then falls;
- PE fund raising and investment activity is subject to the boom and bust cycle and very sensitive to the credit market conditions[40].

Gilligan and Wright provide an extensive review of the various studies empirically investigating the above aspects as well as others. They find that capital and R & D expenditure falls after a buyout, but MBOs enhance new product development. Accounting and management control systems are also improved. Patent citations are improved, although the number of patents filed is not increased. The patent portfolios become more focused. Together these two findings suggest that LBOs focus their portfolio companies' R & D efforts on winners[41].

How important is the discipline of debt?

The disciplinary effect of high leverage is argued as a key mechanism for mitigating the agency costs of managerial control. In an LBO this beneficial effect of high leverage may be confounded by other sources of effective management monitoring, for example by the buyout specialist or by improved managerial performance-related incentives. How do we disentangle these effects? Leveraged recapitalization is a transaction in which high levels of debt are substituted for equity that is bought out from the shareholders. Management of the recapitalized firm, however, remains in place. While the discipline of high leverage is common to recapitalization and LBO, the former lacks the discipline of close monitoring and other organizational disciplinary mechanisms associated with the LBO. Firms that are similar but undergo a recapitalization or LBO may differ in their post-transaction performance because of the absence of non-leverage disciplinary mechanisms[42]. The case study at the end of this chapter compares the performance of an LBO and that of a leveraged recapitalized firm. This case shows that high leverage alone cannot generate the corporate governance changes that lead to improved shareholder value performance. It is also likely that buyout specialists may substitute their own monitoring for leverage so as to loosen the stringency of debt conditions[43].

How important is organizational change?

Another perspective on the importance of governance and organizational changes is provided by the performance of target firms after failed MBO bids. If the superior performance of MBOs is due to buyout specialists and managers exploiting their privately held information about the undervaluation of the target firm, this information can be exploited by the managers themselves, even when the governance changes introduced by the buyout specialist are not

Table 11.6 Long-term returns (%) to private equity investors in MBOs

Type of LBO fund	Pre-1996 vintage			Post-1996 vintage		
	Number of funds	IRR % inception	IRR % 10 years	Number of funds	IRR % inception	IRR % 10 years
Small MBO				28	6.5	11.7
Mid-MBO	33	15.8	13.5	120	14.9	14.6
Large MBO	26	18.2	27.3	42	21.5	16.8
FTSE All-Share			1.2			1.2
FTSE 250			5.6			5.6

FTSE indices are Financial Times (London) Stock Exchange indices. FTSE All-Share is the widest market index and FTSE 250 represents 250 mid-capitalization firms on the London Stock Exchange.
Source: Adapted from PricewaterhouseCoopers & Capital Dynamics, *BVCA Private Equity and Venture Capital Performance Measurement Survey 2008*, from www.bvca.co.uk.

available. In a study of 120 unsuccessful MBOs Ofek found no operating performance improvement in the targets[44]. Moreover, the abnormal returns to shareholders two years after the MBO bid failure were not different from zero. Management turnover following unsuccessful MBOs was also insignificantly higher than normal.

This study again suggests that performance improvements in LBOs are the result of multiple changes to the buyout target. These include increased debt discipline, closer monitoring, higher levels of managerial incentives, closer alignment of managerial and investor interests, and clearer expectations and goals concerning the level of future cash flows, operating performance, debt repayment, time to exit and the exit-level value.

UK evidence: investor returns and operating performance

Internal rates of return to private equity investors, net of fees and costs, depend on the investment stage, i.e. whether early-stage venture capital, development or expansion, or late-stage LBOs. BVCA, the British venture capital and private equity association, has reported returns over different holding periods for different types of LBOs, shown in Table 11.6. While details of the computational procedures are not available, it appears that all three buyout funds outperformed the market indices. Further, this outperformance increases with the size of the MBO equity investment. It must, however, be borne in mind that MBO investments may carry a much higher systematic risk than the market indices, since they carry higher leverage. Whether the performance differential between MBO funds and market indices is sufficient to compensate for any additional systematic risk is not clear. These returns also depend on the 'vintage', that is, the year the fund is raised. The table shows the performance of funds of two different vintages, but vintage does not yield higher returns in all categories of MBOs.

Performance of MBOs may be assessed over the short and the long term. Wright and Coyne (1985)[45] found from a study of 111 MBOs up to 1983 that they showed improvement in profitability, trading relations, and cash and credit control systems, and also evidence of new product development. In a more recent study of 251 buyouts and 446 non-buyouts, Wright *et al.* found that buyouts outperform non-buyouts in terms of return on assets and return on equity in years 3 to 5 after the buyout but not in the first two years, since that period may represent a turnaround phase. They also report significant productivity improvements[46].

Evidence on the performance of MBIs is mixed. A survey reported by Wright and his colleagues of 58 buyins of private companies found that MBIs did more restructuring than MBOs. Operating profit was worse than forecast in 53% of cases[47]. Cost of finance and

Table 11.7 Long-term IRRs (%) to private equity investors in buyout funds

Buyout funds/ benchmark index	Number of funds	In 2008	Over 3 years	Over 5 years	Over 10 years
Buyout funds	431	−31.0	3.5	10.8	11.6
MSEI	–	−46.9	−17.5	−7.5	−7.2
HSBC Small Company	–	−56.3	−16.1	−2.1	0.8

Source: European Private Equity and Venture Capital Association (EVCA), Pan-European Private Equity Performance Benchmarks Study, 2008, Brussels, Belgium. EVCA's web address: www.evca.eu

discovery of unexpected problems were the most serious problems faced by MBIs. However, BIMBOs appear to have been more successful. In a study of the 300 MBIs it had backed, 3i reported that BIMBOs had increased from less than 25% of MBI deals in 1990 to 50% in 1993[48]. The study suggests that BIMBOs have become more effective than pure MBIs, since the involvement of the existing management provides the incoming manager with more reliable information, and the existing managers who remain part of the management team contribute equity, and are therefore better motivated.

In a recent study of operating performance by portfolio companies, Acharya and Kehoe find from a sample of 66 UK buyouts made between 1996 and 2004 and exited during 2000–07 the following:

● PE deals of large, mature houses outperform their quoted sector peers on average, controlling for both sector risk and leverage.
● Outperformance is correlated with stronger operating performance than peers, mainly because of improved profit margins.
● Employment growth is slower than that of quoted peers.
● Top management change happens quickly, with CEOs changed in 39% of deals within 100 days and, during the PE ownership, in 69% of deals.
● Smaller boards with a third of directors representing the PE firm meeting quite frequently provide robust governance for the portfolio companies[49].

Continental European evidence

Table 11.7 provides the current year and long-term returns to buyout funds to the end of 2008 along with the comparative performance of the returns to the Morgan Stanley Euro Index (MSEI) index and the Hongkong and Shanghai Banking Corporation (HSBC) small European company index. The buyout funds substantially outperform the benchmark indices.

Future of the LBO market in the US and Europe

Many US-based LBO firms, faced with such intense competitive pressures, changed their strategy. The nature of the targets changed, and LBO sponsors moved towards building up clusters of related businesses that could leverage the synergies – scale, scope and learning economies – within each cluster. Thus at the end of the 1990s financial buyers started to resemble strategic buyers. Moreover, LBO firms also began to invest in Europe and Latin America, where extensive corporate restructuring has provided new opportunities for their financial and deal-making skills. Further, LBOs have also become less geared than in the early 1980s. Thus in recent years the game has changed. The credit crunch during 2007–09 has made high leverage deals even more difficult to finance.

LBO firms fine-tune their strategies

With increasing competition and pressure from lenders, buyout firms have altered their competitive strategies in a number of ways. Far from relying on smartness in spotting undervalued businesses and cleverness in financial engineering, buyout firms have had to develop their resources and capabilities to give them a competitive advantage. They have to add strategic value to the buyouts. This has led to the buy-and-build or leveraged build-up strategies discussed in Chapter 6. Other strategies include:

- high-technology buyouts;[50]
- joint-venture LBOs, in which the buyout specialist shares equity ownership with a strategic buyer or the divesting parent;[51]
- club deals, with several private equity firms buying out the target;
- private investment in public equity (PIPE), where private equity firms take minority stakes in publicly listed companies.[52]

These strategic moves represent radical departures from the traditional buyouts that targeted low R & D industries and firms, mature companies with stable cash flows to support high-leverage, low-business risk profile, etc. Whether buyout specialists can develop the necessary resources and capabilities to operate high-risk new-technology businesses remains to be seen. Buyout specialists seem to be moving nearer to the venture capital end of the private equity spectrum.

Buyouts in early years were sold off or taken public through IPOs. With the new strategies, however, they need to be kept in the stable longer for leveraged build-up strategies to work, or for real option-type investments in high-technology areas to bear fruit. Historically, buyouts have been perceived as an organizational efficiency tool to streamline organizational processes, downsizing and cost paring. The new challenges, however, require a new entrepreneurial mindset that regards buyouts as a vehicle for renewal, revitalization and strategic innovation.[53]

PE firms attracted a great deal of negative publicity during 2007 and 2008, centred on their 'slash and burn' approach to creating value, and the wealth accumulated by private equity 'barons'. A new code of conduct has been drawn up in the UK to increase the transparency of the way in which PE firms conduct their business. In future LBOs will be subject to even more critical scrutiny than in the past.

CASE STUDY

The tale of two stores: Safeway and Kroger

Denis compares the LBO of Safeway by KKR and the leveraged recapitalization of Kroger which were remarkably similar supermarket chains in the US in 1986. Safeway's (Kroger's) sales revenue was $20bn ($17bn), market capitalization $2.2bn ($1.8bn), number of stores 2365 (2882). Safeway had 90% of its employees unionized whereas Kroger had 59%. Both companies had underperformed the grocery store industry over the years 1976–85 in terms of operating income to total assets. Both firms undertook some restructuring in response, but the results were modest. Their industry relative under-performance continued.

The LBO and recap (high-leverage transactions, HLT)

In July 1986, Safeway, in the face of a rival offer from Dart Group, accepted an LBO offer from KKR and a group of Safeway managers. The offer valued the company at $4.2bn with a 58% premium over the pre-takeover contest price. The financial structure of the LBO was: 63% bank credit; 24% long-term debt; 3% KKR equity investment, 7% loan from KKR partners and 3% other sources. Some 4% of the equity investment came as subscription from the management. In addition, managers were given the option to purchase additional shares at the same subscription price of $2 per share. Shortly after the buyout the managers increased their ownership to 10% by exercising the options. Debt now accounted for 96% of the market value of Safeway's capital. It had increased from 41%.

In September 1988, the Haft family controlling Dart attempted a takeover of Kroger. KKR made a counter-offer with a 62% premium, valuing Kroger at $5bn. The Kroger board rejected the offers and pursued a leveraged recapitalization (recap) plan to increase borrowing and using the proceeds to buy back equity. The resulting financial structure was: 60% bank credit, 20% of loan notes, 14% subordinated debenture and 6% bank working capital facility. The recap increased the total debt to firm value ratio from 42% to 91%. This increase is remarkably similar to that achieved by Safeway LBO. Employee ownership of shares in Kroger increased to 25%.

Post-deal changes

- In Kroger, officers and directors increased their fractional share stake from 1.4% before the recap to 3% but their dollar stake fell from $62m to just $22m. In contrast, at Safeway, the fractional stake ($ stake) increased from 0.7% ($25m) to 10.3% ($19m).
- In Kroger there was little change in the 14-member board of directors. The board held 1.8% of Kroger equity with outside members having 0.06%. At Safeway, the board shrank from 18 directors to five, of whom three were KKR general partners. Total board equity was 93%, of which KKR held 90% and the CEO and vice-chairman of Safeway held 3%.
- Executive compensation at Kroger consisted of: salary, bonus on average of 56% of salary, stock options and direct share ownership. In Safeway, it was: salary, bonus at 110% of salary, stock options and shares. The structure of the stock option and share components was to make them more sensitive to the company's stock price changes in Safeway than in Kroger. Thus executive compensation was closely tied to stock performance. In Safeway, as the CEO put it: 'If our managers don't hit 90% of their plan, they get no bonus. If they hit their plan they get half their potential bonus they can earn and if they beat their plan by 20% they get the other half. So there is a big incentive to beat the plan.'

Post-deal performance

- Both firms improved their operating performance. Safeway increased its EBITDA to assets by 69% from the year before to four years after the deal. Kroger increased by 49%. Kroger's assets and number of stores represented a small change of 3% but the number of employees grew by 12%. At Safeway, the decline in these variables was very substantial between 31% to 53%.
- Whereas capital expenditure to assets declined by 46% at Kroger, it increased by 24% from the year before to four years after the deal.
- Safeway reversed the LBO and went public in April 1990.

- The post-deal market-adjusted abnormal returns were 24% for Kroger (over 4.3 years), 483% for Safeway (over 6.2 years) (see Chapter 4 on abnormal returns methodology). The dollar abnormal returns were $170m for Kroger shareholders and $653m for Safeway shareholders. Total dollar gains including the HLT premium was $1.5bn for Kroger and $2.1bn for Safeway shareholders.

Discussion questions

1 What is the distinction between an LBO and a leveraged recap?

2 What changes happened at Kroger and at Safeway after the HLT?

3 What are the performance indicators after the HLT?

4 What is the linkage between post-HLT changes and performance?

Source: D. J. Denis, 'Organizational form and the consequences of highly leveraged transactions, Kroger's recapitalization and Safeway's LBO', *Journal of Financial Economics*, **36**, 1994, 193–224.

Overview and implications for practice

This chapter discusses the evolution, characteristics and consequences of leveraged buyouts (LBOs). An LBO is an acquisition financed with very high levels of debt compared with equity.

- Many specialist firms, called LBO sponsors or private equity firms, emerged in the 1980s to carry out LBOs. The largest LBO in history was that of RJR Nabisco in 1989 for $25bn. European and UK LBO growth is of more recent origin.

- LBO targets come from a variety of sources – corporate divestitures, public companies going private, bankrupt companies, secondary buyouts.

- LBOs are funded by sponsors by raising debt capital 'funds' and contributing their own private equity. Private equity funds are also set up in the form of partnerships, with general partners managing the funds and overseeing the LBO investees.

- Value creation in LBOs comes from tax subsidy on debt, heavy use of cheaper debt, and changes in management and corporate governance structures. The general partners are active monitors and sit on the LBO boards.

- Sponsors need to exit most of the LBOs because of the need to repay the fund contributors. Exit can be in the form of a trade sale to a strategic buyer, another LBO sponsor, initial public offerings (IPOs), or a return to the stock market, i.e. reverse LBO.

- LBO is considered a dual revolution in corporate finance and corporate governance. We review evidence on the returns generated by buyout funds in the US, Europe and UK. Returns to PE funds in the US seem to be low relative to public market benchmarks, but seem to be high in the UK and Europe.

- Because of competitive pressures and rising acquisition target prices, private equity firms increasingly seek to add strategic value by following other strategies, such as buy and build. They now look more like conglomerates and strategic buyers.

- Level of debt in recent HLTs are also much lower than in the deals from the 1980s. The credit crunch will drive leverage levels even further.

Review questions

11.1 What is an LBO? What is its general financial structure?

11.2 What are private equity firms' competitive advantages in the takeover market over other buyers?

11.3 What are the different types of LBO and their characteristics?

11.4 Compare the LBO market in the US and Europe.

11.5 What are the sources of LBO targets? How does the source affect the pricing of an LBO?

11.6 What is an LBO exit? What are the alternative exit strategies?

11.7 What kind of targets makes good LBOs?

11.8 What are the different sources of funds for an LBO?

11.9 What is a junk bond?

11.10 Discuss the LBO and high-yield bond market in European countries.

11.11 What are the sources of value creation in an LBO?

11.12 Does debt provide a good discipline over management?

11.13 Comment on the sources of fee revenue to PE firms, and whether they create a conflict of interest between general and limited partners.

11.14 Do you agree that PE firms' corporate governance is superior to that of public companies? Will this be so in the future?

Further reading

J. Gillighan and M. Wright, '*Private Equity Demystified: An Explanatory Guide*' (London: Institute of Chartered Accountants in England and Wales, 2008).

S. Kaplan and P. Strömberg, 'Leveraged buyouts and private equity', *Journal of Economic Perspectives*, **23**(1), 2009, 121–146.

P. Strömberg, 'The new demography of private equity', in A. Gurung and J. Lerner (Eds), *Globalization of Alternative Investments Working Papers Volume 1: Global Economic Impact of Private Equity 2008* (New York: World Economic Forum, 2008), pp. 3–26.

The Economist, 'The great tech buy-out boom', 25 February 2006.

Notes and references

1. M. Jensen, 'The eclipse of the public corporation', *Harvard Business Review*, **5**, 1989, 61–74.
2. G. P. Baker and G. D. Smith, *The New Financial Capitalists: Kohlberg Kravis and Roberts and the Creation of Corporate Value* (Cambridge: Cambridge University Press, 1998), pp. 2–3.
3. A. Rappaport, 'The staying power of the public corporation', *Harvard Business Review*, **1**, 1990, 96–104.
4. The following provide a flavour of the literary output: Connie Brook's *Predator's Ball*; James B. Stewart's *Den of Thieves, Merchants of Debt*; Moira Johnston's *Takeover, The New Wall Street Warriors*; Judi Bevan's *The Insiders*. The movies *Wall Street*, featuring an Oscar-winning performance by Michael Douglas as the ruthless Wall Street financier Gordon Gekko, who extols greed as good, and *Other People's Money*, featuring Danny DeVito, the diminutive, doughnut-crazed and determined financial buyer, represent Hollywood's tribute to the new financial capitalists of the 1980s. On the other hand, under the irresistible charm of *Pretty Woman* Julia Roberts, Richard Gere mellows from a ruthless raider into a caring capitalist.

5. See P. Strömberg, 'The new demography of private equity', in *The Global Economic Impact of Private Equity Report 2008* (hereafter the Global PE Report), World Economic Forum, Figure 1b.

6. See P. Cornelius, B. Langelaar and M. van Rossum, 'Big is better: growth and market structure in global buyouts', *Journal of Applied Corporate Finance*, **19**(3), 2007, 109–116.

7. M. Zenner, M. Matthews, J. Marks, and N. Mago, 'The Era of Cross-Border M & A: How Current Market Dynamics are Changing the M & A Landscape'. *Journal of Applied Corporate Finance*, **20**(2), Spring 2008, 84–96.

8. See Roundtable on 'Steering LBOs beyond financial engineering', *Mergers and Acquisitions*, November/December 1994, 23–30.

9. *Mergers and Acquisitions, 1996 Almanac*, March/April.

10. The statistics in this and the previous paragraph are taken from the Centre for Management Buy-out, Research, *Quarterly Review of Management Buy-outs*, Summer 2001. The figures for continental Europe are approximate and based on interpretation of Figure 2.1 of the *Review* and converted from € into $ at the rate of $1 to 1€. Although approximate, these figures are a good indicator of the trend in value of LBOs. Figures for the UK have been converted at the rate of $1.5 to £1. Again, the converted figures, albeit approximate, still reveal the trend in LBO deal values.

11. See S. Sudarsanam, *Creating Value from Mergers and Acquisitions: The Challenges* (Harlow, Essex: FT Prentice Hall, 2003), Ch. 12.

12. Centre for Management Buy-out Research, *Quarterly Review of Management Buy-outs*, Summer 2001, 41–42.

13. The percentages of management buyouts and buyins from different sources for continental Europe (for the UK) are: family and private companies 40% (42%); divestiture by foreign parent 7% (7%); divestiture by local parent 26% (18%); public to private 2% (3%); receivership 2% (11%); secondary buyout 14% (12%); and others 10% (7%).

14. CMBOR, 'Management buyouts', *Quarterly Review*, Spring 2002, Table A34.

15. J. Morris, 'Privates on parade fail to pass muster', *Euromoney*, June 2002.

16. L. Saigol, 'Investors map out an alternative exit', *Financial Times*, 3 July 2002.

17. Tertiary buyouts and quarternary buyouts to recycle LBO firms among PE firms have been increasing in recent years. This kind of exit has become more important than IPOs. See Q. Carruthers, 'Keeping it in the family', *Acquisitions Monthly*, March 2007, 36–37. Thus any stigma about these exits may be diminishing.

18. Other examples include the buyout of TDC, a Danish telecom company, for $15bn and Sun Guard Data Systems, a financial technology firm, for $11bn. See *The Economist*, 'The great tech buy-out boom', **378**(25), February 2006, 65–66.

19. See *Texas Pacific Group – J. Crew*, Harvard Business School case study (HBS 9-808-017)

20. A second lien is secured on the same assets on which a prior charge exists. Its collateral is therefore weaker.

21. R. Doumar, 'All set for a record European LBO', *Acquisitions Monthly Supplement*, October 2000, 56–58. This kind of whole-business financing is a form of structured finance.

22. See E. Thornton, 'Private equity's white-knuckle deal', *Business Week*, 17 September 2007.

23. S. Kaplan and J. Stein, 'The evolution of buyout pricing and financial structure in the 1980s', *Quarterly Journal of Economics*, **108**, 1993, 313–358.

24. E. I. Altman and B. J. Karlin, *Defaults and Returns in the High Yield Bond Market: The Year 2007 in Review and Outlook*, Special report from the New York University Salomon Center, Leonard. N. Stern School of Business, February 2008, Figure 25.

25. See European High Yield Association, *European Quarterly High Yield and Leveraged Loan Report*, first quarter 2009, Figure 13, downloaded from www.ehya.com.

26. M. Wright, B. Chiplin and S. Thompson, 'The market for corporate control, divestments and buyouts', in M. Bishop and J. Kay (Eds), *European Mergers and Merger Policy* (Oxford: Oxford University Press, 1993). pp. 96–133.

27. M. Wright, S. Thompson, B. Chiplin and K. Robbie, *Buy-ins and Buy-outs* (London: Graham & Trotman, 1991), Table 4.6.

28. *Ibid.*

29. *Ibid.*

30. G. Baker and C. Montgomery, *Conglomerate and LBO Associations: A Comparison of Organizational Forms*, Harvard Business School Working Paper, 1994.

31. See P. Strömberg, *The Global PE Report, ibid.*, Table 4.

32. For a further discussion of the different types of fees and the basis of the estimated fees reported here, see A. Metrick and A. Yasuda, 'The economics of private equity funds', Yale University working paper, September 2008.

33. Adding to the mystique of private equity is the origin of the 20% rule. Metrick and Yasuda (see previous footnote) say 'The exact origin of the 20 percent focal point is unknown, but previous authors have pointed to Venetian merchants in the middle ages, speculative sea voyages in the age of exploration, and even the book of Genesis as the source.'

34. See Metrick and Yasuda, *ibid.*, Table 7.

35. NVCA News Release dated 10 June 2002, obtained from the NVCA website (www.nvca.org).

36. P. A. Butler, 'The alchemy of LBOs', *McKinsey Quarterly*, No. 2, 2001, from www.mckinseyquarterly.com.

37. See NVCA Yearbook 2008, downloaded from www.nvca.org.

38. See L. Phalippou and O. Gootschlag, 'Performance of private equity funds', *Review of Financial Studies*, **22**(4), 2009, 1747–1776.

39. Returns to shareholders in LBOs have generally been high. DeAngelo and DeAngelo found in their study of 72 going-private LBOs that the average premium was 56% to target shareholders. Hite and Vetsuypens also provided evidence that leveraged MBOs generate positive returns to the divestor shareholders. See H. DeAngelo and L. DeAngelo, 'Going private: The effects of a change in ownership structure', in J. M. Stern and D. H. Chew (Eds), *The Revolution in Corporate Finance* (Oxford, UK: Blackwell, 1986); G. Hite and M. Vetsuypens, 'Management buyouts of divisions and shareholder wealth', *Journal of Finance*, **44**(4), 1989, 953–970.

40. S. Kaplan and P. Strömberg, 'Leveraged buyouts and private equity', *Journal of Economic Perspectives*, **23**(1), 2009, 121–146

41. J. Gillighan and M. Wright, *Private Equity De-mystified: An Explanatory Guide* (London: Institute of Chartered Accountants in England and Wales, 2008).

42. R. T. Kleiman and K. Nathan, 'Was heavy debt a good disciplinarian for recapped firms?', *Mergers and Acquisitions*, November/December 1992, 18–25.

43. J. F. Cotter and S. W. Peck, 'The structure of debt and active equity investors: The case of the buyout specialist', *Journal of Financial Economics*, **59**, 2001, 101–147.

44. E. Ofek, 'Efficiency gains in unsuccessful management buyouts', *Journal of Finance*, **49**(2), 1994, 637–654.

45. M. Wright and J. Coyne, *Management Buy-outs* (London: Croom Helm, 1985).

46. M. Wright, N. Wilson and K. Robbie, 'The longer term effects of management-led buy-outs', *Entrepreneurial and Small Business Finance*, **5**(3), 1999, 213–234.

47. Wright, Thompson and Chiplin, *ibid.*

48. 3i, *The Changing Face of Management Buy-ins* (London: 3i Group plc, 1994).

49. See V. Acharya and C. Kehoe, 'Corporate governance and value creation: Evidence from private equity', 2008, downloadable from www.cgi.org.

50. K. Robbie, M. Wright and M. Albrighton, 'High-tech management buyouts', *Venture Capital*, **1**(3), 1999, 219–239; A. Serwer, 'The deal of the next century: The Silver Lake partners are wagering on a whole new way to invest in infotech – the biggest, baddest LBO fund ever to hit Silicon Valley, *Fortune*, **140**(5), 1999, 154–159.

51. J. W. Bartlett, 'The joint venture LBO: A strategic balancing act', *Mergers and Acquisitions*, November/December 1990, 48–50.

52. See M. Goldstein, 'Private equity's public moves', *Business Week*, 8 October 2007.

53. M. Wright, R. E. Hoskisson and L. W. Busenitz, 'Firm rebirth: Buyouts as facilitators of strategic growth and entrepreneurship', *Academy of Management Executive*, **15**(1), 2001, 111–125.

Acquisition decision process: organizational, psychological and governance perspectives

Objectives

At the end of this chapter, the reader should be able to understand:

- the alternative models of the organizational processes involved in acquisition decision-making;
- the limitations of the rationalist perspective of the process;
- how managerial biases influence acquisition behaviour;
- how executive compensation may provide wrong incentives for acquisition;
- how the M & A function may be organized;
- the characteristics of an effective acquisition function; and
- the role of the acquisition function in specific acquisition deal structuring.

Introduction

Previous chapters have described the framework for a strategic analysis of acquisitions and mergers. This framework is useful in evaluating the choice of acquisitions and mergers as a means of achieving the firm's strategic objectives, and it leads to the selection criteria for screening potential candidates for acquisitions and mergers. In this chapter alternative perspectives on the acquisition decision process within firms are presented.

An understanding of the acquisition decision process is important, since it has a bearing on the quality of the acquisition decision and its value creation logic. Success of post-acquisition integration is determined at least partly by the thoroughness, clarity and forethought with which the value creation logic is blueprinted at the acquisition decision stage. Under certain circumstances the deficiency of the decision process can diminish the chance of a successful acquisition.

Not all firms regard the M & A function as a separate function distinct from corporate development or corporate strategy. In some firms, however, separate M & A functions exist to provide an internal capability to undertake acquisitions on behalf of the firm as a whole, or on behalf of business units that lack such a capability. In this chapter we develop a framework for effective organization of the M & A function within acquisition-active firms. The aim of this framework is to develop the acquisition function as an important organizational capability and as a core competence of the firm. We describe the various components of the acquisition function. Such a function serves as a repository of the firm's M & A-related skills, knowledge and capabilities. It also serves as a gatekeeper for ideas for M & A generated by the different parts of the firm and by external advisers. In the context of specific acquisitions the acquisition function provides the strategic direction, organizes the resources for teams responsible for deal-making, directs those teams, and ensures that deal-making leads to acquisitions that deliver the firm's strategic objectives and shareholder value.

Acquisition decision-making process: organizational perspective

Haspeslagh and Jemison[1] contrast two perspectives of acquisition decision making – the rationalist and the organizational processes. Figure 12.1 delineates the conventional rationalist view of acquisition decision-making. This view is based on hard economic, strategic and financial evaluation of the acquisition proposal, and estimates the potential value creation based on such an evaluation. The acquisition justification is articulated in terms of the strategic goals, how the acquisition will serve these goals, and the sources of value gains. An important aspect of the rationalist procedure is the emphasis on quantification of expected costs and benefits of the acquisition.

In the rationalist view, the acquiring firm is a black box, and the acquisition decision emerging out of the black box is a unified view held by the firm. Any discord among the various players within the firm, such as top managers, operating managers and different functional managers, has been neatly ironed out. The resulting decision will then command the wholehearted commitment and loyalty of those players. Thus acquisitions are the result of coldly rational decision processes, with the acquiring firm regarded as an undivided, homogeneous decision unit.

The organizational process perspective

The process perspective differs from the rationalist model in that it considers the organizational context as relevant at both the pre-acquisition decision-making and the post-acquisition integration stages. The process perspective adds the soft dimension to the rationalist, strategy-oriented approach and takes a peep into the black box.

In the process perspective the acquisition process starts with an idea and progresses through acquisition justification. The acquisition decision-making process is a complex one,

Figure 12.1   The rationalist view of the acquisition decision process

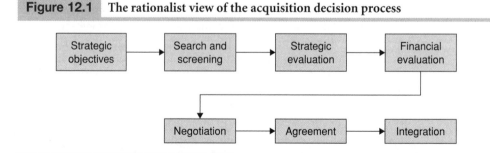

giving rise to a number of problems. This process therefore has to be carefully managed, and the firm must have the necessary organizational structure for such management. The acquisition decision process in a large firm is characterized by four potentially debilitating factors. The four factors are not mutually exclusive and indeed are interrelated:

- fragmented perspectives on the acquisition held by different managers;
- escalating momentum in decision-making, which may dilute the quality of the decision;
- ambiguous expectations of different managers about the benefits of the acquisition; and
- diversity of motives among managers in lending support to the acquisition.

Impact of the process characteristics

The fragmented perspectives arise from the fact that evaluating an acquisition is a complex, multidisciplinary exercise. Specialists from different functional areas, such as finance, R & D, marketing, operations, legal affairs, personnel, environmental audit and antitrust law, are involved in making such an evaluation. Each of these specialists analyzes the separate aspects of the acquisition with an essentially narrow focus. Sometimes, where the acquirer lacks specialists in certain areas, outside consultants such as environmental specialists may be co-opted into the evaluation team.

Communication among these different specialist groups may be limited. Integration of the narrow specialist perspectives becomes difficult as the complexity of the acquisition and the number of specialists increase. As a result, the top management in charge of the acquisition may focus on easily and quickly communicated issues, and on quantified factors. Where outside specialists such as investment bankers are brought in, the problem of fragmented perspectives is accentuated.

The danger of such a narrow perspective is that the more subtle and soft issues that are relevant to the success of post-acquisition integration may be given scant attention.[2] For example, the acquisition may be conceived by the top management without the active involvement of the operational-level managers, although the latter may have much greater familiarity with the proposed acquisition.

Further, an acquired firm is normally a bundle of different capabilities and opportunities. Not all the managers involved in deciding upon the acquisition may be fully aware of them, or their impact on the acquirer's competitive strength. Thus they develop a partial view of the potentialities of the acquisition (see Exhibit 12.1).

Exhibit 12.1

BTR learns after the acquisition of Hawker Siddeley

BTR was an experienced and successful acquisitive British conglomerate. It acquired Hawker Siddeley (HS), an engineering company, in a £1.55bn hostile bid in 1991. Though the bid was made after an intensive study of HS lasting several months, BTR nevertheless found that it did not know everything about HS. It dropped its proposal to create a global electrical engineering business, suggesting that HS knew more about its businesses than BTR. BTR also slowed its pre-bid integration plan until it learnt more about HS.

Source: Adapted from A. Baxter and A. Bolger, 'Godfathers get control', *Financial Times*, 11 March 1992

Acquisitions often generate a momentum of their own, even in friendly mergers. Hostile takeovers, in addition, can generate a hothouse atmosphere. Managers often find the acquisition process full of excitement, and are propelled by the thrill of the chase.[3] Moreover, acquisitions may create the need for external advisers such as investment banks. These external advisers may have an incentive in closing the deal, especially if their fees are not fixed in advance, but are success related. Such an incentive structure will add to the pressure on acquiring firm managers (see Chapter 19).

There are also other kinds of pressure on managers making acquisition decisions. They may have staked a great deal of their prestige on the acquisition, and will be reluctant to pull out for fear of being stigmatized by this 'failure'. On the other hand, success in an acquisition may increase their career prospects and compensation levels by increasing the size of businesses under their control (see Chapter 3 on the managerial motives for mergers and Chapter 4 on the empirical evidence for managerial motives).

Managers may also fear that, if the acquisition decision-making is prolonged, word may get out and the firm's competitors may make a pre-emptive bid, thus increasing the chances of an auction for the target and raising the eventual bid premium. Moreover, disclosure of the acquisition move may trigger resistance from stakeholders such as employees where the acquisition is motivated by efficiency and rationalization considerations, and may lead to job losses. In EU countries works councils have in many cases to be consulted about the proposed acquisition.

The acquisition proposition has to be 'sold' internally to different managers. In selling the idea, managers who are championing, and who perhaps stand to gain most from, the acquisition may play up the attractions to those managers whose consent is needed, while playing down the potential problems associated with the acquisition. This information asymmetry can lead to different managers developing different expectations of the value of the acquisition.

This expectational ambiguity may be used tactically by the acquisition sponsor to sell the idea and win support from other managers. After the deal, resolution of such ambiguity is left to operating managers, who may not have been involved in the negotiations. While ambiguity is useful in developing political coalitions and evolving a consensus in favour of the acquisition, it hinders a smooth post-acquisition integration process.

The essentially political process of selling the acquisition proposal generates multiple objectives from different players in that process. In the post-acquisition phase these objectives lead to conflicting claims on priorities and resource allocation, thereby diminishing the effectiveness of the integration process. For example, the same acquisition may aim to create value through capacity rationalization, product development, merging of distribution networks or vertical integration. Where different managers are responsible for bringing about these changes, they may have to agree on how fast and in what sequence these must be achieved.

The acquirer's normal resource allocation planning styles have a significant impact on the quality of acquisition decision-making. Companies with a robust allocation style can handle acquisition decisions much more effectively. Characteristics of a robust style of resource allocation include a long-term strategic orientation, firm commitment of the top management, an analytical rather than a political approach, and consensus rather than dominance by individual managers.

Acquisitions are often high-profile corporate events, both within the acquirers and outside in the capital markets and possibly in the media. They often prove irresistibly tempting for high-profile CEOs who wish to pursue 'dash for growth' strategies driven by grand visions for their company. In this grand pursuit the hubris-ridden CEOs may make acquisitions that are poorly thought out, overpaid for, and shoddily integrated. They may not allow their organization to pause for breath and assimilate the acquisitions already made before pushing it into the next deal. The acquisition trail then suddenly stops, pushing the acquirer into financial distress or bankruptcy. This is the story of Worldcom, Tyco, Vivendi, Marconi and Deutsche Telecom, to name but a few of the 1990s' hyperactive acquirers that turned from supernova into black holes in short order. The 'tycoon factor' is often a symptom of a weak organizational structure, a subservient board of directors and poor acquisition capability. It is not unknown for two high-profile CEOs to get together over dinner and agree a merger, then leaving it for vice-presidents to rationalize it in terms of value creation. Such 'seat of the pants' deal-making may in some cases and for some time be successful, but a more enduring value creation strategy is perhaps to develop an effective acquisition function within the firm.[4]

Acquisition decision process: psychological perspective

Hitherto we have assumed a rationalist perspective: that is, top managers of firms make their acquisition decisions to maximize shareholder value after due consideration of the risks and returns to alternative corporate strategies, albeit subject to organizational process constraints. The agency model of shareholders as principals and managers as their agents, and the dichotomy between their interests and the scope for self-serving behaviour of managers, introduces psychological issues about human behaviour in general, and specifically in the context of the relation between shareholders and managers. In addition to the proclivity of managers towards self-serving behaviour, there are other behavioural traits rooted in individual psychology giving rise to biases in individual managers such as the CEO, and in social psychology giving rise to collective biases among groups of individuals such as the board of directors.

The traditional agency model has been both challenged and extended by researchers who have formulated a behavioural agency model. Taking into account the behavioural biases of managers may result in dramatic revision of conclusions based on the traditional agency model. For example, overoptimism or overconfidence on a CEO's part may lead to more risky corporate strategy choices than the risk aversion implied by the traditional model. Under the latter, the firm has to correct for this risk aversion with appropriate monetary incentives that reward risk-taking, e.g. stock options whose value increases non-linearly with the underlying stock value. Under the behavioural agency model, however, overoptimistic or overconfident managers may be risk-preferring, thereby obviating the need for stock options. Indeed, stock options may reinforce the behavioural bias of managers, causing excessive risk-taking.

Another perspective that may shed light on the factors that allow firms to undertake value-destroying mergers and acquisitions is rooted in the individual psychological attributes and behaviour of the CEO and in the collective social dynamics of the board of directors. The behavioural corporate finance literature has identified several psychological traits of CEOs, including:

- hubris;
- overconfidence; and
- overoptimism.

Hubris is arrogant pride whereas overconfidence is excessive confidence in one's ability. Both overconfidence and overoptimism suggest an unrealistically high level of confidence or optimism. When managers consider taking over another firm, hubris causes managers to underestimate the risks inherent in acquisitions, leading to overvaluation of the target and an excessive takeover premium. March and Shapira find that managers are *overconfident* and consider themselves able to distinguish between gambling, i.e. where the chances of win or loss are uncontrollable, and risk-taking, i.e. where uncertainty can be reduced by skill or information.

Overoptimistic individuals also underestimate the likelihood of hazards affecting them. Heaton, and Malmendier and Tate find that overoptimistic managers often show an upward bias in their cash flow forecasts for investment projects[5]. The impact of these behavioural biases is that CEOs may underestimate the risk of the acquisitions they make, and overpay for them.

What are the sources of CEOs' biases? In terms of personality, CEOs who reach the top of the managerial hierarchy are, by definition, confident high achievers. Their firms' past successes may lead to their being identified as the architects of such success. CEOs themselves may claim, and vigorously encourage, such attribution, even if many other factors may have contributed to success, giving rise to self-attribution bias. The mirror image is that they attribute firm failures to other factors or simple 'bad luck'. They may also assiduously cultivate their image as the movers and shakers and architects of their firm's success.

In the context of mergers, managers may suffer from biases such as self-attribution bias: that is, claiming too much credit for the firm's success in an acquisition while blaming 'uncontrollable' external factors for the firm's failure, reflecting the attitude *'heads I win but tails it is just bad luck'*. Self-attribution bias may allow managers to continue to operate the same policies as in the past, since they were successful. Far from being denigrated, their inordinate claim may be legitimized by the cultural milieu in which powerful and charismatic CEOs are often portrayed as heroic, larger-than-life corporate saviours[6]. Success of the firm is attributed to the CEO as an individual rather than to the organization as whole. The media tend to love winners and often attribute corporate success not to a faceless, but nevertheless purposeful and efficient, organization, but to a charismatic leader of that organization because of the human element involved, and it is easier to tell stories with clearly identifiable human actors[7]. Successful CEOs often gain 'celebrity' status and start to believe in their own invulnerability and infallibility[8]. This can lead to an overconfident behaviour bordering on arrogance, self-glorification and self-aggrandizement of top managers such as the CEO.

Nothing succeeds like success: the 'halo' effect

In his insightful and entertaining discourse on the various delusions that business managers fall prey to, Rosenzweig identifies the 'halo effect' as one among them[9]. The halo effect arises when, if a person excels in one endeavour, he is deemed capable of similar accomplishment in another endeavour even though, on objective verification, this attribution may not be valid. The success of a firm overall may be attributed to success in carrying out every activity that contributes to that success, e.g. innovation, marketing, human resource management, *on the basis of the overall success alone*. The downside of the halo effect is that, when the firm's performance declines, it is deemed to have performed badly in all those activities. Further, instead of tracing success in activities to success overall, the analyst bases his evaluation of these activities on the overall success. Thus the halo effect precludes an objective analysis of the cause-and-effect relationship, i.e. what contributes to success.

From halo to hubris

The halo effect is closely related to attribution bias, which we discussed earlier. If the success of a firm is attributed to, or is claimed by, a charismatic CEO, the true determinants of that success will not be known. A firm's good performance may be due to a myriad of internal and external factors, including luck, but may be attributed by observers to the CEO and, by inference, to his outstanding qualities as a corporate leader. Misattribution may arise from a genuine difficulty in disentangling the multiple causes of that performance, from laziness and avoidance of the search for these multiple causes, from naïve belief in one visible cause, or from a desire to tell a good story without the distraction of the minutiae. Misattribution due to the halo effect can be a source of hubris.

Rovenpor examines the role that four CEO personal characteristics – preference for organizational growth, belief in synergy, need for power, and self-confidence – play in encouraging companies to engage in mergers and acquisitions[10]. Rovenpor finds that these four CEO characteristics are highly and positively related to the level of M & A activities. There is a thin line between confidence and overconfidence. Jack Welch, the former CEO of GE, notes the thin line between self-confidence and hubris. After describing GE's disastrous acquisition of Kidder Peabody, Welch says: 'There is only a razor's edge between self-confidence and hubris. This time hubris won and taught me a lesson we'd never forget.'[11] This suggests that behavioural biases can provide the tipping point between optimal and excessive risk-taking by top managers.

Overconfident managers may be particularly attracted to high-tech acquisitions, being opportunities to demonstrate their capability in 'creating miracles'. Available empirical evidence points to the negative value impact of different behavioural biases. Acquisitions driven by managerial hubris destroy acquirer shareholder value. Managerial overconfidence induced by glamour stock rating leads to a risky acquisition strategy, excessive acquisition premium, and value destruction for acquirer shareholders. Overconfident managers are more likely to conduct mergers – in particular, value-destroying mergers – than are rational CEOs.

Malmendier and Tate test the proposition that overconfident CEOs overestimate their ability to generate value from acquisitions and overpay for target companies, resulting in value-destroying mergers. These predictions are tested using two proxies for overconfidence: CEOs' personal over-investment in their company and their press portrayal. They find that the odds of making an acquisition are 65% higher if the CEO is classified as overconfident. The effect is largest if the merger is diversifying and does not require external financing. The market reaction at merger announcement is significantly more negative than for non-overconfident CEOs[12].

Leaders often exhibit overoptimism, either because of an intense desire to succeed or to inspire the 'troops' to fight hard and win. Such optimism may again engender unrealistic overstatement of the benefits of an acquisition and an understatement of the problems in achieving those benefits. Overoptimism may also lead to attaching higher probabilities to future favourable states of the world, e.g. high economic or industry growth or new technological breakthroughs, and lower probabilities to the adverse states, thereby making acquisitions more attractive or more attractive at certain times than they would be on a more sober understanding of the world. Such overoptimism, combined with overconfidence in their own ability to manage risks, may induce managers to venture ahead of other firms – i.e. be first movers – even though technological and market uncertainties are unlikely to be resolved soon. Overoptimism may often be manifested in grandiose visions of the future and the firm's positioning in that future. The disastrous merger of AOL and Time Warner (TW) was crafted on the basis of exuberant optimism about Internet broadband as a transformative technology, and visionary faith in its potential[13].

Psychologists who have studied individual and group decision-making have identified several other behavioural biases that may dilute the quality of decisions made by CEOs. Kahneman and Tversky, in their path-breaking studies of decision behaviour under uncertainty, identify a number of such biases:[14]

- *Representativeness* – the decision-maker draws upon another situation in which a successful decision was made to validate the decision in the present context, even though the former may have only superficial similarity to the latter: for example, a past successful acquisition is used to justify the case for another, seemingly similar acquisition.

- *Availability* – undue generalization is made on the basis of a more recent event than distant ones, even though the objective probability of the former measured over long periods may be much less: for example, a current economic boom is regarded as likely to endure, even though past history of economic cycles would indicate that a slowdown is more likely. The behaviour of home mortgage borrowers and lenders just before market crashes indicates such biased expectations based on recent experience.

- *Anchoring* – people, in estimating the future value of an event or transaction, start with an anchor and then adjust it to reach a final figure. Persons with successful recent experience would anchor their estimate of future transaction on the value of that recent transaction. In the case of serial acquirers, recent success in their acquisitions would serve as anchor, and the value of the next acquisition would be based on that success.

- *Prospect theory* – people tend to adopt more risky positions after losing a gamble than after winning, in the hope of recovering their loss. A poor, value-destroying acquisition may lead to managers persisting in their acquisition strategy and choosing even more risky acquisitions to recover lost ground[15].

Self-delusion and overcommitment to deal-making

CEOs often launch the bid for a target because they want to acquire it. Given this initial commitment they are predisposed to see what they want to see[16]. They will selectively use information that reinforces the validity of their decision to acquire, by relying on representativeness and availability heuristics. Moreover, any discordant facts or revelations that might call for questioning or abandoning the acquisition may be dismissed as non-representative. This behaviour is characteristic of self-delusion.[17]

Commitment to a deal often turns into overcommitment from which it is difficult to *walk away*, even when there is a cause and an opportunity to do so, for example during the pre-negotiation due diligence stage. Haunschild, Davis-Blake and Fichman, in their experimental study of commitment in the acquisition process, find evidence that personal responsibility for proposing the acquisition, competition for the target and a publicly announced acquisition bid all lead to escalating commitment, even in the face of emerging signals that the acquisition is likely to destroy value[18]. The decision-maker is thus in denial and has low tolerance of cognitive dissonance. All three conditions for escalation are associated with the loss of face or power or authority that may follow a decision to walk away. The commitment escalates, even during the due diligence stage, which normally should allow the bidder to walk away without loss of face, since the purpose of due diligence is to allow reassessment of risk in making the acquisition, and a perfect opportunity to walk away. Negative signals thrown up by due diligence may be dismissed as non-representative. Thus self-delusion trumps rational risk assessment.

Overoptimism may also be engendered by the social process at work within organizations. As Lovallo and Kahneman note, as they outline the 'organizational pressures' to conform and to be optimistic: 'Organizations also actively discourage pessimism, which is often interpreted as disloyalty. The bearers of bad news tend to become pariahs, shunned and ignored by other employees. When pessimistic opinions are suppressed, while optimistic ones are rewarded, an organization's ability to think critically is undermined. The optimistic biases of individual employees become mutually reinforcing, and unrealistic views of the future are validated by the group'. This process may explain why non-CEO directors on the board may often fall in line with CEO's overoptimism and thus fail to rein in the CEO.[19]

In a survey of 250 senior managers involved in M & A deals, Bain & Company found the following[20]:

- 50% (of respondents) said that their due diligence had overlooked significant problems;
- 50% found the targets had been dressed up to look good;
- two thirds said their approach routinely overestimated synergies from the acquisition;
- only 30% were satisfied with their due diligence process; and
- a third acknowledged that they had not walked away from deals, despite nagging doubts.

Nothing succeeds like excess? The overconfidence effect

Often the pressures on firms to merge arise from both internal and external factors. As noted above, competition for a target increases the commitment to make an acquisition. Another form of competition also gets the CEO's adrenalin pumping overtime. In an atmosphere in which the firm's rivals are making acquisitions, not to make matching acquisitions will project the executives as corporate wimps. Jeffrey Pfeffer, a foremost scholar of organizational behaviour, identifies three forces that drive firms to merger even though the vast majority of mergers and acquisitions create little value or destroy value[21]:

- Executive ego leading to hubris and overconfidence – mergers get attention from analysts, and sometimes from the media, and the ego-driven CEO likes that attention[22].
- Executives find mergers exciting, i.e. they enjoy the thrill of the chase; mergers often seem like a faster and less risky solution to problems than solving those problems internally. 'Mergers have sex appeal.'
- In a world in which everyone else is doing a deal, who wants to be left out?

This may explain imitative acquisitions and crowd-like behaviour causing waves.

Narcissistic CEOs and acquisitions

Behavioural biases such as overconfidence and overoptimism may themselves be rooted in the personalities of the CEOs or other top executives. Clinical psychologists have identified a personality disorder called narcissism. Narcissus is a Greek mythological character who fell hopelessly in love with his own image and pined away to death. The lesson is that excessive self-love is self-destructive.

Manfred Kets de Vries, a trained clinical psychologist and management professor who has specialized in leadership development in organizations, differentiates between different forms of narcissism, from 'healthy self-esteem' to 'self-destructive egotism'. He argues that 'a moderate measure of self-esteem contributes to positive behaviours such as assertiveness, confidence, and creativity, all desirable qualities for an individual in any walk of life, but particularly so for business leaders. At the other end of the spectrum, however, extreme narcissism is characterized by egotism, self-centredness, grandiosity, lack of empathy, exploitation, exaggerated self-love and failure to acknowledge boundaries . . .', and within an organization 'the combination of a leader's overly narcissistic disposition and his or her position of power can have devastating consequences'[23].

CEO narcissism may find manifestation in frequent and high profile acquisitions based on grand visions. Chatterjee and Hambrick argue that 'corporate chieftains with supersized egos favour grandiose and high risk strategies . . . acquisitions . . . , large scale product launches and aggressive international expansion . . . they can hit big but they can also miss big'[24]. In recent years there have been many examples of such narcissistic behaviour by Chairmen and CEOs leading to massive value destruction and great misery for thousands of employees and investors of the corporations they led[25].

Figure 12.2 Number of acquisitions and number of overconfident CEOs. Data based on S&P 500 companies

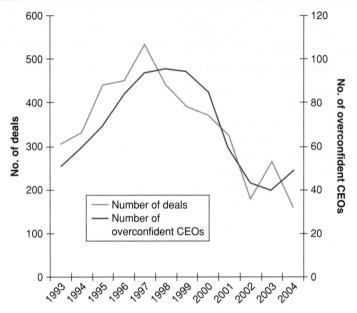

Source: Data based on S&P 500 companies

The behaviour of Jean-Marie Messier the CEO of the French conglomerate Vivendi Universal who through a series of grandiose and expensive acquisitions led his company to the largest loss in French corporate history and to the brink of bankruptcy, streaks of narcissism[26]. His rise and fall because of arrogant self-belief and the sense of being special are described in our Case study in Chapter 7[27].

Sudarsanam and Huang find a close correlation between the number of overconfident CEOs and the number of M & A deals in the US during the same period (see Figure 12.2)[28]. They define a CEO as overconfident if he fails to exercise his stock option that is at least 67% in the money during the year prior to acquisition announcement. A risk-averse CEO may be expected to exercise such options when they are so deep in the money. The delay in exercise is treated as a measure of the CEO's high confidence that the future performance, and hence its share price, will be even higher, and the value of the stock options will be even greater[29].

Psychological traits such as overconfidence cannot be directly observed, but only inferred. However, several empirical studies have used variables that may be considered reasonable proxies for overconfidence to examine its impact on shareholder value following acquisitions. Media profile can give rise to celebrity status and overconfidence, as argued above. Serial acquirers are likely to be overconfident because they have done many deals before and can ride on their success. Longholder is a definition of a overconfident CEO, based on a CEO not exercising deep-in-the-money stock options (see discussion of Figure 12.2 above). Low book-to-market ratio (the reciprocal of high market value of equity to its book value) is generally used as a measure of the glamour status of the firm's stock. Self-importance is measured by the CEO's compensation relative to other executives' compensation. Media profile is the profile of a CEO in media accounts of that CEO. Thus both CEO-level indicators, e.g. CEO

Table 12.1 Impact of overconfidence on shareholder gains to acquirers[30]

Study (year of publication)	Country (sample period)	Acquirer's share performance (%)	Proxy for overconfidence
Hayward and Hambrick (1997)	US (1989–92)	−4 [11 days] −11 [1 year]	• Past performance • Media appraisal • CEO self-importance
Rau and Vermaelen (1998)	US (1980–91)	−4.04 [3 years]	• Book-to-market ratio
Kohers and Kohers (2001)	US (1984–95)	0.92[a] [2 day] −18.68[a] [3 years]	• Book-to-market ratio
Sudarsanam and Mahate (2003)	UK (1983–95)	−1.39[a] [2 days] −8.71 [3 years]	• Book-to-market ratio
Doukas and Petmezas (2006)	UK (1980–2004)	1[a] [5 days]	• Serial acquisition
Malmendier and Tate (2005)	US (1980–94)	−0.5 [3 days]	• Longholder • Media appraisal

Except for Sudarsanam and Mahate, who employ, buy and hold abnormal returns (BHARs), all studies use cumulative abnormal returns to measure shareholder value gains (see Chapter 4 for definitions of these return metrics).
The period in brackets is the period over which performance is measured.
[a]Indicates significance at 1%

self-importance and non-exercise of stock options, and firm-level indicators of performance, e.g. book-to-market ratio, are used to infer CEO overconfidence.

Table 12.1 lists the results from various studies that examine the impact of overconfidence on acquirer share price performance around acquisition announcement or over the longer term following it. From this table we find that overconfidence is in general associated with value-destroying acquisitions in either the short or the long term.

The imperial overstretch

Moeller, Schlingeman and Stulz find that large acquirers make more value-destroying acquisitions than small acquirers[31]. They attribute this to hubris of large acquirers. Large acquirers pay higher bid premia to acquire their targets, although bid premium does not significantly influence bid success. Large acquirers also experience $ synergy losses, i.e. the $ abnormal returns to the portfolio of bidders and targets. Moeller *et al.* estimate three-day abnormal dollar returns to the bidder-target combined are −$56m when the bidder is large and $5m when the bidder is small, both statistically significant. Large acquirers thus '*hit big and miss big*', as noted by Chatterjee and Hambrick[32].

Imitative acquisitions: institutional theory perspective

The behavioural biases and narcissism may explain takeovers that top corporate managers *initiate* but what about the takeovers that they *imitate*? DiMaggio and Powell (1983) argue that institutions become similar over time through the process of institutional *isomorphism* as organizations adopt/adapt innovations and practices of other institutions to become more like them[33]. The motivation behind isomorphism may differ. Organizations may adopt practices either because those practices will increase their economic efficiency and therefore their competitive positioning in the input or output markets or because the practices confer social legitimacy. Adoption of such practices may be taken for granted in the institutional environment of those organizations thereby compelling their adoption. Failure to adopt would result in loss of social legitimacy and the associated power. Thus organizations differ in their motivation to adopt – economic efficiency or social legitimacy. These motivations are not always mutually exclusive.

The dynamics of isomorphism also depend on the institutional environment and the key players within organisations. DiMaggio and Powell identify three channels of isomorphic change: 1. coercive, 2. normative, and 3. mimetic. Coercive isomorphism is through some external pressure such as a law or a mandatory regulation, e.g. the European Union Takeover Directive enforced in 2006. The external pressure may also be generated by the key stakeholders of the organization forcing it to adopt, e.g. a firm not being takeover-active, when its competitors are, may attract adverse comment from analysts and investors that the company's top management lack dynamism and the ability to exploit growth opportunities. Normative isomorphism is voluntary and due to convergence through socialization. Mimetic isomorphism is a mechanism for the organization to cope with environmental uncertainty by following early adopters and derive the comfort of being 'one of a crowd'.

Institutional theory also considers that organizations may resist external pressures to homogenize themselves because of inertia or their own history, i.e. due to path dependency. Key actors in such institutions 'realise considerable gains from the maintenance of those institutions' and therefore have a vested interest in resisting change[34]. On the other hand, other players may challenge these vested interests and force the key players to adopt. Changes adopted under different dynamics may not be of the same quality or effectiveness. Adoption may be perfunctory and superficial, enough to gain legitimacy without being purposeful or effective.

Firms may therefore engage in high profile acquisitions to gain legitimate competitive advantage as well as in their quest for purely social legitimacy. Even when top managers act out of the latter motivation they may project the former as their apparent motivation. Me-too acquisitions may often be driven by the quest for social legitimacy rather than by competitive strategy.

Acquisition decision-making process: compensation incentive perspective

Conflicts of interest between shareholders and managers in the agency model of the firm may be managed in a number of different ways: internally through efficient board monitoring and control, or through large shareholder monitoring, and externally through the threat or actual incidence of hostile takeovers. Among the tools available for internal control are appropriately designed compensation contracts for the CEO and other executives. Such contracts include various forms of compensation – cash salary, cash bonus, long-term incentive plans (LTIPS) that grant the firm's stock, and stock option grants. Both stock and stock option grants are subject to performance benchmarks and vesting periods. They become exercisable after vesting periods of, say, three to five years. These different compensation components bring about different degrees of alignment to shareholder interests.

Cash salary has little relation to shareholder value. Similarly, cash bonus based on annual accounting performance benchmarks, i.e. revenue or profits, is not directly related to share price to the extent that share price does not reflect accounting performance. Values of stock and stock option grants are obviously determined by the share price. The components also offer different risk incentives to the executives in terms of reward and retribution for risk-taking. Salary and bonus encourage risk avoidance, since managers endanger these by taking too much risk with the firm's future financial performance. Since stock grant value goes up and down with the share price, if a risky decision drags the share price down the value of the grant also goes down. This suggests that stock grants may discourage risk-taking. Finally, stock option has value only if the share price rises about the exercise (which at the time of the grant is often the current share price). Above the exercise price the stock option value increases exponentially. Stock option value is more volatile than that of the firm's stock, but an option holder gains far more from the upswing of the share price than he or she loses from the downswing. A stock option is often described as a punt on volatility. Thus, far more than any other compensation element, stock option is designed to encourage risk-taking.

In this section we discuss the relation between executive compensation and acquisition from opposite angles:

- how acquisitions affect compensation; and
- how compensation affects acquisition behaviour.

We also review the empirical evidence from some recent studies for the impact of stock options on acquisition risk.

Does executive compensation increase with acquisition?[35]

Acquisition can affect current or future compensation of the top management in several ways. In recent years CEOs and other top managers have been paid bonuses for acquisition completion, thus providing incentives for managers to complete deals even if in the long run they destroy value. Acquisition also increases firm size, and it is well documented that firm compensation increases with firm size. Managers may also increase firm risk by undertaking high-risk acquisitions and gain from the stock options they have awarded themselves[36]. Thus while compensation affects the nature of acquisitions, it is also, in turn, influenced by acquisitions. Table 12.2 summarizes a number of empirical studies of the impact of acquisition on executive

Table 12.2 Impact of corporate acquisition on executive compensation[37]

Study, country and sample period	Major Results
Lambert and Larcker (1987), US (1976–80)	• Increases in executive compensation and wealth observed only if acquisition increases shareholder wealth
Firth (1991), UK (1974–80)	• Acquisition leads to increase in managerial remuneration owing to increased firm size
Khorana and Zenner (1998), US (1982–86)	• *Ex ante* compensation-to-size sensitivity makes large acquisition more likely • *Ex post*, large acquisitions have a small positive effect on total compensation • Good acquisitions increase compensation, whereas bad acquisitions do not reduce compensation
Bliss and Rosen (2001), US (1986–95)	• Mergers increase compensation, mainly because of firm size effect • Compensation increases even if mergers cause acquiring bank's stock price to decline • CEOs make fewer wealth-reducing mergers when they own more stock
Grinstein and Hribar (2004), US (1993–99)	• More powerful CEOs gain more in acquisition-related bonus • Bonuses larger with larger deals • Deal announcement performance in stock returns unrelated to variation in compensation
Harford and Li (2005), US (1993–99)	• CEO's total pay and overall wealth increase substantially following an acquisition • In poorly governed acquirers, CEO's pay following merger insensitive to performance • CEO's wealth increases even if he or she makes a poor acquisition
Coakley and Iliopoulou (2006), UK (1998–2001)	• Less independent and larger boards award CEOs significantly higher bonuses and salary following M&A completion, consistent with CEO power

---

Exhibit 12.2

'Have done the deal, give me my bonus!'

In April 2006 Boston Scientific bought Guidant, a rival medical device manufacturer, for $27bn. Following the deal completion, five Boston Scientific executives have received special bonuses, some potentially worth more than last year's salary. The CFO, the strategy coordinator, the general counsel, the human resources chief and a public relations executive were awarded bonuses worth at least $1.98m in cash, plus options and deferred stock grants. The awards come at a time of renewed public scrutiny of corporate compensation. Compensation experts cautioned that rewarding executives for completing deals raises governance questions, and could be seen as premature, given the often poor record of mergers in creating value for shareholders. The largest cash payment offered was to Mr Best, which at $625,000 is equal to his salary for last year. Boston early in 2006 outbid rival Johnson & Johnson's agreed deal with Guidant, a maker of implantable devices such as pacemakers. Paul Hodgson, a researcher at the Corporate Library, a corporate governance watchdog, said: 'The psychology of the boards and compensation committees is they justify it to themselves completely as "We've done a fantastic job", instead of thinking to themselves: "This is when the real work starts."' Charles Rudnick, a spokesman at Boston Scientific, said many people across a 'broad cross-section' of the company received bonuses following the deal.

Source: Adapted from C. Bowe, 'Boston Scientific executives win bonuses for deal', *Financial Times*, 14 May 2006

---

compensation. The studies reveal a positive link between good acquisitions (those that add value) and executive compensation. But bad acquisitions do not impact at all or, perversely, they increase compensation. This is consistent with the self-attribution bias discussed earlier: managers claim reward for good performance but probably disclaim responsibility for bad performance. Where compensation is sensitive to firm size, this incentivizes managers to go for larger acquisitions.

In some recent deals the CEO and other top executives were paid deal completion bonuses, as shown in Exhibit 12.2. Such bonuses are not related to the success of the acquisition in terms of value creation, but are paid merely for executing a transaction. The rationale for such payments is weak, since making acquisition where it will serve the company's interests is part of the business of a company. Such incentive for mere deal-making offers a perverse incentive for managers to undertake acquisitions that may even destroy value.

How does executive compensation affect acquisition behaviour?

Table 12.2 provides some evidence that size-sensitive compensation encourages large acquisitions. Given the risk incentive characteristics of stock options, one can expect that a higher proportion of executive compensation in the form of stock options will encourage more risky acquisitions. Several studies in the US and in the UK provide evidence to support this expectation. Sudarsanam and Huang find that, in the 1990s and the beginning of the

Figure 12.3 Average total compensation of a CEO and the stock market level in the US

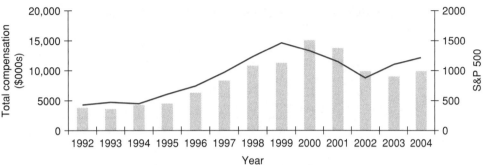

*Note: The bars are compensation levels, and the line is the S&P 500 index level.
Source: Adapted from 'Executive compensation and managerial overconfidence: Impact on risk taking and share-holder value in corporate acquisitions', *International Mergers and Acquisitions Activity Since 1990: Recent Research and Quantitative Analysis*, Sudarsanam, S. and Huang, J. (eds. Gregoriou, G. N. and Renneboog, L. 2007), pp. 223–260.

Figure 12.4 Average stock option compensation of a CEO and the stock market level in the US. The bars are compensation levels, and the line is the S&P 500 index level

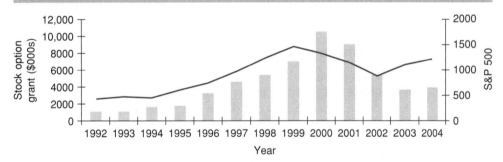

*Note: The bars are compensation levels, and the line is the S&P 500 index level.

new millennium, the average total compensation of US S&P 500 company CEOs (including salary, bonus, stock grants and stock options) (the bar chart) closely tracked the S&P stock market index (the line), as shown in Figure 12.3[38]. This reflects a high proportion of stock grants and stock options in the total compensation.

Figure 12.4 shows how the average stock options value tracked the S&P 500 index. Figure 12.5 shows that the average acquisition deal value and average stock option value received by CEOs are closely aligned.

Thus during the fifth merger wave in the US, stock market level, executive compensation, stock option compensation and M & A deal value were all highly correlated. The correlation between average acquisition target size and stock option compensation was high (0.92). Thus the risk incentive for undertaking acquisitions and, in particular, large acquisitions was quite strong[39]. This reflects the link between stock options and increased risk-taking in acquisitions reported in several recent studies[40].

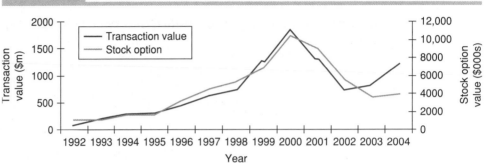

Figure 12.5 Average CEO stock option compensation and average acquisition size

Executive compensation and target board behaviour

The compensation and other payoffs, e.g. jobs after the takeover, are likely to influence the behaviour of target CEOs and other senior executives, as well as that of independent directors on the target company board. One major consideration for target CEOs and board members is the prospect of losing their jobs. This fear may stiffen the resistance of the target board. Of course, such resistance may be constrained by the board's fiduciary duties discussed above. Offering monetary payoffs as well as non-monetary incentives such as a suitable executive position in the merged entity or a place on the acquirer board may prove very persuasive in winning a favourable recommendation from the target. We review these arguments and the related literature in more detail in Chapter 21 on takeover defences.

Managerial ownership and acquisitions

In addition to compensation, equity ownership of CEOs and directors in their firms can align their interests with those of shareholders. It may therefore be expected that acquirers in which top managers hold a significant proportion of shares would perform better than those without such ownership. From their analysis of 363 takeovers in the UK during 1985–96, Cosh, Guest and Hughes report that 'acquirers whose CEOs own a larger proportion of equity . . . carry out acquisitions which perform significantly better in terms of both long run returns and operating performance and that these impacts are stronger at lower levels of board owner-ship reflecting diminishing returns to alignment at higher ownership levels'. These results are also similar to those observed for a sample of family-controlled Canadian firms in recent takeovers[41].

Acquisition decision-making process: governance structure impact

There are other aspects of corporate governance that are important to the acquisition process, and these need to be taken into account in designing an effective organizational process for acquisitions. First of all, the board of directors of the acquirer must be in tune with the cor-porate strategy of the firm and the role of acquisitions in that strategy. If there is any discord among the directors, or if the acquisition team (the A team) does not prepare a convincing case for an acquisition, it may be scuppered, with loss of face and authority for the manage-ment, generating a perception of drift within the firm. There may also be certain erosion of credibility with the external constituencies such as the stock market (see Exhibit 12.3).

Exhibit 12.3

Directors don't like to mix their Coke with breakfast cereal and Gatorade

Douglas Daft was appointed as CEO to restore the fortunes of Coca-Cola after the problems that a contamination scare had caused in Europe. In November 2000 the company was still undergoing substantial restructuring when Daft proposed a $15bn takeover of Quaker Oats (QO). The bid was based on the strategy of widening the range of non-alcoholic beverages Coca-Cola (CC) would be selling. QO had earlier rejected an all-share exchange offer from CC's inveterate rival Pepsi and faced a potential bid from a French dairy, water and biscuit company. There was thus the possibility of an auction for QO. It looked like CC was being bounced into the fray to pre-empt QO being acquired by its rivals.

The board of directors of CC were divided over the merits of the bid. One of them, the legendary Warren Buffet, hated auctions, which can lead to an exorbitant price being paid for the acquisition. The timing of the bid was regarded as inopportune, since CC was already caught up in a massive restructuring. The directors felt that CC shareholder value had a lot of potential on its own once the restructuring was completed. The board therefore did not approve of the bid.

The stock market reaction to the bid was very unfavourable, with analysts at Salomon Smith Barney downgrading the CC stock, which fell by about $5 to $57. Another analyst felt the timing was horrible. There were also worries that the deal would face antitrust obstacles because of the overlap between CC's own sports drink, Powerade, and QO's Gatorade.

When the directors declined to sanction the bid, questions arose about who was running CC – Daft or the board.

Sources: A. Edgecliffe-Johnson and P. T. Larsen, 'Coke board to decide if takeover plan is sweet enough', and B. Liu, 'Questions raised over Daft's control', *Financial Times*, 21 and 23 November 2000

What difference does the board make to acquisition performance?

The acquire board's fiduciary duties to the corporation and, in many countries, to the shareholders should, in theory, constrain self-interested or wayward behaviour of directors. Breach of these duties may expose directors to shareholder law suits and class action, e.g. in the US. When the post-acquisition performance of the company declines, the directors may be held to account. We review below the studies that show that bad acquisitions are more likely to lead to CEOs and directors losing their jobs. Target boards have even more onerous responsibilities, as discussed in Chapter 21.

Independent or subservient board?

As seen in Exhibit 12.3, acquisitions represent major and strategic decisions, and directors are likely to play an important role in shaping and executing them (see Chapter 3 on the various dimensions of corporate governance). In doing so, directors have a fiduciary duty to the corporation and its shareholders in the US, to the corporation in the UK, and to shareholders and other stakeholders in many continental European countries (see Chapter 18 on takeover regulation). It may therefore be expected that an independent and vigilant board will ensure that acquisitions made by their firms increase shareholder value. The extent of board independence from executive directors is an empirical issue, but there are reasons to believe that the 'good old boy network' is still alive and well in the US. In continental Europe interlocking shareholdings and directorships, i.e. directors adorning one another's boards, characterize the corporate governance system even more[42]. When Tyco, the aggressively acquisitive US conglomerate, collapsed amidst allegations of fraud by the CEO, Dennis Kozlowski, in 2002, the old board was quickly cleaned out and a new board was created.

A CEO derives his or her power from a variety of sources, including the legal position as the chief executive. Such *de facto* power relative to that of the board of directors depends on the CEO's past record of success, personality, whether the directors were chosen by him or her and therefore owe a debt of gratitude, and access to corporate information that may not be available to the directors. A deferential board will not be able to challenge and restrain an arrogant CEO. To the extent that the directors themselves bask in the reflected glory of a successful CEO, they may even share the same overconfidence and, far from restraining the CEO's overweening ambition, may aid and abet it. The board as a whole may exhibit overconfidence and overoptimism, leading to more risky acquisitions. In a study of the riskiness of acquisitions made by UK firms during 1993–2000, Sudarsanam and Gao find that there is a positive association between proxies for overconfidence, including high media praise received by the board, and high risk acquisitions[43].

Board monitoring of acquirers

Over the years, attempts have been made by regulators and law makers to enhance the oversight role of the board. For example, starting with the Cadbury Code of Corporate Governance in 1992, several subsequent committees have recommended further strengthening the board's independence of the CEO, culminating in the Code of Best Practice that is now part of the listing regulations of the London Stock Exchange. Several scandals involving CEOs of major US corporations such as Worldcom, Tyco, Adelphia, Enron and Imclone, who were indicted and imprisoned on charges of fraud or embezzlement of corporate funds, revealed the weaknesses in board monitoring and led to the enactment of the Sarbanes-Oxley (SOX) Act to make directors more accountable to their corporations rather than to the CEOs. Nevertheless, two stalwarts of the international corporate governance movement, Robert Monks and Professor Michael Jensen, consider that US corporate boards are still subservient, especially in comparison with the UK boards[44].

Continental Europe has a range of corporate governance structures. In the two-tier system obtaining in Germany, Austria, the Netherlands, Sweden and other countries the executive board is monitored by a supervisory board. In countries such as the Netherlands, managers are well entrenched behind some impregnable defences such as structured regimes and friendly shareholding trusts (see Chapter 21 on takeover defences for a more detailed discussion) and insulated from shareholder pressures to deliver value to shareholders from their acquisition decisions, although in recent years these defences have been breached by activist shareholders, or corporate governance reforms have eroded them (see Chapter 21 on defences against takeovers).

Byrd and Hickman empirically tested the view that an independent board would result in value-creating acquisitions[45]. They identified outside directors who were independent, for a sample of US bidders, during 1980–87. They found that bidding firms in which independent outside directors held at least 50% of the seats had significantly higher announcement date abnormal returns than other bidders. This evidence is consistent with effective board monitoring of tender offer decisions. Byrd and Hickman also reported that the relation between bidder returns and the proportion of independent directors is non-linear, with these returns falling at high levels of independent board membership. Thus there is an optimal level of independence of the board. For the UK, Sudarsanam and Mahate report that a higher proportion of non-executive directors significantly increases long-run shareholder gains to acquirers over three years, but duality, i.e. CEO and board chairman being the same person, reduces the gains[46]. Thus board independence has a beneficial impact on post-acquisition performance of acquirers.

Do directors respond to adverse market reaction to acquisitions?

We have seen substantial evidence that stock markets react, on average, negatively to takeover announcements. If this is a signal of the value-destroying nature of the proposed acquisition, acquirer directors can act to prevent it going through. Is the board's response a function of its independence? Donna Paul finds that highly independent boards are more likely to terminate bad takeover bids. Moreover, where bad bids are completed, independent boards are also more likely to induce more restructuring of the acquirer, e.g. downsizing. Thus board vigilance can prevent bad bids, or mitigate the value destruction from such bids, by inducing corrective post-acquisition actions[47].

Institutional monitoring and acquisitions

Independent long-term institutional investors (ILTI) with large ownership stakes also prevent such bad deals evoking negative stock market reaction from being completed. For every 1% negative reaction the odds of the bid being withdrawn increase by 0.55% compared with an unconditional withdrawal likelihood of only 16% in US deals. Concentrated holdings by the top five ILTI are associated with a 20% increase in three-year buy-and-hold abnormal returns and 5% higher post-acquisition ROA and 1% higher EPS forecast by analysts. These investors also reduce the chances of a potentially value-destroying deal being undertaken[48].

What happens to bad acquirers?

Do CEOs and their crony directors who make value-destroying acquisitions 'get away with it'? Empirical evidence from the US and UK shows that there is a time of reckoning, and the CEO and director turnover is high after bad acquisitions. Kenneth Lehn and Mengxin Zhao investigate the CEO turnover within five years after acquisitions and bids that are cancelled[49]. In firms where the CEO was replaced, the announcement period returns to the preceding acquisitions were highly negative and much lower than those for firms where the CEO was not replaced. Three-year post-acquisition buy-and-hold abnormal returns (see Chapter 4 for definition of BHARs) are also negatively related to turnover. CEOs who cancel value-reducing acquisitions are significantly less likely to be replaced than CEOs who proceed with similar acquisitions. These results indicate that internal governance, takeovers and the bankruptcy process discipline managers who make value-destroying acquisitions.

Sudarsanam and Mahate find, from an analysis of a large UK sample of acquisitions during 1982–95, that good post-acquisition shareholder value performance (measured by BHARs over three years) improves the chances of the CEOs, chairmen and directors retaining their jobs. They report that hostile acquirers create more value than friendly acquirers, and the board turnover is higher after value-destroying friendly takeovers. For example, the job retention rates (in %) for CEOs and chairmen in the three years after an acquisition are:

	In acquisition year	After year 1	Year 2	Year 3
Friendly	100	87	69	53
Hostile	100	94	78	61

Thus bad acquirers' top managers seem to be paying a price for undertaking poor acquisitions[50]. Such a fate befell the top executives of Alcatel when its acquisition of Lucent turned out to be poorly conceived/executed (see Exhibit 12.4).

Role of the board in reigning in managerial biases: deal champion vs devil's advocate

Given the behavioural biases of managers, and the pressures on them to pursue acquisitions, acquisition proposals may gain an irresistible momentum unless speed-breakers are built into the acquisition decision-making process. Such speed breakers will have an unenviable job to

---

Exhibit 12.4

Alcatel and Lucent telecoms don't fit. The engineer loses his job

In 2006 Alcatel, the French telecom equipment company, and its American rival Lucent merged to create Alcatel-Lucent, the world's largest provider of fixed-line telecoms equipment. But two years later the merger hadn't worked. Alcatel-Lucent dumped both its chairman and chief executive in a bid to cement a still-fragile merger after a series of profit warnings and market share decline. Chief Executive Pat Russo was to leave before the end of 2008, and Serge Tchuruk, the architect of the 2006 merger, would leave in October. The move came weeks after shareholders heaped criticism on top directors following a string of profit warnings and a collapsing share price, and approved measures that would make it easier to oust them.

'These departures are not a total surprise,' said Exane analyst Alexander Peterc. 'It is a good thing that the company can now move forward and put behind it the differences between the Lucent parts and Alcatel side,' he added.

Henry Schacht, a former Lucent chief executive until Russo took his job in 2002, would immediately resign from the board. Alcatel-Lucent said both Tchuruk and Russo had themselves decided to resign, and it was also initiating a process to change the composition of the board to a smaller group that would include new members. For Tchuruk, who climbed the corporate ladder to become head of oil group Total before joining Alcatel in 1996, and engineered a restructuring of the sprawling Alcatel empire into the core telecoms activities, the merger with Lucent was meant to crown his career as it pulled the equipment firm back to the front line of global competition with Nortel, Nokia Siemens Networks and Ericsson.

Tchuruk said, 'It is now time that the company acquires a personality of its own, independent from its two predecessors'.

Source: Downloaded and adapted from www.infotech.indiatimes.com on 29 July 2008

do – pouring a bucket of cold ice on the heat, passion and often excitement among top executives that the prospect of an acquisition may create. Nevertheless, they are required, to ensure that acquisition strategies and specific acquisition proposals pass the enhanced scrutiny imposed by the speed-breakers. Directors can institutionalize a devil's advocate whose function is make a serious case as to why the deal should not be done, or suggest constructively how a deal might be improved. This may be the job of independent directors, or some other mechanism that is answerable to them. Where members of the board play the devil's advocate, this should not be seen by the outside world as a divided board at war with itself, but as part of a robust acquisition decision-making process.

Shareholder activism and corporate acquisitions

In our review in Chapter 3 of the multiple perspectives on M & A, we briefly discussed the impact of corporate governance on the acquisition process. In recent years institutional shareholders and other investors have resorted to active initiatives to force the investee companies to take shareholder concerns into account and modify their investment, financing, dividend and strategic plans, including acquisitions and divestitures. Shareholder activism covers a range of approaches to shareholder monitoring and pressuring of managements and boards. In the US activism was pioneered by many public sector pension funds, such as CalPERS. The activist approaches include a discreet dialogue with the target firms' directors, 'naming and shaming', voting against the resolutions put forward by the management, and proxy fights. A new band of activists joined the fray a few years ago. These are the hedge funds, which often take a short-term position in companies that are underperforming, and whose performance may be improved by changes to the board, for example to increase it independence, or CEO turnover – the CEO may have led the firm badly, or have been responsible for value-destroying decisions. They have also launched campaigns to put firms in play, stop a firm entering into deals with friendly acquirers, or to stop a firm making an acquisition.

Activism by hedge funds differs from that of the traditional funds such as mutual funds and pension funds, in terms of their investment horizon and the short-term focus of their campaigns. They also differ in terms of campaign style, which is more aggressive and confrontational, and in forcing issues into the public domain. Even though hedge funds may have only a small stake in the target companies, their vigorous campaigns often generate enough bad publicity for the target companies that their managements are forced to respond. There have been several high-profile cases where activist shareholders have succeeded in forcing out CEOs, for example in Bob Bordelli Home Depot over his excessive compensation contracts, in forcing ABN-AMRO to consider the rival bid from the RBS-led consortium of banks and insurers in 2007, and in forcing Deutsche Boerse to abandon its hostile bid for the London Stock Exchange in 2005.

Activists often intervene in a merger to oppose the sale completely or on the terms accepted by the vendor (target) management, or to oppose the purchase completely or on the terms proposed by the bidder. Since there is *prima facie* suspicion on the sell side that the agreed price is too low, and on the buy side that it is too high, the aim of the activist is to alter the price in its favour. Where the activist is opposed to the deal itself, for example what is perceived as a strategically inappropriate bid, then the aim is to make the management abandon the deal altogether.

In a study of 25 proposed mergers in the US that attracted hedge fund intervention, Brattton finds that such interventions are quite effective. Only five were closed on the original terms. Seven closed after price concessions and 13 did not proceed at all to completion. He also notes that out of the 10 buy-side deals eight were terminated. One was completed, but the activist gained a board seat. Only one was completed without change of terms. On the sell side the outcomes were more diverse. Only five were terminated without a higher price on the table. Thus, although this sample is small, it suggests that bidders face greater pressures to abandon the deals than target managements, who are only forced to sell at much better prices[51]. The case study at the end of this chapter describes how hedge funds with small stakes started a revolt against Deutsche Boerse's management and supervisory board over the hostile takeover bid for the London Stock Exchange and forced its abandonment.

Overview of the impact of corporate governance

Acquisition teams must pay careful attention to ensure that the acquisition programmes are consistent with the expectations of the board of directors. The composition of the board has a significant influence on the quality of the acquisition decision, and on the shareholder value outcome of the acquisition. Similarly, the board of the target of a bid also has an important influence on the bid outcome. The bidder must very carefully consider the board character-istics of the target, and craft a bid strategy to minimize any resistance from that board and to enhance the chances of bid success.

Our five-stage model of the M & A process envisages that the risk of value destruction from acquisition can arise in stages other than deal-making and negotiation. This suggests that the risk is substantially organizational in origin, and management of that risk therefore depends on organizational structures and their strengths. A good acquisition function is part of an effective organization for acquisitions.

Managing acquisition decision-making

In some companies the M & A decision process may be separately established from the normal corporate planning function. The need for a separate acquisition function depends on the expected level of acquisition activity, the complexity and variety of the anticipated acqui-sitions, and the prior acquisition experience of managers sponsoring or implementing acqui-sitions. The acquisition function, if separate, is likely to be located at the corporate level. At the business unit level individual acquisitions have to be handled by the business unit managers, but subject to approval and monitoring by the corporate-level senior managers. Even in firms where a separate acquisition function is deemed unnecessary because of the current or expected low-level of takeover activity, many of the principles and characteristics of the acqui-sition function described below are still relevant to managing the acquisition decision process well.

The M & A function: what it is and how it is organized

In many companies the corporate-level acquisition function is a dedicated function, for example a corporate M & A group. The acquisition function performs several roles. Essentially it acts not as a supreme authority on acquisition decisions, but as a conduit and catalyst for promoting acquisitions as a means of achieving the firm's broad corporate and business strat-egy objectives.

The M & A group (for convenience called the Acquisition or A team) serves as a focal point and as a clearing house for ideas emanating from within and outside the firm. Over time it becomes a repository of learning, experience and distilled wisdom in acquisition-related matters and skills in identifying acquisition opportunities, evaluating them and negotiating deals. Finally, the group team serves as an internal consultant to acquisition task forces concerned with specific acquisitions. The acquisition team must be composed of managers with the required experience and authority, so that the team commands the respect of the operational managers and the board of directors to whom it will make its recommendation. The team must also be accessible to managers in its role as a diffuser of acquisition learning and knowledge.

Marrying the business model and acquisitions

The most important function of the A team is to evolve an acquisition programme and develop the organizational capability to carry out the broader business/corporate strategy of the firm. It must have a deep understanding of the firm's business model and the sources of its current and future competitive strengths. It must also have knowledge of the mismatch between the firm's need for, and lack of, resources and capabilities for achieving its competitive strategic goals. The A team evaluates the place of M & A in the broader corporate and business strategies of the firm, as well as making a balanced evaluation of M & A and the alternative modes of market entry and growth, such as organic growth, joint ventures and strategic alliances. It needs to assess the comparative riskiness of these alternative modes of implementing the firm's business model. Acquisition programmes must be evaluated within a balanced scorecard framework and their contribution towards converting the firm's vision and strategy into operating results. The acquisition function can also proactively identify potential growth opportunities for the firm through M & A.

Creating the acquisition capability

The A team can enhance the firm's acquisition making capability by:

- evaluating the acquisition justification, the blueprint for acquisition-led strategies from the shareholder and long-term competitive advantage perspectives;
- coordinating the various functions within the firm involved in the broad acquisition programme;
- developing the internal acquisition deal-making, post-acquisition integration and acquisition-related training capabilities;
- developing the necessary database on past acquisitions, their weaknesses and strengths, successes and failures, and communicating the lessons from the past for future acquisitions to the rest of the organization;
- developing the capability to evaluate and manage risks in M & A transactions;
- evaluating the need for and choice of external advisers such as investment bankers, accountants, lawyers, strategy consultants or environmental consultants; and
- coordinating the efforts of internal acquisition team and the external advisers on a continual basis as part of the acquisition programme.

The accumulation of acquisition-related expertise and skills within the corporate acquisition function is itself a distinctive capability, which can confer a competitive advantage in the market for corporate control[52]. By increasing the credibility of the acquisitions that the firm makes, its acquisition function can ensure that overpayment to targets is avoided and the chances of a successful integration are improved. This requires that the acquisition function be backed up by robust systems and processes capable of learning from the past and applying this learning effectively to the current acquisition project (see Chapter 23 on organizational learning in the context of M & A). It must also be adequately resourced.

Managing the acquisition decision process

As described above, the acquisition decision process in organizations is far from a model of perfect rationality. The waywardness and excesses of the process can, however, be curbed by a robust acquisition function. It can ensure that expected benefits of the acquisition are not inflated by the optimism of the sponsoring manager or CEO, and that the cost of capital for the proposed acquisition adequately covers the risk. With its holistic perspective on acquisitions the function can unify the fragmented perspectives of managers at different hierarchical levels, and across different functions and divisions. Thus managers can be made to 'sing from the same hymn book'. A key to this is the ability of the A team to articulate the rationale and motivations for an acquisition programme or a proposed acquisition.

While ambiguity of expectations can be tactically exploited by the champions of an acquisition programme, it will spell disaster in the post-acquisition period. For example, a merger that is touted as a friendly merger or a merger of equals, or one that will not lead to substantial job losses, may in fact turn out otherwise, not by an unfortunate turn of events but by devious design. The A team can ensure that assumptions beneath the value creation model are explicitly articulated and evaluated for realism and feasibility of accomplishment.

As noted above, M & A deals can generate a lot of euphoric excitement among managers conceiving them and those who promote them. Both within the firm and externally in dealings with the acquisition targets and merger partners these deals may trigger a flash flood of adrenalin that carries everything in its path. Querulous voices are swamped by this flood, or attributed to timorous souls without imagination or capacity to grasp the grand vision. The A team can stem the flash floods and restore a calmer flow of ideas.

In many cases the acquisition champions may argue very eloquently why a deal should be done on strategic grounds, even though the value 'numbers don't add up'. These arguments may often rest on speculative real-option-type acquisitions. When these options are taken into account, the acquisition becomes seductively attractive. In such situations the A team must play the devil's advocate role with even greater vigour. If the numbers do not add up, the most disciplined thing is to walk away[53]. This discipline in screening speculative acquisitions is not to kill them but to ensure that the underlying strategic and value creation scenarios are well articulated and subjected to rigorous scrutiny.

Other issues concerned with a specific acquisition the A team can assess include:

- the timescale for the enhancement of business processes and organizational learning, so that a realistic post-merger integration programme can be designed;
- whether the acquirer and target firms have the organizational structures, systems, communication capabilities and cultural framework for organizational learning where it drives the value creation logic of the acquisition; and
- whether the proposed acquisition passes the test of shareholder value criterion.

Assessing and managing risks

An important part of the A team's job is to assess the risk associated with the acquisition programme as a whole, and with a specific acquisition. This can be carried out by simulating alternative scenarios for the outcome of the proposed acquisition. It must incorporate the results of any due diligence of the target into the valuation and risk appraisal models. Although due diligence is often specific to a given acquisition, the A team can develop generalized strategies for managing the outcome of due diligence and mitigating the risks that due diligence is likely to reveal. Risk assessment includes incorporating the costs of externalities such as environmental costs, potential litigation and shareholder class action.

Managing the deal-making

The A team has overall responsibility for managing the deal-making stage. This stage is discussed in detail in Part Three of this book, including bid strategies and tactics:

- choice of external advisers;
- crafting bid strategies and tactics;
- planning and making the approach to selected targets;
- assessing the target response;
- determining the bid premium range;
- scanning the radar for potential 'showstoppers';
- developing strategies and tactics to eliminate risk to deal completion;
- defining the lines of attack if the bid becomes hostile;
- day-to-day conduct of the bid; and
- communication with the media, important shareholders and regulatory authorities.

Building the negotiating team

The A team should also have excellent negotiating skills and experience. The foremost aim of deal-making is to reach a win–win deal that leaves both parties satisfied. This requires a fine understanding of the psychological motivations of the various players in the acquisition game, and the ability to exploit them so as to reach a deal. Both fear and greed play a part in motivating the two managements to arrive at a settlement. The negotiating team (N team) is often put together by acquirers for specific deals, with the responsibility for team-building resting with a lead function such as corporate development. See Chapter 20 for further discussion.

Survey evidence on the M & A function

In a 2004 survey of US and European (including UK) companies, KPMG finds that M & A departments[54]:

- are in 95% of cases centralized multidisciplinary teams of three to eight personnel, with large firms (>$5bn revenue) having larger groups;
- report to the CEO or CFO;
- cover a range of transactions, including M & A, strategic alliances and joint ventures;
- contribute about 50% to pricing and valuation, negotiating terms and conditions, deal execution and management of the deal process (other groups contributing are from the central office and operating units);
- get involved in integration in only 22% of cases;
- generate 80% of new deal opportunities; and
- share resources with other functions such as legal services, finance, human resources, business units, investor relations, and health and safety.

On average about 48 deals are initially sourced; 20 survive the initial screening and nine due diligence, and five are completed, giving a hit rate of 10%. Sourced deals have to pass hurdles along the way to completion, with 52%, 70% and 79% passing each stage conditional on passing the previous stage. Each stage takes about five to eight weeks. The M & A group is also involved in making financial forecasts and valuation in nearly half the cases.

The M &A department has a high level of responsibility (between 53% and 76% of cases) in tracking expected synergies, reviewing deal assumptions, tracking integration costs, follow-up assessments and holding sessions for lessons learned and best practice.

Survey evidence on the acquisition process

There is little direct evidence in support of the organizational process perspective developed by Haspeslagh and Jemison[55], but a survey by Hunt *et al.* provides some useful indirect evidence[56]. As regards the acquisition-planning stage, we find the following characteristics:

- Acquisition targeting is haphazard.
- The acquisition motive is often emotional rather than cold, clinical and rational. The chairman or chief executive's whims and prejudices often dictate the need for and the pace of acquisition, as well as the choice of target. In some cases machismo and hubris provide the motive force.
- Acquisitions are often opportunistic – an 'it was there and we grabbed it' approach.
- The decision to pursue a target is by no means neat and tidy.

Exhibit 12.5 provides a recent example of the dangers of such opportunism in deal-making, and the price that companies and their shareholders have to pay for it.

Exhibit 12.5

Fortis breaks ABN AMRO and then goes broke

In 2008, three European governments agreed a €11.2bn ($16.3bn) bail-out of Fortis, the Belgian-Dutch bank-cum-insurance group. The immediate crisis was sparked by turmoil in the credit markets. But the roots of the Belgo-Dutch group's troubles could be traced directly to its decision, in spring 2007, to participate in the break-up bid led by Royal Bank of Scotland for ABN AMRO, its larger Dutch rival. Fortis was then a medium-sized European banking and insurance group in a rapidly consolidating industry. By participating in the ABN AMRO deal it hoped to transform itself into one of the largest financial institutions in northern Europe. For Maurice Lippens, Fortis's mercurial chairman, and Jean-Paul Votron, its hyperactive chief executive, the opportunity to take control of ABN AMRO was just too tempting to pass up. The idea of a largely Belgian institution taking charge of the bank of the Dutch establishment also carried enormous symbolism, as the Belgians were still the butt of many Dutch jokes. However, a year later, Fortis's dream of dominating banking and insurance in Belgium, the Netherlands and Luxembourg – and of participating on equal terms in the future consolidation of Europe's financial services industry – lay in tatters. In a desperate effort to shore up confidence among savers and shareholders, it was forced to accept a partial nationalization whereby the Benelux governments each bought 49% of Fortis's banking subsidiaries in their countries in return for an €11.2bn capital injection. Fortis's stake in ABN Amro will be sold, and the rest of the group seems likely to be dismembered as banks and insurers pick off its best businesses. Mr Lippens resigned, and Mr Votron went in July. The bank, advised by Morgan Stanley, explored the possibility of selling itself to either BNP Paribas of France or ING of the Netherlands. However, no bidder was willing to take on Fortis without some form of government insurance against future losses on the bank's €42bn portfolio of mortgage-backed securities. Bankers were also concerned that shareholders might threaten to veto a takeover deal, adding to

the uncertainty among savers. BNP offered to pay about €1.60 per Fortis share
– well below Friday's €5.20 closing price – and demanded protection from up
to €6bn of future losses. ING, meanwhile, was mainly interested in acquiring
Fortis's stake in ABN AMRO. In the end the governments concluded that a direct
capital injection into Fortis was more sensible. Such a move would prevent the
bank from being forced to sell assets at fire sale prices. It also removed any
uncertainty that Fortis would receive the cash, thereby reassuring savers. The
Fortis crisis is a disaster for the bank's shareholders, who have pumped more
than €14bn in fresh capital into the group over the past 12 months, but who were
holding shares in an institution with a market capitalization of just €12bn. Fortis's
quest for growth did not begin with the ABN AMRO deal. For much of the previous decade the group had been looking to grow and escape its crowded and
low-growth domestic market. The product of an early attempt at cross-border
consolidation between a Dutch banking and insurance group and a Belgian
insurer, it had long been known as a dysfunctional institution. Mr Votron, a
former Citigroup executive who took charge in 2004, promised to change all
that, setting targets to expand outside the Low Countries. But when ABN AMRO
came into view, Fortis executives could not resist the temptation. How they must
now be wishing they had!

Source: Adapted from P. Larsen, 'Fortis's woes lie with ABN Amro break-up', *Financial*
Times, 29 September 2008

The deal negotiation phase bears the imprint of escalating momentum and expectational
ambiguity. Clinching a deal is not a hard-nosed, rational economic process, but one where
non-financial factors also play a role. In some deals the two negotiators develop trust, and
believe they could do business with each other. Thus intuition and judgement play a part.

Negotiating teams are generally small (average size of under three persons), including the
chairman, the finance director and the managing director of the subsidiary relevant to the
acquisition. Bidders, especially the less experienced ones, rely much on their advisers, who
have different incentives to close the deal. Sometimes the bidder is hustled into closing a deal
by the investment bank adviser.

Tight secrecy in planning and negotiating is considered necessary to prevent either rivals
or the staff of the target finding out about the deal. This secrecy may be one of the reasons for
the due diligence audit being somewhat superficial. Even in friendly bids (they made up 80%
of the sample), pre-acquisition audit neglects detailed human resources aspects. Financial/
legal audit is done in 98% of the acquisitions or more, and engineering/production audit in
40% of the cases.

Management or personnel audit is done in only 37% of the buys. Even in those cases the
audit is less concerned about the target's human resource capabilities than about remuneration, pension rights, etc.: in other words, the pecuniary aspects. The rather limited nature of
the audit results in some nasty surprises after the acquisition, even in some friendly deals.
Some 35% of the acquirers find dishonest presentation, lax or no management controls and
poor management calibre in target companies.

Many acquirer negotiating teams realize that they should engage in credible and honest
dialogue, give only those assurances they could deliver after the acquisition, and communicate
without ambiguity the benefits to either side from the acquisition. Thus they try to minimize
expectational ambiguity.

Deutsche Boerse CEO and Chairman pay with their jobs for lesson on shareholder activism!

In 2005, Deutsche Boerse AG (DB), that owned the German stock exchange in Frankfurt, made a hostile bid for the London Stock Exchange. The bid was not welcomed by many of the institutional shareholders of DB. After a protracted revolt mounted by activist hedge funds and supported by traditional investment funds, DB abandoned the bid but soon thereafter both Werner Seifert, the chairman of DB's management board (the CEO) and Rolf Breuer, Chairman of DB's supervisory board, resigned their positions.

The bid for LSE

On 13th December 2004, the Werner Seifert, DB's CEO announced that it was seeking to acquire the London Stock Exchange (LSE) and made a bid at 530 pence a share in cash for the latter. The bid valued the LSE at £1.3bn, at a 23% premium to the closing price of LSE shares two days earlier. However, the LSE management responded that the bid under-valued the company and rejected it immediately. LSE maintained its hostility to the bid in subsequent months.

Strategic logic of the bid

The LSE, the UK's national stock exchange and DB, the German national stock exchange were at the time of the bid amongst the largest stock exchanges in the world. At the end of 2003, only the New York Stock Exchange, Tokyo Stock Exchange and NASDAQ in the US were larger in terms of the value of the equity stocks listed than the European rivals. The LSE was the larger of the two exchanges when measured by either equity listing volumes or value of equities traded (£2.2bn vs DB's 0.7bn). However, it was the smaller of the two exchanges, in terms of its market capitalization (£1.1bn vs DB's £2.93bn) and turnover (£226m vs £836m). It was much less profitable (profit after tax of £53m vs £145m).

The LSE had benefited from a buoyant market in secondary listings for oversees companies looking to raise finance from European investors. Thus LSE was a magnet for overseas companies thereby increasing its revenue from the trading in these overseas companies' stocks.

Consolidation was seen by DB as inevitable and a combined exchange would be in pole position to attract future partners, such as OMX Nordic Exchange, the Scandinavian stock exchange group or national exchanges. There was also the potential threat of a takeover by one of the American exchanges as they sought to gain access to the European market.

Value creation logic

The strategic drivers were expected to convert into financial drivers and create value. DB looked to derive significant synergies from a unified IT infrastructure, from head office cost efficiencies and from revenue increases as a result of larger trading volumes across a more diversified set of trading platforms. DB planned to improve revenue streams by cross selling products to participants on each exchange. Merger would also help reduce the development cost of new IT systems. Trading platforms were associated with a high fixed cost of development and a reduction in the number of trading platforms would not only reduce the aggregate development cost but also spread it over a much larger number of terminals. This would help reduce trading costs for participants further, whilst also reducing the enlarged entity's own cost base. Finally, DB saw LSE as the key European player in the fight to attract liquidity from other European and international exchanges. The forecast merger synergies were: cost savings (€75m) and revenue enhancement (€25m) per annum to be realised by 2008.

Market reaction to the DB bid

Analysts' opinion in general was that the acquisition would destroy value for DB shareholders as the 530p offer price was too high. Analysts favoured a share buyback as a better alternative strategy to enhance shareholder value for DB shareholders. However, given the stakeholder perspective under which German companies operated, shareholder value maximization was not the primary objective for a German company. Deutsche Bank analysts were exceptional in arguing that the bid would create substantial value for all parties involved but it was known that the bank was one of DB's bankers and Rolf Breuer had been the CEO and chairman of the bank.

Shareholder revolt

The initial offer proposal was made to the LSE on 13th December 2004. On 16th January 2005, a small hedge fund based in London, The Children's Investment Fund Management (TCI), called on the DB management to drop the acquisition plans and consider alternative ways to generate value for shareholders. Over the coming weeks, Atticus Capital, Fidelity Investments and Merrill Lynch, amongst others, joined TCI in voicing their disapproval of the offer.

Since the IPO of DB on the Frankfurt exchange in 2001, the composition of DB's shareholders had changed dramatically, as shown in Tables 1 and 2.

Table 1 Ownership (%) of DB by region of investor origin at year end

Investor origin	2006	2005	2004	2003	2002	2001	2000
Germany	16	10	35	41	47	68	100
United Kingdom	29	42	24	24	23	12	0
United States	48	27	26	26	22	12	0
Other countries	7	21	15	9	8	8	0

Table 2 Ownership (%) of DB by type of shareholders at year end

Investor type	2006	2005	2004	2003	2002	2001	2000
Private investors	2	3	4	4	2	2	0
Institutional investors	98	97	93	93	76	47	0
Strategic investors	0	0	3	3	22	51	100

Tables 1 and 2 show the changing ownership structure of DB following the reform of German financial markets and tax rules allowing for divestment of large holdings by German banks and companies. In 2000, all of the equity in DB was held by German strategic investors, mainly wealthy German families, banks or corporations. However, demutualization of the exchange through DB's IPO in 2001, and the gradual shift to UK and US

→

institutional investors, brought with it different types of owner. In October 2002, Deutsche Bank sold its 9.3% stake to institutional investors, removing the blocking power of long term German strategic investors. The major institutional shareholders in DB (as at 1st March 2005) were: five hedge funds (owning 16%) of the DB shares, five traditional mutual funds (15.5%), one investment bank (2%), and three banks (4.2%). Among these were one German mutual fund and one bank (6%).

Why did they revolt?

The shareholder revolt at DB initially occurred because of the perception that the offer for the London Stock Exchange would be value destructive. However, it subsequently encompassed dissatisfaction over governance at DB, the lack of timely and effective communication between the company and its shareholders, and the seeming indifference of DB's top management to shareholder concerns.

TCI felt that the offer price was too high and gave away too much of the synergy benefits to the shareholders of LSE. The proposed acquisition was therefore not the best strategy to unlock value for shareholders and a share buyback would be the more appropriate route. TCI's manager Christopher Hohn said 'repurchase of the company's own shares by Deutsche Boerse would be far superior in value creation.'

Corporate governance

The persistent refusal of the DB executive board to put the takeover bid to a shareholder vote inevitably switched the activists' focus from the takeover bid to the wider issue of corporate governance. Atticus Capital fund manager David Slager said that 'The acquisition appears to us to be motivated by empire building. If they were purely motivated by shareholder interests, they would put the acquisition to a vote.' Harris Associates told the *Financial Times* in March 2005 that in its opinion, shareholders should have the right to vote on major acquisitions. This view was also shared by the mutual funds that joined the hedge funds in calling for the removal of the CEO and supervisory board members at an extraordinary general meeting.

TCI complained that the supervisory board of DB was unrepresentative of the investors of the company (see tables above). Many of the members of the board were selected from other German companies or shareholders of DB. In December 2004 the number of shareholder representatives who were German was 16 compared to five non-Germans. Both Fidelity Investments and Merrill Lynch argued that the supervisory board was in place to ensure that the management was acting in the best interests of shareholders. However, by allowing the CEO to continue with his proposal, and even back his plans to continue with a hostile takeover if the LSE continued to reject its 530p offer price, the supervisory board was failing in its duty to shareholders.

Corporate governance in DB

As a German enterprise, the corporate governance system of DB follows the dual board structure mandated by German law. As a publicly listed company with over 500 employees, codetermination regulations decreed that a third of DB's board must be representatives of the employees of the company. In contrast, the LSE governance system followed the

Anglo-American model of a unitary board with independent directors to represent shareholder interests. DB's supervisory board characteristics did not match the change in shareholder nationality, with most shareholder representatives still emanating from the boards of major German banks such as Deutsche Bank. This, the activists alleged, possibly made the management board complacent as they felt well protected by a friendly supervisory board.

Communication with shareholders

The activists were dismayed by DB management's indifference towards their concerns. They were also perplexed that the DB board was oblivious of their threat to block the takeover bid and to the positions of the SB and MB members themselves. It was not until a couple of days before the offer was rescinded by DB, in April 2005, that Rolf Breuer, Chairman of SB, attempted to open discussions with investors to allay their concerns and reassure them that the takeover of the LSE would enhance the long term value of Deutsche Boerse. However, by this time the ill feeling felt by the activists was running far too deep. They had already started to call for a complete overhaul of the board. A number of the activist investors involved had even commenced nomination of potential new directors for restructured management and supervisory boards. The Chairman of the supervisory board was ultimately responsible for meeting with shareholders and entering into dialogue with them. But it was the CEO Werner Seifert that undertook this responsibility. This was catastrophic for the management of the Boerse, as he was the champion of the takeover strategy. The high acquisition price was merely the catalyst for activist pressure to be directed at DB. Ultimately it was poor governance, inadequate communication and arrogant insensitivity to shareholder concerns that caused the investors to escalate their insurrection.

On 20th February 2005, the ten largest shareholders in DB announced that they planned to force the resignation of the CEO, Werner Seifert, over his refusal to listen to shareholders' concerns. Three days later, DB announced positive annual results but in the process confirmed its intention to continue with the acquisition despite growing unrest amongst its shareholders. As a result, Fidelity Investments called for an extraordinary general meeting in which the activists planned to remove not only the CEO, but also the Chairman of the supervisory board, and replace the remaining members. Lord Rothschild, Chairman of Rothschilds Investment Bank, was selected by TCI as the candidate to replace DB's chairman Rolf Breuer should they succeed in ousting him from the company.

On 1st March 2005, DB obtained an injunction through the German courts that would prevent dissident shareholders from completely scuppering its plans to buy the LSE. At the same time, its CEO called for shareholders to engage in peace talks with the Chairman in an attempt to find a way out of the problem that had arisen. This was rejected out-of-hand by Fidelity Investments. On 7th March 2005, DB announced it was withdrawing its offer for LSE due to the fierce unrest amongst the majority of its shareholders. The collapse of the bid did not appease the activists. They continued to call for the resignation of the CEO, and on 27th April 2005, Lord Levene resigned from his position on the supervisory board after the CEO refused to bow to the activists' demands.

On 9th May 2005, the CEO Werner Seifert announced that he was resigning with immediate effect. At the same time, Chairman Rolf Breuer announced that he would stand down at the end of the year. DB announced that the resignations were accepted in order to soothe the shareholder unrest and to benefit the long term future of the company.

It is remarkable enough that the activists were led by such a small investor as TCI. But it is even more impressive given that the governance regime in Germany very much protects the boards of companies in issues such as takeovers. The effectiveness of the shareholder revolt was a surprise for many commentators as shareholders traditionally had little impact on strategic decisions of this kind in German companies. 'It definitely came as a surprise that the critical shareholders so clearly prevailed,' says Herbert Bayer, a member of the German exchange's supervisory board. Ultimately, Seifert and Breuer paid the price for their own mistakes and behaviour bordering on hubris.

Discussion questions

1 What is the strategic logic of the DB bid for LSE?

2 What is the value creation logic?

3 What were the grounds on which the institutional shareholders of DB opposed the deal and what alternative did they suggest for value creation?

4 Comment on the attitude and behaviour of the CEO and the supervisory board of DB.

5 How could the fiasco of a failed bid have been averted by DB management?

6 What are the lessons for acquirer managers and directors from this case?

Source: S. Sudarsanam and T Broadhurst, 'Corporate Governance Convergence in Germany Through Shareholder Activism: Impact of the Deutsche Boerse bid for London Stock Exchange', Cranfield School of Management working paper (available from the author). For the sources of the quotes in the case see the working paper.

Overview and implications for practice

This chapter provides an organizational perspective on the process of acquisition decision-making in acquiring companies.

● This process is not always a clinical, rational process, and it is subject to many political currents prevailing in an organization. The personal motivations of decision-makers also influence the nature and quality of acquisition decisions.

● A number of factors impart a momentum to acquisition decision and deal-making that individual players may find difficult to control. Companies and key decision-makers need to be conscious of these pressures and pulls, and not allow them to overwhelm the logic of the deal. Otherwise the deal will turn out to be a suboptimal one and lead to value destruction.

● The psychological perspective provides an insight into managerial biases such as hubris, overconfidence and optimism, which may cause CEOs and directors to undertake value-destroying acquisitions. It is the role of the board of directors to set up 'devil's advocate' mechanisms to insure against overoptimistic proposals for acquisitions.

● Executive compensation arrangements may provide perverse incentives for making acquisitions even if they will not create value. Such incentives need to be monitored and guarded against.

- This emphasizes the importance of establishing an acquisition function, or the A team. The A team has responsibility for a range of activities that arise when a firm employs acquisitions as a means of achieving its corporate strategy aims.

- The A team has a role in developing acquisition programmes to deliver the strategic goals, in proactively looking for acquisition opportunities, in providing internal consulting expertise to divisions, in coordinating the acquisition-related activities, and in developing the necessary capabilities and resources for an acquisition function that confers a competitive advantage.

- The A team can regulate the acquisition decision process to minimize the impact of the dysfunctional attributes of that process identified earlier.

- The A team has to play the devil's advocate from time to time so that over-optimistic acquisition proposals are not accepted.

- Corporate governance structures such as an independent board have an important influence on the acquisition process, target selection, bid outcome and shareholder value. Corporate governance at both the acquiring and potential target firms needs to be considered carefully in developing acquisition programmes and specific acquisition plans.

- Once the decision has been made, the bidder has to carry out deal structuring and negotiation in a way that minimizes risks not only to deal consummation but also to the achievement of the strategic and value creation objectives.

- The deal negotiation teams must be carefully put together with the necessary resources and capabilities to accomplish these objectives.

- The A team must develop the capability for risk evaluation of acquisition programmes.

- In the various chapters in Part Three we discuss the various aspects of deal structuring and negotiation.

Review questions

12.1 What are the differences between the rationalist view and organizational view of the acquisition process?

12.2 Why is it important to understand the organizational processes in the acquisition decision context?

12.3 What insights does a psychological perspective on managerial biases provide? In what ways can a firm mitigate these biases?

12.4 What is the link between executive compensation and acquisitions decision-making?

12.5 What are the roles of the acquisition team?

12.6 How does a well-organized acquisition function cope with the problems in the organizational process of acquisition decision making?

12.7 What is the relevance of corporate governance to the acquisition process?

12.8 What is a win–win strategy? What other strategies can the bidder adopt?

12.9 If you were considering making an acquisition, how would you draw up the ideal target profile?

12.10 Should negotiation cover post-acquisition issues? Why?

12.11 What is the importance of building up negotiation skills and resources?

Further reading

M. Hayward, V. Rindova and T. Pollock, 'Believing one's own press: The causes and consequences of CEO celebrity', *Strategic Management Journal*, **25**, 2004, 637–653.

D. Jemison and S. B. Sitkin, 'Acquisition: The process can be a problem', *Harvard Business Review*, **64**, March/April, 1986, 107–116.

U. Malmendier and G. Tate, 'Who makes acquisitions? CEO overconfidence and the market's reaction', *Journal of Financial Economics*, **89**, 2008, 20–43.

D. Paul, 'Board composition and corrective action: Evidence from corporate responses to bad acquisition bids', *Journal of Financial and Quantitative Analysis*, **42**(3), 2007, 759–784.

P. Rosenzweig, *The Halo Effect and the Eight Other Business Delusions that Deceive Managers* (New York: Free Press, 2007).

S. Sudarsanam and A. Mahate, 'Are friendly acquisitions too bad for shareholders and managers? Long term value creation and top management turnover in hostile and friendly acquirers', *British Journal of Management*, **17**, 2006, S7–S30.

Notes and references

1. P. Haspeslagh and D. Jemison, *Managing Acquisitions: Creating Value through Corporate Renewal* (New York: Free Press, 1991), Chapter 1. See also D. Jemison and S. B. Sitkin, 'Acquisition: The process can be a problem', *Harvard Business Review*, **64**, March/April 1986, 107–116.
2. This may reflect the managers' availability bias (defined and discussed further below).
3. Such excitement and thrill may cloud the managers' judgement and value destruction may attend upon acquisitions undertaken in those circumstances. Managers may also knowingly undertake value-destroying acquisitions in order to get high on such excitement and thrill. Such a behaviour is an agency cost to the shareholders. I wish to thank Professor Hersh Shefrin of Santa Clara University in California for suggesting this perspective and for other comments on this chapter.
4. Seat of the pants deal-making suggests managers rely on their gut feeling, instincts and intuition. This is a manifestation of the 'affect heuristic'. See below for further discussion of heuristics and biases and H. Shefrin, *Behavioral Corporate Finance*, (New York: McGraw-Hill, 2007).
5. See R. Roll, 'The hubris hypothesis of corporate takeovers', *Journal of Business*, **12**, 1986, 371–386 on hubris, J. March and Z. Shapira, 'Managerial perspective on risk and risk taking', *Management Science*, **33**, 1987, 1404–1418 on overconfidence and J. Heaton, 'Managerial optimism and corporate finance', *Financial Management*, **31**, 2002, 33–45 and U. Malmendier and G. Tate, 'CEO overconfidence and corporate investment', *Journal of Finance*, **60**, 2005, 2661–2700 on overoptimism biases among top managers.
6. See R. Khurana, *Searching for a Corporate Saviour: The Irrational Quest for Charismatic CEOs* (Princeton, NJ: Princeton University Press, 2002). Khurana describes the process of CEO selection, and how this places a premium on the candidates' charisma.
7. See P. Rosenzweig, *The Halo Effect and the Eight Other Business Delusions that Deceive Managers* (New York: Free Press, 2007), Chs 2 and 3. He pokes fun at the tendency of the media to 'overaccentuate' good performance and damn poor performance. The glorification of Percy Barnevik, CEO of the Swedish-Swiss power generation equipment company, in the 1990s and his damnation following his fall from grace illustrate this point. Rosenzweig cites two journalists from *Fortune*: 'Barnevik was never as good as the rave reviews he received in the 1990s, nor was he half as bad as the recent damning press coverage might suggest' (p. 49). It appears that the media are interested in the 'here and now' view of history rather than a long-term view that allows for cycles of good and bad performance. The lesson for CEOs is that they should heavily discount the 'here and now' view of themselves as portrayed by the media, and keep the wise counsel of cyclicality: 'what goes around, comes around'.
8. M. Hayward, V. Rindova and T. Pollock, 'Believing one's own press: The causes and consequences of CEO celebrity', *Strategic Management Journal*, **25**, 2004, 637–653 argue that media accounts of chief executive officers (CEOs), which confer celebrity, may lead them to attribute the glowing achievements to their disposition or volition, rather than to situational factors: i.e. they 'believe their own press'. The greater a CEO's celebrity, the more likely it is that the CEO will claim personal credit for the firm's performance, and the more likely it is that the firm's stakeholders will grant the CEO greater control over organizational activities and decision processes (p. 645). Media-conferred celebrity may accentuate CEOs behavioural

biases, making them more overconfident and more committed to the strategies that made them a celebrity. Sudarsanam and Gao find that the media profile of the board of directors as whole also leads to more risky acquisitions (see S. Sudarsanam and L. Gao, *Executive Compensation and Directors' Media Profile: Impact on Risk Taking and Value Creation in UK High-Tech and Low-Tech Acquisitions*, Cranfield School of Management Working Paper, 2007). J. Pfeffer, *What were they thinking?* (Boston: Harvard Business School Press, 2007), notes that 'the belief in the potency and importance of the CEO has been driven, in part, by the business press, which has made CEOs into almost rock-star figures'. He notes the growth of the CEO-as-celebrity cult promoted by the media (pp. 185–186). Mr Sandy Weil who built up his travellers insurance group forayed into Wall Street by first acquiring the prestigious Salomon Brothers and then in 1998 merged with one of the largest commercial banks in the world, the Citicorp. In his auto-biography, co-written by Judah Kraushaar, Weil reveals himself as 'a man desperate to be revered as the architect of an industry-changing merger. When the media flooded into the press conference and cameras started flashing, he recalls, he felt like a *rock star*'. Weil was 'always happier doing deals than making them work' (*The Economist*, 14 October 2006, p. 113).

9. P. Rosenzweig, *ibid*.

10. See J. Rovenpor, 'The relationship between four personal characteristics of Chief Executive Officers (CEOs) and Company merger and acquisition activity', *Journal of Business and Psychology*, **8**(1), 1993, 27–55.

11. J. Welch, *Jack, what I've learned leading a great company and great people*, (with J. Byrne), (London: Headline, 2001). p. 229.

12. See U. Malmendier and G. Tate, 'Who makes acquisitions? CEO overconfidence and the market's reaction', *Journal of Financial Economics*, **89**, 2008, 20–43. N. Kohers and T. Kohers, 'Takeovers of tech-nology firms: Expectations vs reality', *Financial Management*, **30**, 2001, 35–54 for US acquisitions and Sudarsanam and Gao (2007) for the UK report that overconfidence is correlated with more risky, high-tech acquisitions. Hayward and Hambrick (1997) report that hubris is associated with value-destroying acquisitions (see note 30 for reference).

13. A respected portfolio manager, Gordon Crawford, reflecting on the AOL-TW merger said of Jerry Levin, the CEO of TW and one of the prime movers behind the deal: 'This was a breathtaking deal. Everyone was surprised by it. But it turned out to be the wrong company at the wrong time and at the wrong price. *The crux of the issue here is Levin's ego. . . . Levin got caught up in his self-image as a leading thinker about trans-formative technology*' (R. Bruner, *Deals from Hell, M&A Lessons that Rise above the Ashes* (New Jersey: Wiley, 2005), p. 278) (*italics added*). Crawford does not fault Levin's vision about The internet, but about the timing of the deal, the choice of merger partner, and the price paid to realize the vision.

14. A. Tversky and D. Kahneman, 'Judgement under uncertainty: Heuristics and biases,' *Science*, 185, 1974, 1124–1131.

15. For a discussion with numerous examples of these behavioural biases among corporate managers in different decision contexts including M & A, see H. Shefrin, *ibid*.

16. J. Pfeffer, *What were they thinking? Unconventional wisdom about management* (Boston: Harvard Business School Press, 2007).

17. D. Lovallo and D. Kahneman, 'Delusions of Success: How Optimism Undermines Executives' Decisions', *Harvard Business Review*, July 2003, (56) 57–58. Lovallo and Kahneman refer to managers who see busi-ness opportunities through 'rose-colored glasses,' as in effect 'setting themselves up for failure.'

18. P. Haunschild, A. Davis-Blake and M. Fichman, 'Managerial overcommitment in corporate acquisition processes', *Organization Science*, **5**(4), 1994, 528–540.

19. D. Lovallo and D. Kahneman, *ibid*.

20. G. Elton and R.-M. Eddigen, 'Top tips to make the best acquisition or not', *Financial Times*, 27 May 2006.

21. J. Pfeffer, *ibid*., Ch. 24. Chatterjee and Hambrick argue that 'corporate chieftains with supersized egos favour grandiose and higher risk strategies . . . acquisitions . . . , large scale product launches and aggressive international expansion . . . they can hit big but they can also miss big.' See A. Chatterjee and D. Hambrick, *It's all about me; Narcissistic CEOs and their effects on company strategy and performance*, Working Paper, Pennsylvania State University, 2006.

22. The case of Vivendi illustrates such adventurous tendencies (J. Johnson and M. Orange, *The Man who Tried to Buy the World: Jean-Marie Messier and Vivendi Universal* (London: Penguin Books Ltd., 2003). Jean-Marie Messier transformed a water company into an international high-tech conglomerate through successive acquisitions. He was granted the title of the 'perfect Frenchman' by the French media. However, after the telecom bubble burst in 2000, Vivendi fell into substantial financial difficulties. Jean-Marie

Messier was sacked, and convicted of fraud. 'Without his (Messier's) vision and personality – a strange blend of French technocratic arrogance, wannabe Hollywood showmanship and investment banker charm – Vivendi Universal would never have come into existence. Without Jean-Marie Messier's weakness – a love of deal-making, self-promotion, obfuscation and risk – the dream of a French champion might have survived' (Johnson and Orange, 2003, p. 3).

23. M. Kets de Vries, *The Leader on the Couch: A clinical approach to changing people and organizations*, (San Francisco, USA: Jossey-Bass), 2006, pp. 24–25.

24. A. Chatterjee and D. Hambrick (2007), 'It's all about me: Narcissistic CEOs and their effects on company strategy and performance', *Administrative Science Quarterly*, 52, 2007, 351–386. The authors provide empirical evidence that their proxies for CEO narcissism increase the chances of value destroying acquisitions.

25. The 'rogues' gallery' of such leaders includes: Gary Winnick, Chairman of Global Crossing, who made $735m from his stock holding in the company in the four years of his leadership while the company collapsed into bankruptcy; Kenneth Lay, Chairman of Enron. Jeffrey Skilling, the CEO, and Andrew Fastow, the CFO, were all convicted of fraud and other felonies; Dennis Kozlowski, the CEO of Tyco, was convicted of fraud, conspiracy and grand larceny for looting his own company of $600m; and Bernie Ebbers, the CEO of Worldcom, was found guilty of accounting fraud amounting to $11bn. He was sentenced to a 25 year prison term. All these leaders 'ignored the rules of civilized organizational behaviour' since 'narcissists often develop a sense of entitlement, believing that they deserve special treatment and that rules and regulations only apply to others.' (Kets de Vries, *ibid.*, pp. 28 and 39).

26. See Kets de Vries, *ibid.*, pp. 33–39.

27. Jean-Marie Messier was granted the title of the 'perfect Frenchman' by the French media. However, after the telecom bubble burst in 2000, Vivendi fell into substantial financial difficulties. Jean-Marie Messier was sacked and convicted of fraud. 'Without his (Messier's) vision and personality – a strange blend of French technocratic arrogance, wannabe Hollywood showmanship and investment banker charm – Vivendi Universal would never have come into existence. Without Jean-Marie Messier's weakness – a love of deal-making, self-promotion, obfuscation and risk – the dream of a French champion might have survived' (J. Johnson and M. Orange, *The Man Who Tried to Buy the World: Jean-Marie Messier and Vivendi Universal*, (London: Penguin Books Ltd), 2003, p. 3.

28. S. Sudarsanam and J. Huang, 'Executive compensation and managerial overconfidence: Impact on risk taking and shareholder value in corporate acquisitions', in G. N. Gregoriou and L. Renneboog (Eds), *International Mergers and Acquisitions Activity Since 1990: Recent Research and Quantitative Analysis* (Amsterdam: Elesevier, 2007), pp. 223–260.

29. We follow Malmendier and Tate (2005)'s definition of overconfidence.

30. See M. Hayward and D. Hambrick, 'Explaining the premium paid for large acquisitions: Evidence of CEO hubris', *Administrative Science Quarterly*, 42, 1997, 103–127; P. R. Rau, T. Vermaelen, 'Glamour, value and the post-acquisition performance of acquiring firms', *Journal of Financial Economics*, 49, 1998, 223–253; N. Kohers and T. Kohers, 'Takeovers of technology firms: expectations vs. reality', *Financial management*, 30, 2001, 35–54; S. Sudarsanam and A. Mahate, 'Are friendly acquisitions too bad for shareholders and managers?: Long term value creation and top management turnover in hostile and friendly acquirers', *British Journal of Management*, 17, 2006, S7–S30; J. A. Doukas and D. Petmezas, 'Acquisitions, overconfident managers and self-attribution bias', working paper, 2006, Old Dominion University, US; U. Malmendier and G. Tate, 'Who make acquisitions?: CEO overconfidence and the market's reaction', *Stanford Research Paper*, October 2005, 1798.

31. S. Moeller, F. Schlingemann and R. Stulz, 'Firm size and the gains from acquisitions', *Journal of Financial Economics*, 73, 2004, 201–228, Tables 6 and 7.

32. See footnote 14 *ante*.

33. P. DiMaggio and W. Powell, 'The Iron Cage Revisited: Institutional Isomorphism and Collective Rationality', *American Sociological Review*, 1983, 48, 147–160.

34. P. DiMaggio and W. Powell, 'Introduction', in W. Powell. and P. DiMaggio (Eds), *The New Institutionalism in Organizational Analysis* (Chicago, IL: University of Chicago Press), pp. 1–38.

35. This section draws upon the following study: S. Sudarsanam and J. Huang (2007), *ibid.*

36. This link makes executive compensation and firm risk endogenous variables within the control of top managers.

37. See R. A. Lambert and D. F. Larcker, 'Executive compensation effects of large corporate acquisitions', *Journal of Accounting and Public Policy*, 6, 1987, 231–243; M. Firth, 'Corporate takeovers, stockholder

returns and executive rewards', *Managerial and Decision Economics*, **12**, 1991, 421–428; A. Khorana and M. Zenner, 'Executive compensation of large acquirors in the 1980s', *Journal of Corporate Finance*, **4**, 1998, 209–240; R. Bliss and R. Rosen, 'CEO compensation and bank mergers', *Journal of Financial Economics*, **61**(1), 2001, 107; Y. Grinstein and P. Hribar, 'CEO compensation and incentives: Evidence from M&A bonuses', *Journal of Financial Economics*, **73**(1), 2004, 119–143; J. Harford and K. Li, 'Decoupling CEO wealth and firm performance: The case of acquiring CEOs, *Journal of Finance*, **62**, 2007, 917–949; J. Coakley and S. Iliopoulou, 'CEO compensation for bidders in UK M&As', *European Financial Management*, **12**(4), 2006, 609–631.

38. See S. Sudarsanam and J. Huang (2007), *ibid.*

39. Another measure of risk incentive is the vega of stock options. It is the change in value of the stock option for a unit increase in stock price volatility. The correlation between vega and mean transaction value was also high (0.83), indicating a high risk incentive for undertaking large acquisitions. For further details of the definitions and computational procedures see Sudarsanam and Huang (2007), *ibid.* Figure 12.4 shows how the average stock options value tracked the S & P 500 index. We also find in Figure 12.5 that the average acquisition deal value and average stock option value received by CEOs are closely aligned.

40. S. Datta, M. Iskandar-Datta, and K. Raman, 'Executive compensation and corporate acquisition decisions', *The Journal of Finance*, **56**(6), 2001, 2299–2336 and M. Williams and R. Rao 'CEO stock options and equity risk incentives', *Journal of Business Finance and Accounting*, **33**(1&2), 2006, 26–44 report a link between stock option value and acquisition-related risk increase, and S. Sudarsanam and K. Huang, 'Managerial incentives and overconfidence: Impact on risk-taking and acquirer value creation in mergers and acquisitions', *Financial Management Association (USA) Annual Meeting*, 2006, and Cranfield School of Management working paper report a positive link between vega and increase in such risk. Many other studies report that stock options encourage more risk-taking in other contexts, such as financial leverage. See Sudarsanam and Huang (2007), *ibid.*, for a review.

41. See A. Cosh, P. Guest and A. Hughes, 'Board share-ownership and takeover performance', and W. Ben-Amar and P. André, 'Separation of ownership from control and acquiring firm performance: The case of family ownership in Canada', both in *Journal of Business Finance and Accounting*, **33**(3&4), 2006, 459–511 and 517–543 respectively.

42. A. Hill and B. Benoit, 'Ending boardroom backscratching', *Financial Times*, 25 November 2002.

43. See S. Sudarsanam and L. Gao (2004), 'Value creation in UK high technology acquisitions', *Financial Management Association (USA) Annual Meeting*, New Orleans, October 2004 and Cranfield School of Management Working Paper.

44. See R. Walkling, 'Round table on *US Corporate Governance: Accomplishments and Failings: A Discussion with Michael Jensen and Robert Monks*,' *Journal of Applied Finance*, **18**(1), 2008, 133–147.

45. J. W. Byrd and K. A. Hickman, 'Do outside directors monitor managers? Evidence from tender offer bids', *Journal of Financial Economics*, **32**, 1992, 195–222.

46. S. Sudarsanam and A. A. Mahate, 'Are friendly acquisitions too bad for shareholders and managers? Long term value creation and top management turnover in hostile and friendly acquirers', *British Journal of Management*, **17**, 2006, S7–S30. The authors find these board structure variables among several that impact significantly on long-term shareholder value gains. The sample consists of 519 acquisitions of UK target firms during 1983–95. The impact of board independence on corporate performance, in general, of UK firms is also confirmed by J. Dahya and J. J. McConnell, 'Board composition, corporate performance and the Cadbury Committee recommendations', *Journal of Financial and Quantitative Analysis*, **42**(3), 2007, 535–564.

47. D. L. Paul, 'Board composition and corrective action: Evidence from corporate responses to bad acquisition bids', *Journal of Financial and Quantitative Analysis*, **42**(3), 2007, 759–784.

48. See X. Chen, J. Harford and K. Li, 'Monitoring: Which institutions matter', *Journal of Financial Economics*, **26**, 2007, 278–305.

49. K. M. Lehn and M. Zhao, 'CEO turnover after acquisitions: Are bad bidders fired?', *Journal of Finance*, **61**(4), 2006, 1759–1811. Of the 714 CEOs in the US who made the sample acquisitions during 1990–98, 407 were replaced in disciplinary turnovers, and of these 225 were replaced by internal governance, 142 by takeovers, and 40 by bankruptcy. Interestingly, the authors note that governance structure variables do not account for the observed relation between value destruction and CEO turnover. R. Scholten reports a similar relation between value-destroying acquisitions and subsequent CEO turnover for the 1980s and 1990s in the US. Despite the decline in hostile takeovers in the latter period the relation holds good, suggesting that internal control devices – CEO stock ownership, independent board, block shareholder

monitoring – act as effective disciplinary mechanisms. He reports that CEO ownership, unsurprisingly, reduces the chances of his/her displacement but does not protect fully against disciplinary displacement. See R. Scholten, 'Investment decisions and managerial discipline: Evidence from the takeover market', *Financial Management*, **34**(2), 2005, 35–61.

50. See Sudarsanam and Mahate, *ibid.*, Table 9. They also report similar retention rates and negative relation to poor post-acquisition performance for all board directors in their Table 8. These rates are broadly comparable to those reported by Lehn and Zhao, *ibid.*, when allowance is made for their longer, i.e. five-year, post-acquisition period.

51. See W. B. Bratton, 'Whither hostility?', in G. N. Gregoriou and L. Renneboog (Eds), *Corporate Governance and Regulatory Impact on Mergers and Acquisitions* (Amsterdam: Elsevier, 2007) pp. 103–130. Bratton notes that activist investors may often have both bidder and target shares in their portfolios, and therefore may be constrained from pushing too hard on either side to the point of breaking the deal.

52. See R. N. Ashkenas, L. J. DeMonaco and S. C. Francis, 'Making the deal real: How GE Capital integrates acquisitions', *Harvard Business Review*, January/February 1998, 165–178, on acquisition integration skills as a core competence. The integration issues are discussed in Chapter 22.

53. R. G. Eccles, K. L. Lanes and T. C. Wilson, 'Are you paying too much for that acquisition?' *Harvard Business Review*, July/August 1999, 136–146.

54. KPMG International, *Benchmarking M&A Teams*, Publication number: 211–810, June 2005. 221 firms, including some of the largest firms from the US and Europe, participated in the survey.

55. *Ibid.*

56. J. Hunt, S. Lees, J. J. Grumbar and P. D. Vivian, *Acquisitions: The Human Factor* (London: London Business School, 1987).

CHAPTER 13

Target selection for acquisition

Objectives

At the end of this chapter, the reader should be able to understand

- the various steps involved in the target selection process;
- how to develop target selection criteria;
- how to identify potential targets using a range of strategic screening tools;
- alternative acquisition strategies, their sources of value, their riskiness and limitations;
- the importance of timing acquisitions;
- target characteristics that dictate the relative attractiveness of potential targets; and
- how to rate potential targets on a range of desirable attributes, and rank them for selection.

Introduction

In Stage 1 of our five-stage model of the M & A process the firm has to choose an acquisition strategy to deliver its corporate strategy objectives. These objectives are derived from an analysis of the firm's current business environment, how this environment is likely to evolve, its current strategic position and its business model, the strategic opportunities available with changes in the business environment, the relative attractiveness of these opportunities, what the desired post-acquisition strategic positioning is, and how the firm's business model should change to accommodate such positioning. A useful starting point is therefore a thorough analysis of the business environment using the PEST framework introduced in Chapter 3 and how the PEST forces are likely to evolve. A review of the firm's current strategic positioning in light of this expected evolution and the strategic moves it should make to respond to, or even shape, this evolution is undertaken. Industry-level analysis of the six forces shaping its competitive structure is the next step in making strategic choices. The place of acquisition in implementing these choices, and whether acquisition is the best instrument for implementation, need to be justified. The target selection process then proceeds to identify the optimal target through further screening steps. This chapter describes this process, and the analytical tools that may be used at different stages of the process. A simple procedure for constructing a desirable target profile and ranking feasible targets is outlined and illustrated. We also discuss opportunistic bids and their advantages and disadvantages.

Target selection process

Figure 13.1 shows the various analyses and the decision points in the target selection process. Even though a firm's corporate or business strategy may be premeditated or emergent (see Chapter 3 for a discussion of these alternative views), it is reasonable to assume that before

Figure 13.1 **Target selection process**

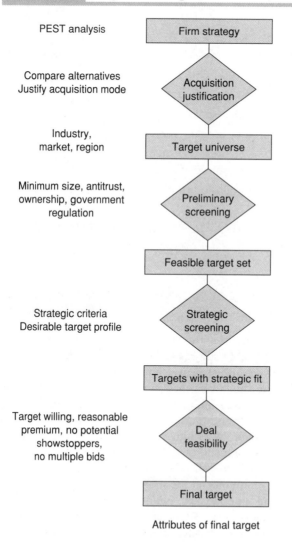

PEST analysis — Firm strategy

Compare alternatives
Justify acquisition mode — Acquisition justification

Industry, market, region — Target universe

Minimum size, antitrust, ownership, government regulation — Preliminary screening

Feasible target set

Strategic criteria
Desirable target profile — Strategic screening

Targets with strategic fit

Target willing, reasonable premium, no potential showstoppers, no multiple bids — Deal feasibility

Final target

Attributes of final target

- Best strategic fit to acquirer
- Transactionally feasible
- Not overpriced
- Minimum risk to deal completion

embarking on an acquisition the firm develops its strategy, and that the choice of acquisition is to implement the strategic objectives in a value-maximizing manner.

After determining the appropriate acquisition strategy to deliver its corporate strategy objectives, the firm needs to identify potential targets that will satisfy the acquisition objectives. The process of target selection starts with defining the universe of potential targets and filtering these through various criteria or tests to narrow the search, as shown in Figure 13.1. The various filters are in the form of strategic criteria, strategic fit, deal feasibility etc. The final stage of the process yields a target that the firm will be most comfortable making a bid for. This sets the scene for the deal structuring and negotiation stage of our five-stage model.

This process has to be handled with care, since inappropriate target selection entails not only wasted effort and resources but also potential value destruction, because such a target, far from delivering the objectives of the acquisition, may cause negative synergy and grief. Potential regulatory roadblocks such as antitrust investigation (see Chapter 17) and other showstoppers are often associated with the choice of particular target. They have to be anticipated, and countervailing strategies put in place, to be activated if necessary. This process also involves assessment of *ex ante* risk at various stages of target selection, deal-making and post-acquisition integration. Informed by this assessment, the firm can select those targets that will minimize these risks. In the discussion below we indicate the nature and sources of these risks.

Strategic choices and acquisition

The broad strategic choices are delineated in the Ansoff products–markets matrix in Figure 13.2. The quadrants reflect the types of acquisition discussed in Chapters 5 to 8 that a firm can undertake. Market penetration is by horizontal acquisition, whereas product extension is by related acquisition. Cross-border acquisition actualizes market extension, and conglomerate acquisition results in diversification. The strategic choice of the firm can be implemented through acquisition.

The application of this model to the acquisition strategy of a commercial bank is illustrated in Figure 13.3. Depending on its corporate strategy, it can make acquisitions to deepen and strengthen its presence in its existing market, enter a related product market, enter a new

Figure 13.2   Strategic direction of acquisition: Ansoff's matrix

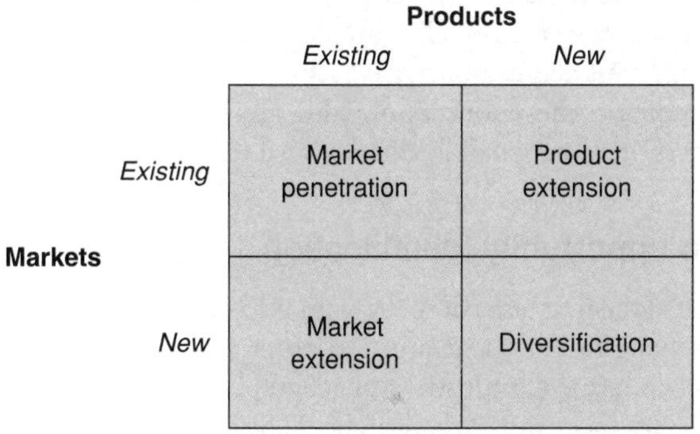

Source: I. Ansoff, 'Strategies of diversification', *Harvard Business Review* 25(5), Sept–Oct, 1957, pp. 113–125.

Figure 13.3 Acquisition strategy of a bank and its post-acquisition corporate portfolio

Post-acquisition portfolio of bank

Acquisition strategy		Horizontal	Horizontal
	Market penetration	Larger domestic bank	International bank
	Market extension	Related products Mortgage, consumer credit, asset management	Unrelated products Insurance, car dealership, real estate

Figure 13.4 Sources of value in different value types

Post-acquisition portfolio

Acquisition strategy		Horizontal	Cross-border
	Market penetration	Scale economy Market power Network externality No excess capacity	Global brands Scale economy Cost efficiency Proximity to customers
	Market extension	**Related** Scope economy Umbrella branding Market power	**Unrelated** Corporate branding Managerial synergy Financial synergy Risk reduction

geographical market, e.g. in neighbouring countries, or enter unrelated lines of business. The resulting post-acquisition corporate portfolio is shown in the figure. Figure 13.3 shows some of the various value sources in different acquisition types.

Each acquisition type is pregnant with different sources of value gains to the acquirer, although they are not all mutually exclusive. For example, common branding can add value to different acquisition types (see Chapter 7 on the limits of value creation from corporate branding). These sources of value are shown in Figure 13.4, and are discussed, along with others, in more detail in Chapters 5 to 8.

Bid opportunity identification

One of the first tasks of the A team is to locate potential targets and prepare a shortlist of those satisfying the firm's acquisition criteria. The search for potential targets may be narrow or wide in terms of industry and geography. In the case of horizontal or vertical integration the industry spectrum of the search will be narrow, but, depending upon the global strategy of the firm, it may span several countries. In the case of conglomerate acquisitions one may scan both diverse industries and numerous countries.

Opportunity identification is often facilitated by intermediaries. Business brokers, accounting firms, stockbrokers and investment bankers may be able to suggest potential targets. These intermediaries may provide additional services, such as preliminary soundings of the targets. The A team also needs to undertake its own detailed research of the target industries and target companies.

In the case of target industries the same as or related to the bidder's, its line managers will be aware of the relative performance of those industries and their competitors. This internal database may be supplemented by research based on external sources of information. Publicly available information, such as company annual reports, industry surveys, trade journals, stockbrokers' circulars in the case of stock-market-listed targets, and credit ratings of targets from rating agencies such as Dun & Bradstreet, may be used to assess the relative attractiveness of industries and companies.

Assessing industry attractiveness

This may be assessed as using a variety of analytical frameworks, such as:

● industry dynamism-market position matrix; and
● five or six forces model, introduced in Chapter 3.

These frameworks may be used to assess the positioning of the post-acquisition firm relative to its pre-acquisition position. In the light of the evidence of industry clustering of mergers, presented in Chapter 2, a firm considering acquisition as a strategic move needs to anticipate the reaction of current or potential competitors to its move. *Competitor neglect* leads to over-estimation of the competitive advantage period, the strategic benefit of the acquisition, and the expected value creation. In analyzing the potential *competitor reaction*, the game-theoretic approach outlined in Chapter 3 is useful. Figure 13.5 delineates this. The timing and strength of competitor reaction determine the competitive advantage period that an acquirer can hope to enjoy, and hence the value of the acquisition.

Figure 13.5 **Industry dynamism, competitor reaction and post-acquisition positioning of acquirer**

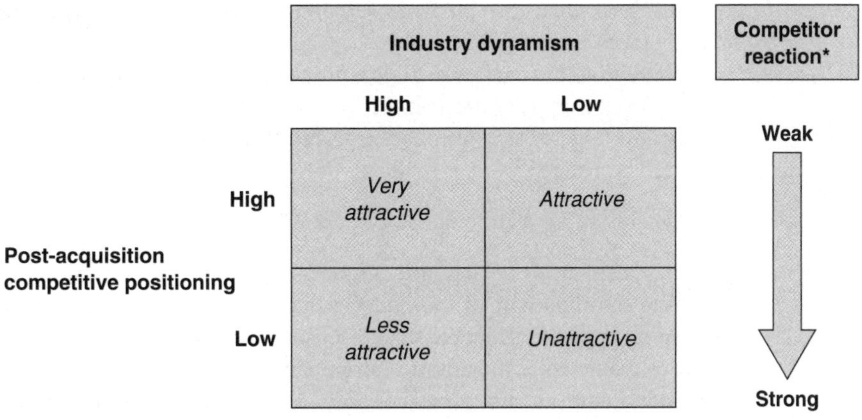

*Although we refer to competitor reaction, the reaction of *any* of Porter's five forces is relevant to the post-acquisition competitive positioning.

Blind spots in competitor analysis and their implications for acquisition pricing

In making acquisition decisions the competitor reaction scenario needs to be given explicit and careful consideration. Further, the firm needs to consider how such reactions can be blunted through appropriate isolating mechanisms, such as a unique configuration of the resources and capabilities of the merged entity passing the VRINS test. The benefits of any acquisition must be evaluating potential competitor reaction and the cost and probability of effective isolating mechanisms as well as the duration of their effectiveness.

Competitive reaction is likely to be more robust industries with excess capacity, high competitive pressure and limited growth prospects, and in oligopolistic industries where competitors can observe one another's moves. It is also more probable where the acquisition logic is driven by exploitation of known resources and capabilities than when it is driven by exploration for new resources and capabilities.

Competitor reaction based on models such as game theory rely on assumptions of economic rationality on the part of all the players: that is, they seek to maximize their monetary payoffs and information symmetry – the payoffs to, and the competitive moves of, players are observed by all the players. Where there is information asymmetry, or where the players deviate from rationality, it is difficult to predict the contingent behaviour of rivals. Behavioural decision literature suggests that players may suffer from 'blind spots', leading to the behavioural biases referred to in the previous chapter, e.g. overconfidence, limited framing and escalation of commitment[1].

In new and emerging businesses such threats may be less muted because of the 'expanding cake'. In such businesses competitor reaction may convert a unique growth opportunity into a shared opportunity, for example two pharmaceutical companies acquiring two similar biotechnology companies that could lead to the discovery of therapies for the same disease. As we shall see in Chapter 14, shared real options are less valuable than unique real options. While competitor reaction through imitative acquisition may be strong, the firm may nevertheless set up *isolating mechanisms* or entry barriers discussed in Chapter 3 to dilute its impact. Competitor reaction can also be mitigated when acquisition is undertaken to implement a new business model – 'blue ocean strategy' – that is difficult for established players to imitate, thereby isolating the move from damaging competitor reaction[2]. Isolating mechanisms that a firm contemplates need to be 'stress tested' for their robustness, and must not be based on comforting self-delusions born of overconfidence or over-optimism (see Exhibit 13.1 on how isolating mechanisms can be built).

Effective isolating devices include a unique post-acquisition configuration of the acquirer's and target's resources and capabilities to create VRINS-compliant competences. Acquisition strategy and target selection must be geared towards creating such isolated competitive positioning. The synergy value is made up of two components:

Synergy value = Unique component + Imitable component

Isolating mechanisms enlarge the unique component and minimize the imitable component. The unique component of the added value is more appropriable by the acquirer than the imitable component. The deal structure and post-acquisition integration processes can contribute to maximizing the unique component.

In identifying an attractive industry, the six forces model discussed in Chapter 3 is useful. Table 13.1 summarizes the broad approach to assessing the impact of these forces, and illustrates some of them for a hypothetical acquisition of a competitor. A large acquisition can significantly alter the industry structure, and those affected include not only the current

Exhibit 13.1

Paccar thrives in isolation

Strategy means building isolating mechanisms against the competitive forces, or finding a position in the industry where the forces are weakest. Paccar is in the market for heavy trucks, which is structurally challenging. Many buyers operate large fleets, or are large leasing companies, with both the leverage and the motivation to drive down the price of one of their largest purchases. Most trucks are built to regulated standards and offer similar features, so price competition is rampant. Capital intensity causes rivalry to be fierce, especially during the recurring cyclical downturns. Unions exercise considerable supplier power. Truck buyers face important substitutes for their services, such as cargo delivery by rail.

In this setting Paccar, a Washington-based company with about 20% of the North American heavy-truck market, focuses on one group of customers: owner-operators – drivers who own their trucks and contract directly with shippers or serve as subcontractors to larger trucking companies. Such small operators have limited clout as truck buyers. They are also less price sensitive because of their strong emotional ties to and economic dependence on the product. They take great pride in their trucks, in which they spend most of their time. Paccar has invested heavily to develop an array of features with owner-operators in mind: luxurious sleeper cabins, plush leather seats, noise-insulated cabins, sleek exterior styling, and so on. At the company's extensive network of dealers, prospective buyers use software to select among thousands of options to put their personal signature on their trucks. These customized trucks are built to order, not to stock, and are delivered in six to eight weeks. Paccar's trucks also have aerodynamic designs that reduce fuel consumption, and they maintain their resale value better than other trucks. Paccar's roadside assistance program and IT-supported system for distributing spare parts reduce the time a truck is out of service. All these are crucial considerations for owner-operators, who pay Paccar a 10% premium, and its Kenworth and Peterbilt brands are considered status symbols at truck stops.

Paccar illustrates the principles of positioning a company within a given industry structure. The firm has found a portion of its industry where the competitive forces are weaker – where it can avoid buyer power and price-based rivalry. And it has tailored every single part of the value chain to cope well with the forces in its segment. As a result, Paccar has been profitable for 68 years straight, and has earned a long-run return on equity above 20%.

Source: Adapted from M. Porter, 'The five competitive forces that shape strategy', *Harvard Business Review*, January 2008, p. 89

competitors but also other players representing the different forces. The reaction of these players depends on their threat perception and their ability to respond with a countervailing acquisition or other strategies such as an alliance or greater investment in advertising, R & D, etc. For a more detailed framework for analyzing these forces the reader is referred to textbooks on strategic management[3].

Table 13.1 Impact of acquisition on acquirer's competitive forces environment

Competitive force	Pre-acquisition strength	Post-acquisition strength	Post-acquisition strength after force reaction relative to pre-acquisition
Current rivalry	Strong	Moderate	No change
Threat of suppliers	Weak	Weaker	Stronger buying power
Threat of buyers	Strong	Moderate	Moderate
Threat of substitutes	Weak	Weak	Weak
Complementors	Not relevant	Not relevant	Not relevant
New entrants	Strong	Weak	Weak

It is important to understand whether these forces will strengthen or weaken as a result of the acquisition, and to understand the reaction of those players whose competitive position is threatened by the acquisition. The emerging configuration has to be assessed for its attractiveness. In the illustration the acquisition leads to a temporary increase in market power, but that is offset by an imitative acquisition by the acquirer's rivals, leaving the level of rivalry intact. On the other hand the acquisition can lead to a stronger bargaining power against suppliers, and the pre-acquisition threat from suppliers is moderated by the acquisition. The probability of these benefits fructifying needs to be rigorously tested[4]. Potential new entrants may be deterred by having to face a stronger acquirer. The other forces – threat of substitutes and complementors – are unchanged by the acquisition. Overall, the acquisition seems to improve the acquirer's competitive environment owing to a benign reconfiguration of the competitive forces. Similar analysis can be undertaken for other types of acquisition outlined above. Greater feel for the relative importance of the *change in the forces* can be generated by using a scoring system to award points on any relevant scale, say 1 to 5, and then estimating the weighted average scores of the pre- and post-acquisition configurations.

Change in competitive position and value creation

The above framework helps an acquirer understand the sources of incremental value, e.g. increased buyer power and reduced threat from buyers, which represent the strategic drivers of that synergy value. The strategic drivers must be quantified in terms of *changes in* market share, revenue, costs, investments, cost of capital etc., and then need to be converted into financial drivers, as shown in Chapter 14 on target valuation.

From industry analysis to target selection

Within the target industry there may be several potential target firms. Not all of them will satisfy the strategic and value creation objectives of the firm. A screening device for finding the target with the best fit is to identify the key competences that the post-acquisition firm will need to achieve its objectives, and then match these against the resources and capabilities that the firm and the different targets bring to the merger. Figure 13.6 shows this matching process, and how targets with the best fit may be located.

Having identified a strategically attractive target industry and a shortlist of potential targets in that industry, a profile of the targets in terms of their strengths and weaknesses must be drawn up. This profile should cover, *inter alia*, the following aspects:

- quality of management in terms of strategic thinking, effective implementation of strategic plans and delivering performance;

Figure 13.6   Required R & C and targets with best fit

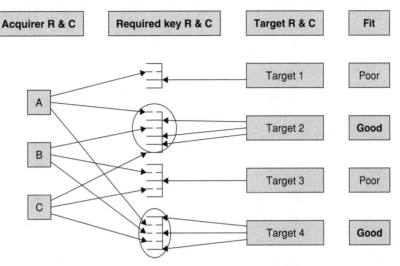

*Note: A, B and C represent the acquirer's R & C. The arrows to the broken lines in the middle show the R & C the acquirer brings to the merger, and those to the unbroken lines show the R & C the target brings. The more arrows in a merger, the better is the fit.

- industry status of the target company, the level of competition in the industry, and the company's competitive strengths;
- future technological and competitive evolution of the industry, and the target's ability to cope with this change; and
- the target's financial and stock market performance.

Such an evaluation of the strengths and weaknesses helps the A team formulate the appropriate strategy for negotiating with the target management, or for launching a hostile bid, if necessary. Valuation of the targets under the bidder's management may then be undertaken as described in Chapter 14. Such a valuation, including a sensitivity analysis under varying assumptions of future scenarios about target performance, provides the bidder with a price range over which to negotiate with the target or vary the terms of a public offer.

Scope for overvaluation of the acquisition must be limited by a disciplined search for a deep understanding of the limitations on the various sources of value in different acquisition types. Some of these are illustrated in Figure 13.7. Scoping the sources of value and its limits can often lead to crafting better acquisition strategies that extend these limits. In horizontal acquisitions driven by cost efficiencies, once scale reaches beyond the minimum efficient scale (MES), further gains dry up. In businesses characterized by positive feedback and network externality effects, limits to scale are much weaker. In cross-border acquisitions, scale economies are more difficult. Foreign direct investment (FDI) rules may also restrict the gains by limiting ownership, control or flexibility to hire and fire the work force.

Another important consideration is the time scale for the realization of expected synergies. Some value sources are easier to realize than others because of complexities and the scale of the changes the merging organizations have to undergo before synergies can be realized. Any post-acquisition integration process often leads to the discovery of new sources of synergies, and in other cases to the painful acceptance that the anticipated synergies are indeed

Figure 13.7 Limits on sources of value in different acquisition types

Post-acquisition portfolio

	Horizontal	**Cross-border**
Market penetration	Past MES* – no gain Antitrust Diseconomies Imitable?	Brands don't travel Scale economy limited FDI** restrictions Cultures incompatible
Market extension	**Related** Good brand diluted by poor brand Antitrust	**Unrelated** Agency costs, inefficient internal capital markets, conglomerate discount, investors can replicate

Acquisition strategy (left)

*Minimum efficient scale; **Foreign direct investment.

Figure 13.8 Risk of realization of different value sources

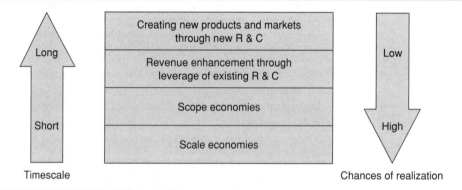

Timescale (Long/Short) — Chances of realization (Low/High)

Creating new products and markets through new R & C
Revenue enhancement through leverage of existing R & C
Scope economies
Scale economies

illusory. In view of this, the probability of achieving the expected synergies has to be carefully evaluated. Figure 13.8 illustrates the time scales and risk of non-realization in different acquisition types.

A measure of the risk associated with different value sources may be gained from the survey of managers involved in acquisitions. Table 13.2 shows different sources of cost savings and revenue enhancement that may be achieved from a merger. Available evidence suggests that cost savings and revenue enhancements are not easy to realize. The elusiveness of synergies receives support from a recent survey of 420 corporate executives. Only 51% of the respondents reported achieving expected revenue synergies and 45% achieved cost synergies. Only 40% could complete post-acquisition integration as quickly as possible with minimal stress.

Many M & A practitioners and observers consider that revenue enhancement is more difficult to achieve than cost savings. According to Robert Pozen, chairman of a large asset management firm in the US, 'revenue synergies tend to be particularly suspect and hard to deliver . . . Investors tend to respond positively to acquisitions that involve cost reductions . . . But revenue synergies are viewed as being in the realm of speculation'. Professor Robert

Table 13.2 Sources of revenue gains and cost savings in acquisitions

Revenue enhancement through:	Cost reduction through:
Acquiring new customers in existing markets	Head count reduction
Entering new markets	More efficient buying and merchandising
Pooling marketing resources and sales forces	More efficient supply chain management
More efficient customer services and back-up	Improved manufacturing processes
Acquiring new distribution channels	Efficient new product development process
Launch of new products	Outsourcing
Cross-selling	More cost effective R & D

Table 13.3 Comparative analysis of bidder's and target's SWOT

Bidder's strength	Bidder's weaknesses
● Strong market position	● No new products, unproductive R & D
● Strong brand	● Mature market

Target's strength	Target's weaknesses
● Strong R & D	● Little expertise in clinical trials
● Strong patent bank	● Little marketing expertise
	● Financially weak

Bidder's opportunities	Bidder's threats
● Fill in product pipeline and grow to blockbusters	● Strong competition from generic sellers
● Rejuvenate its R & D capability	● Rivals can acquire target and gain competitive advantage
	● Technology and market risk

Target's opportunities	Target's threats
● Piggyback on bidder's brand to grow	● Delay in bringing product to market
● Raise its R & D game	● Shared real options, pre-emption by rivals
	● Copycat R & D

Bruner, a leading academic authority on M & A, has a similar take: 'Revenue-increasing synergies from cross-selling, for example, are notoriously hard to capture as many of the banking conglomerates have discovered' (Ernst & Young, 'Corporate Portfolio Management Roundtable', *Journal of Applied Corporate Finance,* 20(2), Spring 2008, pp. 12–14. See also S. Sudarsanam, *Creating Value From Mergers and Acquisitions: The Challenges,* (Harlow, UK: FT Prentice-Hall, 2003), p. 559 for evidence based on a managerial survey that revenue enhancement is more difficult than cost savings).

SWOT analysis of the fit between firm and its acquisition target

We can carry out a comparative SWOT (strengths, weaknesses, opportunities and threats) analysis of the firm and its target, highlighting whether these are complementary or reinforcing. A good fit requires that each firm offset the other's weaknesses with its strengths, and threats with its opportunities. Table 13.3 illustrates the mapping of each firm's strengths, weaknesses, opportunities and threats, and exploring of their complementarity, where the bidder is a mature pharmaceutical firm and the target is a young, innovative, smaller competitor, e.g. a biotech company. Such a comparison helps to project the combined firm's SWOT and assess *ex ante* whether this projected profile is attractive from the bidder's point of view.

Another use of the SWOT analysis is to prepare for deal negotiation. Since it reveals each firm's SWOT and how they complement each other, it also points to the relative bargaining power of the two when negotiating a deal. This depends not only on the current configuration of SWOT, but also on who will gain more from a reconfiguration after the acquisition. We return to the use of comparative SWOT in deal structuring and negotiation in Part 3 of the book.

Platform strategies

Young, fast-growing industries are characterized by a large number of small firms. Consolidating a number of such firms to achieve critical mass in terms of scale and scope economies is often an attractive business strategy. Even in industries where there are large players, consolidating the small players that compete with them may provide these small firms with the necessary scale, financial resources and market share to turn into more credible competitors. Consolidation of this type differs from the consolidation of large firms in a mature industry that we dealt with in Chapter 5.

Consolidation takes a variety of forms, and has been described as a roll-up, add-on, bolt-on, buy-and-build or platform acquisition. Fill-in is another type of consolidating acquisition by a company seeking to fill in the gaps in its product line. These names are pretty descriptive of the underlying strategy, and highlight a major motivation for consolidation, namely, to scale up to reach a certain critical mass and achieve the benefits associated with size, such as scale and scope economies.

Fragmented industries contain a large number of very small firms selling a single product or a small range of related products. The markets they serve may be niche markets or geographically limited. They are often described as 'mom and pop' businesses. These businesses may be selling mature products, or they may be start-up firms. Examples of industries that may be characterized as fragmented include business services, professional service firms, construction companies, oilfield services, health services, software development companies, real estate, automobile parts, food and retailing. Exhibit 13.2 provides examples of how acquisition is used as a strategic tool to achieve growth through consolidation.

Exhibit 13.2

Roll on for a roll-up

AccuStaff Inc. made 21 acquisitions in 1996 to consolidate temporary professional and technical employment firms offering diverse services and geographical spread; to increase scale to support investment in information systems and associated technology.

Century Business Systems in the US is a provider of business services to small and medium-sized firms. It follows a strategy of enlarging its geographical coverage of the markets in these services by adding on small regional operators to create a large national company providing accounting, financial, employee benefits and consulting services in an integrated format to small and medium-sized businesses. Century's strategy is based on the opportunity provided by the growing trend of businesses to outsource professional services. In 1998 Century made 38 acquisitions, and followed this up with another 20 acquisitions in 1999.

UK-based Wolseley stepped up its roll-up strategy in distribution of building supplies through mostly small to mid-sized companies using US platform companies Stock Buidling Supply and Ferguson Enterprises. It made 24 acquisitions in 2006 and 21 acquisitions in 2005.

Brown & Brown undertook 23 acquisitions in 2004, 15 in 2005 and 11 in 2006 to implement its strategy of buying up mid-sized regional players in the insurance brokerage and risk management services. The industry is highly fragmented, and B & B is one of several firms following a roll-up strategy.

Sources: *Mergers and Acquisitions,* February 2000 and 2005 to 2007

Value creation logic of consolidation

The value creation logic is not very different from that of the consolidation of large firm horizontal mergers. It will be recalled from Chapter 5 that we classified the sources of value creation broadly as:

- cost savings;
- revenue enhancement; and
- new growth opportunities.

Consolidation of fragmented industries allows cost savings through both scale and scope economies, and possibly learning economies, in periods after consolidation. As seen from the examples of consolidation in Exhibit 13.2, consolidating firms acquire not only firms selling the same products but also those selling complementary products, thereby enabling the accomplishment of scope economies. Scale and scope economies in production, marketing, sales, and inbound and outbound logistics increase with increasing consolidation. The small size of consolidators means that they may be well below the minimum efficient scale (MES) of production in manufacturing businesses. Thus there is scope for them to reap scale economies at the plant level. They may also be able to reap firm-level economies in support services such as logistics, marketing and R & D, and in IT investments[6].

The market extension from small niche or subregional to regional and then to national markets gives the consolidator the opportunity for revenue enhancement. The increased size and visibility of the consolidated firm also provides opportunities for brand building, and the fixed costs of advertising, marketing and brand building can then be spread over a larger volume and wider range of products. The larger firm size may enable the consolidator to compete on more equal terms with established competitors and gain market share. Value creation through substantial market power increase seems unlikely because of the small size of the acquisitions, although when rolled up these are intended to give the consolidator a reasonable market share. In most of the consolidations, for example in business services or mature industries, revenue growth through exploiting network externality again seems unlikely (see Chapter 5 for a discussion of network externality, NWE, as a source of growth and value). However, in the case of consolidation of high-technology growth companies such as those carried out by Cisco, network externality may have contributed to revenue growth.

Consolidation of firms in more mature industries may be less likely to provide for real-option-type growth opportunities. These are broad-brush evaluations of consolidation as a source of value in different industries.

Consolidation and build-up of resources and capabilities

Apart from exploiting the existing, but probably meagre, R & C of the firms being consolidated, the consolidator will be able to build new R & C. The increasing firm size allows the firm to buy new and valuable skills and talents by hiring highly trained and qualified human resources that small fragmented firms will find it hard to access. Given the small size of each bolt-on or platform acquisition, organizational learning and diffusion of capabilities may be much easier to accomplish than in the case of larger acquisitions. Integration of the acquired firm may also be a less arduous task (see Chapter 22 on post-acquisition integration).

Consolidation of fragmented industries can be carried out by different techniques. These differ in terms of the players, their motivation, strategy for growing the acquired businesses and the exit route.

The following are the different types of consolidation:

- add-on or bolt-on acquisition;
- platform acquisition or leveraged build-up;
- buy–build–operate (BBO);
- buy–build–sell (BBS);
- IPO roll-up.

An add-on or bolt-on is a strategy based on acquiring small operating companies that would complement the acquirer's existing businesses and increase its operating scale to a critical mass. In a platform strategy the firm chooses the market or segment that it wants to build its competitive strength in and makes an initial acquisition, which then serves as a platform for carrying out the competitive strategy. This platform is used as a lever to make subsequent acquisitions and strengthen it. This strategy is also known as leveraged build-up. One of the earliest leveraged build-ups was carried out by Kohlberg Kravis and Roberts (KKR) in 1989. The strategic objective, as in the case of the bolt-on strategy, is to remain as a significant competitor in the chosen market in the long term. The BBO strategy is similar to the bolt-on and platform strategies but with the difference that firms use the acquisitions to leverage their existing resources and capabilities and build up new resources and capabilities to gain competitive advantage. All the above strategies follow a dedicated and consistent acquisition programme to grow in size and competitive strength.

The BBS strategy aims to put together, through acquisitions, firms lacking in competitive strengths because of their small size. When these acquisitions are integrated and built into a competitively stronger business the consolidator sells it, and realizes a profit on its investment. The sale may be a trade sale to another operating company, e.g. a competitor or a diversifying acquirer, or to the management in a management buyout. The IPO roll-up consolidation involves bundling a number of related businesses through quick-fire acquisitions and getting the consolidated business listed on a stock exchange through an initial public offering[7].

Serial acquisitions

Consolidation requires serial acquisitions. Serial acquisitions are thus part of a premeditated consolidation strategy. Serial acquisitions also provide the acquirer with the opportunity to learn from the preceding acquisitions about the problems of making and integrating acquisitions, and these lessons, if internalized by the acquirer's organization, can enhance its capacity to make successful acquisitions. Thus successful acquisition-making becomes the firm's core competence. Of course, no two acquisitions are alike, and the learning process must intelligently differentiate between similar and dissimilar acquisitions, and apply the lessons judiciously rather than indiscriminately. The organizational learning issues in M & A are dealt with in more detail in Chapter 23.

Serial acquisitions may be announced by a firm as its sustained competitive strategy. This may have the advantage of a firm commitment that deters its rivals from imitative acquisitions, thereby maintaining its competitive advantage. However, this depends on how the rivals react. The serial acquirer may therefore wish to preserve its flexibility by waiting for its rivals' reactions before embarking upon further acquisitions in the series. If the rivals' reactions are robust, then the firm may follow a less aggressive and more accommodating strategy that will avoid a 'no-holds-barred' war, and cease its acquisition programme. In Chapter 14 we illustrate how the real options framework can be used to model the choice between strategic commitment and flexibility, and how valuable such flexibility is.

Empirical evidence on serial acquisitions

When a firm engages in serial acquisitions as part of its long-term strategic positioning, it is reasonable to surmise that, at the outset of the series, its investment opportunities are quite high. As it makes successive acquisitions to carry out its strategy, these opportunities get exhausted, and the marginal returns from follow-on acquisitions fall off. When the returns turn negative it is an indication that such opportunities exist no more. If the scenario plays out, we shall observe that high returns to acquirers from initial acquisitions in the series are followed by lower returns to later acquisitions.

Klasa and Stegemuller find that 25% of acquisitions during 1982–99 in the US are in the form of serial acquisitions, defined as those made by the same acquirer over a period separated by 24 months of no acquisitions before and after the series. 1285 acquisitions were made in 487 sequences compared with 3796 acquisitions out of sequence. They estimate the buy-and-hold abnormal returns (in %) for the first, middle and last acquisition in a sequence as follows:

	Year −1	Year +1	Year +2	Year +3	Year +4
First acquisition	17	25	21	−10	15
Mid acquisition	32	3	−21	−27	−28
Last acquisition	−3	−14	−24	−20	−19

Klasa and Stegemoller find that investment opportunities do diminish from before the first acquisition to after the last one[8].

Sudarsanam and Huang (2008) examine the performance of serial acquirers that make at least five acquisitions from the first acquisition over a five-year period. They find, in a sample of 2527 US acquisitions from 1993 to 2004, 149 serial acquirers making 1223 acquisitions. They observe that the three-day abnormal returns at bid announcements are positive at the first acquisition, and no different from those of non-serial (occasional) acquirers, but as the series progresses these returns fall and turn negative. The abnormal returns to the fifth and later acquisitions in a series are also significantly lower than those of non-serial acquirers.

Figure 13.9 Cumulative returns over treasury bill for serial acquirers

*Note: **SAQ** (a) is the value-weighted returns of the serial acquirers portfolio minus the one-month Treasury bill return. **OCA** (b) is the value-weighted returns of occasional acquirers portfolio minus the one-month Treasury bill return. **MKT** (c) is the excess return on the market portfolio, which is the value-weighted return on all NYSE, AMEX, and NASDAQ stocks (from CRSP) minus the one-month Treasury bill return. In order to facilitate our comparison, the full index levels of these three portfolios are re-based to 100 on January 1, 1994.

This pattern is consistent with diminishing marginal returns to later acquisitions. It is also consistent with later acquisition stirring up the six competitive forces we discussed earlier[9]. It is also consistent with more acquisitions adding to complexity and making the integration effort more demanding[10].

What is the cumulative impact of serial acquisitions on acquirers' shareholder value? Sudarsanam and Huang estimate the three-year abnormal return to a portfolio of serial acquirers and compare it with the abnormal return to a control portfolio of non-acquirers and the return to the US stock market. The abnormal return is over the one-month US treasury bill rate. Figure 13.9 shows that serial acquirers seem to outperform occasional acquirers and the stock market[11,12].

Deal considerations

Having considered potential targets from a strategic point of view, we next consider certain deal attributes that may make one target more desirable than others. Further, the timing of an acquisition may also influence the value gains from it.

Buying public or private targets?

Several empirical studies have found that acquirers of private companies make significantly higher value gains at announcement, as well as in the post-acquisition period, than those of publicly listed companies. From a very comprehensive sample of 4429 acquisitions by Western European firms during 1996–2001, Faccio, McConnell and Stolin find that[13]:

- the cumulative abnormal return around announcement to acquirers is −0.4% for public targets and 1.5% for private company or subsidiary business acquisition (subsidiary businesses being generally unlisted and hence 'private'; and
- this listing effect prevails in all sample years and most sample countries.

Officer, Poulsen and Stegemoller also find superior returns to private company acquisitions with US data: for a sample of 735 private and 1944 public company targets during 1995–2004 the acquirer's three-day abnormal returns are respectively 3.8% and −1.3%[14,15].

This superior performance of acquirers of private companies is, however, not sustained in long-term returns. Over a three-year post-acquisition period their abnormal returns are either zero or negative. For the UK, and the same period, acquirers of both public and private targets experience significant value losses, but these are larger in the former case (−0.6% versus −0.4% respectively)[16]. Thus the initial value gains from acquiring private targets are not sustained over the longer term.

Among the reasons for this superior performance of private company acquirers are the following:

- *No free-ride and hold up*: Private companies have concentrated ownership, often held by the founder and his family. In a public company with dispersed ownership individual shareholders can hold up tendering their shares, and thereby reduce the chances of a successful bid unless the premium offered to target shareholders is high. In a private company such free-riding is not possible, thereby reducing the bid premium.
- *Liquidity discount*: For owners a takeover is a way of encashing their equity invested in the target firm. The offer price from the bidder reflects this liquidity discount, and is therefore lower than for a public target whose shares are traded on a stock market. This effect should be larger for a relatively large target. Available empirical evidence suggests that the median liquidity discount may be as high as 17%[17].
- *Post-acquisition monitoring*: Since the owners of the target, in a stock-for-stock deal, become block shareholders in the acquirer, they can monitor the latter's performance. The stock market reaction on announcement reflects this expected positive influence. If this were true we would expect to see higher acquirer returns on stock offers than on pure cash offers. Since stock exchange acquisitions of private companies are a small fraction of cash acquisitions this cannot be a very strong reason for the higher value gains.

Moeller, Schlingemann and Stulz report that over a three-year post-acquisition period large (small) acquirers of private firms generate 0.3% (−0.3%) monthly abnormal return, the difference being significant. In the three-day announcement period the small (large) acquirers generate 2.14% (0.7%). Thus while large acquirers generate significant positive gains in both periods, small acquirers experience gains in the short term but losses in the long term. Moreover, in both the short and the long term all stock acquirers experience larger gains than all cash acquirers with private targets, whereas the opposite is true of public company returns. This is consistent with the monitoring benefit of the target owners becoming block shareholders of the acquirer. (see their Tables 5 and 8). In the UK, non-cash acquirers of private targets perform worse than cash acquirers over three years, indicating no evidence of such monitoring benefit. There is also no value gain from reduction in valuation risk through stock exchange offers[18].

Private targets are more valuable because they are private!

The information asymmetry model regards lack of information about private targets as a source of valuation risk, and therefore induces acquirers to pay a lower premium and earn superior returns than with public targets. An alternative view is that certain types of acquirer, for example with requisite familiarity because of business or geographic proximity, or prior acquisition experience of private firms, may prefer to acquire private rather than public targets. Similarly, to avoid competition from other potential bidders they may prefer private targets. Thus the choice of private versus public targets may not be random, but contingent on the characteristics of the target and bidder. Using these arguments, Capron and Shen build a model to predict the choice of a private or public target, and another to predict expected returns conditional on target and acquirer characteristics, such as acquirer nationality, pre-merger profitability and payment method, and including a factor to correct for the endogeneity of the target choice variable[19]. They then compare the predicted announcement period abnormal returns for private or public target acquirers estimated for each of these two subsamples with those they might have earned had they bought the other type of target: that is, if a firm that bought a private target had instead bought a public target.

The authors find that the difference in returns between what the acquirers are predicted to earn, given their actual target choice, and what they might have earned if they chose the other type of target is highly significant. For example, the predicted return for acquirers of public (private) targets when buying such targets is −0.7% (4%) compared with −12% (−5%) if these acquirers had bought a private (public) target instead. This means that buying the wrong type of target would have cost the acquirers, on average, about 11% (9%). Thus by making the choice that they did, these sample acquirers are increasing shareholder value, confirming a strategic fit between them and their actual target type. These results conform to the theory that private company information is a strategic factor, and companies that are endowed to exploit this factor can create more value than acquirers that lack such endowment.

Small versus large targets

Smaller targets are easier to integrate after acquisition. The cost to the acquirer of misvaluation is less when the target is smaller. On the other hand, the expected synergies are also smaller with smaller targets. Several empirical studies show that the smaller the target is relative to the acquirer, the larger are the announcement period returns to acquirers. This result is, however, not uniform across studies[20]. The size effect is also not similar across public and private company targets. Acquirers generate significant positive abnormal returns when they buy large private targets, and significant negative returns with large public targets[21].

Timing

A takeover bid may be made on an opportunistic impulse because a seemingly attractive target company is being offered as a takeover candidate. Often companies with a poor performance record, limited growth opportunities or management succession problems when the founder manager retires look for potential acquirers and become available for acquisition. Sometimes a company may be bounced into a bid because of an acquisition move made by a rival.

Unplanned takeover bids may turn out, serendipitously, to be winners. However, there is an element of risk in such acquisitions that the underlying value creation logic may be glossed over, or the target may be overvalued and a high bid premium paid, or the post-acquisition integration problems may not be foreseen. It is therefore important to undertake acquisitions only after much deliberation, and as part of the firm's strategic planning. While not forgoing opportunistic bids, the A team needs to ensure that they satisfy the same rigorous criteria for value creation as the more deliberately chosen bids. Exhibit 13.3 provides a cautionary tale.

Exhibit 13.3

'Don't blame me! I didn't know a credit crisis was coming!'

In July 2007 the board of Royal Bank of Scotland (RBS) faced a critical decision. For the previous two months an RBS-led consortium had been pursuing a break-up bid for ABN AMRO (ABN), the Dutch bank. But a Dutch court had just ruled that ABN AMRO was allowed to complete a controversial deal to sell its US subsidiary – a business that RBS coveted. After a brief deliberation the RBS board – led by Sir Tom McKillop, chairman, and Sir Fred Goodwin, chief executive – chose to press ahead with the ABN Amro bid for €72bn.

The true cost of that decision became clear in April 2008 when the bank launched the largest rights issue in European history for £12bn to repair its battered balance sheet. RBS executives attempted to blame the rights issue – and losses of £5.9bn on complex debt securities held on the bank's balance sheet – on the recent turmoil in the capital markets. Sir Tom said the market's slide in March had forced RBS to recognize additional losses and raise fresh capital. But, in retrospect, the precarious state of RBS's balance sheet, and a substantial proportion of its write-downs, can be traced back to the decision to push on with the ABN AMRO deal. At the end of 2006, before it launched the bid, RBS's core Tier 1 ratio – a measure of shareholders' equity as a proportion of the bank's balance sheet – was slightly more than 5%. But RBS's share of the ABN takeover, which was paid for largely in cash, reduced that ratio to just 4%. RBS's total losses on debt securities, amounting to £8.8bn, about a third of which come from ABN, were written off. RBS is far from unique in the banking sector in taking writedowns and being forced to raise new capital. But the scale of RBS's losses, and the capital it needs to rebuild its reserves, are much more significant than they would have been without ABN.

Sir Tom acknowledged that *the timing of the deal was wrong*, but suggested the board could not have foreseen the impact the turmoil in the markets would have on the business. 'Looking back we purchased ABN at a point when bank valuations were way higher than they were today. That is unfortunate. You could call that misjudgement. Who would have known what was going to happen?' RBS's shareholders, some of whom argued that Sir Tom and Sir Fred should step aside, had overwhelmingly voted in favour of the deal in mid-August 2007, well after the turmoil in the markets had already become apparent. As a result of the losses, RBS was expected to embark on a cost-cutting plan to eliminate thousands of jobs.

Following the rights issue, the calls for the chairman and the CEO Sir Fred to go became vociferous. Sir Tom insisted that the board and executive team were collectively responsible for the bank's position, and would work together to turn it round. Sir Tom also dismissed accusations that the board had failed to curb Sir Fred's acquisitive urges. 'This is an extremely strong board,' he said: 'there are no patsies on this board.' Soon both the CEO and chairman were gone!

In contrast to RBS, which had to be rescued by the UK government in a bailout, Barclays, which had been outbid by RBS for ABN, did not seek or accept any government bail-out offer. Barclays had a fortunate escape. RBS bought ABN not only at the top of the stock market but also in an auction against Barclays. A double dose of winner's curse indeed!

Source: Adapted from P. Larsen, 'RBS finds out the true cost of the ABN AMRO deal', *Financial Times*, 23 April 2008

Buying in a recession

If buying at the top of a stock market cycle is that bad, is it a good idea to buy after a market crash or at the bottom of a cycle? There are several advantages to this timing strategy:

- The acquirer is in a buyer's market rather than a seller's market with the collapse of the M & A market; this enhances the bidder's bargaining power.
- The acquirer is not making the acquisition under peer pressure to 'keep up with the Jones', and therefore can consider carefully what it is buying, and why.
- With increased bargaining leverage, the bidder can secure a more thorough due diligence and avoid any nasty post-acquisition surprises: this reduces acquisition risk and potentially its cost of capital.
- Assuming the bidder has not already exhausted its war chest in reckless acquisitions during the boom, its liquidity is likely to be large enough to finance an attractive acquisition.
- As witnessed during 2008–09, the credit crunch that normally accompanies a recession might have hit financial buyers that rely on high levels of debt more harshly than strategic buyers.
- The acquisition premium is much lower than at the top of an M & A boom[22].

Profiling desirable targets

Following the various stages described in Figure 13.1 we can develop a desirable target profile. This is a multidimensional profile, and there may be several targets with a good strategic fit, and satisfying the deal feasibility criteria. Some of the attributes of a desirable target are shown in Figure 13.10. Table 13.4 provides a more detailed description of these attributes. These not only contribute to the acquirer achieving its strategic and value creation objectives, but also mitigate risk of deal failure. Among the strategic attributes are:

- right product/geographical market; high market share, benign market structure (not very competitive); market leadership; good scope for cost savings;

Figure 13.10 Oh, What a lovely target!

Table 13.4 Desirable target profile

Strategic attributes
- Right product/geographical market; high market share, benign market structure (not very competitive); market leadership, good scope for cost savings
- Provides platform for future growth; fragmented with scope for roll-up strategy; mature market ripe for consolidation

Resource attributes
- Product complementarity, allowing cross-selling
- Marketing capabilities; R & D capabilities; information system capabilities; high-calibre management/staff
- Product/process excellence

Deal attributes
- No onerous contractual relations between target and other parties
- Available for acquisition, and target management willing to sell
- Ownership structure favourable to deal, e.g. no entrenched owners with blocking vote
- Thorough due diligence possible, and highly transparent information about target available
- Low deal-breaking risk
- No chance of a multiple bid/auction
- Not too pricey!

Post-acquisition attributes
- Under-performer with scope for efficiency improvement and cost-cutting
- Competitors cannot replicate acquisition strategy
- Low integration risk; easy-to-integrate people, systems, IT and culture
- Costs of sharing resources not too high

- strong platform for future growth; fragmented with scope for roll-up strategy; mature market ripe for consolidation.

Showstoppers include contractual arrangements, for example with suppliers or distributors, antitrust investigation, shareholder law suits. Good due diligence reduces the valuation risk. Multiple bids lead to auctions and increase the acquisition price. Post-acquisition attributes are also important to consider, since they affect the realizability of the strategic objectives, and may destroy the value creation logic of the deal.

Scoring the targets

The desirable target profile can be used to score the shortlisted targets on their attributes. It is important to remember that the attributed must be evaluated for what they can do to the merged entity rather than to the target as a stand-alone entity. Figure 13.11 illustrates the scoring approach. The scoring is necessarily subjective, but can be founded upon the analytical frameworks described earlier, and made as rigorous as possible. It can be on a scale of 1 to 3 or 1 to 5 where fine-grained analysis is possible. The score for each group of attributes is calculated, and these can be summed to give the overall score for each target. Where attributes have unequal strength or relevance to the merger, a weighted sum of the overall score can be computed, with the weights reflecting these differential contributions.

We illustrate the scoring approach with a hypothetical bank seeking to acquire a target firm. After going through the elaborate target-screening process it has arrived at a shortlist of three possible targets, called A, B and C, and needs to choose one for making a takeover bid. It assigns scores to different attributes in each of the four categories in Table 13.5. Here an equal

Figure 13.11 Scoring potential targets

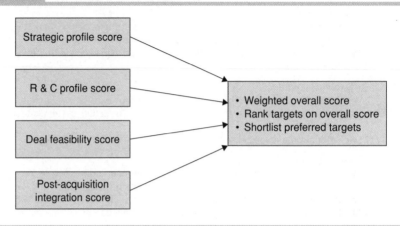

Table 13.5 Comparative profiling of alternative acquisition targets

Target attributes	Bank A	Bank B	Bank C
Strategic			
In high-growth domestic markets	3	2	1
Presence in high-growth regional markets	2	3	1
High retail banking share	1	2	3
High corporate banking share	2	3	1
Good scope for value chain leveraging	3	2	1
Strategic profile score	*11*	*12*	*7*
Resources and capabilities			
High managerial competence	2	3	1
Scope for cross-selling products	2	1	3
Marketing and IT capabilities	1	2	3
Excellent risk management capabilities	3	2	1
Young, well-qualified staff	3	2	1
Resource profile score	*11*	*10*	*9*
Deal feasibility			
No chance of multiple bids/auction	1	2	3
Available for friendly acquisition	2	3	1
Scope for thorough due diligence	3	2	1
Low deal-breaking risk	3	2	1
Low regulatory risk, i.e. antitrust	1	2	3
Deal feasibility profile score	*10*	*11*	*9*
Post-acquisition integration			
Adequate prudential capital	3	2	1
Scope for efficiency – slimming branch network	2	1	3
Low risk of replication of acquisition by rivals	3	1	2
Low integration costs	3	2	1
Post-acquisition integration risk score	*11*	*6*	*7*
Overall target profile	*43*	*39*	*32*
Maximum profile score	*57*	*57*	*57*

weighting scheme is used, but different weights may be attached to different attribute categories. For example, if the four categories are given weights of 4, 3, 2 and 1 (total of 10), the maximum weighted score is 147 and the target weighted scores will be:

Bank A – 108
Bank B – 106
Bank C – 80

On both equal and differential weighting, C is a poor target. A is the best target, but it is only marginally superior to Bank B. The acquirer must therefore focus on the first two banks and seek further information to determine the greater attractiveness of one of them. We have illustrated the choice of one among three potential targets, but this formal analysis can be extended to a larger number of potential targets before shortlisting them.

Due diligence

Any target selection based on publicly available information but not upon any information made available by the target firm must be screened further, based on any due diligence undertaken by the firm. Information revealed by the due diligence process modifies the profile of the target company, making it less or more desirable. Due diligence also allows the bidder to make a more realistic assessment of the riskiness of the deal, and negotiate stronger deal-protection clauses in its agreement with the target management. Such clauses will include stronger indemnities and warranties (see Chapter 19 on the role of lawyers in securing these). Further discussion of the due diligence process and its limitations is deferred to Chapter 20 on bid strategies and tactics.

CASE STUDY | How Beecham approached its merger with SmithKline Beckman

The merger of Beecham, the UK pharmaceutical and consumer products company, with the US pharmaceutical company Smith Kline Beckman (SKB) was formally approved by the shareholders of the two companies in June 1989. A new company SmithKline Beecham (SB) was created. But the idea that Beecham needed to merge with a US partner had been sown in late 1986 when Robert Bauman, an American, was appointed CEO of Beecham. He hired the strategy consulting firm Booz Allen to study the future growth options for Beecham and the concept of an integrated healthcare company, selling both prescription and over the counter (OTC) drugs and healthcare products emerged. With the appointment of new board of directors, Bauman started to explore how this strategy could be put into effect.

In December 1987, Beecham directors agreed to pursue potential partners in the US the largest pharmaceutical and healthcare products market in the world. Without entering the US market Beecham, which had more than two-thirds of its sales in Europe, would not be able to compete effectively with other pharma companies, especially the American ones. In the late 1980s, because of enormous competitive pressures as well as pressures from increased buyer power, regulatory relaxation in favour of generic producers, etc. the pharma companies were underperforming the stock market and they had to find new ways of enhancing their competitive advantage and their bargaining power against buyers,

→

etc. Beecham had to increase its research and marketing capabilities substantially especially in the US. An important objective was to enhance these resources by pooling those of Beecham and those of an American firm. In 1988, Beecham executives including Bob Bauman made visits to potential US pharmaceutical candidate companies. Beecham also considered alternatives to mergers.

Among the options considered were the following:

- Forming a strategic alliance for co-marketing specific products in the US, adding significantly to its sales strength. Beecham could contract with research laboratories to co-develop its new compounds, thereby speeding up the drug discovery process.
- Buy several small companies. By acquiring several small companies and folding them into Beecham's existing US operations, it can build critical mass. Beecham, given its financial constraints, could make only small acquisitions. Building critical mass would take a long time, losing valuable time to its rivals in a fast-consolidating industry.
- Make a large acquisition. While overcoming the small acquisitions problems, this option would run up against a weak Beecham balance sheet. Beecham did not want to pursue an acquisition that could turn hostile and increase the acquisition cost.
- Be acquired or spin-off the two businesses. The threat of a competitor making a take-over bid before Beecham management had a chance to pursue any of these options still loomed. Moreover, the potential acquirer must be someone to Beecham's liking.
- Do a merger of equals (MOE). Financially and strategically this was the best answer since it would require an exchange of shares with no control premium being paid to either partner. The MOE would increase Beecham's scale in the US.

Beecham realized that a MOE was a very complex transaction. Many previous MOEs had run into problems and the long-term strategic success of MOEs was doubtful. Many of them faced post-merger integration problems and for several years after the merger, the two partner companies would operate separately, thereby destroying the chances of value creation that had provided the merger justification in the first place (see Chapter 20 for further discussion of the problems with MOEs).

In pursuing each of these options the consultants identified 23 US and European pharmaceutical companies and organized them into three possible combinations:

- a major company acquisition;
- acquiring just part of a business; and
- merger of equals, i.e. with similar stock market values.

Each company was assessed for strategic fit with Beecham's criteria to become an integrated healthcare company. In pharmaceuticals the deal would broaden its core anti-infective franchise, adding products in the antifungal and antiviral areas. Would it strengthen the cardiovascular and central nervous system therapy areas? In the OTC medicine market, would it add to Beecham's scale and extend its presence to areas such as analgesics? Would the deal give Beecham the scale and marketing capacity to compete in both pharmaceuticals and OTC medicines on a global scale, including in the US, Germany and Japan? Can Beecham gain a research base in the US?

Beecham also had to test any possible deal on the 'do-ability' criteria:

- Could Beecham afford to pay for the acquisition and what effect would it have on earnings dilution and leverage? (See Chapter 16 on paying for the acquisition.)

- Was it technically possible?
- What would the reaction of shareholders and management of the two companies be?

After vetting the initial list of 23 potential candidates, Beecham's Executive Management Committee shortened the list to just six, including SKB and Stirling Drug. SKB was rated low on do-ability because its stock market value was much higher than Beecham's, thus disallowing an MOE. Stirling had just been acquired by Eastman Kodak (this turned out to be a disaster for Eastman but that is another story).

Beecham board, however, decided that MOE was the best option to pursue among the shortlisted candidates. However, they felt that MOE with any of the candidates had a zero probability. But by July 1988, the poor performance of SKB had taken its toll and its market capitalization had fallen closer to that of Beecham, around $4bn. The deal was then done as an MOE. Thus timing was all and the rest became history.

Discussion questions

1 What was Beecham's growth strategy after the appointment of Bob Bauman?

2 What were the strategic criteria for entering into a partnership with another firm?

3 What options did Beecham consider to implement its strategy?

4 What were the obstacles to each of these options?

5 What is a merger of equals? What are the likely problems with it?

6 Comment on the way the acquisition process was organized in Beecham.

Source: R. P. Bauman, P. Jackson and J. T. Lawrence, *From Promise to Performance: A Journey of Transformation at SmithKline Beecham* (Boston, MA: Harvard Business School Press, 1997), pp. 51–55.

Overview and implications for practice

This chapter describes the target selection process, and the various factors that influence the strategy, type of target and timing of acquisition. A flow chart provides an overview.

- The first step in the target selection process is the strategic choice the firm makes and the strategic direction it will follow as a result of the acquisition.
- The business portfolio of a firm will be reshaped as a result of the acquisition type chosen by the acquirer.
- We describe the different sources of value in different acquisition types, the likely sources of value in each type, the limitations, and the time scale for realizing value.
- We describe the process of identifying bid opportunities, and highlight the need for avoiding blind spots and competitor neglect in evaluating the strategic attractiveness of potential targets.
- Firms must think of ways of establishing isolating mechanisms as part of their strategic analysis so that the acquisition can lead to strong and sustained competitive advantage.
- A template is provided for evaluating the match between the acquirer and potential targets in terms of their resources and capabilities.

- Platform strategies require serial acquisitions, and the value creation potential of serial acquisitions is considered. We report empirical evidence that suggests diminishing returns to later acquisitions in a series.

- Target characteristics such as their size, whether they are private or public etc. are analyzed to evaluate their attractiveness.

- Timing of acquisitions is an important determinant of value creation, and we provide examples of mistiming and consequent value destruction.

- A template is provided for profiling desirable potential targets and ranking them for selection.

Review questions

13.1 What are the stages in a target selection process?

13.2 What is the relationship between a firm's strategic choice and the type of acquisition it makes?

13.3 Describe the sources of value in different acquisition types, and the limitations and risks attached to them.

13.4 What is the impact of Porter's five forces on the post-acquisition competitive positioning of the acquirer? What is the impact of complementors?

13.5 What are isolating mechanisms? Suggest ways in which an acquirer can set up such mechanisms. How durable are they likely to be?

13.6 What do you understand by comparative SWOT analysis? How will you apply it to target selection?

13.7 What is a platform strategy? How is it expected to create value?

13.8 Why is a small or unlisted company more attractive as a target than a large or public company?

13.9 How important is timing for the success of an acquisition? Why?

13.10 What are the various attributes of a desirable target, and what is the rationale for these attributes?

Further reading

M. Bhagai, S. Smit and P. Viguerie, 'M & A strategies in a downmarket', *McKinsey Quarterly*, September 2008.

G. Cullinan, J. Le Roux and R. Weddigen, 'When to walk away from a deal', *Harvard Business Review*, **82**(4), 2004, 96–104.

M. Faccio, J. McConnell and D. Stolin, 'Returns to acquirers of listed and unlisted targets', *Journal of Financial and Quantitative Analysis*, **41**(1), 2006, 197–220.

S. Klasa and M. Stegemoller, 'Takeover activity as a response to time-varying changes in investment opportunity sets: Evidence from takeover sequences', *Financial Management*, **36**(2), 2007, 19–43.

Notes and references

1. E. J. Zajac and M. H. Bazerman, 'Blind spots in industry and competitor analyses: Implications of interfirm (mis)perceptions for strategic decisions'. *Academy of Management Review*, **16**(1), 1991, 37–56.

2. See W. Chan Kim and R. Mauborgne, *Blue Ocean Strategy: How to Create Uncontested Market Space and Make the Competition Irrelevant* (Boston, MA: Harvard University Press, 2005).

3. For example, see D. Besanko, D. Dranove, M. Stanley and S. Schaefer, *Economics of Strategy* (John Wiley & Sons, 2007), R. Grant, *Contemporary Strategy Analysis* (Oxford, UK: Blackwell Publishing, 2008) or

J. Barney and W. Hesterly, *Strategic management and competitive advantage* (Upper Saddle River, NJ, USA: Pearson Prentice Hall, 2008). This is not an exhaustive list.

4. For examples of targets being potentially squeezed by buyer power see G. Cullinan, J. Le Roux and R. Weddigen, 'When to walk away from a deal', *Harvard Business Review*, April 2004, 96–104.

5. See J. Cummings, 'Upfront: M & A synergies? Don't count on it', *Business Finance*, www.bfmag.com. We discuss the cross-selling challenges in Chapter 23 on post-acquisition integration. Also see P. Duclos, R. Luzardo and Y. H. Mirza, 'Re-focusing the sales force to cross-sell', *McKinsey Quarterly*, December 2007.

6. C. W. L. Hill, 'Differentiation versus low cost or differentiation and low cost: A contingency framework', *Academy of Management Review*, **13**(3), 1988, 401–412.

7. For a sample of US IPO roll-ups, Brown, Dittmar and Servaes find that these firms deliver poor stock returns; their operating performance mimics that of comparable firms, but does not justify their high initial valuations. However, if the managers and owners of the firms included in the transaction remain involved in the business as shareholders and directors, operating and stock price performance improve, and future acquisitions are better received by the market. Higher ownership by the sponsor of the transaction leads to a reduction in performance, consistent with the view that the sponsor's compensation is excessive. See K. Brown, A. Dittmar and H. Servaes, 'Corporate governance, incentives, and industry consolidations', *Review of Financial Studies*, **18**, (2005), 241–270. Michael Madden observes that many high-profile roll-ups have gone awry, fuelling the charge that consolidators are 'financial cowboys' looking for a quick killing. Many IPO roll-ups are also quite expensive in terms of transaction costs, which include management and underwriting fees, offering expenses, legal and accounting expenses, etc. In some cases these costs accounted for between 7% and nearly 20%. See M. D. Madden, 'The slap-dash roll-up sits on shaky ground', *Mergers and Acquisitions*, November/December 1999, 26–30. See P. Carroll and Chunka Mui, 'Seven ways to fail big. Lessons from the most inexcusable business failures of the past 25 years', *Harvard Business Review*, September, 2008, 82–91. They say roll-up consolidations are disastrous!

8. S. Klasa and M. Stegemoller, 'Takeover activity as a response to time-varying changes in investment opportunity sets: Evidence from takeover sequences', *Financial Management*, **36**(2), 2007, 19–43, Table XII. On buy and hold abnormal returns see Chapter 4, and for the benchmarks used refer to the paper.

9. S. Sudarsanam and K. Huang, 'Are CEOs bidding for higher pay? Evidence from firms that make serial acquisitions', Cranfield School of Management working paper, March 2008. Croci and Petmezas, with a US sample of acquisitions during 1990–2002, report that announcement period abnormal returns are significant and positive for the first five bids in a series, but later acquisitions generate negative returns. See E. Croci and D. Petmezas, 'Why do managers make serial acquisitions? An investigation of performance predictability in serial acquisitions', SSRN–id727503 (1) downloaded from www.ssrn.com. For similar diminishing returns with UK data, see R. L. Conn, A. Cosh, P. M. Guest and A. Hughes (2004), 'Why must all good things come to an end? The performance of multiple acquirers', Working paper, Judge Business School, Cambridge University, UK.

10. H. Barkema and M. Schijven, 'Toward the full potential of acquisitions: The role of organizational restructuring', *Academy of Management Journal*, **51**(4), 2008, 696–722.

11. SAQ is the value-weighted returns of the serial acquirer portfolio minus the one-month Treasury bill. OCC is the value-weighted returns of the occasional acquirer portfolio minus the one-month Treasury bill. MKT is the excess return on the market portfolio, which is the value-weighted return on all NYSE, AMEX and NASDAQ stocks (from CRSP) minus the one-month Treasury bill rate. In order to facilitate our comparison, we set the full index levels of these three portfolios to 100 on 1 January 1994. For SAQ and OCC the acquirer stock is placed in the portfolio at announcement, and then held in the portfolio for three years when it leaves the portfolio. For further details see Sudarsanam and Huang, *ibid*.

12. This evidence is consistent with results reported by D. Harding and S. Rovit, *Mastering the Merger* (Boston, MA: Harvard Business School Press, 2004). In a sample of 110 US acquirers making at least 20 deals during the sample period 1986–2001, constant acquirers outperformed those making acquisitions only during recessions, the growth phase or the period in between in an economic cycle. Continuous acquirers in Europe (sample of 52) outperformed early acquirers in an economic cycle, and both outperformed late acquirers. The sample sizes are small, and the study does not provide tests of significance of the intra-group differences (see Figures A-2 and A-3, p. 183).

13. M. Faccio, J. J. McConnell and D. Stolin, 'Returns to acquirers of listed and unlisted targets', *Journal of Financial and Quantitative Analysis*, **41**(1), 2006, 197–220. They conclude that this listing effect is still strong after controlling for other relevant factors. For the US, see J. Ang and N. Kohers, 'The takeover market for privately held companies: the US experience', *Cambridge Journal of Economics*, **25**, 2001,

723–748, who report 1–2% significant two-day CARs for all private targets, whereas for public companies the CAR is either negative or insignificant. R. Masulis, C. Wong and F. Xie, 'Corporate governance and acquirer returns', *Journal of Finance*, **62**(4), 2007, 1851–1889; S. Chang, 'Takeovers of privately held targets, methods of payment and bidder returns', *Journal of Finance*, **53**, 1998, 773–784; and K. Fuller, J. Netter and M. Stegemoller, 'What do returns to acquiring firms tell us? Evidence from firms that make many acquisitions', *Journal of Finance*, **57**, 2002, 1763–1793. For UK studies reporting similar results, see A. Antoniou, D. Petmetzas and H. Zhao, 'Bidder gains and losses of firms involved in many acquisitions', *Journal of Business Finance and Accounting*, **34**(7&8), 2007, 1221–1244; P. Draper and K. Paudyal, 'Acquisitions: Private vs public', *European Financial Management*, **12**, 2006, 57–80.

14. M. Officer, A. Poulsen and M. Stegemoller, 'Target-firm information asymmetry and acquirer returns', *Review of Finance*, **1**, 2008, 1–27.

15. For a sample of 6224 UK acquisitions during 1986–2008, S. Sudarsanam and L. Barbopolous find that five-day announcement period abnormal returns are: 1.4% (private targets), 1.5% (subsidiary targets), and −0.8% (public targets), all significant at 1%. See their Cranfield School of Management working paper, 'Determinants and shareholder wealth effects of choice of earnout as acquisition payment currency', 2009.

16. See A. Antoniou *et al.*, *ibid*. Note that this sample consists only of multiple, i.e. repeat, acquirers.

17. See Officer *et al.*, *ibid*., Table II. The 75% percentile is 52%. Discount is measured with four different value multiples (deal value to total assets, deal value to net income, deal value to EBITDA, and deal value to sales) for industry-, size-, and profitability-matched portfolios of publicly traded targets.

18. See S. Moeller, F. P. Schlingemann and R. Stulz, 'Firm size and the gains from acquisitions', *Journal of Financial Economics*, **73**, 2004, 201–228, and Antoniou *et al.*, *ibid*.

19. L. Capron and J. C. Shen, 'Acquisitions of private vs public firms: Private information, target selection and acquirer returns', *Strategic Management Journal*, **28**, 2007, 891–911. The data for the study are based partly on a multinational survey of US and European (mainly French and UK) acquirers for acquisitions carried out during 1988–92. This study differs in its strategic factor rationale for private acquisitions from the others reviewed here, with a predominantly finance focus.

20. Relative size of target to acquirer is normally one of several 'control' variables used in multiple regressions of returns to acquirers on explanatory variable. These are too numerous to list here. For example, see Faccio *et al.* or Masulis *et al.* cited in footnote 11 *ante*.

21. See Officer *et al.*, *ibid*., Tables VI and VII, where target size is measured relative to the acquirer's. This result may be due to large public targets having greater negotiating power against bidders, and the free-rider problem is much more severe in large public targets than in large private targets, where large block shareholdings are more likely. On the free-rider problem, how it affects takeover premium and acquirer returns, and how it may be mitigated by large shareholders in targets, see Chapter 18 on takeover regulation.

22. See M. Baghai, S. Smit and P. Viguerie, 'M & A strategies in a downmarket', *McKinsey Quarterly*, September 2008. The authors note that companies often 'freeze' in a downturn, more so than in an upturn (60% compared with 40%), and forgo many value-creating acquisition opportunities.

PART 3

Deal structuring and negotiation

The previous part of the book was concerned primarily with the development of corporate strategy, and the organization of the acquisition function within the firm. The outcome of the processes described in that part is the specific target selection. Once a firm has made this selection, it has to negotiate the merger transaction or make a takeover bid. The aim is to make a deal that will satisfy the strategic objectives of the firm, and create value. The deal structuring and negotiation process is very complex, and involves various interconnected steps. Deal structuring depends on whether the bid is friendly or hostile. In a friendly deal the negotiation between the bidder and target management teams can alleviate some of the risk through a degree of trust and willingness to allow an extensive due diligence. However, the process is still not free of ambiguity, hard bargaining and opportunistic game playing. Understanding and exploiting the psychology of the negotiation process are important for a successful deal.

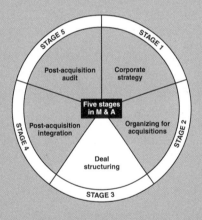

The terms of the merger or acquisition deal will depend upon the riskiness of the acquisition as perceived by the bidder. To start with, there is information asymmetry between the bidder and target. The bidder may fear a skeleton tucked away in every target cupboard. Due diligence may help dispel such fear, but the due diligence process is never as thorough as the bidder may wish, since it does entail cost to both the bidder and the target if due diligence is exhaustive, even if it is feasible. Due diligence may reveal some of the potential risks to the bidder, which may demand appropriate warranties and indemnities to minimize the impact of these risks. The deal-structuring process may also encounter many showstoppers or deal killers, which need to be anticipated and avoided. These are the broad parameters of the acquisition decision-making and deal-structuring process. We discuss the important and specific elements of this process, including valuation, financing, managing the regulatory impact, managing the relationship with external advisers, crafting hostile bid strategies, and developing responses to robust defences employed by a hostile bid target in the following chapters.

Chapter 14 sets out the valuation models, and Chapter 15 examines the impact of accounting rules, not only on structuring the deal but also on how the performance of the combined entity will be reported in the financial reports. The choices available to a bidder to pay for the acquisition and the criteria for choosing among them are discussed in Chapter 16. Chapter 17 describes the relevance of antitrust rules that may prevent a deal, the various regulatory regimes, and how they create regulatory risk. Regulation of takeover bids is the subject of Chapter 18. We compare the regimes in different countries.

Chapter 19 discusses the roles played by a range of advisers, the contribution they make, how they are remunerated, and the potential conflicts of interest between bidder and target firms on the one hand and their advisers on the other. Chapter 20 is concerned with bid strategies for both friendly and hostile takeovers, and how effective they are. The final chapter in this part, Chapter 21, examines the range of defensive strategies that targets of hostile bids pursue, and how effective they are.

Through this part we emphasize the problems that firms may encounter in deal-making. It is often a tiring process, with its own momentum, tug-of-wars, brinkmanship, etc. Once the deal has been successfully done, and the two firms or businesses come under single ownership or control, the next challenge is to integrate them in an effective way so that the journey 'from promise to performance' can be concluded. This we take up in Part Four.

CHAPTER 14

Target valuation

Objectives

At the end of this chapter, the reader should be able to understand:

- the traditional earnings, asset and cash flow models, their conceptual bases and assumptions;

- the value drivers in earnings-, asset- and cash-flow-based models, and how they are influenced by the underlying economics of the acquisition;

- non-traditional multiples as valuation models;

- the impact of intellectual or knowledge assets on valuation;

- the concepts of real options, strategic adaptability and managerial flexibility;

- the differences between traditional models and real option models; and

- the limitations of the models, and the caveats in using them for acquisition pricing.

Introduction

Valuation of the target in an acquisition is an important part of the process of determining the consideration to be offered to the target shareholders. The value that the bidder places on the target sets the maximum or 'walk away' price that the bidder can afford to offer the target shareholders. This price is only one point in a range that the bidder should derive to guide negotiation. The value of the target from the bidder's point of view is the sum of the pre-bid stand-alone value of the target and the incremental value the bidder expects to add to the target's assets. The latter may arise from improved operation of the target or synergy between the two companies. Added value may also come from profitable target asset disposals, as in a bust-up takeover.

Valuation of the target requires valuation of the totality of the incremental cash flows and earnings. The expected incremental value may be reflected in the earnings and cash flows of both the target and the bidder in the post-acquisition period. The incremental earnings and cash flows may include those arising from reduced corporation tax liability. They also include the effects of combining and leveraging the target's and the acquirer's resources and capabilities.

Valuation of a target is based on expectations of both the magnitude and the timing of realization of the anticipated benefits. Where these benefits are difficult to forecast, the valuation of the target is not precise. This exposes the bidder to valuation risk. The degree of this risk depends on the quality of information available to the bidder, which in turn depends upon whether the target is a private or a public company, whether the bid is hostile or friendly, the time spent in preparing the bid, and the pre-acquisition due diligence and audit of the target.

There are several models employed by firms to evaluate targets. These may be broadly divided into those based on (1) earnings and assets multiples and (2) discounting of accounting earnings or cash flows. The earnings and assets multiples are less information intensive than the discounting models, and less rigorous, although they can be shown as attempting to capture the underlying earnings or cash flow discounting process. In this chapter we describe how these models can be applied in target valuation. As discussed in chapter 3, in recent years new models have been developed to take into account the sequential nature of many corporate investments, with the initial investment being an option on subsequent investments. Such options allow managers to determine if and when subsequent investments will be made and, if the investment is already made, if and when it may be abandoned. This managerial flexibility adds value to corporate investments such as acquisitions and divestitures. These options are called real or strategic options, and valuation models developed for valuing financial assets have been extended to valuing real options. This chapter provides an introduction to how real options may be valued. Real option valuation again is fraught with great imprecision, and therefore increases valuation risk.

Value from acquisitions is derived from cost or efficiency savings and revenue enhancement, while maintaining costs and real options (see Table 5.1 on these sources in the context of horizontal mergers, but they apply in varying degrees to other types of acquisition discussed in Chapters 6–8 and 11). While the first two may be valued using traditional valuation tools, these tools fail to capture the essence of real options. We need new tools for valuing real options.

Sources of value in acquisitions

As has been articulated in previous chapters (see Chapter 3 and Chapters 5–8 and 11), value in acquisitions may be broadly derived from various cost efficiencies (scale, scope and learning economies), revenue enhancement (through leveraging each merging company's current resources, such as brands or distribution channels) and future growth opportunities (through leveraging each other's resources to create future competitive advantages). These sources are depicted in Figure 14.1, which relates strategy drivers to sources of value in acquisitions. The competitive strategy underlying the acquisition determines the relative importance of the three different sources of value. In a single acquisition there may be primary and secondary sources of value[1].

Value creation versus value appropriation

Value creation needs to be distinguished from value appropriation by the acquirer. Value creation depends on the robustness of the corporate strategy that drives the acquisition, and on the validity of the specific acquisition strategy chosen to implement that strategy. An acquirer having undertaken such an acquisition may nevertheless find that it is not able to appropriate an adequate share of that added value to yield the required rate of return. Of course, where there is no value creation, there is little to appropriate, and the deadweight transaction costs will inevitably lead to value destruction for the acquirer. Thus value creation is a necessary, but not a sufficient, condition. The sufficient condition is that both value creation and value appropriation take place.

Figure 14.1   Value creation in acquisitions with different strategy drivers

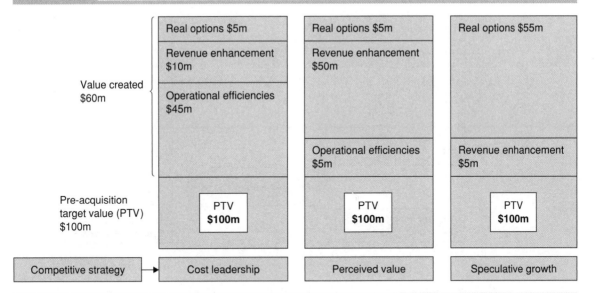

The ability to appropriate depends on:

1   whether the synergies are unique to the bidder and target;
2   whether there are several targets for each bidder;
3   whether there are several bidders for each target;
4   whether the offer price is subject to any regulatory determination; and
5   the relative bargaining strengths of the bidder and target.

Factor 1 means the appropriation is subject to bilateral negotiation. Under factor 2 the targets will compete down the takeover price. Under factor 3 targets can play off one bidder against another: the competition among targets and bidders under these circumstances may be actual or potential. The last factor, while reflecting the impact of factors 1 to 3, may also reflect the behavioural imperatives of each party to negotiate a deal even if there is little appropriation, for example when managers seek to make a deal to satisfy their ego, from overconfidence, or because of the bandwagon effect (see Chapter 2 on the bandwagon effect and Chapter 12 on the psychological impulses driving M & A deals). This factor depends not only on the relative contribution of the target and bidder to synergies but also on an understanding that each has about its own contribution as well as that of the other firm. Such an understanding, while difficult to accomplish, given that information asymmetry between bidder and target normally characterizes M & A valuation and negotiation, can nevertheless lead to realistic deal negotiation strategies. Figure 14.2 shows examples of value appropriation and overpayment by the bidder.

Connecting strategic drivers and financial drivers

Mergers and acquisitions are aimed at strengthening the competitive advantage of the acquirer or the target, or of both merging firms. But such enhanced competitive advantage needs to be reflected in incremental value creation. Further, the value sources are rooted in the

Figure 14.2   Value appropriation in acquisitions

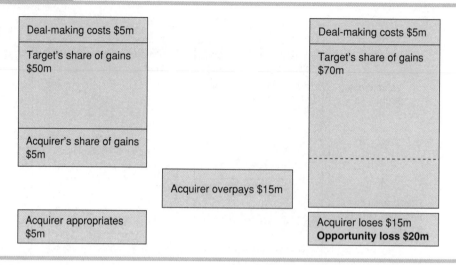

Figure 14.3   Connecting strategic drivers and value drivers

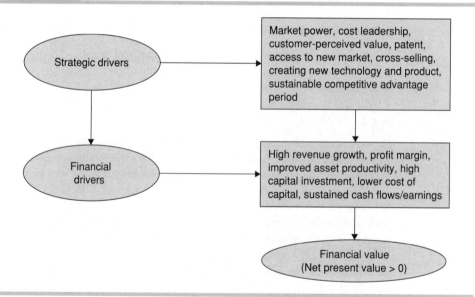

business model leading to such advantage and driving the merger. Figure 14.3 depicts the relation between strategic drivers and financial drivers. Valuation models rely on financial drivers, and where there is disconnect between strategic drivers and financial drivers, valuation can lead to under- or over-estimatation of incremental value. In general, since strategic drivers are often articulated in vague and unquantified terms, value drivers such as revenue growth, profit margin and incremental investment are also measured with imprecision. This results in misevaluation of the merger benefits, and mispricing of the deal.

Disconnect between strategic and value drivers is due to poor specification of the business model underpinning the merger, and to poor articulation of its implications for revenue, costs, investments, risk and cost of capital. Strategies may often be expressed in grandiloquent terms based on excessive optimism about the world, the economy, the industry and the firm's own prospects. An important reality check on such exuberance is to convert the strategic drivers into financial drivers and financial value, and see whether the financial numbers such as growth rate, CAP and profit margin are way too optimistic[2]. Another caveat is that financial drivers don't always reflect the full range of strategic drivers. For example, valuation of a merger driven by revenue enhancement through common branding or cross-selling may fail to reflect the resulting synergies and bidders may place undue emphasis on cost efficiencies. Similarly, a merger resting on speculative real options may be justified on the basis of cost efficiency and revenue growth. Exhibit 14.1 provides an example of such disconnect. While most mergers may combine all these different sources of synergies, establishing a clear and transparent link between strategic and financial drivers is an important step in the valuation process.

Exhibit 14.1

Disconnect between strategic and value drivers: merger of Hewlett-Packard and Compaq

In February 2001 HP and Compaq (C hereafter) filed their merger agreement. The strategic logic of the merger was:

- HP and C had been strong in enterprise computing and IT-services businesses, but neither company was dominant across the board; the merged company would be a major force in enterprise computing and perhaps among the top three in services; with customers looking for fewer technology vendors, the merged entity could provide a wider range of products and services to them.
- HP's three primary business lines were: (1) imaging and printing; (2) computing, including desktops, notebooks, servers and storage products; and (3) services. It was very strong in 1 but weak in 2 and 3.
- C's primary divisions were: (1) access, consisting of commercial and consumer PCs; (2) enterprise computing; and (3) global services. Although its direct distribution model (in response to Dell's successful direct distribution model) had lowered costs, access still operated at a negative margin.
- C was market leader in fault-tolerant computing and industry-standard servers, but HP was not present in the former and weak in the latter. C was not strong in the UNIX market, but HP-UX was a top supplier. C was the world's leading supplier of storage systems, and HP was strong in high-end servers.
- The merged company would be a dominant leader in servers and be well positioned to *exploit the fast-growing trend of storage area networks* in the storage market. By combining these complementary server and storage lines the new company could reduce costs, *offer a comprehensive array of products for enterprise customers*, and more effectively allocate R & D for growth in enterprise computing.

The above description clearly indicates that the two companies were seeking to exploit product complementarities and cross-selling opportunities, and operate a 'one-stop shopping' technology vendor model. These may normally be expected to lead to significant revenue enhancement and even real-option-type

→

opportunities in enterprise computing. Thus *the merger seems to be driven by more than cost savings alone*.

The merger agreement enumerated several opportunities for savings in admininstrative/IT costs, cost-of-goods sold, sales management, R & D efficiencies, purchasing and marketing amounting to $2.5bn per year by mid-2004. Management also stress-tested this estimate and stated that even revenue loss as high as $21bn (five times the expected revenue loss) would only just wipe out the cost savings. Management also expected that the cost synergies, when realized, would lead to substantial improvement in operating profit margins from 2003.

Management underplayed the revenue enhancement opportunities and focused almost exclusively on cost efficiencies as the strategic drivers. This understated both potential value-added and the risk attached to the synergies, since revenue enhancement is probably a more risky source of synergy than cost efficiency. A correct valuation model needs to incorporate all incremental sources of value and the incremental risk.

Source: R. Bruner, 'The merger of Hewlett-Packard and Compaq (A): Strategy and valuation', Darden Business Publishing, University of Virginia, case no UVA-F-1450, 2004

Valuation models

We first present the traditional valuation models that are appropriate for valuing the first two components. We then discuss real option models.

Traditional valuation models

With these models, the earnings or assets of the target are estimated after taking into account any changes the acquirer plans to make to the operations and asset structure of the target in the post-acquisition period. The estimated earnings or assets are capitalized into target value using an appropriate benchmark earnings or assets multiplier. The choice of this benchmark multiplier is very important, and can present problems when the target is a private company or a multi-business firm. These multiples are single-number valuation tools, but are derived from the economic fundamentals of the firm. We start with the residual income models that lead to the earnings and asset multiples.

Residual income models[3]

Starting from the fundamental premise that the equity value of a firm is the present value of its future dividends discounted at the appropriate risk-adjusted discount rate, we can derive the simple Gordon growth valuation model:

$$\text{Equity value at time } t = \frac{\text{Dividend at time } t+1}{K^e - g} \tag{14.1}$$

where K^e is the cost of equity capital and g is the expected constant dividend growth rate. For example, if company X is expected to pay a dividend of $1 next year, this dividend is expected to grow indefinitely at the rate of 6%, and the cost of equity is 16%, the firm's equity value now is $10. The ratio of dividend to current share price is the dividend yield, i.e. 10%.

We can express the Gordon model in terms of earnings and return on equity at $t = 0$:

$$\text{Equity value} = \text{BE}_0 + \frac{\text{NI}_1 - K^e \cdot \text{BE}_0}{1 + K^e} + \frac{\text{NI}_2 - K^e \cdot \text{BE}_1}{(1 + K^e)^2} + \frac{\text{NI}_3 - K^e \cdot \text{BE}_2}{(1 + K^e)^3} + \ldots \quad (14.2)$$

where NI_t = net income for equity holders for year t and BE_{t-1} = book value of equity at $t - 1$. The firm or asset value is expressed similarly (BE at the end of $t - 1$ is the same as at the beginning of t). Since asset value is the sum of the capital from equity and debt, the following formula uses the after-tax profit for both these capital providers rather than just net income for equity:

$$\text{Asset value} = \text{BA}_0 + \frac{\text{NOP}_1 - K^w \cdot \text{BA}_0}{1 + K^w} + \frac{\text{NOP}_2 - K^w \cdot \text{BA}_1}{(1 + K^w)^2} + \frac{\text{NOP}_3 - K^w \cdot \text{BA}_2}{(1 + K^w)^3} + \ldots$$

$$(14.3)$$

where NOP_t = net operating profit after tax (NOPAT) for year t and K^w = weighted average cost of equity and debt (see below on weighted average cost of capital). BA_{t-1} = book value of assets represented by sum of equity and debt at $t - 1$.

Equation (14.2) is based on the clean surplus relation (CSR) among book value of equity, net income and dividend[4]. The interpretation of the above formulae is simple. Equity/asset value equals the book value of assets in place plus the value due to future growth, at a rate of return in excess of the dollar cost of capital. The growth component specifies the conditions under which growth creates value. The net income, NI_t, must exceed the opportunity cost of using the assets for equity, $K^e \cdot \text{BE}_{t-1}$. The excess is known as residual income (RI). Similarly, profit made by the company from all assets, NOP_t, should exceed the opportunity cost of using them, $K^w \cdot \text{BA}_{t-1}$. If the assets do not generate returns in excess of the relevant cost of capital, there is no value addition.

The important question, therefore, is under what competitive conditions can the acquirer generate returns in excess of the cost of capital? Another aspect of the above equations is that the growth component can extend over several years. Each growth term on the right-hand side represents the value addition from maintaining the competitive edge in that year. Competitive equilibrium is reached when profit equals the dollar cost of capital. Value destruction happens when the profit fails to match the latter. It is now clear why RI models are also called economic profit or abnormal returns models. Economic profit arises from economic rents that a firm enjoys, and economic rent depends on its superior competitive position. In competitive equilibrium firms can earn only the minimum return, i.e. the risk adjusted cost of capital. Return in excess of that is 'abnormal', and can arise only from superior competitive positioning.

Equity value to book value of equity (EVBV)

The above value equations can be transformed into asset multiples as follows:

$$\frac{\text{Equity value}}{\text{Book value}} = 1 + \frac{\text{ROE}_1 - K^e}{1 + K^e} + \frac{(\text{ROE}_2 - K^e)(1 + g_1)}{(1 + K^e)^2} + \frac{(\text{ROE}_3 - K^e)(1 + g_1)(1 + g_2)}{(1 + K^e)^3} + \ldots$$

$$(14.4)$$

where ROE_t is return on equity $= \text{NI}_t / \text{BE}_{t-1}$, and g_t is percentage growth in book value (GBV) of equity BE from $t - 1$ to t, i.e. $(\text{BE}_t - \text{BE}_{t-1}) / \text{BE}_{t-1}$. The equation tells us that a firm has equity-to-book value of 1 when the return on equity equals the cost of capital in every period. Suppose company A's ROE is 10% and its equity cost of capital is 15%. Then it does not generate any value, because returns from its investments are not sufficient to recover the cost of capital. Its equity-to-book value will be less than 1.[5] An acquirer of A may be able to improve its performance and its ROE and deliver shareholder value. The difference $(\text{ROE} - K^e)$ is the abnormal return, and represents the value spread. This spread will be high when a firm enjoys any competitive advantage, but will be competed away if it fails to maintain that advantage.

Market or price to book ratio

The ratio equity value/book value, when expressed on a per share basis, is known as the price-to-book (PTBV) ratio. This is done by dividing both the numerator and denominator by the number of shares at issue at the time of calculation of the ratio. It is also known as market-to-book ratio (MTBV), since equity value is the share price times the number of shares at issue of the firm. PTBV or MTBV exceeds 1 when RI is positive, at least in some periods in the future, and the sum of the present values of the spreads in Equation (14.4) is positive. Since MTBV depends on the competitive conditions in a sector there is a wide variation in sector MTBVs.

We can derive a similar formula for equity plus debt to book value of total assets. In the latter case, the return on assets ROA should exceed the weighted average cost of capital in every period in the future. With competition eroding profit margins, ROE (ROA) as well as the growth rate g will decline over time. This is competitive attrition of profitability. Exhibit 14.2 shows the application of the equity multiple to valuing an acquisition target. Here, $(1 + \text{CGBV}_t) = (1 + g_1)(1 + g_2) \ldots (1 + g_t)$.

Exhibit 14.2

Fast Mover (FM) makes value out of Sluggish target

Sluggish Company has £100m of assets at book value and depreciates them over 4 years @ 25%. It generates ROE of 10% on book value, and its cost of capital is also 10%.

	Year 1	Year 2	Year 3	Year 4
Book value at start	£100	£75	£50	£25
Earnings	£10	£7.5	£5	£2.5
ROE (%)	10	10	10	10

Since abnormal (abn.) ROE, i.e. (ROE – K^e), is zero, its equity-to-book value is just one. Now FM Company acquires Sluggish, makes its assets (and its managers) sweat to generate higher earnings as follows with cost of equity unchanged:

	Year 1	Year 2	Year 3	Year 4
Earnings	£20	£15	£10	£2.5
ROE (%)	20	20	20	10
Abn. ROE (%)	10	10	10	0
Growth in book value (GBV) (%)	0	−25	−33	−50
1 + CGBV	1	0.75	0.50	0.25
Abn. ROE (1 + CGBV)	10	7.5	5	0
Present value factor	0.909	0.826	0.751	0.683
PV of abn. ROE (1 + CGBV)	9.09	6.20	3.76	0
Cumulative PV of abn. ROE	19.1			
Equity value to book	119.1%			

Fast Mover can increase the value of Sluggish by 19%.

Price/earnings ratio

Price/earnings ratio (PER), also known as the earnings multiple, expresses the relation between a firm's earnings for equity, NI, and its equity market capitalization. This can be derived from the equity value model above[6]. It can be shown that

$$\frac{P_0}{\text{NI}_0} = \left(\frac{1 + K^e}{K^e}\right)\left[1 + \sum\left(\frac{\Delta\text{RI}_t}{(1 + K^e)\text{NI}_0}\right)\right] - \frac{\text{Dividend}_0}{\text{NI}_0} \tag{14.5}$$

where $\sum$ is over $t = 1$ to ∞ and ΔRI_t is change in RI from $t - 1$ to t. This shows that PER:

- increases with growth in RI ($\Delta\text{RI}_t > 0$) and therefore in NI; and
- declines with increase in the cost of capital, K^e, and therefore risk.

It is also a positive function of the length of time over which residual income increases.

In practice the equity value is proxied by the market value of the company's equity:

$$\text{Price/earnings ratio} = \frac{\text{Market value of equity}}{\text{Earnings for equity}}$$

$$= \frac{\text{Share price}}{\text{Earnings per share (EPS)}}$$

We can relate the MTBV and PER ratios:

$$\begin{aligned}
\text{MTBV} &= P_0/\text{BE}_0 \\
&= (\text{NI}_0/\text{BE}_0) \times (P_0/\text{NI}_0) \\
&= \text{ROE}_0 \times \text{PER}_0
\end{aligned}$$

Thus the higher the PER, the higher the MTBV, for a given ROE. If PER is 20 and ROE is 10%, MTBV will be 2. For the period 1974–2004 in the US Lundholm and Sloan report PER ranging from 5 to 20. This suggests a range for ROE of 10% in 1974 to about 9% in 2004[7]. During takeover bids, the PER is often argued by both offerors and targets to indicate whether the price being offered is generous or inadequate.

Investors generally employ alternative definitions of the PER: the historic and the prospective. The historic PER relates current market value of equity to the earnings of the most recent accounting year. Prospective PER relates the current market value of equity to the earnings expected to be reported at the end of the current accounting year. Prospective PER requires a forecast of prospective earnings[8].

Interpretation of the PER

The PER is a function of three factors, as Equation (14.5) indicates:

- investors' expected return for equity investment in the firm, i.e. the equity cost of capital, which in turn rests on the riskiness of the firm's earnings, K^e;
- the expected return on the investments made by the firm, ROE; and
- the length of time the firm can earn returns on its investments in excess of the investor-required return, i.e. the speed to establishment of competitive equilibrium.

Meaning of growth

As is clear from Equations (14.4) and (14.5), the value of a firm increases with growth of the firm, but that growth must be accompanied by positive RI. Therefore valuable growth comes from the firm's ability to invest in projects, including acquisitions, yielding higher returns than the investors' required return. This ability depends upon the competitive advantages the firm possesses: for example, a low-cost production process, product differentiation through branding, exclusive access to a distribution network, or privileged access to raw materials. The profitable growth phase does not last for ever, and is terminated by the emergence of competitors. However, the longer the competitive advantage can be maintained, the greater the value of the firm to its shareholders (see Chapters 5–9). The *competitive advantage period* (CAP) is therefore a critical variable for acquirers to estimate. In Equations (14.4) and (14.5) CAP may be defined as the length of time T over which $RI_t > 0$ for $t = 1, T$. In equilibrium, $RI_t = 0$ for all t. Where RI increases over time ($\Delta RI_t > 0$), the firm is operating with increasing returns to scale, e.g. a firm with network externality (see Chapter 5 for a discussion). Acquirers often see growth in sales from their acquisitions, but not profitable growth, or may assume a prolonged CAP. Such errors lead to value destruction.

Estimating target equity value using the RI model

We can use Equation (14.2) to estimate the equity value of a target firm. This requires forecast of RI_t. Analysts, for example on the IBES database, often forecast the EPS for two years, from which RI can be estimated. Since analysts' earnings forecasts are available for two years ahead, the forecast horizon used is two years, and the terminal value (TV) is the present value at the end of year 2 of all the RI from year 3 onwards. To estimate TV we need to make some assumptions about how RI will behave after year 2. Several possible assumptions are possible: RI stays level, i.e. no growth; or RI grows at a constant rate, g; or it is eroded, and reverts to the mean for all firms in the economy over a period.

Assuming a forecast horizon of 2 years,

$$TV_{t=2} = \frac{RI_{t=2}}{K^e} \text{ (in the case of level perpetuity)}$$

$$= \frac{RI_{t=2}(1+g)}{K^e - g} \text{ (in the case of constant growth rate } g \text{ for RI beyond year 2)} \quad (14.6)$$

$$\text{Equity value}_0 = BE_0 + \frac{RI_1}{1+K^e} + \frac{RI_2}{(1+K^e)^2} + \frac{TV_2}{(1+K^e)^2}$$

This requires an estimate of the cost of equity K^e and BE_t for $t = 0$ and 1. BE_0 is the book value of equity per share taken from the firm's most recent financial statements, and BE_1 needs to be forecast.

Residual income model with earnings attrition

A level or constant-growth assumption for the RI may be unrealistic when RI is eroded by competition. If RI regresses towards the mean as a result, then future long-term RI will be less than the near term RI. Equity value P_0 is then

$$P_0 = BE_0 + \sum_{t=1}^{T-1}\left[\frac{NI_t - K^e BE_{t-1}}{(1+K^e)^t}\right] + \frac{NI_T - K^e BE_{T-1}}{(1+K^e - \omega)(1+K^e)^{T-1}} \quad (14.7)$$

where the RI persistence parameter is ω ($0 \le \omega \le 1$). Here profit attrition sets in after T periods. The higher the profit persistence, the higher is the value of the firm[9].

Exhibit 14.3 shows how the attrition rate affects the amount of value creation. With moderate attrition the value of Exotic can be raised by 126%. With more serious attrition of 40% this falls to 85%, and with high attrition of 60% it declines further to 66%. As argued earlier, profit attrition depends on the evolving competitive structure of Exotic's industry after the acquisition. The acquisition price that Acme can offer Exotic will therefore be constrained by the expected attrition.

Exhibit 14.3

Valuing a target firm using the RI model

Acme Inc. evaluates a potential target company, Exotic Inc., using the model in Equation (14.7) above. It has gathered the following values for the parameters:
$BE_0 = \$100$ per share; $NI_1 = \$30$; $NI_2 = \$35$; $NI_3 = \$40$; $NI_4 = \$50$;
$D(ividend)_1 = \$10$; $D_2 = \$15$; $D_3 = \$20$; $BE_1 = \$120$; $BE_2 = \$140$; $BE_3 = \$160$
$K^e = 15\%$; $\omega = 0.60$; $T = 4$ years
Substituting in Equation (14.6):
$P_0 = \$184.94$
Value addition $= P_0 - BE_0 = \$84.94$
This represents 85% value addition and a market-to-book value (MTBV) of 1.85.
If ω is low at 0.40 (high profit attrition), MTBV is 1.66 (66% value added).
If ω is low at 0.80 (low profit attrition), MTBV is 2.26 (126% value added).

Estimating target value using the PER model

Application of the PER model proceeds in the following steps:

1 Examine the most recent profit performance of the target firm and the expected future performance under the current target management.
2 Identify those elements of revenue and costs that will be raised or lowered under the acquirer management.
3 Re-estimate the target's future, post-acquisition earnings for equity shareholders on a sustainable basis. These earnings are known as sustainable or maintainable earnings.
4 Select a benchmark PER.
5 Multiply the sustainable earnings by the benchmark PER to arrive at a value for equity.

Past performance of the target firm

In examining the recent profit and loss accounts of the target, the acquirer must carefully consider the accounting policies underlying those accounts. Particular attention must be paid to areas such as treatment of extraordinary items, interest capitalization, depreciation and amortization, pension fund contribution, and foreign currency translation policies. Where necessary, adjustments for the target's reported profits must be made, so as to bring those policies into line with the acquirer's policies. For example, the acquirer may write off all R & D expenditure, whereas the target might have capitalized the development expenditure, thus overstating the reported profits.

Re-estimating the target earnings

This goes beyond adjustments needed to bring the two companies' accounting policies into harmony. Re-estimation reflects the improvements in the target operation that the acquirer plans to make after the acquisition. For example, the combined operation of the two firms may be expected to lead to higher prices or lower cost of sales, thus improving the gross profit margin. Reduction of sales and administration costs resulting from the acquisition may lead to improved net profit margins.

The acquirer's post-acquisition management plans for the target, based on the acquisition logic, determine the extent of cost saving or revenue enhancement. The assumptions behind the plans, such as higher output prices, lower input costs or reduced selling and adminis-tration costs, must be carefully vetted and must reflect the genuine capabilities of the two firms and not just wishful thinking. The costs of achieving the planned operational efficiencies must be allowed for in estimating the purchase price. For example, rationalization of produc-tion or sales force may lead to redundancy costs or relocation costs.

In estimating the future earnings for equity shareholders, the capital structure – that is, the proportion of debt and equity in financing the acquired firm – is an important consideration owing to the tax deductibility of interest on debt. Where the target firm is going to be funded differently from its pre-acquisition capital structure, the equity shareholders' earnings will be different. In general, an increase in gearing will increase those earnings and K^e.

Since equity earnings are estimated post-tax, the impact of accumulated trading losses must be taken into account in estimating the corporation tax on profits. In many countries, such as the UK and US, there are strict rules for offsetting past losses against future profits, and these rules are discussed below. Provided the conditions are satisfied, past losses reduce the effective rate of corporation tax. Some of the adjustments that the acquirer has to make to the target earnings, such as redundancy costs and tax savings due to accumulated tax losses, are of a transitory nature. Since the PER model requires an estimate of sustainable earnings, one sol-ution to the estimation problem is to identify and value the transitory components separately. Their value can then be incorporated in the purchase price.

Selecting the benchmark PER

Various PER benchmarks are available:

- the target's prospective PER at the time of the bid;
- the PER of firms comparable to the target;
- the target's sector average PER;
- the PER reflected in the M & A transactions in the same sector in recent years; or
- the PER reflected in the M & A transactions of similar size in recent years[10].

In choosing the benchmark we must ensure its comparability in terms of risk and growth. It is the risk–growth configuration of the target post-acquisition and not its historic profile that forms the basis of comparison. The benchmark is normally adjusted to reflect this expected configuration. Such an adjustment is often a matter of subjective judgement, since the relation between PER and risk and growth is, in practice, only imperfectly understood. Sustainable earnings estimated in the previous step are then capitalized at the adjusted benchmark PER to give a target value.

Determining the purchase price

Estimation of the sustainable post-acquisition earnings of the target involves a concomitant appraisal of the investment needed to sustain those earnings. This appraisal helps the acquirer identify those target assets that are not needed and can be disposed of, as well as the new investment to be made, such as new plant and equipment. The proceeds of such disposals reduce the purchase price. Acquirers are often faced with the obligation to top up employee pension schemes, and this can add substantially to the acquisition cost. Trustees of such pension schemes negotiate hard with potential acquirers (see Exhibit 14.4). In recent years several bids have failed because of bidders' failure to meet the trustees' demands.

Exhibit 14.4

Pension top-up a 'poison pill'

ICI, a leading UK chemical company, became the target of takeover bids in June 2007. The size of the employee pension scheme's deficit and the ability of a potential acquirer of the company to provide additional funds to cover this deficit were of major concern to ICI pension fund trustees. They insisted on a central role in any takeover talks between the UK chemicals group and Akzo Nobel, the Dutch conglomerate. The trustees' demand came as ICI rejected a takeover proposal from Akzo valued at £7.2bn (€10.6bn). A spokesman for ICI's pension trustees said: 'We would have expected to have an early and direct conversation with anyone wanting to replace ICI as owner of the company'. He highlighted the power of the trustees to determine the size of the deficit, which could range from £500m up to £2.2bn, depending on their view of a bidder's financial strength and their confidence in the bidder's willingness to fund long-term promises to pensioners. The scheme's liabilities were more than £9.2bn, against a market value of its assets of £6.5bn, according to the company. He said: 'If faced with someone who hasn't talked with us, we would have to form a different, harsher view [of the owner]. That would be another factor in determining the size of the deficit. 'If we perceive the promise [of whoever sponsors the pension scheme] is legally and financially weaker, that would increase the size of the deficit. It would be better to have an up-front conversation.'

Source: Adapted from S. Davoudi and K. Burgess, 'Pensions warning to ICI bidder', *Financial Times*, 18 June 2007

Where rationalization is contemplated by the acquirer, the associated costs must be added to the purchase price if they have been excluded from the computation of sustainable earnings. It must be remembered that profits on asset disposals and refund of pension fund surpluses are generally subject to corporation tax, and rationalization costs are tax deductible. The cost of new investments must be added to the purchase price.

Example of valuation using the PER model

Target is the subject of a takeover bid from Bidder. Both Bidder and Target operate a number of car dealer franchises, but in different parts of the UK. Bidder's rationale for the merger is as follows:

● The two companies' operations are complementary in terms of dealerships of different manufacturers and geographical spread.
● The merger will help each company diversify its product range and geographical coverage.
● The increased size of the merged firm will help increase its bargaining power and improve its purchasing terms *vis-à-vis* the manufacturers.

Table 14.1 Income statement of Target (£m)

Turnover	1500
Cost of sales	1380
Gross profit	120
General and administration expenses	60
Associate company loss	5
Operating profit (earnings before depreciation and amortization, EBITDA)	55
Depreciation and amortization (DA)	15
Earnings before interest and tax (EBIT)	40
Interest payable	8
Earnings before tax	32
Corporation tax @ 30%	10
Earnings for ordinary shareholders	22

Table 14.2 Balance sheet of Target (£m)

Fixed assets		
Plant, property and equipment	300	
Investment in associate	30	330
Current assets		
Stocks	120	
Debtors	110	230
Total assets		560
Current liabilities		
Accruals	20	
Creditors	160	180
Long-term loans		90
Ordinary shareholders' funds (1m shares)		290
Net asset value per share (pence)	290	

- Bidder can improve the profitability of Target through improved management and selling techniques.

Any added value from the acquisition that Bidder hopes to achieve must stem from this rationale (see the earlier discussion of strategic and financial drivers). Target's forecast income statement and its forecast balance sheet for the next accounting year-end without the takeover by Bidder are shown in Tables 14.1 and 14.2 respectively. These are assumed to have been derived from Target's historic financial statements and the incumbent management's plans for Target. In practice, these plans are unlikely to be publicly disclosed.

The forecast earnings of Target in Table 14.1, when multiplied by the company's prospective PER, yield its stand-alone value. Target's prospective PER before the bid is 10. This gives a pre-bid Target value of £220m that may be assumed to be also its market value. For its shareholders to gain from the acquisition Bidder needs to run Target better than the latter's incumbent management, and enhance its value from the stand-alone level. This can be done by increasing Target's earnings growth after acquisition, and this requires that Target's operational efficiency be improved or its competitive positioning be strengthened to generate higher revenues.

Bidder expects to make the following changes after acquisition, with impact on the revenues, costs and assets of Target:

- Increase both volume and sales. Forecast revenue growth is 8% per annum.
- Reduce cost of sales. Forecast profit margin (earnings before interest and tax/sales) is 4%, raised from the current 2.67%.

Table 14.3 Pro forma income statement of Target under Bidder (£m)

Turnover	1620
Cost of sales	1474
Gross profit	146
General and administrative expenses	61
Operating profit (earnings before depreciation and amortization, EBITDA)	85
Depreciation and amortization (DA)	20
Earnings before interest, tax (EBIT)	65
Interest payable	8
Corporation tax @ 30%	17
Earnings for ordinary shareholders	40

- Sell off loss-making associate investment at book value.
- Sell Target's head office premises, as they will be redundant.

Although some of the planned improvements of Target will benefit Bidder and add to its own earnings, and therefore its valuation, in this example all the benefits are attributed to Target and incorporated in its earnings[11].

Table 14.3 provides the pro forma income statement for Target under Bidder's management. The projected post-acquisition earnings for Target are much higher than the pre-acquisition earnings. The average PER of its direct competitors is 12 and the sector average is 9.

In choosing among the alternative benchmark PERs, Bidder evaluates the underlying growth expectations and riskiness of Target, its competitors, and the average firm in the sector. Such an evaluation is done using traditional financial statement variables or stock-market-based historic returns and risk measures. From a careful evaluation, Bidder concludes that Target's risk and growth profile is better than that of the sector average firm. Bidder is also confident that its post-acquisition plan for Target will raise its performance to that of its competitors. Thus the appropriate benchmark PER is 12.

Bidder estimates that, in order to achieve the projected level of sustainable earnings, it has to invest in new showrooms, an inventory control system, and a new dealer network. This capital expenditure is projected at £90m. Additional working capital investment to sustain the higher level of sales is £20m. Thus total new investment is expected to be £110m. This investment, to be spread over the following five years, is stated at its present value (see later). Since Bidder's post-acquisition plan involves rationalization, the expected redundancy costs are £20m.

Bidder plans to divest the loss-making associate company investment for the book value of £30m. Further, Target's current head office will be closed and its functions transferred to Bidder's head office. The head office property is therefore redundant, and will be disposed of for £70m after any capital gains tax. The maximum value of Target to Bidder is made up as shown in Table 14.4.

Table 14.4 Value of Target to Bidder (£m)

Value of the sustainable earnings from the PER model	480
(prospective earnings of £40m in Table 14.3 × 12)	
Plus	
Associate company divestment	30
Sale of Target head office	70
Less	
New fixed asset investment	90
Additional working capital investment	20
Redundancy costs	20
Value of Target to Bidder	450

Target's pre-acquisition value was £220m. Thus from Bidder's view, potential added value from the acquisition is £230 million. Any control premium that Bidder has to pay must not exceed this added value, and must fall short of it if Bidder shareholders are going to gain from the acquisition. This represents added value of more than 100%, and calls for critical and serious scrutiny of the assumptions about the growth rates and efficiency savings, both in operating costs and in new investments. As we saw in Chapter 4, while targets make substantial gains from takeovers, only a small minority receive 100% premium. There must therefore be strong justification for paying a high premium. Recent deals of a similar nature involving similar companies can provide a benchmark for assessing a reasonable premium, although the idiosyncrasies of specific deals have to be taken into account.

Limitations of the PER model

The PER model estimates the post-acquisition earnings for the target for a single period, and assumes that this level will be maintained. There is no explicit recognition of the time pattern of earnings growth. For example, operating profit margin may increase from the current 2.67% to the projected 4% over a five-year period. The revenue growth rate of 8% may be feasible in the first post-acquisition year, but competition may erode that growth quickly. Thus it may not be a sustainable growth rate. The acquirer needs to make realistic estimates of future revenues, costs, investments etc. Moreover, the model does not directly consider the investor-perceived risk of the target firm's earnings. Problems also arise in the selection of the benchmark PER, as indicated above. Despite these limitations, the PER model provides a valuation based on the capital market consensus view of the value of earnings. It is widely used by the investment community, and makes for ease of communication during a bid.

Enterprise value multiple

In recent years analysts have used an alternative measure of valuation. The ratio, enterprise value/earnings before interest and tax (EV/EBIT) or its 'cash flow' variant, enterprise value/ earnings before interest, tax, depreciation and amortization (EV/EBITDA), has been employed. It is called enterprise value multiple (EVM). EBIT represents the pre-tax return to both shareholders and debt holders. Since most firms are overwhelmingly funded by equity and debt, the sum of equity and debt values represents the value of the firm or enterprise. Depreciation and amortization are non-cash expenses deducted in deriving EBIT. Adding them back, we get EBITDA, which is widely regarded as a measure of operating cash flow. Tables 14.1 and 14.3 show the EBIT and EBITDA before and after acquisition of Target. As in the case of PER, the EVM requires an appropriate benchmark.

Sum of parts valuation

Where a target firm has several distinct businesses differing in their competitive environment and performance, it makes little sense to value the firm as a whole using a single multiple PER or EVM.

More fine-grained valuation can be obtained by valuing each individual business and then summing up the individual values. Targets with multibusiness portfolios often feel that the overall firm valuation does not truly value the underlying businesses correctly, i.e. the firm is valued at a 'conglomerate discount' (see Chapter 7 on conglomerate discount). They are therefore keen to establish that 'sum of parts' (SOP) valuation gives a more realistic firm value. Acquirers that may buy the target and then unbundle it to divest some of the acquired businesses may also find SOP valuation more insightful of the true value of their purchase, and what the unbundled business would likely fetch if they were divested. Another reason for SOP valuation is that valid benchmark multiples may be easier to obtain at the business level than at the firm level for a multi-business firm. Exhibit 14.5 shows the use of sum of parts valuation based on EV/EBITDA in a merger of two companies.

Exhibit 14.5

Sum of parts valuation

Each firm is valued as the sum of the values of the component businesses. Each component business must be clearly identifiable and independent market-listed comparator firms need to be available to serve as benchmarks. Each business is then valued using the appropriate market multiples discussed above for the relevant comparator companies. To arrive at a range of values analysts use high and low multiples of the comparator companies. The SOP valuation based on EV to sales revenue (EV/S) ratio in the case of an Internet services company and EV/EBITDA in the case of a multimedia company is shown below. Revenue or EBITDA figures are generally taken from the most recent financial statements of the merging companies.

Internet services (IS)

	Sales Estimate	Comparator EV/S	Value $
Online services	$500m	8	4.0bn
E-commerce & advt	$400m	50	20.0bn
Enterprise solutions	$100m	14	1.4bn
ISP market value			$25.4bn

Multimedia (MM)

	EBITDA Estimate	Comparator EV/EBITDA	Value $
Networks	$200m	20	4.0bn
Publishing	$100m	15	1.5bn
Music	$ 60m	15	0.9bn
Filmed entertainment	$110m	18	2.0bn
Cable systems	$350m	24	8.4bn
MM market value			$16.8bn
IS+MM total firm value (high)			$42.2bn
IS+MM total firm value (low) (calculations using low multiples, not shown)			$30.0bn

The market multiple of 50 for the E commerce business shows a high valuation of the E-commerce business. Since SOP valuation depends on market multiples as benchmarks the choice of these multiples is critical to a realistic valuation.

Asset-based valuation

The best known of the asset-based models is Tobin's q, which is the ratio of the market value of a firm to the replacement cost of its assets. The replacement cost of an asset is the cost of acquiring an asset of identical characteristics, such as the production capacity of a plant:

$$\text{Tobin's } q = \frac{\text{Market value of a firm}}{\text{Replacement cost of its assets}}$$

For example, if the market value of a firm is £500m and the replacement cost of its assets is £250m, its q is 2. The excess value may also be regarded as the value of the option to exploit these opportunities. The value of a firm is thus made up of two components:

Firm value = Replacement cost of assets + Value of growth options

This relationship is similar to the one between firm value, book value of assets and the value of residual income we discussed above[12].

Tobin's q can also be used as a valuation tool in the same way as the PER. Selection of a benchmark q is, however, much more difficult than in the case of the PER. The asset structures of firms could differ considerably, even if they are in the same business. Moreover, evaluation of the underlying growth options is not easy. Growth options facing different firms in the future are not always identical. For example, two oil exploration and production companies operating in different parts of the world may have different growth opportunities. In some other sectors, such as property, although valuation of the firm's individual assets can be done more easily, there is nevertheless the problem of valuing the growth options.

There are other limitations in the use of Tobin's q for valuation purposes. In the UK, assets reported in company accounts are valued not at replacement cost, but mostly at historic cost. Although frequent revaluations allow reported firm asset values to approximate to their replacement cost, this practice is not consistently followed by all firms, since revaluation under current accounting rules is not mandatory. Thus asset figures reported by UK companies are a mixture of historic and current cost values. Similar problems may arise in other countries.

As regards the numerator of the q ratio, the market value of the firm is the sum of the market values of all the financial claims on the firm, such as equity and debt. Since corporate debt in the UK is generally not traded, market value of debt is difficult to ascertain. Often analysts use the sum of the market value of equity and the book value of debt, but this is only an approximation to the firm market value.

A widely used approximation to q in practice is the market-to-book value of equity (MTBV) derived earlier. This ratio is also known as the valuation ratio. For Target this ratio under its pre-acquisition management is 0.76, derived from the stand-alone market value of Target at £220m and its net worth of £290m in Table 14.2. This ratio level suggests that Target's assets are seriously undervalued by the stock market, thus offering Bidder the scope for enhancing the valuation ratio. MTBV is interpreted broadly the same way as the q ratio.

Valuation using other multiples

In addition to earnings and asset multiples, analysts use other multiples, such as price to sales revenue or price to cash flow. In each case the variables are measured per share. Cash flow is in theory the free cash flow (see the discounted cash flow model below), but in practice it is proxied by EBITDA. Price to sales is used to value young businesses, where earnings or cash flow data are not available, that is, when the firm makes losses in the initial years of its life. Multiples used by analysts are in some cases sector specific. Although they are handy, and reflect some measure of performance, it requires a leap of imagination to assume that they are highly correlated with the real value drivers – profits, cash flows and dividends. For example, advertising agencies may be valued as a multiple of billings, cable television as a price per subscriber, hotels as sale price per room. Price to sales was used to value start-up companies such as Amazon.com, a company that did not make any profit for its shareholders for several years. (See Exhibit 14.5 for the use of a related measure, EV/S.) This provides a cautionary tale since no matter how big the revenue, what fattens shareholder wallets is not revenue, but cash flows and dividends[13]. In the case of Amazon.com all its value was based on capitalization of future growth opportunities in the form of real options (see below on real option valuation). Mobile telecom companies have been valued as price per subscriber, ignoring the cost of building up the networks and the cost of attracting, retaining and servicing the subscribers. Thus multiples based on variables far removed from cash flows to investors must be carefully used.

Discounted cash flow model

The earnings-based models described above can be transformed into a cash-flow-based valuation model. The numerator of the equity value model is expressed in terms of free cash flow to equity holders (FCFE) in each period. This cash flow model is known as the equity residual model, since the FCFE is the residual cash flow after meeting the claims of debt holders, e.g. interest. The numerator of the asset value model above can be expressed in terms of the free cash flow to the firm (FCFF), i.e. to both equity and debt holders. We now describe how the FCFF (a.k.a. the WACC) model is used to derive the value of target's equity.

The discounted cash flow (DCF) model is applied in the following steps:

1 Estimate the future cash flows of the target, based on the assumptions for its post-acquisition management by the bidder over the forecast horizon.
2 Estimate the terminal value of the target at the forecast horizon.
3 Estimate the cost of capital appropriate for the target, given its projected post-acquisition risk and capital structure.
4 Discount the estimated cash flows to give a value of the target.
5 Add other cash inflows from sources such as asset disposals or business divestments.
6 Subtract debt and other expenses, such as tax on gains from disposals and divestments, and acquisition costs, to give a value for the equity of the target.
7 Compare the estimated equity value for the target with its pre-acquisition stand-alone value to determine the added value from the acquisition.
8 Decide how much of this added value should be given away to target shareholders as control premium.

In preparation for the forecast of target cash flows under the bidder's management, the historic cash flow statements of the target must be examined. As with the sustainable earnings forecast discussed earlier, the cash flow forecast is based on assumptions about the changes to the operation of the target to be introduced by the bidder. In particular, these assumptions relate to the value drivers.

Value drivers and cash flow forecast

Value drivers are those key revenue, cost or investment variables that determine the level of a firm's cash flows, and hence its value to the shareholders. We can identify six key value drivers[14]:

- forecast sales growth in volume and revenue terms;
- operating profit margin;
- new fixed capital investment;
- new working capital investment;
- the competitive advantage period (CAP); and
- the cost of capital.

Competitive advantage period

The time to competitive equilibrium when the acquirer's competitive advantage is eroded depends on factors such as replicability, imitability, cost of developing countervailing competitive advantage by its rivals, and the payoffs to being a second or third mover (see Chapters 3, 5 to 8, and 11). If the competitive opportunities are shared, and not unique to the acquirer, and the rivals can replicate the resources and capabilities that gave the acquirer the first-mover advantage, the competitive equilibrium may be quickly established. As we noted in our discussion of merger waves (Chapter 2), given the proliferation of me-too acquisition strategies by rivals, any presumption of unassailable competitive positioning through acquisitions may be unwarranted.

Empirical evidence suggests that such a positioning may last four to five years before reversion to the mean. Palepu *et al.* show, for a sample of European firms from 1989–2005, that many value drivers are mean-reverting, as shown in Figure 14.4[15]. This evidence suggests that maintaining relatively high-growth sales rates is a formidable challenge. This is consistent with the evidence seen earlier that revenue enhancement is quite a daunting task for acquirers (see Chapter 5). Maintaining high profitability is also a great challenge. The rapid emergence of competitive equilibrium must therefore be factored into the assumptions behind valuation models.

What lengthens the CAP?

CAP can be eroded by any of Porter's five forces, or by the erosion of complementors (see Chapter 3 on these models): buyer power may increase, substitutes may appear, current competitors may unleash a ferocious counter-attack, new competitors may enter, or complementors may suffer a similar fate, and their loss of competitive advantage then contaminates the merged entity's competitive advantage. Figure 14.4 suggests that any or all of these forces may be causing the mean reversion. Where these potential threats take a long time to materialize, the merged entity can enjoy a long and fruitful CAP. CAP is lengthened by the robust *isolating mechanisms* that we discussed in Chapter 13.

The bidder's post-acquisition management plan normally aims at altering the above value drivers, so that additional value can be created from the acquisition. Alteration of the value driver levels depends upon the value creation logic underlying the acquisition. Changes in the driver levels are often interdependent. For example, higher sales growth may be achieved only by increasing expenditure on marketing, advertising or product development, or by additional investment in fixed assets and current assets. These changes in the value drivers are then translated into a forecast of cash outflows and inflows.

Operating cash inflows, arising from the operations of the firm, are after-(corporation) tax cash flows but before payment of interest on borrowing that has been used to finance the target. Any changes in the effective tax rates as a result of a reduction in potential corporate tax liabilities should be added to the cash inflows. Examples of such incremental tax benefits include writing off the accumulated tax losses of the acquired company against its future, post-acquisition profits, or any saving from stepped-up depreciation under certain tax regimes. Cash outflows are due to additional fixed capital and working capital investments.

Figure 14.4   (a) **High sales growth reverts to mean; (b) high ROE reverts to mean**

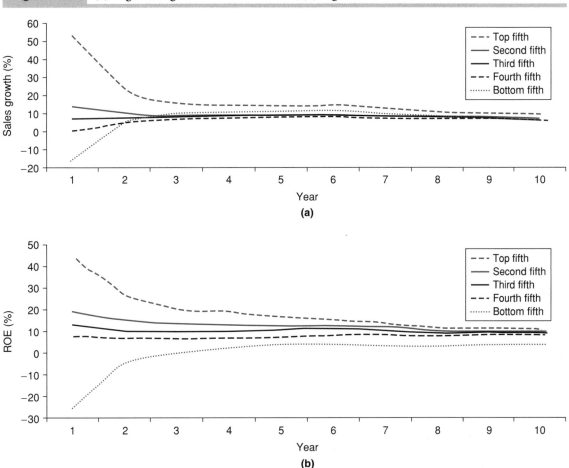

Source: K. G. Palepu, P. M. Healy, V. L. Bernard and E. Peek, *Business Analysis and Valuation* (Cincinnati, OH: South-western College Publishing, 2007), Chapter 6 and Appendix.

After-tax operating cash flows net of investment cash outflows are called free cash flows (FCFF or just FCF) (see Chapter 3 on the interpretation of FCF).

Target cash flows are generally forecast for the next five to ten years. In general, the longer the forecast horizon, the less accurate is the forecast. Where CAP is short, it can form the forecast horizon. The terminal value (TV) of the target at the end of that period based on FCFs thereafter also needs to be forecast. Often this terminal value is based on the assumption of perpetual free cash flows at the same level of operations as in the last year of the forecast period. The level perpetual cash flows are then capitalized at, i.e. divided by, the cost of capital to yield the terminal value. The forecast FCFs, when discounted, provide the acquirer with the present value of the target as a whole. From this firm value, debt is subtracted to give the equity value. TV can also be based on assumptions about the rate of sustainable growth. For most industries and firms sustainable growth rate may be just the economy's growth rate of 3–5%. Overconfident/over-optimistic managers may project much higher rates, but such projections need to be exposed to very rigorous and sceptical scrutiny. A healthy dose of scepticism is warranted by the mean reversion phenomenon, although, as Figure 14.4 suggests, high per-formers seem able to sustain their *relative* (not *absolute*) high performance over several years.

Cost of capital

The cost of capital is the weighted average cost of capital (WACC), estimated from the target's pre-acquisition costs of equity and debt. If, after the acquisition, the risk profile of the target changes, perhaps because of product or market diversification of the target, the cost of equity and of debt will change. The pre-acquisition cost of capital has therefore to be adjusted to reflect this change in risk. Further, if the post-acquisition capital structure for the target differs from its pre-acquisition structure, the WACC has to be adjusted for the difference. Thus:

$$\text{WACC} = K^e E/V + (1 - T^c)\, K^d\, D/V + K^p\, P/V\, P \tag{14.8}$$

where K^e = cost of equity;

$\quad K^d$ = cost of debt;

$\quad K^p$ = cost of preference shares (relevant if capital structure includes preference shares);

$\quad E$ = market value of equity;

$\quad D$ = market value of debt;

$\quad P$ = market value of preference shares;

$\quad T^c$ = corporation tax rate;

$\quad V = E + D + P$, the value of the firm.

In general P is a negligible source of capital, and in the following discussion of WACC we focus on cost of equity and cost of debt.

Estimating the weighted average cost of capital

This requires estimation of the costs of the various components of long-term capital, includ-ing equity, preference shares and debt. As regards equity, earning yield (earnings/share price) and dividend yield (dividend/share price) do not fully reflect the opportunity cost of equity to the shareholder. The capital asset pricing model (CAPM) may be used to estimate the historic cost of equity for the target. The CAPM estimates the investor-required return as the sum of a risk-free rate and a risk premium based on the overall market risk premium and the risk of the stock in relation to the market. This risk is known as the systematic risk, and a measure of that risk is known as beta, β (see Chapter 4 for a discussion of beta and its importance to deter-mining security returns).

$$\text{Equity cost of capital, } K^e = R_F + \beta\,(R_M - R_F) \tag{14.9}$$
$$= \text{Risk-free rate} + \text{Equity risk premium}$$
$$\times \text{Beta on equity stock}$$

Equity risk premium = Expected return on market, R_M − Risk-free rate, R_F

Equity beta = Sensitivity of stock return to market return

$$= \frac{\text{Covariance of stock with market returns}}{\text{Variance of the market return}}$$

Beta is estimated by an econometric procedure using historical share price data. For public companies betas are also readily available from investment advisory services in different countries, such as Value Line in the US, and the Risk Measurement Service of the London Business

School in the UK. For a private company the beta of a similar public company may be used. The risk-free rate is in practice the return on a short-dated (say 90 days) government Treasury bill, or the return on a government Treasury bond. The market is generally proxied by a broad-based stock market index such as Standard & Poor's in the US and the Financial Times All-Share Index in the UK.

The pre-acquisition expected return on equity for the target needs to be adjusted for a possible change in the target beta after the acquisition. This adjustment, necessitated by changes in the underlying operating characteristics of the target due to the acquisition, is somewhat subjective, since the relation between the operating characteristics of a firm and its betas is not definitively understood.

Having estimated the individual components of cost of capital, we then weight them by the proportion of each type of capital in the capital structure of the target. The relevant capital structure is the post-acquisition capital structure contemplated by the bidder.

Estimating the cost of equity

Although the empirical validity of the CAPM has been questioned by numerous studies, and alternative asset pricing models have been proposed and tested (see Appendix 4.1 in Chapter 4 on CAPM and the other models), CAPM still remains the workhorse of the valuation industry and discussed in textbooks on corporate finance. One of the important issues in employing the CAPM is the equity risk premium (ERP), which is the difference between the expected return on the market portfolio and the risk-free rate.

Estimates of the ERP have been made by numerous researchers, some using time-series data stretching back to the beginning of the 20th century! Estimates for some countries are presented in Table 14.5.

Apart from these historic estimates, many researchers have also made 'forward looking' estimates based on some measure of expectation of stock market earnings/dividend growth

Table 14.5 Historical ERP around the world 1900–2005

Country	Based on long bond rate	Based on Treasury bill rate
Australia	7.1	6.2
Belgium	2.8	2.6
Canada	4.5	4.2
Denmark	2.9	2.1
France	6.8	3.9
Germany*	3.8	5.3
Ireland	4.1	3.6
Italy	6.6	4.3
Japan	6.7	5.9
Netherlands	4.6	3.9
Norway	3.1	2.6
Spain	3.4	2.3
Sweden	5.7	5.2
Switzerland	3.6	1.8
U.K.	4.4	4.1
U.S.	5.5	4.5
Average	4.8	4.0
World	4.7	4.0

Note: The numbers are geometric averages. Arithmetic averages are generally higher than geometric averages.
Source: E. Dimson, P. Marsh and M. Staunton, (2006) 'The Worldwide Equity Premium: A Smaller Puzzle', *EFA 2006 Zurich Meetings Paper. AFA 2008 New Orleans Meetings Paper*, downloaded from http://ssrn.com/abstract=891620.

rates. In this regard, the dividend growth model and the residual income model have been put to service. These efforts yield the implied expected cost of equity for the market as a whole, from which the ERP can be calculated by subtracting the risk-free rate. ERP is model sensitive[16]. In general, historic arithmetic average overestimates future ERP, and geometric average underestimates it. It is better to work with a reasonable range of ERP and test the sensitivity of value estimates to the choice of ERP and therefore the cost of equity. Both ERP and the risk-free rate vary from one country to another.

Cost of debt

Cost of debt is generally different from the coupon rate when the face value of debt is different from its market value. It also varies with the maturity of debt, in general increasing with increasing maturity. The rate at which a firm can borrow is influenced by the firm's default risk. Debt rating agencies such as Standard & Poor's, Moody's and Fitch rate corporate debt and the debt-issuing companies, and the rating category is a reflection of the expected default risk. The ratings go down from AAA through AA down to BBB, and further down to C, D etc. The lower the rating, the greater is the likelihood of default, and the higher is the coupon to attract debt investors (see Table 14.6).

Moody's long-term obligation ratings are opinions of the relative credit risk of fixed-income obligations with an original maturity of one year or more. They address the possibility that a financial obligation will not be honoured as promised. Such ratings reflect both the likelihood of default and any financial loss suffered in the event of default.

The rating category is closely linked to the expected default risk and the cost of debt, which is measured as a base rate plus a spread. The base rate is the London Interbank Offered Rate (LIBOR), and the spread depends on the rating category. The spread increases non-linearly as the rating is lowered. The default risk also increases similarly.

BBB is an important category, because it represents the minimum investment-grade bond. Under the law in the US, certain prudential financial institutions are not allowed to invest in corporate bonds with a rating lower than BBB. Categories below BBB are variously referred to

Table 14.6 Long-term fixed income bond rating definitions

Moody's	S & P/Fitch	Definition
Aaa	AAA	Highest quality, with minimal credit risk
Aa	AA	High quality and subject to very low credit risk
A	A	Upper-medium grade and subject to low credit risk
Baa	BBB	Moderate credit risk – medium-grade with certain speculative characteristics
Ba	BB	Have speculative elements and subject to substantial credit risk
B	B	Speculative and subject to high credit risk
Caa	CCC	Of poor standing and are subject to very high credit risk
Ca	CC	Highly speculative and probably in, or very near, default, with some prospect of recovery of principal and interest
C	C	Lowest-rated class of bonds, and typically in default, with little prospect for recovery of principal or interest

Definitions are from Moody's and are broadly similar to S&P's and Fitch's ratings.
Moody's appends numerical modifiers 1, 2 and 3 to each generic rating classification from Aa to Caa. The modifier 1 indicates that the obligation ranks in the higher end of its generic rating category; the modifier 2 indicates a mid-range ranking; and the modifier 3 indicates a ranking in the lower end of that generic rating category.
S & P correspondingly appends +, no sign or – to the alphabets.

as 'junk', 'sub-investment', 'speculative', or 'high yield'. Sub-investment grade bonds have to pay considerably higher spreads to compensate investors for higher default risk. For example, in December 2000 (following the financial markets' collapse) spread was about 2500bps (basis points) for CCC, 500bps for BB, 250 for BBB and 200 for A. Spreads widen very substantially for grades below BBB. The calculations above provide only the coupon, that is, the nominal interest rate on the bond. Cost of debt itself may be higher or lower than the coupon, depending on the level of interest rates in the economy as reflected in the LIBOR. For example, the bond yield will be less if the interest rates have risen and more if they have fallen. In our WACC calculations we need the cost of debt represented by the expected yield, and the coupon may or may not be a good proxy for that.

One way to calculate the cost of debt is to use the CAPM to estimate the systematic risk of corporate debt. The statistical procedure is the same as for estimating equity beta. However, because corporate debt is either untraded or traded infrequently, such estimation may result in debt beta estimates subject to a lot of error and therefore unreliable. An alternative method is to break down the excess of the coupon over the risk-free rate into its various components due:

- systematic risk, which may include economy-wide default risk
- firm-specific risk, which may include firm-level default risk; and
- liquidity risk, i.e. the secondary market in debt is not deep and investors cannot disinvest without selling at a high discount.

Attempts to estimate disaggregate the coupon have not so far yielded universally agreed conceptual and procedural models. Nevertheless, it is intuitively plausible that high levels of leverage will increase the systematic risk of debt, i.e. debt beta[17]. Some estimates for debt beta range from 0 at low levels of leverage debt to about 0.20 or 0.30 at high leverage levels. It also follows that low credit rating will be associated with high debt beta[18].

Determining the purchase price

The value of target free cash flows to the bidder is

$$\text{TGTVAL}_a = \sum_{t=1}^{T} \frac{\text{FCF}_t}{(1+\text{WACC})^t} + \frac{\text{TV}_T}{(1+\text{WACC})^T} \tag{14.10}$$

where TGTVAL_a = target value after the acquisition;
FCF_t = free cash flow of target in period t;
TV_T = terminal value of target at $t = T$;
T = terminal period for forecast, and $t = 1 \ldots , T$.

The total value of the target to the bidder may also include the proceeds of sale of assets and divestments, reorganization costs or pension fund deficits discussed earlier. These sale proceeds and pension fund deficits must be calculated on an after-tax basis. From the target value, the debt of the target must be subtracted to yield the target equity value to the bidder. The actual consideration paid to target shareholders must fall short of this value if the bidder shareholders are to receive any gains from the acquisition.

DCF valuation of a target: example

Table 14.7 projects the free cash flows for Target over the five years ($T = 5$) following the acquisition in 2010. It assumes that the operating cash inflows from year 6, i.e. 2016, will be constant, and at the same level as in year 5. No new investment in fixed assets or working

Table 14.7 Valuation of Target equity using forecast free cash flows (£m)

	2011	2012	2013	2014	2015	2016
Sales	1620.0	1750.0	1890.0	2040.0	2204.0	2204.0
Operating profit	64.8	70.0	75.6	81.6	88.2	88.2
– Corporation tax	21.4	23.1	24.9	26.9	29.1	29.1
– Additional fixed assets	20.4	22.0	23.8	25.7	27.8	0.0
– Additional working capital	4.8	5.2	5.6	6.0	6.5	0.0
Free cash flow (FCF)	18.2	19.7	21.3	23.0	24.8	59.1
PV of FCF 2011 to 2015						78.0
PV of terminal value @ 2015						319.0
TGTVAL$_a$						397.0
+ Divestment of associate						30.0
+ Sale of Target head office						70.0
– Redundancy costs						20.0
– Long-term loans						90.0
Value of Target equity to Bidder						387.0

capital is needed after year 5. The terminal value of Target at the end of year 5 is therefore the capitalized value of this level perpetuity of free cash flow (£59.1m) at the post-acquisition WACC of Target. The forecast assumes the following values for the five value drivers:

- Expected sales growth = 8% per annum for 2011 to 2015 and 0% growth thereafter.
- Operating profit margin = 4% of sales.
- Additional fixed capital = 17% of incremental sales.
- Additional working capital = 4% of incremental sales.
- Cost of capital (WACC) = 11%.

It is further assumed that Target expends the depreciation provision each year to maintain its operating capacity at the pre-acquisition level. In the example, the depreciation provision is therefore not added back to operating profit in deriving the FCF or to fixed asset investment.

The estimated Target value of £387m to Bidder compares with the pre-bid market value of £220m, its stand-alone value. Thus the added value expected from the acquisition is £167m. This is the maximum control premium that Bidder can afford to pay to Target shareholders. This maximum will be reduced by bid costs, which could be substantial if the bid were to become hostile.

Terminal value, TV$_T$

The DCF model back end-loads corporate value with the present value of TV$_T$ accounting for 80% of Target value. TV$_T$ can vary widely (and wildly), depending on whether the growth assumption is optimistic, realistic or pessimistic. In the above example we have assumed that cash flows beyond 2015 will not grow, but will remain perpetually the same as in 2015. We assume a 'sudden death' scenario in which the Bidder loses all competitive advantage after 2015. Other assumptions are possible. For example, a three-stage model might include a high-growth stage lasting, say, five years, a declining growth phase over the next five, and then a stable growth period when Bidder grows at the same sedate pace as the economy. It is easy to extend the DCF model to accommodate such an extended valuation horizon. The terminal value assumption is quite critical, and must be chosen with a thorough understanding of the current and, even more importantly, the future competitive dynamics of the market in which Bidder will be selling its goods and services.

Table 14.8 Impact of growth assumptions beyond TV on value of Target to Bidder

	FCF growth rate after 2015			
	8%	*3%*	*0%*	*−20%*
PV of TV$_T$ (£m)	1169	438	319	113
TGTVAL$_a$ (£m)	1247	516	397	191
(TV$_T$/TGTVAL) @ 2010 (%)	94	85	80	59
Net value to Bidder	1237	506	387	181
Maximum £ premium	1017	286	167	−39

We can demonstrate the importance of paying critical attention to estimating the terminal value by varying our assumptions for beyond 2015. Target value to Bidder under various scenarios is shown in Table 14.8. The very high growth assumption at 8% indefinitely implies some degree of increasing returns to scale, and can be due to Bidder enjoying network externality benefits. Where Target can grow at a high a rate and settle at the long-run equilibrium for a mature economy, say 3%, its competitive advantage, though temporary, is not completely eroded. Target may achieve a high growth, but severity of competition may flatten its growth rate after five years down to 0% (our base case). Finally, competitors may retaliate so fiercely as to quickly erode Target's competitive advantage at the rate of 20% per year. The appropriateness of each assumption depends on the anticipated competitive rivalry, as well as on the competitive reactions of buyers and sellers. The scenario analysis, by raising questions about the post-acquisition competitive advantage and its durability, can aid realistic acquisition pricing.

Sensitivity analysis of the DCF valuation

Given the uncertainty surrounding the forecast process, it is sensible that the acquirer examine how sensitive the target value is to any variation in the assumptions. This kind of analysis highlights those critical value drivers that the acquirer needs to focus on. In particular, the assumptions behind the critical drivers need to be robustly justified. Forecasting their post-acquisition levels also demands greater accuracy. The impact of changing some of the value driver forecasts while maintaining the others is illustrated in Table 14.9. The value of the acquisition appears most sensitive to improvement in operating profit margin and increase in the discount rate. The key to value creation is not sales growth but enhanced profitability and return on assets. Reducing cost of capital through the right choice of acquisition financing is also critical to value creation.

Assessing sustainable growth

We can reverse-engineer the DCF model to figure out the rate of growth of FCF after the forecast horizon, which can justify a given acquisition premium. The stand-alone value of the

Table 14.9 Sensitivity of Target value to value drivers

1% increase in	*Change in equity value (£m)*
Sales growth rate	4.4
Operating profit margin	126.0
Fixed asset investment	−5.2
Discount rate	−41.9

target in our example is £220m. If Bidder aims to pay a 50% premium, the purchase price will be £330m. Assuming the 8% growth in sales in the first five years can be achieved, what is the growth rate beyond that will yield a Target value of £330m? This requires the corporate value of Target to be £340m (allowing for assets divestments, redundancy costs and long-term loans in Table 14.7), and TV_T should be £441.48m. This implies an FCF growth rate of

$$441.48(0.11 - g) = 59.1$$

$$g = 0.11 - 59.1/441.48 = -2.4\%$$

Thus FCF growth after year 5 can decelerate by 2.4% per year, and Bidder can still afford a premium of 50%.

The DCF model is much more information intensive than the multiple models, but also much richer in its analysis. It allows for a detailed sensitivity analysis. While the problems of forecasting free cash flows and estimating the cost of capital remain, the DCF model is conceptually and analytically more sophisticated.

Adjusted present value (APV) model

In the above DCF model we forecast cash flows to the firm and discounted them at WACC to arrive at the firm value, but inclusive of the benefit of leverage reflected in WACC. An alternative DCF model in Equation (14.10) is the APV:

Value of firm = Value of firm if it were fully equity financed
+ The value of tax benefits of debt

Thus firm value is estimated in two steps. To calculate the value of a 100% equity-funded firm we need the cost of equity of such a firm. This cost of equity is also called the unlevered cost of equity to distinguish it from the levered cost of equity.

$$\text{TGTVAL}_a = \sum_{t=1}^{T}\left(\frac{\text{FCF}_t}{1 + K^{\text{ue}}} + \frac{\text{TV}_T}{1 + K^{\text{ue}}}\right) + \sum_{t=1}^{T}\left[\left(\frac{\text{Tax benefit}_t}{1 + K_d}\right)_t + \left(\frac{\text{TV of tax benefit}_T}{1 + K_d}\right)_T\right] \quad (14.11)$$

In Equation (14.11) K^{ue} = cost of unlevered equity; Tax benefit$_t$ = coupon on debt times the corporation tax rate at t; and K_d is the cost of debt, which may be different from the coupon (see above for discussion of cost of debt).

From Equation (14.11) we can see that the operating cash flows to the firms are discounted at the unlevered cost of equity. It is also known as the cost of capital for the firm's assets, and is independent of the way the firm finances its assets, i.e. of its leverage. The tax benefits are separately valued.

Since the APV model estimates firm value and the benefit of debt separately, it is particularly useful when leverage changes over time. In the case of LBOs (see Chapter 11), private equity firms raise leverage substantially after buyout. The pre-buyout equity beta is therefore an inappropriate measure of the cost of equity, which consequently increases after buyout. WACC falls with increased leverage, since lower cost debt is substituted for high cost equity (see Equation (14.8) above).

Equation (14.9) above estimates the levered cost of equity from the observed stock returns of the company as a function of levered equity beta. To arrive at the asset cost of capital we calculate the asset beta, i.e. we calculate the unlevered beta. This procedure is known as delevering the equity beta. We then substitute the estimated asset beta in the CAPM equation to calculate the cost of unlevered equity, K^{ue}. The following formulae are used for this purpose:

$$\beta_{Asset} = \beta_{Levered\ equity}\ [E/(D+E)] + \beta_{Debt}\ [D/(D+E)] \tag{14.12}$$

$$\beta_{Levered\ equity} = \beta_{Asset} + (D/E)\ (\beta_{Asset} - \beta_{Debt}) \tag{14.13}$$

β_{Asset} is invariant to leverage, and it measures the pure business risk. $\beta_{Levered\ equity}$ increases with business risk and leverage. This effect may be offset by increasing β_{Debt} as leverage increases. Using Equation (14.12) we can estimate the asset beta, given the current leverage. To recalculate the levered equity beta if leverage increases, we can use Equation (14.13). This is shown in Exhibit 14.6.

Valuation for private equity buyouts

As discussed in Chapter 11, private equity firms expect to exit their investments within defined periods in order to return the capital to equity investors. They forecast possible exit dates, e.g.

Exhibit 14.6

Estimating asset beta, levered equity beta and WACC when leverage increases

Suppose Lowlev is the target of a private equity buyout. Currently it is 25% funded by long-term debt, and 75% by equity. The equity has a beta of 1.5 and the debt beta is 0.10, reflecting the low leverage. The risk-free rate is 3% and the market risk premium (MRP) is 5%. Corporation tax rate is 30%.

The buyout will be financed with 80% long-term debt and 20% equity. Debt beta is assumed to rise to 0.30 because of the high leverage.

We can use Equation (14.8) (ignoring preferred shares) to calculate WACC, Equation (14.9) to calculate cost of equity and cost of debt, Equation (14.12) to calculate asset beta, and Equation (14.13) to calculate the levered equity beta when the leverage is raised. The various calculations are shown below for before and after the buyout.

	Before		After
Debt/(Debt + Equity)	0.25		0.80
Debt/Equity	0.33		4.00
Levered equity beta	1.50	1.15 + (0.80/0.20) (1.15 − 0.30) = (using Equation (14.13))	4.55
Debt beta	0.10		0.30
Asset beta = 1.5 × 0.75 + 0.10 × 0.25 (using Equation (14.2))	1.15	Unchanged	1.15
Cost of debt = 0.03 + 0.10 × 0.05 =	0.035	Cost of debt = 0.03 + 0.30 × 0.05 =	0.045
Cost of equity = 0.03 + 1.5 × 0.05 = (using Equation (14.9))	0.105	Cost of equity = 0.03 + 4.55 × 0.05 =	0.2575
WACC = 0.105 × 0.75 + 0.035 × 0.7 × 0.25 = (using Equation (14.8))	0.0849 8.49%	WACC = 0.2575 × 0.20 + 0.045 × 0.7 × 0.80 =	0.0767 7.67%

The effect of leverage is to reduce WACC from 8.49% to 7.67%, a saving of 0.82%. As seen in Table 14.9, the dollar effect of such reduction can be substantial.

three or five years from the date of investment in a portfolio company. They then work out the return to equity investors conditional on that exit. For this purpose they normally estimate the internal rate of return (IRR) to their investment in the LBO target during the investment holding period. To calculate the IRR, they forecast a possible exit value of equity. For this purpose one can use the DCF model described earlier. In this case the terminal value becomes the exit value. Instead of using the DCF to estimate the exit value, PE firms often use an exit multiple: for example, the FCF of £24.8m at the end of 2015 (exit in 5 years) is converted into exit value by using an FCF multiple (say 12) in Table 14.7, i.e. £298m. This is then used in the IRR calculation. Intermediate cash flows that the PE firm receives from the portfolio company (see Chapter 11, Exhibit 11.8) are also factored into the IRR model. PE investors normally aim for an IRR of 25–30% per year.

Cost of capital for different synergy sources

It may be argued that cost efficiencies, revenue enhancement and real options give rise to risks of varying magnitudes, and therefore merit different cost of capital. In general, cost savings do not fundamentally alter the business profile. Similarly, when the merged firms' revenue grows, but they remain in the same lines of business, the business/asset risk of the business does not change. If the merged entity diversifies into related or unrelated businesses to achieve revenue enhancement, there is likely to be a change in asset risk. This needs to be modelled, and revised asset beta can be used to calculate equity beta assuming the expected leverage level.

Valuation of private companies

While the principles of valuation of private companies are the same as for public companies, an important difference is that for private company targets we do not have the benchmark valuation provided by the stock market. Use of the PER model or the discounted cash flow model requires that we locate a stock market proxy for the private company. This proxy must be as similar as possible to the target. Often the proxy is matched by industry or sector and size to the target. The proxy's PER or its cost of capital may then be used to value the target.

Even where the proxy is well matched to the target in terms of industry and size, the proxy PER needs to be discounted for the potential non-marketability of target shares before it can be applied to the target. Similarly, the cost of capital has to be raised to compensate for this additional risk.

Compared with a public company that is often widely researched by investment analysts, information about the private target may be sparse. Forecasting the future cash flows is thus a more difficult exercise. Offsetting this disadvantage is the fact that private company bids are almost always friendly, with easier access to the target's management information.

Impact of tax on target valuation

In the past, some of the acquisitions were driven by tax factors. For example, a target with accumulated trading losses (called tax losses) that could be offset against the acquirer's profits would be an attractive target. The acquirer could reduce the tax liability for the group after acquisition. Because of subsequent changes in the tax law in the UK, use of tax losses is now subject to strict conditions.

The trading losses can be carried forward only for offset against future profits of the same company. That is, there is no immediate transfer of losses and profits between the target and the acquirer after the acquisition. Further, there should be no major change in the target's trade in the period three years before and three years after the change of ownership. The practical implication of this rule is that the acquirer has to run the same business of the target as before, turn that company around, and then use the tax losses to reduce future tax liability. Tax law provisions in the UK also restrict the carryback by the target of losses incurred after a change of ownership to the pre-change periods[19].

Accumulated capital losses of a target cannot be set against a chargeable capital gain (i.e. a gain liable to capital gains tax, CGT) made by another member of the group. It is also difficult to buy a target with accumulated capital losses, and transfer to it from the acquirer assets pregnant with capital gain, thus offsetting the gain against the losses. In pricing a target the buyer therefore has to examine very carefully whether the potential tax benefits can be reliably factored into the valuation. Tax rules differ widely across countries, and so merit careful consideration of each country's rules.

Real options framework for valuing targets

The abnormal earnings models, the multiples and the DCF all suffer from an important shortcoming. Corporate investments may often involve a series of investments. The above models assume that not only the initial investment but also all subsequent stage investments are irreversible. For example, investment in a patent will necessarily be followed up with investment in product development and marketing. However, often the subsequent investments rely on the outcome of early-stage investments. For example, production decisions will be made on the basis of results from clinical trials of a patented drug. The subsequent stages may even not be undertaken if information from the early-stage investment is adverse. That is, management gains an option from the first-stage investment on the follow-on investments. Further, managers have the flexibility to time their investments, and to adapt to emerging new information such as an alternative drug from a competitor.

Examples of such contingent investments are research and development, advertising, pilot marketing, licences for oil exploration, and geological testing for mineral reserves. In some cases managers may make an initial investment, knowing well that they can exit or abandon that investment. Acquisitions generally include a range of such options. These options available to corporate managers may be modelled using decision trees in conjunction with the DCF.

We can use the decision tree model (DTM) to derive the NPV of the initial investment. For this we calculate the NPV of each decision branch, starting with the final stage. We weight each branch's NPV by the probability of its occurrence. We then trace these NPVs backwards to the prior decision nodes, and finally to the first decision. For example, suppose we have a two-stage investment decision problem. The first stage is a small pilot investment, and the second stage is investment to scale up. There are two outcomes from the second stage (see Figure 14.5). The favourable outcome has an NPV of $100 in a strong economy with a probability of 60%. The unfavourable outcome has an NPV of $20 in a weak economy with a probability of 40%. If the firm is committed, no matter what the outcome is, the NPV is $52, the probability-weighted average of the NPVs of the two outcomes. When this overall second-stage NPV is discounted to the time of the initial decision, the NPV is, say, $40 (discounted at 30%). If the initial investment is £46, then at the first stage the NPV becomes −$6. So the project is not worthwhile.

If, however, the firm makes the second-stage investment on the basis of the information available after the first stage, for example about the unfavourable outcome of the first stage, then it will not make the investment. Thus the second-stage negative NPV investment will be

Figure 14.5 **Real options in a multi-stage investment**

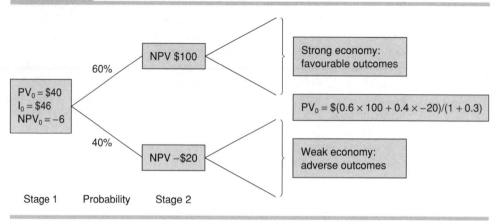

avoided. The overall second-stage NPV is then $60 and, discounted back, we find that the initial investment is a break-even decision.

While a decision tree is useful as a way of mapping out alternative decision choices contingent on outcomes of prior decisions, it is restricted to dichotomous outcomes at each stage rather than a continuous range of outcomes. Moreover, the discount rate assumed is constant for all outcomes and over different time periods. These shortcomings are avoided in the real options models derived from the Black–Scholes (BS) option-pricing model first developed for application to financial options, that is, options written on financial assets such as stocks, bonds and currencies. To understand the real options valuation we need an understanding of the model.

Call and put options on financial assets

A call option gives the buyer of that option the right, but not the obligation, to buy the asset on which it is written at an agreed price (the exercise price) at maturity of the option contract (in the case of a European option) or any time before maturity (in the case of a US option). The price of the option is called the option premium. A put option gives the buyer the right, but not the obligation, to sell the asset at the agreed price at or before maturity. An investor buys a call option when he or she expects the asset to increase in value beyond the exercise price. An investor buys a put when he expects the asset to decline in value below the exercise price. Appendix 14.1 provides an introduction to financial options and illustrates alternative valuation approaches.

Financial options and real options

A real option is an option to buy or sell an investment in physical or intangible assets rather than in financial assets. Thus any corporate investment in plant, equipment, land, patent, brand name, etc. can be the assets on which real options are 'written'. Purchase of a brand is an option on the related product or service. A licence to explore for oil is an option on oil.

Table 14.10 Types of real options: where do they exist?

Option type	Description	Typical context
Growth	Early investment to open up future markets	Investments in multiple-generation products; bolt-on acquisitions
Abandonment	Resale or exit from loss-making investment or one with no prospects	New product introduction; mineral licences; brand names
Switch	Allows switch in output mix with same inputs or in input mix for same outputs	Investments with scope economies in production, marketing, technology
Alter scale	Option to expand or contract output	In cyclical or fashion industries

Source: L. Trigeorgis, *Real Options: Managerial Flexibility and Strategy in Resource Allocation* (Cambridge, MA: MIT Press, 1996), Table 1.1.

Many investment projects have call and put option features. Investment in R & D is a call option, since it may lead to 'buying', i.e. investing in, a second-stage production facility. Any exploratory investment in a growth opportunity such as the Internet or biotechnology is a call option. An investment that can be sold if it does not meet the investor's expectations may be regarded as a put option, such as a mine that is abandoned when the price of gold falls and is unlikely to recover.

In addition to the examples of real options cited above, we can identify many other types of real options. These are listed in Table 14.10. A compound option combines two or more of these options. For example, in a bust-up takeover the acquirer plans to break up the target and sell some of the businesses while retaining others. The potential sale represents a put option to the acquirer. The search for real options is not a Holy Grail. Investment and financing decisions are replete with such options, if only managers do not miss the wood for the trees. Many of these options drive acquisition strategies[20].

Valuation of real options

The Black-Scholes option pricing model (BSOPM) may be used to value real options[21]. We first show such a valuation application, and then discuss the limitations and caveats in valuing real options using the BSOPM. The variables in the model when applied to real options are as follows:

C = the first-stage investment;

S = present value of the second-stage investment;

t = the time to making the second-stage investment, i.e. how long that opportunity will be open or how long the second-stage investment can be deferred;

X = present value of the cost of the second-stage investment;

Dividend = intermediate costs to keep the second-stage investment opportunity open, e.g. maintenance costs, rents;

σ = the volatility of the value of the second-stage investment.

The risk-free rate has the same connotation as in the financial asset case. Exhibit 14.7 shows how a small acquisition can be acceptable when considered as an option on subsequent growth opportunity rather than as a stand-alone investment.

Exhibit 14.7

Real options in small exploratory acquisitions

Fashion Experience (FE) plc is considering buying a small designer firm for £12m. The present value of cash flows from the acquisition is expected to be £10m. Thus, on its own, the investment is a negative-NPV one. However, FE considers that the target is a really exciting new design force that will transform the fashion industry for years to come. However, it will take years for the designs to be developed and tested, and for them to find a large market. While the current designs may be produced on a larger scale, FE thinks it is prudent to wait and learn more about the market. It can for now buy the target and wait to expand until more information is available.

FE has researched the potential sales and profits if the designs become popular in five years, and the investment to produce on a sufficiently large scale. It has the following data:

- The present value (PV) of cash flows from a large manufacturing project if undertaken now (S) is £15m.
- The investment cost for the large project, X, is £20m.
- FE estimates that the variability of the project's value is 28.3%.
- Time to expiry of the option to expand is five years.
- Risk-free rate is 6%.

If the large project were undertaken today it would also be a negative-NPV project.

Using the BSOPM we find that the option to expand within the next five years is £3.8m. This is the price of the option to make the large investment in the next five years. To buy this option, FE has to buy the target now, and this purchase has an NPV of −£2m. By buying the target and losing £2m FE gains an option with a value of £3.8m. So the net value of the acquisition is £1.8m. FE decides to make the acquisition. For FE the acquisition is exploratory, and an opportunity for learning. One of the most important, and the most difficult, parameters to estimate is the volatility. The timing for exercising the option is also critical. Both depend on how the fashion industry will evolve, and how turbulent its evolution will be.

Real option as a learning opportunity: 'They also win who only stand and wait'[22]

While waiting to make the second-stage investment the company is gathering information that flows from the first-stage investment, e.g. about feasibility of technology, and from the outside world, e.g. the size of the potential market or the price of the output, say, gold or a drug or a regulatory change. This learning covers learning what the company's resources and capabilities are, and how they can be adapted to the environmental changes (a process of self-discovery) as well as learning about the environment (intelligence gathering)[23].

Real options and game theory

What is the option value that a firm has acquired when there is competition? How soon will the competitors catch up and acquire similar options? Real options may give rise to unique non-imitable claims on the underlying second-stage investment opportunity, or they can be replicated by competitors, in which case the opportunity is shared. This is a fundamental issue in competitive strategy, and not peculiar to the real options framework[24]. However, the real options framework may be used to shed light on the value implications of shared options.

Whether competitors enter and spoil the game for the first mover depends on whether the claims on the growth opportunities are shared, and also on the entry barriers and what the first option holder does to forestall such entry. The game theory framework can be used to figure out how the game will be played with shared opportunities, and entry and pre-emptive strategies of different players. One way we can model the threat of entry is to incorporate an estimate of competitive erosion (proxied by 'dividend' payment in the BSOPM). Where there is more than one competitor this attrition can be increased to reflect such competition on the option value, as in the case study at the end of the chapter. See Appendix 14.1 for valuation of a dividend paying stock.

Another way to model competitor reactions and value strategic flexibility is to use the DTM described earlier. Suppose Serial Acquirer (SA) has a programme of acquisitions to build its competitive strength, and the value of each acquisition is path-dependent and influenced by the reaction of SA's competitors. The decision tree and the payoffs to SA following each acquisition are shown in Exhibit 14.8. This extends the acquisition series from two acquisitions in Exhibit 3.6 to five.

Exhibit 14.8

Valuing serial acquisitions as a compound real option

Serial Acquirer (SA) is valued currently at $t = 0$ at $1000. It plans an acquisition programme to make one acquisition each year for the next five years, starting at $t = 0$. SA's value may increase by 60% if its main competitor (we ignore other competitors for simplicity) does not replicate its acquisition, and it may decline by 20% if it does. The probability of the up or down value change is 50%. After each acquisition SA can evaluate whether a further acquisition is value creating or value destroying by comparing its value at that time with the net present value (NPV) of the acquisition's payoffs one year ahead. If the NPV is less than its value then no acquisition is made, and its value is unchanged: i.e. SA exercises its option to abandon further acquisitions. If the NPV is greater than its value, SA makes the next acquisition. This procedure is repeated at $t = 0$ to 4. No acquisition is made at $t = 5$ or thereafter.

Each acquisition, whether made by SA or by its rival, costs $100 each. SA's risk-adjusted cost of capital is 10%. The DTM below shows the value outcomes following the decision made at each node. The formulae for calculating these values are listed in the notes to the DTM. For simplicity, the subscripts t and up/down are not attached to the variables at nodes $t = 1, 5$. The valuation model is the discounted present value of the probability-weighted upward and downward value outcomes. SA is the payoff equivalent to its value before the acquisition times (1 + the growth rate). V is calculated starting with SA at $t = 5$ by discounting its probability-weighted up and down values at the cost of capital and subtracting the acquisition cost. This procedure is rolled back to $t = 0$. While SA is value rolled forward, NPV and V are values rolled back, one node at a time[25].

By exercising its option to make further acquisitions contingent upon the rival's reaction and its impact on its own valuation, SA may increase its current value from $1000 to $1135. If it stops with the first acquisition its current value will fall to $991. Thus although the first acquisition is likely to destroy value it provides valuable options to continue with the acquisition programme.

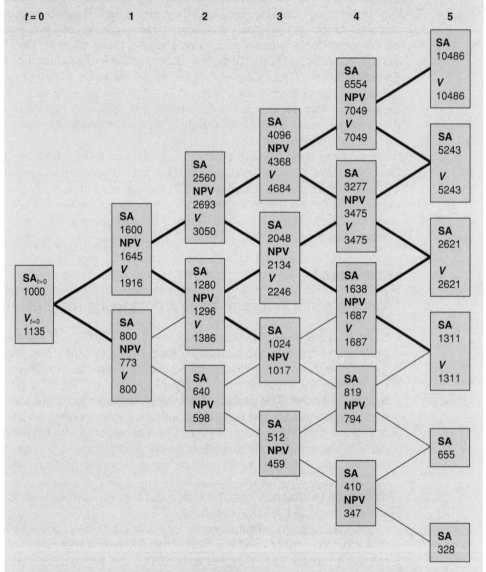

1. SA's acquisition programme: one acquisition/year at $t = 0$ to 4. Acquisition cost (AC) $100 each
2. Each rectangle a decision node at $t = 0$ to 5
3. Upward branch = SA makes acquisition but rival does not; downward = SA and rival both acquire
4. Value growth multiple: 1.6 for up and 0.8 for down
5. $SA_t = SA_{t-1} \times$ growth e.g. $SA_1 = \$1600 = 1000 \times 1.6$ or $\$800 = 1000 \times 0.80$
6. NPV = PV of SA one year ahead less AC e.g. $NPV_{t=1} = (0.5 \times SA_{up} + 0.5 \times SA_{down})_{t=2}/(1.1) - AC$
7. At each decision node decision rule: acquire if NPV > SA e.g. at $t = 1$ NPV of $1645 > SA_{up}$
   of $1600, so acquire. On the down branch, NPV of $773 < SA_{down}$ of $800. So do not acquire
8. $V_t = [(0.5 \times V_{up} + 0.5 \times V_{down})_{t+1}/1.1 - AC]$ at $t = 0$ to 4. $V = SA$ if no further acquisition is made
9. Thick branches follow optimal acquisitions
10. Thin branches follow 'no acquisition' by SA

Limitations of real option valuation models

Extrapolation of the BSOPM model to real options and strategic options is fraught with problems. Many of the assumptions that underlie financial options do not hold in the real options context. Data such as volatility are difficult to estimate, since the underlying investment opportunities are not traded. By their very nature many of these are of an exploratory nature, and historical data about them will not be available. Many other differences between financial and real options make valuation of real options using BSOPM less reliable (see Table 14.11).

Table 14.11 Comparing financial and real options

Financial option	Real option
Requires no ongoing investment to maintain asset value	May require managerial and organizational effort
Provides a proprietary claim on asset	Competitors may have or acquire similar claim, e.g. competing R & D programmes
Exercise price is fixed	Exercise price, i.e. cost of follow-on investment variable
Underlying asset value identical for all option holders	Asset value depends on the option owners' resources and ability to leverage
Secondary markets provide liquidity and pricing mechanism	Secondary markets non-existent or imperfect

CASE STUDY

'They also lose who only stand and wait' – when option value is eroded by competition

Biogen is a biotechnology company with a patent on a drug called Avonex. It has received US Food and Drug Administration (FDA) approval to treat multiple sclerosis. The patent gives the firm legal monopoly for 17 years. Biogen, however, is strapped for cash and wants to shop its patent and invest the proceeds in further research. Major Pharma (MP) is considering buying the firm because of its patent for the MS drug. There is no other drug with Biogen.

MP has analyzed the situation as an acquisition opportunity. How much is Biogen worth? The following data are used to value Biogen as a real option since the patent would give MP the opportunity to manufacture the drug if the market conditions are favourable in the next 17 years. If the drug is produced on a commercial scale and marketed today, the investment cost is \$2.875bn (X). The present value of cash flows from that project is \$3.422bn (S). Although immediate investment is a positive \$547m NPV decision, MP wants to know whether waiting until more marketing and other information is available will create more value. There is the risk that competitors may come up with alternative me-too drugs and erode MP's competitive advantage. The risk-free, 17-year Treasury bond rate is 6.7%. Time to expiry of the option is 17 years (t). MP estimates the variability of the expected present value S as 22.4% (σ^2). With a single potential competitor, the option value will be eroded evenly at 1/17 per year. This is the expected cost of delay (similar to dividend yield). Estimation of σ is often taken from the volatility of the stock of a company similar to the follow-on project. It is the variability of the value of the follow-on manufacturing project. Analysts may be able to estimate this variability through simulation.

These data, used in the BS model, give an option value of $907m compared with a static NPV of $547m. This suggests that MP will increase the value of its acquisition if it waited to exercise the second-stage investment option. If we assume that with more competitors the attrition rate will double to 2/17, the option value is $255. In this case MP will be nearly $300m better off by buying Biogen now and manufacturing straight away, unless it can think of other ways of challenging potential competitors and keeping them at bay, e.g. erecting entry barriers or threat of nasty and expensive litigation.

Discussion questions

1 What defines a real option? Can Biogen acquisition be regarded as a real option?

2 Comment on the way the real option model has been employed and data inputs estimated.

3 What is the interaction between competitive strategy and real options? Suggest other ways of capturing this interaction in the BS model.

Source: Adapted from A. Damodaran, 'The promise of real options', *Journal of Applied Corporate Finance*, **13**(2) Summer 2000

Overview and implications for practice

This chapter has described different techniques for the valuation of target companies on the basis of three broad sources of value: cost efficiency savings, revenue enhancement, and real options.

- Abnormal earnings valuation models rely on book value of assets, cost of capital, accounting earnings and an estimate of economic profit to estimate firm value. Terminal value is an important component of value, and needs to be estimated after taking account of the period of sustainable competitive advantage.

- Price to earnings ratio, market value of assets to book value of assets and market value of assets to their replacement cost are other widely used valuation models. The multiples, while conceptually related to growth and risk, do not explicitly allow for either.

- In using multiples the choice of a benchmark multiple is important, and needs to be carefully chosen and, if necessary, adjusted for differences between a target and the benchmark.

- Several, more exotic, multiples have been used in recent years. Their link to value is rather tenuous.

- Cash-flow-based models are conceptually more robust than multiples, and allow for explicit inclusion of a number of drivers. Six drives can be identified. Cash flow models are information intensive and require forecasts of cash flows. Terminal value assumptions are even more critical in the cash flow model than in the case of the abnormal earnings model.

- The above traditional models are inappropriate to value real options. The use of the Black–Scholes option-pricing model was illustrated in situations where the acquisition represents a tentative and exploratory investment that may trigger a follow-on investment conditional on better information.

- The real options model, while difficult to apply in practice, nevertheless provides a useful framework for analyzing factors that influence value.

- The interaction between real options and game theory offers considerable insights into competitive equilibrium, how to preserve competitive advantage, and valuation.

- All valuation models suffer from varying degrees of imprecision and unreliability. Many of the assumptions underlying these models are subjective and somewhat arbitrary. Thus using a range of values from alternative models for target valuation is prudent and sensible.

- Having priced the target, the bidder has to decide on the method of payment. One of the important considerations in choosing the method is its impact on the reported profits of the group after the acquisition. This impact depends on the accounting rules used to account for the acquisition. We discuss acquisition and merger accounting in the next chapter and the method of payment in Chapter 16.

Review questions

14.1 What are the different sources of value in acquisitions?

14.2 What is the abnormal earnings model? What are the determinants of value in that model?

14.3 What is the importance of the terminal value in the model?

14.4 Describe the price/earnings ratio (PER). In what sense is it a valuation model?

14.5 What are the important caveats in using the PER?

14.6 How do accounting rules and practices affect the usefulness of PER as a valuation model?

14.7 What is Tobin's q, and how is it different from the market-to-book value of equity?

14.8 What are the limitations of using q or market-to-book as a valuation model?

14.9 What are the value drivers in the discounted cash flow model? What is the significance of the terminal value assumption?

14.10 What is a real option, and how does it compare with a financial option?

14.11 What are the different types of real options?

14.12 What are the problems in applying a financial option valuation model to a real option?

14.13 What is the effect of competition on real option valuation?

Further reading

J. Berk and P. DeMarzo, *Corporate Finance* (New York: Pearson Addison-Wesley, 2007) , Part VII.

T. A. Luehrman, 'Investment opportunities as real options: Getting started on the numbers', *Harvard Business Review*, July/August 1998, 51–67.

K. G. Palepu, P. M. Healy, V. L. Bernard and E. Peek, *Business Analysis and Valuation* (London: Thomson Learning, 2007).

H. Smit and L. Trigeorgis, *Strategic Investment: Real Options and Games* (Princeton, NJ: Princeton University Press, 2004), Chapters 1 to 6.

Notes and references

1. In acquisitions driven by cost leadership, the lower post-acquisition cost may increase sales and market share and contribute to revenue enhancement, depending on the price elasticity of demand for the firms' products. Similarly, where revenue enhancement through product differentiation is the primary driver, there may be cost efficiencies resulting from the increased operating scale. Thus the sources of value may not be mutually exclusive.

2. See R. G. Eccles, 'Are you paying too much for that acquisition?', *Harvard Business Review*, July–August 1999, 136–146.

3. This section draws on K. G. Palepu, P. M. Healy, V. L. Bernard and E. Peek, *Business Analysis & Valuation* (London: Thomson Learning, 2007), Chapter 7. See also R. Lundholm and R. Sloan, *Equity Valuation and Analysis* (New York: McGraw-Hill Irwin, 2007), Ch. 10.

4. CSR means that closing equity book value = opening equity book value + net income during year – dividends. This assumes that the increase (surplus) in the book value of equity at the end of the fiscal year is due only to retained profits. In practice there are a number of accounting adjustments that may distort CSR, e.g. reserves created on the balance sheet without affecting the income statement. In such cases the surplus is said to be 'dirty'. See R. Lundholm and R. Sloan, *ibid*. These authors demonstrate that the RI valuation model is robust to such accounting distortions, since any bias in the book value of equity creates an opposite bias in the residual income estimate: for example, higher book value increases the cost of capital and reduces the residual income over several periods. Equation (14.3) assumes CSR at the assets' level.

5. Where the firm maintains the policy of 100% payout of its net income as dividends, $g_t = 0$ for all t. Even then the firm can add value if residual income is positive. MTBV will increase if $ROE_t > K^e$. Where the firm retains some of its net income, then it will add to firm value in a multiplicative way. On the other hand, if $ROE_t = K^e$, even 100% retention of net income will not add value, and the equity-to-book value will be just 1.

6. See Lundholm and Sloan, *ibid.*, p. 234.

7. See Lundholm and Sloan, *ibid.*, section 11.5.

8. Analysts' forecasts are available for publicly listed companies of many countries in databases such as IBES on Thomson Financial.

9. This model was developed by Dechow, Hutton and Sloan. For a discussion see J. Stowe, T. Robinson, J. Pinto and D. McLeavey, *Equity Asset Valuation* (Hoboken, NJ, USA: Wiley, 2007), p. 273.

10. Bidders or their financial advisers often benchmark their chosen PER against PERs observed in recent takeovers of comparable firms, e.g. targets from the same sector. For examples, see R. Bruner, 'The merger of Hewlett-Packard and Compaq (B): Deal design', Darden Business School case (UVA-F-1451).

11. One can use the valuation approaches illustrated in this chapter to value Bidder before and after the acquisition of Target.

12. Tobin's q has been used in the acquisition context to spot undervalued companies. In the early 1980s many firms were selling at q values below 1: that is, at a discount to their assets at replacement cost. This discount was seized upon by many predators, who bid for those undervalued companies. *Business Week* captioned one of its articles 'The q-ratio: Fuel for the merger mania' (24 August 1981), reflecting the wild spirit of the times.

13. A. Damodaran, *The Dark Side of Valuation* (New York: Financial Times Prentice Hall, 2001).

14. See A. Rappaport, *Creating Shareholder Value* (New York: Free Press, 1986) on the first five.

15. K. G. Palepu, P. M. Healy, V. L. Bernard and E. Peek, *Business Analysis and Valuation* (London: Thomson Learning, 2007), Chapter 6 and its Appendix. Figure 14.2c shows net operating profit after tax (NOPAT) to sales margin. For US data from 1979 to 1998 firms with high sales growth of the order of above 50% per annum experienced a similarly rapid decline to the average growth rate of just below 10%; within the third year ROE fell from nearly 30% to nearer 15% over six or seven years for the top quintile firms in their sample. While top performers maintained their lead over several years, it was gradually eroded. These numbers are the author's interpretations of these graphs.

16. For the UK this ranges from 2 to 5.4 (arithmetic) and from 1.7 to 4.1 (geometric). See the Report of the inquiry into the price regulation of Stansted Airport, October 2008. For publication details of the cited studies see that report at www.competitioncommission.org.uk.

17. In the extreme, if a firm finances all its assets with debt, the debt beta will equal the asset beta, and if it is financed only with equity, the equity beta will equal the asset beta. Thus debt risk must have a systematic risk component.

18. On the use of debt betas in calculating the WACC in merger situations, see S. Gilson, 'Seagate technology buyout', Harvard Business School case 9-201-063, 2004. This case illustrates how asset beta can be calculated from observed equity and assumed debt betas, and also how asset beta can be relevered to arrive at equity beta appropriate for any level of gearing.

19. T. Scott, 'Tax planning', in *Company Acquisitions Handbook* (Croydon: Tolley Publishing Co. Ltd, 1996).

20. K. W. Smith and A. J. Triantis, 'The value of options in strategic acquisitions', in L. Trigeorgis (Ed.), *Real Options in Capital Investment: Models, Strategies and Applications* (Westport, CT: Praeger, 1995), 135–149.

21. T. A. Luehrman, 'Investment opportunities as real options: getting started on the numbers', *Harvard Business Review*, July/August 1998, 51–67.

22. Adapted from John Milton, *Paradise Lost*.
23. A. E. Bernardo and B. Chowdhry, 'Resources, real options and corporate strategy', *Journal of Financial Economics*, **63**, 2002, 211–234; B. Kogut and N. Kulatilaka, 'Capabilities as real options', *Organization Science*, **12**(6), 2001, 744–758.
24. T. A. Luehrman, 'Strategy as a portfolio of real options', *Harvard Business Review*, September/October 1998, 89–99; E. Bowman and G. T. Moskowitz, 'Real options analysis and strategic decision making', *Organization Science*, **12**(6), 2001, 772–777; H. T. J. Smit, 'Acquisition strategies as option games', *Journal of Applied Corporate Finance*, **14**(2), 2001, 79–89.
25. See Exhibit 3.6 for the application of the valuation formulae used here.

Appendix 14.1 | Real options in mergers and acquisitions

A firm contemplating acquisitions is faced with several choices concerning the timing, future expansion or growth opportunities following an initial acquisition, and, if the acquisition turns out to be bad, faces the decision to abandon it either wholly or partially. The timing of an acquisition may be determined by uncertainty about interest rates, technology and market size for the post-acquisition entity's products and services. Timing may also be influenced endogenously by the strategic moves, including acquisitions made or likely to be made by the firm's rivals. It is also influenced by the firm's competitive strategy towards rivals, that is, being a first mover or a me-too follower. Delaying an acquisition may often be a sensible decision, since during the waiting period some of the uncertainties may be resolved, or capital market conditions may turn favourable, for example a fall in interest rates or a rise in the stock market.

An acquisition may often be in the nature of a platform on which to build a larger and more valuable business through subsequent investments in the form of greenfield production or further acquisitions. The platform or buy-and-build strategy discussed in Chapter 13 is an example of such an approach. Buying a company with just a patent for a drug or a manufacturing technology may be another. The platform acquisition or acquisition of a firm with no profits or cash flows, and only the patent as an asset, may by itself be a negative-NPV decision but, in conjunction with the value generated by the follow-on investments, may be a substantial value creation proposition. How do we value such platform acquisitions?

Having made an acquisition, a firm may find that either the whole of the acquisition or parts of the acquired firm generate negative synergies. In this event the acquirer may be better off by divesting the acquired firm wholly or partially. Such divestitures depend on the liquidity in the corporate assets market as well as the timing of the divestitures. If, for example, the whole of the acquired firm can be divested, the exit value of that business reduces the cost and risk of an acquisition. The exit or 'abandonment' option is therefore valuable. How can we value this option?

Alternative approaches to option valuation

There are broadly three approaches to valuation of real options:

● **Replicating portfolio approach:** Valuing a call (put) option by valuing a hedge or replicating portfolio made up of a long (short) position in the underlying asset on which the option is written and a short (long) position in a risk-free bond of the same maturity as the option itself. A short (long) position involves the sale (purchase) of the security. The payoffs to the hedge portfolio are identical to those of the option in a given state of nature. The hedge portfolio replicates the end-of-holding-period payoffs to the option, and hence is known as a replicating portfolio. For example, in valuing a call option written on a stock (S), we can construct a portfolio of delta (Δ) number of the shares of the stock and selling a risk-free bond (B).

- **Risk-neutral probability:** The risk-neutral probability (RNP) discounts the payoffs to the option at the risk-free rate rather than the risk-adjusted discount rate used in the conventional DCF model. The advantage of this approach is that no assumption regarding investors' risk preference, e.g. risk aversion or risk seeking, needs to be made. Since with risk-neutral investors the appropriate discount rate is the risk-free rate, which is publicly available information, this makes valuation easier. Moreover, the appropriate discount rate for valuing the asymmetric cash flows of options is not easy to determine. This approach involves estimating the risk-neutral probabilities from the data.
- **Black–Scholes–Merton model:** Popularly known as the Black–Scholes (BS) model, this approach uses mathematically derived formulae based on stochastic calculus and assumptions about the evolution of asset prices over time. Originally derived for valuing options on corporate stock (stock options), this model has been applied to value an enormous range of derivatives written on other assets, such as commodities, currencies and bonds. It has also been used to value real options. The application of this model is illustrated in Chapter 14.

Valuation of a call option using the replicating portfolio approach

A call C is written on stock S with a current price of $\$S$ with an exercise price of $\$E$. Assume that the time to expiry of the option is one year. The stock price can go up to S_u or down to S_d (see Figure 14A.1). We can issue bonds with a face value of $\$B$ or invest in them.

Suppose we buy Δ units of S and borrow $\$B$ (may be regarded as B units of $\$1$ bond), such that the payoffs to this portfolio in both up and down states are the same as the payoffs to the call option, C_u and C_d. Then we solve the following equation to get Δ and B:

$$\Delta S_u + (1 + R_f)\, B = C_u \text{ and } \Delta S_d + (1 + R_f)\, B = C_d \tag{14A.1}$$

$$\Delta = \frac{C_u - C_d}{S_u - S_d} \qquad \text{and } B = \frac{C_d - S_d\, \Delta}{1 + R_f} = \frac{C_u - S_u\, \Delta}{1 + R_f} \tag{14A.2}$$

The value of the call option is

$$C = \Delta S + B \tag{14A.3}$$

Where the exercise price is above the value of the underlying stock, the option will not be exercised and its value is zero. Thus the value of the call option at maturity is

$C_u = \text{Maximum of } [S_u - E, 0]$ in the up state and
$C_d = \text{Maximum of } [S_d - E, 0]$ in the down state.

Figure 14A.1 One-period binomial option and its payoffs

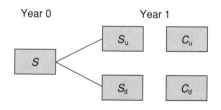

Illustration

Suppose $S = \$100$, $E = 120$, $S_u = \$140$, $S_d = \$80$ and $R_f = 5\%$. The probability that S will go up is 60% and that it will go down is 40%. The risk-adjusted cost of capital for the firm is 16%.

Then

$$C_u = \text{Max} \,[140 - 120, 0] = \$20; C_d = \text{Max} \,[80 - 120, 0] = \$0$$

$$\Delta = (20 - 0)/(140 - 80) = 0.3333, \text{ i.e. the investor buys } 0.3333 \text{ shares of } S$$

$$B = \$(20 - 0.3333 \times 140)/(1 + 0.05) = -\$25.35$$

The investor borrows $25.35 and buys 0.3333 of S to construct the notional hedge portfolio.

$$C = \Delta S + B = 0.3333 \times 100 - 25.35 = \$7.98$$

This is the value at time 0 of the call option on the stock S.

Valuation of call and put options using the risk-neutral probability (RNP) approach

The hedge portfolio depends on locating a portfolio that will have the same payoffs as the options. If the future payoffs to the option are known, why can't we just discount them with the risk-adjusted cost of capital for the option? After, this is the traditional DCF approach. The problem associated with this approach is that the discount rate for an option is more difficult to estimate than the discount rate used in the DCF models to estimate NPVs. A much simpler approach is to weight the payoffs to the options with risk-neutral probabilities and discount the weighted payoffs to arrive at the option value at the current time. Discounting with RNP avoids the problem of estimating the risk-adjusted discount rate for the option.

RNP assumes a virtual world in which investors do not, by definition, require a premium for bearing risk. Hence discounting by a risk-free rate. Where do we find the RNPs? Here we do a little conjuring trick. RNP is the probability that the investor will receive with certainty what is an uncertain payoff. Suppose the objective probability of receiving $100 is 70% (30% for zero payoff). The expected payoff, i.e. the probability-weighted payoff, is $70. Will an investor buy this opportunity for $70 (ignoring time value of money)? An investor may want to pay, say, $60 to buy the opportunity: that is, her risk premium is $10. This investor is risk averse and demands a risk premium of $10.

An alternative question to the investor is at what probability of winning she will be prepared to pay the expected payoff and not demand a risk premium. Suppose the probability of winning is 60% rather than 70% (probability of losing is 40% rather than 30%); she may not demand a risk premium, that is, she will bet $60. So what we have done here is estimate the probability that, when used to weight the payoffs, will convert those uncertain payoffs into their certainty equivalent (CE). The $ payoffs remain the same, but the probability weighting has changed. The probability attached to the favourable outcome, i.e. payoff of $70, is reduced, and the probability attached to the unfavourable outcome, i.e. payoff of $0, is increased. With these revised probabilities the investor has 'lost' her risk aversion and is happy to forgo a risk premium! How do we estimate the RNP and use it to value options?

The current stock price S is known with certainty. The future payoffs are:

S_u with objective probability of $\text{Pr}(S_u)$
S_d with objective probability of $\text{Pr}(S_d)$ or $\{1 - \text{Pr}(S_u)\}$

$$S = \frac{\text{Pr}(S_u)S_u + \text{Pr}(S_d)S_d}{(1 + k)} \qquad (14\text{A}.4)$$

where k is the risk-adjusted discounted used traditionally in the DCF model.

The RNP(S_u) and RNP(S_d) can now be calculated from the following relations:

$$S = \frac{\text{RNP}(S_u)S_u + [1 - \text{RNP}(S_u)]S_d}{(1 + R_f)} \tag{14A.5}$$

$$\text{RNP}(S_u) = \frac{S(1 + R_f) - S_d}{S_u - S_d} \tag{14A.6}$$

Illustration

For the options discussed earlier:

$$\text{RNP}(S_u) = \frac{100(1 + 0.05) - 80}{140 - 80} = 41.667\%$$

$$\text{RNP}(S_d) = (1 - 0.41667) = 58.33\%$$

Compare these with the objective probabilities 60% and 40%. When weighted with these probabilities, the expected payoff is $116 (= 140 × 0.6 + 80 × 0.4). When discounted at the cost of capital of 16%, the current value of the stock is $100, equal to the observed stock price. The CE value, on the other hand, is $105 (= 140 × 0.4167 + 80 × 0.5833). This CE is appropriately discounted at the risk-free rate of 5% to yield a current value of $100. So both methods give the same value, but the RNP method does not require estimate of the risk-adjusted cost of capital.

Value of the call option = 0.41667 × $20 + 0.5833 × 0 = $8.33

Valuation using the Black–Scholes model

As noted above, this model is based on stochastic calculus, and rests on the following assumptions:

- The option payoff is contingent on the value only of the underlying asset.
- The price of an asset on which the option is written is normally distributed.
- The option can only be exercised at maturity.
- The future exercise price is known with certainty, and is constant.
- A replicating portfolio of the asset and risk-free bond can be identified.
- The process of asset price evolution over time is known.

Many of these assumptions do not hold strictly in the real world. The BS option pricing model (BSOPM) was also developed to value European options, which can be exercised only at maturity.

C, the value of a European call option, is

$$C = S\,N(d_1) - E\,e^{-rt}\,N(d_2) \tag{14A.7}$$

Alternatively,

$$C = e^{-rt}\,[S\,e^{rt}\,N(d_1) - E\,N(d_2)] \tag{14A.8}$$

where $d_1 = [\ln(S/E) + (r + \sigma^2/2)t]/\,\sigma\sqrt{t}$
$\qquad d_2 = d_1 - \sigma\sqrt{t}$
$\qquad S$ = current stock price
$\qquad E$ = exercise price at maturity
$\qquad \sigma^2$ = annual variance of the continuous return on stock S
$\qquad r$ = annually compounded risk-free rate (normally on a zero coupon risk-free bond of maturity t)
$\qquad t$ = time to expiry of the option

The exponential term, e^{-rt}, is the discount factor, and discounts the exercise price to the present value.

Call value $= S\,N(d_1) -$ Present value of $E \times N(d_2)$

$N(d_1)$ and $N(d_2)$ represent the cumulative standard normal probability distributions (with a mean of 0 and standard deviation of 1). $E \times N(d_2)$ is the exercise price times the probability that it will be paid, that is, that the option will be exercised in a risk-neutral world. $N(d_1)$ is the probability that the stock value at t, i.e. $S\,e^{rt}$, is at least equal to E. In the BS model they measure the risk associated with the volatility of the value of S. σ is the standard deviation of the distribution of S. It is often proxied by the stock return volatility in the case of options written on stocks.

Illustration

Valuing a call option on a stock

Suppose Wild Goose Chase (WGC) Company stock is selling for $10, and a call option on the stock is available. The exercise price is $10. This European call has a maturity of one year. The risk-free rate (the government Treasury bill rate for one year) is 12%. The standard deviation (σ) of the annual returns on WGC is 10%.

$$d_1 = \frac{\ln(S/E) + (r + \sigma^2/2)t}{\sigma\sqrt{t}}$$

$$= \frac{\ln(10/10) + (0.12 + 0.005)1}{0.10 \times 1}$$

$$= 1.25$$

$$d_2 = d_1 - \sigma\sqrt{t}$$

$$= 1.25 - 0.10 = 1.15$$

We use normal probability distribution tables to get $N(d_1)$ and $N(d_2)$[1].

$N(d_1) = 89.4\%;\ N(d_2) = 87.5\%$

$C = \$10 \times 0.894 - \$10 \times 0.887 \times 0.875 = 8.94 - 7.76 = \$1.18$

So the value of the call is $1.18. This value will change with the value of the various parameters in the BS model.

Valuing a put option on a stock

The value of a European put option on a non-dividend paying stock is

$$P = E\,e^{-rt}\,N(-d_2) - S\,N(-d_1) \tag{14A.9}$$

The notations are as above.

Illustration

Suppose we want to value a put option written on Downhill stock with a current stock price of $50, exercise price of $30, standard deviation of annual returns of 40%, expiry period of 1 year and risk-free rate of 10%. Then

---

[1]Such tables can be found in textbooks on corporate finance or valuation. The function NORMDIST in Microsoft Excel can also be used to estimate these probabilities.

$$d_1 = \frac{\ln(S/E) + (r + \sigma^2/2)t}{\sigma\sqrt{t}}$$

$$= \frac{\ln(50/30) + (0.10 + 0.08)1}{0.40 \times 1}$$

$$= 1.25 + 0.45$$

$$= 1.73$$

$$d_2 = d_1 - \sigma\sqrt{t}$$

$$= 1.73 - 0.40 \times 1 = 1.33$$

$$N(-d_1) = N(-1.73) = 0.042; \ N(-1.33) = 0.092$$

$$P = \$30 \times 0.905 \times 0.092 - \$50 \times 0.042$$

$$= \$2.5 - \$2.1 = \$0.4$$

The put is valued at $0.4.

Valuation of a dividend-paying stock

The effect of dividend payment by a company on whose stock the option is written is to reduce the value of that stock. We adjust the current stock value by the present value of the future dividend. For example, in the above WGC illustration, if the present value of the dividend payable in 6 months is $0.94 ($e^{-0.12 \times 0.5}$) at the risk-free rate of 12%. So S becomes $9.06, and the value of the call falls to $1.03 from $1.18.

$$d_1 = \frac{\ln(S/E) + (r + \sigma^2/2)t}{\sigma\sqrt{t}}$$

$$= \frac{\ln(9.06/10) + (0.12 + 0.005)1}{0.10 \times 1}$$

$$= 0.26$$

$$d_2 = d_1 - \sigma\sqrt{t}$$

$$= 0.26 - 0.10 = 0.16$$

$$N(d_1) = 0.6026; \ N(d_2) = 0.5636$$

$$C = \$10 \times 0.6026 - \$10 \times 0.887 \times 0.5636$$

$$= 8.94 - 7.76 = \$1.03$$

Valuation of American options

In contrast to the European options, which can be exercised only at maturity, American options allow exercise at any time to maturity. For this reason these options are more valuable than European options. In the case of a dividend-paying call option, early exercise avoids the dilution of the stock value, and hence an American option will be exercised early. In the case of non-dividend-paying stock the American option is optimally exercised only at maturity, and hence has the same value as its European counterpart.

From financial option to real option valuation

While all the three approaches to financial option valuation can be extended to valuation of real options, we illustrate real option valuation using the BS model because of its simplicity, although this also makes the model somewhat unrealistic. Real investments share many of the characteristics of financial options, but there are also substantial differences. In the chapter we illustrate the application of the valuation tools to real options, and also note the differences between financial and real options, and how these differences may affect the valuation of real options.

Acquisitions as games and real options

Some acquirers make one-off acquisitions, whereas others use them as their primary engine of growth. In Chapter 13 we described platform or buy-and-build acquisition strategies. They represent compound options, or options on options, since following the exercise of the first option to acquire the acquirer may have options to make subsequent acquisitions. Serial acquirers thus exercise compound options. Smit and Trigeorgis classify acquisitions into several types as shown in Figure 14A.2, based on their option characteristics.

The value of an acquisition is endogenously determined by the competitive reactions of the acquirer's rivals (and the other of Porter's five forces). For simplicity we focus here on the rival's reactions to an acquisition. Such reactions may be contrarian, e.g. the rival lowers its output, or reciprocal, e.g. the rival lowers the price to match any price reduction by the acquirer. Compound options exercised over a period of time may increase the overall value of the firm possessing those acquisitions, but they also alert rivals and allow them to mount counterstrategies to prevent exercise of further options by the first mover unless the first option is a 'killer op(tion)' that massively pre-empts the rivals' counter-attacks. Serial acquisitions that evoke competitors' me-too acquisitions may be modelled and valued as real options using the binomial tree approach (see Exhibit 14.8 in the chapter).

Figure 14A.2 Types of acquisition, defined by option characteristics

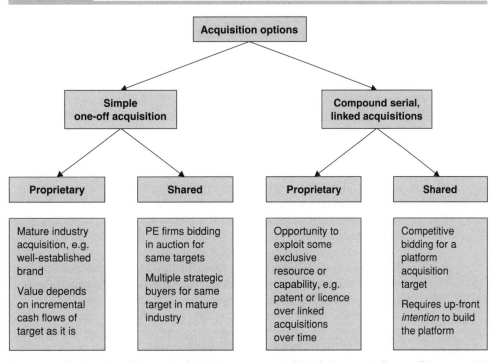

Source: H. Smit and L. Trigeorgis, *Strategic Investment: Real Options and Games* (Princeton, NJ: Princeton University Press, 2004), Figure 8.4

CHAPTER 15

Accounting for mergers and acquisitions

Objectives

At the end of this chapter, the reader should be able to understand:

- the differences between pooling accounting and purchase accounting;
- how these differences impact on the combined entity's income statement and balance sheet;
- why accounting rules have changed to favour purchase accounting;
- how purchase method affects the reported numbers and their reliability;
- whether stock markets value accounting policy choices in accounting for acquisitions and goodwill; and
- the relationship between goodwill and valuation.

Introduction

When mergers and acquisitions take place, the combined entity's financial statements have to reflect the effect of the combination. In many countries, accounting regulations require that the accounts of companies that are members of a group be prepared in the form of group accounts. In the year of the business combination the consolidation of the new subsidiary with the parent is carried out using different sets of accounting rules, depending upon the nature of the combination: that is, whether it is treated as a pooling or uniting of interests, or as purchase. The two sets of rules are known as pooling of interests and purchase accounting. In the UK they are called merger accounting and acquisition accounting respectively. More recently, the International Accounting Standards Board (IASB), an independent professional accounting body that has developed internationally agreed accounting standards, has used the term 'acquisition method' to replace acquisition or purchase accounting.

The choice of accounting method can have a dramatic impact on the combined entity's post-combination financial performance and condition, as reflected in its consolidated accounts. If stock markets react to the reported accounting performance, market valuation of the combined entity and its shareholders' wealth may be affected. If companies foresee such an impact, they may structure their acquisition deals in such a way as to qualify for their preferred method of accounting, and seek to influence reported performance and thereby the firm valuation. The new rules for accounting for goodwill require any erosion in the value of goodwill ('impairment') to be estimated and charged against income. These rules may have created incentives and scope for manipulation of such estimates and hence the projected post-acquisition performance of the acquirer.

Accounting rules may influence not only the presentation of post-combination performance but also the economics of the deal resulting in the combination. In this chapter we set out the pooling and purchase accounting rules, the disadvantages and advantages of each from the acquirer's point of view, creative accounting in the acquisitions context, and the recent efforts at reforming and harmonizing the accounting rules for business combinations. We also trace the evolution of the concept of goodwill as a business asset, and how this evolution has affected the way it is accounted for. We highlight how the new rules for the treatment of goodwill impact on interpretation of post-acquisition performance of acquirers.

Consolidated accounts

In the EU, the US and other countries, group accounts have to be prepared in the form of a consolidated set of accounts, as if the parent company and its subsidiaries constituted a single entity. In the EU, since 2005, publicly listed companies have to prepare their financial statements in accordance with International Financial Reporting Standards (IFRS) promulgated by the IASB and mandated by EU law. In recent years there has been considerable convergence of the accounting standards for business combinations and the treatment of goodwill between the US and the rest of the world. The recent US Statements of Financial Accounting Standards (SFAS) 141 and 142 have brought this convergence much closer. Both IFRS 3 and SFAS 141 now stipulate a single method of accounting for business combinations, the acquisition method. Goodwill treatment has also become more uniform.

Types of business combination

A business combination can be classified as either: (1) an acquisition or (2) a merger. In International Accounting Standard (IAS) 22 the term 'purchase' is analogous to acquisition, and 'uniting of interests' is analogous to merger. According to IAS 22 an acquisition is a business combination in which one of the enterprises involved, the acquirer, obtains control over the net assets and operations of another enterprise, the acquiree, in exchange for transfer of assets, incurrence of a liability, or issue of equity. A uniting of interests is a combination in which the shareholders of two enterprises combine control over the net assets and operations of those enterprises and continue to share in the risks and benefits attaching to the combined entity. Both acquisition and merger are distinct from a transaction in which one company buys only the assets of another, e.g. property in a sell-off by the latter.

In an acquisition the acquiring company purchases the interests of the acquired company's shareholders in their company. The latter cease to have any material interest thereafter. In a merger the two groups of shareholders continue to maintain their interest in their companies, but also have an interest in the other company: that is, they pool their interests. Hence the US terms 'purchase' and 'pooling' for an acquisition and a merger respectively. In this chapter we use the terms 'merger', 'pooling of interests' or 'uniting of interests' interchangeably, and similarly with 'acquisition' and 'purchase'. In common parlance an acquisition is often referred to as a takeover, indicating that one of the parties to the combination is the dominant partner.

In the uniting of interests neither party can be identified as an acquirer. It is substantially a 'merger of equals'. However, even in transactions described as a merger of equals, it may still be possible to identify an acquirer (see Chapter 20 for further discussion of merger of equals).

Accounting for business combinations

Table 15.1 sets out the differences between merger and acquisition accounting in both holding company and consolidated accounts as per Financial Reporting Standard (FRS) 6 issued by the Accounting Standards Board (ASB) in the UK. The holding (parent) company is the enterprise that obtains control of the other enterprise, which is then legally its subsidiary. Consolidated accounts treat the holding company and its subsidiary as if they formed a single economic unit. This accounting framework is used irrespective of the substance of the transaction, i.e. for both mergers and acquisitions.

The presumption behind merger accounting is that the shareholders of the merging companies pool their interests and continue to retain their interests in their companies, albeit now jointly. Merger accounting seeks to preserve this continuity. This principle of continuity also means that the profits and accumulated reserves of the two firms can be pooled without regard to the date of the merger. It is as though the two firms had always existed together under joint ownership. For this reason, the prior-year accounts are restated for comparison.

In the case of acquisition accounting the acquired firm's assets are restated to their fair values at the acquisition date. Under this method the rule that the prior-year accounts are not restated may often lead to a sudden increase in the acquirer's assets and profits, thus painting a flattering picture of dramatic growth. This merely reflects the fact that in the year of acquisition and thereafter the reported accounting results include those of two companies, whereas in the previous year they include only the acquirer's.

Fair value is based on an arm's length transaction. Since merger accounting presumes that the merger is not such a transaction, the assets of the companies or the payment for the deal need not be stated at fair values. On the other hand, an acquisition is regarded as an arm's length purchase deal, and both the acquired assets and the purchase consideration are recorded at fair values. A consequence of this is that the difference between these fair values and book nominal values needs also to be recognized. Where the consideration includes

Table 15.1 Differences between merger accounting and acquisition accounting

Merger accounting	Acquisition accounting
(a) In holding (parent) company accounts	
Investment in subsidiary recorded at nominal value of issued shares	Recorded at fair value of acquisition
No share premium arises	Share premium normally results and is recorded
(b) In consolidated (group) accounts	
Subsidiary's pre-merger reserves included in group reserves and available for dividend payment	Excluded from group reserves and not available
Group accounts reflect subsidiary's profit for full merger year	Only profit from date of acquisition
Subsidiary assets consolidated at pre-merger book values	Fair values
Provision for future losses/reorganization costs not allowed	Allowed
Goodwill not recognized	Recognized
Previous year's accounts restated as if merger in effect then	Not restated

shares, the difference between the fair (market) value and the nominal value of the shares issued must be recognized as share premium.

The excess of fair value of consideration over the fair values of the separately valued assets is called goodwill. Goodwill represents the cost of the acquired firm to the acquirer over and above the values of the individual assets of the firm, and is an intangible fixed asset. Goodwill is essentially derived from certain competitive advantages the firm has over its rivals. It consists of the firm's reputation, excellence of research and development or after-sales service, quality of management, locational advantage, market power, its unique, probably inimitable, resources and capabilities, etc. The accounting treatment of goodwill has been one of the most controversial areas in financial reporting and is considered in detail below.

Example of merger and acquisition accounting

The above rules are applied to the case of the business combination between Big Fish and Small Fry. The combination results from a successful offer for Small Fry by Big Fish. Small Fry becomes the wholly owned subsidiary of Big Fish. The details of the offer and the pre-offer balance sheets of the two companies are given in Exhibit 15.1 Part (a). Exhibit 15.1 Part (b) shows the consolidation of Small Fry's accounts into Big Fish's under merger accounting and acquisition accounting.

In Exhibit 15.1 Part (b) the share premium is the excess of the market value of Big Fish shares (£1225m) over their nominal value (£700m). Goodwill is the excess of the fair value of Big Fish's offer of £1225m over Small Fry's net assets of £1020m after revaluation of its fixed assets.

In this example we note the following points of difference between the two methods of accounting:

- Acquisition accounting gives rise to goodwill of £205m and a share premium of £525m, and increases the value of the acquired fixed assets by £190m.

Exhibit 15.1

Big Fish offer for Small Fry

Part (a)

Offer details: Big Fish issues 700 million shares in a one-for-one share exchange offer. The nominal value of both shares is £1. The market value of Big Fish shares at the unconditional date (see Chapter 18 on this date), is 175 pence per share. The fair value of the fixed assets of Small Fry is £750m. The balance sheets of the companies (£m) are:

	Big Fish	Small Fry
Fixed assets	820	560
Net current assets	330	270
	1150	830
Share capital	800	700
Profit and loss account	350	130
	1150	830

Part (b)

Holding company and consolidated (group) balance sheets of Big Fish Group (£m)

	Holding Company	Small Fry	Group
Merger accounting			
Fixed assets	820	560	1380
Investment in Small Fry	700		
Net current assets	330	270	600
	1850	830	1980
Share capital	1500	700	1500
Profit and loss account	350	130	480
	1850	830	1980
Acquisition accounting			
Goodwill at cost			205
Fixed assets	820	750	1570
Investment in Small Fry	1225		
Net current assets	330	270	600
	2375	1020	2375
Share capital	1500	700	1500
Share premium	525		525
Revaluation surplus		190	
Profit and loss account	350	130	350
	2375	1020	2375

- Merger accounting increases the group profits of Big Fish from £350m to £480m, since the profits of Big Fish and Small Fry are pooled.

These differences have important implications. With acquisition accounting:

- goodwill now has to be 'dealt with';
- the share premium account has a restricted use – Big Fish cannot easily use it as a means of writing off goodwill, and in the UK needs the permission of the court to do so;
- the increase of £190m in the value of fixed assets compared with the merger accounting figure increases the annual depreciation charge and potentially reduces reported profits in the post-acquisition period;
- Big Fish cannot access the £130m reserves of Small Fry if it wishes to pay a larger dividend to its shareholders, unlike under merger accounting.

All of these appear to make acquisition accounting a less attractive choice than merger accounting for acquirers.

Criteria for merger accounting

The continuity and pooling principle behind merger accounting is reflected in the conditions normally imposed for a business combination to qualify for that treatment. Under UK FRS 6 a business combination satisfying the following five conditions would be accounted for by merger accounting:

- None of the combining parties is portrayed as either acquirer or acquired. This suggests a genuine pooling of interests.

- Post-combination management is based on the consensus of the combining parties. This provides that the combination serves the interests of all combining parties.
- No party is so large as to dominate the combined entity. This requires a combination of near equals.
- Non-equity consideration is only an immaterial part of the fair value of the total consideration paid. This ensures that material resources do not leave the group, and that continuity of ownership is maintained.
- None of the parties retains interest in only a part of the combined entity: that is, becomes a minority interest. This again suggests a genuine pooling of interests.

Other combinations should be accounted for by acquisition accounting[1].

Criticism of merger accounting

Merger accounting has been critiqued on both conceptual and practical grounds. Conceptually, the notion that the two merging entities should be treated as if they had been a single entity before the merger is inconsistent with the business strategy driving mergers. As discussed in Chapter 3 under the strategy perspective, an important rationale for mergers is to change the firms' competitive profile. The change in competitive profile means that the future will represent a break from the past in terms of the firms' resources and capabilities and performance. Second, non-restatement of assets and liabilities in current values at the time of the merger transaction means that the consolidated financial statements of the merged entities do not disclose either the true resources and capabilities of the two firms, e.g. goodwill and certain intangible assets, or their true valuation, e.g. tangible assets still shown at historic costs. Third, the consolidated financial statements do not fully reflect the cost of one firm buying the resources and capabilities of the other. Thus the investment in these assets is not fully revealed, and this prevents a correct evaluation of the post-merger performance.

In practice, in most mergers it is possible to identify a dominant partner. Combinations of near equals, while observed in practice, nevertheless represent a small proportion of all mergers and acquisitions. The existence of merger accounting and its putative benefits in terms of favourable post-merger performance has also distorted the incentives for managers to structure M & A deals, and has encouraged them to 'buy' pooling. Business combinations that are in substance acquisitions or takeovers have often been dressed up as mergers. This has been described as 'dirty pooling'[2].

Acquisition method

In the 1990s accounting standard setting bodies around the world considered these conceptual and practical deficiencies of merger accounting and attempted to reform the rules. In 2001 the US Financial Accounting Standards Board (FASB) did away with pooling altogether in its Statement of Financial Accounting Standard (SFAS or FAS) 141 for business combinations. Thus purchase accounting became mandatory. In 2004 the International Accounting Standards Board (IASB) followed suit, and prohibited merger accounting in its IFRS 3 for business combinations. The EU enforced IFRS for all listed EU companies from 2005. Thus there has been convergence in this area between US and international accounting standards. Acquisition or purchase accounting is now referred to as the 'acquisition method' of accounting for business combinations.

IFRS 3 defines a business combination as follows:

A transaction or other event in which an acquirer obtains control of one or more businesses. Transactions sometimes referred to as 'true mergers' or 'mergers of equals' are also business combinations.

Presumption of control

Control is generally presumed to exist when the parent owns, directly or indirectly through subsidiaries, more than half of the voting power of an entity. In exceptional circumstances, however, it may be possible to demonstrate clearly that such ownership does not constitute control. Control also exists when the parent owns half or less of the voting power of an entity when there is [IAS 27 (2008).13]:

(a) power over more than half of the voting rights by virtue of an agreement with other investors;
(b) power to govern the financial and operating policies of the entity under a statute or an agreement;
(c) power to appoint or remove the majority of the members of the board of directors or equivalent governing body, and control of the entity is by that board or body; or
(d) power to cast the majority of votes at meetings of the board of directors or equivalent governing body and control of the entity is by that board or body.

The definition and guidance on control is intended to identify whether an entity has sole control over one or more other entities.

Current rules for accounting for business combination

According to the IASB, the objective of IFRS 3 is to enhance the relevance, reliability and comparability of the information that an entity provides in its financial statements about a business combination and its effects. It does that by establishing principles and requirements for how an acquirer:

- recognizes and measures in its financial statements the identifiable assets acquired, the liabilities assumed, and any non-controlling i.e. minority interest in the acquiree;
- recognizes and measures the goodwill acquired in the business combination or a gain from a bargain purchase; and
- determines what information to disclose to enable users of the financial statements to evaluate the nature and financial effects of the business combination.

Applying the acquisition method

A business combination must be accounted for by applying the acquisition method, unless it is a combination involving entities or businesses under common control, in which case accounting treatments similar to pooling may be employed[3]. IFRS 3 presumes that 'one of the parties to a business combination can always be identified as the acquirer, being the entity that obtains control of the other business (the acquiree)'. The standard establishes principles for recognizing and measuring the identifiable assets acquired, the liabilities assumed, and any non-controlling interest in the acquiree. Any classifications or designations made in recognizing these items must be made in accordance with the contractual terms, economic conditions, acquirer's operating or accounting policies and other factors that exist at the acquisition date. Each identifiable asset or liability is measured at its acquisition-date fair value. Any non-controlling interest in an acquiree is measured at fair value or as the non-controlling interest's proportionate share of the acquiree's net identifiable assets. Only those contingent liabilities that are an obligation of the acquired entity at acquisition date and can be measured reliably are recognized.

Assets that the acquiree had not recognized prior to the acquisition, e.g. patents, trademarks, brands or customer relationships, probably because they had been internally developed, may nevertheless be recognized as of the acquisition date at fair values to the acquirer. Intangible assets are recognized if they satisfy the criteria of separability or contractual or legal criteria. IFRS 3 provides a number of examples of identifying intangibles assets[4]:

- market related, e.g. trademarks, newspaper mastheads, Internet domain names;
- customer related, e.g. customer lists, customer contracts;
- artistic related, e.g. plays, books, lyrics, video and audio material;
- contract based, e.g. licensing, construction contracts, franchise, use rights, e.g. for water; and
- technology based, e.g. patented technology, computer software, database.

The acquirer, having recognized the identifiable assets, the liabilities and any non-controlling interests, has to identify any difference between:

(a) the aggregate of the consideration transferred, any non-controlling interest in the acquiree and, in a business combination achieved in stages, the acquisition-date fair value of the acquirer's previously held equity interest in the acquiree; and

(b) the net identifiable assets acquired.

The difference is recognized as goodwill. If the acquirer has made a gain from a bargain purchase, that gain is recognized as profit in the income statement. The consideration transferred in a business combination (including any contingent consideration) is measured at fair value.

IFRS 3 requires acquirers to separately identify and value a range of intangible assets other than goodwill. The list of intangible assets that need to be recognized separately is extensive, and includes a host of things such as patents, brands, trademarks and computer software. Their valuation is to be carried out under International Accounting Standard (IAS) 38 (Intangible Assets), which deals with valuation of intangibles. Assets of the acquired entity should be measured at fair values at the date of acquisition, reflecting the conditions at that date[5]. The fair value of an intangible asset is the amount the entity would have paid for the asset at the acquisition date in an arm's length transaction between knowledgeable and willing parties, on the basis of the best information available. To the extent that fair value exceeds the book value of the acquired company's assets, their values are 'stepped up' in the combined balance sheet. This step-up strengthens the balance sheet and makes it look much stronger than with pooling.

The standard prohibits provisions for reorganization costs and future operating losses. Costs of reorganization and integration of the acquired business should be dealt with as post-acquisition costs unless there exists an obligation at the acquisition date to incur those costs. Acquisition-related transaction costs, e.g. finder's fees, advisory fees, professional consulting fees, are expensed – that is, charged to the income statement of the acquirer, and not added to the goodwill as was done previously. The rules under FAS 141 are broadly similar[6].

Accounting for goodwill

As seen above, acquisition accounting gives rise to goodwill. In theory, goodwill can be negative: that is, the fair value of consideration can fall below the fair value of the net assets purchased. This represents a smart, bargain buy for the acquirer, and IFRS3 requires that negative goodwill be immediately recognized as part of the profits of the acquirer in the year of acquisition. In practice, negative goodwill is rare, so we shall concentrate on positive goodwill. We must remember that goodwill 'emerges' as a residual figure, as the excess of fair value paid by the acquirer over the fair value of assets acquired (see Exhibit 15.1 Part (b) for the calculation of goodwill).

The fair value of consideration, such as cash, equity or debt security, is far more easily ascertainable than the fair value of assets received. The latter is assessed from the acquirer's point of view. This means that there is scope for manipulation of the fair value of the assets, and hence of the estimated goodwill.

IFRS3 (as well as FAS 141) now require that acquired goodwill be capitalized and placed on the acquirer's balance sheet. Both standards prohibit amortization but require the acquirer to carry out, post-acquisition, an annual impairment test. If this test shows erosion of goodwill, the amount of impairment is written off to the income statement. The current view is that goodwill is not a wasting asset, but one with indefinite life. Its value does not deteriorate in a systematic way, and therefore amortization is not necessary. However, changes in the firm's competition position may lead to impairment of goodwill, and therefore such impairment needs to be measured and treated as an expense[7]. This view of goodwill marks a reversal of the long-held view that goodwill was a wasting asset like plant and equipment, and hence had to be systematically amortized to match revenue and costs. Goodwill in the post-acquisition financial statements is now accounted for under IAS 36 (Impairment of Assets) or SFAS 142 (Goodwill and Other Intangible Assets). Prior to these standards, goodwill, being considered a wasting asset, was amortized over 20–40 years. We illustrate below the impact of amortization on the balance sheet strength and profit performance of the acquirer, and also that of impairment.

Impact of goodwill amortization or write off

The disadvantage of the amortization procedure from the acquirer's point of view is that the annual goodwill charge reduces the reported post-acquisition profit. The Big Fish acquisition of Small Fry illustrates this outcome (see Exhibit 15.1 Part (b)). If Big Fish keeps goodwill on its group balance sheet (i.e. capitalizes it) and amortizes it over, say, 20 years, there is an annual charge and reduction in profits of £10.25m per year. For companies preferring not to have their reported 'bottom line' (earnings per share) hit, this treatment is bad news. The impairment charge, on the other hand, avoids annual reduction in profits and earnings per share, but may produce more volatile year-to-year profits (see Exhibit 15.2 below on the massive goodwill impairment suffered by companies in recent years).

Impact of acquisition method on earnings per share and other profit performance measures

Analysts use measures such as return on assets (profit before interest and tax/total assets) or return on equity (net after tax profits/shareholders' funds). Under merger accounting both these measures will be higher than under acquisition accounting. This is because acquisition accounting inflates the asset or equity base and reduces the profits through amortization. Since acquisition accounting also requires revaluation of Small Fry's assets, the post-acquisition depreciation charge may also be higher and the reported income lower. For example, in Exhibit 15.1 Part (b), the group accounts show fixed assets of £1380m under merger accounting but £1570m under acquisition accounting. If we assume straight-line depreciation over 10 years, the increase in annual depreciation charge is about £19m ([£1570m − £1380m]/10). Together with the annual goodwill amortization charge of £10.25m calculated above, the extra charge to the income statement is £29.25m per year for the next 10 years.

At the same time the group's total assets are £1980m and £2375m under merger and acquisition accounting respectively, i.e. an increase of £395m. Compared with merger accounting, acquisition accounting reports total assets £395m larger and profits £29.25m lower. This is a double whammy. Acquisition accounting may thus project a poorer accounting performance than merger accounting. We can demonstrate a similar effect with return on equity.

Analysts often use the change in earnings per share (EPS) of an acquirer after an acquisition to assess whether it will create value. An acquisition may be earnings-dilutive, i.e. EPS declines, or earnings accretive, i.e. EPS increases. Earnings dilution is treated as signalling potential value creation (for further discussion of these concepts and their interpretation see Chapter 16 on payment methods). Acquisition accounting with goodwill amortization of £10.25m each year leads to greater EPS dilution in the short term.

Absence of goodwill amortization under the new standards (IFRS 3 and SFAS 141) means that the reported earnings per share may be higher than where amortization is applied. In our example, under the acquisition method, the annual goodwill amortization charge of £10.25 will be avoided, and an immediate earnings dilution is less likely. As a result, most acquisitions will result in earnings per share accretion rather than dilution. Thus post-acquisition EPS of the acquirer may not be a good indication of value creation or value destruction[8].

The acquisition method will generally reduce profit performance measures such as return on assets (ROA) because of the increase in the asset base. For the same reason these profit measures are also a truer reflection of the firm's underlying profitability, since the asset base now includes a more comprehensive range of firm's assets. The reduction in profit measures following an impairment charge may also provide a more timely indicator of the erosion in the firm's competitive position. While annual amortization is somewhat arbitrary, since the charge may not be highly correlated with the erosion in goodwill, the impairment rule may also allow acquirers considerable discretion in the estimation and timing of the impairment charge, as we discuss below.

One beneficial aspect of acquisition accounting is its impact on risk measures such as debt to total assets. Since group debt is largely unaffected by the choice between merger and acquisition accounting but the asset is enlarged, debt/total assets will be reduced, and acquisition accounting reports the group as a less risky business.

Valuation of goodwill

Goodwill is a tricky item to value for accounting purposes. IFRS 3 defines it as the excess of the fair value of the purchase consideration over the fair values of separately identifiable tangible and intangible assets. Valuation errors may arise in valuing the consideration, as well as in valuing these assets of the target company. To the extent that non-goodwill assets are subject to amortization but goodwill is not, acquirers may be tempted to allocate more of the target firm value to goodwill than to these wasting assets. Thus scope for manipulation of reported profits does exist.

Todd Johnson and Kimberley Petrone identify six components of goodwill estimates[9]:

1 excess of the fair values of assets recognized by the target in its pre-acquisition financial statements over their book values;
2 fair values of the assets not so recognized, e.g. intangibles that fail to meet the recognition criteria under extant accounting rules;
3 fair value of the 'going concern' or stand-alone element of the target's existing business, i.e. the target's pre-existing, stand-alone goodwill;
4 fair value of the synergies from combining the acquirer's and acquiree's businesses, i.e. the goodwill that the combination is expected to create;

5 overvaluation of the consideration offered by the acquirer, e.g. overvaluation of stock during stock market bubbles; and

6 overpayment due to competition for the target.

The first two components are errors due to the accounting and measurement deficiencies in the target. The last two may overstate the true goodwill that the acquirer can generate from the combination. Item 3 reflects the stand-alone goodwill, and should not be attributed to, or paid for by, the acquirer. Item 4 is the correct measure of the synergistic goodwill. It stems from the ability of the merging companies to leverage their resources and capabilities to create sustainable competitive advantage and value. In practice, these various elements may be confounded and lead to gross over- or underestimation of the purchased goodwill. Thus valuation of the target company's assets is fraught with measurement error.

Incentives to manipulate the goodwill estimate

Accounting-performance-based managerial compensation contracts obviously increase the incentives for managers to prefer earnings-increasing accounting methods over those that lead to earnings dilution. Even if the compensation contracts are stock market return-based, managers have incentives for similar preference if they believe that earnings-increasing accounting methods will lead to positive stock market rating. For example, in the 1990s (when goodwill had to be amortized) many acquirers of high-technology target firms allocated part of the purchase price to in-process R & D and reduced the goodwill[10]. This practice was subsequently disallowed by the FASB. Now that goodwill does not have to be amortized unless there is impairment, the opposite incentive to inflate goodwill and reduce the value of other depreciable assets may also exist. The purchase price may be allocated in such a way as to deflate the values of the tangible and other intangible assets and inflate the size of goodwill.

Valuation of intangibles is a very difficult exercise based on highly imprecise assumptions about the contribution of such intangibles to value, the rate of attrition of their value and the length of their useful life. Ramanna discusses the allocation of the purchase price of $7.1bn paid by Cisco Systems for Scientific-Atlanta in 2005[11]. Cisco followed FAS 141 and broke down the purchase price as follows:

- Intangible assets $1.95bn; In-process R & D $0.09bn; net tangible assets $1.29bn; goodwill $3.76bn

Intangible assets were made up of:

- Customer relationships – Cisco estimated a useful life of 7 years for this asset and valued it at $1.35bn;
- Technology – Cisco valued the patented and unpatented technology, trade secrets and computer software at $0.55bn, based on a useful life of 3.5 years;
- 'Other' – Cisco valued this at $0.05bn with a useful life of 2 years.

Since goodwill is a residual figure, the quality of its estimate crucially depends on the reliability of the values allocated to the intangible and tangible assets. Given the substantial valuation uncertainties associated with intangible assets, it may not be difficult for acquirers to generate plausibly low values for separately identifiable intangibles and plausibly high valuation of goodwill[12].

Carla Hayn and Patricia Hughes examine the factors that could predict goodwill impairment write-offs for a sample of US acquirers before and after the introduction of SFAS 142. They find that 'goodwill write-offs lag behind the economic impairment by an average of three to four years. For a third of their sample companies, the delay can extend upto ten years'! While some delay in recognizing impairment is unavoidable because such impairment may be temporary and therefore reversed, the substantial delay of up to 10 years 'may reflect the exercise of management discretion in timing goodwill write-offs to meet certain reporting objectives'[13].

Accounting rules in the UK during the 1980s, prior to FRS 7, allowed the acquirer to take into account future trading losses and reorganization costs that the acquirer expected to incur in managing the acquired company *after* the takeover. The acquirer could make provisions for such losses and costs, which reduce the fair value of the assets acquired, and increase the goodwill figure. The advantage of manipulating these costs and losses upwards is that the depreciation charge in respect of the acquired tangible assets in future periods will be reduced, and the reported profits of the group inflated. Further, excess provisions can be released into the profit and loss account directly, again inflating the post-acquisition group profits[14]. With the benefit of these 'lax' rules to account for goodwill, UK acquirers were said to be able to offer higher premia for US targets than their US rivals, constrained by goodwill amortization rules in the US. A research study by Ivancevich provided some evidence that UK firms in fact paid higher premia for US targets, leading to larger goodwill[15]. The absence of a mandatory goodwill amortization, albeit subject to annual impairment test, may encourage acquirers to overpay for their acquisitions.

Some major UK companies fiercely opposed FRS 7, the standard on the fair valuation of assets and liabilities of the acquired entity, on the ground that a proper valuation of the acquired business required the expected future costs of reorganization and future operating losses to be assessed at the time of acquisition and incorporated in the valuation. Although this argument had some merit, the new standard did reduce the scope for acquirers to manipulate the provisions and inflate their future profits. It is for the latter reason that FRS 7 received much support from the users of accounts in the investment community[16].

The impairment test requirement may also increase the manipulation of the goodwill. Both the estimate of impairment and the allocation of goodwill impairment to different segments are subjective, and hence subject to potential manipulation. While, conceptually, reflecting the impairment of an assets in the company accounts may be realistic, extensive manipulation of impairment estimated will make such accounts less reliable. This will make performance assessment of an acquisition difficult. Watts has therefore criticized SFAS 142 as allowing arbitrary adjustments to reported profits[17]. Following the stock market crash of 2008, goodwill, which formed a very large proportion of the acquisition prices paid during the M & A boom of 2004–07 is likely to be impaired. However, how much impairment should be recognized and charged to the income statement depends on the view that acquirers take about whether the impairment is transient, and will be restored when normal market conditions return. This divergence of opinion is shown in Exhibit 15.2.

Risk of goodwill overestimation

In our discussion of the various components of purchase premium and goodwill, we noted the large scope for measurement errors. One of these components is market overvaluation of the acquirer's stock. Another is overpayment for the target because of competitive bidding. Synergistic goodwill may also be overestimated in the absence of a thorough due diligence, and because of information asymmetry between the acquirer and target. Some of the deals done during the late 1990s at the top of the M & A and stock market boom provide salutary examples of such overestimation and subsequent massive write-down of goodwill, as Exhibit 15.3 shows.

Exhibit 15.2

Impaired goodwill divides the Europeans and Americans

There are two possible approaches for those businesses that know that an impairment charge is looming. Some take it all in one go, getting the bad news out into the open and dealing with the consequences in one fell swoop. Others prefer to take a series of small charges, arguing that accepting one sizeable impairment charge would not reflect the true value of their company in anything other than the exceptional economic circumstances, effectively banking on the market returning to health before they have to take their full course of impairment charges. To date, North American businesses appear to be taking the 'single hit' approach, whereas European businesses appear to favour the more conservative 'small steps' approach.

According to a recent study by KPMG in the US, goodwill impairment in 2008 more than doubled to US$339.6 billion, with the median charge going up tenfold. The number of companies in the US study that had impairment in 2008 increased to nearly 20%, up almost threefold from the previous year. The North American approach may in some way be due to the pressure exerted by agencies such as the SEC, which expected to see more goodwill impairment charges due to the state of the stock market. The message seems clear: the regulators are watching, and will want a good explanation for why impairment charges may appear smaller than expected.

Will European regulators take a similar tack? They probably will sharpen their focus on this issue, demanding more in-depth explanations around the impairment-testing process. The problem they will run into is the problem affecting everyone else currently involved in this area – i.e. that valuation is not an exact science, and that it has never been more difficult than it is now to ascribe a value to an entity. There is no suggestion of any wrongdoing here. Rather, there are grey areas on top of grey areas, making life difficult. As one example, self-generated goodwill (arising from things such as synergies across business units) can be used to compensate for the impairment of goodwill arising from an acquisition, depending on the level of impairment testing. How can the extent to which one compensates for the other be gauged? Similarly, business forecasts constitute a significant portion of the valuation process, and while these may sometimes be over-optimistic, it can be very difficult to actually prove that this is the case. Businesses that argue most vociferously against impairment appear to treat impairment and worsening economic conditions as two separate issues. It is somewhat disingenuous for some companies to report that they are being adversely affected by the economic downturn but not translating that into an impairment charge. This is where businesses can quickly get into the grey area of interpreting the guidance around goodwill. Some regulators, like the SEC, have already stated their position on goodwill impairment treatment. European businesses may soon find that their own regulators will gear up to take a similar stance. Until then, our transatlantic difference of opinion may continue unabated.

Source: Adapted from *M. Castedello*, 'Goodwill impairment in 2009', downloaded from www.kpmg.co.uk

Exhibit 15.3

High-flying acquirers run out of goodwill

At the height of the M & A boom in 1999 and 2000 many multimedia companies made mega-acquisitions. The primary driver of these deals was the creation of new technologies and markets, based on the convergence of media technologies – the Internet, mobile telephony, cable television, satellite communication, etc. Much of the investment was in the nature of real options on future technologies, markets and growth opportunities (see Chapter 14 on valuing real options). This was reflected in the high valuations of the target companies, much of it unsupported by physical assets. The acquirers paid very high prices for goodwill. When the boom ended, many acquirers got the bill for their irrational exuberance. They were forced to write off the goodwill or restructuring charges:

- AOL-Time Warner $54bn
- JDS Uniphase $48bn
- Clear Channel $20–30bn
- Worldcom $17bn
- Vivendi Universal $16bn
- Nortel Networks $12bn

These represented substantial chunks of the purchase price: for example, AOL's acquisition of Time Warner cost $165bn. This represented the biggest charge in corporate history. The losses reported by Vivendi were the largest in French history.

Source: Adapted from R. Waters, 'Media chiefs forced into a balancing act', *Financial Times*, 10 May 2002

As Exhibit 15.3 also shows, goodwill impairment can be colossal following the economic and stock market meltdown in 2008, i.e. $340bn in 2008, which was more than double that in 2007! Such impairment of goodwill can have a very serious consequence for the company's ability to adhere to its contractual obligations to lenders in the form of debt covenants. Since goodwill write-off will lower the asset and equity bases, companies writing down goodwill may find themselves in violation of debt covenants such as debt to equity or debt to total assets[18].

Overview and implications for practice

In this chapter we have described the accounting rules for reporting acquisitions and mergers. Essentially these rules are concerned with: (1) the valuation of the consideration paid by the acquirer, the valuation of the assets, and the estimation of goodwill; and (2) the treatment of goodwill.

- Goodwill – the excess of the purchase price over the cost of the net assets purchased – is often a large cost in many acquisitions. It is an intangible asset that reflects the target firm's competitive advantage and future growth opportunities, either on its own or in combination with the acquirer. Goodwill is not directly estimated.

- Accounting treatment of goodwill may vary across countries, although in recent years there has been substantial convergence. The International Financial Accounting Board and the US Financial Accounting Standards Board have issued recent standards to account for business combinations and goodwill accounting that are broadly similar.

- Choice of accounting method impacts on post-acquisition accounting performance measures, such as return on assets or debt to equity, and acquirers therefore have incentives to choose a 'favourable' accounting method. But such a choice generally has no cash flow implications.

- Under these standards pooling has been abolished, and acquisition method (previously called acquisition or purchase accounting) is now a single mandated accounting method for business combinations. The standards have also abolished amortization, and now require at least annual impairment testing of goodwill. Impairment is expensed.

- There is scope for acquirers to manipulate asset valuations in acquisitions to project a favourable post-acquisition performance.

- High risk attaches to estimation of goodwill and intangibles in acquisitions. Many acquirers have had to write off huge amounts of goodwill after their recent acquisitions.

Review questions

15.1 Why is accounting for a business combination important?

15.2 What are the different types of accounting relevant to business combinations?

15.3 What is pooling accounting? What is purchase accounting?

15.4 What are the major differences between the two methods of accounting?

15.5 What is goodwill? How is it estimated for accounting purposes?

15.6 What impact does choice of accounting method have on post-combination accounting statements?

15.7 How can you, as an analyst, make post-combination evaluation across companies comparable?

15.8 What are the incentives for managers to manipulate accounting numbers derived from accounting for business combinations?

Further reading

R. Dobbs, B. Nand and W. Rehm, 'Merger valuation: Time to jettison EPS', *McKinsey Quarterly*, downloaded from www.mckinseyquarterly.com, 2008.
C. Hayn and P. Hughes, 'Leading indicators of goodwill impairment', *Journal of Accounting, Auditing & Finance*, **21**(3), 2006, 223–266.
L. Johnson and K. Petrone, 'Is goodwill an asset?', *Accounting Horizons*, **12**(3), 1998, 293–303.

Notes and references

1. There are similar restrictive preconditions for pooling in the US under Accounting Principles Board Opinion 16, which preceded FAS 141, and in other countries.
2. IFRS 3 has stopped the 'abuse' of merger accounting by eliminating it as an option. David Tweedie, the head of the IASB said, while presenting the proposal, 'There are very few real mergers', and that 'companies routinely attempt to flout the rules to their advantage. We have got some cheaters'. See L. Smy, 'IASB proposals for Europe will hit mergers', *Financial Times*, 6 December 2002.

3. Deloitte, 'Business combinations and changes in ownership interests', *A Guide to the Revised IFRS 3 and IAS 27*, 2008, p. 14 (downloaded form www.iasplus.com).

4. IFRS 3 also lists examples of non-identifiable intangibles: assembled workforce and future growth.

5. International Accounting Standards (IAS) are predecessors to IFRS, and many of them are still operational. IASs are also the responsibility of the IASB.

6. We provide a broad overview of the accounting rules in this chapter. For more advanced discussion of the accounting standards readers should turn to the IASB, FASB or other national accounting standard-setting bodies. Leading financial accounting textbooks also deal with the issues related to accounting for acquisitions, accounting for goodwill, and fair valuation of assets and liabilities in the context of M & A and the differences in accounting rules. IASB and FASB undertake projects from time to time to bring about greater convergence between their respective standards. Interested readers can follow up the progress of such projects and new emerging new accounting rules by looking up the websites of these regulators, www.iasb.co.uk and www.fasb.org.

7. In the US the abolition of pooling in 2001 was furiously opposed by companies. N. W. C. Harper, R. S. McNish and Z. D. Williams, 'The high stakes battle over M & A accounting', *McKinsey Quarterly*, **3**, 2000, 185–189. This opposition was pacified only when the FASB conceded that goodwill need not be amortized on a regular basis but only in the event of impairment revealed by the annual impairment test. On the politics of goodwill treatment see K. Ramanna, 'The implications of unverifiable fair-value accounting: Evidence from the political economy of goodwill accounting', *Journal of Accounting and Economics*, **45**, 2008, 253–281.

8. See R. Dobbs, B. Nand and W. Rehm, 'Merger valuation: Time to jettison EPS', *McKinsey Quarterly*, downloaded from www.mckinseyquarterly.com on 26 April 2008.

9. L. T. Johnson and K. R. Petrone, 'Is goodwill an asset?', *Accounting Horizons*, **12**(3), 1998, 293–303. The authors use the excess of purchase price over the book value of target equity as a proxy for goodwill. This difference is called 'purchase premium'.

10. B. Browning, 'Maximising R&D write-offs to reduce goodwill', *Mergers and Acquisitions*, September/October 1997, 29–30. See also R. H. Herz and E. J. Abahoonie, 'Innovations to minimise acquisition goodwill', *Mergers and Acquisitions*, March/April 1990, 35–40, on other deal structures to minimize goodwill.

11. K. Ramanna, *The politics and economics of accounting for goodwill at Cisco Systems*, Harvard Business School case 9-108-021, 28 September 2007.

12. The strong lobbying against FASB's initial proposal to abolish pooling accounting and replace it with only purchase accounting plus amortization is an indication of managers' incentive to avoid earnings dilution, since such earnings may be related to managerial compensation. Following FASB's exposure draft proposing the change, many firms strongly lobbied politicians in the US Congress to annul the amortization requirement. The result was SFAS 141, which mandated purchase accounting plus periodic impairment testing and no amortization. See K. Ramanna, *ibid.*, for empirical evidence of lobbying and how it changed the accounting rules. For an alternative and more benign interpretation of the lobbying activity, see the comments on the paper by D. Skinner, 'Discussion of "The implications of unverifiable fair-value accounting: Evidence from the political economy of goodwill accounting"', *Journal of Accounting and Economics*, **45**(2–3), 2008, 282–288. See also K. Ramanna and R. Watts, 'Evidence on the effects of unverifiable fair-value accounting', Harvard Business School working paper, 2007.

13. C. Hayn and P. J. Hughes, 'Leading indicators of goodwill impairment', *Journal of Accounting, Auditing & Finance*, **21**(3), 2006, 223–266.

14. For examples of these creative accounting feats, see P. S. Sudarsanam, *The Essence of Mergers and Acquisitions* (Hemel Hempstead: Prentice Hall, 1995), Chapter 10.

15. D. M. Ivancevich, 'Acquisitions and goodwill: The United Kingdom and the United States', *International Journal of Accounting*, **28**, 1993, 156–169. See also F. D. S. Choi and C. Lee, 'Merger premia and national differences in accounting for goodwill', *Journal of International Financial Management and Accounting*, **3**(3), 1991, 219–240; and M. L. Davis, 'The purchase *vs* pooling controversy: How the stock market responds to goodwill', *Journal of Applied Corporate Finance*, **9**(1), 1996, 50–59.

16. *Accountancy*, October 1994.

17. R. L. Watts, 'Conservatism in accounting Part I: Explanations and implications', *Accounting Horizons*, **17**, 2003, 207–221. See also K. Ramanna and R. Watts, 'Evidence on the Effects of Unverifiable Fair-Value Accounting', 2007, downloaded from www.ssrn.com

18. M. Rapoport and J. Weil, 'Goodwill write-downs give lenders leverage', *Wall Street Journal Europe*, 24 September 2002.

CHAPTER 16

Paying for the acquisition

Objectives

At the end of this chapter, the reader should be able to understand:

- the historical pattern of the alternative methods of paying for acquisitions;
- the factors relevant to the choice of payment currency by bidders and target companies;
- the potential earnings dilution in share exchange offers;
- the various models of choice between cash and share exchange;
- how payment currency is used to manage valuation risk;
- the empirical evidence on shareholder value consequences of payment currency;
- the impact of payment currency on post-acquisition operating performance; and
- the criteria for the choice of payment currency.

Introduction

Under the takeover regulation in the UK, in certain circumstances the bidder is obliged to make a cash offer or attach a cash alternative to an all-share exchange offer (see Chapter 18). This means that the payment method is determined partly by the nature of the bid being made, and partly by the share purchases made by the bidder prior to the bid. Payment currency, whether in the form of cash, shares or debt securities, is, however, a matter of importance to the bidder for other, non-regulatory, reasons.

These reasons include the choice of accounting policy that the bidder wishes to employ to account for the acquisition (see Chapter 15), the availability of finance to make a cash offer, tax considerations, the bidder's liquidity position, and its gearing. The choice of payment currency is also a risk management tool that may mitigate valuation errors made by the bidder or the target. It is determined as a trade-off among these, often competing, factors. The choice is also a matter of negotiation between the bidding and target companies, since it determines who will control the post-merger entity.

This chapter describes the characteristics of alternative payment methods, and their advantages and disadvantages from the bidder's and target shareholders' points of view. The recent innovations in acquisition financing, such as equity-based derivatives and deferred consideration to mitigate potential valuation errors, are also described. Different payment methods generate different levels of benefits to the bidder and target shareholders. Empirical evidence on the use of different payment currencies in actual takeovers, and their impact on the returns to shareholders of bidders and targets, is provided.

Methods of payment for acquisitions

The principal methods of payment are shown in Table 16.1. A share exchange offer is also known as stock-for-stock exchange, since common stockholders of the target exchange their stock for the acquirer's common stock, or as an all-paper offer.

Payment methods in the UK in the 1990s and 2000s

Figure 16.1 shows the number and value of M & A deals in the UK during 1990–2007. The targets are all publicly listed companies. It shows that use of shares increased during the 1990s wave, and slightly dominated the use of cash. Mixed offers substantially dominate both pure cash and pure share deals. Its dominance from 1994 to 2000 and its sudden collapse in 2001 track, with a short lag, the rise and fall of the UK stock market proxied by the FTSE All Share Index. Interestingly, during the millennial boom (2003–07) it is cash that has dominated, perhaps reflecting the greater liquidity in the credit markets and the increasingly powerful role played by private equity acquirers. Pure equity offers are dominated by mixed and cash offers.

Payment methods in European deals

Figure 16.2 provides a similar historical record of payment methods in the EU, excluding the UK. It shows the trends in the total deal values by different payment methods. In contrast to the UK, shares and mixed offers clearly dominate cash offers during 1995–99 before the crash in 2000. In the millennial wave, however, it is mixed offers and cash that slightly dominate pure equity offers. Moreover, during 2005–07 all methods show a rising trend, perhaps reflecting a combination of factors – rising stock markets, highly liquid credit markets and the increasing role of private equity. Again in contrast to the UK, mixed and pure equity offers seem to lead stock market (proxied by the FTSE Western European Stock Index) rise and fall.

Table 16.1 Principal methods of payment for acquisitions

Bidder offers	Target shareholders receive
Cash	Cash in exchange for their shares
Share exchange	A specified number of the bidder's shares for each target share
Cash-underwritten share offer (vendor placing/vendor rights)	Bidder's shares, then sell them to an investment bank or stockbroker for cash (vendor placing) or to the bidder shareholders (vendor rights)
Loan stock	A loan stock/debenture in exchange for their shares
Convertible loan or preferred shares	Loan stock or preferred shares convertible into ordinary shares at a predetermined conversion rate over a specified period
Deferred payment	Part of consideration after a specified period, subject to performance criteria

Figure 16.1 Total value of UK M & A by payment method, 1990–2007

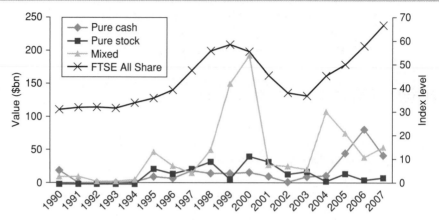

Targets are UK public companies.
All deals completed and acquirers hold more than 50% of the target share after transaction.
Only deals of which transaction value is disclosed included.
Deals categorized according to announcement year.
Deal value in 2007 US dollars.
US Consumer Price Index – All Urban: All Items is used to adjust for inflation.
Source: Thomson Reuters.

Figure 16.2 Total value of M & A in EU by payment method, 1990–2007

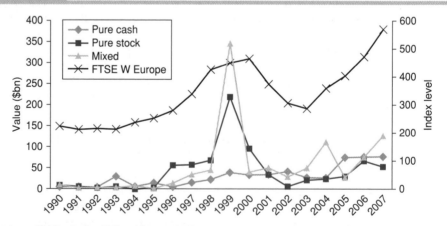

Targets are EU (excluding UK) public companies.
All deals completed and acquirers hold more than 50% of the target share after transaction.
Only deals of which transaction value is disclosed are included.
EU means: 27 current members plus Switzerland.
Deals are categorized according to the announcement year.
Deal value in 2007 US dollars.
US Consumer Price Index – All Urban: All Items is used to adjust for inflation.
Source: Thomson Reuters.

Figure 16.3   Average value of M & A in EU by payment method, 1990–2007

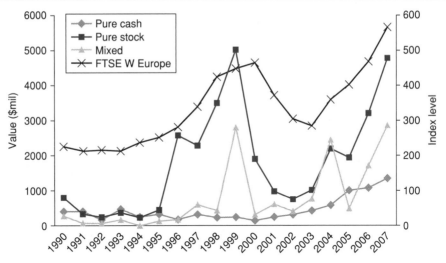

Targets are EU (excluding UK) public companies.
All deals completed and acquirers hold more than 50% of the target share after transaction.
Only deals of which transaction value is disclosed are included.
EU means: 27 current members plus Switzerland.
Deals are categorized according to the announcement year.
Deal value in 2007 US dollars.
US Consumer Price Index – All Urban: All Items is used to adjust for inflation.
Source: Thomson Reuters.

Figure 16.3 depicts the trend in payment currencies by the average deal value. We find that pure stock offers and mixed offers clearly dominate cash offers from 1995 to 1999, and even during the millennial wave. The European stock markets track the use of these stock-based payment currencies closely, but with a slight lag. Thus in larger deals acquirers tend to use stock or mixed offers, especially during periods of stock market boom[1].

Payment methods in the US

A similar pattern is observed in the US for the 1990s, with a surge of stock exchange and mixed offer deals between 1995 and 1999 before the huge crash in 2000. Figure 16.4 shows the trends in total deal values by payment method for the US.

We find that cash deals also increase and decrease the same way, but not to the same extent, as pure stock and mixed offers during 1995–2000, slightly extending the bull run longer than the other two. An interesting feature of the millennial wave is that cash begins to dominate stock and mixed offers. The preference for stock and mixed offers when the stock market is high is borne out in Figure 16.4, but this relation breaks down in the new millennium. During 2004–07 cash becomes more dominant, even though the stock market is still rising[2]. As with the European trend, this may be due to increasing private equity role in M & A in the last few years, and the high liquidity in credit markets.

Many of the megadeals of the 1990s, such as Vodafone's acquisition of Mannesmann, Worldcom's acquisition of MCI, the AOL–Time Warner merger and Daimler-Benz's merger

Figure 16.4   **Total value of US M & A by payment method, 1990–2007**

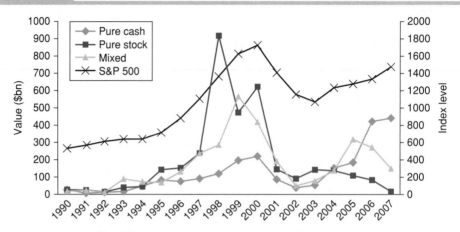

Target companies are US public companies.
All deals are completed, and the acquirers hold more than 50% of the target share after the transaction.
Only deals of which transaction value is disclosed are included.
Deals are categorized according to the announcement year.
Deal value is in 2007 dollars and US Consumer Price Index – All Urban: All Items is used to adjust for inflation.
Source: Thomson Reuters.

with Chrysler, were financed with equity. Both the high valuation of the acquirer's stock in these cases and the large cost of raising cash to finance the acquisitions made stock exchange offers quite attractive. The high stock value appreciation of the targets prior to the bid and the bid premium meant that cash offers might have resulted in immediate tax liability to target shareholders, and this was avoided by stock exchange offers, as we discuss below. Overall, in the 1990s there was high correlation between the use of stock or mixed offers and the stock market movement, consistent with our expectation that high stock market levels provide acquirers with the incentive to capitalize on the high value of equity. After 2001, however, this pattern is no longer as strong as before. There is a greater use of cash, even when the stock market level is high, and a decline in the use of stock or mixed offers.

There are other factors that may influence the choice of payment method. Accounting, tax and financial strategy considerations may be relevant to this choice. The accounting considerations have been dealt with in Chapter 15. Tax and bidder's financial strategy are considered next.

Tax aspects of acquisition financing[3]

Acquirers can structure the acquisition financing in a way that maximizes the tax reliefs, thereby increasing the value of the offer not only to the target company shareholders but also to themselves. Tax rules differ from one jurisdiction to another, and financing through finance subsidiaries in an offshore financial centre may reduce the overall tax burden on the acquirer. Any tax saving through efficient structure can then be used to increase the bid premium to the target, thereby enhancing the chances of bid success. Tax consequences of an acquisition or merger are closely linked to the method of financing it, and to the proportion of acquirer stock or cash or other securities in the payment currency. In auction situations, which have become increasingly common (see Chapter 20 on bid strategies), pricing of targets is highly competitive, and a keen evaluation of the tax aspects of the deal can make a critical difference to the competitive advantage of a bidder.

Tax rules in EU countries

Some of the important considerations in EU countries are as follows[4].

Transfer tax and value added tax

- Tax on the transfer of ownership differs between shares and assets and among different types of assets, e.g. real estate, intangibles. In general, transfer of shares is taxed at a lower rate than transfer of assets: for example, in the Netherlands there is no tax on shares, but 6% on real estate company share transfers or transfer of real estate. Thus buying a company may be cheaper than buying its assets.
- Sales or value added tax on share or asset transfer may also be a relevant consideration in structuring a deal.

Amortization and depreciation of assets

- Cost of goodwill and other intangibles may be tax deductible in some EU countries but not others. Tax relief is available for amortized goodwill in many European countries, e.g. the UK, Germany, the Netherlands and Belgium. This is goodwill attached to assets purchased, rather than goodwill that arises in consolidated accounts. In the UK after the adoption of IFRS 3 (see Chapter 15 on accounting for acquisitions) goodwill is not amortized, but a 4% writing-down allowance (WDA) can be claimed against goodwill.
- Tax relief may be available for higher depreciation as a result of asset step-up. However, in the UK asset step-up of the acquired company has no tax implication.
- In some countries, e.g. the UK, asset acquisitions, in contrast to share acquisitions, can result in asset revaluation and a higher tax allowance.

Tax efficient financing structure

- It may be tax efficient to 'push down' debt from the country of the acquisition vehicle to that of the target to exploit tax deductibility of interest or deductibility at a higher corporation tax rate: for example, the UK corporation tax rate of 28% and the US rate of about 42% (combined Federal and state taxes) suggest that debt should be raised by a US-based entity. However, anti-avoidance rules in different countries may limit such push-down. Further, when the funds are re-lent to the acquiring entity, the subsequent interest payments may be subject to withholding taxes and anti-avoidance provisions.
- Under thin capitalization anti-avoidance rules, debt may not be treated as such if it is not at interest rates appropriate for arm's length transactions, but as equity, and interest paid on that debt may not be tax deductible. Any excess interest above such rates may be treated as dividend distribution, and denied tax deductibility.
- In some EU countries there are 'earnings stripping' rules that impose limits on the level of debt financing by related parties, and interest paid above such limits may not qualify for tax deduction. The limits may be numerical, for example 3 to 1 for debt to equity in Spain and the Netherlands and 1.5 to 1 in France, where intra-group interest paid may not exceed 25% of EBITA. In some countries, where the debt to equity is too far above the corresponding group ratio the interest on the excess does not qualify for tax deduction, e.g. Germany, France and the Netherlands.

- While the issue costs, such as investment banking fees of debt, may be tax deductible, issue costs of equity may not be, for example in the UK. This makes financing of cash acquisitions with debt more attractive than with equity.
- Tax treatment of intragroup loans is based on transfer pricing rules and comparison with terms in arm's length loans, e.g. the UK.

Treatment of pre-acquisition tax losses

- Can pre-acquisition tax losses of the target be offset in the future against the bidder's or the merged entity's profits? What are the restrictions on such carry-forward of tax losses?
- The target company may be restructured prior to the acquisition so as to reduce the taxable capital gain to the target or its shareholders. However, there may be restrictions on such restructuring.
- Many countries have change-of-control rules that may eliminate or restrict the use of historic tax losses of the target to offset current or future tax liabilities, thereby reducing their value to the acquirer.

Withholding taxes

- In the case of cross-border acquisitions, dividends and interests payable to the foreign owners of targets may be subject to withholding or other forms of double taxation. Interest payments are subject to such a tax, but not dividends, in the UK and Germany. The opposite is the case in the Netherlands. In France, Italy and Spain both dividends and interest are subject to withholding tax. Double taxation treaties (DTTs) between countries often eliminate withholding taxes. Many EU countries, e.g. Spain, exempt dividend and interest payments to other EU resident companies.
- DTTs have a bearing on the country of location of acquisition vehicles. In general, where the country of the acquisition vehicle has a DTT with the country of the operating business, dividends or interest paid to the former by the latter may be tax exempt.

What is the impact of deal structure on vendor shareholders?

- Target shareholders may be liable for capital gains tax immediately on deal completion in some countries but can defer the tax in others, e.g. the UK.
- In the case of asset sales, followed by distribution of proceeds to vendor shareholders, there may be double taxation, i.e. CGT paid by the vendor and income tax by the vendor shareholders. A tax-efficient structure can avoid such double taxation.

In considering the impact of taxation on the form of payment to target shareholders, the bidder has to take into account both the possible capital gains tax liability at the time of the takeover and the income tax liability on the dividends or interest paid by the acquirer after the acquisition. The tax issue must also be tackled within the acquirer's own tax strategy, since interest on loan stock is normally corporation tax deductible, whereas dividends are not. We illustrate some of the relevant tax issues in the UK and the US.

US capital gains tax rules

Section 368 (a) (1) provides a list of corporate acquisitions and mergers that can be organized in a tax-free manner. While in some transactions voting shares of the acquirer must be the sole consideration, in others the US Internal Revenue Service (IRS) allows partial consideration in the form of non-voting shares, cash, debt or other assets. In this case voting shares should account for a 'substantial' proportion of the consideration. Certain types of disposals of the shares received by the target shareholders may nullify the tax-free treatment. The acquiring corporation in a tax-free merger normally inherits the tax basis and tax attributes of the target, but there are restrictions on the availability of the tax losses in the target to the acquirer.

Under the IRS Code, for an acquisition to be non-taxable (tax-free merger), it must satisfy the 'continuity of interest' condition[5]:

- At least 50% of the target's shares must be exchanged for stock in the merged entity. The stock portion of offers satisfying this condition can be deemed taxable or non-taxable for personal tax purposes.
- Consideration other than the acquirer's stock, e.g. cash (called 'boot'), may be taxable.
- All compensation is taxable if an offer contains less than 50% stock. If a shareholder receives taxable compensation, the shareholder must pay a tax on any capital gain he or she realizes in the acquisition.
- The capital gains tax is deferred if the shareholder receives stock in a non-taxable offer. Whether an offer is taxable or not is often agreed by the bidder with the IRS. This deferment is similar to the roll-over of the gain in the UK.
- Amortized goodwill is now tax deductible.
- In the US, under the Tax Reform Act of 1986, in taxable mergers asset basis step-up increases the tax relief.
- Asset acquisitions, in contrast to share acquisitions, can result in asset basis step-up and a higher tax allowance.
- In the US, acquirers and vendors can elect share acquisitions to be treated as asset acquisitions, under Section 338 of the IRS Tax Code, to benefit from the basis step-up.

Income and corporation tax after acquisition

The advantage of issuing loan stock as consideration is that the interest on it is corporation tax deductible (see above for restrictions on this). Thus the acquirer is able to reduce its tax liability. The target company shareholder who accepts loan stock is, however, subject to income tax on the interest he or she receives.

Payment method may also affect the tax paid by the merged entity. In the UK, when a company acquires the share capital of another, any revaluation of the target's assets has no tax implication, since the asset step-up does not alter the capital allowance the target was entitled to. Use of the target's previously accumulated tax losses, i.e. losses that can be offset against future profits or profits of other members of a group to which the company belongs, to reduce the overall tax liability by the acquirer, is now subject to stringent conditions such as continuity of business for three years on either side of the acquisition. Such tax losses are therefore difficult to translate into higher profits and cash flows for the acquirer.

In the US the continuity of interest rule applies to corporate tax[6]. In a non-taxable offer the target firm's unused tax credits and loss carry-overs can be deducted against the combined firm's future taxable income, because target shareholders maintain substantial ownership. In a taxable offer ownership rights are considered sold, and the bidder is allowed to step up the depreciation basis of the purchased assets. Step-ups allow the acquirer to reduce its future taxable income and the tax liability. However, the 1986 Tax Reform Act largely eliminated the tax benefits from step-up, and imposes annual limits on the amount of carry-forward net operating losses (NOL) that can be offset against post-acquisition taxable income of the target.

Tax due diligence, indemnities and warranties

These are important in the purchase of shares, since the buyer inherits the tax exposure of the target firm i.e. its liabilities including contingent liabilities and tax liabilities. Warranties may need to be preceded, where possible, by due diligence of the tax affairs of the target and the consolidated tax group to which it belonged. Due diligence should cover exposures to federal, state and local income and other taxes in both share and asset purchases. Indemnities and warranties may not be available from publicly listed targets or targets bought from receivers and liquidators.

Tax and acquisition deal structure

The structure of a deal is determined by the acquirer also taking into account the corporate law provisions, the accounting rules for mergers and acquisitions, and any antitrust consideration. Thus tax considerations are not the sole determinant of the legal structure of an acquisition. However, the legal structure chosen will have tax implications, and therefore will influence the valuation of merger benefits and target pricing. The acquirer's financial strategy and other considerations, e.g. control, also influence the choice of payment currency and hence the legal structure and the tax consequences.

Impact of bidder's financial strategy

A company's financial strategy has many strands. Maintaining a reasonable gearing ratio and the credit rating by rating agencies such as Moody's is one of them (see below for a discussion of the impact of credit rating). Ensuring adequacy of lines of credit from banks is another. Taking advantage of any tax provisions to reduce the cost of capital is also relevant. Finally, timing of security issues to exploit favourable market conditions is an important consideration. The choice of payment currency for an acquisition is based on a trade-off of these often conflicting criteria, which are discussed below.

Where the bidder has an already high gearing ratio, issue of loan stock to pay for the acquisition is less attractive than a share exchange offer, which will reduce that ratio. Moreover, the operating cash flows of the combined entity and its cash flow or earnings cover for the debt interest must be sufficient and sustainable. These considerations also apply when the bidder raises bank finance to make a cash offer. The source of loan finance differs in the two cases, but the related obligations are the same.

Issue of loan stock or drawing on the firm's credit lines may cause the acquirer to breach loan covenants stipulating a maximum debt-to-equity ratio or a minimum interest cover. Such a breach is a source of potential financial distress for the acquirer. The acquirer may suffer a credit rating downgrade that increases the cost of both existing and new debt. Of course, the tax deductibility of debt provides the acquirer with an opportunity to enhance the earnings per share (EPS) for its existing shareholders, and thereby the value of the company. This rationale drove some of the high-leverage buyouts of the 1980s and 1990s, as we discussed in Chapter 11.

Earnings dilution in a share exchange

A share exchange, in contrast to a loan stock or a leveraged acquisition, imposes its own 'cost', in that the enlarged shareholder base can lead to a decline in EPS in the year of acquisition, or

Table 16.2 Pre-bid data for Bidder and Target

Company	EPS (p)	PER	Share price (£)	No. of shares (m)	NI (£m)	Market capitalization (£m)
Bidder	10	20	2	20	2	40
Target	10	10	1	20	2	20

EPS = earnings per share; PER = price/earnings ratio; NI = net after-tax income for ordinary shareholders.

for several years thereafter. Let us assume that Bidder (B) makes a share exchange offer for Target (T). The two companies have the pre-bid data shown in Table 16.2.

B offers 1.5 of its own shares for each T share. The exchange ratio (ER) is 1.5. The number of B shares after acquisition will be 20 million of the old shares plus 30 million of the new shares. The combined earnings of B and T are £4m. Thus the EPS will be 8 pence, compared with B's EPS of 10 pence before the bid. Thus its earnings are diluted by 20%.

Assuming the share value of B does not change, the bid premium that B offers to T shareholders is 200%:

$$(\text{B share value} \times \text{Exchange ratio}) - \text{Pre-bid value of T share} = £2 \times 1.5 - £1$$

B may avoid dilution by offering one B share for each T share. The post-acquisition EPS will then be 10p. In this case, the bid premium is 100%. Can B afford such a high premium as 200, or 100%? The answer to this question lies in the view that the stock market is likely to take of the virtues of the acquisition. This view is expressed in terms of the earnings multiple after the acquisition: that is, the post-acquisition PER. This is the rate at which the EPS of the combined entity (BT) will be capitalized to give the market value of that entity. A bidder has to take into account this post-acquisition value in determining the ER.

For any given value of expected post-acquisition PER it is in the interest of the target to bargain for as high an ER as possible. The bidder's incentive is to keep the ER as low as possible. However, there is usually a range of ERs over which both can gain, both can lose, or one can gain at the expense of the other. These possible outcomes are shown in Table 16.3 for three different expected post-acquisition PERs of 10, 15 and 20 for B's acquisition of T.

The gain or loss to each shareholder group is:

For B: gain $= (N_B/N_{BT}) \times V_{BT} - V_B$

For T: gain $= [(N_T \times ER)/N_{BT}] \times V_{BT} - V_T$

Table 16.3 Relationship between post-acquisition price/earnings ratio (PER) and the exchange ratio (ER)

Pre-bid market value of B = £40m and T = £20m. BT's combined earnings = £4m

ER	Company	Post-acquisition value of B and T at PER (£m)		
		10	15	20
0.5	B	26.6	40.0	53.3
	T	13.4	20.0	26.7
1.0	B	20.0	30.0	40.0
	T	20.0	30.0	40.0
1.5	B	16.0	24.0	32.0
	T	24.0	36.0	48.0

Source: Table 16.2.

where N_B and N_T are the pre-bid numbers of shares in B and T, and V_B and V_T are their prebid market values. N_{BT} and V_{BT} are the corresponding figures for the post-acquisition firm, BT.

$$V_{BT} = \text{Post-acquisition PER of BT} \times \text{BT's combined earnings}$$

For example, if PER = 20 and ER = 0.5, V_{BT} = £80m, N_B = 20m, N_T = 20m, N_{BT} = 30m, then B's and T's shares of V_{BT} are £53.3m and £26.7m. Gain to B = £13.3m and gain to T = £6.7m.

It will be recalled from Chapter 14 that a company with a high PER is valued highly, owing to high expected future earnings growth or low risk, or both. The forecast PER applied by the stock market determines the value of BT. At a PER of 15 this value is £60m, the same as the sum of the pre-bid values of B and T. This suggests that the acquisition does not create added value for the shareholders. It has a neutral value creation impact.

At a forecast PER of 10, the same as Target's pre-bid PER, BT's value will be £40m, implying that the acquisition is actually value destroying by £20m. The combination of B and T leads to negative synergy. On the other hand, with a PER of 20, the same as B's pre-bid level, BT's value will be £80m. The added value from the acquisition is £20m. It can be seen that this added value comes from the capitalization of T's earnings at 20 not at 10.

Bootstrapping

The phenomenon whereby shareholder value increases by the application of the bidder's higher PER to the target's earnings is known as bootstrapping. Is bootstrapping based on the bidder's pious hope, or on stock market inefficiency, or on the market's expectation of synergy? Unless the stock market is convinced of the strategic value creation logic of the acquisition, a PER of 20 is unlikely to be applied. Assessment of such logic was discussed in Chapters 5–9. What does capitalization at 20 mean? It means that the market expects that the earnings growth of the target after acquisition will match that of the bidder: that is, that it will be twice as fast as in the pre-bid period. If this growth is not achieved, bootstrapping will be a short-lived delusion, and BT's value will decline (see Tables 16.5 and 16.6 and discussion of the impact of different growth rates for T on BT's earnings per share below).

Sharing acquisition gains between bidder and target

The exchange ratio, ER, determines how the overall added value at any PER will be shared between B and T shareholders. From Table 16.3 we can see that, for any given PER, the bidder can avoid losing by choosing an appropriate maximum ER. Similarly, by negotiating for a minimum ER, T can also avoid losing. For example, with a PER of 20, B will lose if ER is 1.5. At 15, it loses with an ER higher than 0.5. On the other hand, T loses when PER is 10 and ER is 0.5.

The case of PER = 15 and ER = 0.5 is an interesting one, since neither B nor T loses. 15 is the average between the PERs of B and T. An ER of 0.5 is the ratio of T's share value to B's share value. Thus when the bidder expects no synergy, it cannot afford a higher ER than a simple ratio of the target's to the bidder's share price, in order to prevent loss of value from the acquisition. This means that no bid premium is paid to the target. The bidder can justify a bid premium only if the acquisition produces some synergy, and if this synergy is credibly translated into a higher PER than the average of the pre-bid PERs.

The various combinations of expected post-acquisition PER and bidder's choice of ER are shown in Figure 16.5, derived by Larson and Gonedes[7]. The 'Bidder' line represents the *maximum* ER that the bidder can afford for a given forecast PER. The 'Target' line represents the *minimum* ER acceptable to target shareholders if they are not to lose from the acquisition. For the acquisition to be beneficial to both B and T shareholders, it must lie in the first quadrant of Figure 16.5.

| Figure 16.5 | Impact of PER and ER on the wealth gains of Bidder and Target shareholders – Larson–Gonedes model |

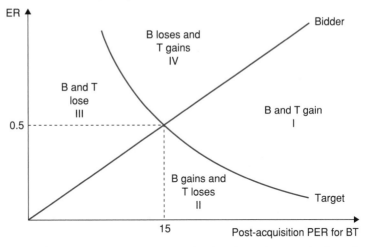

Source: K. Larson and N. Gonedes, 'Business combination: An exchange ratio determination model', *The Accounting Review*, **44**, 1969.

Table 16.4 ER and shareholder wealth outcomes

Larson–Gonedes ER zone	*% of sample deals across studies*
I – both B and T gain	50
II – B gains and T loses	5
III – B and T lose	14
IV – B loses and T gains	31

Source: See studies reviewed above.

Empirical tests of Larson and Gonedes's model, summarized in Table 16.4, show that in nearly half of the sample cases studied acquisitions fall into the first quadrant, indicating that both bidder and target shareholders make gains from the acquisition[8]. This pattern also points to bidders overpaying in nearly 45% of the acquisitions (Quadrants III and IV). One possible reason is that they overestimate the earnings growth rates for both bidders and targets. Another may be that acquirer managers expect the market to attribute the acquirer's high PER, a possible case of managerial hubris.

Wealth transfers from targets to bidders are very rare (only 5%). Both B and T losing (the merger is value destroying for both) happens in 14% of the deals. These are bad deals. In 31% of cases there is wealth transfer from bidders to targets. These may overall create value, but bidders seem to overpay.

Earnings dilution versus accretion

Earnings are said to be diluted when the acquirer's post-acquisition EPS is lower than its pre-acquisition value. Accretion is the opposite change. Table 16.5 illustrates the calculation of the extent of dilution or accretion for the preceding acquisition. It is clear that dilution increases with increase in the number of acquirer's shares, and this in turn depends on the ER, which,

Table 16.5 Impact of exchange ratio on earnings per share dilution and accretion

Exchange ratio	No of shares post-acquisition	Net income post-acquisition	Post-acquisition EPS (£)	Accretion (A)/ Dilution (D)
0.5	30m	4m	0.13	30% (A)
1.0	40m	4m	0.10	No A/D
1.5	50m	4m	0.08	20% (D)

Source: Table 16.2.

in turn, is dictated by the implied bid premium. When expected PER is that of B, therefore, the bidder can offer a lower price and hence a smaller premium, and ensure that EPS is accretive. For example, for a PER of 20 and a customary target premium of 30% (see Chapter 4 on the level of abnormal returns to targets in numerous studies), the acquisition price is £26m (= £20m × 1.30) and £1.30 per share. ER is 0.65. New B shares issued number 13m, the total number of BT shares is 33, and BT's EPS will be 12p. Thus the deal is EPS accretive at a 30% premium because of bootstrapping. Bootstrapping can work up to an ER of 1.

Choosing purchase price and exchange ratio to avoid earnings dilution

The above analysis is based on EPS in the year of the merger. The exchange ratio based on just one year's EPS may be misleading, since it may not reveal the extent of the earnings dilution in the following post-acquisition years. Table 16.6 shows earnings dilution over five years following a merger. We use the data from Table 16.2 for the year of the merger, year 0, and estimate the EPS for the five post-acquisition years, year 1 to year 5. B's high PER of 20 indicates that its earnings growth rate is expected to be much higher than that of T (PER of only 10). We assume that B's earnings will grow at 20% per annum, whereas T's earnings will grow at just 10%. The bid premium is 100%, and T is therefore valued at £40m (ER = 1 and 20m new B shares issued). We also assume that B's share price will remain unchanged.

Table 16.6 Earnings dilution in stock exchange offers after the acquisition

	Year 0	Year 1	Year 2	Year 3	Year 4	Year 5
Panel A: BT's net income (NI) assuming B's EPS grows at 20% and T's NI at 10%						
B's EPS (pence)	10.00	12.00	14.40	17.28	20.74	24.88
B's net income (NI) (£m)	2.00	2.40	2.88	3.46	4.15	4.98
T's NI (£m)	2.00	2.20	2.42	2.66	2.93	3.22
BT's NI (£m)	4.00	4.60	5.30	6.12	7.08	8.20
Panel B: EPS dilution and the maximum number of shares to T to avoid dilution (100% premium, ER = 1, T valued at £40m, new B shares issued = 20m)						
BT's EPS (pence)	10.00	11.5	13.25	15.30	17.70	20.50
Dilution (%)	0.00	4.2	7.99	11.49	14.68	17.63
Maximum number of shares to T (m)	20	18.33	16.81	15.41	14.31	12.95
Panel C: EPS accretion and the maximum number of shares to T to avoid accretion (Nil premium, ER = 0.5, T valued at £20m, new B shares issued = 10m)						
BT's EPS (pence)	13.33	15.33	17.67	20.39	23.59	27.33
Accretion (%)	33.33	27.75	22.71	18.00	13.74	9.85

Table 16.7 Post-acquisition earnings growth to avoid dilution (100% premium)

	Year 0	Year 1	Year 2	Year 3	Year 4	Year 5
BT's NI (£m)	4.00	4.80	5.76	6.91	8.30	9.95
BT's EPS (pence)	10.00	12.00	14.40	17.28	20.74	24.88

BT's EPS = BT's NI/(Old B shares + new B shares). Comparison of row 1 in Panels A and B shows that the merged firm BT's EPS is lower than B's pre-acquisition EPS. The dilution as a percentage of B's EPS is shown in row 2 of Panel B. Dilution = $100 \times$ (B's EPS − BT's EPS)/B's EPS. Row 3 of that panel shows the maximum number of shares in BT that B could offer to T to avoid any dilution, i.e. for BT's EPS = B's EPS.

$$\text{Maximum number} = \left(\frac{\text{BT's NI}}{\text{B's EPS}}\right) \text{Number of B's pre-merger shares.}$$

In Panel B of Table 16.6, while the ER based on year 0 data is 1 to 1, that based on year 5 earnings forecast is 0.65 (= 12.95/20). In determining the ER, B therefore needs to take into account the expected growth in B's earnings as well as in T's earnings after the acquisition. If the target is expected to grow at a slower rate than the bidder, ER based on year 0 data will be excessive, and lead to significant earnings dilution. Comparison of panels B and C of Table 16.6 shows that, for a given level of expected earnings growth of the bidder and target, the premium paid also determines whether the acquisition is earnings dilutive or accretive. BT's earnings may experience accretion rather than dilution when B avoids paying a premium. The higher the premium, the larger is the ER and the higher the rate of earnings dilution.

Another important factor is that, for any given level of premium paid, the rate of post-acquisition earnings growth determines whether the acquisition is earnings dilutive or accretive. Table 16.7 shows that, with the target's expected earnings growth at 20%, the acquisition becomes earnings accretive even with a 100% premium and T priced at £40m, i.e. ER = 1. Starting from year 0 NI of £4m, BT's NI grows at 20%, and EPS also grows at the same rate. There is neither dilution of nor accretion to B's pre-acquisition earnings (compare BT's EPS in Table 16.7 with B's EPS in Panel A of Table 16.6).

For B, several options to avoid dilution are available:

- Improve the post-acquisition earnings growth rate of T, say, to 20%, the same as B's.
- Reduce the premium paid and hence the ER.
- Base ER on realized performance of T, i.e. use deferred payment terms (see below on earn-outs).

Impact of goodwill on earnings dilution

Where B's purchase price for T includes a substantial amount of goodwill, and the goodwill is amortized over a period of, say, 20 years, the EPS would be further diluted (see Chapter 15 on accounting for goodwill). For example, suppose the purchase price is £40m and the number of BT shares is 40m (see Table 16.6, Panel B). If goodwill amounts to £10m, the annual amortization is £0.5m, and BT's EPS would fall by 1.25 pence per share. In years 0 to 2 this will reduce EPS by about 10–13%. Analysts, however, may disregard the dilution caused by goodwill amortization in assessing the impact of share exchange offers, since it is also common to cash-financed offers.

Under IFRS 3 and SFAS 142 goodwill cannot be amortized in the case of public company acquirers (see Chapter 15), but is subject to annual impairment test. Where impairment is material it will be charged to the income statement. Such impairment introduces significant subjectivity in impairment estimates, and can thus make EPS estimates less reliable. This also affects EPS dilution. Compared with the annual amortization rule, the impairment rule is likely to result in more EPS accretion than dilution. This can be illustrated with the data in Table 16.3 above. Let us assume that there are no synergies in the merger of B and T. In this case the expected PE will be 15 and the optimal ER will be a maximum of 0.5. If, however, B pays a 50% premium, i.e. £10m, and acquisition price of £30m (see under column 15 in Table 16.3), this represents a goodwill of £10m (assuming the targets' other assets are not revalued). If this is amortized under the old rules over, say, 10 years, the reduction in BT's net earnings will be £1m and EPS will be diluted to 7.5p (£3m/40m shares). Without amortization BT's net earnings will be £4m and EPS will remain at 10p, i.e. no dilution. Thus non-amortization under the new rules may mask the overpayment (it is overpayment because the merger is devoid of any synergy), rendering the EPS a less reliable measure.[9,10]

Valuation risk and payment currency

In negotiating the payment currency, the bidder and target have different and opposing incentives. If B finds it difficult to value the target, offers cash and, post-acquisition, discovers some skeletons in T's cupboard, the entire loss falls to B's shareholders. If B had offered a share exchange, T shareholders would have stayed on to share the loss. Thus the downside of the valuation risk is mitigated by a share exchange.

On the other hand, if B is confident that post-acquisition PER will be 20, in a share exchange with an ER of 0.5, T will end up with a gain of £6.7m (see Table 16.3). If B could make a cash offer with a bid premium of only, say, £4m, it would appropriate the extra value for its own shareholders. Thus, if B expects good times to roll after the acquisition, it has the incentive to offer cash.

T shareholders also have contradictory incentives. They also face the valuation risk that B is already overvalued[11], or that B will mess up the acquisition. In this event they will prefer cash to avoid the downside risk. But they forgo the upside potential that they would enjoy if they accepted a share exchange and stayed on to enjoy the good times. This leads to the rather perverse situation that just when B offers paper, T wants cash, and vice versa.

Adverse selection and stock-for-stock exchange

The valuation risk arises from what the economists call information asymmetry: that is, each side believes that the other side knows something more. Information asymmetry leads to adverse selection, i.e. selection of a target whose real value is worse than what it appears to be. It is also called 'buying a lemon'. The acquirer may worry about buying a lemon as much as the target shareholders about accepting the bidder's shares in consideration.

The bidder can alleviate its own adverse selection problem by offering a share exchange rather than cash. In Hansen's model, common stock due to its contingent pricing effect reduces the target valuation risk for the bidder by forcing the target shareholders to share the risk[12]. The bidder can also mitigate the target's adverse selection problem with a generous share exchange ratio. This may take the form of higher ER if the bidder's stock price falls below an agreed threshold.

As we have seen, this may result in perceived earnings dilution and even value loss for B's shareholders. It is for this reason, *inter alia*, that share exchange offers are often greeted with bidder's share price decline (see the empirical evidence on market reaction to stock exchange offers below). In conditional offers, bidders may limit the ER to avoid excessive dilution of earnings as well as dilution of control to the target shareholder.

Equity derivatives and risk management in equity offers

Share exchange offers are vulnerable to the valuation risk from short-term price movements. The true value of the offer from the target shareholders' point of view in the long run depends not only on any initial overvaluation but also on the success of the acquirer in creating value out of the acquisition. A number of derivative securities attached to the share exchange offer addresses the short-term lemons problem between merger agreement and closing of the deal, whereas derivatives such as contingent value rights (CVRs) seek to solve the long-term post-acquisition performance failure problem. These derivatives are agreements between bidders and targets to provide price protection against adverse price movements of the bidder stock. For this reason these offers are also known as conditional stock exchange offers. These derivatives increase the chances of a successful stock-for-stock deal by assuring the target shareholders of the value of the consideration they receive. In hostile bids, and in multiple bidder contests for the same target, attaching such derivatives to the stock exchange offer may make it more attractive to target shareholders[13].

Dangers of unprotected SEX: wear a cap or a collar!

SEX is the stock exchange ratio between the bidder shares and the target shares in a stock-for-stock exchange. Where the SEX is fixed, any adverse price movement of the bidder's stock reduces the value of the offer to the target. To avoid this problem of uncertainty of offer value associated with a fixed SEX, the bidder may make a fixed-value offer. Under this the SEX is adjusted when the bidder share price moves out of an agreed range during an agreed period (see Exhibit 16.1 below).

Fixed exchange rate and fixed value pricing of target

Share exchange offers are broadly of two kinds:

- fixed exchange rate offers; and
- fixed value offers.

Fixed SEX pricing of the target offers both parties the advantage of certainty, and the acquirer is able to calculate in advance the resulting dilution in the post-acquisition ownership. However, the value of the offer to the target depends on the bidder's stock price movement. If the decline in the bidder stock is steep, the offer value may be pushed too low to be acceptable to target shareholders, and the deal may fall through. For example, in 1996 ACC Corp. terminated the discussion to be acquired by LDDS Communications (later renamed Worldcom and then MCI after Worldcom's emergence from bankruptcy). On the other hand, if the bidder's stock price is too high, the bidder may feel it is overpaying and abandon the bid.

In a fixed-value offer, also known as floating rate offer, at closing of a deal the exchange is completed at whatever SEX is required to yield the agreed fixed value. Fixed-value offers enhance the target's protection, but the acquirer is faced with uncertainty about the number of shares it will issue, and what the dilution effect of the acquisition will be.

The pricing period, both length and timing, may be a bone of contention between bidder and target. A lengthy period increases uncertainty to the bidder, and the timing of the end of the period needs to be agreed so that the shareholders will have the information to judge the offer and vote accordingly. Further, arbitrageurs, who take speculative positions in firms involved in merger negotiations, may depress the bidder's stock price. The bidder would not want its stock price to experience a free fall that raises the SEX too high.

Collars, caps, ceilings and floors

The dangers of unprotected SEX are thus clear. The following options have been designed to offer protection:

- Floor to a fixed SEX pricing – if the bidder price falls below the floor the fixed rate is adjusted upwards and the bidder has to issue more shares.
- Cap to the SEX subject to a floor – the acquirer who is reluctant to issue too many shares may impose an absolute limit on, or cap, the additional shares to be issued.
- Collar – a fixed rate price subject to both a floor and a cap.

There are two types of collar:

- a fixed SEX ratio over a certain range of the acquirer's stock price limited (collared) at both the top and bottom ends so that the target receives a fixed value. This means the ER is adjusted down or up to hold the offer value constant outside the range;
- a fixed-value offer over a range of the acquirer's stock price, but the ER is fixed at either end of the range. This means that below the bottom of the range the value to the target falls and above the top of the range it rises with the ER[14].

The collar range typically captures about 10–20% of the price fluctuations during the pricing period, but need not be symmetrical.

Exhibit 16.1 provides an example of the way the ER is adjusted to provide protection to buyer and seller. In the Banc One bid for American Fletcher the fixed value was $60 per share over an agreed range. Further Exhibit of the use of caps, floors and collars, and how they affect the payoffs to bidders and targets, is in the case study at the end of this chapter.

Termination and walk-away options

Merger agreements may also provide for either party to terminate and walk away from the deal when the price of the deal has fallen unacceptably low (from the target's point of view) or risen unacceptably high (from the bidder's point of view). Walk-away rights may be used in combination with collars and exercised when the bidder's stock price goes outside the range of protection offered by the collar provisions for the exchange ratio adjustment. To offset the target's walk-away rights the bidder may ask for 'top-up' rights that allow it to increase the exchange ratio and the offer value to close the transaction. For example, in the BankAmerica Corp. merger with Continental Bank of Illinois in 1994, Continental's board could have walked away if the BankAmerica stock price fell below a certain floor. This right was subject to the latter's right to top up the share offer so that Continental would receive the floor price.

Since companies invest a great deal of time and resources in negotiating mergers, walk-away rights, when exercised, may cause substantial losses. In volatile markets with a high volume of arbitrage trading the price pressure on the bidder may trigger the walk-away option and cause the deal to collapse. However, with the top-up right the bidder may choose to abandon a bid rather than pay a highly dilutive price[15].

Exhibit 16.1

Banc One tackles American Fletcher's lemon problem

In January 1986 Banc One (BO) entered into an acquisition agreement with American Fletcher (AF). The agreement stipulated that BO would exchange a certain number of its common stock for each share of AF stock. The number of shares depended on the average BO share price, P, for a 10-day period ending six days before the merger closing. The exchange ratio (ER) formula is as given below:

Number of shares exchanged	Price (P) range for BO stock
2.15 shares	if $P < \$27.9$
60/BO share price	if $\$27.9 < P < \$34.1$
1.76 shares	if $P > \$34.1$

This formula would ensure that AF shareholders would receive $60 worth of BO stock in its price range of $27.9 and $34.1, but within this price range they receive more BO shares to compensate for any fall in the value of the latter.

The payoff curve is a *Travolta* and the ER curve is *Egyptian*. Here BO limits the ER to 2.15, even when its stock prices falls below $27.19, and the target shareholders bear the risk of reduced payoff. By the same token, by putting a floor under the ER at 1.76 BO allows AF shareholders to enjoy the windfall if BO stock price rises beyond $34.1.

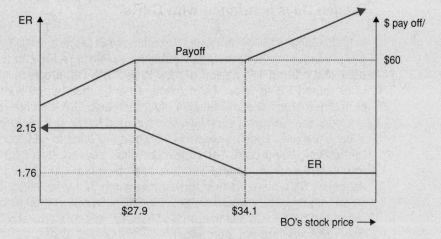

Source: Adapted from data in J. F. Houston and M. D. Ryngaert, 'Equity issuance and adverse selection: A direct test using conditional stock offers', *Journal of Finance*, 52(1), 1997, 197–219

Contingent value rights (CVRs)

The lemon problem facing the target shareholders in a share exchange extends beyond the consummation of the merger deal. Since the offer value depends on the future performance of the post-acquisition entity, target shareholders may need protection conditional on such future performance. CVRs are commitments by the acquirer to pay additional cash or securities to the target shareholders if the share price of the combined company does not exceed a specified level at some future point, e.g. a year after the acquisition is completed. CVRs are part of the acquisition currency and may be traded on the open market, thereby allowing the target shareholders to cash out early. The promised stock price may be at or below the lower collar level.

For the acquirer, the immediately dilutive effect of a collar is avoided, since CVR is based on long-term performance and not on short-term volatility of the acquirer's stock price. However, if the acquirer fails to achieve the stipulated post-acquisition performance level, CVR may become an expensive albatross, and in the run-up to the expiration of the CVRs may create large contingent liabilities[16]. In its merger with Dow Chemical's Merrel division Marion failed to hit the performance target, and ended up repurchasing the CVRs at a premium for $1bn. Exhibit 16.2 shows the structure of the CVR issued by General Mills, the US food company, in connection with its acquisition of Pillsbury, the US subsidiary of the UK food and drinks firm, Diageo plc.

CVRs may also leave acquirers vulnerable to speculative arbitrage between the CVR and the underlying stock. In the Viacom acquisition of Paramount Communications Corporation in 1994 Viacom sweetened the offer of $69 a share cash and stock by another $20 in the form of warrants, debentures and CVRs. CVRs had a floor of $36 and a ceiling of $48. In the wake of the acquisition arbitrageurs ('arbs') purchased 80% of the takeover derivatives at low, fire-sale prices as the target shareholders were cashing in the CVRs early. They also bought Viacom

---

Exhibit 16.2

Diageo buys insurance with CVRs

In 2000 General Mills (GM) was negotiating with Diageo plc (DP), a UK company, the purchase of the latter's US subsidiary, Pillsbury (PB), in a stock-for-stock deal, and offered 141 million of its shares. With GM stock selling at $42.55 the offer valued PB at $6bn. DP's management, while happy with the offer, were concerned about the future value of GM's stock. GM then offered DP its CVRs.

Under the CVR plan each GM share issued to DP stockholders would receive in cash the difference between $42.55 and the price of GM stock one year after the deal's closing date. The maximum cash payable was $4.55. If GM's stock traded at the target date at $40, the cash payable was $2.55. If the stock price fell below $38, there was no further insurance. If it was $36, the value received by DP shareholders would be $40.55 ($36 + $4.55). Although DP would not be protected below GM's stock price of $38, DP accepted the stock exchange plus CVR offer, and agreed the merger.

The CVR is equivalent to a combination of buying a put option (option that gives the right but not the obligation to sell the stock) with an exercise price of $42.55 and selling a put option with an exercise price of $38 (see Chapter 14 on call and put option valuation). Between these two prices the long (bought) put position is in the money and increases in value to $4.55. Below $38 the long position increases further in value, but the short (sold) position is out of the money and loses value in step, dollar for dollar, with the gain in the long position. Thus the net gain from the two puts below $38 is zero, i.e. the insurance is limited to the range $42.55 to $38. The payoffs are shown in Figure 16.6.

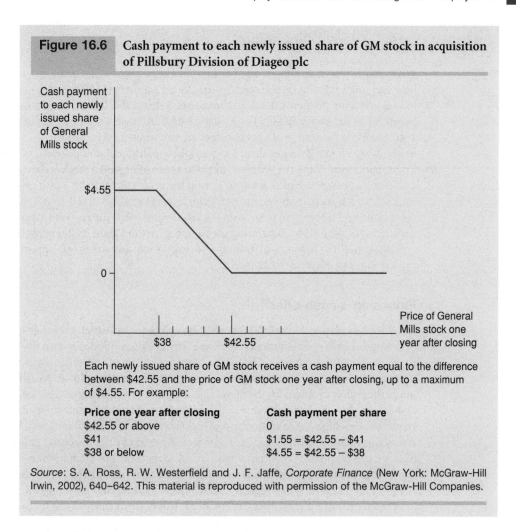

Figure 16.6 Cash payment to each newly issued share of GM stock in acquisition of Pillsbury Division of Diageo plc

Each newly issued share of GM stock receives a cash payment equal to the difference between $42.55 and the price of GM stock one year after closing, up to a maximum of $4.55. For example:

Price one year after closing	Cash payment per share
$42.55 or above	0
$41	$1.55 = $42.55 – $41
$38 or below	$4.55 = $42.55 – $38

Source: S. A. Ross, R. W. Westerfield and J. F. Jaffe, *Corporate Finance* (New York: McGraw-Hill Irwin, 2002), 640–642. This material is reproduced with permission of the McGraw-Hill Companies.

stock. As the stock price rose, arbs' profit on their long stock position increased, but profit on their long put position on the CVR declined. As a result of the speculative buying Viacom's stock price increased, further increasing the arbs' profits. As the CVR approached expiration, the arbs began to sell the stock and lock in their profits. The price decline that followed was at the same time increasing the value of the CVRs and the chance of Viacom having to pay out to honour the CVRs. Viacom ended up paying $82m to retire the CVRs[17].

In Europe CVRs have been employed in a few acquisitions, listed below. The contingency can be other factors than just the bidder's stock price[18]. In each case CVR will be triggered if the minimum performance is not achieved.

Year	Bidder	Target	Contingency
1996	AXA	UAP	Bidder share price
2000	France Télécom	Equant	Bidder share price
2001	Hewlett-Packard	Indigo NV	Minimum revenue growth over set period
2005	Lufthansa	Swiss Intl Airlines	Below performance of comparable airlines

Payment currency versus financing

While the bidder may choose one (or more) of several payment methods, a separate issue is how such methods will be financed. In the case of a pure (i.e. 100%) stock exchange offer, the bidder will issue its own stock[19]. In the case of a debt offer it can issue its own loan stock or bonds. Thus the two coincide. For a pure cash offer, however, a range of financing options is available. Here the source of cash becomes an important consideration. Some of the financing methods are seemingly equivalent: for example, a loan stock offer is similar to selling the stock in the market and using the proceeds to make a cash offer, and a stock exchange offer is similar to making a seasoned equity issue and using the proceeds to make a cash offer. Nevertheless, each source has its own implications for the leverage of the merged entity, the cost of capital, the monitoring it brings to bear upon the acquisition itself, the regulatory burden, facilitating the success of the bid etc. Separating the payment method from its financing allows the bidder greater flexibility in terms of timing and exploiting any arbitrage opportunities between capital markets, currency markets etc.

Financing a cash offer[20]

A bidder may choose to make a cash offer in preference to a stock exchange offer for a variety of reasons. A cash offer is more certain, and its value does not depend on the post-acquisition performance of the acquirer. There is no need for complex and difficult-to-value derivatives to insure against acquirer's stock price decline. It is simple to evaluate. A cash offer thus eliminates the lemon problem for the target shareholders. Fishman argues that a cash offer is made by bidders who attach a high value to the target of their bid and signal their confidence that the target will be a high-value company under their control. On the other hand, bidders, who are not so sure, cannot afford to pay cash and would prefer to offer a security exchange. Thus cash bids are pre-emptive against potential rival bidders[21]. Eckbo, Giammarino and Heinkel also derive the result, from modelling the information asymmetry between bidder and target and their negotiating games, that higher-valued bidders increase the cash component of their offer[22].

A bidder making a cash offer can finance it from one or more of the following sources:

- internal operating cash flow or cash flow from prior asset disposals (the 'war chest');
- a pre-bid rights issue (i.e. seasoned equity issue or SEO);
- a cash-underwritten offer, e.g. vendor placing or vendor rights (see Table 16.1 for definition);
- a pre-bid loan stock/ bond issue, including junk bonds;
- bank credit.

The bidder's internal operating cash flow is perhaps the cheapest and easiest source, since it avoids both the transaction costs of raising finance and the delay in doing so. However, except for relatively small acquisition targets, a bidder is unlikely to have enough internal cash flow.

SEO or cash underwritten offer

An SEO is often made by a firm with a well-defined acquisition programme. In May 2008 Carlsberg, the Danish brewer, in partnership with Heineken, won a tough battle to acquire the UK brewer Scottish and Newcastle (S & N)[23]. It made a rights issue of DKr 30.5bn (€4.1bn) to finance the acquisition, that is, to replace a bridging loan of DKr 28.7bn it had taken, and maintain its investment grade rating. Carlsberg priced the one-for-one rights issue at 40% discount to its current price. Analysts and investors fearing earnings dilution were, however, disappointed with the size of the issue, and had expected Carlsberg to minimize it through property and S & N's non-core asset disposals.

In a cash-underwritten offer the bidder offers stock exchange to the targets, but target shareholders can sell the received stock to realize cash. Thus it is somewhat similar to a rights issue, but it may be more flexible in that the underwriting can be made conditional upon the bid succeeding. Thus if the bid fails, the bidder is not left with a surplus of cash, although the underwriters may have to be paid a commitment fee.

Such an SEO may also have another adverse consequence. An SEO to raise the cash so as to make a cash acquisition and a stock exchange offer have similar effects on the acquirer's debt to equity ratio. They may, however, have different impacts on its share price in the post-acquisition period. Where target shareholders exhibit trading inertia, they are unlikely to sell the acquirer's stock that they receive as consideration when the deal is completed. If this puts less price pressure on the acquirer's stock, the post-acquisition return to acquirer shareholders will be less adverse. Trading inertia is a function of the shareholder composition of the target. Baker, Coval and Stein argue that institutional investors (IIs), especially those that are exempt from CGT on selling the acquirer's stock, exhibit less inertia than individual investors[24]. They develop a measure of inertia according to which over 70% of individual stockholders of targets suffer from inertia whereas only 30% of IIs do. Thus in stock exchange offers to targets with relatively high concentration of inertial shareholders, acquirers suffer much less stock price decline. The authors also contend that price decline after SEOs is much larger than in stock exchange offers, making the latter a more attractive way of financing an acquisition.

The City Takeover Code in the UK allows the underwritten cash alternative to a UK share offer to be 'shut off' earlier where the cash alternative is for more than 50% of the maximum offer value (Rule 33.2 of the Code). Normally, it is shut off after the first closing date: that is, Day 21 (see Chapter 18 on takeover regulation). Since underwriting expenses are related to the period over which the underwriting commitment is kept open, the cash-underwritten offer may be cheaper than a rights issue. Moreover, some 'core' underwriters are also paid a success-related commitment fee, which further reduces the cost of the cash-underwritten alternative if the bid fails[25].

Another advantage of a cash-underwritten offer is that the early shut-off can add to the pressure on target shareholders to accept the offer, and thus improve the chance of a success-ful bid. Such an offer is much more tax efficient from the target shareholders' perspective, since shareholders with different exposures to potential CGT liability can choose either the cash or the paper offer, so as to minimize their tax liability. Further, it serves as a signal to the market that the bid is supported by financial institutions.

Leveraged cash financing

One of the most important considerations in this form of financing is the ability of the bidder to service the debt obligations: that is, periodic interest payments and capital repayment. The bidder may rely on alternative sources of cash flows for this purpose:

● operating cash flows; or
● cash proceeds from sales of the target's assets.

A careful forecast of the future operating cash flows from the target under the bidder's management must be made to assess the debt-servicing capacity. Where the bidder expects to asset-strip the target in order to realize immediate cash flows to pay off the debt, careful consideration must be given to laws, e.g. the CA 2006 provisions, prohibiting a public company from providing financial assistance to purchase its own shares. Where the target becomes a wholly owned subsidiary, this prohibition may not apply. Where the target is a private company, subject to certain conditions target assets may be used to finance the acquisition. There are provisions in countries such as Italy and Spain that prohibit the use of the target's assets to finance the acquisition (see Chapter 18).

The high gearing that results from this method of financing may be of concern to the bidder. There have been numerous cases of highly leveraged acquisitions causing the decline and downfall of acquirers, such as the collapse of the UK telecom equipment firm Marconi in 2001 after its speculative acquisitions in the US, paid for with cash, both internal and borrowed. One attraction of leverage is that the related interest payment is tax deductible, thus enhancing future EPS.

Types of debt

In raising cash via debt, the bidder generally chooses a mixture of different types of debt, which differ in terms of their seniority of claim against the assets and profits of the firm, maturity, riskiness and pricing, i.e. the interest rate. These types and their salient characteristics are listed below:

- Secured bank debt – in the form of revolving credit facility or term loan amortized over its life; syndicated to a group of lenders; relatively cheap, flexible and available in small amounts, <$100m; requiring collateral and covenants; short average life of maximum five years and floating interest rate feature that increases uncertainty to borrower.
- Mezzanine debt – secured but second-ranking loan with floating rate plus sweeteners such as warrants; typically 8–10 year maturities; no secondary market to trade; expensive, and subject to restrictive covenants.
- Corporate bonds including high-yield or junk bonds – long maturities from 7 to 30 years and no amortization; generally fixed rate; deep global markets and more liquid than bank debt; diversified investor base and raised profile among institutional investors; subject to investor sentiment; more expensive than bank debt; not feasible for amounts less than $100m.
- Bridge loans – short-term bank loans to be replaced by high-yield bond or equity.
- Convertible bonds – treated as debt until conversion; cheaper financing than straight debt because of option to convert; diversified investor base; high speed of execution; need for rating; until conversion, treated as debt.

Pricing is stated in terms of the 'spread' or the margin over some benchmark interest rate at which the lenders are able to raise funds for lending: the more risky the debt, the higher is the spread. Debt seniority reduces the risk and therefore the price of debt. Riskiness is assessed on the basis of the debt to equity ratio, debt to total assets ratio or interest cover, i.e. ratio of operating profit or cash flow to annual interest charge. Operating cash flow is measured by earnings before interest, tax, depreciation and amortization (EBITDA). EBITDA is an indicator of the borrower's ability to service the debt: that is, pay interest when due and retire the debt at maturity or, in a term loan, repay according to an amortization schedule. Operating profit is EBIT. EBITDA-to-debt or EBIT-to-interest ratios are widely used indicators of debt risk.

Debt rating and financeability

Rating of debt securities by rating agencies Standard & Poor's (S&P), Moody's or Fitch IBCA (Fitch) is important, and determines not only whether debt can be raised but also at what price (see Chapter 11 on bond rating in the context of junk bonds). Acquirers are concerned about the impact of their choice of acquisition financing on the rating of their existing debt, as well as on that of future debt. They therefore need to have spare debt capacity that preserves their rating. Sweden's largest utility company, Vattenfall, made a number of acquisitions in Germany and Poland to take advantage of the deregulation of utilties in Europe, spending more than SKr40bn ($3.89bn) in 2000. These acquisitions financed with debt, however, strained Vattenfall's balance sheet, raising debt to levels too uncomfortable for rating agencies Moody's and S&P. They put Vattenfall on credit watch as a prelude to possible debt downgrade. The company said, 'We don't want to issue paper (debt securities) while we are on the watch list'[26].

Banks can contribute to the different layers of the debt package. Loans are often syndicated to spread risk among banks. Arranging banks take responsibility for arranging the loans and then syndicating them, initially to co-arrangers and then by general syndication. The banks commit themselves to providing the finance if needed by the borrower, and are paid commitment fees; then they receive interest for the loans they actually provide. Exhibit 16.3 exemplifies the structure of debt financing of an acquisition.

The debt capacity of the acquirer for different layers of debt is determined by reference to the combined forecast EBITDA of the merged firms, i.e. by (size of debt layer/EBITDA). The following credit ratios illustrate the basis of the credit decisions by lenders:

- Senior debt/EBITDA   4 to 5
- Subordinated debt/EBITDA   1 to 1.5
- Total debt/EBITDA   5 to 6.5
- EBITDA/Interest   3 to 3.5
- (EBITDA – Capital expediture)/Interest   1.5

In the case of rated debt, the financial strength indicators that rating agencies employ need to be forecast for the post-acquisition period, and the acquirer must ensure that they fall within the range appropriate for the rating that it seeks. In general, the stronger these indicators are, the higher is the rating accorded by the agencies. Rating agencies normally consider not just the first post-acquisition year (when such indicators may be low, since merger synergies take time to be realized) but the indicators over three to five years. The indicators must converge towards the acceptable range over that time. Debt rating influences the coupon that the borrower has to pay and the credit spread it implies, that is, the difference between the coupon rate and risk free rate. This spread is a function of:

- the default risk of the borrower;
- the illiquidity risk, i.e. the risk that the lender/investor cannot sell the loan/bond in a secondary market without loss; and
- the systematic risk, i.e. the risk of default on an economy-wide basis.

Table 16.8 lists the different rating categories employed by Standard & Poor's (S & P), Fitch and Moody's, and some of the financial metrics used by Moody's in its rating methodology[27]. As can be seen, higher-rated borrowers have higher profit margin and interest cover and lower debt as a percentage of EBITA and equity. Companies target a particular credit rating for their debt, e.g. AA or BBB, and then forecast the borrowing cost. Given this borrowing cost they work out the financial metrics. If the forecast financial metrics fall outside the relevant range they then need to adjust the level of borrowing and the cost of debt. This process involves some trial and error exercise. Rating agencies consider other judgemental factors than just the forecast financial ratios, such as management quality, asset quality,

Table 16.8 Debt rating by rating agencies and financial metrics by rating category

	Rating category		Financial metrics (Moody's)			
	S & P/Fitch	Moody's	EBITA margin	EBITA/Interest	Debt/EBITDA	Debt/Equity
Investment grade	AAA	Aaa	18.9	24.5	0.6	21
	AA	Aa	14.0	8.9	1.6	38
	A	A	14.8	8.4	1.9	40
	BBB	Baa	13.5	5.0	2.6	46
Sub-investment grade	BB	Ba	13.3	3.2	3.1	52
	B	B	10.0	1.4	5.3	73
	C	C	2.7	0.4	7.6	102

Source: Adapted from Moody's Financial Metrics™ Key Ratios by Rating and Industry for Global Non-Financial Corporations: 2008, January 2009 (downloaded from www.moodys.com). Figures in the Debt/Equity column are rounded to the nearest integer.

recovery in the event of default, whether the cash flows of the borrowing entity are ring-fenced, debt covenants etc. Thus financeability of a deal crucially depends on debt rating.

For example, suppose an acquirer wishes to finance its acquisition of the target firm with debt. It sets up the acquisition vehicle Newco that will issue bonds to raise the cash to finance the acquisition. Newco aims for a rating of A. Its post-acquisition financial metrics, which it must achieve, can be read off the table:

- EBITA margin 14.8%
- Interest cover 8.4 times
- Debt to EBITA 1.9 times and
- Leverage 40%

The acquirer may be able to reach these benchmarks within a period that a rating agency may consider acceptable.

Credit spread is a monotonic function of the rating. In general, the difference in spreads is expressed as basis points (bps) (1bps = 0.01%).

The ratios in Exhibit 16.3 represent the maximum level of debt based on the first post-acquisition year's forecast EBITDA. Depending on the amortization schedule for some debt layers, e.g. Term loan 1, these ratios become stronger and the credit quality of debt improves with increasing EBITDA, provided the cash flow forecasts are achieved by efficient post-acquisition management meeting its strategic and financial objectives. The risk level of debt may also depend on the type of funding that replaces the bridging component, i.e. whether it is high-yield debt, convertible bond or equity. The comfort levels for debt depend on the nature of the business, i.e. whether cyclical, highly volatile, etc. More stable cash flows permit a more aggressive, high-leveraged financing. Aggressive leverage levels raise the financial risk to lenders and the interest rate spread, as illustrated by the experience of lenders to Endemol, the inventor of the big-time TV reality show *Big Brother* (see Exhibit 16.4).

The bridge loan may be subject to interest rate step-up, at intervals typically of three to six months. This raises the cost of the bridge loan, and encourages the borrower to seek the replacement funding expeditiously. Transition from a bridge loan to a security issue is not free of event risk, such as delay in obtaining antitrust approval. Any potential debt downgrade may also make issue of new debt security more expensive, if not impossible. These risks characterized the bridge loan financing of Bayer's acquisition of Aventis CropScience in December 2001, and the subsequent attempt at replacing it with bond financing[28].

Exhibit 16.3

Structure of acquisition financing with debt

B has made a successful bid for T with a cash offer of $5000m, and finances the offer with debt, including a bridging loan of $1600m, as shown below. A bps or basis point is one hundreth of a per cent.

Type of debt	Amount ($m)	Interest rate	Bankers' fees ($m)	
Revolving credit	300	LIBOR + 250 bps	2.00%	$6.00
Term loan 1	1300	LIBOR + 250 bps	2.00%	$26.00
Term loan 2	1800	LIBOR + 325 bps	2.00%	$36.00
Bridge loan	1600	11%	4.50%	$72.00
	5000			$140.00

The revolving credit facility is for eight years and is amortized over that period. The bridge loan is a short-term facility, to be replaced within a year by alternative funding sources. These may be subordinated high-yield debt (see Chapter 12), or mezzanine debt, or equity in the form of a rights issue, or placing. LIBOR is the London Inter-Bank Offered Rate at which prime banks are able to raise funds in money markets. The fee of 4.50% for the bridge loan includes the fee for arranging the replacement funding for the bridge loan.

Exhibit 16.4

Leveraged loan makers hit by credit crunch

A consortium of three investors – Mediaset, Sirius Satellite Radio and Goldman Sachs Capital Partners – bought Endemol in June 2007 for €3.1bn. The deal was financed by €2bn of senior debt, €250m of second lien lower-ranking debt, and €345 of mezzanine debt, which was provided by ABN AMRO, Barclays Capital, BNP Paribas, Goldman Sachs and Merrill Lynch. The loans turned sour with the credit crunch, and in May 2008 the banks were preparing to sell the debt at 20% discount and faced a loss of €400m. The banks had provided the leveraged loans at the height of the debt market at what, in retrospect, was an excessively high EBITDA multiple of 8.5.

Source: A. Edgecliffe-Johnson and A. Sakoui, 'Reality check for Endemol lenders', *Financial Times*, 10 May 2008

Debt financing and bid strategy

Bidders may choose to use debt financing in order to gain an advantage over potential competitive bidders. A low leverage allows the bidder the financial slack to raise the necessary financing for its bid quickly, whereas a high leverage constrains the bidder. Thus a bidder can time its takeover bid when it enjoys this slack. A low-leverage bidder also signals a stronger commitment to a takeover bid than a highly levered competitor. Such a commitment may persuade the target managers (or target shareholders in a tender offer) to accept its bid more readily than a bid from a rival, more highly levered, bidder. Following the success of the bid, the acquirer may lever up[29].

Impact of bank financing on merger valuation

Bhardwaj and Shivdasani test whether the source of cash for a cash offer signals the quality of the acquisition. They find, for a sample of cash tender offers in the US, that bank financing has a favourable impact on the stock market reaction to the tender offer announcement. This is attributed to the monitoring of the acquisition decision by the lending banks. Under this monitoring, the higher the bank debt, the higher are the returns to bidders on announcement[30]. Martynova and Renneboog provide similar evidence on the source of cash for a cash offer (see Figure 16.7).

Figure 16.7 shows that the way the bidder raises the cash to finance its acquisitions provides a signal to the stock market. Where the funding comes from the internal cash flow (cash financing in Figure 16.7), bidder's cumulative abnormal returns over the window −60 to +60 days around bid announcement are worse than when debt financing is used. There is a striking similarity between pure equity offers (equity payment/equity financing, with no need for

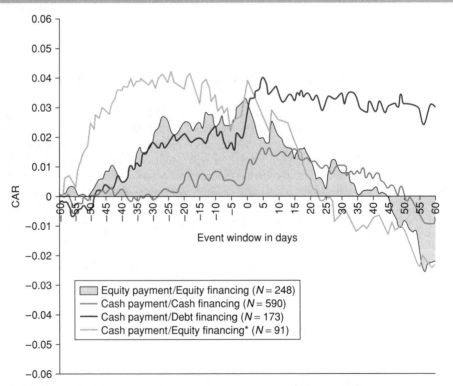

Figure 16.7 Shareholder value effects of different sources of cash in all cash European acquisitions

Source: M. Martynova and L. Renneboog, 'What determines the financing decisions of corporate takeovers? Investor protection, asymmetric information or method of payment?', *Journal of Corporate Finance*, 15(3), 2009, 290–315, Figure 8

external sourcing) and all cash offers funded by equity issue (equity financing). In both cases the bidder's stock rises in the run-up to the bid and falls thereafter, and the two methods of payment closely track each other. Thus the market reaction is conditional not merely on the method of payment but also on the source of funding of that method. Debt financing of a cash offer is more favourably received, possibly because of the disciplinary effect of debt financing, consistent with the free cash flow model of agency conflict[31].

Financing with loan stock

This differs from the leveraged cash offer in that the loan stock is the consideration for the bid, and is offered to the target shareholders. They swap their shares in the target for the loan stocks of the bidder. Further, the transaction cost of a direct loan stock is lower than that of a leveraged cash buyout. To the target shareholders a loan stock minimizes the problem of information asymmetry since, as in a cash offer, they are assured of a definitive sum on redemption of the stock. For some target shareholders accepting loan stock may mean an unwanted shift of their portfolio weighting against equity. Further, acceptance of loan stock means loss of control over their company.

Financing with convertibles

Use of convertibles in acquisition financing is less common than that of straight loan stock. Convertibles may be preferred stock (CPS) or loan stock (CLS). They represent a bundle of two underlying securities – the straight preferred or loan stock, and an option on the shares of the company. Valuing a convertible is rather complex, and may be done with a mathematical model such as the Black–Scholes option pricing model[32]. Under UK tax rules a convertible is not a qualifying corporate bond. Target shareholders can therefore 'roll over' their capital gains and avoid immediate CGT. The particular tax treatment of convertibles in other tax jurisdictions needs to be taken into account by the bidders in their plan to finance with convertibles.

Because of the call option element and the prospect of high-equity returns on conversion, the interest rate for the straight component of convertibles is lower than in pure corporate bonds of similar risk or rating. This means that the dilutive effect of interest payment on post-acquisition earnings will be smaller than in the latter case.

Deferred consideration financing

As discussed earlier, both bidders and target shareholders face valuation risk in negotiating a price and the payment currency in a takeover. One way of mitigating this risk is to make the consideration payable to the vendors contingent upon the future performance of the target under their own management. This method, called 'earn-out', is used to finance acquisitions of private companies operating in the service or high-technology sectors, such as advertising agencies or software development businesses. In such cases the value of the company often depends on the intangible asset of human creativity and the flair of one or two individuals. Retaining the target management after acquisition to ensure that the target performs as expected by the acquirer may be a key consideration[33]. Valuing such companies, however, is immensely difficult. Earn-out provides a solution when price negotiation between buyer and seller stalls[34].

In an earn-out, consideration to the vendor is made up of the following:

- an immediate payment in cash or shares of the acquirer; and
- a deferred payment contingent upon the target-turned-subsidiary achieving certain pre-determined performance levels.

Exhibit 16.5

Torex offers earn-out deal to McKeown

Torex, a UK firm supplying software to retailers, acquired McKeown, specializing in the supply of software to the UK's National Health Service, in November 2001 in order to focus on the lucrative and fast-growing healthcare sector. The acquisition would add 150 employees to Torex's 1800 staff and augment sales by 5%.

The purchase consideration included an earn-out element conditional on agreed targets being met:

- Cash paid immediately   £7.5m
- Discretionary earn-out at end of first year   £2.0m
- Discretionary earn-out at end of second year   £2.5m
- Maximum consideration   £12.0m
- Total consideration if earn-out targets missed   £11.0m

Earn-out consideration to be paid in cash or shares.

Source: A. Wendlandt, 'Torex expands into healthcare with acquisition', *Financial Times*, 23 November 2001

The performance level may be expressed in terms of sales revenue or pre-tax profits.

The structure of a typical earn-out acquisition is as follows. B acquires the shares of a fellow TV programme maker, C, under an earn-out deal. C's 2009 pre-tax profits are £1.5m. B estimates that future pre-tax profits of C will be £2.5m in 2010, £3m in 2011, and £3.5m in 2012. B will make an initial payment of £10m, and an earn-out payment in cash at the end of 2006. The earn-out formula is twice the excess of pre-tax profits over £2m from 2004 to 2006. Maximum earn-out payment will be £6m. The total consideration is therefore £16m. A recent earn-out deal is described in Exhibit 16.5.

The earn-out element may be paid in shares or loan notes as well as cash. The tax position of the vendors under the UK rules with regard to the deferred element is somewhat complex. The tax law makes a distinction between ascertainable and unascertainable contingent payment. If the amount is fixed and known at the time of the acquisition, that amount is immediately liable for CGT.

If the payment is contingent upon future profit levels, it is not ascertainable. In this case the right to receive that payment (called 'chose in action') is treated under the UK tax regime as an asset, and the value of that right is included as part of the consideration for the shares and thus becomes liable for CGT immediately. Where the earn-out payment is paid in shares of the acquirer, the right to receive those shares is treated as if shares have been received, provided the transaction has a commercial justification. In this event the vendor may claim roll-over relief for any accrued capital gains, with the approval of the Inland Revenue. Earn-outs may be less attractive if future tax rates, when the earn-out part of the consideration will be received, are likely to be higher[35]. Similar tax implications in other countries need to be addressed when using earn-out.

Earn-outs are not free of problems. The culture shock of transformation from owning and managing an independent company to running a subsidiary under the control of a larger firm may be quite traumatic. For the buyer, an earn-out is a way of retaining the vendor's talents.

Table 16.9 Advantages and disadvantages of earn-out

Advantages	Disadvantages
(a) For acquirer	
● Vendor's talents retained	● Conflict of motives between vendor and buyer
● Valuation risk reduced	● Vendor given autonomy and buyer's integration plan delayed
● 'Buy now and pay later' reduces financing need.	● Vendor, after becoming rich, may lack motivation
● Provides hedge against warranty and indemnity claims (see Chapter 20)	● Management succession after earn-out may cause problems
(b) For vendor	
● Increases personal wealth	● Loss of control
● Career opportunities may be brighter	● Pressure for short-term results
● Buyer can fund future growth of business	● Culture shock of working in a large, 'bureaucratic' company

However, the vendor may lack motivation, or may try to maximize short-term profits to the detriment of the long-term interests of the buyer. These and other advantages and disadvantages are given in Table 16.9.

The earn-out agreement must carefully spell out how profits will be measured, to avoid problems of interpretation. The vendor may also be concerned that, when the earn-out payment is due, the buyer might be unable to pay. So the vendor will look for some security to ensure payment. Despite these problems, a survey of earn-outs in the UK has found that both acquirers and vendors are largely satisfied. Hussey surveyed 27 acquirers and 33 vendors and found that 87% of the acquirers regarded their earn-out deals as mainly or highly successful. While most vendors considered the personal wealth gain as important, they also regarded job challenge and job satisfaction as important motivating factors[36]. In Germany almost 20% of transactions involving medium-sized enterprises include an earn-out element. Acquisition targets are generally firms with new products, technologies or patents not yet introduced to the market. Targets considered 'people businesses' are also subject to earn-out terms. Earn-outs may also complicate post-acquisition restructuring, since it may erode the autonomy that the target may need to deliver the expectations of the earn-out. Further, loss of autonomy may create a moral hazard problem, since the target's performance can no longer be unambiguously measured (see Chapter 6 on moral hazard)[37].

Earn-outs are generally used in small or medium-sized deals. They are difficult to use in public company acquisitions, because the target managers generally own only a fraction of the firm equity. In the US, during 1997–2001, the total number and value of M & A deals, and the earn-out component of the value were respectively 737, $94bn and $22bn. The earn-out value represents 24% of the deal value[38]. In a European sample of 4342 acquisitions during 1997–2000 Faccio and Masulis report 478 with earnouts[39].

Factors determining financing method choice

Availability, cost and speed of execution of the financing arrangement are major concerns to bidders, who are anxious to clinch their bid and consummate the acquisition. We have alluded to information asymmetry and valuation risk as important determinants of the choice between cash and stock exchange offers. Minimizing the tax liability to both the acquirer and the target shareholders is also a relevant factor. The effect of payment currency on post-acquisition earnings dilution often influences the bidder's choice. Accounting rules such as pooling and purchase accounting have in the past driven many deals to be financed with stock exchange offers (see Chapter 15).

Among other factors relevant to the choice among different payment currencies, and in particular between cash and equity offers, are the following:

● Bidder's liquidity, i.e. free cash flow and cash and other liquid securities.
● The recent stock price performance of the bidder. If this performance is good, that makes the bidder's shares a more attractive currency.
● Pre-acquisition leverage of the bidder and target. If this is high, a stock exchange offer that reduces the leverage is preferable.
● The nature of the business being acquired. If it is a highly volatile business, or if its value depends on real options on innovation, new technology, new product or market development, a stock exchange offer that makes the bidder and target share the business risk is preferable.

Importance of corporate control considerations

Managers who own significant shares in the acquirer, and are reluctant to give up control or share it with the acquirer, may opt for a cash or a loan stock offer rather than a share exchange offer that leads to dilution of their control. The extent of control dilution depends on the relative sizes of the acquirer and the target. When the acquirer is very large relative to the target, dilution is of little concern. Where the acquirer's share ownership includes large block shareholders they will also be concerned with control dilution, and may oppose a share exchange offer.

The ownership and control structure of the target firm may also affect the target's preference for a payment currency. Where the target managers or large block shareholders of the target want to retain a measure of control of the combined entity, they will opt for a share exchange. In the case of mergers of equals, the two management teams and the two shareholder groups wish to share control. Hence cash or loan stock is not preferable to a share exchange offer.

Empirical evidence on factors influencing payment currency choice

Several US studies have empirically investigated the importance of the above factors for the payment currency choice. Martin found that the higher the acquirer's future growth opportunities, the more likely it was to make a stock for stock offer. When the acquirer managers' share ownership is neither too large nor too small they are more reluctant to offer, for fear of diluting their control[40]. Amihud *et al.* also found a positive association between managerial ownership in the acquirer and the likelihood of a stock offer[41]. Ghosh and Ruland find a similar association. Bidders are also more likely to make stock offers when the stock market and their own stock returns have been high recently. Where bidders have high liquidity, the chance of stock offers decreases. It also decreases with larger institutional blockholdings. Ghosh and Ruland found that target managers with larger stock ownership seemed to strongly prefer stock offers. They also reported that these managers were more likely to retain their jobs after acquisition when they received stock rather than cash offers[42].

There is also evidence from Ghosh and Jain that leverage of the combined entity increases significantly following mergers, and that this increase in debt is positively correlated with shareholder wealth increase at the time of bid announcement. The debt increase is a result of past unused debt capacity, although this result is not very strong. Ghosh and Jain found that tax benefits, such as higher depreciation reliefs from asset step-up or target's losses and investment credits being carried forward to the offset against the acquirer's profits, are small[43]. Brown and Ryngaert modelled the payment currency choice of a bidder as a trade-off between reducing valuation risk (through a cash offer) and avoiding the capital gains liability (through a stock offer) to the target. Their empirical analysis supported this model[44].

For the UK, the evidence from 1980–90 is similar. Salami and Sudarsanam found that cash offer was more likely than stock or mixed offers when the target was relatively small and bidder's leverage, free cash flow and cash position were high. Recent high stock market returns also make a stock offer more likely. There is some weak evidence that if the potential capital gains to target shareholders are high, the payment currency is more likely to be equity. The presence of large block shareholders discourages equity issues. With low levels of top management share ownership the bidder is more likely to offer equity, but as this increases, bidders switch to a cash offer[45]. Gregory also found support for the influence of many of these variables[46].

For Europe, Faccio and Masulis examine the choice determinants for a large sample of 3667 deals, including as targets listed firms, private companies and corporate subsidiaries during 1997–2000: 60% of the targets are UK targets, 80% of the deals are for cash, 11% are for mixed currency and 8% are for pure stock. Several factors significantly influence whether a cash or a stock exchange offer will be made:

- impact of bidder's collateral (positive), leverage (negative), and asset size (positive) significant;
- when the bidder has special access to bank borrowing due to interlocking directors, making cash financing more likely; and
- unlisted targets and corporate subsidiaries making stock financing less likely, suggesting bidder aversion to creating a new blockholder and diluting its control of the firm.

Table 16.10 summarizes these factors and their likely influence on the bidder's payment currency choice. These factors are, however, not mutually exclusive.

Influence of payment currency on outcome of hostile takeover bids

We noted earlier in this chapter that bidders may choose cash as a way of pre-empting rival bidders. There is also evidence that a hostile offer has a higher probability of success if it is financed with cash rather than with paper. Thus payment currency may be an important tactical weapon in prosecuting hostile takeovers. We discuss the various bid strategies and tactics in detail in Chapter 20.

Empirical evidence on the impact of payment method on financial performance

Franks *et al.*, in their extensive study of payment methods and their impact on shareholder returns for the UK and the US for the period 1955–85, reported a negligible use of convertibles in the UK, but a significant use in the US[47]. They found that shareholders of target companies earned a risk-adjusted abnormal return of 30% in all cash offers and 15% in all share offers in the month of bid announcement (see Chapter 4 for abnormal returns methodology). For the bidder shareholders the returns were 0.7% and 21.1% respectively. The returns for 'cash or equity' for the same month were close to all-cash offers, and for 'cash and equity' offers the returns were higher than in pure equity offers.

Salami found similar results for a later sample of over 500 UK acquisitions during 1980–90[48]. For the bidders, cash and equity offers generated little abnormal return, although in mixed offers combining equity and cash bidder shareholders experienced negative returns.

Table 16.10 Factors influencing choice among acquisition financing methods

Factor	Which payment method is preferred
(a) Risk and valuation considerations	
High valuation risk to bidder (target)	Bidder (target) prefers share (cash) offer
Target a highly cyclical business	Share offer to reduce financial risk to bidder
Target value depends on uncertain or unknown future growth opportunities	Share offer to reduce financial risk to bidder
Target unlisted/overseas listed/subsidiary	Share offer to reduce financial risk to bidder; targets prefer cash
Bidder keen to exploit its high current share valuation	Share offer
Bidder already highly (poorly) leveraged	Share (debt or leveraged cash) offer to reduce (increase) leverage to optimal level
(b) Maximizing tax benefits	
High capital gains tax to target shareholders	Target prefers share offer to achieve tax-free merger
Bidder can use accumulated tax losses and investment credits of target	Stock offer to comply with continuity of interest tax rules
Bidder can step up target's asset values to gain higher depreciation tax relief	Cash offer
Exploit additional debt capacity of bidder/target and tax subsidy on debt	Loan stock or leveraged cash financing to increase post-acquisition leverage
Tax-free mergers in the US	Require minimum % of share exchange consideration
(c) Corporate control considerations	
Bidder management does not want to dilute control by creating a new block of shareholders	Loan stock or leveraged cash financing Cash offer to unlisted and subsidiary targets
Target managers want to retain control	Share exchange offer or earn-out payable in bidder shares
Merger of equals	Can only be stock exchange
Long-form statutory merger (USA)	Often stock exchange
Tender offer + short-form or long-form freeze-out merger	TO generally cash followed
(d) Deal execution considerations	
Bidder keen to deter rival bidders	Cash offer
Need for speed in deal execution	Cash or leveraged cash offer
Bidder's free cash flow and liquidity high	Cash offer
Target unlisted and shareholders wish to exit	Cash offer
Target overseas and shareholders averse to foreign securities	Cash offer
Mandatory bid or Rule II bid under UK Takeover Code	Cash or Share offer with cash alternative (see Chapter 18 on the Code)
(e) Capital market conditions	
Credit crunch	Cash offer using internal free cash flow Share exchange offer Earnout

Table 16.11 Abnormal returns (%) to acquirers by payment method[49]

Study and sample period	All cash	Mixed	All stock
Moeller et al. (2004) (US) 1980–01	1.38	1.45	0.15
Bouwman et al. (2003) (US), 1979–98	0.88	2.33	−0.79
Bradley and Sundaram (2004) (US), 1990–2000	0.83		−1.29
	0.71		1.39
Faccio et al. (2006) (Europe), 1996–01	0.30	−0.66	−1.81
	1.17	2.14	3.90
Martynova and Renneboog (2006) (Europe), 1993–2001	1.03	1.03	0.66

The first row in Bradley and Sundaram and in Faccio et al. reports returns to public targets, and the second row to private targets. In other studies the returns are mixed. A blank means the study does not report any result. See Chapter 4 on abnormal returns methodology.

The relative superiority of cash offers in the returns to shareholders is also observed in other countries, such as France[50].

This pattern of superior returns to cash acquirers is replicated in more recent studies in the US as well as in Europe. Table 16.11 shows the abnormal returns (%) around announcement dates. One interesting point is that in the case of private targets, in contrast to public targets, stock acquisitions outperform cash acquisitions, in both the US and Europe. In general, acquirers earn higher returns from private than from public company acquisitions (see Chapter 13 for a review of the evidence). This is explained as an illiquidity discount to the private targets. Since private target shareholders should gain greater liquidity in cash offers than in stock offers, the expected order of performance of the acquirer would be cash and stock offers. What we observe is the opposite. Thus increased liquidity to private targets may not explain the latter pattern. An alternative explanation is that acquirers do better in private target acquisition because such targets have concentrated ownership, and this, when converted into acquirer's equity, creates large block shareholders that can better monitor the acquirer in the post-acquisition period. This corporate governance benefit cannot materialize in cash acquisitions but only in stock acquisitions. The superior returns to acquirers in stock acquisitions of private targets are consistent with this rationale.

Figure 16.8 shows the abnormal returns to targets and acquirers with different payment methods. Targets achieve considerably higher returns in cash and mixed methods than in stock exchange acquisitions over −60 to +60 days around deal announcement. By day +60 the difference is as much as 15–20%. Bidder shareholders also do better in cash offers than in stock and mixed offers. In the pre-bid period both stock and mixed bidders enjoy significant run-ups, relative to cash bidders, but post-announcement these gains are quickly wiped out, and they end up underperforming the cash bidders. Thus both target and bidder shareholders experience larger wealth gains in cash, than in mixed or stock, acquisitions.

Many other US and UK studies have reported broadly similar results for cash and equity offers[51]. In terms of post-acquisition operating performance, however, Heron and Lie do not find any significant difference between cash and stock exchange acquirers for a sample of US acquisitions during 1985–97[52].

If, as documented by the several studies cited above, cash offers generate significantly more value than stock exchange offers, why do acquirers choose the latter? One answer is that acquirer managers are motivated by considerations other than shareholder value enhancement. However, these managers may have information on the basis of which they rationally prefer one method over another. In an interesting empirical study of the returns to cash acquirers and stock acquirers, Emery and Switzer estimated the returns to the optimal payment method predicted from an expectations model comprising the various motivational

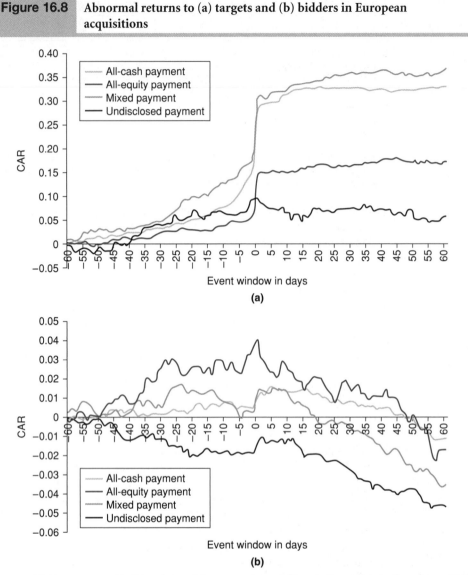

Figure 16.8   **Abnormal returns to (a) targets and (b) bidders in European acquisitions**

Source: M. Martynova and L. Renneboog, 'Mergers and acquisitions in Europe', in L. Renneboog (Ed.), *Advances in Corporate Finance and Asset Pricing* (Amsterdam: Elsevier, 2006)

factors listed in Table 16.10[53]. This model also allowed them to estimate the returns to the wrong payment currency. An innovative feature of the expectations model is the inclusion of a measure of private information that the acquirer managers have. They then compared the actual announcement period abnormal returns with the expected returns from the optimal choice and the expected returns from the wrong choice.

Emery and Switzer's results, based on a US sample of completed acquisitions during 1967–87, show that managers correctly chose the method with the higher expected abnormal return. Further, bidders making cash acquisitions earned higher returns than if they had made a stock offer. Emery and Switzer also reported that managers' choices were motivated by the target shareholders' personal tax liability and the need to minimize the valution risk, as indicated in Table 16.10. This study suggests that acquisition currency choices are not as irrational as the previous empirical research suggested. This area, however, needs further research to establish which of several motivations dominate the payment currency choices.

Performance of earnout acquirers and stock acquirers with collars[54]

Kohers and Ang compare the abnormal returns to earn-out acquirers with those of cash and stock acquirers. Earn-out acquirers outperform the latter in terms of two-day abnormal returns when acquiring private targets (corporate subsidiaries): 2.2% (2.1%) for earn-out acquirers compared with 1.8% (1.5%) for cash acquirers and 1.13% (2.0%) for stock acquirers. Such outperformance is even greater when the targets are associated with greater information uncertainty about their value, e.g. high-tech or service sector targets, consistent with the rationale that earnout reduces risk to the acquirer owing to information asymmetry. Sudarsanam and Barbopoulos, analyzing a large UK sample of acquirers using different payment methods including earn-outs, find similar results: 1% for non-earn-out acquirers and 1.5% for earn-out acquirers, the difference being statistically significant[55].

Officer finds that straight stock acquirers earn a three-day median abnormal return of −2.0%, whereas stock acquirers with collar protection perform better: with a fixed exchange rate collar −0.9%, and with a fixed price collar −0.8%. Targets in these deals receive similar returns, between 13.8% and 14.3%. Thus offering protection reduces the information risk to the targets, and the bidder avoids having to compensate them excessively for this risk. This may explain the collar offers' superior value creation.

Why do acquirers perform worse in stock exchange offers?

There are several possible reasons. One of them is that the acquirer's stock is overvalued, and in the post-acquisition period this is corrected, and the stock declines in value. Another is that in the pre-acquisition period, and in preparation for a stock exchange acquisition, potential acquirers massage their earnings to improve their stock price performance. This allows these acquirers, especially, in stock acquisitions to lower the ER they need to offer to win a takeover. Following the acquisition, however, these acquirers reverse the earnings management and report lower earnings. This reversal may lead to acquirer value decline, but this may not happen immediately, since the reversal may take several years.

Earnings management

Louis tests whether potential acquirers indulge in earnings management, and how it affects the acquirer's stock return performance before and after its acquisition. Using discretionary abnormal accruals as a measure of earnings management, Louis finds[56]:

- strong evidence that acquiring firms report significant positive abnormal accruals in the quarter preceding stock-swap takeover offers;
- no evidence that the market reaction over the three days around a stock swap announcement is correlated with prior earnings management.
- a significantly negative correlation between the discretionary accruals and the abnormal return over a longer event, i.e. day −21 day to day +1 around merger announcement;
- stock-for-stock acquirers largely responsible for the long-run negative performance of acquiring firms; and
- a significant negative correlation between the discretionary accrual and the stock-for-stock acquirers' long-term performance.

The results suggest that the long-term underperformance of acquiring firms (see Chapter 4 for evidence) is attributable to the reversal of the effects of prior earnings management[57].

Impact of M & A on bondholder returns

Since bondholders' and stockholders' interests are not always aligned some acquisitions may benefit the acquirer's or the target's bondholders, but harm stockholders of these firms. For example, a diversifying acquisition reduces the riskiness of the combined firm and its default risk, thereby benefiting the bondholders. This is called the *co-insurance* effect, since the merger reduces the variability of the merged firm's cash flows (compared with those of the pre-merger firms), and the assets of each firm are now available as collateral for the other firm's debt[58].

Several US studies have over the years reported that abnormal returns to acquirer bondholders are insignificant, significant and negative, and significant and positive. However, in a recent paper, Billett *et al.* report that, in the case of below-investment-grade target bonds, target shareholders experience significantly positive abnormal returns whereas acquirer bondholders experience negative abnormal returns. Additionally, target bonds have significantly larger returns when the target's rating is below the acquirer's, when the combination is anticipated to decrease target risk or leverage, and when the target's maturity is shorter than the acquirer's[59]. This evidence is consistent with the debt co-insurance effect, since the merger enhances the quality of the lower rated debt for the benefit of holders of such debt.

In a recent study of the wealth effects of European acquisitions on bondholders, Renneboog and Szilagyi, however, report announcement period median abnormal returns[60]:

Bidders:
Bond return 0.81% (significant at 1%)
Stock return 0.34% (not significant)

Targets:
Bond return 0.33 (not significant)
Stock return 9.6% (significant at 1%)

CASE STUDY

Choosing the better acquirer: MCI faces a dilemma!

In February 2005, MCI, the US telecom company, was the target of a fierce battle between Verizon and Qwest. Both these bidders were also operating in the telecom sector that had been hit by the collapse of the telecom bubble in 2000 and the slowdown in the US economy. MCI had only recently emerged from the trauma of bankruptcy. Prior to its bankruptcy it was known as the infamous Worldcom that had grown at break-neck speed through ill-advised acquisitions. Worldcom's CEO Bernie Ebbers was convicted of fraud and received a long prison sentence. MCI was also subject to competitive pressure on many of its overseas operations.

The industry background

The industry characteristics were:

● It is made up of companies offering a range of products, services and technologies e.g. traditional copper wire telephony, fibre optic telephone and broadband services, the Internet and mobile telephony;

- companies were growing by consolidation i.e. acquisitions to cut costs, increase customer base to reap scale economies and network externalities, and create new growth opportunities through innovation in technologies, products and services;
- undergoing technology shift from analogue to digitial, from wired to wireless and from narrow band to broad band;
- customer preference for one-stop shopping for video, internet, data transmission, etc. providing the rationale for telecom firms to become full-service communications powerhouses through mergers;
- there was strong competition in the various segments of the market from both US operators and international firms leading to substantial price pressure;
- the industry was subject to federal regulation by the FCC, state regulation in the US states and regulation in the countries in which the companies, especially MCI, operated.

The comparative financial and business profiles of the three companies

	MCI	Verizon	Qwest
Sales ($bn)	21	71	14
Operating income ($bn)	−3.2	13.1	−0.3
Net income ($bn)	−4	7.8	−1.8
Debt	5.9	39.2	17.3

MCI operated in three businesses:

- Enterprise markets selling communications and network solutions to large multinational companies and government agencies and serving customers through partnership with third party network solutions providers.
- Sales and Service to small and medium corporate customers and consumer operations such as telemarketing and direct response marketing.
- International and wholesale markets serving businesses, government agencies and telecom carriers outside the US.

MCI operated in 200 countries and had the most extensive international communication network of 100k miles. It provided managed network services to customers.

Compared to MCI, both Verizon and Qwest were largely US-based operators. Verizon's wireline services yielded a revenue of $38bn in 2004 and its wireless services $28bn. The revenues from its information services ($3.5bn) and international businesses ($2bn) were much smaller. Qwest's revenue in 2004 was overwhelmingly from its wireline US operations ($13.3bn) compared to $0.5bn from wireless and $40m from information services.

Verizon was a telecom giant with a market capitalisation of $97bn and Qwest was an emerging player with a market capitalisation of $7bn of a similar size to MCI (market capitalisation of $8bn). In terms of assets, competencies and overlap of resources and capabilities, Verizon offered a much stronger fit to MCI than Qwest. Qwest had a similar history of very rapid growth in the dotcom era through acquisitions, and subsequently crashed. Like Worldcom, Qwest was investigated for fraud and accounting irregularities and its debt had been downgraded to 'junk' status by the rating agencies. Like Bernie Ebbers, Joseph Nacchio, the CEO of Qwest was indicted for fraud and, in 2007, convicted.

→

For MCI the merger aims would be to ensure continued survival after the bankruptcy, grow its international business again, expand into new markets, become part of a nation-wide wireless network and keep up with rivals like SBC Communications which were also consolidating (SBC was bidding to acquire AT&T). For Verizon, the merger rationale was that it would give access to MCI's blue chip international clientele and the government business, and enhance its global presence. The threat of rivals consolidating was also an important consideration. These were also the attractions of the merger for Qwest. In addition, the merger was likely to strengthen its balance sheet and improve its debt rating. It would be able to enter new markets both in the US and globally.

On 14 February 2005, Verizon entered into a definitive Merger Agreement (see Chapter 20 on merger agreements) with MCI. Its bid was for $6.75bn including a cash dividend payable by MCI of $4.10 on deal completion but reduced by any dividend paid in the time to completion. Qwest entered the fray as a rival bidder with a bid of $8bn. Both bids were mixed cash and stock bids and both included collars for the stock part of the bid. The MCI board considered the Qwest bid riskier and favoured the Verizon bid although it was a lower bid. Analysts were surprised at this. One MCI shareholder launched a class action suit against the MCI board for favouring an 'inferior' bid. MCI therefore had to make a strong case for its preference.

On 16 March 2005, Qwest made a higher offer of $8.4bn:

- $26 per share, $10.50 in cash (including the already paid dividend of $0.40) plus $15.50 in its shares. Value of stock consideration based on Q's stock price of $4.15.
- If average Q stock price over 20 days preceding transaction close not equal to $4.15 then:
  - Between $3.74 and $4.14, ER adjusted *up* to deliver $15.50 in stock consideration.
  - Between $4.15 and $4.57, ER adjusted *down* to deliver $15.50 in stock.
  - If Q stock price > $4.57, then ER = 3.392.
  - If Q stock price < $3.71, ER = 4.1444.

On 29 March 2005, MCI received a revised higher offer worth $7.6bn from Verizon:
Verizon (V)'s offer:

- $23.50 per share of MCI stock, $8.75 in cash (including a cash dividend of $5.60) plus $14.75 in its shares.
- ER not less than 0.4062 but exact ER determined by the ratio, $14.75/average of V's common stock prices over 20 trading days ending on the third day prior to effective acquisition date. This is intended to secure for MCI shareholders V shares worth $14.75.

Meanwhile MCI paid a $0.40 dividend. The Merger Agreement was amended to increase the break-up fee payable by MCI to $240m from $200m and MCI would also reimburse V $10m for its expenses. Further, if MCI changed its recommendation favouring V, then V could cause MCI to call a shareholder meeting to consider V's offer.

The bidding war then hotted up further. MCI and Qwest entered negotiations to have the Qwest offer raised. On 31 March it raised its bid:

- $27.50 per share made up of cash of $13.50 (excluding the paid dividend) and stock valued at $14.
- No collar above $4.15 thus allowing MCI shareholders to benefit from any upside potential.
- Downside collar lowered to $3.32.

- $2bn worth equity offered would be placed with third party investors and the proceeds used to increase the cash component.

These terms were designed to increase the cash component relative to the share component and assuage MCI shareholders' concerns about the value of Qwest shares.

Given the pressures from its shareholders, MCI was still open to negotiations with Qwest and said it might declare the latter's offer superior if it was raised. On 21 April 2005, Qwest raised its offer further to $30 (excluding the cash dividend of $0.40) with a cash offer of $16 and a stock offer of $14 and threatened to withdraw if it was not declared superior. The revised offer at $9.8bn consisted of an ER of 3.373 subject to a collar:

- between $3.32 and $4.14, ER adjusted up to deliver $14 in stock (Q can at its option deliver all or a portion of this value protection in cash);
- below $3.32, ER = 4.217 (Q can deliver all or a portion of this value protection in cash provided the minimum ER is 3.373);
- if Q share price > $4.15, then ER = 3.373.

The stock offer value was protected upto 20% decline in Q's share price. But upside potential was not limited. MCI then declared the offer superior but the auction was far from over.

On 1 May 2005, Verizon raised its bid to $8.4bn:

- Cash dividend of $5.60 reduced by the $0.40 dividend paid in February 2005, *plus*;
- ER of either 0.5743 or the quotient of $20.40 divided by the average of V's common stock price over the 20 trading days ending in the third day prior to the effective acquisition date, whichever is higher; V reserved the right to pay in cash the consideration due if the ER > 0.5743.

On receiving this offer, MCI declared it superior to Q's offer of 21 April 2005. Upon this, Q declared that it would not raise its bid any further. In June 2005 one of the institutional investors filed a proxy statement opposing the merger recommendation by the MCI board ahead of the MCI shareholders' meeting. In October 2005, MCI shareholders approved the merger.

Discussion questions

1 What is the industry background to the takeover bids from Verizon and Qwest?

2 What is the merger rationale in each case?

3 Comment on the payment terms of the bids from Verizon and explain the motivation behind them.

4 Comment on the payment terms of the bids from Qwest and explain the motivation behind them.

5 What is the rationale for MCI to prefer Verizon over MCI?

6 Comment on the auction process and how it benefited MCI shareholders?

Sources: The 2004 annual reports of the three companies for financial data and various filings under Rule 425 of Securities and Exchange Act 1934 with the SEC, including Qwest's letters of 31 March and 21 April 2005 to MCI and MCI's 10-Q form of 9 May 2005 downloaded from SEC's Edgar database.

Overview and implications for practice

This chapter has examined the alternative methods of financing an acquisition. Historically, cash has generally been the most popular method, although when the stock markets are high there is often a shift to share exchange or mixed offers. The use of debt securities is relatively unpopular.

● The choice of payment currency depends upon a variety of considerations, including the tax implications, concern about earnings dilution, and the impact on financial risk.

● Payment by stock exchange is a means of reducing the valuation risk to the acquirer. This may increase the valuation risk to target shareholders.

● To protect the value of the offer in stock exchange offers, derivatives such as collars and contingent value rights may be used.

● The exchange ratio is chosen by acquirers to avoid post-acquisition earnings dilution. Both immediate period and long-term dilution need to be taken into account. Expected post-acquisition valuation influences the exchange ratio.

● Corporate control considerations are important in the choice of payment method.

● Deferred payment is a way of reducing valuation risk, but raises difficult questions about performance measurement, managerial motivation, the need to delay restructuring, etc.

● The payment currency often has a significant influence on the outcome of contested bids.

● Bidders choose the payment method to increase the chances of a successful bid. Target companies, as part of their defensive tactics, attack the method of payment. These defensive tactics and others are discussed in Chapters 20 and 21.

Review questions

16.1 What are the different methods of paying for acquisitions?

16.2 Do you think stock market conditions inlfuence the choice of payment currency? Why?

16.3 What is the relevance of tax to payment currency choice?

16.4 What is the impact of the bidder's financial strategy on payment currency choice?

16.5 How does earnings dilution occur in a share exchange offer?

16.6 What is bootstrapping? How does it influence payment method?

16.7 How can acquirers avoid earnings dilution?

16.8 What are equity derivatives in the context of takeovers? How are they used for risk management?

16.9 What is an underwritten rights issue? Compare it with a direct cash offer to the target shareholders.

16.10 How important is credit rating to the choice of payment method?

16.11 What is earn-out? Under what circumstances is it useful as a payment method?

16.12 Are corporate control considerations important to payment method? How?

16.13 Why do cash acquisitions generate larger shareholder gains than equity offers?

Further reading

C. Bouwman, K. Fuller and A. Nain, 'Stock market valuation of mergers and acquisitions', *Sloan Management Review*, **45**(1), 2003, 9–11.

R. Dobbs, B. Nand and W. Rehm, 'Merger valuation: Time to jettison EPS', downloaded from www. mckinseyquarterly.com, 2008.

M. Faccio and R. Masulis, 'The choice of payment method in European mergers and acquisitions', *Journal of Finance*, **60**(3), 2005, 1345–1388.

R. Hansen, 'A theory of choice of exchange medium in mergers and acquisitions', *Journal of Business*, **60**, 1987, 75–95.

K. Martin, 'The method of payment in corporate acquisitions, investment opportunities and management ownership', *Journal of Finance*, **51**(4), 1996, 1227–1246.

M. Martynova and L. Renneboog, 'What determines the financing decisions of corporate takeovers? Investor protection, asymmetric information or method of payment?', *Journal of Corporate Finance*, **15**(3), 2009, 290–315.

Notes and references

1. The pattern in the UK differs from that in continental Europe. Pure stock offers dominate cash offers throughout 1994–2005, whereas in 2006 and 2007 cash slightly dominates pure stock offers. Mixed offers dominate both through all these years. Thus for larger deals mixed offer is the most preferred method, followed by pure stock. Further, the link between stock market level and payment currency in an average deal is more tenuous than in the case of continental Europe. This suggests that bigger deals are not necessarily financed with an equity or mixed offer.

2. A similar picture emerges when average deal value is examined. During 1995–99 both stock and mixed offers increased enormously, but cash increased to a smaller extent. Between 2001 and 2004–05 mixed offers and stock exchange offers hit another peak, before declining steeply by 2007. Average cash offers rose during this time, and in 2007 the average cash deal was larger than the average stock or mixed offer deal.

3. This section draws upon *The KPMG Guide to M & A Tax*, published in association with the *Acquisitions Monthly*, August 2007, and the various issues of the KPMG publication *Taxation of Cross-Border Mergers and Acquisitions*, 2008 edition, downloaded from www.kpmg.co.uk. This section is necessarily a brief overview of the tax issues. For a more detailed discussion of these issues see the KPMG publication.

4. S. Mathieson, 'Amersham in two-shot power play', *Corporate Finance*, **157**, December 1997, 63–64; S. Weston, 'Structure the merger for maximum tax efficiency', *Corporate Finance, Global M & A Yearbook*, January 2000, 50–51.

5. D. T. Brown and M. D. Ryngaert, 'The mode of acquisition in takeovers: Taxes and asymmetric information', *Journal of Finance*, **46**(2), 1991, 653–669. See also Faccio and Masulis below (footnote 41).

6. Brown and Ryngaert, *ibid.*

7. R. D. Larson and N. J. Gonedes, 'Business combination: an exchange ratio determination model', *Accounting Review*, **44**, 1969, 720–728.

8. In the US study by Conn and Nielsen, 51% of the deals fell into the first quadrant one month after deal completion. In 14% of the cases both lose. In 45% of the sample cases, bidder shareholders experience wealth losses. Cooke *et al.* tested the LG model with a UK sample of 95 acquisitions during 1984–88 and adjusted the price movement of the bidder and target firms for stock market movements as well as for market risk, i.e. beta (see Chapter 4 for a description of beta). They found that about 49% of the sample acquisitions created value for both firms' shareholders. In about 14% of the cases they both lose, and in 47% of sample cases the acquirer shareholders experience wealth losses. These wealth losses to acquirers are consistent with evidence from other stock return-based studies extensively reviewed in Chapter 4. See R. L. Conn and J. F. Nielsen, 'An empirical test of the Larson–Gonedes exchange ratio determination model', *Journal of Finance*, June 1977, 749–759, and T. Cooke, A. Gregory and B. Pearson, 'A UK empirical test of the Larson–Gonedes exchange ratio model', *Accounting and Business Research*, **24**(94), 1994, 133–147. This paper also modifies the LG formulae (see note 9 *ante*) to adjust stock prices for market movements.

9. If B overpays even more and offers an ER of 1.5, i.e. a premium of £20m, then annual amortization will be £2m and BT's net earnings will decline to £2m and its EPS will be diluted to £2m/50m shares = 4p. Without amortization EPS will be £4m/50m or 8p. Once again, the extent of EPS dilution will be

significantly understated, rendering it unreliable. For further discussion see R. Dobbs, B. Nand and W. Rehm, 'Merger valuation: Time to jettison EPS', *The McKinsey Quarterly*, downloaded from www. mckinseyquarterly.com on 26 April 2008. If, following the merger, BT recognizes the absence of synergy and the overpayment, it may have to carry out an impairment test that will reveal the fictitious nature of the goodwill, and BT will have to write it off.

10. It is not clear how far the stock market marks down acquirers that experience earnings dilution. Harding and Rovit find some evidence that dilutive deals outperform accretive deals in terms of total shareholder return to the acquirers, benchmarked against their sector indices. See D. Harding and S. Rovit, *Mastering the Merger* (Boston, MA: Harvard Business School Press, 2004, Figure A-6, p. 187). They argue that this may be because dilutive acquisitions involve high-growth targets, whereas accretive deals may rely on cost-cutting. The stock market pressure on dilutive acquirers may lead them to achieve synergies.

11. S. Myers and N. S. Majluf, 'Corporate financing and investment decisions when firms have information that investors do not have', *Journal of Financial Economics*, **13**, 1984, 187–221.

12. R. G. Hansen, 'A theory for the choice of exchange medium in mergers and acquisitions', *Journal of Business*, **60**, 1987, 75–95. Within the same adverse selection framework, E. Eckbo, R. Giammarino and R. Henkel, 'Asymmetric information and the medium of exchange in takeovers', *Review of Financial Studies*, **3**, 1990, 651–675, derive the result that high-value bidders, i.e. bidders whose post-acquisition value will be high offer cash, and low-value bidders offer equity as a way of risk sharing. Officer *et al.*, *ibid.*, find evidence supportive of the Hansen model in their analysis of methods of payment by US acquirers. Where the targets are young companies at development stage (or are relatively intensive of intangible assets), and hence subject to high valuation risk, the announcement period abnormal return to acquirers is 6% (10%) compared with returns with non-development stage (less intangible-intensive) targets of −6% (5%). The differences are statistically significant. Thus acquiring high-risk targets with stock generates more value than acquiring them with non-stock consideration. See their Table IV.

13. B. Wasserstein, *Big Deal: The Battle for Control of America's Leading Corporations* (New York: Warner Books, 1998), pp. 624–629. See also C. Garcia-Peri, 'Using equity derivatives in M & A', *Corporate Finance*, **187**, June 2000, 27–28.

14. Micah Officer calls these fixed exchange (FEX) and fixed payment (FP) collars. They are also referred to as *Egyptian* and *Travolta* (after the Hollywood dancing superstar) because of the rising pyramidal shape and the sinuous shape of the target payoff curves. In a sample of 1127 stock deals in the US during 1991–99 Officer finds 66 FEX (6%) and 133 FP (12%) collars, and reports that the use of collars reduces the probability of renegotiation of the deal terms. See M. S. Officer, 'Collars and renegotiation in mergers and acquisitions', *Journal of Finance*, **59**(6), 2004, 2719–2743. Valuation of the collars can be done using the option pricing framework because of the contingent nature of the payoff.

15. See Chapter 20 on bid strategies for a discussion of termination fee, material adverse change (MAC) and other provisions in merger agreements, which may constrain either party from walking away from a deal.

16. R. Bruner, *Case Studies in Finance: Managing for Corporate Value Creation* (New York: Irwin, 1994), Chapter 45.

17. T. N. Amobi, 'Price protections in stock-swap transactions', *Mergers and Acquisitions*, **32**(2), 1997, 22–29.

18. See M. Shaw, G. Davies, M. Bardell and S. Hawes 'Bridging the value gap: The takeover of British Energy', Herbert Smith LLP, *www.practicallaw.com/0-385-2836*.

19. A bidder, instead of issuing new equity, may choose to buy back its shares ahead of a bid and reissue it to target shareholders. To buy back the shares, it needs cash. This method is therefore effectively a cash offer. However, the rationale for this exercise is that it avoids the earnings and control dilution that accompanies a new share issue. Further, the buy-back often raises the share price, thereby making the stock exchange more attractive. There may also be tax advantages to this two-stage process if target shareholders demand a higher price to compensate them for any CGT in a straight cash offer. See R. S. Wilber, 'Why do firms repurchase stock to acquire another firm?', *Review of Quantitative and Financial Analysis*, **29**, 2007, 155–172.

20. This section is also relevant to mixed offers that include a non-trivial amount of cash.

21. M. Fishman, 'Preemptive bidding and the role of the medium of exchange in acquisitions', *Journal of Finance*, **44**(1), 1989, 41–57. For the UK empirical evidence in support of pre-emption, see P. Cornu and D. Isakov, 'The deterring role of the medium of payment in takeover contests: Theory and evidence from the UK', *European Financial Management*, **6**(4), 2000, 423–440.

22. B. E. Eckbo, R. M. Giammarino and R. L. Heinkel, 'Asymmetric information and the medium of exchange in takeovers: Theory and tests', *Review of Financial Studies*, **3**(4), 1990, 651–675.

23. R. Anderson, 'Carlsberg unveils $6.3bn rights issue', *Financial Times*, 16 May 2008.

24. See M. Baker, J. Coval and J. C. Stein, 'Corporate financing decisions when investors take the path of least resistance', *Journal of Financial Economics*, **84**, 2007, 266–298. The model assumes a downward-sloping curve for the acquirer's stock. In economic terms, a two standard deviation increase in target institutional ownership in the sample studied reduces the acquirer's five-day announcement period return by 1.76 percentage points, taking it from its unconditional mean value of −2.23% down to −3.99% when II ownership is included in the model. The authors show that potential CGT liability does not explain the greater inertia of individual shareholders. This is consistent with the evidence that choice of stock exchange as a payment currency is not influenced by the potential CGT liability of target shareholders (see our earlier discussion of tax issues in M & A in this chapter). The authors argue that an SEO involves the shareholders having to make an 'active' decision to buy the stock or not, whereas in an exchange offer they may 'buy' the acquirer's stock by default.

25. *Acquisitions Monthly*, October 1987.

26. S.-L. Boyes, 'Vattenfall polishes the silverware', *Corporate Finance*, **199**, June 2001, 35.

27. Other metrics employed by Moody's are: EBITA/Average assets; FFO+Interest/Interest; FFO/Debt; RCF/Debt; Operating margin; CAPEX/Depreciation and Revenue volatility. FFO is funds from operations and RCF is retained cash flow. See Moody's, *ibid.*, for definitions.

28. D. Firn and R. Bream, 'Bayer to gain €6bn in finance deal', *Financial Times*, 13 December 2001. EchoStar's $26bn acquisition of Hughes Electronics from General Motors in 2001 was hit by similar worries (P. T. Larsen, 'Hughes is downgraded to junk status', *Financial Times*, 31 October 2001).

29. See E. Morellec and A. Zhdanov, 'Financing and takeovers', *Journal of Financial Economics*, **87**, 2008, 556–581, for further development of this model. They also cite evidence that, post-takeover, the leverage of the merged entity increases, and argue that this is supportive of their model.

30. A. Bharadwaja and A. Shivdasani, 'Valuation effects of bank financing in acquisitions', *Journal of Financial Economics*, **67**, 2003, 113–148. It could be argued that banks' and bidder shareholder interests are not always aligned, and that banks may influence bidder managers to make acquisitions that serve their interests, e.g. risk-reducing diversifying acquisitions. The evidence is, however, more consistent with robust monitoring by banks to the benefit of shareholders.

31. See M. Jensen and W. Meckling, 'Theory of the firm: Managerial behaviour, agency costs and ownership structure', *Journal of Financial Economics*, **3**(4), 1976, 305–360.

32. On valuation of convertibles, see S. Ross, R. Westerfield and J. F. Jaffe, *Corporate Finance* (New York: McGraw Hill, 2002), Chapter 24 (see Chapter 14 on the Black–Scholes model).

33. In some cases preventing the defection of key managers to rivals or to set up their own shop, rather than retention, may motivate an earn-out. See J. Marino, 'Resisting defection', *Mergers and Acquisitions*, **43**(10), 2008, 60–61.

34. S. J. Sherman and D. A. Janatka, 'Engineering earn-outs to get deals done and prevent discord', *Mergers and Acquisitions*, September/October 1992, 26–31.

35. In the UK, prior to 2008, 'taper relief' was given from CGT when business assets held for several years were disposed of, e.g. the 40% normal rate was reduced to 10%. In 2007 this was changed to a flat rate of 18%, irrespective of the length of time the investment was held. This increased the incentive to sell for cash rather than for deferred consideration to beat the deadline for the change.

36. R. Hussey, 'Maintaining the honeymoon time' and 'Problems and priorities when you look after baby', *Accountancy Age*, 1 and 8 March 1990.

37. C. Blumberg, 'Earn-outs: solution or problem?', *Corporate Finance*, **189**, August 2000, 31–32. See also B. Craig and A. Smith, 'The art of earnouts', *Strategic Finance*, June 2003, 45–47, and M. Gundersen, 'Seller, beware: In an earnout, the buyer has doubts; the seller has hopes', *Business Law Today*, **14**(4), March/April 2005.

38. *Mergers and Acquisitions, Almanac*, February 2002. N. Kohers and J. Ang, 'Earnouts in mergers: Agreeing to disagree and agreeing to stay', *Journal of Business*, **73**(3), 2000, 445–476 provide evidence that earn-outs are rarely used in public company takeovers in the US. In their sample of 938 acquisitions with earn-out during 1984 to 1996, 96% are non-public targets, i.e. private companies or divested subsidiaries. The earn-out component as a proportion of the deal value is 45% (average value $10.4m) for private companies and 33% ($27.2m) for divested subsidiaries. See also M. Officer, A. Poulsen and M. Stegemoller, 'Target-firm information asymmetry and acquirer returns', *Review of Finance*, **1**, 2008, 1–27, who report that the proportion of earn-outs in their sample is about 9%.

39. M. Faccio and R. W. Masulis, 'The choice of payment method in European mergers & acquisitions', *Journal of Finance*, **60**(3), 2005, 1345–1388.

40. K. J. Martin, 'The method of payment in corporate acquisitions, investment opportunities and management ownership', *Journal of Finance*, **51**(4), 1996, 1227–1246.

41. Y. Amihud, B. Lev and N. G. Travlos, 'Corporate control and the choice of investment financing: The case of corporate acquisitions', *Journal of Finance*, **45**(2), 1990, 603–616.

42. A. Ghosh and W. Ruland, 'Managerial ownership, the method of payment for acquisitions and executive job retention', *Journal of Finance*, **53**(2), 1998, 785–798.

43. A. Ghosh and P. C. Jain, 'Financial leverage changes associated with corporate mergers', *Journal of Corporate Finance*, **6**, 2000, 377–402. See also A. J. Auerbach and D. Reishus, 'The effects of taxation on merger decision', in A. Auerbach (Ed.), *Corporate Takeovers: Causes and Consequences* (Chicago, IL: University of Chicago Press, 1988), who report that tax factors were not a major factor. C. Hayn, 'Tax attributes as determinants of shareholder gains in corporate acquisitions', *Journal of Financial Economics*, **23**, June 1989, 121–153, finds some evidence of tax benefits.

44. Brown and Ryngaert, *ibid.*

45. A. R. Salami and P. S. Sudarsanam, 'Financing corporate acquisitions: Relevance of the accounting policy choice', Cranfield School of Management Working Paper, 2000.

46. A. Gregory, 'Motives underlying the method of payment by UK acquirers: The influence of goodwill', *Accounting and Business Research*, **30**(3), 2000, 227–240.

47. J. Franks, R. Harris and C. Mayer, 'Means of payment in takeovers: results for the UK and the United States', in A. J. Auerbach (Ed.), *Corporate Takeovers: Causes and Consequences* (Chicago, IL: University of Chicago Press, 1988).

48. A. Salami, *Determinants and Financial Consequences of the Method of Payment in Corporate Acquisitions*, unpublished PhD thesis, City University Business School, London, 1994.

49. See S. B. Moeller, F. P. Schlingemann and R. Stulz, 'Firm size and the gains from acquisitions', *Journal of Financial Economics*, **73**, 2004, 201–228; C. Bouwman, K. P. Fuller and A. Nain, 'Stock market valuation and mergers', *Sloan Management Review*, 2003; M. Bradley and A. Sundaram, 'Do acquisitions drive performance or does performance drive acquisitions?', SSRN working paper, 2004; M. Faccio, J. McConnell and D. Stolin, 'Returns to acquirers of listed and unlisted targets', *Journal of Financial and Quantitative Analysis*, **41**(1), 2006, 197–220; M. Martynova and L. Renneboog, 'Mergers and acquisitions in Europe: the fifth takeover wave', in L. Renneboog (Ed.), *Advances in Corporate Finance and Asset Pricing* (Elsevier: Amsterdam, 2006) pp. 13–75.

50. E. Eckbo and H. Langohr, 'Information disclosure, method of payment and takeover premiums', *Journal of Financial Economics*, **24**, 1989, 363–403.

51. See Y. Huang and R. A. Walkling, 'Target abnormal returns associated with acquisition announcements, payment method, acquisition form and managerial resistance', *Journal of Financial Economics*, **19**, 1987, 329–349; N. G. Travlos, 'Corporate takeover bids, methods of payment and bidding firms' stock returns', *Journal of Finance*, **42**(4), 1987, 943–963; P. Draper and K. Paudyal, 'Corporate takeovers: Mode of payment, returns and trading activity', *Journal of Business Finance & Accounting*, **26**(5&6), 1999, 521–558; and D. R. Peterson and P. P. Peterson, 'The medium of exchange in mergers and acquisitions', *Journal of Banking and Finance*, **15**, 1991, 383–405. They attribute higher gains to targets in cash offers to the need to compensate for capital gains tax. Also Amihud *et al.*, *ibid.*, find that in some exchange offers shareholder gains for acquirers are less when managerial shareholding is smaller. Thus managerial alignment with shareholder interests moderates the negative wealth impact of equity financing. Several studies reviewed in Chapter 4 on acquisition performance report superior performance for cash offers relative to exchange offers. Among them are: Rau and Vermaelen, Loughran and Vijh, Gregory, Sudarsanam, Holl and Salami, and Sudarsanam and Mahate. See Appendix 4.2 in Chapter 4 for details of these references.

52. R. Heron and E. Lie, 'Operating performance and the method of payment in takeovers', *Journal of Financial and Quantitative Analysis*, **37**(1), 2002, 137–155.

53. G. W. Emery and J. A. Switzer, 'Expected market reaction and the choice of method of payment for acquisitions', *Financial Management*, **28**(4), 1999, 73–86.

54. See Kohers and Ang, *ibid.* and Officer, *ibid.*

55. See S. Sudarsanam and L. Barbopoulos, 'Determinants and shareholder wealth effects of choice of earnout as acquisition payment currency', Cranfield School of Management working paper, 2009.

56. H. Louis, 'Earnings management and the market performance of acquiring firms', *Journal of Financial Economics*, **74**, 2004, 121–148. See also M. Erickson and S. Wang, 'Earnings management by acquiring

firms in stock for stock mergers', *Journal of Accounting and Economics*, **27**, 1999, 149–176 for similar earlier evidence.

57. For a much smaller UK sample, A. Botsari and G. Meeks, 'Do acquirers overstate earnings prior to a share for share bid?', *Journal of Business Finance and Accounting*, **35**(5/6), 2008, 633–670 report earnings management by acquirers in the year before the announcement. On the alternative methodologies for estimating earnings management through accounting accruals see Louis, *ibid.*

58. This also means that stockholders are correspondingly exposed to greater risk. This co-insurance can lead to wealth transfer from stockholders to bondholders. The former can avoid or mitigate this if the merged entity levers up to a level where the merged firm's risk is no lower than that of the pre-merger firms. Bondholders who anticipate this may insist on event risk covenants to protect themselves. In this case wealth transfer may occur from acquirer to target shareholders.

59. M. Billett, T. King and D. Mauer , 'Bondholder wealth effects in mergers and acquisitions: New evidence from the 1980s and 1990s', *The Journal of Finance*, **59**(1), 2004, 107–135. They also report that event risk covenants to protect bondholders became more widespread in the 1990s.

60. See Table 2 of L. Renneboog and P. Szilagyi, 'How do mergers and acquisitions affect bondholders in Europe? Evidence on the impact and spillover of governance and legal standards', Tilburg University working paper, 2006.

CHAPTER (17)

Antitrust regulation

Objectives

At the end of this chapter[1], the reader should be able to understand:

- the economic rationale for merger regulation;
- the nature, structure and characteristics of antitrust regulatory systems in Europe and the US, as applied to mergers;
- the broad set of rules that govern the investigation of mergers, and the criteria for allowing or disallowing mergers;
- how the hierarchy of jurisdiction operates in the EU;
- the scope for jurisdictional conflict and arbitrage, and the trend towards cross-jurisdictional cooperation among countries;
- the shortcomings of different antitrust regimes; and
- how firms can minimize the regulatory risk to their deals.

Introduction

It is axiomatic that competitive markets promote consumer welfare, economic efficiency, innovation and economic progress. Antitrust regulation is concerned with regulating the structure of markets and the conduct of firms competing in those markets, to ensure they are competitive. It covers the formation and behaviour of cartels ('trusts', hence the name 'antitrust'); whether firms become dominant in terms of their market power; whether, if already dominant, they abuse their dominance to disadvantage their competitors and consumers; and whether they act in ways to impede competition. Mergers by their nature increase the size of firms, and horizontal mergers (see Chapter 5) may also substantially increase the merging firms' market share relative to what they enjoyed pre-merger and relative to other remaining firms. Other types of merger, such as vertical and conglomerate (see Chapters 6 and 7 respectively), can also enhance market power. Merger regulation is concerned with evaluating whether specific mergers do indeed lead to increased market power, whether they will lead to less competitive markets, and whether there are countervailing competitive constraints to offset the anticompetitive aspects of such mergers.

The history of antitrust regulation goes back to the Sherman Act of 1890 in the US, but merger regulation within the rubric of antitrust regulation was formally initiated by the Clayton Act of 1914. This legislation has since been followed by other Federal Acts that have focused on the antitrust aspects of mergers and acquisitions. In more recent years antitrust regulation, including merger regulation, has been enacted in many other countries and regions of the world.

Mergers of enterprises operating within the EU have been, since 1990, subject to EU-level merger regulation. This regulation was promulgated with the aim of achieving a 'one-stop shop' clearance of mergers. The result is that there is now a hierarchy of merger regulation in the EU, with very large mergers having an EU-wide impact being examined by the European Commission (EC), while smaller mergers with their impact predominantly within a single member state are investigated by that state's own antitrust regulator.

In the UK, mergers have been the subject of antitrust regulation since 1965, during which period the UK government's policy has gone through distinct phases. While the main thrust of the antitrust regulation has been the maintenance of effective competition, many other issues of public interest have been, from time to time, considered relevant in determining whether a merger should be allowed. The US system provides a contrasting approach to antitrust regulation in terms of investigative procedure, judicial review, institutional arrangement and theoretical approach to issues of definition of market, monopoly, etc.

Globalization of product and services markets, as discussed in Chapter 8, has increased cross-border takeover activity. This has increased the scope for multiple antitrust jurisdictions over a proposed merger, and for jurisdictional friction among different national and regional regulators. Smart antitrust lawyers and their corporate clients have also played the jurisdictional arbitrage game in the absence of a commonality of procedures, timetables and conceptual approaches to antitrust regulation.

Another development is the privatization of previously government monopolies. This has been accompanied in many countries by the setting up of sector-specific regulators, such as Ofcom (the Office of Communications) and OFWAT (the Water Services Regulation Authority) in the UK. Mergers involving such privatized companies have to be cleared by these regulators and/or by the antitrust regulators.

Intervention of the antitrust regulator, at either the UK or the EU level, may cause a bid for a UK public company to be abandoned, at least for the duration of the antitrust inquiry. Antitrust regulation in different countries is not grounded in pure economics, but is more often an exercise in political economy. Enforcement has also been influenced by the ideological predilections of governments from time to time, as well as by nationalist sentiments, if not xenophobia, in the case of cross-border acquisitions. Regulatory uncertainty increases the risk to deal execution and to the expected value creation from a merger. Companies contemplating mergers must carefully evaluate their antitrust implications and the regulatory risk and cost to those deals. They need to evolve strategies to minimize the risk and the cost of a deal being blocked on antitrust grounds.

In this chapter we describe the antitrust regimes in Europe, the UK, the USA and several European countries. We also outline the developments in other countries, and describe the evolution of an international approach to antitrust regulation to accommodate the accelerating globalization of product markets, cross-border M & A (see Chapter 8), and the desire of countries to set up transparent and credible antitrust architectures. We discuss the consequences of the merger regulatory process for takeover bids, their strategic rationale and value creation potential.

Economic rationale for antitrust regulation

Antitrust regulation of mergers is based upon the expectation that mergers may have harmful effects for consumers and other stakeholders because they can confer market power on the merging firms. Such accretion of market power may allow theses firms to distort competition. The harmful effects of mergers may be manifested in lower output, higher than competitive market prices, lower quality of product or services, and excessive profits for the merging firms. Together, these reduce consumer welfare (consumer surplus). The aim of antitrust regulation is to prevent mergers that may have these harmful consequences, or at least mitigate the latter as much as possible. To understand the nature of these harmful effects of mergers we need to formulate the theories of harm.

Theories of harm in merger regulation

Increase in market power depends on the type of merger. In Chapters 5 to 7 we developed the framework to understand horizontal, vertical and conglomerate mergers, and indicated that market power increase was most likely in horizontal mergers of firms selling the same or broadly similar products with the same functional use. Vertical mergers can also give firms market power if the vertically integrated firm can exploit its control of inputs or outlets to deny its competitors access to these. Such denial is known as *foreclosure*. In Chapter 7 we discussed how conglomerate mergers could increase market power when conglomerates confronted one another in different product markets and, over time, appreciated their mutual dependence and hence learned to coexist and exercise competitive *forbearance*. Conglomerates can also exploit some common resources and capabilities, e.g. corporate brands, financial expertise, or lower cost of capital to increase their market power. Such exploitation is facilitated by the *portfolio effects*. Market power accretion from vertical foreclosure and portfolio effects is likely to be weaker than that from horizontal mergers, since the latter, by definition, eliminates a competitor. For these reasons, leading antitrust regulators have developed detailed guidelines to assess the harmful effects of horizontal mergers.

Theories of harm in horizontal mergers

The harms comprise:

- unilateral effects due to the merged entity exercising its market power independent of its competitors' behaviour or response;
- coordinated effects due to the reduction in the number of competitors and the increased scope for tacit or explicit collusion (oligopolistic coordination) among them, e.g. in maintaining high prices to the detriment of consumers. 'Coordinated interaction is comprised of actions by a group of firms that are profitable for each of them only as a result of the accommodating reactions of the others'[2].

We discuss these in turn, and illustrate them with cases of mergers that give rise to these effects.

Unilateral effects

A merger, by increasing the market power of the merging firms, may enable them to increase prices and lower their output, thereby reducing consumer welfare. In the pre-merger period any price increase by one might have driven its customers to shop at the others. This loss of customers might have rendered such price increase unprofitable, depending on how critical this loss is[3]. But these customers would now be deprived of the opportunity to choose between them, and the pre-merger competitive constraint would be relaxed after the merger, allowing the merged firm to raise its prices or reduce its output. Lack of competitive constraint may also reduce the incentive to innovate. Unilateral effects are likely to be important in markets where the number of sellers is already small, e.g. three sellers reduced to two ('3 to 2') (see Exhibit 17.1). Although this increases seller concentration, exercise of market power by the merged firm does not depend on any coordination with other firms in the market. It should be noted, however, that other firms in the market may also benefit from the increased concentration and price rises initiated by the merged firm, since they may also be able to raise their prices[4]. Even when the products of the merging firms are not homogeneous but are close substitutes, the unilateral effect can be felt by the consumers of the two products. However, a mere reduction in the number of competitors is by itself not a reliable indicator of unilateral effects.

Exhibit 17.1

We are merged and stronger. So you better pay more!

The Federal Trade Commission (FTC), the US antitrust regulator, challenged the merger of two makers of ultrasonic non-destructive testing (NDT) equipment used for quality control and safety purposes in many industries. For many customers the products of the merging firms were their first and second choice, and evidence showed that the two firms were frequently head-to-head rivals. The merger would have eliminated the effect of this strong and beneficial competition on pricing and innovation. The elimination of competition increased the probability that the merged firm could raise prices to its customers. Moreover, customers might also be deprived of the benefits of innovation from the firms competing with each other. To settle the FTC's claim that the proposed merger was illegal, the companies agreed to divest the buyer's NDT business.

Source: An FTC Guide to Mergers: Competitive Effects, downloaded from www.ftc.gov on 8 June 2009

Coordinated effects

Coordinated effects arise from the increased scope for the merged firms and their rivals to engage in tacit or explicit collusion to avoid or reduce their competitive rivalry, e.g. by not competing on price. They may also coordinate their capacity decisions, thereby reducing the output and causing welfare loss to the consumers. In general, a highly concentrated market structure with a small number of large competitors allows them to recognize their interdependence and the benefits of friendly coordination. However, not all such markets manifest coordinated behaviour, and some oligopolistic market structures are highly competitive. Successful coordination typically requires competitors to:

- reach an agreement that is profitable for each participant;
- have the means to detect cheating (that is, deviations from the agreement); and
- have the ability to punish cheaters and reinstate the agreement (FTC, 1997).[5]

This formulation recognizes that competitors must have both incentives to cooperate and the disincentive to refrain from cheating on the consensus. Further, where cheating occurs, it must be capable of being detected and punished. Otherwise, cheaters will be doubly rewarded: that is, they benefit from the restraints of their consensus-abiding competitors as well as their own consensus-breaking behaviour. They gain at the expense of both the consumers and their fellow producers!

The necessary conditions for tacit collusion to occur have been formulated by the Court of First Instance (CFI) in its 2002 judgement overturning the EC's prohibition of the Airtours–First Choice Holidays merger[6]:

- ability – firms 'have the ability to align their behaviour in the absence of an explicit agreement to do so';
- incentive – 'they have sufficient incentives to maintain this conduct' and a mechanism is available to punish the firms that deviate from the expected conduct; and
- sustainability – 'coordination should be sustainable in the face of other market pressures; e.g. the entry of a 'maverick' producer who does not understand the rules of the club, or chooses brazenly to break them.

The EC's horizontal merger guidelines, published in 2004, reflect these as tests for identifying collusive behaviour. A merger, if it is to result in collusive behaviour, should create or enhance the above conditions for coordinated effects (see Exhibit 17.2).

Exhibit 17.2

They're a rum thing, these coordinated effects

The FTC challenged a merger between the makers of premium rum. The maker of Malibu Rum, accounting for 8% of market sales, sought to buy the maker of Captain Morgan's rums, with a 33% market share. The leading premium rum supplier controlled 54% of sales. Post-merger, two firms – the market leader and the merged firm – would control about 95% of sales. The Commission challenged the merger, claiming that the combination would increase the likelihood that the two firms could coordinate to raise prices. Although a small competitor, the buyer had imposed a significant competitive constraint on the two larger firms, and would no longer play that role after the merger. To settle claims that the merger was illegal, the buyer agreed to divest its rum business.

Source: *An FTC Guide to Mergers: Competitive Effects*, downloaded from www.ftc.gov on 8 June 2009

Theories of harm in vertical mergers

As discussed in Chapter 6, vertical mergers bring under common ownership and control firms operating in successive stages of the supply chain. If the merger leads to supply chain efficiencies and these are passed on to consumers, then they enhance consumer welfare. However, when a firm acquires its input supplier (backward integration) or when it acquires its market access channels (forward integration), it can gain market power against its competitors or those of the acquired firm, if, pre-merger, one of the merging firms had been a supplier or distributor to the competitors. Exercise of such power may result in the merged firm denying, or raising the cost of, access to inputs (*input foreclosure*) to its downstream rivals. In the case of forward integration, such power may result in the merged firm denying, or raising the cost of, access to distribution channels (*customer foreclosure*) to its upstream rivals[7].

Theories of harm in conglomerate mergers

Forbearance, as noted in Chapter 7, is an example of coordinated effects in conglomerate mergers. Conglomerate mergers of firms selling complementary products may also give rise to:

- bundling effects, i.e. sale of product A is bundled with the sale of product B;
- portfolio effect, i.e. where customers buy B when they buy A.

In the case of bundling, a firm can use its market power in the market for A to sell B, and vice versa. Thus a merger of the two firms can increase the merged firm's market power in both markets[8]. In the case of the portfolio effect the merged firm may have a wider range of products than competitor firms selling only A or B.

Several theories of harm may be concurrently relevant in some cases:

- different effects on the same competitive aspect, e.g. unilateral and coordinated effects on price;
- same effects on different competitive aspects, e.g. unilateral effects on price and on quality; or
- different effects on different aspects, e.g. unilateral effects on price and coordinated effects on capacity.

Theories of harm may also apply over different timescales, e.g. short-run unilateral effects on price and long-run coordinated effects on capacity[9].

Assessing the effects of mergers on competition

Antitrust regulators are mindful of the unilateral and coordinated effects of mergers. They face four challenges in evaluating these effects in particular mergers:

- identifying reliable indicators of the likelihood of these effects;
- assessing the *counterfactual*;
- assessing the competitive constraints that may prevent or mitigate these effects; and
- assessing the countervailing benefits of otherwise anticompetitive mergers.

There may not be a single indicator of overwhelming reliability. In practice, regulators look at a battery of such indicators.

The substantive test

Regulators test whether a merger will impact negatively on competition and induce the harmful effects that we discussed under theories of harm above. These tests are known as *substantive tests* of merger effects, and vary among merger control regimes. Broadly, they are:

- substantial lessening of competition (SLC) test;
- significant impediment to effective competition (SIEC) test;
- the market dominance test; or
- a combination of market dominance and SLC or SIEC.

The SLC test originated in the US, where mergers, whose effects 'substantially lessen competition or tend to create a monopoly' are prohibited. It was incorporated into the UK Enterprise Act 2002 (EA 2002). Both the Office of Fair Trading (OFT) and the Competition Commission

(CC) in the UK apply this test. The EC adopted the SIEC test in 2004, replacing its earlier market dominance test, which was severely criticized by the Court of First Instance (CFI) in three cases in 2002[10]. However, the EC has not abandoned the market dominance test but uses it as one of the indicators to SIEC, rather than a self-contained test on its own. According to the EC, 'significant impediment to effective competition generally results from the creation and strengthening of a dominant position'. The concept of 'collective dominance' is also regarded by the EC as relevant to assessing the coordinated effects that might lead a merger being a SIEC. Thus the concept of market dominance now plays a complementary, rather than a central, role in EC's substantive test.

Market definition

One of the major tasks for the merger regulator is to define what constitutes the relevant market. Such a definition is necessary before the harmful effects, and the competitive constraints on such effects, can be assessed. Markets may be defined in terms of:

- products; and
- geography.

Products will include close substitutes with a high cross-elasticity of demand, i.e. demand for product A rises with rise in the price of product B. Geographical demarcation takes into account import penetration of the domestic market. Some products are traded in global markets such as oil, gas, fertilizers, even electricity. Markets are more competitive when import penetration from different exporting countries is high. In the case of services, geographic proximity of the service providers will be important, and the ease with which customers can switch from one provider to another will be a criterion to decide the local market (see Exhibit 17.3 for the use of isochrones to determine a geographical market).

Indictors of potential SLC

Before identifying a SLC, regulators may often have to define the relevant markets in which a merger gives rise to it. Several analytical approaches are available for market definition:

- Demand-side substitution, i.e. whether consumers can easily switch from one product to another to serve the same end-use. In this case the market will consist of both products. Demand substitution imposes switching costs on customers, which need to be factored into models of such substitution.
- Supply-side substitution, that is, whether suppliers of different products that are not demand-side substitutes can switch their production to supply the products of the merging firms, i.e. the ones whose price has increased, perhaps as a result of a merger or for other reasons. Supply-side substitution imposes switching costs on producers, which need to be factored into models of such substitution.
- The hypothetical monopolist test for the profitability of a significant price increase by a hypothetical monopolist in the market. Also known as the *SSNIP* test, it measures the change in profitability as a result of a 'small but significant and non-transitory increase in price'. Such a price increase will be unprofitable if consumers of the monopolist's product can switch to other products, i.e. there is demand-side substitution[12]. Any product that is a candidate for such substitution then belongs in the same market.

Indicators of a potential SLC include high market concentration, high market shares of the merging firms, or a large increase in market concentration. The analytical tools include analysis

Exhibit 17.3

Own two cinemas within 20 minutes' drive-time? That's a monopoly![11]

In 2005 the UK's Competition Commission investigated the acquisition of A3 Cinema Limited and its sole operating entity, Ster Century, by Vue Entertainment Holdings (UK) limited. Vue and Ster were respectively the third and fourth largest multiplex cinema operators in the UK. The CC considered whether the merger would have any adverse effects at the national level. Since Vue's national market share increased by only 2.2 percentage points to 16%, the CC judged that this would not have a substantial impact on Vue's negotiating position with screen advertisers, contractors and distributors, or the suppliers of food and drink at concession points within the cinemas.

The CC concluded that the product market was no wider than cinema exhibition, and that the geographic market was local. To assess the local impact the CC considered the four markets where both firms had multiplexes pre-merger. Without the merger, Ster was likely to have continued as a viable competitor to Vue, either alone or after sale to a purchaser other than Vue. This is a *counterfactual* based on *status quo ante* (see below for definition).

In each of the local markets cinemas that fell within a 20-minute drive-time *isochrone* of the acquired cinema were considered. This is the area within which it is possible to drive to the cinema in 20 minutes or less. Vue argued that it competed with cinemas outside the isochrone. It was in only one city, Basingstoke in southern England, that there was high expectation of an SLC. The two cinemas there shared the same customer catchment area and, pre-merger, competed directly. The merger therefore created a local monopoly.

Having found SLC in Basingstoke, the CC required divestiture of one of the cinemas to remedy the SLC there.

Source: Adapted from The Competition Commission, *Annual Report 2005/2006*. This can be downloaded from www.competition-commission.org.uk

of pre- and post-merger market shares of merging firms, say, the four-firm concentration ratio (CR4), the Herfindahl–Hirschman Index (HHI), change in CR4 or HHI.

The HHI is a measure of market concentration of sellers, which takes into account the market shares of all the sellers in the market and not just the top four sellers in CR4.

$$HHI = \sum ms_i^2$$

where ms_i is the market share of seller i in the market and $i = 1, n$, where n is the total number of sellers. Market share is expressed as a percentage. For a monopoly, i.e. a single firm with a market share of 100%, HHI is 100^2 or 10,000. For two firms with equal market shares of 50% it is 5000, and so on. Thus a higher number indicates greater concentration. In horizontal mergers, regulators consider different thresholds of post-merger HHI and ΔHHI, the post-merger increase in HHI, to judge whether SLC or SIEC is likely. For example, with the EC and UK regulators, the following thresholds (Shown in Table 17.1) would trigger concern[13]: In different mergers several other characteristics of products and consumers need to be taken into account before a satisfactory market definition can be reached[14].

Table 17.1 Herfindahl–Hirschman index as anti-competitive indicator

Post-merger HHI (ΔHHI)	Concentration level	Anti-competitive concern
< 1000	Not concentrated	Little concern
> 1000 (250)	Moderately concentrated/ concentrated (UK)	Significant concern
> 2000 (150)	Highly concentrated	Significant concern/ cause for concern (UK)

These interpretations are not hard and fast rules, and are often tempered by other factors.

The counterfactual

Possible counterfactuals include:

- the *status quo* (*status quo ante*), i.e. the current (pre-merger) competitive conditions in the case of anticipated (completed) mergers;
- the possibility that one of the merger firms may have exited in some way, perhaps through bankruptcy ('the failing firm' scenario) or through divestiture due to its change of corporate strategy (see Chapter 10 on the rationale for divestitures);
- in the event of exit, who might have bought those assets, e.g. a competitor of the exiting firm or a new entrant? The competitive constraints may be different in each case.

The last two scenarios depend on expectations shaped by the dynamics of market evolution: for example, what tactics might the acquiring firm adopt if denied the opportunity to acquire the target? How might other firms in the market react if the proposed merger is not allowed[15]? These scenarios must also be predictable over a foreseeable period, which could be, for example, two years. Exhibit 17.3 above shows how the counterfactual was determined in the case of a cinema merger.

Competitive constraints on merging firms

Having determined that a merger being investigated would give rise to SLC, regulators consider the competitive constraints that prevent it so doing. Among these constraints are:

- buyer power, i.e. whether buyers can switch their demand to another supplier or substitute product – for example, supermarket chains have considerable buyer power against food and grocery suppliers
- the reaction of current competitors of the merging firms to the merger, i.e. whether they will challenge the merged firm by lowering prices and increasing supply, e.g. foreign suppliers with excess capacity to increase their supply;
- the potential entry of new competitors, i.e. whether there are potential competitors with credible resources to enter;
- low entry barriers, e.g. the capital cost of investment to new competitors is low; and
- supply substitution – for example, producers of products with similar production technology may be able to switch their production to products of the merging firms and increase competition.

Regulators need to assess whether these constraints are currently operative and, if not, whether they will be operative within a reasonably foreseeable period, say two years. If they will not come into effect within a reasonable period, the regulator will not give such constraints much weight.

Countervailing benefits

While competitive constraints mitigate SLC, countervailing benefits offset the cost of an SLC to the consumers or other stakeholders. Two defences of mergers that may otherwise lead to counterveiling benefits are:

- efficiency; and
- failing firm.

Some mergers may generate cost efficiencies due to operational synergies or greater innovation in the future. Innovation can lead to new technologies, new processes and new products that can increase both consumer and social welfare in the future. Regulators are generally sceptical of arguments in favour of these efficiencies because they are uncertain, and subject to overoptimism or hype by the merging firms. These claims are not easily susceptible to independent verification. The burden of proof therefore lies with the merging parties.

The failing firm defence is that, without the merger, the target company may fail, i.e. go bankrupt. If this happens, it will cease to present any competition to the acquirer, and the concentration of the market will increase[16]. Regulators will consider whether the exit of the firm through failure is inevitable, whether there are buyers for the failing company's assets, whether sale of those assets to such buyers will be less anti-competitive than the proposed merger, and whether exit of the failing firm itself may be less anti-competitive than the merger[17].

Merger regulation in the European Union[18]

The Treaty of Rome incorporates a strong emphasis on the maintenance of competition within the Community (the terms Community and Union are used interchangeably in this chapter and elsewhere in this book). The EU rules are designed to prevent distortion of competition in the Common Market through cartels and abuses of dominant market positions. Article 81 of the EC Treaty (the *anticartel* rule) aims at preventing arrangements among enterprises that have the effect of distorting competition. Article 82 (the *antidominance* rule) is designed to preclude firms from abusing their dominant position so as to restrict competition and interstate trade.

Both Articles 81 and 82 have been held by the European Court to have application in the merger area, but their scope is not well defined, since they were not originally designed for regulation of mergers. To remedy this shortcoming a new regime of merger regulation was installed in September 1990. Articles 81 and 82, however, still have force in certain types of business combination, such as joint ventures.

EU merger policy evolution

'Concentration' is the somewhat ambiguous word used in EU competition law parlance to cover merger, acquisition and takeover, whether they involve acquisition of controlling or minority interests in shares or assets. Some joint ventures may also be considered as concentrations. Until the promulgation of the new merger control regulation in 1990, the Commission had applied Articles 81 and 82 to prevent or modify mergers. There was no system specifically designed to screen and regulate mergers, and no single authority to implement that system. This deficiency goes back to the Treaty of Rome.

Two landmark cases decided by the European Court somewhat remedied the situation – *Continental Can* (1973) and *Philip Morris* (1987)[19]. The decisions extended the application of

Article 82 and Article 81 respectively to mergers. Prior to the Philip Morris case it was thought that Article 81 did not apply to agreements to buy shares, such as in acquisitions and mergers. Similarly, the Continental Can case decision laid down the principle that, if a company that already held a dominant position in the Common Market sought to take over a competitor, it would amount to abuse of its dominant position, thereby attracting Article 82.

The Merger Regulation

The European Community Merger Regulation (ECMR), referred to below as Merger Regulation (MR) 4064/89, came into effect on 21 September 1990. In 2004 this was replaced by Council Regulation 139/2004 (see below for a discussion of the circumstances behind the new regulation). The regime lays down size and other criteria for concentrations (including mergers) that will be subject to screening by the Director General (DG), Competition of the European Commission (hereafter EC or Commission). It sets up a procedure for notification, and also a timetable for the Commission's deliberations. It seeks to minimize the overlap between EU and national antitrust regulations and procedures. A concentration can arise in any of the following circumstances:

- Two or more previously independent undertakings merge.
- One undertaking acquires, through purchase of shares or otherwise, direct or indirect control of another.
- Persons who already control at least one undertaking acquire direct or indirect control of another.

Direct or indirect control, derived from rights, contracts or other means, confers the possibility of exercising decisive influence on an undertaking. This means that even a minority stake can be deemed to lead to *de facto* control if the minority holder exercises decisive influence[20]. Once a person has acquired decisive influence over an undertaking, a concentration generally occurs. However, arrangements that confer decisive influence for a temporary period only are unlikely to be considered as bringing about concentration. What constitutes decisive influence is reviewed by the Commission on a case-by-case basis, but it may occur at shareholding levels as low as 20%.

The ECMR exempts certain types of shareholding, such as investment by security firms, and certain types of control, such as that of administrators in receivership, from the definition of concentration.

Concentration with a Community dimension (CCD)

A 'concentration' will fall under the EC's jurisdiction only if it has a 'Community dimension'. Thus, for a transaction to fall under the ECMR, it must be a concentration and must have a Community dimension. A CCD is defined in terms of three turnover size thresholds – global, Community wide and country. These are designed to catch large concentrations that are not limited to a single member state, but have Community-wide impact.

Under the ECMR, a CCD is present when:

- the *combined worldwide turnover of all* the companies involved totals €5bn or more; and
- the *aggregate EU turnover of each* of at least two of the companies is €250m or more; unless
- each of the companies concerned achieves *more than two-thirds* of its total EU turnover *within one and the same member state.*

An example is shown in Table 17.2. Although each company achieves about 72% of its EU turnover in its home country, they are from different countries. So the merger is a CCD. If we

Table 17.2 UK plc bids for German AG

Company	Turnover (€m)		
	World	EU	Home country
UK plc	4000	2500	1800 (72%)
German AG	3000	1500	1100 (73%)

alter the scenario and assume that German AG is also a British company, then the two-thirds rule is infringed, and the merger will fall under UK jurisdiction. The first threshold seeks to exclude mergers between small and medium-size firms. The second seeks to exclude small acquisitions by large firms, or those with only small EU-wide impact. The third applies subsidiarity by allowing mergers with largely national impact to be investigated by national antitrust agencies.

Alternative thresholds for CCD

In 1998 the ECMR was amended to provide alternative thresholds to define CCD. A concentration that does not meet the original thresholds in the first definition is a CCD where:

- the *combined worldwide turnover* of the undertakings concerned is more than €2500m;
- the *combined Community-wide turnover* of each of at least two of the undertakings concerned is more than €100m; and
- in each of *at least three member states*,
- the *combined turnover* of all the undertakings concerned is more than €100m; and
- the *turnover of each* of at least two of the undertakings concerned is more than €25m; unless
- each of the undertakings concerned achieves *more than two-thirds* of its aggregate Community-wide turnover within *one and the same member state* (the two-thirds rule).

The following example illustrates the application of the alternative thresholds. Suppose two companies, X and Y, plan to merge. Their turnovers under alternative scenarios are shown in Table 17.3. In the scenario in Panel A, X and Y satisfy all of the alternative thresholds, making their merger a CCD. In Panel B, X has no turnover in France and therefore the merger is not

Table 17.3 Turnover of merging firms X and Y (€m)

Company	UK	Germany	France	EU	World
Panel A Merger is CCD					
X	600	200	200	1000	1500
Y	500	300	100	900	1200
Panel B Merger not CCD					
X	600	400	0	1000	1500
Y	500	250	150	900	1200
Panel C Merger not CCD					
X	700	200	100	1000	1500
Y	650	300	50	900	1200

a CCD. In the third scenario in Panel C, both X and Y have more than two-thirds of their EU turnover in the UK: so the merger is not a CCD.

The alternative definition generally has lower thresholds but envelops mergers where the merging firms have much more evenly spread Community operations. The alternative definition thus seeks to capture smaller mergers with wider Community impact than the first definition. The two-thirds rule still ensures that mergers with overwhelming impact within a single member state are investigated by that member state. A merger that is not a CCD but nevertheless has impact on several member states can then be investigated by more than one member state.

In appraising whether a CCD is compatible with the common market, the EC will determine whether the CCD will create or strengthen a 'dominant position' in any market and, therefore, significantly impede effective competition in the common market. In this determination, the merged entity's market share of more than 40% is generally regarded as indicative of dominance, and is likely to trigger Phase II investigation. Market share below 25% is generally, but not always, regarded as not likely to cause SIEC[21].

The Commission has exclusive jurisdiction over CCDs, except in certain circumstances permitted under the Regulation (see below). This avoids the need for companies involved in CCDs to satisfy antitrust authorities in different EU countries. As we have seen, this elimination of multiple jurisdictions is known as the 'one-stop shopping' principle. The thresholds have been arrived at as a compromise between advocates of Community-wide merger regulation, who see merit in one-stop shopping, and the reluctance of some member states to cede too much power to Brussels.

Mergers with a Community dimension must be notified by the participating companies to the European Commission 'prior to their implementation and following the conclusion of the agreement, announcement of the bid, or the acquisition of a controlling interest'[22]. A bidder can approach the Commission for confidential advice prior to making an offer, and obtain a non-binding preliminary opinion. Figure 17.1 shows the timeline for investigation, and the outcomes of such investigation in two phases. In Phase I, if it needs more information from the companies, the EC can 'stop the clock', i.e. suspend the investigation. For example, the Commission stopped the clock on its review of the Omya/Huber merger in 2006 while awaiting more and accurate data[23]. The clock would restart when the companies have supplied the required information[24]. If the Commission initiates Phase II proceedings, a bid covered by the City Code immediately lapses (see Chapter 18). Under the fast track (Short Form Notification) procedure, mergers that are unlikely to raise serious competition concerns, e.g. the parties have very little overlap in their businesses, are cleared at the end of Phase I.

Evolution of the substantive competition assessment in the EU

Until 2002 the EC relied on the structural characteristics of markets to infer the adverse impact of mergers on competition. The Commission had blocked the proposed £950m acquisition of the UK company First Choice Holidays by another UK company, Airtours, in 1999. The decision was based on the economic theory of 'collective dominance' by oligopolists to the detriment of consumers. Under this model the oligopolists would collude, and avoid any price competition. The merger would have reduced the number of tour operators in the UK from four to three, thereby increasing the scope for collusion and collective dominance, and Airtour appealed this decision to the court. In June 2002 the Court of First Instance (CFI) overturned the blocking decision.

In October 2002 the CFI piled even more agony on the EC's merger control regime. It declared that the Commission had been wrong to block the merger between Schneider and

Figure 17.1   Timeline for Phase I and Phase II investigations by European Commission

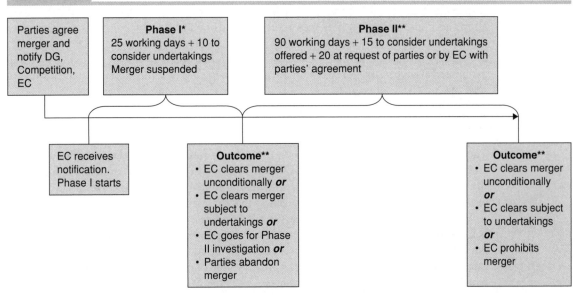

*In Phase I, extension may be to consider a member state's request for reallocation. Derogation from suspension may be given in rare cases, e.g. bankruptcy.

**In Phase II, where parties offer undertakings within 55 working days, there is no 15-day extension. Clearance means the merger is compatible within the Common Market.

Legrand, the French electrical groups (see Exhibit 17.9 below on this merger). The Court, in a harsh judgement, concluded that 'the Commission's economic analysis is vitiated by errors and omissions which deprive it of probative value'. It also found that the Commission had committed a 'serious infringement of the rights of the defence' by failing to clearly spell out to the companies what its concerns were. Two days later the CFI again overturned the Commission's decision to block the €1.7bn bid of Tetra Laval, the Swedish packaging group, for its French rival Sidel[25].

Collective dominance theory challenged

Following these judicial setbacks, the EC re-conceptualized the substantive test in 2004. While retaining collective dominance as a useful indicator of the potentially harmful effects of a merger, the EC adopted the SIEC, which goes beyond collective dominance, as shown in our earlier discussion. The 2004 horizontal merger guidelines now require consideration of both actual and potential competition, the competitive constraints on collusive behaviour and the efficiency gains from mergers as well as the harmful effects[26]. In the same year Council Regulation 139/2004 replaced the original Council Regulation 4064/1989. The articles referred to in this chapter and elsewhere in the book are from 139/2004 unless indicated otherwise.

Assessment of the harmful effects of vertical mergers and conglomerate mergers also needs to take into account the competitive constraints on foreclosure and portfolio effects following the judgements of the CFI and the European Court of Justice (ECJ) in *Tetra Laval/Sidel* and of the CFI in *General Electric/Honeywell*[27].

Remedies for anticompetitive features of a proposed merger

If the EC makes an SIEC finding either in Phase I or in Phase II, it may prohibit the merger altogether. Alternatively, it may seek remedies that can alleviate those aspects of the merger that cause the SIEC. The merging parties can offer undertakings to the EC ('plea bargaining') to remedy the anticompetitive aspects of the proposed merger, thereby avoiding its being prohibited. Two possible remedies for curing the merger of its anticompetitive infirmities are possible:

- behavioural; and
- structural.

The EC may consider either or both as appropriate or feasible. It may also prescribe a remedy either from among the undertakings the parties have offered or based on its own analysis of the merger aspects that lead to SIEC. A structural remedy normally involves the divestiture of the offending parts of the merged business that threaten the most SIEC.

With a behavioural remedy the parties to the merger undertake to avoid any predatory behaviour that would be detrimental to their customers, as well as being unfair competition. For example, the firms may offer to engage only in an arm's length relationship with the merger partner. The parties may agree to provide input or customer access to their competitors which might be concerned about foreclosure. They might agree to erect 'firewalls' or 'Chinese walls' to prevent access to information in the merging partner that gives it an advantage over its own competitors. The appropriate undertakings, whether structural or behavioural remedies, may be negotiated by the EC, which then seeks the views of affected third parties about the proposed remedies. The EC may modify the remedies in response to such views if necessary.

Exhibit 17.4 shows how the EC designed both a structural and behavioural remedy to clear one merger. A merger may also be cleared at the end of Phase II without any strings, as shown in Exhibit 17.5.

Exhibit 17.4

'Thou shalt not have too much power', EU tells Veba and Viag

In 2000 the Merger Taskforce investigated the merger between Veba and Viag, the German electricity companies. The power sector in Germany had recently been liberalized, and to ensure the competition was not stifled by a duopoly between a merged Veba and Viag and their rival RWE, the European Commission gave the merger a conditional approval against undertakings given by the merging companies to divest several of their holdings in eastern Germany. VEAG, a major electricity producer jointly controlled by the merging firms and RWE, was thus transformed into an independent power producer. The undertakings also provided for improvements to the rules governing access to the transmission network operated by the two leading groups. In dealing with the case, the Commission worked closely with the German Federal Cartel Office (Bundeskartellamt), which simultaneously investigated and cleared the merger of RWE and VEW, subject to similar undertakings.

Source: European Commission, *European Economy, Supplement A, Economic Trends*, No. 12, December 2001

Exhibit 17.5

Big with merger? Mind your bigger rivals!

On 4 March 2009 the European Commission approved the proposed acquisition of v. d. Linde Arzneitmittel GmbH (v.d. Linde) by Sanacorp Pharmahandel GmbH (Sanacorp), both wholesale distributors of pharmaceutical products in Germany. Sanacorp is active Germany-wide in the wholesale distribution of a full range of pharmaceutical products to pharmacies. v.d. Linde also specialises in the wholesale distribution of pharmaceuticals to pharmacies, with a geographical focus on North-Rhine Westphalia. Through the proposed acquisition Sanacorp would complement its geographical coverage in the distribution of pharmaceuticals throughout Germany: v.d. Linde, a relatively small player on the German market, is only well established in North-Rhine Westphalia, where Sanacorp currently has only minor operations.

The Commission found that the transaction would have only a limited impact on the market structure of the distribution of pharmaceuticals in Germany under any possible geographic market consideration. While becoming the second largest player in Germany, and the third in North-Rhine Westphalia, Sanacorp would face strong competition from four large distributors active throughout Germany: Phoenix Pharmahandel AG, Andreae-NorisZahn AG, Gehe PharmaHandel GmbH and Noweda eG.

Source: Adapted from European Commission, Press release dated 4 March 2009, downloaded from http://ec.europa.eu/competition/mergers/news.html

Conflict of jurisdictions

There are at least two types of jurisdictional conflict that conceivably can arise in the operation of the Merger Regulation. The first is conflict between the European Commission and the member states. The second is conflict between the EU and non-EU countries, such as the US or Japan. We discuss the latter, and the recent international cooperation attempts to harmonize national merger control regimes, after discussing the various national/regional merger regimes.

Although the aim of the Regulation is to avoid multiple antitrust investigations of the same concentrations, in practice both the Commission and the antitrust authority of a member state can claim jurisdiction in a particular case. Articles 9 and 21 of the Regulation allow member states to claim jurisdiction under certain circumstances. Under Article 9 the Commission may refer a merger to the national authority upon a claim by that authority that the merger threatens to create or strengthen a dominant position impeding effective competition in 'a distinct market' within the member's territory, *provided the Commission finds the claim justified*. An example of this transfer of jurisdiction is given in Exhibit 17.6. This clawback provision is known as the 'German clause', so called because the Germans, not willing to trust the Commission's competition credentials too much, insisted on it.

Under Article 21 member states may intervene and claim jurisdiction to protect 'other legitimate interests' not already subject to Community rules. This is a rare occurrence[28]. Such interests include public security, media plurality and prudential rules affecting, for example,

> ### Exhibit 17.6
>
> ## The Czechs can check better
>
> In 2008 REWE, active in food and non-food wholesale and retail, travel and tourism in a number of European countries, notified its proposed acquisition of a Czech target, Plus Discount . In the Czech Republic, REWE operated under the brand names 'Penny' (171 discount shops) and 'Billa' (181 stores in the supermarket sector). Plus Discount was active in the Czech Republic in the retail of everyday consumer goods, and operated 146 discount shops under the brand name 'Plus'.
>
> The main horizontal overlaps between REWE and Plus Discount related to the retail market for everyday consumer goods through modern distribution channels (hypermarkets, supermarkets and discount stores) in the Czech Republic. The Czech Competition Authority (CCA) requested referral of the notified transaction to it because the transaction would affect competition in a number of local retail markets within the Czech Republic, which present all the characteristics of distinct markets and which do not constitute a substantial part of the Single Market. The transaction would threaten to significantly affect competition in these markets. The EC found that the conditions for referral under Article 9(2)(a) of the EC Merger Regulation were met. Although, according to Article 9(3), the EC had discretion to refer only that part of the case relating to the affected distinct markets concerned, the EC considered that due to the local character of the retail markets in the Czech Republic, the CCA would be better placed to investigate the impact of the concentration. For efficiency reasons, and in order not to split the proposed transaction, the Commission decided to refer the entire case to the Czech Republic.
>
> *Source*: Adapted from 'Mergers: Commission refers proposed acquisition of Plus Discount by REWE to Czech Competition Authority', EU press release IP/08/1102, 19 May 2008. More information on the case available at: http://ec.europa.eu/comm/competition/mergers/cases/index/m102.html#m_5112

banks. Where the concentration is not a CCD, Articles 81 and 82 cannot be invoked by the Commission. However, it can be investigated by the national antitrust authorities[29].

Assessment of the Merger Regulation

While concentrative joint ventures that are similar to mergers fall under the Merger Regulation, cooperative joint ventures that resemble cartel arrangements attract Article 81 of the EC Treaty. The distinction between the two types is often difficult to make. Further, definitions of 'controlling interest', 'corporate group', for the purpose of calculating the turnover thresholds, and 'markets', where the proposed concentrations are likely to impede effective competition, are areas of some ambiguity.

The Regulation has a provision for vetting concentrations on grounds which may include contribution to 'technical and economic progress' and 'social cohesion'. It is not clear that these have influenced the Commission's decisions. The performance of ECMR is shown in Table 17.4. Prohibition rate amounts to just 0.5%. If a Phase II inquiry is initiated, the conditional probability of a merger being prohibited is 12.8% (= 24/188). Thus a Phase II inquiry,

Table 17.4 Notifications and decisions under the Merger Regulation during 1990–May 2009

Decision type	Number	Percentage
All notifications on which decision made	3984	100
Phase I clearance – no commitments	3555	89.2
Phase I clearance – with commitments	182	4.6
Phase II initiated	188	4.7
Phase II clearance – no commitments	46	1.2
Phase II clearance – with commitments	89	2.2
Prohibited (Art 8.3)	20	0.5
Order restoring effective competition (Art 8.4)	4	0.1

125 notifications withdrawn are excluded. 52 were decided as outside the scope of ECMR. Under Art 8.4 of the ECMR. 139/2004, the Commission can order dissolution of the concentration already implemented.
Source: Adapted from 'Notifications and decisions under the Merger Regulation during 1990–May 2009', European Commission, downloaded from http://ec.europa.eu/competition/mergers/statistics.pdf, June 2009.

as may be expected, increases the chances of a merger being prohibited quite significantly. This may reflect the tendency for Phase II to be initiated when a merger raises serious anti-competitive concerns. Nevertheless, the regulatory regime does not appear to be aggressive.

The UK merger control regime

Regulation of mergers is part of the UK government's competition policy, aimed at maintaining effective competition in product markets within the UK, or a substantial part of it. Although restrictive trade practices have been subject to government scrutiny since 1948, mergers became the explicit focus of government competition policy only in 1965, with the enactment of the Monopolies and Mergers Act. This Act adopted an administrative means of merger control in the form of a Monopolies and Mergers Commission (MMC). The 1998 Competition Act replaced the MMC with the Competition Commission (CC) to investigate a merger when a merger is referred by the Office of Fair Trading (OFT)[30].

The UK has no mandatory merger notification system. Currently, merger investigation in the UK is a two-stage process. Under the Enterprise Act 2002 (EA 2002) the first stage/phase is a preliminary screening by the OFT[31]. This stage may lead to a reference to the CC (the second stage/phase) of mergers that merit a more detailed investigation. The CC undertakes such an investigation and makes a finding, whether or not the merger has led, or might be expected to lead, to a *substantial lessening of competition (SLC)*. This substantive test was a major change, introduced into the UK regime by EA 2002. Where it finds the merger might lead to SLC, it can accept or impose remedies rather than prohibit the merger. CC has the legal power to require information from the parties that will assist in its investigation. Unlike the pre-1998 system, CC's decisions are binding, and are not required to be accepted by the Secretary of State[32].

Although the UK system is a two-phase system, there is a crucial difference between the UK and the EU and US merger control regimes. In the latter, both the first- and second-phase investigations are carried out by the same agency, whereas in the UK two independent entities, the OFT and the CC, carry them out. Unlike the EU regime, a merger can be lawfully consummated prior to an OFT decision. However, once the OFT makes a reference, 'standstill' provisions will apply, and further implementation of the merger will be suspended.

Office of Fair Trading

The OFT is an independent competition watchdog, and monitors all merger proposals or actual mergers in the UK. It is now headed by a chairman assisted by an independent advisory board and run by a chief executive. From its initial screening of a merger or a proposal, the OFT has to determine whether 'a relevant merger situation has been created' and, if so, whether this has resulted, or may be expected to result, in a *substantial lessening of competition* within a market in the UK for goods and services. Such a situation exists when all of the following conditions apply[33]:

- Two or more enterprises cease to be distinct.
- (a) The combined market share of the merging firms in the supply (or purchase) of goods or services of any description, supplied in the UK or a substantial part of it, will exceed 25% (the *market share test*); or
  (b) the value of the turnover in the UK of the acquired enterprise exceeds £70m (the *size test*).

OFT's interpretation of whether firms cease to be distinct takes into account whether one of the merging firms exercises material influence over policy of, or control over, the other. Such control may be *de facto*, i.e. over policy, or *de jure*, i.e. in the form of controlling interest. It may be direct or indirect. Material influence may be presumed when a firm holds 25% or more of the voting rights in the other[34].

Although a qualifying merger situation may be identified by the OFT, not every such situation is referred to the CC. The OFT judges each case on its merits, and has to weigh whether sufficient reasons for a reference exist. The criteria that it applies to screening qualifying mergers are broadly similar to those discussed earlier in this chapter[35].

There is no statutory obligation for the merging firms to notify the OFT of their merger. The OFT endeavours to complete its assessment quickly, having regard to the timetable for a public company bid under the City Code on Takeovers and Mergers. Under this Code, a bid lapses on its being referred to the CC (see Chapter 18).

The Competition Commission

The CC is an independent advisory body headed by a full-time chairperson, and includes a number of part-time commissioners made up of businesspeople, academics, lawyers, economists, accountants and other specialists. The first task of the CC upon a referral is to establish whether the merger situation qualifies for investigation. It must then determine whether the merger, as a whole or in parts, has resulted, or may be expected to result, in SLC in the UK, or in any relevant market within the UK. The process of determining relevant markets within the UK is described earlier in this chapter.

The CC's deliberations are investigative and not adversarial. The investigations are carried out by small inquiry groups made up of three to five members with relevant expertise. Informality and flexibility characterize the CC's proceedings. The CC first publishes an issues statement, and after taking evidence through formal hearings of the parties to the merger and third parties with interest in the merger (e.g. customers, suppliers), and gathering further evidence from site visits, customer surveys, econometric analysis, specific interest groups etc., it publishes its provisional findings. Where it provisionally decides that there is an SLC from the merger, and that it may be eliminated by remedies, the CC also publishes a remedies notice to allow for the merging firms and other affected parties, e.g. downstream customers of the merging firms, to comment on the possible remedies for the SLC identified. Taking into account these views, the CC publishes its final report of the findings of its inquiry along with, where appropriate, the remedies it is imposing.

The CC may reach one of three conclusions:

- The merger does not result in SLC, and can therefore be allowed to proceed or stand.
- The merger has resulted, or may be expected to result, in SLC, and should therefore be prohibited.
- The merger, although resulting in SLC in some relevant markets, can be allowed, subject to the adverse effects on competition in those markets being remedied.

In making its determination the CC can take into account relevant customer benefits from the merger, e.g. lower prices, higher quality, greater choice, greater innovation. It also can make public interest findings, where appropriate, for the attention of the Secretary of State[36].

Timeline for OFT and CC investigations for completed mergers

In the case of completed mergers that are notified to the OFT or come to its knowledge, the OFT has four months to make its decision. Figure 17.2 shows the timeline for both Phase I and Phase II inquiries in the UK. Clearance means that the merger has not resulted, or may not be expected to result, in SLC. In the absence of the mandatory pre-notification system, the burden of spotting completed mergers in time lies upon the OFT. Once a reference is made, further implementation of the merger comes to a standstill unless the CC consents otherwise[37].

OFT investigation under a merger notice

The EA 2002 (Merger Prenotification) Regulations 2003 provide for voluntary pre-notification of a publicly announced merger bid to the OFT, and a time-bound screening process by it. Under this fast-track procedure the OFT must make its reference recommendations within 20

Figure 17.2   Timeline for OFT and CC investigations in the UK

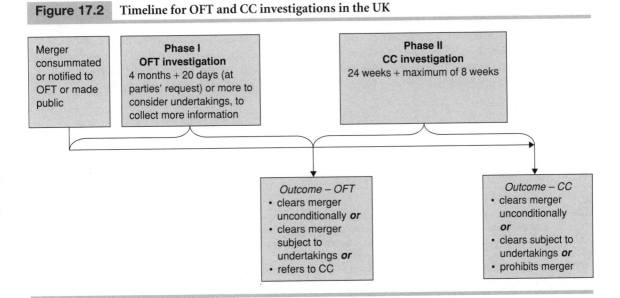

working days (the consideration period). However, where relevant information has not been provided, a maximum of 30 working days is allowed. Once the merger is referred, the CC inquiry follows the same timetable as for completed mergers (see Figure 17.2).

Informal advice and undertaking in lieu (UIL) of reference

The OFT can also be approached by potential acquirers and targets for informal advice before making a formal and public bid. This enables the merging parties to assess the likelihood of a referral and modify their merger proposal if necessary. The confidential advice is, however, not a guarantee against subsequent reference, since a reference can be made only after the merger has been announced and there has been an opportunity for the OFT to seek views from third parties[38]. Moreover, this process does not altogether remove the uncertainty about potential reference to the CC, and takes much the same time as formal notification.

The OFT may accept binding and enforceable divestment undertakings from the merging companies in lieu of making a reference. The undertakings must be appropriate to remedy the effects that might lead to the SLC. Where the offeror can give acceptable undertakings, a reference to the CC can be avoided and disruption of the bid timetable minimized. Table 17.5 provides examples of clearance of a merger by the OFT after obtaining UILs.

With a behavioural remedy, the parties to the merger undertake to avoid any predatory behaviour detrimental to their customers as well as being unfair competition. For example, the firms may offer to engage only in an arm's length relationship with the merger partner. The appropriate undertakings, whether relating to structural or to behavioural remedies, may be negotiated by the OFT[39]. Upon acceptance of these, the OFT monitors compliance with the undertakings and enforces them. The divestments covered by the undertaking must be carried out before a deadline.

Often the remedies offered by the merging firms may be inadequate, or the remedies demanded by the OFT or the CC too stiff. Exhibit 17.7 exemplifies this approach.

First- and second-phase investigations and outcomes

Even when a merger qualifies for CC investigation, a reference is not a forgone conclusion, since the OFT can avoid a reference for a variety of reasons, and has the power to negotiate remedies to remove any SLC. The different outcomes of CC inquiries during 2005–09 are shown in Table 17.6. It is clear that when a reference is made to the CC, the probability of the merger being prohibited outright is very small. Of the investigated (referred) mergers, 52% (38%) did not give rise to SLC. The most preferred remedy is divestiture on its own,

Table 17.5 UILs to escape reference to the CC

Year	Merging firms	What is acquired	What is divested
2006	Hilton/Ladbroke/Jack Brown	141 licensed betting offices	4 offices
2006	Boots/Unichem	958 pharmacies	98 pharmacies
2007	Inchcape/European Motor	52 motor vehicle franchises	1 franchise
2007	Co-op/United Co-operatives	£2bn target (7 overlapping businesses)	Supermarkets/pharmacies etc.
2008	Dunfermline Press/Trinity Mirror	8 newspaper titles	1 title
2009	Global/Gcap	Classic FM, 71 analogue radio stations	4 stations, 1 license

Source: Based on information available from www.oft.gov.uk

Exhibit 17.7

Regulator finds hospital remedy a bitter pill to swallow!

In early 2000 BUPA, the UK's largest private health insurer, made a £230m agreed bid for private hospital and health service operator Community Hospitals Group (CHG). The acquisition would have made BUPA, with 40% of the health insurance market, the largest hospital operator, with a 27% market share. The proposed deal was opposed by the British Medical Association and the Consumers' Association. It was a vertical integration, and the fear among these groups was that BUPA would use its position as a health insurer to channel its customers to CHG hospitals at the expense of rival operators, or offer unfavourable deals in its hospitals to other health insurers. The vertical integration could therefore be anticompetitive. There was also some overlap in hospital service between BUPA and CHG, an element of horizontal merger.

In an attempt to avert a referral to the CC, BUPA argued that the insurance and hospital businesses were run separately, i.e. at arm's length, and that vertical integration would lead to lower insurance premiums. It also offered to dispose of six CHG hospitals that overlapped with BUPA's own hospitals. This remedy was, however, not acceptable to the OFT, and the bid was referred to the CC in June 2000.

The CC recommended rejection of the proposal in December 2000, as the acquisition would have given BUPA a dominant position in private insurance and hospital markets, reducing competition and potentially increasing prices. The Secretary ordered Schroder Salomon Smith Barney, which had acquired a 26.8% stake in CHG on behalf of BUPA, to sell that stake. The CC report said that the separation of the two businesses – the Chinese walls between them – would not be an effective safeguard against increased vertical linkages. The deal might have been saved if BUPA had agreed to demerge its insurance business, but this prescription was unpalatable to it.

Sources: F. Guerrera, 'BUPA acquisition of CHG blocked', *Financial Times*, 8 December 2000; C. Batchelor, 'BUPA's bid for CHG lapses after referral', *Financial Times*, 13 June 2000

Table 17.6 Outcomes of CC investigations 2005–09

Year*	Number completed	No SLC	SLC + divestiture	SLC + behavioural	SLC + divestiture + behavioural	Prohibited
2009	4	1	0	1	0	2
2008	12	5	4	2	1	0
2007	9	4	5	0	0	0
2006	10	7	2	0	1	0
2005	13	8	1	2	0	2
Total	48	25	12	5	2	4

*Year from April to March. 18 of the referred mergers were cancelled during this period. Thus the total number of referrals is 66, of which 25, or 38%, did not give rise to an SLC.
Source: CC Annual Reports 2005 to 2009.

or in combination with behavioural remedy. In such cases, once an SLC is found by the CC, a divestiture of those parts of the merged firms that cause the SLC is required.

During 2006–08 344 mergers were investigated by the OFT under EA 2002. This was about 9–14% of the annual number of UK companies acquired. Of these, 83 were pre-notified. Forty of the cases were referred to the CC, accounting for about 12% of the qualifying cases[40]. Given that only about 6% of the referred and completed cases are prohibited by the CC (see Table 17.6), the proportion of UK mergers that are completely stopped is tiny[41]. However, a significant proportion of mergers screened by the OFT will not survive unscathed. They will be subject to remedial divestitures when cleared and, in a smaller proportion of cases, subject to behavioural remedies. These remedies may reduce the attractiveness of the acquisition to the acquirers. This outcome has important implications for the value creation logic of mergers that managers contemplate.

Enforcement of remedies

Both the EC at the EU level and the OFT and the CC at the UK level have statutory powers to impose remedies. Once these are agreed, they also have the powers to enforce them. In the case of divestitures, the regulators have to ensure that the buyers of the divested businesses have the financial and other resources to maintain them as viable businesses. They also need to be independent of the merging firms. Regulators therefore stipulate that the buyers must be acceptable to them. They also lay down deadlines for the divestiture. To ensure that divestiture takes place as intended by the regulator, a divestiture trustee may be appointed. In the UK, since mergers are mostly investigated after completion, to implement the divestiture remedy it is important that the to-be-divested business be run separately from the rest of the merged businesses. Thus 'hold-separate' is often one of the undertakings that the merging firms should offer the CC and comply with.

How effective are the merger controls?

From time to time regulators subject themselves to some independent assessment of their procedures, as well as the effectiveness of their decisions and remedies where mergers are allowed subject to remedies. In a study of the UK regime carried out by Deloitte and Professor Stephen Davies, 10 cases decided by the OFT and the CC are analyzed in detail[42]. The report of this analysis finds as follows:

- Subsequent market developments raised doubts about the overall soundness of the decision in two cases.
- In the unconditionally cleared DS Smith/Linpac merger there were a series of price rises post-merger. This suggests coordinated effects: the relevant markets exhibited characteristics that academic literature would regard as consistent with potential for tacit or explicit collusion; some customers, however, did not regard the price rises as due to the merger.
- In the EWS/Marcroft case, where the CC found an SLC, there was evidence that the extent of competitive constraints had been understated and entry barriers overstated by the regulator.
- In the remaining six cases market developments did not raise substantial doubts about the soundness of the decisions.

This report, albeit based on a very small sample, shows that regulators take a view of the future developments in markets and base their decisions on probabilities of coordinated effects, competitive constraints etc. Nevertheless, in the majority of cases the regulatory decisions seem to be supported by subsequent market developments[43].

Challenging regulatory decisions

As we have seen, the rulings of the EC under the ECMR are subject to judicial review at the CFI and the European Court of Justice. In the UK, the Competition Appeals Tribunal (CAT) performs the oversight function. In the *Somerfield plc and Wm Morrison Supermarkets plc* case, the CC cleared the merger in 2005 after finding SLC but subject to divestiture of 12 specified stores. Somerfield appealed against this decision to the CAT, and argued against the specification of the stores. The CAT, however, upheld the CC decision. The CAT's adverse decisions often lead to improvement in assessment procedures or rigour of analyses. For example, following the challenge to OFT's decision not to refer the merger of iSoft and Torex, the CAT reminded the OFT that its role was 'primarily that of a first-stage screen to identify where competition concerns *may* arise'. It therefore raised questions about the standard of test for referral applied by the OFT. In light of this judgement, the OFT amended its guidance in 2004[44].

Merger regulation in the US[45]

The US has the longest tradition of antitrust regulation, starting with the Sherman Act of 1890. This Act declared illegal contracts and combinations that restricted interstate trade or trade with other countries, and any attempt at monopolizing this trade a criminal offence. The Sherman Act was not particularly suitable for the prevention of prospective mergers and monopolies, especially in the form of acquisition of stock to gain control of companies.

The Clayton Act 1914 was passed to overcome the shortcomings of the Sherman Act, and was later extended by the Celler–Kefauver Act 1950 to make it more effective in dealing with mergers. Section 7 of the Clayton Act prohibits full or partial acquisition by a commercial corporation of the stock or assets of another engaged in commerce in the country, if the effect of such an acquisition may be *to substantially lessen competition or tend to create a monopoly*. The prohibition applies to horizontal, related and conglomerate acquisitions.

The various statutory rules are enforced by the Federal Department of Justice (DOJ) and the Federal Trade Commission (FTC). Prospective mergers have to be notified to these agencies. Both agencies then investigate and, if necessary, initiate proceedings in Federal courts. The FTC also has various appeal procedures involving the administrative law courts and the independent FTC commissioners. In the past the two agencies were engaged in oneupmanship of competitive enforcement, but have now agreed a truce and division of labour, with each agency focusing on selected sectors[46].

In addition to the above Federal regulation, individual states have their own antitrust laws applying to mergers that would not affect interstate trade. The state attorney-general can bring a suit in the state courts. Affected parties can bring or join proceedings under both Federal and state laws. This contrasts with the EU and the UK position, where affected parties cannot bring a legal action to force the European Commission or the OFT to investigate a merger. Antitrust enforcement in the US has in the past fluctuated from great vigour to deep indifference, depending upon the political current of the times.

Merger control procedures in the US

Merger transactions in which the parties have significant assets or sales are regulated by the Hart–Scott–Rodino Act (HSR). HSR requires such parties to notify the DOJ and the FTC of the transactions, and to observe prescribed waiting periods before completing them. Like the EU's Merger Regulation, HSR stipulates a threshold test of applicability based on the size of

Figure 17.3 Timeline for FTC/DoJ investigations in the US

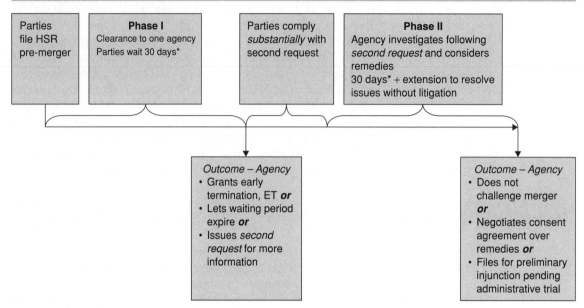

* Fifteen days in Phase I and 10 days in Phase II in the case of cash tender offer or bankruptcy.

the parties, but HSR has an additional test based on the transaction size, similar to the UK's, for a qualifying merger:

- *size of person test*: one of the parties has global sales or assets of $100m or more and the other party has at least $10m or more (these amounts are adjusted each year for change in the US GNP); and
- *size of transaction test*: the acquirer acquires either 15% of the target's voting stock or assets or the value of the voting stock and assets exceeds $50m (this is adjusted each year for change in the US GNP)[47]; and
- either the acquirer or the acquired has commercial activities within the US[48].

After the notification, the proposed merger is 'cleared' to one of the agencies. Like the Merger Regulation, HSR is also a two-phase process, with an initial filing and a '*second request*' for more elaborate information. Figure 17.3 shows the timeline for the merger review process in the US. Agency is either the FTC or the DoJ.

Figure 17.4 shows the number of HSR notifications during 1998–2007, falling from a high in 2000. Part of the reason for the fall is the raising of the notification threshold from $15m to $50m in 2001 and subsequent indexing for US GNP growth. In 2007 it was $59m.

Figure 17.5 shows that very few notifications get past Phase I. Over the same period, second requests were only about 3% of all notifications, the maximum being 4.3% in 2002. These figures are not dissimilar to those for Phase II investigation by the EC (4.7% over 1990–2009: see Table 17.4 above).

Competition theory behind the US antitrust approach

The economic models and the substantive tests applied by the US regulators are broadly similar to those described at the beginning of this chapter. *Substantial lessening of competition*

Figure 17.4   Number of notified transactions under HSR Act

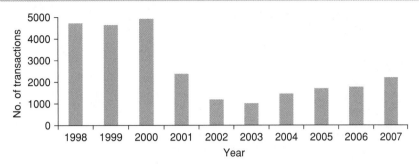

*Note: Fiscal year is from 1 October to 30 September.
Source: Federal Trade Commission (Bureau of Competition) and Department of Justice (Antitrust Division), Hart–Scott–Rodino Annual report, fiscal year 2007, Figure 1. Downloaded from www.ftc.gov

Figure 17.5   Percentage of HSR notices resulting in second request

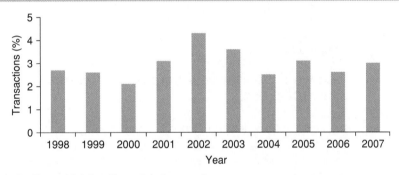

Source: As for Figure 17.1, but Figure 2 in the report

and tendency to create a monopoly are the essential substantive tests of the impact of a merger on competition. The basic model of industry structure and its impact on competition within an industry applied by the US regulators is contestability of markets. In this dynamic model, industry structure is subject to change because of the challenge posed by potential new entrants. Contestability is high where entry barriers are low and the number of potential entrants is large. The contestability model does not presume that oligopolistic structure is *prima facie* evidence of successful collusive behaviour, or that the transformation of industry structure into an oligopoly would, *per se*, substantially lessen competition. As noted above, the UK has adopted the SLC test, and the EU has moved very close to it with its SIEC test.

Remedies and enforcement under Clayton Act

Like the EU and UK regulators, FTC or DoJ negotiates the remedies and, if acceptable, signs a consent agreement. These remedies include both structural remedies, i.e. divestiture, and behavioural remedies. But, unlike the EU and UK regulators, the US regulators need to file an administrative complaint for trial before an administration judge, and to prevent the

Table 17.7 FTC merger enforcement actions, 2004–09

Fiscal year	Consents	Federal injunctions	Admin. complaints	Abandoned	Total
2009	8	5	*	2	15
2008	13	1	1	6	21
2007	14	3	*	5	22
2006	9	0	7	0	16
2005	9	1	0	4	14
2004	10	1	1	3	15
Total	63	11	9	20	103

*In addition to filing for an injunction, FTC also filed an administrative complaint. Fiscal year is from 1 October to 30 September. For 2009 data are up to February.

parties from implementing their merger may seek a preliminary injunction in Federal court. Table 17.7 shows the FTC merger enforcement actions over the years 2004–09. It is clear that in 60% of the cases where FTC takes enforcement action the mergers are 'cleared', subject to remedies. The proportion of abandoned mergers is quite significant, about 27%. Thus US deal-makers have to factor in this risk, although only a tiny proportion of US mergers get into Phase II (see Figure 17.5 above). Exhibit 17.8 provides examples of the various outcomes of Phase II investigations in the US.

Exhibit 17.8

Can we have lots of superpremium vodka please? Absolut(ly) not!

In 2008 FTC challenged Pernod Ricard SA's proposed $9 billion acquisition of V&S Vin & Spirit as harmful to competition among suppliers of 'superpremium' vodka. The proposed deal would have merged the two leading brands, Absolut and Stolichnaya, and allowed Pernod to raise prices profitably on both brands. Additionally, the markets for cognac, domestic cordials, coffee liqueur and popular gin would be subject to anticompetitive effects, because sensitive pricing and promotion information for Beam Global Brands, a competitor in these product markets, would be available to Pernod after the acquisition as a result of Beam's joint venture with V&S. FTC settled the charges by requiring Pernod to divest its distribution interests in Stolichnaya Vodka, and to erect a firewall to prevent the sharing of any competitively sensitive information from Beam Global Brands with Pernod employees.

In 2008 FTC issued an administrative complaint charging that the acquisition of CCC Information Services by Mitchell International, for $1.4 billion, would be anticompetitive in the market for 'estimatics', a database system used by auto insurers and repair shops to generate repair estimates for consumers. The transaction would also harm competition in the market for total loss valuation (TLV) systems, used to inform consumers of such loss. The transaction would create a new entity with well over half of the market share for these systems, allowing for unilateral price increases, and facilitating coordination among the remaining smaller competitors in the market. FTC concurrently filed a complaint in the Federal District Court, and the US District Court for the District of Columbia ordered a preliminary injunction and temporary restraining order preventing the parties from consummating the transaction, pending a full administrative trial on the merits.

In 2008 FTC charged that Agrium Inc.'s $2.65 billion proposed acquisition of UAP Holding Corporation would substantially lessen competition in the market for the retail sale of bulk fertilizer and, in some cases, related services by farm stores, in several local markets in Michigan and Maryland. The acquisition would eliminate important competition between Agrium and UAP, allowing Agrium to unilaterally increase prices, and increasing the likelihood that the remaining competitors would engage in coordinated interaction, to the detriment of fertilizer buyers. FTC ordered divestiture of five UAP farm stores in Michigan, and two Agrium stores in Maryland.

In 2007 FTC challenged Kyphon Inc.'s $220 million proposed acquisition of the spinal assets of Disc-O-Tech Medical Technologies Ltd and Discotech Orthopedic Technologies (collectively Disc-O-Tech) as anticompetitive in the market for minimally invasive vertebral compression fracture treatment products in the US. Disc-O-Tech's Confidence products promised real benefits to patients in treating these painful fractures in a minimally invasive way, and threatened Kyphon's near-monopoly on treatment options. FTC's consent order required that Kyphon divest all assets, intellectual property and development rights related to the Confidence brand to an FTC-approved buyer.

Source: Federal Trade Commission, Enforcement database, downloaded from www.ftc.gov/bc/caselist/merger, June 2009

Antitrust regulation in continental Europe[49]

This section provides a brief overview of the regulation in some EU countries, to indicate the diversity of approaches. Merger controls in continental European countries differ in terms of their approach, their institutional structure, and the zeal with which antitrust regulation is enforced. Almost all EU countries have mandatory notification systems. All of them apply turnover threshold tests to trigger investigation, but Spain also has market share tests. Countries differ in terms of whether the transaction is suspended for the duration of the investigation or whether other constraints apply. Table 17.8 provides a comparative overview of merger control regimes in six major countries that are M & A active. In five of these countries a standstill rule applies. In four countries ministers are not directly involved in clearing or blocking mergers. Substantive assessment test tends to be SLC or SIEC. Some countries allow efficiency and national interest defence.

Critique of merger control regimes

There are some areas of merger regulation that still remain contentious. As we have noted above, the EU's reliance on market structure and the application of market dominance as a test for the potential anticompetitive effects of a merger was subject to judicial criticism, and the EU modified its substantive test as a consequence, and its investigative procedures. Antitrust regulation aims to protect consumer welfare. An alternative perspective is that it

Table 17.8 Merger control regimes in continental European countries

Country	Major law	Pre-merger notification	Thresholds	Review by 1. Phase 1 2. Phase 2	Timetable* 1. Phase 1 2. Phase 2	Substantive test
France	Commercial Code New Economic Regulations Act 2001	Mandatory notification but no time limit; standstill	Based on turnover: worldwide > €150m; in France > €50m	1. Minister 2. Competition Council	1. 5 wks + 3 wks 2. 3 mths 3. Minister, 4 wks	SLC; efficiency defence; international competitiveness
Germany	Act Against Restraints of Competition (GWB) 2007	Mandatory; standstill	Based on turnover: worldwide > €500m domestic > €25m	Both by Federal Cartel Office (BKartA)	1. 1 mth 2. 4 mths Remedies discussed	Creating or strengthening dominance; market share based; efficiency defence
Italy	Competition Act 1990	Mandatory; standstill may be ordered	Based on turnover: domestic > €440m aggregate or target > €44m; annually adjusted for GDP growth	Both by Antitrust Authority (AGCM)	1. 30 days + 30 2. 45 days + 30	Creating or strengthening of dominance to SLC; competitive constraints considered
Spain	Antitrust Law 2007	Mandatory; standstill; no deadline except for public bids	Based on turnover and market shares; 30% market share or domestic turnovers > €240m and €60m	Both by National Competition Commission (CNC)	1. 1 mth + to resolve undertakings; 2. 2 mths	SLC; ministers can overturn on public interest
Netherlands	Competition Act	Mandatory; standstill	Based on turnover; combined > €113m Dutch > €30m; lower thresholds in health care sector	Both by Competition Authority (NMa)	1. 4 wks from receipt of information; 2. 13 wks NMa can impose remedies during both phases	SIEC as in ECMR; efficiency defence
Sweden	Competition Act 2008	Mandatory; no time limit; standstill	Turnover based; worldwide > SEK4bn; domestic > SEK 100m each	Competition Authority (CA); Stockholm City Court can prohibit if CA brings action	1. 25 days + 10 for remedies; 2. 3 mths +	SIEC similar to ECMR; national interest defence

* wk = week; mth = month; ECMR = EC Merger Regulation 139/2004; Standstill means the concentration is suspended during the waiting period. In all countries mergers falling under ECMR are not screened by the national competition authority.

should aim to maximize total welfare, even though some consumers may be hurt. For example, a merger that generates large efficiencies may at least in the short term harm some consumers. Carleton, who is a leading academic and has served with the DoJ, argues that 'it is better to pursue public policies that maximize output and then worry about distributional questions, rather than to pursue inefficient policies'[50]. A pure consumer surplus test favours short-run price reductions over long-run efficiency gains. As noted above, regulators, for reasons of difficulty of forecasting far ahead, and the uncertainty attached to such forecasts, tend to limit their horizons to a reasonable period of say two years. Efficiency gains that arise beyond this period may therefore be ignored. But the short-run view allows the regulator to monitor the effects of mergers with greater confidence.

Regulators have to take a view about future market developments, e.g. market entry and exit, capacity decisions of rivals, changes in international trade regimes etc., but again the view is limited to a reasonably foreseeable period. While this is justifiable on grounds of practicality and relatively more certainty, it also means that this view may under- or overestimate the competitive threats and harmful effects of a merger in the future.

Market definition often raises very tricky questions of reliability. By necessity, regulators rely on a range of techniques to define markets, but these techniques are nevertheless subject to error. Considerable judgement is often involved in making market definition decisions. Inaccurate market definition may again under- or overestimate the effect of a merger on consumers. Defining markets in rapidly technologically evolving industries poses another problem. Another difficult area is 'whether antitrust strikes the right balance between encouraging the sort of market power that provides an incentive for innovation and discouraging the sort of market power that inhibits innovation'[51].

Regulatory risk to M & A deals

While the statistics suggest that the number and proportion of deals eventually prohibited by the CC in the UK or the EU under the ECMR are small, this may not be much comfort to deal-makers. Although many regulators have timetables for investigations, these may be extended to gather further information. There is still a significant element of uncertainty about the eventual outcome of antitrust investigation and the remedies that may have to be offered to win clearance. Such remedies may often unscramble the strategic and value creation logic of the deal.

In recent years the decisions of the regulators have been subject to more judicial scrutiny than in the past, and in some cases the decisions have been overturned on substantive or procedural grounds. This judicial intervention increases uncertainty as well as the cost of litigation, although in the long run it may improve the regulatory process and increase certainty by providing a body of case law. The direct and indirect costs of participating in antitrust investigations also have to be taken into account in evaluating acquisitions that have a significant risk of a long investigation whose outcome is uncertain. Where the deal has been concluded and is then blocked, the costs are even greater (see Exhibit 17.9). A blocked acquisition bid may render the firm vulnerable to predators. The intrusive investigative process also lays bare the company's business strategies, its weaknesses and strengths.

Risk due to multiplicity of jurisdictions

As we have seen, there is a considerable variation in the merger regulatory systems. The tests for invoking the different jurisdictions increasingly rely on global and/or regional turnover

Exhibit 17.9

Happily merged until the EU casts Schneider and Legrand asunder

In July 2001 Schneider Electric, the French electrical equipment maker, acquired a 98% stake in fellow French company Legrand, in the same line of business. This cost Schneider €5.4bn. As permitted under the French takeover regulation, Scheider did not make the acquisition conditional on clearance by antitrust authorities. In October 2001 the acquisition was blocked by the European Commission because of the combined group's large market shares in electrical equipment in a number of countries, such as France and Italy. Although Schneider had offered €400m in disposals as a remedy, the Commission prohibited the merger.

It ordered Schneider to dispose of its 98% Legrand stake. Schneider's rivals, e.g. Siemens and General Electric, showed interest in acquiring Legrand, sniffing a potential bargain because of the forced nature of the disposal. In February 2002 Schneider reported a net loss of €986m, due mainly to the provision of €1.4bn, representing the fall in the value of Legrand. This direct cost understated the total cost, including the earlier acquisition cost, the antitrust lobbying cost, advisory fees, the cost of disposal, and the knock-on effect on Schneider's current businesses.

The French takeover regime, which allowed the deal to proceed despite a possible full investigation by the EC, contributed to the problem. Nevertheless, confidential prenuptial guidance from the EC ahead of the acquisition might have saved Schneider the cost and embarrassment of the forced divorce.

For Schneider and Legrand, however, there was prospect of a happy ending when the Court of First Instance overturned the EC's decision (see earlier discussion in the chapter). If the EC then decided not to launch a fresh investigation into the deal, Schneider would not have to sell Legrand. But it would be obliged to pay a break-up fee of €180m to a consortium of investors to whom Legrand was going to be 'unmerged' (see Chapter 20 for details of break-up fees). But the bliss was short lived. In December 2002 the EC started a four-month investigation, and Schneider sold Legrand to the consortium for €3.6bn compared with the €5.7bn it had paid to buy the company. In addition to this loss, the company also incurred the direct and indirect costs of first merging, then 'unmerging' and litigation. The disruption to the two businesses also added to these costs.

Schneider then sued the EC for damages of €1.66bn. In 2007 CFI upheld the claim, ruling that the regulator's mistakes were so grave that Schneider deserved compensation. It did not, however, uphold the group's full claim, saying Schneider was in part to blame for the losses.

Source: F. Guerrera, 'Brussels blocks Schneider deal with Legrand', *Financial Times*, 11 October 2001; R. Minder, 'Schneider counts the cost of Legrand adventure', *Financial Times*, 28 February 2002; F. Guerrera and M. Arnold, 'Schneider to sell Legrand to consortium', *Financial Times*, 3 December 2002; T. Buck and P. Yuk, 'EU to pay damages over merger deal veto', *Financial Times*, 11 July 2007

thresholds. This means a deal can be caught up in several jurisdictions at the same time. In the EU the hierarchy of merger control rules demarcates jurisdictions between the EU and the member states, but there are instances when several member states can investigate the same merger. A merger can be cleared by one authority but blocked by another. Until the judicial setbacks that it suffered in 2002, the European Commission was steadily raising its stature as a tough regulator, overcoming the initial perceptions as a 'soft touch'. The tough posture that the Commission adopted in the Boeing–McDonnell Douglas case was therefore something of a revelation to the US corporations[52].

Differences between antitrust regimes arise for a variety of reasons. They may differ not only in the substantive tests they apply to determine the harmful effects of mergers, but also in terms of the current and future competitive constraints[53]. There may be divergence in the conceptual models employed by the US and EU regulators, as vividly demonstrated in the General Electric (GE)–Honeywell merger proposal. This deal was cleared by the FTC but blocked by the EU. One of the major issues for the EU on which its blocking decision turned was the ability of GE to bundle the aircraft engine, aviation electronics and aircraft leasing operations so as to gain a competitive advantage over its rivals. The bundling model supposes that firms cross-subsidize their products and services to maintain their competitive advantage in the markets for these (see Chapter 8 for an evaluation of this model). When the EU blocked the GE–Honeywell deal, the reaction from not only GE but also the US regulators was quite scathing, and somewhat disdainful of the economic theories underpinning the EU regime.

Multiplicity of jurisdictions increases the transactional risk to firms undertaking mergers. It also provides opportunities for these firms to arbitrage between these jurisdictions to get clearance from one regulator so that other regulators will follow suit. Rivals of merging firms can also play this game, by complaining to another authority to investigate the deal. In the AOL–Time Warner merger being investigated by the FTC, Disney with similar interests in media and cable television complained to the European Commission, which was regarded as being more aggressive. Even though the deal was not stopped, the complaint might have forced changes in the merger proposal[54]. A multiplicity of jurisdictions can lengthen the bid time and create considerable uncertainty in deal completion.

International Competition Network[55]

It is clear from the foregoing analysis of merger control in different jurisdictions that there are similarities in competition theories and analytical approaches, but there are also substantial differences, which often lead to friction and cause much uncertainty for stakeholders in mergers that have international effects. There is thus much need for greater convergence among these jurisdictions.

In October 2001 the US and 13 other jurisdictions around the world created the International Competition Network (ICN). The ICN now includes 107 member agencies from 96 jurisdictions. It seeks to provide a forum for antitrust agencies to address antitrust enforcement and policy issues of common interest, and formulate proposals for procedural and substantive convergence. It has set up merger working groups that develop and propose recommended practices. For example, recently ICN members adopted three new recommended practices for merger analysis:

- competitive effects analysis in horizontal merger review;
- unilateral effects;
- coordinated effects.

Stock market reaction to merger references

Franks and Harris investigate the shareholder wealth impact of the OFT references to the MMC, using monthly abnormal returns for a sample of about 80 UK takeover bids[56] (see Chapter 4 on abnormal returns methodology). MMC referrals lead to wealth losses of 8% in the referral month for target shareholders. They lose further in the report month when the MMC report is adverse. Thus most of the gains to targets on bid announcement that are subsequently lost might have arisen from increased market power of the merging firms. Both referrals and MMC reports have a broadly neutral impact for bidder shareholders.

In a recent analysis of the stock market reaction for a sample of 50 mergers between 1989 and 2002, Arnold and Parker estimate daily abnormal returns surrounding referral by the OFT, the MMC/CC decision[57], and all the relevant events between bid announcement and bid closing (called 'overall' return). They find that sample bidders make insignificant 1% returns overall, but when the MMC/CC prohibits the mergers they experience −7% returns (significant at 1%). Their returns are insignificant in the case of accepted mergers. Target firms gain 14% overall, 21% in mergers that are eventually allowed, and only 5% when they are prohibited. The overall gain of 14% is less than what targets normally experience (see Chapter 4, Table 4.4). Prohibition thus reduces gains to both bidders and targets, suggesting that at least some of these gains may have been due to potential in market power[58]. Thus we have consistent evidence that substantial increase in market power is a source of value to shareholders in some mergers, but they are likely to be precluded from these gains when antitrust authorities intervene to prohibit such mergers[59].

CASE STUDY

William Hill takes a bet on Stanley Leisure and swallows OFT remedy

On 18 June 2005 William Hill (WH) plc, a leading UK licensed betting office (LBO) operator acquired the LBOs of Stanley Leisure plc (SL). The merger brought together the second and fourth largest LBOs by shop count in the UK. The Office of Fair Trading (OFT) investigated the impact of the merger on the competition. The issues for the OFT were:

- the relevant market in which the competitive impact should be assessed;
- the market structure of the relevant market/s;
- nature of competition among LBOs;
- theories of harm;
- any counterfactual considerations; and
- buyer power that might constrain the merging firms from exercising their market power.

Relevant market/s

The companies supplied betting services and competed in some areas. Telephone and Internet betting was not considered part of the relevant market as such betting catered for a different clientele who placed larger bets on average and needed to have access to a telephone, or a computer and Internet, and a credit card. Geographically, the relevant markets considered were both national and local. Local markets were defined as falling within a radius of 400 metres or 800 metres around both firms' LBOs. The OFT considered those localities where the number of facias (shops) fell 3-to-2 or 2-to-1 within a 400m radius and 2-to-1 within a 800m radius.

Market structure and the impact of the merger

The number of LBOs owned by different companies and their gross revenues in the UK LBO market at the time of the acquisition are shown in the table below:

Company	Shop count	% of supply	Gross win (£m)	% of supply
Ladbroke	1941	23	600–700	20–30
William Hill	1613	19	500–600	15–25
Coral	1176	14	350–450	10–20
Stanley	561	7	100–200	0–10
Betfred/Done	500	6	50–100	0–10
Tote	460	5	50–100	0–10
Others	2249	26	600–700	20–30
Total	8500	100	2550–2650	
Wm Hill + Stanley	**2174**	**26**	**650–750**	**25–35**
HHI	1433–1470		1600–1700	
ΔHHI	250		150–250	

HHI is the Herfindahl-Hirschman Index and ΔHHI is the increase in HHI resulting from the merger. William Hill would become the largest supplier of LBO services after the merger controlling 26% of the betting shops. However the overlap between the two was limited since WH was strong in the South East whereas SL was strong in the north west of the UK. The overlaps based on different local market definitions were:

Geographic definition	Reduction in facias	Number of LBOs
400m radius	2-to-1	41
400m radius	3-to-2	26
800m radius	2-to-1	12
Total		79

Nature of competition

Pricing of a bet is in the form of odds on or against a win. Competition on setting the odds was limited since most bets were placed at the starting prices that were common across all LBOs especially in the case of horse and greyhound racing that accounted for 80% of the bets although the LBOs competed in setting the odds on other types of events, e.g. football games. Thus in general, LBOs competed mainly on non-odds dimensions, e.g. branding, quality of outlet, product range, stake limits and opening hours. There was also competition in relation to staff bonuses and the terms and conditions attached to the bets.

Theories of harm

These were considered at both the local and national levels. The OFT was concerned that the reduction in the number of facias might result in reduction of competition in non-odds terms of the services. It received very little quantitative evidence of the reduction in odds or non-odds competition but some evidence was produced by a third party that staff received higher bonuses when the number of LBOs in an area was higher, pointing to keen local competition. WH staff training also emphasised the local competition dimension. At the national level, Stanley was not considered a strong competitor with a strong brand and had failed to invest.

Barriers to entry

New entrants had to get betting office licenses and invest in premises and in building up their brands. The OFT considered that these were not low enough to alleviate competition concerns at the local level.

Counterfactual

There was no indication that either company would exit the LBO market in the absence of the merger. So this was not relevant.

Buyer power

Individual customers of the LBOs were not in a position to exercise any power against the companies. Thus competition concerns would not be mitigated by such power.

The OFT decision and remedy

After considering the above aspects of the merger situation, the OFT decided that the acquisition might be expected to result in an SLC in those localities where it resulted in a reduction in a number of facias within a 400m or 800m radius, as shown in the table above.

Upon this finding, WH offered, and the OFT accepted, undertakings in lieu (UIL) of a reference to the Competition Commission to divest the LBOs identified by the OFT. Thus the divestiture remedy was chosen to address the SLC that the acquisition had given rise to.

WH sold 78 shops to Tote between September and December 2005.

Discussion questions

1 What is the nature of the business affected by the acquisition of SL by WH?

2 What is the competitive structure of the industry prior to the acquisition?

3 What were the OFT's approaches to the investigation of the impact of the acquisition? What analytical tools did it use?

4 What was the OFTs' finding?

5 What was the remedy to address the consequences of the finding?

Source: Adapted from Deloitte LLP, 'Review of merger decisions under the Enterprise Act 2002', Report prepared for the Competition Commission, Office of Fair Trading, and the Department for Business, Enterprise and Regulatory Reform, 18 March 2009. Public version available from www.oft.gov.uk

Overview and implications for practice

This chapter has provided an introduction to the rules and regulations governing mergers and acquisitions in the US and the EU from the antitrust perspective.

- Various theories of the harm that may arise as a consequence of mergers, and the techniques used for detecting them, are discussed.

- There is a hierarchy of these regulations, divided between the EU and the national authorities, based on the principle of one-stop shopping.

- The EU investigates and decides on concentrations with a Community dimension (CCD). These are mergers affecting several EU member countries and not one country only.

- National antitrust regulations govern mergers with overwhelming competitive effect in one and the same member country.

- EU and other countries, especially the US, have in some cases overlapping jurisdiction. This increases the scope for jurisdictional conflict and the risk and cost of a merger deal.

- The US antitrust regulations under the Clayton Act have similarities with and differences from the UK and EU regimes.

- Different regulators apply different economic models to assess whether a merger is anti-competitive. This has caused friction in some cases; but recent years have seen greater convergence of substantive tests for harmful effects.

- In many countries of the EU and other European countries merger control regimes have been set up recently, and there is much uncertainty surrounding the operation of these regimes.

- In the UK and the rest of the EU major changes have been introduced into the procedures and/or the conceptual basis of what is anticompetitive. These changes have also increased the uncertainty, at least in the short term.

- Judicial intervention, long an essential part of the US regime, may become an increasing part of the European regimes too. This may lengthen the time for resolution of merger control issues, and increase uncertainty and the cost of mergers.

- The regulatory risk needs to be carefully considered when contemplating acquisitions.

Review questions

17.1   What do you understand by antitrust regulation?

17.2   What are the various theories of harm from mergers? In horizontal mergers? In vertical mergers? In conglomerate mergers?

17.3   What are the objectives of antitrust policy? Should they be restricted to just competition grounds?

17.4   What is the structure of the antitrust regime in the UK, EU and the USA? Contrast and compare.

17.5   What are the criteria used by the UK and EU regulators to investigate mergers?

17.6   What are the remedies available to cure mergers of antitrust aspects?

17.7 What are the alleged shortcomings of the EU regime?

17.8 How do antitrust regulations in Europe and the US compare? What are the similarities and differences?

17.9 What does the stock market reaction to merger referrals and decisions say about sources of value and risk to the deal?

17.10 What is the impact of a bid being subject to multiple antitrust jurisdictions?

Further reading

D. Carleton, 'Does antitrust need to be modernized?', *Journal of Economic Perspectives*, **21**(3), 2007, 155–176.
The Economist, 'Oceans apart: Mergers and dominant firms', 3 May 2008.
The Federal Trade Commission and Department of Justice, *Horizontal Merger Guidelines*, 1997.
M. Furse, *The Law of Merger Control in the EC and the UK* (Oxford, UK: Hart Publishing, 2007).

Notes and references

1. I am a member of the Competition Commission (CC) in the UK, and have benefited from the comments of Anthony Pygram at the CC on this chapter. However, the views expressed in this chapter are my own, except where they are explicitly attributed, and do not reflect the views of the CC or Anthony Pygram. I am also responsible for any factual or interpretational error in discussing the CC's role as a regulator in this chapter.
2. The Federal Trade Commission (FTC) and the Department of Justice (DoJ) (hereafter just FTC), *Horizontal Merger Guidelines*, 1997, p. 17.
3. *Critical loss analysis* is among several analytical tools employed by antitrust regulators to assess the pre- and post-merger competition in a market.
4. See European Commission (EC), Guidelines on the assessment of horizontal mergers under the Council Regulation on the Control of Concentrations between undertakings, Official Journal, C31, 5.2.2004, 5–18.
5. See note 2.
6. Case T-342/99, *Airtours plc v Commission* (2002) Downloadable from http://eur-lex.europa.eu/LexUriServ/LexUriServ.do?uri=CELEX:61999A0342:EN:HTML
7. Vertical mergers may give rise to other anti-competitive effects, not discussed above. They may, notably, 'allow the merged firm to gain access to commercially sensitive information about the upstream or downstream activities of non-integrated rivals, allowing it unilaterally to compete less aggressively in the downstream market or to otherwise put rivals at a competitive disadvantage. Less commonly, a vertical merger may have the effect of restoring upstream monopoly power; this could occur where a monopoly input supplier could not extract high prices from downstream firms before a merger because it could not credibly commit not to supply their competitors' (Competition Commission and Office of Fair Trading (CC & OFT hereafter), *Merger Assessment Guidelines*, joint consultation document, April 2009).
8. It may be argued that by strengthening the competitive position of the merged firm in the market for B, where it is relatively weak, the merger actually *strengthens* competition. In this sense, a conglomerate merger can be *pro-competitive* rather than *anti-competitive*.
9. CC & OFT, *ibid.*, para 4.12.
10. These landmark cases decided by the CFI include: *Airtours/ First Choice* 1999; *Schneider/ Legrand* 2001; *Tetra Laval/ Sidel* 2001. Other important cases are: *General Electric/ Honeywell* 2001; *Sony/ BMG* 2004. For a discussion of these cases and the judgements of the CFI, see M. Furse, *The Law of Merger Control in the EC and the UK* (Oxford, UK: Hart Publishing, 2007), Ch. 8.
11. I served as a member of the inquiry group at the Competition Commission for this merger.
12. Demand substitution depends on the product's own price-elasticity of demand as well as the cross-elasticity of demand for the substitute product to which demand is switched. 'An own-price elasticity of −1 means that a 5 per cent increase in the price of the product results in a 5 per cent decrease in the quantity sold of that product. Demand is said to be elastic when the own-price elasticity is more negative than −1: that is, when a 5 per cent increase in price leads to a greater than 5 per cent fall in the quantity sold. Demand is inelastic when the elasticity is less negative than −1 (i.e., is closer to zero). Similarly a cross-

price elasticity of +1 means that a 5 per cent increase in the price of product A results in a 5 per cent increase in the quantity sold of product B. For products A and B to be substitutes, the cross-price elasticity between them must be positive (as an increase in the price of one product leads consumers to substitute to the alternative product). For products A and B to be complements, cross-price elasticity between them must be negative (as an increase in the price of one product leads consumers to buy less also of the alternative product because they are complementary, i.e., are consumed together)' (CC & OFT Guideline, April 2009, fn 46). Estimates of elasticity, demand substitution and supply-side substitution are made with econometric models using past price and volume data.

13. FTC in the US has broadly similar thresholds: >1000 plus Δ100 and >1800 plus Δ50 raise significant concerns. >1800 plus Δ100 more likely to 'create or enhance market power or facilitate its exercise'. See FTC, *Horizontal Merger Guidelines, ibid.*, p. 15.

14. These include: asymmetry of impact on competitors, whether products are intermediate products rather than consumer products, chains of substitution, captive production etc. For a further discussion of these see CC & OFT, *ibid.*

15. See Furse, *ibid.*, p. 42.

16. Moreover, there may be other social costs arising from the failure. Allowing the target to be acquired can mitigate some of these adverse outcomes. The acquisition, by preserving the productive capacity of the target, avoids a welfare loss to the society.

17. See CC & OFT, *ibid.*, paras 4.27 to 4.33, for further discussion of the failing firm doctrine and how it is applied by the UK regulators.

18. This regime has been extended to cover the European Economic Area, broader than the EU.

19. See P. S. Sudarsanam, *The Essence of Mergers and Acquisitions* (Hemel Hempstead: Prentice Hall, 1995), Chapter 6, for further details of these cases.

20. For example, in the *Anglo American Corporation/Lonrho* (case M.754), a 27.5% stake by Anglo American in Lonrho was considered enough to exercise decisive influence. In making this determination the EC took into account other factors, such as ownership dispersion among other shareholders.

21. By the same token, even very high market share may not lead to the merger being blocked after Phase II investigation. See *Danish Crown/Vestjyske Slagterier* (case M.1313), which, despite a 80% market share, was cleared.

22. Article 4 of ECMR 139/2004. Deals not fulfilling these conditions, but where there is an agreement in good faith to conclude such a deal, may also be pre-notified. EC may grant derogation from suspension of the notified concentration under Article 7 taking into account the impact on one or more of the merging parties, e.g. bankruptcy, but this is rare. Out of 3984 notified concentrations from 1990 to May 2009, only 103 (just 2.6%) received such derogation (source same as in Table 17.1).

23. The suspension decision was challenged by the parties to the merger. The Court of First Instance, however, upheld EC's right to suspend. See case T-145/06 of the CFI and EU Memo 09/49 dated 4 February 2009.

24. 'EU stops clock on Pfizer–Pharmacia deal', *Economic Times*, 20 November 2002.

25. See Francesco Guerrera's articles in the *Financial Times*, 'Ruling on Airtours will affect EU competition policy' (7 June 2002), 'Monti's trials' (13 June 2002), 'Brussels "wrong" to block French Merger' (23 October 2002) and 'Tetra Laval pushes Brussels over takeover' (20 November 2002). For further discussion of these cases see M. Furse, *ibid.*, Ch. 7.

26. The changes also included many procedural reforms, e.g. flexibility in the timetable for extensions if parties ask for them, a stronger focus on economic analysis of data to support the EC's conclusions, more rigorous analysis etc.

27. See Furse, *ibid.*, pp. 180–187, for a discussion of these judgements.

28. Only 8 out of 3984 notifications from 1990 to May 2009 have been decided under Article 21 of ECMR 139/2004 (source as in Table 17.1).

29. Where a company becomes the target of multiple bids, both the EU and a member state may exercise jurisdiction over the different bids, with the result that they may be investigated with different and potentially inconsistent criteria. This situation is illustrated by the bids by the Hong Kong and Shanghai Banking Corporation and the UK's Lloyds Bank for the UK target Midland Bank in 1992. The HSBC bid fell within the ECMR, and the EC cleared it within two weeks, but the Lloyds bid fell under the UK jurisdiction. The UK first-phase agency, the Office of Fair Trading, decided to refer it to the second-phase investigator, the Monopolies and Mergers Commission (MMC). So HSBC stole a march over Lloyds, and Lloyds abandoned the bid. Midland was taken over by HSBC. See J. Love, 'The operation of the EC mergers policy: the Midland Bank takeover', *Journal of General Management*, **20**(1), 1994, 29–43.

30. Until June 2003 it was the Secretary of State who, acting upon the OFT recommendation, referred mergers.

31. The OFT was created under the Fair Trading Act 1973 (FTA), which has now been replaced by the Competition Act 1998 and the Enterprise Act 2002 as regards its responsibilities, powers, organizational structure etc.

32. Except where the case has been referred to the CC by the Secretary of State on specified public interest grounds. In such circumstances he has to accept the CC's competition assessment, but can reach his own view of the public interest issues raised, and his own decision on any remedy, if necessary.

33. At least one of them is likely to be a UK or UK-controlled company.

34. A share of less than 15% may, if other factors indicate so, confer material influence. See Office of Fair Trading, *Substantive Assessment Guidance*, 2003. For further discussion of the criteria for qualifying mergers see Furse, *ibid.*, Ch. 10. Also see the CC & OFT, *ibid.*, 2009, for the current thinking of these two UK competition authorities on competitive assessment processes.

35. For more detailed statements of these criteria and their rationale, see OFT, *Substantive Assessment Guidance*, 2003, *ibid.*

36. When there is an adverse finding, the CC can consider whether to modify its proposed remedy to retain any relevant customer benefits from the merger. The CC has a limited role in making public interest findings when the Secretary of State asks it to consider a specified public interest issue when referring a merger on public interest grounds. Its public interest findings are, however, not binding on him or her.

37. See Section 77 of EA 2002. Similar restriction applies to anticipated mergers under section 78.

38. See OFT, *Interim Arrangements for Informal Advice and Pre-notification Contacts*, 5 January 2007. Downloaded from www.oft.gov.uk.

39. UILs involving behavioural remedies are used relatively rarely by the OFT.

40. Source of these statistics is the merger statistics annexe to the OFT annual report 2007–08. This may be downloaded from www.oft.gov.uk. These statistics may differ from those in Table 17.6 because of differences between the number of cases referred to the CC and the number of inquiries completed by it, number of mergers cancelled etc. Some merger inquiries by the CC are not completed in the same year as their referral by the OFT.

41. This is confirmed by evidence from previous periods. Over 1998 to 2001 the OFT examined 1511 cases, of which 915 qualified for investigation. Of the qualifying mergers, 42 (4.6%) were referred to the CC. 207 cases were pre-notified under the fast-lane scheme described above. In 2001 (2000 figures), of the 10 (14) investigations made by the CC, five (two) were held against the public interest, two (four) were abandoned, and three (four) were held not against the public interest. For evidence from an earlier period, see J. Fairburn, 'Evolution of merger policy in Britain', in M. Bishop and J. Kay (Eds), *European Mergers and Merger Policy* (Oxford: Oxford University Press, 1993), pp. 239–277. He reports that, between 1965 and 1986, out of a total of 3540 qualifying mergers only 107 (3%) were referred to the MMC. Of these, 33 (31%) were abandoned by the bidders. For 1989 to 2002 Arnold and Parker report that qualifying mergers were 3165 (32% of all UK reported mergers). Of these, 1.6% were referred to the MMC/CC, which made adverse findings in 0.7% and no adverse finding in 0.6% of the cases. 0.3% of the cases were abandoned by the bidders. Behavioural, structural remedies were applied by the MMC/CC in 0.2% and 0.3% of the cases, and 0.2% were prohibited. For 1989 to 2002, Arnold and Parker report that qualifying mergers were 3165 (32% of all UK reported mergers). Of these, 1.6% were referred to the MMC/CC, which made adverse findings in 0.7% and no adverse finding in 0.6% of the cases. 0.3% of the cases were abandoned by the bidders. Behavioural, structural remedies were applied by the MMC/CC in 0.2% and 0.3% of the cases, and 0.2% were prohibited. See M. Arnold and D. Parker, 'UK competition policy and shareholder value: The impact of merger inquiries', *British Journal of Management*, **18**, 2007, 27–43. Thus the vast majority of mergers and acquisitions do not raise serious competition issues, and only a tiny proportion of qualifying mergers are actually investigated. An even smaller proportion are prohibited.

42. See Deloitte LLP, 'Review of the decisions under the Enterprise Act 2002', 18 March 2009, public version available from www.competition-commission.org.uk. See the executive summary of the report for overview.

43. The EC also commissioned LEAR to develop appropriate methodologies to assess post-decision developments in markets affected by a merger and evaluate the soundness of EC decisions. The authors apply various methodologies to a single case, *Pirelli/BICC*, and conclude that the decision to clear the merger was sound, as judged by the stock market reaction, post-decision customer surveys etc. See Laboratorio di

economia, antitrust, regolamentazione (LEAR), 'Ex-post review of merger control decisions', 2006, down-loaded from http://ec.europa.eu/competition/mergers.

44. See Furse, *ibid.*, pp. 258–261 and 275–278 for a further discussion of these cases.

45. For a detailed discussion of the legal and economic bases of the US antitrust regime see E. Giellhorn and W. E. Kovacic, *Antitrust Law and Economics* (St. Paul, MN: West Publishing Co., 1994), Ch. IX.

46. P. Spiegel, 'Antitrust agencies in division of labour', *Financial Times*, 6 March 2002.

47. On 13 January 2009 the thresholds were $13m (for original $10m), $65.2m ($50m) and $260.7m ($200m). The adjusted amounts each year can be found in the HSR website, www.ftc.gov/bc/hsr/introguides/guide2.pdf, and this can be linked from the FTC website www.ftc.gov.

48. The rules on who should file the notification and who is exempt are rather complex. For an introduction to these rules see HSR Premerger Notification Program Introductory Guide II *To File or Not to File, When You Must File a Premerger Notification Report Form.* This can be downloaded from the FTC or HSR web-sites. See previous footnote.

49. This section draws upon *A Practitioner's Guide to Takeovers and Mergers in the European Union* (Old Woking: City & Financial Publishing, 2001), various chapters.

50. See D. Carleton, 'Does antitrust need to be modernized?', *Journal of Economic Perspectives*, **21**(3), Summer 2007.

51. See Carleton, *ibid.*

52. N. Aktas, E. de Bodt, M. Levasseur and A. Schmitt, 'The emerging role of the European Commission in merger and acquisition monitoring: The Boeing-McDonnell Douglas case', *European Financial Management*, **7**(4), 2001, 447–480.

53. *The Economist*, 'Oceans apart: Mergers and dominant firms', **387**, 3 May 2008, p. 89. This article discusses political, economic and historical reasons for differences.

54. R. Byrne, 'Merger-busting gets harder in Europe', www.thestreet.com/_yahoo/markets/rebeccabyrne.

55. See Department of Justice press release, 'International competition network adopts recommended practices to improve merger analysis and presents reports on unilateral conduct issues', 5 June 2009, downloaded from www.usdoj.gov. For more information about the ICN see www.internationalcompetitionnetwork.org.

56. J. Franks and R. Harris, 'Shareholder wealth effects of UK takeovers: Implications for merger policy', in M. Bishop and J. Kay (Eds), *European Mergers and Merger Policy* (Oxford: Oxford University Press, 1993), pp. 134–161. They report that the average gain for target shareholders when the bids for their companies are cleared by the MMC is 38% over the period from 12 months before to one month after the report. This suggests that, where bids are not rejected by the MMC, the gains to the merger may arise from sources other than increased market power. In the case of rejected mergers, the target shareholders gain only 9% over the same interval. For the bidders, the return over the period from 12 months before to one month after the MMC report is not significant.

57. M. Arnold and D. Parker, *ibid.*

58. Forbes investigates the abnormal returns to bidder shareholders around three dates – bid announcement, MMC referral and MMC decision dates – using a sample of 53 UK bids and daily returns. The impact of referral on returns is not significant, whereas bidders whose bids are cleared by the MMC enjoy a significant 0.3% over three days and 0.81% over 21 days surrounding the MMC decision. Bidder share-holders whose bids are stopped by the MMC experience non-significant gains over the same periods. Thus Forbes' results are broadly in line with those of Franks and Harris. See W. Forbes, 'The shareholder wealth effects of Monopolies and Mergers Commission decisions', *Journal of Business Finance and Accounting*, **21**(6), 1994, 763–790.

59. This is consistent with the results of a small sample analysis of 20 mergers from 1991 to 1995 subjected to EC investigation under ECMR, where EC's 'serious doubts' or announcement of a suspension decision adversely affected the companies' share prices. See U. Brady and R. Feinberg, 'An examination of stock price effects of EU merger control policy', *International Journal of Industrial Organization*, **18**, 2000, 885–900.

CHAPTER 18

Regulating takeover bids

Objectives

At the end of this chapter, the reader should be able to understand:

- the importance of takeover regulation for the orderly conduct of takeovers;
- the salient features of the UK self-regulatory system;
- the evolving EU takeover regulations and the US regulation;
- how takeover regulations differ in other countries;
- the major characteristics of these different regimes;
- the implications of takeover regulations for takeover bid and defence strategies; and
- the economic rationale for takeover regulation, and its impact on takeover activity, value creation and value sharing from takeovers.

Introduction

In Chapter 17 we discussed the statutory regime governing the antitrust and public interest aspects of mergers. This chapter describes the framework within which takeover bids are conducted. We start with the UK framework, since it is the oldest takeover regulatory regime, and forms the philosophical basis of the more recent European Union Takeover Directive[1]. This framework, in the form of the City Panel on Takeovers and Mergers and its rule book, the City Code on Takeovers and Mergers, is concerned mainly with bids for public companies. Bids for private companies are regulated by the provisions of the UK Companies Act 2006 (CA2006). The EU Directive on Takeovers, which seeks to provide a EU-wide framework for bids, together with its shortcomings, is discussed. After describing the UK and the EU regimes for takeovers, we compare their counterparts in the US and in some major European countries. Since the EU Takeover Directive has been substantially based on the principles of the UK Takeover Code, an understanding of the UK regime is particularly useful in understanding the evolution of takeover regulation in Europe.

Rationale for takeover regulation

In Chapter 3 we introduced the market for corporate control as a mechanism for allocating corporate resources to different management teams that can deploy them more efficiently and create value for shareholders and enhance social welfare. Hostile takeover is an important tool in this reallocation process, and can correct managerial failure. It can also correct managerial entrenchment, i.e. when managers run a company in their self-interest rather than in the interests of shareholders. Whether the market for corporate control can perform this efficiency-enhancing role depends on the way takeovers are regulated. This regulation is quite distinct from antitrust regulation, which we discussed in the previous chapter. A robust takeover regulation should facilitate orderly control transfers, by eliminating obstacles in the form of entrenched managers, skewed ownership rights, corporate structures that reduce transparency and obscure the relation between ownership and control, etc.

The importance of regulating the bid process

In a takeover bid involving an offer by the bidder to purchase shares from the target company shareholders there is much scope in principle for manipulative tactics from both the bidder and the target management. Some of these tactics are as follows:

- selective release of information during a bid;
- special deals with the larger target shareholders denied to the smaller ones;
- creating a false market in either bidder or target shares;
- insider dealing; and
- frustrating action by the target management, which denies the target shareholders the opportunity to accept a fair offer.

Thus the target company shareholders, especially the multitude of small shareholders, may be the victims of 'sharp practice' unless the process is properly policed. Further, the bid process, if prolonged inordinately, will render the target management unable to manage the firm. Such an incapacitation is to the detriment of managers, staff, shareholders, suppliers and customers of the target firm. Thus a definitive time-bound process is desirable.

Takeover regulation in the UK

A takeover is a means of achieving a controlling interest in the target company. A public offer extended to all the target shareholders is only one way in which the controlling interest can be passed on from the existing to new shareholders. Other transactions that could also result in control transfers include private contract; issue of new shares by the target; redemption of target shares; share capital reconstruction; and schemes of arrangement.

Since shares in private companies are not widely held, the need for regulation of takeover bids is much less for them than for public and listed companies. In the UK the regulatory body for takeovers of public companies is the City Panel on Takeovers and Mergers (the Panel), administering the City Code on Takeovers and Mergers (the Code).

The EU Takeover Directive and the Panel jurisdiction

Under the Directive on Takeover Bids (the Directive hereafter in this chapter), the Panel has both exclusive and shared jurisdiction over mergers, as shown in Figure 18.1[2]. Under the

Figure 18.1 **The Takeover Panel jurisdiction over takeovers**

*Note: The securities may be listed on an unregulated market, such as the Alternative Investment Market (AIM) in the UK. The test of location of the central management is known as the residency test.
**Note: There are several cut-off dates for choice of jurisdiction under this condition. Refer to the City Panel for further details. UK jurisdiction includes the Channel Island and the Isle of Man.

Directive, the scope of jurisdiction of a member state is based on the location of the registered office and the regulated exchange on which the target company's securities are listed. EEA is the European Economic Area, which includes the EU and non-EU European countries, e.g. Switzerland and Norway. In the UK the Code also applies to private companies that fulfil certain criteria, e.g. they have been listed on the London Stock Exchange in the previous 10 years. It is obvious that shared jurisdiction is a matter of some complexity. In some cases the target companies can ask for the Panel's jurisdiction, but the Panel may refuse.

Scheme of arrangement

A scheme of arrangement (SoA) is carried out under Sections 903 to 918 of the Companies Act (CA) 2006. It is a scheme between the target company and its shareholders, and requires the cooperation of the target. A takeover proposal may be the subject of a scheme. Such a scheme, when agreed by three-quarters in value of shareholders, needs to be sanctioned by the court. Once sanctioned, the scheme is binding on all shareholders, thus obviating the problem of minority shareholders after acquisition. Thus it is easier to squeeze out the minority share-holders and convert the acquired company into a private company that facilitates the use of its assets to finance its acquisition. For leveraged buyouts (LBOs) this is a particularly attractive route to access the assets of the target company and use them to pay down the acquisition related debt.

The bidder also saves 0.5% stamp duty, because the old shares are cancelled rather than sold. For UK companies with many US shareholders, a scheme of arrangement allows the bidder to avoid filing a registration statement with the US Securities and Exchange Commission[3]. SoAs are friendly deals. Dissident shareholders must hold more than 10% of the voting shares to block a squeeze-out in a conventional takeover, whereas under an SoA they need more than 25% to do so. Thus activist shareholders with small stakes will find it more difficult to challenge a merger (see Chapter 13 on shareholder activism and its impact on takeovers).

Because of the involvement of the court, a scheme is tedious, time consuming and expensive. For this reason, mergers by schemes of arrangement were much less frequent than public offers under the Code. For example, in their study of UK mergers during 1955–85, Franks and Harris find only 121 schemes of arrangement, compared with 1693 public offers[4]. However, in recent years SoAs have again become more popular because of their attractions, as noted above. In 2002 only eight companies worth £11.5bn were acquired using such schemes, whereas in 2007 the arrangement was used for 47 companies worth £58bn, including 28 of the 36 takeovers worth more than £250m[5]. The Panel, taking note of this trend, has modified several of its rules to bring the SoAs under its purview (see below).

The Takeover Panel: its origin and structure

The Panel was promoted by the Bank of England in response to rising concern about some of the market 'rigging' and manipulative activities of bidders and target managements. It came into being in 1968. It was created as a self-regulatory, non-statutory authority, a character it retained until 2006. Its aim is to provide a speedy response to takeover situations, and to ensure a fair and orderly transfer of ownership of companies in the stock market. Its philosophy is to promote best practice rather than minimally acceptable conduct among those involved in takeovers. This philosophy permeates the six General Principles and 38 Rules of the Code.

The Panel is both a rule-making and a rule-enforcing body. Until recently the legislative and enforcement functions were not clearly separated. In response to criticism that its rule-making process was obscure, and lacked transparent public participation, the Panel created a Code Committee to carry out the legislative function after due public consultation. The Panel's enforcement function encompasses adjudication of disputes between parties to a takeover by the Executive, and this adjudication is subject to two layers of review – by the Hearing Committee and a by Takeover Appeals Board (TAB). The rulings of the Hearing Committee are binding on the parties unless and until overturned by the TAB.

The membership of the Panel includes representatives of investment institutions, their trade associations, banks, the accountancy profession and industry. The chairperson and two deputy chairpersons are appointed by the Panel. The Panel Executive is headed by the Director-General, normally on secondment from an investment bank, and is staffed by a mixture of permanent Panel employees and those seconded from the City firms.

The day-to-day work of the Panel is carried out by the Panel Executive, whose decisions and interpretations of the Code can be challenged before the Hearings Committee. There is also a right of appeal from this Committee to the TAB, which is headed by a chairman and two deputy chairmen with experience of high judicial office. The major part of the Executive's work is to provide guidance when companies contemplate an action covered by the Code, and the Panel encourages early consultation. The surveillance team monitors market dealings in the shares of companies in the offer period, or may go into it. This team focuses on enforcing compliance with the disclosure requirements of the Code.

The Panel's role has been recognized and its jurisdiction over takeovers supported by the court and other self-regulatory organizations such as the Stock Exchange. In the landmark Datafin case in 1986, which involved two rival bids for McCorquodale, Datafin challenged the Panel ruling. The Court of Appeal held that the proceedings of the Panel were subject to judicial review. This review does not amount to an appeal. The focus of the review is to ensure that the Panel has observed its own rules and procedures fairly. The effect of this ruling (the *Datafin doctrine*) is to prevent any tactical litigation in challenge of the Panel's rulings while a bid is in progress. This position of the court has been affirmed in further cases in 1988 and 1992.

The Panel's authority is also recognized by the UK government and regulatory bodies under the Financial Services and Markets Act (FSMA) 2000, which came into effect in 2001. The Panel can receive information from the Department for Business Innovation and Skills (formerly known as the Department of Trade and Industry or DTI) that the latter obtains in the course of an investigation, and can use this information to form its own rulings.

The rules of the Financial Services Authority (FSA), the apex regulator of financial services in the UK under FSMA, and other organizations such as the Securities and Futures Authority or the London Stock Exchange, provide that the firms authorized to carry on investment business should not act for clients or with professionals who are not prepared to comply with the Code ('the cold shoulder rule'). Further, practitioners in breach of the Code may be deemed by the FSA as not 'fit and proper' to carry on investment business. Such a judgement may lead to loss of authorization to carry on investment business. Nevertheless, there is scope for jurisdictional overlap and friction between the FSA under FSMA and the Panel (see discussion below).

Following the Takeover Directive (see below for a discussion of this), which has now been incorporated into the UK Companies Act 2006, the Panel has gained some statutory powers:

- to require disclosure of documents and information;
- to require compensation to be paid to target shareholders; and
- to seek enforcement orders from the courts.

Considering the 100% compliance with its rulings under the pre-statutory regimes, the Panel has indicated that it does not expect that it will need to exercise these powers.

Under CA 2006, rulings of the Panel have binding effect, parties to a takeover are not able to sue each other for breach of a rule-based requirement, and a transaction, once completed, may not be unpicked[6].

The City Code

The Code operates principally to oversee conduct of bids, and to ensure fair and equal treatment of all shareholders in relation to takeovers. The Code is not concerned with the financial or commercial advantages or disadvantages of a takeover. Nor is it concerned with competition and other public policy issues, which are the province of antitrust authorities (see Chapter 17). The Code represents the collective opinion of professionals involved in takeovers as to good business standards, and how fairness to shareholders can be achieved.

Further, the Code seeks to achieve a fair balance between the interests of the offeror (the bidder) and of the offeree (the target) company and its shareholders. The Code has jurisdiction over bids for UK resident public companies (both listed and unlisted) and certain statutory, chartered and private companies. These private companies must have been, in the previous 10 years, listed at any time on the Stock Exchange or involved in the sale of their equity share capital, or must have had dealings in their shares advertised. (For a more detailed description of the jurisdiction, see the Code.)

The Code is based on six general principles and 38 rules. These rules are clarified by notes, which accompany them. The Panel promulgates new rules or provides new interpretation of existing rules in response to developments in the takeover market. Speed and flexibility of such response are the hallmarks of the self-regulatory system that the Panel embodies.

The principles

Prior to the implementation of the Directive the Code had 10 General Principles but now has six, which are summarized as follows[7]:

- There must be equivalent treatment of all holders of securities of the same class in takeover bids; if a person acquires control of a company, the other holders of securities must be protected.
- Adequate information must be provided in a timely manner, and advice to enable holders of securities to reach a properly informed decision on the bid; where the offeree board advises holders of its securities, it must give its views on the effects of the takeover on employment, conditions of employment and location of the company's place of business.
- The board of the offeree company must act in the interests of the company as a whole, and must not deny the holders of securities the opportunity to decide on the merits of a bid.
- False markets must not be created in the offeree's securities, or those of any other company concerned by the bid.
- The offeror must announce a bid only after ensuring that the cash consideration, if offered, can be fulfilled, and taking all reasonable measures to secure the implementation of any other type of consideration.
- The offeree must not be hindered in the conduct of its affairs for longer than is reasonable by a bid for its securities.

As regards the fifth principle, the Code imposes responsibility for compliance not only on the offeror but also on the financial adviser (see Exhibit 18.1 below).

The rules

The 38 rules flesh out these principles, to give direction to concerned parties and their advisers in specific situations. The rules impose obligations as well as enjoining certain courses of action. Where a particular situation is not covered by a rule, the Panel will apply the relevant general principle to arrive at its ruling. At all times in the interpretation of the rules, the Panel seeks compliance with their spirit, and not merely their letter. A brief summary of some of the more important rules now follows. This summary carries the health warning that it should be used only as a signpost to the rules, and not as a substitute.

- *Possible offers (Rule 2.4)*. The panel can order, at the target's request, the bidder to '*put up or shut up*', i.e. make a firm offer or announce it will not be making an offer within a specified time. In the latter case the bidder cannot make another offer for at least six months, or 12 months in the case of excessive siege by the potential bidder (see Exhibit 18.3 below).
- *Preconditions to offers (Rule 2.5)*. The only preconditions allowed are for regulatory reasons.
- *Mandatory bid (Rule 9)*. When a person or a group acquires 'interests' carrying 30% or more of the voting rights of a company, it must normally make a cash offer (or a share offer with a cash alternative) to all other shareholders at the highest price paid in the previous 12 months. Similarly, if the holder of 30% or more of the voting rights adds to that holding in a year, a mandatory bid is generally required[8].
- *Mandatory cash offer (Rule 11.1)*. When an offeror purchases shares carrying 10% or more of the voting rights in the offer period, or in the previous 12 months, or any class of shares under offer during the offer period, the offer must include a cash alternative at the highest price paid by the offeror.
- *Mandatory securities offer (Rule 11.2)*. When an offeror purchases offeree shares carrying 10% or more voting rights in exchange for securities during or within three months prior to the commencement of the offer period, it must make a securities exchange offer to all holders of offeree securities of the same class. A cash alternative may also be required if the vendors are not obliged to hold on to the shares until the offer period concludes.
- *Uniform price offer (Rule 6.2)*. If the offeror buys shares in a target company at a price above the offer value, the offer must be increased to that price.

- *Minimum level of consideration (Rule 6.1).* This is the highest price paid by the offeror for any target shares during the three months prior to commencement of the offer period, or even earlier if the Panel deems it necessary. The offeror may seek dispensation if the target share price has collapsed substantially as a result of new public information about the target.
- *Independent advice for target shareholders (Rule 3).* The target management must obtain competent and independent advice on the offer, and communicate it to its shareholders with its own views. This assumes particular importance in MBOs (see Chapter 11). Where the offeree board is split, the minority board view must also be communicated.
- *Equality of information (Rule 20.1).* All shareholders must be given the same information (see Exhibit 18.3 below).
- *Information for employees (Rule 30).* Offerors should provide bid information to employee representatives or employees at the same time as the offer document is mailed. Similarly, the offeree board also must provide timely information to its employee representatives or employees.
- *Equality of rival bidders (Rule 20.2).* Prospective rival bidders should have access to the same information from the target company (see Exhibit 18.3 below).
- *Equality of treatment (Rule 16).* Special deals with favourable conditions for selected shareholders are banned. Irrevocable commitment to sell should not confer any valuable benefits on the person giving them.
- *Integrity of information (Rule 19).* Profit forecasts and asset valuations must be made to high standards and reported on by professional advisers, who must declare their responsibility.
- *No frustrating action (Rule 21).* The target company cannot undertake any frustrating action during the offer unless shareholders approve. This is one of the most distinguishing characteristics of the UK regime (see discussion of the European Takeover Directive art. 9 below).
- *Disclosure and prohibition of share dealings (Rule 8).* There are no restrictions on the offeror, its concert parties or associates during an offer period; but there are stringent disclosure requirements for share dealings during an offer. Financial advisers to target companies are prohibited from buying or facilitating the purchase of target shares during an offer.
- *Timetable for a bid.* In general, offers must close 60 days after the posting of the offer document. Parties must observe other deadlines in the offer period (see later).
- *Impact of antitrust actions (Rule 12).* A bid lapses if it is referred for Competition Commission or European Commission Phase II investigation. Bids must be made subject to this condition (see Chapter 17 on antitrust investigations).
- *Break-up fee (inducement fee) (Rule 21.2).* The Panel must be consulted where an inducement fee or a similar arrangement is proposed. The offer document must disclose any such fee payable by the offeree. Such break-up fees, and break-up fees when the target breaches the 'no-shop' agreement, must not exceed 1% of the offer value[9].
- *Twelve-month moratorium (Rule 35).* No renewal of a failed bid is allowed for 12 months unless a rival bid for the target emerges, or the renewed offer is recommended by target management. This prohibition does not apply to bids cleared by the Competition Commission or the European Commission when the offeror can renew the bid within 21 days.

Determination of control

The Code's mandatory bid rule (Rule 9) embodies a concept of effective control defined in terms of the threshold of 30% of voting rights. When effective control of their company changes hands, the shareholders must be given the opportunity to decide whether they want to continue to hold their shares in the same company. The term 'interest in shares' includes

Exhibit 18.1

Contracts for differences make a difference

In 2004 BAE Systems made an offer for Alvis and obtained irrevocable commitments from a number of investment funds that had bought CFDs referenced to Alvis' shares amounting to 16% of its share capital. Some of the funds agreed to request physical settlement of the CFDs and then assent all shares so received to BAE. Other funds consented to the counterparty to their CFDs giving BAE irrevocable commitment to accept BAE's offer in respect of the Alvis shares it held to hedge the CFDs.

Source: A. Ryde and R. Turnill, 'Share dealings: Restrictions and disclosure requirements', in *A Practitioner's Guide to the City Code on Takeovers and Mergers 2008/09* (Woking, UK: City & Financial Publishing, 2008), p. 72 (hereafter the *Practitioner's Guide*)

physically held shares as well as derivative contracts that confer the right to buy the shares, e.g. options, and those where the holder of the contract does not acquire the shares physically. A *contract for difference* (CFD) is one such derivative contract, in which the buyer only settles the difference between the 'contract price' and the current price of the share on which the contract is written. However, a CFD can also allow for physical delivery of the share in settlement. The counterparty to the CFD in general hedges the contract by buying the share, and may also cast the vote as instructed by the CFD buyer. Thus the CFD buyer has interest in shares carrying voting rights, although not physically owning the shares See Exhibit 18.1 on how CFDs affect the calculation of 'interest'. When this interest is committed to the bidder, the aggregate interest of the bidder in the target shares increases.

The Code also covers voluntary bids made when the effective control threshold has not been breached. Table 18.1 compares the conditions attached to mandatory and voluntary bids under the Code.

Table 18.1 Conditions for mandatory and voluntary bids

Mandatory bid	Voluntary bid
Required if bidder has acquired interests in 30% of target's voting shares or, if already owning interests of 30% or more, has increased the holding (Rule 9)	Made when bidder has not breached mandatory bid threshold
Offer extended to all target shareholders	Offer extended to all target shareholders
Offer must be cash or with cash alternative at the highest price paid in the previous 12 months	Offer need not be cash unless bidder breaches the mandatory cash offer rule (see the summary of rules above)
Offer must become unconditional when acceptances lead to bidder holding more than 50% of voting rights in target	Bid may be conditional on a higher minimum of acceptances
Offers for voting non-equity shares must be made	Not required, but offer cannot be declared unconditional unless acceptances for at least 50% of total voting rights are received Offer conditions must be objective and not subject to offeror directors' judgement
Offer cannot be subject to 'no material adverse change' (MAC), consents from other parties or clearances from regulators	Offer can be made subject to such conditions (see case study on Panel ruling on MAC at end of chapter)

In a voluntary offer the offeror may set a high minimum acceptance such as 90% for the offer to become unconditional, but can reserve the right to waive this condition and declare the offer unconditional even at 51% acceptance level. Moreover, a minimum acceptance level of 90% is often advantageous, as it could allow the successful offeror to buy out the minority compulsorily under CA 2006 (see below for further discussion). A 90% acceptance level would also enable the acquirer to qualify for merger accounting (see Chapter 15 for details). Ownership of 90% also allows the acquirer to take the target company private, although the minority can move the court to challenge that resolution. With 95% ownership the dissenting minority cannot move the court. If the target becomes a private company, restrictions on target providing financial assistance to the acquirer to buy its shares are few.

Acquisition of 75% voting rights is also useful from tax, financing and control perspectives. The target can form part of a 75% tax group, with significant tax advantages to the acquirer[2]. Any special resolution to convert the target into a private company is passed more easily when the acquirer already owns 75% of voting rights. Such a conversion may be a prelude to the target providing financial assistance to the offeror. This assistance may be used to finance the acquisition itself. If the acquisition is being financed by debt, with the target's assets providing security for the borrowing, the offeror's lenders may want a 90% acceptance. This increases the offeror's control over those assets, for example through the ability to buy out the minorities. The increased control enhances the security to lenders. Further, if more than 25% of the target shares are still in public hands, they may, under the London Stock Exchange rules, still be listed, with a consequent loss of control to the acquirer.

Setting a high minimum acceptance level means the offer may perhaps have to be kept open longer, with the outcome of the bid more uncertain. However, a voluntary offer is much more flexible, and conditions under the Code are less stringent. A mandatory offer is generally to be avoided if possible. During the years 1991–2001 (year ending 31 March) the number of proposals screened by the Panel was 1459. Of these only 110 (7.5%) were Rule 9 mandatory bids. During 2002–08 the number of proposals was 894, of which 59 (6.6%) were Rule 9 bids[10]. It is a moot point what purpose the mandatory bid rule serves if it is so minimally used. We return to this question below when we discuss the impact of takeover regulation on takeover activity.

Implications of price, payment method and mandatory bid conditions under the Code

It is clear that these rules begin to bite long before a bidder makes the bid announcement, in the case of cash purchases exceeding 10% of target's voting equity, 12 months before announcement. Potential bidders must carefully evaluate share purchases in potential targets as part of the acquisition strategy. In general, such purchases are likely to be made at lower prices than the subsequent formal offer price. However, the opposite situation may also arise if the target share price slides in the run-up to the formal bid. More important perhaps is the lack of flexibility in choice of payment currency that such a purchase might impose, i.e. a cash alternative has to be added even in a voluntary offer.

Other constraints of the mandatory offer for the firm's post-acquisition integration plans must be considered. Where such integration presupposes 100% control, a mandatory offer is inappropriate. Post-acquisition restructuring may be much more difficult after a mandatory bid that leaves a large minority in place where it requires approval by, say, 75% of voting shares. Since a mandatory bid reduces the chances of using the target's funds to finance the acquisition, the acquirer's financing costs may be higher than in a voluntary bid. The absence of group tax benefits at less than 75% control may also raise the acquisition cost. A mandatory offer is also perhaps more expensive, since the bidder may not be able to invoke conditions

Table 18.2 Bid timetable under the Code

Announcement day	The bidder announces the offer with all terms and conditions
Posting day (Day 0)	Offer document must be posted within 28 days of offer announcement
Day 14	Last day for target recommendation to its shareholders and for response to offer document
Day 21	First offer closing day. Offer may be extended. Offeror may buy target shares in the market above 30% under voluntary offer rules
Day 35	End of grace period for acceptance when offer went unconditional on Day 21
Day 39	Last day for target to release new information, e.g. profit forecast
Day 42	1. If offer had become unconditional as to acceptances on Day 21 this is the last date for fulfilling all other conditions 2. After this day target shareholders can withdraw their acceptances if offer was not declared unconditional on Day 21
Day 46	Last day for bidder to revise and post offer terms, e.g. raise offer price, or release new information, e.g. dividend forecast
Day 60	Final closing date, i.e. last day of offer period. Bid either fails or is declared unconditional as to acceptances
Day 81	Last day for clearing all other conditions attached to bid
Day 95	Last day for delivery of consideration if offer went unconditional on Day 60 and Day 60 is not extended.

such as material adverse change (MAC) to 'wriggle out' of an offer. It is therefore not altogether surprising that the mandatory bid in the UK has been as popular as the plague.

The bid timetable

It is the objective of the Code that the bid process should be brought to a definitive conclusion within a predictable time frame, in general of no more than three months. The reasoning behind this stance is that any protracted siege of the target will detract from the target management's task of managing the company, and may create uncertainty for managers, employees, customers and suppliers, and lead to loss of value for shareholders. The Code therefore lays down milestones on the timetable for a hostile bid. This timetable is shown in Table 18.2.

Where an offer becomes unconditional as to acceptances, it must also become unconditional in all respects not later than 21 days thereafter. The Code also allows another 14 days for the payment of consideration from the day the offer becomes wholly unconditional. The timetable can be extended at the discretion of the Panel. For example, if there is any delay in the Office of Fair Trading (OFT) decision to refer the bid to the Competition Commission (CC), the Panel can 'stop the clock', thus allowing the bid to proceed after the OFT has cleared the bid. Where a competing offeror for the target emerges, its bid timetable is available to the first offeror. The withdrawal right given to the accepting target shareholders increases their leverage and helps them get a better price in the event of multiple bids for the target.

The Code recognizes that bidders and target companies may camouflage their intentions and actions before and during an offer. It therefore employs the concepts of 'concert party' and 'associate' in defining the obligations and responsibilities of parties to a takeover. 'Persons acting in concert comprise those who, pursuant to an agreement or understanding (whether formal or informal) actively cooperate, through the acquisition by any of them of shares in a company, to obtain or consolidate control of that company' (the Code Definitions). The obligations under the Code are extended to the concert parties. For example, in determining whether a mandatory bid has become necessary, the share purchases by the offeror's concert parties will be taken into account.

The term 'associate' is intended to cover all persons (whether or not acting in concert) who directly or indirectly own or deal in the shares of the offeror or the offeree company in an offer, and who have an interest or potential interest in the outcome of the offer (see the Code for a more comprehensive definition). Associates may include subsidiaries, professional advisers such as investment banks, directors and their close relatives, and company pension funds. Ownership or control of 5% of shares may lead to a rebuttable presumption that the holder is an associate. Associates have the obligation to disclose their dealings in the offeror or target company securities and any arrangements concerning those securities such as an indemnity.

Bid timetable with competing bids

When a rival bidder enters the fray for the same target, the timetable of the first bidder cannot run its course, since it will preclude an auction, and the target shareholders will be the losers. Hence the first bidder's timetable is extended by the Panel by extending Day 46 and correspondingly Day 60. For example, in the Ferrovial Consortium bid for BAA, the UK airports operator, in 2006, Day 46 passed but there was a rival Goldman Sachs-led consortium (GS) bid that was yet to announce its bid formally. The Panel extended Day 46 and Day 60 so that Ferrovial could post a revised offer in case GS outbid its current offer. Not to have extended the timetable would have denied BAA shareholders the opportunity of a much higher premium from the winner of the auction. In the event GS did make a formal higher bid but was, in turn, trumped by Ferrovial's final bid.

If, on Day 46, two rival offers are outstanding and neither is a final offer, the Panel now runs an open auction under Rule 32.5. In this process each bidder is granted a set period within which to respond to any revised offers announced by the competing bidder, but the Panel can 'guillotine' the time period of the auction. In the Corus steel acquisition there were two rival bidders, and the Panel accelerated the auction by specifying the maximum number of rounds that would be allowed, i.e. nine (see Exhibit 18.2).

Exhibit 18.2

Tata lands a knock-out punch in round 9

In 2006 Corus, the Anglo-Dutch steel maker, was the object of a heated bidding bout between Tata Steel Limited (Tata) from India and Companhia Siderugica Nacional (CSN) from Brazil. On 20 October Tata and Corus announced an agreed bid, to be implemented by a scheme of arrangement. Three days earlier CSN had approached Corus with a competing higher bid, and on 11 December it announced an offer, subject to the condition that the Tata scheme lapsed or was withdrawn. Corus shareholders were to vote on the Tata scheme on 20 December. The Panel required CSN to post its offer document to Corus shareholders.

The Panel set 30 January 2007 as the end date for an auction, but on 30 January neither bidder declared its offer final. The auction then entered the accelerated phase, with the Panel specifying a maximum of nine rounds. Bids were made in private to the Panel and then communicated to the bidders. In the first eight rounds the bidders made fixed price bids, but in the ninth they could make a formula bid, i.e. a specified amount in cash they would pay more than the other bidder's highest offer, subject to a maximum bid. The auction ended when Tata submitted a winning bid of 608p compared with its offer of 500p before the auction. The final bid valued Corus at £6.7bn. The Tata scheme was approved by the court in early 2007. CSN's bid was 603p.

Was the outcome a sweet triumph or a winner's curse for Tata, which paid 20% more for Corus than before the auction? In a recent interview Ratan Tata admitted that his company persisted in the auction, since pulling out would have hurt national pride: forays of Indian business houses into foreign markets through acquisitions had generated much pride and euphoria in India! In another, he admitted 'he might have gone too far too fast'*.

Source: The Panel Statements 2007/4 and 2006/24; * *Hindustan Times*, 11 May 2009

A detailed discussion of the application of the Code rules is beyond the scope of this book. A flavour of the pragmatic way in which the Panel interprets these rules and the general principles is provided from a selection of cases decided by the Panel in Exhibit 18.3.

Exhibit 18.3

Panel decisions in a selection of bids

Quality of profit forecast

During the hostile bid by Dixons Group for Woolworth Holdings in 1986, Woolworth produced a profit forecast. The Panel ruled that this was not up to the Code standards, and that the Panel had not been consulted as required by the Code. The Panel required the deficiencies in the statement to be made good, and accordingly extended Day 39. The Panel also expressed surprise at the advice given to Woolworth by Rothschilds, its financial adviser (Panel Statement 1986/25).

Highest price to all

Guinness won the bid for Distillers in 1986. It had an undisclosed concert party arrangement with Pipetec of Switzerland, which bought Distiller's shares on behalf of Guinness during the bid, but at a higher price (731 pence) than was on public offer (630.3 pence cash alternative). The concert party was only discovered during the DTI fraud investigation into Guinness. It breached the Code that the highest price should be extended to all target shareholders. The Panel ordered Guinness in July 1989 to pay some £85m compensation to Distillers' shareholders, including interest (Panel Statement 1989/13).

Independent advice for target

In the 1997 bid by Abbey National for Cater Allen, Dresdner Kleinwort Benson (DrKB) was appointed to act as investment bank adviser to Cater Allen.

However, DrKB had a close, recent and continuing advisory relationship with Abbey National, having been one of its advisers since Abbey's flotation. The Panel considered DrKB would not be an appropriate person to give independent advice to Cater Allen, and emphasized the importance of the adviser not only being, but also being viewed objectively as, independent. Cater Allen therefore appointed another adviser (Panel Statement 1997/9).

'Put up or shut up'

When a potential offeror has announced a possible offer, there is no fixed deadline in the Code for that potential offeror to clarify its intentions to make a firm offer. This would depend on the reaction of the offeree company, and on the readiness of the potential offeror. A prolonged time lag, however, creates uncertainty, and possibly a false market in the offeror and offeree shares. To end the uncertainty, one of the parties could approach the Panel to impose a deadline. Wolverhampton & Dudley Breweries (WDB) was the subject of two rival approaches by Botts and Pubmaster in early 2001. After several months of talks WDB approached the Panel in April 2001 to end the process. The Panel ruled that each party must either announce an offer ('put up') for WDB by 1 June 2001 or announce it would not proceed with an offer ('shut up'). An offer was then made before the deadline (Panel Statement, 2001/6). Depending on whether the target had been under prolonged limbo, a six- or 12-month moratorium on any subsequent offer would apply to the potential offeror.

Virgin is special!*

In April 2006 NTL, the cable operator, made an offer for Virgin Mobile (VM), in which Virgin Enterprises (VE), a member of the Virgin Group, had a 71% interest. VE entered into a separate agreement to license the Virgin brand to NTL. Because of the conflict of interest between VE and non-VE shareholders of VM, the Panel required the licence deal to be approved by a simple majority of independent shareholders, i.e. holding the 29% stake. In addition, the independent directors of VM stated that the deal terms were arm's length commercially negotiated and reasonable. A similar statement was made by VM's independent financial adviser.

Time stands still at the Panel!

In 2008 WPP Group plc notified its offer for Taylor Nelson Sofres plc (TNS) to the European Commisison, and was awaiting its decision on Phase II investigation. This decision would be known only by 23 September. Day 39, the last day for TNS to release its final defence document, however, fell on 9 September. The Panel therefore ruled that 'Day 39' would be deemed to be the second day after the announcement of the EC decision. 'Day 46' and 'Day 60' were also extended as a consequence (Panel Statement 2008/40).

Source: * *Practitioner's Guide, ibid.*, p. 178

Statutory rules

As noted earlier, schemes of arrangement are carried out under sections 903 to 918 of CA 2006 (previously under sections 425–427 of CA 1985). CA 2006 also requires an acquirer to notify the target of purchases resulting in a holding of 3% or more of the voting shares within two days. Any 1% change above that threshold needs to be similarly notified. The use of a public company target's resources to provide financial assistance to pay for the acquisition is generally prohibited (sections 677–679). Proposed compensation payments to directors in connection with a takeover for loss of office that occurs because of a takeover must now be disclosed in the annual directors' report (sections 215–219).

When the share stake build-up is carried out through nominees, CA 2006 gives companies the right to require disclosure of the true owners of the shares (section 793). Failure to respond to a notice is an offence punishable by imprisonment or a fine. A company may also assume power, in its articles, to disenfranchise those shares or appeal to the court to do so. An offeror who has 90% of its offer accepted can then compulsorily purchase the remaining 10% of the shares that are the subject of the offer (sections 974–982). This provision helps the acquirer to get rid of any unwanted minority. Offerors and offerees providing documents not compliant, as regards their contents, with Rules 24 and 27 of the Code may be guilty of a criminal offence.

The FSMA 2000 requires offer documents, which are investment advertisements, to be approved by authorized persons (section 21). In a securities exchange, listing particulars must be published and be free of defective particulars. The FSMA prohibits misleading statements and practices. The Company Securities (Insider Dealing) (ID) Act 1985 prohibits a person who has received price-sensitive information about an offer or contemplated offer from a person connected with a company from dealing in shares in the target company. It is a criminal offence not only to deal, but also to counsel or procure others to deal. Under the Criminal Justice Act 1993 it is a criminal offence for an individual who has information as an insider, such as a director, to deal in securities whose price would be significantly affected if the insider information were made public. It is also an offence to encourage insider dealing and to disclose inside information to others with a view to their profiting from it.

Market abuse rules under FSMA 2000

The FSMA, which came into effect in December 2001, provides a comprehensive supervisory regime for the UK capital markets and financial services industry. The FSMA has created a new civil regime to punish market abuse. The supervisory authority under the Act is the Financial Services Authority (FSA). The FSA can take disciplinary or enforcement action against a person committing market abuse, or encouraging another to behave in a way that will amount to market abuse by the first person.

The takeover market is one of the markets covered by FSMA. The Authority can take disciplinary action against a financial adviser for breach of the Code at the Panel's request as if he or she had breached the Authority's rules.

In particular, the FSA's enforcement policy is that it will not normally intervene in takeovers unless the Panel's powers are inadequate to address the market abuse. Furthermore, where it does intervene, it will do so only after the process is over. The Authority has given certain provisions of the Code a 'safe harbour' status under which compliance with certain provisions of the Code would not amount to market abuse. The Authority and the Panel have also developed operational arrangements, made public, with the objective of ensuring that there is minimum disruption to the takeover timetable where market abuse may be occurring[11].

The London Stock Exchange rules

The regulations of the London Stock Exchange (LSE) concern the following:

- the announcement of takeover bids;
- the need for shareholder approval for large transactions;
- the content of offer documents and notification to the LSE; and
- the content of listing particulars when securities are issued in consideration.

LSE's Listing Rules divide acquisitions, disposals, takeovers and mergers into size classes. Size is expressed as a percentage of the target's net assets or profits, or the consideration paid or gross capital in relation to the offeror's net assets, market capitalization or gross assets (for the detailed criteria for size classification, see the London Stock Exchange Listing Rules). The LSE imposes one or more of the following obligations on the offeror in class transactions: notify the Regulatory Information Service (RIS) at the LSE, send a circular to the offeror shareholders with details of the offer, and obtain their approval for the transaction at a general meeting. As the class size of a transaction increases, the obligations become more onerous.

A reverse takeover is one where the size ratio exceeds 100%. This means that in an acquisition the target is larger than the listed offeror, and thus control of the offeror may pass to the target shareholders. When a reverse takeover is announced, the offeror's listing is suspended pending approval by the offeror shareholders at an extraordinary general meeting. If the takeover is approved, the company will have to apply for listing as a new applicant. In that event, the company would normally produce listing particulars conditional on shareholder approval so that listing can be granted immediately following the approval.

The various size classes and their respective obligations under the LSE Listing Rules are shown in Table 18.3. The Listing Rules stipulate deadlines for the dispatch of notification and circulars, and for shareholder approval. Where shareholder approval is required, as for a Class 1 or reverse takeover bid, the offeror must take care not to invite the obligation to make a mandatory bid, since it cannot be made conditional upon such approval (Rule 9.3 of the Code). Listing particulars are required if offeror share capital is increased by 10% or more as a result of an equity financed offer.

If a public company offeror (target) indemnifies an associate purchasing offeror (target) shares against losses, such an arrangement is a criminal offence, as it amounts to extending unlawful financial assistance to buy its own shares under CA 2006[12]. In some deals merging partners enter into arrangements to pay break-up fees to compensate the other party for undertaking the trouble of entering the merger agreement. It also compensates to some extent for any opportunity loss suffered by one party if the other party is taken over by a rival bidder. The Code limits the break-up fee to a reasonable amount, in general 1% of the deal value (see Chapter 20 for more on break-up fees).

Table 18.3 Transaction type and obligations

Class (size)/transaction	Obtain shareholder approval?
Class 3 (less than 5%)	No
Class 2 (less than 25%)	No
Class 1 (more than 25%)	Yes
Reverse takeover	Yes
Related party transaction[a]	Yes

[a] Transactions in which directors may have a conflict of interest.
Source: Based on information from London Stock Exchange, Financial Services Authority (FSA)'s handbook can be downloaded from http://fsahandbook.info/FSA/html/handbook/significant transactions.

European Union Takeover Directive

The EU's attempt at evolving a takeover regulatory mechanism has had a long and chequered history. More than 12 years in the making, the Takeover Directive (the Directive) was finally passed by the European Parliament in late 2003 and became effective in May 2004. Member states were required to implement it by May 2006. In the UK the Directive became part of CA 2006. Some provisions of the Directive aroused considerable opposition from member countries, such as Germany, Sweden, France and the Netherlands, while it was being formulated[13]. The obstacles to a Directive generally centred on:

- the restraints on frustrating action;
- the limited role of employee consultation; and
- the *breakthrough* provision to break down the target firm's pre-bid defences.

As noted above in our discussion of the Code in the UK, employee representatives or employees directly must be informed of the offer and the target defence as early as possible. The offer document has to spell out the impact of the proposed acquisition on employment, conditions of employment and the location of the place of employment. The Directive reflects the difficult political compromises that the EC had to reach to get it on the statute book over the provisions, since of the spirit of nationalist protectionism, if not xenophobia, is still alive and well in many member states (MS)[14]. The Directive now allows 'opt-out' of, as well as 'opt-into', some of the contentious provisions. MS are allowed to opt out of articles, but companies in those states may be allowed to opt back into them, and the same companies can also opt out against offerors from EU states, which are not subject to the same restrictions on grounds on non-reciprocity, a kind of revolving door approach!

Multiple voting rights allow companies to issue dual class shares and limit disproportionately the voting rights attached to certain classes of shares (see Chapter 9). After privatization of state enterprises, many member states retained a 'golden share' to veto any unwelcome takeovers of the privatized companies. In Scandinavian countries and in France the ability to limit voting rights has provided effective defences against hostile takeovers. The Germans themselves had special voting arrangements in Volkswagen offering a similar protection[15]. Many member states also wanted to preserve management's ability to frustrate hostile takeovers. Germany complained that the lack of an international level playing field would render European companies more vulnerable to hostile takeovers than their counterparts in other countries such as the US, and companies in certain member states more vulnerable than those in other member states[16]. Against these objections from MS, the Directive emerged.

The Directive contains 21 articles dealing with:

- general principles with which the rules formulated by member states must comply;
- the supervisory authority;
- mandatory bid rules;
- obligations to make relevant information available, the scope of information, timing of information release, documents to be released, etc.;
- the conduct of bids, how long the offer period is, when a bid lapses, how bids can be revised, conditions for revoking bids, etc.;
- the responsibilities of target management, the limits on frustrating actions, communicating its opinion on the implications of the bid for employees and business locations;
- consultation with employees (article 14, see discussion under UK takeover regulation above); and
- sanctions for violation of the Directive.

General principles and supervisory authority

The six general principles in article 3 are those that now appear as part of the UK Code, and are discussed above. Each MS will have to establish a supervisory authority for takeover offers, and it may be a private body. As we have seen, in the UK it is the City Takeover Panel. In article 4 the Directive defines the scope of the jurisdiction in terms of exclusive and shared jurisdiction, as illustrated in Figure 18.1.

Major articles of the Directive

Among the 21 articles, some of them will have quite far-reaching effects in term of whether a level playing field will be established in the market for corporate control in Europe. Table 18.4 summarizes the major articles and their implications. The BTR rule is the most radical of the provisions, since it not only disenfranchises security holders of their voting rights, and thus amounts to breach of contract and violation of extant property rights, but also goes against the grain of many continental European corporate structures and traditions. It can also be argued that since voting structures reflect the contractual choices made by investors in securities, it

Table 18.4 Major provisions of the Takeover Directive

Article no. and title	Main provisions	Implications
5. Mandatory bid rule (MBR); equitable offer rule	Crossing a control threshold requires mandatory bid; offer at highest price paid by offeror in 6/12 months pre-bid; offer in cash or liquid securities; mandatory cash offer if offeror acquires 5% or more during 6/12 months prior to or during bid.	'Control' not defined; threshold determined by member states (MS) where target is registered; threshold can vary across MS. MS can vary equitable price.
9. Board neutrality	Prohibits target taking frustrating action post-offer without shareholder approval; target board can seek alternative bids; offeree board to give its opinion on offer and its effects on company, shareholders and employees.	Binds on both management and supervisory boards; MS can opt out of article; restricts issue of shares that will impede offeror from acquiring control; *neutrality affects post-offer defences.*
11. Breakthrough rule (BTR)	Once bid is public, any restriction in target company articles on transfer of securities disapplied against offeror; when a general meeting decides on article 9 defensive measures, any restriction of voting rights disapplied; multiple voting rights limited to one vote per share; if offeror holds 75% of capital carrying voting rights, restriction on voting rights, transfer of voting rights or appointment of board members disapplied; such offeror can convene a general meeting at short notice.	Restrictions on transfer of securities and certain voting and other rights *unenforceable*; converts multiple voting right securities into one-share-one-vote; multiple voting security holders *disenfranchised*; equitable compensation payable to security holders for their losses; MS can opt out; *most radical of all articles in Directive*; BTR affects *pre-offer defences.*
12. Opt-out rule; reciprocity rule	MS can opt out of articles 9 and 11; companies in those MS can opt back in but can disapply articles if offeror is from another EU state or has its securities listed in EU and not subject to same restrictions.	This article will prevent harmonization of EU takeover rules; may increase protectionism by MS; MS can discriminate between competing bidders.
15 & 16. Minority squeeze-out and sell-out	Where offeror, after a bid for all holders of offeree securities, holds 90% of voting rights it can require minority holders to sell at a fair price; minority shareholders can require offeror to buy their securities at a fair price; three-month time limit for exercise.	MS can increase squeeze-out/sell-out threshold to maximum 95%.

Exhibit 18.4[17]

Grids locked in Spanish electricity merger!

In September 2005 Spanish Gas Natural (GN) made a €23bn public bid for the shares of Endesa, the Spanish electricity company, and was rejected by Endesa. In February 2006 EON, the German power company, made a competing €29bn bid for Endesa, at a 30% higher price than offered by GN. A few days later the Spanish regulator, CNE, imposed 19 conditions on EON, including divestments that could break up EON, with the obvious goal of putting up a barricade against the takeover of Endesa by EON. It also seemed that the ruling party in the Spanish government was playing for time to see the regional elections in Catalonia out of the way. The European Commission warned the Spanish government that the restrictions it had imposed were illegal. Then the Spanish government relented. When finally EON was allowed to continue its bid on Endesa, it was confronted with the joint attempt of the Spanish building conglomerate Acciona and Italian power provider ENEL to frustrate its bid by making a competing bid at a slightly higher price. The Spanish Securities and Exchange Commission, CNMV, allowed Acciona/ENEL to make a competing bid after six months, provided that EON's bid had failed by then. EON opposed this decision of the Spanish supervisory authority, which would allow the Spanish/Italian combination to announce a future bid (at a higher price), thus seriously reducing the chance that EON's bid would be accepted. Eventually, EON decided to withdraw its bid and enter into a settlement with Acciona and ENEL.

amounts to unreasonable interference in the contracts between firms and their security holders to have them disenfranchised. The UK government opted out of article 11 for this reason (see below for further discussion of the case for and against the mandatory rule, equitable price and the BTR).

The Directive may not create a level playing field for all bidders in a control contest. One bidder, normally a local company, may be preferred by a member state, thereby unfairly discriminating against a bidder from another Member State (see Exhibit 18.4).

Since mandatory bids are not common across member countries of the EU, the Directive will bring about greater uniformity, although the control thresholds and the 'equitable price' at which the mandatory bid must be made are left to the member states. The offeror must offer cash or a cash alternative unless it offers liquid securities traded on a regulated market in a member state. Unlike in the UK Code, the cash alternative kicks in when the offeror or any concert party buys offeree shares for cash during a period of *three* months including the offer period, and the minimum cash purchase is 5%.

The rationale for articles 5, 9 and 11[18]

The overall rationale for the Takeover Directive is the same as we set out at the beginning of this chapter: that is, to ensure an efficient market for corporate control. It is for this reason that the Directive is based substantially on the principles that underlay the UK Code. However, continental European countries present a very different picture from the UK in terms of corporate ownership, governance, and the relative importance of stock markets. In particular, continental European companies exhibit a very high degree of ownership concentration, the presence of controlling shareholders in many cases with majority control, a greater divergence between voting and non-voting shares, a greater incidence of multiple voting rights attached to a share, pyramidal shareholding that allows control of large corporate groups with relatively small ownership stakes, cross-shareholding etc. (see Chapter 12 on the corporate governance aspects of takeovers in Europe). In addition, in some countries managers are also able to refuse transfer of ownership to potential 'insurrectionists', or freeze their voting rights at low levels.

Thus the scope for managerial entrenchment, oppression of minorities and wilful avoidance of the discipline of hostile takeovers is probably much greater in continental Europe than in the UK. Since desperate situations call for desperate remedies, some of the provisions proposed in the earlier versions of the draft Directive were too drastic for many member states. We focus here on three of the articles in the Directive that aroused much opposition on its journey into the statute book.

Article 5 imposes the mandatory bid rule. Where a bid will lead to change of control, non-controlling shareholders should be given the opportunity to judge the bid and decide whether they should remain shareholders of the target firm or exit on acceptable terms. Where in the pre-bid period the ownership of the target firm was dispersed, the holding of say 30% of voting shares represents a substantial shift in control to the new block holder. Although large block holdings of shares can align the interests of controlling block holders and the remaining shareholders, where voting rights are skewed the private benefits, e.g. perks, power, status, may exceed the cash flow benefits to the controlling block holders. In this case the alignment breaks down, and the controlling block holders, typically commanding a majority of the voting rights, can oppress the non-controlling shareholders, typically the minority.

Removal of such real or potential oppression is what motivated the sell-out rule (see Table 18.4). The mandatory bid rule creates greater transparency in the ownership control process, leading to better-informed decisions by target shareholders on the merits of the bid and protecting shareholder rights. Article 5, by imposing the highest price rule, also increases transparency and further strengthens shareholder rights. The constraints on the payment currency also increase fair dealing between the bidders and target shareholders. These facilitate a more orderly reallocation of corporate assets to a new management group.

The rationale for article 9 imposing the board neutrality rule is that it is for the shareholders, as owners of the target company, to decide on the merits of a bid, and not for managers, who may block a value-creating acquisition for self-serving purposes, including the continued enjoyment of the private benefits of control. On the other hand, where shareholders are poorly informed about the benefits of the proposed acquisition, managers as better-informed agents can act for such shareholders and, armed with various frustrating devices, can extract higher value from the bidder than the shareholders themselves. Thus these two arguments are based on the 'bad agent' versus 'good agent' perspectives of the agency relationship between shareholders and managers. Several institutional factors, e.g. robust corporate governance regime, alert board monitoring, shareholder activism, managers compensation structure that aligns managerial and shareholder interests etc., may prevent the agent from becoming 'bad', and may even transform him or her into a 'good' agent. Board neutrality inclines to a sceptical view of managers' goodness, and seems to conclude 'why take a chance?' Thus, board neutrality abstracts from choice between good and bad manager views, and leaves the decision to or not to accept a bid firmly in the hands of shareholders. It is therefore conducive to a smoother functioning of the market for corporate control.

The case for the BTR is much more complicated. Corporate control should be commensurate with the risk carried by investors, and share capital with its exposure to maximum risk

---

Exhibit 18.5

Breaking through the disproportionate risk barrier

Ericsson, the Swedish telecom company, has a dual class share structure – A class and B class shares. Each A class share carries 1000 times the voting rights of each B class share, although both carry the same cash flow, i.e. dividend, rights. A shares have the overwhelming majority of votes but less than 10% of the cash flow rights. Under current rules A shares have a decisive say on whether Ericsson should accept an acquisition offer. Under the (proposed) proportionality principle and the breakthrough provision, a bidder that acquires all the B shares can gain control, since it can break through the rights of the A shares, which bear less than 10% of the risk capital. Elimination of the power of the dual-class structure may, however, lead to pyramid structures (see Chapter 9 on these) not covered by the Directive.

Source: L. Bebchuk and O. Hart, 'A threat to dual class shares', *Financial Times*, 31 May 2002

---

should carry the control rights (see Exhibit 18.5)[19]. This proposition is based on the proportionality principle that risk should equate to control rights. BTR also rests on the merits of the 'one-share-one-vote' (OSOV) principle. On the face of it, this has an attractive appeal to one's sense of democracy and egalitarianism. There are arguments in favour of OSOV as a value-increasing structure: for example, when a controlling block shareholder enjoys private benefits of control, and in the process destroys firm value to the disadvantage of other shareholders, OSOV can restrain such behaviour. On the other hand a large block shareholder can monitor the management more efficiently and thereby enhance firm value, to the benefit of dispersed shareholders. Thus the case for OSOV is conditional on controlling shareholder behaviour and the incentives for such behaviour.

A second objection to BTR is that ownership rights – both cash flow rights and voting rights – are contractually determined. Those investors who wish to have only cash flow rights may buy shares with lesser voting rights than those who wish to exercise control, but they do so willingly. Of course controlling shareholders may run the firm to serve their own interests rather than those of shareholders with only cash flow rights. This risk is inherent in the division of cash flow and voting rights, and the values of these rights may reflect this risk. It is therefore intrusive of the rule to force the shareholder to abandon their contracts and accept a less or more favourable dispensation[20].

But firms run for their private benefits, by controlling shareholders with concentrated voting rights, may be run in an economically inefficient way, and elimination of such inefficiency will not only benefit the other shareholders but also enhance social welfare. The welfare argument therefore has to establish that dispensing with concentrated voting rights *ex post* is justifiable in terms of compensating benefits, e.g. a more efficient market for corporate control.

Implementation of the Directive

Almost all the EU member states have now implemented the Directive. However, several countries have taken advantage of the opt-out provisions (see Table 18.4 above). In a review of the progress of implementation of the Directive, the EC found that, as of February 2007:

- board neutrality rule was implemented in 18 MS, but it had already existed there. Five MS introduced or intended to introduce the reciprocity exception to this rule;
- no MS chose to impose neutrality where it was not already applied;
- the vast majority of MS had not imposed the breakthrough rule but made it optional for their companies. Thus a mere 1% of listed companies in the EU would apply this rule on a mandatory basis;
- company level opt-outs and opt-ins are reversible and therefore do not represent a permanent move towards adoption of the articles; and
- the majority of MS allowed their companies to discriminate against offerors on reciprocity basis;

The review concludes on a sombre note: 'A large number of MS have shown reluctance to lift takeover barriers'[21].

Regulation of takeover bids in continental Europe[22]

Many continental European countries have in recent years introduced rules and guidelines incorporating some of the principles and rules of the UK Takeover Code. Most of the countries that have introduced them have opted for a statutory system. Among these are Austria, Belgium, Finland, France, Italy and Spain. Until recently, the Netherlands operated a non-statutory merger code, but this has now been superseded by a statutory code. Similarly, Germany, until recently, operated a voluntary code but now has a statutory code. In this section the regulations in some European countries are outlined. The reader must bear in mind that the following description is indicative and not exhaustive.

Table 18.5 summarizes the salient features of the regulatory rules and laws in five countries that have witnessed in recent years considerable takeover activity – France, Germany, Italy, the Netherlands and Sweden. Germany, France and Italy, together with the UK, are the largest economies in the EU. All these countries have mandatory bid requirements, but the shareholding level that constitutes *de facto* control varies around 30%. Neutrality of target management towards a bid is emphasized. So is the duty to avoid frustrating action, but the constraint on the latter varies. None of these countries allows the target company to finance the acquisition of its own shares. All of them allow minority squeeze-out, but the threshold stake for exploiting this provision varies from 90% in Sweden, 95% in France, Germany and the Netherlands to 98% in Italy. In some of these countries takeover regulation has been revised to incorporate many of the principles and practices underlying the UK Takeover Code. But in some of these countries there is much greater emphasis on employee consultation through works councils and labour organizations. In spite of the convergence of takeover regulation, several obstacles to hostile takeovers in the EU remain. These were referred to in Chapter 8 on cross-border acquisitions, and are discussed further in the context of bid strategies in Chapter 20 and defence strategies in Chapter 21.

In addition to the disclosure of share dealings during offer periods many countries have imposed disclosure requirements at much lower levels of share acquisitions. In the UK, the Companies Act 2006 requires disclosure above 3%. In France, Germany, the Netherlands and other countries disclosure has to be made when share acquisitions reach thresholds ranging from 5% to 75%. These disclosures make the share acquisition process quite transparent, and can alert target managers to impending takeover bids, friendly or hostile.

Table 18.5 Summary of the major provisions of takeover regimes in selected continental European countries

France

- General Regulation (Règlement Général) amended to implement Directive. Squeeze-out at 95%. Supervisory authority – Autorité des marchés financiers (AMF). Decisions may be appealed to Paris Court of Appeal.
- Control of a company can be achieved by: (1) voluntary takeover offer, (2) mandatory offer, and (3) mergers and related transactions without purchase of shares. Hostile bids are voluntary offers.
- Mandatory bid threshold 33% of capital/voting rights or creeping acquisition of 2% in a year above 33%. AMF can grant exemption on several grounds. Indirect control through other companies and concert parties taken into account.
- Mandatory bid not subject to any level of acceptance. Takeover offers generally irrevocable. Non-mandatory bids may be conditional on acceptance level. Banks guarantee financial ability to implement offer; AMF can authorize simplified offer procedure; market purchase of shares allowed.
- Offers filed with AMF and publicly announced. AMF reviews offer terms and price, decides conformity and approves offer document. AMF fixes timetable for offer. Deadlines for offer publication, offer opening and defence document cleared by AMF. Normal deal closure 56 days later; timetable adjusted to competing offer.
- Some restrictions on share purchases during offer, the price paid and share dealings by associates. Dealings in offeror and target shares to be disclosed to AMF daily; target shareholders can withdraw acceptances until closing date.
- Target has to consult its work council. Offeror obliged to appear before it; otherwise may lose voting rights in target. In cases of conflicts of interest, and in squeeze-out, target must secure fairness opinion.
- Pre- and post-offer defences available. Cross-shareholdings common; targets must obtain shareholder approval for post-offer defences. Reciprocity test applied; free warrants can be issued by target as poison pill.

Germany

- Takeover Act (TA). Stock Corporation Act and Securities Trading Act also relevant. Supervisory authority, Bundesanstalt für Finanzdienstleistungsaufsicht (BaFin) to approve offer document.
- TA covers stock corporations and partnerships limited by shares. All target shareholders to receive equal treatment and information, and given time to make informed decision. Disclosure of share acquisitions at a range of thresholds from 5% to 75% required.
- Mandatory bid threshold 30% of target voting rights. Cash or liquid stock as consideration. Price must be adequate based on average target stock prices. Mandatory cash offer if 5% target stock bought in previous 6 months. Squeeze-out at 95%.
- Any higher price during offer period or 1 year after bid closure to be offered to all accepting shareholders.
- Prompt publication of offer and offer document content laid down by TA. Bidder liable for correctness and completeness. Public offer notified to target. Confirmation from a financial institution of ability to implement included.
- Conditions on offers allowed but must be objective, e.g. bidder shareholders' approval.
- Bid timetable from offer announcement for submission of offer document to BaFIN, offer period of 4 to 10 weeks. Another 2 weeks for remaining shareholders to accept.
- Target management has to comment promptly on offer and exercise neutrality, and take no frustrating action, but shareholders can approve of defensive action during 18 months prior to offer; creation of multiple voting rights abolished in 2003. Measures approved by supervisory board can be taken; target can opt into articles 9 and 11 of Directive but also disapply them under reciprocity rule. Searching for white knight allowed but no break-up fee from target assets.
- Offeror and target to inform works councils or employees.

Italy

- Financial Services Act 1998, Takeover Act 2007 implementing the Directive and rules of Commissione Nazionale per le Società e la Borsa (CONSOB), the Italian stock exchange authority.
- Concern companies with listed shares and unlisted but widely publicly distributed shares. CONSOB has to authorize public offers.
- Mandatory bid required where: (1) direct or indirect acquisition of 30% in a listed company; (2) by chain (cascata) principle if through an intermediate holding company 30% of target is acquired, acquirer obliged to make public offer for holding company first and, if successful, for target (creeping or incremental bid); (3) acquirer already with 30% has added more than 3% in previous 12 months; (4) when bidder has 95% to buy out the minority (squeeze-out). CONSOB can exempt from mandatory offers, e.g. in context of restructuring.
- Equal treatment of all shareholders in paying control premium. Concert parties counted in.
- Voluntary preliminary bid for at least 60% of target shares may be made subject to CONSOB verification and certain conditions about prior purchases and approval by majority of target shareholders.

Table 18.5 *continued*

- Bid timetable – 15–30 days for CONSOB to authorize offer document. Offer period starts 5 days after publication and open for 25–40 trading days. CONSOB can extend to maximum of 55 days. With rival bid, timetable aligned with the rival's.
- Voluntary offer irrevocable but can be conditional, e.g. minimum acceptance level. No conditions in mandatory bids.
- Target management can initiate pre-bid defences, e.g. poison pills, with shareholder approval. No restrictions on pre-bid defences. Board neutrality post-offer. Breakthrough implemented. Reciprocity defence allowed but shareholders must approve. Target shareholders can revoke acceptance to accept rival offer. Target defence document needs CONSOB approval.
- No restrictions on share purchases during offer period, but offer price adjusted to any higher purchase price. Offer price increase at least 2%.

Netherlands
- Financial Supervision Act 2006. Decree on Public Offers 2007 implements the Directive. Supervisory authority is Authority for Financial Markets (AFM) and the Enterprise Chamber of Amsterdam Court.
- Rules apply to a public offer for shares of listed companies. Public offer must be made within 12 weeks of announcement. Offer period 35 weeks. Offer memorandum approved by AFM. It must indicate financing for bid. In a public offer all shareholders treated equally.
- Mandatory bid threshold 30%. Mandatory public offers irrevocable.
- Bidder and target can deal in their securities, subject to public disclosure of transactions.
- Bid timetable – announcement, offer memorandum (OM) filed with AFM within 12 weeks, AFM approves within 10 days, offeror publishes OM, offer kept open for 4–10 weeks. Shareholders accepting offer can withdraw if offer period extended.
- Squeeze-out at 95%. In mergers, in contrast, squeeze-out at 70%.
- Labour organizations and works councils should be consulted. Works councils of both bidder and target can render advice. Management should inform works council of its decision.
- Opted out of articles 9 and 11, but Dutch companies can opt in. They can also opt for reciprocity.

Sweden
- Takeover Act 2006 implementing the Directive, Takeover Rules and Financial Instruments Trading Act 1991 apply. Financial Supervisory Authority (FSA), OMX Nordic Exchange Stockholm (OMX) and Securities Council (SC) supervise. SC's role similar to UK Panel's. Before public offer, offeror must agree with OMX to abide by takeover rules.
- Foreign acquirers set up a Swedish subsidiary to make acquisition to facilitate squeeze-out.
- Various disclosure thresholds at 5–90% of target stakes. Mandatory bid above 30%. Concert party taken into account. If in previous 6 months cash purchases made, cash alternative must be offered ('cash trap'); financing arrangement for offer must be in place.
- Bid timetable – set by offeror. Offer kept open for 3–10 weeks. Offeror can buy target shares, subject to disclosure. Offer must be increased if purchase price higher. Offer price must be highest paid in 6 months prior to offer.
- Conditional non-mandatory offers allowed, e.g. 90% minimum acceptance. If offer is unfulfilled, accepting shareholders can revoke acceptance in favour of competing offer.
- Offeror and target required to inform own trade unions/employees. Acquirer shareholder approval exceptional.
- If bid fails, offeror can rebid, but if in following 9 months it pays a higher price than offer price, acceptors in the first offer must receive 'top-up' compensation.
- Frustrating action through market manipulation of offeror or target shares not allowed. Cross-shareholdings and multiple voting rights common. Companies can opt into breakthrough rule. Board neutrality in force, but target can solicit rival bids, and must consider unsolicited rival bids.

Takeover regulation in the US

In the US, companies are incorporated in the states of the US and not under a Federal law. Mergers and acquisitions are therefore carried out under state laws. There are broad types of merger that are common to the states, whose laws may nevertheless allow or disallow certain types of merger. The Federal securities laws, e.g. the Securities and Exchange Act, and stock exchange rules, e.g. NYSE rules, impact on mergers and acquisitions, because in the case of publicly listed targets mergers and acquisitions necessarily involve the sale of their securities for cash to the acquirer or the exchange of securities for those of the acquirer. In this section we provide a brief overview of the different merger types, tender offers under the Williams Act, and how mergers are often combined with tender offers in multi-stage mergers.

Merger process[23]

A merger is a procedure in which two or more 'constituent corporations' merge *with or* into a single corporation that is also one of the participating 'constituent corporations'. The constituent corporation into which the other corporations are merged survives, and is hence called the 'surviving corporation' (Kenyon-Slade, *ibid.*, p. 15). Shareholders of constituent corporations may have to approve of the merger. A merger of two firms may be effected with or without an intermediary acquisition vehicle (often nicknamed Newco), a 100%-owned subsidiary of the acquirer. Where a Newco is not interposed, the target firm becomes the subsidiary of the acquirer, which is one of the constituent corporations. With a Newco the acquirer is not a constituent corporation. This is useful, since the acquirer can vote its 100% shares in Newco to approve of its merger with the target, without having to secure *its own* shareholder approval. Consideration for a merger can be the acquirer's stock, other securities, cash or other assets. The non-stock consideration is known as the 'boot'.

Mergers can be organized in different ways:

- Negotiated long-form stock-for-stock merger
  - Acquirer issues new stock as consideration, and requires approval of target shareholders.
  - Acquirer may also require its own shareholder approval where it issues shares, amounting to 20% or more of its outstanding shares, as consideration.
  - Newly issued shares must be registered with the Securities and Exchange Commission (SEC), and this causes delay.
  - Where the firms merge into a single surviving Newco, both acquirer and target shareholders must approve such a merger.
  - The process may take three to four months for a Certificate of Merger to be issued.
- Tender offer (TO)
  - Acquirer makes a tender offer to target shareholders as per the procedure under the Williams Act (see below).
  - Proportion of target shares sought in the TO may be for less than or more than 50% or at least 90%.
  - Share exchange offers are tender offers in which the acquirer's stock is issued as consideration.
  - Share exchange TOs take longer than cash TOs, but the SEC has since 2000 allowed '*early commencement*' of such TOs to minimize delay.
- Cash tender offer plus back-end freeze-out merger[24]
  - TOs can be the first stage of a two-stage merger to overcome delays in long-form negotiated mergers; the second or back-end stage is either short-form freeze-out merger or the long-form freeze-out merger.
  - Consideration for first-stage TO is cash.
  - Short-form freeze-out requires at least 90% tender from target shareholders; minority shareholders are then 'squeezed out'; it is often part of a negotiated merger agreement with target management that supports the TO.
  - TO made conditional on 90% minimum tender.
  - Only feasible in states that allow short-form freeze-out merger.

- TO plus short form may be completed in little over 20 business days.
- TO plus long-form freeze-out more difficult where target has anti-takeover provisions, e.g. supermajority approval, poison pills.

While the merger *process* as described above is important, and must be carefully conducted to minimize delays and increase the probability of a successful merger, the merger *structure* also needs to be given due consideration.

Merger structure

This is concerned with which participating constituent corporations will be merged, and into which other, and which of them will be the surviving corporations. Merger structure is often chosen to achieve a tax-free status for the target shareholders. But tax benefits to the acquirer, e.g. in the form of step-up of acquired assets for corporation tax purposes, are also important. Tax-free mergers in general must include a high proportion of the acquirer's stock as consideration, although the proportion of boot allowed depends on the merger structure (see Chapter 16 on the tax aspects of payment methods).

Strategic considerations will determine which firm survives. For example, to preserve its corporate brand value, the acquired firm will be retained and Newco will be merged into it. The extent of post-merger integration planned will also influence the merger structure. In the case of a *merger of equals* (MoE), both participating corporations are merged into Newco as the only surviving corporation. This may be done since it avoids the feeling of being dominated by one or the other participating corporation if it were merged into the other, and *perceived* dominance is antithetical to the *assumed* spirit of equality.

Some of the alternative merger structures are shown in Figure 18.3. Panel A shows a statutory merger. In Panel B the target is merged into Newco, which survives (forward triangular merger). In Panel C the opposite happens, and the target survives (reverse triangular merger). Panel D shows a consolidating merger appropriate for MoE[25]. Where there are any minorities facing a freeze-out, they have appraisal rights so that they receive fair consideration for their shares. Dissenting shareholders of constituent corporations, instead of participating in a merger, may exercise their appraisal rights instead.

Regulation of tender offers

Tender offers are regulated under the Williams Act (WA) 1968 by the Securities and Exchange Commission. The WA imposes obligations on both offerors and targets, and prevents secret accumulation of large stakes by requiring acquisitions of 5% or more of the voting shares to be disclosed within 10 days. The WA defines when a tender offer commences, and sets out the information to be disclosed, including the source of funds for and the purpose of the offer. Tender offers must be open for 20 business days, and revised offers kept open for another 10 business days.

The 'best price' and 'all holders' rule requires that the bidder buy the tendered shares at the best price during the offer, and that the tender be open to all shareholders. During the offer, shares cannot be bought by the offeror except in pursuance of the offer itself. The bidder can revise the terms of the offer, including the offer price. WA makes any fraudulent act, including insider trading in connection with the offer, illegal.

WA imposes obligations on targets in their response to tender offers. It requires the target to inform its shareholders of its position on the tender offer within 10 business days. Target management must disclose any conflict of interest, and also refrain from materially misleading statements. This parallels the obligations of targets under the City Code (see above).

Figure 18.3   Merger structure in the US

A: Target merged into acquirer (statutory merger)

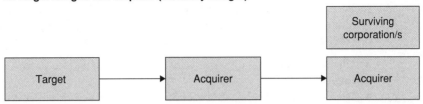

B: Target merged into Newco, which remains subsidiary of Acquirer (forward triangle)

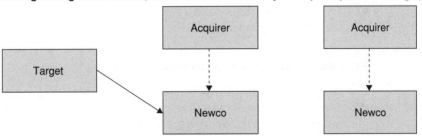

C: Newco merges into Target, which becomes subsidiary of Acquirer (reverse triangle)

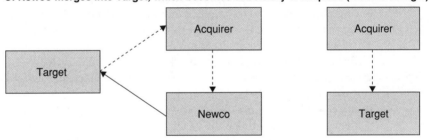

D: Acquirer and Target merged into Newco (statutory consolidation)

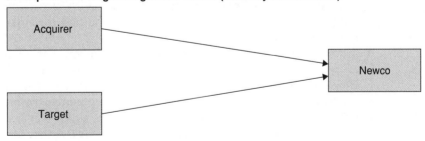

*Note: Solid arrow indicates the direction of merger of one company into another. Broken arrow indicates a subsidiary relationship.

Since in the US companies are incorporated under state laws, the structure of an acquisition is a matter partly of state law and partly of Federal law. Some state laws have recently made tender offers more difficult by allowing certain defensive devices by target companies, such as shark repellents and poison pills (see Chapter 21).

Although united in the spirit of protecting shareholder autonomy in deciding on the merits of a takeover offer, the UK Code and the WA tender offer provisions differ in major respects:

● The Code is far more prescriptive of the conduct of various parties, including the financial advisers.
● The Code allows dealing in shares during the offer period, whereas the WA does not.
● The Code is far more prohibitive of frustrating action than the WA, but this is partly because frustrating action in the US is covered by the state anti-takeover laws.
● The Code has a *maximum* offer period, whereas WA has a minimum period for a TO, but it can be kept indefinitely open.

Principal clauses in a merger agreement

The merger agreement (MA) between participating firms prepares the ground for undertaking the merger process, as well as providing for the merger structure. There are several other important issues that are covered by MA. Among these are:

● the confidentiality agreement, including a 'standstill provision', e.g. acquirer agrees not to buy voting securities in target for an agreed period;
● target board agrees to recommend merger or tender offer followed by short-form freeze-out;
● representations and warranties, e.g. preparation of financial statements in accordance with US securities laws; that target has received third-party consents to consummate merger; that there is due compliance with all required SEC filings etc.;
● covenants, e.g. target will refrain from any major capital expenditure; deal protection covenants (see below);
● material adverse change (MAC) conditions, e.g. market out condition, which would permit the acquirer to terminate the TO if acquirer's share price or target's share price or share prices in general move significantly adversely, say 15–20%;
● merger agreements that include MAC conditions often also contain MAC exception or exclusion conditions. These define the circumstances in which the buyer cannot invoke the MAC and walk away. Thus while stringent MAC favours the buyer, stringent exceptions favour the seller;
● material adverse effect (MAE) is related to MAC and refers to certain events that have an adverse effect on the target. MAE enables the buyer to walk away if a defined event has a MAE. However, sellers may counter this buyer-friendly condition by stipulating 'disproportionate effect' exception. That is, while a MAE may have occurred, the buyer can only walk away if the MAE has had a disproportionate effect on the target compared to, say its peers in its industry. See Exhibit 18.6 involving MAE and how the Delaware Court interpreted it;
● while MAC favours the buyers, exception to MAC such as MAE, e.g. general deterioration in market conditions favours the seller since the buyer cannot invoke the MAC. For buyers, the disproportionate effect clause allows them to dilute 'the exception to the exception' since if material adverse effect falls disproportionately on the seller, the buyer can excuse itself from the obligation to complete the deal. However, the buyer then has to establish not only that there is a MAE on the seller but that it is also disproportionate;
● break-up fee in the event of one party terminating the MA.

Exhibit 18.6

MAC and MAE – wheels within wheels!

A recent Delaware Chancery Court decision addressed the analysis to be undertaken with respect to the disproportionate effects language. On September 29 2008, the Delaware Chancery Court rendered its decision in *Hexion Speciality Chemicals, Inc. et al* v. *Huntsman Corp.*, C.A. No. 3841-VCL (Sept. 29, 2008). Hexion, a portfolio company of Apollo Global Management, agreed to acquire Huntsman, a chemical company, pursuant to a merger agreement executed in July 2007. The merger agreement included a 'no MAE' condition to closing. The merger agreement defined Material Adverse Effect to exclude events resulting from changes in general economic or financial market conditions, except to the extent such event has had a disproportionate effect on Huntsman and its subsidiaries, taken as a whole, as compared to others in the chemical industry. In holding that no MAE had occurred, the Court found that the exception to the MAE definition had to first be tested before testing the exception to the exception. The Court found that Huntsman had not suffered an MAE, and accordingly, determined that the Court need not reach the question of whether its performance had been disproportionately worse than the chemical industry taken as a whole. Hexion had argued that Huntsman had suffered an MAE principally as compared to other chemical companies. However, the Court found that, as compared to prior years, Huntsmans financial condition, business and results of operations, while decreasing, had not suffered an MAE. Accordingly, its position as compared to other chemical companies was irrelevant. Notably, the Court reaffirmed that absent clear language, the burden of proof with respect to an MAE rests on the party seeking to excuse its performance, and that Delaware courts have never found a Material Adverse Effect to have occurred in the context of a merger agreement.

Source: D. DeChiara, R. Porter, M. Abascal, 'MAC Survey: A Nixon Peabody study of current negotiation trends of Material Adverse Change clauses in M&A transactions', 29 October 2008, downloaded from www.nixonpeabody.com

In long-form stock-for-stock mergers the MA may cover the board and managerial positions after the merger, the exchange ratio between acquirer and target shares in consideration, how the ratio will be adjusted for adverse relative share price movements (see Chapter 16 on fixed value and fixed exchange ratio offers), and agreement to redeem poison pills (see Chapter 20).

Deal protection covenants include:

- 'no-shop' clause, which prevents the target from shopping for alternative acquirers;
- 'no-talk', which prevents target from entertaining unsolicited rival bidders;
- share or 'crown-jewel' lock-up, which provides acquirer with options to buy new share allocations in target or on target's valuable assets if target breaches the MA and recommends a rival offer; and
- break-up fees to be paid by the party breaching the MA and causing the deal to collapse.

Takeover regulation and takeover activity

The City Code, in conjunction with the SARs and the Companies Act 1989 in the UK, requires extensive disclosures of share acquisitions by actual or potential bidders. Our brief review of takeover regulation in some continental European countries as well as the US indicates a similar emphasis on transparency of share dealings even before actual takeover bids. Takeover regulations prohibit discriminatory price offers. In many regimes the offer price has to be the maximum the offeror has paid in the months, often up to 12 months, prior to the offer. They also require that any post-offer share purchases be at no less than the offer price. Do such disclosure and best price requirements raise bid premia and reduce the profitability of acquisitions, and hence reduce the incentive for potential bidders to undertake acquisitions?

Several countries also require a mandatory bid to ensure that target shareholders are given the opportunity to decide whether they wish to remain shareholders when effective control of the target has passed on to the bidder. Further, both mandatory and voluntary bid offers have to be extended to all target shareholders. Do these rules overprotect target shareholders, enhance their leverage against bidders, and lead to high bid premia? Do they deter profitable and value-creating takeovers? If value-creating acquisitions are deterred, the result may be a welfare loss to the economy as a whole. We attempt below to answer the above questions.

Grossman and Hart put forward the 'free-rider' model of the relationship between the ownership structure of a target firm and the incentive for bidders to make bids[26]. In this model, which assumes the US system of strong minority shareholder rights, the target is owned by a multitude of small shareholders (an atomistic shareholder structure). Each shareholder, believing his or her own decision has a trivially small effect on the probability of success of a particular bid, will have an incentive to decline the bid offer if he or she expects other shareholders to accept. In this way, the shareholder expects to participate in the post-acquisition performance improvement of the target effected by the acquirer.

Each shareholder thus expects to free-ride on the accepting decisions of his or her fellow-shareholders. Further, the shareholder free-rides on the acquirer, since he or she benefits from the efforts of the acquirer in researching the enhanced profit potential of the target and in realizing that potential after the acquisition. If all target shareholders expect to free-ride, the bid will fail and there will be no ride for anyone. This free-riding behaviour will therefore deter any value-increasing bid. That is, there is no incentive for any potential bidder to incur the costs of researching value-creating takeover opportunities and the bid-related costs (see Chapter 20), if he or she has to pass all the added value to a bunch of free-riders.

Grossman and Hart argue that the WA disclosure requirements in the US aggravate the free-riding problem, since they prevent the potential bidder from accumulating a substantial stake (the toehold) ahead of a public bid. This also applies to the UK and continental European countries that have low disclosure thresholds (see above including Table 18.5). A toehold allows the bidder to retain some of the value improvements it brings about after acquisition. This compensates it for the cost of making the acquisition. Grossman and Hart suggest a remedy for the free-riding problem – diminished rights for minority shareholders of the target after being acquired by the bidder. Such diminution of rights allows the bidder to retain some of the benefits of acquisition.

In the UK, the free-rider problem may be much less serious. According to Yarrow, protection of minorities in the UK against oppression by the majority shareholder is much weaker[27]. Moreover, the Companies Act 2006 allows an acquirer that has purchased 90% of the target shares to compulsorily acquire the minority. Thus the incentive for free-riding appears to be small. Indeed, it may be the small shareholder who perhaps needs protection from being locked into a minority position. The Code rules on equality of treatment and information disclosure, as well as the prohibition of partial bids except in very restricted circumstances, restore some balance in favour of the small shareholders. Yarrow therefore argues that the UK regulatory regime does not provide any disincentive to profitable takeover bids[28]. On the Continent, similar minority squeeze-out rules again reduce the free-rider incentive. For this reason, German companies welcomed the new takeover law[29].

The assumption of atomistic shareholding underlying the Grossman and Hart model is also weakened by the presence of substantial block shareholdings by institutional shareholders and large block shareholders in continental European companies. Moreover, the presence of arbitrageurs (see Chapter 19), who exploit the difference between the market and offer prices of the target shares, leads to accumulation of large block shareholding. Insider trading, though prohibited by law, also allows such large block accumulation. Thus these deviations from the Grossman and Hart assumption may mitigate the impact of free-riding and allow for a greater level of takeover activity[30]. We have seen in Chapter 2 evidence of high, almost frenzied, takeover activity from time to time during merger waves. This suggests that the free-rider problem may have been considerably mitigated by the above countervailing factors.

While takeover regulation may not have deterred takeover activity, it may have reduced the profitability of acquisitions because of the high premia acquirers are forced to pay through best price requirements. This interpretation is consistent with the poor post-acquisition value creation performance documented in Chapter 4.

CASE STUDY

UK Takeover Panel doesn't buy the big MAC

The material adverse change (MAC) argument has been put forward by bidders to either abandon their bid altogether or to revise the offer terms to their advantage. WPP, the UK advertising group, made a £5.55 per share bid for Tempus, a media-buying agency, valued at £434m well before the 11 September 2001 bombing of the World Trade Center in New York. The impact of that terror attack was to diminish the business prospects of advertising firms. WPP therefore argued that Tempus's prospects had been severely hit by the turmoil following 9/11. It therefore felt that it should pull out of its offer for Tempus. In October 2001 WPP approached the Takeover Panel for a ruling allowing it to withdraw its offer. This raised an important issue of interpretation of the concept of material adverse change and the Takeover Code's Rule 2. Any ruling would have significant repercussions for the conduct of takeovers in the UK in future. It was also a test of the Panel's authority.

Two of the Codes rules are relevant to this case. Note 1 on rule 2.7 says that 'a change in general economic, industrial or political circumstance will not justify failure to proceed with an announced offer; to justify a decision not to proceed, circumstances of an exceptional and specific nature are required'. Rule 13 prohibits the attachment of subjective conditions to an offer, and note 2 on this rule says: 'An offeror should not invoke any condition so as to cause the offer to lapse unless the circumstances which give rise to the right to invoke the condition are of material significance to the offeror in the context of the offer'. The Panel Executive had to decide whether WPP's claim of material adverse change was consistent with these rules. Tempus argued that there were no grounds for allowing the material adverse change condition to be invoked. From Tempus's point of view WPP's withdrawal might have pushed its share price down to £2.50. If Tempus were to issue a profit warning following 9/11, WPP's case that the material adverse change was specific to the target might have been strengthened. Tempus, on the other hand, could argue that the

→

impact on its profits was still industry and not company specific. The two sides were therefore engaged in a fierce battle of attack and evasion. In the meanwhile, the European Commission's Merger Control division cleared the merger, and WPP's hope of avoiding the bid now rested on the Panel ruling. Analysts expected that WPP itself would report annual profits sharply down from an earlier estimate of £540m to £490m.

On 25 October 2001 the Panel Executive ruled that WPP could not drop the bid on the ground of material adverse change. WPP then appealed the decision to the full Panel. The Panel had to decide whether WPP had established that the prospects of Tempus had undergone an MAC that was also material to WPP in the context of its offer for Tempus. On 1 November 2001 the Panel took the view that meeting the MAC test specified in the Code required 'an adverse change of very considerable significance striking at the heart of the purpose of the transaction'. In the Panel's view, change in circumstances must be judged not in terms of short-term profitability but in terms of their effect on the longer-term prospects of the offeree company.

WPP thus lost the appeal, and proceeded with the offer. WPP, while wanting to get out of the bid, also bought Tempus stock after 9/11. This seems to weaken WPP's case, but the Panel did not attach much importance to this purchase. The Panel's ruling was a lesson 'for any directors mounting a takeover bid who still harboured illusions about relying on general get-out clauses'. It set a standard that MAC had to be real big MAC.

Discussion questions

1 Was WPP right in invoking the MAC clause to abandon its bid?

2 Do you agree with the Panel's decision and the reasons for it?

3 How important is the ruling for the takeover regulatory mechanism?

Sources: Panel Statement 2001/15; C. Pretzlik, 'WPP's best hope may be that Tempus fugit'; R. Tomkins, 'Row delays resolution of WPP/Tempus takeover'; *Financial Times* 12 and 24 October 2001 respectively

Overview and implications for practice

This chapter has described the statutory and non-statutory framework for the regulation of takeovers in the UK. Alternative takeover and merger procedures have been examined.

- The City Panel on Takeovers and Mergers operates its Code, and polices bids for public companies. The advantages and disadvantages of this uniquely non-statutory and self-regulatory system in the UK have been described. Takeovers in the UK are also significantly influenced by statutory rules.

- In 2004 the European Commission enacted the Takeover Directive, whose features included the equality principle, mandatory bid, prevention of frustrating action without shareholder approval, a larger role for employees to consult and express their views, the breakthrough rule to prevent concentrated voting rights blocking takeovers, etc.

- The Directive also defines the scope of jurisdiction of a national authority, and the circumstances of shared jurisdiction.

- The Directive allows member states to opt out of the board neutrality and breakthrough provisions, and they can in turn allow companies in those countries to opt into those provisions; companies can also selectively opt out of these provisions against bidders not subject to similar provisions; this reciprocity rule seeks to maintain a level playing field.

- Takeover regulation in the US covering the different forms of statutory mergers under state laws and the tender offer provisions under the Williams Act are discussed.

- Merger agreements allow both buyers and sellers to protect themselves against opportunistic behaviour by the other party, and include clauses such as 'no-shop', MAC, break-up fees, etc. These clauses need to be carefully negotiated, although the extent of protection that can be secured by them depends on the relative bargaining power of buyers and sellers, and the external market conditions, such as highly active M & A market, credit market conditions, etc.

- Takeover regimes in major continental countries are outlined to enable the reader to appreciate the variety of approaches to such regulation.

- Similarities and differences among the regimes in the US and Europe are highlighted.

- Takeover regulation may influence the economic incentives for potential bidders to make profitable bids and hence the level of takeover activity. Takeover regulations in different countries appear to prevent free-riding by minority shareholders that might otherwise eliminate incentives for takeover activity. While not deterring takeover activity, some of the regulations may still increase takeover costs and reduce gains to shareholders.

Review questions

18.1 What is the rationale for takeover regulation?

18.2 What are the principles of the UK Takeover Code? What is the rationale for these principles?

18.3 What is a mandatory bid? Is it necessary?

18.4 What is frustrating action? Is it necessary?

18.5 What is the importance of a bid timetable?

18.6 Compare and contrast the EU Takeover Directive and the UK Code.

18.7 What is the rationale of the board neutrality and breakthrough rules in the Directive?

18.8 What is the rationale for the opt-in and opt-out provisions and for the reciprocity rule?

18.9 Compare and contrast the US takeover regulation with the UK Code and the Takeover Directive.

18.10 How do buyers and sellers minimize deal risk using the merger agreement?

18.11 Compare and contrast the regulations in the continental European countries.

18.12 Does takeover regulation help or hinder takeover activity? How and why?

Further reading

A Practitioner's Guide to Takeovers and Mergers in the European Union (Old Woking: City & Financial Publishing, 2008).

S. Grossman and O. Hart, 'Takeover bids, the free rider problem and the theory of the corporation', *Bell Journal of Economics*, **11**(1), 1980, 42–64.

C. Mayer and J. Franks, 'Different votes for different folks', *Financial Times*, 19 October 2006.

Notes and references

1. The UK outlined its principles for regulating takeover in 1959 with the 'Notes of Amalgamation of British Business' after several notorious takeover bids. At that time shareholders had very little say in influencing bid outcomes. See A. Farrell, 'Why continental European takeover law matters', in G. Ferrarini, K. Hopt, J. Winter and E. Wymeersch (Eds), *Reforming Company and Takeover Law in Europe* (Oxford: Oxford University Press, 2004).
2. Directive 2004/25/EC. See the introduction to the Code on jurisdiction. These criteria also apply to Societas Europaea, which is a public limited company that can be set up by merger of two or more European companies, or with one of them as a holding company of the others. For further details see www.companieshouse.gov.uk.
3. B. Masters, 'Delay to Expro ruling points to M&A troubles', *Financial Times*, 23 June 2008.
4. J. Franks and R. Harris, 'Shareholder wealth effects of corporate takeovers: The UK experience 1955–85', *Journal of Financial Economics*, **23**, 1989, 225–249.
5. B. Masters, *ibid.*
6. Sections 945 and 956 of the Act.
7. One of the 10 was about takeover defences: *No action which might frustrate an offer is taken by a target company during the offer period without shareholders being allowed to approve it.* Under the Directive target management's ability to mount defences is subject to a complex set of 'opt-in' and 'opt-out' rules. It remains a highly contentious issue among member states (see discussion of the Directive below).
8. Mandatory bids can be dispensed with under certain conditions, e.g. by independent shareholders under the 'whitewash' procedure. See the Code for details.
9. 'No-shop' agreement obliges the target not to look for alternative offerors, probably in an attempt to find a more agreeable acquirer or to leverage a higher bid premium. See below for such a clause in US merger agreements and Chapters 20 and 21 on break-up fees and their role in bid and defence strategies.
10. Calculations based on statistics from the Panel's annual reports.
11. For a further discussion of the impact of FSMA and FSA on the Code and the Panel's operations see V. Knapp and A. Marsh, 'Application of the market abuse regimes to takeovers, *Practitioner's Guide, ibid.,* pp. 305–321.
12. This prohibition does not apply to private companies under CA 2006. Therefore a plc must re-register itself as a private company before its assets can be used to finance its acquisition.
13. P. Betts, 'Europe's capitalists survey a level playing field', *Financial Times*, 31 May 2001.
14. See S. Cox, 'Takeover makeover', *Utility Week*, 14 July 2006, on the frustrating implications of article 12 for cross-border acquirers in the utility sector.
15. The state of Lower Saxony had, since 1960, a blocking shareholding in VW to block any unwanted takeover of that company. The EC challenged this 'VW law', and the Court of First Instance held in 2007 that the law limited free movement of capital and must be abolished (*Financial Times*, 24 October 2007).
16. G. Schröder, 'Shaping industry on the anvil of Europe', *Financial Times*, 29 April 2002.
17. See G. Kemperink and J. Stuyck, 'The thirteenth company law directive and competing bids', *Common Market Law Review*, **45**, 2008, 93–130. The authors develop extensive arguments to show the Directive's failure to create a level playing field for competing bidders. See also *The Economist*, 2 September 2006, 380, 8493, p. 66.
18. Discussion of the arguments for and against these articles is necessarily brief. For a more detailed analysis, including supporting empirical studies, see the collection of articles in Part III, Corporate governance: The market for corporate control and the level playing field, in Ferrarini et al., *ibid.*
19. The Winter Report develops arguments concerning breakthrough further. See J. Winter, 'Report of the high level group of company law experts on issues related to takeover bids', January 2002, Annex 2 in Ferrarini et al., *ibid.*
20. The UK government opted out of the breakthrough rule for this reason, but allows companies to opt in. See C. Mayer and J. Franks, 'Different votes for different folks', *Financial Times*, 20 October 2006, for further discussion of the relative merits of OSOV and the breakthrough rule.
21. Commission of the European Communities, *Report on the Implementation of the Directive on Takeover Bids*, Commission Staff working document, 21 February 2007.
22. This section draws upon various chapters in *A Practitioner's Guide to Takeovers and Mergers in the European Union*, 4th edition (Old Woking, UK: City & Financial Publishing, 2008). The section is

necessarily a highly condensed view of the laws, regulations and practices in various countries. The reader is advised to consult the publication for more detailed discussion and precise description.

23. This section draws upon S. Kenyon-Slade, *Mergers and Takeovers in the US and UK* (Oxford: Oxford University Press, 2004).

24. On coercive tender offers as a takeover strategy, see Chapter 20.

25. In a reverse merger a large 'acquirer' is merged into a relatively small 'target', which issues its stock as consideration to the big firm shareholders. In substance it is the big firm that is in control, since its share of ownership of the combined entity is much larger than that of the 'acquirer', although it is the small firm that survives. A reverse merger is often used to circumvent burdensome charter requirements such as supermajority provisions (Kenyon-Slade, *ibid.*, p. 19).

26. S. Grossman and O. Hart, 'Takeover bids, the free rider problem and the theory of the corporation', *Bell Journal of Economics*, **11**(1), 1980, 42–64.

27. G. K. Yarrow, 'Shareholder protection, compulsory acquisition and the efficiency of the takeover process', *Journal of Industrial Economics*, **34**(1), 1985, 3–16.

28. Yarrow, *ibid.*

29. A. Major, 'Minority shareholders face a squeeze', *Financial Times*, 17 June 2002.

30. A. Roell, *Regulation of Takeovers*, London School of Economics Discussion Paper 003, 1987.

CHAPTER 19

Advisers in takeovers

Objectives

At the end of this chapter, the reader should be able to understand:

- the range of advisers involved in M & A deal-making;
- their different roles and responsibilities;
- the importance of investment bankers to the deal-making process, and the range of services they provide;
- conflicts of interests between advisers and their clients, how compensation contracts create and resolve conflicts; and
- empirical evidence on the value of investment banks' services to bidders and targets.

Introduction

Although takeovers have increased substantially in recent years, for many companies these happen very infrequently. Thus, except in the case of large firms that are also frequent acquirers, firms are unlikely to have the in-house expertise necessary for carrying out an acquisition, and will have to seek the help of outside advisers. Further, since takeovers are subject to antitrust and other regulatory rules, advisers who are familiar with those rules and can guide the firm in their proper observance are indispensable. Since an acquisition involves transfer of ownership of shares or assets, the contracts to accomplish that transfer should be drawn up very carefully by expert lawyers. Directors of bidder and target boards have a fiduciary duty to their corporation and shareholders. In discharging their duty they must be seen to be acting diligently and with due care, and often seek fairness opinions from investment banks as to the fairness of the offer terms. The process of obtaining such fairness opinions itself can be a source of conflicts of interest among investment bankers, their M & A clients, and the shareholders of those clients. We review the empirical evidence concerning the purpose and effectiveness of these opinions.

Valuation of the target is an important aspect of an acquisition, requiring a great deal of skill and judgement as to the future prospects for both the acquirer and the acquired firms. This exercise calls for an understanding of the strategic aspects of the acquisition, and of valuation models. It also requires a detailed understanding of the operations of the target firm as well as the acquirer. This again may demand contributions from outside experts.

This chapter describes the different advisers who may become involved in a takeover. The paramount role of the investment banks in the US and UK is detailed. Their responsibilities and relationship to acquirers and targets are described. The role of other advisers, such as corporate lawyers, accountants, strategy consultants, investor relations and public relations consultants and environment consultants, who may also participate in an acquisition or a defence in a contested bid, is also discussed.

Role of advisers in acquisitions

A takeover may involve the use of one or more of the following advisers:

- investment banks;
- lawyers;
- accountants and tax advisers;
- stockbrokers;
- investor relations/public relations consultants;
- strategy and human resources consultants;
- environment consultants;
- actuaries;
- intellectual property consultants such as patent agents; and
- risk evaluation and management consultants.

In addition, business brokers or specialist acquisitions consultants may often be used by companies to locate potential acquisition targets.

The need for any of the above advisers in a takeover deal depends upon the extent of in-house expertise available to the company, the regulatory requirements, and the level of complexity of the deal. For example, the acquisition of a private company or the division of another firm may not require the services of a stockbroker or an investor relations adviser. Some acquisitions may not give rise to any environmental concern. Small deals may often be concluded with the help of the firm's accountants, and without the involvement of an investment banker.

The needs of a bidder for external advice are of a different character from those of a company defending itself against a hostile bid. Some of the advisers, such as investment banks, specialize in advising hostile bidders or targets. Advisers also differ in the range of services they offer.

The advisory services in acquisitions and corporate restructuring have become increasingly competitive, with advisers offering an overlapping range of services: for example, accountants offer corporate finance advice, and their strategy consulting arms offer strategic evaluation advice. Lawyers have also encroached upon the role traditionally played by investment banks. Nevertheless, in the UK, at least in bids for public companies, the role of the investment bank is still paramount. In the 1990s banks adopted the business model of 'financial supermarkets' or 'one-stop shopping' to provide a wide range of services and products. The model exploits scope economies through common distribution channels, cross-selling in different product markets, satisfying customer demand for the convenience of one-stop selling, etc. Giant global banks were formed on this basis, including J. P. Morgan Chase, Citigroup, Morgan Stanley, UBS, Credit Suisse, Deutsche Bank and Merrill Lynch. These banks became financial supermarkets.

Role of investment banks

The services that investment banks offer include corporate finance services, stockbroking, fund management and securities trading. Corporate finance services include valuing companies and businesses, as well as arranging packages to finance a deal. An investment bank can act for either the bidder or the target, although some have developed expertise for one or the other role: for example, Goldman Sachs built a great reputation in defending targets in hostile bids. Investment banks normally act in an advisory capacity. However, often in the UK they have acted as principals – for instance, in underwriting a cash offer or in financing a deal, e.g. stapled financing (see Chapter 11 on investment banks' private equity operations).

Services offered by an investment bank in its capacity as an adviser for a bidder are as follows:

- finding acquisition opportunities, e.g. locating an acquisition target;
- evaluating the target from the bidder's strategic and other perspectives; valuing the target; providing 'fair value' opinion;
- devising an appropriate financing structure for the deal, covering offer price, method of payment and sources of finance;
- advising the client on negotiating tactics and strategies for friendly/hostile bids or, in some cases, negotiating deals;
- collecting information about potential rival bidders;
- profiling the target shareholders to 'sell' the bid effectively; helping the bidder with presentations and 'road shows';
- gathering feedback from the stock market about the attitudes of financial institutions to the bid and its terms;
- identifying potential 'showstoppers', such as antitrust investigation by the Competition Commission in the UK, the European Commission or the Federal Trade Commission in the US, and helping prepare the bidder's case in such investigation;
- helping prepare offer document, profit forecast, circulars to shareholders and press releases, and ensuring their accuracy;
- dealing with the takeover regulator, e.g. the City Panel in the UK (see Chapter 18); and
- coordinating all other advisers.

Services offered to targets are as follows:

- monitoring target share price to track potential bidders and provide early warning to target of a possible bid;
- crafting effective bid resistance strategies, e.g. dividend increase;
- valuing the target and its component businesses to negotiate a higher offer price; providing fair value opinion on the offer;
- helping the target and its accountants prepare profit forecasts;
- finding white knights or white squires to block hostile bids;
- arranging buyers for any divestment or management buyout of target assets as part of its defensive strategy;
- getting feedback from the financial institutions concerning the offer and the likelihood of its being accepted; and
- negotiating with the bidder and its team.

The various bid and defence strategies are discussed extensively in Chapters 20 and 21. In devising these strategies the investment bank will rely on the other advisers in the team. For example, in preparing the case in an antitrust investigation, the role of economic consultants and lawyers is crucial. In preparing profit forecasts, the accountants assume the dominant role. In defending the bidder's strategic rationale or in picking holes in that for the defence, the role of the strategy consultant is important.

Fair value opinion (FO)

Investment banks provide 'fair value' opinions, which bidders and targets often invoke in support of their decisions, and in recommending these decisions to their respective share-holders. Over the period 1998–2007 several US investment banks offered FOs. The number and value of completed US M & A deals with their opinions are as follows in 1998 to 2007[1]:

- Goldman Sachs (434 deals; value of deals $2.1 trillions or tn)
- Morgan Stanley (378 deals; value $1.7tn);
- Merrill Lynch (366; 1.6tn);
- J. P. Morgan (440; $1.4tn);
- Credit Suisse First Boston (450; $1.3tn);
- Citigroup (311; $1.3tn);
- Lehman Brothers (280; $1.1tn).

These statistics raise the question of the true purpose of FOs. Very often the banks that advise the bidders on the deal and receive advisory fees, much of which is contingent on deal success, also provide FOs. Fee for these opinions is a proportion of the overall fees received by the banks. In a detailed study of FOs in the US, Kisgen, Qian and Song report that that the average fee paid by an acquirer for all investment bank services is $5.1m, whereas the fee for FOs alone is only $0.9m for bidders and $0.7m for targets[2]. Thus the incentive to complete a deal can compromise the integrity of the fairness opinion.

Fairness opinions may be used by acquirer and target managements to cover themselves against potential charges of lack of diligence and due care and loyalty to the corporation, and failure in their fiduciary duty[3]. If so, they provide a legal protection (the '*legal protection*' hypothesis). On the other hand the process of securing a fairness opinion, with investment banks bringing their expertise to assess the logic, value creation potential and fairness of the offer terms, can lead to improvement in the quality of the deal and thereby enhance share-holder value (the '*transaction improvement*' hypothesis). Kisgen *et al.* test these two hypotheses in the case of acquirers, and find that the securing of FOs:

- improves the probability of deal completion, and the probability is larger when the opinion is provided by the only adviser and when that adviser has a lower reputational capital;
- reduces the bid premium by 4.3%, and by 13% when two advisers are involved and they provide fairness opinion;
- reduces the premium more when the top-tier bank provides the opinion than when it is from a low-tier bank; and
- reduces the three-day abnormal returns to acquirers by 2.3%, and that this value decline is greater when the opinion is provided by the only adviser or by a low-tier bank (see Chapter 4 on the methodology for calculating abnormal returns).

These results are less consistent with transaction improvement than with a desire of the acquirer managers to secure legal cover.

A third hypothesis is that acquirers and targets seek 'fairness' opinions that would buttress their own position *vis-à-vis* the bid: that is, a high-value opinion is offered to bidders who are keen to complete the deal, and a low acquirer value opinion is offered to targets who are keen to defeat a hostile bid (the *rubber stamp* hypothesis). The 'rubber stamp' opinion is merely another weapon in the hands of corporate managers in their battle for or against a bid, and, as such, will hardly convince either company's shareholders. It appears that investors therefore consider that fairness opinions are conflicted and not very credible[4]. In response to much criticism of FOs, the National Association of Securities Dealers has issued a ruling that calls for more disclosure, forcing member firms to disclose if they will receive a 'success fee' at the completion of the deal, and also make public whether or not they have had other relationships with the target company as an intermediary or lender[5].

Fairness opinions in the UK

Unlike in the US, where FOs are not required by law, in the UK they are required under the Takeover Code by the offeree company (Rule 3.1 of the Code) and by the offeror board in the event of a conflict of interest between the board and the shareholders and in the case of reverse takeovers (see Chapter 18 on these) (Rule 3.2. of the Code). Where the takeover bid requires the bidder shareholders' approval, e.g. under the London Stock Exchange rules on class transactions (see Chapter 18), bidders cite the fair value opinion of their investment bankers. Rule 3.3 states that certain advisers are disqualified from providing FOs. The Panel will not regard, as an appropriate person to give independent advice,

> a person who is in the same group as the financial or other professional (including a corporate broker) to an offeror or who has a significant interest in or financial connection with either an offer or offeree company of such a kind as to create a conflict of interest (Rule 3.3).

Moreover, advisory fee contracts may also create a conflict of interest, thereby disqualifying an adviser from offering independent advice. The Code cites an offeree adviser who receives the advisory fee only when the bid fails as exemplifying such a conflict. In all cases of doubt about conflicts of interest the Panel must be consulted.

Fairness opinion in other countries

Fairness opinion is required or is part of M & A practice in several other countries. In Germany, Switzerland and Austria the boards of target firms must issue a written opinion on the offer, in which they comment on, among other points, the type and amount of the consideration and the consequences for the target's shareholders[6]. However, the legal regulation of fairness opinions is rather different. German target boards are not required to obtain and disclose FOs, whereas both actions are mandatory in Austria. In Switzerland, FO is not required, but once targets have obtained an FO, disclosure is compulsory. In 2005 Germany passed a law incorporating the business judgement rule (BJR) similar to the US. Following that, the use of fairness opinions has increased. Legal protection of the target's management is an important determinant in the use of FOs. Since Germany passed the Business Judgement Rule, a significantly higher share of target boards has obtained at least one fairness opinion. Issue of such opinions does not influence the stock market returns to targets. In Switzerland, where there is a conflict of interests between targets and bidders and the targets include FOs, the negative stock market reaction is less than when targets do not include them. In Austria, where FOs are mandatory, there is little stock market reaction[7].

Other roles played by investment banks

Investment bankers play the 'ears and eyes' of the bidders and targets in gauging the mood of the market during bids. Because of the large block holdings of institutional shareholders, it is especially important that a persuasive case for the bid or for the target independence be made to these investors. In many cases the outcome of a bid hinges on the decisions of institutional shareholders.

Assessing market sentiment about the bid or the defence is necessary to modify the tactics and offer terms. Some investment banks have longer antennae than others in reading these sentiments. Investment banks with security trading or stockbroking arms are probably better equipped in this regard, since this helps the banks stay close to the ground. Alternatively, the stockbrokers who are normally part of the advisory team to a bidder can collect market intelligence.

Many investment banks operate risk arbitrage departments (known as arbitrageurs or 'arbs'), in order to exploit the differentials between market and offer prices[8]. Such risk arbitrage associated with M & A is a significant source of income to arbs. When Bear Stearns reported a decline of 27% to $250m in its institutional equities trading revenues in the first quarter of 2002, it attributed this decline to the lack of arbitrage opportunities resulting from low M & A activity[9]. This kind of securities trading again enables an investment bank to sharpen its market intelligence capabilities (see Chapter 20 for further discussions of merger arbitrage).

Many of the takeover defence techniques developed by US investment banks during the 1970s and 1980s – soliciting white knight bidders, sale of crown jewels, demergers, Pac-Man defence, etc. – were subsequently used not only by US banks but also by the native investment banks in other countries as hostile takeover became more common, even in countries such as Germany and France that had traditionally frowned upon it as an unseemly display of corporate pugnacity.

Investment banks and conflicts of interest

In many countries the use of investment bank advisers on M & A deals is a matter of choice for the bidders and targets. For example, in the US many companies prefer not to engage them[10]. In the UK the City Takeover Code (the Code) (Introduction to General Principles, 2000) accords a special place to investment bank financial advisers. Rule 3 of the Code requires the boards of both the bidder (offeror) and the target in the case of takeover bids, where directors face a conflict of interests, e.g. where the two firms share directors to obtain competent independent advice. It also requires target (offeree) companies to obtain independent competent advice on any offer, and the substance of such advice must be communicated to their respective shareholders.

The Code places special responsibility on them in the conduct of bids for public companies. Financial advisers must do the following:

- Comply with the Code.
- Ensure that an offeror and the offeree company and their respective directors are aware of their responsibilities under the Code and comply with them.
- Ensure that the Panel is consulted whenever necessary.
- Cooperate fully with any enquiries made by the Panel.
- Avoid conflicts of interest.

In playing 'minder' to their clients, investment banks should therefore observe the Code with scrupulous care. There have been several instances where they have overzealously transgressed the Code and earned reprimands from the Panel, as evidenced in Exhibit 18.3.

Conflicts of interest may arise, especially where the bank is a financial conglomerate with a market-making or fund management or stockbroking arm. The scandals on Wall Street in the early 2000s, with investment analysts making fraudulent stock purchase recommendations or

Exhibit 19.1

Get the banker and gag the analyst?

During the negotiation of the merger of America Online (AOL) and Time Warner, both companies were assembling a larger advisory team of investment banks, although the negotiation itself was being carried out by the two CEOs, Steve Case and Gerald Levin. The part played by any of the investment banks was unusually small. AOL's share price fell sharply, and the companies felt that the deal was not being sold properly on Wall Street. So more bankers were needed to rectify this problem. However, an alternative view was that 'by buying up investment bankers, both companies will also be able to tie up the banks' analysts from issuing any critical research notes'.

Source: Adapted from W. Lewis, 'Turning the tables on rivals', *Financial Times,* 18 February 2000

being paid success fees for their input to corporate M & A advisory work, also raised questions about the integrity of the advice or research generated by investment banks. Although these different activities are separated by putative Chinese walls, these walls have exhibited remarkable porosity. Companies may be keen to buy the silence of critical investment analysts by enlisting the investment banks they work for (see Exhibit 19.1).

A past advisory role may also conflict with the current role, as when Goldman Sachs acted for Vodafone in its hostile bid for Mannesmann (see Exhibit 19.2). Rule 3.3 of the UK Code requires that financial advisers be independent. They must also avoid potential conflicts of interest, e.g. one part of multi-service bank acting for the bidder and another for the target. If the bank had acted previously for one of the parties and had come into 'material confidential information', a conflict of interest is created when it acts for another party.

Exhibit 19.2

Mannesmann catches out Goldman Sachs

In November 1999 the UK mobile telecommunications company Vodafone AirTouch made an over €100bn hostile bid for Mannesmann, the German telecommunications and engineering group. Goldman advised Vodafone. Earlier in October Mannesmann had bought the UK mobile operator Orange, and Goldman had acted as adviser to Hutchison Whampoa, the main shareholder in Orange. Mannesman complained in the High Court in London that Goldman was in a position to misuse confidential information given to Hutchison during the Orange acquisition. Klaus Esser, chairman of Mannesmann, said that he was 'concerned that Goldman Sachs explicitly promised us not to advise Vodafone or anybody else on an unsolicited bid and then did the contrary'. Goldman was therefore forced to withdraw from Vodafone's advisory team while the case was heard. One unidentified Goldman executive said the case was 'excruciatingly embarrassing'. He further added, 'Investment banks are always managing these conflicts but the thing is not to get caught out. We have been caught out.' Goldman believed it had acted entirely properly.

Did Goldman Sachs play on both sides of the game?

In early 2005, the New York Stock Exchange (NYSE) made an agreed takeover bid for the electronic stock trading company, Archipelago Holdings, for $4bn. As per the terms of the deal, Archipelago would own, post-merger, 30% of the combined entity. It seemed that Goldman Sachs was advising both sides of the deal. One of the members of NYSE, representing several other members, then filed a lawsuit alleging that 'the 30 per cent allocation to Archipelago share-holders was too high, and that this was because of favoritism by senior NYSE executives, several of whom are veterans of Goldman Sachs'. John Thain, CEO of NYSE, had recently been President of Goldman that was also a stockholder in Archipelago. It was also alleged that Goldman had a conflict of interests since it held shares in the target company while holding stakes in one of the leading market makers on NYSE. Many Wall Street rivals of Goldman such as Merrill-Lynch were furious that it was working for both sides. NYSE denied this and maintained that Goldman was merely a 'facilitator'. Goldman was paid $3.5m by each company for this role. Citigroup provided a fairness opinion to NYSE and also disclosed that it had suggested the acquisition to NYSE much earlier imply-ing Goldman was receiving undue credit for the deal.

The law suit was settled by NYSE in December 2005 under which the 30 per cent allocation remained. However, another investment bank was appointed to make an independent evaluation of the merger, and send a fairness opinion to the judge overseeing the case, and to all 1,366 NYSE members. Investment banks Lazard and Greenhill & Co were also barred from undertaking the work as they had advised on the original transaction.

Source: W. Lewis, R. Atkins, J. Mason and A. Cane, 'Mannesmann legal move hits Vodafone's hostile bid plans', *Financial Times,* 16 November 1999; J. Authers, 'NYSE settles suit over Archi-pelago takeover', *Financial Times*, 16 November, 2005; D. Wighton and J. Authers, 'NYSE merger report raises fresh questions', *Financial Times*, 24 November 2005.

Compensation terms for investment bankers

It is thus well recognized that there is much scope for conflicts of interest between companies and their investment bank advisers. There is indeed a wide perception that investment bankers' interests are seriously misaligned with those of their corporate clients. It is held that 'industrialists, egged on by fee-hungry investment bankers, find it more exciting to trade in companies than to focus on operational management'. The term 'pinstripe plunder' captures the late 1990s excesses on Wall Street[11].

A major reason for this is that the M & A advisory service, especially for large deals, is oligopolistic, with only a small number of banks with the resources and capabilities. Com-panies shop around among this limited number of bankers. It is therefore unsurprising that a bank adviser acting for an acquirer in one deal becomes an adviser to its predator in another. The league table of investment bankers compiled by trade journals and databases such as the SDC Thomson database is based on the number and size of deals they have advised, and cor-porate clients contemplating hiring their financial advisers use these league tables to pick their preferred advisers. Hence a place on the league table is hotly contested by bankers, who are prepared to forgo fees to be able to land deals and keep their league position or break into it[12].

Table 19.1 League table of investment bank advisers in M & A deals, 2008

Bank	Deal value ($bn)	No. of deals	Average ($bn)	Disclosed fees ($m)	No. of deals (fee disclosed)	Average ($m)
Goldman Sachs	550	213	2.6	837	47	17.8
J. P. Morgan	424	186	2.3	811	41	19.8
Citi	374	134	2.8	394	17	23.2
Merrill Lynch	335	145	2.3	450	17	26.5
Morgan Stanley	298	144	2.1	465	23	20.2
UBS	253	131	1.9	436	25	17.4
Credit Suisse	243	167	1.5	187	13	14.4
Barclays Capital	236	123	1.9	371	25	14.8
Deutsche Bank	219	93	2.4	362	23	15.7
Lazard	179	104	1.7	271	14	19.4

Table 19.1 shows the league table in 2008 for US deals. The average deal size among the listed 10 banks is between $1.5bn and $2.8bn. In some deals the advisory fee received by the banks is disclosed. The average fee per deal is between $14m and $27m. This is a one-year snapshot picture. Over the 10-year period 1999–2008, in the US, the fee per deal ranges from $10.7m to $18m (in nominal $)[13].

Bankers are agents of the companies in the course of a deal. This relationship creates an agency problem between the two. How do companies ensure that bank advisers as agents perform their tasks in the best interests of their principals? The fee structure may be a device to alleviate the agency problem. Robyn McLaughlin identifies three types of compensation contract in tender offers that are made directly by bidders to target shareholders[14]:

- fixed fees independent of deal outcome;
- contingent fees as either:
  - share-based fees as a function of the number of shares purchased, e.g. a fee of $0.2m plus $0.08 per share acquired – the contingent element may also be a step function, increasing with different levels of shares acquired; or
  - value-based fees, either total value or incremental value fees, e.g. a flat fee of $0.125m plus 0.5% of the value of the completed transaction (total fee incentive) or $0.125m flat fee plus 2.5% of the value above $20 per share for a completed acquisition (incremental fee incentive).

Most contracts provide for a minimum fee if no transaction takes place, and many target contracts in hostile offers contain a provision paying a bonus if the hostile offer is defeated. There are also often special fees for successfully completed defensive measures, such as share repurchases, special dividends and spin-offs. In hostile takeovers target contracts may not explicitly contain an incentive to defeat any and all offers, since that may expose target managers to shareholder legal action for failure to encourage adequate bids.

Share-based contracts create incentives for both target and bidding firm bankers to complete the transaction, although neither has the incentive to optimize offer value. Bankers will prefer this contract type if the completion probability is high and the probability of higher bids is low. With total value fee, both target and bidding firm bankers have strong incentives to complete a transaction, and some incentive to seek higher bids if a higher price does not reduce the associated probability of offer success. Incremental value fee contracts motivate bankers to complete a transaction, but only at a price higher than the first offer. Thus different contract types have different degrees of misalignment between shareholders' and bankers' interests.

Incidence of different compensation contract types

For a sample of 132 target firms and 195 bidding firms involved in tender offers from 1980–85, Robin McLaughlin found that over 80% of the investment banker fee in an average contract was payable only if the acquisition was completed[15]. Typically, the fee for the target banker was a function of offer value and that for the bidder banker a function of the number of shares purchased. This structure created potentially perverse incentives. In the case of targets there was a conflict between the bank's duty to seek high valuation and its incentive to complete the deal. In the case of bidders there was no incentive to minimize the price paid.

In the 1992 follow-up study McLaughlin found, with a US sample of 161 target and 241 bidder contracts during 1978–86, that fixed fees were used infrequently (8% of sample target contracts and 6% of the bidders). Bidding firm and target firm contingent contracts relied on different measures of outcome, with most bidder fees based on the number of shares acquired (80%) and most target fees based on acquisition value (71%). The contingent portions of these fees averaged 80% of total fee. Average banker fees in the sample of completed transactions was 0.59% of value for bidders and 0.79% for targets.

For a larger and more recent sample of 372 US mergers (offers made in agreement with, and recommended by, target management) and 388 tender offers, Raghavendra Rau observes in the acquirers' contracts that 39% fees in mergers are contingent and 66% in tender offers, the latter being more uncertain of success[16]. Moreover, in tender offers, first-tier banks charge 73% of their fees as contingent, whereas second- and third-tier banks charge 61% and 64% respectively. This differential is consistent with top-tier banks signalling their superior quality by charging a higher proportion of their fee as contingent, and with top-tier bankers more eager to complete the deals. In friendly mergers, however, the three tiers of banks did not differ in their deal completion rates. This suggests that tender offers, being more contentious, require more dexterity and resources to complete, and top-tier banks are more likely to exhibit these. The top-tier banks are the bulge bracket banks – Morgan Stanley, Salomon Brothers, Goldman Sachs, Lazard Freres and First Boston (now part of Credit Suisse).

In the UK, information on investment banker contracts is not generally available. However, it appears that up to a deal size of $1bn, the fee is 0.75% and above that it is 0.50%. This is a ballpark figure, and varies significantly from one bank to another and one deal to another. This fee structure suggests total value contingent fee contracts. In the case of hostile bid defence the contingent fee may be at least 1.5%, with a large part of the total fee payable regardless of success or failure. The fee is higher, as one senior banker explained to the author, because when the target company appoints the investment bank, it is clear that if the defence fails, the target company and its management will fall. The company therefore wants the best advice possible: if it wins, the price of advice would have been worth it (they survived!) and if it loses the bidder picks up all of the target obligations, including the adviser fees! Thus the target is relatively price insensitive. While there may be alignment of interests between managers and bankers in this type of contract, it may not be in the best interests of target shareholders, who may ultimately bear the cost of an expensive defence. Exhibit 19.3 shows the structure of compensation contracts for the bidder and target advisers in the merger of Hewlett-Packard and Compaq announced in September 2001. The bidder's contract with Goldman Sachs is a fixed-price contract contingent on the success of the bid, whereas Compaq has a contingent-fee contract with fee dependent on the value of the deal.

Regulation of success fee contracts for financial advisers

In the takeover bid for Argos, the UK catalogue retailer, by Great Universal Stores (GUS), Argos agreed to pay a success fee to its financial adviser Schroders (now part of Citigroup with

Exhibit 19.3

Some bankers have greater incentives than others to close the deal and cost shareholder value

In September 2001 Hewlett-Packard (HP) and Compaq (C) announced a merger of equals, valuing Compaq at $25bn. It was a share exchange merger, with an exchange ratio of 0.6325 and a premium of 14% to C. HP retained Goldman Sachs (GS) as its financial adviser, and C hired Salomon Smith Barney (SSB) as its adviser. Both banks had had previous engagements with both companies. GS had been a manager of HP's debt issues in 2000 and 2001. Each adviser also provided a fairness opinion (FO) to its client. Each adviser carried out various analyses based on the Merger Agreement, previous 5 year 10K reports, internal financial analyses, and forecasts from the company managements, discussions with senior management etc to assess the offer. GS's fairness opinion on the exchange ratio was: 'It is our opinion, . . . the exchange ratio is fair from a financial point of view to HP.' SSB also provided a similar opinion for C's shareholders.

The fee for GS was:

- $5m upon execution of the Merger Agreement; and
- $28m on completion of the deal.

The fee for SSB was quite different. SSB was to receive:

- $0.5 at engagement;
- $9.5m upon completion of the merger agreement; and
- 0.25% of deal value less $10m received as above.

Both contracts were contingent. However, a greater portion of the GS fee depended on completion ($28m out of $33m total fee). For a deal completed at $25bn, SSB would receive:

$0.5m + 9.5m + (0.25 \times 25bn - $10m) = $62.5m$, almost double the fee for GS.

In terms of incentives, SSB had a greater incentive to complete the deal, but also at as high a price as possible. GS's fee was unrelated to the eventual deal value. It had no incentive to help HP minimise the acquisition price. The SSB contract provided an incentive to maximize the value of the deal to C.

Source: Darden Business Publishing, University of Virginia, 'The merger of Hewlett-Packard and Compaq (B): Deal design, case UVA-F-1451, 2004

Salomon Smith Barney) in the event the hostile bid was defeated. This was later challenged by GUS before the Takeover Panel (see Chapter 18), but the Panel Executive ruled that Schroders had not been influenced by the success fee, and the fee did not breach the Code. However, in 1999 the Panel stated its position that arrangements that reward an adviser to the offeree dependent on failure of a hostile offer, irrespective of the offer price, give rise to, or create the perception of, conflicts of interest. In these circumstances the adviser will normally be disqualified from acting as independent adviser under Rule 3. This does not preclude the use of such an adviser.

Connected market-makers (and from October 1997 principal traders) belonging to multi-service financial firms, e.g. firms with M & A advisory, corporate finance and securities trading functions, may be exempt from a detailed disclosure of their dealings, required of others acting in concert, so that their normal course of business is not impeded. But the Panel seeks to ensure, through Rule 38, that covert purchases of target shares are not made through the exempt market-maker, and it regards violation of that rule seriously.

Bank reputation and alignment of interests

It may be surmised that banks that have built up high reputation over the years will be keen to ensure that their compensation contracts align their own and their corporate clients' interests. Thus the misalignments we have discussed above may be mitigated by bank reputation. For targets, McLaughlin finds no evidence of any reputational impact on bid outcome or on the bid premium. For bidders, it is the low-reputation bankers that reduce the premium offered, thereby increasing the returns to bidder shareholders[17].

Investment banks often provide support to their M & A clients in the following ways:

- buying shares in either the bidder or target;
- underwriting a share exchange offer so as to provide a cash alternative to target shareholders;
- arranging finance for a cash bid;
- financing the acquisition as a principal; or
- providing stapled financing to buyers in auctions although they act for the seller.

Share support operations are allowed under the Code, subject to disclosure rules and the rules governing the maximum price, uniform price and mandatory cash offer described in Chapter 18. In buying the target shares on behalf of the bidder, timing is very important. In addition to supporting the bidder and enhancing the probability of a successful bid, the advisory banks, in buying stakes in targets, may seek to maximize their profits even at the expense of their bidder clients. Having bought the target stake, the advisers may exert influence on the targets to accept the offer, thereby ensuring that they can unwind their target stake profitably. They can also induce targets to offer break-up (termination) fees to the bidders, again increasing the chances of bid success[18]. Advisers, having built up their target stakes ostensibly for the purpose of helping the bidders, may subtly influence the bidders to up the premium, which in turn can raise the chances of bid success. These arguments point to divergence of interests between a bidder and its investment bank adviser that buys target stakes. This divergence may result in bidders overpaying for their targets or concluding deals that are value destroying, as Exhibit 19.4 shows.

Investment banks underwriting a share offer to provide a cash alternative have the deal sub-underwritten by other financial institutions, although they may retain some of the exposure

---

Exhibit 19.4

Bidder bank advisers buying target stakes: helping their clients or helping themselves?

Bodnaruk, Massimo and Simonov investigate, with a large sample of US deals in which the bidders' investment bank advisers buy stakes in the target firms just before deal announcement, whether they do so in their own self-interest or to further the bidders' interests. They assess the impact of such stakes on the probability that the investee company becomes the target of a bid, the probability of bid success, the bid premium, and termination fee payable by the target.

In the sample, bidders' advisers have target stakes in 26% of the deals. This stake on average represents 0.63% of target market capitalization, amounting to an investment of $14m. The authors find that the advisers' stakes:

- increase the probability of the investee becoming a target (from 4% to 6%), consistent with the advisers using their privileged access to the acquirer to build up their stake in potential targets;
- are associated with the bidders paying a higher premium, i.e. 5.5% more on average, to targets in which the advisers hold stakes than to targets without such stakes;
- make target termination fees more likely; and
- reduce the probability of bid failure significantly by 28% from 24% to 17%.

These results are not conclusive evidence of a conflict of interest, since it is in the bidders' interest that their bids are successful. However, the authors also report that, on average, targets with advisory stakes:

- are overvalued by 10%; and
- experience, in the first post-acquisition year, decline in profit margin, ROE and ROA of around 2%.

This suggests that the acquisitions of targets with advisory stakes are value destroying.

Further, the returns for advisory banks from investing in targets significantly exceed the returns from a pure arbitrage strategy, based only on public information and bereft of the privileged information and ability to influence deal structure and outcome that the advisory banks enjoy (see Chapter 20 on merger arbitrage):

Advisory bank investment strategy*   4.1% (net of risk adjustment)
Merger arbitrage strategy*   0.5% (net of risk adjustment)

Advisory banks can take positions in targets ahead of bid announcements, thereby benefiting from the increase in target share values upon those announcements, whereas non-advisory banks investing in the same targets do so using only non-privileged information. This advantage translates into superior returns to advisory banks. The authors report the returns based on these investment strategies:

Advisory banks' returns when they invest in targets   3.4%
Non-advisory banks' returns when they invest in targets   1.9%

These results suggest that:

advisers exploit their privileged position, not only by acquiring positions in the deals on which they advise, but also by directly affecting the outcome of the deal in order to realize higher capital gains from their positions. These results are, however, also consistent with the alternative explanation: that the bidder's board hires a deal-advocate/adviser with high-powered incentives to get the deal done.

Source: Adapted from A. Bodnaruk, M. Massa and A. Simonov, 'Investment banks as insiders and the market for corporate control', *The Review of Financial Studies*, 22 2009, 4989–5026. The sample comprises 10,458 M & A announcements during 1984–2003, of which 4,280 involve an adviser to either the target or the acquirer, or to both.
*The investment strategy assumes a short position in bidder's stock and long position in the target's stock.

themselves. The underwriting may be a conventional rights issue type, or contingent upon the success of the bid. The differences between these two forms of underwriting are discussed in Chapter 16.

Arranging acquisition financing requires a good deal of placing power from the investment bank. The success of this effort will depend upon the reputation of the bank in its corporate finance role in general, and its track record of supporting good acquisitions. While even small investment banks can successfully place the bidder's securities to raise funds, a bank that chooses to finance a part or whole of the deal itself needs a 'deep pocket'. This is where being part of a larger banking group may be of great competitive advantage[19]. In recent years many commercial banks without a strong M & A advisory business have gained significant market share in that market and have enticed acquirers through their ability to arrange both acquisition and non-acquisition financing. They have used their prior lending relationship with the acquirers, developed through commercial operations, to offer attractive loan terms. They have also used low loan pricing of non-acquisition financing as a *loss leader* to win both acquisition-financing mandates and M & A advisory mandates (see Exhibit 19.4). Investment banks see their ability to cross-sell M & A advice and providing finance as a source of competitive advantage and profits[20].

Exhibit 19.5

Beware of banks bearing gifts of cheap loans!

Commercial banks that seek to develop lucrative M & A advisory services in their portfolios of banking services use their ability to make loans at attractive rates to the acquirers to win the mandate to act as their M & A advisers. The loans they make may be part of the acquisition financing, i.e. to pay for the acquisition, or may be loans for post-acquisition ('general purpose') financing of the acquirer's operations or investments. Acquisition financing is generally more transparent than non-acquisition financing, since the former is disclosed as part of the acquisition-related disclosures. Thus any underpricing of the loans is more likely in non-acquisition loans than in acquisition financing. Such underpricing normally takes the form of lower credit spread (see Chapter 16 on credit spreads). Underpricing in the primary (i.e. new loan) market means that the risk of lending to the acquirer is not fully reflected in the spread. Such underpricing is therefore likely to be reflected in a steeper discount at which such loans are traded in the secondary market, since the lead lenders have sacrificed credit quality to attain their M & A-related objectives. If the spreads on non-acquisition financing are lower than on acquisition financing, and in the secondary market non-acquisition debt is traded at a greater discount than the acquisition-related debt, the implication is that the non-acquisition debt is a *loss-leader*.

Linda Allen and Stavros Peristiani examine whether banks that have a prior lending relationship with acquirers behave in a way that suggests that they leverage that relationship to win M & A mandates from those acquirers. Using non-acquisition-related loans as loss-leaders would be consistent with the relationship banks' seeking to leverage their ability to make/arrange attractive loans to the acquirer to win the M & A mandates.

→

Allen and Peristiani examine the pricing of both types of syndicated loan led by relationship banks that also act as M & A advisers (called 'agent banks' by the authors) in the year after the merger, and compare it with the pricing of similar, syndicated loans led by relationship banks that have no M & A relationship. They find that:

● non-acquisition loans by agent banks surge in the year following the merger, whereas such loans by non-agent banks do not surge, thus pointing to the link between an advisory role in a merger and the lending to the acquirer that follows;

● primary market spreads on acquisition-related loans are significantly higher, both economically and statistically, than on non-acquisition (general purpose) loans;

● spreads on acquisition-related loans arranged by agent banks are about 36 basis points (0.36%) higher than the spreads for non-acquisition loans granted by non-agent banks – thus acquisition financing is not underpriced;

● non-acquisition loans are underpriced, i.e. they have smaller spreads in the primary market;

● this underpricing is followed by significantly larger price declines when these loans begin trading in the secondary market;

● loan market participants are particularly concerned about the poorer credit quality of non-acquisition loans extended by merger advisers, and therefore they are sold at steep discount; and

● non-acquisition loans arranged by bank advisers are sold at an average discount of around 11% points in their first week of trading.

This pattern of loan pricing indicates that banks use non-acquisition financing as a loss-leader to win lucrative advisory mandates.

Source: Adapted from L. Allen and S. Peristiani, 'Loan underpricing and the provision of merger advisory services', *Journal of Banking and Finance*, **31** 2007, 3539–3562.
The sample consists of 9294 non-agent loans and 503 agent loans during 1994–2003.

Investment banks and takeover auctions

In the US in the last 20 years, auctions for sale of companies or divisions have become much more frequent. Where the directors of a company have put up a sale sign in the face of a hostile or unsolicited bid they have the fiduciary duty to run an auction among competing bidders, as decided in one of the landmark cases in the US, *Revlon vs Pantry Pride*, concerned with directors' fiduciary duties in the takeover context. This duty does not extend to the target directors having to actively solicit rival bidders.

The auction process and its various stages are described in more detail in Chapter 20. Investment banks play an important role in organizing the auction, in exploiting their knowledge of the industry of the target to identify potential bidders, their networks to line up such bidders, and their expertise in running successful auctions for the seller. Their clients expect that they will ensure a keen contest so that the sale price is maximized. On the bidder's side, investment banks help bidders to understand the auction game, and play it in such a way as to not only win the bidding war but also avoid the *winner's curse* of overpayment. Thus the auction context

Exhibit 19.6

Stapled financing and conflict of interest

An investment bank is running an auction on behalf of a corporate vendor. The value of the deal is $10bn. The bank, being a sell-adviser, stands to make a fee of $50 million at, say, 0.5% of deal value from the seller. If the sell-adviser can also provide the staple financing, it can add $130m to $150m at 1.3–1.5% of the amount financed, i.e. the deal value, from the buyer, for a total of $180–$200m in fees for a single deal. The sell-adviser stands to makes three times as much fee from the buyer as from the seller! This becomes problematic when there is another bidder who offers $10.5 billion but will not use the staple financing. Here, the sell-adviser/stapled-lender will make only $52.5m. But the seller will receive $500m more in sale proceeds. So there is a powerful incentive to skew the auction, assuming that skewing the auction is possible. All of this presupposes, however, that the deal goes through and the stapled-lender can actually syndicate the loans or sell the bonds for an amount equal to what they lent minus the 1.3–1.5% financing fee. During a credit crisis such a fee structure increases the incentive for the adviser not to pull the financing, thereby allowing the deal to go through! At such times even sellers will not mind the conflict of interest, since without the stapled financing there will be no deal on the table!

Source: C. Foulds, 'My banker's conflicted and I couldn't be happier: The curious durability of staple financing', *Delaware Journal of Corporate Law*, 34(2), 2000

provides a good test of the mettle of investment bankers' ability to add value on both sides, because the outcome is more uncertain and less easy to manipulate than in a negotiated deal.

Investment banks running the auction for the targets often extend financing to potential buyers. There is scope for conflict of interest between the target and its financial adviser. Moreover, the target board, to satisfy its *Revlon* duties, has to avoid such conflict of interest. There are arguments in favour of staple financing such as speed, level playing field among potential bidders, more certainty of consummation of a bid, etc. Investment banks receive considerably higher fees from underwriting the stapled financing than from advising the seller (see Exhibit 19.6). Thus they may have an incentive to skew the auction in favour of buyers who would take up its stapled financing offer[21].

Responsibilities of investment bank advisers

While the city Code imposes the responsibility of care on the advisers involved in takeover bids for public companies, the extent of any liability for loss or damages to those who rely on the information and opinion provided by the advisers is a matter for the courts to decide. There have been a few instances where contravening the Code, or negligence in the provision of information during a bid, has been very costly to merchant banks and other advisers, as described in Exhibit 19.7. The duties owed by investment bank advisers to various parties to a merger are defined by the advisory contracts they sign, and by case law. Several cases in the US exposed investment banks to claims from third parties, shareholders of the clients advised by them, and to trustees in bankruptcy if, following a merger, the firm goes bankrupt (see Case study at the end of this chapter).

Exhibit 19.7

Investment banks' risk exposure

Hill Samuel breaks the Code and pays the price

T & N made a £257m bid for AE, which was advised by investment bank Hill Samuel. T & N lost the bid by a margin of 1% after some hectic dealings in AE shares just before the bid closed. Hill Samuel and Cazenove, the stockbrokers, were censured by the Panel for not disclosing indemnity agreements with third parties to buy AE shares to prevent T & N winning. The Panel then waived the 12-month moratorium and allowed T & N to bid again immediately. T & N won with a higher bid of £278m and sued Hill Samuel to recover the difference of £21m. In January 1990 Hill Samuel settled with T & N out of court.

Wall Street bulge bracket bankers exposed to lawsuits for not so fair opinion

In June 1987 long-time Dallas banking rivals Republic Bank Corp. and InterFirst merged to form First RepublicBank. Fourteen months later the merged bank went bust and filed for bankruptcy. For work connected with the failed merger, Wall Street banks Goldman Sachs and Morgan Stanley charged an estimated $13m in fees, commissions and expenses, and about $6.5m of it for rendering fairness opinion. When the merged bank collapsed it was revealed that the bankers had information at the time of the merger that Republic had wildly over-valued its loan portfolio by $1bn, but they had ignored this vital information in rendering their fairness opinion. The shareholders and bondholders lost heavily, and the Federal Deposit Insurance Corporation spent $3bn in a bailout. Following the bank failure shareholders filed lawsuits in state and Federal courts against the two banks, as well as the failed bank's executives and directors.

Sources: *Financial Times*, 4 January 1990; W. P. Barrett, *Forbes*, 1 October 1990 respectively

Empirical evidence on the impact of investment bankers on bid premium and shareholder wealth

One important question that companies engaging in takeovers and mergers would ask is what difference the choice of an adviser makes to the outcome or cost of a bid. Bankers can contribute in one of two ways or both:

- by identifying and brokering superior value creating mergers (the *better merger* hypothesis); and/or
- by outsmarting the banker to the opponent in a deal (the *superior bargaining* hypothesis).

For a sample of 114 US acquisitions, Bowers and Miller divided the advising banks into top-tier and bottom-tier banks, and compared the market model abnormal returns to the shareholders of both bidders and targets at the time of bid announcement (see Chapter 4 on the abnormal returns methodology)[22]. They found that the total returns to the two companies' shareholders were indeed higher when at least one of them chose a first-tier bank. However, they found no evidence that first-tier bankers brought superior bargaining expertise to acquisition negotiations. The shareholders of either company did not gain from the choice of a first-tier bank, even when its wits were pitted against a second-tier bank in the opposite camp.

Sudarsanam and Salami carried out a similar test of the two hypotheses with a sample of nearly 1100 UK acquisitions during 1985–94[23]. They found support for the better merger hypothesis. Acquisitions in which both parties were advised by top-tier banks generated significantly higher returns to target shareholders (over 20 days before deal announcement to its completion) than deals in which both were advised by bottom-tier banks (33% versus 24%). For the bidders there was no significant difference. The combined shareholder returns were significantly higher with top-tier than with bottom-tier banks (7% versus 2.3%). This translated into an average total gain of £29m for the first group and only £1m for the second group. Sudarsanam and Salami also found that the investment bank reputation made a difference to a hostile bid outcome. When targets chose a top-tier bank, their chances of defeating the hostile bids were much higher than when they were advised by bottom-tier bankers. The reputation of the bidder bank, however, was not relevant to bid outcome. Thus it is targets that in the UK lose through inappropriate choice of investment banker rather than bidders lose through their choice. This result contradicts the result for US tender offers reported by Rau[24].

Rau examined the short- and long-term returns. Over three days around bid announcement, tender offers advised by top-tier banks generated superior returns to those by third-tier banks (3.5% compared with 0.2%). However, in tender offers there is a strong negative relation between average contingent fee paid to the adviser and the abnormal returns earned by the acquirer over 6–18 months after offer completion. Thus paying high contingency fees may hurt tender offer acquirers, because the adviser may be too focused on deal completion and encourage them to pay high prices for targets rather than craft a value-creating deal.

In a study of 308 takeover contests during 1989–99, including those in which several bidders participated in an auction and those that were bilaterally negotiated between the target and acquirer, Boone and Mulherin compare the abnormal returns to bidders advised by prestigious banks and lower-tier banks[25]. They find that the former are significantly higher than the latter. However, where the target is advised by a top-tier bank the returns to bidders are significantly lower, suggesting that the successful bidder was not allowed to get away with low-balling. Thus prestigious investment banks are not associated with overpayment by their bidder clients, and seem to help their target clients extract higher offers from bidders.

To summarize these empirical results, top-quality bankers may add value to deals. Thus companies may benefit from their search role to find value additive mergers. However, they are perhaps of less value at the deal negotiation stage. This may be because compensation contracts do not structure incentives for value extraction during negotiation. On the contrary, in tender offers the incentives may allow bankers to push for deal closure rather than for value extraction. Alternatively, bankers may be serving the interests of managers (their immediate paymasters) rather than the distant shareholders. These studies emphasize the need to structure bankers' incentives carefully so that they are aligned to the interests of shareholders.[26]

The above studies have relied on a market-share-based proxy for investment banker quality. From the acquirer's point of view a better screening criterion in the choice of its investment bank adviser may be whether in the past deals advised by the bank the acquirers have created value. This criterion is also of greater relevance to acquirer shareholders. A recent study shows that investment banks with superior returns in their past deals are able to repeat such performance through their various skills, e.g. target selection or deal negotiation. Such performance persistence is not related to their market share. Thus the latter may be a less reliable guide to the choice of investment bank advisers[27].

Lawyers

Among the other advisers, lawyers are almost always involved in acquisitions of both private and public companies. Lawyers play an important role in drafting agreements and coordinating paperwork. They manage this process to completion and thereafter. They can also play a negotiator's role or facilitate negotiation. They play an important part in a due diligence audit undertaken as part of an acquisition, although other specialists such as chartered surveyors and risk insurers may be co-opted in carrying out these tasks (see Table 20.2 on the various types of due diligence and their motivation). They play a critical role in designing efficient legal structures in appropriate jurisdictions.

The important elements of a legal due diligence audit are as follows:

- property investigation, e.g. establishing legal title and valuation;
- assessment of the target company's liabilities, both current and contingent, e.g. liabilities for unpaid tax or pension fund deficits, redundancy payments, pending litigation and obligations imposed by environmental protection laws or practices; and
- assessment of risks and insurance cover arranged by the target, e.g. insurance of physical assets, and insurance of liabilities such as product liability or directors' and officers' liability.

Warranties and indemnities

When the due diligence points to the potential risks in proceeding with the transaction, the bidder will look for some form of risk insurance or purchase price reduction, or a combination of both. A warranty is a contractual representation by the vendor that, if it is untrue, entitles the purchaser to claim for damages. For example, a warranty may be to the effect that the vendor company's title to its properties is good, or that the company's latest accounts are true and accurate. A warranty allows the bidder to elicit crucial information. A vendor can reduce the extent of warranties through fair disclosures, thereby reallocating risk to the buyer.

An indemnity is similar to a warranty, but provides that the vendor will compensate the buyer in the event of any loss under specified circumstances. For example, an indemnity may cover potential but undisclosed tax liabilities. Carefully drafted warranties and indemnities provide risk insurance, and may raise the comfort level of the bidder in proceeding with the deal. The lawyers' role in negotiating appropriate warranties and indemnities to allocate the risk between the bidder and the vendor is therefore critical. They can also advise the bidder in negotiating an appropriate price reduction in lieu of a warranty or indemnity, or if the vendor is unwilling to agree to one.

Role of lawyers in bid strategy and takeover defence

Lawyers in the UK have a lower profile in public company takeovers than their US counterparts. In the 1980s the latter enjoyed as much visibility as the investment bank superstars. For example, Martin Lipton of the US law firm Wachtell, Lipton, Rosen and Katz is the progenitor of the famous poison pill defence, one of the most potent of the defensive devices available to targets in the US (see Chapter 21 for definition and illustration of the effect of poison pills). Most of the significant innovations in the hostile takeover business have come from lawyers[28].

In the UK, lawyers Freshfields invented the 'vitamin pill' for Consolidated Goldfields (Consgold) in its defence against Minorco. When faced with a £3.2bn hostile bid from

Minorco in 1989, Consgold pledged to pay its shareholders a cash dividend of £6 gross per share if the company did not meet a target earnings per share figure of 400 pence cumulative over the following three years. The £6 was to be tied to the issue of special preference shares carrying rights to vote the promised dividend. If the target EPS were met, the special shares would become worthless. Consgold did beat off the predator, although it employed other more effective defence ploys. Consgold was in the same year taken over by Hanson.

Lawyers play an important role in preparing the case to be presented to antitrust regulators, for example, the Competition Commission or the FTC in connection with any antitrust investigation. Although the Code specifically emphasizes that its appeal proceedings must be conducted in a non-judicial manner, lawyers do get involved in preparing the arguments presented to the Panel. While lawyers have traditionally been paid by the hour, there is a greater trend towards some form of success fee to relate lawyers' input to the value added. But the contingent fee is still a relatively small part of the total lawyer's fees[29].

Accountants

Accountants carry out the due diligence investigation, which may often be wide ranging and cover pre-purchase review, purchase investigation and acquisition audit. A pre-purchase review provides limited information about the target, its industry and the reasons for sale, but it is not a substitute for a strategic evaluation. The principal aim of the purchase investigation is to identify significant matters relevant to the valuation of the target, or the warranties and indemnities to be obtained. Such matters cover the target's accounting policies and financial projections, and the key commercial assumptions behind those projections.

The acquisition audit, available only in the case of a private company target, examines the quality of the company's accounts, and contains the investigating accountant's assessment of that quality. Based on this, the buyer can seek an appropriate warranty from the seller.

Accountants are also involved in preparing profit forecasts, which are then used by the bidder or target to strengthen their argument for or against the bid. As noted in Chapter 18, such forecasts must be prepared to the highest standards of care and accuracy. The financial adviser takes responsibility for observing these standards. Financial advisers, in giving fairness opinion, may rely on the accountants.

Other advisers

Stockbrokers play an important role as a channel of communication, through their circulars, of bid-related information between the parties to a bid and the investors. They also become involved in market purchases of shares during a bid. Further, where bid financing involves the issue of new securities, they act as sponsors to the issue. Finally, they may also underwrite a share exchange offer to provide the cash alternative.

Strategy consultants may be called in to evaluate the attractiveness of the target company from the bidder's strategic criteria, and to assess the value creation logic of the bid. More recently, owing to burgeoning environment protection laws in different countries, acquirers are concerned about the potential costs of complying with those laws, and the liabilities arising from the past failure of the target to comply. The latter influences the purchase price or, alternatively, forms the basis of indemnities from the target. The cost of failing to perform an environmental audit can often be high.

Public and investor relations

Both public relations (PR) and investor relations (IR) consultants play a crucial role in contested takeovers. IR is about convincing the shareholders and potential investors of the merits of the bid or of defence. PR has a much wider remit, since the targets for a PR exercise are not only shareholders but also the press, employees, politicians and regulatory bodies. The two terms are often used interchangeably. A large number of UK companies employ PR consultants in their corporate advisory team as part of their long-term bid defence plans.

During a contested bid, putting over the bid and defence arguments powerfully and effectively is quite important. PR consultants are used in the preparation of offer and defence documents and in the wording of letters to shareholders, so that the arguments are presented clearly and persuasively. Use of advertising in the print media as well as television and radio is also done with the advice of PR consultants.

Specialist PR consultants often field questions during a bid on very difficult and sensitive questions. For example, an optimistic profit forecast from a target company with a lacklustre performance in the past will naturally arouse much scepticism, if not derision. It is then for the PR person to make a convincing case for the forecast. PR consultants also 'tutor' company executives who are not used to the limelight to face the media with poise and conviction.

A PR person also advises on bid tactics, and on effective counterattacks against the other side. PR consultants have increasingly become part of a bid or defence advisory team, but their activities need to be regulated so that they are always in compliance with the Code.

CASE STUDY

What are investment banks' duties and to whom are they owed?

As described in the chapter above, investment banks (IBs) carry out several functions. In carrying out these functions, IBs may become liable to various parties for:

- negligent misrepresentation or professional negligence in offering 'bad' advice to the client;
- negligent misrepresentation or breach of fiduciary duty to the client, its stock holders or a trustee in the post-deal bankruptcy of the client company;
- fraud or violation of securities laws to the party opposite the client in a transaction, e.g. a seller or a buyer.

Claims by a client or its stockholders

Since there is a contractual agreement between an IB and its client, a claim by the client for negligent misrepresentation flows from the contractual rights of the client. The IB acts as the client's agent. Thus there is a principal–client relationship between them. But does the adviser owe the same duty to the stockholders of the client as their 'agent's agent'? In 1990, the case *Scheider* v. *Lazard Freres & Co* arose from the 1988 leveraged buyout of RJR Nabisco Inc by the private equity firm KKR against a competing MBO bid by Ross Johnson the target's incumbent CEO. Former shareholders of RJR Nabisco alleged that the bank was negligent in its analysis and advice on the relative merits of the two rival bids for the target. In its defence, Lazard argued that it had been retained by the special committee of the target board and the stockholders did not have a valid claim against it.

A New York State appellate court, however, held that the special committee was effectively an agent of the stockholders. The bank, therefore, owed a duty of care to them as their 'agent's agent'. The bank's agency responsibility extended to the principal's principal. This judgement ran counter to prior law regarding the liability of an IB to its client's stockholders.

Claims by trustee in bankruptcy

The 1996 case *In re Daisy Systems Corp.* in California centred on the duty of Bear Stearns (BS) that advised Daisy in its 1988 hostile acquisition of Cadnetix Corp. Financing was also to be arranged by the bank. The combined company, Dazix, subsequently failed due to operational and financial problems and went into bankruptcy in 1991. The trustee in bankruptcy sued BS for breach of fiduciary duty, negligent misrepresentation and professional negligence and alleged that the bankruptcy resulted from its advice to pursue a hostile tender offer and its failure to arrange financing for it.

Although BS won at the district court level, this judgement was reversed on appeal. The US 9th Circuit Court of Appeals ordered a trial on questions of fact concerning the breach of fiduciary duty and professional negligence claims. The jury found that BS owed a fiduciary duty to Daisy and had not breached that duty. However, the jury held BS liable for professional negligence. The court appeared to adopt a standard by which IBs could be held responsible for analysis of risks and benefits, and the business and operational effects of a deal, beyond what the engagement letters between the client and the bank specified.

Claims by a third party

In 1998 Ron Perelman, the well known deal maker of the 1980s and the 1990s, sold camping equipment maker, Coleman, owned by his holding company, Coleman (Parent) Holdings Inc, to Sunbeam Corp for $1.5bn in exchange, substantially, for the Sunbeam stock. Following the acquisition and the accounting problems that emerged, Sunbeam filed for bankruptcy in 2001. Perelman sued Morgan Stanley, Sunbeam's adviser on the deal, for fraud and conspiracy, and for violation of securities laws. Perelman argued that he had relied on the bank's reputation as one of the world's top investment banks whom he himself had engaged in the past.

A Flordia jury, in 2005, decided in Perelman's favour. It awarded $1.5bn including $850m in punitive damages to Coleman Co against Morgan Stanley. This verdict followed the pre-trial judge's ruling that the bank had failed to produce required emails on a timely basis during the discovery phase. This ruling was controversial. The judgement was overturned on appeal.

Discussion questions

1   What is the nature of the relationship between an investment bank and the client it advises?

2   What is the doctrine of 'agent's agent'? Whom does it benefit?

3   Does the adviser's duty or responsibility extend to a trustee in bankruptcy of the client?

4   What is the importance of the investment bank's reputation in cases such as the Perelman case?

5   How can investment banks protect themselves against such claims?

Source: M. J. Mihanovic, 'Legal perils mount for M & A advisers', *Mergers & Acquisitions* November 2005, 37–41.

Overview and implications for practice

In this chapter, the roles played by different advisers in acquisitions have been described, and the central role of investment banks in UK public company bids highlighted.

- The responsibilities of advisers, especially of the investment banker, under the Code are extremely stringent.

- The risk faced by investment banks when they fail to meet these responsibilities entails both direct and indirect costs to their reputation, and forfeiture of competitive advantage.

- There is scope for conflict of interest between bidding and defending companies, and their advisers, causing companies to overpay for their acquisition or defend their companies 'to the last shareholder' while a more value-enhancing decision may be to accept an offer.

- Compensation contracts for investment bankers may create perverse incentives to do a deal at the wrong price. Companies can minimize these conflicts by drawing up contracts carefully, avoiding too much emphasis on contingent payments.

- Acquisition financing provided by the acquirer's advisory bank to the acquirer may also be a source of conflict.

- In auction situations stapled financing offered by the seller's bank advisers to the bidders may also create a conflict of interests.

- So what are the checks against such incentives for opportunism on the part of investment banks? The most important is that the banks have to safeguard their reputation capital. A bank that persistently displays opportunism will soon run out of opportunities.

- Empirical evidence shows that top bankers may add value by being able to craft better mergers than their lower-ranking counterparts, but there is little evidence in the US and UK that they manifest superior bargaining skills to extract more in negotiations.

- Acquirers need to choose appropriate measures of investment bank adviser performance in past deals as screening criteria to improve the chances of value creating acquisitions.

- We also discussed the role of other M & A professionals, such as accountants and lawyers, whose compensation terms present less of a challenge, since these are generally not contingent on deal completion.

Review questions

19.1 Who are the different advisers involved in takeovers?

19.2 What services do these advisers offer?

19.3 How important is the role of investment bankers? What are their responsibilities?

19.4 What is an arbitrage in the merger context?

19.5 What are the sources of conflict of interest between companies and their advisers?

19.6 Do compensation contracts create conflicts of interest? How?

19.7 What is a success fee? How does it help the target, the bidder and the bank adviser?

19.8 Does investment bank reputation deter opportunism and conflict of interests?

19.9 What do empirical studies say about the role of investment banks?

19.10 How important are the roles of lawyers, accountants and investor relations advisers?

Further reading

L. Allen and S. Peristiani, 'Loan underpricing and the provision of merger advisory services', *Journal of Banking & Finance*, **31**, 2007, 3539–3562.

P. R. Rau, 'Investment bank market share, contingent fee payments and the performance of acquiring firms', *Journal of Financial Economics*, **56**, 2000, 293–324.

Notes and references

1. *Mergers & Acquisitions*, Fairness opinion league tables, February 2008, p. 80.
2. See D. Kisgen, J. Qian and W. Song, 'Are fairness opinions fair? The case of mergers and acquisitions', *Journal of Financial Economics*, **91**, 2009, 179–207, Table 3. The sample period is 1994–2003, with a sample of 1509 acquirers and targets, of which 947 (307) acquirers (targets) do not secure fairness opinions.
3. For several landmark cases defining the scope of the business judgement rule, tests of the duty of care and loyalty and evidence of observance of director's fiduciary duties including *Smtih vs Van Gorkham* in 1985 see S. Kenyon-Slade, *Mergers and Takeovers in the US and UK: Law and Practice* (Oxford: Oxford University Press, 2004), section 4.46.
4. See Kisgen *et al.*, *ibid*. Makhija and Narayanan report similar results for a sample of 1927 US M & A deals over the period 1980–2004. They conclude that 'boards seek fairness opinions for the legal cover they provide against shareholders unhappy with the deal's terms'. The relatively better performance of top-tier banks in reducing bid premia or avoiding abnormal wealth losses is consistent with these banks' desire to preserve their reputational capital. See A. Makhija and R. Narayanan, 'Are fairness opinions in mergers and acquisitions conflicted?', Ohio State University working paper, 2008, downloaded from www.ssrn.com. In most of these studies top-tier and low-tier banks are defined in terms of market share in the M & A advisory market.
5. See K. MacFadyen, 'Regarding fairness opinions pros ask, what's fair?', *Mergers & Acquisitions*, January 2008, 24–25. For an extensive discussion of fairness opinions, and whether they should be legally regulated, see the references provided in footnote 320 of T. Paredes, 'Too much pay, too much deference: Behavioral corporate finance, CEOs, and corporate governance', *Florida State University Law Review*, **32**, 2005, 673–761.
6. See S. Lobe and N. Schenk, *Fairness Opinions and Capital Markets: Evidence from Germany, Switzerland and Austria*, European Capital Markets Institute, ECMI Research Report No. 4, January 2009, Brussels.
7. Bugeja provides evidence for Australia that where the valuation opinion is offered by the firm's own auditors i.e. those with existing business dealings with targets the market reaction is significantly negative. See M. Bugeja, 'The 'independence of expert opinions in corporate takeovers: Agreeing with directors' recommendations', *Journal of Business Finance & Accounting*, 32, 9&10, November/December 2005.
8. J. P. Williamson, *The Investment Banking Handbook* (New York: John Wiley, 1988).
9. G. Silverman, 'Wall St seeks M & A revival', *Financial Times*, 21 March 2002.
10. H. Servaes and M. Zenner, 'The role of investment banks in acquisitions', *Review of Financial Studies*, **9**(3), 1996, 787–815.
11. S. Tully, 'Betrayal on Wall Street', *Fortune*, 14 May 2001; P. Martin, 'Wizards unmasked', *Financial Times*, 23 March 1999; J. Plender, 'Globalisation's troops', *Financial Times*, 21 December 2001 give a critical view of the role of investment bankers in the press.
12. *The Economist*, 'Are league tables to blame for the industry's ills?', 3 May 2008, 387, p. 93.
13. Based on author's calculations from tables on pp. 52–53, *Mergers & Acquisitions*, February 2009.
14. R. M. McLaughlin, 'Does the form of compensation matter? Investment banker fee contracts in tender offers', *Journal of Financial Economics*, **32**, 1992, 223–260.
15. R. M. McLaughlin, 'Investment-banking contracts in tender offers', *Journal of Financial Economics*, **28**, 1990, 209–232.
16. P. R. Rao, 'Investment bank market share, contingent fee payments and the performance of acquiring firms', *Journal of Financial Economics*, **56**, 2000, 293–324.
17. McLaughlin, *ibid.*, 1992. Bank reputation is measured by a ranked index of its involvement in security issues in previous years.
18. M. Officer, 'Termination fees in mergers and acquisitions', *Journal of Financial Economics*, **69**, 2003, 431–467, provides empirical evidence that target termination fee increases the probability of bid success.

19. Linda Allen *et al.* provide evidence that acquirers seek merger advisers who can also provide/arrange acquisition financing. See L. Allen, J. Jagtiani, S. Peristiani and A. Saunders, 'The role of commercial bank advisers in mergers and acquisitions', *Journal of Money, Credit and Banking*, **36**, 2004, 197–215.

20. G. Silverman and C. Pretzlik, 'US banks say lending is vital for attracting fees', *Financial Times*, 6 December 2001.

21. For a further discussion of the advantages of stapled financing, the various sources of conflict, and whether they are equally serious in good times and during credit crisis, see C. Foulds, 'My banker's conflicted and I couldn't be happier: The curious durability of staple financing', *Delaware Journal of Corporate Law*, **34**(2), 2009.

22. H. Bowers and R. Miller, 'Choice of investment banker and shareholders' wealth of firms involved in acquisitions', *Financial Management*, Winter 1990, 34–44.

23. P. S. Sudarsanam and A. Salami, *Does It Matter Who Your Banker Is? Impact of Investment Bank Reputation in Takeovers*, Cranfield School of Management Working Paper, October 2001.

24. Rau, *ibid*.

25. A. Boone and J. Mulherin, 'Do auctions induce a winner's curse? New evidence from the corporate takeover market', *Journal of Financial Economics*, **89**, 2008, 1–19.

26. A senior investment banker who reviewed this chapter said: 'Acquiring clients often complain, after a deal is done, that the fee is large, or that there's a conflict of interest in being paid on a contingency basis. However, it is very difficult to get clients to agree to a smaller but non-contingent fee. Sooner or later somebody has to pay for the thousands of man-hours that bankers put into failed deals where they get no fee. Clients are just as eager to work on large contingency fees rather than smaller, non-contingent fees as the bankers!'

27. J. Bao and A. Edmans, 'Do investment banks have skill? Performance persistence of M&A advisers', SSRN paper –id952935, July 2009

28. J. P. Williamson, *The Investment Banking Handbook* (New York: John Wiley, 1988); J. Ivey, 'Lawyers at the sharp end', *Corporate Finance*, **210**, 2002, 20–23.

29. R. Sengupta, 'This is the hour of our discontent', *Financial Times*, 27 August 2001.

CHAPTER 20

Bid strategies and tactics

Objectives

At the end of this chapter, the reader should be able to understand:

- the range of bid strategies and tactics available to bidders;
- the factors that shape the choice among these strategies;
- how takeover laws and regulations influence bid strategies and tactics;
- the role of hedge funds and other activist shareholders;
- the limitations and risks associated with alternative strategies; and
- the various players, including arbitrageurs, who may scupper the bid.

Introduction

A bid strategy is a plan to acquire another company in order to achieve the predetermined business and corporate strategy objectives of the acquirer. In Chapter 3 the place of acquisitions in the overall strategic planning of a firm was discussed. A thorough strategic analysis of acquisitions is a precondition for an effective and successful acquisition programme. Flowing from this general framework of an acquisition programme are individual takeover bids. The objective of a bid strategy is to acquire a suitable target, satisfying the acquisition criteria dictated by the objectives of the firm's acquisition programme. In Chapter 13 a framework for identifying potential targets was presented. In this chapter we describe a process by which companies may develop their bid strategies.

Having identified a suitable target, the bidder must adopt the appropriate tactics during the progress of the bid. Bid tactics are a game plan to consummate a bid for a specific target, and should be played according to the legal framework and the regulatory regime policing the conduct of bids. Europe, under the Takeover Directive ('the Directive'), designated national agencies to oversee the takeover process. In the UK, bids for public companies are subject to the City Takeover Code ('the Code'). In addition to takeover regulation, corporate law in many countries determines the design of mergers, the processes and conditions for mergers. In the US, mergers are governed by state corporate laws, and tender offers are regulated by the SEC under the Williams Act (see Chapter 18 on takeover regulation). The impact of these laws and regulations on the terms and timing of bids is discussed in this chapter. Bid strategies and tactics need to be adapted to the potential or actual responses of the target company. The defensive strategies and tactics available to a target company are discussed in Chapter 21. Bid strategies available in the US and continental European countries and the associated constraints are discussed.

Bid strategies

Market timing

Proactive or reactive bids?

A very important strategic decision a firm has to make in seeking acquisitions is whether to be proactive or reactive, i.e. whether to be a first mover or a me-too acquirer. A first mover may have several motivations to be so. Assuming a limited pool of targets of varying desirable target profiles, a first mover can cherry-pick the best of these targets. Second, a first mover may be able to buy at a lower price than follow-on buyers, because the first buyer's purchase may become a floor for subsequent deals, since bidders and their financial advisers often benchmark the price they offer in a deal against the prices paid in recent similar deals (see Chapter 14). Third, a first mover may wish to prevent a rival from gaining competitive advantage by 'locking up' a desirable target by buying it first. This motive is effectively an anticipatory reaction to what its rivals might do to its disadvantage. Thus being a first mover has several competitive and financial advantages.

On the other hand, being a second mover may also have advantages in new and fast-evolving industries, where the true value of a target to an acquirer is difficult to assess in both strategic and financial terms. In such industries the first mover may be acting in haste, e.g. in buying start-ups. Dotcom and biotechnology acquisitions in the 1990s often ended up as disasters. Of course, this assumes that the second mover allows a decent interval following the first mover's acquisition, and uses that interval as a learning opportunity to fine-tune its own acquisition plan. The second mover can also take the time to counter the first mover effectively through strategies other than acquisition, e.g. a joint venture (see Chapter 9 on JVs).

Merger waves and bid timing

In Chapter 3 we discussed mergers as games. We considered merger waves and industry clustering as manifestations of sequential games, and examined the relative advantages of being a first mover or a copycat follower in such games. The available empirical evidence shows that early movers in merger waves experience larger value gains than late movers and those that buy at the peak of the M & A market boom[1]. This evidence is observed for both US and European merger waves. Therefore it appears that the balance of advantage lies with first movers in merger waves. This may be partly because, as the merger wave gets under way and the takeover market gets hot, later acquirers are paying a high premium. However, this does not explain why acquirers buying after the collapse of the wave also underperform. This may be because, by then, the acquirers buy their targets cheap, but they also buy the left-overs!

Join the fray as white knight or hostile bidder?

The choice between being a first mover and a second mover arises in a *sequential game*, where the second mover observes the first mover and decides on its countermove. In this game the two bidders bid for different targets at different times. But the game can also be a *simultaneous game*: that is, one bidder for a target is joined by another for the *same target*. This situation is called a *multiple bidder* situation. In such situations it is often the case that one of the bidders is a hostile bidder and the other is a friendly bidder, defined as such by the attitude of the target management. A friendly bidder may be a white knight, solicited by the target to act as a saviour from the hostile bidder. Often the firm may not be the first to spot an attractive opportunity. The target may have been 'in play' explicitly as the object of other bids, or it may have been stalked by a potential predator that has built up a toehold in the target. Moreover, the likelihood of a rival bid either by a white knight or by a competitor provoked by the firm's bid, and the value of the target to the competitor, must be factored into the firm's bidding strategy. Exhibit 20.1 shows acquisitions of biotechnology companies pointing to both sequential and simultaneous games.

Exhibit 20.1

Mergers are therapeutic for Big Pharma!

In early 2009 there was a scramble among drugmakers to acquire biotechnology companies in the US. One of the targets was CV Therapeutics (CVT), facing a friendly offer from Gilead Sciences, a competitor, and a hostile bid from Astellas, the Japanese drugmaker. Astellas was then in partnership with CVT to market Lexiscan, one of CVT's top-selling cardiovascular drugs, and had been looking to take control of the entire company to fill out its product portfolio and its pipeline of drugs in development. But after repeatedly rejecting Astellas's advances, CVT announced that it had agreed to sell itself for $1.4bn to Gilead, a biotech company that developed drugs to treat cancer and a range of viral and infectious diseases. Astellas, which had offered $1.1bn, then capitulated, dropped its hostile takeover bid, and said that it was a 'disciplined acquirer and [did] not see value for Astellas's stockholders in CVT at the price level of the sale' to Gilead. Tokyo-based Astellas said it also planned to drop a lawsuit it had filed in Delaware against CVT and its directors.

Several massive mergers were struck between global pharmaceuticals companies in 2009, including Pfizer's $68bn deal to buy Wyeth, and Merck's $41bn deal to buy Schering-Plough. Recent transactions involving biotech companies, however, have been harder fought, partly because of richer valuations that are based on better prospects for biotech companies' innovative drug platforms and pipelines. Global drug giants are eager to control biotech assets, but the tough equity markets have not knocked biotech sellers' expectations down enough to make for easy takeovers. Roche had pressed Genentech over an unsolicited takeover offer since July 2008 before Genentech agreed in March 2009 to an offer worth $46.8bn, or $95 a share. Bristol-Myers Squibb's effort in 2008 to buy ImClone, its longstanding partner, failed after ImClone said it deserved a higher bid, and eventually secured one from Eli Lilly, a white knight. Astellas withdrew its offer the same day Canada's Agrium, a fertilizer maker, launched a $3.3bn hostile exchange offer to buy key US rival CF Industries as part of another three-way takeover battle. But while CVT was able to find a suitable 'white knight' bidder to top Astellas's unwanted offer, the affections between CF, Agrium and Terra remain unrequited so far. CF has rejected a bid of about $69 a share from Agrium, a top competitor in the North American crop nutrient business, and has instead raised its own unsolicited bid for smaller rival Terra Industries.

Source: J. MacIntosh, 'Astellas drops hostile bid for CV Therapeutics', FT.com, 16 March 2009

Buying in an auction

Increasingly, target companies sell themselves or their subsidiaries in an auction. Unlike the previous two types of game, such an auction is a closed-bid, multi-bidder game. In the US, as noted in Chapter 18 on takeover regulation, a target board, having become the subject of an unsolicited cash tender offer and having decided to sell the firm, is under the *Revlon* duty to conduct an auction[2]. Target boards are also under increasing shareholder pressure to sell in an auction to maximize shareholder value from the sale and not make *sweetheart* deals to sell to favoured bidders, probably as a *quid pro quo* for side 'payments' to target directors.

In an auction the target firm hires a financial adviser to conduct the auction, and the adviser is chosen on the basis of its experience and expertise in running successful auctions (see Chapter 19 on the role of the financial adviser in this context). The various steps involved in the auction procedure are described below.

Auction process[3]

As we have seen from some of the exhibits above, LBO sponsors buy their targets in auctions. The vendors engage financial advisers to manage the auction process. The selection of the advisers is made using several criteria, e.g. expertise, previous experience, success rate in auctions, ability to provide 'stapled financing'. An auction involves several phases:

- due diligence and preparation;
- refining preliminary valuation, preparing of data and developing a marketing strategy, finalizing the offering memo, assembling the list of buyers to contact, and preparing the confidentiality letter;
- marketing of the target to potential buyers;
- contacting buyers, executing confidentiality agreements, distributing confidential information, preparing data room, soliciting and evaluating preliminary bids, preparing draft sale agreement, and shortlisting potential buyers;
- investigating buyers;
- doing buyer due diligence, presentations, arranging data room access and site visits, distributing draft definitive merger agreement (DMA), soliciting final bids;
- negotiations;
- evaluating final bids, negotiating with selected buyer and signing DMA;
- financing and closing;
- getting regulatory approvals if necessary, securing seller shareholders' vote if necessary, and closing the transaction.

Sellers invite both strategic and financial buyers, i.e. PE firms, which need longer to arrange financing than strategic buyers. To accelerate financing, the financial advisers handling the auction may, with the consent of the vendor, offer to finance the purchase and provide tentative terms of such financing to qualified bidders. The vendor must ensure that its financial advisers, while offering stapled financing to the bidders, do not compromise their duty to the vendor[4]. Such financing may also elicit greater interest from potential buyers. For this reason it is called 'stapled financing'. As part of the negotiation process bidders ask for termination fees to raise the cost to the vendor of shopping around. The DMA may include 'no shop', 'antitrust out', and 'material adverse change' clauses[5]. The auction process may take up to six or seven months to run through all the phases. Investment bankers receive a retainer, e.g. $100k for a $100m deal and $150k for a $1bn deal, and a success fee of 1.1% of deal size up to $1bn, 0.75% up to $2.5bn, and 0.4% above that level.

From an initial list of potential buyers, which in some cases could be over 100, the financial adviser will shortlist more serious and likely bidders. This list may include both strategic and financial buyers. Strategic buyers often dislike auctions because of the time and resources needed, and the uncertainty. Financial buyers reckon that many strategic buyers will drop out. They of course worry about price ratcheting in an auction, and the 'curse of the winner' – that is, win the prize but at too high a price! For high-value targets, PE firms form a consortium to bid and compete with similar consortia. For the vendor, consortia increase the chance of sale of such targets, but also reduce the number of bidders and hence the sale price[6].

In a recent study of auctions for public companies in the US, Boone and Mulherin report the following numbers in each category in their sample of 145 auctions[7]:

	Mean	Maximum	Median
Potential buyers contacted	13.8	150	3
Potential buyers signing confidentiality agreement	5.8	50	2
Bidders submitting private offers	1.5	6	1
Bidders making public offers	1.2	2	1

Source: Adapted from A. Boone and J. Mulhern, 'Do auctions induce a winner's curse? New evidence from the corporate takeover market', *Journal of Financial Economics*, **89**(1), 2008, 1–19.

Thus while a large number are contacted in some auctions, the median number of contacts is only three, and the median number of potential buyers signing confidentiality agreements is also low at two. Thus the auction process in a majority of cases involves just two or three serious potential buyers.

Buying distressed firms

Buying a distressed firm may be thought of as a smart deal, since such companies may be available at 'bargain basement' prices. However, low price cannot be the only consideration, since low price also represents high risk. The acquirer also has to factor in the cost of turning the target company around. The turnaround effort may also be a distraction, and a drain on the managerial and financial resources of the acquirer. For these reasons, a bidder has to carry out extremely rigorous due diligence before buying a distressed target. Empirical evidence is not very encouraging for acquirer shareholders[8].

Pre-bid stake building in target

After a specific target has been identified, the potential bidder may start to build up a significant stake in it (the toehold). In the UK, the disclosure rules for share purchases of 3% or more under the Companies Act 2006 must also be taken into account. Pre-bid stake building has both advantages and disadvantages, as shown in Table 20.1. Because of the stringent

Table 20.1 Advantages and disadvantages of toehold

Advantages	Disadvantages
● Puts pressure on target to negotiate	● Bid intentions revealed. Target put 'in play' and target price driven up
● Improves chances of securing majority control in a bid	● If 10% or more purchased for cash within 12 months, bid may have to be for cash at the highest price paid (see Chapter 18 on the Code)
● A large toehold may deter potential rival bids and prevent high bid premium	● If bid fails, bidder stuck with unwanted investment
● If outbid, the stake could be sold at a profit	
● Cash underwriting of offer less expensive, since toehold already bought	

Percentages refer to proportions of target voting shares.

disclosure rules, toehold build-up cannot be done on a quiet prowl. Nor can it be done on the sly using nominees, since the target can notify the nominees to reveal the beneficial owners or disenfranchise the shares (see Chapter 18). In many continental European countries, such as Germany, when share acquisitions cross certain thresholds starting from 5% they have to be disclosed, although the speed of disclosure varies. Slower disclosure allows the bidder to build a significant stake without revealing its hand. In the US, acquisition of 5% or more of the beneficial interest in any class of shares needs to be disclosed to the SEC on Schedule 13D within 10 days if the acquisition is for the purpose of gaining control of the target. The disclosure includes the acquirer's identity, source of funds, purpose of the transaction, and any contractual or other relationship with the target. Such acquisition through market purchased is known as 'street sweep', and aims at building a 'beachhead' (toehold) to facilitate a subsequent tender offer.

Toehold, bid premium and bid outcome

Toehold has been suggested by Grossman and Hart as a possible solution to the free-rider problem discussed in Chapter 18[9]. A toehold allows the bidder to enjoy the post-acquisition value creation accruing to the related shares, and thus provides an incentive to make takeover bids. Of course, the benefits of toehold must exceed the target search and bid costs. The larger the toehold, the greater is the added value from the acquisition accruing to the bidder.

The implications of toeholds for the probability of a subsequent bid either by the toeholder or by a third party, for the probability of a successful bid and for the bid premium have been discussed by several researchers using the game theory and information economics frameworks. Shleifer and Vishny predict that a toehold will increase the probability of a subsequent bid and reduce the premium in such a bid[10]. Hirshleifer and Titman examine the relation between toehold, bid premium and the probability of success in a tender offer[11]. Their model predicts that toehold will have a positive impact on success probability (see Exhibit 20.2). A negative relation between toehold and average bid premium in takeovers is also implied.

In contrast to the previous two models, Choudhury and Jegadeesh argue that a toehold is used by the bidder to signal the post-acquisition value of the target[12]. A large toehold signals

---

Exhibit 20.2

Can Friends stick to Resolution to save their merger?

In July 2007 UK insurance companies Resolution and Friends first announced their £8.5bn all-share, nil-premium merger. Shareholder reaction was lukewarm, opening the situation up to other parties. Other bidders began almost immediately to evince interest in making rival offers. Standard Life, the UK's fifth biggest insurer, then threw its hat in the ring and, like Friends, it would be able to fund its new business using Resolution's ability to generate cash from its closed life funds. Then it was revealed that Hugh Osmond had been building a stake in Resolution through Pearl, a rival to Resolution. Pearl held 16.5% and made no offer. 'We rule nothing in and nothing out,' said Pearl. In the developing auction scenario, Pearl's toehold would give it a strong strategic leverage.

Source: Adapted from J. Hughes and K. Burgess, 'Standard Life could gatecrash merger', *Financial Times*, 20 September 2007

high value. This model predicts that as toehold increases, the subsequent bid premium also rises. The empirical evidence for these models is discussed below.

Showstoppers

The firm must look for any potential 'showstoppers' or 'deal-killers' that can thwart the bid. Of these impediments, the most important is the antitrust regime. In the UK, before announcing a bid, the bidder can obtain confidential guidance from the Office of Fair Trading (OFT) as to the chances of the bid being referred to the Competition Commission (CC). After announcing its bid, a bidder may use the OFT's fast-track procedure to obtain an OFT decision within 35 days. Similar confidential guidance and fast-track clearance procedures are available under the EU Merger Regulation (see Chapter 17). In the US, where, following the Second Request investigation, FTC/DoJ decide to seek injunction and file for administrative trial, the process can take an indeterminate time.

If a bid is referred by the OFT or the European Commission for full investigation, under the City Code the bid lapses. It may be relaunched within 21 days under the Code if the CC or the Commission clears the bid, but this may take up to four months or more. Thus valuable time may be lost by the bidder, giving an opportunity to rival bidders or time for the target management to bolster their defences. A careful vetting of the bid proposal for any antitrust implications is therefore necessary. Financial buyers such as private equity firms are often in a more advantageous position, since their acquisitions pose fewer antitrust problems than bids by strategic buyers (see Chapter 11 on financial buyers).

Other showstoppers could be litigation initiated by the target as a defence strategy (see Chapter 21). The potential for such an action must be considered as part of the bid strategy. Contracts between a target and its suppliers or customers may often contain clauses that allow cancellation or renegotiation rights when there is change of control (see Exhibit 20.3). The affected parties may also exploit change of control as an opportunity to renegotiate terms to their advantage. Bond covenants often contain 'change of control' clauses obliging the target firm to renegotiate the interest rate payable on the bonds, or to buy them back if they carry a put option.

Exhibit 20.3

CSC comes hard on (I)Soft partner

On 16 May 2007 the UK IT group iSoft (IS) announced an agreed merger valued at £140m with its Australian rival IBA Health (IBA). IBA was the largest healthcare software provider in Australia, providing IT services to clinics, hospitals and care homes in 22 countries, although it had no clients in the UK. With the merger it would have gained a foothold in the UK. Computer Sciences Corporation (CSC), a US firm, was iSoft's partner in a £6bn IT upgrade for UK's National Heath Service. CSC said that it would not consent to a change of control at iSoft, and refused to give its backing to the deal. Greg King, IBA's Sydney-based head of business development, said CSC had not given any reasons for its move, and both iSoft and IBA were seeking clarification. He added that IBA was perplexed by CSC's decision, since IBA had been working well with CSC for the last few months. He added that IBA and IS were working on complex projects, and while he could not say there were not issues that needed resolving, they were not significant barriers. IBA had no plans to withdraw its bid, but it hoped to resolve any issues. Mr King also hinted that CSC had been taking undue advantage of IS's troubles in the past over accounting irrgularities and refinancing.

IS shares plunged 19% to 41 pence. In Sydney, IBA fell 2%. The value of the share exchange deal to IS investors would be equivalent to 58.1 pence a share. IS's share price, well below the offer price, suggested strong market scepticism about the deal going through.

Source: Adapted from E. Fry, 'iSoft takeover hits hurdle', *Financial Times*, 29 May 2007

Under the Takeover Directive both bidders and targets must inform and/or consult trade unions representing employees or employees themselves. Thus employee concerns will need to be taken into account (see Exhibit 20.4). Where employee share option schemes hold shares in the target firm, or employee pension funds are invested in the target firm, the takeover has to be made acceptable to the trustees. In the US several states have constituency statutes obliging target management to consider the interests of employees and other stakeholders alongside shareholder interests in their decision to accept a bid or not. In the UK the new pension regulatory regime, set up to protect employee pension interests, can block a bid until necessary top-up funds are made available by the bidder to cover any potential pension fund deficit (see Chapter 14 on the impact of these regulations on target valuation).

Exhibit 20.4

Suez and GdF go into labour but take 2½ years to deliver

In February 2006 the French government promoted the merger between Suez, an electricity company, and Gaz de France (GdF), a gas company, to avoid a takeover of Suez by Enel, the Italian energy company. The merger met with both shareholder and trade union resistance for the next 2½ years. Many shareholders feared the consequences of a merger, believing it was imposed by the government on a reluctant GDF to save the private group from a hostile bid. In January 2007 the court ruled that GDF needed to give unions more information, potentially delaying the deal. In May 2007 Nicolas Sarkozy became president, and said he would review the merger plan. In December 2007 GDF sued the unions for delaying tactics on talks. In May 2008 the GDF works council gave a mandatory opinion that allowed the shareholder vote to go ahead.

Investors in both companies in July 2008 overwhelmingly approved the merger that would create GDF Suez, ranking as Europe's second biggest producer of electricity, the continent's biggest gas transport and distribution group, and a world leader in the liquefied natural gas market. It would have consolidated annual sales of €74bn ($117bn) and be valued at between €90bn and €100bn.

Source: Adapted from P. Hollinger, 'GdF Suez merger overcomes two years of political road-blocks and diversions', *Financial Times*, 17 July 2008

Getting the board on board

A bid strategy must command the wholehearted support of all bidder directors. Similarly, the strategy must also have the support of the large and influential shareholders. Where the board is divided, the bidder team will find it very difficult to sell the deal to the target board and its shareholders, and to other stakeholders, e.g. investors. In 2001 Carly Fiorina, the newly appointed CEO of Hewlett-Packard (HP), and Capella, the CEO of Compaq, proposed a merger of equals. The proposal was initially endorsed by HP board director Walter Hewlett, representing the Hewlett family trust's shares in HP. Subsequently, however, Hewlett, supported by the Packard family trust also a shareholder in HP, bitterly and publicly opposed the merger on grounds of poor strategic fit, weak value creation logic, potential merger integration problems, and the negative stock market reaction to the deal announcement. His opposition was so fierce that in the end the shareholders of HP voted for the merger with only 50.1% of their votes, a wafer-thin majority[13].

Exhibit 20.5 provides another example of a merger, sound on strategic grounds, being blocked by key shareholders and top managers in at least one of the merging companies.

Exhibit 20.5

Porsche on the fast lane but Volkswagen overtakes

In 2009 Porsche (P), the German luxury sports car maker, had accumulated ownership of 51% of shares and enough cash options on Volkswagen (VW) shares to take the ownership to 75%. The motivation for this accumulation was the merger of VW with P. In accumulating the stake, P had also incurred debt of €9bn, which strained its financial health. In contrast VW was in good financial condition, and even lent €700 to P. Ferdinand Piëch who was the CEO of VW, but was also a family shareholder of P. His strategy was to merge P with VW. Despite his large shareholding in P, he would not be allowed to run it, because of the agreement among all family shareholders of P that no family member could be a member of its management board. However, the 71-year-old Mr Piëch could realize his dream of running P by merging it into a division of VW!

P's mounting financial difficulties, caused by the slump in demand for luxury cars such as Porsche, provided Mr Piëch with the opportunity to turn the tables on his family rivals and Porsche's management. So rather than Porsche taking over VW, he then proposed that VW take over Porsche. At the end of the day this would still lead to the combination of VW and Porsche, but with VW and Mr Piëch in the driving seat. P now felt that it had become a prey to VW rather than its predator earlier! Mr Piëch's cousin Wolfgang Porsche, P's chairman, and Wendelin Wiedeking, its chief executive, were fighting to keep VW at bay by trying to find new allies to provide urgently needed funds to secure P's independence. To this end, they turned to Qatar Investment Authority.

However, in 2009 the firms merged, forming a holding company to hold shares in both VW and Porsche! Porsche had lost the race to be winner!

Source: P. Betts, 'Porsche and VW are spinning out of control', 'Feud threatens Porsche's empire-building ambitions', 24 April 2009 and 30 June 2009; D. Schäfer, 'Porsche and VW agree merger', 6 May 2009, all from *Financial Times*

Bid tactics

The objectives of bid tactics are as follows:

- to win control of the target;
- to minimize the control premium paid to target shareholders;
- to minimize transaction costs;
- to make a 'win–win' deal with target management if possible (see below); and
- to smooth post-acquisition integration.

The transaction costs include: professional fees paid to advisers and specialist consultants; printing and advertising; and antitrust authority fees. For cash-underwritten offers, the underwriting fee could be substantial. Stamp duty and value-added tax may also be payable.

In the case of a bid for a UK public company, except in very unusual cases the bid must be concluded within 60 days from the posting of the offer document. As noted in Table 18.2, there are other deadlines to be met within this timetable. While the bidder may carefully plan the opening moves in the bid game, subsequent moves are determined by the target's responses. To some extent these responses may have been foreseen. But the bidder must still be alert, adaptive and nimble in counteracting the target's responses. In the US, recourse to litigation and proxy fights may be a way of circumventing the takeover defences (see below for further discussion).

Responsibilities of bidder directors

Under the general principles and rules of the Code, directors are responsible for the conduct of a bid. They should act in the interests of their shareholders, employees and creditors (see Chapter 18). Under the law, directors have a fiduciary duty to act in the best interests of their company. They should ensure that the bid is conducted in accordance with the law and the Code. They should maintain a high standard of integrity in providing information relating to the bid. In the US, directors owe a fiduciary duty of loyalty and care to the corporation *and* the shareholders. Under the Business Judgment Rule (BJR) they can also consider the interests of other constituencies. In continental European countries such as Germany and Holland with a co-determination system, directors are obliged to take into account employee interests in carrying out acquisitions and mergers. In other countries the boards are required to inform, and consult with, trade unions and employee representatives.

Where the board is split, the dissenting director/s may have to seek independent legal or financial advice, and also inform the company's financial advisers. Since directors will be in possession of price-sensitive information about the bid, their dealings in the securities of the bidder and the target need to be carried out and disclosed in accordance with the Code, the insider dealing laws and the rules of the London Stock Exchange (see Chapter 18 for a discussion of these).

In bidder companies, a campaign committee including some executive and non-executive directors may often be formed, and responsibility for the day-to-day conduct of the bid may be delegated to the committee. However, the board as a whole still remains responsible. 'Delegation does not mean abdication'[14]. In the US the whole board must have participated in exercising its judgement and not just some of the directors, in order to qualify for the protection of the BJR.

Developing a negotiation strategy

Clarity of objective of negotiation – to obtain the best deal acceptable to both sides while satisfying the goals of the acquisition – is critical. For this purpose the negotiating (N) team must gather as much information as possible about the target business, individuals involved on both sides, other opportunities in the market, and terms of similar deals done by the bidder or by other firms to provide a benchmark. The team must grasp what motivates the seller, its managers and shareholders, and understand the key issues for the vendor – highest price, longevity of firm, ensuring employee interests, continued involvement in the firm after takeover. Often key stakeholder groups have to be identified, and the deal must be structured to win their acceptance: otherwise the deal may be killed as happened in the Deutsche Boerse bid for London Stock Exchange (see Chapter 12 Case Study).

The N team must be briefed on:

- who the adversaries are, their strengths and weaknesses, their preferences and prejudices, and the results of due diligence, if any;
- the valuation of the target, the basis of valuation, the range of acceptable price to negotiate, and how to adjust the price for factors that come to light during the negotiation;
- a range of options and the trade-offs between them, e.g. cash consideration for a lower price, higher price for an earn-out arrangement, lower price for some post-acquisition involvement in management; and
- criteria – when is the negotiation deemed successful? What is the benchmark?

The N team must be ready to make concessions during negotiations, time the concessions – not too late, not too soon – and use concessions to win concessions.

Types of negotiation strategy

Alternative strategies and tactics are available to choose from: for example, win–win, where compromises are made to ensure that both companies feel they have gained something from the deal; or win–lose, where the bidder attempts to extract the last pound of flesh from the target, i.e. the 'take no prisoner' approach. The choice of strategy/tactic depends on the complexity of the acquisition, the attitude and motivation of the target managers, the relative strengths and weaknesses of the two parties, how badly the bidder needs the target, etc. Although some strategy planning ahead of negotiation is necessary, the negotiating team should be nimble enough to adapt its strategy and tactics to the emergence of new problems and opportunities.

Understanding the negotiation process

Negotiation is not an unambiguously rational process, and requires both an understanding of the perspectives of the other party to the negotiation and an appreciation of the emotions driving the negotiators. The end objectives of negotiation are often a mixture of pecuniary gains and non-pecuniary or psychological gains. The negotiators may often appeal to the greed, fear and ego of the leaders of the merging firms. Fear arises from the threats faced by the firm in the absence of a deal. SWOT analysis is a useful tool in understanding the weaknesses of the other party, and the threats it faces (see Chapter 13 on comparative SWOT analysis of bidders and targets). This can be linked to the familiar concept in negotiation literature known as the best alternative to no agreement (BATNA). For example, the BATNA for a target firm may be an unwanted and unloved existence as an independent firm, or being taken over

Figure 20.1 Negotiation parameters and limits

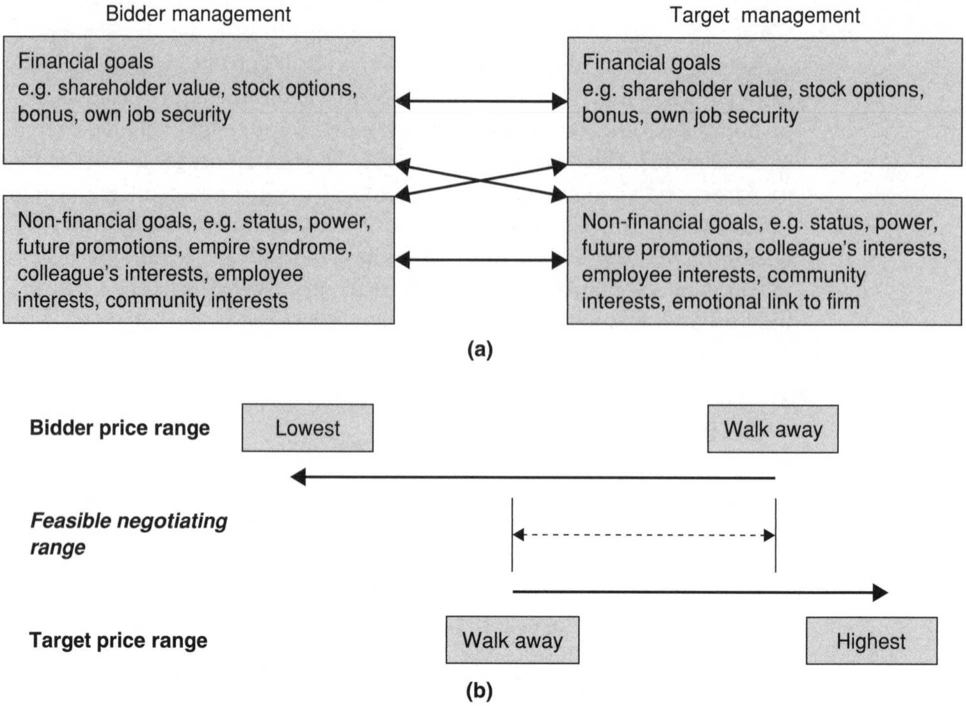

by a predator. For a bidder, BATNA may be the loss of competitive advantage and shareholder value decline, possibly causing the bankruptcy of the firm.

Clues to a firm's BATNA may often emerge from the probing of its negotiating team by the other team. Understanding by each team of the other's BATNA helps fine-tune the terms of the deal to its best advantage. Given that negotiations may often happen at both the rational and emotional levels, BATNA must be assessed at both the firm level – i.e. what is best for the firm? – and the negotiators' level – i.e. what is the best for the negotiators? This understanding can provide a powerful lever to persuade the other team to accept the deal on the table. There are therefore many trade-offs that negotiators must explore in reaching acceptable terms for a deal. The interactions between the financial and non-financial parameters of the two negotiating teams are shown in Figure 20.1a. Figure 20b shows how wide apart the two teams are, and what the feasible negotiation range is as regards the price. The 'walk-away' price equals the value of BATNA for each team. The interaction between financial and non-financial parameters allows creative exploration of acceptable trade-offs during the negotiation stage. Deals may collapse because of insufficient appreciation of the other party's non-financial motivation for doing a deal (see Exhibit 20.6).

An important characteristic of a win–win deal is that it is perceived by each party to be so, even though the reality may be different. For example, one type of merger deal is the so-called merger of equals. In practice, however, in such deals there is a barely concealed dominant partner that in effect takes over the weaker partner. The $40bn merger of Daimler-Benz and Chrysler in 1998, cited earlier, was touted as a merger of equals, but the dominant partner was Daimler-Benz. The deal was dressed up as a merger of equals so that it could win acceptance by a number of important stakeholders, e.g. top managers and large minority shareholders of

Chrysler. This illustrates how presentational, face-saving considerations, essentially psychological props, facilitate the conclusion of a deal. Sometimes an MoE may be *avoided* to satisfy the acquirer manager's ego (see Exhibit 20.6).

Exhibit 20.6

'You can pay less but I get your job'

In June 2004 J. P. Morgan Chase (JPM) and Bank One (BO) of Chicago completed their friendly $58bn merger. While the two CEOs – Bill Harrison of JPM and Jamie Dimon of BO – celebrated the merger, a leading class-action law firm, Milberg Weiss, slapped down a suit claiming that Mr Harrison had the chance to pay $7bn less than he did for BO. It had been reported in the *New York Times* that Mr Dimon had offered to sell BO for its market value if he was given the top job at the combined group immediately. Instead, JPM agreed to pay a 14% premium to the market price, $7bn, in exchange for Mr Harrison keeping the reins for two years. It appeared that during the negotiations the two sides discussed the relationship between price and management positions. 'There was a spectrum of outcomes in terms of premium and governance,' said one adviser. In simple terms, Mr Dimon *seemed* to say, 'The sooner I get the job the less you have to pay'.

Is this a clash of two egos, lending credence to the claim that many US chief executives treat the companies they run purely as vehicles for their personal aggrandisement and enrichment? There is no doubt that personal ambitions of senior executives play a big role in determining which companies buy which and at what price. Indeed, the question of who gets what job is such a key factor in most mergers that there is a special term in sanitised investment banking-speak: *social issues*. Usually the arguments over social issues are kept private. Sometimes they become embarrassingly public.

Back in 1998 a proposed £110bn merger between two UK companies, Glaxo Wellcome and SmithKline Beecham, fell apart at the last minute because of a disagreement between the drug giants' bosses, Sir Richard Sykes and Jan Leschly. Attempts were made to dress it up as a clash about culture and structure. But it was clear they just could not agree who would get the jobs. And it was only when Mr Leschly announced his retirement two years later that the deal could be done.

In the JPM–BO case Mr Dimon clearly wanted to take over immediately as CEO of the combined group, while Mr Harrison was determined to stay at the helm to steer the merger through. It could also be seen as part of the normal debate over whether a deal should be treated as a merger of equals (MoE) or a takeover. In a takeover the target's management and shareholders give up control over their company, and receive a control premium from the acquirer. In an MoE control is shared, and so there is a smaller premium, if at all. The lawsuit alleged that JPM shareholders should have been told about Mr Dimon's nil-premium offer and given the chance to decide whether Mr Harrison was worth an extra $7bn.

Source: Adapted from D. Wighton, 'Lawsuit ruins merger celebration', *Financial Times*, 2 July 2004

Figure 20.2 One-to-one or one-to-many availability of bidders and targets, and relative bargaining strength

No of bidders	No. of targets	Nature of synergy	Who has advantage?
Single	Single	Unique synergy	Advantage to both
Single	Several	Unique synergy	Advantage to bidder
Several	Single	Unique synergy	Advantage to target
Several	*Several*	*No unique synergy*	*Advantage to both*

*Note: 'Unique' means only one bidder (one target) has the set of resources and capabilities (R & C) to provide a unique configuration of R & C with a target (a bidder), although several such targets (bidders) may be available.

Framing the deal and assessing target reaction

Insufficient appreciation of the opponent's view of the decision problem and overconfidence in one's own ability to win could lead to a collapse of negotiation. In negotiations, the cognitive power to see a problem from the other side (called *perspective taking*) and the emotional power to understand and feel the other side's aspirations and expectations (called *empathy*) are important. Perspective taking is a useful intellectual discipline, and empathy can break the ice when negotiations get stubbornly stuck because of emotional intransigence[15]. Another style often used in negotiation is the '*good cop, bad cop*' routine, with some negotiating team members playing the good cop, showing some empathy with the other side, while others act as bad cops, adopting a less compromising posture.

Negotiators need to assess the relative bargaining strengths and weaknesses of the merging firms. These are determined partly by the configuration of bidders and the universe of targets they have chosen the target from. These configurations are shown in Figure 20.2. It also shows the configurations where neither, either or both of bidder and target doing a deal have a negotiating advantage. In understanding each other's BATNA, an understanding of such a configuration would be useful. Our earlier discussion of the Boone and Mulherin study suggests that even in the case of auctions the number of potential bidders is quite limited. Thus one-to-many mapping is much less likely than one-to-one between bidder and target.

Negotiating takeover price and premium

Pricing the target and determining the takeover premium are matters of negotiation between the bidder and target. In general, each side will have done its own valuation of the target as a stand-alone entity and as part of the acquirer contributing to synergy and value creation. The estimate of synergy depends on a lot of assumptions, and these may not be the same between the two sides. The negotiation price range would coincide perfectly if both made identical assumptions for all future conditions. However, such coincidence may be just that! It is part of the negotiation exercise to get these assumptions out into the open, so that valuation using the same models can be harmonized. Then the arguments move from the set of assumptions to the validity of those assumptions. Here each side may be biased, with the target being more optimistic and the bidder more pessimistic. Of course, the bidder should not overdo the pessimism, since that prompts the question 'Why merge at all if there is not much value to be created?'

Negotiators normally benchmark their valuations and takeover premia against those applied in recent mergers of similar size, of similar status, e.g. 'best of breed' companies but in different sectors, or in the same industry/sector. Arguments about the appropriate benchmark will then ensue!

Agreeing the value that is likely to be created is only the first step in determining the takeover price and takeover premium. The next step is to agree how the pie will be divided between the bidder and the target, i.e. how the added value will be appropriated between the bidder and the target.

Negotiating a friendly bid

A bid may be friendly, hostile or opportunistic. In a friendly bid the bidder wins the support of the target management, which then recommends the bid for acceptance by the target shareholders. In a hostile bid such a recommendation is not forthcoming, and the two companies have to slug it out. A friendly bid is less expensive than a hostile bid, since it can be concluded sooner; less risky, because of the greater access to information about the target in 'due diligence' (see below); and smoother. This smoothness is conducive to a more successful post-acquisition integration. Where the target top management is an essential part of the bidder's post-acquisition strategy, a hostile bid must be counted out. A hostile bid, of course, demands of the bidder much greater tactical dexterity and staying power, since it is likely to last longer.

Where the bidder has the support of the target board it may be able to obtain their irrevocable commitment to sell their shareholdings to the bidder. Such a commitment is included in their recommendation to their shareholders, thereby signalling their support for the deal. This may be persuasive in some cases, although target shareholders need to be convinced that their directors are doing so in the interests of the target company and its shareholders, and in their own.

Playing the white knight

A white knight (WK) is a bidder that enters the fray as a friendly bidder to a target already facing a hostile bidder. A WK bid is a reactive and not a proactive bid. The justification is often that, in rescuing the target in distress, the WK can gain a favourable deal from the beleaguered target in terms of price, access to information, large break-up fee, asset or stock lock up, etc. While these advantages may be plausible, the decision to enter the fray still needs a hard strategic justification. A simple test of a strategic rationale for making a counter-bid is why the WK had not thought of bidding for the target earlier. Given that the WK bid is a 'me-too' bid at best, it is likely that the hostile first bidder has a stronger strategic rationale and value creation potential than the WK. The value creation logic may often be concocted, and the WK may end up paying too much for the target[16]. Often WKs enter the fray after negotiating compensation payments if their bid fails[17,18].

When a target is in play, the potential bidder faces an opportunity as well as a threat. Such a target is very vulnerable, and may be persuaded by a friendly overture to recommend a bid. On the other hand, a competitive bid with two or more rival bidders may develop, pushing the bid premium inexorably high. Increasingly, target companies and their advisers shop around to find alternative buyers, and run auctions to find the best bidder. In an auction situation the risk of overpayment is high, resulting in the 'winner's curse'. A white knight may not be spared this curse[19].

Assessing the target for a friendly deal

In general, a bidder seeks to obtain the recommendation of the target management. In approaching the target with a friendly overture, the bidder must assess the possible target management response. This assessment includes an appreciation of the key players in the target in terms of the following:

- personalities;
- motivations for sale, e.g. retirement, lack of management or resources to develop target business;
- relation to the target, e.g. whether they are founder-managers with a sentimental attachment to the firm and its workforce;
- their independence quotient (IQ);
- post-acquisition expectations, e.g. whether they expect to continue to play a role of similar status and authority as now;
- stake in the target; and
- preference for payment currency, cash or shares.

Not all of the above considerations may be relevant to a public company target. Many vendors, especially the directors of family firms, may be concerned more with the post-acquisition plans of the bidder for the firm, its managers and workforce than with the size of bid premium being offered.

Merger of equals

To clinch a friendly deal, a bidder may often agree to a merger of equals. Examples of such mergers are BP-Amoco, Glaxo-Smith Kline Beecham and Daimler-Chrysler. A merger of equals, generally financed with a stock exchange offer, facilitates:

- smooth post-acquisition integration;
- continued commitment of both managements to the common destiny of the merged entity;
- easier acceptance of the bid by target management; and
- a lower bid premium.

The deal may be described, not always accurately, as a 'nil-premium' merger.

A merger of equals (MoE) may often hide, behind its warm and sentimental semantics, a skewed power structure, with clearly discernible acquirer and acquired. Thus in substance the deal is a takeover, and not a merger of equals. In the post-acquisition period the veneer is stripped away, and the fiction of a merger of equals gives way to the situation where one firm dominates the other. The MoE may be harmless – 'just a dream' in the minds of the target management – or an expedient tool in the hands of the acquirer[20].

A bidder that makes a big play about a merger-of-equals deal while concealing its real intention loses credibility, and exposes itself to legal challenge by shareholders aggrieved by such deception. In prosecuting its 1998 acquisition of Chrysler for $40bn, the German prestige car maker Daimler-Benz (DB) structured the deal as 'a merger of equals'. In October 2000 Jürgen Schrempp, DB's CEO, admitted that it had always been his intention that the deal would be an acquisition by Daimler. This led a large shareholder, Kirk Kerkorian, to launch a $8bn claim against Daimler-Chrysler for fraud[21].

Empirical evidence from the US suggests that target CEOs in mergers of equals may be trading power for premium, by negotiating shared control in the merged firm in exchange for a lower shareholder premium[22]. Exhibit 20.6 above provides an example of such a trade-off. For the acquirer this is good news provided it does not create post-merger problems alluded to above.

Post-acquisition integration and deal negotiation

The deal negotiation process often develops its own dynamics, with adversarial posturing, oneupmanship etc., which can derail the purpose of the deal and the objectives of negotiation. The overall strategic objectives of the acquisition and the nature of the proposed acquisition broadly condition post-acquisition objectives. Post-acquisition objectives encompass the following.

- The reasons for buying the target – people, technical capabilities, market position, brand name.
- The source of value – cost reduction means excess of similar resources, revenue enhancement means under-utilized resources that can generate higher revenue, and growth options mean a need for future resources.
- The degree of integration required – how much autonomy should the acquired have? What is being integrated – functions, systems, processes?
- The imposition of acquirer's goals and objectives, systems, procedures, values, performance benchmarks on acquired firm or a merger of equals and shared vision, learning together, co-evolution of the merging partners.
- The need to retain key management and staff of the acquired.

Negotiation needs to aim to eliminate any risk, not only to deal completion but also to the attainment of the acquisition goals. Due diligence (DD) is an instrument of achieving this aim. It may reveal potential sources of risk, and allow the negotiators to devise remedies to cure the deal of those risks. The objectives of DD are:

- to confirm the expectations of the buyer about the target's performance, prospects, assets, liabilities, strengths and weaknesses;
- to identify critical areas in the target that the buyer needs to focus on in furtherance of his objectives in making the acquisition;
- to identify critical areas of concern that may increase risk to the buyer;
- to identify and formulate appropriate remedies and solutions to any problems revealed by due diligence; and
- to identify areas where access for due diligence has been denied, and critically evaluate the risk.

Due diligence

Traditionally DD was restricted to the legal and contractual aspects of assets and liabilities, or to the representations in accounting statements, the bases of preparation of these statements, etc. Accountants and lawyers carried it out. Increasingly, however, the scope of DD has increased to cover a wider range of issues. Table 20.2 lists and describes the main characteristics of these different types of DD, and their motivation.

Human resource, and especially culture due diligence, is often one of the most difficult areas in due diligence. Until recently HR audit was done not up-front while the deal was

Table 20.2 Types, scope and motivation of due diligence (DD)

Type	Areas investigated	To assess
Commercial	• Competitive position • Customer and supplier relations • Regulatory • Industry growth • Patents	• Core competences and how inimitable they are • Competitive strengths and weaknesses • Opportunities and threats • Potential synergies • Value of target
Operational	• Production technology • Processes and systems	• Assess efficiency • Need for new technology • Need for investment
Financial	• Historical information • Management information system	• Target past performance • Scope for cost savings • Target value
Tax	• Current and potential tax liabilities • Availability of tax losses	• Potential risks and costs • Need for warranties and indemnities
Organizational and cultural[23]	• Structure, mission and values • Power distribution • Management style • Contribution to competitive advantage	• Impact on post-acquisition integration • Key integration issues • Risk of integration failure
Human resources	• Compensation and incentives • Pensions • Importance of human resources to target • Morale and commitment • Employee and union relations • Labour contracts • Training and development	• Unfunded pension liability • Key players and motivation • Their expectation and fears from acquisition • What they will settle for • How to deal with unions
Information system	• Performance • Cost • Complexity	• IT fit and compatibility • Key integration issues • Target value
Legal	• Contractual agreements • Problems, e.g. product liability • Environmental liabilities	• Potential risks and costs • Need for warranties and indemnities • Discount on target value

negotiated, but after deal closure. However, practice has changed over the years. Scott Moeller[24], in a survey of M & A deals closed in 2003, finds that there 'is early involvement of human resources (HR). Key person identification, retention strategies and cultural issues are all critical to successful takeovers.' A study by Towers Perrin, a HR consultancy, found in 2000 that HR departments were typically not involved in pre-deal or due diligence activities. Their later study in 2004 found that HR professionals were being brought into the M & A process earlier: in 2000 only 40% had any meaningful involvement in pre-deal or due diligence stages, but by 2004 the figure had jumped to 62%[25].

Limitations of and on DD

As can be expected, the buyer and seller will differ in the scope and variety of DD, and the need for it. The buyer will like extensive DD and the seller quite skimpy DD. For the seller, DD can be quite disruptive. It may also rely on disclosures to mitigate the need for warranties and indemnities demanded by the buyer after DD. The time available for DD may not be long enough to permit as detailed an investigation as the buyer would like. In the case of public companies DD may be perhaps restricted to publicly available documentation. With hostile

Exhibit 20.7

One Plus but a lot of minuses

Smith & Nephew (S&N) acquired the Swiss company Plus Orthopaedics in 2007 for SFr 1.1bn (£531m). The deal was agreed in March and completed in June 2007. The UK healthcare group's due diligence had failed to identify that Plus was using unethical sales practices. S&N stopped them, and stood to lose $100m (£51m) of annual sales. In April 2008 S&N announced this, and a 5% cut in forecast pre-tax profits for 2008, triggering a 13% drop in its share price. This was not a case of complex fraud. It involved widespread sales practices that S&N, an 'industry leader', should have known about. For S&N, Plus was a consolation prize after it had been outbid in auctions for Switzerland's Centerpulse in 2003 and Biomet of the US in 2006. The case highlighted the risk of cross-border deals, and underscored the difficulty of conducting due diligence when assets are acquired in a hurried auction. S&N shares had been enjoying a premium over peers, owing to the new CEO Mr Illingworth's management, but now he had to restore stock market confidence.

Source: Adapted from C. Hughes, 'Smith & Nephew's management premium in jeopardy', *Financial Times*, 2 May 2008.

bids, the bidder is unlikely to gain any access to the target for DD purposes. Cultural due diligence is a particularly difficult area because of the need to observe the behaviour of people in an organizational setting over a period of time. Despite all these limitations, DD is still a useful way of discovering more about the target companies.

The importance of a thorough due diligence audit of the target in a takeover is vividly brought out by the acquisition of Swiss company Plus Orthopaedics by UK's Smith & Nephew (see Exhibit 20.7). The scope for due diligence audit may be very limited in public company acquisitions, overseas acquisitions and hurried auctions.

In 2002 Bain & Company surveyed 250 international executives with M & A responsibilities. Half the participants said their due diligence processes had failed to uncover major problems, and half found that their targets had been dressed up to look better for the deals. Two-thirds said they routinely overestimated the synergies available from their acquisitions. Overall, only 30% of the executives were satisfied with the rigour of their due diligence processes. Fully a third admitted they hadn't walked away from deals they had nagging doubts about[26].

A proper due diligence allows the buyer to assess the risks, and allow for them in pricing the acquisition. In 2008 WellCare Health Plans (WCG), the Florida-based managed care services provider, was discreetly inviting potential acquirers' interest even though it was under investigation by the Federal Bureau of Investigation with regard to how it priced different health plans between subsidiaries, among other points. By allowing extensive due diligence by potential buyers, WCG sought to enable them to assess the size of any potential damages following the investigation, and factor the cost into the offer price[27]. Due diligence can also bring pleasant surprises when the bidder discovers the target's hidden strengths and opportunities. In this case the bidder may be able to realise more value from the acquisition than implied in the offer price.

The Sarbanes-Oxley Act, passed in 2002 to improve corporate governance and board monitoring of corporations in the wake of the massive scandals such as Enron, Worldcom and

Tyco, has raised the bar in terms of the due diligence acquirers have to undertake for their target firms[28].

Hostile bid tactics

A hostile bid requires a battle plan detailing the various lines of attack, outflanking moves and counterattacks. An important element of the plan is surprise. In this respect the initial advantage certainly lies with the hostile bidder, and surprise is more easily achieved in a voluntary bid without pre-bid stake building than in a mandatory bid in which the bidder has already built up a 30% stake. Timing of the various moves, such as revision of the offer terms, must be made in accordance with the bid timetable laid down by the City Code.

In a hostile bid the bidder has to rely on external advisers to a much greater extent than in a friendly bid. In particular, the services of investment banks with special expertise in hostile bids, lawyers, PR consultants, and stockbrokers who can convey and influence the market sentiment in favour of the bid will be indispensable. The role of the investment bank adviser is of the utmost importance under the Code (see Chapter 19).

Lines of attack

The various lines of attack that a hostile bidder may in general follow are outlined in Table 20.3. The first move of talking to the target is often made to coincide with any unpropitious or vulnerable time for the target. The target may have just announced or be just about to announce poor profits, or even losses. It may be in the middle of a restructuring programme with depressed earnings. The target may be in a cyclical industry and currently at the bottom of that cycle.

Table 20.3 Lines of attack in a hostile bid

Line of attack	Nature of attack
The advisory team	Select advisers with experience of hostile bids well ahead of bid
Strong bid rationale	Justify bid rationale, and articulate benefits clearly to bidder and target shareholders
Timing (see Chapter 18 on the Code rules and Table 18.2)	Announce bid when target is vulnerable. Post offer document early to reduce target response time. Revise offer terms after Day 39. Release own results by Day 46. Choose offer closing date to maximize pressure on target shareholders. Choose when to 'shut off' cash alternative (see Chapter 16)
Denounce target's performance	Attack target's flawed strategy, inept management, poor past performance, unrealistic profit and dividend forecast. Highlight any 'hocus-pocus' in target's accounts to reduce its credibility
Lobby target shareholders	Present bid case to institutional shareholders. Try for irrevocable acceptances from large shareholders
Market purchases (see Chapter 18 for the Code rules)	Buy in the market up to 10% within offer price. Otherwise, offer price has to be raised/cash alternative has to be offered
Public relations	Lobby politicians to minimize adverse political fall-out. Project virtues of bid in the press. Communicate bid benefits to employees, their pension fund trustees and trade unions to win support for bid
Offer terms (see Chapter 16 on payment methods)	Tailor consideration to suit target shareholder profile. Include cash alternative. Underwrite cash alternative to raise credibility of offer. Offer payment terms to appeal to arbitrageuers

Table 20.4 Hostile bids and their outcome in the UK

Period to March 2001–08	Number of proposals	Hostile at start No. (% of proposals)	Hostile at close No. (% of start)	Hostile lapsed No. (% of close)
Total	1092	123 (11.3)	80 (65)	32 (40)
Annual average	136.5	15.4	10	4

Hostile means the offer is not recommended by the target management either at bid announcement ('start') or at the end of the offer period.
Source: City Takeover Panel annual reports.

Subject to the constraints of the Code, the bidder must fine-tune the time of release of new information, revision of offer terms, extension of the closing date and market purchases, so as to put the maximum pressure on the target management and shareholders. An early release of information may give the target the chance and time to respond robustly. Early market purchases may signal that the bidder is not confident of winning the bid. Analysis of the target shareholder profile is important in choosing the appropriate medium for communication, in effective presentation of arguments for the bid, and in tailoring the consideration.

Hostile turning into friendly or recommended bid

Initial resistance by the target management may be just an opening gambit in a protracted game. After that posturing, target management in many cases negotiates a higher premium, a higher exchange ratio in share exchange offers, or a more attractive post-acquisition managerial position: for example, board membership of the acquirer may be negotiated, and the bid is completed on a friendly note. Thus hostility is merely a tactical ploy for target management to extract better terms from the bidder. This view is supported by the data from the City Panel in Table 20.4. The proportion of hostile bids among the takeover proposals for UK public companies is about 11.3%. Of such hostile bids, 65% remain hostile until the end of the offer period. Thus a third of the hostile proposals are converted into 'friendly' during the offer period[29]. Bid failure probability is high at 40% if the bid remains hostile.

Institutional investors and bid outcome

Institutional shareholders' shareholdings in public corporations have increased over the years, and they now hold a very high proportion of public companies' equity: for example, in the UK this is well over 60%, and in the US over 50%. It is therefore important to understand their role in influencing takeover outcomes. For bidders, it is vital that they 'sell' their takeover bid to their own institutional shareholders and those of the target company. In practice, bidders conduct 'road shows' to sell their deals. Institutional shareholders are not a homogeneous group, and their investment strategies are not all the same. Traditional funds are generally long-term investors, although they will not be averse to accepting attractive takeover premia and voting against the incumbent target management. Hedge funds, on the other hand, are much more short-term and opportunistic investors.

One of the important factors influencing the voting behaviour of institutional investors is their cross-shareholding in the bidder and the target. Matvos and Ostrovsky find that, in a given merger, mutual funds that hold shares in both the acquirer and the target are more likely to vote for the merger than those that hold shares only in the acquirer. Furthermore,

Exhibit 20.8

Swings and roundabouts for institutional investors

The merger of Bank of America (BAC) and FleetBoston Financial (FBF) was announced on 27 October 2003. Many institutional investors (IIs) held shares in both firms, and their gains and losses estimated over seven days around announcement are as follows.

BAC shares held by IIs	861m
% of BAC shares owned by IIs	57.5
FBF shares held by IIs of BAC	647m
% of FBF shares held by IIs of BAC	61.5
Loss of institutional shareholders of BAC on BAC shares	$5.28bn
Gain of institutional shareholders of BAC on FBF shares	$5.56bn
Net gain	$280m

In this case, although the IIs lost on their holdings in the acquirer, this was more than offset by their gains from FBF. Thus they have the incentive to vote for the merger. If they held shares only in the acquirer BAC they would not have the same incentive!

Source: see footnote 30

this effect is present only in 'bad' mergers, i.e. negative announcement effects. These funds vote for such mergers, while other shareholders do not. Cross-ownership thus increases the probability of getting a bad merger done, but also that of a higher number of bad mergers proposed by managers.[30] What is the reason for this voting behaviour? Cross-holding institutions, while losing on their acquirer holding, are able to offset the loss with gains from their holding in the target, as shown in Exhibit 20.8. Bidders must therefore pay attention to such ownership patterns.

Hedge fund activism in takeovers

Hedge funds, as noted in Chapter 2, have become key players in many takeover situations. They often force bidders to abandon what they consider to be potentially value-destroying mergers. They have also brought pressure on targets defending against hostile bids which they consider to be value enhancing. Thus bidders (and targets, but see Chapter 21 on their problems) have to be aware of the demands of hedge fund investors and make sure they are supportive of the bid (see Exhibit 20.9)[31].

Beware of the arbs!

Increasingly, arbitrageurs play a significant role in infuencing the outcome of a bid. Arbitrageurs ('arbs') are short-term speculators that buy target company stock when the bid is announced. Unless the market expects a higher bid, stock in the target often trades at a discount to the offer price, reflecting the uncertainty about deal consummation. If the deal is completed, arbs make a profit on the spread, the difference between the purchase price and the eventual offer price in a successful deal. If the bid fails, arbs make a loss. By the end of a

---

Exhibit 20.9

No nod or a wink from Knight Vinke for VNU's acquisition strategy

In 2005 hedge fund Knight Vinke led a campaign against the Dutch publisher VNU's acquisition strategy, and forced it to abandon it. Subsequently, VNU itself was acquired by private equity firms in an LBO.

In 2008 Centaurus, the UK hedge fund, and Paulson, an American hedge fund, joined forces against the business strategy and performance of Corporate Express, the office supplier. Its attempt to merge with a white knight, Lyreco, a French rival, when faced with a hostile bid from Staples, the US office supplies company, was abandoned following the shareholder pressure generated by hedge funds. In the end Office Supplies agreed terms with Staples.

---

successful offer a large portion of the target shares is in the hands of arbs. In a medium-sized deal this may be as much as 50%. Many leading investment banks, such as Goldman Sachs, run risk arbitrage desks.

Arbs: allies or adversaries?

Arbs trade in the target's stock on margin, and therefore incur interest costs on margin loans. In their keenness to have the deal completed and minimize these costs they pile the pressure on targets and their advisers, often relying on 'bluff and posturing'. This may work to the advantage of bidders, but bidders also have to pay heed to their preferences in structuring the offer. Arbs obviously run the risk of bid failure, and the return they get must compensate them for this risk, as well as for the financing costs and the opportunity cost of speculation, i.e. what return they would have earned from an alternative investment. Arbs' profits are a function of:

- the spread, i.e. the bid premium;
- the risk of deal failure; and
- the duration of the bid – the longer it takes, the costlier the arbs' position is.

While a contested deal enhances the bid premium, it also reduces the chances of a successful deal. Multiple bids increase both the bid premium and the probability of one of the bids succeeding. So the more the merrier for the arbs. Agreements with clauses that allow a bidder to walk away, e.g. material adverse change (MAC), may attract friendly bidders such as WKs. Thus arbs have to pay a lot of attention to deal detail. These transactions also increase the power of the arbs, and their influence on the progress of multiple and contested deals. Smart bidders could also turn the arbs' vulnerability to their advantage and leverage their pressure on targets to win favourable deals.

Risk of deal failure or delay in consummation may arise from regulatory intervention. For example, a prohibition by an antitrust regulator or a prolonged investigation or litigation in the US can force the arb to close its open position at a loss. Thus correctly estimating the likelihood of an antitrust investigation, its length and the likelihood of eventual clearance and the terms of clearance is vital for profitable arbitrage. Arbitrage departments run by investment banks may also create conflicts of interest if they arbitrage stocks of clients that they advise on acquisition or defence. This led arbitrageurs from Salomon Smith Barney in London to leave the bank and set up an independent business[32].

Table 20.5 Disastrous losses to arbitrageurs in major deals

Bidder	Target date	Announcement date	Withdrawal dates	Arb's take in target (%)	Estimated loss in 2004 ($bn)
General Electric	Honeywell	23 Oct 2000	2 Oct 2001	53.4	2.8
American Home Products	Monsanto	1 Jun 1998	13 Oct 1998	45.2	2.3
British Telecom	MCI	1 Nov 1996	10 Nov 1997	40.2	1.9
Tellabs	CIENA	3 Jun 1998	14 Sep 1998	33.7	1.2
Staples	Office Depot	4 Sep 1996	2 Jul 1997	44.5	0.6
Abbot Labs	ALZA	21 Jun 1999	16 Dec 1999	45.8	0.5

Source: Adapted from M. S. Officer, 'Are performance based arbitrage effects detectable? Evidence from merger arbitrage,' *Journal of Corporate Finance*, **13**(5), 2007, 793–812.

Both cash offers and stock exchange offers can stimulate arbitrage. In a cash offer the arb buys the target stock and waits for the offer to close, and receive the cash proceeds. In an exchange offer the arb buys the target stock and short-sells the bidder stock. When the offer closes, the received bidder stock is used to close the short position. Baker and Savasoglu estimated that arbitrage in cash and stock financed offers during 1981–96 could yield a monthly risk-adjusted return of 0.6–0.9%[33]. With a UK sample, Sudarsanam and Nguyen found annual returns of 6–11% for arbitrage strategies[34]. For small target shareholders arbs provide a safer exit than if they were to wait until deal completion, but they may miss out on any upward revision of the offer price.

Merger arbitrage losses and implication for deal closure

Merger arbitrage can turn into huge losses when arbs have taken a large position in the target (in a cash offer) or target and bidder (in a share exchange offer) if the merger proposal or tender offer is withdrawn. Officer provides some estimates of such losses (called *arbitrage disasters*) for some well-known US deals (see Table 20.5)[35]. What is striking is the large size of these holdings. Given this size, and the disastrous losses that accompany deal failures, it is a reasonable conjecture that arbs' interests are best served by deal completion, and that they will seek to influence both bidders and targets to bring deals to closure.

Factoring in competitive bids

Risk of stimulating rival bids is present in both friendly and hostile bids when one bidder puts the target 'in play'. The possibility of a rival bidder joining the fray needs to be carefully appraised ahead of the bid launch. In the case of horizontal or related acquisitions the likely rival bidders following similar strategies may be easy to identify. In the case of conglomerate bidders this becomes difficult. Where potential bidders include financial buyers and overseas buyers, figuring out potential rival bidders becomes daunting. Nevertheless, a bidder must constantly scan the radar to see the emergence of likely rivals.

Where rival bidders do emerge, the tactics to be adopted need to be carefully thought through. Pre-empting rival bidders with break-up fees, asset lock-ups, stock lock-ups, etc. are possible tactics, but they must be consistent with the target directors' fiduciary responsibilities. Both the chances of rival bids and the chances of success in the face of rival bids need to be evaluated. The incidence of multiple bids is not very common – about 8–10% of deals. Nevertheless, the entry of a rival such as a white knight (WK) increases the chances of bid failure (see Chapter 21 on the effectiveness of various takeover defences, of which WK is one).

Bid strategies and tactics in the US[36]

In Chapter 18 we described the statutory merger procedure under various state incorporation laws in the US and the tender offer (TO) procedure under the Federal Williams Act (WA). Statutory mergers are normally friendly, negotiated deals. When a target firm management refuses to negotiate a friendly deal, the bidder may turn to a hostile TO. However, not all TOs are hostile. In many cases a TO is part of a merger agreement, and is supported by the target management. In the two-step transaction, if the bidder acquires 90% of the outstanding stock of the target it will usually have the power to approve the second-step, short-form freeze-out merger without shareholder approval. Where the bidder secures over 50% voting rights but not over 90% in a TO, it may still aim for long-form freeze-out merger, but will hit takeover defences such as supermajority and standstill provisions that require the target board and target shareholder vote to eliminate. The bidder has to carefully weigh the chances of achieving a short-form or long-form freeze-out.

In an exchange offer, to make it non-taxable from the target shareholder point of view, the bidder must acquire 80% of the target stock. There may be the remaining minority shareholders. In a merger the minority shareholders have appraisal rights to approach the court if they are not offered a fair price[37]. Some forms of statutory merger may need bidder shareholder approvals, whereas others do not, e.g. a forward triangular merger (see Chapter 18 on different merger types).

The WA requires information disclosure, fair treatment of shareholders, a timetable, and share-dealing restrictions on tender offers. If the bidder wishes to avoid these onerous conditions it must avoid making a tender offer. On the other hand, a TO shortens the time for merger when it is combined with a short-form freeze-out merger. WA lays down eight tests to determine whether a series of transactions constitute a tender offer. Purchase of shares in the marketplace, called 'street sweep', may under certain circumstances be construed as a tender offer, e.g. offer of a premium over market price, or solicitation of a substantial percentage of shares. Such actions, unless avoided, may force the buyer into an unintended and undesirable tender offer. US companies have a range of defensive mechanisms against unsolicited and hostile bids.

A *bear hug* is a publicly announced unsolicited proposal to the target management to enter into a negotiated merger. A bear hug, by revealing that the company may become a bid target, draws in speculative target share purchases, e.g. by arbitrageurs who will sell to the highest bidder. It also alerts the target to a potential tender offer and gives it time to prepare its defences. Because of its surprise element, a bear hug has also been called a *Saturday Night Special*.

Target's anti-takeover defences

In the next chapter we describe the range of anti-takeover defences put in place by US firms in more detail. Some of these are:

● shark repellants – structural defences in the company's charter or by-laws;
● poison pill or shareholder rights plans that increases the cost to the bidder enormously;
● supermajority provision requiring 80–85% of the board to approve of a merger;
● fair price to all shareholders, i.e no coercive back-end-loaded two-tier offers;
● standstill agreement that freezes the voting rights of ownership in excess of a specified level, e.g. 15–20%; many state 'voting rights' statutes mandate such freezing, but allow target shareholders to vote to opt out.

A bidder needs strategies and tactics to overcome these if it wishes to launch a hostile bid. Bidders can seek to negotiate friendly merger agreements that may provide for the redemption of poison pills. In a friendly deal the bidder can count on the support of the target management to win the shareholder vote to waive the shark repellents or opt out of state anti-takeover laws such as 'fair value' or 'voting rights' statutes.

Detoxing the poison pills and overcoming other defences

Having chosen, or been forced by target management's resistance, to launch a hostile bid, the bidder needs to weaken the target defences and improve the chances of success of the bid. Hostile bidders then resort to:

- legal challenge to the anti-takeover defences in place, or the actions taken by the target board in response to a takeover bid;
- a proxy fight to replace the target directors so that the poison pills can be redeemed and other impediments removed;
- a high premium offer for more than 90% of the target shares to, if successful, force a freeze-out merger on the minority; the supermajority provision will be overridden once the bidder accumulates 90% stake; and
- enlisting shareholder activists to support the TO and bring pressure to bear on the target board.

Legal challenge to anti-takeover defences[38]

Anti-takeover defences are in general protected by the Business Judgment Rule (BJR), which allows corporate board directors a great deal of discretion in the discharge of their functions *as directors*. This protection is available to directors who observe:

- the fiduciary duty of care by exhibiting diligence, rational purpose and reasonableness; and
- the fiduciary duty of loyalty by exhibiting *bona fide* and disinterestedness.

In the US, directors owe fiduciary duty to both the corporation *and* the shareholders[39]. The US courts have in general shown great deference to directors' business judgement. The courts have consciously refrained from second-guessing the validity of business decisions, and from substituting their own views retrospectively for the judgement of directors.

While takeover defences are generally protected by BJR, the courts, over the years, have held target directors to greater accountability and have circumscribed the discretion under BJR. They have applied increasingly stringent standards in reviewing the actions of target directors. BJR is a process-oriented rule: that is, the process by which directors reach their decisions is an important element in the determination of whether their actions/decisions are protected by BJR.

While respecting the freedom provided by BJR to directors, courts have also imposed stringent tests for the due exercise of their business judgement. *Unocal* imposes the two-stage test in the context of the defensive moves taken by target directors:

- they must have reasonable grounds for believing that the proposed takeover poses a threat to the corporation and its shareholders (the *reasonableness test*); and
- the actions taken by them against the threat are *reasonable* in relation to that threat (the *proportionality test*).

In *Unitrin* the court evolved the *entire fairness* test, under which the directors' actions must be *bona fide* and not tainted by any self-dealing, and they must aim to receive a *fair price* for their shareholders through their actions. Thus *fairness in price* and *fairness in dealing* are the elements of this test to be satisfied.

The *Blasius* standard lays down that target directors' action to impede the exercise of stockholder voting power – for example, impeding, as in that case, the hostile bidder's attempt to commence a written consent solicitation procedure to expand the target board and fill it with its own nominees – would be protected only if the board demonstrated a '*compelling justification*' for such action.

The burden of proof shifts from one test to another. For the *Unocal* test it is for the plaintiff to establish that target directors breached their fiduciary duty, whereas for the *entire fairness* test it is for the defendant target directors to demonstrate that their actions were entirely fair. Where directors' defensive actions fail these tests, their actions may not be protected by BJR. In some cases the courts have ordered the defendants to redeem poison pills. Thus hostile bidders challenging the targets' defences have the burden of proof that the target board failed the *Unocal* test and have to make sustainable charges under the *entire fairness* test.

As noted earlier under 'Buying in an auction', the *Revlon* judgement imposes a duty on target directors to run an auction among competing bidders. This puts the hostile bidder on a level playing field with the target's preferred bidder or a white knight[40].

Tender offer plus proxy fight

Control of a corporation may be accomplished by capturing the board through a proxy fight, or by obtaining written consents. In a proxy fight the insurgent shareholders gather enough shareholder votes to replace a majority of the board of directors with the insurgents' 'slate' of alternative nominees. An insurgent may also solicit written consents from shareholders and avoid a shareholder meeting. There is no acquisition proposal, and target shareholders are not being solicited to sell their shares but to cast their proxy votes or give written consents to change the board in favour of the insurgents' slate. A proxy fight may often be a preparation for a hostile takeover bid, as shown in Exhibit 20.10[41].

Exhibit 20.10

Microsoft's proxy fight is search engine for Yahoo shareholder support

Microsoft (MS) made a $42bn ($31 per share) offer to Yahoo, the Internet search engine company, in February 2008, but the bid was expected to be rejected by the latter, since 'what was on the table massively undervalued the company'. Reports suggested that Yahoo would be unlikely to consider seriously an offer of less than $40 per share. That would add $12bn to the price MS had to pay. MS had seen the value of its own shares fall 12% since it made the bid. Yahoo was trading at about $19 just before MS's bid. MS considered a proxy contest to replace Yahoo's board at its annual meeting in June. Steve Ballmer, MS chief executive, signalled his company's determination not to take no for an answer. MS had a team of advisers in place for any proxy fight, as did Yahoo to secure shareholder votes in favour of the current board.

Source: Adapted from C. Nuttall and R. Waters 'Microsoft to target Yahoo investors', FT.com, 11 February 2008

Exhibit 20.11

Largest break-up fees in 2007 in the US

Target	Acquirer	Deal value ($bn)	Target fee in $m (% of deal value)	Acquirer fee in $m (% of deal value)
Equity Office Prop	Blackstone	40.7	720 (1.8)	
TXU Corp	Investor Group	32.1	1000 (3.1)	1000 (3.1)
Caremark Rx Inc	CVS Corp	26.3	675 (2.6)	
Phelps Dodge Corp	Freeport-McMohan	25.8	750 (2.9)	188 (0.7)
First Data Corp	KKR	25.7	700 (2.7)	
Altel Corp	Atlantis Holdgs	25.1	625 (2.5)	625 (2.5)

Source: Adapted from Mergers & Acquisitions, February 2008, 26

Avoiding multiple bids

In a negotiated deal, to pre-empt rival bidders the first bidder may enter into various agreements with the target management:

- 'no shop' and 'no talk' to prevent the target management from 'shopping' the company or talking to unsolicited bidders;
- asset lock-up, giving the acquirer the right to buy a significant asset of target company;
- stock lock-up, giving the acquirer the right to buy newly issued target stock up to 20% of its outstanding shares;
- break-up fees, as discussed above (see Exhibit 20.11 for some recent US deals involving break-up fees).

Reverse break-ups are payable by *bidders* to targets if they walk away. Exhibit 20.11 shows such fees payable by US acquirers. The table shows that reverse break-up fees are not always paid, and often are of the same size as the fee payable by targets. In the recent credit crisis many private equity firms walked away because of the problems in raising debt funds for LBOs. When Apollo Management walked away from its offer to buy Huntsman it had to cough up more than the reverse break-up fee of $325m. Huntsman sued Apollo for breach of contract and, following a long litigation, Apollo and its and its creditors paid $1bn to the target. Reverse break-up fees force the bidders to share some of the risks of deal collapse for reasons beyond the control of targets, e.g. prolonged antitrust investigation[42].

The *Revlon* duties imposed by the Delaware Supreme court (see Chapter 22) mean that the above devices need to be consistent with the target directors' fiduciary duty, and satisfy the criteria that:

- directors have no conflict of interest in agreeing to these; and
- they are being used to get the best possible deal for the shareholders, or they protect the long-term interests of the company.

The court may also look upon these acquirer-protective devices favourably if the target is engaged in a strategic combination rather than being sold to acquirer. Thus stock exchange offers that maintain continuity of interest may be more in tune with this criterion than a cash offer.

Toehold acquisitions

As in the UK, acquisitions of significant stakes require to be disclosed. Schedule 13D filing with the SEC is required if the purchase exceeds 5% of the target's stock within 10 days of acquisition. Acquisitions exceeding 15% are not allowed without clearance under the Hart–Scott–Rodino (HSR) Antitrust Improvement Act (see Chapter 17). These disclosure requirements mean that secret accumulation of a substantial stake in the target before a tender offer is made is difficult, and may invite arbitrageurs to start accumulating stock. They may also alert a target shareholder to an imminent bid and drive up the target share prices and the subsequent bid premia. Toehold acquisitions in excess of certain thresholds also attract the stringent 'fair value' and 'voting rights' statutes, thus effectively limiting their strategic value (see above).

Empirical evidence on bid strategies and value creation

In this section we review the empirical evidence concerning the effectiveness of various bid strategies and tactics, and their shareholder wealth effects. Given the importance of hostile takeover as an instrument for the efficient functioning of the market for corporate control, we examine the evidence for the superiority of the value creation performance of hostile acquirers.

In their study cited earlier in this chapter, Boone and Mulherin do not find that winners of multi-bidder auctions suffer 'winner's curse', since the three-day announcement period abnormal returns to bidders in both auctions and negotiated single-contact deals were the same, −0.7% (on abnormal returns see Chapter 4). They conclude that 'breakeven returns to bidders in corporate takeovers stem not from the winner's curse but from the competitive market for targets that occurs predominantly prior to the public announcement of bids.'

Evidence for the impact of bidder's toehold on the returns to target shareholders is somewhat ambiguous. Franks reported that toehold has little impact for his small sample of brewing industry takeovers, whereas in the Franks and Harris study target shareholders gain from bidder's toehold[43]. The latter result is consistent with the Choudhury and Jegadeesh model prediction[44]. Sudarsanam *et al.* provided evidence that toehold reduced the returns to target shareholders, consistent with the prediction of Shleifer and Vishny[45].

For a sample of over 200 contested bids in the UK during 1983–89, Sudarsanam found that bidder's toehold had no significant influence on the outcome[46]. However, the presence of large institutional block shareholders helped the hostile bidder. This probably reflects the success of shareholder lobbying. The most decisive factor in favour of the bidder, though, is the method of payment. Consideration in the form of pure equity or equity plus cash favours the target, and reduces the chances of a successful bid. If the consideration includes cash, the bidder stands a better chance of winning. Given the problem of valuing a securities exchange offer (see Chapter 16), an equity offer often evokes a strong attack from the target management. A cash offer reduces the scope for such attack. Jenkinson and Mayer also provide evidence, from a smaller sample of 42 contested UK bids, that a cash offer is more effective than an equity or mixed offer in facilitating a successful bid[47].

Cost of bids

Takeover bids, especially hostile bids, are very expensive affairs for bidders as well as for targets. In addition to the fees paid to the advisers, there are other transaction costs, such as fees paid to the regulators and the costs of printing, mailing and advertising. If the cash alternative is underwritten, then the bidder pays the underwriting and arrangement fee to the merchant bank and the sub-underwriters. All these make up the direct costs of a bid, but there are also opportunity costs. The latter include, in the case of a failed hostile bid, loss of face, a strategy in shambles, and diminished credibility in future bids. The smell of defeat lingers on. In the case of a successful bid the opportunity costs may be in the form of departure of target management, fear and anxiety among staff, and their reduced morale (see Chapters 4 and 22). Opportunity costs also include the corporate resources, such as top management time diverted to the prosecution of the bid. As discussed in Chapter 12, acquirer directors and CEOs also run the risk of losing their jobs following a value-destroying acquisition.

How important is the bid premium?

Bidders may consider a high bid premium an effective tactical tool to influence the bid outcome. Hoffmeister and Dyl found that bid premium had little impact on the bid outcome, whereas Walkling reported a positive impact, in line with Hirshleifer and Titman. In a more recent US study Moeller, Schlingemann and Stulz find no evidence of bid premium influencing outcome[48]. In hostile bids the premium is higher than in friendly bids, but hostile bids have a much lower probability of success. Thus, by itself, high premium may be insufficient to achieve success.

In Walkling and Edminster there is evidence of a decline in the average bid premium as the bidder's toehold increases[49]. Stulz *et al.* found that the bidder's toehold reduced the wealth gains to target shareholders[50]. Both these results are consistent with the Shleifer and Vishny and Hirshleifer and Titman models[51].

Does a high bid premium lead to value destruction? In recent US takeovers during 1980–2001 the average (median) premium paid for public targets was 68% (61%) by large acquirers and 62% (52%) by small acquirers. A high premium is generally treated as evidence of overpayment, sometimes due to bidder managers' hubris or overconfidence. As noted in Chapter 12 while discussing these biases, large acquirers pay higher bid premia but also experience significant value destruction over a three-year post-acquisition period compared with value creation by small acquirers (see Chapter 4). Antoniou, Arbour and Zhao find that, for a large UK sample, acquirers that pay a high four-week premium do not underperform those paying relatively low premiums in the three-year post-acquisition period. Although they do not analyse the impact of acquirer size on bid premium and post-acquisition abnormal returns, they report that there is little difference in these returns between relatively large and relatively small acquirers, i.e. relative to targets. Thus evidence on the link between high premium and post-acquisition shareholder value performance is inconclusive[52].

Shareholder wealth effects of hostile and friendly acquisitions

Recent empirical evidence from large-sample studies points to superior returns for acquirer shareholders in hostile acquisitions compared with friendly deals. As discussed in Chapter 4, a number of US studies have demonstrated empirically that tender offers generate significantly larger wealth gains than mergers. Both bidder and target shareholders experience these superior gains in tender offers (see Tables 4.1 and 4.2). Further, tender offers outperform mergers in creating long-term value for shareholders. It must be remembered that mergers are friendly deals, and tender offers often (but not always) are hostile deals. Thus it appears that hostile takeovers generate more value for acquirers and targets than friendly mergers.

White knights are found to generate less shareholder value than hostile bidders. In a large sample of 519 UK acquirers including WKs, single friendly, single hostile and hostile acquirers from multiple bids, Sudarsanam and Mahate found that abnormal returns over three post-acquisition years to single hostile acquirers are significantly larger than returns to the other types. White knights' returns are similar to those of single friendly and multiple hostile bidders. For the US, two studies show that WKs destroy more shareholder value than hostile acquirers, and suggest overbidding[53].

For the UK the difference is as much as 12–16% in the two-year post-acquisition period[54]. Thus acquirer shareholders seem to receive larger returns from hostile acquisitions. It is also well documented that target shareholders experience substantially larger wealth gains in hostile than in friendly deals. Thus, overall, the value created may be larger in hostile than in friendly deals.

Are hostile bids disciplinary?

Evidence on the pre-bid performance of targets does not point to any pronounced under-performance by targets[55]. Thus hostile bids are not always aimed at inefficient managers. However, inefficiency can be conceptualized as errors of commission as well as errors of omission. Errors of commission are those misjudgements that target managers have made in terms of corporate and business strategy, such as disastrous acquisition, for example Lasmo's acquisition of Ultramar in 1992 in the UK, which wiped out £1bn of shareholder value. Errors of omission are just failures to realize that the corporation they have been running can be run and managed to yield better shareholder value. This is a failure to exercise all the real options that the target firm's assets have conferred upon its managers. It may be a failure of vision. The function of hostile bids is to identify missed opportunities, redirect target assets to the highest value use, and thereby create value for shareholders[56]. This evidence strengthens the case for allowing hostile takeovers and against attempts to deter them.

Hey! What happened to those nice folks, the hostile predators?

In the 1990s hostile takeovers in the US became a relative rarity, for several reasons. The decline in hostile takeovers is reflected in Figure 20.3. A major reason is the passage of anti-takeover laws in several states (see Chapter 17) and the invention of potent anti-takeover devices such as poison pills. This forced many would-be hostile bidders to make friendly approaches to target managements. Overcoming the anti-takeover defences required other tactics, such as lawsuits and proxy fights (see Chapter 21). A second reason is that increasingly robust corporate governance regimes and greater institutional activism were probably making hostile takeover, as a disciplinary device, somewhat redundant.

Bid strategies and tactics in continental Europe: impact of the Takeover Directive

A variety of factors limit the incidence of hostile bids in many countries on the continent, although in the 1990s such bids became more common. Martynova and Renneboog report that only 6.7% of their sample of 2257 European mergers and acquisitions during 1993–2001 were hostile bids[57]. Corporate governance structures such as differential voting rights, management's ability to limit voting rights, pyramid corporate ownership structures, the absence of one-share-one-vote, two-tier boards that cannot be easily changed by an acquirer, the presence of employee representatives on supervisory boards, resistance from trade unions, the obligation to negotiate with the target boards before launching an offer, and the low disclosure

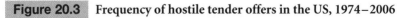

Figure 20.3 Frequency of hostile tender offers in the US, 1974–2006

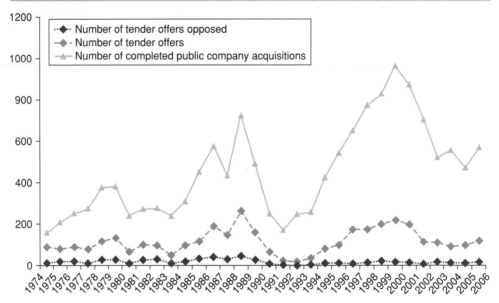

Source: W. W. Bratton, G. Gregoriou and L. Renneboog (eds.), 'Whither hostility?', *Corporate Governance and Regulatory Impact on Mergers and Acquisitions* (Elsevier Inc, 2007), pp. 103–129

thresholds for target share acquisitions are some of the factors that render hostile bids very difficult[58]. The Takeover Directive, by allowing national opt-outs from articles 9 (mandatory bids) and 11 (the breakthrough rule), has preserved very much the *status quo ante*.

Any of these could be formidable showstoppers for any hostile takeover. Thus negotiated and friendly bids are perhaps the most important, if not the only, bid strategy available. Moreover, other constituencies than the shareholders of the two companies involved and their managers may have to be satisfied. Similarly, when Cadbury Schweppes acquired Orangina-Pampyril in 2001, it discussed the acquisition with the target company works council as required under the French takeover code (see Chapter 18). It agreed not to make any job cuts for about two years after the acquisition. It obtained the cooperation of the workforce[59]. The Mittal takeover of the French steel company Arcelor in 2006 brings into focus many of the issues involved in European, and French in particular, takeovers (See case study below).

CASE STUDY

Mittal breaks Arcelor's steely defence and becomes the Emperor of Steel!

In January 2006 Mittal Steel, controlled by Lakshmi Mittal and his family with steel manufacturing and iron ore mining operations in Europe, Asia and the US, made an audacious bid for Arcelor the French steel maker also with manufacturing operations in Europe, Asia and the Americas. Although Mr Mittal had contacted senior executives of Arcelor, and discussed future cooperation, no serious discussion of a merger of the two companies seems to have taken place. Lakshmi Mittal had a dinner with Guy Dollé, the CEO of Arcelor, and the merger idea was discussed (or only mentioned according to Mr Dollé).

The initial bid and Arcelor reaction

The bid was for €18.6bn ($24bn) and the consideration was in Mittal Steel's shares and cash. The public announcement of a bid took Arcelor by surprise. It evoked a hostile response not only from Mr Dollé and Joseph Kinsch the chairman of Areclor but also from French politicians including the Prime Minister, Mr de Villepin, and the finance minister, Thierry Breton, and the prime minister of the Duchy of Luxembourg, Jean-Claude Juncker, in which Arcelor was the largest employer and the Duchy was a large shareholder. Luxembourg was naturally concerned about any potential job losses from any restructuring of Arcelor following the acquisition by Mittal.

Mittal Steel's history

Lakshmi Mittal founded the eponymous Mittal Steel. It had grown rapidly in the previous 10 years to become the largest steel producer in the world. Mittal had grown through acquisition mainly by buying bankrupt or underperforming steel companies in the US and in Central and Eastern Europe, Mittal's strategy was to acquire distressed government-owned steel manufacturers or those that were being privatized. From rather obscure origins in his family steel business in India and the steel mill he operated in Indonesia, Lakshmi Mittal had emerged with astonishing speed to head a sprawling steel empire. His rise to the top of the steel pyramid, was, in the words of *The Economist*, 'a result of opportunism, a bold eye for a deal and an ability to turn around failing firms'.

The strategic rationale for the bid

The steel industry was highly fragmented with steel manufacturing in many countries around the world having been for decades in the state sector before being privatised. In many countries, governments regarded steel as a national strategic industry and therefore one that should not be allowed to fall into the hands of foreigners. The fragmented nature of the industry meant that steel manufacturers had relatively weak bargaining power against both mining companies that provided the iron ore for steel manufacture and the user industries such as the large automobile manufacturers and white goods manufacturers. The top three iron ore companies – CVRD, BPH Billiton and Rio Tinto – controlled 70% of the supply market and the top five automobile companies controlled 70% of the user market. Similarly, the white goods manufacturers were also becoming concentrated. Compared to these markets, the top five steel companies controlled less than 20% of the market. Thus steel manufacturers were between a rock and a hard place. They were squeezed by enormous buyer power and even more enormous seller power.

Size was therefore becoming a strategic imperative for steel manufacturers. This would allow scale economies as well as enhance their bargaining power against both miners and the users. In recognition of this the industry was consolidating on a global scale through M & A and alliances (see Exhibit 5.3 on this trend prior to the Mittal bid for Arcelor). Both Mittal Steel and Arcelor had grown through acquisitions and mergers. Arcelor resulted from the merger of three companies in France, Spain and Luxembourg. Lakshmi Mittal was a passionate advocate of global consolidation and believed that further consolidation of the steel sector was necessary and inevitable.

The combined market share of the merged entity would be about 10% based on the 2005 data (60m tonnes by Mittal and 40m tonnes by Arcelor).

→

At the time of the Mittal bid in January 2006, Arcelor was a widely-held company, the largest shareholder, Romain Zaleski with 7.8% and the Duchy of Luxembourg with 5.6%. On the other hand, only 12% of Mittal stock was in the hands of shareholders outside the Mittal family. Lakshmi Mittal was the Chief Executive Officer (CEO) and son Aditya Mittal was the Chief Financial Officer (CFO). His daughter was also on the board of directors. By May 2006, about 20% of Arcelor had passed into the hands of hedge fund arbitrageurs who would play a significant role in swinging the battle in favour of Mittal (on merger arbitrage see above).

Arcelor's defensive tactics

After the initial hostile and dismissive reaction of the CEO, Guy Dollé, to the Mittal bid, Arcelor began to construct its defences. It:

- enlisted political allies – French and Luxembourg prime ministers and other politicians who were upset by the Mittal bid spoke against it;
- attacked the offer terms;
- attacked the dominance of the Mittal family in ownership and management and its 'weak' corporate governance;
- promised to improve shareholder value through a share buyback for $5bn;
- put the shares in Dofasco, its Canadian subsidiary, into a special trust to prevent Mittal from selling it in the event of a successful bid;
- negotiated a white knight merger with the Russian steelmaker Severstal, 90% owned by Mr Alexey Mordashov. This combination would have a total output of 70m tonnes with annual sales of $59bn. Arcelor would buy Mr Mordashov's stake in Severstal and his other steel and mining interests. In return Mr Mordashov would have a 32% in the combined entity; and
- wooed institutional investors in Arcelor to support the merger with Severstal and its defensive moves against Mittal.

Market reaction to these defensive moves was unenthusiastic if not downright hostile. It was felt that the defensive strategies were guided less by the merits of Arcelor's independence or by the business logic of the merger with Severstal than by the incumbent top management's desire to entrench themselves and to avoid giving serious consideration to the Mittal offer.

Mr Dollé's responses indicated that he had been miffed by the hostile bid. His irate response was a series of statements mocking Mittal as a company and its offer tinged with barely concealed hauteur. He called the bid 150% hostile and ridiculed the management of Mittal because Aditya Mittal was on the management board. He spoke with lofty condescension about Mittal and its being run by lots of Indians and said Arcelor was *parfum* whereas Mittal was just '*eau de cologne*'. Mr Dollé called the Mittal offer 'monkey money'. Such ill-concealed snootiness won few admirers for Mr Dollé and probably turned Mittal into an underdog and won him and his company much sympathy.

Shareholder revolt

Arcelor had argued that the corporate governance structure of Mittal was not consistent with best practice since the ownership was dominated by the family, and Aditya Mittal at the very young age of 30 was on the management board of the company. The implication was that Arcelor shareholder interests would not be best protected if they exchanged their shares for those of Mittal. Analysts contrasted the alleged flaws in Mittal Steel with the governance of Severstal. Weaknesses of the corporate governance practices in Russian companies were well known. Analysts argued that it was strange that Arcelor top management had greater faith in governance standards of a Russian company than in those of a company listed on the Amsterdam and New York stock exchanges. One institutional investor described Severstal's corporate governance as 'the Chernobyl of corporate governance'. Colette Neuville, head of ADAM a French lobby group for minority shareholder rights, doubted that the governance of a Russian conglomerate listed in Moscow was better than that of Mittal listed in Amsterdam and New York where listing requirements were especially stringent.

The industrial logic of the merger with Severstal was also seriously questioned. Jutta Rosenbaum of Commerzbank argued that the planned deal with the Russians was inferior to a merger with Mittal. The assets owned by the two companies were similar but Mittal had a more extensive distribution network, wider geographic reach, and more market power. Severstal's unlisted assets had also been overvalued. Ms Neuville also asked why Arcelor considered Severstal's mining assets valuable while complaining about Mittal's mining assets.

Many investors also had concerns that after the merger Mr Mordashov would soon be able to control the merged entity and be in a position to take over the entire company. If after the merger the buyback went to plan, his initial 32% stake would grow to 38%. Although under the Luxembourg takeover law, anyone with a 33% stake would have to make a full bid for all the remaining shares, thus allowing minorities to sell out, the Duchy's regulator had waived this requirement for Mr Mordashov. Thus, he would be gaining effective control but without offering the remaining shareholders a way to escape that control. Although Arcelor said these concerns were unfounded since there was a stand-still agreement that Mr Mordashov would not increase his stake for the next four years, shareholders remained sceptical.

Arcelor also sought to change the way the proposed merger with Severstal was to be voted on by the shareholders. The company required that shareholders would be able to veto the merger only if at least 50% of the shareholder base voted against it. This was an unusual voting procedure since normally it is the majority of the votes cast that would count for approving or not approving a proposal. Shareholders felt that Arcelor was changing the rules and treating shareholder rights shabbily. This kind of gerrymandering also raised questions about the motives of Mr Kinsch and Mr Dollé. Mr Zaleski, the largest shareholder in Arcelor, decided to vote against the merger with Severstal and instead support Mittal. Given the strong resentment of shareholders against the Arcelor management it was becoming apparent that the proposal to merge with Severstal was going nowhere.

The decision to put Dofasco into a trust was also seen as a ploy to lock away one of Arcelor's crown jewels and deny Mittal the opportunity to divest it in the event of a successful bid. Mittal had agreed with ThyssenKrupp, the German steelmaker, that, in the event of a successful takeover of Arcelor, Dofasco would be sold to it. Arcelor's move was to throw the spanner in this agreement and weaken the bid strategy of Mittal. One institutional investor in Arcelor called the move a 'disgrace'. The plan for a buy-back also lacked credibility since it was hastily conceived in the light of the hostile bid from Mittal.

→

Role of hedge funds

Hedge funds that owned 20% of the Arcelor stake now became quite active. They put pressure on the company by writing to call for it to agree to the merger with Mittal. They were orchestrated by Goldman Sachs, the investment bank adviser to Mittal.

Mittal's tactics

Wilbur Ross, a veteran American financier, who had sold the International Steel Group in the US to Mittal in 2005, and was a non-executive director of Mittal, called the Dofasco plan 'a screwball idea' aimed at 'ensuring that Mr Dollé can keep control of his cherished plaything (Arcelor)'. Lakshmi Mittal kept a low profile and did not respond to the barbs aimed at him by Dollé. Mittal let his own track record as a consolidator and the robust strategic logic of scaling up through the merger to speak for themselves. Concerns raised by Arcelor about the corporate governance weaknesses in Mittal were not enough to detract from this perception of the soundness of the proposed acquisition.

However, Mittal did respond to the concerns about the dominance of his family in the ownership and control of the merged entity and the offer terms were revised.

Revised terms

Mittal raised its offer to €25.8bn. Mittal family ownership in the merged entity was reduced to 43% and Lakshmi Mittal did not initially assume the role of CEO which went to Roland Junck, a veteran of Arcelor. Kinsch became the chairman of Arcelor Mittal as the merged firm was called. The merger agreement provided that Lakshmi Mittal would become board president without any operational responsibility. The board and senior management positions were divided equally between representatives from the two companies.

Mr Dollé did not find a place in the new company. Kinsch adjusted to the new regime, uttered soothing words about the merger and called it a 'marriage of reason'. He hoped that it would turn into a 'marriage of hearts'. In 2007 ThyssenKrupp sued Arcelor Mittal for not honouring Mittal's commitment to sell Dofasco and challenged its placing in a trust. However a Dutch court threw out that lawsuit and analysts considered Dofasco a valuable asset fitting well with Arcelor Mittal's North American operations. Thus what was set as a trap by Arcelor in its defence against Mittal turned out to be an unintended gift!

Fairly soon after the deal closure, in November 2006, Lakshmi Mittal became CEO replacing Roland Junck. The merger agreement was modified to accommodate this change and it was not a surprising change since Lakshmi Mittal had always been a hands-on operational man. Moreover, he had won the takeover battle. As one commentator put it, 'history is made by the winning side. They are the guys who write the rules'. Moreover, the change also seemed to respond to investor, especially US investor, wishes to see him take a more dominant role. Joseph Kinsch justified the change: 'We are making these changes to clarify the leadership of the company'. He described Mr Mittal as 'one of the most experienced and successful executives in the steel industry'. In February 2008 the group reported $19.4bn profits on sales of $105bn, up 27% on the two firms' aggregated profits in the previous year. Mr Mittal's 43% stake made him worth $19bn the fifth richest man in the world (*The Economist*, 16 February 2008).

Discussion questions

1 What is the strategic rationale for the takeover bid by Mittal Steel for Arcelor? How does it stem from the competitive structure of the industry?

2 How did Lakshmi Mittal's vision for the steel industry impact on the takeover bid?

3 What were the takeover defence tactics of Arcelor?

4 Why were they, in the end, ineffective?

5 Comment on the tactics of Mittal?

6 Comment on the management changes post-deal closure.

Sources: P. Marsh, 'Arcelor's chief calls Mittal bid "150%" hostile', 30 January 2006; W. Munchau, 'Why France must relax its corporate control', 6 February 2006; P. Marsh, 'Mittal comes under pressure to improve bid for Arcelor', 17 April 2006; P. Marsh, 'ThyssenKrupp suffers Dofasco setback in court', 24 January 2007; all from *Financial Times*. 'Treating shareholders as pig iron: Steel', 3 June 2006; 'Little love lost', 1 June 2006; 'Mittalic magic: Face value', 16 February 2008; all from *The Economist*. S. Reed, 'Blood, steel and empire building', *Business Week*, 13 February 2006; D. Mukerjea, 'Mittal's bid: The INSIDE story', 5 May 2006, downloaded from www.rediff.com; N. Schwartz, 'Emperor of steel', *Fortune*, 24 July 2006; P. Glader, 'Mittal founder becomes CEO', *The Wall Street Journal*, 7 November 2006.

Overview and implications for practice

In this chapter we describe the important elements of takeover bid strategies and tactics.

● Market timing is an important strategic as well as a tactical factor. The timing of takeover bids during merger waves is explained, and empirical evidence in support of early moves is provided.

● Alternative acquisition strategies include friendly bids, merger of equals, hostile bids, and white knight bids. The disadvantages of playing a white knight must be seriously considered.

● With the help of external advisers, the acquisition team has to anticipate potential showstoppers and develop countervailing strategies. These showstoppers include labour and union opposition, rebel directors, and hedge fund activism: they are to be prepared for and countered.

● The role of arbitrageurs has to be factored into bid strategy. Similarly, the probability of rival bids to trigger an auction must be taken into account.

● Building a stake in the business ahead of a bid has advantages and disadvantages.

● Different legal and regulatory jurisdictions may not allow certain strategies.

● Bid strategies must anticipate target defence strategy and prepare for different target defences.

● Various counter-strategies to overcome strong defences in the US are considered.

● The decline in hostile bids is explained in terms of various statutory and non-statutory obstacles. Improved corporate governance is a possible factor in such decline.

Review questions

20.1 What is a bid strategy? What are its objectives?

20.2 What is the role of an internal acquisition team (the N team)?

20.3 What are the advantages and disadvantages of building up a stake in a potential target company?

20.4 Compare the advantages and disadvantages of making a friendly bid rather than a hostile bid.

20.5 What is a merger of equals? What does it mean for takeover premium, negotiation and post-acquisition integration?

20.6 What are the different hostile bid strategies?

20.7 Who are arbitrageurs? What is their role in the M & A process?

20.8 Which bid strategies are likely to succeed on the basis of empirical evidence?

20.9 What are the different strategies available to bidders in the US?

20.10 What is the significance of rivals entering the contest for a target?

Further reading

A. Boone and J. Mulherin, 'Do auctions induce a winner's curse? New evidence from the corporate takeover market', *Journal of Financial Economics*, **89**, 1–19, 2005.

K. Carow, R. Heron and T. Saxton, 'Do early birds get the returns? An empirical investigation of early mover advantages in acquisitions', *Strategic Management Journal*, **25**, 563–585, 2004.

W. Fruhan, 'The company sale process', *Harvard Business School* case 9-206-108, 2008. *The Economist*, 'Inside a deal: Psychology', 3 May 2008.

Notes and references

1. See K. Carow, R. Heron and T. Saxton, 'Do early birds get the returns? An empirical investigation of early mover advantages in acquisitions', *Strategic Management Journal*, **25**, 2004, 563–585, and G. McNamara, J. Haleblian and B. Dykes, 'The performance implications of participating in an acquisition wave: Early move advantages, bandwagon effects and the moderating influence of industry characteristics and acquirer tactics', *Academy of Management Journal*, **51**, 2008, 113–130. In the first paper the acquirer returns are higher in related acquisitions, in growth industries, and when they are financed with cash. In the second paper returns are lower for acquirers buying at the top of the wave. The first-mover gains are limited to those in stable industries. For other studies reporting similar early-buyer advantages see M. Martynova and L. Renneboog, 'Mergers and acquisitions in Europe', in L. Renneboog (Ed.), *Advances in Corporate Finance and Asset Pricing* (Amsterdam: Elsevier, 2006), pp. 13–75.

2. More precisely, the *Revlon* duty of the target board, when the sale would involve 'change of control', is to obtain 'the highest value reasonably attainable for the shareholders'. For further discussion see Chapter 21 on defence strategies.

3. This section draws on W. Fruhan, 'The company sale process', Harvard Business School case 9-206-108, 16 April 2008. This procedure applies to both public and private company sale in the US. Since strategic buyers are uncomfortable in participating in auctions, the seller often conducts the auction on a *sequential* basis, with exclusive negotiation with each bidder in turn. In the UK, since bids for public companies are regulated by the City Code, this procedure is less relevant. Where there are two bidders or more, the City Panel can arrange an auction to find the winning bidder, as shown in Exhibit 18.2.

4. Under Rule 3 of the UK's Takeover Code a bank adviser to the target cannot provide the stapled finance for the offer (see Chapter 18 on the Takeover Code). See Chapter 12 for further discussion of stapled financing, and the conflicts of interest between targets and their financial advisers.

5. 'No shop' prevents the target from finding alternative, more attractive bidders. 'Antitrust out' allows the deal to fall through if blocked by antitrust regulators, without any penalty to either party. MAC allows either party to abandon the merger if there is a material adverse change to the companies. For further discussion see Chapter 17 on antitrust regulation.

6. See 'Banks cannot resist the perilous lure of private equity', *The Economist*, 14 October 2006. This article also highlights conflicts of interest between banks and PE firms, since banks both provide finance to, and also compete through their PE arms, with PE firms. Because of their anti-competitive effect, the Department of Justice in the US and the European Commission have investigated these 'club deals'. See Chapter 17 on the antitrust issues.

7. They also study a sample of 163 negotiated deals. As would be expected, the mean number of contacts is only 1.1, with a maximum number of contacts being just 3. See A. Boone and J. Mulherin, 'Do auctions induce a winner's curse? New evidence from the corporate takeover market', *Journal of Financial Economics*, **89**, 2008, 1–19, Table 1.

8. See M. Carapeto, S. Moeller and A. Faelten, 'The good, the bad, and the ugly: A survival guide to M&A in distressed times', Mergers and Acquisitions Research Centre, Cass Business School, City University, London. They find that acquirers of distressed and bankrupt targets enjoy positive abnormal returns on the days surrounding the announcement, an indication that the market views the acquisition as creating value for the acquirer. However, analysis of the long-term operating performance shows that acquirers of distressed and bankrupt targets struggle to realize value as their performance deteriorates as a result of the acquisition.

9. S. Grossman and O. Hart, 'Takeover bids, the free-rider problem and the theory of the corporation', *Bell Journal of Economics*, **11**, 1980, 42–64.

10 A. Shleifer and R. Vishny, 'Large shareholders and corporate control', *Journal of Political Economy*, **94**(31), 1986, 461–488.

11. D. Hirshleifer and S. Titman, 'Share tendering strategies and the success of hostile takeover bids', *Journal of Political Economy*, **98**(2), 1990, 295–324.

12. B. Choudhury and N. Jegadeesh, 'Pre-tender offer share acquisition strategy in takeovers', *Journal of Financial and Quantitative Analysis*, **29**(1), 1994, 117–129.

13. See R. Bruner, 'The merger of Hewlett-Packard and Compacq (A)', University of Virginia, Darden Publishing House case study UVA-F-1450, 2004.

14. PRONED, *Takeover Bids: A Guide for Directors* (London: Promotion of Non-executive Directors, 1988), p. 6.

15. See *The Economist*, 'Inside a deal: Psychology', 3 May 2008, 387, p. 99, describing an experimental study by Adam Galinsky of negotiation styles and their impact on outcomes. The study shows that perspective taking is far more effective than empathy, with Professor Galinsky arguing that 'a large amount of empathy can actually impair the ability to reach a creative deal'.

16. A. Banerjee and J. E. Owers, 'Wealth reduction in white knight bids', *Financial Management*, Autumn 1992, 48–57.

17. Access to privileged information or payment of break-up fees is also subject to regulatory constraints. In the UK the target is obliged under the Code to treat rival builders equally in terms of access to information. Further, directors' fiduciary responsibility to consider rival offers fairly may erode some of the advantages the WK may enjoy because of its friendly disposition. Break-up fees are also subject to regulatory constraint. Under the Code it is normally restricted to 1% of deal value. Excessive break-up fees that have the effect of shutting out competitive bids may fall foul of target directors' fiduciary duties to their shareholders (see below for the US rules on break-up fees). In the competitive bid for P & O Princess Cruises, the target agreed a break-up fee of $62.5m against a deal value of £3.2bn for the favoured bidder, Royal Caribbean Cruises, and the rival bidder, Carnival Corporation, complained to the Takeover Panel.

18. While Boone and Mulherin, reviewed earlier in this chapter, report that acquirers in multi-bidder auctions do not suffer from winner's curse, they do not test whether white knights experience greater wealth losses than hostile bidders. See below for empirical evidence.

19. N. Varaiya, 'Determinants of premium in acquisition transactions', *Managerial and Decision Economics*, **8**, 1987, 175–184.

20 Bernd Ratzke and Tom Kelly, Head and Trainer of the HVB Akademie, the HR development and training division of HypoVereins Bank Group in Germany, characterize it as a 'just a dream'. See G. Stahl and

M. Mendenhall (Eds), *Mergers and Acquisitions: Managing Culture and Human Resources* (Stanford, CA: Stanford University Press, 2005), pp. 178–179.

21. T. Burt, J. Mason and U. Harnischfeger, 'Tracinda gains more support for lawsuit', *Financial Times*, 29 November 2000.

22. J. Wulf, 'Do CEOs in mergers trade power for premium? Evidence from "mergers of equals"', *Journal of Law, Economics and Organization*, **20**, 2004, 60–101.

23. On the various approaches to cultural due diligence, and assessing whether cultural differences are a source of risk to the integration process and the goals of the merger, see S. Cartwright and S. McCarthy, 'Developing a framework for cultural due diligence in mergers and acquisitions', in G. Stahl and M. Mendenhall (Eds), *Mergers and Acquisitions: Managing Culture and Human Resources* (Stanford, CA: Stanford University Press, 2005).

24. See S. Moeller, 'Studying M&A targets', *Financial Times*, 5 October 2006.

25. The Towers Perrin report can be found here: www.towersperrin.com/.../USA/2007/200705/The_Importance_of_LeadershpFMTTVD_EF_Apr30.pdf

26. Cited in G. Cullinan, J. Le Roux and R. Weddigen, 'When to walk away from a deal?', *Harvard Business Review*, April 2004, 96–104.

27. See N. Damouni, S. Damouni and Y. Morris, 'WellCare in the midst of market check to gauge potential deal with select industry players – sources', *Financial Times*, 8 May 2008 (downloaded from www.ft.com).

28. See Corporate Executives Board, 'The Effect of Sarbanes-Oxley on the M&A Process', April 2004, downloaded from www.cfo.executiveboard.com.

29. See L. Saigol and J. McIntosh, on the pressures on target managements to turn 'friendly' when facing a hostile bid; 'Number of hostile bids the highest in a decade', *Financial* Times, 28 July 2008.

30 See G. Matvos and M. Ostrovsky, 'Cross-ownership, returns, and voting in mergers', *Journal of Financial Economics*, **89**, 2008, 391–403. This type of voting creates a conflict between institutional investors and acquirer-only investors, and the conflict arises only in mergers with negative returns in the acquirer. It is in the interest of both shareholder groups to pass mergers with positive announcement returns. It is not clear whether and how such conflicts should be addressed. Cross-ownership could also have an impact on which mergers are proposed to begin with.

31. Hedge funds often take positions in companies in an effort to change the governance of the target firms. They win board seats or other concessions, e.g. change in corporate strategy. Bratton finds, for his sample of 130 US firms subject to hedge fund onslaught, that their efforts succeed in 82% of the cases. See W. Bratton, 'Whither hostility?', in G. Gregoriou and L. Renneboog (Eds), *Corporate Governance and Regulatory Impact on Mergers and Acquisitions* (London: Elsevier, 2007), pp. 103–130.

32. See A. Wendtlandt, 'Merger arbitrage begins to lose appeal', *Financial Times*, 4 May 2000.

33. M. Baker and S. Savasoglu, 'Limited arbitrage in mergers and acquisitions', *Journal of Financial Economics*, **64**, 2002, 91–115. See also F. Cornelli and D. D. Li, *Risk Arbitrage in Takeovers*, London Business School Working Paper, December 1999, for a theoretical treatment of risk arbitrage.

34. See S. Sudarsanam and D. Nguyen, 'UK Evidence on the Profitability and the Risk-Return Characteristics of Merger Arbitrage', Cranfield School of Management, UK, working paper, 2009. The return is gross of any short sale costs.

35. See M. Officer, 'Are performance based arbitrage effects detectable? Evidence from merger arbitrage', *Journal of Corporate Finance*, **15**(5), 2004, 793–812.

36. This section draws upon B. Wasserstein, *Big Deal: The Battle for Control of America's Leading Corporations* (New York: Warner Books), Chapters 14–18; R. S. Gilson and B. S. Black, *The Law and Finance of Corporate Acquisitions* (Westbury, New York: The Foundation Press, 1995), Chapters 16–19; and S. Kenyon-Slade, *Mergers and Acquisitions in the US and UK* (Oxford: Oxford University Press, 2004), various chapters.

37. See T. Bates, M. Lemmon and J. Linck, 'Shareholder wealth effects and bid negotiation in freeze-out deals: Are minority shareholders left out in the cold?', *Journal of Financial Economics*, **81**, 2006, 681–708. They note that 'minority claimants and their agents exercise significant bargaining power during freeze-out proposals. Overall, our results suggest that legal standards and economic incentives are sufficient to deter self-dealing by controllers during freeze-out bids.'

38. See Chapter 21 for a more detailed discussion of takeover defences, the BJR, and the various cases alluded to here.

39. This contrasts with the UK, where directors owe their fiduciary duty exclusively to the corporation. In the Netherlands the board owes a duty to the corporation, and also to stakeholders other than shareholders, such as employees, customers etc.

40   The City Code rule requiring equality of treatment of rival bidders by targets has a similar levelling effect.

41. AT&T's acquisition of NCR in 1990 was preceded by a proxy fight in which a third of NCR's board was replaced. This brought around the other directors to negotiate a merger with AT&T at a higher price. Where the hostile bidder has secured proxies or has written consents for more than 50% of the target shareholder vote, target directors may see the writing on the wall and become more amenable to negotiation.

42. See A. Davis, 'Strategic reverse course', *Mergers & Acquisitions*, February 2009, p. 26.

43. J. Franks, 'Insider information and the efficiency of the acquisition market', *Journal of Banking and Finance*, **2**, 1978, 379–393; J. Franks and R. Harris, 'Shareholder wealth effects of corporate takeovers: The UK experience 1955–85', *Journal of Financial Economics*, **23**, 1989, 225–249.

44. Jegadeesh and Choudhury, *ibid.*

45. S. Sudarsanam, P. Holl and A. Salami, 'Shareholder wealth gains in mergers: Effect of synergy and ownership structure', *Journal of Business Finance and Accounting*, **23**(5&6), 1996, 673–698; Shleifer and Vishny, *ibid.*

46. S. Sudarsanam, 'The role of defensive strategies and ownership structure of target firms: Evidence from UK hostile takeover bids', *European Financial Management*, **1**(3), 1995, 223–240.

47. T. Jenkinson and C. Mayer, *Takeover Defence Strategies* (Oxford: Economic Research Associates, 1991).

48. J. Hoffmeister and E. A. Dyl, 'Predicting outcomes of cash tender offers', *Financial Management*, Winter 1981, 50–58; R. Walkling, 'Predicting tender offer success: A logistic analysis', *Journal of Financial and Quantitative Analysis*, **20**(4), 1985, 461–478; Hirshleifer and Titman, *ibid*; and S. Moeller, F. P. Schlingemann and R. M. Stulz, 'Firm size and the gains from acquisitions', *Journal of Financial Economics*, **73**, 2004, 201–228.

49. R. Walkling and R. Edminster, 'Determinants of tender offer premium', *Financial Analysts Journal*, **27**, 1985, 27–37.

50   R. Stulz, R. Walkling and M. H. Song, 'The distribution of target's ownership and the division of gains from successful takeovers', *Journal of Finance*, **45**(3), 1990, 817–833.

51. Shleifer and Vishny, *ibid.*; Hirshleifer and Titman, *ibid.*

52. S. Moeller, F. P. Schlingemann and R. M. Stulz, *ibid.* Their measure of bid premium is 50 day target value difference to announcement day. For the UK see A. Antoniou, P. Arbour and H. Zhao, 'How much is too much: Are merger premiums too high?', *European Financial Management*, **14**(2), 2008, 268–287. Interestingly, they report that the combined announcement period abnormal returns to bidders and targets are positive and significant, suggesting market expectation of synergies. According to the authors, since these synergies are already capitalised at announcement, the acquirers experience zero post-acquisition abnormal returns. A high premium, where driven by expected synergies, may lead to deeper restructuring of the merged firms, e.g. larger job losses, than a low premium, since the high premium acquirer has to work harder to justify the high price paid for the target. For a test of this proposition see H. A. Krishnan, M. A. Hitt and D. Park, 'Acquisition premiums, subsequent workforce reductions and post-acquisition performance', *Journal of Management Studies*, **44**(5), 2007, 709–732. Laamen argues that a high premium may reflect target valuation difficulties and not overpayment. For a sample of 458 acquisitions Laamen finds that, although high premia are paid for R & D-related assets, these acquirers do not suffer negative abnormal returns. See T. Laamanen, 'On the role of acquisition premium in acquisition research', *Strategic Management Journal*, **28**, 2007, 1359–1369.

53. P. S. Sudarsanam and A. Mahate, 'Are friendly acquisitions too bad for shareholders and managers? Long-term value creation and top management turnover in hostile and friendly acquirers', *British Journal of Management*, **17**, 2006, S7–S30. For the US, WKs generate more shareholder value losses than friendly and hostile acquirers, and targets of WKs also experience higher returns than those of friendly and hostile acquirers. This suggests that WKs are overbidding. See C. Niden, 'An empirical examination of white knight corporate takeovers: Synergy and overbidding', *Financial Management*, **22**, 1993, 28–45; C. Carroll, J. Griffith and P. Rudolph, 'The performance of white knight management', *Financial Management*, **27**, Summer 1998, 48–56.

54. See Sudarsanam, Holl and Salami (1996), Gregory (1997) and Sudarsanam and Mahate (2003), cited in Chapter 4.

55. J. Franks and C. Mayer, 'Hostile takeovers and the correction of managerial failure', *Journal of Financial Economics*, **40**, 1996, 163–181. They find that hostile bids lead to higher top management turnover and significantly more sales of the acquired firms' assets than friendly bids. These point to sub-optimal exploitation of the targets' assets in the pre-acquisition period.

56. See O. Kini, W. Kracaw and S. Mian, 'The nature of discipline by corporate takeovers', *Journal of Finance*, **59**, 2004, 1511–1552, who find that target's market-to-book value was lower than that of friendly targets.

Since this metric is a measure of the future investment opportunities, their finding is consistent with the failure of vision.

57. M. Martynova and L. Renneboog, 'Mergers and acquisitions in Europe', in L. Renneboog (Ed.), *Advances in Corporate Finance and Asset Pricing* (Amsterdam: Elsevier, 2006), pp. 13–75. They also note that hostile bids had become more popular in the 1990s than in the 1980s.

58. F. Barca and M. Becht (Eds), *The Control of Corporate Europe* (Oxford: Oxford University Press, 2001); J. Franks and C. Mayer, 'Ownership and control of german corporations', *Review of Financial Studies*, **14**(4), 2001, 943–977.

59. R. Minder and A. Jones, 'Cadbury surmounts Orangina obstacle', *Financial Times*, 24 August 2001.

CHAPTER ㉑

Defences against takeovers

Objectives

At the end of this chapter, the reader should be able to understand:

- the nature of corporate takeover battles;
- the range of strategies and tactics that targets of hostile takeover bids can pursue;
- the regulatory and other constraints on the choice of these strategies in different countries;
- the effectiveness of such strategies; and
- how corporate governance and ownership structures influence takeover defences.

Introduction

In Chapter 20 we described the various strategies and tactics that a bidder could deploy in winning control of the target firm. In this chapter we discuss how the target management can counter these. When target company managers decide to resist a bid for their company, the chances of successful resistance depend upon the defences available, the regulatory and shareholder constraints on their use, and their cost. We referred to many of these, and their impact on bid strategies and tactics, in the last chapter. This chapter discusses takeover defences in more detail. In the UK, the City Code imposes very stringent constraints on the target management's choice of defensive strategies and tactics. Despite these constraints, target managements do employ a variety of strategies and tactics, and some have been pretty effective too.

In the US and in many continental European countries anti-takeover defences are quite formidable. We also report the available empirical evidence on the use and effectiveness of defensive strategies. Evidence on the impact of bid resistance on the wealth position of target shareholders is presented.

Bid resistance motives

Managers of companies that become the targets of bids have to decide whether to accept them on a friendly basis, or resist them and turn them into hostile bids. For either course of reaction there is a variety of motives. Managers may honestly believe that remaining independent is the best way to serve the interests of their shareholders and other constituencies, such as employees and local communities. Managers may regard resistance as a tactical posture to extract the maximum bid premium from the bidder for the benefit of the shareholders. Less unselfishly, they may resist because they fear losing their jobs, status, power, prestige and other psychological perquisites of their jobs when taken over. Available evidence on management turnover in targets after takeover suggests that this fear is not wholly misplaced (see Chapter 12 on post-acquisition management turnover).

Acceptance of a bid by managers may again be because it secures them a better deal in the post-acquisition dispensation. The target management may be allowed an acceptable degree of autonomy. They may be allowed to keep their power and perks. They may even be elevated to the parent's board as a reward for their meekness in accepting the overwhelming logic of the bid, and their loyalty in recommending the bid to the target shareholders. Less selfishly, managers may consider takeover by the favoured bidder the best option available to the target. In practice, it is difficult to disentangle the selfish from the disinterested motive. In the US the Business Judgment Rule and the standards imposed by the courts for its due exercise mean that target boards have to abide by their fiduciary duty to the corporation and the shareholders.

An important factor that may influence the target's willingness to agree to a takeover is the compensation to be received by the target CEO and his executive team. Change-of-control clauses in most executive compensation contracts lead to the vesting of their stock options and stock grants so that they can exercise the options immediately and sell the target stock to the bidder. In addition, the target managers may also receive golden parachute payments. A 'golden parachute' is a contract to compensate the management for loss of office in the event of a takeover of the firm. On top of these, in many deals these managers also receive cash bonuses to compensate them for loss of office. These payments can add up to several million dollars, and provide an important incentive not to resist the takeover bid to maximize shareholder value. On the other hand, it may be argued that these managers, knowing that they will receive a significant payoff, will fight hard on behalf of their shareholders, consistent with the rationale for the golden parachute. Target managers can also trade off some of the golden parachute for a job with the acquirer, as shown in Exhibit 21.1.

From the target shareholders' point of view, bid resistance may be a mixed blessing. While resistance raises the bid premium and the returns, it also reduces the chance of the hostile bid succeeding. Thus for the target shareholders the optimal course is to provide sufficient incentives to their managers to resist to the point where the bid premium is maximized, without endangering the chance of a successful bid. Devices such as 'golden parachutes' are designed to achieve this optimal result. However, as Exhibit 21.1 shows, golden parachutes may be used by the managers for their own, rather than shareholder, interests. Where shareholder power is high relative to the managers', they are able to secure a higher premium to the detriment of bidder shareholders[1].

Bid defence strategies

The best form of defence is being prepared. Eternal vigilance is indeed the price of independence for a company that is a probable takeover target. However, the best-laid strategic defensive plans might go awry, and the company, having become a target, needs battlefield tactical plans. One can thus divide defensive strategies into pre-bid and post-offer categories. Each of these categories of defence encompasses an extensive range of weapons.

Exhibit 21.1

What's in it for me?, ask target CEOs

Hartzell, Ofek and Yermack investigate the payoffs to target CEOs for a sample of 311 US acquisitions during 1997 to 1999. In addition to the above types of payments, the target CEO receives last-minute cash payments. For their sample, the authors find that the sum of capital gains on their stock, pre-merger golden parachutes and last-minute cash payments averages between $8m and $12m (median $4m to $5m), amounting to between 10 and 16 times the pre-takeover cash compensation.

More than 50% of the CEOs are employed by the buyer post-takeover, and 57% of these become CEOs. However, the vast majority of them leave within three years. Negotiated cash payments are lower for those CEOs who remain in employment than for CEOs who leave. CEO benefits, such as positions with the buyer or special bonuses, have a negative effect on the bid premium received by the target's shareholders. This suggests that there is some conflict of interest between the CEO and shareholder interests. The benefits received by the CEOs are less than the forgone additional bid premium. This leads to gains for bidder shareholders.

Source: Adapted from J. C. Hartzell, E. Ofek and D. Yarmack, 'What's in it for me? CEOs whose firms are acquired', *Review of Financial Studies*, **17**(1), 2004, 37–61

Pre-bid defences

Pre-bid defences that may be set up by the potential target fall into two broad categories. Internal defences are decisions/actions to alter the internal structure or nature of operations of the firm. External defences are actions taken to influence outsiders' perceptions of the firm, and to provide early warning signals about potential predators. These various defences are listed in Table 21.1[2].

If hostile bids are driven by the desire to create shareholder value, the best defence available to a firm is to ensure that its operations and strategies deliver cost efficiencies, high profit margins, and high earnings per share. This in itself may not be enough to increase the market valuation of the firm. The firm must engage in a consistent programme of educating the shareholders, analysts and media that its policies are indeed value enhancing. Where the company experiences setbacks due to the economic cycle, or the restructuring it has undertaken, it must make a credible case to the analysts and investing institutions that the setbacks are indeed temporary. The use of investor relations consultants in this context is discussed in Chapter 19.

The company needs to keep a close watch on unusual share price movements or share purchases to see whether any potential predator is building up a toehold. Under the Disclosure and Transparency Rules (DTR) of the UK Financial Services authority (FSA), in the case of shares listed on a regulated UK stock exchange:

- a person holding voting rights reaching, exceeding or falling below 3% must notify the issuing company within two trading days of the requirement to notify arising[3];
- the holding may be through direct or indirect holding of shares, or through derivative financial instruments, e.g. options, futures, swaps and other derivatives;
- such a person must also disclose the above information publicly as soon as possible; and

Table 21.1 Pre-bid defensive strategies against hostile takeovers

Action	Result
(a) Internal defences	
Improve operational efficiency and reduce costs	Improved EPS, higher share prices and firm value
Improve strategic focus by restructuring, divestment, demerger, equity carve-out, etc.	Improved EPS and higher firm value. Asset stripping by bidder difficult
Change ownership structure, e.g. dual-class shares, high gearing, share buyback, poison pill	Control by bidder difficult. Scope for LBO limited
Change management structure or incentive, e.g. staggered board, golden parachute	Predator control delayed and bid cost increased
Cultivate organizational constituencies, e.g. unions and workforce	Useful alliance against bidder; share support from pension funds/ESOPs; support of workers' councils
(b) External defences	
Cultivate shareholders and investors, e.g. use investor relations advisers to inform about company's performance, prospects and policies	Ensures loyalty and support during bid of key shareholders
Inform analysts about company strategy, financing policies and investment programmes	Share undervaluation risk reduced and bid cost raised
Accept social responsibility to improve social image; use constituency statutes to advantage	Public hostility to predator roused
Make strategic defence investment, e.g. joint venture/mutual shareholding in fellow targets	Predator control blocked
Monitor the share register for unusual share purchases; force disclosure of identity of buyers	Early warning signal about possible predators

EPS = earnings per share; LBO = leveraged buyout; ESOP = employee share ownership plan.

- for the purpose of such disclosure, holdings of parents and of those of its controlled undertakings must be aggregated.

These disclosure rules impose obligations on the holder of voting rights in a UK-listed company. Section 793 of the UK Companies Act 2006 enables the company to flush out the true owners behind the nominees. A UK public company may require any person whom the company 'knows or has reasonable cause to believe' to be or to have been in the preceding three years interested in *any* (not just over 3%) of its shares to confirm or deny the fact and reveal the identity of the person who has acquired his or her interest. Irrevocable commitments obtained by a potential offeror from target shareholders would be covered by this section, as are concert parties and nominees. A reply to a section 793 notice must be given within any 'reasonable time as may be specified in the notice'. Failure to respond to the notice may be punished with imprisonment or fine, and the related shares may be disenfranchised. While these legal and regulatory rules allow firms to 'out' potential bidders, they must be used to advantage by potential targets, who might otherwise be caught by default.

Some of the defensive actions listed in Table 21.1 are not available in all countries. For example, in the UK the London Stock Exchange does not allow companies with dual-class shares (i.e. with differential voting rights) to be listed, although there are still a small number of old listed companies with such a share structure. But this is one of the more common defences in continental Europe (see below).

Poison pills are relatively common in the US (see below under Takeover defences in the US). They refer to shareholder rights plans that confer upon the target shareholders the right to subscribe at a heavy discount to shares in the target (flip-in pill) or to the shares of the success-ful bidder (flip-over pill). The aim of these toxic arrangements is to increase the cost of the acquisition. Poison pills of this kind are unknown in the UK, where the term is used loosely to denote any arrangement to raise the cost to a potential bidder, e.g. pension deficits that the acquirer may have to top up.

Equally rare in the UK is a staggered board of directors, only a few of whom are replaced each year. Thus the acquirer may have to wait several years before it succeeds in shaping the board 'in its own image'. An ESOP is an arrangement involving an employee benefit trust, which, with financial assistance from the employer, acquires substantial quantities of employer shares or securities for subsequent allocation to employees. Companies can use an ESOP to see shareholding accumulate in comparatively friendly hands. In the event of a hostile takeover an ESOP may play a crucial role in defence[4]. Under UK company law, however, use of an ESOP as a poison pill is not permitted[5]. In the US, ESOPs were used in takeover defence in the 1980s.

With a highly leveraged capital structure, control of the company can be maintained with a relatively small equity holding. High gearing, with possible restrictive covenants on existing debt, may discourage a heavily leveraged buyout (on LBO, see Chapter 11), since post-acquisition asset disposals to raise the cash to pay off the acquisition-related borrowing will be constrained. Thus financial engineering is unlikely to be profitable for the bidder.

Share repurchase also leads to increased gearing, and often to higher EPS and net asset value per share, with a possible increase in the share price of the company. Moreover, it reduces the number of shares that could fall into the hands of predators. Repurchase during a bid requires the approval of the shareholders under Rule 37 of the Code (see Exhibit 21.2 below).

Post-offer defences

In the UK, under the Code, the offer period is in most cases limited to 60 days from the posting of the offer document by the bidder, adding urgency to the target's tactics (see Table 18.4). Further, Rule 21 of the Code imposes upon the target management the obligation to get the approval of their shareholders for any frustrating action, which is defined widely to include the following:

- issue of shares, or options or securities convertible into shares;
- disposal or acquisition of assets of a material amount – normally 10% of the target's assets;
- contracts made except in the ordinary course of business; and
- golden parachutes arranged at the onset of a bid, or when it is imminent.

Despite the above constraints, a range of tactics is still available in contested bids, as shown in Table 21.2. In addition to Rule 21 of the Code, other rules of the Code are also relevant to the target's defensive strategy. Rule 19 requires that each document issued to shareholders must satisfy the highest standard of accuracy, and that the information contained must be adequately and fairly presented. Advertisements must in most cases be cleared by the Panel, and must avoid arguments and invective.

Profit forecasts are required by Rule 28 to be compiled with scrupulous care, and the target's financial adviser and accountant must ensure that they are so prepared. The reporting accountant's consent to the forecast must accompany it. The Panel monitors these forecasts long after the end of the bid, to see whether there was any deliberate distortion of the forecasts in the light of information available at the time the forecasts were made. Similarly, under Rule 29, asset valuations must be supported by an independent valuer. The actual use of the various defensive strategies in some of the hostile bids in the UK is described in Exhibit 21.2.

Exhibit 21.2

Post-offer defensive strategies in UK hostile bids

Share buyback

When faced with a hostile bid from the French cement maker Lafarge in February 2000, Blue Circle Industries (BCI), its UK rival, announced a share buyback programme for £800m. The bid was worth £3.4bn. The bid failed.

Report improved performance

In the above bid battle, BCI also reported much improved profit forecast for its Asian businesses. BCI highlighted the relatively poor performance of Lafarge, and accused it of wanting the better-performing Asian assets of BCI.

Seeking a white knight

In 2000 Wickes, the do-it-yourself retailer, was the subject of a hostile bid for £327m from its UK rival Focus Do It All (FDIA). The offer was pitched at 430 pence per share, and represented a 78% premium. Wickes rejected the bid as opportunistic, because the stock market had undervalued old economy companies like Wickes as inadequate. It started looking for a white knight (WK). Analysts felt Wickes could accept an agreed bid from a WK at 470 pence. FDIA's bid failed.

Divestitures, lobbying large shareholders

In June 2001 Wolverhampton & Dudley Breweries (WDB) received a hostile £453m bid from Pubmaster (PM), which owned a chain of public houses ('pubs'). In its vigorous defence against the bid WDB adopted the following defence strategies:

- share buyback of £200m at a price not less than the average price over five days prior to the close of the PM bid;
- sell some of its pubs and non-core assets to raise £100m;
- promise increased dividends;
- sue PM, alleging it had passed secret commercial data to rivals;
- force PM into an embarassing admission of errors in its press releases about WDB's accounting for exceptional charges;
- lobby large shareholders, winning support from holder of 11% of shares in WDB.

The bid failed, but it was a narrow escape for WDB, with PM winning acceptances for 47% of WDB shares.

Table 21.2 Post-offer defences against hostile takeover bids

Defence	Description and purpose
First response and pre-emption letter	Attack bid logic and price; advise target shareholders not to accept
Defence document	Praise own performance and prospects; deride bid price and logic, form of finance and predator's track record
Profit report/forecast	Report or forecast improved profits for past/current year to make offer look cheap
Promise higher future dividends	Increase returns to shareholders; weaken predator's promise of superior returns
Asset revaluation	Revalue properties, intangibles and brands; show bid undervalues target
Share support campaign	Look for white knight or white squire; enlist own employee pension fund or ESOP; attempt to block control
Regulatory appeal	Lobby antitrust/regulatory authorities to block bid (see Chapter 17)
Litigation	To enforce antitrust rules or force disclosure of nominee shareholders; litigation to frustrate an offer is not allowed under the City Code Rule 21.
Acquisition and divestment	Buy a business to make target bigger or incompatible with bidder; sell 'crown jewels'; organize a management buyout; bid cost higher and bidder strategy thrown into disarray
Unions/workforce	Enlist to lobby regulators or politicians and to attack bidder's plans for target
Customers/suppliers	Enlist to lobby antitrust authorities or to show relations with them will be jeopardized if predator wins
Red herring	Attack predator on peripheral matters
Advertisement	Media campaign to discredit bid

Source: Adapted from P. S. Sudarsanam, 'Defensive strategies of target firms in UK contested takeovers', *Managerial Finance*, **17**(6), 1991, 47–56.

Impact of defensive strategies

The chances of a successful defence against a hostile predator are more than even. In a sample of 238 contested bids covering the period 1983–89 and accounting for about 24% of all bids for UK public companies, 147 (62% of sample) successfully defended themselves. However, of these only 112 (47% of sample) remained independent, with 35 falling to the embrace of white knights[6]. Table 21.3 reports the frequency of use of 23 defensive strategies, based on the same sample. Blocking is the use of any device, e.g. recapitalization, to raise obstacles/cost to the bidder.

Statistical test of the effectiveness of these strategies indicated that only the following strategies made a significant positive contribution to a successful defence:

- entry of a white knight;
- lobbying friendly shareholders;
- support of the unions; and
- litigation.

Divestment had a significantly negative impact on defence. Advertising also did not help the targets in their defence, as its impact was not statistically significant. It appears that advertising during bids containing perhaps too much rhetoric and hyperbole lacks credibility. The remaining strategies, such as profit forecasts and increased dividend announcements, made no difference to the outcome of hostile bids.

Table 21.3 Frequency of use of defensive strategies in UK contested bids

Strategy	Times used	Frequency (%)
Knocking copy	157	66
Profit forecast	106	45
Increased dividend	102	43
Antitrust lobbying	79	33
Friendly shareholders	62	26
Profit report	51	21
White knight	46	19
Divestment	40	17
Regulatory appeal	36	15
Asset revaluation	32	13
Good news	29	12
Acquisition	29	12
Blocking	23	10
Red herring	22	9
Political lobbying	18	8
Union support	16	7
Pre-emption letter	15	6
White squire	13	6
Litigation	13	6
Customer support	12	5
Advertising	10	4
Management change	10	4
Bidder shareholder appeal	6	3

Based on a sample of 238 contested bids.
Source: Adapted from P. S. Sudarsanam, 'Less than lethal weapons: Defence strategies in UK contested takeovers', *Acquisitions Monthly*, January 1994, 30–32.

Takeover defences outside the UK

Hostile bids are most prevalent in Anglo-Saxon countries. These countries differ among themselves in the regulation of takeover bids[7]. The defences available to target companies in hostile bids therefore also differ. In countries on the Continent and in Japan, hostile bids are very rare. The reasons for the absence of hostile bids are both cultural and institutional. Here we take a brief overview of the takeover defences in some continental European countries and the US to give the reader a flavour of the differences among countries.

Takeover defences in continental Europe

There are substantial differences between continental European countries and the UK or the US in the defences available to target companies. In general, hostile takeovers are much more difficult to win, because of the panoply of effective defences that targets can deploy. The differences arise from philosophical, cultural and statutory factors. There is a clear distinction between the Anglo-Saxon tradition, where the shareholders' interests predominate over the interests of other stakeholders, and the continental tradition.

In the continental tradition these stakeholders often have an equal claim. In many continental countries the board of directors has a responsibility to their company rather than just to their shareholders. The former requires that directors take account of the interests of shareholders, employees, customers and the local communities in making their decisions. This broader responsibility is reflected in both company statute and corporate practice. For example, Dutch company law reflects the philosophy that 'the balance of power should not unduly favour the shareholders. It must also take into account the interests of other stakeholders such as employees'[8].

A detailed examination of the barriers is made in Chapter 8 on cross-border acquisitions, but here their role as defences against unwelcome bids is highlighted. These barriers consist of legal and regulatory rules, institutional arrangements, and cultural attitudes. The degree to which they are strong, and impede takeovers, varies from one country to another. Employees are given varying rights in different countries in the context of takeovers. In Denmark, Germany, Luxembourg and the Netherlands they are represented on supervisory boards, and therefore have a say in determining whether a bid will be accepted. Under the Takeover Directive now implemented by EU member states, worker unions/workers have to be directly informed by both bidders and targets. More stringent requirements for consultation with employees are in place in countries such as France.

One share, one vote (OSOV) is not a principle adhered to in all countries. Issue of non-voting shares is common. In France, listed companies may limit transferability of shares by contract or by articles of incorporation. Among all the EU countries, managements in the Netherlands have the greatest freedom to issue shares with limited voting rights. Dutch companies can issue priority shares, which confer on the holders a substantial degree of control over the issuing company. Often these shares are issued to an institution whose directors may include the managing or supervisory directors of the issuing company itself. Preference shares with limited financial rights, i.e. to cash flow such as dividend, but full voting rights may be issued to a trust office, whose main purpose is to serve the interests of the company and its business. Non-voting depository receipts, which separate the voting rights from the financial rights, are also issued. An administration office holds the shares, exercises the voting rights, and issues the depository receipts. Binding appointment of directors can be made either by a change in company statutes or by vote of the priority shareholders. Ordinary shareholders are then deprived of the ability to appoint their own directors.

Kabir *et al.*'s empirical study of the use of defensive strategies by 177 Dutch companies found that 79 firms issued priority shares, 70 issued depository receipts, 64 made binding appointments, and seven firms restricted the voting rights. Only 16 firms remained unprotected by any of these defensive measures[9]. Under recent corporate governance reforms, embodied in the *Code Tabaksblat* effective from January 2004, many such devices are losing their potency. Priority shares to block mergers instigated by activist shareholders have also been challenged in the Enterprise Chamber[10]. In countries such as France and Spain voting rights can be limited by charter, whereas in Germany this right is no longer available for listed companies.

Large or 'structure' companies in the Netherlands are required to have supervisory boards, which wield tremendous powers to dismiss managing directors, adopt annual accounts, and veto certain important management decisions. The directors of the supervisory board have a responsibility to shareholders, but the interests of the company can override this responsibility. As a result, Dutch public companies are better protected from hostile takeovers than their counterparts in most European countries.

In continental countries managers also enjoy a high degree of protection. In Germany the management board of directors is appointed by the supervisory board for a fixed term of up to five years. During that time they can be removed only for clear breaches of duty, gross incompetence, or by vote at a shareholders' meeting for good reason. Removal of the supervisory board members requires the approval of 75% of the votes of shareholders.

Exhibit 21.3

Role of banks In German takeovers

- In the Krupp bid for Hoesch, Deutsche Bank (DB) chaired the supervisory board of Hoesch and supported the bid, even though it was opposed by the head of the management board.
- In the Pirelli bid for Continental, DB again chaired the supervisory board and voted a large number of proxy shares. It was closely involved in shaping Continental's attitude to the bid. It opposed the bid, but supported merger talks between the two companies. When the head of the management board opposed the merger, DB was instrumental in removing him.
- In Krupp's hostile bid for Thyssen in 1997, the German banks DB and Dresdner Bank, advising Thyssen along with Goldman Sachs, attracted widespread condemnation from trade unions and steel workers of the two companies and politicians for aiding and financing the 'Wild West' tactics of Krupp. Krupp abandoned its bid and later pursued a friendly merger with Thyssen.

Source: J. Franks and C. Mayer, 'Ownership and control of German corporations', *Review of Financial Studies*, 14(4), 2001, 943–977; P. Norman, 'Krupp, Thyssen under pressure to agree to steel merger', *Financial Times*, 24 March 1997

Shareholders cannot dismiss supervisory board members appointed by the workforce. The veto that employee representatives have under the German co-determination system may thus be an effective poison pill for any would-be acquirer.

The corporate governance structure plays an important role in Germany, where only a relatively small proportion of public companies are listed on the stock exchange. The banks play a crucial role as lenders, equity holders and share depositories. Shareholders often deposit their shares with banks, which then exercise the proxy votes on behalf of these shareholders. Although shareholders can direct the depositories to vote according to their wishes, in practice the proxy votes are determined by the banks' own preferences.

German banks also have representation on the supervisory boards, sometimes as chairmen. Franks and Mayer note that banks' power is especially strong in companies with widely dispersed shareholding, precisely the companies where a hostile bidder has a good chance of success by appealing direct to small shareholders[11]. The power of banks to restrict or allow takeovers is demonstrated in Exhibit 21.3. Banks facilitated the accumulation of large hostile stakes, often without disclosure[12].

Ownership structure as takeover defence

Continental European countries are characterized by block ownership of shares and voting rights. Among seven such countries – Belgium, Austria, Germany, the Netherlands, Spain, Italy and Sweden – the percentage of listed companies with a blocking minority of at least 25% of the votes ranges from 64% in Sweden to 94% in Belgium. The percentage of listed companies under majority control for the same countries varies from 26% in Sweden to 68% in Austria. In contrast, in the UK the percentages are 16% and 2.4% respectively, and for the New York Stock Exchange they are 5% and 1.7%. Moreover, indirect pyramidal ownership control can also effectively block transfer of ownership of companies at the lower levels of the

---

Exhibit 21.4

White squires board Air Berlin flight to 'no hostile bid' land

By March 2009 Air Berlin's share price had fallen by about 40% as the airline industry struggled to cope first with the surge in fuel prices in the first half of 2008 and subsequently with the deepening recession. TUI Travel, the London-listed leisure group that is majority-owned by Germany's Tui, entered a strategic alliance with Air Berlin by acquiring a 19.9% stake for €64.8m at a significant premium to its current share price. Separately, ESAS Holding, a Turkish conglomerate, acquired a stake of 15.3% in Air Berlin. ESAS, which owned Pegasus Airlines, the second largest Turkish carrier, would have one seat on Air Berlin's board. Under the strategic cooperation deal with Tui Travel Air Berlin will take a 19.9% stake in Tui's struggling German airline operations Hapag-Lloyd Flug and Tuifly. The two deals would help the troubled German carrier, Europe's third-largest budget airline, to deter hostile bidders as its stock languished near record lows.

Source: Adapted from G. Wiesman and K. Done, 'Two new investors buy into Air Berlin', FT.com, 29 March 2009

---

pyramid. Given such concentrated ownership structures, it is difficult for hostile bidders to achieve control[13]. Moreover, shares placed in the hands of friendly white squires can also provide protection against hostile bids, as shown in Exhibit 21.4. The transaction is the latest in a growing trend among German companies to find so-called *anchor investors* to protect them from predators. Recession is hammering corporate profits and pushing asset prices down to bargain levels. Daimler announced around the same time that a state-owned investment company from Abu Dhabi was taking a 9.1% in the German car maker, reeling from a fall in car demand.

The above examples show that defences against hostile bids for continental companies can be formidable. These are reinforced by the unfavourable attitude of German companies and shareholders to hostile bids. The adversarial nature of hostile bids is perhaps anathema to the more consensual continental tradition. This is reflected in the fact that German companies generally avoid making hostile bids for companies in other countries. The breakthrough rule in the Takeover Directive can help a hostile bid in those member states that have not opted out of it, such as Italy, or where companies in those countries have opted back into BTR, e.g. Spain. In most of these countries companies can prevent the BTR on the reciprocity ground.

With the implementation of the Takeover Directive (see Chapter 18), taking frustrating action after announcement of a bid in many countries now requires shareholder approval. Since shareholder meetings cannot be held without a long delay, such actions may not be easily pursued. Moreover, the regulations impose a duty of neutrality on target managers. Thus effective defence is not what the target can do after the offer but in anticipation of one, even though it may be uncertain to materialize.

Here the European countries offer a range of weaponry. Among these is the cross-shareholding very common in many countries, although in some there are limits to such shareholding, e.g. say 10% in Italy. In 2001 Renault and Nissan, the French and Japanese automobile manufacturers, bought shares in each other to set up a takeover barrier. Table 21.4 summarizes some of the important rules governing takeover defences in six European countries.

Table 21.4 Pre- and post-offer defences in some continental European countries

France

- *Pre-bid:* Incorporate as limited partnership with listed shares (SCA); limit voting rights, e.g. to 8%, but if bidder gets two-thirds of voting rights it can remove limits; defensive cross-shareholding between companies; shareholders' agreement giving 'right of first refusal'

- *Post-offer:* General Regulation embodies principles of free competition between offers, equality of treatment between target shareholders, loyalty, transparency and integrity of takeover market enforced by Autorité des marchés financiers (AMF); defensive actions taken must serve company's interests; frustrating action approved by shareholders in the previous 18 months require their confirmation during offer period; issue of warrants as poison pills possible, but should not interfere with offeror's right to make increased offer; shopping for alternative bidders allowed; target can issue warrants allowing all shareholders to buy shares on preferential terms after approval at a general meeting; warrants used as threat to force negotiation; target must announce intention to issue warrants before expiry of offer period; restrictions on frustrating action relaxed when used against offerors failing reciprocity test; AMF to judge whether reciprocity correctly invoked

Germany

- *Pre-bid:* Not possible to limit voting rights or issue shares with multiple voting rights in listed companies; previously authorized new share issue possible but subject to pre-emption right; new issue must be in company's best interests; limited share buyback possible, but subject to shareholder approval, and only to avert severe and imminent damage to corporation; sale of crown jewels needs shareholders' prior consent; conversion of bearer shares into registered shares requires each shareholder consent; poison pills, i.e. shareholder rights, illegal; voting rights limitation or multiple voting rights for a share by listed companies not allowed after June 2003; shareholder represented members of the supervisory board can be staggered, but it is rare

- *Post-offer:* Management board must act in best interests of the corporation; Takeover Act does not allow frustrating measures except with shareholder approval 18 months before; supervisory board can authorize measures; companies can opt into mandatory and breakthrough articles, and having opted in can opt out on reciprocity grounds; searching for WK allowed but no break fee can be paid; share buybacks only in extreme cases of threat to corporation; BaFin, the regulator (see Chapter 18), can regulate advertising; if BTR opted in, acquirer must compensate for loss of voting rights

Italy

- *Pre-bid:* No restrictions on pre-bid defence; share buyback of up to 10%, share issue to employee stock option plans, cross-shareholding between parent and subsidiary, and going private all allowed; limits on voting rights not allowed; golden parachutes to top executives allowed; warrants to current shareholders can be issued

- *Post-offer:* Passivity Rule forbids frustrating action during offer period; any frustrating action, e.g. new share issues, subject to at least 30% share capital approval; shopping for other bidders allowed; scope of frustrating action defined by CONSOB, the stock exchange authority (see Chapter 18); directors violating Passivity Rule subject to fine; breakthrough rule implemented as per Takeover Directive but may be waived on reciprocity condition; CONSOB determines whether offer subject to equivalent restrictions and breakthrough rule; acquirer must compensate for loss of voting rights under BTR

The Netherlands

- *Pre-bid:* Takeover Directive implemented; opted out of BTR but companies can opt in; BTR will not affect companies under Large Company Regime (LCR); under LCR, supervisory board and works councils control management board composition more than shareholders; companies can take frustrating action, including share transfer restrictions, subject to shareholder approval; many of the old defences, e.g. issue of bearer depository receipts and poison pills type priority shares, have become weaker; if acquirer gains 75% of issued share capital can break through priority shares and gain control of management and supervisory board

- *Post-offer:* Targets can invoke reciprocity to apply anti-takeover defences; priority shares issued during offer period not counted for the breakthrough; hostile bidder and target must negotiate potential offer for 14 days before bidder announces a public offer; minimum acceptance period for a hostile takeover extended from 30 days to 8 weeks

Spain

- *Pre-bid:* Takeover Directive implemented in 2007; articles of association can include anti-takeover provisions; voting rights can be limited; supermajority allowed; qualifying criteria for directors may be specified; information about these defences available at the Securities and Exchange Commission or in company annual reports

Table 21.4 *continued*

- *Post-offer:* directors must always act in the interests of the corporation; targets can opt out of their own defences, such as restrictions on transfer of shares, limited voting rights; they can opt into the breakthrough rule; such neutralization of defences must be approved by shareholders at a general meeting; Passivity Rule forbids frustrating action, e.g. new share issues, sell-offs, buyback or extraordinary dividends without shareholder approval; board can use 'fiduciary out' to breach Passivity Rule; shareholders can authorize breach of Passivity Rule on reciprocity ground; acquirer must compensate for loss of voting rights under BTR

Sweden

- *Pre-bid:* Takeover Act 2006 implements the Takeover Directive; substantial cross-shareholding; shareholder agreements giving first refusal rights on share sales; staggered board makes board changes by acquirer difficult unless two-thirds of voting rights acquired; restrictions on disinvestment in subsidiaries or sale of assets

- *Post-offer:* Board neutrality implemented; board must act in the interests of company and all its shareholders; frustrating actions subject to approval by shareholders meeting; can seek competing offers and has a fiduciary duty to consider unsolicited offers; no obligation to shop

Source: Various chapters from *A Practitioner's Guide to Takeovers and Mergers in the European Union* (Old Woking: City & Financial Publishing, 2008) (valid as at 1 February 2008); Freshfields Bruckhaus Deringer, '*New public takeover regime in the Netherlands*', April 2005, downloaded from the www.freshfields.com.

The spread of 'Wild West' defence techniques to the staid and cosy world of continental mergers is illustrated by the Pac-Man defence that Elf mounted against its French-Belgian rival, TotalFina, in 1999. When faced with a hostile stock exchange offer, Elf launched a lawsuit, but more importantly it made a leveraged cash bid for TotalFina and raised the cash in record time. Although the Pac-Man defence failed to stop Elf's acquisition, it raised the bid premium quite substantially.

The unsettled nature of takeover regulation, and the statutory character of such regulation in many countries, also increase the scope for tactical litigation. In the TotalFina versus Elf case the companies went to court challenging the bid and counterbid. In the case of the ABN-AMRO takeover in 2007 the company's decision to sell LaSalle in the US was challenged as an unlawful takeover defence in the Dutch courts, which upheld the decision.

Hedge funds, shareholder activism and takeover defence

In recent years target firms in some European countries have come under enormous pressure to lower their defences and accept takeover bids. Hedge funds have played a key role in this activist shareholder phenomenon, although traditional investment funds have also initiated action or joined forces with pace-setting hedge funds. Exhibit 21.5 describes how a hedge fund

---

Exhibit 21.5

Hey! Barbarians are not outside the gate but inside!

Hedge funds used their awesome power to teach Dutch corporate managements a few lessons in 'corporate democracy' in 2006 and 2007. Dutch companies such as Ahold, Stork, VNU and ABN AMRO (ABN) were targets of shareholder activism spearheaded by hedge funds based in the UK and US.

The pressure on ABN started when the London-based hedge fund The Children's Investment (TCI) Fund, which had taken a 1% stake in the bank, attacked the bank's performance in February 2007. Since 2000 ABN's cumumulative stock return had been zero, excluding dividends, compared with 40% on average generated by its competitors. TCI attacked both the Chairman of the supervisory board, Arthur Martinez, and the CEO of the management board, Rijkman Groenink, for poor management. TCI called for a shareholders' meeting, and for shareholders to vote on the break-up of the bank, or a merger. It should also immediately cease any plan to acquire the Italian banking group Capitalia.

This stirred the interest of a number of potential acquirers. Barclays Bank, Britain's third-largest bank, announced in March that it was in exclusive talks with ABN. On 12 April a consortium of European banks comprising the Royal Bank of Scotland (RBS), Spain's Santander and Fortis of Belgium communicated its interest. The consortium members were interested in ABN's different businesses to strengthen their own competitive positions in wholesale, Asian, Benelux and American banking markets. Thus if the RBS-led consortium bid succeeded, a break up of ABN was inevitable. On 23 April Barclays announced a recommended all-share bid for €67bn. The 3.225-to-1 share exchange deal would have led to a new bank, and Barclays would have owned 52% of it. Moreover, ABN would sell its US banking operation, LaSalle, to Bank of America (BoA) and raise €21bn in cash. This business was not of interest to Barclays, but to RBS it was. The consortium construed this sale as a poison pill to make ABN unattractive. VEB, the Dutch Investors' Association, representing 20% of ABN shareholders including some investment funds, concurred and challenged the LaSalle sale without shareholder approval. Then on 25 April the consortium proposed a €72.2bn offer comprising 70% cash and 30% in RBS shares, conditional on ABN not selling LaSalle.

On 3 May the Enterprise Chamber of the Amsterdam court ruled that the La Salle sale must be put to shareholder vote. On 13 July the Dutch Supreme Court overturned that ruling, deeming the sale within the management's power. Although a setback, this did not deter the consortium, and it pitched its offer at €38.4 (compared with €39 previously) for ABN minus LaSalle, thus effectively raising the offer for ABN. Barclays responded with a higher bid, valuing ABN at €68bn, but this offer fell in value as Barclay's share spiralled down on worries about its exposure to the subprime crisis. The consortium offer went unconditional on 10 October with a 99% acceptance.

Although the consortium members won, soon the credit crisis overtook them. RBS had to go cap in hand to the UK government in 2008 for a rescue package, and had to raise new equity for £12bn. Fred Goodwin, the CEO of RBS, who had gained a reputation for his aggressive takeover style and the nickname 'Fred the Shred', lost his job after having been subjected to a great deal of public criticism for the way he had led the bank.

Many of the famed and impregnable defences of Dutch companies against hostile takeovers, e.g. issue of preferred shares to friendly foundations, were unavailable against hedge fund insurgents, who challenged incumbent managers as *shareholders not as hostile bidders*. Dutch managements realized too late that the barbarians were not outside the gate but inside!

Source: A. Durchstag, 'Project Arran: The battle for ABN AMRO', *Acquisitions Monthly*, December 2007, 2–4; *Barbarians at the Gate: The Fall of RJR Nabisco* is a 1990 book about the LBO of RJR Nabisco, written by Bryan Burrough and John Helyar. In 1993 it was made into a movie.

initiated a campaign against ABN AMRO that culminated in the largest-ever financial services mergers and the second-largest takeover in Europe. Hedge funds played a key role in scuppering the Russian steelmaker Severstal's white knight rescue of Arcelor and strengthening Mittal's bid against the target in 2007.

Takeover defences in the US

Between the US and the UK there are some similarities but also major differences in takeover regimes. There are many similarities between the US and many continental European countries in takeover defences. As described in Chapter 18, in the US, tender offers are regulated under the Williams Act (WA) 1968 by the Securities and Exchange Commission (SEC). WA imposes obligations on both offerors and targets, and prevents secret accumulation of large stakes by requiring disclosure of purchases when they take the shareholding in the target company to above 5%. For the WA requirements as regards offer price, timetable and share dealings that bidders must satisfy, see Chapter 18. WA is neutral between friendly and hostile tender offers. By contrast, state anti-takeover laws are aimed at protecting corporations and shareholders against aggressive hostile takeover tactics.

Evolution of state anti-takeover laws[14]

Since in the US companies are incorporated under state laws, these laws have considerable impact on takeover defences. After the takeover binge of the 1980s, many states amended their laws to shift the balance of power against the predator and in favour of the target management and shareholders. State laws may in some cases render takeovers difficult to accomplish. They may permit the use of certain defensive devices by target companies subject to the *Unocal* enhanced scrutiny and the *Blasius* 'compelling justification' standards and the *Revlon* duty (see Chapter 18).

State anti-takeover laws have evolved through three generations. The first generation ran afoul of the 'blue sky' rule that state laws should not encroach upon the Federal law (the Supremacy Clause of the US Constitution), in this case the WA, e.g. in terms of notice period, and more onerous disclosures than required by WA. Some state laws empowered state officials to interfere in the tender offer process, e.g. ordering administrative hearings, causing delay in hostile bids. Some first-generation statutes could regulate takeovers involving investors and corporations not resident in a state. They therefore fell foul of the interstate Commerce Clause, i.e. they unduly burdened the conduct of interstate commerce. The second-generation laws therefore responded to the judicial restraints on the first generation. The third generation introduced business combination laws that prevented acquirers of certain levels of stakes in target companies from merging with the latter. Table 21.5 shows the laws belonging to different generations[15]. It cites only one state act to illustrate the law in each category, but several US states have passed similar laws.

Defensive strategies and tactics by US targets

Although several state anti-takeover laws afford substantial protection, they also allow companies to opt out. Moreover, the anti-takeover laws are not enough to understand the range of firm-specific defensive strategies and tactics. Ruback identifies a number of pre-offer and post-offer defences that target managements in the US have used[16]. These are shown in Table 21.6.

The above defensive strategies encompass many others. Asset restructuring covers asset lock-up, sale of 'crown jewels' and 'Pac-Man defence'. Liability restructuring includes

Table 21.5 Three generations of anti-takeover laws in the US

First generation: Management-friendly anti-takeover statutes
Purpose: to prevent merger without incumbent management support
Example: Illinois Business Takeover Act
Characteristics
- Unduly protective of incumbent management; allowed inefficient management entrenchment; conflicted with WA provisions in terms of timing, filing and disclosure requirements; extra-state jurisdiction of state law infringed Commerce Clause
- Struck down by US Supreme Court in *Edgar v. MITE Corp* for violating both Supremacy and Commerce clauses

Second generation: Control share acquisition, super-majority, fair price, anti-greenmail and constituency statutes
2.1 Control share acquisition: To protect shareholders against coercive takeovers; to facilitate collective shareholder response when share acquisitions reach control thresholds
Example: Indiana Control Share Acquisition Act, 1986
Characteristics
- Automatic suspension of voting rights if acquirer crosses certain threshold, e.g. 20%
- Majority of disinterested shareholders to vote to reinstate rights
- To effect freeze-out merger, acquirer must offer same price as for control shares
- Corporations can opt out by charter amendment; minorities given appraisal rights
- US Supreme Court upholds Indiana law in *CTS Corp v. Dynamics Corp of America* as protecting independent shareholders and enhancing WA
2.2 Super-majority and fair price: Mandate supermajority approval for effecting back-end freeze-out merger; mandate fair price requirement – price paid and payment currency for target shares in back-end mergers should at least equal that paid in control reaching purchases
Example: Maryland Fair Price 1983
Characteristics
- Prohibit an acquirer who has purchased more than a specified percentage of target shares, e.g. 10% or 20%, from effecting back-end freeze-out merger unless approved by shareholders and the board (see next point)
- The back-end transaction must be approved by a supermajority (at least two thirds) of votes of 'disinterested' shareholders or by the 'continuing directors' of the target board
- The price paid in the back-end merger is at least equal to a statutory formula-based price
- Corporations can opt out by charter amendment

2.3 Disgorgement statutes: To deter greenmail payments by targets to raiders by requiring them to return profits made on sale of their acquisition of target shares to the target
Example: Ohio Revenue Code 1990
Characteristics
- Acquirer of 20% or more of target voting rights must disgorge to the target any profit made on sale of that shareholding within 18 months
- Any greenmail payment to shareholder holding more than 10% may require board and majority shareholder approval in states such as New York
- Corporations can opt out
2.4 Constituency statutes: To protect interest of non-shareholder constituencies
Example: New York Business Corporation Law
Characteristics
- Directors allowed to consider factors other than those immediately associated with corporate and shareholder issues, e.g. interests of employees, creditors and customers, the economy, community, short- and long-term interests of corporation and its shareholders
- Directors allowed greater latitude in deploying defensive measures against hostile bidders
- Delaware has no constituency statute, but its Supreme Court has held in *Unocal* that directors may consider the impact of a bid on constituencies like those listed above

Third generation: Business combination statutes
Purpose: To strike a balance between free market in shares and need to limit abusive takeover tactics
Example: Delaware Business Combination Act (Section 203)
Characteristics
- Prevents two-stage coercive tender offers followed by freeze-out mergers unapproved by target board
- Prevents LBOs being financed by the assets of the target corporation
- Delay merger between a target and an unwanted buyer ('interested stockholder') who has acquired 15% or more target voting stock for three years unless this standstill is waived by the board of directors and a supermajority (two thirds) of independent shareholders excluding the interested stockholder
- 85% stockholder exempted from three-year moratorium; blocking minority only 15%
- Act cannot be used by target board to favour one bidder over another
- Act provides for exemptions from moratorium and for opt-out by corporations

Table 21.6 Pre- and post-offer defences in the US

Pre-offer	Post-offer
• Staggered board of directors • Supermajority approval of merger • Fair price requirement • Issue of poison pill securities • Dual-class recapitalization	• Targeted repurchase (greenmail) • Standstill agreement with potential predator • Litigation • Asset restructuring • Liability restructuring • Organize white knight counter-bid

Source: Adapted from R. Ruback, 'An overview of the takeover defense economy', in A. Auerback (Ed.) *Mergers and Acquistions* (Chicago: University of Chicago Press, 1988)

recapitalization to increase leverage, ESOPs and stock lock-up. In an asset lock-up the target agrees to sell to a friendly buyer those parts that the predator might covet in the event of a bid. In a Pac-Man defence the target turns on the predator and makes a counter-bid. A stock lock-up involves the issue of shares to a friendly party, so as to prevent the predator from gaining a controlling stake. As noted in Chapter 17, if an acquisition falls within the scope of the Hart–Scott–Rodino Antitrust Improvement Act 1976 (HSR Act), the bidder has to file its pre-merger notification on announcing the tender offer. The HSR Act imposes a waiting period of 30 days before the bidder may accept the tendered shares. The proposed acquisition may be challenged on antitrust grounds by the Federal Trade Commission (FTC) or the Department of Justice under Section 7 of the Clayton Act. The target can sue to obtain injunctive relief to restrain an acquisition that would violate Section 7.

Poison pill

Poison pill, i.e. a shareholder rights plan, is regarded as one of the most potent of target defences. They can be put in place very quickly, since the board of directors does not require shareholder approval to institute them. There are two types of poison pill:

- the *flip-in*, where the target has a shareholder rights plan to issue its own shares to its share-holders at a heavy discount to the current market price; and
- the *flip-over*, where the target shareholders received the right to buy the bidder's shares following the acquisition at a heavy discount to the bidder share's current market price.

The overall effect of the pills is to increase the cost to a hostile acquirer of the acquisition. Exhibit 21.6 shows the relevant calculations.

Exhibit 21.6

How the poison pill works its way to the bidder's wallet

Flip-in pill

Let us assume the following data for a target: number of shares outstanding 100m; current share price $10; purchase price for a flip-in right $30; the target stock will be issued at a 50% discount; trigger level for pill 20% of target shares. The acquirer now reaches 20% of target stock and the pill is triggered. Other shareholders own 80%.

Immediately after the flip-in event, rights become exercisable:
With 1 right, holder can buy 6 new shares ($30/$5 per share @ 50% discount to market price).
When the rights are fully taken up the ownership of target will become:

Original shares held by non-acquirer shareholders	80m
New shares acquired under flip-in pill	480m
Shares held by acquirer	20m
Total number of shares	580m
% of shares held by acquirer after flip-in	3.4%
% of shares held before	20%

To maintain the same level of ownership as before the acquirer has to hold 116m shares, and therefore has to buy 96m more shares.

After the pill the share price of the target will be ($10 × 100m shares + $5 × 480m)/580 = $3.4bn/580 = $5.86 per share. 116m shares will cost the acquirer $680m.

Flip-over pill

Assume the same data as above, except that the acquirer stock price is $20. Target shareholder can buy each new bidder share at $10. Number of new bidder shares issued is 80m shares × 3 shares for every right per share = 240m.

Original shares held by acquirer in the bidder	100m
New shares issued to target shareholders under flip-over pill	240m
Total number of shares in bidder	340m
Acquirer's % ownership before	100%
Acquirer's % ownership after	29% (= 100/340)
Bidder's share price may settle at ($20 × 100m + $10 × 240)/340 = $12.94	
Loss to acquirer ($20 − $12.94) × 100m	= $705.9m

Source: Adapted from S. Kenyon-Slade, *Mergers and Takeovers in the US and UK* (Oxford: Oxford University Press, 2004), pp. 343–344

Because of the cost of the pill, bidders have to either negotiate with the target board an agreed merger and have the pill redeemed, or pursue alternative tactics, e.g. litigation or proxy fight (see Chapter 20 for further discussion).

Empirical evidence on takeover defences in the US

The 1980s produced a merger wave of unprecedented intensity, and also spawned a cottage industry of academic research into the circumstances, characteristics and impact of takeover defences in the US. These studies (many of them of great methodological and conceptual sophistication) are too numerous to list or individually review. Sudarsanam has reviewed these studies and summarized the major conclusions of these studies concerning the types and effectiveness of strategic (pre-bid) and tactical (post-offer) defences[17]. Table 21.7 summarizes the pre-bid defences and Table 21.8 the post-offer defences.

Table 21.7 Strategic (pre-bid) anti-takeover defences

Defence	Description	Broad conclusions
Poison pills	First and second generation, flip-over and flip-in, back-end plans, poison puts to allow security holders to sell them back to target company	Wealth effect small/insignificant. Takeovers not deterred. Higher takeover premium for targets. Puts protect creditors and managers. Poor performers adopt poison pills
Corporate charter amendments	Staggered board, supermajority, dual class capitalization, anti-greenmail	Ineffective as takeover deterrents. Target shareholder wealth effect insignificant, especially if amendments subject to shareholder approval
Re-incorporation	Shift incorporation to a state with favourable anti-takeover regime, e.g. Delaware	Only some firms prefer this anti-takeover protection. Where it aids takeover defence, shareholder wealth decreased. Wealth effect ambiguous
Financial restructuring	Exchange offers, dual-class recapitalization, leveraged recapitalization, ESOP	ESOPs have negative effect on takeover activity and depress firm value of takeover targets
Golden parachute (GP)	Compensation to management for loss of office in the event of corporate control change	May cause management alignment or entrenchment. Adoption may signal takeover vulnerability. Excess GP subject to tax. Wealth effect ambiguous

Source: Adapted from S. Sudarsanam, 'Corporate governance, corporate control and takeovers', in C. Cooper and A. Gregory (Eds), *Advances in Mergers and Acquisitions*, Vol. I (New York: Elsevier Science Inc., 2000), pp. 119–155.

Table 21.8 Tactical (post-bid) defences

Defence	Description	Broad conclusions
Greenmail and standstill agreement	Buy out potential predator at a premium, with agreement not to exceed holding above agreed level	Early studies report wealth losses to target shareholders, suggesting entrenchment. Recent studies refute entrenchment. Standstill reinforces entrenchment
White knight	Arrange friendly rival to hostile bidder	White knight shareholders suffer wealth losses
White squire	Sell large share block to friendly investor	
Recapitalize	Debt for equity swap, buy back shares, open market and targeted share repurchases	Ownership changes result in shareholder wealth losses
Litigation	Challenge bid in court for antitrust violation, breach of trust, etc.	Evokes competing bids. High premium if successful. If bid is withdrawn targets suffer wealth losses
Pac-Man defence	Counter-bid for hostile bidder	Very rarely attempted
Asset restructuring	Acquisitions, sell-offs	Asset restructuring results in shareholder wealth losses

Source: Adapted from S. Sudarsanam, 'Corporate governance, corporate control and takeovers', in C. Cooper and A. Gregory (Eds), *Advances in Mergers and Acquisitions*, Vol. I (New York: Elsevier Science Inc., 2000), pp. 119–155.

Board monitoring of targets in acquisitions

Brickley and James tested the hypothesis that board monitoring and the takeover market were substitutes[18]. They compared the level of independence of the board in the US states with and without laws prohibiting bank acquisitions. In the event of substitution, the proportion and number of outside directors, a proxy for board independence, would be higher in the former states. Brickley and James, however, found that boards were significantly more independent in those states that had no anti-takeover laws. They did not find any significant difference in ownership concentration, between the two groups of states, which could act as a substitute for either the takeover market or strong board monitoring.

Shivdasani investigated the interaction among board monitoring, ownership structure and hostile takeover in the US[19]. For a sample of completed and abandoned hostile takeover attempts that occurred during 1980–88 Shivdasani found that, relative to a control sample of non-targets, outside directors unaffiliated to the management represented a higher proportion of directors, but had a smaller ownership stake in targets. On the other hand, block shareholders owned a higher percentage of firm shares in targets than in non-targets. Hostile takeover likelihood was increased by low outside director ownership, but augmented by unaffiliated block ownership. Shivdasani's results support the hypothesis that board monitoring and hostile takeovers are substitute corporate governance mechanisms, whereas block shareholding and hostile takeovers are complementary mechanisms.

As regards insider ownership, Mikkelson and Partch showed that targets in the US had significantly lower insider shareholdings than non-targets, but that the probability of offer success was directly, but insignificantly, related to officers' and directors' holdings[20]. It is not clear whether this result supports management alignment with shareholder interests. Shivdasani also found that high CEO share ownership reduced hostile takeover likelihood. Cotter and Zenner provided evidence that the probability of a successful tender offer was directly related to the shareholding of directors and senior managers in target firms and to the capital gains to the top executive, on his shareholding[21]. Cotter *et al.* examined the role of the target firm's independent directors during tender offers. They found that target shareholders gained more with independent boards. Such boards also used the presence of poison pills and target resistance to their shareholders' advantage, to enhance target shareholder wealth[22].

CASE STUDY | **State anti-takeover laws in the US and how they protect targets**

As noted above, state anti-takeover laws in the US allow target companies a wide range of protective devices against hostile bidders. For the ill-prepared bidders these amount to booby traps. The degree of protection offered and the ability of the bidders to overcome the defences vary from one state to another. The experience of ArvinMeritor Inc (AM) in its failed 2003 bid for Dana Corp (Dana) incorporated in the state of Virginia, illustrates how formidable these defences are.

The acquisition, if successful, would have been a strategically significant transaction in consolidating the auto parts industry since the two companies produced a range of products and systems for vehicle manufacturers in North America with 90,000 employees worldwide and with combined sales of $17bn. AM had made a number of non-public approaches to Dana, its larger competitor, but these had been rebuffed.

In July 2003, AM announced that it was launching a hostile tender offer (TO) at $15 per share and an enterprise value of $4.4bn. The TO was conditioned on the removal of the restrictions arising from the Control Share Acquisitions Act (CSA) and the Affiliated Transactions Act (AT). Dana also had in place a poison pill. Dana's directors formally advised their shareholders to reject the offer. In the following months, AM made only limited progress with its TO and then increased its offer to $18 per share. It also filed a bill of complaint in a state court in Virginia seeking injunctive relief for alleged breaches of their fiduciary duty by Dana's directors. It also sought a declaratory judgement that Dana's anti-takeover measures were improper. AM failed in all these attempts and withdrew its TO in November 2003 as well as its lawsuit challenging Dana board's actions. The aborted takeover bid cost AM $16m in banking, legal and other costs.

AM's failure may have been due to a number of factors such as potential antitrust challenge to the takeover, inadequate offer price or divergence of opinions between AM and Dana over the strategic rationale for the acquisition. But Dana's incorporation in Virginia and the elaborate protective envelope against hostile takeovers that its laws threw around firms incorporated there, were also possible contributory factors. The laws comprising Virginia's anti-takeover regime at the time of the bid were:

- Control Share Acquisitions Act (CSA) – Once a hostile bidder acquired beneficial ownership of greater than 20% of a target's stock, the bidder's right to vote its shares (acquired before and after crossing that threshold) is extinguished. The voting rights are reinstated only by the affirmative vote of two-thirds of the outstanding shares not held by the bidder. Thus the bidder is effectively disenfranchised. A Virginia corporation can 'opt-out' of the CSA by providing for it in its bylaws. However, Dana's directors could amend the bylaws without shareholder approval and reinstate the restriction any time. Although AM could have, under the CSA, asked the target shareholders to reinstate its voting rights at a special meeting, a majority of disinterested shareholders of Dana would have been required to vote in favour of that proposal. However, this procedure was in practice not meaningful, given the target board's hostility and its recommendation to its shareholders, and the time and expense involved. AM therefore did not pursue this line of attack and instead filed the lawsuit very early in the TO process.

- Affiliated Transactions Act (ATA) – Under this law, certain transactions are prohibited for a period of three years if they result in the acquisition of more than 10% of any class of target's shares. These transactions included merger, share exchange or asset transaction with the acquirer. Such a long term restriction would delay an acquisition and nullify its strategic rationale. It would also discourage practices such as two-tier coercive offers and 'greenmail'. The bidder may seek to remove this restriction before crossing the threshold (majority of disinterested directors need to approve) or thereafter (two-thirds of such disinterested shareholders and majority of disinterested directors to approve). Another way to gain exemption from the ATA is if the bid terms meet the ATA's fair price mechanism, i.e. the offer is at a premium over the price of the target's securities in the previous two years.

- The Poison Pill Statute – Virginia law allows directors to install poison pill plans without shareholder approval and these plans can be discriminately applied to individual shareholders subject only to the standards for director conduct. This standard is based on a 'good faith business judgment'. Directors must use the poison pills 'in the best interests of the corporation'. Also permissible under Virginia law is the 'dead hand' pill that allows it to be redeemed only by continuing directors. Thus, even if the bidder replaces some of the directors of the target with a staggered board of its own nominees they will be unable to vote in favour of redemption. The 'dead hand' of the departed directors would still maintain the pill intact. In Dana, the flip-in pill was tied to the acquisition of 15% or more of its shares by a hostile bidder. Dana's directors could also have modified their pill to make it a dead hand pill.

- The Business Judgment Rule (BJR) – The Virginia statute differed from similar statutes in other states (see discussion above) in the standard imposed on directors in exercising their business judgement. Whereas in other states this was subject to the fiduciary duty of care and loyalty (see Chapter 20 for discussion of BJR) to the corporation and a fiduciary duty to their shareholders, under Virginia law, the duty and the test are significantly different. In most other states, the test is based on an objective 'prudent or reasonable person' standard. In Virginia the test is based on whether the directors' decision was made in 'good faith'. The test would be satisfied if the directors followed a due process. The substance of their decision was not relevant for this test since in one of its decisions ('*Willard*'), the Virginia Supreme Court affirmed the process-over-substance approach. Thus any hostile bidder challenging the target directors under the Virginia BJR would not be able to rely on a flaw in the target directors' business judgement but only on the process which those directors had followed.

Overall, the anti-takeover statutes enable target firms to frustrate hostile takeovers effectively. Although in recent years hedge funds and activist investors have brought pressure on US firms to remove poison pills and other anti-takeover devices, they still remain in place. One study reported that more than 70% of the US public companies staggered their boards. The combination of staggered boards and poison pills especially of the 'dead hand' variety is a truly formidable defence.

Discussion questions

1 How did the anti-takeover laws help Dana Corp defeat the hostile bid from ArvinMeritor?

2 Comment on the relative effectiveness of the different laws.

3 Compare the state anti-takeover laws in the US with the EU Takeover Directive? What are the similarities?

4 Compare the state anti-takeover laws in the US with the UK Takeover Code.

Sources: K. Smith, 'The booby traps in state anti-takeover laws', *Mergers & Acquisitions, The Dealmaker's Journal*, July 2004, 39, 7, 23–27; R. Sidel, 'Staggered terms for board members are said to erode shareholder value, not enhance it', *The Wall Street Journal*, 1 April 2002.

Overview and implications for practice

- When faced with a potential or actual hostile takeover bid, target company managers may resist the bid, both for their own reasons and in order to negotiate better terms for shareholders.

- They can set up takeover defences in anticipation of a hostile bid, or adopt defensive tactics once the bid has been made. The pre-bid defences are of a strategic nature.

- Pre-bid defences can rely on changes to the firm, and to the relationship with its organizational constituencies, or rely on external defences by changing the relationship or perceptions of outside stakeholders.

- Post-offer defences, once a hostile offer has been made, may be subject to regulation, as under the UK Takeover Code. Nevertheless, in the UK a range of tactical defences are available to target firms. Empirical evidence points to some of them being effective in defeating hostile bids. Over 23 defensive tactics may be available.

- Defences available to continental European targets vary from country to country, although takeover regulations are increasingly converging to restrict frustrating action without shareholder approval.

- Defences on the continent include restricted voting rights, ability to issue shares to friendly parties, shareholder agreements, and cross-shareholding.

- Takeover defences, both strategic and tactical, available in the US are reviewed and summarized. They are more wide ranging than in the UK.

- Empirical evidence from numerous US studies shows that many of them are not effective in defeating hostile bids, but can raise the value of the bids to target shareholders.

- Targets must review their vulnerability to hostile bids, examine the reasons for such vulnerability and take action to minimize it. They can put in place some pre-bid defences to negotiate from a stronger position than otherwise.

Review questions

21.1 What are the different motives for managers to resist hostile takeover bids?

21.2 What are the different types of defence available to UK target companies?

21.3 How difficult is it for UK targets to mount effective defences? What are the obstacles to doing so?

21.4 How effective are the post-offer defences in the UK?

21.5 What are the costs associated with successful and failed defences?

21.6 What defences are available to targets in European countries on the Continent?

21.7 Do countries differ in the defences available to targets in Europe?

21.8 What defences are available to target companies in the US?

21.9 How effective are the defences in the US?

21.10 What is the case for restricting defensive actions?

Further reading

A. Davis, 'A pre-emptive defence', *Mergers & Acquisitions, The Dealmaker's Journal*, March 2009, 22–23.

R. Kabir, D. Cantrijn and A. Jeunink, 'Takeover defences, ownership structure and stock returns: An empirical analysis with Dutch data', *Strategic Management Journal*, **18**(2), 1997, 97–109.

T. Moeller, 'Let's make a deal! How shareholder control impacts merge payoffs', *Journal of Financial Economics*, 76, 2005, 167–190.

R. Ruback, 'An overview of the takeover defence economy', in A. Auerbach (Ed.), *Mergers and Acquisitions* (Chicago, IL: University of Chicago Press, 1988).

Notes and references

1. See T. Moeller, 'Let's make a deal! How shareholder control impacts merger payoffs', *Journal of Financial Economics*, **76**, 2005, 167–190.

2. P. S. Sudarsanam, 'Defensive strategies of target firms in UK contested takeovers', *Managerial Finance*, **17**(6), 1991, 47–56.

3. For non-UK issuers the notification period is four trading days, and higher thresholds apply at each 5% interval up to 30%, and then at 50% and 75%.

4. D. Reid, *ESOPS: Employee Share Ownership Plans in the UK* (London: Butterworths, 1990), p. 26.

5. D. Carnell, 'ESOP: Opportunities knock', *Accountancy*, February 1990, 105–107.

6. P. S. Sudarsanam, 'Less than lethal weapons: Defence strategies in UK contested takeovers', *Acquisitions Monthly*, January 1994, 30–32.

7. D. A. De Mott, 'Comparative dimensions of takeover regulation', in J. Coffee, L. Lowenstein and S. Rose-Ackerman (Eds), *Knights, Raiders and Targets* (Oxford: Oxford University Press, 1988).

8. P. Verloop, *Acquisitions Monthly*, 1991. Also see *A Practitioner's Guide to Takeovers and Mergers in the European Union* (Old Woking: City & Financial Publishing, 2008).

9. R. Kabir, D. Cantrijn and A. Jeunink, 'Takeover defences, ownership structure and stock returns: An empirical analysis with Dutch data', *Strategic Management Journal*, **18**(2), 1997, 97–109.

10. M. Steen, 'Hermes finds ASMI defence hard to swallow', *Financial Times*, 15 May 2008.

11. J. Franks and C. Mayer, 'Ownership and control of German corporations', *Review of Financial Studies*, **14**(4), 2001, 943–977.

12. T. Jenkinson and A. Ljungqvist, 'The role of hostile stakes in German corporate governance', *Journal of Corporate Finance*, **7**, 2001, 397–446.

13. For further discussion of the impact of block shareholding on hostile takeovers see M. Becht, 'Reciprocity in takeovers', in G. Ferrarini, K. Hopt, J. Winter and E. Wymeersch (Eds), *Reforming Company and Takeover Law in Europe* (Oxford: Oxford University Press, 2004). Becht gives several examples of control structures referred to here.

14. This section draws upon S. Kenyon-Slade, *Mergers and Takeovers in the US and UK* (Oxford: Oxford University Press, 2004), Chapter 3.

15. Some authors divide these into five generations.

16. R. Ruback, 'An overview of the takeover defence economy', in A. Auerbach (Ed.), *Mergers and Acquisitions* (Chicago, IL: University of Chicago Press, 1988).

17. S. Sudarsanam, 'Corporate governance, corporate control and takeovers', in C. Cooper and A. Gregory (Eds), *Advances in Mergers and Acquisitions*, Vol. I (New York: Elsevier Science Inc., 2000), pp. 119–156.

18. J. A. Brickley and C. M. James, 'The takeover market, corporate board composition and ownership structure: The case of banking', *Journal of Law and Economics*, **30**, 1987, 161–180.

19. A. Shivdasani, 'Board composition, ownership structure and hostile takeovers', *Journal of Accounting and Economics*, **16**, 1993, 167–198.

20. W. Mikkelson and M. Partch, 'Managers' voting rights and corporate control', *Journal of Financial Economics*, **25**, 1989, 263–290.

21. J. F. Cotter and M. Zenner, 'How managerial wealth affects the tender offer process', *Journal of Financial Economics*, **35**, 1994, 63–97.

22. J. F. Cotter, A. Shivdasani and M. Zenner, 'Do independent directors enhance target shareholder wealth during tender offers?', *Journal of Financial Economics*, **43**, 1997, 195–218.

PART 4

Post-acquisition integration and organizational learning

Having carried out the first three stages of the acquisition process – strategic planning, organizing for acquisitions and deal negotiation – the acquirer now embarks upon the next important stage of integrating the two organizations to achieve the strategic aims of the acquisition. The strategic logic of the acquisition, i.e. sustainable value creation, dictates both the extent and the pace of integration. Some acquisitions require quick and complete absorption of the acquired firm. Others may allow the firms to co-evolve over a period of time and become integrated slowly. In Chapter 22 we present a model of acquisition integration. Integration involves changes in organizational structures, people and cultures of the merging firms. Human aspects and organization behaviour assume a critical role in the integration process. We highlight the obstacles to effective integration, and signpost the critical success factors. Chapter 23 covers the fifth stage of our five-stage model, and discusses organizational learning as an integral part of the M & A process. We draw upon the insights of organizational learning theory, and discuss the conditions under which effective learning about M & A can take place. We highlight the importance of systems, processes and incentives in promoting organizational learning, and the limits to such learning. The role that internal audit can play in facilitating and ensuring effective learning is emphasized.

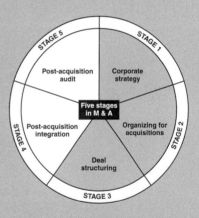

Chapter 24, the final chapter, revisits the themes and findings that emerge from the previous chapters. It provides the 'take away'. It highlights the challenges that the M & A process poses to would-be acquirers, whether experienced or callow, throughout all its five stages, and provides some guidelines for meeting the challenges.

CHAPTER 22

Organizational and human aspects of post-acquisition integration

Objectives

At the end of this chapter, the reader should be able to understand:

- the alternative acquisition integration approaches, and what criteria guide the choice among these;
- the alternative political, cultural and change management perspectives on integration;
- the problems that may arise in the integration process and evidence of these problems; and
- the lessons to be learnt from the evidence on successful and failed integration efforts.

Introduction

When the acquisition deal has been closed, the job of realizing the strategic and value creation objectives of the deal starts. Depending on the type of acquisition made, its strategic rationale and value creation logic, the companies involved in the merger have to be integrated in varying degrees. The extent of integration is defined by the need to maintain the separateness of the acquired business. Integration of two organizations is not a matter of just changing the organization structure and establishing a new hierarchy of authority. It involves integration of systems, processes, procedures, strategy, reporting systems, etc. Above all, it involves integration of people. It may often require changing the organizational culture of the merging firms, possibly to evolve a new one to deliver the strategic objectives of the merger.

Mergers driven by efficiency considerations and need for consolidation of operations, downsizing, etc., affect a large number of people. Their world is being turned over by the merger. This may generate fear, anxiety, resentment, anger and hostility towards the merger and the acquirer's integration plans. These feelings have to be handled sensitively to ensure a sense of fairness not only among those who have to leave but also among those fortunate enough to retain their jobs.

Integrating organizations may require people to change their mindset, cultures and behaviours. Cultural issues have therefore to be addressed during the integration process. It is also a politically surcharged process, since it often involves redistribution of power between the merging firms. Conflicts of interest and loyalty may hinder an effective integration process. There is empirical and survey evidence that many acquirers do not successfully integrate their acquisitions. The reasons for such failure are varied.

From strategy to integration

We started with the acquirer's strategy and, following the deal, have now reached the integration stage. The relationship between strategy and integration is shown in Figure 22.1. Ahead of deal closure, acquiring teams develop some integration plan and, where deals are friendly, integration teams made up of managers from both the acquirer and target are formed and tasked with preparing an integration blueprint. This plan may be modified by the details of the agreement made, e.g. board membership, no redundancy for two years, retention of senior positions by acquirer or target managers, the policy for selecting the right people for jobs that overlap, etc. The integration plan may be further fleshed out in the light of the knowledge that the acquirer gains about the target after the agreement, since the pre-acquisition due diligence by necessity would not be complete.

Effectiveness of post-acquisition integration: the VRINS test again

As we discuss below, the extent of integration of the acquired firm with the acquirer depends on the strategic objectives of the acquisition and its value creation logic. Since an acquisition is intended to create a sustainable competitive advantage and, through that, enhanced corporate or shareholder value, an effective integration process should ensure that the acquisition achieves those objectives. It is useful to recall the VRINS test described in Chapter 3 for the effectiveness of the integration process (see Figure 3.9). If the acquisition is founded upon

Figure 22.1   From strategy to integration and learning

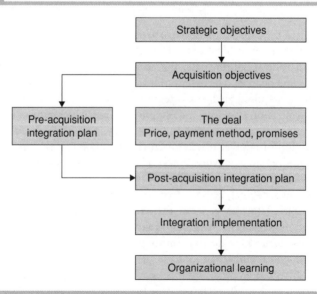

Figure 22.2   Acquirer and target organizational components

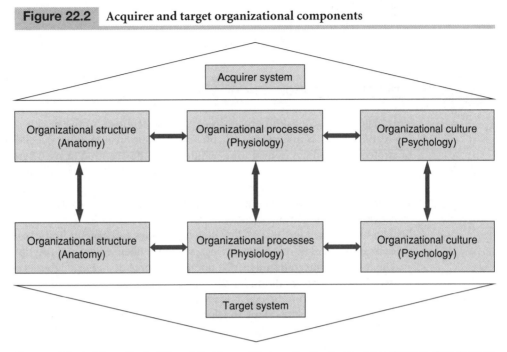

Source: Adapted from B. de Wit and R. Meyer, *Strategy Synthesis: Resolving Strategy Paradoxes to Create Advantage* (London: Thomson Learning, 2005), Figure 4.3

sound strategic logic, and the deal was done on the most advantageous terms in terms of acquisition price, risk reduction etc, an effective integration process should lead to value creation: that is, it will reconfigure the merged firms' R & C in such a way as to satisfy the VRINS test. Where the process is messed up, it fails the test, defeats the acquisition intent, and destroys value.

A pertinent question to ask is 'What is being integrated?' Are we 'integrating' the merging firm's structures, processes or people? A firm is an organized ecosystem with interactive components that affect, and are affected by, the members of that organization. It can be conceptualized as being made up of structure, process and culture, representing its anatomy, physiology and psychology respectively. Figure 22.2 shows these components of both the acquirer and target.

Structure refers to the 'clustering of tasks and people into smaller groups' in some meaningful way to achieve an efficient division of labour that will facilitate the firm's accomplishing of its corporate or business objectives, e.g. output-based, functional, geographic, supplier-based structure[1]. Organizational processes refer to 'the arrangements, procedures and routines used to control and coordinate various people and units within the organization', e.g. reporting system, budgeting, planning and control procedures. In addition to formal processes there may be informal processes, gossip, personal networking, informal negotiation etc. Finally, organizational culture refers to the shared beliefs, value systems and preferences that guide the behaviour of the organization members. Within a common organizational culture there may be subcultures representing other shared interests and values, e.g. professional or ethnic identity[2]. The national culture within which an organization functions may influence the organizational culture. Post-acquisition integration may involve integration of any or all of the three components. Moreover, integration of similar components, e.g. structure, may affect the relationship between the other components: for example, changing the structure may affect the process, which in turn may affect behaviour and cause culture clashes.

A post-acquisition integration model

This stage of the acquisition process is a major determinant of the success of the acquisition in creating value. As indicated in Chapters 5–8, value creation often depends on the transfer of strategic capabilities between the acquirer and the acquired firms. There are four broad sources of added value, of which three involve some capability transfer between the acquiring and the acquired firms. These three require operational resources pooling, or functional skills transfer, or general management skills transfer. The fourth is size related and derives from the increased size of the combined entity relative to the pre-combination firms. These capabilities/benefits are outlined in Table 22.1[3]. These capabilities and benefits lead to one or more of the three broad sources of value: cost savings, revenue enhancement and real options.

The extent of integration depends upon the degree of strategic interdependence between the two firms as a precondition for capability transfer and value creation. The timing of integration also depends on the type of capability being shared or transferred. Rationalization of operating capacity is often done much faster than the transfer of functional or management skills.

Strategic interaction versus autonomy

The strategic value creation logic behind the acquisition dictates the extent to which the capabilities of the two firms need to be merged within a single organizational structure or maintained within the boundaries of the firms. Haspeslagh and Jemison model the trade-off between the need for strategic interdependence and the need for autonomy for the acquired firm[4]. This trade-off is represented by Figure 22.3. At the two extremes are complete preservation and complete absorption. Most acquisitions require a mixture of interdependence and autonomy. This taxonomy leads to four types of post-acquisition integration: portfolio management, preservation, symbiosis and absorption.

Under absorption, integration implies a full consolidation of the operations, organization and culture of both firms over time. In a preservation acquisition there is a great need for

Table 22.1 Types of strategic capability/size benefits in value-creating acquisitions

Category of capability/benefit	Specific capabilities/benefits transferable
Operating resource sharing	Sales force, manufacturing facilities, trademarks, brand names, distribution channels, office space, etc.
Functional skills	Design, product development, production techniques, material handling, quality control, packaging, marketing, promotion, training and organizational routines
General management	Strategic direction, leadership, vision, resource allocation, financial planning and control, human resource management, relations with suppliers, management style to motivate staff
Size benefits	Market power, purchasing power, access to financial resources, risk diversification, cost of capital reduction

| Figure 22.3 | Strategic interdependence and organizational autonomy |

Need for strategic interdependence

		Low	*High*
Need for organizational autonomy	*High*	Preservation	Symbiosis
	Low	Holding company	Absorption

Source: P. Haspeslagh and D. Jemison, *Managing Acquisitions* (New York: The Free Press, 1991), pp. 139–140

autonomy. The acquired firm's capabilities must be nurtured by the acquirer with judicious and limited intervention, such as financial control, while allowing the acquired firm to develop and exploit its capabilities to the full. In a symbiotic acquisition the two firms initially coexist but gradually become interdependent. Symbiosis-based acquisitions need simultaneous protection and permeability of the boundary between the two firms[5].

Acquiring company managers select an appropriate integration approach that will lead to exploitation of the capabilities of the two firms for securing sustainable competitive advantage. In an absorption approach operational resources need to be pooled to eliminate duplication. An acquisition aimed at reducing production capacity in a declining industry dictates an absorption approach. In a preservation approach the acquirer nurtures the acquired firm through a series of interactions that bring about positive changes in the ambition, risk-taking and professionalism of the acquired company's management group. In addition to nurturing, the acquirer uses the acquisition as a learning opportunity that may be central to a strategy such as platform building (see Chapter 13 on consolidating acquisitions). Such acquisitions may thus be exploratory and need preservation. Acquisitions by private equity firms may be underpinned by the preservation approach (see Chapter 11).

In a holding company relationship the investment by the parent is passive, and more in the nature of a financial portfolio motivated by risk reduction and reduction in capital costs; the parent seeks no interaction among the portfolio companies. Thus in Figure 22.3 organizational autonomy for holding-company-type acquisitions may not be a relevant concept. The line between preservation and holding company types may not be quite distinct in some acquisitions.

In a symbiotic integration no sharing of operational resources takes place, but there may be a gradual transfer of functional skills and other capabilities. A telecommunications firm acquiring a computer firm in order to create multimedia products needs to preserve each firm within its boundary, but also to allow interaction across the boundary. Strategic capabilities transfer encompasses numerous interactions between the two firms at different levels, and requires management of the interface between the two organizations and the personnel of the two firms. The interactive process is also a process of mutual learning and consequential adaptation of the original acquisition blueprint to the realities of the two firms.

Exhibit 22.1

Baxter acquisition of American Hospital Supply

Integration guiding principles:

- Organization will be based on what is best for the business.
- The best people will be retained, regardless of affiliation.
- The merger must achieve early and visible benefits, but in an orderly fashion.
- The organization will decentralize if necessary to serve customer interests.
- The need to do integration right will be balanced against the need to do it expeditiously.
- Executives from both sides will participate in integration at every step.
- Employees of both companies will be treated in an open and honest fashion, and will be kept informed.

Source: Schweiger and Lippert, *ibid.*, p. 35

Identifying the capabilities to be transferred is not enough. A proper atmosphere conducive to this transfer needs to be created. Where the capabilities to be transferred are not properly identified, owing to deficiencies of the pre-acquisition decision-making or poor due diligence (described in Chapters 13 and 20 respectively), or the necessary atmosphere is not created or the interface is mismanaged, value destruction rather than value creation may result from the integration process.

Aligning strategies, structures and cultures

The goal of integration is to create an organization capable of achieving the strategic objectives of the acquisition. The two firms need to share these objectives, but they must agree not only on the destination but also on the roadmap for the journey, and the logistical and organizational configuration of the firms undertaking the journey. This requires the 'hard' side of aligning strategy and structure but also the 'soft' side of aligning the organizational culture and strategy (see Exhibit 22.2 below). The extent to which such alignment needs to be accomplished is determined by the integration type chosen.

Articulating the principles behind the integration approach

Acquirers often set out the principles that will guide their integration effort for the benefit of both the acquirer and target company managers and employees. These are intended to bind the integration effort, and to reassure employees, target employees in particular, for whom a merger is time of uncertainty and anxiety. Exhibit 22.1 lists the principles set out by Baxter when it acquired American Hospital Supply.

Political and cultural perspectives on integration

Schweiger *et al.* proposed a model of integration in which the value chains (see Chapter 3) of the acquirer and the acquired need to be reconfigured in order to achieve the value creation objectives of the acquirer[6]. Such a reconfiguration has three dimensions: technical, political and cultural. The technical reconfiguration is similar to the capabilities transfer model discussed above, with an impact on the different components of a value chain.

However, the value chain represents more than a technical configuration. It is also a configuration of social interaction and political relationships. These represent the informal processes and systems that influence people's ability and motivation to perform. A manager's position, power and influence may not be fully captured by his or her formal and official title. In carrying out integration the acquirer should have regard to these political relationships, if acquired employees are not to feel slighted or unfairly treated.

The culture of an organization is embodied in its collective value systems, beliefs, norms, ideologies, myths and rituals. Carlos Ghosn, the CEO of Nissan, which has an alliance with Renault of France, has said that '*the most fundamental challenge of any alliance or merger is cultural*'[7]. Culture can motivate people, and can become a valuable source of efficiency and effectiveness. Cartwright and Cooper suggest four different organizational culture types, as shown in Table 22.2 (see also Figure 22.4) [8]. The four culture types have as their patron gods Zeus (power), Apollo (role), Athena (task) and Dionysus (person) in Charles Handy's delightful pantheon of management[9].

Cartwright and Cooper, in subsequent work, suggest that the following factors are likely to be important in determining merger outcomes[10]:

- the degree of cultural fit that exists between the combining organizations, given the objectives: that is, whether the mode of acculturation is one of cultural integration, displacement or maintenance of cultural autonomy;

Table 22.2 Types of organizational culture

Type	Main characteristics
Power	Essentially autocratic and suppressive of challenge; emphasis on individual rather than group decision-making
Role	Bureaucratic and hierarchical; emphasis on formal rules and procedures; values fast, efficient and standardized customer service
Task/achievement	Emphasis on team commitment; task determines organization of work; flexibility and worker autonomy; needs creative environment
Person/support	Emphasis on equality; seeks to nurture personal development of individual members

Figure 22.4 Organizational culture types and their characteristics

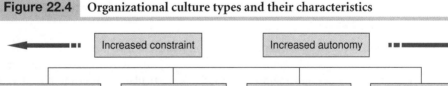

Source: S. Cartwright and S. L. Cooper, *Managing Mergers, Acquisitions and Strategic Alliances: Integrating People and Cultures* (Oxford: Butterworth-Heinemann, 1996), p. 50

- the impact of the event on the individual: that is, the degree and scale of stress generated by the merger process and its duration.

Poor culture fit or incompatibility is likely to result in considerable fragmentation, uncertainty and cultural ambiguity, which may be experienced as stressful by organizational members. Such stressful experience may lead to their loss of morale, loss of commitment, confusion and hopelessness, and may have a dysfunctional impact on organizational performance[11].

Impact of organizational culture on integration process and acquisition performance

Cultural dissimilarity between the combining organizations may be underestimated or overlooked in the pre-acquisition stages although, increasingly, culture audit may be part of due diligence. This dissimilarity may influence the integration process, as well as its effectiveness and success in value creation. Differences in culture may lead to polarization, negative evaluation of counterparts, anxiety and ethnocentrism between the top management teams (TMT) of the acquired and acquiring firms[12]. These alienating emotions may take time to abate before genuine integration can happen. Several empirical studies of culture difference and TMT turnover, information system integration and stock market performance of the acquirer indicate a negative influence[13]. Thus similarity of organizational cultures seems to reduce the risks in post-acquisition integration. Cartwright and Cooper argue that mergers between certain culture types can be disastrous[14].

David and Singh considered acquisition culture risk, which is a measure of cultural incompatibility or distance between the acquirer and the acquired firms, and which is capable of impeding the efficient integration of the two[15]. In assessing the advisability of an acquisition the acquirer must, in addition to strategic issues, consider cultural risk. There is in general a cultural distance between the two firms. They often differ in organizational culture, and may also differ in professional (e.g. scientist versus accountant) and national culture. Acquisition culture risk, however, depends on the following contingencies:

- Whether operational integration occurs. Different types of synergy imply different degrees of risk. Operational integration increases the risk.
- The division being integrated. Within a firm there are subcultures: for example, a task-oriented research and development division compared to a role-oriented service division.
- The mode of integration adopted by the acquirer.

Alternative perspectives on cultural similarity: culture is socially constructed

The above discussion is premised upon a structural view of culture: that is, the structure of an organization's culture is preset and is static. An alternative view is that culture is a dynamic phenomenon, and members claiming a particular cultural identity may re-create another cultural identity. Kleppestø postulates that culture is a socially constructed entity, and that its construction is contextually determined. Culture is not a structure but a *process*. All human beings need to classify themselves and others into various social categories. Groups and group identities are self-created to give meaning and substance to situations in which members find themselves. They differentiate 'them' (other groups) from 'us', thereby lending focus and cohesion to the group. Members of such a group share certain common traits, perceptions and cognitive structures, and show 'consistency through time and space'. Social construction of identities is also a defensive mechanism to confront any threats facing the members who seek, and help create, these identities[16].

The implication of this perspective is that culture clashes at the post-acquisition integration stage cannot be inferred from a delineation of the structure of merging firms' pre-merger cultures. Thus any mapping of these cultures may not have much predictive value as regards the nature of culture clashes during integration. New cultures may mutate during that process, based on new identities of managers and employees, socially constructed to meet the threats, e.g. target employees faced with potential job loss or relocation. Members of such newly constructed culture groups may rely on stories and anecdotes about the commonality of their interests, perceptions and behaviours in the past to give legitimacy to their own group.

A corollary and sanguine view of the social construction of identities and cultures is that such construction may be opportunistic, fluid, and contingent upon the persistence of the threat that begot it. Acquiring firms can find ways of 'deconstructing' such new-found identities by understanding the stimulus for their creation, and endeavouring to remove any perceived threat. 'Conflicts here and now could be defocused by future oriented perspective . . . Future oriented stories will also have a function of creating new joint identities, reducing anxiety and creating positive identities'[17].

National cultural differences and cross-border acquisition integration

National cultural stereotypes are often attributed to organizations and individuals. They also inform the interpretation of people's behaviour by others. But such interpretation may differ quite dramatically from the self-interpretation of those people, thereby possibly giving rise to misunderstanding, rudeness and confrontation. Figure 22.5 illustrates how certain characteristics of bidder and target groups may be perceived differently by each other. Such incomprehension may often arise from national or ethnic or cultural stereotyping[18]. Exhibit 22.2 shows how uninformed mutual perceptions can often influence attitudes towards integration and the merger.

Countries differ in terms of their cultures, which may be represented on four dimensions defined by Hofstede: attitude towards and acceptance of power imbalances, uncertainty

Figure 22.5   **Mutual incomprehension of acquirer and target people**

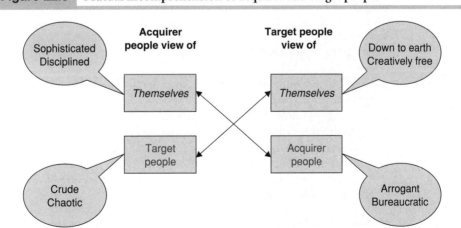

Exhibit 22.2

Rational Germans rattle the flexible French

In 2004 Air Liquide, the French industrial gases group, acquired two-thirds of its German rival Messer Griesheim and formed Air Liquide Deutschland (ALD). The newly combined business became a breeding ground for cross-cultural misunderstanding and resentment. Just beneath the surface conflicting work styles, national stereotypes and insecurity about the future threatened to undermine the new entity. The management team, under Mr Sieverding, ALD's CEO, decided to take swift action to identify and resolve the problems.

With the help of JPB, a specialist consulting firm, it interviewed employees and identified 12 'emotional viruses' that could weaken the merger. Among these 'viruses' were a strong *belief by both sides in their own superiority*, a fear of job losses at Messer, and anxiety at Air Liquide that its *flexible* management style would be deadened by German *rationality*.

National differences are intertwined with differences in corporate culture, says Ulf Tworeck, an expert in cross-border deals at the Frankfurt office of Mercer Delta, the organisational consulting firm. 'The most difficult [mergers] are between northern and southern Europe,' says Mr Tworeck, who worked on the Messer Griesheim acquisition and is a past consultant to Eon, the German power company, and to its current bid target, Endesa of Spain. 'The way Endesa operates is virtually completely opposite to how Eon is run,' he says. Eon, for example, is more meticulous about preparing for and recording meetings and decisions.

Source: Adapted from A. Maitland, 'A good merger is all in the mind', *Financial Times*, 15 March 2006

---

avoidance, masculine/feminine characteristics, and individualism/collectivism. Using these and other dimensions of national culture, measures of cultural distance or cultural incompatibility may be constructed. The empirical studies of the impact of culture distance show the following:

- Higher uncertainty avoidance of the acquired company's national culture strengthens the positive link between autonomy for the target and profitability one year after acquisition.
- In highly individualistic societies a lower level of integration leads to higher productivity growth.
- In a study of British and French acquisitions, the US, British and French acquirers adopted different integrations measures depending on national culture: for example, French acquirers tended to exercise higher formal control than did US and British acquirers. In terms of uncertainty avoidance France scored higher than the US and the UK.
- Too much control exercised by the acquirer over the acquired firm's operations depressed economic performance[19].

Exhibit 22.3 shows how differences between national and organizational cultures influence the integration approach.

Exhibit 22.3

Reckitt Benckiser is cultured in its approach to diversity

In November 1999 Reckitt Benckiser, the household cleaning materials group, was formed from a merger of Reckitt, a British company, and Benckiser, a German company. Bart Becht, a Dutchman, became CEO of the combined firm, and was determined to prevent culture clashes between the merging partners from wrecking the merger, as they had many other cross-border mergers. He aimed to develop a common set of core values – achievement, teamwork, entrepreneurship and commitment. Although most of these values came from Benckiser, teamwork was very much a Reckitt one. Thus integration would involve marrying these different cultures and moving the new organization towards a shared culture and commitment to common values. Mr Becht admitted that 'marrying the cultures of the two groups will take longer than putting the new organisational structure in place or combining the two computer systems'. Even those who were competent but did not match up to the four values would have to go.

Source: Adapted from M. Urry, 'Bart Becht is strong on values', *Financial Times*, 16 March 2000

Cultural diversity: source of strength or weakness?

Companies differ in their tolerance of cultural diversity. For example, Electrolux, the Swedish multinational, made numerous acquisitions in different countries. Its integration approach was to accept and even preserve the cultural identity of the acquired companies. It tended to retain target firm executives, unambiguously giving them operational control, negotiating performance goals, and relying on them to cooperate and integrate themselves voluntarily with the rest of the group[20].

Diversity enables a firm to tolerate ambiguity, and endows the firm with resilience. To the extent that people using different cultural frameworks frame and analyze problems differently, the firm is able to generate richer perspectives on those problems. Similarly, diversity generates greater creativity in formulating a wider range of solutions. The interaction and co-evolution of cultures within the firms may engender newer and more creative cultural prototypes for the future. Therefore integration should not smother diversity in an effort to craft a homogeneous monoculture and in the process forgo the dividends of diversity.

Psychic distance paradox

Very explains this paradox that 'operations in countries that are psychologically close to each other are not necessarily easy to manage, because the perception of similarity prevents executives from apprehending critical cultural differences. The easier it looks, the harder it is in reality!' This theory is a challenge to the view that cultural differences impede the effectiveness of integration and the achievement of the acquisition objectives. Schoenberg, in his survey research, finds that national cultural differences do not have a significant impact on acquisition performance[21]. What acquirers need to learn is that there is something to learn from differences. Thus openness, humility and receptivity allow acquirers to capitalize on diversity and put it to creative use. To quote Carlos Ghosn again, 'If one does not believe anything can be learned from one's new partners, the venture is doomed to fail'[22].

Strategic change and culture change: which drives what?

According to Nahavandi and Malekzadeh, targets' and acquirers' perceptions of their own culture and that of the other side often dictate the outcome and direction of any culture change[23]. In this view, culture would drive performance. Thus culture change may often be a precondition for both organization structure change and strategic change. Thus merging firms, where dictated by the merger imperative, must consciously and proactively seek to transform the cultures of their organizations. While the existing culture may have been appropriate for the time when the firm was performing well, because of its market power, it would not serve its strategic purpose when faced with a severe competition. A bureaucratic culture appropriate for a mature business may prove disastrous when the firm has to become innovative and risk-taking. While customer focus may not be important to a dominant player in a market, it becomes a condition of survival in a highly competitive market. Behavioural change, at both the personal and organizational levels, may often be a necessary first step towards achieving the strategic change that provides the logic of the merger.

Cultural integration approaches are dependent upon the strategic interdependence between the merging firms and the extent of cultural difference between them, as shown in Figure 22.6. Thus low strategic interdependence requires no intervention, or just enough intervention to avoid dysfunctional conflict. High strategic interdependence, on the other hand, may require either imposition of the dominant culture or a conscious programme to evolve a new culture that draws on the best of both firms. Before choosing the form of cultural integration the integration team must investigate the impact that cultural differences will have on effective integration, and on the achievement of the strategic and value creation goals of the acquisition. Where differences may be a source of value, the integration process needs to carefully preserve different cultures and nourish them. Where differences may impede integration, a strategy for dealing with these differences must be in place.

Figure 22.6   Strategic interdependence versus cultural diversity

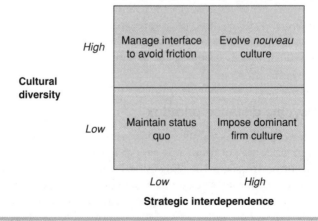

Figure 22.7   Approaches to cultural integration and associated risk

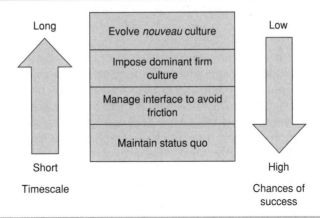

Different integration approaches will happen over different timescales. They also have different probabilities of success, as shown in Figure 22.7. Cultural integration is thus an important determinant of the integration risk and overall acquisition risk.

In some cases an entirely *nouveau* culture needs to be created to supplant the legacy cultures of the merging firms. Although this has the virtue of neutrality between the rival claims of the merging firms' cultures, such a creation may run into the combined opposition of both firms' workforces, and take longer to initiate and sustain. Nevertheless, without a fresh cultural paradigm the strategic objectives of the merger may never be realized in full. Exhibit 22.4 describes how culture change became an important instrument for delivering

---

Exhibit 22.4

Simply Better culture for a Simply Better company

In the middle of 1988 Bob Bauman, the new American CEO of Beecham, the British public company, initiated merger discussions with Smith Kline Beckman (SKB). Beecham was a long-established firm, with operations in pharmaceut- icals and consumer products, including popular home remedies and cosmetics. The consumer products division was market driven, and more profitable than the pharmaceutical division, which was focused more on research than on the market for drugs. The two divisions had distinct and often antagonistic cultures – one was brand driven and the other research driven.

SKB was a pharmaceutical company, but also operated clinical laboratories. It was much more focused than Beecham. At the time of the merger the two companies had similar market capitalization (about $5.6bn), sales revenue (about $4bn), number of employees (about 36,000 to 42,000) etc. The merger was consummated in the middle of 1989 as a friendly, nil-premium merger of equals (see Chapter 20 on the concept and implications of a merger of equals). A new UK-listed company, SmithKline Beecham (SB), was created, with Bob Bauman the CEO of Beecham becoming the CEO of SB, and Henry Wendt, the

→

CEO of SKB, becoming the non-executive chairman of SB. The immediate board composition of SB reflected the friendly nature of the merger, and included executives from both Beecham and SKB.

The merger was a defensive strategic move by the firms, faced with escalating costs of pharmaceutical R & D, blockbusters due for patent expiry, buyer pressure from governments and health management organizations and pharmacy benefit managers in the US, and 'me-too' drugs from other pharmaceutical competitors. The firms not only had to cut costs but also cross-sell each other's products in the US, where SKB was strong, and in Europe, where Beecham was strong. Further, they had to leverage each other's resources and capabilities in R & D, drug discovery, accelerating the drugs to markets and selling.

The two merging companies had been in business for 150 years, and differed in their cultures in a number of ways:

SKB	Beecham
Scientific/academic	Commercial/competitive
Pharmaceutical/strategic	Brands/operational
Long product cycles/planning horizons	Short cycle, retail environment
Strategic/visionary	Pragmatic/tactical
Traditional	Hierarchical chain of command
People oriented	Numbers oriented
Technology/product orientation	Market orientation
Inertia/bureaucracy	Rigidity/formality
'Don't look bad'	'Don't make a mistake'

Both
Paternalistic, creative dependency, risk averse

A year after the merger, although substantial integration of various functions had been achieved, the top management of SB felt that the changes were not enough to deliver the strategic goal of being a leading healthcare company. The cultures of the organizations had not evolved to become one that would deliver the goal. A new, homogeneous culture had to be created:

Strategy	Culture	System
Pharmaceutical peer leader	*Simply Better*	*Simply Better Way*
Most effective marketer	Customer focus	Customer-driven process
Leader in new products	Innovative	Continuous improvement
Most efficient producer	Performance focused	Eliminate waste
Best managed	People, integrity	Training, communication
Cross-sector linkages	Sharing	Teamwork

To bring about culture change, SB received external advice, studied Japanese companies, organized workshops and training, communication strategies and involved employees in the *Simply Better* transformation programme. The six cultural goals above became the values of SB, and by early 1994 SB declared that the merger promises had been fulfilled. Thus ended the journey from Promise to Performance.

Source: Adapted from R. Bauman, P. Jackson and J. Lawrence, *From Promise to Performance, A Journey of Transformation at SmithKline Beecham* (Boston, MA, Harvard Business School Publishing: 1997), Chapters 7 and 8.

the strategic change that drove the merger between the UK pharmaceutical and consumer products firm Beecham and the US pharmaceutical firm Smith Kline Beckman (SKB) in 1989 to become the UK firm SmithKline Beecham (SB).

Cultural profiling and assessment of cultural compatibility

The first step towards cultural integration and aligning culture to strategy is the profiling of the cultures of the merging firms. This would be informed by the information collected by the acquirer in the pre-bid period and during the due diligence exercise (see Chapter 13 on cultural due diligence). Further information may have been collected in the course of signing up the merger agreement. In friendly deals the merging firms often begin preparation for integration and form joint integration committees before the deal is implemented. For example, when Hewlett-Packard and Compaq signed their merger agreement, they prepared for post-merger integration in advance of deal completion. Their integration office consisted of 450 dedicated employees supported by advisers and headed by key executives from both companies reporting directly to Carly Fiorina, HP's CEO[24].

The next step is to evaluate the compatibility of the cultures and identify the areas of potential conflict. Third, a cultural awareness programme through education, workshops and working together needs to be set up. For example, Novell Inc. used a 'merger book' containing 2000 questions covering the hiring and firing practices, management styles, pay programmes, worker attitudes and other general cultural considerations[25]. Often, as observed in the case of SmithKline Beecham (see Exhibit 22.4 above), mere cultural compatibility is inadequate to meet the strategic objectives of a merger. A new culture has to be evolved.

The people map developed by Eric Abrahamson provides a useful framework for approaching the culture change problem[26]. It starts with what employees already have, and the integration has to revive, reuse and redeploy. These include personal, social and psychological attributes:

- knowledge and skills – what people already know and what they are good at doing; these are easier to adjust;
- demeanour and networks – demeanour is 'the impression or perception that an employee creates in other people he/she interacts with; network is everyone you know or who knows you and is often vital to get a job done'; these are harder to adjust;
- aptitudes, values and traits – these are psychological and motivational; these are largely fixed.

A change programme needs to match these to the goals of integration, and devise appropriate change techniques to adjust people's characteristics so that integration leaders can successfully redeploy and recombine them. Where change is not possible, hard decisions about replacement may be necessary.

Change management perspective on post-acquisition integration

Nature of change

Business organizations are faced with change in their external environment all the time. In response to this change, firms adapt themselves. Change, however, can be either evolutionary or revolutionary, depending on the scale and discontinuity it represents from the firm's prior position. Evolutionary change is small and incremental change that may not strain the firm's adaptive system and resilience. On the other hand, some changes in the environment may be fundamental and often cataclysmic, straining the adaptive capabilities of a firm to breaking point and causing it to collapse in irretrievable failure. In our environmental analysis of merger waves in Chapter 2 we identified a number of discontinuous changes of a political, technological and social nature causing such waves. Often long periods of success in coping with evolutionary change may engender both structural and cultural inertia in a firm, which ill-prepares it for surviving massive discontinuous changes. Thus managing evolutionary change and managing revolutionary change require different configurations of strategy, structure, culture and personal attributes of leaders[27].

Attitudes to change

While the need to change is a Darwinian imperative of survival, there is no guarantee that the challenged species will be excited by the prospect of change or embrace it with enthusiasm. The selfish genes of the human animal may, however, predispose it to accept change, albeit reluctantly. Thus in an organizational change context attitudes to change may vary, and management of change requires an understanding of this diversity, as well as a strategy to minimize it. Resistance to major, especially, discontinuous changes may be high. Perhaps 20% of the people are 'change friendly', 50% are fence-sitters trying to figure which way to go, and 30% are resistant and antagonistic to change, possibly adopting the survival strategy of a dinosaur[28].

M & A as a change process

Mergers and acquisitions are major change events in the lives of corporations and those employed by them. The changes occasioned by acquisitions are often wide ranging. They may change strategies, operations, cultures, the relationships among the staff and managers, team relationships, power structures, incentive structures and job prospects. They may require individuals to change their lifestyles, behaviour, personal beliefs and value systems. Acquisitions, as noted above, create anxiety and fear and, are often traumatic and wrenching events for those who might lose their jobs, for those who wield the axe, and even for those that are spared the axe, since they might be afflicted with survivorship guilt. The turbulence associated with acquisitions may impact on career loyalty, organizational loyalty, job involvement and job satisfaction[29].

Given the scale of change that an acquisition may cause in both merging firms, change management concepts may be employed to inform the post-acquisition integration effort. These concepts include[30]:

- assessing speed of change, e.g. incremental or discontinuous, as discussed above;
- establishing clear leadership;
- clarity of communication;
- maintaining customer focus;
- making tough decisions;
- dealing with resistance; and
- taking focused initiatives.

The change management programme in M & A involves three types of change – change of the acquired firm, change of the acquiring firm, and change in the attitude and behaviour of both to accommodate coexistence or fusion of the two organizations. Changing an organizational structure may be difficult, since managers and employees identify psychologically with it, and for this reason may engender resistance to change, fear and resentment against enforced change. Resentment may take the form of lack of commitment to change, failure to implement the change programme, and even subtle sabotage. Such behaviour may be part of a defensive strategy. Resistance to change is not always dysfunctional or irrational. Often the 'change agents', through lack of empathy and understanding, may provoke resistance. Resistance, when correctly interpreted, can also contribute to more effective change than proposed by the integration managers[31].

Acquisitions may often result in the breach of implicit employee contracts such as expectations of future benefits or benign work conditions. They consist of 'personal compacts', the mutual obligations and commitments that exist between employees and the company. Such compacts include formal, psychological and social components. Breaches of these contracts, or fear of such breaches, may intensify hostility to change[32]. To make change acceptable, the acquirer must offer, to those affected, payoffs that are demonstrably superior to their existing payoffs, or the payoffs that might have been, had their organization continued in the old familiar way. Change must be seen to be in the interests of the affected. Such a perception is as much a matter of substance as of the transparency of the process delivering change. In the case of underperforming target companies, there may be dissatisfaction with the present and therefore greater readiness to accept the imperative of change. However, while for some change is an opportunity, for others it may be a threat. Senior managers with their stock options may see change as an opportunity to El Dorado, but lower-level employees may regard it as a threat.

Building a winning coalition

For the merger proposition to be widely accepted, and the vision and goals of the merger to be internalized by people in both merging organizations, the integration team must start with those internal leaders who, once they are persuaded of the merits of the mergers, can influence others. This initial coalition can then envelope others who look to these leaders, and the coalition becomes stronger and more effective. The coalition building process consists of:

- focused initiatives targeted on 'opinion makers and shapers';
- identifying key stakeholders and their expectations;
- identifying those who have power/influence; and
- developing strategies for
  - managing their expectations;
  - communicating with them; and
  - forming a 'coalition of the willing' to change.

Opinion leaders are not the same as titular leaders whose names appear on the organization chart. 'Real' leaders may be the 'power behind throne' by virtue of seniority and experience, family relationship etc., e.g. the founder of a company who does not hold any powerful position in the company. Similarly, the psychological leaders are those who have no formal power but who are widely regarded as the 'wise guys' because of their maturity, disinterestedness and moral authority[33]. The coalition can demonstrate the will for integration, and help alleviate cultural and other forms of resistance.

Human resource management issues during integration

In the course of integration the merging firms have to confront the following issues:

- changing the board of directors;
- choosing the right people for the right positions;
- management and workforce redundancy;

- aligning performance evaluation and reward systems; and
- key people retention.

Board-level changes

Board-level positions may have to be revamped to align directorial expertise with the emerging needs of the post-merger business. The new board should be change leaders so that they can carry out the change process dictated by the merger. Often such top-level change is both symbolic and a credible signal of the changes to be made at lower levels. Board-level changes could also be inspirational for the rest of the organization. This is particularly so where the merging partners had experienced performance problems, which triggered the merger. It is not unknown for disagreements over board representation for the merging companies, or over who will be the CEO and who will be chairman of the merged business, to cause the collapse of merger negotiations. Any compromise merely to secure a merger agreement will, in the post-merger period, come back to haunt the merged entity, perhaps permanently debilitating it. On the other hand, top management change (TMT) may often be regarded by the acquirer as a way of 'clearing out the old lot' and putting 'our people in control' to speed up the integration, but it can lead to loss of important capabilities[34] (see Exhibit 22.5).

Who will do which senior job?

In all integration types there will be rival claims for senior executive positions such as the chairman, CEO, CFO, COO, heads of divisions, heads of functions such as R & D, etc., if both merging firms had these positions prior to the merger. The choice of the right person for the right job is important, because otherwise the success of the merger will be jeopardized. Equally importantly, the choice is often a signal about the style, culture and intent of the new management. Such choices based on tribal affiliations of the acquirer or on non-transparent processes will lead to perceptions of bias and lack of good faith. The disappointed managers may linger, nurturing resentment and grievance, and slackening their commitment to the merged firms, or may leave. Accent on merit is as important as the integrity of the process of managerial appointments. Early managerial appointments may alleviate the anxieties of the concerned managers, but speed is far less important than the transparency of the process.

Head count reduction

In an absorption-type integration, with its emphasis on efficiency savings through consolidation of duplicate functions or production sites, head count reduction is perhaps inevitable. With legal regulations such as the Transfer of Undertakings Protection of Employment Act (TUPE) in the UK, similar legislation in the EU, and protective legislation in other countries, employees have to be treated with some minimal decency. However, managing head count reduction should be driven not by legal minimalism but by transparently genuine concern for the welfare of the people being made redundant. Companies often arrange for counselling, training and outplacement programmes to alleviate the distress to the employees.

Aligning performance measurement and reward systems

Where the merging firms have different approaches to measuring and rewarding performance, attempts to align the evaluation and incentive systems may evoke hostile responses from the staff adversely affected by such changes. The balance between basic compensation, i.e. salary,

Exhibit 22.5

Ferrero departs and leaves a trail of doubt about synergies

Crédit Agricole (Agricole) acquired Crédit Lyonnais (CL) in 2003. Just six months later Dominique Ferrero, CL's former chief executive, left Agricole abruptly, casting doubt on the bank's ability to deliver the main benefits of the deal. An analyst at Citigroup, Smith Barney, said: '[The] management changes at Crédit Agricole may increase the market's scepticism on the group's ability to deliver on targeted merger synergies.' About two-thirds of the €760m ($936m) of synergies promised by the two managements when the €19.5bn deal was announced were to come from the enlarged group's corporate and investment banking (CIB) division. These businesses were being integrated by Mr Ferrero, who left after a personality clash with Agricole managers. People close to Agricole said they had found that his assertive style had hindered the integration process, and one analyst said he was 'unmanageable'. Others saw his departure as evidence of Agricole's determination to assert control over a bank for which it paid a substantial control premium. Lyonnais's former chairman, Jean Peyrelevade, one of the main architects of the merger, was asked to resign in September 2003 in connection with the Executive Life scandal.

Citigroup said the simultaneous resignation of Mr Ferrero and Marc Antoine Autheman, the former head of Agricole's investment bank, 'may leave the group without any "bankers" with vast experience in CIB integration processes'. The division would be run by Edouard Esparbes, who ran the largest of the 44 regional banks that controlled Agricole. He was one of the most vocal critics of the merger, and was not an investment banker. However, another analyst said it was impossible to tell what impact Mr Ferrero's departure would have. The strategy in CIB was based more on aggressive cost-cutting than on the more complicated task of revenue growth. Nevertheless, a UBS analyst said: 'The departure of Ferrero, who was seen as a safe pair of hands, may raise the spectre of more aggressive and less Lyonnais-friendly rationalisation, and with its potential revenue losses.' These, he predicted, would be €100m in 2004. Agricole shares fell 1.4% on announcement.

Source: Adapted from C. Pretzlik, 'Ferrero departure casts doubt on merger', *Financial Times*, 16 December 2003

and performance-related compensation, i.e. bonuses, stock options, etc., may differ between the two firms, and altering the balance to introduce more pay-to-performance sensitivity may engender resentment and resistance. However, changing the performance evaluation and reward system may be a necessary element in evolving a new culture, because of its power to motivate staff and influence their behaviour.

Disparity between remuneration systems often characterizes cross-border mergers involving US companies, with their reliance on stock options and other performance-related compensation schemes. When Daimler-Benz merged with Chrysler in 1998 there were stunning differences in the compensation arrangements between the American managers and their German counterparts. For example, the 10 members of the Daimler-Benz management board earned $11m between them in the year before the merger, whereas the top five managers in

Chrysler alone earned about $35m. Chrysler CEO Bob Eaton and the president, Bob Lutz, earned $10m and $16m respectively. After the merger a far more level playing field, based on stock options, was created[35]. Differences in evaluation and reward systems may generally be quickly resolved, and empirical evidence suggests that, for possibly this reason, such differences do not affect post-acquisition performance[36].

Key people retention

The uncertainty during a merger often leads senior managers to end it by leaving. Others may leave because they regard the future envisaged by the merger, in terms of culture, business model, compensation system, etc., with dread or distaste. A merger is also the time when the firm's competitors attempt to capitalize on the uncertainty and lure away the 'stars', as happened in many investment banks undergoing mergers. For example, when Deutsche Bank acquired Bankers Trust, the entire telecom advisory group was poached by Credit Suisse First Boston (CSFB). In the aftermath of the merger between SmithKline Beecham and Glaxo Wellcome many leading scientists left the merged firm GSK to join rival firms. Such departures have to be factored in while contemplating the merger and in executing the integration. Key people retention may be achieved through devices such as 'golden handcuffs', i.e. special bonuses or stock options or generous earn-outs, etc. Often these people, probably already wealthy, may be tempted to stay not with offers of more wealth but with positions of power and prestige that reflect their merit.

Managing conflicting expectations

Mergers are characterized by expectational ambiguity, as noted in Chapter 12. As in the Indian fable of five blind men describing an elephant, each manager may see only a part of the whole merger and its objectives, and may expect different outcomes from it. In addition, expectations of outside stakeholders such as shareholders and the stock market analysts may differ from those of internal stakeholders such as top management and employees. Expectations may also differ as to the timescale for delivery of merger benefits, and this divergence generates additional pressures on the integration process. Realistic mapping of expected benefits and the integration timetable is as important in managing these pressures as credible communication strategies to keep the external and internal stakeholders on board. During the integration of Beecham and Smith Kline and Beckman (see Exhibit 22.4 above) aggressive milestones were set deliberately to create a sense of urgency and maintain the momentum for change. The goal was not only to realize the savings necessary to retain their credibility with the financial markets, but also to get the merger out of the way quickly to build a new and better healthcare company. However, the SmithKline Beecham (SB) management 'were setting up what would be an ongoing conflict between speed to satisfy financial markets and time required to guarantee organizational ownership. It was a conflict that would plague them throughout the entire process'[37].

The merger integration process may often be based on incorrect assumptions about the thinking, behaviour and expectations of people from the two organizations. Such assumptions, if acted upon, may create mistrust and suspicion rather than the trust and goodwill necessary for effective integration. Integration should also accommodate, as far as is compatible with the goals of the merger, the preferences of the two companies, and their managers and staff. Tools available for measuring these preferences may be part of the integration process in drawing up and implementing merger integration plans. Integration is a transitional process, and requires the creation of a 'thinking environment' that minimizes the impact of incorrect assumptions, mistrust and emotional reactions[38]. Exhibit 22.6 describes the role played by HR

Exhibit 22.6

Critical role of HRM in M & A

Tata Consultancy Services (TCS) is one of India's foremost IT services companies, boasting a clientele of world-class corporations. It has made a number of cross-border acquisitions around the world. Ajoy Mukherjee, Vice President and Global Head of HR at TCS, describes the role HR plays at various stages of the M & A process in his company.

'Our experience reinforces the belief that the success of every M&A activity depends on aligning the people, organisational and cultural assets of the new entity. Finessing the soft issues is the most complex component of any integration process and has the strongest influence on a deal's long-term success.

'A dedicated human resource integration team would act as the effective change agent to ensure smooth transition. Due diligence can involve assessing the culture of the organisation that has been identified for the acquisition. Does the organisation have a compatible culture? How do management styles differ? Are there potential HR financial issues – for example, an underfunded pension plan, or post-retirement issues? One of the first critical areas that HR should be involved in is assessing the potential compatibility of cultures. This could involve reviewing an array of things such as leadership style, mission, vision and values of the organisation, team strength, performance and reward management systems, customer focus and organisational capabilities.

'Integration planning is an important phase when the HR professionals' skills in project management and change management are critical to the merger or acquisition. HR is usually involved in a wide range of planning issues such as talent management, retention initiatives, determining transition strategies to move people to new roles; provide training and re-skilling, outplacement processes and policies, determining the new management team, the direction for the new organisational culture, the leadership style for the new organisation, designing the communication strategy for staff, appointment criteria for new positions, development of the contract terms of employment for the new entity and determining work environment and work location issues.

'Communication is the key mantra to a successful M&A deal and HR typically has a huge role to play in the communication process. Employee concerns and cultural issues need to be addressed as early as possible to ensure smooth transition. The first three- to six-month period pre- and post-announcement of the deal is critical in the communication process of every successful M&A. Addressing key employee issues at the earliest creates a sense of satisfaction and acceptance in the minds of the people. This can help establish a sound foundation for ensuing merger integration activity. In the end, it never hurts to over-communicate.

'The challenge of cultural integration is another crucial aspect. As organisations scout for cross-border acquisitions, cultural integration becomes far larger than creating a single culture. Cultural sensitivity and harmony among the multicultural workforce assumes a primary consideration in the integration process. Induction programmes, cultural sensitisation workshops, visits to near-shore facilities and continuous HR interventions are very critical to ensuring cultural harmony. Flexibility is the keyword here'.

Source: A. Mukherjee, 'HR has key role in IT company mergers', *Financial Times*, 2 December 2008

in the cross-border acquisitions made by one of India's world-class IT services companies. The company assigns a comprehensive role to HRM at various stages of the M & A process.

Problems in integration

Since pre-bid acquisition justification is generally based on limited information about the true financial, strategic and organizational strengths and weaknesses of the target, it seldom corresponds fully to post-acquisition reality. This means that pre-bid expectations usually have to be modified in response to this reality, and the integration process should be flexible enough to accommodate this response.

Haspeslagh and Jemison trace integration problems to three possible sources: determinism, value destruction, and leadership vacuum[39]. Determinism is a characteristic of managers who believe that the acquisition blueprint can be implemented without change, and without regard for ground realities. They tend to forget that the blueprint was based on incomplete information, and is often a wish list to accommodate the political compulsions of decision-making in the acquirer. They do not consider that the implementation process is one where mutual learning between the acquirer and the acquired takes place, and that the process is essentially adaptive in the light of this learning (see Exhibit 22.7 on shared learning).

Determinism leads to a rigid and unrealistic programme of integration, and builds up hostility from managers on both sides when they do not share the blueprint's assumptions about the capabilities to be transferred, or the timescale for the transfer. Such a hostility engenders a non-cooperative attitude among managers, vitiating the atmosphere for a healthy transfer.

Where the integration experience of managers and other personnel in the two organizations is contrary to their expectations, they may feel that they stand to lose from the acquisition. Thus at a personal level the acquisition is value destroying. Value in this context includes both pecuniary and non-pecuniary, psychological compensations that managers have earned in the past. Value destruction may take the form of reduced remuneration in the post-acquisition firm, or loss of power, or of symbols of corporate status. For example, the target firm managers may be given positions that fail to acknowledge their seniority in the pre-acquisition target, or their expertise.

Finally, the management of the interface requires tough and enlightened leadership from the top managers of the acquirer. Where the integration task is delegated to the operational managers of the two firms, without visible involvement or commitment of the top management, the integration process can degenerate into mutual wrangling and recrimination. Top management must be on hand to iron out the inevitable frictions that arise between groups of managers in the integration process.

Sharing and transferring resources and capabilities

Many of the resources and capabilities that form the basis of the acquisition, and need to be leveraged, have first to be shared and internalized by both firms. This sharing involves transfer between one merging firm and the other. However, such transfers may be impeded by the vary nature of these resources and capabilities. As discussed in Chapter 3, resources and capabilities may be the result of the firm's evolutionary process. Their evolutionary path dependence determines not only whether they can be effective when transplanted into another corporate body, but also whether they can be prised apart from the parent. Similarly, since the transferred resources and capabilities are not part of the recipient's evolutionary trail, they may face transplant rejection.

Exhibit 22.7

Target will learn, sure! But acquirer can learn too

In September 2006, as the German group Linde closed its £8.2bn ($15.6bn) takeover of the UK's BOC to create the world's largest industrial gases company, it was about to experience a subtle linguistic change. English would become the official company language. Wolfgang Reitzle, Linde's dapper chief executive, said the change of language was just one of many changes that Linde faced. Normal takeover practice would suggest that when a company buys a competitor it quickly imposes its own culture and management on the target. Instead, Mr Reitzle decided to use the BOC deal to question everything at Linde, from the way it is run to its legal status. 'Nothing stays as it was. It is a complete redesign. It is the maximum that you can create as a change,' he said. The deal, which Mr Reitzle called the 'biggest reorganization' of a German blue-chip company, showed how a chief executive could use disruptive events such as a merger to push through necessary reforms of the acquirer. As both BOC and Linde would be radically affected by the deal, he was keen to approach it more as a merger than as a takeover. In part, this was due to size: BOC's market capitalization exceeded Linde's over the several years that the deal was being planned. Its gas business was also much bigger. The approach also underlines what amounts to a new humility over takeovers in German boardrooms about learning from acquired companies.

Deals during the previous wave of cross-border acquisitions at the turn of the century have been frequently afflicted by poor integration and weak operational performance. The new management structure of Linde – announced alongside a new corporate identity, new reporting structure and new headquarters – would have people from both companies at the top. 'We are approaching this as a merger. The selection criteria will not be: does somebody come from BOC or Linde? It will be: who is the most suitable?' insisted Mr Reitzle. The changes were likely to go right to the top, with BOC managers expected to join the executive board. The supervisory board was also likely to be revamped, although this would take much longer. BOC's chief executive, who was expected to retire, was likely to join the following year. Mr Reitzle said, 'There is momentum in the organization, and it leads me to the conclusion that we will make the integration – and wherever we think we can learn from BOC, we will.'

Source: Adapted from R. Milne, 'A cultural shift in the gas works', *Financial Times*, 6 September 2006

Integrating innovation capabilities

Acquiring new innovation capabilities to create new products or markets, or to leverage extant innovative capabilities to stronger competitive advantage in existing markets, is often an important acquisition goal. If so, how successful is the integration process in achieving it? In Chapter 4 we reviewed the evidence on the post-acquisition innovative performance, and found some evidence of innovation becoming a casualty of acquisition. In Chapter 5 we discussed some of the contingent factors that may improve post-acquisition success in innovation. Among these are[40]:

- the extant intellectual capital endowment of the acquirer and the type of that capital; the type of IC, whether human, social or organizational, affected the scope of innovation, whether exploitative or exploratory;
- the breadth and width of innovative capability the acquirer has; the prior expertise of the acquirer in a similar or dissimilar knowledge domain to that of the acquired firm affects the probability of subsequent innovations.

The choice of integration mode may also affect the post-acquisition innovation capability. The acquirer has to strike a balance between coordinating the acquired firm to exploit its current innovations and allowing it enough autonomy to preserve its ability to carry on with its exploratory capabilities. Too much coordination may stifle the latter. Puranam, Singh and Zollo find that structural integration decreases the likelihood of new products from targets that have not launched products before acquisition, and for all firms after acquisition[41]. The trade-off between structural coordination and autonomy, however, depends on the strategic rationale of the acquisition – that is, whether it aims at exploitation or exploration as the source of value, and where both are desired the timescale for each to be realized. This means that the innovation trajectory of the acquired firm needs to be carefully managed so that the stampede for exploitation does not crush the tender shoots of exploration (see Exhibit 22.8 for a symbiotic acquisition).

Exhibit 22.8

Preserving CAT's antibodies, a symbiotech integration

In January 2007 AstraZeneca acquired Cambridge Antibody Technology (CAT). The challenge for the Anglo-Swedish pharmaceuticals group was in integrating its £702m biotech acquisition: how to take advantage of ground-breaking science for new drugs while preserving entrepreneurial talent. Integration is a sensitive and difficult issue, especially so in biotechnology, which is somewhat dependent on an informal network, key talent, agility and a lack of bureaucracy. 'It's not going to be smooth sailing; there will be issues, and there have been already,' said Hamish Cameron, an AstraZeneca veteran parachuted in to replace Peter Chambre, CAT's outgoing chief executive. CAT's 300 employees – who, in keeping with the informal spirit of biotech culture, could go to work in jeans and a T-shirt, with some even sporting piercings and interesting hair colours – were five months into the process of becoming a research and development arm within the vast AstraZeneca network.

Mr Cameron planned to double the size of CAT over the following three years, but said that if the process of expansion was not managed properly, and CAT got swallowed up inside AstraZeneca, all the key scientists would leave, and the company's culture would be destroyed. To stave off a wave of staff defections – and crucially key talent – AstraZeneca established a first-year retention bonus across the company. But after the acquisition, the turnover of staff went up 'beyond the annual 8–12%'. The companies were not strangers, following a two-year alliance in the areas of respiratory and inflammation research.

But despite the links, Mr Cameron closed the door to AstraZeneca when he took over. He said, 'I sent a signal back to AZ saying this was a well-run public company with all processes in place that didn't need immediate help and then I put a bit of distance between us. My immediate priorities were making people here feel comfortable with their new contacts and establishing the operating model.' CAT is now a wholly owned subsidiary that has retained its name, company profile and even corporate colours – none of its functions has been merged. It has its own board, which reports to AZ. 'A member of the clinical team of CAT was reporting into AZ and not a member of AZ's global clinical function,' said Mr Cameron.

CAT is responsible for the discovery and early development of antibody therapeutics, up to the moment of demonstrating efficacy in patients, or somewhere in the second phase of drug discovery. Then the process moves to full-scale development at AZ. Its research into new drugs has expanded into the areas of cancer and heart disease, as well as respiratory and inflammatory complaints. Mr Cameron was keen to allay fears that AZ planned to put CAT into a technology box, asking it to deliver nothing but antibodies and giving it no say in its future development. 'Ten per cent of the R&D budget is set aside for CAT to invest in as part of its own decision-making process. This gives it the space to invest in things that are too risky for AstraZeneca.' Post-acquisition, CAT no longer had to make judgements and evaluate risk based on finding the 'leanest way through', a traditional culture of cash-strapped biotech firms. But Mr Cameron said that the company's annual budget would be managed tightly to make sure the same atmosphere of creativity and motivation was kept intact.

AZ teams were collaborating with CAT's employees over the best understanding of current science, and discussing how operating models should be built. 'We use a "no-veto" model, which means you put these scientists together in a room and they cannot come out until they agree – one or other party can't trump the other,' said Mr Cameron. 'There is a danger you default to a low common denominator, but the best route is usually teased out.' If Mr Cameron had his way, CAT would in 10 years be more than twice the size, and a well-known centre of excellence in biopharmaceuticals, delivering a broad range of antibody therapeutics. 'There is an enormous emotional engagement in the biotech sector of feeling your success is related to the success of the company in a very direct way,' he said. 'Over the next two to three years CAT's culture will change, but the point is that CAT will change it.'

Source: Adapted from S. Davoudi, 'Pioneer in need of protection', *Financial Times*, 29 January 2007

In addition to these considerations of the acquirer knowledge base and organizational integration mode, there is also a need to consider the impact of the incentives for innovation on the acquired and acquirer firm innovators, at both the individual and team levels. Acquired firm inventors may not have the incentive to continue to be as productive as before, because in the enlarged merged entity they may not receive as much as recognition and reward as in a smaller target firm, and because of moral hazard that allows them to shirk and slacken

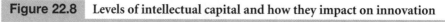

Figure 22.8 Levels of intellectual capital and how they impact on innovation

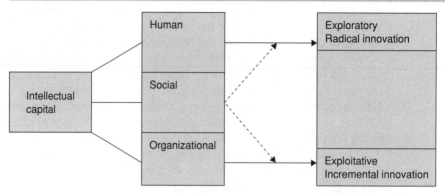

*Key: Solid lines: direct positive effect. Dashed lines: interactive positive effect.
Source: M. Subramaniam and M. A. Youndt, 'The influence of intellectual capital on the types of innovative capabilities', *Academy of Management Journal*, 48(3), 2005

without being penalized for it. Moreover, appropriating all the fruits of their inventions in the larger merged entity is more difficult than in the smaller target firm. For these reasons, acquired firm inventors have less incentive to maintain their innovative performance. Kapoor and Lim find evidence that in the semiconductor industry the number of patents (a proxy for inventive intensity) filed by inventors in acquired firms falls compared with those in non-acquired firms, whereas prior to acquisition these firms experienced similar patent filing intensity (the total number of granted patents filed by an inventor with a focal firm in a given year)[42]. In the post-acquisition period the number of patents filed in both acquirer and acquired firms falls, but their trajectories converge, suggesting that disincentive effects may wear off. However, the gap between the acquired and non-acquired control firms remains significantly wide.

Subramaniam and Youndt illustrate the types of IC and their individual and interactive effects on innovation (see Figure 22.8)[43]. In the context of acquisitions we have to consider two bundles of IC – the acquirer's and the target's. Thus the direct and interactive effects become much more complex to understand and manage. The choice of integration model is likely to have a significant effect both on the direct effects and on the timescale for integration, as demonstrated by Puranam *et al.*, 2006[44].

Integrating brands

The challenge of integrating brands was discussed in Chapter 5. Corporate brand strategy is not an important component of most companies' M & A deliberations[45]. Post-merger product branding strategies may be varied:

- *global brand* – the island brand architecture with brands maintained in islands, e.g. PepsiCo;
- *one message* – umbrella architecture with a corporate brand, e.g. HSBC;
- *one offer* – ladder architecture with a hierarchy of brands of different price and quality, e.g. Bridgestone;
- *best fit* – network architecture, network of independent but linked brands, e.g. BMW.

The challenge is to choose the right 'post-acquisition branding strategy and appropriate brand identity before moving to the design of the architecture of the merged portfolio'[46].

Can your and our computer systems talk to each other? Information system integration

Information system (IS) integration is a critical, but often neglected, part of the overall integration programme. IS compatibility between acquirer and acquired companies must be seriously considered, even at the pre-deal or due diligence stage[47]. This is particularly important in mergers that seek to leverage each company's information on customers, markets or processes with that of the other company, as in a banking and insurance merger or in the merger of two banks. The compatibility of IS must be considered as thoroughly as any strategic, operational, organizational or political issue. IS integration in M & A depends on a mix of both technical and organizational factors. New system designers have to consider the impact of the strategic objectives of the transaction on the integration cost in terms of financial, information and human resources[48]. Organizational culture compatibility must be considered alongside IS synergies[49]. Culture clash may damage the cooperation and commitment of the very group that may be instrumental in determining the success of the IS integration and ultimately the merger itself. Exhibit 22.9 exemplifies the problems faced by Monsanto and Pharmacia & Upjohn Inc. in carrying out IS integration as part of the $23.3bn merger.

Exhibit 22.9

IS integration might SAP the Monsanto–Pharmacia merger

In December 1999 Monsanto Co. and Pharmacia & Upjohn Inc. announced their plan to merge and become a global pharmaceutical giant. Monsanto had implemented SAP AG R/3 more than three years earlier, and designed it to be flexible enough to handle any potential merger. Analysts, however, felt that the two companies would face formidable IS integration problems. Two of their competitors had recently undergone a merger, and integration 'had brought them to their knees'. They gave up integration and maintained separate structures for the previously independent organizations. Another analyst said: 'CEOs stand up to talk about the economies of scale and how they're going to combine their sales forces and jointly sell their products. But in order to do any of that, these companies have to achieve some level of integration of their information systems. And it is a very difficult thing to do.'

In another merger the CEO painted a picture of a sales representative being able to go to a customer, take a single order for products of both companies, and deliver the products in one shipment with a single invoice. Unfortunately, they learned that each company had its own management information system. The merged company then settled on a new order management system, and a six-month project turned into one that was expected to take three years. Monsanto, however, expected to benefit from its integration experience of its two 1998 acquisitions.

Source: C. Sliwa, 'Drug giant's merger to bring systems integration hurdles', *Computerworld*, 3 January 2000

Stages in the integration process

The three stages are:

- pre-deal closure;
- stabilization; and
- resources and capabilities sharing/transfer

Although 'post-acquisition integration' suggests that the integration process should start once the acquisition deal has been closed, this may be too late for effective integration. Integration is about implementing a deal in such a way as to achieve its strategic and financial objectives. However, not anticipating the problems and risks of the integration stage may lead the acquirer to do a deal that is doomed to fail. A proper evaluation of the risk associated with the acquisition should therefore start well before the deal is signed up, from the target selection stage or at least from the due diligence stage (see Chapter 20). Some companies in recent years have started forming integration teams composed of managers from both bidder and target once the merger deal has been signed. For example, in the friendly merger of Glaxo and Smith Kline Beecham in 2000, integration teams were set up following the merger agreement, but the consummation of the merger was delayed by US antitrust investigations for more than a year. The due diligence investigations also need to be carried out, keeping in view the need for as much information about the target as possible. This information would then be used by the acquirer to formulate its post-acquisition integration strategies. In some companies an integration manager takes part in the deal-making stage, and in the due diligence process.

Following this deal-making stage the acquirer needs to prepare for integration. The transition stage is also the stabilization stage. At this stage the acquirer must take stock of the acquired firm. In some cases, before any functional or general management skills can be transferred, the operations of the target may have to be strengthened by infusing fresh capital, say, for working capital purposes. Merging firms' managers may be too distracted by the integration process to 'keep an eye on the ball', i.e. they may neglect to 'mind the store' and its customers, who will then turn to the firms' competitors, perhaps for good.

Customer retention while integration proceeds

Integration generates uncertainty and anxiety, not only for employees of the merging firms but also for their customers. Integration cannot be used as an excuse to take the customers for granted and neglect their demands and expectations. More than employees, customers generally have a choice – to take their custom to the merging firms' rivals, who will be happy to grab those customers. Integration of the sales forces of the acquirer and the target needs to be managed with this paramount consideration. Sales forces are also the main communicators of the purpose and benefits of the merger to the customers. This requires that they be properly briefed on these matters adequately, clearly, and as soon as possible after the deal. Whether sales forces should be integrated or not depends on the strategic and value creation logic of the merger. Integration that ensures customer retention is imperative to the revenue growth that is often touted as one of the strategic drivers of a merger[50].

The interface between the two firms has to be managed carefully, and an interface management team may be set up. This team, made up of a senior manager of the acquirer, the head of the acquired firm and some support staff, must identify what capabilities can and need to be transferred, and in which direction.

Often the morale of managers in the acquired firm may be low, without a sense of direction or purpose. The interface managers have the important function of restoring the confidence of these managers by instilling a new and vigorous sense of the purpose that underlies the acquisition. They also need to restore an external, market focus so that the competitors are put on notice that the acquired firm is back in business. Effective integration of the sales forces, if ordained by the strategic interdependence of the merging firms, is a vital instrument in achieving such focus.

The third stage of the integration process involves the actual capability transfer. The mode of transfer and the length of the transfer process depend upon the type of integration – preservation, symbiosis or absorption. Each integration mode is characterized by specific tasks, which lie at the heart of the process.

Project management approach to integration

Post-merger integration involves integration of systems, processes and activities at different levels of the organization. Such integration therefore needs to be coordinated so that effective overall integration is achieved[51]. Integration of some subsystems, e.g. information system capabilities (see Exhibit 22.9 above), may often take longer than that of others, e.g. purchase functions or operations. A project management approach is therefore needed to effect integration.

A project management approach involves:

- setting up clear goals;
- proclaiming an inspiring theme for change and what it means, and repetitive invocation of the theme to win 'buy-in' from the merging firms' managers and staff;
- definition of 'where and what we will be' at the end of the project;
- a coordination body to oversee the transition and accept overall responsibility;
- a leader or leaders drawn from both merging firms, who have the experience and expertise in integration and the authority – often integration team leaders in major acquisitions may be at the board or other senior level;
- formation of task forces to plan the project activities, and teams to carry these out;
- proper delineation of lines of authority, reporting, accountability between the coordination body, the task forces and activity teams;
- proper resourcing of the project management bodies, task forces and teams in terms of people with relevant background, experience, commitment to change, and drawn from both merging firms;
- mechanism for feedback and mid-course correction;
- setting up milestones and realistic timescales for achieving them; and
- rewards for achieving milestones, and punishment for project slippage.

Importance of leadership

As noted above, the integration project leader must have the expertise and authority. Effective integration leaders are also likely to be 'strong general managers who have excellent decision-making instincts and are comfortable working cross-functionally. They will also be courageous, politically astute and capable of influencing corporate opinion'[52]. They must command the respect of both the top management and the integration teams. They must have cultural sensitivity.

In addition, integration leaders must be those who can connect to the individuals and teams in the organizations, whom people trust as a good leader, must be an architect of those conditions that encourage members to identify with and become part of the merged entity, inspire and support members through resources, training and emotional support so that members raise their game[53]. To win buy-in from the employees and managers of the acquired firm the integration process must be transparent, fair and credible in terms of actions, and not just rhetoric. The integration leader, and the process he or she leads, must inspire trust in the midst of uncertainty, fear and anxiety.

Building trust between the acquirer and target managers and employees depends on a range of factors. From the target members' point of view, these include the characteristics of the takeover situation[54]: takeover friendliness, power equality between the firms, prior target performance, cultural similarity and prior positive interaction history between the firms, their managers and employees. The characteristics of the acquisition process also influence the creation and maintenance of trust: how much autonomy is retained by the target firm, the integration speed, cultural tolerance and sensitivity, job security and reward enhancement and communication quality.

From the acquirer's point of view, target firm members' behaviour and attitude contribute to trust-building:

- organizational commitment, willingness to take risks, acceptance of change, willingness to subordinate personal goals to organizational goals;
- job performance, communication quality and level of cooperation.

It is clear that trust building is a dynamic and two-way process, although the acquirer has the greater onus of initiating the process of trust building. For example, an acquirer displaying a 'conquerer syndrome' is almost certain to kill any trust even before it begins. 'Building trust is difficult. Rebuilding it is even more difficult[55].'

Importance of high-visibility symbols and celebrating milestones

Post-merger integration is generally a long, drawn-out process. To maintain the momentum of change and preserve the commitment of the people involved, the transition authority needs to display high-visibility symbols of change, and celebrate 'wins' to convince the firms of the progress towards the merger goals. Clear and frequent communications about the progress being made are necessary to maintain the momentum and avoid 'integration fatigue'. It is also important that top management's commitment and enthusiasm for the integration process are visible and inspiring.

Is there need for speed? Internal and external influences

There are opposing views of the need for speedy implementation of the integration programme. While speed may terminate the uncertainty associated with the process, this by itself need not be a virtue. The advantage of speed depends on prior planning, the quality of the pre-acquisition due diligence, the nature of the acquisition and its complexity, and the need for mutual learning between companies about their resources and capabilities and how they can be leveraged. Integration of processes and procedures may not take as long as integration of softer intangibles. Functional integration may be done more quickly than integration of R & D, if the target's R & D is to be preserved. Cultural integration or new culture evolution, i.e. integration of mindsets, takes longer than integration of systems and processes. Jürgen Shrempp, the CEO of Daimler-Benz, who led the merger with Chrysler, remarked after the merger integration, 'It'll take ten years to integrate people's minds'[56]. But Chrysler was divested in less than 10 years, as the acquisition turned out to be a massive failure!

Among the external factors are the imperative of customer retention (see discussion above) and the strategic focus of the acquisition, i.e. whether the acquisition is driven by market deepening, market extension or diversification. For example, market deepening in the form of a horizontal merger may require speedy integration. Investor pressure may force companies to short-circuit the integration process, with serious and adverse long-term consequences for the firm and its investors and other stakeholders. It is therefore important to *manage investor expectations* and shape them to accommodate the imperatives of a well-thought-out integration process. This challenge can be met only when the acquirer communicates clearly to the external stakeholders the logic of the acquisition, its challenges, its approach to integration, and a realistic timescale for delivering the value creation objectives of the acquisition. As in the case of internal communication within and between merging firms, this external communication must also be credible and transparent. 'Walking the talk' is important to inspire trust. The talk must be sober and not extravagant in its promises, either in magnitude or in timing. Top managers' psychological biases such as hubris and overconfidence, discussed in Chapter 12, often drive them to extravagance and hyperbole[57].

Thus the value of speed depends on the internal interactions between the merging firms and the external interactions between the firms, their markets, customers, investors and other stakeholders. There is no one speed that fits all. Not surprisingly, empirical evidence on the merit of speed is inconclusive[58].

What do managers think about acquisition integration and performance? Survey evidence

In Chapter 4 we reviewed the empirical evidence on the success of acquisitions from different stakeholder perspectives. The picture that emerges from that review is somewhat mixed in terms of profit performance of acquirers and the returns to shareholders of those companies. Whereas, on average, mergers do not seem to deliver the promised land, this average picture masks a substantial minority of successful performers. The interesting questions are, therefore, what factors contribute to success, and what factors cause failure?

We now seek to provide some answers to these questions. The answers are based both on survey evidence of managers' own assessment of success or failure and on their identification of critical success factors. While one can glean a list of these critical success factors from different acquisition experiences of companies, such a list has no universal validity, since each acquisition may have its own idiosyncratic characteristics.

Survey evidence on acquisition performance

From time to time, surveys of corporate managers have been carried out to elicit their assessment of the acquisitions they have undertaken in the recent past, and of the factors contributing to their success or failure. A survey has one advantage over the statistical methodology presented in Chapter 4, in that the acquisition decision-makers are asked to make their own assessments of their decisions. Moreover, they are also asked to provide the reasons for their decisions, and for the outcomes. These can only be inferred from a statistical study.

However, a survey is also more subjective, and often based on small samples. It is in the nature of a confessional, and often done some time after the event. It is by no means a 'fly on the wall' account, and depends on the quality of recapitulation that the respondents are capable of. Subject to these limitations, a survey provides some useful insights into

Table 22.3 Causes of acquisition failure and success: Coopers & Lybrand study

Cause of failure	Cause of success
Target management attitudes and cultural difference (85%)	Detailed post-acquisition integration plans and speed of implementation (76%)
No post-acquisition integration planning (80%)	Clarity of acquisition purpose (76%)
Lack of knowledge of industry or target (45%)	Good cultural fit (59%)
Poor management of target (45%)	High degree of target management cooperation (47%)
No prior acquisition experience (30%)	Knowledge of target and its industry (41%)

The numbers in parentheses represent the percentage of interviewees who cited this cause.
Source: *Making a Success of Acquisitions* (Coopers & Lybrand 1993)

managerial decision-making. Coopers & Lybrand, the accounting and consulting firm, now part of PricewaterhouseCoopers (PwC), carried out a study in 1992 of the acquisition experience of UK companies[59]. In-depth interviews with senior executives of the UK's top 100 companies, covering 50 deals worth over £13bn, formed the basis of analysis. The study covers large acquisitions with a minimum value of £100m by some of the largest companies in the UK during the recession years of the late 1980s and the early 1990s. Some 54% of the acquisitions were regarded as failures by the interviewed executives. This level of perceived failures is consistent with the 49% and 48–56% failure rates reported in earlier surveys in 1973 and 1988 by *Business International*. Coopers & Lybrand also investigated the causes of failure and success of acquisitions, and the executives' responses are shown in Table 22.3.

Cultural difference reflected the way that the decisions were made in the acquirer and target companies (see above on organizational culture). Some respondents felt that the target managements lacked self-motivation and entrepreneurial instincts. Such managements were also accustomed to a hierarchical decision-making structure, or one in which decisions were made by committees. Hostile bids were thought to have hindered a good cultural fit between the acquired and the acquirer.

Lack of knowledge of the target and its industry was blamed on a poor pre-acquisition audit (see Chapter 23 on organizational learning). The warranties received by the acquirer did not in some cases cover the problems found. Lack of adequate pre-acquisition planning led to loss of valuable time in integration. Where such planning had been done, the actual synergies exceeded what were anticipated.

Survey evidence on acquisitions and the human factor

Mergers and acquisitions are often change events that presage a massive dislocation in the professional and private lives of managers and other staff of the companies, especially those of the acquired company. Both the uncertainty associated with the event and the actual changes it brings about can cause fear, anxiety and stress. Cartwright and Cooper found that potential sources of merger stress included loss of identity and job security, and changes in personnel and work practices, resulting in cultural incongruence[60].

The extent of these merger-related negative feelings and their impact on the merger outcome depend on two factors:

- the degree of culture fit that exists between combining organizations, given the 'terms of marriage' (see Table 22.3) – that is, whether merger presupposes cultural integration or displacement or preservation of cultural autonomy; and
- the impact of the event on the individual – that is, the degree and scale of stress generated by the merger process and its duration. The long-term stress may have an adverse impact on the physical health, psychological well-being and performance behaviour of the individual.

These two factors are also interrelated, since cultural incompatibility may result in considerable fragmentation, uncertainty and cultural ambiguity, and consequently stress[61].

Cartwright and Cooper carried out a questionnaire-based survey of the middle managers of two UK building societies being merged, one much smaller than the other[62]. The survey aimed to assess the degree of cultural incompatibility between the two societies, and the extent to which the organizational commitment, job satisfaction, and physical and psychological health of those involved were affected by the merger. The questions related to organizational culture, organizational commitment, job satisfaction, potential stress sources and mental health.

A total of 157 middle managers responded to the questionnaire, a response rate of 52%. The merging partners were regarded as culturally compatible and similar. They were also strategically well matched. Cultural integration was smooth. Nevertheless, the merger was stressful for both groups of managers, especially the smaller society's managers. Overall job satisfaction was maintained. An important lesson from this study is that cultural congruence is no guarantee that merging company staff will welcome the merger and become committed to its goals. The human factor still needs to be addressed with a great deal of care and sensitivity.

Faced with uncertainty, managers and workers may be prepared to jump ship. They may be lured away by the competitors. The integration programme must assuage staff anxieties, but also develop a key personnel retention policy. Executives from an acquired firm are an intrinsic component of the acquired firm's resource base, and their retention is an important determinant of post-acquisition performance. There are strong economic motives for initiating acquisitions, but there are also strong social processes at work that may seriously affect the outcomes[63].

Human resources perspective on post-merger integration

A Conference Board survey of 134 senior executives in human resource management in the US support many of the conclusions of the above UK surveys[64]. Over 67% of these executives rated merger integration programmes in their companies successful or highly successful. However, in terms of stock market performance one year after merger, only 53% of the companies with successful merger integration performed better than their competitors. In companies with less successful programmes only 30% outperformed their competitors, and 46% performed worse. Thus even when merger integration is internally perceived to be successful, the outsider perceptions may not fully reflect that success.

The survey identifies the following factors as contributing to success:

- prior M & A experience;
- major involvement of the top management, e.g. CEO, president or chairman;
- a formalized integration plan, process or procedure for the merger – the earlier the planning the better;
- integration teams with both buyer and seller firm representatives;
- a commitment to measure success of integration programme; and
- not letting discord fester and delaying remedial action.

The survey found substantial differences between the buyer and seller companies. For example, 87% of the HR executives reported differences in leadership style and CEO personality between the merging firms. In a range of 31 characteristics covering leadership, culture, organization and personnel practices, on most issues the firms were found to be different. However, initial differences did not inhibit their resolution or negate integration success, provided the integration programme was sensitized to these, and included steps to resolve the differences.

Some of the unexpected findings of the survey are instructive[65]:

- Merger of equals is more of a myth than reality.
- Downsizing is not a barrier to successful integration.

The survey flags up a few warning signs:

- There was 'disconnect' between the rhetoric of employees being the most important assets and lack of open and prompt communications with the workers and their involvement in the merger process.
- Communication campaigns lacked prominence.
- Leadership differences, ego, power, turfmanship and control problems and culture change efforts were areas of concern.
- In some cases a culture of fairness was lacking in the distribution of jobs and positions.
- The due diligence process was not deep enough to find out who were the key to operations, or sales relationships, or had critical knowledge or trade union relations.

Critical success factors

Hunt *et al.* identified the factors that contribute, in the opinions of the acquiring and acquired company managers, to success or failure of the acquisition[66]. They divided these factors into context and buyer behaviour factors. The importance of the context factors, as perceived by the participating managers, is indicated in Table 22.4. A further analysis of the behaviour factors identified as making varying contributions to the success of an acquisition is shown in Table 22.5.

Prior acquisition experience is not absolutely critical. This assessment echoes the Coopers & Lybrand conclusion that only 30% of managers regard it as contributing to acquisition failure (see Table 22.3)[67]. This is not altogether surprising, since some of the spectacular company failures of the 1980s and the 1990s were active acquirers (see Chapter 4). It is the quality of experience that matters, not a high tally of repeated follies. Indeed, a rapid-fire

Table 22.4 Contextual determinants of acquisition success

Contextual factor	Critical	Helpful	Neutral
Pre-acquisition audit	Yes		
Whether target is healthy	Yes		
Prior acquisition experience		Yes	
Relatively small target		Yes	
Friendly not hostile acquisition		Yes	
Clear implementation plan			Yes
Small target + acquisition experience			Yes

Table 22.5 Buyer behaviour determinants of acquisition success

Factors associated with successful acquisitions	(%)	Factors associated with unsuccessful acquisitions	(%)
Honourable rhetoric	59	Assurances broken	39
Clear vision communicated	68	No clear vision	67
Buyer management earns credibility and respect	55	Buyer management fails to impress	72
Perceived business benefit to acquirer	64	No perceived business benefit to acquirer	44
Interface well regulated	77	Lax interface	58
Changes with people focus	59	Changes confined to business	61
Incentives and benefits to target staff improved	68	Incentives and benefits to target staff reduced	67

The numbers are the percentages of successful or unsuccessful acquisitions where the factor contributed to the outcome.

acquisition strategy prevents consolidation and learning from previous acquisitions (see Chapter 23).

The size of the target and the tone of the acquisition (i.e. hostile or friendly) are quite relevant. A small target may enable the acquirer to be generous to the target company managers and staff, but it could also engender condescension and insensitivity. An acquirer may also pay less heed to the value creation logic because it can afford to, in small acquisitions. In hostile acquisitions the target top management may be the first casualties of battle, but a sensible acquirer can win the loyalty of the remaining staff with new incentive structures and a more promising future for the acquired company.

The lack of a clear implementation plan has little influence on the outcome. Determinism, the belief that a pre-acquisition plan is right whatever the realities in the target company, is often inimical to good integration. Open-mindedness and willingness to learn, on the other hand, promote good integration. Perhaps the lack of a clear plan facilitates such learning for many successful acquirers.

The two critical factors – pre-acquisition audit and the health of the target company – are interrelated. An indifferent quality of such audit is probably due to the escalating momentum of the acquisition decision process. Neglect of the human audit also appears to contribute to failure. An interesting result of the survey is that many factors hitherto considered critical to successful acquisitions, such as pre-acquisition planning, are indeed not so. One possible reason for this is that the acquirer's weaknesses in some contextual factors can be made up by its behaviour during the negotiation and integration stages.

The behaviour factors are largely self-explanatory, and consistent with the caveats derived from the Haspeslagh and Jemison model. Honesty, sensitivity, competence and willingness to share with the target staff the benefits of the acquisition are the important contributors to success. Truth should not become the first casualty of an acquisition. The need for competent management of the interface is also highlighted by the survey (see Exhibit 22.10 for an illustration).

In a survey of 250 managers involved in acquisition integration, Bain & Co identified the factors contributing to integration success. The respondents rated early tackling of cultural issues the most important (percentage of respondents rating 83%). Other highly important factors are:

- a 'best of both' policy in choosing people for jobs in merged entity (81%);
- value focus of the integration programme (80%);

Exhibit 22.10

Fine art of tech mergers

In late 2002 EMC was known only for one product – data storage disk drives. In 2003 Joseph Tucci, the CEO, announced that EMC had bought Documentum, a document management company, for $1.7bn and VMware, a pioneer in the software that manages computers. Analysts were wondering what these acquisitions had to do with storage! But by late 2006 EMC had completed 17 deals worth $4.7bn in an ambitious diversification drive. Software now made up 37% of the revenues, at $9.6bn. EMC had hit earnings targets for 13 quarters in a row. It was at 20 in the *Business Week* 50 list of top performers. An analyst said about the performance of the company, 'Investors point to tech acquisitions and say it's unclear if they really work. EMC has been fairly unique in being able to do them successfully.'

To refocus EMC as a company that managed information rather than just store it, Tucci followed a 'string-of-pearls' approach as opposed to game-changing acquisitions. Most of EMC's acquisitions were also small niche leaders for under $100m. Tucci was also after talent. Fifteen of the 17 CEOs of its target companies stayed with EMC.

In 2003 Tucci chose Joseph Walton, then head of EMC's services unit, as the 'integration czar' and gave him a warning: 'Don't mess it up. I am going to spend a lot of money, and I don't want you to crush their DNA.' Walton came up with a process that was part art, part science. The science was the easier. Walton set up an integration team that, after doing a couple of deals, created a playbook of processes for the preclose period, the day of closing and the 100 days thereafter. It laid out procedures for transition in leadership, business processes, computer systems, and sales. The team used Six Sigma techniques to constantly improve the process, and tracked the acquisition performance for six quarters to ensure it made steady progress.

The art was in keeping people happy and engaged. Immediately after a deal, Walton's team and the leaders of the acquired company customized an integration plan. After several months the target was joined with other acquisitions to create new business units. To help the former CEOs, an executive mentor was assigned to each. Walton also conducted cultural awareness sessions with the acquired company employees. The former CEOs were also encouraged to pursue growth opportunities by combining EMC's various business units.

Despite the impressive acquisition track record, investors were rather lukewarm towards EMC stock.

Source: Adapted from S. Hamm, 'The fine art of tech mergers', *Business Week*, 10 July 2006

- extensive communication by leaders (74%);
- establishing clear performance criteria and tracking them (70%);
- pre-deal planning and ensuring integration plan is aligned to strategy (65%).

Speed of integration is not recognised as critical (42%), perhaps for the reasons discussed above.[68]

Spanish conquistador arrives in England:
Santander the new Armada?

In July 2004, the Spanish banking group, Grupo Santander, one of the largest banks in the world, announced a takeover bid for the UK personal financial services company, Abbey National (ANL). The bid valued Abbey at £8.5bn. Santander offered one of its shares and 31p as consideration for each Abbey share. It was a friendly deal that closed on 12 November when Abbey was de-listed and became part of the Santander group. Although the friendly nature of the deal allowed Santander to carry out some due diligence during the negotiation and deal closing phases and plan for the post-acquisition integration, with the deal closure the time for implementing the integration plan had come.

The background to the acquisition

Grupo Santander

Grupo Santander was a leading commercial bank with an extensive retail banking network in Spain and in South America. It was a family business that had grown very fast through a series of acquisitions to become the 11th largest bank in the world by market capitalization of €45bn at the end of 2003. It had the goal of becoming one of the largest ten banks in the world.

Abbey National

Abbey was a mutual building society specializing in home mortgages and personal banking and savings products before being de-mutualised and turned into a privatized company in 1989 with a listing on the London Stock Exchange.

Abbey had expanded from core mortgage to non-core businesses in order to diversify its revenue and profit streams. It operated Abbey National Treasury Services (ANTS), a wholesale banking business, and Abbey National Life (ANL) life assurance business. ANTS lent money to corporates and invested in corporate debt. These diversification moves were received well by shareholders and investors and its share price reached 440 pence in March 1995 compared to 154 pence at conversion into a company. Its diversification goals became more ambitious and it set a target of 40% contribution to profits by its non-core businesses. In February 1998, after the announcement of its 1997 profits of £1.3bn, Abbey's share price reached 1220 pence and in April 1999 it peaked at 1435 pence.

In the meanwhile, Abbey's share of new UK mortgage lending had been declining, from 16% in 1989 to under 9% in 2004. Its diversification strategy was taking a toll on its bread-and-butter mortgage business. Its declining mortgage market share was causing concern among analysts. A merger seemed a way out of its problems. In October 2000, Abbey's attempt at a merger with Bank of Scotland was rebuffed. It then rejected an offer from Lloyds TSB, Abbey's giant UK rival for £18.6bn.

The bank's share price was 317p in March 2001. The main contributor to this decline was ANTS which had burned its fingers by lending to companies like Enron which, after revelations of fraud by its high level executives including the chairman, CEO and CFO, and their subsequent conviction, filed for bankruptcy. ANTS had lent £115m to Enron and held £1.3bn in junk bonds by September 2001. In June 2002 the rating agency

→

Standard & Poor's reflected the serious deterioration in the financial profile of Abbey by downgrading its debt from AA to AA– (see Chapter 16 on junk or high yield debt and credit rating).

The Abbey clean-up and takeover bid

Ian Harley, the CEO, resigned in July 2002 and was replaced in October by Luqman Arnold, a former President of the Swiss giant UBS. Prior to his appointment, Abbey was the subject of feverish takeover speculation. The new CEO announced a new strategic direction – back to the core. It would focus on Personal Financial Services (PFS) rather than on being a diversified group. This meant divestiture of non-core businesses at fire-sale prices and huge write-off of losses. In February 2004, Abbey's 2003 results showed losses ten times larger than analysts had expected. Its credit rating fell further to A+ and the share price fell 12% on a single day. ANL was still suffering from lack of liquidity and required fresh capital injection of £373m. By July 2004, the finances of the Abbey were becoming more stable and it was becoming more of a takeover target. On 26 July 2004 the Abbey board announced its recommendation for Santander's cash and shares bid valuing Abbey at £8.5bn, £10bn less than the offer from Lloyds TSB, Abbey's big UK rival three years earlier. Santander's bid was approved by both companies' shareholders in October 2004.

So what was in store for this Spanish *conquistador*? Santander seemed to be leading a new Spanish Armada to the shores of England, this time with greater success. For a bank seeking to become a global force in retail banking, the capture of Abbey was an important prize. But this prize came with lots of problems – among them the turnaround of Abbey before it could become a valuable part of Santander.

Santander's strategy for Abbey

Santander had prepared well for its bid called Operation Jack. It had transferred a team of over 40 people to the UK to win acceptance for the bid among analysts, media, trade unions and the regulator, the Financial Services Authority (FSA). This team was also responsible for the due diligence of Abbey and post-acquisition planning, which would allow Santander to carry out post-acquisition integration quickly.

At deal closure, Abbey represented 34% of the combining group's assets and 40% of its loan book. However, Abbey's profits of £273m accounted for only 8% of Santander's group profits. This disproportionately low share of Abbey in the Grupo profits was at once a challenge and an opportunity.

Santander's global strategy for managing a multinational portfolio of retail banks was 'multi-local'. Each bank operated as a separate division as opposed to the bank operating as a single integrated global bank, e.g. HSBC. The acquired banks would operate under the Santander brand but brand transitioning was not done immediately. Abbey's brand was retained for several years until 2009 before being completely replaced by the Santander brand. The centre provided certain functions, e.g. audit and risk management, but the national retail banks were managed by local teams with their deep knowledge of the local market, their local brand strength and knowledge of how local business opportunities could be exploited. For Santander the challenge was to *turnaround-stabilise-and-grow* Abbey.

Due diligence, SWOT analyses and defining the challenges

In preparation for its acquisition, the Santander team had carried out significant due diligence involving many senior managers of Abbey and their counterparts in Santander to discuss areas of responsibility and areas of serious concern, e.g. the Life division of Abbey. Santander, therefore, brought a good knowledge of Abbey's organizational and management structure to the integration process. Some SWOT analysis of the Abbey's strengths and weaknesses had been done. Santander recognised that Abbey had had a traumatic experience as a bank and had folded back into a PFS provider. Santander's strategy was to re-convert Abbey into a bank and this required that Abbey managers and staff needed to change their outlook and culture to make this reinvention possible.

The integration plan and its implementation

Santander appointed Francisco Gómez-Roldán (GR), the CFO of Santander since 2002, as the new CEO of Abbey. The chairman of Santander, Emilio Botín described GR as 'an expert in banking. He carried out the restructuring of Banesto and Argentinia. He's what you call a crack player'. Botín also laid out Santander's target for Abbey's growth: 'we're going to put this franchise back to where it was. It had 12% (mortgage) market share. Now we are at 10% and we aspire to increase that with new products'.

The vision and mission

GR's first day message spelt out the vision: 'I want Abbey to be one of the most efficient and most profitable banks in the UK personal financial services market place . . . Shareholder value will be the driving force behind everything we do'.

His mission was to achieve this. He said: 'I know this to be achievable'. He added: 'It was vital to build a true performance culture' in Abbey by increasing 'individual accountability and responsibility and reward everyone for their results and achievements'. GR listed his main priorities:

- Firm up the transition plan for improvements to be made to Abbey's operations to both increase its revenues and cut costs;
- Enhance sales revenue through improving channel efficiency; although intermediaries, telephone and electronic channels were important, there would be renewed emphasis on the 'unique role' of the branch distribution network; branches would get closer to their customers to increase cross-sale of products such as insurance, unsecured personal loans and credit cards to help customers manage their finances better;
- Develop the small and medium enterprise (SME) market which in the UK was very attractive;
- Reduce costs – Abbey's cost to income ratio was around 60%, about 8% higher than the industry average; the aim was to get this down to low 40s; the main tool for achieving such drastic cost reduction was the implementation of Santander's leading-edge core IT platform, Partenon in Abbey by 2007.

The cultural challenge was emphatically communicated by GR: 'Grupo Santander is a winning bank. Santander's culture is a winning culture. I want to see that positive culture start to permeate Abbey to make Abbey one of the leading players in the UK market'.

→

He acknowledged that this was going to be a 'challenging but exciting time for Abbey' but ended on an upbeat note: 'I'm really looking forward to it with confidence and I hope you are too'.

Changes to management structure

GR quickly formed a new executive committee, Exco, that was made up of a number of Abbey executives but with four non-executive directors from Santander; some Abbey executives, e.g. the IT director were made redundant and a few others left after the takeover. Three business divisions and four support divisions were created.

Given the mission to increase market share, there was great emphasis on strengthening the customer-facing front office. The staff reductions and staff re-locations were carried out so as to strengthen the sales function and the message was that 'the front office was of paramount importance and that everyone else was at risk'. Otherwise, head count reduction proceeded apace with a target of removing approximately 3,000 jobs. Each department was given a target for head count costs.

Cost and revenue teams were set up with a brief to agree and present future integration plans. There was a great sense of haste. GR was a man in a hurry and speed was imperative to achieve Abbey's turnaround. As one executive put it, 'time spent debating was time not implementing'. Spending limits and tighter cost control focus were introduced. At the end of the first 100 days post-acquisition, Abbey's employees were well aware of the new austere regime. Internal communication emphasised costs, sales and profits more than under the previous management.

Abbey's logo was changed to include Santander's white flame against a bright red background. This made clear that Abbey had changed direction and become much stronger as it belonged to the global banking giant, Santander.

How well did Santander's acquisition perform?

In October 2005, Santander announced a more ambitious plan for Abbey expanding beyond the PFS focus prevailing at the time of the acquisition to take on the five largest UK banks in such areas as current accounts, consumer finance and lending to small and medium-sized enterprises. As a result Santander expected Abbey, which had been losing market share in recent years, to raise revenues by 5 to 10 per cent annually over the following three years. Santander said it would achieve the target for cost savings envisaged at acquisition even before it switched over the IT systems to Partenon. The savings would require further job losses, though, Santander executives said, redundancies would not be on the scale of the 4,000 staff cut since the merger. Santander reported a 52 per cent jump in pre-tax profit for the nine months to the end of September 2005.

In October 2006, Santander, by then Spain's largest bank, revealed a 28 per cent year-on-year rise in net attributable income at the nine-month stage, driven by buoyant lending and cost controls in its main markets. The bank said profits for the year to end to September were €4.95bn, slightly ahead of analysts' forecasts. Revenues were up 17 per cent at €16.9bn, reflecting 20 per cent growth in net interest income and a 17 per cent rise in net income from fees. Abbey contributed €743m to profits, up 31 per cent, as the pace of new lending picked up. Overall costs at the UK bank were reduced by 10% to 54.3% of revenues, to help drive a five-point reduction at the whole group to 47.6 per cent.

Santander's results confirmed a trend at Spanish banks that analysts had identified as among the most profitable in the world.

The Spanish conquest continues

Flushed with its success over the acquisition of Abbey, Santander went on to make further acquisitions in the UK retail banking – Alliance & Leicester (A&L) and Bradford & Bingley (B&B) in 2008 – and built up one of the largest branch networks in the UK with 1300 bank branches. In May 2009, Antonio Horta-Osorio, chief executive of Santander in the UK, said that public awareness of the Santander name had climbed to 80 per cent from 20 per cent in 2004, helped by Santander's sponsorship of the British Grand Prix and partnership with Formula One champion Lewis Hamilton. 'Customers feel comfortable with Santander and see it as a safe haven in the UK,' he said. He added that rebranding and the introduction of Santander's IT system Partenon into A&L and B&B would mean that by 2010 customers would be able to use any of Santander's 1300 branches. The move would kill off some of the UK's best known banking brands.

Discussion questions

1 What was the rationale for Santander's acquisition of Abbey National?

2 What was its strategy for making a success of the acquisition? What were the sources of value creation?

3 How did it carry out its due diligence and develop its integration plan?

4 Comment on the vision and mission of Santander for the acquisition.

5 How important was the culture issue and how did Santander address it?

6 Comment on the communication approach of Santander during integration.

7 Was the acquisition a success? What contributed to it?

Sources: S. Moeller, 'Santander is coming to town, The acquisition of Abbey National by Grupo Santander', Case study no 305-512-1, 2005 (available from the European Case Clearing House at www.ecch.com); From *Financial Times*: P. Larsen, 'Santander unveils plan for Abbey', 26 October 2005; P. Larsen, 'Bank deal points the way for Europe', 1 September 2006; M. Mulligan, 'Santander's revenues 17% up at €16.9bn', 27 October 2006; J. Croft, 'Santander to rebrand UK operations', 27 May 2009.

Overview and implications for practice

We have described in this chapter the organizational dynamics and human aspects of the post-acquisition integration process.

● The acquisition integration process may be undermined by a variety of pitfalls, thereby destroying the acquisition's value creation potential.

● Value potential in acquisition is realized or destroyed at the implementation stage.

● Integration approaches must be tailored to the target and the value creation logic, e.g. absorption or symbiosis. This determines the speed and extent of integration.

- There must be continuity between deal negotiators and those implementing it, so that the aims of the acquisition are preserved.
- Merger integration may be regarded as a change process, and needs to be managed, drawing upon the principles and practice of change management.
- Organizational change involves changes in the politics of the merging organizations as well as their culture.
- Changing the cultures of the merging firms may be necessary for the acquisition's strategic objectives. Strategy, organizational structure and organizational culture must be aligned during the integration process to deliver sustainable value creation.
- Integration may be managed as a project to integrate structures, cultures, systems, processes and procedures. Task forces, transition teams and project teams may be set up to manage integration of these.
- Any integration plan the acquirer has must be capable of being modified to accommodate ground realities when the process starts.
- The integration process is fraught with uncertainty, fear and anxiety among target company staff, which may lead to withdrawal of their commitment and lack of morale. The acquirer's implementation team must handle these concerns with tact, sympathy and understanding in order to instil confidence in and trust between the two companies' personnel.
- The acquirer must communicate its plans and expectations for the acquisition clearly, and at the earliest possible moment, so as to allay the anxieties of the target personnel.
- Transparency of the integration process and honesty in communication are critical to effective integration.

Review questions

22.1 What are the objectives of post-acquisition integration?

22.2 What is capability transfer? What are the different capabilities that may be transferred or shared in a merger?

22.3 What is strategic autonomy? Why is it important to the acquisition integration process?

22.4 What is the importance of organizational, political and cultural issues to integration?

22.5 What are the different types of organizational culture, and what is their relevance to the integration process?

22.6 Are national cultural differences as important as organizational cultural differences in cross-border acquisitions?

22.7 Is acquisition integration a change management programme? How?

22.8 What is the relevance of the project approach to post-merger integration?

22.9 What are the major problems in post-merger integration?

22.10 Fast integration or slow integration? Which is more appropriate? Under what conditions?

22.11 What do surveys say about the chances of acquisition success?

22.12 What do the surveys say about critical success and failure factors?

22.13 How important are the human factors to the success of integration? Why?

22.14 What is the relation between integration success and the prior stages of the acquisition process?

Further reading

K. Basu, 'Merging brands after mergers', *California Management Review*, **48**(4), 2006, 28–40.

S. Christofferson, R. McNish and D. Sias, 'Where do mergers go wrong,' *McKinsey Quarterly*, January 2005.

P. Puranam, H. Singh and M. Zollo, 'Organizing for innovation: Managing the coordination–autonomy dilemma in technology acquisitions', *Academy of Management Journal*, **49**(2), 2006, 263–280.

D. Schweiger and R. Lippert, 'Integration, the critical link in M & A value creation' in G. Stahl and R. Mendenhall (Eds), *Mergers and Acquisition: Managing Culture and Human Resources* (Stanford, CA: Stanford University Press, 2005).

P. Very, *The Management of Mergers and Acquisitions* (Chichester, UK: John Wiley, 2004).

S. Wall, 'Looking beyond the obvious in merger integration', *Mergers & Acquisitions*, March 2005.

Notes and references

1. B. de Wit and R. Meyer, *Strategy Synthesis: Resolving Strategy Paradoxes to Create Competitive Advantage* (London: Thomson Learning, 2005), pp. 76–78.
2. For more detailed definitions and examples, see de Wit and Meyer, *ibid*.
3. P. Haspeslagh and D. Jemison, *Managing Acquisitions* (New York: Free Press, 1991), pp. 139–140.
4. Haspeslagh and Jemison, *ibid*.
5. Schweiger and Lippert propose a broadly similar integration template consisting of: consolidation; standardization, i.e. transfer of best practice from one to the other firm; coordination, e.g. as a holding company; and intervention, e.g. to turn around the target firm or to prevent value destruction. See D. Schweiger and R. Lippert, 'Integration: The critical link in M & A value creation', in G. Stahl and M. Mendenhall (Eds), *Mergers and Acquisitions: Managing Culture and Human Resources* (hereafter Stahl and Mendenhall) (Stanford: Stanford University Press, 2005), Ch 2.
6. D. Schweiger, E. N. Csiszar and N. K. Napier, 'A strategic approach to implementing mergers and acquisitions', in G. Von Krogh, A. Sinatra and H. Singh (Eds), *The Management of Corporate Acquisitions* (New York: Macmillan, 1994), pp. 23–49.
7. See Stahl and Mendenhall, *ibid*., p. xvi.
8. S. Cartwright and C. L. Cooper, *Mergers and Acquisitions: The Human Factor* (London: Butterworth-Heinemann, 1992), Chapter 5.
9. C. Handy, *Understanding Organisations* (London: Penguin, 1993), Chapter 7.
10. S. Cartwright and C. L. Cooper, 'The psychological impact of merger and acquisition on the individual: A study of building society mergers', *Human Relations*, **46**(3), 1993, 327–347.
11. D. Carey, 'Lessons from master acquirers: A CEO roundtable on making mergers succeed', *Harvard Business Review*, May/June 2000, 153.
12. A. L. Sales and P. H. Mirvis, 'When cultures collide: Issues in acquisition', in J. R. Kimberly and R. E. Quinn (Eds), *Managing Organisational Transitions* (Homewood, IL: Irwin, 1984), pp. 107–133.
13. See D. M. Schweiger and P. K. Goulet, 'Integrating mergers and acquisitions: An international research review', pp. 61–91, in C. Cooper and A. Gregory (Eds), *Advances in Mergers and Acquisitions* (New York: Elsevier Science, 2000) for a review of these studies.
14. Cartwright and Cooper, *ibid*., 1992.
15. K. David and H. Singh, 'Sources of acquisition culture risk', in G. Von Krogh, A. Sinatra and H. Singh (Eds), *The Management of Corporate Acquisitions* (New York: Macmillan, 1994), pp. 251–292.
16. See S. Kleppestø, 'The Construction of Social Identities in Mergers and Acquisitions', in Stahl and Mendenhall, *ibid*., Chapter 6.
17. See B. Ekelund and A. Aske, 'Executive Commentary on Chapter 6', commenting on Kleppestø's paper in the same volume.
18. See P. Very, *The Management of Mergers and Acquisitions* (Chichester: John Wiley, 2004), p. 110.
19. See Schweiger and Goulet, *ibid*., for a review of these studies (See also Chapter 9.)
20. S. Ghoshal and P. Haspeslagh, 'Electrolux: The acquisition and integration of Zanussi', in J. Henry and A. Eccles (Eds), *European Cases in Strategic Management* (London: Chapman & Hall, 1993).
21. R. Schoenberg, 'The influence of cultural compatibility within cross-border acquisitions: A review', in C. Cooper and A. Gregory (Eds), *Advances in Mergers and Acquisitions* (New York: Elsevier Science, 2000), pp. 43–60.
22. See P. Very, *ibid*., p. 113, on the psychic paradox. See C. Ghosn, 'Introductory comments', in Stahl and Mendenhall, *ibid*., p. xvi.

23. A. Nahavandi and A. Malekzadeh, 'Acculturation in mergers and acquisitions', *Academy of Management Review*, 13, 1988, 79–90.

24. See R. Bruner, 'The merger of Hewlett-Packard and Compaq: Deal design', University of Virginia case study UVA-F-1451, 2004, Exhibit 6.

25. T. A. Daniel, 'Between trapezes: The human side of making mergers and acquisitions work', *Compensation and Benefits Management*, **15**(1), 1999, 19–37.

26. E. Abrahamson, *Change Without Pain: How Managers Can Overcome Initiative Overload, Organizational Chaos and Employee Burnout* (Harvard, MA: Harvard University Press, 2004).

27. M. Tushman and C. O'Reilly III, 'Ambidextrous organizations: Managing evolutionary and revolutionary change', *California Management Review*, **38**(4), 1996, 8–30.

28. Daniel, *ibid.*, suggests these figures.

29. A. H. Reilly, J. M. Brett and L. K. Stroh, 'The impact of corporate turbulence on managers' attitudes', *Strategic Management Journal*, **14**, Special Issue, 1993, 167–179.

30. T. J. Galpin and D. E. Robinson, 'Merger integration: The ultimate change management challenge', *Mergers and Acquisitions*, **13**(4), 1997, 24–28. See also S. W. Bridges, *Managing Transitions: Making the Most of Change* (Reading, MA: Addison-Wesley, 1991).

31. See J. Ford, L. Ford and A. D'Amelio, 'Resistance to change: The rest of the story', *Academy of Management Review*, **33**(2), 2008, 362–377.

32. P. Strebel, 'Why do employees resist change?', *Harvard Business Review*, May/June 1996.

33. See S. Wall, 'Looking beyond the obvious in merger integration', *Mergers & Acquisitions*, March 2005, 41–45.

34. On the detrimental impact of TMT see M. Zollo and H. Singh, 'Deliberate learning in corporate acquisitions: Post-acquisition strategies and integration capability in US bank mergers', *Strategic Management Journal*, **25**, 2004, 1233–1256.

35. D. Waller, *Wheels on Fire: The Amazing Story of the DaimlerChrysler Merger* (London: Coronet Books, 2001), p. 254.

36. D. Datta, 'Organizational fit and acquisition performance: Effects of post-acquisition integration', *Strategic Management Journal*, **12**, 1991, 281–297.

37. Bauman, Jackson and Lawrence, *ibid.*, p. 97.

38. Alan Frost, with many years of experience of merger integration, suggested to me the importance of creating the 'thinking environment', and drew my attention to N. Kline, *Time to Think* (London: Ward Lock, 1999).

39. Haspeslagh and Jemison, *ibid.*, Chapter 7.

40. The relevant studies are: J. C. Prabhu, R. K. Chandy and M. E. Ellis, 'The impact of acquisitions on innovation: Poison pill, placebo or tonic?', *Journal of Marketing*, **69**, 2005, 114–130 (see footnote 15 in Chapter 4); M. Subramaniam and M. A. Youndt, 'The influence of intellectual capital on the types of innovative capabilities', *Academy of Management Journal*, **48**(3), 2005, 450–463 (see footnote 36 in Chapter 5). These authors use a questionnaire-based survey of CEOs/presidents and VPs of HR, marketing and R&D to gather data on both IC types and innovation capabilities. R. Kapoor and K. Lim, 'The impact of innovations on the productivity of inventors at semiconductor firms: A synthesis of knowledge-based and incentive-based perspectives', *Academy of Management Journal*, **50**(5), 2007, 1133–1155 (see footnote 37 of Chapter 5). These authors use patent filing frequency as a measure of inventiveness.

41. P. Puranam, H. Singh and M. Zollo, 'Organizing for innovation: Managing the coordination-autonomy dilemma in technology acquisitions', *Academy of Management Journal*, **49**(2), 2006, 263–280. See footnote 37 of Chapter 5.

42. R. Kapoor and K. Lim, 'The impact of innovations on the productivity of inventors at semiconductor firms: A synthesis of knowledge-based and incentive-based perspectives', *Academy of Management Journal*, **50**(5), 2007, 1133–1155.

43. M. Subramaniam and M. Youndt, *ibid.*

44. P. Puranam, H. Singh and M. Zollo, *ibid.*

45. R. Ettenson and J. Knowles, 'Merging the brands and branding the merger', *Sloan Management Review*, **47**(4), 2006, 39–49.

46. K. Basu, 'Merging brands after mergers', *California Management Review*, **48**(4), Summer 2006, 28–40.

47. M. Buck-Lew, C. E. Wardle and N. Pliskin, 'Accounting for information technology in corporate acquisitions', *Information and Management*, **22**(6), 1992, 363–369.

48. F. Giacomazzi, C. Panella, B. Pernici and M. Sansoni, 'Information systems integration in M & A: A normative model', *Information and Management*, **32**(6), 1997, 289–302.

49. Y. Weber and N. Pliskin, 'The effects of information systems integration and organisational culture on a firm's effectiveness', *Information and Management*, **30**, 1996, 81–90; S. S. Robins and A. C. Stylianou, 'Post-merger systems integration: The impact of IS capabilities', *Information and Management*, **36**(4), 1999, 205–212.

50. See M. Bekier and M. Shelton, 'Keeping your sales force after the merger', *The McKinsey Quarterly*, 4 January 2005, suggest a number of ways of ensuring sales forces integrate effectively.

51. A. Braganza and P. Janes, 'Unbundle processes to deliver acquisition value', *Management Quarterly*, **15**, April 2002, 18–24.

52. M. Shelton, 'Managing your integration manager', *The McKinsey Quarterly*, 4 January 2005.

53. On the leadership qualities that would make an effective integration leader, see S. Sitkin and A. Pablo, 'The neglected importance of leadership in mergers and acquisitions', in G. Stahl and M. Mendenhall (Eds), *Mergers and Acquisitions: Managing Culture and Human Resources* (Stanford, CA: Stanford University Press, 2005), pp. 208–224.

54. See G. Stahl and S. Sitkin, 'Trust and mergers and acquisitions', in Stahl and Mendenhall, *ibid.*, pp. 82–102.

55. H. Engeli, 'Executive Commentary on Chapter 4', in G. Stahl and M. Mendenhall (Eds), *Mergers and acquisitions, Managing culture and human resources* (Stanford, CA: Stanford University Press, 2005, 107).

56. Waller, *ibid.*, p. 260.

57. See S. Christofferson, R. McNish and D. Sias, 'Where mergers go wrong', *The McKinsey Quarterly*, 4 January 2005, on how acquirers overestimate synergies, especially revenue growth.

58. See Schweiger and Goulet, *ibid.* For a discussion of the contingent nature of speed see M. Cording, P. Christmann and D. King, 'Reducing causal ambiguity in acquisition integration: Intermediate goals as mediators of integration decisions and acquisition performance', *Academy of Management Journal*, **51**(4), 2008, 744–767. They argue that speedier integration facilitates internal reorganization goal achievement, and may reduce employee resistance. Homburgh and Bucerius develop and test a model of the interactive influence of internal relatedness and external relatedness, and find that speed is most beneficial when the merging firms are internally highly related and the external relatedness is low. See C. Homburgh and M. Bucerius, 'Is speed of integration really a success factor of mergers and acquisitions? An analysis of the role of internal and external relatedness', *Strategic Management Journal*, **27**, 2006, 347–367.

59. Coopers & Lybrand, *Making a Success of Acquisitions* (London: Coopers & Lybrand, 1993).

60. Cartwright and Cooper, *ibid.*, 1993.

61. *Ibid.*

62. *Ibid.*

63. A. A. Canella Jr and D. C. Hambrick, 'Effects of executive departures on the performance of acquired firms', *Strategic Management Journal*, **14**, Special Issue, 1993, 137–152.

64. The Conference Board, *Post-merger Integration: A Human Resources Perspective*, Research Report 1278-00-HR, 2000.

65. M. L. Marks and P. H. Mirvis provide some recent illustrations consistent with these findings in 'Making mergers and acquisitions work: Strategic and psychological preparation', *Academy of Management Executive*, **15**(2), 2001, 80–94.

66. J. Hunt, S. Lees, J. J. Grumbar and P. D. Vivian, *Acquisitions: The Human Factor*, London Business School Working Paper, 1987.

67. Coopers & Lybrand, *ibid.*, 1993.

68. Bain & Co. Survey; D. Harding and S. Rovit, *Mastering the Merger* (Boston, MA: Harvard Business School Press, 2004).

Post-acquisition audit and organizational learning

Objectives

At the end of this chapter, the reader should be able to understand:

- the importance of measuring acquisition performance that is directly related to the strategic objectives of the acquisition;
- the social context of learning, and how many psychological and behavioural factors may deter learning;
- the various performance metrics, and how they are related to the strategic value creation logic of the acquisition;
- the role of post-acquisition audit in ensuring that acquisitions deliver what they promise, and in generating lessons for the future;
- how organizational learning can improve the odds of success of future acquisitions;
- the conditions for effective organizational learning; and
- how organizational learning capabilities can be enhanced.

Introduction

We have so far covered the first four stages of the M & A process – strategy development, organizing for acquisitions, deal-making and post-acquisition integration. Important questions remain. How did the acquisition go? How assiduously do acquirers assess their acquisition performance? Do acquirers assess performance in terms of measures more directly affected by the strategic logic of their acquisitions than shareholder returns? In this chapter we review surveys of acquirers' assessment of their success in terms of these measures. Is there a systematic post-audit process that provides the basis for learning from successes and failures in acquisitions? We report on the extent of performance assessment among acquirers, again relying on survey evidence.

Another important question is about how previous acquisitions influenced the way the current acquisition has been prosecuted. Given the enormous takeover activity, and the consistent evidence that a large minority or even a majority of acquisitions fail to create value, it appears that acquirers have a great potential to learn from their experience, but generally fail to realize that potential[1].

Companies that have the right strategy of growth through acquisition and necessary organizational capabilities to manage their acquisitions efficiently and effectively can sustain their competitive advantage for longer and create value for their stakeholders. For acquisition-making to evolve into a firm's core competence, it must also possess robust organizational learning capabilities. Developing such learning capabilities is thus part of the M & A core competence-building effort by multiple or serial acquirers. It is, or ought to be, a part of their competitive strategy.

Organizational learning theories suggest that past experience can have both positive and negative feedback effects, and that there are certain conditions that facilitate optimal learning from the past. How organizational learning is applied to new acquisition depends on the ability of the firm to create the necessary organizational memory and also diffuse the learning throughout the organization. In addition to codifying learning and knowledge about past acquisitions there must be an active learning process that juxtaposes the past with the present. In this chapter we examine the performance measurement issues and the post-acquisition audit process. We examine the impact of learning on the current acquisition performance. We suggest ways of establishing and strengthening organizational learning capabilities in the acquisition context.

Do acquirers assess acquisition performance?

As noted in Chapter 2, M & A activity is a multi-trillion dollar activity in the US and Europe. This suggests that companies regard acquisitions and mergers as a means of achieving their competitive strategy goals, such as market leadership, cost leadership, or being the first mover with new products or markets. Given this critical role of acquisitions in corporate competitive strategies, we need to find out whether they deliver the promised land. Our review of post-acquisition performance, based on accounting, productivity and stock market measures of performance, points to a substantial number, or even the majority, of acquirers failing to create value for their shareholders.

This evidence points to the failure of many acquisitions to create the competitive advantages that they are designed to. This failure should be reflected in more fundamental measures than profits, cash flows or stock returns. Acquisitions may perform well against these benchmarks and yet may fail to deliver visible performance success, such as shareholder wealth enhancement.

In Chapter 13 (see Table 13.2) we referred to a survey by KPMG, the consulting firm, of 107 global corporations that were also active acquirers. It revealed that less than 45% had carried out a formal post-deal review, although many of these deals involved substantial investments[2]. Several of the respondents were active acquirers, yet they seemed to regard formal reviews as non-essential to the M & A process. These companies were not learning from past acquisitions in crafting their future acquisition strategies or pursuing specific acquisition targets. Another survey of US companies on performance measurement during merger and acquisition integration also showed that only 45% of respondent companies included performance tracking and reporting in their integration plan, while 42% did partially[3]. Only 44% measured integration success, while 33% measured only partly and 23% did not measure performance success at all.

These figures may partly explain the statistical results that more than half of the acquirers fail to generate value from acquisitions. They also suggest that in a majority of active acquirers there are no systems, processes or procedures to ensure organizational learning. It seems that each acquisition experience is lost in organizational amnesia, so that history repeats itself.

Recent survey evidence from Bain & Co. also highlights the fact that failure to create value arises from errors made at different stages of the M & A process. Percent of respondents rating this as contributing to failure[4]:

- poor strategic fit (45%) and overestimated synergies (66%) (Stage 1);
- lack of organizational checks and balances that could have taken on board 'doubts' (Stage 2) (36%) and poor due diligence capabilities (Stage 2) (50%);
- lack of discipline during the deal-making stage (Stage 3) (34%); and
- weak integration models (Stage 4) (61 to 67%).

This means that M & A audit and organizational learning should encompass all of the first four stages of the M & A process. Appropriate performance metrics and benchmarks should be developed for each of these stages as part of organizational learning.

What are the performance metrics?

Acquisitions must be judged against criteria derived from their own strategic and value creation drivers. The value drivers are:

- cost reduction;
- revenue growth; and
- the acquisition of new resources/capabilities to exercise exploratory real options (see Chapter 3 on merger perspectives and Chapter 14 on target valuation).

It is inappropriate to measure performance using the wrong criterion. Revenue growth may come from increased market share or through cross-selling of products enjoying scope economies. Acquisition of new products/technologies can create real options on future growth opportunities. The KPMG report referred to earlier lists the proportion of sample acquirers enjoying a range of revenue-enhancing benefits in varying degrees (see Table 13.2). It is interesting that fewer acquirers realize revenue enhancement benefits than cost reduction benefits, consistent with other evidence that revenue enhancement is more difficult to accomplish than cost reduction (see Chapter 5). Acquisition delivered new customers and new markets for less than half of the sampled firms. Only a third of these firms, or even fewer, achieved revenue growth from new marketing, product development and new distribution channels. While delivery of cost reduction benefits is on a wider scale than revenue benefits, it is derived mostly from head count reduction, buying and merchandising and supply chain efficiencies. In another survey almost 70% of the mergers failed to achieve revenue enhancement synergies, and one-quarter of the sample of 92 acquirers overestimated cost synergies by 25%. In another 15% of cases they overestimated by a smaller magnitude. A 25% overestimate could knock off as much as 5–10% of the target value of $2.5bn to the acquirer[5].

Performance measures for real options

Many acquisitions are driven by the search for new technology. While some of the target companies may have reached a stage of product development and marketing to generate revenue, others may be still at a start-up stage. These are acquisitions driven by the race for the future and not just by the race for the world (see Chapter 5). Performance criteria for such acquisitions need to reflect the trajectory of these acquisitions towards fulfilling these future strategic objectives. For example, in technology development the criteria may include targets for product schedule, product content, employee retention/turnover and product cost. These criteria, when met, are expected to lead to a successful market entry. For example, Texas Instruments, in its acquisition of new technology or a development team, used the product development time line as a primary performance measure. Specific goals and milestones were set and tracked, e.g. prototype by month M1 and development model by month M2[6].

In general, performance criteria need to be set up and their fulfilment within a timetable agreed by the integration team with the functional teams. Milestones are set up so that any project slip-up can be quickly noted and mid-term correction applied to the integration process in terms of extra resources or time. The criteria cover the critical elements of the integration programme, such as market share growth, customer and employee retention or IT systems integration. When the criteria for these critical activities are not met, the integration and the acquisition itself may not be fruitful (see Chapter 22 on post-merger integration).

Performance measurement for intellectual assets

As discussed in Chapter 22, intellectual assets increasingly represent a major source of value to companies, and hence are of great importance to acquirers. Under the resource-based view of acquisitions, mutual leveraging of the resources and capabilities of the acquirer and the target is necessary to gain competitive advantage that will pass the VRINS test (see Chapter 3 on this test). Acquirers must therefore devise appropriate performance metrics that will indicate whether the merger leads to enhanced resources and capabilities of the merged entity relative to those of the merging firms. Moreover, metrics to assess the creation of new R & C also need to be devised.

These resources and capabilities are increasingly not in the form of physical or financial assets but in the form of knowledge or intellectual assets, which also include intellectual property for which a legal claim is already registered, e.g. patents, trademarks. Whether intellectual property acquired in an acquisition is leveraged to create value has to be audited, for example whether patents are effectively exploited to gain competitive advantage. Other intellectual assets, e.g. reputation, customer loyalty, are much less amenable to valuation. Nevertheless, tracking the contribution they make to post-acquisition value creation is an important element of the post-acquisition audit[7].

Performance measurement in the presence of causal ambiguity

Causal ambiguity (see discussion in Chapter 3) makes the establishment of a cause-and-effect relation between resources and capabilities and performance outcomes difficult. There is a multitude of ways in which to combine and recombine resources and combinations, and the same combination might yield different results contingent upon other, often unmeasurable and latent, factors. This ambiguity arises because a completely specified model of the cause-and-effect relation may not be possible. This is particularly the case where intangible resources or capabilities, which are often tacit, reside in individuals, groups and their interactions. Moreover, the one-to-many and many-to-one relations between intra-firm causes and effects may also reduce the reliability of performance measurement. These are multiplied in the case of inter-firm leveraging of resources and capabilities (see Figure 3.9 and related discussion).

Given causal ambiguity, performance may be measured at intermediate stages, since ambiguity is much less between adjacent stages. Cording, Christmann and King propose this approach in their study of integration of horizontal acquisitions. Two intermediate goals, i.e. internal reorganization and market expansion, are identified as the links between four integration decisions and acquisition performance measured in terms of a three-year post-acquisition abnormal stock returns (see Chapter 4 on this methodology). These links are shown in Exhibit 23.1. In their empirical analysis the authors report that this approach provides a stronger explanation of the link between intermediate goal of market expansion and final goal of stock return performance.

Exhibit 23.1

Intermediate goals between integration decisions and acquisition performance

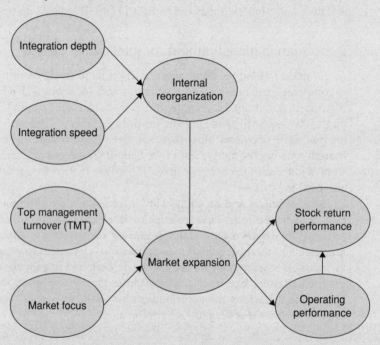

The intermediate stage is the reorganization of the acquirer and the acquired in preparation to achieve the intermediate goal of market expansion, i.e. revenue enhancement. It is then linked to operating performance, which in turn is linked to stock return performance. Stock return performance is also directly influenced by stock market perceptions based on, *inter alia*, non-operating performance measures, competitor reaction etc. Several other factors may influence the links at each stage, e.g. prior acquisition experience, relative size of the acquired firm, acquirer's and target's pre-merger performance, and any serial acquisition strategy of the acquirer.

Source: Adapted from M. Cording, P. Christmann and D. King, 'Reducing causal ambiguity in acquisition integration: Intermediate goals as mediators of integration decisions and acquisition performance', *Academy of Management Journal*, **51**(4), 2008, 744–767

Financial and non-financial performance measures

In addition to measures such as cost savings or revenue growth, or softer items such as customer retention, the impact of the acquisition on the financial performance indicators, such as return on capital employed of the business unit into which the acquired company is integrated, needs to be measured. Such accounting-based financial measures are still short of measures that reflect the acquisition's impact on shareholder value. Measures such as economic value added, i.e. excess profit generated by an activity after allowing for the cost of capital used to generate that profit, are only infrequently used, but offer potential for relating an acquisition to shareholder value[8] (see Chapter 14).

As shown in Exhibit 23.1, performance in achieving intermediate goals may also be measured as part of the integration process, as suggested in Chapter 22. It must, however, be remembered that a clear link between intermediate goal performance and the value creation performance needs to be established. Thus even when a cost reduction or market share target is reached, it is by no means certain that this will result in overall value creation in terms of shareholder return or economic value added. In a survey by KPMG, the consulting firm, of M & A teams around the world and how they measured performance, 67% of the M & A teams measured acquisition success in terms of EPS growth and 42% by IRR. Only 17% considered share price increase and 8% analysts' recommendations[9]. While EPS growth is an important indicator, whether it translates into shareholder value increase is not clear. IRR is a useful measure of value added, but needs to be benchmarked against the firm's cost of capital to determine whether the acquisition has resulted in shareholder value gains. The survey indicates that shareholder value gain is used as a direct performance metric in only a very small number of cases. Yet the vast majority of the surveyed M & A teams believed the M & A deals they had been involved in in the previous three years had created value.

Post-acquisition performance audit

Jeffrey Pfeffer notes that companies don't make the effort to learn from past mergers. He advises companies to 'do something unusual – go back and revisit past merger decisions, admit when they turned out badly, figure out why and learn so you and your colleagues don't keep making the same mistakes over and over'[10]. A robust post-acquisition audit can contribute to effective learning and successful acquisition programmes. The major elements of such an audit are as follows:

- acquisition-specific audit rather than as part of the normal internal audit;
- audit team well briefed on the strategic and value creation objectives, and on any predetermined time scale for accomplishing them;
- avoiding inadequate assessment of performance due to poor performance metrics or constrained time scale for delivery of performance;
- ensuring appropriate and different benchmarks for different types of acquisition made (see discussion above);
- performance benchmarks representing a balanced score card covering:
  - short-term and long-term objectives;
  - financial, business process and organizational learning objectives driving the acquisitions; and
- clear identification of reasons for success or failure.

As seen above, performance tracking of acquisition integration is not undertaken by a large number of acquirers. After completion of integration the responsibility for performance passes to the business unit making the acquisition or into which the acquired company is integrated. The important issues are whether, and for how long, the contribution of the acquired business to the acquirers' strategic and value creation objectives is tracked, and whether such a contribution is subject to separate audit as part of the long-term acquisition evaluation and organizational learning programme.

Internal audit departments, while carrying out their normal period audit, may be able to assess the acquisition's contribution. Nevertheless, it appears that no separate audit of the acquired business and its contribution is carried out in major US and European companies except as part of a routine audit of the parent business unit. In a survey of the role of internal audit in M & A in 22 major US and European companies carried out in 2000–01, Selim, Sudarsanam and Levine found only a minority of companies with post-acquisition audit tailored specifically to assess the acquired business contribution[11].

Several factors account for this lack of post-acquisition audit. With the integration of the acquired business the acquisition trail has gone cold. Separate information about the acquired business is no longer available. It is subsumed under the performance information about the acquiring business unit. In any case, since the acquiring business unit is now responsible for the acquired business, separate assessment of the acquired business may no longer be necessary. Plausible as these reasons are, the lack of a separate post-acquisition audit of the acquired business's contribution eliminates the opportunity for organizational learning.

Does acquisition experience enhance acquisition success?

With increasing frequency of acquisitions by firms, can they learn from their past deals? How important is the past as a guide to the future? Are frequent acquirers more successful in creating value from acquisitions than infrequent ones? Gregory, in a study of UK acquirers' post-acquisition performance measured by shareholder returns, found that experienced acquirers did generate significantly higher returns[12]. This result is consistent with acquirers learning from their past experience of deal-making. On the other hand, with US data of acquisitions from 1948–79, Lubatkin failed to find a significant link between acquisition experience and performance[13]. Other US-based studies similarly failed to find a positive relation between acquisition experience and acquisition performance[14]. In our review of serial acquisitions as part of an acquisition strategy in Chapter 13 we found that serial acquirers created value most from the earlier acquisitions in a series, but later acquisitions in a series experienced diminishing returns[15]. Sudarsanam and Huang, however, find that overall for the acquisitions in a series the three-year abnormal returns are positive, and such acquirers outperform relevant benchmarks[16]. These results seem to present a paradox. There are several plausible explanations:

- Serial acquirers do not learn from earlier acquisitions, thereby generating diminishing returns; they are either bad learners or there are obstacles to learning.
- Serial acquirers do learn how to make better acquisitions, but they also have to contend with increasingly fierce retaliation from the competitive forces, e.g. Porter's five forces, which fear the accrual of power of the serial acquirer.
- The stock market anticipates the whole serial acquisition programme, and capitalizes the value of that programme at the time of the first acquisition in the series, so that the abnormal returns are the highest at the start and diminish subsequently. This does not negate the value of learning, but takes into account the competitive force reaction.

Barkema and Schijven propose a model of effective integration of serial acquisitions through periodic reorganization of the acquirers[17]. Firms gain experience and expertise in integrating their acquisitions as they make repeat acquisitions. With their first acquisition firms seek to minimize the dislocation caused by integration, and hence seek organizational fit between the acquirer and the acquired by restructuring only the latter. They therefore fail to realize fully all the anticipated synergies. This amounts to a local optimum, and may be dictated by the limited experience of the acquirer and the acceptance of a 'satisficing' solution rather than a maximizing solution to the integration problem. This behaviour manifests 'bounded rationality'.

As the firm makes more acquisitions it gains more experience of integration, but may nevertheless continue to apply the old model of integration, thus diminishing the 'cognitive effort'. The acquirer makes incremental, rather than radical, changes. Initially, at least, an acquirer tends to disregard more radical possibilities for integration such as recombining both acquirer and acquired firm's subunits. This limited and localized search for integration solution to realize synergies is likely to result in underperformance of the acquirer since it is missing out on all the potential synergies that are possible and probably underpinned the acquisition and the premium paid. With more acquisitions, the acquirer suffers from coordination problems until it reaches a crisis point that forces it into an organizational restructuring aimed at achieving a 'global solution'.

In this model, organizational restructuring punctuates an acquisition sequence, and allows the acquirer to learn about effective integration and become prepared for more acquisitions in the future, consistent with the theory of punctuated equilibrium in organizational learning[18]. However, the new learning may soon become routinized in the organization's attempt to improve the efficiency of the integration process, and be applied indiscriminately to every future acquisition. To the extent that no two acquisitions are very similar, since each acquired company is different, such mechanistic integration effort is again bound to lead to another crisis after a few acquisitions. Barkema and Schijven therefore hypothesize a long term acquisition–organizational restructuring cycle. An acquisition's contribution to firm performance therefore depends on its place in a sequence of acquisitions. In this model the deficiencies of the acquirer's integration effort, based on local optima, over the first few integrations are exposed, and organizational restructuring provides the opportunity for it to learn to design and apply globally optimal solutions, i.e. across all organizational subunits of both the acquirer and the acquired businesses, and improve acquisition performance. Thus integration is 'not a one-shot game'.

An implication of this model is that while individual acquisitions as well as a short sequence of acquisitions may underperform, a long sequence that straddles organizational restructurings may be successful, provided, of course, that the restructurings happen at the opportune times and effectively resolve the integration problems.

Organizational learning perspectives

There are different perspectives on how organizations learn from their past activities. Such learning becomes embedded in organizational routines through repetitive engagement in the same activities. Such routines are not only reflected in the organizational members' behaviour, but may also dictate how they react to the external stimuli[19]. Adaptive learning is the process of matching the current routine against the external challenge, evaluating the match, and modifying the routine if necessary to ensure adequacy of the response. Thus adaptive learning is a dynamic process, which adapts its own content to increase its relevance, and the ability to adapt is itself part of the learning. Adaptive learning, to be effective, requires a discriminatory ability to choose the appropriate experience from the content of past learning, and discard the inappropriate. This defines the distinction between *knowledge* (the state of knowing) and *adaptive learning* (the judicious application of knowledge).

In the acquisition context knowledge both about past acquisitions done by the acquirer and about how that knowledge is adaptively applied to problem-solving when new acquisitions are undertaken may influence the success of subsequent acquisitions.

Transfer theory of organizational learning

Psychologists describe the influence of a prior event on the performance of a subsequent event as the transfer effect. Positive transfer refers to a prior event facilitating the superior performance of the following event, and negative transfer inhibits subsequent performance. Transfer effects are reflected in differences in performance between a prior event and a subsequent event. The presence of significant transfer effects testifies to the impact of learning. When events are similar the transfer effect is probably positive, whereas it may be negative when the events are dissimilar. In the acquisition context this inference leads to the expectation that similar (not the same as related) acquisitions are more likely to result in superior performance of follow-on acquisitions, whereas dissimilar ones will result in inferior performance[20].

Can old dogs learn new tricks?

Human beings, through the accumulation of experience over time, formulate mental models of their world, and this model specifies the cause-to-effect relationship between their efforts and outcomes. Managers use their mental model to understand new tasks such as post-acquisition integration. Initially they fit the environment of the new task to their legacy mental model and derive forecasts of outcomes, e.g. effective integration, given their and their team's efforts as inputs. This approach is consistent with bounded rationality. However, the complexity of the task environment requires that managers transcend the bounds of such limited rationality and learn to adapt their mental model to the demands of the new task. Nevertheless, managers may be too attached to their mental model to abandon it. Thus they may search for solutions to the problems raised in integrating a new acquisition within the bounds of their experience, even if the new acquisition has considerable dissimilarity from earlier acquisitions. Causal ambiguity may aggravate the problem if it causes the managers to construct their mental model based on poorly understood cause-to-effect relationships in earlier acquisitions (see Chapters 3 and 22 for the relevance of causal ambiguity to acquisitions). Thus past experience of acquisitions is no guarantee that the integration team can judiciously apply that experience to the challenges of new acquisitions.

You may learn wrongly from the past

While past experience may be a useful guide to the future acquisition, such utility may be limited if the future acquisitions are substantially different from those of the past. Behavioural learning theory predicts that individual behaviour may be conditioned by two kinds of influence: present and past environmental influences. The present influences are called *antecedents*, and the past ones are called *consequences*. Past experience may predispose people to view new situations as similar to those of the past. This induces a biased perspective, caused by cognitive bias. This blinds a person to the obvious as well as subtle differences between the past and the present. This person lacks discrimination, and wrongly generalizes the past to the present. The opposite error is that antecedents similar to the consequences are treated as dissimilar. This represents a tendency to find uniqueness in a new acquisition where none exists. In acquisition situations both errors are likely. Acquirers must therefore be wary of the 'experience trap'. It appears that managers do not adapt their past learning to new situations enough or in good time to improve their project management decisions. Their experience seems to blinker them to take a limited perspective of the new challenges. Sengupta and his team suggest a number of ways to improve the experience-learning cycle so that experience is continually updated by new learning[21]:

- Provide systematic cognitive feedback to managers so that they can realize their errors in good time.
- Focus on goals that promote desired behaviour rather than on performance targets.
- Provide feedback tools that combine previously used models and heuristics so as to combine experience with new learning.
- Ensure that forecasts for the project are well calibrated, and not based on unrealistic projections.
- Customize learning for each project; don't blindly follow 'best practice' from other companies.
- Develop project 'flight simulators' to train experienced managers for project-specific tasks so that potential problems can be anticipated and specific responses to them can be considered in advance.
- Allow managers to revise targets if necessary, so that they avoid being forced to work to overambitious targets, resulting in their dysfunctional behaviour.

Exhibit 23.2 shows how previous experience is modified in the light of the emerging characteristics of new acquisitions. Björkman, Tienari and Vaara explain the lessons from this study as follows:

- Sociocultural integration is context-specific; it is characterized by ambiguity as to cause-to effect; and whether past experience is relevant or not is determined by the dominant coalition of the managers in the merged firm.
- Context specificity is illustrated by the change in the HQ policy and the change in the corporate language, but the retention of shared vision statements.

Exhibit 23.2

Something good, something bad: lessons from past acquisitions

The Swedish-Finnish bank Merita Nordbanken (MNB) merged with the Danish bank Unidanmark (Unidan) in 2000 to form Nordea. Both banks had been formed through several prior mergers, and the lessons learnt from the integration of these mergers were available at the time of the MNB merger with Unidan. The mergers that resulted in MNB and Unidan are shown in the diagram below.

It is clear that the integration approach in the case of Nordea reflects some of the elements of the approaches adopted by MNB and Unidan in the previous stage of their acquisitions. The arrangement for top managers to split their time between Sweden and Finland was appropriate for a merger of equals, but considered inappropriate, since Nordea planned to project itself as a Nordic bank and needed a single headquarters (HQ) (Virtual HQ) where all top executives of the various businesses would meet for two days a week, and Stockholm was the only option, given its central location among all Nordic capitals. Moreover, the earlier travelling HQ model had resulted in high travel costs and executive time.

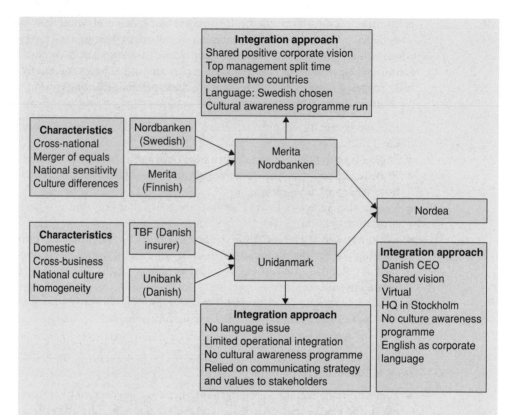

After the negative spin-off from the choice of Swedish as the corporate language in the MNB merger, English was agreed for that role.

There was no culture awareness programme early on, perhaps reflecting the prior Danish experience, where it was not an integration issue, and the fact that the new CEO was Danish. The Danish members of the corporate management felt that 'one should focus on the future and not spend too much time on "irrelevant" cultural differences'. This lack of a specific cultural training programme received mixed responses among Nordea's top managers. Interestingly, one senior Danish manager in charge of a major business unit said, 'I have learnt that one should be more aware of the cultural differences before starting this kind of process'. Later a Group Identity and Communication unit led by a Danish top manager was given a prominent role in developing a set of corporate values and diffusing it throughout Nordea. The HR function involved in the culture awareness programmes earlier came to be involved late in this process. Neither Finnish nor Swedish executives who had experience of the programmes had any overall responsibility for sociocultural integration projects in Nordea. The shared corporate vision element was regarded as a positive aspect of the earlier integration approaches, and was therefore readily incorporated into the Nordea integration approach.

Source: Based on I. Björkman, J. Tienari and E. Vaara, 'A learning perspective on sociocultural integration in cross-national mergers', in G. Stahl and M. Mendenhall, *Mergers and Acquisitions, Managing Culture and Human Resources* (Stanford, CA, USA: Stanford University Press, 2005), pp. 155–175

- The impact of cultural awareness programmes was not universally considered to be valuable, especially by managers who had not been exposed to such programmes.
- What learning is carried forward from previous integration experience depends on the dominant actors who judge the relevance of that experience. The model that prevailed in the Nordea case was the Unidan model of value awareness rather the MNB model of cultural awareness. The lessons from the latter were not exploited in the subsequent Nordea case. The corporate memory storing the prior experience of sociocultural integration by the MNB managers was not drawn upon.

Corporate memory seems to be fragmented, and different groups involved in a merger may draw upon different fragments for application to future mergers.

Exploitative and exploratory learning

James March distinguishes between exploration and exploitation in organizational learning[22]. Accumulated knowledge can be adapted to solve problems with considerable similarity to those solved in the past. This represents exploitation, and companies may become quite efficient at such exploitation. On the other hand, firms may also adapt their learning to solve problems 'off the beaten track'. Where the ecological balance between the firm and the environment remains subject to small variations, exploitation may be adequate for firm survival. Where such a balance is vulnerable to unanticipated and violent turbulence, exploration becomes the key to long-term survival. Examples of situations appropriate for exploitation are mature markets with stable demand patterns, and acquisitions in the same industry. Examples of situations where exploration is appropriate are markets with unpredictable technological shocks, and acquisitions representing real options.

> Effective selection among forms, routines or practices is essential to survival, but so also is the generation of new alternative practices, particularly in changing environments . . . The essence of exploitation is the refinement and extension of existing competences, technologies and paradigms. Its returns are positive, proximate and predictable. The essence of exploration is experimentation with new alternatives. Its returns are uncertain, distant and often negative[23].

Both uncertainty and the time to realization of benefits are smaller in exploitation than in exploration. These advantages of exploitation, combined with structural and cultural inertia, may predispose a firm to limit itself in its search for growth opportunities or solution to integration problems. More importantly, the firm may lack the capacity to adapt its learning to novel and unfamiliar opportunities. Further, the firm may develop a cognitive bias, treat the unfamiliar as the familiar, and misapply exploitative routines and competences to exploratory situations[24].

Organizational learning modes: the social context

Organizational learning is a process in which individual members of the organization learn from the established organization codes, and these codes are modified by interaction with the individuals. This mode of learning creates a dynamic equilibrium between the organization and the individual, characterized by mutual reinforcement and renewal. However, the source of renewal may often lie outside the firm, i.e. new experiences arising from the ecological interaction with the outside world such as the competitors. Openness to learn from this interaction *without* and the ability to influence mutual learning *within* can ensure the long-term survival of the firm. Over-emphasis on exploitation may shut out this source of self-renewal.

An implication of this limitation is that firms may often benefit from acquisitions that are indeed off the beaten track, i.e. unrelated acquisitions. This questions the received wisdom of the 1990s that firms should 'stick to the knitting'.

Organizational identity, organizational knowledge and learning

Organizational learning may be affected by the organization's extant knowledge domain, and what members of that organization consider to be its identity[25]. Members of an organization may cherish its identity, regard themselves as individuals closely defined by that collective identity, and jealously guard it against challenges posed by organizational change. Any new knowledge graft may be rejected by current members of the firm, because they identify themselves with a different body of knowledge that defines their identity, e.g. as scientists or technologists. Thus organizational identity and organizational knowledge interact. The two may interact in such a way as to lead members to resist learning new skills, routines and perspectives. In the context of a merger whose *raison d'être* is learning and leveraging each other's skills and capabilities, such an interaction can impede effective and successful integration. For example, members of a technology-based firm with a proud lineage of innovations may be reluctant, and find it difficult, to learn the marketing and business development tools and skills that are necessary to turn their technology into commercially viable products. Such resistance can lead to unsuccessful merger integration, as seen in Exhibit 23.3[26].

Exhibit 23.3

This old dog doesn't like to learn marketing tricks

TekMar, Inc. began as a dedicated research laboratory of a large US electronics firm in the early 1940s. The division's scientists achieved significant technological and scientific breakthroughs, and national acclaim. The dominant mindset of the organization was great pride in its status as a top scientific team, and an attitude of 'technology push'. The organizational behaviour was characterized by internal creative processes that focused on designing and developing cutting-edge technology, even without an obvious commercial application. It was 'science for science's sake'. By the late 1980s the parent company had been acquired, and Tekmar was spun off as a free-standing firm that had to earn its keep. It was now responsible for its revenues and funding its research. The old mindset had to change to cope with this existential challenge.

TekMar's need for new market-oriented knowledge, skills and behaviour was now a compelling imperative. In 2000–01 the management formed a Venture Management Group (VMG) of executives, among whom were experienced market professionals with strong skills in venture development, spotting commerical opportunities and funding. Creation of VMG meant power was slipping from scientists to business unit managers, to the centralized VMG. From a 'technology push' mindset the organization had to make a seismic culture shift to a 'market pull' attitude. The scientists could now win research funding if they could demonstrate the market relevance of the ouput of their research. VMG could now tell the scientists how to do their job! The knowledge use would now have a different focus from before the graft. Knowledge use practices before and how they should change after the graft are as exemplified below (note that M&BD is Marketing and Business Development):

	Before	After
Practice dimension	Scientific practices	Changes in M&BD practices
Locus of knowledge use	Aiming for scientific brilliance	Adapt technology over multiple markets
Search for tech applications	Scientific challenge as primary criterion	Hiring external market experts; based on customer needs
Customer interaction	Negligible	Motivating customers to buy company's technology promise
Knowledge sharing	Informal, independent and localized, mentoring	Regular sharing between business units based on mutual benefits

The key dynamics of deterrents to change through knowledge grafting are shown in the figure below.

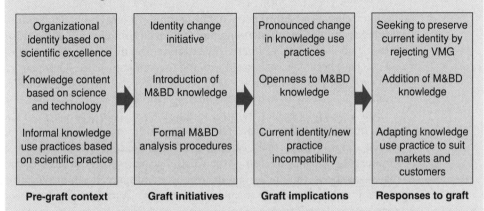

Pre-graft context	Graft initiatives	Graft implications	Responses to graft
Organizational identity based on scientific excellence	Identity change initiative	Pronounced change in knowledge use practices	Seeking to preserve current identity by rejecting VMG
Knowledge content based on science and technology	Introduction of M&BD knowledge	Openness to M&BD knowledge	Addition of M&BD knowledge
Informal knowledge use practices based on scientific practice	Formal M&BD analysis procedures	Current identity/new practice incompatibility	Adapting knowledge use practice to suit markets and customers

The grafting effort ended as a failure. 'The intersection of organizational identity, knowledge and practice hindered the development of new knowledge and undermined the broader strategic transformation effect.'

Source: Adapted from R. Nag, K. Corley, and D. Gioia, 'The intersection of organizational identity, knowledge and practice: Attempting strategic change via knowledge grafting', *Academy of Management Journal*, **50**(4), 2007, pp. 821–847

From this case study, Nag and his co-authors draw several implications for organizational learning:

● Organizational identity frames or creates meaning for the knowledge use practices of organizational members.
● Difficulties of organizational change emerge from collective ways of thinking and doing among organization members.
● Deterrents to change occur at the intersection of identity ('who we are'), knowledge ('what we know') and practice ('what we do').

Organizational learning can be based on both direct experience, i.e. actual acquisitions the firm has made in the past, and indirect or vicarious experience, i.e. acquisitions made by other firms. In other words, firms can learn not only from their own mistakes but also from the mistakes of their competitors. The merger waves discussed in Chapter 2 point to firms seeking to base their strategies on vicarious experience, i.e. on the 'me-too' strategy. The failure of many acquirers to create value suggests that vicarious learning may be valuable. Baum and Li find that acquisitions by multi-unit chain organizations such as supermarkets and department stores in different geographical locations in the US can be explained by vicarious learning. They imitate the location choices of other visible and comparable chains' most recent acquisitions[27]. While a firm can learn vicariously from its competitors' acquisition location decisions, it is not clear how much it can learn about the sources of success or failure of those acquisitions purely from vicarious learning. Thus direct experiential learning may be a richer and more valuable source of learning for some aspects of the acquisition process.

Organizational learning modes: forms of learning

Learning comes in different forms:

- tacit/informal; and
- explicit/formal.

Tacit learning is embedded in the organization's routines and habits without any articulation. It is behavioural in manifestation rather than to be found in any codified instruction manuals. It resides in individuals within the organization who through their past exposure to the transactions have become impregnated with the relevant knowledge. The organization draws upon this learning by co-opting these individuals whenever the need to apply the learning arises. For example, a person with previous negotiating experience is recruited to the negotiating team.

Explicit learning comes from the codification of past experiences in the form of codes, rules, instruction manuals, etc. The background to the experience, how the experience was gained and with what results can be included in the codified information. The lessons from these experiences may be clearly articulated. The persons on whose experience the code draws may be removed from the learner in both time and space. It can therefore be passed on 'hand to hand' rather than from 'memory to memory'. Transmission of learning is not through anecdotes and folklore, or tales of heroism and hubris.

Empirical evidence on organizational learning and acquisition performance

Zollo and Leshchinskii carried out a study of the impact of acquisition experience, codification of past acquisition experience along with the extent of integration for a sample of 47 US bank acquirers during 1964–96[28]. The acquisition experience variable takes into account acquisitions going back to 1964. In the absence of codification, acquisition experience would represent tacit learning. The extent of integration influences the relevance of learning from the past. Codification is proxied by tools such as spreadsheets, due diligence checklists, HR affiliation manuals, etc. Zollo and Singh[29] reported that acquirers with well-specified and codified integration processes have significantly improved accounting returns on assets and long-term shareholder abnormal returns (see Appendix 4.1 in Chapter 4 on abnormal returns methodology). They conclude that firms learn from their past acquisition experience to the extent that they codify that experience. However, learning from codification is not linear, with learning becoming less effective at high levels of codification. This may happen because the relevance of past acquisition experience to current deals may be limited. Codification may have inhibited exploratory adaptation of organizational learning.

Applying the principles of behavioural learning theory to corporate acquisitions, Haleblian and Finkelstein examined 449 US acquisitions from 1980 to 1992[30]. They tested for both the positive and negative effect of past acquisition experience in its interaction with similarity or dissimilarity of current acquisition to previous acquisitions. Performance was measured by abnormal returns to acquirer shareholders. The main conclusions of this study are as follows:

- Acquisition experience has both positive and negative effects on performance.
- In a majority of cases, when a firm's current acquisition was dissimilar to its prior acquisitions, acquisition experience had a negative effect for slightly and moderately experienced acquirers.
- The best performers appeared to be either those without experience, who therefore did not make an inappropriate generalization error, or those who used their substantial experience in a discriminatory way.
- Firms making multiple acquisitions within the same industry benefit from generalizing their past experience.

In their subsequent paper, Finkelstein and Haleblian tested the transfer theory to find negative transfer effects for a sample of 96 organizations engaged in serial acquisitions during 1970–90. They measured performance by abnormal stock returns, as in the previous study. Transfers appeared to reduce the performance of follow-on acquisitions. They concluded that prior acquisition knowledge is often misapplied to a subsequent, albeit similar, target. Thus prior acquisition experience needs to be applied carefully, after sifting the similarities and dissimilarities between the successive targets[31].

Hayward tested the proposition that the impact of learning was non-linear. In this view, too much similarity may not be a good thing. Diverse acquisition experience may yield rich inferences about the causes of acquisition performance. Thus dissimilarity may be more beneficial to the acquirer, and lead to greater value creation. For a sample of 214 acquisitions made by 120 US firms between 1990 and 1995 Hayward found that a firm's acquisition performance measured by abnormal returns was higher when prior acquisitions:

- were not highly similar or dissimilar, measured by the frequency of prior acquisitions in the same four-digit industry of the target;
- had led to small losses; and
- were neither too close nor distant in time[32].

When firms undertake a series of highly similar acquisitions they risk entering the experience trap and suffering adverse performance. When the series of acquisitions are dissimilar, they lack the specialist knowledge about how to select and integrate them. Learning is more likely when prior acquisitions incur small losses, prompting refreshed search for an acquisition to which their prior experience is still germane. Thus moderate attempts at exploratory adaptation of learning from past acquisitions are more effective than simple exploitation or excessive exploration. Moderate frequency of acquisitions is also more conducive to effective learning than a frenetic or languid pace.

Learning to learn

These studies suggest that both tacit knowledge and codified knowledge about past acquisitions are useful in improving the chances of value creation in acquisitions. Codification seems to generate additional value. However, any extrapolation or generalization of the past experience to present acquisition evaluation or integration needs to be conditioned by the similarity or dissimilarity between the past and the present. Thus firms have to develop discriminatory capabilities that will allow them to generalize intelligently from past acquisitions to the current one. An experimental attitude to new acquisitions may lead to superior performance provided it is not excessively so. While learning is perhaps good, learning about how to apply that learning is even better. Acquisition-making as a core competence depends on both.

Impediments to organizational learning

While over-generalization presupposes the existence of corporate memory, firms may choose not to build up that memory on the ground that each acquisition is unique. They will then be guilty of overdiscrimination between successive acquisitions. The lack of a centralized and ongoing function responsible for archiving the past, and for diffusion of learning, impedes effective learning. Functions such as internal audit responsible for post-acquisition audit may not be involved at earlier stages of the acquisition process. In this case there is little continuity of perspectives through all the stages of the process. This may lead to fragmented learning about different stages, and impede internal communication as well as the emergence of holistic perspectives encompassing the different stages. Organization members may also fail to learn, owing to the absence of incentives for learning or fear of scapegoating. Managers may also be in denial concerning the reasons for past acquisition failures, and this inhibits them from applying the lessons from such failures.

Where an organization's key resources and capabilities are embedded in inherited routines and practices, or in groups and individuals, learning by sharing or transfer may be more difficult. These teams and groups may also want to guard the knowledge they have accumulated jealously as a source of bargaining power and privilege. In the case of groups and individuals at the receiving end of the transfer process, learning may have to be preceded by unlearning the past routines and practices[33]. Such groups may reject new learning, displaying a 'not invented here' syndrome. Acceptance of new learning from the acquirer or acquired groups is also to concede superiority and power. Many of these behavioural traits that adversely affect learning are seen in Exhibit 23.3 above.

Greenberg, Lane and Bahde identify a number of other impediments to organizational learning in the M & A context[34]:

- *Language.* For example, the use of specialized language, or use of the same language by people of different nationalities with different nuances and subtleties, prevents transfer of information between the merging partners or a common interpretation of the same events or phenomena. Consequently, the acquirer cannot learn fully about the value creation potential of the target.
- *Physical space.* For example, a lack of geographical proximity may prevent members from developing the informal relationships that could facilitate sharing of information.
- *Organizational structure for learning.* For example, the absence of a dedicated sub-unit of the acquirer, composed of members with experience of evaluating and managing the acquisition process; the absence of the target firm's organization structure, which allows sharing of information with the acquirer's team. The lack of such structures may lead to poor assessment of the target's capabilities and their fit to the acquirer's capabilities. Differences in organizational structure between acquirer and target may also impede assessment of fit, for example when the two firms have different product development processes. The structure and composition of the integration team influence learning. The lack of a structural link between the due diligence team and the integration team results in the latter being deprived of the knowledge accumulated during due diligence about the target's strategy, culture, structure and financial performance. The inability of the integration team to link up with

other organizational members may result in failure to enlist their cooperation, enable joint action or spread the learning about the integration.

- *Motivation*. Most acquisitions do not fuel the desire among organizational members to learn about each other in order to integrate their organizations. Employees are often demotivated by worries about their jobs and their roles, and look out for their own interests. Sharing of knowledge is also inhibited by resistance to sharing and learning. Performance appraisal and compensation systems do not encourage members to share with, or learn from, their new colleagues.

Feedback plays an important role in the learning process. However, its purpose should be to correct and improve practice and thereby contribute to learning, and not as a tool in performance assessment. The latter is likely to deter organizational members from honest communication of errors. Noisy feedback that blurs the cause-to-effect relationship of actions and outcomes during the M & A process is unlikely to help members learn. Such feedback may also be used by some members to confirm their own biases and carry on with their actions, whereas a corrective action may be needed: for example, poor integration outcomes may be blamed on external factors rather than flawed integration models. Overconfident managers may also overlook negative feedback[35], and more so if the feedback is noisy.

Organizing for learning

In large firms with frequent acquisition activity, the corporate development (CD) function may be responsible for the strategic planning stage of the M & A process, generating the business model and evaluating acquisition as the preferred mode of implementing the business model. In this, CD may act in tandem with the relevant business units initiating the acquisition or responsible for operating the acquired business. Task forces may have been set up to evaluate the business model and the place of M & A in the model. In specific acquisition planning CD may delegate the work to a specialist acquisition (A) team. This team may be made up of business unit experts, and experts drawn from different functional areas. This team may also employ external advisers to fashion the acquisition strategy. The A team and its advisers may be put together for a specific acquisition programme or deal.

The A team may coordinate and oversee the deal structuring and negotiation stage. A smaller team may be responsible for negotiating the deal (the N team). The members of the N team act on the brief provided by the A team and CD. After deal closure, the N team may disband, and responsibility for post-merger transition and integration may be passed on to specially set-up transition management or integration project teams. These teams prepare integration plans and pass them on to the operating units for implementation. At this stage the A team may also be disbanded. The post-integration performance of the acquiring business unit may be monitored by the CD, and the unit's performance may be subject to a specially tailored post-acquisition audit or to a more general audit of business unit performance in the normal audit cycle of the firm.

The M & A process as described appears to be a series of linked activities. Each activity may be imbued with the overall strategic purpose and value creation logic of the acquisition, but there is also scope for these activities to be disjointed and disharmonious. This is not uncommon, as Jean-Pierre Garnier, the former CEO of GlaxoSmithKline, points out[36]:

> 'Another issue common with mergers and acquisitions is a lack of continuity. Very often, different teams are involved with the initial target acquisition stage, the deal-making stage and the postintegration stage. Companies tend to spend a lot of time at each stage but what commonly happens is that not enough attention is spent on the interfaces between them. Sometimes, the team in charge of postmerger integration has only a vague idea of what the target acquisition team had in mind when deciding on the merger'.

Our integrated five-stage model emphasizes the danger of this, and seeks to avoid it.

Any meaningful post-acquisition audit process needs to be anchored in the integrated perspective of M & A. Such an audit also needs to project the successes and failures at every stage of the M & A process. A deep understanding of these will facilitate adaptive learning, allowing firms to assess similarities and dissimilarities between past acquisitions and proposed acquisitions. Past acquisitions and proposed acquisitions can be mapped across the first four stages. Acquirers can then apply the lessons from past acquisitions in a discriminatory way. Both exploitative learning and exploratory learning may be enhanced by this approach to post-acquisition audit.

The survey evidence cited above indicates that acquirers are not well organized for organizational learning. An important challenge is to create the structures, systems and processes that can promote such learning. While CD can become the repository of such learning, it may not be detached enough from the M & A process to permit an objective audit.

Internal audit and organizational learning

Some of the problems associated with organizational learning may be alleviated by an ongoing post-acquisition audit system. The internal audit (IA) function may be one of the functions that can contribute to this process, although in most companies IA's role is limited to due diligence, transition management and post-acquisition audit, generally as part of the normal annual audit cycle. Its role has thus been reactive rather than proactive[37]. Nevertheless, IA has a vantage position to develop a holistic view of M & A audit, the capacity to develop the appropriate methodologies for auditing the different stages, to carry out an objective audit, and act as the repository of organizational learning. IA can:

- contribute to codification of past acquisition-related activities;
- communicate both successes and failures in acquisitions effectively so they become embedded in organizational procedures, systems, cultures and routines;
- highlight the weaknesses in systems and processes, and help the business units and functions improve these systems and processes;
- create a well-calibrated feedback mechanism for organizational learning;
- facilitate single-loop learning, i.e. understanding the reasons for failure of expectations; and
- facilitate double-loop learning, i.e. question the assumptions underlying the acquisition strategy and programme and its expectations[38].

The involvement of internal auditors (IAs) in many companies up front in due diligence and risk management also facilitates their involvement in the organizational learning process. Such involvement gives internal auditors a better opportunity to observe all the stages of the acquisition process and develop a holistic perspective of the acquisition process than other functions such as finance and IT. Increasingly, many active acquirers, such as Nations Bank (now Bank of America) and Wells Fargo have realized the benefits of drawing upon the expertise of IAs, and of involving them in many stages prior to and after due diligence[39] (see Exhibit 23.4).

Acquisition-making as a core competence

Given the complexity of the various stages of acquisition, and the cost of failure of acquisitions, which is now well documented, firms that can carry out successful acquisitions are likely to enjoy competitive advantage over firms that mess up their acquisitions. Developing a

Exhibit 23.4

Internal auditors in Wells Fargo step beyond due diligence (DD) and post-audit

Since 1987 Wells Fargo (WF) has completed more than 200 acquisitions, as well as numerous purchases of assets. In these acquisitions and purchases the Wells Fargo Audit Services (WFAS) have played an extremely beneficial role. WFAS's involvement begins well before the due diligence stage, and extends beyond the legal closure of the transaction. WFAS works to support corporate development. The various stages at which WFAS become involved are described below.

Prior to due diligence, IAs:

- approach the due diligence for any upcoming deal as a project management task;
- gather extensive intelligence about the target company, and develop a 'hit list' of issues that should be addressed during due diligence;
- assess whether the teams that will carry out due diligence are adequately staffed; and
- determine whether each team's role, list of objectives and scope have been clearly defined.

During due diligence, IAs:

- carry out due diligence of the target organization's internal audit;
- assess the target's compliance and control environment, e.g. regulatory reviews and weak spots, external audit reports;
- provide oversight of the due diligence process to ensure the M & A process functions as intended; and
- assist other groups in their due diligence programmes.

After due diligence, IAs:

- prepare a DD report and receive all other teams' DD reports;
- summarize significant issues to help management resolve them before the deal is signed;
- highlight the financial impact of issues on deal-pricing, e.g. anticipated write-offs; revenue enhancement and cost-saving opportunities; growth assumptions; and
- assist and oversee the pre-deal close and post-close transition phases.

dedicated acquisition function, and in particular an integration function, can achieve a number of advantages. It can:

- lighten the burden on the acquiring business unit manager, and avoid his or her being distracted from running the business during the integration;
- avoid the top management involvement in firefighting, problem-solving and refereeing;
- build confidence and trust in acquired company managers, so that retention rate is improved; and
- codify the M & A experience to facilitate organizational learning.

The case study below illustrates the organizational learning process in the context of acquisitions. Well-established systems and processes for organizational learning will further strengthen the core competence.

Learning from past acquisitions

In 1999, SC Johnson (SCJ), a family-owned company in the US, generated $4.2bn in revenue and employed 9500 people across 60 countries. The company is a leading manufacturer of branded consumer household products. In January 1998, SCJ acquired Dow Brands consumer products for $1.125bn. This was a major acquisition for SCJ and over 50 people were involved in carrying out the acquisition. Ray Johnson led a debriefing process to learn from the company's substantial acquisition. Many of those attending the debriefing may have attended acquisition conferences or learned the technical aspects of the activity.

The purpose of the debriefing was to present a holistic view and clarify what worked for SCJ. The debriefing process covered the following:

- Early evaluation process – what does the company want to acquire? What is the strategic fit of the target?
- Valuation and negotiation – is the acquisition affordable? What is the bidding process and how is it handled?
- Closing – how does it work with the antitrust authorities, Federal Trade Commission?
- Integration – how does it optimize its internal processes for acquisition integration?

During the integration phase, a vice president led an integration team of 12 full-time people representing the functional heads of human resources, marketing, sales, logistics, technology, etc. When necessary, the HR director brought in other experts in benefits, compensation or communication.

Some of the learning points that emerged during debriefing were as follows:

- Closing process – when is the time for the SCJ's negotiators to talk to the SCJ's family owners and determine what could be the deal breakers in their negotiation with the acquisition target.
- Integration process – the procedure to identify where all the target's transaction records are kept.
- How SCJ can use cultural integration surveys in the acquired company to help understand where efforts are necessary to improve integration.
- Integration process needs right talent with the right skills and the right resources to succeed:
  - a small highly experienced group is better than a large, inexperienced team – not good for the team to learn on the job;
  - select the best people with the skill for the job and not the only ones available;
  - team skills are different for different stages, e.g. benefits compensation aspects and building trust require people with different skills and expertise;
  - pacing the team members, especially the core members is important;
  - the team and the firm must celebrate milestones to keep the team energized.

Discussion questions

1 What is the purpose of the debriefing that Ray Johnson conducted?

2 What lessons did SCJ learn about its acquisition of Dow?

3 Does SCJ's learning provide a holistic view of its acquisition?

4 Is debriefing an effective learning tool? Think of other tools.

Source: The Conference Board, *Performance Measurement during Merger and Acquisition Integration*, Research Report 1274-00-RR, 2000

Overview and implications for practice

In this chapter we focused on the fifth stage of the M & A process. Our concern is not about an individual merger or acquisition, but about the M & A programme, in which firms become serial acquirers in pursuit of their corporate and competitive strategies.

- The serial nature of acquisitions raises the scope for learning from previous acquisitions and incorporating that learning in the various stages of future acquisitions. Our focus is therefore on organizational learning.

- Some empirical studies provide evidence that acquisition experience has a positive impact on acquisition performance in terms of shareholder value gains. Therefore frequent acquirers have the incentive to improve organizational learning, and in turn their acquisition performance, further.

- Many other studies have shown that acquisitions, on average, fail to generate shareholder value.

- This points to a lack of learning. Indeed, we have provided survey evidence that a majority of acquirers do not track the performance of their acquisitions.

- While acquisition experience, and the tacit learning that goes with it, may improve learning, explicit learning through codification of past experience seems to add even more value.

- Acquirers should be careful not to over-generalize past acquisition experience in evaluating or implementing current acquisitions.

- Acquirers must develop critical capabilities to apply their learning from past acquisitions in a selective and discerning way. The opposite error of over-discrimination, i.e. treating every new acquisition as unique and dismissing the past as irrelevant, should also be avoided.

- There are several impediments to organizational learning about past acquisitions. Many of these are rooted in the social context of organizational learning, and many behavioural factors, including social identity, influence the willingness to learn.

- Learning activities and admissions of errors may be used for scapegoating or 'witch-hunting' if an acquisition goes terribly wrong.

- While accountability is important, it should not obstruct the process of learning.

- Internal audit function has a number of strengths that allow it to play a crucial role in organizational learning. The audit function can provide means of centralizing codification and diffusion of learning to give a holistic view of the M & A process.

- When properly institutionalized, organizational learning can give firms in which being acquisition led is a crucial plank of their corporate strategy, a core competence and a competitive advantage.

- Such firms need to ensure that an institutional learning approach is put in place to increase the odds of acquisition success.

- Without effective organizational learning, the five-stage acquisition process is incomplete, and future acquisitions may not create value.

Review questions

23.1 What is the importance of measuring post-acquisition performance?

23.2 What are the problems that hinder effective performance measurement?

23.3 What are the different ways in which performance can be measured?

23.4 What is post-acquisition audit? How important is it to acquisition success?

23.5 What is organizational learning?

23.6 What is the relevance of organizational learning to acquisitions?

23.7 What distinguishes exploration from exploitation of learning?

23.8 What are the impediments to organizational learning in the acquisition context?

23.9 What role can internal audit play in facilitating and ensuring organizational learning?

23.10 How relevant is learning from past acquisitions to future acquisitions?

23.11 Think of ways of improving organizational learning and its effect on future acquisitions.

Further reading

A. Gupta, K. Smith and C. Shalley, 'The interplay between exploration and exploitation', *Academy of Management Journal*, **49**(4), 2006, 693–706.

M. Hayward, 'When do firms learn from their acquisition success? Evidence from 1990–95', *Strategic Management Journal*, **23**, 2002, 21–39.

G. Selim, S. Sudarsanam and M. Lavine, 'The role of internal auditors in mergers, acquisitions and divestitures: An international study', *International Journal of Auditing*, **7**, 2003, 223–245.

J. Ullrich and R. van Dick, 'The group psychology of mergers & acquisitions: Lessons from the social identity approach', in C. L. Cooper and S. Finkelstein (Eds), *Advances in Mergers and Acquisitions* (Amsterdam: Elsevier, 2007), 1–15.

Notes and references

1. M. L. A. Hayward, 'When do firms learn from their acquisition experience? Evidence from 1990–1995', *Strategic Management Journal*, **23**, 2002, 21–39.

2. KPMG, 'Unlocking shareholder value: the keys to success', *Mergers and Acquisitions, A Global Report*, (London: KPMG, 1999), p. 7.

3. S. Gates, *Performance Measurement during Merger and Acquisition Integration*, Report 1274-00-RR, (New York: The Conference Board Inc., 2000), p. 12.

4. Bain & Co. survey; D. Harding and S. Rovit, *Mastering the Merger* (Boston, MA: Harvard Business School Press, 2004), Figure 3.1.

5. S. Christofferson, R. McNish and D. L. Sias, 'Where mergers go wrong', *The McKinsey Quarterly*, 4 Janury 2005.

6. S. Gates, *ibid.*, p. 16.

7. On how firms realize value from their intellectual assets and intellectual property see J. L. Davies and S. S. Harrison, *Edison in the Boardroom* (New York: John Wiley & Sons, 2001).

8. M. Sirower and S. O'Bryne, 'The measurement of post-acquisition performance: Towards a value-based benchmarking methodology', *Journal of Applied Corporate Finance*, **11**(2), 107–121.

9. KPMG International, 'Benchmarking M & A teams', June 2005, Figure 22, downloaded from www.kpmg.com

10. J. Pfeffer, *What Were They thinking? Unconventional Wisdom about Management* (Boston, MA: Harvard Business School Press, 2007), p. 165.

11. G. Selim, S. Sudarsanam and M. Lavine, 'The role of internal auditors in mergers, acquisitions and divestitures: An international study', *International Journal of Auditing*, **7**, 2003, 223–245.

12. A. Gregory, 'An examination of the long-run performance of UK acquiring firms', *Journal of Business Finance and Accounting*, **24**, 1997, 7–8.

13. M. H. Lubatkin, *A market model analysis of diversification strategies and administrative experience on the performance of merging firms*, unpublished PhD dissertation, University of Tennessee, 1982, cited in Haleblian and Finkelstein, see note 13 below.

14. J. Haleblian and S. Finkelstein, 'The influence of organizational acquisition experience', *Administrative Science Quarterly*, **44**, 1999, 29–56.

15. For an earlier study see C. Loderer and K. Martin, 'Corporate acquisitions by listed firms: The experience of a comprehensive sample', *Financial Management*, Winter 1990, 17–33. They find that serial acquirers generate less shareholder value from their second and subsequent than from their first. Although the authors conjecture that this pattern may be due to partial stock market anticipation of follow-on acquisitions, it is also consistent with organizational learning failure.

16. This evidence is consistent with results that Bain & Company, Inc. in its Global Learning Curve study report. See D. Harding and S. Rovit, *Mastering the Merger* (Boston, MA: Harvard Business School Press, 2004). For a sample of 1693 US, European and Japanese firms making 11,049 acquisitions during 1986–2001, the authors report that frequent acquirers had higher one-year CAPM-adjusted abnormal returns than less frequent acquirers. Further, among US acquirers making at least 20 deals during the sample period, constant acquirers outperformed those making acquisitions only during recessions, the growth phase or the period in between in an economic cycle. Continuous acquirers in Europe outperformed early acquirers in an economic cycle and both outperforming late acquirers (see Figures A-1 to A-3, pp. 180–183).

17. H. Barkema and M. Schijven, 'Toward unlocking the full potential of acquisitions: The role of organizational restructuring', *Academy of Management Journal*, **51**, 2008, 696–722.

18. For a summary of the ambidexterity versus punctuated equilibrium approaches to organizational adaptation see A. Gupta, K. Smith and C. Shalley, 'The interplay between exploration and exploitation', *Academy of Management Journal*, **49**(4), 2006, 693–706. See further discussion below.

19. R. R. Nelson and S. G. Winter, *An Evolutionary Theory of Economic Change* (Cambridge, MA: Belknap Press, 1982). This view also represents a stream of the resource-based view of competition (see Chapter 3).

20. S. Finkelstein and J. Haleblian, 'Understanding acquisition performance: The role of transfer effects', *Organization Science*, **13**(1), 2002, 36–47.

21. See K. Sengupta, T. Abdel-Hamid and L. Wassenhove, 'The experience trap', *Harvavd Business Review*, February 2008, 94–101.

22. J. G. March, 'Exploration and exploitation in organizational learning', *Organization Science*, **2**(1), 1991, 71–87.

23. March, *ibid.*, pp. 72 and 85.

24. The literature on organizational adaptation considers two alternative models of adaptation based on March's theory of the exploitation versus exploration dichotomy. Ambidexterity is a synchronous pursuit of both. Punctuated equilibrium models adaptation as a cyclical process alternating between exploitation and exploration. These represent 'radically different mechanisms for organizational learning' and require different organizational structures. According to March the two may be incompatible, since each is self-reinforcing, i.e. exploration often leads to failure, which in turn prompts even more exploration, thereby creating a *'failure trap'*. In contrast, exploitation may lead to early success, which in turn reinforces the

pursuit of further exploitation, thereby creating a *'success trap'*. However, other scholars have argued that under certain organizational conditions, e.g. separate domains of activity that are only loosely coupled, and with no constraint on resources devoted to either exploitation or exploration, the two may be beneficially combined. For an overview of this debate see A. Gupta, K. Smith and C. Shalley, 'The interplay between exploration and exploitation', *Academy of Management Journal*, **49**(4), 2006, 693–706.

25. For a review of the social identity approach (SIA) to the problems of post-acquisition integration see J. Ullrich and R. van Dick, 'The group psychology of mergers and acquisitions: Lessons from the social identity approach', in C. L. Cooper and S. Finkelstein (Eds), *Advances in Mergers and Acquisitions* (Amsterdam: Elsevier, 2007), 1–15.

26. The case is adapted from R. Nag, K. Corley and D. Gioia, 'The intersection of organizational identity, knowledge and practice: Attempting strategic change via knowledge grafting', *Academy of Management Journal*, **50**(4), 2007, 821–847.

27. J. A. C. Baum and S. X. Li, 'Making the next move: How experiential and vicarious learning shape the locations of chains' acquisition', *Administrative Science Quarterly*, **45**(4), 2000, 766–801.

28. M. Zollo and D. Leshchinskii, *Can Firms Learn to Acquire? Do Markets Notice?*, INSEAD Working Paper, May 1999.

29. M. Zollo and H. Singh, 'The impact of knowledge codification, experience trajectories and integration strategies on the performance of corporate acquisitions', *Strategic Management Journal*, **25**, 2004, 1233–1256.

30. J. Haleblian and S. Finkelstein, 'The influence of organizational acquisition experience on acquisition performance: A behavioural learning perspective', *Administrative Science Quarterly*, **44**(1), 1999, 29–49.

31. Finkelstein and Haleblian, *ibid.* See Loderer and Martin, *ibid.*, for evidence consistent with these conclusions.

32. Hayward, *ibid.*

33. 'Unlearning' is not easy, 'especially if a firm has a long history of success using old patterns of behavior and if those old patterns of behaviour are reflected in its organizational structure, formal and informal controls, and compensation policies': J. Barney and W. Hesterly, *Strategic Management and Competitive Advantage: Concepts and Cases* (Upper Saddle River, NJ: Pearson Prentice Hall, 2008), p. 127.

34. D. N. Greenberg, H. Lane and K. Bahde, 'Organizational learning in cross-border mergers and acquisitions', in G. Stahl and M. Mendenhall (Eds), *Mergers and Acquisitions: Managing Culture and Human Resources* (Stanford, CA: Stanford University Press, 2005), pp. 53–76.

35. See J. Russo and P. Schoemaker, 'Managing overconfidence', *Sloan Management Review*, Winter 1992, who observe that 'overconfidence persists in spite of experience because we often fail to learn from experience' (p. 10).

36. J. Garnier, 'Introductory comments', in G. Stahl and M. Mendenhall (Eds), *ibid.*, p. xvi. See also D. N. Greenberg *et al.*, *ibid.*, on the failure to integrate learning from different stages of the M & A process.

37. See survey evidence from Selim, Sudarsanam and Lavine, *ibid.*

38. On the roles that IA can play at different stages see N. Dounis, 'The auditor's role in mergers and acquisitions', *Internal Auditor*, June 2008, 61–63.

39. J. Trampe, 'Thriving on change, the internal auditor's role in mergers and acquisitions', *Journal of Accountancy*, **185**(4), 1998, 33; L. Nygaard, 'Beyond due diligence', *Internal Auditor*, April 2002, 37–43 (on the internal auditors' role at Wells Fargo).

Meeting the challenges of mergers and acquisitions

Objectives

At the end of this chapter, the reader should be able to understand:

- the overview of the five-stage model of the M & A process;
- the importance of the inter-stage linkages;
- the need for both foresight and hindsight in developing an effective acquisition programme;
- the overview of the challenges to successful acquisitions at each of the five stages; and
- some of the ways in which acquirers can organize themselves to meet these challenges.

Introduction

We reviewed the historical trend in mergers and acquisitions in Chapter 2. This review shows that M & A activity reached phenomenal levels in the most recent of several historical merger waves. Corporations in the US and Europe spent nearly $3 trillion at the height of the 1990s merger wave. In the new millennium another M & A wave peaked in 2007 at $2.4 trillion in the US and Europe combined. This level of corporate expenditure on M & A points to the importance of M & A to the competitive strategies of corporations. The rising tide of M & A over the past two decades has been accompanied by well-documented and widespread evidence that most mergers and acquisitions fail to create value for the acquirer shareholders. We reviewed in Chapter 4 the extensive empirical evidence from the US, the UK and several other European countries. In particular, the majority of them fail to create value when tested against the criterion that the benefits from acquisitions exceed that cost of capital invested in them, especially over the long term, although we noted a number of methodological limitations of empirical studies dealing with long-term returns to shareholders.

To examine the issues that potentially contribute to acquisition failure and value destruction we developed a model of mergers and acquisitions, which regards merger or acquisition as a *process* rather than as a *transaction*. This process-oriented conceptualization yields a five-stage process model of M & A. The five stages of the model comprise:

1 corporate strategy development;
2 organizing for acquisitions;
3 deal structuring and negotiation;
4 post-acquisition integration; and
5 post-acquisition audit and organizational learning.

In this chapter we revisit our discussion of these stages in the preceding chapters.

Importance of the five-stage model

Acquisition driven by some business models such as conglomerate diversification seem to destroy more shareholder value than others. This points to the weakness of the business model that some of the acquiring firms follow[1]. Even though there is evidence that related acquisitions create more value than unrelated or conglomerate ones, the picture is not quite uniform. This means that there may be other factors that limit the success of this business model. In Chapter 5 we discussed the limits to related acquisition as a corporate strategy for competitive advantage and value creation. Our review in Chapter 6 of vertically integrating mergers again highlights the limits to the value creation potential of this business model. While there is limited evidence that short-term shareholder gains are positive, there is little evidence so far on the long-term gains or on the operating performance of vertical acquirers. In the case of industry-blurring vertical integration, the business model may have both overestimated the market opportunities for the merged firms and underestimated the technological risks in the evolution of new multimedia technologies. The excessive optimism inspired by this business model led many companies in the 1990s to overpay for their acquisitions and destroy value. That the business models driving many past acquisitions may have been flawed is evidenced not only by the increasing levels of divestitures of various types we observed in Chapters 2 and 10 but also by the positive stock market reaction to them. However, behavioural biases may prevent managers from divestitures that are sufficiently large or timely.

Even seemingly similar business models, e.g. conglomerate acquisitions by strategic buyers, discussed in Chapter 7, and portfolios of businesses put together by LBO sponsors and private equity firms, discussed in Chapter 11, may lead to different value creation outcomes because of differences in the way they are financed, and in the corporate governance systems of acquires. In one type of organization the capital allocation process, i.e. the internal capital market, seems to function more efficiently than in the other. Thus organization structure and the internal political processes play an important role in allocating capital to acquisitions efficiently, and in monitoring how the allocated capital is utilized to deliver shareholder value. In addition to sound business strategy for sustainable competitive advantage, a firm must also have the internal organization structure that ensures not only the soundness of the strategy but also the acquisition competence to deliver value from that strategy.

Organizational characteristics contribute to creating the acquisition competence in mergers and acquisitions by shaping the way firms develop their acquisition programmes and specific acquisition strategies. As discussed in Chapter 12, acquisition decision-making in firms may not always be a coldly rational process driven by the value creation imperative. It is often driven by organizational dynamics and political processes that override the economic rationale of the business model. It is also hostage to managerial biases such as hubris or overconfidence, both at the individual CEO level and collectively in the board of directors. The various components of corporate governance – the independence of the board of directors, the activism of large shareholders, monitoring by lenders, incentives for top managers that align the interests of managers and shareholders – can contribute to the effectiveness of the acquisition decision-making process. In Chapter 13 we provided a template for screening potential targets, combining the important attributes of the different stages of the acquisition process to generate useful screening criteria.

We discussed in Chapter 22 the importance of the organizational dynamics and the human aspects of acquisitions, again in the context of post-acquisition integration. Chapter 23 highlighted the obstacles to efficient organizational learning about acquisitions. Lack of effective post-acquisition audit and other obstacles were discussed in detail.

Our review of acquisition performance in Chapter 4 also suggests that acquisitions may be seen as value creating overall, but that the shareholders of the acquired companies not only gain all of the additional value an acquisition creates, but also gain by wealth transfers from the acquirers. In simple terms, acquirers overpay for their acquisitions and in the process destroy value for their shareholders. In certain types of acquisition both acquirer and acquired companies' shareholders gain, depending on the transactional characteristics of such acquisitions. This means that acquirers need to pay as much attention to how they structure the acquisition deal in terms of valuation, payment method, etc., and how they handle the deal negotiation, as to the strategic and organizational aspects of M & A. We described the deal-structuring and negotiation aspects of M & A in Chapters 14 to 21, and identified the risks involved at this stage of the M & A process.

Importance of understanding the inter-stage linkages

Our five-stage model represents a circle of stages in the M & A process. These stages are obviously interlinked, in that one stage follows another in a decision-making and chronological sequence. But the stages are linked in a more important, evolutionary sense. Without efficient consummation of the following stages the earlier stages will stand unfulfilled. The test of successful conception of a business model lies in the ultimate and fruitful delivery of value. In the case of serial acquisitions that form a coherent programme of acquisitions to implement a business model, the test is the ultimate delivery of value at the end of the programme rather than at the end of a single acquisition. The five-stage circular model completes this linkage between past acquisitions. The success of M & A requires understanding of all the stages in the process, and the inter-stage linkages.

The implication of the inter-stage linkages conceptualized by the five-stage circular model is that the M & A process needs to be both forward looking and backward looking in order to be successful. Chapter 23 has cited academic and practitioner evidence that it is common for companies to neglect the continuity of these stages, and to fail to manage the interfaces between them (see the comments of Jean-Pierre Garnier, the former CEO of GlaxoSmithKline). There is therefore a need for considerable and sophisticated *look-ahead* capabilities within organizations active in acquisitions. At each stage of the process the consequence of the actions taken at the stage and their impact on the following stages need to be given explicit consideration and be carefully evaluated. Business models developed in a rarefied atmosphere of hype, overconfidence and over-optimism dictate the kind of acquisitions made and the premium paid. A business model whose sources of value creation are poorly understood will fail to create the organizational conditions or external conditions necessary for realizing that value.

A firm that lacks an effective organization for making acquisitions may make acquisitions whose rationale is poorly understood and communicated to the key constituencies within and outside the firm, and lead to sloppy deal structuring and negotiation. A deal negotiation process that is not well informed about the underlying business model and the source of expected value creation may result in a deal that inhibits smooth post-acquisition integration.

Figure 24.1 **Foresight and hindsight loops in M & A**

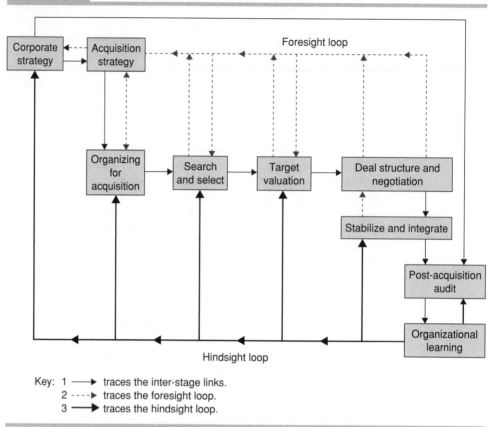

Key: 1 ⟶ traces the inter-stage links.
2 ----▶ traces the foresight loop.
3 ⟶ traces the hindsight loop.

But this failure may have arisen not merely at the deal-making stage but may be traced to the lack of an effective organization for acquisition-making. A successful acquirer therefore needs to combine both foresight and hindsight.

The foresight and hindsight loops

Figure 24.1 revisits the five-stage model and shows the importance of foresight and hindsight learning. The foresight loop is concerned with whether acquiring firms look ahead to see the risks in subsequent stages of the acquisition process, and modify their expectations and deal terms and evolve appropriate integration plans. If the foresight loop reveals risks disproportionate to the benefits of the proposed acquisition, the wise thing is to abandon the proposal. A real options analysis of the availability of 'follow-on' investments to capture the value of emerging growth opportunities, discussed in Chapter 3 and in other chapters, is part of the foresight loop. This loop allows the acquirers to develop a holistic and integrated view of the proposed acquisition or an acquisition programme in general.

The hindsight loop is concerned with post-acquisition audit and organizational learning. It identifies the reasons for success and failure; evaluates the organizational systems, processes and procedures for their contribution to success and failure; and draws up the lessons. The hindsight loop is not merely an archival process but must play a proactive role in diffusing organizational learning, and in enhancing the quality of the acquisition programme. It feeds into the foresight loop by alerting managers responsible for developing and executing acquisitions to the potential risks, and sharpens the foresight loop. It can transform acquisition-making into a valuable core competence of the organization.

The process integration tools in M & A

While a holistic perspective must inform all activities in the five-stage model, two stages, in particular, require an all-embracing vision. These are valuation of the acquisition, and post-acquisition integration. At the valuation stage the potential sources of value and risk need to be carefully mapped out. This requires an understanding of the strategic drivers of the acquisition, the acquirer's resources and capabilities, the target firm's resources and capabilities, and how these will be leveraged to create new sources of competitive advantage. In translating this strategic evaluation into value for stakeholders the valuation model needs to evaluate the risk of *not* achieving the strategic aims, and the risk of value erosion, rather than merely value creation from the acquisition. This imposes upon the firm the need to look ahead to see the potential risks not only from inappropriate deal structure but also from shoddy post-acquisition integration. Over-optimistic forecasts of acquisition benefits and underestimation of potential risks are both enemies of good acquisition. Avoiding both errors requires that the acquirer have a thorough understanding of all the five stages of the M & A process. Bad strategy and bad acquisition integration cannot be offset by clever financial calculus and smart financial engineering.

Post-acquisition integration similarly requires a thorough understanding of the strategic motives for the deal, the assumptions underlying the valuation model, the terms of the deal, and the explicit and implicit expectations of stakeholders in the merging firms. Post-acquisition integration is not a compartmentalized activity that picks up when the deal has been closed and signed. It must be informed by the events that occurred in the previous three stages, and must have regard to the performance criteria against which integration success will be judged in the fifth stage. Integration should be a creative process of transformation to a better and stronger firm, with resources and capabilities that either of the merging firms on its own would have had difficulty creating. However, efficient post-acquisition integration cannot fix a deal based on poor strategic logic and unrealistic deal valuation assumptions that led to an excessive takeover premium.

Challenges in competitive strategy planning

Acquisitions are a means to achieving the corporate strategy aims of improving the firm's competitive positioning in its chosen markets on a sustainable basis. They are an important means of accessing those resources and capabilities that are critical to the attainment of those aims. Before embarking on acquisition as a way of implementing their corporate strategy, managers need to establish whether the business model that embodies the firm's corporate strategy is well developed and widely understood. The key questions relating to this understanding are as follows:

- Are the sources of the firm's current and future competitive strengths clearly identified?
- How sustainable and unique will these competitive strengths be?
- How difficult will it be for the firm's current and potential competitors to replicate this strategy?

- Will the competitive strategy create value, meeting the criterion of the benefits exceeding the cost of capital?

An important consideration in developing competitive strategies and business models is the expected reaction of the firm's competitors. As our discussion of merger in Chapter 2 shows, firms may adopt given strategies as either first movers or 'me-too' followers. Both approaches have associated risks as well as opportunities. In some situations the first mover gathers the 'winner-takes-all' booty, but the risk of failure may be high. The second mover can reap the benefit of vicariously learning from the mistakes and failures of the first mover. In the competition to exploit new or emerging technologies the temptation to be the first mover may often be overwhelming. The organizational decision processes need to be sensitized to the risks and costs of failure, and be capable of a reasoned evaluation of these and not be seduced only by the elusive prize of a 'winner-takes-all' outcome. Blind spots regarding competitor reaction to an acquisition must be studiously overcome (see Chapter 13).

From our review of the various competitive strategies in Chapters 5 to 10, we need to keep in view the limitations of these business models. Strategies for revenue enhancement must factor in not only competitor reactions and their 'me-too' replication of similar strategies, but also the constraints on cross-selling the merging firms' products. We have provided empirical evidence that revenue enhancement is often difficult to achieve, and that revenue synergies are most often grossly overestimated and underachieved. Another danger with revenue enhancement is that it may often be achieved by sacrificing the bottom line, i.e. by forgoing control of costs that reduce the profitability of any revenue growth that is actually accomplished. Similarly, cost leadership strategies should not lead to cutting the muscle and the bone and not merely the flab. This will lead to revenue decline rather than revenue enhancement. The circularity between cost efficiency and revenue decline requires that the trade-off between the two be achieved in a way that leads to a virtuous circle of lower costs, leading to higher sales volume, higher revenue and lower costs.

In horizontal mergers, studied in Chapter 5, from the resource-based view of acquisitions, harnessing these sources of value requires redeployment of the merging firms' resources and capabilities. Empirical literature on the effect of mergers on cost savings through scale efficiencies and on market power suggests that accretion of market power is difficult to achieve, and scale economies may be easily exhausted and copied by rival firms following me-too mergers. Recent and large-sample studies show that resources and capabilities redeployed include marketing resources such as sales forces, brands and general marketing capabilities, manufacturing, R & D, general management and financial resources, but the impact of resource redeployment on financial performance shows that such impact is limited. Redeployment of some marketing resources may actually be detrimental to acquirers. This suggests that resource redeployment is a hazardous business, and the odds on success may not be high. This is so even when the resources transferred are well defined, such as brands. We have little evidence on how resource redeployment to generate real options influences post-acquisition performance, but the odds against performance enhancement are probably even longer.

Vertical merger is optimal when it generates the best trade-off between the technical and coordination efficiencies compared with the buy decision, as argued in Chapter 6. Where relative coordination costs exceed the relative technical efficiency benefits, outsourcing is preferable to vertical merger. The recent trend towards outsourcing was reviewed. However, outsourcing may also fail and be strategically risky. Survey evidence suggests that outsourcing is not always optimal. We considered a more recent type of vertical integration that combines the vertical chains of firms operating in different industries. Vertical mergers of this type tend to blur industry boundaries. Examples of such mergers in recent times include those in the financial services industry, e.g. bancassurance mergers, and those in multimedia industries, e.g. mergers of Internet, cable, movie and music businesses. Industry-blurring mergers pose challenges in technology and market development as well as in organizational integration, which may destroy rather than create value in such mergers. In cross-border acquisitions there are a variety of barriers to takeovers in many European countries, and problems of post-acquisition integration are more complex in cross-border acquisitions than in purely domestic ones. Survey evidence shows that cross-border acquisitions are successful in more than half the cases. But a number of empirical studies of shareholder value gains, cited in Chapter 8, provide no consistent evidence of such gains.

Is acquisition necessary?

Given the risks associated with M & A, the firm must consider the alternatives to acquisitions as a means of achieving its strategic objectives. Acquisition may be preferred to organic growth of the necessary resources and capabilities if there is compelling need for speed to get the existing products to new markets or to create new products and markets. On the other hand, organic growth avoids takeover premia, the risks in deal negotiation and structuring, and the risk of failure of post-acquisition integration. Similarly, the acquisition option needs to be evaluated against the alternative of strategic alliances including joint ventures. Strategic alliances have their own risks, as discussed in Chapter 9. A balanced evaluation of alternative modes of market entry and growth must be made prior to the choice of the acquisition mode, taking into account the relative costs and benefits of these alternatives.

Challenges in organizing for acquisitions

The personal motivations and psychological biases of decision-makers also influence the nature and quality of acquisition decisions. A number of factors impart a momentum to acquisition decision and deal-making that the individual players may find difficult to control. Companies and key decision-makers need to be conscious of these pressures and pulls, and not allow them to overwhelm the logic of the deal; otherwise the deal will turn out to be a sub-optimal one and lead to value destruction. This emphasizes the importance of establishing an acquisition function, or the A team. The A team has responsibility for a range of activities that arise when a firm employs acquisitions as a means of achieving its corporate strategy aims. The A team has a role in developing acquisition programmes to deliver the strategic goals, proactively looking for acquisition opportunities, providing internal consulting expertise to divisions, coordinating the acquisition-related activities, and developing the necessary capabilities and resources for an acquisition function that confers a competitive advantage. In developing acquisition ideas and programmes the A team needs to consult with and coordinate all the relevant functions, business units and top management involved.

The A team can regulate the acquisition decision process to minimize the impact of the dysfunctional attributes of that process identified earlier. The A team has to play the devil's advocate from time to time so that over-optimistic acquisition proposals are not accepted, or the acquisition process is not driven by the grandiose vision or overweening ambitions of the CEO, reducing acquisitions to a one-man show. Independent members of the board should also play the 'devil's advocate' and not put too much trust in a visionary, charismatic or narcissistic CEO. There needs to be a robust pre-acquisition audit to pick flaws in the acquisition strategy and say '*the Emperor has no clothes*'. There is a need for the corporate equivalent of a

Shakespearean fool who can mock royal vanities, remind corporate emperors of their fallibility, and warn against imperial overstretch (see Chapter 12).

Once the decision has been made, the bidder has to carry out deal structuring and negotiation in a way that minimizes risks not only to deal consummation but also to the achievement of the strategic and value creation objectives. The deal negotiation teams must be carefully put together to accomplish these objectives. Negotiation strategies and tactics should be deployed to achieve a win–win deal that will strengthen post-deal integration and thereby deliver the acquisition objectives and result in value enhancement. Since trust is an important factor in fostering effective post-acquisition integration, trust-building among top management teams has to start during deal structuring and negotiation. Trust is not inspired by 'talk' but by 'walking the talk'. Honourable intent must be reflected in honourable behaviour.

To develop acquisition-making as a core competence the firm needs to establish:

● the internal acquisition deal-making, integration and post-audit capabilities;
● a good corporate memory of past acquisition successes and failures informing current acquisition programme.

The other conditions that can contribute to the creation of an effective acquisition function are:

● the firm recognizing strong acquisition function as an important capability, and a source of competitive advantage and value creation;
● the firm allocating enough resources to strengthen this function; and
● the acquisition function being benchmarked against the best.

Challenges in deal structuring and negotiation

In Chapters 14 to 21 we identified a range of potential risks concerned with the deal-structuring and negotiation stage. Selection of an acquisition team lacking in balance of expertise from operations, law, human resource management and other relevant functions to carry out negotiation or hostile bids if necessary and engaging advisers with little relevant experience or standing may lead to a costly and aborted acquisition attempt. The A team must set realistic negotiation parameters and benchmarks for negotiation, but ensure that the deal-making momentum does not breach these parameters. Information is the key to successful deal-making. Inadequate due diligence and not factoring in potential showstoppers and delays may lead to risk of failure of the bid, as well as cost escalation in terms of the bidder managers' time and organizational resources, and also in terms of the cost of advisers. Among these showstoppers are the unexpected antitrust investigations and the inability of the acquirer and the target firms to enlist the support of key shareholder groups and other constituencies such as suppliers. The increasingly strident role of activist investors such as dedicated activist funds and hedge funds will have to be factored into the acquisition campaign. Effective strategies to counteract activist pressures and win their buy-in need to be crafted ahead of the campaign. Due diligence traditionally was restricted to accounting and legal issues. It must be extended to cover a wider range of issues identified in Chapter 20, including commercial and human resources due diligence.

Advisers, especially investment bankers, must be chosen in such a way as to ensure that the preferences of the advisers are aligned with those of the bidders and target firms. Incentive contracts that create conflicts of interest with the advisers need to be avoided. Target valuation must be based on realistic expectations about whether the business model driving the acquisition will deliver the expected long-term competitive advantage, and how it may be sustained.

There must be a keen awareness of the competitive forces that may quickly erode any competitive advantage that the acquisition creates.

Depending upon whether the bid is friendly or hostile, bid strategies and tactics differ. Researching the target for its strengths and weaknesses is the foundation of an effective bid strategy. Acquisition criteria derived from the company's corporate and competitive strategies help screen targets. The internal organization for an acquisition, the A team, has a range of functions from bid opportunity identification to developing acquisition strategy and communication. Alternative acquisition strategies include friendly bids, merger of equals, hostile bids and white knight bids. The disadvantages of playing a white knight must be seriously considered. The role of arbitrageurs has to be factored into bid strategy. Similarly, the probability of rival bids to trigger an auction must be taken into account. Building a stake in the business ahead of a bid has advantages and disadvantages that need to be carefully weighed. Different legal and regulatory jurisdictions may not allow certain strategies, and local knowledge directly obtained or through local advisers will help evolve strategies appropriate to each jurisdiction. Bid strategies must anticipate target defence strategy and prepare for different target defences.

The payment method has a critical role in M & A. It influences the deal negotiation process and the chances of its successful outcome. It is also important in allocating risk between the acquirer and acquired firm shareholders. Since, as discussed in Chapter 16, stock exchange offers create less value for shareholders than cash offers, making a stock exchange offer merely to satisfy extraneous considerations, for example, to effect mergers of equals, requires careful justification. On the other hand, a stock exchange offer to ensure that valuation risk is shared between the buyer and seller may be a substantive and justifiable decision. Stock exchange offers may create the illusion that the acquisition is not 'costly', since no cash payment is made. This may lead to an excessively generous share exchange ratio in favour of the selling firm's shareholders, and also to value destruction rather than value creation, as observed in Chapter 16. In determining the exchange ratio, the bidder must foresee how the stock market will value the post-acquisition entity. To ensure that such a valuation is high requires that the acquisition be based on strong value creation fundamentals, and the bidder must tell a credible story to the stock market about the benefits of the acquisition. While deferred payment is a way of reducing valuation risk, it raises difficult questions about performance measurement, managerial motivation, the need to delay restructuring, etc.

Challenges in post-acquisition integration

The post-acquisition integration stage is intended to implement the acquisition's strategic and financial goals. In practice, there may be a 'disconnect' between the previous stages and this stage, because there is a lack of continuity between the A team that developed the acquisition strategy and guided the negotiation on the one hand, and the integration teams, mainly involving operations managers, on the other. The disconnect may also arise from poor articulation of the strategic goals, and of how organizational transformation would achieve them. There may also be a lack of clarity about the new organizational structure, and how the merging organization would fit into that new structure. These may give rise to fragmented perspectives and expectational ambiguity, discussed in Chapters 12 and 22.

Integration approaches must be tailored to the target and the value creation logic, e.g. absorption or symbiosis, as discussed in Chapter 22. This determines the speed and extent of integration. An inappropriate integration mode is likely to endanger the whole acquisition rationale, and destroy value.

Merger integration may be regarded as a change process, and needs to be managed by drawing upon the principles and practice of change management. Organizational change involves changes in the politics of the merging organizations as well as their culture. Strategy, organizational structure and organizational culture must be aligned during the integration process to deliver sustainable value creation. The integration process is fraught with uncertainty, fear and anxiety among target company staff, which may lead to withdrawal of their commitment and lack of morale. The acquirer's implementation team must handle these concerns with tact, sympathy and understanding in order to instil confidence in and trust between the two companies' personnel.

Integration may be managed as a project to integrate structures, cultures, systems, processes and procedures. Task forces, transition teams and project teams may be set up to manage integration of these. The lack of a project management approach to integration may result in the goals of the acquisition not being achieved, in costly errors that are not spotted and corrected in good time, or in costly delays. Such delays may have both direct costs associated with the extended dislocation from the merging firms' normal businesses and indirect costs associated with the time that the firm's competitors gain. A poor management approach is characterized by:

- the absence of performance benchmarks and milestones for evaluating integration progress;
- poor project management capabilities, with the project management team being inadequately resourced;
- the absence of continuity in the project management teams from acquisition team to completion;
- skewed project management teams that exclude managers from the acquired firm;
- weak communication strategies for internal and external stakeholders;
- an over-ambitious timetable for integration that leads to missed deadlines, loss of morale or shoddy implementation;
- a lack of robust feedback about implementation of the prior stages and timely 'feed-forward' to the next stages[2];
- the absence of a plan to allow for mid-course correction.

While the firms are preoccupied with the integration process, they may take their eyes off the ball and neglect their normal businesses and their customers. The merging firms must continue to maintain their external market, customer and supplier focus so that relationships with these key constituencies are not severed. The uncertainty created by the integration process may lead to the key personnel leaving, or being poached by competitors in order to weaken the merging firms. The dislocation caused by integration of the merging firms is a good opportunity for competitors to lure their talented staff and disgruntled customers. Appropriate human resource management policies aimed at key person retention need to be in place during the integration process. Communication with the key persons to ensure that the post-acquisition organization will recognize and reward their contribution is also important.

The integration process is a major element in developing a firm's core acquisition competence. Important questions arise in this context:

- Does the integration experience contribute to organizational learning and the development of a core competence?
- Does the integration process draw on the corporate memory of past successes and failures?
- Does the integration process renew the memory to make it ever relevant?
- Does the process provide for feedback loop among strategy, acquisition, deal making and integration to create an interconnected M & A programme?

Challenges in post-acquisition audit and organizational learning

This stage represents perhaps the least researched and understood of the five stages in our model. There may be several reasons for the shortcomings at this stage. We provide survey evidence in Chapter 23 that a majority of acquirers do not track the performance of their acquisitions. Firms may often not undertake acquisition-specific audit, but include the acquired business in normal internal audit. The audit may, if carried out, provide inadequate assessment of performance owing to poor performance metrics or an over-ambitious timescale for delivery of performance. As a result, there may be no clear identification of the reasons for success or failure. The post-acquisition audit process may also be characterized by a lack of effective strategies to communicate the lessons from acquisitions to managers, not only managers of business units concerned but also managers and directors concerned with acquisitions and corporate strategy. These attitudes depend on the culture of the organization, its openness to learning, how harsh the attitude of top management to failure is, etc. The firm may lack the incentives for learning. The audit process may be perceived as an exercise in scapegoating rather than as a means of collective organizational self-learning.

The scope of the audit often defines its quality. Some of the important issues that arise are as follows:

- Have the deals been audited for delivering their promises?
- Is there a separate acquisition audit, or is it part of the normal internal audit?
- Does the audit ensure appropriate benchmarks for type of acquisition made?
- Does the audit create a well-calibrated feedback mechanism for organizational learning?
- Are lessons from both successes and failures in acquisitions communicated effectively so that they become embedded in organizational procedures, systems, cultures and routines?
- Does post-audit lead to a more effective acquisition process and organizational capability that confers a competitive advantage?

Organizational learning

Our concern here is not about an individual merger or acquisition but about the M & A programme in which firms become serial acquirers in the pursuit of their corporate and competitive strategies. The serial nature of acquisitions raises the scope for learning from previous acquisitions and incorporating that learning in the various stages of future acquisitions. Our focus is therefore on organizational learning. Some empirical studies provide evidence that acquisition experience has a positive impact on acquisition performance in terms of shareholder value gains. Therefore frequent acquirers have the incentive to improve organizational learning further and, in turn, their acquisition performance. Many other studies have shown that acquisitions by acquirers with prior acquisition experience fail to generate shareholder value. This suggests both positive and negative learning effects of prior experience.

While acquisition experience and the tacit learning that goes with it may improve learning, explicit learning through codification of past experience seems to add even more value. Acquirers, however, should be careful not to over-generalize past acquisition experience in evaluating or implementing current acquisitions. Acquirers may apply their previous acquisition models mechanically without regard to the idiosyncrasies that the new acquisitions exhibit. They must develop critical capabilities to apply their learning from past acquisitions in a selective and discerning way. The opposite error of over-discrimination, i.e. treating every new acquisition as unique and dismissing the past as irrelevant, should also be avoided. There are several impediments to organizational learning about past acquisitions.

While accountability is important, it should not obstruct the process of learning. When properly institutionalized, organizational learning can give firms for which acquisition-led growth is a crucial plank of their corporate strategy a core competence and a competitive advantage. Such firms need to ensure that an institutional learning approach is put in place to increase the odds of acquisition success. Without effective organizational learning, the five-stage acquisition process is incomplete, and future acquisitions may not create value.

Notes and references

1. P. Carroll and C. Mui, after researching 750 corporate failures of companies with assets over $500m during 1981–2005 in the US, find that wrong corporate strategy was a key factor responsible for 355 of these. Several of the mistaken strategies are deployed in the M & A context, e.g. the synergy mirage, pseudo-adjacency (i.e. faulty scope economy assumptions) and rushing to consolidate. See P. Carroll and C. Mui, '7 ways to fail big', *Harvard Business Review*, September 2008, 82–91.
2. See D. Greenberg, H. Lane and K. Bahde, 'Organizational learning in cross-border mergers and acquisitions', in G. Stahl and M. Mendenhall (Eds), *Mergers and Acquisitions, Managing Culture and Human Resources* (Stanford, CA: Stanford University Press, 2005), pp. 53–76. Feedback and feed-forward are related to our concepts of foresight and hindsight loops.

INDEX

accounting 233, 466–81, 603
  amortization 474, 480
  audits 621
  carve-outs 293
  cash flow 480
  conglomerate acquisitions 191
  cross-border acquisitions 231, 233
  European Union 467, 478
  fair value 468
  goodwill 473–9
  leveraged buyouts 324
  payment 483, 487
  performance 101–3, 106, 474–5
  spinoffs 288–9
  target valuation 430
  United Kingdom 467–80
  United States 233, 467, 478
adjusted present value (APV) model 446–7
adverse selection 161
advisers 6, 373, 375
  accountants 603, 621
  consultants 621
  decision-making 352
  hostile bids 603, 646
  investment banks 6, 25, 26, 28, 32, 309, 604–19, 622–3
  investor relations consultants 670
  lawyers 603, 620–1
  public and investor relations 622–3
  stockbrokers 621
  strategy and tactics 604, 621
  takeovers 602–26
anchoring 358
Ansoff's matrix 391
antitrust 54–7, 528–67
  Competition Commission 533–4, 546–7, 577, 633
  competitor neglect 393
  competitor reaction 393
  concentrations 538–9, 544
  conflicts of jurisdiction 543–4
  core competences 19
  cross-border acquisitions 221, 529
  dominant position 541–2
  economic perspective on mergers 50
  European Union 36–7, 221, 529, 537–45
  globalization 529
  horizontal mergers 129, 132, 140, 530
  hostile bids 646–7

  hypercompetition 69, 70
  industry analysis 54–7
  International Competition Network (ICN) 559
  joint ventures 250, 251, 252, 537, 544
  leveraged buyouts 308, 326–7, 329, 344–5
  Office of Fair Trading 533–4, 546, 547–51
  oligopolies 553
  private equity market 309–10
  privatization 529
  real options 453
  regulation 530–3, 557–9
  resources and capabilities 4–5, 141–2, 149, 150
  stock market reaction 560–2
  strategic alliances 248
  strategy 62–5
  sustainability 69–71
  target selection 391, 394–6
  United Kingdom 27, 528–36, 545–51
  United States 18, 33, 529, 551–5
  vertical mergers 123
  wave patterns 33
asset-based valuation 436
audits 9, 353, 621, 745–6, 758, 775

barriers to takeovers 54, 57, 230–4
benchmarking 88–91, 94–9, 187, 289, 290, 424, 430, 448
best alternative to no agreement (BATNA) 637–8
beta 93–4
Black-Scholes model 460, 462–4
Black-Scholes option pricing model (BSOPM) 451
bootstrapping 492
brand-driven acquisitions 144–5
buy-and-hold abnormal returns (BHAR) 115, 116

calendar time portfolio returns (CTPR) 116
call option 460–4, 463
capital asset pricing model (CAPM) 91–3, 114
Carhart four-factor model 115
carve-outs 292–6
cash 103, 105, 107, 203, 480
  accounting 480
  conglomerate acquisitions 203
  leveraged buyouts 324, 337
  payment 483, 483–6, 490, 502–3, 517
  target valuation 420, 437
causal ambiguity 146–7, 743–4

competencies 758–60
  antitrust 19
  contracting out 165
  integration 8, 774
  organization 351–2
  United States 19
Competition Commission 533–4, 546–7, 577, 633
competition *see* antitrust
conflicts of interests 6, 250, 323, 362, 607–8, 611
conglomerate acquisitions 181
  accounting 191
  antitrust 185
  benchmark 196
  capital market, internal 186–7, 203–8
  cash flow 203
  corporate governance 187, 192, 201, 203
  corporate refocusing 271
  discount 191–2, 196–8, 201–2, 307
  diversification 181–203
  divestiture 196, 199, 272–3
  economic perspective 188–9, 196, 200–1, 203
  employees 188
  Europe 180, 183–4, 200
  finance 186–7, 189–90, 194, 195
  information technology 187
  investments 184–5, 189, 203–8
  leveraged buyouts 307, 337–8
  management perspective 192–4
  market power 185
  organization 188–9, 194–5
  performance 107, 108, 194, 202–3, 198, 202
  resource-based view of 187–9
  scope economies 181
  shareholder value 180–216
  strategy and tactics 67
  tax 191, 201
  United Kingdom 27, 201
  United States 19, 33, 181–3, 184, 198, 201
  value 196–201
  waves of merger activities 180, 182, 198, 204
consolidated fragmented industries 132, 149–50
contingent value rights (CVRs) 497, 499–501
contracting out 157, 165
corporate governance
  agency costs 72–3, 74, 342
  conglomerate acquisitions 187, 192, 201, 202
  decision-making 366–72
  directors 366, 367
  finance 73–4
  hostile bids 362
  leveraged buyouts 309, 337, 343–4
  managers 74–5
  performance 362

  shareholder value 363
  spinoffs 286
  target selection 366
  United States 367–8
corporate refocusing 270–305
costs
  accounting 473
  agency 72–3, 74, 342
  of capital 440
  capital markets 187
  corporate governance 73
  debt 342, 442–3
  defences 675
  diversification 189–90
  economic perspective on merger 50–1, 53–4
  of equity 441–2
  horizontal mergers 131–9
  hostile bids 649–50, 655–6
  investments 160–1
  joint ventures 251, 253–4, 257
  performance 741
  strategy and tactics 62, 630
  vertical mergers 159–64
cross-border acquisitions 217–44
  accounting 231, 233
  antitrust 221, 529
  barriers to takeovers 230–4
  diversification 233, 239–40
  employees 230, 235
  European Union 30–1, 219, 220, 222–4, 230–4
  foreign direct investment 218, 224, 225, 228
  fungibility 226
  hostile takeovers 230
  innovation 239–40
  integration 234–5, 703–4
  investments 218, 228, 263
  joint ventures 228
  management 235, 239
  performance 236–40
  privatization 221
  resources and capabilities 224
  restructuring 218, 221
  tax 230, 233, 235
  technology 221
  United Kingdom 234, 236, 240–1, 265
  United States 218–20, 221, 222, 233, 261
cultural perspectives 700–9, 726–8
cumulative abnormal returns (CAR) 115, 116

debt 73–4, 297, 342
  amortization 504–6
  conglomerate acquisitions 191

debt (*continued*)
  leveraged buyouts 307–8, 325–8, 337, 342
   payment 504–8
   target valuation 437, 442–3
decision-making 351–88
  advisers 352
  compensation incentive 362–6
  conflicts of interest 362
  corporate governance 366–72
  due diligence 377
  Germany 378–82
  governance 366–72
  management 372–5
  organization 5, 50, 79, 86, 352–5
  psychology 355–9
  resource allocation 354
  shareholder value creation 355
  target valuation 450
defences 607, 620–1, 669–92
Denmark, leveraged buyouts in 334
derivatives 497–500, 502–3
directors 366, 367, 636, 637, 673, 677, 712
discounted cash flow model (DCF) 437–49
diversification 196–201
  carve-outs 296
  conglomerate acquisitions 181–202
  costs 189–90
  cross-border acquisitions 229, 239–40
  divestiture 239–40
  economic perspective 50–4, 184–5, 199–200
  Europe 22–4, 183–4
  finance theory 189–90
  horizontal mergers 145
  innovation 239–40
  investments 189
  management 78, 193–4
  organization 194
  performance 108, 149, 238–9
  research and development 239
  scope economies 134
  shareholder value 185
  spinoffs 296
  United States 17–18, 181–3, 238–9
divestiture
  see also carve-outs, spinoffs
  conglomerates 196, 199, 270
  corporate refocusing 271–5, 298–301
  corporate sell-offs 275–81
  defences 675
  diversification 199
  European Union 22–4
  forms 274–5
  joint ventures 255

leveraged buyouts 310, 323, 336–7, 338, 345
  management 274
  management buyouts 334
  shareholder value creation 272–5
  tax 276
  United Kingdom 26, 28–30, 279–80
  United States 19, 20, 21, 22, 272, 277
downsizing 296
due diligence 7, 621
  audits 758, 759
  decision-making 377
  hostile deals 7
  integration 643–7, 700, 722
  negotiations 641, 643–6
  organization 358
  target selection 411
  United Kingdom 645
  United States 645, 759
dynamic capabilities 69–71

earnings dilution 493–6
earn-out 509–11, 517
EBIT 504
EBITDA 504–6
economic perspective on mergers 51–4, 80
  antitrust 50
  conglomerate acquisitions 188, 196, 199–200, 201
  costs 50–1, 53–4
  diversification 52, 184–5, 188
  learning, economy of 51–2
  market power 50
  scale and scope economies 50–1, 52
  strategic alliances 247–50
  wave patterns 31
employees 65, 81
  audits 377
  conglomerate acquisitions 188
  contracts 104, 163
  cross-border acquisitions 234
  employee share ownership plans 673
  integration 8, 711–16, 726–8, 774
  key personnel retention policy 8, 714, 729, 774
  management 711–12, 714–16, 774
  ownership change 104
  performance 104–5, 106, 712–14
  remuneration 712–14
  strategy and tactics 63
  United Kingdom 673
  vertical mergers 162
enterprise value multiple 434–5
environment 32–3, 621

Europe *see also* European Union, individual countries (e.g. France)
  antitrust 555
  conglomerate acquisitions 180, 183–4, 200
  corporate refocusing 271
  defences 676–83
  diversification 183
  hostile bids 657–8
  leveraged buyouts 310, 315–19, 332–5, 344–5
  management buyouts and buyins 332–4
  performance 100–1
  regulation 588–90, 657–8
  shareholder value 281
  spinoffs 282, 284–6
  strategy and tactics 657–8
European Union 22–6, 36–7, 132, 219–20
  accounting 467, 478
  antitrust 36–7, 219, 220, 537–45, 555, 556
  Concentration with a Community dimension (CCD) 539–41
  cross-border mergers and acquisitions 30–1, 219, 220, 220–4, 226–7, 228
  defences 679
  distribution 23–4, 36–7
  divestitures 22–4
  European Monetary Union 24, 34, 221, 224, 225
  exemptions 265
  horizontal mergers 530
  hostile bids 657–8
  integration 24
  joint ventures 250, 537
  merger regulation 263, 537–45, 555–7
  payment 483, 484–5
  privatization 25, 26
  regulation 76, 569–70, 583–90, 627, 635, 657–8
  restructuring 21
  Single Market 21, 31, 32, 34, 37, 221
  technological changes 25, 221
  wave patterns 22–6, 31
event clustering 116
event study methodology 113

fair value 468, 605–6
Fama–French three factor (FFTF) model 93, 114–15
finance 49, 72–8, 86
  see also costs, payment for the acquisition
  agency 73–4, 191–2
  conglomerate acquisitions 184–5, 189–92, 194
  corporate control, market for 75–6
  corporate governance 74–5
  diversification 189–92
  hostile takeovers 74–5
  investment banks 611–12
  leveraged buyouts 337–8

real options 76–8, 450–5, 459–65
  shareholder value 67
  target valuation 451
five stage model 3–9, 54–7, 391, 765–9
foreign direct investment 397
France
  defences 677
  divestiture 281
  employment 658
  joint ventures 257
  leveraged buyouts 332
  negotiations 634
  strategy and tactics 658–63
free cash flows (FCF) 439
free-rider problem 596–7
FSMA 2000 581
fungibility 145, 226

game theory and competitive moves 57–61, 77–8, 452–3
Germany
  accounting 233
  banks 33, 678
  capital gains tax 33
  carve-outs 294
  conglomerate acquisitions 201
  corporate governance 678
  cross-border acquisitions 226–7, 228
  decision-making 378–82
  defences 677–9
  divestiture 281
  integration 704–5, 717
  leveraged buyouts 332, 334
  negotiations 635
  poison pills 678
  restructuring 33
  spinoffs 285
golden parachutes 670

halo effect 356
Herfindahl-Hirschman Index (HHI) 535
high buys low strategy 39, 41
historical overview of mergers and acquisitions activity 15–48
horizontal mergers 124–6, 131–3, 122–55
  antitrust 129, 133, 137, 530
  capabilities 130–1
  collusion 127
  costs savings 131–9
  diversification 145
  information technology 125
  investments 137
  learning economy 137–9
  in mature industries 124–6

horizontal mergers (*continued*)
   performance 107, 108, 147
   restructuring 126, 132
   scale and scope economies 133–7, 149
   shareholder value 123–55
   strategy and tactics 65–6
   United Kingdom 27
hostile bids 629, 658–63
   advisers 603, 646, 646
   antitrust 646–7
   arbitrageurs 648–50
   corporate control 75
   costs 649–50, 655–6
   cross-border acquisitions 230
   defences 669, 671
   due diligence 7
   European Union 657–8
   finance 74
   investment banks 646
   junk bonds 329
   management and 74, 109, 655–7
   negotiations 641–3
   payment 513
   performance 657
   strategy and tactics 646–7, 651, 657–8
   United Kingdom 26, 647, 649, 655–7, 674–5
   United States 19, 649, 651–5, 657
   white knights 649
hubris 355, 356–8
hypercompetition 69

imitation (institutional theory) 361–2
industry attractiveness 393
information symmetry 496
initial public offers 91, 295, 322, 345
innovation 62, 90, 103–4, 239–40, 251, 271
integration 8, 234–5, 773–4
   audits 729, 745–6
   capabilities 696–8, 716
   cross-border acquisitions 235–6, 703–4
   cultural perspectives 700–9, 726–8
   directors, changes in board 712
   due diligence 700, 722
   employees 8, 712–14, 726–8, 774
   European Union 24
   information systems 8, 721
   key personnel retention policy 8, 714, 729, 774
   learning 751
   management 8, 698, 701–2, 709–16, 723–6, 773–4
   negotiations 637–9
   organizational 694–739, 773–4
   performance 702, 712–14, 725–6
   project management 8, 723–5
   resources 698, 716

   reward systems 712–14
   shareholder value 696, 698
   stages 722–3
   strategic 696–8, 706–7, 773
   teams 722–3
   United Kingdom 704, 727
   United States 157–9, 162–4
   vertical mergers 157–9, 162–5
International Accounting Standards (IAS) 467, 475
International Competition Network 559
investments 6–7, 137, 140, 160–2, 187
   banks 6, 33, 34, 309, 604–19, 622–3
   conglomerate acquisitions 184–5, 189, 203–8
   costs 160–1
   cross-border acquisition 218, 218, 224–5, 226, 228, 263
   diversification 189
   horizontal mergers 141
   integration 697
   joint ventures 250, 253, 261
   leveraged buyouts 307–14, 328–32, 344–5
   management 187
   real options 77–8, 450–5, 459–65
   strategic alliances 247, 249
   target valuation 420, 451
   vertical mergers 162
isomorphism 361–2
Italy 230–1, 232, 235, 314, 332, 679

Japan 201, 233, 237, 250, 251
joint ventures 247–61
   antitrust 250, 251, 252, 537, 544
   concentrative 538–9, 544
   conflicts of interest 250
   cooperative 250, 251–2, 261
   costs 251, 253–4, 257
   cross-border acquisitions 228
   divestiture 255
   equity (EJV) 249
   European Union 250, 261, 537
   exit 258
   innovation 251
   investments 250, 253, 261
   management 257–9, 261–2
   negotiation 256
   non-equity (EJV) 249
   performance 259–62
   real options model 254–6
   shareholder gains 257
   tax 250
   technology 251
   United Kingdom 251, 254
   United States 251, 254, 257
junk bonds 307, 328–9

lawyers 603, 620–1
learning 137–9, 775–6
  adaptive 747–8
  audits 758
  economic perspective on mergers 51–2
  exploitative and exploratory 751–8
  horizontal mergers 137–9
  integration 751
  organizational 9, 741, 747–58, 775–6
  performance 754–5
  real options 452
  scale economies 138
  strategic alliances 248
leveraged buyouts 306–50
  accounting 324
  agency costs 339–40
  antitrust 309–10, 485–6
  buyin management buyout (BIMBO) 314, 344
  cash flow 324, 337
  conflicts of interest 314, 323
  conglomerates 307, 337–8
  corporate governance 309–10, 337, 342
  corporate refocusing 271
  debt 307, 325–8, 337–8, 342
  defences 673
  divestitures 315, 323, 336–7, 338, 339
  Europe 314–19, 329, 333–5, 334–5
  exit 320–3, 332, 339
  finance 306, 337–8
  initial public offers 322, 345
  interest, repayment of 326–7
  investment 307–8, 320–3, 345
  investor buyout 309, 313, 318
  junk bonds 307, 328–9
  limited liability partnerships 309–10
  liquidation 320
  management 308–13, 320–3, 323–32, 337
  management fees 326
  management buyins and buyouts 309, 313–14, 317, 320, 335–6
  organization 306–7, 324–8, 336–41, 342–3
  payment 504
  performance 338–44
  private equity 307, 309–10, 323–32, 337–8
  public to private buyouts 318
  raiders 307
  restructurings 314, 323
  secondary buyouts 323–4, 325
  shareholder value 307, 315–19, 337–44
  specialists 307–8, 323–4, 337, 342–3
  sponsors 320, 323–4
  strategy 345
  subordinated debt 325–6
  tax 323, 338–9

  United Kingdom 26, 315–18, 332, 343, 673
  United States 20, 315–19, 322, 328–9, 338–9
  wave patterns 306–7, 315–16
like buys like strategy 41
long-horizon studies 114

management 49, 78, 87, 108–9, 189–91, 201, 239
  see also management buyins and buyouts
  agency model of the firm 78
  brand 129–30
  compensation 235
  conglomerate acquisitions 192–4, 196
  corporate control 75–6
  corporate governance 74
  cross-border acquisitions 234–5, 236, 239
  decision-making 351–416
  defences 669, 670–3, 676–83
  diversification 78, 189–92
  divestiture 274
  employees 711–16, 729, 774
  finance 74, 76–7
  hostile bids 75, 109, 655–7
  integration 8, 697, 701, 709–16, 723–6, 773–4
  investments 187
  job security 109
  joint ventures 257–9, 261–2
  key people retention 714
  leveraged buyouts 308–13, 318, 320–2, 337–8
  negotiations 641–3
  payment 511–13
  performance 194, 513–18
  remuneration 109, 191
  shareholder value 108–9
  strategic alliances 249
  takeovers 76, 109
  target valuation 430
  United States 110
  vertical mergers 163
management buyins and buyouts 334–6
  buyin management buyout (BIMBO) 314
  corporate refocusing 271
  divestiture 274
  Europe 332–4
  exit 334
  institutional investors 335
  leveraged buyouts 309–10, 317, 322, 332–5
  management incentives 335–6
  organizational change 342–3
  performance 342–4
  United Kingdom 334, 343–4
  United States 20
market model 114
market to book ratio 426
market-adjusted model 114

mature industries
    horizontal mergers in 124–6
mean-adjusted model 114
minimum efficient learning scale (MELS) 138, 139
moral hazard 161

Nash equilibrium 58–60
negotiations 6–7
    directors 635, 636
    due diligence 641, 643–6
    France 634
    Germany 635
    hostile bids 641–3
    integration 637–9
    joint ventures 256
    management 641–3
    payment method 773
    strategy and tactics 637–43
    United Kingdom 647
Netherlands 677
network externality 128–9, 401
New Zealand, cross-border acquisitions in 233
Norway, leveraged buyouts in 312

oligopolies 16, 27, 33, 50, 57, 553
organization 5–6, 50, 79–80, 194, 351–88
    see also decision-making
    conglomerate acquisitions 194
    decision-making 5, 50, 79, 86, 352–5
    diversification 194
    due diligence 374
    identity 752–4
    integration 694–739, 772–3
    knowledge 752–4
    learning 9, 741, 747–58, 775–6
    leveraged buyouts 306–7, 323–32, 336–41, 342–3
    management 79–80, 374
    management buyouts 343–4
    negotiations 374
    strategy 64–5
outsourcing 170–7
overconfidence 355, 359

payment for the acquisition 482–527
    accounting 482, 487
    call options 509
    cash 482, 483–6, 490, 503–9, 513–15
    collars, caps, ceilings and floors 498
    convertibles, financing with 509
    corporate control 512
    currency 483, 490, 496–7, 512–13
    debt, types of 504
    Europe 483–5
    exchange 490–6, 497–8

goodwill 495–6
hostile bids 513, 658
    leveraged buyouts 504
    leveraged cash financing 503–9
    loan stock, with 509
    management 511–13
    negotiations 772–3
    performance 513–18
    share exchange offers 483, 483–6, 490–6, 517–18
    strategy 490
    tax 486–90, 503, 509, 510
    United Kingdom 483, 502–3, 509, 513–17
    United States 485–6, 513–15
performance 91–101, 127, 200, 297, 741–2
    see also benchmarking
    accounting 474–5
    audits 745–6, 775
    capital markets 90
    carve-outs 293
    cash flow 103, 107
    conglomerates 107, 108, 194, 196, 198, 202
    consolidated fragmented industries 149
    corporate governance 362
    corporate refocusing 271
    costs 741
    cross-border acquisitions 236–40
    diversification 108, 149, 238–9
    employment 104–5, 106, 712–14
    Europe 100–1
    horizontal mergers 108, 149
    hostile bids 657
    joint ventures 261–2
    learning 754–5
    leveraged buyouts 338–44
    management 194
    management buyins and buyouts 343–4
    measurement 742–7
    operating 101–7, 149, 202, 343–4
    payment 517
    real options 742–3
    shareholder value 91–101, 741, 745
    spinoffs 290
    target valuation 430
    technology 742–3
    United Kingdom 98–9
    United States 94–8
PEST analysis 33–4, 35, 389
poison pills 672–3, 678, 685–6, 689
price earnings ratio 93, 427–8, 429–34
price to book ratio 426
privatization 25–6, 28, 30, 33, 34, 37, 221, 404–6, 529
prospect theory 358
psychic distance paradox 705–6

psychology
  decision-making 355–9
  narcissism 359–61
public and investor relations 622
put option 461–2, 463

Q theory 32

real options 77–8, 254–6, 450–5, 459–65, 742–3
reference portfolio 115
refocusing 270–305
regulation 568–601
research and development 34, 134, 135, 137, 239
residual income models 424–5, 428–9
resources and capabilities 4–5, 141–7
  antitrust 4–5, 141–2, 145, 146–7
  conglomerate acquisitions 187–8, 194
  cross-border acquisitions 224–30
  decision-making 354
  horizontal mergers 129–30, 141–7
  integration 696–8, 717–18
  performance 147
  strategy 63–5
rubber stamp hypothesis 605–6

scale economies 51, 57, 133–7, 138, 149, 150
  Scandinavia 239
  scope economies 52–3, 134–7, 181
  secondary buyouts 320–2, 339
  sell-offs see divestiture
  share exchange offers 482, 483–6, 490–6, 517
seasoned equity issue (SEO) 502–1
self-delusion 358–9
sell-offs 275–81
serial acquisitions 402–4
shareholder value 2–3, 88, 91, 166–7, 180–216,
    420
  abnormal returns methodology 113–16
  activism 371–2
  benchmarking 88–91
  carve-outs 293–4
  corporate refocusing 270
  decision-making 355
  diversification 185
  divestiture 272–5, 279–81
  finance 86
  horizontal mergers 123–55
  investment banks 622–3
  joint ventures 261–2
  leveraged buyouts 307, 315–19, 336–44
  management 108–9
  performance 91–101, 741, 745
  spin-offs 289–92

strategy and tactics 655–7
  target valuation 420
  United Kingdom 28
short-horizon studies 114
showstoppers 633
significant impediment to effective competition (SIEC)
    test 533–4
six forces model 56–7, 393, 394
Spain 333–4, 585
spinoffs 282–92, 296, 298–301
SSNIP test 534
Statements of Financial Accounting Standards (US)
    (SFAS) 467, 475
stockbrokers 621
strategic alliances 77, 245–69
  see also joint ventures
strategies 62–9, 80, 86, 196, 621–2, 627–68
  advisers 604, 621
  antitrust 62–6
  bids 627–68
  business 71–2
  conglomerates 67, 196
  corporate 71–2
  defences 669–92
  directors 636
  employees 63
  Europe 657–8
  France 658–63
  horizontal mergers 65–6
  hostile bids 646–7, 651, 656–7
  lawyers 620–1
  leveraged buyouts 345
  negotiations 637–43
  payment 490
  resources of firms 63–6
  restructuring 62
  shareholder value 655–7
  target selection 391–400
  United Kingdom 647, 655
  United States 651–5
substantial lessening of competition (SLC) 533,
    534
substantive tests 533–4
success of mergers and acquisitions 86–119
Sweden 281, 315, 321, 332, 334, 587, 678
SWOT analysis 399–400, 637

takeover regulation 568–601
  EU 569–70, 583–8
  Europe 588–90
  takeover activity and 596–7
  UK 569–82, 597–8
  US 590–5

target selection 389–416
  antitrust 391
  deal consideration 404–8
  due diligence 411
  platform strategies 400–2
  process 390–1
  profiling 408–11
  serial acquisitions 402–4
  strategy 391–400
  UK 411–13
target valuation 419–65
  abnormal earnings model 449
  accounting 430
  benchmark 424, 430, 433, 448
  Black-Scholes Option Pricing Model 450, 451, 462–4
  call options 451, 460–2
  capital asset pricing model 440
  cash flow 420, 437
  debt 438, 442–3
  decision-making 450
  discounted cash flow model (DCF) 437–49
  dividends 451
  earnings 424–34
  equity value to book value of equity (EVBV) 425–6
  financial drivers 421–3
  financial options 451
  Gordon growth valuation model 424
  investments 420
  models 424–48
  net present value (NPV) 449
  options 420, 449–55
  performance, past 429
  price earnings ratio (PER) 427–8, 429–34, 448
  purchase price, determining 430–1, 443
  put options 450–1, 461–2
  real options 450–5, 459–65
  shareholder value 420
  sources of value 420–4
  strategic drivers 421–3
  tax 448–9 430, 437, 448–9
  United States 451
tax
  capital gains 33, 433, 488–9
  carve-outs 293
  conglomerate acquisitions 191, 201
  corporation tax 489
  cross-border acquisitions 230, 233, 235
  divestiture 276
  Germany 33
  income tax 489–90
  joint ventures 250
  leveraged buyouts 323, 338–9, 340
  offset 447

  payment 486–90, 503, 509, 510
  reliefs 489
  spinoffs 282, 287, 288–9
  target valuation 430, 437, 448–9
  United Kingdom 489, 510
  United States 488–9
  wave patterns 33
technology 34
  barriers 231
  conglomerate acquisitions 187
  cross-border acquisitions 221
  European Union 25, 221
  horizontal merger 125
  information 32–3, 125, 160, 187
  joint ventures 250, 251
  performance 742–3
  vertical mergers 160
terminal value 445
toe-hold 632
tracking stock 296–8
trade-off 163
trading stock 296–8
transnational acquisitions *see* cross-border acquisitions

United Kingdom 26–30
  accounting 466–81
  antitrust 27, 528–37, 546–7
  Big Bang deregulation of financial services 28
  call options 451, 460–2
  capital gains tax 489
  carve-outs 293
  City Code on Takeovers and Mergers 569, 572–7, 607–8, 612–13, 627, 646–7
  City Panel on takeovers and Mergers 569–70, 571–2, 579–80, 597–8
  Competition Commission 533–4, 546–51, 577, 633
  conglomerates 27, 201
  cross-border acquisitions 233–4, 240–1, 265
  defences 671–5, 676
  deregulation 28
  directors 636, 637, 673, 712
  diversification 25, 28
  divestiture 26, 28–30, 279–80
  due diligence 643–6
  Financial Services Authority (FSA) 671
  hostile bids 26, 646–7, 657–8, 674–5
  information, access to 636
  institutional investors 28
  investment banking 33, 607–8, 611–12
  joint ventures 255
  leveraged buyouts 26, 315–18, 332, 334, 343–4, 673
  London Stock Exchange 582, 637
  management buyouts and buyins 335, 343–4

United Kingdom (*continued*)
  Monopolies and Mergers Commission 27
  negotiations 636
  Office of Fair Trading 546, 547–51, 577, 633
  oligopolies 27
  payment 483, 484, 502–3, 509, 513–17
  performance 98–9
  poison pills 672
  privatization 26, 28, 30, 33
  regulation 569–82
  restructuring 28
  shareholder value 28, 279–80
  spinoffs 282, 283, 286–8, 296
  strategic alliances 250
  strategy and tactics 647, 655
  target selection 411–13
  tax 489, 510
  undertaking in lieu (UIL) 548
  utilities, deregulation of 240–1
  wave patterns 22, 25–6, 26–30
United States 18, 33, 297
  accounting 233, 467, 478
  antitrust 18, 33, 529, 551–5
  capital gains tax 488–9
  carve-outs 294
  Clayton Act 17, 18, 551, 553–4
  conglomerates 19, 33, 181–4, 198, 201
  consolidated fragmented industries 21
  core competencies 19
  corporate refocusing 270
  cross-border acquisitions 218–20, 222, 235, 261
  defences 683–90
  disclosure 655
  diversification 17, 18, 19, 181–3, 240
  divestitures 19–20, 21, 272, 277
  due diligence 759
  economic perspective on mergers 17–18
  hostile bids 19, 657, 659
  investment banks 34, 607, 610, 622–3
  joint ventures 250, 255, 257
  leveraged buyouts 20, 315–19, 322, 328–9, 338–9,
    344–5
  management 110
  management buyouts 20, 334
  monopolies 16, 33, 553
  oligopolies 16, 33, 553
  OPEC oil crisis 18
  payment 485–6, 513–15
  performance 94–8
  poison pills 672–3, 678, 685–6, 689
  privatization 33
  public companies 182
  raiders 28
  regulation 590–5
  remuneration 712–14
  restructuring 17
  savings and loans associations 328, 339
  scandals 233
  shareholder value 280, 656–7
  Sherman Act 17, 551
  spinoffs 282, 288–9
  strategy and tactics 651–5
  target valuation 451
  tax 488–9
  technologies, new 21
  wave pattern of takeovers in 16–22, 31

valuation *see* target valuation
vertical mergers 156–79
  antitrust 165, 532–3
  bancassurance 157, 167–8
  contracting out 157, 165
  costs 159–64
  employment contracts 163
  information technology 160
  innovation 159
  integration 157–9, 162–4
  Internet 157
  investments 160
  long-term contracts 160–2
  make or buy decisions 158–9
  management 163
  revenue enhancement 165, 169
  technology 165
  trade offs 163
  value creation 165
VRINS test 68–9, 394, 696–8

wave patterns of mergers and acquisitions 15–41, 49,
    86
  antitrust 33
  behavioural models 39–41
  clustering of mergers 34, 36–7, 41–2
  conglomerate acquisitions 180, 182, 198, 199, 204
  economic analysis of 32–3
  emerging markets 30
  environmental analysis 32–3
  European Union, in 22, 25–6
  leveraged buyouts 306–7, 315
  Q theory 32, 39, 41
  rational models 32–3
  reason for 31
  tax 32–3
  United Kingdom, in 22, 25–6, 26–30
  United States, in 16–22, 31
white knights 628–9, 641–2, 648, 649, 671
workforce *see* employees
works councils 354